A HISTORY OF EARLY VEDĀNTA PHILOSOPHY

PART TWO

A History of Early Vedānta Philosophy

HAJIME NAKAMURA

Translated into English by

HAJIME NAKAMURA,
TREVOR LEGGETT
and others

Edited by
SENGAKU MAYEDA

PART TWO

(English translation of Volumes III-IV of the *Shoki No Vedanta Tetsugaku*)

MOTILAL BANARSIDASS PUBLISHERS
PRIVATE LIMITED • DELHI

First Edition: Delhi, 2004

(The English edition of the *Shoki No Vedanta Tetsugaku* by Hajime Nakamura published in 2004 by Motilal Banarsidass Publishers (P) Ltd., Delhi, by arrangement with the copyright holder c/o Iwanami Shoten, Publishers, Tokyo.)

ISBN: 81-208-1963-2

Also available at:

MOTILAL BANARSIDASS
41 U.A. Bungalow Road, Jawahar Nagar, Delhi 110 007
8 Mahalaxmi Chamber, 22 Bhulabhai Desai Road, Mumbai 400 026
120 Royapettah High Road, Mylapore, Chennai 600 004
236, 9th Main III Block, Jayanagar, Bangalore 560 011
Sanas Plaza, 1302 Baji Rao Road, Pune 411 002
8 Camac Street, Kolkata 700 017
Ashok Rajpath, Patna 800 004
Chowk, Varanasi 221 001

Printed in India
BY JAINENDRA PRAKASH JAIN AT SHRI JAINENDRA PRESS,
A-45 NARAINA, PHASE-I, NEW DELHI 110 028
AND PUBLISHED BY NARENDRA PRAKASH JAIN FOR
MOTILAL BANARSIDASS PUBLISHERS PRIVATE LIMITED,
BUNGALOW ROAD, DELHI 110 007

PREFACE

The purpose of the present work is to trace the development of early Vedānta philosophy before Śaṅkara. Fairly well known to the academic world is the Vedānta philosophy of Śaṅkara and his successors, but pre-Śaṅkara Vedānta has been little explored and this work aims at filling the gap.

The Japanese original of this work was my doctorate thesis submitted to the University of Tokyo in 1942. From 1936 to the end of 1941 I was engaged in post-graduate research at the University under the guidance of the late Dr. Hakuju Ui, finally submitting a thesis, entitled "A History of Early Vedānta Philosophy," on pre-Śaṅkara Vedānta philosophy, which was accepted by the University in 1943. Just after World War II it was difficult to arrange publication, but it finally appeared in four volumes, published respectively in the years 1950, 1951, 1955 and 1956.

After that I made some piecemeal English translations of certain sections, some of which appeared in foreign journals, but there seemed not much possibility of completing the task. However Professor Daniel H. Ḥ. Ingalls urged me to make a complete translation into English, and was kind enough to recommend the project to Harvard-Yenching Institute, whose director Professor John Pelzel generously interested himself in the matter. In 1967 and 1968 the Institute offered a grant towards the work of translating.

I count myself fortunate that with the help of many scholars I shall be able to bring the task to completion before long, though it has been an exacting one, almost amounting to a new work, with some chapters being re-written in English.

I wish to express my sincere gratitude to those who have kindly given me their collaboration in various points. This all too brief acknowledgement must suffice to express a deep appreciation of their generosity with time and trouble.

February, 1998.

Hajime Nakamura

Some portions of this work were formerly published in English, mostly in foreign journals, as follows:

1. "Early Vedāntic Scholars Subsequent to the Brahma-sūtra", *Studies in Indo-Asian Art and Culture, Commemoration Volume on the 69th Birthday of Acharya Raghu Vira*, vol. I, ed. by Perela Ratnam, New Delhi, The International Academy of Indian Culture, 1972, pp. 165-170.
2. "Tibetan Citation of Bhartṛhari's Verses and His Date", *Studies in Indology and Buddhology, Presented in Honour of Prof. S. Yamaguchi*, Kyoto, Hozokan Publishing Company, 1955, pp.122-136.
3. "Some Notes on the Māṇḍūkya-Upaniṣad and the First Chapter of the Māṇḍūkya-Kārikā", 『暁城趙明基博士追慕　仏教史学論文集』, 韓国ソウル, 東国大学出版部 1988, pp. 1-18.
4. "The Vijñānavāda Theory as Presented in the Fourth Chapter of the Māṇḍūkya-Kārikā", *Proceedings of the First International Sanskrit Conference*, Rashtriya Sanskrit Sansthan, vol. IV, 1981, pp. 185-206.
5. "Bhartṛhari and Buddhism", *Journal of the Ganganatha Jha Kendriya Sanskrit Vidyapeetha, Kshetresa Chandra Chattopadhyaya Felicitation Volume*, Allahabad, vol. XXVIII, Jan.-April, part II, 1972, pp. 395-406.
6. "Buddhist Influence upon the Vākyapadīya", *Journal of the Ganganatha Jha Kendriya Sanskrit Vidyapeetha, Ganganatha Jha Centenary Volume*, Allahabad, vol. XXIX, parts 1-4, 1973, pp. 367-388.
7. "Bhartṛhari the Scholar", *Indo-Iranian Journal*, vol. IV, no. 4, 1960, pp. 282-305.

In this Part Two, I added some appendices, which were written by me on Śaṅkara in English:

1. "A Conflict between Traditionalism and Rationalism: A Problem with Śaṅkara", *Philosophy East and West*, vol. XII, no. 2, July, 1962, pp. 153-161.
2. "Meditation in Śaṅkara, translated by T. Leggett", *The Journal of Religious Studies, Panjabi University*, vol. VII, no. 1, Spring, 1979, pp. 1-18.
3. "A Review of V. M. Apte's Brahma-sūtra Shankarabhāshya", *Journal of the American Oriental Society*, vol. LXXXI, no. 2, April-June, 1961,

pp. 141-142.

4. "An Interview with Śaṅkarāchārya, *The Jagadguru*, compiled by V. Raghavan", Madras, Jayachadra, June, 1965, pp. 55-70. ("Japanese Professor's Interview in the Achary's Call", *Madras Discourses*, 1957-1960, part I, compiled by V. Ramakrishna Aiyer, Madras, B. G. Paul & Co., 1971, pp. 227-237.)

On Śaṅkara, I published other papers:

1. "Practice of Selfless Action", *The Integral Philosophy of Sri Aurobindo, A Commemorative Symposium*, edited by Harisas Chaudhuri and Federic Spiegelberg, London, George Allen and Unwin, Ltd., 1960, pp. 223-230.
2. "Approches to the Upaniṣads: Swami Nikhilananda's The Upanishads", *Philosophy East and West*, vol. XI, no. 4, January, 1962, pp. 245-253.
3. Foreword to *Śaṅkara's Upadeśasāhasrī, critically edited with Introduction and Indices by Sengaku Mayeda*, Tokyo, Hokuseido Press, 1973, pp. ix-x.
4. "Weisheit und Erlösung durch Meditation, Ihr Sinn in der Philosophie Schankaras, Munen Muso, Ungegenständliche Meditation", *Fetschrift für Pater Hugo M. Enomiya-Lassalle SJ zum* 80 *Geburtstag*, hrg. von Gunter Stachel, Mainz, Matthias-Grunewald-Verlag, 1978, S. 52-63.

Some portions of the first volume of this work were formerly published in English, and they are mentioned in PREFACE (Part One, pp. viii-xi). Still there are some others that fell out of memory. Here I mention them:

1. "The Concept of Brahman in the Brahma-sūtra", *The Indo-Asian Culture*, published quarterly by the Indian Council for Cultural Relations, vol. XI, no. 2, Oct. 1960, pp. 176-186.
2. "Yājñavalkya and Other Upaniṣadic Thinkers in a Jaina Tradition", *The Adyar Library Bulletin, Dr. V. Raghavan Felicitation Volume*, vols. 31-31, 1967-1968, pp. 216-228.
3. "Bhāskara, the Vedāntin, in Buddhist Literature", *Annals of the Bhandarkar Oriental Research Institute, Golden Jubilee Volume*, vol.

XLVIII-XLIX, 1968, pp. 119-122.

4. "Kārṣṇājini and Kāṣakṛtsna", *The Journal of Oriental Research*, Madras, 1973, pp. 11-19.
5. "The Brahma-sūtra", *The Encyclopaedia of Sikkhism*, ed. by Harminder Singh Kohli, Patiala, Panjabi Universtiy.

ABBREVIATIONS AND SELECTED REFERENCES

AAA.	*Abhisamayālaṃkārāloka*, edited by Unrai Wogihara.
ABhI.	*Annals of the Bhandarkar Institute*, Poona.
Adyar L.B.	*Adyar Library Bulletin*, Madras.
AKV.	*Abhidharmakośavyākhyā*, edited by Unrai Wogihara.
Ān.	Ānandajñāna.
ĀnSS.	Ānandāśrama Sanskrit Series, Poona.
ĀpDhS.	*Āpastamba-Dharma-Sūtra.*
Aufrecht : *Bodl.Cat.*	Th. Aufrecht : *Catalogus Codicum MSS. Sanscriticorum Bibliothecae*, Bodleiane, Oxoni, 1859-64.
Aufrecht : *CC.*	Th. Aufrecht : *Catalogus Catalogorum*, 1891 ; II, 1896 ; 1903.
AV.	*Atharva-Veda.*
BB.	Bibliotheca Buddhica, Leningrad.
BCA.	*Bodhicaryāvatāra.*
BCAP.	*Bodhicaryāvatārapañjikā*, BI.
BEFEO.	*Bulletin de l'Ecole Francaise d'Extrême Orient.*
Belvalkar : *SSG.*	S. K. Belvalkar : *An Account of the different existing Systems of Sanskrit Grammar*, Poona, 1915.
Belvalkar : *Lectures.*	S. K. Belvalkar : *Shree Gopal Basu Mallik Lectures on Vedānta Philosophy*, Part 1, Poona, 1929.
BenSS.	Benares Sanskrit Series.
Bhag.G.	*Bhagavadgīta.* (Commentaries on it are cited from the edition by Wāsudev Laxmaṇ Shāstrī

	Paṇsīkar, NSP.).
Bhāgavata-Purāṇa.	*Le Bhāgavata Purāṇa on histoire poëtique de Krichṇa*, traduit et publiès par M. Eugène Burnouf, tome I-III, Paris, 1840-47. tome IV et V publiès par M. Hauvette-Besnault et. P. Roussel, Paris, 1848 et 1898.
Bhāmatī.	*The Brahmasūtra-Śaṅkarabhāṣyam with the Commmentaries Ratnaprabhā, Bhāmatī* and *Nyāyanirṇaya*, edited by Mahādeva Shāstri Bākre, NSP., 2nd edition, Bombay, 1909.
Bhandarkar *Coll. Works.*	*Collected Works of Sri R. G. Bhandarkar*, 4 vols. Government Oriental Series, Bhandarkar Oriental Research Institute, Class B, 1-4, Poona, 1933.
Bhāskara ad *BS.*	Bhāskara : *Brahmasūtra-bhāṣya,* ChowkhSS. 1903, 1913, 1915.
Bhattacharyya : *AS.*	*The Āgamaśāstra of Gauḍapāda*, tr. by Vidhushekhara Bhattacharyya, Calcutta, University of Calcutta, 1943.
BI.	Biblotheca Indica.
Br.	*Brāhmana.*
Bṛhad. Up.	*Bṛhadāraṇyaka-Upaniṣad.*
Bṛhad. Up. Vārttika.	Sureśvara : *Bṛhadāraṇyaka-Upaniṣad-Bhāṣya-Vārttika*, ĀnSS. No.16.
BS.	*Brahma-sūtra.*
BSOAS.	*Bulletin of the School of Oriental and African Studies*, London University.
BSS.	Bombay Sanskrit Series.
Bodhisattvabhūmi.	edited by Unrai Wogihara.
Buddhacarita.	*The Buddhacarita*, edited by E. H. Johnnston, Panjab University Oriental Publications, No.32.
Caraka-saṃhitā.	edited by Moti Lal Banarsi Das, Lahore, 1929.
Catuḥśatikā.	edited by Haraprasad Shasri, Memoirs, Asiatic Society of Bengal, Vol.III.

Chānd.Up.	*Chāndogya-Upaniṣad.*
ChowkhSS.	Chowkhambā Sanskrit Series, Benares.
Dasgupta : *HIPh.*	S. Dasgupta : *History of Indian Philosophy*, 5 Vols.
Deussen : *AGPh.*	P. Deussen : *Allgemeine Geschichte der Philosophie* I, 1-3, Leipzig, 1894f.
Deussen : *SV.*	P. Deussen : *System des Vedānta*, Leipzig, 1883.
D.N.	*Dīgha-Nikāya.*
Ghate : *The Vedānta.*	V. S. Ghate : *The Vedānta, A Study of the Brahma-sūtras with the Bhāṣyas of Śaṃkara, Rāmānuja, Nimbārka, Madhva* and *Vallabha*, Government Oriental Series, Class C, No.1., Poona 1926.
GK.	*Gauḍpādīya-Kārikā*, ĀnSS. No.10.
GOS.	Gaekwad's Oriental Series, Baroda.
Guha : *Jīvātman.*	Abhayakumar Guha : *Jīvātman in the Brahma-sūtras*, published by the University of Calcutta, 1921.
HOS.	Harvard Oriental Series, edited by Ch. A. Lanman.
IBK.	*Indogaku Bukkyogaku Kenkyu* (*Journal of Indian and Buddhist Studies*), Tokyo.
Ind.Ant.	*Indian Antiquary.*
IHQ.	*The Indian Historical Quarterly*, edited by Narendra Nath Law.
Jacob : *Concordance.*	Colonel G. A. Jacob : *A Concordance to the Principal Upanishads and Bhagavadgītā*, 1891.
JAOS.	*Journal of the American Oriental Society.*
JASB.	*Journal of the Asiatic Society of Bengal.*
JBRAS.	*Journal of the Bombay Branch of the Royal Asiatic Society.*
JORM.	*Journal of Oriental Research Madras.*
JRAS.	*Journal of the Royal Asiatic Society of Great Britain and Ireland.*

Kauṣ.Up.	*Kauṣītaki-Upaniṣad.*
KF.	O. Böhtlingk : *Sanskrit-Wöterbuch in Kürzerer Fassung*, St. Petersburg, 1879-89.
Laṅk.	*The Laṅkāvatāra-sūtra*, edited by Bunyu Nanjio.
MadhyK.	*Mūlamadhyamaka-Kārikās* (*Mādhyamika-sūtra*) *de Nāgārujuna avec la Prasannapadā, commentaire de Candrakīrti*, publiēe par L. de la Vallēe Poussin BB.IV, St. Pétersbourg, 1913.
Māṇḍ.Up.	*Māṇḍūkya-Upaniṣad.*
Mahābhāṣya.	*The Mahābhāṣya*, edited by F.Kielhorn, BSS. Nos. 18-22, 26, 28-30, 1906 ff.
Mahadevan : *GP.*	T. M. P. Mahadevan : *Gauḍapāda, A Study in Early Advaita*, Madras, 1952.
MAV.	*Madhyāntavibhāga.*
MAVṬ.	*Madhyāntavibhāga-Ṭīkā*, edited by Susumu Yamaguchi.
Max Müller : *ASL.*	F. Max Müller : *A History of Ancient Sanskrit Literature*, London 1859.
MBh.	*Mahābhārata*, Bombay Edition.
Mhvyut.	*Mahāvyutpatti*, edited by Unrai Wogihara.
Mit.	*Mitāksharā, A Gloss on Śri Gauḍapāda Āchārya's Māṇḍūkya Kārikās*, edited by Paṇḍita Ratna Gopāla Bhaṭṭa, Haridās Sanskrit Series, No.1, Benares 1910.
M.N.	*Majjima-Nikāya.*
MSA.	*Mahāyānasūtrālaṅkāra*, édité par Sylvain Levi, Bibliothēque de l'École des Hautes Études, tome 159, Paris, 1907.
Muṇḍ.Up.	*Muṇḍaka-Upaniṣad.*
Mvr.	*Madhyamakavṛtti.*
MW.	Sir Monier Monier-Williams : *A Sanskrit-English Dictionary*, Oxford, 1899.
Naiṣkarmyasiddhi.	ed. by G. A. Jacob, BSS. No.38,1.
Nṛs.Pū.Tāp.Up.	*Nṛsiṃha-pūrva-tāpanīya-Upaniṣad.*

Nṛs. Ut. Tāp. Up.	*Nṛsiṃha-uttara-tāpanīya-Upaniṣad.*
NSP.	Nirṇaya Sāgara Press, Bombay.
Nyāyabinduṭīkāṭippaṇī.	ed. by Th. Stcherbatskoi, BB.XI, St. Petersburg, 1909.
Nyāyabhāṣya.	ĀSS. No.91, 1922.
Nyāyamañjarī.	VizSS. No.5, 1895.
Nyāyasūtra.	W. Ruben: *Die Nyāyasūtras*, Leipzig, 1928.
Pañcapādikā.	VizSS. Vol.II, 1891, 1892.
Prameyakamalamārtaṇḍa.	NSP. 1912.
Prapañcahṛdaya.	ed. by T. Gaṇapati Sāstrī, TrivSS. No.45, 1915.
Prasthānabheda.	ĀnSS. No.51, 1928.
Proc. I (II, III) OC.	*Proceedings and Transactions of the First (Second, Third) Oriental Conference.*
PW.	O. Böhtling und R. Roth: *Sanskrit-Wörterbuch nebst allen Nachträgen*, St. Petersburg, 1855-1875.
Radhakrishnan: *IPh.*	S. Radhakrishnan: *Indian Philosophy*, 2 vols, London, 1923, 1927.
Ṛ.V.	*Ṛg-Veda.*
Ś.	Śaṅkara.
SaddhP.	*Saddharmapuṇḍarīka*, edited by Unrai Wogihara and K. Tsuchida.
Ś. ad *BS.*	Śaṅkara: *Brahmasūtra-bhāṣya*, ĀnSS. No.21, 1900.
Ś. ad *Up.*	Śaṅkara's *Bhāṣyas* on *Upaniṣads*, ĀnSS.
Saṃkṣepaśārīraka.	ĀnSS. No.83.
Sarvasiddhāntasanmraha.	ed. by Prem Sundar Bose, Calcutta, 1929.
Śat.Br.	*Śatapatha-Brāhmaṇa.*
SBE.	Sacred Books of the East, Oxford.
Scmidt: *Nachträge.*	R. Schmidt: *Nachträge zum Sanskrit-Wörterbuch in kürzerer Fassung von Böhtlingk*, Leipzig, 1924-1928.
SDS.	*The Sarvadarśanasaṃgraha of Sāyana-Mādhava*, ed. by Vasudev Shastri Abhyankar,

	Government Oriental Series, No.1, Poona, 1924.
SHA.	Sitzungsberichte der Heidelberger Akademie der Wissenschaften, Philosophishce-historische Klasse.
Siddhitraya.	ChowkhSS. No.36, 1900.
Ślokavārttika.	ChowkhSS. 1898-1899.
SPA.	Sitzungsberichte der Preussichen Akademie der Wissenschaften in Berlin.
Śrībhāṣya.	ed. by Vasudev Shastri Abhyankar, BSS. No.68, Bombay, 1914.
Śvet.Up.	*Śvetāśvatara-Upaniṣad.*
Tait.Ār.	*Taittirīya-Āraṇyaka.*
Tait.Saṃh.	*Taittirīya-Saṃhitā.*
Tait.Up.	*Taittirīya-Upaniṣad.*
Tattvasaṃgraha.	*Tattvasaṃgraha of Śāntarakṣita with the Commentary of Kamalaśīla*, ed. by Embar Krishnamacharya, 2 vols. GOS. No.30, Baroda, 1926.
Tibaut : *VS.*	G. Tibaut : *The Vedānta-sūtras*, SBE. vols. 34, 38.
Triṃśikā.	*Deux Traitès de Vasubandhu, Viṃśatikā (La Vingtaine) accompagnèe d'une explication en prose et Triṃśikā (La Trentaine) avec lacunae commentaire de Sthiramati*, publiè par Sylvain Lèvi, Paris, 1925.
TrivSS.	Trivandrum Sanskrit Series.
TT.	Taisho Tripiṭaka, ed. by J. Takakusu and K. Watanabe, Tokyo.
Up.	*Upaniṣad.*
Upadeśasāhasrī.	*Minor Works of Śaṅkarācārya*, ed. by Hari Raghunath Bhagavat, Poona, 1925, pp.295-350.
Vajr.Pr.	*Vajracchedikā-Prajñāpāramitā-sūtra*, ed. by F. Max Müller in "Buddhist Texts from Japan", Anecdota Oxoniensia, Aryan Series, I, 1, 1881.
Vāj.Saṃh.	*Vājasaneeyi-Saṃhitā.*

VākyaP.	*Vākyapadīya*, ed. with the commentary of Puṇyarāja and of Helarāja, BenSS. 1887-1907, 1928-1937.
Vedāntasāra.	O. Böhtlingk : *Sanskrit-Chrestomathie*, Commentaries on it are cited from G. A. Jacob's edition, NSP.
Vedārthasaṃgraha.	*The Vedārthasaṃgraha with the gloss called Tātparyadīpikā by Sundarśanasūri*, ed. by S. Sum. P. S. Rama Misra Sastri, Reprint from the Pandit, 2nd edition, Benares, 1924.
Viṃśatikā.	Cf. *Triṃśikā.*
Viṣṇusahasranāmābhāṣya.	*Minor Works of Śaṅkarācarya*, pp.505-584.
VizSS.	Vizianagaram Sanskrit Series.
Walleser : *DAV.*	Max Walleser : *Der ältere Vedānta, Geschichte, Kritik und Lehre*, Heidelberg, 1910.
Weber : *HIL.*	A. Weber : *History of Indian Literature*,. London, 1892.
Weber : *Ind.St.*	A. Weber : *Indische Studien.*
Winternitz : *GIL.*	M. Winternitz : *Geschichte der indischen Literatur*, 3 Bde. Leipzig, 1908-1920.
Winternitz : *HIL.*	M. Winternitz : *History of Indian Literature*, tr. by Mrs. S. Ketkar and revised by the author, Vol. I, Calcutta, 1927.
WZKM.	*Wiener Zeitschrift für die Kunde des Morgenlandes.*
Yogabhāṣya.	ĀnSS. No.47, 1932.
Yogavāsiṣṭha.	NSP.
YSViv.	Śaṅkarācārya's *Pātañjalayogasūtrabhāṣyavivaraṇa*, Published as No.94 in the Madras Government Oriental Series, Triplicane, Madras, 1952.
ZDMG.	*Zeitschrift der Deutshcen Morgenländischen Gesellschaft.*
ZII.	*Zeitschrift für Indologie und Iranistik.*

CONTENTS

A History of Early Vedānta Philosophy, Part Two

Appendices

PART V

THINKERS SUBSEQUENT TO THE *BRAHMA-SŪTRA*

CHAPTER I
GENERAL REMARKS

Almost nothing is known of the actual circumstances of either the Vedānta or the Mīmāṃsā schools prior to the composition of the *Brahma-sūtra*. And the state of affairs in the Vedānta school for a period of nearly 300 years, from the composition of the *Brahma-sūtra* (400–450) to the appearance of Śaṅkara (first half of 8th-century), is likewise unclear. This period, in fact, has so far been styled Dark Ages. Of writings of the Vedānta school during this period there are now extant only the *Māṇḍūkya-kārikā* traditionally said to be a work by Gauḍapāda and the *Vākyapadīya* written by the grammarian Bhartṛhari.[1] In addition to these two books, however, there must have been an enormous number of other writings turned out in this period, but unfortunately all of them have been scattered or lost and have not come down to us today. It is an unfortunate fact, therefore, that we are unable to know in more detail the thought of the great number of Vedānta philosophers belonging to this period. But as it happens, not a few of the doctrines and sayings peculiar to these pre-Śaṅkara thinkers are mentioned or noted in the works of the later schools, and I believe that by carefully selecting, collecting and studying comparatively these remaining references, we should be able to clarify the general contours of the lost history of thought of this period. To be sure, such studies have already been conducted, but here I would like to take these efforts further by comparing the most recent research, gathering all the new resources and data, and attempting to construct a rough, but systematic, sketch of the history of thought as found in the period under discussion.

One extremely fortunate fact is, that the names of the important thinkers of this period have been listed in the *Siddhitraya*, a work by Yāmunācārya (c.1050), as well as in the *Vedārthasaṃgraha* written by Rāmānuja (c.1050–1157), and in the *Yatīndramatadīpikā* by Śrīnivāsa-dāsa. To begin with, Yāmunācārya has recorded the following.

yady api Bhagavatā Bādarāyaṇena idamarthāny eva sūtrāṇi praṇītāni, vivṛtāni ca tāni parimitagambhīrabhāṣiṇā bhāṣyakṛtā, vistṛtāni ca tāni gambhīranyāyasāgarabhāṣiṇā Bhagavatā Śrīvatsāṅkamiśreṇāpi tathāpi Ācārya-Ṭaṅka-Bhartṛprapañca-Bhartṛmitra-Bhartṛhari-Brahmadatta-Śaṇkara-Śrīvatsāṅka-Bhāskarādiviracitasitāsitavividhanibandhanaśraddhā-vipralabdhabuddhayo na yathāvad anyathā ca pratipadyanta iti tat-pratipattaye ca yuktaḥ prakaraṇaprakramaḥ/(*Siddhitraya*, p.5)

"For the sake of this objective, the *sūtras* were written by Bhagavat Bādarāyaṇa; they were then explained by the author of the *bhāṣya*, which expressed tersely their profound meaning; this was explained in detail by Bhagavat Śrīvatsāṅkamiśra who declared the truth profound as the ocean. Nevertheless people, whose minds have become confused because they relied upon the works, both good and bad, written by the masters Ṭaṅka, Bhartṛprapañca, Bhartṛmitra, Bhartṛ-hari, Brahmadatta, Śaṅkara, Śrīvatsāṅka and Bhāskara, have not understood it correctly and have embraced different views. It is therefore proper to begin [this] treatise (i. e. the *Siddhitraya*) for the sake of a true understanding of those (*sūtras*)".

Rāmānuja also lists the names of the leading masters in the academic tradition of his own school:

Bhagavad-Bodhāyana-Ṭaṅka-Dramiḍa-Guhadeva-Kapardi-Bhāruci-prabhṛty-avigītaśiṣṭaparigṛhītapurātana-Veda-Vedānta-vyākhyānasuvyaktār-thaśrutinikaranidarśito 'yaṃ panthāḥ/ (*Vedārthasaṃgraha*, p.154)[2]

"This path is declared in many holy texts, whose meaning had been made very clear by the ancient commentaries on the Veda and Vedānta, accepted by masters such as the Bhagavats Bodhāyana, Ṭaṅka, Dramiḍa, Guhadeva, Kapardi, and Bhāruci, who have never advocated heretical teachings".

Śrīnivāsa-dāsa was much later than these first two writers, so what he has said may not have so much value as source material, but insofar as he does pass on traditional accounts I think that we should at least look into his work. In his *Yatīndramatadīpikā*, we find the names of the masters of his school listed in this order: Vyāsa, Bodhāyana, Guhadeva, Bhāruci, Brahmānandin, Draviḍācārya, Śrī-Parāṅkuśanātha, Yāmunamuni and Yatīśvara.[3]

The arrangement of names in the lists given above may, it seems, refer either to the order of importance or to the *chronological order* of the masters.[4] And the three accounts we have given above form, for the most part, a mutually consistent tradition. Guided by the arrangement of the names of the scholars listed in the foregoing, we are now able to form a chart of their sequential relation, which we shall show below.

[Śrīnivāsa's Tradition]
Vyāsa
↓
Bodhāyana
↓
Guhadeva
↓
Bhāruci
↓
Brahmānandin
↓
Draviḍārya
↓
Śrī-Parāṅkuśānātha
↓
Yāmunamuni[5]
↓
Yatīśvara (i.e. Rāmānuja)

[Rāmānuja's Tradition]
Bodhāyana
↓
Ṭaṅka
↓
Dramiḍa
↓
Guhadeva
↓
Kapardin
↓
Bhāruci

[Yāmuna's Version of the Orthodox Tradition]
Bādarāyaṇa
↓
Bhāṣyakṛt (i.e. Dramiḍa)
↓
Śrīvatsāṅka
↓
Yāmuna

[Yāmuna's Version of the Heretical Theories]
Ṭaṅka
↓
Bhartṛprapañca
↓
Bhartṛmitra
↓
Bhartṛhari
↓
Brahmadatta
↓
Śaṅkara
↓
Śrīvatsāṅka
↓
Bhāskara

We are now in a position to enumerate, as shown in the chart, the following nine men as thinkers belonging to the period of early Vedānta philosophers prior to Śaṅkara, and thus coming within the purview of the present work.

1. Bādarāyaṇa (i.e. Vyāsa)
2. Bodhāyana
3. Ṭaṅka (Brahmānandin)
4. Dramiḍa (The Commntator, Bhāṣyakṛt)
5. Bhartṛprapañca
6. Bhartṛmitra
7. Bhartṛhari
8. Brahmadatta
9. Śrīvatsāṅka

It can be supposed that Guhadeva was perhaps earlier than Śāṅkara, and that Bhāruci lived around the same time as Sureśvara,[6] but the exact chronological relationship with Śaṅkara is uncertain and I shall put the point aside for the time being.

In the foregoing we have noted the names of early Vedānta thinkers which appeared in the work of the religious system of the Śrī-Vaiṣṇava school, and in the philosophical system of 'Qualified Non-dualism' (Viśiṣṭādvaita), but we have, in addition, the names and dates of others which have been handed down in other sources (the works of the Non-dualistic school, the Buddhist Canon etc.).

Combining all these together, we can know that at least the following fourteen thinkers lived between the time of composition of the *Brahma-sūtra* and the appearance of Śaṅkara. Their names are given below.[7]

Compilation of the *Brahma-sūtra*	c.400-450.
1. Bhartṛhari	c.450-500.
2. Upavarṣa	c.450-500.
3. Bodhāyana	c.500.
4. Ṭaṅka (Brahmānandin)	c.500-550.
5. Draviḍa	c.550.
6. Bhartṛprapañca	c.550.
7. Śabarasvāmin	c.550.

8. Bhartṛmitra c.550-600.
9. Śrīvatsāṅka c.600.
10. Sundarapāṇḍya c.600.
11. Brahmadatta c.600-700.
12. Gauḍapāda c.640-690.
13. Govinda c.670-720.
14. Maṇḍanamiśra c.670-720.
Śaṅkara c.700-750.

The names given in this list are, I believe, in the general order of date. The works of Gauḍapāda and Bhartṛhari, who appear in the list, have survived up to the present, and we shall take up our discussion on then particularly in parts VI and VII respectively. (The works of Maṇḍanamiśra have also been handed down to the present day, but he should be taken to have lived around the same time as Śaṅkara and ought rather to be studied in relation to both Śaṅkara and Sureśvara; therefore in this work we shall confine ourselves to no more than an introduction to the studies on him.) Since no works of the others remain in existence today, we cannot chose but collect and note the quotations or descriptions related to them and their doctrines.

Notes

1) We postpone a detailed examination of these two works to later Parts VI and VII.

2) van Buitenen's edition, 93, pp.128, 251,. in the latter edition the word Bhagavat is not mentioned.

3) *Yatīndramatadīpikā* (Ānss.No.50) p.2. R.Otto, however, has Bhāṇaruci and Draviḍācārya (*Dīpikā des Nivāsa*, S.1), while R.G.Bhandarkar (*Report*, 1883-4, i.e. *Collected Works*, II, p.187) lists Bhāruci and Dramiḍācārya. According to Bhandarkar, again, Yatīśvara is thought to refer to Rāmānuja.

4) In the footnotes to the published edition of the *Siddhitraya*, it is noted that this list of names follows *avasthitikālakrama*.

5) Cf. Gerhard Oberhammer : *Yāmunamunis interpretation von Brahmasūtram 2,2,42-45. Eine Untersuchung zur Pāñcarātra-Tradition der Rāmānuja-Schule*. Österreichische Akademie der Wissenschaften, Philosophisch-historische Klasse, Sitzungaberichte, 274 Band, 4. Abhandlung. Wien usw. : Hermann Böhlaus Nachf. 1971.

6) In the *Mitākṣarā* (a commentary on the law-book *Yājñavalkya-smṛti*) by Vijñāneśvara,

it is noted that Bhāruci, Viśvarūpa, and others advocated different theories concerning the rules for marital relations (R. G. Bhandarkar : *Collected Works* II, pp.252,258, "Age of Marriage and its Consummation"). It is said (Bhattacharyya : *AS.* CIX) that Bhāruci's theories appear in the *Mitākṣarā* on the *Yājñavalkya-smṛti*(I,18 ; II,124) and in Mādhava's *ṭikā* on the *Parāśara-saṃhitā* (II,2.3, BSS. p.510). Bhāruci was prior to Vijñāneśvara who lived in the latter half of the 11th century (Winternitz : *GIL.* III. p. 499). Viśvarūpa is generally considered in India to be another name of Sureśvara (Dasgupta : *HIPh.* II. pp.82-83). It has always been a conspicuous fact in India from ancient times that there exists a close relationship between the study of the Mīmāṃsā and jurisprudence, and since both Bhāruci and Viśvarūpa are mentioned in the Vedānta works and the treatises on law, we may perhaps conclude that when the same personal name is mentioned in these different works, it is probably the same man. In that case Bhāruci would have lived, I take it, around the same time as Sureśvara, in the middle of the 8th century, or not too far from that. Rāmānuja places Guhadeva and Bhāruci after Draviḍa, while Śrīnivāsa puts them before him, but I think we should for the time being adopt the tradition given of by the earlier Rāmānuja.

7) Their respective dates will be discussed in the appropriate chapters in this book.

CHAPTER II

TIBETAN CITATIONS OF BHARTṚHARI'S VERSES AND THE PROBLEM OF HIS DATES

In 1936, Dr. S. Yamaguchi pointed out the fact that some verses of a Vedāntin called Bhadrahari or something near to that are mentioned in the Tibetan version of some philosophical works of later Mahāyāna Buddhism.[1] I wish here to go into this question, collecting Tibetan verses ascribed to this Vedāntin, and collating some of them with Sanskrit originals as I have been able to identify them.

Let us begin with the following verse, cited in the Tibetan version of the *Mahāyāna-sūtrālaṃkāra-ṭīkā*,[2] a commentary by No-bo-ñid med-pa (=Asvabhāva) upon the *Mahāyāna-sūtrālāṃkāra* :

(fr.1) *Bha dri ha ri* [*s*] *ji skad du/*
nam mkhaḥ sa rluṅ ñi ma daṅ//
rgya mtsho gliṅ daṅ phyogs rnams ni/
naṅ gi śes paḥi ṅo bo yi//
cha las phyi rol lta bur ḥdug/
ces bśad pa lta bu yin no//

ḥdzin paḥi don las bzuṅ baḥi don tha mi dad mthoṅ baḥo//shes bya ba ni gzuṅ ba daṅ ḥdzin paḥi rnam par śes pa kho nar zad kyi rnam par śes pa la ma rtogs pa byis pas kun brtags pa mig la sogs pa ḥdsin paḥi don ni yod pa ma yin no shes bya bar te/deḥi phyir don du snaṅ ba thams cad sems kho na yin par ltaḥi/don sems las gshan par ni mi blta ḥo//deḥi tshe ni ḥdiḥi gzuṅ ba la rnam par gyeṅ pa spaṅs la ḥdzin paḥi rnam par rtog pa ḥbaḥ shig lus te/de ni bzod paḥi gnas skabs yin no/

"As was declared by Bhadrahari ... Ether, earth, wind, the sun, the sea, continents and directions ... they exist like external things, having been manifested from the innermost proper portions of the interior intelligence (= *adhyātma-jñāna*)."

Then follows Asvabhāva's annotation, in which he says, "So everything which has been manifested as an object is regarded as nothing but mind, and objects are not regarded as separate from mind." So we can assuredly conclude that Asvabhāva himself recognized in Bhadrahari's assertion something similar to the thought of Buddhist Idealism (*vijñaptimātratā*).

The Sanskrit original of the above-cited Tibetan verse is the following one:

dyauḥ kṣamāvāyur ādityaḥ sāgarāḥ sarito diśaḥ/
antaḥkaraṇatattvasya bhāgā bahir avasthitāḥ// *Vākyapadīya*, III,7,41 (p. 200)[3)]

"Heaven (Space), Earth, Air, Sun, Oceans, Rivers, Positions (Directions) are all parts of an inner Reality, manifested externally". (Iyer's translation, p.172).

(Cf. *antaḥkaraṇadharmo vā bahir evaṃ prakāśate / ibid.*, III, 6, 23. p. 170).

In the *Ārya-laṅkāvatāra-vṛtti* by Jñānaśrībhadra there are the following verses.

(fr.2) *de bas na Bha dra ha ris byed pa bstan pa las smras pa/*
grub daṅ ma grub ji sñed pa/
bsgrub paḥi phyir ni bstan par bya/
rten paḥi rim (23b) gyi raṅ bsin phyir/
de ni byed par brjod pa ho//
ṣes pa ste/byed pa dpyad zin to//

"Therefore it has been declared in a treatise written by Bhadrahari--- In so far as a thing attained or a thing not yet attained should be denoted in order to be established, on account of its essence being the order to be resorted to, it is declared to be an action."

(=*yāvat siddham asiddhaṃ vā sādhyatvenābhidhīyate/*)
āśritakramarūpatvāt kriyeti pratīyate//)[4)]

"Whenever something, finished or unfinished, is presented as something to be accomplished, it is called 'action', because of its having assumed the form of sequence." (Iyer's translation).

(Cf. *kriyāyāḥ pariniṣpattir yad vyāpārād anantaram/*
vivakṣyate yadā tatra karaṇatvaṃ tadā smṛtam//(*Vākyapadīya* III, 7, b, 89. p.237.)

(fr.3)[5)] *tshaṅs par smra ba po bha ta ha ri la sogs pa yaṅ smra ba/*

thog ma med paḥi tshaṅs pa rtag/
yaṅ dag sgra ni yig ḥbru gaṅ/
gaṅ las don dṅos ḥbyuṅ ba daṅ/
ḥgro baḥi rab tu byed pa yaṅ//

(fr.4) *gaṅ yoṅs rtogs pa thams cad la/*
(127a) *snaṅ bar yaṅ ni mi gnas te/*
rtog pa luṅ daṅ rjes dpag pas/
rnam pa du mar kun brtags paḥo//

(fr.5) *ḥdas kyaṅ ḥdu ḥdzi byed pa daṅ/*
dṅos daṅ dṅos med rim mi rim/
bden daṅ brdzun par sna tshogs bdag/
dben pa las ni rab tu snaṅ//

(fr.6) *ḥbyuṅ po rnams kyi naṅ rgyu ba/*
ḥgran daṅ rim duḥaṅ snaṅ ba ste/
thar pa rab tu grol ba de/
grol ḥdod rnams kyis bstan par byed//

(fr.7) *de yi tshor ba gcig po yaṅ/*
rnam pa maṅ por rab tu ḥbyed/
ḥjig pa ḥbyuṅ baḥi me mdag daṅ/
chu yi phuṅ por chu bshin du//

(fr.8) *de phyir da rod rigs gnas pa/*
gsal baḥi groṅ rnams ḥbyur ba ni/
spriṅ rnams char daṅ ldan pa rnams/
rluṅ las ḥbyuṅ ba bshin duḥo//

(fr.9) *gstum gyi gzugs su de snaṅ ba/*
mur smra tha dad rnams la ni/
mchog gi yoṅs su ḥgyur ba ste/
lta ba tha dad kyis ni bciṅs//

(fr.10) *shi shiṅ rigs bdag tshaṅs pa ste/*
de las byuṅ baḥi ma rig pa/
des ni srin po bshin du med/
gaṅ smra mi nus rnam dag go//

(fr.11) *ji ltar nam mkhaḥ rnam dag par/*
rab rib ḥkhrul paḥi skyes bu yis/

ri mo rnam pa sna tshogs kyis/
kun tu gaṅ bar sems pa pa//
de ltar tshaṅs pa bdud rtsi ḥdi/
ḥgyur ba med pa ma rig pas/
rñog pa lta bur byas pas na/
tha dad gzugs su snaṅ ba ste//
(fr.12) *lha sa rluṅ daṅ nam mkhaḥ daṅ/*
ri daṅ chu daṅ phyogs rnams kyaṅ/
naṅ du byed paḥi yaṅ dag gi/
cha rnams phyi rol bshin du gnas//
(fr.13) *tshul ni gcig ñid gaṅ yin las/*
tha dad mthu ni rnam gnas pas/
mthu las tha dad ma yin yaṅ/
tha dad bshin du ḥbyuṅ baḥo//
(fr.14) *tshaṅs sgraḥi ḥdi ni sprul pa ste/*
sgra yi mthu las gnas pas na/
sgra tsam las ni byuṅ ba yaṅ/
de dag ñid du sha bar ḥgyur//
(fr.15) *rab tu byed pa gcig ḥbyed la/*
maṅ por rab tu phye ba pa/
de ni (127*b*) *luṅ ston rtogs pa las/*
tshaṅs pa mchog ni chud par ḥgyur//
shes rgya cher ro//

Translation : Bhatahari and others who are *brahmavādins*, also say :

(fr.3) "The beginingless, eternal *Brahman*, whose essence is Word and syllable (*akṣara*, undestructable)..., from That, things have evolved, and the function of the world also has appeared."

(=*anādinidhanam brahma śabdatattvaṃ yad akṣaram/*
vivartate 'rthabhāvena prakriyā jagato yataḥ// Vākyapadīya I,1.

"The *Brahman* who is without beginning or end, whose very essence is the Word, who is the cause of the manifested phonemes, who appears as the objects, from whom the creation of the world proceeds" (Iyer's translation).

(fr.4) "Whatever has appeared by dint of imaginary assumption (*pari-*

kalpa) dose not abide. Imaginary assumptions appear in various forms by dint of ratiocination (*tarka, vitarka*), scriptural dogma (*āgama*) and reasoning (*anumāna*)." (Cf. *Vākyapadīya* II,v.143, p.140 ; III,4,1-2, p.139 ; III,14,v.199, p.550)

(fr.5) "Separation and connection (*saṃsarga*), being (*bhāva*) and non-being (*abhāva*), order (temporal sequence) and non-order (simultaneity), truth and falsehood, various things are manifested from *Ātman*, the Truth."

(Cf. *avirodhī virodhī vā sann asan vāpi tattvataḥ/*
kramavān akramo vāpi nābhāva upapadyate// Vākyapadīya III,3,66, p. 130) (Cf. II,317, p.214) (III,3,67, Limaye's edition, p.79). (*tattvataḥ* is read *yuktitaḥ* in Limaye's edition.)

The Sanskrit original of the above-mentioned fragment No.5 is found in the commentary by Vṛṣabhadeva upon the *Vākyapadīya.*

vyatīto bheda-saṃsargau bhāvābhāvau kramākramau
satyānṛte ca viśvātmā pravivekāt prakāśate/ Vṛṣabhadeva's commentary on *Vākyapadīya*, Kāṇḍa I (Poona,1966, p.10)

This is an anonymous verse cited in Vṛṣabhadeva's commentary on *Vākyapadīya* (ed. by Carudeva Śāstri, Lahore 1937, p. 7) (Paur Hacker: *Vivarta. Studien zur Geschichte der illusonistischen Kosmologlie und Erkenntnistheorie der Inder*. Akademie der Wissenschaften und der Literatur. Abhandlungen der Geistes- und sozialwissenschaftlichen Klasse, Jahrgang. 1953. Nr.5. S.205.) Dr. Hacker takes this anonymous verse for a later development. Taking the above-cited Tibetan version into consideration, however, the present writer thinks that this verse also should be ascribed to Bhartṛhari. I should like to express sincere gratitude to Dr. Hacker for so kindly sending me copies of his valuable researches. Professor Hacker thinks that the attitude of tolerating contradictory opinions derives from Vṛṣabhadeva, but it virtually derives from Bhartṛhari himself according to Jñānaśrībhadra.

"Non-existence can rationally be neither opposed nor non-opposed [to existence] can be neither existent nor non-existent, neither have sequence nor not have it" (Iyer's translation)

(fr.6) "[It is] the internal cause of beings (*bhūta*), which put forth effort and appear in time (temporal sequence). Deliverance is to be saved and released. This is taught by those who wish for deliverance."

(fr.7) "The sensation (*vedanā*) of it is divided in a uniform and multiform way. It is like water in contrast with the multitude of waters and like flames which flare and vanish." (Cf. *Vākyapadīya* II, 252 ; 480)

(fr.8) "Therefore a man who now belongs to a superior clan becomes [a member] of a distinctive family (*kula*) as when many clouds bearing water are born of winds."

(fr.9) "It appears in three forms. To [those thinkers who adhere to] various extremes, it (=one of these) becomes the supreme one. They are bound by various heretical opinions (*dṛṣṭi*)."

(fr.10) "*Brahman* is *Ātman*, which is to be known by tranquility, and from which ignorance (*avidyā*) appears. By means of it [it] does not exist like *rākṣas* (demons), which are of such a nature as can not be explained."

(fr.11) "Even though *Ākāśa* (Space) is pure, yet obsessed by darkness, people come to regard it as limited and made up of diversified parts ; in the same manner, though *Brahman* is immortal and unmodifiable, yet It appears to be sullied by Nescience and hence diversely modified." (Ganganatha Jha's translation)

(The Sanskrit verse corresponding to this verse and parallel verses are found in several works. We shall discuss it later.)

(fr.12) "Gods (*deva*), earth, the wind, the other, mountains, water and directions are what the internal essential portion has manifested as if they were things external." (Cf. fr.1.)

(fr.13) "Whereas there exist various potentialities (*śakti*) different from the entity of one form, yet that is not different from potentialities. They appear as if they were different."[6)]

(≒*ekam eva yad āmnātam bhinnaṃ śaktivyapāśrayāt* /
apṛthaktve 'pi śaktibhyaḥ pṛthaktveneva vartate // *Vākyapadīya* I, 2.)

"Who has been taught as the One appearing as many due to the multiplicity of his powers ; who, though not different from his powers, seems to be so." (Iyer's translation)

(Cf. *Vākyapadīya* II,v.22,p.78 ; v.25,p.79 ; v.476,p.279 ; III,1,v.20,p.23 ; III,14, v.567.p.714.)

(fr.14) "This is the transformation (emanation) of *śabdabrahman*. Abiding by the potentialities of Words, they become tranquil in themselves, although they have arisen from Words alone."

(≒*śabdasya pariṇāmo 'yam ity āmnāyavido viduḥ/*

chandobhya eva prathamam etad viśvaṃ vyavartata[7] // *Vākyapadīya* I, 121. (I,120. Abhyankar-Limaye's edition, p.11)

"Knowers of tradition (the *Vedas*) have declared that all this is the transformation of the word. It is from the *chandas* that the universe has evolved" (Iyer's translation) (Cf. *Vākyapadīya* II,31.p.82)

(fr.15) "As the one entity is divided into many by means of various creative processes, the highest *Brahman* will be attained by resorting to [the science of] grammar."

(=*yad ekaṃ prakriyābhedair bahudhā pravibhajyate/)*

tad vyākaraṇam āgamya paraṃ brahmādhigamyate// Vākyapadīya I,22)

"That which, though one, is variously interpreted in the different traditions, that supreme *Brahman* is attained by a knowledge of Grammar." (Iyer's translation)

So the problem has been discussed in detail.

(fr.16)(42.138a[8]) *de bṣin du nam mkhaḥi yaṅ nam mkhaḥi kho na ste/*

bro ba la sogs pa du ma daṅ sbyor bas yul tha dad par brtags pa ste/

maṅ poḥi gnas na nam mkhhhaḥi kho naḥo shes bha dra ha ris smras pa ḥo//

"Likewise there exists ether alone for ether, the object (place) is regarded as differing with adjuncts and with desires of various kinds. Although there exist many things in ether, there is ether alone in reality. ... So spoke Bhadrahari."

(=*saṃyogidharmabhedena deśe ca parikalpite/*

teṣu deśeṣu sāmānyam ākāśasyāpi vidyate// Vākyapadīya III,1,15.p.20)

"Once parts are postulated on the basis of the properties of the different objects with which space (*ākāśa*) is in contact, the universal of space also is found in these parts." (Iyer's translation)

(42.138b-139a) *mtshan ñid kyi tshig ces bya ni smra ba rnams kyi rjod paḥi don du ḥbyed pas na rtsod pa yaṅ maṅ ste/yi ge ma gtogs tshig gshan ni//yod pa ma yin brjod pa ni/yi ge thshig ni ma gtogs par*(139 a) *ste/Bhadra haris bśad pa/*

(fr.17) *smras paḥi sgra kyaṅ ḥdus pa ni/*
rigs ni ḥjug par ḥgyur ba ste/
gcig bu yan lag med paḥi sgra/
blo yis rigs su bsdu ba ho//

(fr.18) *thog maḥi tshig ni so sor kun/*
bltos daṅ bcas te de ltar yaṅ/
brjod paḥi phyir ni tha dad blo/
tshul smra rnams kyi rnam pa maṅ//shes te/

"Bhadrahari says:

(fr.17) "Spoken Words, having been gathered, are classified into classes (*jāti*). A single, undifferentiated word is put in a class by the mind [of hearers]."

(= *svā jātiḥ prathamaṃ śabdaiḥ sarvair evābhidhīyate/*
tato 'rthajātirūpeṣu tadadhyāropakalpanā// Vākyapadīya III,1,6.)

"All words first express their own universal which is then thought of as being superimposed on the universals of the meanings." (Iyer's translation)

(fr.18) "The first syllables (*akṣara*) have each of them something to be seen [visible aspect] and express [meaning] in such a way, that the capability [of hearers to interpret them] is multiple. There are many kinds of those expressing ways."

(≒ *ekasminn api dṛśye 'rthe darśanaṃ bhidyate pṛthak/*
kālāntareṇa vaiko 'pi taṃ paśyaty anyathā punaḥ//
ekasyāpi ca śabdasya nimittair avyavasthitaiḥ/
ekena bahubhiś cārtho bahudhā parikalpyate// Vākyapadīya II,138; 139, pp.138-139). (II,136; 137. Limaye's edition, p.27.)

"With regard to the same thing, one's views undergo change. The same person sees the same thing differently at different times. To one and the same word are attributed many meanings by one and the same person or by many persons according to undefined circumstances." (Iyer's translation) (Cf. *Vākyapadīya* II,v.33.p.82)

Bhavya, the Mādhyamika philosopher, commenting upon Nāgārjuna's

Madhyamaka-śāstra IX, 3 cites the following verse:[8]

(a..............

(fr.19) *loṅ ba rkaṅ paḥi tshod dpags kyis/*
ñam ṅaḥi lam du rgyug pa ltar/
rjes su dpag pa gtsor ḥdsin pa/
rnam par ltuṅ ba mi dkaḥo//
..............a)

shes bya ba lta bur ḥgyur ro she na/de ni rigs pa ma yin te/

Avalokitavrata comments upon this as follows:

don de ñid bsal bar bya baḥi phyir slob dpon bha ṅdri ha ris rjes su dpag pa sun phyuṅ baḥi khuṅs bstan paḥi phyir/(a. . . a) *shes bya ba smras te/dper na loṅ ba rkaṅ paḥi tshod dpag gis lam bde ba spaṅs te ñam ṅaḥi lam du rgyug pa śiṅ la sogs pa dag gis brdos pa la rdeg ḥchaḥ śiṅ rnam par ltuṅ ba mi dkaḥ ba de bshin du/ yid ches paḥi luṅ spaṅs pa rjes su dpag paḥi tshod dpag gis rtog ge skam poḥi lam du rgyug pa dag kyaṅ tshe ḥdi la yaṅ ḥkhrul paḥi gcod par ḥgyur la/tshe phyi ma la yaṅ ḥbras bu mi ḥdod par rnam par ltuṅ bar ḥgyur ro shes zer ro/*

The Sanskrit original of the cited verse seems to have been the following:

hastasparśādibādhena viṣame(=girimārge, Comm.) *'py abhidhāvatā/*
anumānapradhānena vinipāto na durlabhaḥ// Vākyapadīya I,42.

"Just as a [blind] man who is running quickly on a dangerous pass [in the mountains] may fall down if he fails to cling by hand, so it is not impossible for a man who chiefly relies upon his own reasoning (lit. inference) to fall down [into a hell]."

The Tibetan version seems to have a free translation for the first quarter of the verse. Bhartṛhari asserted that the knowledge derived from scriptures alone is of absolute value, whereas that derived from other sources is of relative value. He denounced the validity of reasoning. (Cf. *Vākyapadīya* I,30; 31; 41, etc.)

Among the above-mentioned verses, fr.1 and fr.12 are nearly identical to each other. It is likely that the same original verse was cited in a slightly different way, as was mentioned, by the two scholars Asvabhāva and Jñānaśrībhadra, who lived in different periods. It is noteworthy that we can find the apparent Sanskrit originals of some of the fragments in the *Vākyapadīya* of Bhartṛhari. As for some other fragments, also we find in this work verses of similar purport, as has been pointed out by the writer.

Moreover, we should add that a verse which might be regarded as the original of fr.11 is cited in the *Tattvasaṃgrahapañjikā*[9] of Kamalaśīla. In the *Śabdabrahmaparīkṣā* of the *Tattgvasaṃgraha* by Śāntarakṣita, the doctrine which assumes *śabda-brahman* as the world-principle is attacked. Kamalaśīla, the commentator, explains that the author attacks Bhartṛhari's doctrine in the verses beginning with v.128, and that he attacks 'the doctrine of the opponent' (*paramata*) in the verses beginning with v. 144. As an instance of the latter, the writes as follows:

yatoktaṃ

yathā viśuddham ākāśaṃ timiropapluto janaḥ/
saṃkīrṇam iva mātrābhiś citrābhir abhimanyate//
tathedam amṛtam brahma nirvikāram avidyayā/
kaluṣatvam ivāpannam bhedarūpaṃ vivartataḥ//

ji skad du/

ji ltar nam mkhaḥ dag pa la/
rab rib kyis bslad skye bo yin/
rab rib sna tshogs dag daṅ ni/
ldan pa bshin du mṅon par rlom//
de ltar bdud rtsi ḥgyur med paḥi/
tshaṅs pa ḥdi ni ma rig pas/
rñog pa bshin du ḥgyur ba ste/
tha dad ṅo bor rnam par ḥgyur//

she bśad pa lta buḥo/[10]

(In the Sanskrit original of the foregoing Tibetan version, the final word seems to have been *vivartate* instead of *vivartataḥ*.)

Ganganatha Jha's translation:

"This has been thus declared: ... Even though *Ākāśa* (Space) is pure, yet obsessed by darkness, people come to regard it as limited and made up of diversified parts; in the same manner, though *Brahman* is immortal and unmodifiable, yet It appears to be sullied by Nescience and hence diversely modified".[11]

The foregoing verses, moreover, nearly completely correspond to two verses of the *Bṛhadāraṇyakopaniṣad-bhāṣya*[12] by Sureśvara, a disciple of Śaṅkara. (In the latter, *amalam* occurs instead of *amṛtam, prakāśate* instead of *vivartataḥ, upalakṣayet* instead of *abhimanyate*; otherwise the passages completely the same.) These two verses are also cited by Prabhācandra, the Jain scholar, in a passage of the *Prameyakamala-mārtaṇḍa* where he criticizes[13] the doctrine of the *śabdabrahmavādins*. (In this text, *amalam* occurs instead of *amṛtam, bhedarūpaṃ prapaśyati* instead of *bhedarūpaṃ vivartaḥ*). Once again, the same verse is cited by Abhayadeva, the Jain scholar, in his work *Tattvabodhavidhāyini* (p.388), as a doctrine of the *śabdabrahmavādins* (*amalam* instead of *amṛtam, vivartate* instead of *vivartataḥ*.)[14] Most strikingly, in the commentary (*vṛtti*) by Bhaṭṭa-Nārāyaṇakaṇṭha upon the *Mṛgendrāgama*, a very important fundamental scripture of the Śaivas, those verses are ascribed to Bhartṛhari, who is characterized as a *vivartavādin*, as follows:[15]

tathā cāha tatra bhavān Bhartṛhariḥ...

yathā viśuddham ākāśaṃ timiropapluto janaḥ/
saṃkīrṇam iva mātrābhiś citrābhir abhimanyate//
tathedam amṛtaṃ brahma nirvikāram avidyayā/
kaluṣatvam ivāpannaṃ bhedarūpe pravartate//

evaṃ cābhinnam evedaṃ paraṃ brahma paramātmalakṣaṇam, manasāṃ hi saṃsāradharmaiḥ sukhaduḥkhādibhir yogaḥ/paramātmā tu sūrya ivāmbhaḥpratibimbabhedair upādhibhir abhinno 'pi bhinna iva pratibhāti/

The Sanskrit text by Nārāyaṇakaṇṭha seems to be the least corrupt form of the original verse.[16] These verses seem to be of the same purport as the *Māṇḍūkya-kārikā* III,8.

yathā bhavati bālānāṃ gaganaṃ malinaṃ malaiḥ/
tathā bhavaty abuddhānām ātmāpi malino malaiḥ//

"As the sky appears to be soiled with dirt to the ignorant, so appears *Ātman*, too, with impurities, to those who are not enlightened".[17]

The same view was shared by Śaṅkara also.[18]

What is most striking from the view point of the history of ideas is that verses very similar to the foregoing are given by Dignāga, the Buddhist philosopher, in vv.31-32 of his *Trikālaparīkṣā* as follows:[19]

ji ltar nam mkhaḥ rnam dag la/
rab rib kyis ni bslad paḥi mi/
skra śad kyis ni kun gaṅ ltar/
sna tshogs su ni mṅon par rtogs//31
de ltar ḥdir yaṅ rnam śes ni/
rnam par mi ḥgyur ma rig pas/
chu rño̧g bshin du shugs pa ni/
tha dad gzugs su rnam par ḥjug//32

[Some noteworthy differences: *skra śad kyis* (*keśoṇḍukaiḥ*) instead of *mārtābhiḥ*; *ḥdir yaṅ rnam śes ni* (*atrāpi vijñānam eva*) instead of *idam amṛtam* (*amalaṃ*) *brahma*.]

Those verses cited in Tibetan versions should be considered as having probably been ascribed to Bhartṛhari. Reasons:

(1) Tibetan versions mention the name of the author of the verses as Bhadrahari, Bhadrihari, Bhatahari, Bharitehari or Bhaṅdrihari. These names give ample testimony to the supposition that the original Sanskrit name of the author of those verses was a little difficult to transcribe with Tibetan characters, and so the name must have been Bhartṛhari which could easily become corrupted into any one of them.

(2) We can find in the *Vākyapadīya* by Bhartṛhari the Sanskrit original texts of at least 10 of these verses. As for some of the other verses we find similar verses in the same work.

(3) Bhaṭṭa-Nārāyaṇakaṇṭha ascribed fr.11 to Bhartṛhari. Although some or the above-mentioned verses can not be traced in the *Vākyapadīya*, the *Bhartṛhariśataka* or in collections of lyrical songs ascribed to him, it is possible that he might have composed[20] other works which are not extant now or that some of the verses might have been ascribed to him in later days.[21]

There are on the other hand some difficulties in identifying Bhadrahari etc. with Bhartṛhari. However these difficulties will be easily solved by the following considerations:

(1) It is a well-known fact that Bhartṛhari adopted the standpoint of emanation-theory (*pariṇāmavāda*), whereas the standpoint made clear in fr.

11 is, as Nārāyaṇakaṇṭha asserts, manifestation-theory (*vivartavāda*). These two standpoints were strictly distinguished from each other by later Vedāntins.[22] It seems that the author of fr.11 would be different from Bhartṛhari, the author of the *Vākyapadīya*. However, in the days when these verses were composed these two philosophical standpoints were not strictly distinguished from each other. Bhartṛhari himself used the two terms (*pariṇāma* and *vivarta*) as nearly the same meaning,[23] just as the *Brahma-sūtras* used many similes which could be interpreted in different ways.

(2) Hithertofore it has been generally supposed that Bhartṛhari died forty years before I-tsing sojourned in India, following the information given by I-tsing himself.[24] Accordingly Bhartṛhari was regarded by J. Takakusu to have died in 651-652 A.D. If we examine this passage more closely, however, it becomes clear that in I-tsing's information there is something amiss. I-tsing said that Bhartṛhari was a contemporary of Dharmapāla,[25] and yet also that Dharmapāla composed a commentary upon Bhartṛhari's verses.[26] These two are not consistent with each other. Let us discuss this problem.

Dr. Hakuju Ui[27] took the passage as meaning that Bhartṛhari died forty years before the beginning of I-tsing's stay in the Nālāndā monastery. According to his calculation Bhartṛhari died c. 630 A.D. In the above-cited passage, however, he is said to have been a contemporary of Dharmapāla who commented upon the *Prakīrṇaka* of Bhartṛhari. The date of Dharmapāla is well-known; he lived 530-561 A.D. Now, Bhartṛhari must have been somewhat Dharmapāla's senior. Suppose that the former was older than the latter by, say, ten years; the Bhartṛhari should have lived c. 520-630. If we adopt Takakusu's view, he must be supposed to have lived c. 520-652. Needless to say, this supposition is absurd. We are brought to the conclusion that either (1) the information that Bhartṛhari died forty years before I-tsing's arrival is wrong or (2) the information that Dharmapāla commented upon Bhartṛhari's work is wrong. We shall take up this problem in another light. Mr. H. R. Rangaswamy Iyengar[28] made clear the fact that Bhartṛhari lived in an age not so remote from that of Vasubandhu. He asserts as follows:

> "In the second Kāṇḍa of the *Vākyapadīya*, while describing how the science of grammar, which had been almost extinct, was restored and

propagated by the great grammarians, Chandra and Vasurāta, Puṇyarāja, the commentator of the *Vākyapadīya*, mentions several times Vasurāta as the teacher of Bhartṛhari.[29] In the *Kārikā* 490 of the *Vākyapadīya*[30] Bhartṛhari himself seems to refer to his teacher Vasurāta by 'Guruṇā' as is evident from the words of Puṇyarāja prefaced to the verse.[31] Again a Jain writer, Siṃhasūrigaṇi, who may be assigned to the beginning of the sixth century A.D., in his unpublished work, *Nayacakraṭīkā*, a commentary on the *Nayacakra* of Mallavādin the senior[32] which is not now extant, twice mentions Vasurāta the Upādhyāya or Bhartṛhari."[33]

This confirms the statement of Puṇyarāja and establishes that Vasurāta was a great grammarian of the day under whom Bhartṛhari studied, and that Bhartṛhari often held views quite different from those of his master.

"According to Paramārtha, Vasurāta was a Brahmin and brother-in-law of Bạlāditya, a pupil of Vasubandhu.[34] He was well-versed in grammar. He defeated Vasubandhu, through the intervention of Chandra, another great grammarian. This means that Vasurāta, Chandra, and Vasubandhu should be regarded as contemporaries and Bhartṛhari, the pupil of Vasurāta, assigned to the fifth century A.D."

Another piece of evidence of much more importance was discovered by him. In the fifth chapter of Dignāga's *Pramāṇa-samuccaya*, which is devoted to the exposition of the *Apoha* theory, the following two *Kārikās* are found :

thigs pa daṅ ni tshogs pa yi/
chu sogs rnams la rjod byed ni/
graṅs daṅ tshad daṅ dbyibs rnams la/
ltos pa med par ḥjug par byed//
dbyibs daṅ·kha dog yan lag rnams/
khyad par can la gaṅ ḥjug pa/
de yi yan lag la sgra ni/
rab tu ḥjug la dun asma yi//

The above Tibetan verses have been cited as from Mr. Iyengar's article. According to the sDe-dge edition of the Tibetan Buddhist Canons kept by Tohoku University, Sendai, the sentences run as follows :

la lar dṅos su rjod par byed dper na/

grańs dań mtshan ñid dań ni dbyibs/
ltos pa med par rab tu ḥjug/
chu la sogs paḥi thigs pa dań/
ḥdus pa la yań rjod par byed//
la lar yan lag ḥbaḥ shig la ḥjug pa ma yin te/dper na/
dbyibs dań kha dog cha śas kyis/
khyad par byas nas ḥjug pa yin/
sgra yis de yi cha śas la/
rab tu ḥjug pa dmigs ma yin//

Restoration into Sanskrit of these verses might easily correspond to the following verses in the *Vākyapadīya* :

bindau ca samudāye ca vācakaḥ salilādiṣu/
saṃkhyāpramāṇasaṃsthānanirapekṣaḥ pravartate//(*Vākyapadīya*, II, 160.)[35]
saṃsthānavarṇāvayavair viśiṣṭe yaḥ prayujyate/
śabdo na tasyāvayave pravṛttir upalabhyate//(*Vākyapadīya*, II,157.)(II, 156 and 155, Abhyankar-Limaye's edition, p.29)

"A word denoting water applies equally to a drop and to a large mass of it, irrespective of number, size and shape."(III,156.)
"A word which is applied to an object as qualified by a shape, color and parts, cannot be considered to denote only a portion thereof." (Iyer's translation)

This means that either Dignāga took the *Kārikās* from Bhartṛhari's work or both Dignāga and Bhartṛhari took them from quite a different work. But there is no evidence to support the latter alternative. We learn from Jinendrabuddhi, author of *Viśālāmalaṭīkā* on the *Pramāṇa-samuccaya-vṛtti* of Dignāga, that Dignāga is here referring to the views of Bhartṛhari.[36] This evidently supports the former alternative that Dignāga is quoting from Bhartṛhari.

The foregoing are the pieces of evidence set forth by Mr. H. R. Rangaswamy lyengar. But whereas he has pointed out just one Tibetan citation of a verse by Bhartṛhari, we have in addition pointed out many citations of his verses. Taking all these pieces of evidence into consideration, we have to conclude that Bhartṛhari must have lived prior to or at latest contemporary with Dignāga, Asvabhāva (Ṅo-bo-ñid med-pa), Bhavya (Bhāvaviveka) and Dharmapāla.

There has been much dispute about the date of Dignāga.[37] Randle once said that "all that can be said with certainty is that he lived somewhere between 350A.D. and 500A.D."[38] According to most scholars he lived about 500 A.D.[39] Dr. H.Ui fixed his date as c.400-480, on the ground that he must have lived a little earlier than Guṇamati.[40] The latter must have lived prior to Paramārtha's arrival in Kuang-tung in China in 546A.D. and earlier than Sthiramati.[41] Sthiramati must have lived in the sixth century[42] or according to Dr. Ui, c.470-550.[43] Winternitz assigns him to the fifth century.[44] Recently Professor Hikata has surmised that the date of Dignāga is about 440-520.[45]

It is generally accepted that Asvabhāva lived earlier than Dharmapāla and later than Dignāga. He lived, according to Dr. Ui, c.450-530A.D.[46] and, according to Prof. Hikata, c.470-550A.D.[47]

Bhavya was almost contemporary with Buddhapālita (c.400-450?).[48] He is believed to have lived and worked at the beginning of the fifth century A.D.[49] According to Dr. Ui, he lived c.490-570.[50] In any case he was an elder contemporary of Dharmapāla. The date of Dharmapāla has precisely been fixed. He lived 530-561A.D.[51]

So we can assuredly say that Bhartṛhari cannot have lived later than these Buddhist scholars. It has become clear that the statement of I-tsing that Bhartṛhari died some forty years before the date of his record is incorrect.

It is, however, doubtless that Bhartṛhari lived after Vasubandhu, as it is clear from the above-cited material Vasubandhu is generally believed to have lived in the fourth century[52] or in the latter half of the fourth century.[53] According to Dr. Ui, Vasubandhu lived c.320-400.[54] According to Prof. Hikata, he lived c.400-480.[55] Frauwallner asserted the existence of two Vasubandhus, ascribing the elder to 320-380A.D. and the younger to 400-480 A.D.[56] Such has been the extent of the debate about his date.

Referring to the *Vijñānavāda*, Bhartṛhari says:

> *kecid vyāvṛttirūpāṃ tu dravyatvena pracakṣate*/(*Vākyapadīya* III,1,19. p. 22.)

This must refer to later Buddhist Idealists, not to such earlier ones as

Asaṅga and Vasubandhu. If so, the date of Bhartṛhari should not be fixed in a period much earlier than set forth above.

So taking these facts into account, we are brought to the conclusion that Bhartṛhari, the author of the *Vākyapadīya*, must have lived c.450-500A.D.

At the end of this chapter the author should not fail to mention the names of the scholars who kindly helped him in carrying on this study. Prof. Yamaguchi introduced him to Dr. Kensho Hasuba and Dr. Kyogo Sasaki, who went over No-bo-ñid med-pa's works in order to discover the suspected citations of Bhartṛhari's verses. Prof. Josho Nozawa kindly informed him of Bhavya's citation of a verse of Bhartṛhari. Dr. Bunkyo Aoki and Prof. Shinya Kasugai did not spare efforts to give the author valuable suggestions. Here the author wants to express his sincere gratitude to these scholars, without whose kind help this chapter could not have been brought to its present state of completion.

After the above work on Tibetan citations of Bhartṛhari's verses had been completed, some new studies were published. Among the verses ascribed to Bhartṛhari, there are at least 28 verses which cannot be found in the extant *Vākyapadīya*. See V. K.Abbyankar and V.P. Limaye's edition of *Vākyapadīya*, Appendix.

Occasionally Kaiyaṭa and others cite Bhartṛhari's verses, though in abridged form. (Mithilesh Chaurvedi: "Note on a *Kārikā* ascribed to Bhartṛhari", *Journal of the Gaṅganatha Jha Kendriya Sanskrit Vidyapeetha*, Allahabad, vol. XXIX, 1973, parts 1-4, pp.203-209).

Some verses and fragments ascribed to Bhartṛhari have been examined by Sadhu Ram, in *Journal of the Ganganath Jha Research Institute*, vol. XIII, 1956, pp.51-79.

Notes

1) Prof. Susumu Yamaguchi: *Nihon Bukkyogaku Kyokai Nempo*, VIII, Kyoto, 1936, pp. 152-153.

2) His comment upon *Dharmaparyeṣṭi* 5. *Bstan-ḥgyur* of the Peking edition, XLV, 90a,8 -b,1.

3) *Vākyapadīya*, ed. by Paṇḍit Rāmachandra Śāstrī Koṭibhāskara (Benares Sanskrit Series), Benares 1887 f., vol. 2, p.200. According to the citation of the verse by Dr.

Chakravarty, *antaḥkaraṇadharmasya* instead of *antaḥkaraṇatattvasya* (Prabhatchandra Chakravarti: *The Linguistic Speculations of the Hindus*, University of Calcutta, 1933. p.197). The reading of the Benares text corresponds with the Tibetan version.

4) *Vākyapadīya* III, 8 (*kriyāsamuddeśa*), I, p.298 (Benares Sanskrit Series). However, the verse cited by Dr. Chakravarti reads *vyapadiśyate* instead of *pratīyate*. (P. Chakravarti: *op. cit*. p. 237). Another emendation could be *sā pratīyate*.

5) All citations henceforth are taken from the Peking edition.

6) The negative character of the absolute was stressed by Yājñavalkya, the Upanishadic thinker; and later in the *Kāṭhaka-Up*. (II,6,9; 12).

7) It seems that the Tibetan translator took *vyavartata* in the original for *nyavartata*.

8) This verse is not found in the corresponding passage in the Chinese translation by Prabhāmitra of Bhāvaviveka's *Prajñāpradīpa*, Taisho Tripiṭaka, vol. XXX, p.82c). According to Prof. Nozawa it is likely that this verse was omitted by the translator.

9) ad v. 144, p.72 (ed. by Embar Krishnamacharya, Baroda 1926, GOS, 30).

10) The Der-ge edition, Bstan-ḥgyur, vol.293,187b.

11) *The Tattvasaṅgraha of Śāntarakṣita with the commentary of Kamalaśīla*, tr. into English by Ganganath Jha, vol.I, Baroda 1937, p.126.

12) ad III,5,43; 44. p.1246, ĀnSS.

13) p.12b, NSP.

14) The text is not now available to the author, who has read it in E.Frauwallner's "Dignāga und anderes" (*Festschrift Winternitz*, S.237).

15) Hārāṇacandra Śāstrī: "Śabdabrahmavādaḥ". (*G. Jhā Commemoration Volume*, p.93.)

16) As for understanding the meaning of the verse, Ānandajñāna's *ṭikā* upon the *Bṛhad. Up. Vārttika* is highly valuable.

17) The *Āgamaśāstra of Gauḍapāda*, edited, translated and annotated by Vidhushekhara Bhattacharyya, University of Calcutta, 1943, p.53.

18) Ś. ad *Bṛhad. Up*. p.152, *l*.24. . . *na hi bālais talamalinatādibhir vyomni vikalpyamāne talamalinatādiviśiṣṭam eva paramārthato vyoma bhavati* (Ś. ad *BS*. I,2,8. vol. I, p.184; II, 5,7.) *vyomanīva talamalādi parikalpitam* (Ś. ad *BS*. I,3,19. vol.I; p.279, *l*.7.) *ākāśe bālās talamalinatādy adhyasyanti* (Ś. ad *BS*. I,1,1, vol.I, p.11. ĀnSS.). *Upadeśasāhasrī*, II,18,22.

19) The author has cited the verse from the above-mentioned Frauwallner's work.

20) *The Epigrams Attributed to Bhartṛhari*, ed. by D. D. Kosambi (Singhi Jain Series, vol. No.23). Bombay, 1948. This work contains not only the famous three *śatakas*, but also the *Viṭavṛtta, Vijñānaśataka* and many other poems ascribed to him.

21) Professor Louis Renou told the author that, according to information from the late S. Dasgupta the editions of the *Vākyapadīya* published hitherto fore do not contain all the verses of the work, and so it might be possible that those verses not identified by the author are found in unpublished MSS.

22) Paul Deussen : *Allgemeine Geschichte der Philosophie*, I,1,4 Aufl., Leipzig, 1920, S.63f.

23) I have discussed this in a work in Japanese : *Tetsugakuteki Shisaku no Indoteki Tenkai*, p.239 f. Cf. Paul Hacker : *Vivarta*, Akademic der Wissenschaften und der Literatur. Abhandlungen der Geistes- und Sozialwissenschaftlichen Klasse, Jahrgang, 1953, Nr.5.

24) "It is forty years since his death (A.D.651-652)." (J. Takakusu : *A Record of the Buddist Religion as Practised in India and the Malay Archipelago*. Oxford, 1896. p.180)

25) J. Takakusu : *op. cit*., p.179.

26) *Nan hai ji gui nei fa zhuan*(南海寄帰内法伝), *TT*. vol. LIV, p.229.

27) *Journal of Indian and Buddhist Studies*, vol.V, p.130.

28) H. R. Rangaswamy Iyengar : "Bhartṛhari and Dignāga" (*Śrī Ātmānanda Prakāśa*, published by "Jain Atmananda Sabha", Bhavnagar, 1952, p.27f. The author obtained a copy by courtesy of Mr. Muni Jambuvijay).

29) *na tenāsmadguros tatrabhavato* Vasurātād *anyaḥ kaścid imaṃ bhāṣyārṇavam avagāhitum ālam ity uktaṃ bhavati*/(Puṇyarāja ad II,486). *kenacic ca brahmarakṣasānīya Candrācārya-Vasurātaguruprabhṛtīnām datta iti/te* [*taiḥ?*] *khalu yathāvat vyākaraṇasya svarūpaṃ tata upalabhya satataṃ ca śiṣyāṇāṃ vyākhyāya bahuśākhitvaṃ nīto vistaraṃ prāpita ity anuśrūyate*/ (ad II,489).

30) Cf. II,490b : .... *praṇīto guruṇāsmākam ayam āgamasaṃgrahaḥ*/

31) Cf. *ibid.* : *atha kadācit yogato vicārya tatra bhagavatā Vasurātaguruṇā mamāyam āgamaḥ saṃjñāya vātsalyāt praṇīta iti svaracitasya granthasya gurupūrvakam abhidhātum āha*/

32) This Mallavādin should be distinguished from another Jain writer of the same name who is the author of *Nyāyabinduṭippaṇī*.

33) Cf. *Nayacakraṭīkā*, folio 272a : . . .*so 'bhijalpo 'bhidheyārthaparigrāhī bāhyāc chabdād anya iti Bhartṛharyādimatam/Vasurātasya Bhartṛharyupādhyāyasya mataṃ tu* . . . . Cf. ibid., folio 277a : . . .*evaṃ tāvat Bhartṛharyādidarśanam uktam/Vasurātaḥ Bhartṛharer upādhyāyaḥ*/

34) Cf. "A study of Paramārtha's life of Vasubandhu and the Date of Vasubandhu" by J. Takakusu : *JRAS*, 1905, pp.33 ff.

35) The first and the second halves are given in reverse order in the edition of the Benares Sanskrit Series. (p.185)

36) Cf. *Viśālāmalaṭīkā* : Mdo. re, folio 331b.1.6.ff. : *kha cig tu gtso bor cha tshas rnams la ḥjug te/bha rite haris yis smras pa/cha sogs rnams la zes paḥi sogs paḥi sgras. sa la yoṅs su gzuṅ ṅo*/(=*kvacit tu mukhyā avayaveṣu vṛttiḥ/yathoktaṃ Bhartṛhariṇā salilādiṣv iti ādiśabdena pṛthivyādīnāṃ parigrahaḥ*/)

37) According to Tāranātha, Dignāga was a pupil of Vasubandhu (*Tāranātha's Geschichte des Buddhismus in Indian*, übersetzt von Anton Schiefner, St.Petersburg, 1869, S.

131).

38) H. N. Randle: *Fragments from Diṅnāga*. London, 1926, p.3. In another work he says: "Diṅnāga's date shares the uncertainty attaching to that of his master Vasubandhu. He may fall anywhere between 400 and 500A. D."(Randle: *Indian Logic in the Early Schools*. Oxford University Press, 1930 p.27).

39) Moritz Winternitz: *Geschichte der ichenndis Litteratur*, Bd.III. Leipzig, 1920. S.467. Louis Renou et Jean Filliozt: *L'Inde Classique*, tome II. Paris, 1953, p.380.

40) H.Ui: *Indo Tetsugaku Kenkyu*, vol.V, pp.142-145.

41) Cf. *ibid*., p.136

42) Filliozat: *op. cit*., p.380.

43) H.Ui: *op. cit*., p.136.

44) M.Winternits: *History of Indian Literature*, vol. II. University of Calcutta, 1933. pp. 362-363.

45) Ryusho Hikata: "Discussion on the Date of Vasubandhu", (*Miyamoto Commemoration Volume*, Sanseido, Tokyo, 1954, p.321)

46) H.Ui: *op. cit*., p.147

47) R. Hikata: *op. cit*., p.321.

48) J.Filliozat: *op. cit*., p.379.

49) Winternitz: *HIL*. etc. II, p.362.

50) H.Ui: *op. cit*., pp.148-149.

51) H.Ui: *op. cit*., pp.123-132: R. Hikita: *op. cit*., p.321.

52) Winternitz: *HIL* etc. II, p.355f.

53) J.Filliozat: *op. cit*., II, p.380.

54) H.Ui: *op. cit*., vol. I, pp.413-414.

55) R. Hikata: *op. cit*. p.315f.

56) E.Frauwallner: "On the Date of the Buddhist Master of the Law Vasubandhu", Roma 1951. All different views about Vasubandhu's date have been mentioned in this work.

CHAPTER III
UPAVARṢA

SECTION I. INTRODUCTION

Upavarṣa is acknowledged to be the earliest and also the most authoritative of the thinkers of the Vedānta and Mīmāṃsā schools after the final compilation of the *Brahma-sūtra*. He is mentioned twice in Śaṅkara's *Brahma-sūtra-bhāṣya*. The first instance occurs in the commentary to *Brahma-sūtra* III,3,53, where it is said:

> Now since it is established that the *ātman* has the character of participating in bondage and liberation, it is proved that the *ātman* actually exists distinct from the physical body. If indeed no *ātman* distinct from the body were to exist, the Vedic declaration that the fruits of one's deeds will be reaped in a future life would have no basis. Moreover [if it were so], for whom would be taught the doctrine [of the *Upaniṣads*] that *brahman* is *ātman*?
>
> (Question) Has it not already been explained in the first *pāda* at the beginning of the *śāstra* (i.e. *Pūrva-mīmāṃsā-sūtra* I,1,5) that an *ātman* actually exists, qualified to receive and enjoy the fruits of action as taught in the scriptures and different from the body?
>
> (Answer) Certainly it has been so explained. However, that is an explanation by the commentator (*bhāṣyakṛt*); there is no *sūtra* which teaches the actual existence of *ātman*. So now in this passage [of the *Brahma-sūtra*], the *sūtra*-author himself, after first refuting the assertion of the other side (i.e. the materialist), lays it down that *ātman* actually exists. And Ācārya Śabarasvāmin extracts [the argument for the proof of the existence of *ātman*] out of this passage and states it in the passage (ad *Pūrva-mīmāṃsā-sūtra* I,1,5) on the definition of valid cognition (*pramāṇa-lakṣaṇa*). And for the very same reason, when teaching the actual existence of the *ātman* in the first *śāstra* (*prathama tantra*) Bhagavat Upavarṣa confines himself to saying "We shall explain it in

> the *Śārīraka* (i.e. *Brahma-sūtra*)". And since [in this third chapter of the third book of the *Brahma-sūtra*] what is being trated is worship whose special character is religious injunction, the existence or otherwise of the *ātman* is examined in order to show that it is just because *ātman* exists that the whole sacred literature can be authoritative.

Again, in the passage which comments on the text (*Brahma-sūtra* I,3,28) "the entire world arises from Word", Śaṅkara winds up his detailed explanation and then says: "This being so, when it is taught in the *sūtra* that [all things] arise from Word, what is the essential nature of Word"?[1]

Having raised this question, he first states the doctrine of the advocates of *sphoṭa*, who assert that the fundamental substance of Word is none other than a kind of metaphysical substance called *sphoṭa*,[2] against which theory he argues:

> The revered (*bhagavat*) Upavarṣa says: "But words are none other than various letter-sounds (*varṇa*)."

He follows up with a detailed debate as to whether words are letter-sounds of this kind or are *sphoṭa*.

In Śaṅkara's commentary on the *Brahma-sūtra*, it is only in these two passages noted above that Upavarṣa is referred to. Bhāskara, who also wrote a commentary on the *Brahma-sūtra*, mentions Upavarṣa three times. And though there are minor difference, what he says is substantially the same as the account in Śaṅkara.[3] Accordingly we should take it that Upavarṣa was looked upon as an authority by all branches of the Vedānta school generally and also that the words of Śaṅkara represent a correct account of Upavarṣa's doctrines.

Now in the Mīmāṃsā school also, he was respected as a great authority. In the commentary on the *Mīmāṃsā-sūtra* (ad I,1,5) by Śabarasvāmin, a passage from the ancient 'Commentator' (*vṛttikāra*) is preserved and within that quatation the question is raised:

> Now when one says 'cow' (*gauḥ*), what fundamentally is this word? to which the answer is given: The word cow or *gauḥ* is the sound '*g*', the sound '*au*' and the sound '*visarga* (*ḥ*)' — so teaches the revered Upavarṣa.[4]

Then he sets out a detailed argument on the point.

In the passage Śaṅkara refutes the opinion of Upavarṣa and vindicates the theory of *sphoṭa* adopted by the Yoga school. In this case Śaṅkara's standpoint is quite contrary to that in the above-cited passage of the *Brahma-sūtra-bhāṣya*.

The words of Upavarṣa quoted in these places are identical with those given by Bhāskara.[5] We can also say that they are identical in sence with what has been preserved by Śaṅkara. Accordingly we can take it that the words of Upavarṣa have been reliably preserved by these writers.

Taking the accounts of Upavarṣa given above, we shall next set out conclusions arrived at from other source material.

Notes

1) Ś. ad *BS*. (ĀnSS), vol. I, p.299, *l*.7.

2) On *sphoṭa*, see Part VII, Chapter IV, Section III of the present work.

3) *ata eva Upavarṣācāryeṇoktaṃ prathamapāde/ātmavādaṃ tu Śārīrake vakṣyāma iti//* (Bhāskara ad *BS*. I,1,1, p.6). *kaḥ punar atra śabdo 'bhipreto? varṇātmako, lokaprasiddher Upavarṣāgamāc ca//*(Bhāskara ad *BS*. I,3,29, p.62). *gaur ity atra gakāraukāravisarjanīyā iti Bhagavān Upavarṣācārya ity āgamaparaṃparāyātanyāyopapannaṃ ca varṇānāṃ śabdatvaṃ//*(*ibid*., p.63)

4) *atha 'gauḥ' ity atra kaḥ śabdaḥ? gakārāukāravisarjanīyā iti Bhagavān Upavarṣaḥ/* The same sentence is quoted by Śaṅkara in his *Yogasūtrabhāṣyavivaraṇa* (ad III,17, p.264, Madras Oriental Series, 1952) *nanu ca 'gakāraukāravisarjanīyāḥ' iti Bhagavān Upavarṣaḥ/tan na ----- avācakatvāt//*

5) See Note 3. supra.

SECTION II. THE MAN, HIS WORKS AND HIS DATES

Sub-Section 1. Upavarṣa's Status as an Authority

Whenever Śaṅkara, the 'Commentator' (*vṛttikāra*) or Bhāskara refers to Upavarṣa, they always add the honorific title of 'Revered [teacher]' (*bhagavat*).[1] In their *sūtra* commentaries, these writers accord the honorific 'reveres' also to the *sūtra* author himself, but it is very rare for them to accord a term of veneration to other thinkers. We may thus conclude that Upavarṣa was highly respected as an authority throughout the two Mīmāṃsā schools. Above all, from the fact that Bhāskara quotes his theories as 'the tradition from Upavarṣa' (*Upavarṣa-āgama*), we can see both that his doctrines were looked upon as authoritative traditional theories, and that chronologically he lived in a period far distant from that of Bhāskara. Before examining the problem of exactly when Upavarṣa lived, we may first consider his works and writings. For in the absence of definite evidence which could directly determine his dates, the only recourse is to seek indications in his writings.

Note

1) A theory attributed to 'Bhagavān Ācārya' is given in *Śabarabhāṣya* ad II.3.16, and some scholars think that it refers to Upavarṣa. Cf. Aufrecht : *CC*. II, 45, and Note 5 of the next sub-section.

Sub-Section 2. His Works

In the light of what is said by the Commentator (*vṛttikāra*), Śaṅkara and Bhāskara as noted above, it is clear that Upavarṣa wrote commentaries on both the *Mīmāṃsā-sūtra* and the *Brahma-sūtra*. Also, in the *Tantracūḍāmaṇi* by Kṛṣṇadeva, it is noted that Upavarṣa wrote a commentary (*vṛtti*) on the *Mīmāṃsā-sūtra*.[1] And according to the later work called *Prapañcahṛdaya*,[2] Upavarṣa is said to have written commentaries[3] not only on the two *sūtras* but also on the *Saṅkarṣaṇa-kāṇḍa* traditionally recognized as a work by Jaimini. He seems to have regarded these three works as constituting Mīmāṃsā learning in the widest sense and paid great attention to their correlation and unification. While commenting on the *Mīmāṃsā-sūtra*, he said, "We shall explain that point in the *Śārīraka*", so transferring consideration of philosophical questions on the *ātman* to his commentary on the *Brahma-sūtra*. From this it would seem that most of his philosophical thinking was in his commentary on the *Brahma-sūtra*, while with the *Mīmāṃsā-sūtra* commentary he was chiefly concerned to explain ritualistic principles. Consequently it can be supposed that his commentaries would have been comparatively short, and in fact the work *Prapañcahṛdaya* noted above clearly states that his commentary works are brief and concisely written. It is likely that among many commentaries on the *Brahma-sūtra*, the one by Upavarṣa was most famous.[4]

Now we come to the problem of the relation between the Commentator (*vṛttikāra*) and Upavarṣa. It seems likely that the two are different men and that the Commentator looked up to Upavarṣa as an authority.

In the commentary of Śabarasvāmin we see that after dealing with *sūtra* I,1,5, the commentary of the Commentator is presented at length. This commentary is markedly different from what Śabarasvāmin gives as his own comments on the *sūtra*, so that it is clear that different interpretations of the *sūtra* existed already within the Mīmāṃsā school before Śabara's time, and since the above-mentioned words of Upavarṣa appear within Śabara's citation of the words of the Commentator, we can assume that the Commentator and Upavarṣa were two quite different men, with Upavarṣa being much earlier, and revered by the Commentator as an authority.

There are however two facts which seem to stand in the way of such a conclusion. (1) Later Mīmāṃsā scholars regard the Commentator and Upavarṣa as one and the same,[5] and (2) when, as already noted, Śaṅkara briefly quotes some words of Upavarṣa in his *Brahma-sūtra-bhāṣya* III,3,5, his sub-commentators Ānandajñāna and Govindānanda call Upavarṣa 'the Commentator', from which it would appear that the two should after all be regarded as the same.

In spite of this, however, we can not identify them. First of all, as to (1) we can say this : Since in Śabarasvāmin's commentary, in the middle of his long citation from the work of the Commentator, he suddenly remarks "Bhagavat Upavarṣa states ...", we must suppose that Upavarṣa is different from the Commentator. If he had thought they were the same, there would have been no point in saying specifically "Upavarṣa states ...". As to (2), there is the following possibility. Śaṅkara, in his commentary on the *Brahma-sūtra*, frequently quotes and refutes heretical views on the *sūtra*. According to all the sub-commentators, these are the views of the *Vṛtti*-author and can really be taken to refer to the views of the commentary (*vṛtti*) by Bodhāyana.[6] However, whenever Śaṅkara has occasion to quote Upavarṣa, he always approves his doctrines and adds the honorific title of 'Bhagavat'. It can not be supposed that the advocator of heretical doctrines refuted in the *sūtras* and the orthodox thinker who is respected and relied upon are one and the same person. In particular, this was even more impossible in mediaeval India, where the tradition of passing down teachings from master to disciple was highly respected. Again, the work *Prapañcahṛdaya* clearly regards Bodhāyana and Upavarṣa as distinct.[7] Accordingly, form a consideration of the above facts, it must be right to suppose that the two are different men.[8]

It is not clear why they later came to be regarded as identical. But perhaps because Upavarṣa wrote commentaries — which might have been called *vṛtti* and came to be lost or unknown in later centuries — on the two *Mīmāṃsā-sūtra*, he may have come to be regarded as the Commentator (*vṛttikāra*, i.e. Bodhāyana), a completely different person. And from this a tradition arose, it would appear, that Upavarṣa and Bodhāyana were the same man.[9] Since, however, this came to be said only in later centuries, we can not accept it for our purposes here.

Consequently the long extract form the Commentator (*vṛttikāra*) quoted in the commentary (I,1,5) of Śabarasvāmin can not be regarded as the words of Upavarṣa. All we can be sure of is the historical fact that he wrote commentaries on the two *Mīmāṃsā-sūtras*.

In addition we have an account which says that Upavarṣa composed a *sūtra* on the rituals and laws (*dharma*). According to the report by Bhandarkar,[10] Upavarṣa is mentioned twice in the *Āpastambadhvanitārtha-kārikā*, a work by a man called Trikāṇḍamaṇḍana Bhāskara Miśra[11] (12th century or earlier). According to one of those passages, "Upavarṣa and others prescribe that a man, when he has participated in the performance of the fire ceremony, must give alms to 100 Brahmins, but this is not prescribed in the other *sūtras*." And in another passage which discusses the relationship among clans (*gotra*), it is said, "According to the text (*pāṭhataḥ*) of Upavarṣa, etc., the Uśija clan, Vāmadeva clan and Dīrghatamasa clan are Gautama clan. Consequently they can not marry with other clans, but may marry with the Bhāradvāja clan." We can know, therefore, that an Upavarṣa was the author of a *sūtra* related to rituals and laws, which was known prior to the 12th century. But no such *sūtra* ascribed to him has survived to the present day. Whether the Upavarṣa who wrote this *sūtra* is the same as the one of the same name who wrote the commentaries on the two *Mīmāṃsā-sūtras* can not be definitely concluded at the present time.

From the above considerations, we can summarize as follows :

Upavarṣa's Works

1. A commentary on the *Mīmāṃsā-sūtra*.
2. A commentary on the *Saṅkarṣaṇa-kāṇḍa*.
3. A commentary on the *Brahma-sūtra*.

In addition, tradition has it that Upavarṣa wrote *sūtras* on the rituals and laws (*dharma*) but it is not clear whether this is the same Upavarṣa. All of his works have been lost, and only fragments have been passed down to us.

Notes

1) H. Jacobi : *JAOS*. XXXI, 1911. p.17, no.1.

2) The *Prapañcahṛdaya*, ed. by T. Ganapati Sāstrī (TrivSS. XLV, 1915). This work is a compendium of arts and sciences from the standpoint of orthodox Brahmanism. The date of its composition is not clear.

3) According to *ibid*., p.39, Bodhāyana wrote commentaries on the *Mīmāṃsā-sūtra*, *Saṅkarṣaṇa-kāṇḍa* and *Brahma-sūtra*, and tradition says that Upavarṣa simplified these (*tad granthabāhulyabhayād upekṣya kiṃcit saṅkṣiptam Upavarṣeṇa kṛtam*). Thus the author of this work thought that Bodhāyana was before Upavarṣa. However, as we shall consider in the next Sub-section, if we suppose that the *Vṛtti*-author quoted by Śabarasvāmin and the *Vṛtti*-author refuted by Śaṅkara are the same person, Upavarṣa would then be earlier than that. Moreover the *Vṛtti*-author, Śaṅkara and Bhāskara refer to Upavarṣa as an authority next after Jaimini and Bādarāyaṇa, but do not mention Bodhāyana as an authority (and indeed Bodhāyana's name appears for the first time in the writings of Rāmānuja). So I incline to the view that Upavarṣa would be the earlier in date. At any rate it is certain that the dates of the two are not too far apart.

4) *tasyāḥ mīmāṃsāyāḥ śārīrakasya upavarṣādyācāryavinirmitā anekā vṛttayaḥ santi* / *Sarvadarśanakaumudī*, p.113.

5) They are identified not only by Kumārila but also in the *Śāstradīpikā* by Pārthasārathimiśra and its commentary by Rāmakṛṣṇa. That is to say, they state that Upavarṣa is the real name of the *Vṛtti*-author ; there are some scholars who say this theory should be adopted. (V.A. Ramaswami Sastri : "Old Vṛttikāras on the *Pūrva Mīmāṃsā Sūtras*", *IHQ*. vol. X, 1934, pp.432-452, Keith : *The Karma-Mīmāṃsā*, pp.7-8. Further, Professor Gangānāth Jhā, I understand, also gave a report to the same effect at the Fourth Oriental Conference.) See further, Bhāskara ad *BS*. I,3,10. Furthermore Keith (*The Karma-Mīmāṃsā*, p.8) says that in the commentary on the *Mīmāṃsā-sūtra* II,3,1,

Śabarasvāmin quotes the *Vṛtti-author* and calls him '*Bhagavān ācāryaḥ*', and that Kumārila regarded him as Upavarṣa. Since, however, by the time of Kumārila, whom we shall consider later, even the writings of the *Vṛtti*-author had been lost (Cf. Chapter here on Bodhāyana), we are in no position to conclude that the '*Bhagavān ācāryaḥ*' has any connection with Upavarṣa.

6) See the next Chapter.

7) See Note 4 above.

8) H. Jacobi : *JAOS*. XXXI, 1911. pp.1ff ; H.Ui : *Studies in Indian Philosophy*, I, p.164 and P.V.Kane : "Gleanings from the Śabarabhāṣya," *JBBRAS*. 1921, also regard the two as being different men.

9) Cf. Section II in the next Chapter of the present work.

10) R. G. Bhandarkar : *Collected Works*, vol. II, pp.100-102. i.e. Report on Search for Skrt. MSS, 1883-4.

11) R. G.Bhandarkar asserts that because this work is frequently quoted in the Kālanirṇaya by Hemādri (latter half of 13th-century) he must have lived perhaps a hundred, two hundred, or even more years before that.

Sub-Section 3. His Life and His Dates

Details of Upavarṣa's life, his biography and what kind of man he was and so forth, are completely unknown. According to the great collection of stories the *Kathāsaritsāgara* (II,54 ; IV,4), a Brahmin Śaṅkarasvāmin had two sons, the older being called Varṣa and the younger Upavarṣa. It also mentions that Upavarṣa had a daughter named Upakośa. R.G.Bhandarkar has argued that since he is thus listed in a work alongside famous men in the history of Indian culture such at Kātyāyana, Vyādi, Pāṇini etc., he must have himself been an important historical figure[1] ; but even if we admit this, it is still highly questionable whether or not the descriptions of his blood relationships do in fact give us the whole truth. Thus although we can not determine the dates of his life, we can be sure that since he wrote a commentary on the *Brahma-sūtra*, he must have been later than that, and since he was called '*Bhagavat*' by the *Vṛtti*-author (i. e. Bodhāyana), He must have been earlier than Bodhāyana. He probably lived some time between 450-500 A.D.[2] And I do not think there can be any objection to the statement that he came from a family of Brahmins.

As evidenced from the passage in the *Yogasūtrabhāṣyavivaraṇa* already cited, he was respected as an authority by opponents of the Yoga school also. They try to refute the opinion of the Yoga school by invoking the authority of Upavarṣa. It is clear that he was regarded as a great and authoritative thinker by all the Mīmāṃsakas, the Vedāntins, and Yoga teachers in the days prior to Śaṅkara.

Notes

1) R. G. Bhandarkar : *ibid.*, p.104.

2) As we considered in Chapter I, in view of the great number of thinkers coming after Upavarṣa and Bodhāyana, it would be difficult to make the dates of his life any later.

SECTION III. HIS THOUGHT

First of all we can say that since Upavarṣa wrote commentaries on both *Mīmāṃsā-sūtras*, he would have thought that ritual Mīmāṃsā learning and Vedānta learning were both most important parts of orthodox Brahmanism. Since from the very first the *Brahma-sūtra* itself assumes study of the ritual Mīmāṃsā as an indispensable prerequisite,[1] it would not be at all strange that Upavarṣa, who lived in a period not too distant from that time, was learned in both the Mīmāṃsās. So on this point we find a remarkable difference from the cases of Kumārila and Śaṅkara in later centuries. These two later thinkers valued and revered only one side, whether the ritual Mīmāṃsā or the Vedānta, and disregarded the other. Thus in the eyes of those later thinkers the standpoint of Upavarṣa was very incompletely worked out, and the fact that he is nevertheless frequently quoted by them would probably have been because he was already established so firmly as an authority that even in subsequent times he could not be disregarded.

Furthermore, according to what has been preserved by Śaṅkara and Bhāskara, Upavarṣa taught a 'theory of *ātman*' (*ātmavāda*). It is not clear what his *ātman* theory was, but there is a verse quoted in the *Nyāyamañjarī* of Jayanta of the Nyāya school, around 900 A.D., which records the *ātman* theory of 'followers of Upavarṣa' (*Aupavarṣa*)[2] :

> Now the followers of the Upavarṣa line understand the *ātman* to be directly perceptible (*pratyakṣa*). For [the *ātman*] can be known by

'I-consciousness', as some of this school also say.
(*tatra pratyakṣam ātmānam Aupavarṣāḥ prapedire/*
ahaṃpratyayagamyatvāt svayūthyā api kecana//)

In the prose passage which follows, the contents of 'I-consciousness' (*ahaṃpratyaya*) are explained:[3)]

> This 'I-consciousness' exists [in us]. 'I-consciousness' has either a common referent with the physical body [as when] we say "I am fat, I am thin", or a common referent with the knower (the cognizing subject, *jñātṛ*) [whose nature is to say] "I know, I remember".

Accordingly we can see that some time prior to Jayanta, there lived thinkers who valued and respected the doctrines of Upavarṣa. And further, that they did not hold that the existence of the *ātman* was to be inferred by reasoning or verbal proof, nor that its existence should be accepted on the ground that the scriptures teach it, but rather because all men can directly know it through the consciousness of self. In other words, since there exists in every man the self-consciousness that he himself has become thin, or that he himself knows, we can not but admit the existence of the *ātman* as the basis for the formation of such consciousness. The fact "I am conscious" is made to establish the existence of the *ātman*.

The fact that the *ātman* is directly knowable was also taught in the Kumārila school of the later Mīmāṃsā, and was an important tenet, constituting a main point of difference from the philosophical doctrine of the Prabhākara school.[4)] And in the *Vaiśeṣika-sūtra* (III,2,14 ff.) also, there is a proof by the same method of the existence of the *ātman*. And another fact, no less important in the history of thought, is that Śaṅkara adopted without modification this argument of Upavarṣa. From the proposition that anyone can directly know the existence of the *ātman*, Śaṅkara proves the existence of the Supreme Being, *Brahman*.

> ...And since [*Brahman*] is the *ātman* of all, the existence of *Brahman* is established. For all men are conscious of the fact that the *ātman* (the self) exists. No one ever thinks "I do not exist". If indeed existence of the *ātman* were not established, all men would think, "I do not exist". And the *ātman* [that whose existence all men admit] is *Brahman*.[5)]

And in another place, he explains that the inner self (*pratyagātman*) is the object of the 'I-consciousness' (*asmatpratyayaviṣaya*) and that it is directly perceptible (*aparokṣa*).[6]

In this way Śaṅkara thus takes up the thought of Upavarṣa, so that Deussen's assumption[7] that Śaṅkara's commentary on the *Brahma-sūtra* might perhaps be based upon a commentary of Upavarṣa finds some confirmation here. Still, in the context of Śaṅkara's whole philosophical standpoint, this argument for the existence of *ātman*, which Śaṅkara puts forward under the influence of Upavarṣa, really does no more than show the existence of an individual self as the subject of conscious functions, and does not directly prove the existence of *Brahman* or the Supreme Self. The Supreme Self transcends all forms of individuality, and is not the object of the 'I-consciousness'. For the object of 'I-consciousness' (*ahaṃpratyaya*) is confined to the phenomenal world. "By the individual self, which is the object of 'I-consciousness', the conscious subject constituting 'I', all actions are produced."[8]

Though the individual self is in its ultimate essence identical with the Supreme Self, still the Supreme Self is distinct from the 'I-consciousness'. The principle which sets up a self-consciousness of the individual self and makes introspection into self possible is strictly speaking none other than the intellect (*buddhi*), an active organ of the individual self. And if the intellect has the power of an agent, it must be admitted that this intellect is really the object of 'I-consciousness', since it is seen that activity is in every case preceded by 'I-consciousness'. For example, "I go", "I come", "I eat", and "I drink".[9] Thus since 'I-consciousness' is brought into being by the intellect and makes possible all our actions in everyday life, an *ātman* in the highest sense apart from the intellect, that is to say the Supreme Self, would also inevitably transcend the 'I-consciousness'. And as the absolute, this Supreme Self would transcend the subjectivity of the individual consciousness. Direct knowledge of it would be impossible on an ordinary empirical basis. Only the *yoga* practitioner with his self absorbed in meditation (*saṃrādhana*) can see it directly.

Thus though Śaṅkara made use of the argument for the existence of self which derived from Upavarṣa, he had to go further. In the following dialogue, the distinction between the argument for the direct knowledge of *ātman* derived from Upavarṣa and the *ātman* theory of Śaṅkara which goes beyond it appears very clearly.

> (Question) Since the *ātman* is the object of the 'I-consciousness', is it unreasonable [for the Advaita school to assert] that the *ātman* is known only from the *Upaniṣads*? [For everybody must be able to know it directly.]
>
> (Answer) Not so. For [your assertion] is refuted by [the fact that] the *ātman* taught in the *Upaniṣads* is a witness (*sākṣin*). For the *Puruṣa* which is other than the subject of activity is witness of that subject, residing within all beings, homogeneous, one alone, eternal, ever-existent and the *ātman* of all. And *Puruṣa* can never be known either by the injunctive parts (*vidhikāṇḍa*, of the *Veda*) or by teachings based on reasoning.[101]

For Śaṅkara, therefore, the Supreme Self is something which transcends individual self-consciousness, so when on the basis of individual self-consciousness he has just asserted the existence of *ātman*, really in the true context of his philosophy this would be no more than a demonstration of the existence of the mere individual. And the existence of the Supreme Self is essentially something which still remains to be educed from the fact of the existence of the individual. That he nevertheless re-affirmed what had come down from Upavarṣa without limiting it to a demonstration of the existence of the individual self was not in accord with his real position. But it is easy to see why he went on upholding the ancient traditional doctrine of such prima facie anomalous teaching, while himself recognizing a philosophical development which went beyond it. The traditional doctrine from Upavarṣa was at the time so powerful that Śaṅkara had to accept it just as it stood, even though there was some disparity with his own ideas.

In the light of the above discussion on the existence of *ātman*, together with the fact that Upavarṣa was learned in the ritual Mīmāṃsā, it is likely that he believed in the eternal existence of a plurality of individual selves each experiencing variously the results of its own sacrifices and good and bad *karman*. We can suppose, namely, that his views were similar to those of the *Brahma-sūtra*, the Commentator (*vṛtti-kāra*), and Śabarasvāmin and so on.

Now the tradition has it that Upavarṣa taught in his philosophy that what is called 'word' (*śabda*) is its individual letters, for instance '*g*', '*au*' and '*ḥ*' (in the case of '*gauḥ*', cow). This is clearly opposed to the doctrine which postulates behind the word a metaphysical entity which brings it into existence. To give an instance, what he is opposing is the idea of a school which holds that '*gauḥ*' is the essence of the word, and that the individual letter-sounds are artificially differentiated out from that word.

In Śaṅkara's commentary on the *Brahma-sūtra* I,3,28, after citing the words of Upavarṣa already mentioned, he gives an elaborate discussion between the *sphoṭa* theorist (*sphoṭavādin*) and an opponent. Deussen takes this opponent to be the doctrine of Upavarṣa,[11] but the surmise is not correct. As the sub-commentators say, the *sphoṭavādin* here is the doctrine of 'Grammarian' (*vaiyākaraṇa*); and in general in India a reference to a Grammarian as a *sphoṭavādin* must be taken to point to Bhartṛhari. In all the Indian philosophical books, when a *sphoṭavādin* is referred to, the doctrine of Bhartṛhari is always presented.[12] Looking at the doctrine of the *sphoṭavādin* which appears here in Śaṅkara's commentary, there are very many points which are identical with what is said in Bhartṛhari's *Vākyapadīya*,[13] and we can therefore suppose that it is the doctrine of Bhartṛhari, or at least of some Grammarian of that line influenced by Bhartṛhari. Since Bhartṛhari lived round about 500 A.D. and Upavarṣa, as already noted, about 450-500, the latter would probably have been earlier.

Of course, there was a *sphoṭa* doctrine before Bhartṛhari, but it would have been very elementary, and since it was perfected and popularized by him, we can not suppose comparable linguistic and philosophical refinements before him. Again, looking at Śabarasvāmin's commentary on I,1,5, the doctrine that word is a whole is attacked there, but there is no direct reference to *sphoṭa*.

In consideration of all these facts, we can conclude that it is only the statement "words are none other than the various letter-sounds" which comes from Upavarṣa, and that the attack on *sphoṭa* is argument supplied by Śaṅkara. The various sub-commentators also remark that in this passage he is declaring established teaching of his own line based on the tradition of the masters;[14] probably here the words of Upavarṣa are understood as 'the tradition of the masters'. Still, Śaṅkara's refutations of the *sphoṭa* doctrine are not arguments original to Śaṅkara himself, but it seems rather that he here summarized previous refutations of *sphoṭa*.[15]

On these lines we can resolve the apparently contradictory positions taken by Śaṅkara in two of his commentaries. Whereas in the *Brahma-sūtra-bhāṣya* he cites the words of Upavarṣa and combats the theory of the *sphoṭavādins*, in the *Yogasūtrabhāṣyavivaraṇa* he opposes the theory of Upavarṣa and takes up a position quite close to that of the *sphoṭavādins*. The two standpoints are on the face of it contradictory, but in either case he was no more than a commentator on the particular text before him, and did not have to be consistent with the commentary on a different text.

It might be that the difficulties could be sought to be explained away by supposing these to be by two different commentators, but the fact is, that the two commentaries have been transmitted as having been composed by a certain person named Śaṅkara, and the difficulty of reconciliation still remains. But it can be resolved by supposing that the author in either case was just a commentator on that text, who did not mind discrepancy with some other text.

Now from the words of Upavarṣa already quoted, we can assume that he was an expert in grammar. It was an established usage among grammarians, from Patañjali's *Mahābhāṣya* on, to use the word '*gauḥ*' (cow) as the example when discussing the essential nature of words.[16] Kāśakṛtsna was a grammarian;[17] Bhartṛhari, while a grammarian, had also Vedāntic ideas. So it is quite normal that Upavarṣa should have been versed in grammar. Moreover among the philosophers of language following Patañjali, there were two opposing views about the essence of words. One line looked to Upavarṣa as authority, followed by the Mīmāṃsā school and the Śaṅkara and Bhāskara lines of Vedānta; Bhartṛhari was the representative figure of the other line, which held *sphoṭa* to be the essence of word. The Jaina philosopher Prabhācandra in his work *Prameyakamalamārtaṇḍa* clearly describes the two lines represented by Upavarṣa and Bhartṛhari.

In the section[18] analyzing the meaning of a sentence, Prabhācandra examines and rejects the views of the Prābhākara school and Kumārila school (Bhāṭṭa), and then brings up for consideration the views that words alone are real, or that sentences alone are real, both of which he then refutes from the Jaina standpoint.

(1) [The doctrine that word alone is real.][19] It is word alone, whether in worldly use or in the Veda, that has value in bringing about comprehension of meaning. A simple verbal root (*prakṛti*) or suffix (*pratyaya*) to a root can not [cause comprehension of meaning]. For we separate out the verbal root or the constituent affix from the word, and we speak of it in some way to determine what the word is etymologically. And so it is said: "The revered Upavarṣa declares the word 'cow (*gauḥ*)' is the sound '*g*' and the sound '*au*' and the sound of *visarga* (the sound '*ḥ*')." Certainly the letter-sounds (*varṇa*) do not [in themselves] have parts, but just as distinctions can be made of difference in volume or intonation (*mātrā*), in the same way, though the word '*gauḥ*' (cow) has [in itself] no distinctions, [distinctions are made] by separating out the various letter sounds such as 'a' and it formed the basis for the comprehension of the meaning of that word itself.

(2) [The doctrine that the sentence alone is real.] The foregoing position is a doctrine that has been incompletely thought out. For the same argument would show that the sentence is the real thing (*tāttvika*), with the various words being separated out from the sentence to establish their parsing. So whether in worldly usage or in the *Vedas*, it is the sentence alone that is the important thing in bringing about comprehension of meaning. And so it is said: "The words separated out from the sentence are divided according to various views: into two classes, into four classes or into five, just as the root and suffixes etc. are separated out from the word." (*Vākyapadīya*, III,1,1.)[20]

(3) [The Jaina criticism.] We must therefore consider that the word, which is in one point different from its parts such as verbal root etc. and in another point not different, is something conceptual (*prātītika*). It is not that the word is altogether devoid of parts. For just as there could be no basis for knowing what is a letter-sound (*varṇa*) apart from its parts, so there can be no basis for knowing what is a word apart from its parts. And in the same way, the sentence is something which in one point is different from its words, and in another not different ...

In this passage we see that Prabhācandra quotes the words of Upavarṣa as authority for the theory maintaining that it is the word alone, constituted of letter-sounds, that is real, and that a collocation of words constitutes the sentence, whereas for the theory that the sentence alone is real, words and letter-sounds being things abstracted from it, he cites Bhartṛhari. (The quotation from Upavarṣa is identical with that in the commentary (*bhāṣya*) of Śabarasvāmin.) So Prabhācandra would have taken Upavarṣa as holding the view that word alone is real (*tāttvika*). Through the eyes of Prabhācandra we see Upavarṣa and Bhartṛhari as the two great authorities on the philosophical investigation of the nature of words, confronting each other in the history of Indian thought like the two great peaks of their respective systems. And so it is that Prabhācandra, accepting the historical fact and allowing a partial truth to each of the doctrines, clearly declares his own doctrine of 'Indeterminacy' (*syādvāda*, *anekāntavāda*) as a step yet higher.

Notes

1) The present work, Part One, p.409, 'The Relation between the Two Mīmāṃsās'.
2) *Nyāyamañjarī*, Viz. SS. X, p.429.
3) *asty ayam ahampratyayaḥ kaścij charīrasamānādhikaraṇaḥ "stūlo 'ham" "kṛśo 'ham" kaścij jñātṛsamānādhikaraṇo "jānāmy aham" "smarāmy aham" iti/*
4) *Sarvasiddhāntasaṃgraha*, VIII, 37. Keith: *The Karma-Mīmāṃsā*, p.71.
5) Ś. ad *BS*. I,1,1. (vol. I, p.28, *l*.1 ff.)
6) *asmatpratyayaviṣayatvād aparokṣatvāc ca pratyagātmaprasiddheḥ*/Ś. ad *BS*. I,1,1. (vol. I, p.11, *l*.1.)
7) Deussen: *SV*. S.25-26, Anm.17.
8) *tenaiva hy ahaṃkartrā, 'haṃpratyaya-viṣayeṇa pratyayinā sarvāḥ kriyā nirvartyante*/ Ś. ad *BS*. I,1,4. (vol. I, p.69. *ll*.10-11.)
9) Ś. ad *BS*. II,3,38.
10) Ś ad *BS*. I,1,4. (vol. I, p.75, *l*.10-p.76, *l*.4.)
11) Deussen: *SV*. S. 76-80; *Sūtra des Vedānta*, S. 173-176.
12) See the present work, Part VII, Chapter IV, Section III.
13) For example, the doctrine that on the basis of the eternal word, the separate things arise at the time of creation (Ś. ad *BS*. vol. I, p.299, *ll*.8-9.) — Cf. *Vākyapadīya*, I,1; I, 121.

The doctrine that the individual letter-sounds, being cognized, cause seed impressions, and at the time of cognizing the final letter-sound the *sphoṭa* suddenly appears in the cognizing subject. (*ibid*. vol. I, p.300, *l*.9-p.301, *l*.2) — Cf. *Vākyapadīya*, I,85 = *SDS*. XIII, *ll*.189-190.

Denial of independent nature of letter-sounds (*ibid*. vol. I, p.300, *ll*.1-2.) — Cf. *Vākyapadīya* I,73.

The argument that if collocation of the various letter-sounds were the object of a single concept and so the word, then the distinction between *jārā* and *rājā*, *kapi* and *pika*, would not be intelligible. (*ibid*. vol. I, p.305, *ll*.2-5.) — Cf. *Vākyapadīya*, I,93 and Comm. *SDS*. XIII, *l*.160 ff.

The letter-sounds being understood in their order, they manifest the *sphoṭa*, and this *sphoṭa* again manifests the meaning. (*ibid*. vol. I, p.305, *l*.14.) — Cf. *Vākyapadīya*, I,47 ; I,98 ; *SDS*. XIII, *ll*.135-136 ; 144.

14) *ācāryasaṃpradāyoktipūrvakaṃ siddhāntam āha — varṇā iti*/(*Nyāyanirṇaya*, NSP. p. 257.) *ācāryasaṃpradāyoktipūrvakaṃ siddhāntayati — varṇā eveti*/(*Ratnaprabhā*, NSP. p. 257.)

15) The attitude of Śaṅkara himself is definite on the point of rejecting the *sphoṭa* doctrine, but a close examination of the details shows that his own thought is not clear-cut. Following Upavarṣa, he is definite that word is no other than letter-sounds (*varṇa*) ; but as to why one and the same letter-sound (for instance the sound '*a*') is heard differently according to the different utterers of it, he says both that it is heard differently according to differences in the conditioning adjuncts (*upādhi*, externally imposed conditions) from elsewhere, and afterwards he says : "Or again (*athavā*, vol. I. p.302 *l*.16.) the difference in the perception of it is something brought about by the intonation, and not brought about by the letter-sounds, and therefore there is no weakness [in our contention]."
That the doctrine which Śaṅkara gives, following this 'Or again' is the established doctrine (*siddhānta*) of his school is agreed by all the sub-commentators. And so we can assume that he is here giving a synthesis of the conclusions of the various lines of thought which preceded him.

16) *Mahābhāṣya*, vol. I. p.1 ; *SDS*. XIII, *ll*.139-141. And see also Dr. Ui : *Studies in Indian Philosophy*. vol. I. p.93.

17) See the present work, Part One, Part III, Chapter I, Section II "The Philosophy of the *Brahma-sūtra*"

18) *ibid*. p.136, a.

19) From the context, this would be the doctrine of the Kumārila school. That school is termed *abhihitānvayavādin* (one who holds that the various words, expressing their respective meanings, brought together constitute the sentence) and may well have held this theory.

20) Cf. *SDS*. XIII, *ll*. 119-120.

APPENDIX. UPAVARSA'S DOCTRINE OF THE FUNCTION OF LETTER-SOUNDS AS SEEN IN THE *YOGASŪTRA VIVARAṆA* ATTRIBUTED TO ŚAṄKARA

I. Intorduction

Upavarṣa[1] is acknowledged to be the earliest and also the most authoritative of the thinkers of the Vedānta and Mīmāmsā schools after the final compilation of the *Brahma-sūtra*. He is probably about 450-500 A.D. and there seems no reason to doubt the tradition that he was of Brahmin birth. He is mentioned twice in Śaṅkara's *Brahma-sūtra-bhāṣya* (commentary on the *Brahma-sūtra*). First, in the commentary on the sūtra III,3,53, in the discussion on the existence of *ātman*, there is the following:

> Now since it is established that the *ātman* has the character of participating in bondage and liberation, it is proved that the *ātman* actually exists distinct from the physical body .... And for the very same reason, the revered (*bhagavat*) Upavarṣa, when teaching the actual existence of the *ātman* in the first *śāstra* (*prathamatantra*) confines himself to saying "We shall explain it in the *Śārīraka* (i.e. *Brahma-sūtra*)". And since [in this third chapter of the third book of the *Brahma-sūtra*] what is being treated is worship, whose special character is religious injunction , the existence or otherwise of *ātman* is examined in order to show that it is just because *ātman* exists that the whole sacred literature can be authoritative.

Again, in the passage which comments on the text (*Brahma-sūtra* I,3,28) "the entire world arises from Word", Śaṅkara winds up his detailed explanation and then says:

> This being so, when it is taught in the *sūtra* that [all things] arise from Word, what is the essential nature of Word?[2]

Having raised this question, he first states the doctrine of advocates of *sphoṭa*, who assert that the fundamental substance of word is none other than a kind of metaphysical substance called *sphoṭa*,[3] against which theory he replies: The revered (*bhagavat*) Upavarṣa says:

> But words are none other than various letter-sounds (*varṇa*).

He follows up with a detailed debate as to whether words are letter-sounds of this kind or are *sphoṭa*.

In Śaṅkara's commentary on the *Brahma-sūtra*, it is only in these two passages noted above that Upavarṣa is referred to. Bhāskara, who also wrote a commentary on the *Brahma-sūtra*, mentions Upavarṣa three times, and though there are minor differences, what he says is substantially the same as the account in Śaṅkara.[4] Accordingly we should take it that Upavarṣa was looked upon as an authority by all branches of the Vedānta school generally, and also that the words of Śaṅkara represent a correct account of Upavarṣa's doctrines.

On the other hand in the Mīmāṃsā school also he was respected as a great authority. In the commentary on the *Mīmāṃsā-sūtra* (ad I,1,5) by Śabrasvāmin, a passage from the ancient *Vṛtti*-author (*vṛttikāra*) is preserved, and within it the question is raised: "Now when one says cow, what primarily is this word?" to which the answer is given: "The word cow or *'gauḥ'* is the letter-sound *'g'*, the letter-sound *'au'* and *visarga* (*'ḥ'*), so teaches the revered Upavarṣa.[5]

There follows a detailed debate on the point. The words of Upavarṣa quoted in this place are identical with those given by Bhāskara. We can also say that they are identical in sense with what has been preserved by Śaṅkara. Accordingly we can take it that the words of Upavarṣa have been reliably preserved by these writers.

Notes

1) For details, see the chapter on Upavarṣa of the present work.

2) Ś. ad *BS*. ĀnSS. vol. I, p.299,*l*.7.

3) On *sphoṭa*, see Part VII, Chapter IV, Section III of the present work.

4) *ata eva Upavarṣācāryeṇoktaṃ prathamapāde/ātmavādaṃ tu Śārīrake vakṣyāma iti/* (Bhāskara ad *BS*. I,1,1. p.6.); *kaḥ punar atra śabdo 'bhipreto? varṇātmako, lokaprasiddher Upavarṣāgamāc ca/* (Bhāskara ad *BS*. I,3,29. p.62.); *gaur iti atra gakāraukāravisarjanīyā iti Bhagavān Upavarṣācārya ity āgamaparaṃparāyātanyāyopapannaṃ ca varṇānāṃ śabdatvam/* (*ibid*. p.63.)

5) *atha gauḥ ity atra kaḥ śabdaḥ? gakāraukāravisarjanīyā iti Bhagavān Upavarṣaḥ/*

II. Upavarṣa as Cited in the *Yogasūtravivaraṇa*

However, the publication of the recently discovered sub-commentary by

Śaṅkara on the *Yoga-sūtra* commentary (*Yogasūtrabhāṣyavivaraṇa*), in which a statement of Upavarṣa is cited as an authority, has provided new material, and this we shall now present for examination.

Yoga-sūtra III,17:

Word, meaning and concept are confused from being mutually [falsely] superimposed (i.e. seen as identical). By separating them out in meditation, he understands the cries of all living beings.

Vyāsa commentary:

Of these, voice (*vāc*) carries meaning only through letter-sounds (*varṇa*). [Mere vocalization from the throat cannot convey meaning: it becomes meaningful only by assuming the form of letter-sounds.] And the ear has as its object (i.e. understands) only what has been thus modulated in sound (*dhvani*).

The word (*pada*) however is grasped through the concept which brings together and integrates the sounds (*nāda* = *dhvani*) in accordance with their order thus [the meaning of the *sūtra*].

The various letter-sounds (*varṇa*) cannot exist at the same time, and therefore [earlier and later-sounds] are inherently incapable of mutually co-operating. These sounds do not amount to the word [which exists apart from them]: they appear and they disappear. And so what is being taught is, that isolated letter-sounds do not attain the status of a word.

Śaṅkara's comment[1]:

(Opponent) If so, the various letter-sounds would have no operative function, whether with meaning or with a word as their object — how can that be?

(Answer) The various letter-sounds (*varṇa*) cannot exist at the same time, for speech (*vāc*) is uttered in a sequence. [Earlier and later-sounds] are inherently incapable of mutually co-operating, namely since there is no continuing relation, there can be no association between them. These sounds [existing separately] do not attain to the status of a word, and do not make a word manifest, namely, they do not attain to any operative function in regard to a word. They appear and they disappear, so [the various sounds] whether individually or collectively, however the limit of their nature might be extended, will never approach the nature of a word. And so, isolated letter-sounds do not attain the status of a word. Since they do not exist at the same time, it is certain that even in conjunction they do not approach the status of a word. Still less could mere letter-sounds, meaningless as they are, by themselves attain the nature of a word.

(Opponent) Is not speech something cognized by the ear?

(Answer) Not so. For speech is something that makes a meaning understood. It is when something causes understanding of meaning (*artha*) that it is speech.

(Opponent) Then what is this 'speech'?

(Answer) Speech is word. And word is grasped by means of the concept formed from putting together the sounds in their order. Namely, the various sounds arriving at the ear one by one, each implants in the conscious subject (*pratyayin*) a latent impression, and then goes to annihilation. The concept which is made manifest by the final sound is the concept formed of the integration of the sounds in their order, which concept arises from the mind of the conscious subject in whom have been implanted the latent impressions, formed through integration of the sequence from the first letter-sound onwards. What is grasped by that very process of cognition is a word. Since it is cognized directly (*pratyakṣa*), like color and so on, it is not dependent on any other means of cognition.

(Opponent) In the word cow—*gauḥ* — Revered (*bhagavat*) Upavarṣa teach that it consists of the letter-sound '*g*', '*au*' and the terminal aspiration (*visarjanīya* = *visarga*)

(Answer) That doctrine is incorrect. For those various letter-sounds do not directly express any meaning. Why not? Because it is impossible for them to join together. As to why they cannot so join, it is because they cannot exist at one and the same time, for at the time when the sound '*g*' is uttered, the sound '*au*' and the terminal aspiration (='*ḥ*') do not exist. Again, when the sound '*au*' is uttered, the '*g*' and the terminal aspiration do not exist, and at the time of the terminal aspiration, there is no opportunity for the other two sounds. Since therefore the sounds cannot join together, they do not directly express any meaning.

Just as the sounds cannot co-exist, so their latent impressions and the mental functions of recollection arising from them do not occur at the same time, so that these also do not directly express any meaning. For since the role of a latent impression is to bring to expression a mental function of recollection, it expresses only a mental function relating to what has been previously perceived; and what is expressed [through the sounds] is something new not previously perceived.

Again if it is to be accepted that the latent impressions directly express a meaning, that would be to deny the accepted principles "Meaning is understood through word", "The condition of what precedes and what follows is made clear by the verb" and "Since human duty (*dharma*) is given its authority from the word (*śabda*) of the sacred texts, what is not based on the word of the sacred texts is not worth considering".

(Opponent) May it be said provisionally that memory and latent impression, as manifesting the state of other sounds in the future, together are the word?

(Answer) This view also is wrong. Because to say that something will come to that state (*tadbhāvabhāvitva*) can only hold in the case 'when A is, B is; when A is not, then B is not' (i.e. in the case when there exists causal relationship between A and B). If it is taken that the various letter-sounds are the word, then that (idea of future coming to that state) cannot hold. Ordinary people, it is true, have the illusion that the body etc. are *ātman* on the basis of undiscriminating knowledge, and thus think what is not A to be A. But such usage is no basis for determining facts.

Again, since it is established that it is only when there is an active functioning of the organ of speech and the ear that understanding of the meaning [of a word] occurs, it is only when it will come to that state (=express the meaning) that the fact of being a word is established (i.e. when a word expresses a meaning, the word is estabished as such). Therefore (in the utterance of a word) the final letter-sound does not directly express the meaning, because it is no more than a mere sound, just as the first letter-sound for instance [cannot express the meaning].

In the same way, the latent impression of the memory of the final sound also does not directly express a meaning, because it is no more than a mere latent impression of memory, just as the latent impression of the memory of the first sound [of the word] does not express meaning.

(Opponent) [When the word is uttered] the final letter-sound, accompanied by and with the help of the latent impressions produced by the sound already uttered, expresses the meaning.

(Answer) Not so. [On your supposition] understanding of the meaning should become possible with the mere utterance of the final letter-sound. The point is that a man who hears its sound, as the one who is to make the association with the others, will have had impressions implanted in him by letter-sound like the letter '*g*' heard by him at various times in the past. In which case, by the mere utterance of the final sound he should come to understanding the meaning.

(Opponent) The utterance of the first sound is for restricting [the subsequent sounds to one time].

(Answer) Not so. The previously uttered sound and the subsequent sounds being of different times, they cannot co-operate to help each other, so that it cannot be said that there is restriction [of the subsequent letter-sounds].

(Opponent) The theoretical difficulty that for the infallible expression of the word by the sounds, the earlier ones have to be uttered first, applies also to your position. But if we assume that it is the sounds that express the word, then it is right that it is the sounds themselves that directly express the meaning.

(Answer) Not so, for it is accepted that each sound will implant in our organ of intellect a latent impression of itself [which does not give rise to an understanding in the form of a word]. So it is in a knowing subject [the organ of general cognition] in which have been sown, in their sequence, the latent impressions of the syllables, which latter disappear at once, that the word appears. This is which is said to be the expression of a word by its letter-sounds.

Like a lamp, the letter-sounds do not directly act in regard to the word itself (i.e. they do not, any more than a lamp does, act directly in regard to a word to create it).

Since the knowing subject is the possessor (*dharmin*) of its qualities, the latent impressions exist in the one repository of the knowing subject, and it can hardly be thought that there could be any relation of mutual assistance (i.e. between the knowing subject and the latent impressions). As when we perceive, and remember, and wish for desirable things and hate undesirable things [it can hardly be thought that they depend on a single subject]. It cannot be concluded that by the final letter-sound there comes to be any combining together of the previous letter-sounds or the latent memory impressions laid down by them.

(Opponent) For me too, the meaningfulness of letter-sounds is the fact that I understand them as producing a concept in the knowing subject in which have been collected in their sequence the latent impressions, in a formation created by the sounds having been produced in a definite order.

(Answer) Your hypothesis is not correct. For it ends up in rejecting your own assumption. First of all, does the concept (*buddhi*) particularized by the number of latent impressions of the various sounds, have as its content the meaning? Or does it have the word as its content?

(1) If it has the meaning as content, then that concept turns out to be the word itself, for it is that which makes meaning understood.

(2) If its content is the word, then on that assumption too, there is contravention of the principles 'Meaning is the understood from word' and 'As is accepted generally in the world' [it is a contradiction of them].

Therefore it has to be recognized that a word is the content of a single concept, something apart from (independent of) the letter-sounds. So what expresses meaning is neither the final letter-sound accompanied by the latent impressions produced by letter-sounds uttered in the preceding instants, nor the memory of it, nor the latent impression of it. For these stand in need of something to assist the latent impressions, as for instance a concept.

Vyāsa commentary:

However, each individual letter-sound has the capacity to become word: it has stored in it a power to link up in co-operation with other operative sounds, and thus express anything, the later (letter-sounds) being delimited by the earlier [ones] and again the earlier by the later, to indicate some particular thing [bringing the appropriate word into being]. In this way, a number of letter-sounds [uttered] in a sequence are determined in accordance with conventional usage (*saṅketa*) to express a meaning as their object: and some definite number [of letter-sounds thus determined] has the power to express any thing, for instance the letter-sound '*g*' with the letter-sound '*au*' with the terminal aspiration ('*ḥ*') indicate an object (cow) possessing a dewlap and so on.

The appearance of a single concept unifying the succession of sounds arranged in their order, determined in accordance with conventional usage to mean the object — this is the word, settled by custom as what expresses that expressible (i.e. the meaning). The word, as that single thing, has for object a single concept, and is brought out by a single effort [of utterance], has no distinctions in it, and has no order. It is not of the nature of letter-sound, and is manifested by an action of comprehension of the last [uttered] letter-sound.

The sounds uttered in the course of speech, in order to convey something to another, are for the listener determined exactly, in accordance with a general understanding, by the common concept held together by latent impressions of this word, from time without beginning.

Śaṅkara's comment[2]:

Now each individual letter-sound is full of potentialities to express all things. The means by which something is stated is a statement in the form of words. The various words making a statement are full of potentialities to express meanings, as in the wheel each individual spoke has its meaning.

The letter-sound '*g*' for example combines in itself the potentialities to express *go* (cow), *varga* (flock), *agni* (fire), *gagana* (sky) and all such words to link up with other operative sounds: for instance, when *gauḥ* is spoken, it is necessary that the letter-sounds '*g*' and '*au*' and the terminal aspiration ('*ḥ*') should mutually co-operate; when *agni* is spoken, it combines with the other syllable. Therefore one letter-sound, combining with some number of others so as to condition each other, can take the form of any word. Later letter-sounds are delimited by earlier [ones] to indicate some particular thing, namely they are there as expressing a particular word (determine a definite word). Again, the earlier by the later, and those in the middle are delimited by both preceding and subsequent.

In this way a number of sounds [uttered] in order, that order being specifically determined, conform to the relation of preceding and subsequent.

In accordance with conventional usage to express a meaning as their object namely if there is a definite number of letter-sounds [fixed as so many] holding to this order, then it is determined by conventional usage (*saṅketa* = *samaya*) to mean this thing.

According to the conventional usage regarding the letter-sounds, a word is used conventionally. This fact establishes the role of the sounds which make up the word, since the conventional usage of the word depends on the special order of them. What is called the conventional usage of the word is in fact simply the conventional usage of the letter-sounds.

Some definite number [of letter-sounds thus determined] has the power to express any thing, namely when one intends to bring out the particular word 'cow' which conveys something possessing the particular dewlap and so on, the other potentialities for making other words understood are lost and nullified. And correspondingly since one intends to use a special one and bring it into operation, the power of manifesting other words which are not to be used is lost. So the letter-sound '*g*', '*au*' and the final aspiration ('*ḥ*') [in combination] express an object possessing the dewlap etc., manifesting, namely, the word 'cow'.

Settled by custom as what expresses that expressible, these letter-sounds according to the above principle arranged in their order namely used in a particular order, the combination of the sounds arising thus in their special order, manifests a single concept, which is the word, the basis, as it were a support, which expresses what is to be expressed (i.e. the meaning). The letter-sounds do not do so.

"The word as that single thing". — Something like a pot, though single, has many parts, and is experienced as connected with many concept. But a word is not like that. The word is connected with one concept, as is to all. The sounds, however, being more than one and appearing at different times, cannot become the object of a single concept. And if it is sought to reject [the fact that this single word] can be thus grasped by a single concept, his position contradicts what is evident to all.

In this way it is brought out by a single effort [of utterance], namely when there is proper attention to the completion of the concept on the basis of the latent formative powers produced in accordance with the order of the letter-sounds, it flashes out abruptly in the final concept.[3]

It has no distinctions having no parts, and so is not of the nature of letter-sound, and is manifested by an action of apprehension of the last [pronounced] letter-sound, namely manitested by perception of the last sound apprehended in a sequence by the action of the first letter-sound.

The sounds uttered in the course of the speech in order to convey something to another by a speaker are for the listener determined exactly, in accordance with a general understanding by the common concept held together by latent impressions of this word, from time without beginning. The life of the world, whirling on from time without beginning on the wheel of transmigration, is based on understanding meanings through words alone. According to the understanding of its people, under the influence of their latent impressions, words are understood to be fixed just as they are. But the people of the world, bent on the actions of the world impelled by its false forms, hold mistaken ideas about the *ātman*, and in the same way they have mistaken ideas about words.

Word then is something separate, apart from its letter-sounds. For there must be comprehension of it as a single concept (action) since it is what brings about the comprehension, like a lamp. And again, because it is the cause of comprehension of the meaning as regards the object, like the organ of cognition (*buddhi*).

For these sounds have been linked in their sequence by a conscious agent, and also there is the point that they are instruments, like the chisel of a carpenter.

Notes

1) *Pātañjalayogasūtrabhāṣya-vivaraṇam*, Śrīmac-chaṅkara-bhagavatpāda-praṇītaṃ, Madras Oriental Series, 1952, pp. 263-267.

2) *ibid*. p.266.

3) *parisphurati* is an unusual word. In *MW*. only the causative *sphārayati*, to spread, divulges, is given. On the other hand there is *parisphuṭati* or *-sphotati*, which in *MW*. is explained simply as to burst open, *Suśruta*.

III. Significance in the History of Thought

The passage from Upavarṣa quoted in this section is very brief, and the same as the words quoted as from Upavarṣa in Śaṅkara's commentary on the *Brahma-sūtra* and that of Śabarasvāmin on the *Mīmāṃsā-sūtra* . Thus as to content, it adds nothing new.

Nevertheless we can see that important problems are hidden here. First of all, the opponent of the Yoga school, who reverse Upavarṣa, seeks to dispose of the view of the Yoga school by overawing them with authority of Upavarṣa. It can therefore be understood that previous to Śaṅkara there was in the Mīmāṃsā school, the Vedānta school and the Yoga school, a common acceptance of Upavarṣa as an important thinker in his own right.

Second, when we look at his thought, what has come down to us shows that he held as one of his philosophical tenets that a word (*śabda*) is its individual syllables (*varṇa*), such as '*g*', '*au*', '*ḥ*'. This is clearly in opposition to the philosophical line which postulates a metaphysical entity behind word, which establishes it. In concrete terms, his position is the opposite of the school of thought which assumed that *gauḥ* is the fundamental form of the word, with the individual letter-sounds merely artificially separated out from that word.

In Śaṅkara's *Brahma-sūtra* commentary (I,3,28), the above-mentioned saying of Upavarṣa is quoted, and then follows a detailed argument with an opponent, called the *sphoṭa* theorist (*sphoṭavādin*). Deussen takes it that the argument against the *sphoṭa* theorist is that of Upavarṣa.[1] I have already given my view on this.[2]

The surmise is not correct. As the sub-commentators say, the *sphoṭavādin* here is the doctrine of a grammarian (*vaiyākaraṇa*), and in general in India a reference to a grammarian as a *sphoṭavādin* must be taken to point to Bhartṛhari. In all the Indian philosophical books, when a *sphoṭavādin* is referred to, the doctrine of Bhartṛhari is always presented. Looking at the doctrine of the *sphoṭavādin*[3] which appears here in Śaṅkara's commentary, there are very many points which are identical with what is said in Bhartṛthari's *Vākyapadīya*, and we can therefore suppose that it is the doctrine of Bhatṛhari, or at least of some grammarian of that line influenced by Bhartṛhari. Since Bhartṛhari lived round about 500 A.D. and Upavarṣa as already noted about 450-500, the latter would probably have been earlier. Of course, there was a *sphoṭa* doctrine before Bhartṛhari, but it would have been very elementary, and since it was perfected and popularized by him, we cannot suppose comparable linguistic and philosophical refinements before him. Again, looking at Śabarasvāmin's commentary on I,1,5, the doctrine that word is a whole is attacked there, but there is no direct reference to *sphoṭa*.

In consideration of all these facts, we can conclude that it is only the statement 'words are none other than the various letter-sounds' which comes from Upavarṣa, and that the attack on *sphoṭa* is argument supplied by Śaṅkara. The various sub-commentaries also remark that in this passage he is declaring established teaching of his own line based on the tradition of the masters ; probably here the words of Upavarṣa are understood as 'the tradition of the masters'. Still, Śaṅkara's refutations of the *sphoṭa* doctrine are not arguments original to Śaṅkara himself, but it seems rather that here summarized previous refutations of *sphoṭa*.[4]

This supposition is now considerably strengthened. If, as Deussen supposed, the view of Upavarṣa were there being given at length, then surely roughly corresponding views would be cited in the *Yogasūtravivarṇa*. From the fact that this is not the case, it may be seen that the quotation of the words of Upavarṣa was extremely short.

Third, and ideologically an important question, is the fact that though Śaṅkara in his *Brahma-sūtra* commentary uses the words of Upavarṣa to refute the doctrine of the *sphoṭa-vādin*, in his *Yoga-sūtra* sub-commentary he refutes the doctrine of Upavarṣa, to take up a position close to that of a *sphoṭa* theorist. The positions in the two works by Śaṅkara are thus diametrically opposed. How is this to be understood?

One conclusion would be that the two works are by different authors, so that there were two Śaṅkaras. As has been pointed out, however, the ideas we encounter in the *Yoga-sūtra* sub-commentary are fairly close to those of the *Brahma-sūtra* commentary ; in the colophon of the Yoga work it states that Śaṅkara, disciple of Govinda, wrote the work,[5] and some Indian scholars accept the identification.[6]

After all, both these Śaṅkaras are commentators, expounding in accordance with the ancient traditional interpretations.[7] In spite of the contradiction, an Indian way of thinking — in sharp contrast to European ideas — may calmly accept that they are by one and the same author.

Again, in the purely philosophical sense, Upavarṣa's ideas here are concerned with one kind of theory of signs. A *varṇa* like the "*kāra*" of "*ga-kāra*" and so on is in western terms a letter-sound. Buchstabe, and all this is a linguistic and not a philosophical problem, as is attested by the fact that there is no heading for it in a major dictionary of philosophy published in Europe.[8]

Even the erudition of an Eisler has been unable to trace the idea of investigating signs (*Zeichen*) before William of Ockham.[9] Here the consideration of symbolism has a far longer history in India, where we can say it began much earlier. But the ideas such as those of Upavarṣa's opponent, the *sphoṭa* theorist, are recognizable from Plato onward in the West, through the mediaeval realism (*Begriffsrealismus* as against nominalism), and among the philosophers who attacked them were certainly some who held a view resembling that of Upavarṣa. This is a problem in the history of ideas which awaits the attention of scholars, and is a separate question.

But naturally this is the problem for philosophy. In the west semiotics of semiology and so on seem to have become fashionable in recent years. The structuralism of Saussure, the science which deals with the study of organization of signs of different kinds, advocated semiology.[10] The debate over the theory of signs deriving from Charles W. Morris and Carnap, proclaiming semiology as the fundamental science of which linguistics is merely a part — these have to be fully considered. What contribution the ideas of Upavarṣa could make to the future development of the theory of signs in philosophy is a most important question, inviting some young scholar in the future.

Notes

1) Deussen: *SV*. S.76-80; *Sūtra des Vedānta*, S.173-176.

2) Supra.

3) See the present work, Part VII, Chapter IV, Section III.

4) For instance, the doctrine that it is from the eternal Word that at the beginning of the world things come into existence (Ś. ad *BS*. vol. I, p. 299, *ll*,8-9). Cf. *Vākyapadīya*, I,1; I,121; the doctrine that with the perception of each individual syllable a seed is implanted as an impression, and when the final syllable is perceived, the *sphoṭa* suddenly appears in the knowing subject (ibid., vol. I, p.300, *l*.9-p.301, *l*.2). Cf. *Vākyapadīya*, I,85 = *SDS*. XIII, *ll*.189-190; the argument that if the combination of the syllables, as becoming the object of a single concept thereby becomes a word, the distinction between the words *jārā* and *rājā*, *kapi* and *pika*, and other pairs, would be inexplicable (ibid. vol. I, p.305, *ll*. 2-5). Cf. *Vākyapadīya*, I,93 and Comm. *SDS*. XIII, *l*. 160ff; the doctrine that the syllables, when apprehended in their sequence, manifest the *sphoṭa* and that *sphoṭa* again makes manifest the meaning (ibid. vol. I, p.303, *l*.14). Cf. *Vākyapadīya*, I,45; I,98; *SDS*. XIII, *ll*.135-136, 144.

5) *ācāryasaṃpradāyoktipūrvakaṃ siddhāntam āha -varṇā iti*/(*Nyāyanirṇaya*, NSP. p.257) *ācāryasaṃpradāyoktipūrvakaṃ siddhāntayati- varṇā eveti*/(*Ratnaprabhā*, NSP. p.257)

6) *iti Śrī-Govinda-bhagavat-pūjyapāda-śiṣyasya paramahaṃsaparivrājakācāryasy Śrī-Śaṅkara-bhagavataḥ kṛtau Śrī-Pātañjalayogasūtra-bhāṣya-vivaraṇa* .../(p. 232.)

7) Examining the previous passages, we find that Śaṅkara himself is definite on the point of rejecting the *sphoṭa* doctrine, but as to the details we find that his own doctrine is not clear-cut. Following Upavarṣa, he is definite that "word is no other than letter-sounds (*varṇa*)" but as to why one and the same letter-sound (for instance the sound '*a*') is heard differently according to the different utterers of it, he says both that it is heard differently according to the different utterers of it, he says both that it is

heard differently according to differerences in the conditioning adjuncts (*upādhi*) from elsewhere, and afterwards he says, "Or again (*athavā* ... vol. I, p.302, *l*.16) the difference in the perception of it is something brought about by the intonation, and not brought about by the letter-sounds, and therefore there is no weakness [in our contention]." That the doctrine which Śaṅkara gives following this "Or again ..." is the established doctrine (*siddhānta*) of his school is agreed by all the sub-commentators. And so we can assume that he is here giving a synthesis of the conclusions of the various lines of thought which preceded him.

8) For instance, *Historisches Wörterbuch der Philosophie*, Basel/Stuttgart: Schwab & Co. 1971, Band I.

9) Rudolf Eisler: *Wörterbuch der Philosophischen Begriffe und Ausdrücke*, Berlin, E. S. Mittler, 1899. S.914.

10) Philip P. Wiener (ed.): *Dictionary of the History of Ideas*, New York, Scribner, 1973. vol. IV, p.324a.

CHAPTER IV
BODHĀYANA

SECTION I. FRAGMENTS

Bodhāyana was an early thinker who wrote a commentary on the *Brahma-sūtra* and he came to be recognized as an authority by a great number of commentators. It is generally also accepted that Rāmānuja was following the ideas of Bodhāyana when he wrote his own commentary on the *Brahma-sūtra* (*Śrībhāṣya*). In the opening verse of his *Śrībhāṣya*, Rāmānuja says:

(Fragment 1)

> Previous masters have abridged the detailed commentary on the *Brahma-sūtra* which had been composed by Bhagavat Bodhāyana. The words of the *sūtra* will here be explained in accordance with their views.[1]

Thus the commentary of Bodhāyana was traditionally honored in the Rāmānuja line, in which various commentaries were written following the ideas of that work, which can therefore be taken to have had a very profound influence on the doctrines of the line. Śrī Nivāsa also regarded him as second only to the author of the *Brahma-sūtra* (Vyāsa = Bādarāyaṇa).[2] The commentary itself is not extant today[3] apart from fragmentary sayings quoted in Rāmānuja's works. However, even though they are few, each of them expresses some special point of Bodhāyana's thought, so that we can through them get an outline of his teaching. In the *Śrībhāṣya* of Rāmānuja, he is called the "Commentator" (*Vṛttikāra*). We shall accordingly now list the words of this Commentator and examine them. Since each of them presents some special teaching by him in regard to points of interpretation of passages in the holy texts and should thus be considered in relation to the respective texts, the investigation is by no means an easy task.

(Fragment 2)[4]

In his interpretation of the first *sūtra* of the *Brahma-sūtra* (I,1,1), Rāmānuja has the following:

> Therefore, the Commentator (*Vṛttikāra*)[commenting upon the first *sūtra* of the *Brahma-sūtra*], says: "As soon as the rituals have been mastered, the enquiry into *Brahman* [is to be undertaken]." He later will declare that the *Karmd-Mīmāṃsā* and the *Brahma-Mīmāṃsā* together constitute one body of doctrine (*śāstra*), saying: "This *Śārīraka* (i. e. the *Brahma-sūtra*) is combined with the sixteen chapters[5] of the Jaimini School. It is thus established that [the two] constitute one body of doctrine."[6]

(Fragment 3)

> The Commentary (*Vṛtti*) also says: "[In the state of final release, the individual self] is equal to [the highest] light (=*Brahman*) except for cosmic action [universal creation, maintenance and dissolution]"[7]

As is clear from the earlier and later references in Rāmānuja's *Śrībhāṣya*, this passage is according to *Vṛttikāra's* commentary on the *Brahma-sūtra* IV,4,17. (See also the Draviḍa Fragment 4)

(Fragment 4)

In the *Chāndogya-Upaniṣad* VI,8,1, the philosopher Uddālaka Āruṇi is said to have taught his son, Śvetaketu, thus:

> My dear, understand from me the true nature of sleep. When of a person it is said that he sleeps (*svapiti*), then he has become one with Being, he has returned to his self (*svam apītaḥ*). Therefore they say [of him] "he sleeps" (*svapiti*), for he has gone to his self (*svam apītaḥ*).

The interpretation by the Commentator (*Vṛttikāra*) on this text is recorded in the *Śrībhāṣya* (ad I,1,10, p. 176):

> Therefore, the Commentator (*Vṛttikāra*) says: "The passage 'he has become one with Being' is established by the fact that [the beings] become one [with Being] and again are separated [from it]. And the holy text [describing deep sleep] says, '[Just as a man embraced by his beloved wife is aware of nothing external or internal, so this *Puruṣa*] when embraced by the intelligent-self (*prājña ātman*)[is aware of nothing external or internal]'" (*Bṛhad. Up.* IV,3,21).[8]

(Fragment 5)

In explaining the *Brahma-sūtra* I,2,1 Rāmānuja says that the doctrine of the famous sage Śāṇḍilya in the *Chāndgya-Upaniṣad* (III,14) teaches not the individual self but the highest Self and then quotes the Commentator:

> For the Commentator (*Vṛttikāra*) says: "that *Brahman* which is [declared to be] the self of all [by the *śruti* passage, the *Chāndogya-Upaniṣad* III,14,1] "All this is indeed *Brahman*" is the Lord (*Īśa*)."[9]

(Fragment 6)

Commenting on the passage in the *Chāndogya-Upaniṣad* (VII,24,1) which declares "where one sees nothing else, hears nothing else, cognizes nothing else, that is the Infinite (*bhūman*), but where one sees something else, hears something else, cognizes something else, that is the small (finite)", Rāmānuja (ad *BS*. I,3,7) holds that 'Infinite' here is not the individual self but the supreme Self and he quotes the word of the Commentator:

> So the Commentator (*Vṛttikāra*) says: "that infinite [of which *Chānd. Up*. declares] 'But [one should desire to understand] the Infinite alone' is the highest *Brahman*. For [in *Chānd. Up*. Book VII, Sect. 1] first name is mentioned and then a series [word, *manas* etc. up to happiness in Section 22, in which series each successive one is taught as the basis of its predecessor] up to [Sections 23, 24] the Infinite [which being clearly founded in the greatness of the Self terminates the series of dependence] and then [from Sect. 25 on] the *ātman* is taught."[10]

(Fragment 7)

Rāmānuja (in the *Śrībhāṣya* ad *BS*. I,3,32) teaches in regard to the doctrine of Honey-Knowledge (*madhuvidyā*) in the Third Book of the *Chāndogya-Upaniṣad*:

> Here it is teaching that the one who meditates [worships] in accordance with this doctrine becomes the god *Vasu*, the god *Āditya* and the others and he ultimately can reach the highest *Brahman*. Thus the prima facie meaning of the text is meditation on the forms of the sun, but its real meaning is, through the meditation on those forms, to meditate on *Brahman*.

With this explanation, he goes on to quote the teaching of the Commentator:

> And thus the Commentator (*Vṛttikāra*) says: "Verily as to the Honey-Knowledge also, this is applicable. For it is *Brahman* that is to be

meditated on in connection with all these things."[11]

Accordingly, the Commentator believes that the various forms of worship taught in the *Upaniṣads* are really enjoining meditation on *Brahman*. Yet in this connection it is doubtful whether the Commentator was clearly aware of the distinction between *Brahman* as the cause and *Brahman* as effect, as taught by Rāmānuja in this context.

The above seven quotations are the only ones from the Commentator (*Vṛttikāra*) in Rāmānuja's *Brahma-sūtra* commentary, but the interpretations of the Commentator are frequently cited in Śaṅkara's *Brahma-sūtra* commentary, though as heretical ideas. It is true that Śaṅkara himself simply presents them as such, without saying anything as to their source, but all the sub-commentators remark that these are words of the Commentator (*Vṛtti-kāra* or *Vṛttikṛt*).

Let us now examine where they occur, nothing that Śaṅkara does not quote, as does Rāmānuja, the Commentator verbatim, but simply paraphrases him in the course of his own commentary.

It is thus rather pointless to present the contextual passages at full length, and we shall simply mark out for discussion those places where there is a contradiction with Śaṅkara's own theories.

(Fragments 8)

The "*ātman* consisting of bliss" of the *Taittirīya-Upaniṣad* II,1 is dealt with in the *Brahma-sūtra* (I,1,12-19) and Śaṅkara gives the usual interpretation in his commentary on *sūtras* 12-19, but then follows with a very different one.[12] As is clear in the sub-commentaries also,[13] the first interpretation is that of the "Commentator" (*Vṛttikāra*) and the second is that Śaṅkara himself.[14] This interpretation of these *sūtras* by the "Commentator" is exactly the same as Bhāskara's and almost the same as that of Rāmānuja. So it is Śaṅkara's own interpretation, different from that of the others and also rather forced that is probably at variance with the original sense of the *sūtra*. So we may take it that the Commentator's reading of these *sūtras* is the correct one. Whereas in the section of Śaṅkara's own commentary there appear '*Brahman*-with-distinctions' (*saviśeṣaṃ brahma*) and '*Brahman*-without-distinctions' (*nirviśeṣaṃ brahma*), these are not taught in the extract from the Commentator. Thus it seems that the Commentator did not recognize a distinction of two kinds of *Brahman*.

(Fragment 9)

In the *Brahma-sūtra* (I,1,23), according to Śaṅkara, the question is being raised. What is the life-force (*prāṇa*) which is taught in the *Chāndgya-Upaniṣad* (I,2,5)? Rāmānuja and Bhāskara take the passage in the same sense. At the end of Śaṅkara's commentary he has this: "There are some who cites the two texts *prāṇa* of *prāṇa*" (*Bṛhad. Up.* IV,4,18) and "dear child, indeed mind (*manas*) is bound to *prāṇa*" (*Chānd. Up.* VI,8,2)[and take these to be what is referred to].[15] According to the sub-commentators (Ānandajñāna and Govindānanda), the word "some" here indicates the Commentator (*Vṛttikṛt*). Śaṅkara rejects this view of the Commentator.

(Fragment 10)

In his commentary on the *Brahma-sūtra* I,1,25, Śaṅkara mentions another view. "Someone else says: [The word *Gāyatrī*, the metre, as taught in the *Chāndogya-Upaniṣad* IV,12,1 is not some indirect indication of *Brahman* but] by the word *Gāyatrī Brahman* is being directly taught. Because there is the similarity of number, namely that *Gāyatrī* has four feet (*pāda*), each with six syllables, just as *Brahman* has four feet (*pāda*). In the very same way, examples are to be found elsewhere of a word meaning a metre being used to indicate something else by way of a similarity of number. For example, having begun 'indeed this set of five and the other set of five together make ten and that is the highest throw in dice (*kṛta*) '(*Chānd. Up.* IV,3,8) it is said 'that is *Virāj* (the metre of ten syllables) the eater of food' (*Chānd. Up.* IV, 3,8). According to this view, [here] it is *Brahman* itself that is being taught and not the metre. [This is the view.]"[16]

The "someone else" is, according to the sub-commentators[17] (Ānandajñāna and Govindānanda), again the Commentator.

The interpretation here is substantially the same as those of Bhāskara and Rāmānuja. Śaṅkara does not reject it, but allows it with the remark "In any case, in the previous passage it is *Brahman* that is being discussed."

(Fragment 11)

In his commentary on the *Brahmasūtra* I,1,31, Śaṅkara, after giving his general interpretation of the *sūtra*, says "Or again" (*atha vā*) and mentions a different view. The sub-commentators (Vācaspati Miśra, Ānandajñāna and Govindānanda) explain that this view is the doctrine of the Commentator (*Vṛttikāra* or *Vṛttikṛt*). According to this view, the *sūtra* should be taken on the following lines:

> There is also proposed as the meaning of the *sūtra* that even in this section which is teaching *Brahman* it is no contradiction in teaching the characteristics of the individual self (*jīva*) and the principal life-force (*mukhya-prāṇa*) by this word *prāṇa*. How so? *Because there are three* types of worship: namely, worship of [meditation on] *Brahman* is taught with life-force as an attribute, with intelligence (*prajñā*) as an attribute and with self as an attribute. Of these three, the texts "Worship as immortal life; life is *prāṇa*" (*Kauṣ. Up.* III,2), "holding this body it makes it stand" (*Kauṣ. Up.* III,3) and "therefore one should worship this life-force as being *uktha*" (*Kauṣ. Up.* III,3) speaks of the life-force as attribute of *Brahman*. Again, having stated "Let us teach now, by intelligence, all existence becomes one" (*Kauṣ. Up.* III,4) the text goes on "each indeed is a part of intelligence extracted[18] out of it; name is the existent element carried over on to the exterior of words" (*Kauṣ. Up.* III,5), "Man by intelligence mounts on speech; by speech he possesses all names" (*Kauṣ. Up.* III,6), and other texts speak of the attribute as intelligence. Such texts as "In relation to intelligence, these indeed are the ten elements of existence. In relation to existence, they are the ten elements of intelligence. If indeed there were no elements of existence, there would be no elements of intelligence either. If indeed there were no elements of intelligence, there would be no elements of existence. For if there were only one of them, no form at all could stand. They are not separate. Just as the rim of a wheel is supported on the spokes and the spokes on the nave, so the elements of existence are supported on the elements of intelligence and the elements of intelligence supported on the life-force. This life-force is the self of intelligence (*prajñātman*)" (*Kauṣ. Up.* III,8) speak of the attribute as *Brahman*. Thus in the same way this one worship of meditation on *Brahman* is taught as of three kinds according to the attribute of the two limiting adjuncts (*upādhi*) and the attribute as itself.
>
> Elsewhere also, in texts like "Who consists of mind, who takes

life-breath for his body" (*Chānd. Up.* III,14,2) worship of [meditation on] *Brahman* as possessed of limiting adjunct *is taught*. And here [where *prāṇa* is being spoken of] *this is applicable* [namely to conceive *Brahman* by means of the three attributes]. For it is clear from the beginning and end of the passage that one and the same thing is being taught and further that there are the three characteristics — *prāṇa*, *prajñā* and *Brahman*. It is thus established that this passage is speaking of *Brahman*. (The italicized words are those of the *sūtra* itself.)

Rāmānuja, Nimbārka and Madhva[19] also follow this interpretation. Bhāskara, like Śaṅkara, presents the two interpretations but simply refers to the view of the Commentator as that of "others" (*apare*). Śaṅkara seems to have thought this interpretation a possible one.

(Fragment 12)

In his commentary on the *Brahma-sūtra* I,2,23, Śaṅkara first gives one interpretation and then presents another. According to the sub-commentators (Vācaspatimiśra, Ānandajñāna and Govindānanda) the first one is that of the Commentator (*Vṛttikāra*, *Vṛttikṛt*) and Śaṅkara's own view is given in the latter one. The view attributed to the Commentator is as follows:

Moreover we see [in the *Muṇḍaka-Upaniṣad*] that directly after [the passage] "Higher than the highest Imperishable" the creation of [all] things from *prāṇa* down to earth is mentioned [in the passage] "From him is born *prāṇa*" (II,1,3) and then the form of this source of [all] beings (*bhūtayoni*) is said to consist of all evolved things: "His head is fire. His two eyes are the sun and the moon. His two ears are the directions. And his speeches the revealed the *Vedas*. His breath is the wind. His heart is the entire world. The earth is born from his two feet. He alone is truly the inner self of all." (II,1,4)

And this explanation is appropriate only to the Overlord (*parameśvara*) since [the Overlord] is the cause of all evolved things. And this description of form is impossible either of the embodied self which is weak in power or of the *pradhāna*, since these cannot be the inner self of all things. Therefore it is settled that the source of [all] being is none other than the Overlord and neither of the other two.

(Question) Then how is it known that this description of form refers to the source of [all] beings?

(Answer) Because [in this passage, the source of all beings] is the subject. And because the word "He" [in the above passage "He alone is truly the inner self of all"] connects [the passage] with the topic under discussion. Because it is the source of [all] beings that is being discussed, the [whole] passage from "From him is born *prāṇa*" down to "He alone is truly the inner self of all" is concerned with the source of [all] beings. Just as when there is an ordinary conversation about a certain teacher, [someone says] "Study under him; he is a man thoroughly versed in the *Vedas* and the *Vedāṅgas*", it must refer to that same teacher.

(Question) But then, how can a bodily form belong to the source of all beings having attributes of invisibility and so on?

(Answer) This is said in order to show that [it] is the *Ātman* of all beings and not to declare that [it] possesses a body. Therefore, there is no fault. Just as in the passages such as "We are food, we are eaters of food" (*Tait. Up.* III,10,6), so here we must not interpret it literally.

On the other hand, Śaṅkara interprets that passage of the *Muṇḍaka-Upaniṣad* as teaching not the form of the source of all beings but the primeval Person, the evolved (*vikāra-puruṣa*), who according to Śaṅkara should be regarded as identical with *Prajāpati* and *Hiranyagarbha*. In Bhāskara's view, again, the above passage shows that *Ātman* as cause exists assuming the shape of *Ātman* as effect and he goes on to an open attack on Śaṅkara's view.[20] Rāmānuja merely remarks very simply that such a form is appropriate to the highest Self.

(Fragment 13)

After giving his own comment to *Brahma-sūtra* I,4,3, Śaṅkara quotes a different interpretation of I,4,2 and 3, and refutes it. According to the sub-commentator (Govindānanda), the differing view is the "interpretation by the Commentator" (*Vṛttikṛt-vyākhyāna*).

Yet other men explain [the previous *sūtra* and this *sūtra* as follows]: The body indeed is of two kinds, gross and subtle. The gross body is this which is perceived and the subtle body is what will be mentioned. "In entering into another one (i.e. a new body, the individual self) goes enveloped [by the subtle elements, the seeds of the new body]. [This is known] from the question and answer." (*BS*. III,1,1). In a previous passage (*Kāṭhaka-Upaniṣad* I,3,3-4) the two bodies were compared, without distinguishing between them, to a chariot but here (*Kāṭhaka-Upaniṣad* I,3,10-11) the subtle body is indicated by the word "the Unevolved" (*avyakta*). Because the subtle body is capable of being indicated by the word "the Unevolved" (*BS*. I,4,2). And since the operations of bondage and final release of the individual self depend upon it, the subtle body is superior to the individual self (*BS*. I,4,3), just as because the operations of the sense organs depend upon external objects, those objects are superior to the sense organs.

Against this assertion, Śaṅkara presents a counter-question: the two bodies, gross and subtle are the topic of discussion in the previous passages of the *Kāṭhaka-Upaniṣad*, so why would only the subtle body be mentioned in this later passage? In reply, the Commentator says:

We can understand the meaning of what is handed down in the Scriptures but we may not criticize what is handed down in the Scriptures. And the word "Unevolved" (*avyakta*) appearing in the Scripture can refer only to the subtle body and can refer to nothing else, since the gross body is "the Evolved" (*vyakta*).

Śaṅkara, however, rejects this theory as impossible, saying that if we follow such a theory, the *Kāṭhaka-Upaniṣad* would become inconsequential, since the topic would be different in the earlier and later passage. However he does say at the end that he agrees that this passage of scripture has no reference to the primary matter of the Sāṅkhya school, so on this point there is no difference of opinion.

Bhāskara admits both interpretations. Rāmānuja gives only the first interpretation of Śaṅkara and Bhāskara and does not present the interpretation of the Commentator.

Besides the above quotations, a theory of the "Commentator" (*Vṛttikāra*) is preserved in Vācaspatimiśra's *Bhāmatī*.[21]

(Fragment 14)

The *Brahma-sūtra* I,1,1 reads: "Now the *Brahman*-investigation" (*athāto brahmajijñāsā*). Śaṅkara interprets the compound "*brahmajijñāsā*" as "investigation of *Brahman*" (*brahmaṇo jijñāsā brahmajijñāsā*). That is to say, he takes the word "investigation" to be connected in a compound with the genitive (called in ancient Indian grammar the sixth case or *ṣaṣṭhī*) of the word "*Brahman*". On these words of Śaṅkara, the *Bhāmatī* remarks:

> It should be known that the ancient Commentator's [interpretation of the compound as a] compound in the fourth [dative] case: "*brahmajijñāsā*, that is, investigation for *Brahman*"[22] is refuted by the demonstration that the compound is in the sixth case [meaning the investigation of *Brahman*]. (*ṣaṣṭhīsamāsapradarśanena prācām Vṛttikṛtām brahmaṇe jijñāsā brahmajijñāseti caturthīsamāsaḥ parāsto veditavyaḥ*/)

Other sub-commentators, e.g. Ānandajñāna and Govindānanda, also record nearly the same thing. Accordingly, Śaṅkara would have rejected the interpretation of the Commentator. Again Bhāskara[23] clearly rejects this interpretation. Rāmānuja not only reject this interpretation from the standpoint of purport, he takes it, as do Śaṅkara and Bhāskara, to be a compound in the sixth case. Kātyāyana, the grammarian, recognizes such a compound in the fourth case, though Patañjali did not admit it.[24]

Our investigations so far of words of the Commentator (*Vṛttikāra*) quoted in works of the Vedānta amount to only what is given above, but elsewhere, in Śabarasvāmin's commentary on the *Mīmāṃsā-sūtra*, the Commentator (*Vṛttikāra*) is quoted three times (I,1,5; II,3,6; and III,1,6). The last two passages give his opinion on the minor regulations concerning performance of the rituals, but there is also a long philosophical quotation given under I, 1,5, which should be noticed in particular for our study of early Vedānta thought. That is to say, Śabarasvāmin, after his own comment on the *sūtras* I,1,3-5, then quotes a differing interpretation by the Commentator (*Vṛttikāra*) on these *sūtras*, in a very long passage. (In the printed edition of the Bibliotheca Indica, it occupies p.7, *l*.18, to p.18, *l*.6;[25] in Frauwallner's edition, p.24, *l*.16ff.) We add it here as Fragment 15.

(Fragment 15)

The *sūtras* I,1,3-5 are interpreted by Śabarasvāmin as follows:

> Investigation [is to be undertaken] of the authoritative grounds for it (knowledge of *Dharma*). (I,1,3)

When a human sense-organ comes into contact with an existent [object] knowledge arises. This direct perception is not an authority [for knowledge of *Dharma*] because it perceives only what is present. (I,1,4)[26]

But the relation of conjunction between word and its object (meaning) is innate. The knowledge of it (*Dharma*) is enjoined [by the *Veda*]. And that knowledge, relating to things [like *Dharma*] not perceived, is infallible. That knowledge is the authority [for *Dharma*]. For Bādarāyaṇa holds [the injunction of the *Veda*] is not dependent on anything else. (I,1,5)

The interpretation of these *sūtras* by the Commentator, however, is very different. He takes the *sūtras* 3 and 4 as prima facie assertions by an opponent (*pūrvapakṣa*) and understands the *sūtra* 3 to mean "Investigation of the authoritative grounds for it (knowledge of *Dharma*) [is not to be undertaken]"; then making considerable changes in the wording of the *sūtra* 4, he reads *tatsaṃprayoge* for *satsaṃprayoge* and *satpratyakṣam* for *tatpratyakṣam*, so that the meaning becomes "when a human sense comes into contact with it (a present object) the arising of knowledge is right perception. [And the authority for the knowledge of *Dharma* too is among the means of knowledge (*pramāṇa*) based on right perception.] [The words of the *Veda*] are not the authority [for knowledge of *Dharma*]. For [what is taught in the *Veda*] if taken as existent, must be perceived."

In other words, his view is that the first half and the latter half of the *sūtra* are concerned with different things. (Śabarasvāmin avoids this "break-up of the sentence" — *vākyabheda*.) He takes the *sūtra* 5 as giving a refutation against this opponent. The passage from the Commentator is very long; under the *sūtra* 4 he discusses the means of knowledge (*pramāṇa*), incidentally attacking theories of the Vijñāna-vāda school of Buddhism and under the *sūtra* 5 he takes up the real nature of words and the relation joining word to meaning. Professor Strauss has already published his translation and analysis of these points[27] and since the problems are not peculiar to the Vedānta but common to all the philosophical schools in India there is no necessity to consider them further here. But I should like to give a little consideration to the attack on the Buddhist Vijñāna-vāda.[28]

This is a very old specimen of the attack on Buddhism and has already attracted considerable attention. Professor Jacobi showed in his analysis that the arrangement and context of the arguments largely correspond to the sections attacking Vijñāna-vādins in the *Brahma-sūtra* (II,2,28-32) and in the *Nyāya-sūtra* (IV,2,26-37). He believed however that these passages do not attack the Vijñāna-vāda but rather the doctrines of the Mādhyamika.[29] Professor Jacobi performed a great service in calling attention to the facts, but he was mistaken in believing that it was Mādhyamika views that were under attack and today it is generally accepted that it is Vijñāna-vāda which is the target.[30] (This part has been already translated by Dr. Ui.)[31]

Which, then, is the branch of the Vijñāna-vāda whose theories are being attacked here? Little consideration has so far been given to the point, but I am inclined to think that the theories under logical attack here are those from the lines extending from Dignāga up to Dharmakīrti.

(1) First of all, in this passage, as Professor Jacobi has already pointed out, the words held to be the peculiar technical terms of the Vijñāna-vāda, such as *ālayavijñāna*, *pravṛttivijñāna*, *vāsanā*, etc. are not used. There are at the center of *vijñāna* theories of the line of Asaṅga and Vasubandhu, but in the line of Dignāga and Dharmakīrti they were not held to be such important and central concepts.[32] Since the doctrines of Dignāga have not yet been fully gone into, we are unable to form a definitive conclusion ; even supposing that he did set up an *ālayavijñāna* theory,[33] what he emphasized was rather doctrines of cognition and logic, and in India in general he is rather regarded as a thinker in that field, so that his arguments related to the *ālayavijñāna* did not attract interest in India. It is well-known that Dharmakīrti, who developed his doctrines, advocated a theory of Consciousness-Only which differed markedly in import from the Vijñāna-vāda of Asaṅga and Vasubandhu. This is a familiar fact.

(2) On the other hand, the *vijñāna* theory referred to here employs such general technical terms, common to the Indian schools, as direct perception (*pratyakṣa*), intuitive awareness (*buddhi*) and cognition (*jñāna*), and these are a special feature of the Dignāga-Dharmakīrti line.[34]

(3) The concept of "self-awareness (*svasaṃvitti*)" is recognized in this passage. Although the word "self-awareness" is not employed, the self-

introspection of consciousness (*Bewusstsein*) is under discussion here. While it is a problem to determine how far back we can trace the origin of this concept of self-awareness, it was after the time of Dignāga that it came to be discussed in the general history of Indian philosophy.[35] Accordingly, using this as our basis, we can make this supposition: The *vijñāna* theory mentioned here, although we cannot conclude that it is the theory of the Dignāga line alone, was at least being borne in mind when making the attack. This fact becomes one of the criteria for determining the dates of Dignāga.

(Fragment 16)

A theory of the "Commentator" in Bhāskara's Commentary on the *Brahma-sūtra* (ad *BS.* I,4,25, p.85) is mentioned alongside that of the "Author" (*Vākyakāra*):

> The author of the *Brahma-sūtra*, following the *śrutis*, expressed an evolution theory (*pariṇāmapakṣa*) in the *sūtras*. Following the tradition in the *Chāndgya-Upaniṣad*, both the Author (Ṭaṅka) and the Commentator (Bodhāyana ?) have accepted this evolution theory.[36]

Since the Commentator (*Vṛttikāra*) is here given alongside the Author (*Vākyakāra*), the title of Commentator might refer to Bodhāyana, and I have therefore provisionally noted it here.

Notes

1) *Bhagavad-Bodhāyana-kṛtāṃ vistīrṇāṃ Brahmasūtravṛttiṃ pūrvācāryāḥ saṃcikṣipuḥ/ tanmatānusāreṇa sūtrākṣarāṇi vyākhyāsyante//* Further, almost the same passage is recorded in *SDS.* IV, *ll.*273-275.

2) See the Present Part, Chapter I.

3) According to Aufrecht: *CC.* I, 377, a work *Brahmasūtravṛttivyākhyā* by Bodhāyana (a commentary by him?) is listed in the catalogue of Gustav Oppert, 1511, II, 4774, but the details are not clear.

4) *tad āha Vṛttikāraḥ — "vṛttāt karmādhigamād anantaraṃ brahmavividiṣā" iti/ vakṣyati karmabrahmamīmāṃsayor aikaśāstryaṃ — "saṃhitam etac chārīrakaṃ Jaiminīyena Ṣoḍaśalakṣaṇeneti śāstraikatvasiddhiḥ" iti//* (*Śrībhāṣya*, p.2). Almost the same passage appears also in *SDS.* IV, *ll.*277-285.

5) The 12 chapters of the *Mīmāṃsā-sūtra* and the 4 chapters of the *Saṃkarṣaṇakāṇḍa*.

6) Sudarśana-sūri's *Śrutiprakāśikā* has *saṃhitam etac Chārīrakam iti Vṛttikāravacaḥ*

(Sukhtamkar: *WZKM*. 1908, p. 129) and since the same is also said in *SDS*. IV, *l*.284, this too ought to be understood as the words of *Vṛttikāra*.

7) *Vṛttir api "jagadvyāpāravarjaṃ samāno jyotiṣā" iti*/ (*Śrībhāṣya* ad *BS*. I,1,1, p.79). Thibaut (SBE. XLVIII. p.90) translates "with the exception of the business of the world [the individual soul in the state of release] is equal [to the highest self] through light", but I feel it should be understood as I have taken it. On this point, see *BS*. IV,4,17; IV, 4,1, etc. Further, see Draviḍa Fragment 4.

8) *tad āha Vṛttikāraḥ — "satā somya tadā sampanno bhavatīti sampattyasampattibhyām etad adhyavasīyate; prājñenātmanā saṃpariṣvaktaḥ — iti cāha" iti*/

9) *yad āha Vṛttikāraḥ — "sarvam khalv iti sarvātmā brahmeśaḥ" — iti*/ *Śrībhāṣya* ad I, 2,1 (p.238). See Ṭaṅka Fragment 8.

10) *tad āha Vṛttikāraḥ — "bhūmā tv eveti bhūmāparaṃ brahma, nāmādiparamparayātmana ūrdhvam asyopadeśāt" iti*/ (*Śrībhāṣya* ad I,3,7, p.284). Raṅgarāmānuja transmits Fragment 6 as the words of Baudhāyana in the *Chāndogya-Upaniṣad-Prakāśikā* (ad VII, 15,4. ĀnSS p.546).

11) *tad āha Vṛttikāraḥ — "asti hi madhvādiṣu saṃbhavo brahmaṇa eva sarvatra nicāyyatvāt" iti*/ (*Śrībhāṣya* ad I,3,32, p.321).

12) Ś. ad *BS*. I,1,19, vol. I, p124, *l*. 5-p. 132, *l*.3.

13) *Vṛttikāramataṃ dūṣayati — idaṃ tv iti*/(*Ratnaprabhā*). *svamataparigrahārtham ekadeśimatam dūṣayati — idam tv iha vaktavyam iti*/(*Bhāmatī*).

14) Previously, Deussen interpreted that the prior commentary was by Śaṅkara himself and the later commentary was an interpretation of later centuries, but that is an mistake. Ghate: *The Vedānta*, p. 60; Thibaut, Introduction, p. xxxiii, n.; Y.Kanakura: "Über die Interpolation des *Śaṅkarabhāṣya* zum *Brahmasūtra*" (*Festschrift Jacobi*: S. 381).

15) vol. I, p.146, *ll*.2-4.

16) vol. I, p.156, *l*.10- p.157, *l*.6.

17) However, see the sub-commentary on the following *sūtra*.

18) In the printed edition, while there is also "*adūduhat*", I have translated it according to the reading "*udūḷham*".

19) Ghate: *The Vedānta*, p.62.

20) *yo 'yaṃ bhūtayoniḥ kāraṇātmā sa eva kāryātmanāvasthita iti darśayituṃ rūpam upanyasyate/Hiraṇyagarbhasyaitad rūpam iti kecid vadanti/tad ayuktam/prakaraṇavirodhāt*//(Bhāskara ad *BS*. I,2,23, pp.46-47).

21) NSP. p. 38 (ad *BS*. I,1,1). The *Bhāmatī* is a sub-commentary on Śaṅkara's commentary on the *Brahma-sūtra*.

22) According to the sub-commentaries, when it is understood in this way, the word "*Brahman*" now indicates *Brāhmaṇa*, *Brahmā*, etc. Cf. the note 4 in Section II of the

present Chapter.

23) Cf. Yensho Kanakura, "An Unorthodox Branch of the Vedas, Particulary in Regard to Bhāskara," (in Japanese), (Jounal, *Shisō* (*Thought*), 1928, May issue, p.174).

24) T. R. Chintamani : *JORM*. vol. III, 1929, p.55 ; V.A. Ramaswami : *IHQ*. X., 1934, pp. 434 ff. However, according to this, the argument of Chintamani that the dates of the *Vṛttikāra* are between those of Kātyāyana and Patañjali is based on weak grounds (Cf. the argument of Ramaswami).

25) According to Kumārila, what comes before the beginning of the attack on the Buddhist, i.e. up to p.3, *l*.20 (*sa evāsamīcīnaḥ pratyayo nānya iti*/) is the words of the Commentator (*Vṛttikāra*), and what follows is the theory of the *Bhāṣyakṛt* (p.221, v.16) or *Bhāṣyakāra* i.e. Śabarasvāmin (p.224, v.29). However, the publisher of the *Śabara-bhāṣya* (BI.) adds a footnote to the end of p.18 *l*.6, to the effect that up to that point it is the words of the Commentator. Later, Prof. Jacobi conducted his critical research and demonstrated that we should understand that what Kumārila says is wrong and that the previously cited publisher's note should be accepted (H. Jacobi : *JAOS*. XXXI, 1911, pp.15-16). This opinion was accepted by Hakuju Ui (*Studies in Indian Philosophy*, I, p.164) and by Otto Strauss (*Die älteste Philosophie der Karma-Mīmāṃsā*, S.21-22). Gangānātha Jhā asserted that up to p. 24, *l*. 11, i.e. up to the end of the commentary on I,1,5 are the words of the *Vṛttikāra* (*Śabarabhāṣya*, vol. I, 1933, p.9) and the reasons for holding this, he noted, are that Maṇḍanamiśra, in his work the *Mīmāṃsānukramaṇikā*, noted that the Commentator attempted to explain many things (*bahvartha*), but these grounds are too weak. Again, V.A. Ramaswami Sastri, relying on the accounts of Rāmakṛṣṇa's commentary, the *Yuktisnehaprapūraṇī*, on the *Śāstradīpikā*, says that at least up to the beginning of the *ātmavāda* is the writing of the Commentator (*IHQ*. X. 1934, p.432, n.9). The present writer has not had access to that account, but even supposing for the moment that such was recorded, it would be difficult to upset the critical studies of Jacobi noted above.

26) *satsaṃprayoge puruṣasyendriyāṇāṃ buddhijanma tat pratyakṣam animittam vidyamānopalambhanatvāt*/

27) Otto Strauss : *Die älteste Philosophie der Karma-Mīmāṃsā*, (*SPA*., Phil-Hist. Klasse, 1932, XXII, S.469-532).

28) p.8, *l*.21-p.10,*l*.10 (BI).

29) Cf. Jacobi : *ibid*.

30) O. Strauss : *op. cit*. S.11 ; Dr. Ui : *Studies in Indian Philosophy*, I. pp.156-161 ; K. Chaṭṭopādhyāya : "Reference to Buddhist Philosophy in the Vṛttikāragrantha of *Śabarabhāṣya*" (*Jhā Commemoration Volume*, pp.115-127).

31) Cf. note 30.

32) The doctrines of Dignāga have not yet been fully studied, but they appear to differ

greatly from the Vijñāna theories of Asaṅga and Vasubandhu. According to information from Mr. Watanabe, who has read the entire Tibetan translation of the *Pramāṇasamuccaya*, the chief work of Dignāga, the *ālayavijñāna* is not discussed there. So he probably did not teach *pravṛttivijñāna* or *vāsanā* either.

33) See for example Dignāga's *Guan suo yuan lun* (観所縁論) (*Taisho Tripitaka*, XXXI. 888c.).

34) Dignāga's definition of the direct perception is quite famous in the history of Indian logic. (Cf. Dr. Ui : *Buddhist Logic*, p.212 ff.)

35) H. N. Randle : *Indian Logic in the Early Schools*, p.105, n.

36) *sūtrakāraḥ śrutyanukārī pariṇāmapakṣaṃ sūtrayāṃ babhūva/ayam eva Chāndgye Vākyakāra-Vṛttikārābhyām sampradāyamataḥ samāśritaḥ/*

SECTION II. THE MAN, HIS WORKS AND HIS DATES

In the foregoing, we have collected what is still extant of the theories of the Commentator (*Vṛttikāra* or *Vṛttikṛt*), but we still have the problem of whether or not these are all attributable to the same man.

First of all, we shall consider whether or not the Commentator named by Rāmānuja as Bodhāyana and the Commentator mentioned by Śaṅkara are the same person. That these two may have been the same has already been conjectured by Thibaut[1] and from consideration of the fragments listed above, I think we may perhaps accept Thibaut's suggestion as correct. Rāmānuja shows great respect for Bodhāyana's commentary and whenever he quote him it is as a revered authority for his own views ; not once has he opposed those theories. Again, not only Rāmānuja himself but those of his line as well, all regarded Bodhāyana as the greatest authority after the author of the *Brahma-sūtra*.[2] Accordingly, we can say that Rāmanuja's line takes the commentary of Bodhāyana as the most important one. On the other hand, whenever Śaṅkara or Vācaspatimiśra refers to the Commentator, they almost always reject him, and when they do not go so far as that, they merely give his theories as differing views. Then whenever Śaṅkara mentions and refutes some differing theory within the Vedānta school, as noted by the sub-commentators, he clearly records the fact that it is in a theory of the Commentator only in those cases when he is rejecting the view. But in no other case does he list the name of the proponent of the differing theory. Thus for Śaṅkara the Commentator was the most influential thinker among the opponents and he was also the only Vedānta thinker whose name is thought worthy of mention by the sub-commentators.

Now since both sub-commentators on Śaṅkara's commentary and Rāmānuja himself merely say "The Commentator", it must have been obvious to students of that time who was referred to, namely a very important thinker in the early Vedānta school. When we consider this fact, we probably are justified in concluding that the Commentator whom Śaṅkara rejects and the Commentator whom Rāmānuja accepts are the same man, that is, Bodhāyana. And considering how he was honored and respected by Rāmānuja's line, we can well understand why Śaṅkara made such strenuous efforts to refute the theories of the Commentator.

However the problem arises, that the teachings of the Commentator as rejected by Śaṅkara are sometimes but not invariably the same as those quoted in Rāmānuja's commentary. Still, Rāmānuja wrote his commentary on the *Brahma-sūtra* with not only Bodhāyana's commentary but a great number of other commentaries before him ; moreover in some passages he certainly is not following any ancient commentary but clearly putting forward ideas of his own.[3] So the fact that a few of the passages do not agree with Rāmānuja's commentary should present no hindrance to our conclusion that both Commentators should be regarded as the same.

As already pointed out, since the Commentator's arguments refuting Buddhism can be regarded as a commentary on the *BS*.II,2,28-32, this Commentator must have been an expert in the *Brahma-sūtra* and the whole Vedānta teaching. Again a question arises : would there not have been several commentaries in existence styled "Commentaries" (*Vṛtti*) on the *Brahma-sūtra*? The words "Commentary" and "Commentator" certainly must have been used as common nouns around the time of Śaṅkara.[4] However, since in the expression "The Commentator says..." the common noun Commentator (*Vṛttikāra*) is used in the sense of a proper noun without further specification, it seems reasonable that in the case "The Commentator" refers always to a definite individual.

The next question is whether the Commentator referred to in Śabarasvāmin's commentary is Bodhāyana. Prof. Jacobi regarded them as the same[5] and when we look into a work of later centuries, the *Prapañcahṛdaya*, which records the writers and the works of the early Mīmāṃsā and Vedānta schools, we find that in its opening verse it says that Bodhāyana wrote a commentary called *Kṛtakoti* on 20 parts of the Mīmāṃsā and that it was a detailed commentary.[6] (According to the same work, the 20 parts consisted of the *Mīmāṃsā-sūtra*, 12 parts; the *Saṃkarṣaṇakaṇḍa*, 4 parts; and the *Brahma-sūtra*, 4 parts.) Therefore, Bodhāyana like Upavarṣa was familiar with the learning of the ritual Mīmāṃsā and since he wrote a commentary on the *sūtra*, the assumption can be entertained that the Commentator[7] whom Śabarasvāmin quotes may perhaps have been Bodhāyana.

What makes this assumption all the more likely is the fact that the two Commentators lived in nearly the same period. First of all, the Commentator on the *Brahma-sūtra*, according to the words of Yāmuna given above,[8] can be thought to have lived even prior to Bhartṛhari. He cannot have been later than the compilation of the *Brahma-sūtra*[9] (400–450), yet we must take into consideration the fact that Upavarṣa[10] (c. 450–500) lived sometime between them. In that case, this Commentator must all events be placed towards the end of the 5th century A.D. From the other side, the Commentator who wrote the commentary on the *Mīmāṃsā-sūtra* was prior to Śabarasvāmin[11] (c.500), but according to our consideration of fragment 15, he was later than Dignāga. Dignāga probably flourished around 400–480 A.D.[12], so that consequently this Commentator must be thought to have lived c.500 at all events. Accordingly the dates of the two Commentators coincide for the most part. This fact also leads one to think that we may well be right to conclude that the two are the same.

Thus concerning Bodhāyana as a historical personage, we can form the following conclusions:

Dates: Latter part of 5th century A.D.

Works: Commentary on the *Brahma-sūtra* (*Brahmasūtravṛtti*)
Commentary on the *Saṃkarṣaṇakāṇḍa*
Commentary on the *Mīmāṃsā-sūtra* (*Mīmāṃsāsūtravṛtti*)

These three works form one unified composition with inter-connections and were called *Kṛtakoti*.[13] It was a very large and detailed commentary. In particular, the commentary on the *Brahma-sūtra* was a detailed interpretation, a fact which later generations noted and handed down.[14] All these works have been dispersed and lost, and none are available to us today. Since Rāmānuja has quoted from it, the *Brahma-sūtra* commentary might have still been extant until later centuries, but his *Mīmāṃsā-sūtra* commentary was lost early, and had already passed out of existence by the time of Kumārila.[15]

In addition, it is thought that he might have written something like a commentary on the *Chādogya-Upaniṣad*,[16] but at the present time there is nothing more specific about it. Furthermore, Th. Aufrecht noted a tradition that he wrote commentaries also on the *Bhagavad-gītā* and on ten *Upaniṣads*, but it is not clear what this is based upon.[17] Again, we come to the problem of whether or not this Bodhāyana is the same as the Bodhāyana who is said to be the author of the *Gṛhya-sūtra*, *Śrauta-sūtra* and *Dharma-sūtra* which each bear the name of Bodhāyana. Some scholars do maintain that they are one,[18] but these *sūtras* came into existence in quite an ancient period, so that it is more likely that they were written by a different Bodhāyana.

Again, Bodhāyana has been regarded as the same man as Upavarṣa, though in fact the two are different. Prof. S. Kuppuswami Sastri has maintained that Upavarṣa is another name of Bodhāyana.[19] The essentials of his argument are as follows: Vedāntadeśika (also called Veṅkaṭanātha, 14th century), a great figure in the Rāmānuja line, wrote a commentary called the *Tattvaṭīkā* on Rāmānuja's *Śrībhāṣya*, in which he identified Bodhāyana and Upavarṣa.[20]

What is said here in Vedāntadeśika can be confirmed from other directions also. Upavarṣa, as we have already mentioned, wrote a commentary on both the *Mīmāṃsā-sūtra* and the *Brahma-sūtra*, and he recognized the fact that both branches of learning have equal significance as the path which the orthodox Brahmin should follow; this coincides with the thought appearing in Bodhāyana Fragment 2, while on the other hand it differs from Śaṅkara's ideas. Since Upavarṣa was called the *Vṛttikāra*[21] by many scholars of the Middle Ages, there is adequate reason to identify Upavarṣa with Bodhāyana. Perhaps the name Bodhāyana might have been the family name (*gotra*) of Upavarṣa. Philosopher in India have two or three names and it is not rare for one of them to refer to the family or clan (*gotra*). Examples are Kāśyapa, Kaṇāda, Ulūka ; Vātsyāyana, Pakṣilasvāmin ; Ātreya, Brahmānandin, Ṭaṅka ; Akṣapāda, Gautama. The foregoing is the essential argument of Professor Kuppuswami, also adopted by Prof. Dasgupta.[22]

However, I myself feel that this argument is seriously defective from the logical point of view. The central point is the words of Vedantadeśika, but his dates are extremely late, separated from the time of Upavarṣa by nearly a thousand years ; his words are not based upon any tradition of the Viśiṣṭa Advaita school, but rather are derived perhaps from a conjecture of his own. In the passage quoted note 20, he does not say definitely *asti*, but only *syād*. Śaṅkara, whenever he refers to Upavarṣa, always affixes the honorific title of Bhagavat and quotes his ideas as authoritative,[23] while whenever he quotes the theories of the Commentator (*Vṛttikāra*, i.e. Bodhāyana), he either shows a critical attitude or merely gives them as differing theories. Again, as already pointed out, *Prapañcahṛdaya* also has the two as different men. We should therefore probably take them as distinct.

Notes

1) Thibaut : *VS*., Intro. p.xxi.

2) Cf. The present work, Chapter I.

3) *A History of Early Vedānta Philosophy, Part One*, Part IV. Chapter XI, Appendix, Section II. p.455f.

4) Śaṅkara comments on the passege : (ad *BS*. I,1,1) *ata eva na brahmaśabdasya jātyādyarthāntaram āśankitavyam / brahmaṇa iti karmaṇi ṣaṣṭhī na śeṣe, jijñāsyāpekṣatvāj jijñāsāyāḥ /* (vol. I, p.25, *ll*.5-7), and Padmapāda says the following : — *tatra yad anyair Vṛttikāraiḥ brahmaśabdasyārthāntaram āśaṅkya nirasyate na khalu brāhmanajātir iha gṛhyate, pratyakṣasiddhatvāj jijñāsyatvābhāvāt /... brahmaṇa iti karmaṇi ṣaṣṭhī / Vṛttyantare tu śeṣalakṣaṇā vyākhyātā tām nirasyati — na śeṣa iti /* (*Pañcapādikā* p.64) *ato Vṛttikāraprayāso vṛthety āha ... ata eveti / Vṛttyantare śeṣe ṣaṣṭhī vyākhyātā tatrāha brahmaṇa itīti /* (Ānandajñāna's *Nyāyanirṇaya*, ĀnSS. I.p.25). *Ratnaprabhā* also noted the same.

5) Cf. The previously noted article of H. Jacobi : *JAOS*. 1911. Further, earlier than this, Ganghānāth Jhā remarked in his English translation of the *Ślokavārttika*, p.116, that the Commentator was Bhavadāsa, but this supposition is not generally accepted today.

6) *tasya viṃśatyadhyāyanibaddhasya Mīmāṃsāśāstrasya Kṛtakoṭināmadheyaṃ bhāṣyaṃ Bodhāyanena kṛtam / tad granthabāhulyabhayād upekṣya kiṃcid saṃkṣiptam Upavarṣeṇa*

kṛtam// (*Prapañcahṛdaya*, TrivSS. XLV, p.39)

7) Cf. Fragment 15.

8) Cf. The present work, Chapter I.

9) Cf. *A History of Early Vedānta Philosophy, Part One*, Part IV, Chapter I, Section III, p.435ff.

10) Cf. The present Part, Chapter III.

11) Cf. *ibid*., Chapter VIII, Section I.

12) Dr. Ui : *Studies on Indian Philosophy*, V, p.142. Randle (*op. cit*., p.27) has him as being from 400-450 A.D.

13) Yet there also exists a tradition which says that Kṛtakoti is the name of a man. According to the work, *Maṇimekhalai*, a man called Kṛtakoti is listed together with Vyāsa and Jaimini, and it is said that Veda Vyāsa set up 3 *pramāṇas*, Jaimini 6, and Kṛtakoṭi 8. (V. S. Ramaswami Śastri : "Old Vṛttikāras on the *Pūrva Mīmāṃsā Sūtras*", *IHQ*., X. p.433, 1934). Again, even in the *Trikāṇḍaśeṣa, brahmavarga*, vv. 19,23, also, Kṛtakoṭi is taken as the name of an author, but in the *Vaijayantī* (Oppert's ed., p. 95, *l*.308 Upavarṣa is called Kṛtakoṭikavi (according to Jacobi, Lanman Studies : p.165). Moreover, according to the one handwritten version of the *Avantisundarīkathā*, said to be a work by Daṇḍin, Upavarṣa is styled Bodhāyana and Kṛtakoṭi, and his work, the commentary on the *Brahma-sūtra* (*Vṛtti*) likewise entitled the Kṛtakoṭi. Now, Upavarṣa is said to have been the teacher of Vyāḍi, Indradatta, and Kātyāyana (Ashokanath Bhattacharya ; "Brahman and the World", *Journal of Department Letters*, University of Culcutta, XXVIII 1935, p.5). Professor Sargam Lal Pandey maintains the opinion that Upavarṣa, Kṛtakoṭi and Bodhāyana were three different persons, and that in later days the tradition of Rāmānuja identified these three persons as one. (*Pre-Śaṅkara Advaita Philosophy*, Allahabad, Darshan Peeth, 1974, p.162f.)

14) Fragment 1. Further, according to the *Prapannāmṛta* of Anantācārya, it is supposed to have been a very detailed work. (Dasgupta : *HIPh*. III, p.108)

15) As for the evidence for this argument, Kumārila has mistaken the scope of the passage he quotes from the Commentator. Cf. Section I, n.25.

16) Cf. Fragment 16.

17) Aufrecht : *CC*. I. p.377.

18) Guha (*Jīvātman*, p. 29) asserted that since the name Vṛttikāra Kāṇva Baudhāyana appears in the genealogy mentioned in the *Baudhāyana-Gṛhya-sūtra* III,11, he must be the same person.

19) "Bodhāyana and Drāmiḍācārya, Two Old Vedāntins Presupposed by Rāmānuja", by Prof. S. Kupuswami Sastri : *Proc. III*, *OC*, Madras 1924. pp.465-474.

20) *Vṛttikāropajñaṃ svamatam āha —śabdasyeti/apir dūṣaṇasamuccayārthaḥ/atra Śābaram — gaur ity atra kaḥ śabdaḥ? gakāraukāravisarjanīyāḥ iti/Vṛttikārasya Bod-*

hāyanasyaiva hi Upavarṣa iti syān nāma// (*Tattvaṭīkā*, Conjīvaram Oriental Library Institution Series, No. 6, Telugu ed. 1906, Sudarśana Press, Conjīvaram, p.149, *ll*. 7-10.; However, this is reproduced from Prof. Kuppuswami's article previously noted. Cf. Dasgupta : *HIPh.* vol.III, p.105, n. See further note 13 Infra.)

21) Cf. The present Part, Chapter III.

22) Dasgupta : *HIPh.* II, p.43, n.1.

23) Cf. The present Part, Chapter III.

SECTION III. HIS THOUGHT

Bodhāyana was a faithful commentator and scholar of the *sūtras* rather than an original philosophical thinker. His commentaries for the most part stay close to the point and in not a few cases coincide with the commentaries by Rāmānuja and Bhāskara.[1]

He emphasized the absolute sacredness of the *Vedas*. According to him, the scriptures are not open to the criticism of human logical speculation. "We can understand the meaning of what is handed down in the scriptures, but we cannot query what is handed down in scripture" (Fragment 13). To revere and comment on the holy texts, thus of absolute authority, was for him the highest duty. He thought that each word, each phrase of the scriptures merited a study with the whole body and soul. Most of the fragments are concerned with the difference in interpretation of passages in the scriptures and the *sūtras* which summarize them, and sometimes there is no relation to philosophical thought. (Cf. Fragments 9, 14)

Accordingly, his speciality was purely that of commentator and scholar of the scriptures, but since the elucidation of the import of the scriptures is possible only on the basis of some certain and definite philosophical standpoint, there must be a particular intellectual attitude and world-view running consistently through his commentaries. We can pick this out from among some fragments attributed to him.

What we first notice is that his thought is very different from that of Śaṅkara and approaches rather that of Rāmānuja. Śaṅkara spared no effort to refute his interpretations, while the Rāmānuja line paid a good deal of respect to him; thus it does appear that his thought stood in opposition to that of Śaṅkara.

He held that the learning pertaining to the Vedānta and to the Karma-mīmāṃsā were both important for the orthodox Brahmin, and that the two together constituted one doctrinal system (*śāstraikatva*). Directly after completing the study of the rituals, he says, one should take up the "investigation into *Brahman*", i.e. the study of the Vedānta (Fragment 2). Inasmuch as he wrote commentaries on both the *Brahma-sūtra* and the *Mīmāṃsā-sūtra*, it is certain that he believed that the ideal of the orthodox Brahmanic culture could be realized by means of these two. In this respect, his thought is identical with that of Upavarṣa and with a prominent line of thought of the *Brahma-sūtra*. In the phrase current later, he seems to have held a type of thought close to that of "the combination of knowledge and action" (*jñāna-karmasamuccayavāda*). There is a thread of connection also with the thought of Bhāskara and others. Accordingly, Śaṅkara, who had little regard for the significance of the rituals, quite naturally exerted himself to the utmost to refute his commentaries.

Next let us consider his philosophical thought. According to Rāmānuja's account (Fragment 6), he took as his Absolute the principle called "Supreme *Brahman*" (*paraṃ brahma*). The word "supreme" (*para*) in this case is no more than a mere adjective describing *Brahman*, and probably not a concept contrasted with a "lower *Brahman*" (*aparaṃ brahma*). Since Śaṅkara rejects Bodhāyana's theory and sets up a distinction between "*Brahman* with attributes" (*saviśeṣaṃ brahma*) and "attributeless *Brahman*" (*nir-viśeṣaṃ brahma*), it would appear that Bodhāyana himself would not have conceived such a distinction (Fragment 8).

In his view, furthermore, this *Brahman* is identical with the Lord (*īśa*), the Supreme Lord (*parameśvara*) (Fragments 5, 12). (Here too the word "supreme" is no more than a mere adjective.) Again, it is also called the "source (womb) of all things" (*bhūtayoni*) (Fragments 12). Thus *Brahman*, besides being the personal God, is symbolized as like a womb, inasmuch as it causes everything to evolve from within itself. And not merely does it bring about the evolution of all things, but it is the god that dwells within everything, controlling and directing them. Accordingly, the term "inner self of all things" (*sarvabhūtāntarātman*) taught in the *Upaniṣad* (Fragment 12) is fitting, and moreover he himself also calls it "the *ātman* of all things" (Fragment 12). However the idea cannot be yet found in him, which appears in Rāmānuja, that *Brahman* has all the spiritual and physical existences as his body. He denies that the Absolute has a body (*vigrahavat*, Fragment 12). Consequently, he probably thought that *Brahman*, as the *ātman* of all things, was the ultimate root which makes possible all phenomena (Fragment 6). Furthermore, he accepted the teaching deriving from the *Upaniṣads* that *Brahman* has four feet (*pāda*) (Fragment 10), but it is not clear in what sense he understood it.

Now since *Brahman* is "source of all things" and is the ultimate cause for the development of all objects, it is called "cause of all evolved things" (*sarvavikārakāraṇa*, Fragment 12). How then did he think that *Brahman* brings about this evolution? None of his own words on this subject have been transmitted to us, but Bhāskara relates that both he and Ṭaṅka (the *Vākyakāra*) held the "evolution theory" (*pariṇāmapakṣa*) of *Brahman* (Fragment 16). Thus Bodhāyana did not accept the *Māyā* doctrine but would have thought that *Brahman*, a personal existence and thought of as a womb, brings the phenomenal world into existence by evolving it out of itself.

Passing on to his concept of the individual self, he thought that it has two bodies. One of these is the gross body (*sthūlaṃ śarīram*), the body which we perceive ordinarily and which soon perishes when we die. The other is the subtle body (*sūkṣmaṃ śarīram*), which cannot be seen by the naked eye, being composed of very fine elements. When we die, the individual self is enwrapped in this subtle body, which escapes from the physical body, and eventually sets up the next gross body. It is so to say the "seed of the body" In the scripture, the former is called "the evolved" (*vyakta*) and the latter the "unevolved" (*avyakta*) (Fragment 13). Such a concept had already been expounded also in the *Brahma-sūtra* (I,4,2). But what should be carefully noted is the assertion that "the bondage and final release of the individual self relate to the subtle body" and that consequently "the subtle body is superior (*para*) to the individual self." According to him, therefore, the transmigration and final release of the individual self might somehow depend upon the activity of the subtle body, with the individual self quite inactive. If so, the conception of the "individual self" has a remarkable resemblance to the *Puruṣa* of the Sāṃkhya school. In this point, his concept of the individual self is markedly different from that of the *Brahma-sūtra*.

There is little further information about his concept of the individual self. The individual self or the embodied self (*śarīra*) is said to be "feeble in power" (*tanumahiman*, Fragment 12). And in the state of deep sleep, the individual self is united with *Brahman* as Existence ; upon awakening, he thought that it becomes separated from it (Fragment 4). Here his thought is identical with that of Uddālaka (*Chānd. Up*. VI, 8, 1) and the *Brahma-sūtra*.

As to the problem of cognition, he took a realist standpoint, asserting the superiority of objects (Fragment 13). He would have thought that the objects determine the contents of the cognition.

As for the problem of *religious practice*, no special sayings of his have been preserved, but as he had completed the study of both the Vedānta learning and the Karma-mīmāṃsā, he may have recommended the worship of *Brahman* as well as performance of the traditional rituals of orthodox Brahmanism. We may conclude that he certainly advocated the worship of *Brahman* with the aid of various signs and symbols (Fragments 7 and 11). As to final release, the individual self becomes equal to *Brahman*, but does not, he thought, possess the capacity to create, preserve and destroy the world (Fragment 3). Therefore in final release the individual self and the supreme self are not, in his view, completely identical. Here his concept of final release is identical with that of the *Brahma-sūtra*.

Other very important points of his thought are the doctrine of the means of knowledge (*pramāṇa*) as Śabarasvāmin[2] quotes him, and also his discussion of the nature of words, but these are not philosophical ideas peculiar to the Vedānta school but rather doctrines common to the other schools also, so they are omitted here.

In what we have seen above, his thought for the most part coincides with that of the *Brahma-sūtra*, varying in only few important matters. It seems that his intellectual standpoint was nearly that of Upavarṣa, and we have noted not a few resemblances to the ideas of Bhāskara and Rāmānuja. Of the *Māyā* doctrine, not the faintest trace can be found. He refuted with all his power the Vijñānavāda theory which reduces the objects of the outer world to the status of dream experiences[3] (Fragment 15). Thus though he is in the same Vedānta tradition, his thought is in sharp contrast to that of the *Māṇḍūkya-kārikā* and Śaṅkara. He is, furthermore, frequently mentioned only as the "Commentator" without any individual name given, a practice which shows that his authority was accepted by the general run of Vedāntic thinkers of later generations.

Notes

1) However in the section at the beginning of the *Mīmāṃsā-sūtra*, his commentary differs greatly from that of Śabarasvāmin (Cf. Fragment 15). It would seem that perhaps the latter is the more faithful as a commentary.

2) ad the *Mīmāṃsā-sūtra*, I,1,5.

3) The argument in refutation of the Vijñānavāda theory in fragment 15 of the *Vṛttikāra* is stated among the assertions of the *pūrvapakṣa*. This was probably not a refutation directed against the Commentator, but rather an argument which the Commentator provisionally inserted in the *pūrvapakṣa*. Kumārila thought that it was a theory of the Mīmāṃsā school itself. (Cf. Otto Strauss: *Die älteste Philosophie der Karma-Mīmāṃsā*, S.8ff.)

CHAPTER V

ṬAṄKA (BRAHMĀNANDIN)

SECTION I. FRAGMENTS

Ṭaṅka is known as Ācārya Ṭaṅka[1] and by another name Brahmānandin,[2] also shortened to Nandin.[3] Again he is called Atrivaṃśya (descendent of Atri) and also Ātreya.[4] He was widely known by the appellation 'The Author' (*Vākyakāra*).[5] All these refer to one and the same person.

His works have been lost, but sayings of his are quoted fragmentarily in later centuries, and they are listed below with a translation.

(Fragment 1) *Saṃkṣepaśārīraka*, III, 217.

Ātreyavākyam api saṃvyavahāramātraṃ kāryaṃ samastam iti naḥ kathayāṃ babhūva/

satkāryavādaviṣayo na hi doṣarāśir māyāmaye bhavitum utsahate virodhāt//

"There is a saying of Ātreya : 'As effect, everything is merely empirically existent.' The many defects involved in the doctrine of the effect existing potentially in the cause (*satkāryavāda*) cannot really apply to what consists of *māyā*."

The commentator Puruṣottamamiśra as well as Rāmatīrtha takes *saṃvyavahāramātra* as equivalent to *māyāmaya* and interpret 'that which is neither being nor non-being' (*sadasadvilakṣaṇa*) (In the four fragments which follow, there should also be added the commentary of Madhusūdana Sarasvatī for reference, but I have not been able to see the original.)

(Fragment 2) *Saṃkṣepaśārīraka*, III, 218.

Kāṇāda-darśana-samāśraya-doṣarāśir dūrān nirasta iha saṃvyavahāramātre/

Vedāntabhūmikuśalo munir Atrivaṃśyas tenāha kāryam iha saṃvyavahāramātram//

"In [the theory of its being] merely empirical existence, the many faults inherent in the Vaiśeṣika system of philosophy are totally removed. So it is that the descendent of Atri, the sage well versed in the field of Vedānta, says: 'In this [Vedānta teaching, the world as] effect is merely empirical existence.'"

In the previous verse it had been explained that the faults inherent in the doctrine of effect existing potentially in the cause do not exist in the Vedānta, and now it is said in this verse that in the Vedānta there are no such defects as are inherent in the doctrine of no effect existing in the cause (*asatkāryavāda*). (Puruṣottamamiśra's *Subodhinī*)

(Fragment 3) *Saṃkṣepaśārīraka*, III, 219.

ṣaṣṭhaprapāṭhakanibaddham udīritaṃ yat tat satyam eva khalu satyasamāśrayatvāt/

atraiva yat punar uvāca samudraphenadṛṣṭāntapūrvakam ado vyavahāradṛṣṭyā//

"What has been taught in relation to Part Six [of the *Chāndogya Upaniṣad*] is verily the truth, since [Part Six] is concerned with Being. Moreover what is taught in the saying of Ātreya is based on the familiar analogy of the ocean and the foam [on it]."

This is the answer to the suspicion that it is a theory of evolution (*pariṇāma*) that is taught in Part Six of the *Chāndogya Upaniṣad*. (*Subodhinī — nanu Ṣaṣṭhe pariṇāmo 'py ukta iti tatrāha — atraiveti*) What is called the empirical view (*vyavahāradṛṣṭi*) is the doctrine of false superimposition (*vivartavāda*, according to Rāmatīrtha's *Anvayaprakāśikā*). *satyasamāśrayatvāt = sadvastuviṣayatvād*. (Rāmatīrtha : *ibid*.)

(Fragment 4) *Saṃkṣepaśārīraka*, III, 220.

pūrvaṃ vikāram upavarṇya śanaiḥ śanais taddṛṣṭiṃ visṛjya nikaṭaṃ parigṛhya tasmāt/

sarvaṃ vikāram atha saṃvyavahāramātram advaitam eva parirakṣati vākyakāraḥ//

"Therefore The Author, first having described minutely [the doctrine] of transformation, then gradually having abandoned this view and taken up one close to it [the theory of false superimposition],[6] maintains non-duality alone: 'all transformation is merely empirical existence.'"

(Fragment 5) Bhāskara ad the *Brahma-sūtra*, I, 4, 25. p. 85.

sūtrakāraḥ śrutyanukārī pariṇāmapakṣaṃ sūtrayām babhūva/ayam eva Chāndogye Vākyakāra-Vṛtti-kārābhyām saṃpradāyamataḥ samāśritaḥ/ tathā ca vākyam — pariṇāmas tu syād dadhyādivad iti/

"The author of the *Brahma-sūtra*, following the revealed scriptures, presented in his *sūtras* the evolution theory. In commenting on the *Chāndogya Upaniṣad*, both The Author (Ṭaṅka) and the Commentator (Bodhāyana) followed his view, based on the tradition as it is, and also adopted the evolution theory. And thus there is the saying: 'But the evolution [of things] is like the appearance of curds out of milk, and so on '"

This saying, again, is quoted in places in the *Brahma-sūtra* commentary of Rāmānuja, the *Śrībhāṣya*.

(Fragment 6)

At the beginning of his commentary on the *Brahma-sūtra*, Rāmānuja explains meditation taught in the *Upaniṣads*:

"Meditation (*dhyāna*) consists of uninterrupted continuity of remembrance (*smṛti*) like a stream of poured-out oil.... Remembrance comes from what has been seen by the dominance of the impressions of the past." (*Śrībhāṣya* p.9. BSS.)

Then he quotes The Author:

Vākyakāreṇaitat sarvaṃ prapañcitam/vedanam upāsanaṃ syāt tadviṣaye śravaṇād iti/sarvāsūpaniṣatsu mokṣasādhanatayā vihitaṃ vedanam upāsanam ity uktam/sakṛtpratyayaṃ kuryāc chabdārthasya kṛtatvāt prayājādivad iti pūrvapakṣaṃ kṛtvā siddhaṃ tūpāsanaśabdād iti vedanam asakṛdāvṛttaṃ mokṣasādhanam iti nirṇītam/upāsanaṃ syād dhruvānusmṛtir darśanān nirvacanāc ceti tasyaiva vedanasyopāsanarūpasyāsakṛdāvṛttasya dhruvānusmṛtitvam upavarṇitam//

"All this has been explained in full by The Author: 'Knowledge (*vedana*) must mean worship (*upāsana*). For in the sacred scriptures it is used in that sense.' He teaches, namely, that in all the *Upaniṣads*, the knowledge (*vedana*) enjoined as the means to release is worship. [And again The Author] having set out a provisional view (*pūrvapakṣa*), that 'meditation is to be performed once, for when that has been done, the purpose of the scripture will have been achieved, as for instance in the case of the preliminary rite (*prayāj*) etc.' settles the point by saying: 'But in view of the word *upāsana*, it is knowledge repeated again and again which is determined to be the means to release.' [Again The Author] says: 'Worship should be a continuous remembrance, because it has been seen, and the scripture affirms it; knowledge, which is meditation often repeated, is a firm remembrance.'"

The first part of this fragment is cited in *SDS*. IV, *ll*.332-333.

(Fragment 7)

Having explained that in order to gain knowledge one must perform throughout life the various actions (*karman*) prescribed in the scriptures, Rāmānuja quotes from the *Brahma-sūtra* (IV,1,12 and 16; III,4,33) and then goes on:

Vākyakāraś ca dhruvānusmṛter vivekādibhya eva niṣpattim āha — "tallabdhir vivekavimokābhyāsakriyākalyāṇānavasādānuddharṣebhyas saṃbhavāṇ nirvacanāc ca" — iti/ vivekādīnāṃ svarūpaṃ cāha — "jātyāśrayanimittāduṣṭād annāt kāyaśuddhir vivekaḥ" iti/ atra nirvacanam — āhāraśuddhau sattvaśuddhiḥ, sattvaśuddhau dhruvā smṛtiḥ" (*Chānd.Up*. VII,26,2) *iti /vimokaḥ kāmānabhiṣvaṅga iti/"śānta upāsīta"* (*Chānd.Up*. III,14,1) *iti nirvacanaṃ/ ārambhaṇasaṃśīlanaṃ punaḥ punar abhyāsa iti/ nirvacanaṃ ca smārtam udāhṛtaṃ Bhāṣyakāreṇa "sadā tadbhāvabhāvitaḥ"* (*Bhag.G*. VIII, 6) *iti/ pañcamahāyajñādyanuṣṭhānaṃ śaktitaḥ kriyeti / nirvacanaṃ "kriyāvān eṣa brahmavidāṃ variṣṭhaḥ"* (*Muṇḍ.Up*. III,1,4)/ *"tam etam Vedānuvacanena brāhmaṇā vividiṣanti yajñena dānena tapasānāśakena"* (*Bṛhad.Up*. IV,4,22) *iti ca/ satyārjavadayādānāhiṃsānabhidhyāḥ kalyāṇāni/ nirvacanaṃ "satyena labhyas teṣām evaiṣa virajo brahmalokaḥ"* (*Praśna Up*. I,16) *ity ādi/ deśakālavaiṣamyāc chokavast-vādyanusmṛteś ca tajjanyam dainyam abhāsvaratvaṃ manaso 'vasāda iti/ tadviparyayo 'navasādaḥ/ nirvacanaṃ "nāyam ātmā balahīnena labhyaḥ"* (*Muṇḍ.Up*. III,2,4) *iti/ tadviparyayajā tuṣṭir uddharṣaḥ/ tadviparyayo 'nuddharṣa iti/ atisaṃtoṣaś ca virodhīty arthaḥ/ nirvacanam api "śānto dāntaḥ"* (*Bṛhad. Up*. IV,4,23) *iti/*[7]

The Author has taught that continuous remembrance is attained on the basis of discrimination and the other qualities, namely: (1) discrimination, (2) abandonment, (3) practice, (4) performance of rites, (5) right action, (6) no depression, (7) no elation, on the authority of reason and of scripture. Then he defines what are discrimination and the others : (1) discrimination[8] is purity of the body by choosing food not polluted as to kind,[9] location[10] and occasion.[11] On this there is the scripture : "In purity of aliment is purity of mind ; in purity of mind, remembrance is firm" (*Chānd. Up.* VII,26,2). (2) abandonment is freedom from sexual desire. The scripture is "In peace let him meditate" (*Chānd. Up.* III,14, 1). (3) Practice is repeated and habitual performance and for this the Commentator cites authority from tradition (*smṛti*) : "Ever dwelling on that state" (*Bhag. G.* VIII, 6) and (4) performance of rites is practice of the five major observances[12] according to one's ability.For this the scriptural authority is "One who practices the performance of rites is the highest among the men who know *Brahman*"(*Muṇḍ. Up.* III, 1, 4) and "The true Brahmins desire to know it (*ātman*) through sacred recitation, sacrifice, charity, austerity and fasting" (*Bṛhad. Up.* IV,4,22). (5) right action is truth, honesty, compassion, charity, harmlessness and desirelessness. The scriptural authority is in the verses "[This *ātman*] is to be attained by truth" (*Muṇḍ. Up.* III,1,5) and "Theirs is that taintless world of *Brahman*" (*Praśna Up.* I,16). (6) Depression is the lowering and darkening arising in the heart from difficulties of situation or time, or from thinking of causes of suffering ; non-depression is the opposite of it. On this there is the scripture : "This *ātman* cannot be obtained by one without strength" (*Muṇḍ. Up.* III,2,4). Elation is the over-satisfaction arising from the opposite of what has just been described [about depression] and no elation is its opposite. The meaning is that over-satisfaction becomes an obstacle [to meditation]. The authority for this is : "Calm, controlled" (*Bṛhad.* IV,4,23).[13]

(Fragment 8)

The *pūrvapakṣin* (probably the Advaitin) in Rāmānuja's *Śrībhāṣya* explains that nescience (*avidyā*) is destroyed by true knowledge of *ātman*, and after listing a number of passages from the *Upaniṣads* in demonstration, goes on to say :

Now, as will indeed be explained later by the *Sūtra* author : "Nonetheless [the supreme *Brahman* should be meditated upon and worshipped] as the *ātman* [of the worshipper]. [The worshippers of ancient times] confirm it and again [the scriptures] explain [the significance of it]" (*BS*. IV,1,3). And The Author (*Vākyakāra*) in the same way also says: "Nonetheless, one should grasp the fact [that *Brahman*] is *ātman*. Why? Because all things are achieved by it (*ātman*)."(*tathā cāha Vākyakāraḥ ātmety eva tu gṛhṇīyāt sarvasya tanniṣpatter iti/*) Then it is taught that by the cognition that *Brahman* is identical with *ātman* [of all things], the bondage which is illusion will be destroyed, together with its cause."[141]

The same is also recorded in the *Vedārthasaṃgraha* (p. 185):

ato 'ham iti śabdaḥ svātmaprakāraprakāriṇaṃ paramātmānam evācaṣṭe, ata idam ucyate. — "ātmety eva tu gṛhṇīyāt sarvasya tanniṣpatter" ity ādināha. — grahaṇopāsanaṃ Vākyakāreṇa " kāryāvasthaḥ kāraṇāvasthaś ca sthūla-sūkṣmacidacidvastuśarīraḥ paramātmaiveti sarvasya tanniṣpatter" ity uktam, "ātmeti tūpagacchanti grāhayanti ca"* (*BS*. IV,1,3) *iti /*

The part from the asterisk(*) is the commentary by Rāmānuja himself on the words of The Author.

(Fragment 9) *Śrībhāṣya* ad *BS*. I,1,1 (BSS. p. 80).

In all meditations (*vidyā*) on the supreme *Brahman*, the object of worship is to be *Brahman* with attributes and that have the identical fruit. Therefore [the *Upaniṣads* teach that] one may select any one out of the meditations. This has been stated by the author of the *sūtras* himself in such *sūtras* as] "[The attributes such as] bliss etc. of the subject (=*Brahman*) of the attributes [should be applied to other passages which teach *Brahman*]" (*BS*. III,3,11) [and] "one should select [and put into practice] one [of the various meditations on *Brahman*], for their fruits do not differ" (*BS*. III.3,59). The Author too states that *Brahman* with attributes is to be the object of worship and that one out of the various meditations on *Brahman* should be selected: "[The object of worship] is [*Brahman*] united [with various attributes]; for one worships what has attributes." The Commentator (*Bhāṣyakṛt*) gives explanatory phrases like "Even if their existence is imagined in the mind."

Vākyakāreṇa ca saguṇasyopāsyatvaṃ vidyāvikalpaś cokto "yuktaṃ tad-

guṇakopāsanād" iti/bhāṣyakṛtā vyākhyātaṃ ca yady api saccitta ity ādinā//

This fragment is also cited in *Vedārthasaṃgraha* (p. 143). The Commentator mentioned in the above passage is Dramiḍa. Cf. Draviḍa, Fragment 2.

(Fragment 10) *Śrībhāṣya* ad *BS.* I,1,1 (BSS. p.116)

idam eva śarīrātmabhāvalakṣaṇaṃ tādātmyam ātmeti tūpagacchanti grāhayanti ca (*BS.* IV,1,3) *iti vakṣyati. ātmety eva tu gṛhṇīyād iti ca vākyakāraḥ/*

This identity [between the world and *Brahman*] which is characterized by the relationship between the body and ātman will be explained: "Nonetheless [the supreme *Brahman* should be meditated upon and worshipped] as the *ātman* [of the worshipper]. [The worshippers of ancient times] confirm it and again [the scriptures] explain [the significance of it]" (*BS.* IV,1,3). And so The Author says: "It should be understood to be *ātman*".

(Fragment 11) The following passage occurs in the scripture (*Chānd. Up.* VIII.1,1):

"Now in this city of *Brahman* (= the physical body) is the dwelling which is a small lotus-flower (=the heart). Within it is a small space (*daharākāśa*). One should seek after that which is within that space."

In explaining this passage Rāmānuja says (*Śrībhāṣya* ad *BS.* I,3,13. BSS. p. 300):

Therefore it is ascertained that what is stated [in the *śruti* passage] is that the small space is the highest *Brahman*, that the aggregate of desirable qualities such as freedom from evils abides in Him, and that both these should be sought after and desired to be known. The Author also clarifies this in passages such as: "*That which is within that* refers to the desirable [qualities]."

tad etad Vākyakāro 'pi spaṣṭayati tasmin yad antar iti kāmyavyapadeśa ityādinā//

This passage is also a topic of discussion in the *Vedārthasaṃgraha* (p. 180):

Vākyakāraś ca "daharo 'smin antarākāśaḥ kiṃ tatra vidyate yad anveṣṭavyaṃ yad vāva vijñāsitavyam" iti codite. "yāvān vāyam ākāśas tāvan eṣo 'ntarhṛdaya ākāśaḥ" ityādinā asyākāśaśabdavācyasya paramapuruṣasyānavadhikamahattvaṃ sakalajagadādhāratvaṃ ca pratipādya "tasmin kāmās samāhitaḥ" iti apahatapāpmatvādisatyakāmaśabdena satyasaṃkalpatvaparyantaguṇāṣṭakaṃ nihitam iti, paramapuruṣavat paramapuruṣaguṇāṣṭakasyāpi pṛthag vijñāsitavyapratipipādayiṣayā "tasmin yad antas tad anveṣṭavyam" ity uktam iti śrutyaiva sarvaṃ parihṛtam// .....tathā ca Vākyakāravacanaṃ— "tasmin yad anta (*Chānd. Up.* VIII,1, 1) *iti kāmavyapadeśa" iti, kāmyanta iti kāmāḥ apahatapāpmatvādayo guṇā ity arthaḥ//*

It is not clear how much of the first part of this fragment is to be referred to The Author.

(Fragment 12) *Vedārthasaṃgraha* (pp. 249 - 250).

After discussing the fact that *Viṣṇu*, the highest god, has all virtues, it is stated :

Vākyakāraś caitat sarvam āha—"hiraṇmayaḥ puruṣo dṛśyata iti prājñaḥ sarvāntaraḥ syāl lokakāmeśopadeśāt. tathodayāt pāpmanām" ity ādinā, tasya ca rūpasyānityatādi Vākyakāreṇaiva pratiṣiddhaṃ syāt "tadrūpaṃ kṛtakam anugrahārtha[ṃ] tac cetanānām aiśvaryād iti upāsitur anugrahārthaḥ paramapuruṣasya rūpasaṃgraha" iti pūrvapakṣaṃ kṛtvā "rūpaṃ vātīndriyam antaḥkaraṇapratyakṣaṃ tannirdeśād" iti, yathā jñānādayaḥ parasya brahmaṇas svarūpatayā nirdeśāt svarūpabhūtaguṇāḥ tathedam api rūpaṃ śrutyā svarūpatayā nirdeśāt svarūpabhūtam ity arthaḥ. Bhāṣyakāreṇaitad vyākhyātam—añjasaiva[15] *viśvasṛjo rūpaṃ tat tu na cakṣuṣā grāhyaṃ manasā tv akaluṣeṇa sādhanāntaravatā gṛhyate. "na cakṣuṣā gṛhyate nāpi vācā, manasā tu viśuddhena"* (*Muṇḍ.Up.* III,2,8) *iti śruteḥ. na hi arūpāyā devatāyā rūpam upadiśyate. yathābhūtavādi hi śāstram, "mahājanaṃ vāsaḥ"* (*Bṛhad.Up.* II,3,6), *"vedāham etam puruṣam mahāntam ādityavarṇam tamasaḥ parastāt"* (*Śvet.Up*, III,8) *iti prakaraṇāntaranirdeśāc ca. "sākṣina" (?), "sākṣī"* (*Śvet.Up.* VI, 11) *ityādinā "hiraṇmayaḥ"* (*Chānd.Up.* I,6,6) *iti rūpasāmānyāc candramukhavat, na mayaṭ atra vikāram ādāya prayujyate, anārabhyatvād ātmanaḥ — iti//*

And The Author (*Vākyakāra*) explains all this by saying : "That golden person seen [within the sun — *Chānd.Up.* I,6,6] refers to the *Prājña* which resides in everything, since [in the succeeding sentence] it is explained that he controls the desires [of the deities and human beings] of this world (Cf. *BS*. I,1,20), and also because he (the golden person) transcends all evil" and other such passages. And any impermanence and so on of the form of [the golden person] is denied by The Author. He first posits an objection from the *pūrvapakṣa* : "That manifested form is for the benefit [of the living beings], for [the golden person] has supremacy over these conscious beings. Thus it is for the benefit of worshippers that the highest *Brahman* assumes a form, " [to which he says :] "or, indeed, this form which is beyond the senses is directly cognized through the inner organ, since it is so stated in the scriptures." [This] means that just as knowledge (*jñāna*) etc., being declared to be the essence of the highest *Brahman*, must be its essential qualities, so this form, being stated as the essence [of the golden person] by the *śruti*, must be [its very] essence. The Commentator also has explained the point : "The form of the creator of all is directly [grasped] but not by the eyes ; [it is] grasped by the unstained mind which is possessed of other means, since the *śruti* says : [it] is not grasped by way of the eyes, nor by way of the mouth, but by the pure mind" (*Muṇḍ.Up*. III,2,8). Verily, of a divinity which is formless, no form is taught, for the scriptures surely state things as they are ; for elsewhere they state [forms by saying] "saffron-coloured raiment" (*Bṛhad.Up*. II,3,6) and "I know the great person who has the colour of the sun beyond the darkness" (*Śvet.Up*. III.8). For like the face of the moon as it were, "the witness" (*Śvet.Up*. VI,II) and such passages refer to the same form as "[the person] made of gold [who is within the sun]" (*Chānd.Up*. I,6,6). Here, the expression "made of ..." is not applicable to something which undergoes transformation, for *ātman* [which is under discussion] is not something to be formed out of any material.

(Fragment 13)

Tattvaṭīkā by Vedāntadeśika (Telugu edition, Part I. p. 34)[16]

tathā ca Vākyam— "upaniṣaṇṇatvād vopaniṣat" iti. tatra Dramiḍabhāṣyam — "gahane hīyaṃ vidyā saṃniviṣṭā" iti. tasya ca Vāmanaṭīkā — "gahane brahmaṇi upanisaṇṇā" iti/

Furthermore there is the statement [of Ṭaṅka] : "or, because [knowledge] is seated [within it] [it is called] *upaniṣad*. "On this the commentary of Dramiḍa [says]: "Indeed, this knowledge rests in the abyss." And Vāmana's gloss on it [says]: "[It] is seated in the abyss, i.e. *Brahman*."

This explanation is accepted by Śaṅkara. At the beginning of his *Taittirīyopaniṣadbhāṣya* (ĀnSS. p.7) he states:

"upaniṣad" iti vidyocyate/tacchīlināṃ garbhajanmajarādiniśātanāt, tadavasādanād vā, brahmaṇo vopanigamayitṛtvāt ; upaniṣaṇṇaṃ vāsyāṃ paraṃ śreya iti. tadarthatvād grantho 'py upaniṣat//

(Fragment 14)

Commenting on the scriptural passage "This person made of gold who is seen in the sun" (*atha ya eṣo 'ntar āditye hiraṇmayaḥ puruṣo dṛśyate//Chānd. Up*. I,6,6), Raṅgarāmānuja (*Chāndogyopaniṣat-prakāśikā*, ĀnSS. No.63, p.279) says:

ādityamaṇḍalasyāntar hiraṇmayo ramaṇīyo yo yogibhir dṛśyata ity arthaḥ/ "dṛśyate tv agryayā buddhyā sūkṣmayā sūkṣmadarśibhiḥ" (*Kāṭhaka Up*. I,3,12) *iti śrutyaikārthyād dhiraṇmaya iti rūpasāmānyāc candramukhavad iti Vākyakāraḥ/tataś ca hiraṇmayatvam ujjvalatvam ity arthaḥ//*

[The passage] means [the person] seen in the sun-disc by *yogins*, who is "made of gold", that is, beautiful. For "made of gold" means the same thing as [is referred to in the passage of scripture] "seen with the most subtle power of understanding by seers of the subtle" (*Kāṭhaka Up*. I,3, 12). The Author says: "Since it is the same form, like the face of the moon". Hence "made of gold" has the sense of being brilliant.

(Fragment 15) Raṅgarāmānuja, *Chānd.Up.Prakāśikā* (ad I,6,7 ; ĀSS. pp.280-281.)

Explaining the term "*kapyāsaṃ puṇḍarīkaṃ* (*Kapyāsa* lotus)", Raṅgarāmānuja says:

kaṃ pibatīti kapir ādityas, tenāsyate kṣipyate vikāsyata iti kapyāsam/ tathāha Vākyakāraḥ—ādityakṣiptaṃ vā śrīmattvād iti/yad vā kaṃ pibatīti kapir nālaṃ tasminn āsta iti kapyāsam/apacitād api paṅkajān nālasthasya puṇḍarīkasya śobhātiśayaśālitvāt tādṛśam iha vivakṣitam/yad vā kaṃ jalam/āsa upaveśana iti dhātur apipūrvakaḥ/vaṣṭi Bhāgurir allopam avāpyor upasargayor iti vacanād akāralopaḥ/ke jale 'pyāsta iti kapyāsaṃ salilastham ity arthaḥ/evam asyārthatrayasyopapannatayā Vākyakāreṇa siddhāntitatvam abhipretya Bhagavatā Bhāṣyakāreṇa Vedārthasaṃgrahe — "gambhīrāmbhaḥsamudbhūtasumṛṣṭanālaravikaravikasitapuṇḍarīkadalāmalāyatekṣaṇa" ity abhihitam/markaṭajaghanasadṛśapuṇḍarīkasādṛśyādyarthāntaraṃ tv aślīlatvādidoṣaduṣṭatayā Vākyakṛdanādṛtatvād Bhāṣya-kāreṇāpy anādṛtam//

Kapi means [one who] drinks water (*kaṃ pibati*), namely the sun. [The lotus which] is thrown out (*asyate*), that is, struck on and opened by the sun is therefore called *kapyāsa*. The Author similarly states: "(1) [*Kapyāsa* is that] which has been struck by the sun, for it is endowed with beauty; (2) or again, *Kapi* means one who drinks water (*kaṃ pibati*), namely a stalk. Because [the lotus] is seated upon a stalk, [it] is called *kapyāsa*. This is what is intended here, because the lotus seated on a stalk is more beautiful than one which has been cut off; (3) or, *ka* refers to water, and the root *ās* (to sit) is preceded by the prefix *api*. [It becomes *pyāsa*] because there is the declaration that [the grammarian] Bhāguri holds that in cases where prefixes *ava-* and *api-* are added, the first vowel is dropped. [Thus] the term *kapyāsa* means that it takes its seat on water, that is, that it lives in water." Taking into account this threefold meaning thus established [for the word *kapyāsa*] by the Author, *Bhagavat Bhāṣyakāra* (=Rāmānuja) stated in [his] *Vedārthasaṃgraha*[17] [that it means] "Having pure and large eyes like the petals of a lotus, opened by the sun's beams, and on a fine stalk, born in the deep water." But other meanings such as "like the lotus which resembles the rump of a monkey" were ignored by the *Bhāṣyakāra*, since [they] had been ignored by the Author (*Vākyakṛt*) as suffering from such faults as vulgarity of language.[18]

(Fragment 16) Raṅgarāmānuja, *Chānd. Up. Prakāśikā* (ad I,6,7; p. 281.)

Explaining the scriptural passage, "he transcends all evils" (*sa eṣa sarvebhyaḥ pāpmabhya uditaḥ//Chānd.Up.* I,6,7), Raṅgarāmānuja states that even good works (*sukṛta*) are included among evils, and says:

pāpmanaḥ kālajarāmṛtyuśokākayaḥ saṃkhyātatvād iti Vākyakāravacanād alaukikatve saty aniṣṭaphalasādhanatvarūpapravṛttinimittayogāt puṇyasyāpi pāpaśabdābhidheyatvopapatteḥ//

Although it is not ordinary [usage], it is possible that the word "evil" should also express even "good works", for the Author has said : "Time, old age, death, grief and so on are evils because of the fact that they are numbered", and good works are bound up with causes of activity, which by their very nature lead to undesirable fruits.

Notes

1) According to Yāmuna's *Siddhitraya*. Cf. Chapter I.

2) According to Sudarśanasūri's *Tātparyadīpikā* (ad *Vedārthasaṃgraha*, p.153), Ṭaṅka is identical with Brahmānandin (Ṭaṅko Brahmānandī). Professor Pandey think that Ṭaṅka and Brahmānandin are different persons. "Brahmānandin has been identified with a teacher called Ṭaṅka who is well known in the tradition of Rāmānuja. But as the tradition of Advaita is different from that of Rāmānuja it is a proper and traditional requirement to regard them as two separate persons." (Sangam Lal Pandey : *Pre-Śaṅkara Advaita Philosophy, op. cit.* p.203). On the facts as we have them at present it is difficult to come to a definite conclusion.

3) Rāmatīrtha's *Anvayārthaprakāśikā* ad *Saṃkṣepaśārīraka* III,221.

4) Cf. *Saṃkṣepaśārīraka* III,217-219 and the passage in Rāmatīrtha's *Anvayārthaprakāśikā* concerning this. However, he is probably not the same person as the Ātreya mentioned in the *Brahma-sūtra*.

5) *Saṃkṣepaśārīraka* III, 217 ; 220. Thibaut : *VS*. Introduction, p.xxii, n.2.

6) *tannikaṭaṃ vivartaṃ parigṛhya* — (Puruṣottama's *Subodhinī*).

7) *Śrībhāṣya* ad *BS*. I,1,1. p.11, BSS.

8) The following is a citation of Ṭaṅka, but since the Bhāṣyakāra's statements are also cited here it is difficult to differentiate them accurately.

9) For example, some types of meats, etc. are unclean.

10) For example, food which belongs to the *Caṇḍāla*, etc. are unclean.

11) For example, food into which strands of hair have fallen.

12) The five major observances which the patriarch of a house should carry out daily, i.e. (1) the honoring of the deities (*devayajña*), (2) all-souls rite of offering food to spirits and animals, etc. (*bhūtayajña*), (3) the rite of presenting offerings to the ancestors (*pitṛyajña*), (4) the studying and chanting of the *Veda* (*brahmayajña*), and (5) the offering of food to guests, etc. (*nṛyajña*)

13) The first part of this fragment is quoted in *SDS*. IV, *ll*.345-356.

14) *Śrībhāṣya* ad *BS*. I,1,1. p.18. BSS.

15) *añjasā avyavadhānena svābhāvikam ity arthaḥ*/(*Dīpikā*).

16) We were unable to see the original. We cite from S. Kuppuswami Sastri : "Bodhāyana and Dramiḍācārya, Two Old Vedāntins Presupposed by Rāmānuja," *Proc. III. OC*. Madras, 1924.

17) This fragment is identical with a saying in Rāmānuja's *Vedārthasaṃgraha*, ed. by J. A. B. van Buitenen : p.164, *l*. 18.

18) Yādava probably accepted this explanation, but Rāmānuja would not have followed Yādava, having the feeling that this kind of explanation would be a slight to the scriptures. Cf. A. Govindācarya : *The Life of Rāmānuja*. Madras, 1906, p. 32f.

SECTION II. THE MAN, HIS WORKS AND HIS DATES

We know almost nothing about Ṭaṅka's personality or biography. But, considering his works and thought, he probably was a Brahmin scholar.

He wrote a commentary, called '*Vākya*', to the *Chāndogya Upaniṣad*, and in the Vedānta school in general he is called the 'Author' (*Vākyakāra*).[1] This work is not now extant, but as has been indicated, fragments of it have been transmitted in many of the works of the late Vedānta school. From these we can see that the '*Vākya*' consisted of extremely simple statements in *sūtra* style.[2] And Dramiḍa wrote a commentary (*Bhāṣya*) to it.[3] However, since there is no record of Ṭaṅka having written a commentary to the *Brahmasūtra*, it is possible that he did not write anything on that.

He lived after Bodhāyana but before Dramiḍa and Bhartṛprapañca. According to Yāmuna he lived before Bhartṛhari, but other ancient sources place Bhartṛhari at a relatively early period.[4] Thus it is difficult to place Ṭaṅka before Bhartṛhari. As stated previously, Bodhāyana lived at approximately 500 AD. Thus we may infer that Ṭaṅka's dates are about 500 - 550 AD. At any rate, since he is not mentioned by his personal name by later Vedānta scholars, but only as the '*Vākyakāra*', his authority was firmly established and was not of a sectarian nature.

Notes

1) Cf. Fragments 3, 5. This is also clearly indicated in Rāmatīrtha's *Anvayārthaprakāśikā* (ad *Saṃkṣepaśārīraka* III, 217). *kāryakāraṇabhāvādeḥ saṃvyavahāramātratvaṃ Brahmanandinā 'py ācāryeṇa Chāndogyabhāṣye parair uktadoṣāprāptyartham uktam ity āha — Ātreyavākyam apīti//* In the footnote to the *Siddhitraya*, pp. 5 - 6, Ṭaṅka is held to be

a *Vārttikakāra*, but it is not know whether there is a *Vārttika* among his works.
2) Cf. Draviḍa, Fragment 16.
3) Cf. The following chapter.
4) Cf. Chapter I.

SECTION III. HIS THOUGHT

Like Bodhāyana, Ṭaṅka was an annotator of the Upaniṣadic scriptures. He explained difficult passages in the texts (Fragment 15) and presented etymological explanation which he believed to be appropriate. In cases where the scriptural texts are difficult to accept literally, he attempted to clarify the nuances of the context (Fragment 14).

As to philosophical thought, since Bhāskara, Rāmānuja and Sarvajñātman of the Śaṅkara school all base their theories on his philosophical views, he was no doubt putting forward ideas related to these. Śaṅkara, on occasion, also uses his explanations (Fragment 13). It is stated that his *Vākya* to the *Chāndogya-Upaniṣad* consisted of heterogeneous (*anekākāra*) annotations and that because it put forward many theories (*anekapakṣa*), it confused those who tried to understand the true intention.[1] Great differences exist among the theories attributed to him, which thus vary according to the school which transmits them.

(1) *Brahman* and the Phenomenal World

According to Sarvajñātman, Ṭaṅka holds the Advaita doctrine. He holds that only *Brahman* is real (*satya*) and that it is the world-cause (Fragment 3). Everything in the phenomenal world is its effect (*kārya*) and is not real, though it is real just from the empirical standpoint (*saṃvyavahāra-mātra*) (Fragment 1,2,4). That is to say, they appear only temporarily in our worldly life, but in reality are 'consisting of *Māyā*' (Fragment 1). Therefore from the standpoint of absolute truth, it must be said that all things are non-dual (Fragment 4). This philosophical view differs from both the *satkāryavāda* and the *asatkāryavāda*: the deficiencies of those two views do not arise in this Advaita view (Fragment 1, 4). In Ṭaṅka's work, the relationship between *Brahman* and the phenomenal world is likened to the ocean and foam, but this is only a provisional teaching presented in order to lead inquirers into the Vedānta philosophy; his true intention was to teach the Advaita or the false-appearance theory (*vivartavāda*) (Fragment 3, 4).

But according to Rāmānuja, Ṭaṅka propounds the 'evolution theory' (*pariṇāmapakṣa*), and likens the evolution of phenomena from *Brahman* to *dadhi* (coagulated milk) arising from milk (Fragment 5).[2] Hence Bhāskara presents him as not teaching that the phenomenal world is illusory.

According to Rāmānuja, Ṭaṅka's views are as follows: *Brahman* is the *ātman* of all and everything is effected by *Brahman* (Fragment 8). That which exists in the space within the heart (Fragment 11), the golden person seen in the eye (Fragment 12) and so on, which are discussed in the *Upaniṣads*, refer to *Brahman*. Its essence is pure consciousness and may be called *Prājña* (Fragment 12). It is eternal and has a form which is beyond the senses; yet it resides in everything and controls the desires of all deities and human beings (Fragment 12). Thus according to Rāmānuja he held that each of the individual selves corresponds to the body of *Brahman*.

In this way the three writers present three different accounts. Among these, Sarvajñātman's statement that Ṭaṅka emphasized the Advaita view is probably his own wishful explanation: on the other hand, the simile concerning the ocean and foam was probably Ṭaṅka's real meaning. The simile was in general use in the Vedānta school of the early period.

Further, Rāmānuja states that Ṭaṅka propounded the 'qualified Advaita theory' (*viśiṣṭādvaita*), but since the fragment concerning this is extremely brief, it is not clear whether Ṭaṅka actually took the position attributed to him by Rāmānuja. Since Rāmānuja's teacher Yāmuna[3] lists Ṭaṅka first among the thinkers who propound heretical views, it may be supposed that he held views differing from those of the Yāmuna-Rāmānuja group. An example of this can be seen in Fragment 12. That is, Rāmānuja himself recognizes that Ṭaṅka had refuted the view that it is for the sake of devotees that the Overlord manifests forms such as the golden person seen within the eye. If that be the case, Ṭaṅka was not well disposed to the theistic views such as the grace of the Overlord or his manifestations, which were frequently emphasized by Hinduism. Thus although Rāmānuja always explains Ṭaṅka's theories in a manner that brings them close to his own, it cannot be denied that there existed quite a philosophical distance between them. The views held by the two should therefore be distinguished.

Bhāskara's statement is very brief (Fragment 5), but so far as this citation goes, we may assume that he quotes Ṭaṅka directly.

By this kind of critical analysis which attempts to remove the supplementary explanations added by later thinkers, we may conclude that Ṭaṅka probably held to the type of 'evolution theory' which states that it is by evolution (*pariṇāma*) of *Brahman* that the phenomenal world is created. So he probably held views similar to those of the *Bramna-sūtra*. At the same time, he did occasionally use philological explanations which are reminiscent of the qualified Advaita theory or else the pure Advaita theory. On the one hand Śaṅkara vigorously refutes the theories of the commentator Bodhāyana, and on the other hand, Sarvajñātman of the same group as Śaṅkara is citing Ṭaṅka as authority for his own theories. From this fact it is clear that Ṭaṅka's views could not have been completely identical to Bodhāyana's.

(2) Religious Practice

According to Ṭaṅka, human existence is limited by time; it cannot escape old age and death and is always accompanied by pain and grief. He seems to have held that what ordinary people recognize to be good works are included in evil (*pāpman*) from the higher standpoint (Fragment 16). Thus he took the emancipation from transmigratory life of this sort as the highest goal of religious exercise.

He esteemed highly, as means towards the attainment of emancipation, knowledge (*vedanā*) and worship (meditation, *upāsana*). By *upāsana* he means here, continuous meditation, that is, uninterrupted meditation on *Brahman*. This must be carried out repeatedly by practitioners (Fragment 8). As a result of such meditation, direct and clear realization of *Brahman* is attained through the inner organs of perception (*antaḥkaraṇa* = means) of each individual. Hence he is opposed to views such as 'instantaneous enlightenment'.

Now when carrying out this practice, the object of meditation is *Brahman* with attributes, endowed with many virtues (Fragment 9). He holds further that one should select any one of the many types of meditation discussed in the *Upaniṣads* and practice it (Fragment 10). It may be held that he accepts that *Brahman* itself is without form (Fragment 12), but he does not discuss, as does Śaṅkara, directly knowledge of *Brahman* without attributes.

In order to complete the practice of this *Prajñā*-based meditation, a cleansing of mind and body is necessary. For this, seven types of preparation are necessary. These are: (1) to forego unclean food in order to maintain the purity of the physical body; (2) not to be attained to lust; (3) to repeatedly and habitually perform the practice; (4) to practise religious rites; (5) to do good actions; (6) to ward off depression; (7) not to be overcome with exultation (Fragment 7).[4] It was thought by him that meditation on *Brahman* with the foregoing preparations makes possible the attainment of emancipation (Fragment 8). Hence he emphasized the union of thought and action (*jñānakarmasamuccayavāda*), a point on which he differs from Śaṅkara but agrees rather with Bhāskara.

Notes

1) *Subodhinī* (ad *Saṃkṣepaśarīraka*, III, 219) — *nanu tadvākyānām apy anekākāratvāt katham tataḥ siddhāntādhyavasāya iti ced vivakṣitavivekād ity āha — atraiva*······

Anvayaprakāśikā (*l. c.*) — *Brahmānandivākyeṣv anekapakṣapratibhānāt tatra kaḥ siddhānta iti, na niśīyata iti cen, naiṣa doṣaḥ, paramārthanirūpaṇāvasare 'bhihitatvād vivartavādasya siddhāntatvaniścayād* /

2) According to Madhusūdana Sarasvatī's note to the *Saṃkṣepaśārīraka* III,218 -220, Brahmānandin felt that through the appearance theory (*vivarta-vāda*) he could lead people to the pure Advaita theory (*śuddhādvaita-vāda*). Cf. V.Bhattacharyya : *ĀS*.p. cx.)

3) Cf. Chapter I.

4) Cf. Sukhtankar : *WZKM*. vol. XXII, p.328 ; Radhakrishnan : *IPh*. vol. II, p.704.

CHAPTER VI

DRAVIḌA

SECTION I. FRAGMENTS

Draviḍa (also Dramiḍa) is usually referred to in terms of respect as Master Draviḍa (or Master Dramiḍa ; Draviḍācārya or Dramiḍācārya) and within the Vedānta school is known as 'the Commentator' (*Bhāṣyakāra*, *Bhāṣyakṛt*). It is only in fragments that his teachings have been transmitted in the later Vedānta work's. We list them below.[1]

(Fragment 1)

At the beginning of Yāmuna (mid-eleventh century)'s *Siddhitraya*, it is stated :

"These aphorisms (*sūtra*) were explained by the Commentator (*Bhāṣyakṛt*) in terms terse and profound." (The original Sanskrit was presented in Chapter I.)

The Commentator (*Bhāṣyakṛt*) mentioned here indicates Dramiḍācārya as shown in the footnotes.

Further, Rāmānuja, who was Yāmuna's disciple and most important thinker of the Viśiṣṭādvaita school, held Draviḍa in great respect. In his works *Śrībhāṣya* and *Vedārthasaṃgraha*, Rāmānuja frequently cites words of Draviḍa as scriptural basis for his own views.

(Fragment 2)

Śrībhāṣya ad I,1,1 (p. 11).

Together with Ṭaṅka's Fragment 7, which is cited here, the term 'Commentator' (*Bhāṣyakāra*) is also cited.

(Fragment 3)

vṛttir api — "jagadvyāpāravarjaṃ samāno jyotiṣā" iti. Dramiḍabhāṣyakāraś ca — "devatāsāyujyād aśarīrasyāpi devatāvat sarvārthasiddhis syāt" ity āha/Śrībhāṣya ad *BS*. I,1,1 (p. 79).

"[Bodhāyana's] commentary also [states] : In the state of final release, the individual-self is equal to the [highest] light (=*Brahman*) [in respects] other than creating, maintaining [and dissolving] the world. And the Commentator Dramiḍa states : Since [the emancipated individual-self] is in union with the divine, although it has no physical body, like the divine it can accomplish all purposes."

The above passage is probably an explication of the *Brahma-sūtra* IV,4,17. (Cf. also Bodhāyana, Fragment 3.)

(Fragment 4)

If *Brahman* its very self evolves, then it becomes experiencer of pleasure and pain, and so the fundamental distinction between *Brahman* and the individual self will disappear -- to meet this criticism Rāmānuja records that Dramiḍa taught as follows ;

yathāha Dramiḍabhāṣyakāraḥ — *"yathā loke rājā pracuradandaśūke ghore 'narthasaṅkaṭe 'pi pradeśe vartamāno 'pi vyajanādyavadhūtadeho doṣair na spṛśyate, abhipretāṃś ca lokān punar api pālayiṣyati, bhogāṃś ca gandhādīn viśvajanopabhogyān dhārayati ; tathāsau lokeśvaro bhramatsvasāmarthyacāmaro doṣair na spṛśyate, rakṣati ca lokān brahmalokādīn, bhogāṃś ca viśvajanopabhogyān dhārayati" iti* / (*Śrībhāṣya* ad *BS*. II,1,14.)

The Commentator Dramiḍa says thus : Just as in the world a king, though in a place infested by mosquitoes and altogether disagreeable, does not come into contact with these unpleasantnesses because his body is fanned and so on [all the time, by attendants], and he thus protects the whole realm wherever he looks, protecting the people in their enjoyment of fragrance and so on, in the same way the Lord of the world (*lokeśvara*), commanding the chowrie [so to say] of his [absolute] power to wave, protects the *Brahmā*-world and all the other worlds, and protects the beings in their enjoyment of pleasures.[2)]

(Fragment 5)

"And the *Veda* speaks of the principle that action, which is either good or bad, pleases or displeases [respectively] the supreme *Puruṣa* (*parama-puruṣa*), and so the results — pain or happiness — follow from the favour or disfavour of that *puruṣa*. Thus the teacher Dramiḍa : The established teaching of Vedic revelation is that in expectation of securing actual results they seek to please the *Ātman* by various actions and *Ātman* being pleased, they have the power to confer the results."

tathā cāha Dramiḍācāryaḥ —"phalasaṃvidhitsayā[3] *hi karmabhir ātmānaṃ piprīṣanti sa prīto 'lam phalāyeti śāstramaryādā"iti*/(*Śrībhāṣya* ad *BS*. II,2,3.)

Almost exactly the same passage occurs in *Vedārthasaṃgraha* (p.222).

yathāhur vedarāvidagresarā Dramiḍācāryāḥ —"phalasambibhantsayā[4] *hi karmabhir ātmānam piprīṣantīti sa prīto'laṃ phalāyeti śāstramaryādā"— iti. phalasaṃbandhecchayā karmabhir yāga-dāna-homādibhir Indrādidevatā-mukhena tat-tad-antaryāmirūpeṇāvasthitam Indrādiśabdavācyam paramātmānam bhagavantaṃ Vāsudevaṃ ārirādhayiṣanti, sa hi karmabhir ārādhitas teṣām iṣṭāni phalāni prayacchatīti arthaḥ*/

(Fragment 6)

tat tvam asītisadvidyāyām upāsyaṃ brahma saguṇaṃ saguṇabrahmaprāptiś ca phalam ity abhiyuktaiḥ pūrvācāryair vyākhyātaṃ, yathoktaṃ Vākyakāreṇa — "yuktaṃ tadguṇakopāsanāt" iti ; vyākhyātaṃ ca Dramiḍācāryeṇa vidyāvikalpaṃ vadatā — "yady api saccitto na nirbhugnadaivataṃ guṇagaṇaṃ manasānudhāvet tathāpy antarguṇām eva devatām bhajate"— iti. tatrāpi saguṇaiva devatā prāpyata iti/(*Vedārthasaṃgraha*, p.143.)

"It has been explained by previous great teachers that in the knowledge of Being (*sat*) 'Thou art That' (in Chapter 6 of the *Chāndogya-Upaniṣad*), the object to be meditated upon is *Brahman*-with-attributes. As 'the Author of the sentences' says : "[The object to be meditated upon is *Brahman* which is] connected [with various attributes], for that which is possessed of those attributes is meditated upon." And Master Dramiḍa, who declares that one from among the many meditations [taught in the *Upaniṣads*] should be selected, explains this in the following manner ; "He who has his mind set on Being[5] can attain the divinity of interior attributes without pursuing through the mind[6] a multitude of distorted divine attributes."Thus in this passage it is also held that the divinity-with-attributes is attained." (Cf. Fragment 16, and Ṭaṅka Fragment 9.)

(Fragment 7)

evaṃ ca sati mantrārthavādagatā hy aviruddhā apūrvāś cārthāḥ sarve vidhiśeṣatayaiva siddhā bhavanti. yathokaṃ Dramiḍabhāṣye — ṛṇaṃ hi vai jāyate iti śruter iti upakramya yady apy avadānastutiparaṃ vākyaṃ tathā 'pi nāsatā stutir upapadyata iti, etad uktaṃ bhavati sarvo hy arthavādabhāgo devatārādhanabhūtayāgādeḥ sāṅgasyārādhyadevatāyāś cādṛṣṭarūpān guṇān sahasraśo vadan sahasraśaḥ karmaṇi prāśastyabuddhim utpādayati, teṣām asadbhāve prāśastyabuddhir eva na syād iti karmaṇi prāśastyabuddhyarthaṃ guṇasadbhāvam eva bodhayatīti anayaiva diśā sarve mantrārthavādāvagatā hy arthāḥ siddhāḥ/(*Vedārthasaṃgraha*, p.209.)

"And such being the case, the non-contradictory and new topics which exist in the *mantras* and explanations of meaning (*arthavāda*) are all composed only as supplements to the injunctions (*vidhi*). So it is taught in Dramiḍa's Commentary, first because there is a *śruti* text 'debt actually arises', and then even though a sentence is devoted to praise of a great achievement, it would not be reasonable to give praise for what did not exist. What has been said is this : Describing a thousand times the unseen virtues of the rites, namely the pleasing of the divinity, and [the virtues] of their limbs and of the divinity who is pleased, every portion of the explanation of meaning (*arthavāda*) [in the *Veda*] brings to mind a thousand times the praises of the rites. If these virtues did not exist, then such thoughts of praises would not arise. Thus, in order to bring mind such thoughts of praise, the actual existence of the virtues is being declared. Hence it is only in this way that all the meanings which are learned from the *mantras* and the explanations of meaning are established."

(Fragment 8)

yathoktaṃ Dramiḍabhāṣye — tasyājñayā dhāvati vāyur nadyaḥ sravanti tena ca kṛtasīmāno jalāśayāḥ samadā iva meṣavisarpitaṃ kurvantīti/ (*Vedārthasaṃgraha*, p.228.)

"There is a great variety of scriptural texts such as, 'O *Gārgī*, truly, at the command of that Imperishable the sun and moon stand apart.... O *Gārgī*, truly, at the command of that Imperishable people praise those who give, the deities seek the sacrificer the fathers seek tne *darvī*-offering.' (*Bṛhad.Up*, III,8,9). As is explained in Master Dramiḍa's commentary : At His command the wind blows and the rivers flow, the oceans have been confined and they spring like rams rutting".

(Fragment 9)

The 'Commentator' (*Bhāṣyakāra*) is cited in Ṭaṅka's fragment 13.

(Fragment 10)

yathāha Bhāṣyakāraḥ — yathābhūtavādi hi śāstram iti /(*Vedārthasaṃgraha*, p.252.)

"[It is] as the Commentator states ; 'The scriptures, indeed, speak of things as they are'."

(Fragment 11)

On the other hand, the works of the Śaṅkara school, which is opposed to the Yāmuna-Rāmānuja school, also cite Draviḍa as an authority. At the beginning of his commentary (*bhāṣya*) to the *Chāndogya-Upaniṣad*, Śaṅkara has the following ;

om ity etadakṣaram ity aṣṭādhyāyī Chāndogyopaniṣat. tasyāḥ saṃkṣepato 'rthajijñāsubhya ṛjuvivaraṇam alpagrantham idam ārabhyate/

Ānandajñāna annotates this in the following manner :

ṛjuvivaraṇam iti — "ṛju" pāṭhakramānusāri "vivaraṇam" arthasphuṭīkaraṇaṃ prakṛtopaniṣadaḥ yasmin bhāṣye tat tatheti yāvat. atha pāṭhakramam āśrityāpi Drāviḍaṃ bhāṣyāṃ praṇītam, tat kim anenety āśaṅkyāha/

From the above passages we see that Śaṅkara's commentary is a summary of Draviḍa's commentary (*bhāṣya*), a systematic explanation of the texts of the *Chāndogya-Upaniṣad*.

(Fragment 12)

Śaṅkara ad *Chānd. Up*.III,10 (ĀnSS. p.145).

The *Chāndogya-Upaniṣad* III,6-10, in teaching that rewards of those who know the five undying things are progressively doubled, states that in the five cases where the sun moves from east to west, south to north, west to east, north to south, or from below to above, each successively later case requires double the time of the one before it. This contradicts the records of the *Paurāṇikas* (authors of the old legends) concerning the rising and setting of the sun. According to the *Purāṇas*, in the realms of the four protective deities — *Indra*, *Yama*, *Varuṇa*, and *Soma* — the times required for the rising and setting of the sun are equal. Some explanation had to be resolve this contradiction. Śaṅkara states:

> "Concerning this point, the difficulties are resolved by the Master (*ācārya*): *Amarāvatī* (the realm of *Indra*) and the other realms successively require double the time of their predecessor for the passing away [of the sun]; in fact the rising of the sun is its entering into the range of virsion of those living beings who dwell there, and its setting is simply its passing away from that region. In terms of the absolute truth, there is no rising or setting [of it], for if there were no living beings dwelling there, there would be nothing that rises or sets for them, although [the sun] proceeded along the same route. So there could be no such things as entering or leaving their range of vision. In the same manner, in the realm called *Samyamanā* (the dwelling realm of the god *Yama*) [the passage of the sun] is twice as long as that in *Amarāvatī*. Thus it is said that for those who dwell there, [the sun] rises as if it were from the south and sets in the north, as we should conceive it. [This interpretation] should also be applied to the succeeding realms."

Śaṅkara continues his explanation further, but at least we can say that the above section is Draviḍa's theory, without too much fear of contradiction. The Master whom Śaṅkara here takes as an authority is Draviḍa.

> *yady api śrutivirodhe smṛtir apramāṇam, tathāpi yathākathaṃcid virodhaparihāraṃ Draviḍācāryoktam upapādayati*/ (*Ānandajñāna, l.c.*)

(Fragment 13)

Śaṅkara states: "The various scriptures which discuss the creation of the world etc., all are intended to teach at *Ātman* is one." Immediately afterwards he says:

> "And in this connection, one who knows the tradition (*sampradāyavid*) narrates the following tale. It is said that a certain prince, soon after birth, was sent away from his mother and raised in the house of a hunter. Then this prince, not knowing his princely descent, thought that he was a hunter and pursed the profession of a hunter and not that of a king, never [thinking] 'I am a king.' When, however, a very compassionate man, knowing that the prince was worthy of attaining the majesty of a king, informed him that he was a prince, telling him: 'You are not a hunter; [in truth] you are the son of such and such a king, but

on account of circumstances you have come to live in the house of a hunter.' Thus informed, the prince abandoned the idea that he belonged to the hunter caste and the actions proper to it, and realizing 'I am a king' followed the path of his fathers. In the same manner, this *ātman* which is of the same nature as the Highest *Ātman*, being separated from it like sparks shot out from a fire, has entered the dense jungle of the physical body, senses, and the rest. Though not subject to transmigration, it takes on the attributes of transmigration of the body, sense-organs and the rest; without knowing that it is the Highest *Ātman*, it [thinks], 'I am the aggregate of the body and senses,' 'I am lean,' 'I am fat,' 'I am happy,' or 'I am miserable.' Then having been taught by the master: 'You are not of that nature. You are the Highest *Brahman* which does not transmigrate,' it abandons the pursuit of the three kinds of desire[7] and realizes 'I am *Brahman* itself.'" (Ś. ad *Bṛhad. Up*. II,1,20. pp.297-298.)

Śaṅkara takes discussion of the 'one who knows the tradition.' According to Ānandajñāna's note, the passage refers to the theory of Master Draviḍa (*Draviḍācāryasammati*).

(Fragment 14)

Śaṅkara's disciple Sureśvara relates the same story as in the Fragment 13. (*Bṛhadāraṇyakopaniṣadbhāṣyavārttika*, II,1. v.506. p.970 ff.) Here the sub-commentator Ānandajñāna also notes: *Draviḍācārya-pranītām ākhyāyikām avatārayati* /

"Concerning this problem, therefore, some people bring forward appropriate parables about how this desirable thing can clearly be shown." (*śloka* 506)

"For example: a youth, who was the son of a king, became obsessed with hunting through association with hunters." (507)

"His proper pride as king being destroyed, he fell into the delusion [of being a hunter] and went to the forest: dwelling with hunters, he thought, 'I am a hunter'" (508)

"For many long months and years, thinking himself a hunter, he conducted himself accordingly. ... He lost all memory of being of the Royal House, and dwelt with the hunters in their house." (509)

"But having taken an effective medicine, he regained his normal mental capacity ; now following his own nature, he was able to free his spirit from the association with hunters." (510)

"But although abandoning the life of hunter, he could not give up his feeling of being a hunter, because he still had no memories." (511)

"A friend of the father of the prince, who was well-intentioned and knew the truth of the birth, actions, and relationship of the prince, learned [the circumstances] and approached him ; he informed him that from his works, actions, birth, and kingly character [it was clear] that he was a prince." (512 & 513)

"The prince, then realizing 'I am of the Royal House,' recovered his memory and his ignorance about himself disappeared. He abandoned his feeling of being a hunter."(514)

"As the heir of the king, he attained his father's royal status and was crowned. To attain this no action was necessary." (515)

"For it was through delusion that he had falsely imagined himself a hunter, so to attain to the status of prince, he needed only to eliminate that delusion." (516)

"In the same manner, although this (individual self) is *Brahman* itself, the intelligence, sense organs, physical body etc. are held to be *Ātman*, simply because of absence of the realization of *Brahman*." (517)

"Because the individual self does not realize the inner truth, its inner *Ātman* is limited by what belongs to birth-and-death, which are not *Ātman*." (518)

"The one who, with the torch of true knowledge, has fully dispelled the great darkness concerning the inner truth, abandons everything arising from delusion and as *Brahman* itself goes directly to *Brahman*." (521)

"No other means than eliminating ignorance of the inner truth is needed, even slightly, for attaining final release." (522)

It is certain that the tale of the prince raised by hunters originated with Draviḍa, but the above *ślokas* cannot all have been faithful to Draviḍa's presentation. Sureśvara explains Draviḍa's simile as expressing the Advaita view. In *ślokas* 524 and after, he refutes the view that the relationship between the whole (*aṃśin*) and its parts (*aṃśa*). However, from the fact that Śaṅkara states that the previous fragments transmit Draviḍa's views, it is probable that the theories that Sureśvara refutes are, in fact, closer to Draviḍa's. Since Draviḍa's words are also regarded as authoritative by Yāmuna and Rāmānuja, it may be considered that what Śaṅkara says is nearer to the truth. (The tale of the prince who became a hunter is also presented in the *Bṛhad,Up.Vārttika*, *Sambandhavārttika*, v.233, p.71, and in Mādhava's *Sarvadarśanasaṃgraha* XVI, *l*.879 ff. but Draviḍa is not mentioned.)

(Fragment 15)

After discussion of the fact that *Ātman* is not an experiencer of pleasures (*sukhin*), there is the following statement:

> *tasmān nirviśeṣa evātmani sukhitvādayo viśeṣāḥ kalpitāḥ yat tv asukhitvādiśāstram ātmanas tatsukhitvādiviśeṣanivṛttyartham eveti siddham/ "siddhaṃ tu nivartakatvāt" ity āgamavidāṃ sūtram*//(Ś. ad *Gauḍapādīya Kārikā*, II,32. (p.94, *ll*.24-26.)
>
> "For this reason, distinctions such as experiencing pleasure are imagined in the undifferentiated *Ātman*. It is established that the scriptures which state that *Ātman* does not experience pleasures etc., are composed in order to negate distinctions such as '*Ātman* does experience pleasure.' A *sūtra* of one who knows the traditions says: 'It is established by negation'."

Śaṅkara adds no note concerning this 'one who knows the traditions' (*āgama-vid*), but the sub-commentator Ānandajñāna has the following:

> "In connection with the previous discussion, the theory of Master Draviḍa has been mentioned: 'It is established ...' The meaning of the *sūtra* is as follows: Although in regard to *Brahman*, words can not suffice, it is established that the scriptures are the source of knowledge [concerning it], for [the scriptures] negate [the attributes] superimposed [upon *Brahman*], by their teaching of the natural non-existence of duality, namely by their conjoining words like '*sthūla*' (coarse) and so on with the negative particle which shows their non-existence [of such qualities]."
>
> *ukte 'rthe Draviḍācāryasaṃmatim āha — "siddhaṃ tv" iti brahmaṇi*

padānāṃ vyutpattyabhāve 'pi siddham eva śāstraprāmāṇyam abhāvabodhanavyutopanna-nañ-pada-saṃsṛṣṭaiḥ sthūlādivyutpannapadaiḥ svābhāvika-dvaitābhāvabodhanenādhyastanivartakatvād iti sūtrārthaḥ/

The joining of the negative particle to terms such as '*sthūla*', as in Ānandajñāna's note, is mentioned in the following passage of the *Bṛhadāranyaka Upaniṣad*, III,8,8 :

"O *Gārgī*, the *Brahmins* (knowers of *Brahman*) call it the imperishable (*akṣara*). It is neither coarse (*asthūla*) nor subtle, neither short nor long, neither red [like fire] nor moist [like water] ; it has neither shadow nor darkness, neither wind nor space ; without attachments, without taste, without odour, without eyes, without ears, without speech, without mind, without radiance, without breath, without mouth, without measure, without inner, without outer. It eats nothing and no one eats it."

Śaṅkara refers to the words of Draviḍa quoted above as his '*sūtra*', but they are not found in the extant *Brahma-sūtra*. However, Ānandajñāna also refers to the saying elsewhere :

uktaṃ hi – siddhaṃ tu nirvartakatvād iti /(Ān. ad Sureśvara's *Bṛhad. Up. Vārttika*, p.493, ad. v.315.)

(Fragment 16)

In his *Saṃkṣepa-śārīraka* III,217-220, immediately after presenting Ṭaṅka's teaching, Sarvajñātman presents those of Master Draviḍa.

antarguṇā bhagavatī paradevateti pratyagguṇeti bhagavān api Bhāṣyakāraḥ/

āha sma yat tad iha nirguṇavastuvāde saṃgcchate na tu punaḥ saguṇapravāde//(*Saṃkṣepa-śārīraka*, III,221.)

"What the venerable master, the Commentator, speaks of as the highest divinity, the *Bhagavat* with interior attributes, [or] as [the highest divinity][8] having interior (*Ātman*'s) attributes,[9] is consonant with teaching of the attributeless being (the undifferentiated *Brahman*) here, but not with teaching of [*Brahman*] with attributes."

The Commentator Rāmatīrtha takes the Commentator mentioned here to be Master Draviḍa. Further in Madhusūdana Sarasvatī's commentary[10] it is stated : *Brahmanandi-viracitānāṃ vākyānāṃ sūtarūpāṇāṃ bhāṣyakartā*

Draviḍācāryo 'pi/ Cf. also Fragment 6.

(Fragment 17)

atra Bhāṣyakāro Brahmanandi-vākyavyākhyātā Dramiḍācāryaḥ/ (*Tattva-ṭīkā*, Telugu edition, p.138.)[11]

"The Commentator here refered to is Master Draviḍa, the commentator on Brahmanandin's exposition."

(Fragment 18)

jīvam abrahma 'brahmety upāsīta' iti. kriyāviśeṣayogād vā, yathā 'vāyur vāva saṃvargaḥ' (*Chānd.Up*.IV,3,1.) *'prāṇo vāva saṃvargaḥ'* (*Chānd.Up*.IV,3,2.)/ *bāhyā khalu vāyudevatā vahnyādīn saṃvṛṅkte/ mahāpralayasamaye hi vāyur vahnyādīn saṃvṛjya saṃhṛtyātmani sthāpayati/ yathāha Draviḍācāryaḥ — 'saṃharaṇād vā saṃvaraṇād vā sātmībhāvād vāyuḥ saṃvargaḥ' iti. adhyātmaṃ ca prāṇaḥ saṃvarga iti. sa hi sarvāṇi vāgādīni saṃvṛṅkte. prāyaṇakāle hi sa eva sarvāṇīndriyāṇi saṃgṛhyotkrāmatīti//* (*Bhāmatī*, ad *BS*. I,1,4. ed. NSP. p.76.)

"[It states] that the individual self (*jīva*), which is not *Brahman*, 'should be meditated upon as *Brahman*.' Or [it teaches meditations] through special actions. For example, 'the wind is verily the absorber' (*Chānd.Up*.IV,3,1) and 'breath is verily the absorber' (*Chānd.Up*.IV,3, 3.). The external wind deity really absorbs flames, etc., for at the time of the great dissolution of the universe, the wind absorbs and destroys the fire and the rest, and established them within itself. It is as stated by Master Draviḍa : 'Because it collects, or because it encloses, or because it has community of nature [with the flames etc.], the wind is the absorber.' And internally [in regard to individual existence], breath is the absorber. In fact, breath absorbs all things, such as speech, for at the time of death the breath, absorbing all the organs, goes up."

(Fragment 19)

The term 'previous masters' (*pūrvācārya*), which appears in Bodhāyana's fragment, is annotated by Sudarśana Sūri in his *Śrutaprakāśikā* as *Dramiḍabhāṣyakārādayaḥ*.[12]

Notes

1) Master Draviḍa has been the subject of academic studies previously. As will be

explained in the discussion in the Section II, there are numerous passages in Sanskrit literature other than these, in which he is mentioned. However, I am at present unable to examine these sources. But I feel that I have here presented a fairy complete introduction to his theories as presented in the major works of the Vedānta school.

2) A position similar to this, supposed by the same analogy, is given to the opponent in Śaṅkara's commentary on the *Brahma-sūtra* I.1.4, and rejected by Śaṅkara.

3) In some manuscripts it appears as *phalasaṃbibhitsayā*.

4) The reading *phalasaṃbibhitsayā* found in some manuscripts has been felt by editors of the published editions to be wrong.

5) Rāmānuja glosses it as '*saccittah sadvidyaniṣṭaḥ*'.

6) In glossing the phrase '*apahatapāpmatvādikalyāṇaguṇam*', Rāmānuja explains '*yady api daharavidyāniṣṭha iva saccito na smaret*'.

7) *eṣaṇātraya* – the desire for progeny, wealth, and the three worlds. Cf. *putrādyeṣaṇātraya* (Ś. ad *Īśā.Up*. p.5, *l*.7 (ĀnSS.); Cf. also *Bṛhad Up*. IV,4,22; III,5,1.

8) According to the various notes to the *Chānd.Up*.VI,2,1, this indicates '*sat*'.

9) *pratyagguṇeti pratyagātmarūpety arthaḥ*/(Rāmatīrtha's *Anvayārthaprakāśikā*).

10) According to V.Bhattacaryya: *AS*. pp. cx - cxi.

11) I have not been able to see the original. This is cited from S.Kuppuswami Sastri: "Bodhāyana and Dramiḍācārya, Two Old Vedāntins Presupposed by Rāmānuja", *Proc. III, OC*. Madras. 1924.

12) Dasgupta: *HIPh*. vol. III, p.109, n.

SECTION II. THE MAN, HIS WORKS AND HIS DATES

From these fragments it is clear that the Śaṅkara line uses particularly the appellation Draviḍa or Draviḍācārya, where the Rāmānuja line calls him Dramiḍa or Dramiḍācārya.[1] It has been suspected that there were two distinct persons.[2] But Fragment 3 transmitted by Rāmānuja agrees extremely well with Fragment 16 transmitted by the Advaitin Sarvajñātman, and as both sides record that he wrote a cornmentary on a work of the Expositor (*Vākyakāra*) it seems certain that the two are the same man, a thinker looked up to as authoritative by both the Śaṅkara and the Rāmānuja schools.

In the Rāmānuja school especially it is proclaimed that Rāmānuja is a standard-bearer for the thought of Dramiḍa. There still exists a copper plate recording the donation, in the year 1478 of the Śaka calendar (1556 in

Western reckoning) by King Sadāśivarāya of Vijayanagara, of several villages to a temple where an image of Rāmanuja was being installed. It includes this eulogy of Rāmānuja :

"He, who reached the position of the highest teacher, established in the way of the *Veda*, who knew the tradition of Dramiḍa which is the essence of the glory of the *Vedas* ; leader of the teachers who established the doctrines of the six schools, who broke the pride of the *Māyā*-teachers, victorious over objectors, who swept away the arrogance of the glamorous teachers of spells ... "

prapeduṣe Vedamārga-pratiṣṭhitācāryavaryatām / tādṛg- Veda-śikhā-sāra-Dramiḍāgama-vedine / / ṣaḍdarśanārthasiddhāntasthāpanācāryamaulaye / māyāvādimanogarvabhedine jitavādine / / mantravādi-manīṣīndra-vṛndāhaṃtāpa-hāriṇe /
.... *Rāmānujamunīndrāya* .... (*Ep. Ind.* IV, 1896-97, pp.15-16)

He is thought to have written at least two works :

1. Commentary on the *Brahma-sūtras* (*Brahmasūtrabhāṣya*)

According to Yāmuna, this commentary expressed profound meaning tersely.[3] Our Fragment 3 is very likely his commentary on the *Brahma-sūtra*, IV,4.17.

2. Commentary on the *Chāndogya-Upaniṣad* (*Chāndogya-upaniṣadbhāṣya*)

This work was fairly detailed and explained each section of each chapter seriatim. Śaṅkara wrote his commentary on the *Upaniṣad* as a shortened form of this Commentary. (See Fragment 11.)

It is also said traditionally that Draviḍa was the author of a commentary (*bhāṣya*) on the Treatise (*vākya*) by Ṭaṅka on the *Chāndogya-Upaniṣad* ;[4] and in the light of the Fragments, where Draviḍa's words are often quoted immediately after those of Ṭaṅka, this may be taken as certain. Whether this Commentary on Ṭaṅka's work was something other than what is referred to as his Commentary on the *Chāndogya-Upaniṣad*, or whether the two are the same and it was a matter of Draviḍa's writing a Commentary on the *Upaniṣad* borrowing the aid of Ṭaṅka's work — at present there is no clear answer to this question. But probably the second was the case. Moreover, a work called *Vāmanaṭīka* — further notes on his Commentary on Ṭaṅka's work — seems to have been in existence.[5]

His Commentary (*bhāṣya*) became extremely important for the later Vedānta school[6] and he came to be commonly called The Commentator (*Bhāṣyakāra, Bhāṣyakṛt*). The commentary was still extant in the early seventeenth century[7] but is now lost.

Again, looking at Fragment 15, it is seen that he is made out to be the author of a *sūtra*. From the text it is clearly a *sūtra* as Śaṅkara says, the style being extremely terse. Again, according to Ānandajñāna's gloss, there is a reference to the *Bṛhad.Up*.III,8,8. And this *sūtra* in style, character and content is very like the *Brahma-sūtra*, though it is not among the *Brahma-sūtras* as we now have them. Now how is this fragment to be understood? It is only the *Brahma-sūtras* going back to Bādarāyaṇa which are now extant as the *sūtras* of the Vedānta schools, which as commented on by the founders of each of the Vedānta schools are taken as a fundamental text. But one may suppose that the *Brahma-sūtras* were originally compiled by some school adhering to the *Chāndogya-Upaniṣad*, and gradually were added to and broadened to reach the present form, but they were by no means the only *sūtras* on the *Upaniṣads*. And if so it may well be that Draviḍa put together or perhaps edited some *sūtras* other than the *Brahma-sūtras* known to us. But the paucity of material at present does not permit any definite conclusion.

In Śrīdhara's *Smṛtyarthasāra* a Draviḍa is referred to as a *dharma*-teacher, and he is said to be the author of a work called the *Smṛtipradīpa*.[8]

There existed also a Draviḍa who was a scholar of the rituals. Trikāṇḍa-maṇḍana Bhāskara-miśra -- who must be before the 11th century at latest — in his *Āpastambadhvanitārtha-kārikā* refers three times to a Draviḍa, as a commentator on *sūtras* relating to rituals.[9] Bhandarkar took these to be the same man[10] and he thinks that the *Smṛtidīpa* which Trikaṇḍamaṇḍana refers to is probably intended for the *Smṛtipradīpa*. Again Draviḍa is mentioned as a Grammarian.[11] It is not yet clear whether these are the same as the Vedāntin Draviḍa.

Draviḍa is an appellation of one of the indigenous tribes of India and also an area in the south of India, and so the 'Draviḍa teacher' (Draviḍācārya) has been used to mean 'a scholar born of the Draviḍa tribe'.[12] And again the great Śaṅkara, born as he was in the Draviḍa region of the south, has been called Drāviḍa.[13] At present the question of what may have been the connection between Draviḍācārya and the Draviḍa tribe or Draviḍa region is obscure.

From the association of the appellations Draviḍācārya with the Draviḍa tribe and Draviḍa region it has often been claimed that he should be identified with one of the Āḷvār Vaiṣṇava sainits who have a close connection with Draviḍa tribe. But probably he was not one of the Āḷvār.

Mr. Tripāṭhi says that the Draviḍa who was a precursor of Rāmānuja would have been Śaṭhakopa, an Āḷvār. (But his reasons for this do not appear.)[14]

Further S.Kuppuswami Sastri[15] asserts that Master Draviḍa is identical with the Sage Tirumaḷiśai Āḷvār of the Vaiṣṇava sect. As reasons he presents the following: (1) Tirumaḷiśai Āḷvār was the son of the Sage Bhārgava, but was adopted and raised by the *Śūdra* Tiruvāḷan. He studied theology and later became a famous sage. His life agrees well with "the tale of the prince who was raised by hunters," which is attributed to Draviḍa. (2) Draviḍa's statements (fragment 5) agree well with *śloka* 72 of the *Nānmukan tiruvantāti*, which was written by Tirumaḷiśai. (3) The names "Draviḍa" and "Tirumaḷiśai" have phonetic resemblances.

Reason (1), however, can be refuted by the fact that, as will be discussed later, a similar tale already existed in the *Saddharma-puṇḍarīka-sūtra*. As for reasons (2) and (3), the fact of identity cannot be shown simply by resemblences. Further, in view of their dates, they cannot be regarded as identical: Āḷvārs are generally of a later period.

Śaṭhakopa is said to be either of the first half of the 12th century[16] or else of the 8th century.[17] Tirumaḷiśai was a little earlier. But Draviḍa is believed to be long before Śaṅkara.[18] Thus the dates of the two do not agree. But a far weightier reason is the difference in social status. The Āḷvārs were mainly born of humble origins and taught their doctrine of God for the *śūdras* and outcasts. In their ideas can be seen influence of *Mahābhārata* and early *Purānas*, but no connection at all with anything Vedic.

Thus to identify the Draviḍa who as a pure theologian wrote, in Sanskrit, commentaries on the *Brahma-sūtras* which do not admit liberation for *śūdras*, and on the *Chāndogya Upaniṣad*, a sacred text of orthodox Brahnanism, with any of the Āḷvārs, is impossible.[19] Probably the teacher Ḍraviḍa was born of a pure Brahmin family.

According to Yāmuna's *Siddhitraya*,[20] Draviḍa is listed as perhaps the earliest who commented correctly on the *Brahma-sūtras* : Śaṅkara, Sureśvara, Sarvajñātman, Yāmuna, Rāmānuja and so on are at one in quoting his words to attest their own doctrine, and since he is of such authority he should be long before even Śaṅkara. But he is later than Ṭaṅka. For not only is he frequently given as commenting on Ṭaṅka's writings, but where his words are quoted together with Ṭaṅka's,[21] they are always presented in second place as accessory. If Ṭaṅka is taken as about A.D.500-550, then Draviḍa may be dated about 500. It is difficult to make his later while keeping to Yāmuna.

Notes

1) According to the views of the Rāmānuja school, "Dramiḍa" is correct. (Thibaut : SBE. XXXIV, Introduction, p. xxii, n.1)

2) T. M. Tripāṭhi (*The Tarkasaṃgraha*, GOS. no. III, Introduction, p. xvi.) feels that the two are different. He feels the Dramiḍa, as the predecessor of Rāmānuja, is identical to Śaṭhakopa, a master of the Viṣṇu school who was one of the Āḷvār.

3) Cf. Fragment 1. Chapter I, "General Remarks." Further, according to the *Prapannāmṛta* by Anantācārya, Bodhāyana's *Vṛtti* to the *Brahma-sūtra* was a detailed work. In contrast, Dramiḍa's commentary was extremely brief.(Dasgupta : *HIPh.* vol. III, p. 108.)

4) *Bhagavān sarvajño Bhāṣyakāro Nandikṛtagranthabhāṣyakāro Draviḍācāryaḥ* --- (Rāmatīrtha : *Anvayārthaprakāśikā* ad *Saṃkṣepaśārīraka*, III, 221) ; also, fragment 17.

5) Cf. Ṭaṅka, fragment 13.

6) According to Aufrecht : *CC.* III, p.134 the *Dramiḍācāryabhāṣya* is also cited in the *Nyāyasiddhāñjana*, p.134 (*Paṇḍit*, vol. XXIII) by the Vedānta scholar of a later period, Veṅkaṭanātha.

7) Śrīnivāsa lists at the end of his work, the *Yatīndramatadīpikā*, the references upon which that work is based. The *Draviḍabhāṣya* is the first in that list. Hence, he probably actually saw Dramiḍa's work. Rudolf Otto : *Dīpikā des Nivāsa*, S.83.

8) Bhandarkar : *Coll. Works*, II, p.137(=*Report*, 1883-84) ; p.107.

9) Bhandarkar : *Coll. Works*, II, p.102.

10) Bhandarkar : *Coll. Works*, II, p.107.

11) Kṣīrasvāmin mentions a Draviḍāḥ or Drāviḍāḥ ; he is also mentioned in Mādhava's

Dhātuvṛtti.

12) For example, in the *Vārijākṣacarita*, scholars such as Bhīmācārya, Kṛpācārya, Trimaṅgalācārya, et al. are presented as Draviḍācārya.(Bhandarkar : *Coll. Works*, II, pp.134-135).

13) In Sureśvara's *Naiṣkarmyasiddhi*, IV, 43, Śaṅkara's *Upadeśasāhasrī* XVIII, 26 is cited as Draviḍa's. Because the plural form "Drāviḍaiḥ" is used, Walleser (*DAV*. S.2 ; 23, Anm. 2) proposed a Draviḍa group which includes Śaṅkara ; but this probably should be explained as an honorific plural.

14) Cf. note 2.

15) Cf. the previously cited article by S. Kuppuswami Sastri.

16) R. G. Bhandarkar : *Vaiṣṇavism, Śaivism and Minor Religious Systems*, p.50.

17) Farquhar : *Outline*, p.188.

18) Cf. Chapter I of this Part. Concerning Śaṅkara's dates, see the present work Part One pp.43ff.

19) He presents no reasons, but Dasgupta (*HIPh.* vol. III, p.106, n.1) is also opposed to Kuppuswami's explanation.

20) *Siddhitraya*, p. 5. Cf. Chapter I of this Part.

21) Cf. the previous Chapter.

SECTION III. HIS THOUGHT

As can be seen from the fact that Draviḍa wrote commentaries on the *Chāndogya-Upaniṣad* and the *Brahma-sūtra*, he took the authority of the sacred texts as absolute and made them the authority for his own doctrine (Fragment 2 ; *Śrībhāṣya* ad *BS.* I,1,11). In particular as to the metaphysical essence of *Brahman* he regarded the sacred texts as the only source of knowledge. (Fragment 15 - Ś. on *GK* II,32 where *'āhama-vid'*, knower of the scripture, is identified by Ānandajñāna as Gauḍapāda.) According to Draviḍa, these sacred texts (*śāstra*) speak of reality as it is (*yathābhūtavādin* Fragment 10). The holy texts could never be saying what was not right, or not in accordance with truth. The eulogies (*prāśastya*) taught in the *śāstra* must always have an adequate foundation. So he thought that the *śāstra* is a transmitter of truth as it is, in every field whether human affaires or Nature.

He considered that the doctrines of the *śāstras* were to be determined *logically* (conformably to reason). Here the idea 'I believe because it is absurd' (Tertullian's reported '*credo quia absurdum est*') is not admitted. And he included in the sacred texts not only the *Upaniṣad*s but the *Purāṇa*s (Fragment 12 - Ś. ad *Chānd. Up.* III,10). Thus certain *Purāṇas* were already about the sixth century being regarded within the Vedānta schools as a part of the sacred texts, which is a fact noteworthy in the history of Indian culture.

But contradictions came to be recognized between the doctrines of this extended field of *śāstra*, and he labored for a method of dissolving the contradictions and clearing up difficult points. His intellectual standpoint was typically Vedāntic.[1]

What now was his metaphysical position? The thinkers belonging to the line of Śaṅkara stress that he held to non-duality.[2] But those of the Rāmānuja line, on the other hand, taught that he was a predecessor of Rāmānuja, holding to the Viśiṣṭa Advaita.[3] As he was regarded by both the schools as authoritative, probably his doctrine had features in common with each of them, and was not identical with either. We must therefore critically examine the fragments which have come down to us.

Like other Vedāntins, he postulates *Brahman* as the absolute principle. He says *Brahman* is 'creator of all' (*viśva-sṛj*).[4] But he did not set up a distinction between *Brahman*-with-attributes and attributeless *Brahman*, as Śaṅkara emphasized.[5] He stipulates that *Brahman* considered by himself is 'existence' (*sat* : Fragment 6).

Again he calls *Brahman* 'the supreme divinity' (*paradevatā*), looking upon *Brahman* as a personal god ; and he regarded *Brahman* as 'Lord of the world' (*lokeśvara* : Fragment 5), so he never made a distinction between *Brahman* and *Īśvara*, as Śaṅkara did. Probably this doctrine of his derives directly from the thought of Uddālaka in the sixth chapter of the *Chāndogya-Upaniṣad*.

Then he calls this *Brahman* 'supreme divinity having interior attributes' (*antarguṇa paradevatā*). It is a question what 'having interior attributes' could mean, but probably the meaning is 'having the attribute of inner self' (*Ātman*).[6] So it can be taken that he thought of the highest Self and the interior self as having common, or at least similar attributes, but at the same time it is clear that he did not think of the highest Self and the interior self as identical. He says that the individual self and the highest Self are of the same genus (*jāti* : Fragment 13). So according to him, *Brahman* and the interior self are realities different from one another ; they merely belong to the same genus, having common attributes and nothing more.

Brahman is called '*Ātman*' (Fragment 5) but that *Ātman* is not in the sense of individual self, but in the sense of main constituent or subject of all that is, namely the highest Self. And such being the case, it can be said that in fact Draviḍa recognized a unique highest Self (creator-god) and innumerable individual selves, eternally existing and each separate.

What then are the attributes common to *Brahman* and the individual self? There is no record of what he said on this, but very likely they were taken by him to be : the attribute of existence, of spirit, of subjectivity, of eternity, of purity, and so on. These attributes were accepted in the Vedānta schools in general and there is no sufficient reason to suppose that he differed ; but whereas Śaṅkara took the individual self and supreme Self — both having these attributes as absolutely identical, Draviḍa took them as quite distinct individual principles postulating attributes of difference and separation of the two. In this can be seen a characteristic of his thought.

According to Śaṅkara's account of what he said, the individual self is certainly of the same genus as the highest Self, and just as sparks come out from a fire, so separating from the highest Self it enters into this tangled thicket of body, senses etc.[7] This is in the line of one doctrine of the old *Upaniṣad* and is common to a good many other Vedāntins. According to this, the Lord as the highest Self is the absolute source which projects the individual selves, and includes all the individual selves. The highest Self is the ultimate in greatness, and the individual self the ultimate in smallness.

The highest Self, then, of such a special character, is a principle transcending the individual selves. It does not come into a relation of comparison with anything else, and so it is in essence without distinctions.[8] It transcends all dualistic oppositions. Of course in the highest Self, there do exist the aforesaid attributes which are common to the individual self, but he no doubt considered that the non-dual teaching of a *Brahman*-without-differences, without attributes, does not entail any contradiction with the

Upaniṣadic doctrine of *Brahman*-without-differences expressible only negatively, because inasmuch as attributes are ascribable to *Brahman*, their natures transcend limited conceptual determination.[9]

Still, if *Brahman* is a principle different from the individual self, one could not say that this *Brahman* transcends all dualistic differences, and so pressing the point to its logical conclusion, the non-dualist school boldly declared the individual self and the highest Self to be absolutely identical. But Draviḍa probably held the view that even allowing them to be different principles — there being a difference of dimension — since the highest Self is absolute transcending the individual self, no relation of difference could be postulated between them.

Probably it was in view of this characteristic thought of his that the later non-dualists acknowledged him as a pioneer of their own lines. But it has to be said that his fundamental thought is close to the qualified non-duality of the Rāmānuja line.

Brahman, this controller Lord, as a transcendent personal god by his absolute power preserves and controls the *Brahma*-world and all the other worlds. He makes possible the phenomena of nature ; making the created phenomena, he allocates to them their places. (Fragment 8). And for this very reason he is called Lord of the world (*lokeśvara*). But he is not tainted by the deficiencies or evils of those worlds, and he preserved the highest limit of happiness.[10]

His relation to the world is compared to that of a king and the kingdom he rules (Fragment 5). All individual selves are placed in the condition of absolute subordination to the Lord. The theistic doctrine of liberation is presented on the basis of this relation between the Lord and the individual self. Generally speaking, the individual self's puny efforts can not achieve any good vouchsafed by the Lord. Man with his various activities pleases the Lord, and he must pray for His grace. When the Lord is satisfied with the believer's reverent faith and self-sacrificing discipline, He grants the good results as His grace (Fragment 5 etc.).

In the matter of attaining the good which is called liberation, the position is exactly the same. Many of the Indian philosophers think that liberation is attained by one's own knowledge (*vidyā*), and they praise it exultantly, but according to Draviḍa, that knowledge really means standing at peace in *Brahman* (Fragment 18). So it is not something that can be acquired by one's own efforts, but something conferred by the Lord (Fragment 5 etc.).

Since our life (fate) rests wholly in the hand of the Lord, we must get rid of our evil heart, make the heart humble, and practise meditation (worship) on the Lord. This meditation (*vidyā*) is taught in many forms in the *Upaniṣad*s, but according to him, they do not all have to be performed ; it is enough to choose one and perform it (Fragment 6).

Brahman is realized by the mind (*manas*) purified from all taints by performance of this meditation. *Brahman* as it is in itself is not to be grasped by the physical eye at that moment, but it is said to be grasped directly (*añjasā*) in the some way as an object is grasped by the eye (Fragment 9). Thus his doctrine as regards practice is in general the same as Ṭaṅka's.

Now man, by performing this meditation, can finally be liberated by the grace of the Lord, and the individual self thus liberated comes to union with the supreme deity. In that case it does not possess a physical body, but continues its individual existence as before, and like the highest deity it can attain any purpose just as it may desire (Fragment 3). It is in fact equal to the supreme deity. But since it is always different from the supreme deity himself, it does not — liberated though it is — possess the functions of world-creation, sustenance and dissolution. On this point he is at one with the doctrine of the *Brahma-sūtra* and of Ṭaṅka. And it is close to the doctrine of Rāmānuja.

His views are summarized as above insofar as they can be inferred from the fragments. In the light of the above-mentioned philosophical characteristics of his thought, we ought to propose a view about the tale of the prince raised by hunters, attributed to Draviḍa. This tale[11)] was used not only by Śaṅkara, Sureśvara, Rāmānuja, Ānandajñāna, Mādhava and Vijñānabhikṣu, but also by Madhva, and for almost a thousand years held its place as an important illustrative allegory for the Vedānta school. As has been mentioned, the explanations of various thinkers concerning this tale do not necessarily agree. While Śaṅkara made use of by the Advaita school, Sureśvara explains that just as the hunter's son became a prince when he came to know his true essence, so when the individual self comes to know its real essence, it will, without any effort, become the highest Self. Mādhạva explains the tale in connection with somewhat Sāṃkhya-like philosophical explanations.

What then was the purpose of Draviḍa himself in presenting the story? The basic idea is similar to that of the well-known account of the 'prodigal son' in the Fourth Chapter (*Adhimukti*) of the *Saddharmapuṇḍarīka-sūtra*. According to that tale, the son of a 'lord' left his father to dwell in a foreign land. He fell into poverty and began a life of wandering but after fifty years he returned to his father's castle. The father was overjoyed to realize that his son had returned, but he did not make this known to those around him. First he employed his son as a servant and gradually promoted him to a high position. Finally he revealed that the servant was his own son and made him his heir. It was only then that the prodigal son realized that he was the son of his 'lord'.

The explanation is given that the Buddha similarly is comparable to the 'lord', and sentient beings to the children of the lord. For the sake of sentient beings the Buddha gradually propounded more and more profound teachings until finally he vouchsafed the doctrine of One Path, in the *Saddharmapuṇḍalīka-sūtra*. But in fact he had from the very beginning taught the essential meaning of Mahāyāna Buddhism : it was only that the followers had failed to realize it.

This is an extremely rare simile[12] and no other examples of it exist in Indian cultural and literary history, so it is probably that Draviḍa borrowed it from the *Saddharmapuṇḍarīka-sūtra*. In Draviḍa's time the *sūtra* was still widely read in India.[13] After Draviḍa the tale was traditionally handed down in the Vedānta school.

If such a historical relationship can be accepted, one may go on to explain Dvaviḍa's parable in the light of it. In which case, its meaning may be said to be as follows :

For the highest governing-deity, the individual selves are like children. They can receive his love, but because of delusion the individual selves do not know their true nature, and rebel against the governing-deity who is like their father. That is (according to Śaṅkara) because, having their being 'apart from the highest Self', they remain in suffering in the cycle of birth and death. But if once there is an awakening of the individual self, and faith in the highest deity, he exists directly within the grace of the highest deity.

To explain the parable in this way agrees with the general views held by Draviḍa, as previously set out. It also agrees with Śaṅkara's statements. One has the impression that Sureśvara and Mādhava explained it in a meaning much too close to their own respective theories.

Now the fact that the *Saddharmapuṇḍarīka-sūtra* and the Vedānta philosophy use the same parable in a similar sense indicates that in their basic thinking they have similar characteristics. It is worthy of note that there are definite aspects of similarity between the Vedānta philosophy and the teachings of the *Saddharmapuṇḍarīka-sūtra*.[14]

Notes

1) Cf. Fragment 12. Here the 'teacher' taken as authoritative is Draviḍa. *yady api śrutivirodhe smṛtir apramāṇam, tathāpi yathākathaṃcid virodhaparihāram Draviḍācryoktam upapādayati*/(Ān. ad Chānd. Up. III,10.)

2) Fragments 14, 16. See also *advaitam eva Brahmanandigranthe vivakṣitaṃ na pariṇāmādīty etad tad-Bhāsyakṛd-Draviḍācārya-vacanād avasīyata. ity āha—antarguṇeti*/ (Rāmatīrtha: *Anvayārthaprakāśikā* ad *Saṃkṣepaśārīraka* III, 221.)

3) *Vedārthasaṃgraha*, p.154.

4) Fragment 9.

5) It appears from Fragment 16 that distinguishing between the two is the doctrine of Sarvajñātman himself and not that of Draviḍa

6) Fragment 6, 16.

7) Fragment 13. See the ideas of Āśmarathya (in the *Brahma-sūtra*) and *Gauḍapādīya-Kārikās*, III,15.

8) Among scholars the fact has been remarked that Draviḍa is often quoted in the works of Rāmānuja, and as a result it is suggested that Draviḍa thought of *Brahman* as with distinctions, and endowed with countless virtues. But among the fragments, there exists no positive evidence to that effect. Draviḍa's words in Fragment 6 only tell us that he considers *Brahman* as Existence (*sat*).

9) Understood in this way, the phrase 'with internal attribute' would not conflict with Fragment 5.

10) Thus the nature of *Brahman*: Existence-Consciousness-Bliss (*sac-cid-ānanda*), taught in later Vedānta can be said to be present already as an idea in Draviḍa.

11) Cf. Fragments 13,14. This story is mentioned by Bhāskara, Rāmānuja, Ānandajñāna, Mādhava, and Vijñānabhikṣu in their respective works. The purport is more or less the same. The tradition of this story as given by Rāmānuja alone differs slightly. It is likely that Rāmānuja adapted the story to fit in with his own teaching. (Shokei Matsumoto: *Journal of Indian and Buddhist Studies*, vol. XXV, no.1, Dec. 1976, pp.98 102.)

12) It is even taken by scholars to have some problematical relation to the tale in the New Testament, Luke 15. (Winternitz: *GIL*. II, S.233, Anm.2.)

13) For example, since the latest Chinese version of the *Saddharmapuṇḍarīka-sūtra* was translated into Chinese in 601 A.D.; this is probably later than Draviḍa.

14) Cf. Part VI, Chapter III, Section IV and also the author's *Indian Development of Philosophic Thought* (in Japanese), p.14ff.

CHAPTER VII
BHARTṚPRAPAÑCA

SECTION I. FRAGMENTS

Among the Vedānta scholars who lived before Śaṅkara, Bhartṛprapañca must be considered particularly important. He is known as the opponent whom Śaṅkara and Sureśvara attacked most strongly. Although none of his works are now extant, a great many of his statements has been preserved in the works of the Advaita school. From these we can get a fairly clear understanding of his viewpoint. Research concerning his theories has recently shown a marked advance.[1]

His views and comments on the scriptures are presented in Śaṅkara's commentary (*Bhāṣya*) to the *Bṛhad-āraṇyaka-Upaniṣad*, Sureśvara's "Appreciation" (*Vārttika*) to this commentary, and in Ānandajñāna's (also called Ānandagiri) sub-commentary (*Ṭīkā*) to those two works. If we list these passages, we have the following:

(1) Passages cited in Śaṅkara's commentary to the *Bṛhad. Up.*: pp.151, 152, 187, 190, 207, 236, 323, 328, 364, 416, 445, 449, (492), 560, 614, 622, 731[2]

In presenting these passages Bhartṛprapañca's name is not directly referred. They are attributed only to "some persons" (*kecid*) or "other persons" (*apare*). However, in the sub-commentary, in Sureśvara's *Vārttika*, and in the sub-commentary to the *Vārttika*, these are explained as being from Bhartṛprapañca.[3]

(2) Passages cited in Sureśvara's *Vārttika*

In Sureśvara's *Vārttika* Bhartṛprapañca's theories are presented in great detail, but it is in rare cases that Sureśvara himself gives Bhartṛprapañca's name. In most cases we learn that they are citations from Bhartṛprapañca only through Ānandagiri's sub-commentary. The following is a list of passages in which his statements are cited and then discussed and refuted:

pp.532 (*śloka* 490), 572 (*śloka* 693), 623 (*śloka* 947ff.), 639 (*śloka* 1025 ff.), 647 (*śloka* 1065ff.), 659 (*śloka* 1127ff.), 666 (*śloka* 1164), 668 (*śloka* 1175ff.), 671 (*śloka* 1188), 724 (*śloka* 1467ff.), 757 (*śloka* 1644 ff.), 760 (*śloka* 1709ff.), 801 (*śloka* 27), 822 (*śloka* 137), 827 (*śloka* 171 ff.), 829 (*śloka* 181ff.), 837 (*śloka* 225), 839 (*śloka* 232ff.), 851 (*śloka* 302ff. Cf. 340), 876 (*śloka* 46ff.), 890 (*śloka* 21), 919 (*śloka* 195ff.), 928 (*śloka* 248ff.), 989 (*śloka* 15), 1000 (*śloka* 49ff.), 1001 (*śloka* 53ff.), 1004 (*śloka* 72ff.), 1007 (*śloka* 90ff.), 1010 (*śloka* 104ff. Cf. 148ff. 178 ff.), 1115 (*śloka* 14ff.), 1123 (*śloka* 67ff.), 1143 (*śloka* 40ff.), 1154 (*śloka* 41ff.), 1158 (*śloka* 62ff.), 1236 (*śloka* 167ff.), 1240 (*śloka* 5ff.), 1258 (*śloka* 113ff.), 1295 (*śloka* 30ff.), 1361 (*śloka* 14ff.), 1369 (*śloka* 65ff.), 1374 (*śloka* 100ff.), 1000 (*śloka* 49ff.), 1432 (*śloka* 318ff.), 1450 (*śloka* 423f.), 1572 (*śloka* 1088ff.), 1579 (*śloka* 1123-1187ff.), 1590 (*śloka* 1188ff.), 1625 (*śloka* 1386ff.), 1651 (*śloka* 1537ff.), 1666 (*śloka* 1625ff.), 1668 (*śloka* 1639ff.), 1728 (*śloka* 28ff.), 1785 (*śloka* 391ff.), 1843 (*śloka* 741ff.), 1852 (Cf. *śloka* 796ff.), 1879 (*śloka* 965ff.), 1890 (*śloka* 1032ff.), 1953 (*śloka* 28ff.).

From the fact that his theories are discussed in several hundreds of the *ślokas*, we see that they are introduced in rather great detail.

In order to read and understand the above passages cited by Śaṅkara and Sureśvara, we of course must rely on Ānandagiri's sub-commentary.

(3) Fragments of Bhartṛprapañca's commentaries cited in Ānandagiri's sub-commentary

The references in Śaṅkara's commentary and in Sureśvara's *Vārttika* are not direct quotations from Bhartṛprapañca. Śaṅkara, writing in prose, summarized Bhartṛprapañca's comments on passages in the *Upaniṣad*. Sureśvara subsequently revised Śaṅkara's prose into verse-form. Thus the original has always been revised by either Śaṅkara or Sureśvara. However, in Ānandagiri's sub-commentary there are passages which appear to be direct quotations. For example, in explaining Bhartṛprapañca's views, the sub-commentary uses the following stylistic forms : *uktaṃ hi ... iti, yathāhur ... iti, ... ityādi-Bhāṣyam vibhajate, ... iti Bhāṣyenāha*, etc. M. Hiriyanna,[4] taking such passages as fragments of Bhartṛprapañca's works, has collected and published them. Such passages are probably based on Bhartṛprapañca's commentary, but there is still room for doubt as to whether they are direct quotations. Had the original been in verse-form they would undoubtedly have been quoted directly, but since it was in prose, it might have been abbreviated or enlarged. Be that as it may, it goes without saying that these are highly important sources for understanding Bhartṛprapañca's theories.

Notes

1) His role as a thinker has been discussed in The *Tarka-saṅgraha*, ed. by T. M. Tripāṭhi (GOS. no.III), Introduction, pp.xv-xvi ; Radhakrishnan : *IPh.* vol.II, p. 466 ; M. Hiriyanna, taking as a basis the fragments of his works, has clarified in some detail the outline of his thought-system. (M. Hiriyanna : "Bhartṛprapañca ; an Old Vedāntin", *Ind. Ant.* vol., LIII, 1924, p.77-86). Further, Prof. Kanakura has published a detailed study of Bhartṛprapañca's theories as presented in Śaṅkara's *Bṛhad. Up. Bhāṣya*, and of Śaṅkara's objections to them. (*A Study of Vedānta Philosophy*, in Japanese, pp. 24-102). Three decades after I completed this work in Japanese, I obtained Dr.Pandeya's work, in which I find valuable discussions on Bhartṛprapañca. (Sangam Lal Pandey : *Pre-Śaṅkara Advaita Philosophy*, Allahabad, Darshan Peeth, 1974, pp. 209-228). I hope readers will refer to it for further studies.

2) Prof. Kanakura : *op. cit.* p.26.

3) A Japanese translation of important sections is presented in Prof. Kanakura's above-cited work.

4) M. Hiriyanna : "Fragments of Bhartṛprapañca", (*Proc. III OC*. Madras, 1924, pp.439 -450). However, since it is clear that Ānandagiri's own statements also are included in the sources which M. Hiriyanna collected, a critical attitude is necessary when using these as source-material.

SECTION II. THE MAN, HIS WORKS, AND HIS DATES.

Śaṅkara does not mention Bhartṛprapañca's name at all and only criticizes his theories. In the main *ślokas* of his *Vārttika*, however, Sureśvara frequently cites his name[1] and also mentions his commentary (*Bhartṛprapañca-bhāṣya*).[2] His theories are refuted by both Śaṅkara and Sureśvara, but not only is he regarded as an upholder of *Brahman* (*Brahmavādin*),[3] he is also treated with great respect. Sureśvara used honorifics, calling him "the sage Bhartṛprapañca" (*Śrīmad-Bhartṛprapañca*)[4] or "the great sage Bhartṛprapañca" (*Śrīman-mahā-Bhartṛprapañca mahīyas*),[5] or ellipses such as "the great person" (*mahātman*)[6] and "he of great wisdom" (*mahādhī*).[7] Hence his authority was recognized generally by the contemporary Vedānta school. From Sureśvara's standpoint he was a thinker of importance equal to Śaṅkara.

Among his works the following may be cited though no longer extant.

(1) The commentary to the *Bṛhadāraṇyaka-Upaniṣad-bhāṣya* (*Bṛhadāraṇyaka-upaniṣad-bhāṣya*)

According to Śaṅkara and Ānandagiri he wrote a large commentary to the text of the *Bṛhadāraṇyaka-Upaniṣad* transmitted by the Mādhyaṃdina school. This work was generally known as "the commentary" (*Bhāṣya*).[8] With this work as his target, Śaṅkara wrote his own "Commentary to the *Bṛhadāraṇyaka-Upaniṣad*." In comparison with Bhartṛprapañca's commentary, however, Śaṅkara's was shorter, and further more used the text of the *Upaniṣad* transmitted by the Kāṇva school.[9] Now Bhartṛprapañca's work was not the first commentary to the *Bṛhadāraṇyaka-Upaniṣad* ; in fact, it too was written as a critique of older commentaries.[10] This work is no longer extant, but from the fact that Ānandagiri frequently cites from it, an edition probably existed in Ānandagiri's time (13c.).

(2) The commentary to the *Kāṭhaka-Upaniṣad*

According to Gopalayogin's sub-commentary, Bhartṛprapañca also wrote a commentary to the *Kāṭhaka-Upaniṣad.* Since it was verbose but shallow,[11] Śaṅkara separately wrote a shorter commentary to this *Upaniṣad*.[12]

(3) The commentary to the *Īśā-Upaniṣad*

We may infer from Ānandagiri's statements that Bhartṛprapañca also wrote a commentary to the *Īśā-Upaniṣad*.[13]

At the least, we know that Bhartṛprapañca wrote the above three works. It is not known whether he authored any others.[14]

His dates are also not definitely known. It is beyond doubt that he lived before Śaṅkara. According to a statement in Yāmuna's *Siddhitraya*, he belongs to the period after Ṭaṅka, but was earlier than Bhartṛhari. The reliability of this statement may be questioned, but considering the date of the *Brahma-sūtra* and the dates of thinkers before him, we may tentatively state that his period of activity centered about 550 A.D.[15] In such a case he would be later than Bhartṛhari, but since Yāmuna is of the eleventh-century this amount of discrepancy seems unavoidable.

Notes

1) *Bhartṛprapañcaprasthāna*, p.666, v.1164.

2) p.671, v.1188. His *Bhāṣya* is also clearly indicated in p.666, v.1164 ; p.1155, v.46.

3) p.1123, v.67. He is further stated to be "the person who is called the 'Discourser on the *Upaniṣads*' " (*Aupaniṣadaṃmanya*). (Ś. ad *Bṛhad. Up*. p.328 ; *Vārttika*, p.1007, v.90).

4) p. 1843, v. 741

5) p.1789, v.412.

6) p.624, v.950.

7) p.1572, v.1088.

8) Ānandagiri, in citing him in the *Bṛhad. Up. Vārttika-ṭīkā*, prefaces the citations with "It is stated in the *Bhāṣya* ...".

9) Cf. The beginning of Śaṅkara's *Bṛhad. Up. Bhāṣya*, and Prof. Kanakura's "*A Study of Vedānta Philosophy*", pp.24-25.

10) Cf. Note 15).

11) *śabdato bahutvād arthataś ca nyūnatvād//*

12) Gopālayogin's *Ṭīkā* ad Śaṅkara's *Kāṭhakopaniṣadbhāṣya* (ĀnSS.), p. 3.

13) Hiriyanna : *op. cit. Ind. Ant.* LIII, p.78, n.5.

14) In his previously cited article, M. Hiriyanna infers from the *Siddhitraya* that Bhartṛprapañca also wrote a commentary to the *Brahma-sūtra*. However, it cannot be said that all philosophers listed in that passage of the *Siddhitraya* wrote commentaries to the *Brahma-sūtra*. For example, although Bhartṛhari held to Vedānta theories, he did not write a commentary to the *Brahma-sūtra*. The same may be said of Ṭaṅka.

15) In commenting on the term "*brahman*" at the beginning of the *Bṛhad.Up*. I,4,10, it is stated in Śaṅkara's commentary (p.151) that Bhartṛprapañca presented two explanations. Śaṅkara refutes both of them. In Ānandagiri's sub-commentary one explanation is held to be that of the *Vṛttikāra* and the other Bhartṛprapañca's. Further, in the sub-commentary to the *Vārttika* p.671, v.1189, both are held to be "*Bhāṣyakṛt*" and the former is held to be an introduction (*pūrvapakṣa*) leading to the latter (Bhartṛprapañca's) explanation. Since the "*Vṛttikāra*" and "*Bhāṣyakṛt*" mentioned here must be different from those who wrote on the *Brahma-sūtra*, they cannot be used as clues to settling problem of dates. However, we do learn from it that Bhartṛprapañca criticized commentaries existent in his time. Dasgupta (*HIPh*. vol. II, p.43) states that Bhartṛprapañca is mentioned by Bodhāyana, but there is no reason for holding that the "*Vṛttikāra*" refers to Bodhāyana.

SECTION III. HIS THOUGHT

In presenting a detailed explanation of Bhartṛprapañca's theories, Sureśvara states in one passage[1] that they closely resemble Śaṅkara's philosophical views (in particular, the theory of temporary appearance through ignorance) and that the meaning of other passages in Bhartṛprapañca's commentary (*Bhāṣya*) should be explained accordingly. Further, according to Ānandagiri's sub-commentary, his theories are as follows:

> Bhartṛprapañca's views accord with the temporary-appearance theory (*vivartavāda*). They are not against the accepted theories (*siddhāntāviruddha*) of our Vedāna school, but some have misunderstood their true meaning and for those people they are thus discussed.[2] He himself opposed[3] the theory of emanation (*pariṇāmin*) from Brahman.

Yet, was it really as Sureśvara and Ānandagiri explain? This is highly doubtful. Śaṅkara consistently presents Bhartṛprapañca as *a person who asserts heretical views*. Further, Bhartṛprapañca, as presented by Śaṅkara, refuted Śaṅkara's basic doctrines.[4] The content of what Sureśvara describes Bhartṛprapañca's theories does not necessarily agree with Śaṅkara's metaphysics and at times it clearly criticizes the Advaita school.[5] Hence, we must state that the previously presented explanations by Sureśvara and Ānandagiri are not accurate. In the above-cited passage from Ānandagiri there is thc question, "Is it not the fact that Bhartṛprapañca holds to the world-emanation (*pariṇāma*) view?"[6] The person who hurled this question should be seen as having had a more accurate grasp of the situation than Ānandagiri.

Now why do Sureśvara and Ānandagiri state that Bhartṛprapañca presents the temporary-appearance theory? As previously stated, since even Sureśvara adds honorifics to Bhartṛprapañca's name, in Sureśvara's time he must have been greatly respected. So it was that Sureśvara was led to say that his theories were really not much different from the Advaita theories. It is habitual with Sureśvara to state that the theories of Vedānta scholars of venerable authority agree with his own views. This tendency is also marked[7] in the case of his account of "Master Draviḍa".

So it is difficult to suppose that Sureśvara's account is invariably accurate as regards Bhartṛprapañca's theories. It may be thought that his own views and explanations have entered to a considerable degree into Sureśvara's account.

In contrast, Śaṅkara consistently mentions Bhartṛprapañca's theories only where they oppose his own views. Thus, there should be no objection in taking Śaṅkara's account as a basic source for understanding Bhartṛprapañca's views. Together with this, of course, the passage from Bhartṛprapañca's commentary quoted in Ānandagiri's sub-commentary are a primary source. However, since those quotations are extremely brief, there are not a few places where Bhartṛprapañca's views are difficult to ascertain from the quotations alone.

To the extent that it agrees with the above two sources, Sureśvara's *Vārttika* may be used as a source. In cases where it is only Sureśvara that presents particular theories as Bhartṛprapañca's, we do not know what degree of reliability they have. However, if they differ greatly from Śaṅkara's and Sureśvara's views, then in the cases where this difference is outstanding, we can probably safely regard them as Bhartṛprapañca's views. In such a case, however, since we must compare them with Śaṅkara's and Sureśvara's theories, a through study of Śaṅkara's commentary (*Bhāṣya*) and Sureśvara's *Vārttika* to the *Bṛhadāraṇyaka-Upaniṣad* is necessary. Such research has only recently been started in the academic world. Thus we must leave for the future any thorough-going study of the theories that Sureśvara states Bhartṛprapañca's.

Using Śaṅkara's comments and the passages from Bhartṛprapañca's commentary as quoted in Ānandagiri's sub-commentary as our major sources, and using Sureśvara's *Vārttika* in a supplementary sense, we shall present below what can be said fairly certainly to be Bhartṛprapañca's theories.[8]

Notes

1) p.659, v.1127-p.666, v.1164.

2) pp.666-667, Ān. ad vv. 1164, 1165. p. 671, Ān. ad v. 1188.

3) p. 663, Ān. ad v. 1149.

4) Ś. ad *Bṛhad. Up.* p.731.

5) p. 1959, v. 62.

6) *katham upodghātasaṃbandhi tadbhāṣyam vivartānusāri vyākhyātaṃ tadīya bhāṣyāntarasya pariṇāmānusāritvād ity āśaṅkhyāha --- ita iti* /p. 666. Ān. ad. v. 1164.

7) Cf. Part V, Chapter VI, Section I and III.

8) In his previously cited article, Hiriyanna states that the theories discussed in Sureśvara's *Vārttika* are Bhartṛprapañca's. However, as has been indicated in the present work, a great many *Bhedābhedavādin* thinkers existed before Śaṅkara. Thus it is difficult to say simply that those views are Bhartṛprapañca's.

Sub-Section 1. His Theory of Knowledge

Like other Vedāntins, Bhartṛprapañca holds that the Upaniṣadic scriptures are the basis of metaphysical knowledge. However, together with this, he states that the essence of *Brahman* can be known through inference (*anumāna*).[1] A marked characteristic of his thinking is the assertion that even in problems of metaphysics it is possible to present proofs through the inference of formal logic. It is on this foundation that his distinctive philosophical thinking is formed. He regarded the significance of proof concerning metaphysical problems as highly important and pointed out that in the Upaniṣadic scriptures also "proof" (*upapatti*)[2] is discussed. Such views can be seen more in the Nyāya-Vaiśeṣika philosophy than in the Vedānta, and indeed such resemblences to the former can be seen at various points of his philosophy as a whole. Here he is in complete opposition to the views of Bhartṛhari and Śaṅkara who assert strongly that knowledge of *Brahman* or *Ātman* is derived only from the scriptures and who deny the use of inference.

Let us consider what it means to say that the true nature of *Brahman* is known through inference. *Brahman* is a principle transcending sense perception and cannot be perceived directly through the senses. Positive concepts attributable to *Brahman* as the conclusions of inference have to be of such a kind that they are appreciable in the world of sense perception. It is the precondition of the use of analogy (*udāharaṇa*) that its conclusions should be valid in the sense world. But in order to maintain that the nature of *Brahman* is knowable by inference, it becomes necessary to accept concepts resting on the sense world, and the correctness of conclusions based on them. It is then impossible to hold, like Śaṅkara, that all such things are merely illusory. Rather must it be maintained that everything in the phenomenal world has reality. Accordingly, Bhartṛprapañca held that "experiential knowledge" (*anubhūti*, *anubhava*)[3] of things of the phenomenal world is also real. This epistemological view, as we shall see later, determines his metaphysics in general.

To sum up his theory of knowledge : he accepts the validity of all three — the scripture (revelation), inference (analogies), and experiential knowledge (phenomena).

Notes

1) p. 877, vv. 50, 51, 52 ; p.1668, v. 1645.

2) Ś. ad *Bṛhad. Up.* p. 364.

3) *svānubhavād dvaitasyādvaitasya śrutivaśād iṣṭatvād karmakāṇḍaprāmāṇyādi saṃbhavati*/p. 1955, v. 36. Ān. ad. *l. c.* In Vedānta philosophy in general, the term "*anubhava*" means "the direct realization of *Ātman*" but Bhartṛprapañca seems to use it in a different sense. In Buddhism the term means "to take in" and is a basic characterization of the act of "receiving of impressions"(*vedanā*). It may be held that Bhartṛprapañca's usage is closer to this.

Sub-Section 2. *Brahman* and Its Evolution

According to Bhartṛprapañca, *Brahman* as the absolute principle is identical with the Highest Self (*paramātman*).[1] It is unique (*eka*),[2] highest (*para*)[3] and eternal (*nitya*).[4] "That which is full" (*pūrṇa*) which is discussed in the scriptures (*Bṛhad. Up.* V,1,1) is none other than *Brahman*.[5]

On this point he holds just the same view as other Vedāntins, but he further defines it as "consciousness" (*vijñāna*).[6] That *Brahman* is a spiritual principle is an idea found in Vedānta philosophy in general. However one can see a characteristic of Bhartṛprapañca's thought in his not holding it to be pure spirit (*bodha*, *cid*), as Śaṅkara does, but in his using the term "consciousness" which in India generally indicates the differentiated knowledge of individual subjectivity. (In calling *Brahman* "consciousness" (*vijñāna*) he is in agreement with the fourth stanza of the *Māṇḍūkya-kārikā* and the Vedānta theories which Śāntirakṣita attacks). It is the spirit which, without borrowing powers from other principles, emanates the differentiated appearances of phenomena from itself, and which includes differentiated appearances within itself.

In order to clarify this structure further, he states that this *Brahman* is "that whose essence is dual and yet not dual" (*dvaitādvaitātmaka*).[7] Since this is a basic characteristic of his metaphysics, he is called "a teacher of plurality in identity" (*nānātvaikatvavādin*).[8] That is, *Brahman* in one aspect is non-differentiated and non-dual, but from another aspect possesses differentiation and plurality. *Brahman* simultaneously manifests these two contradictory aspects. The two aspects are absolutely real (*pāramārthika*)[9] and we cannot hold, as does the Advaita school, that differentiated appearances are illusory (*mṛṣā*).[10] For example, when the wind blows over the ocean surface, myriads of waves and foam arise. They are the same in being sea-water but as waves and foam they have manifested differentiated appearances. Both are real (*paramārthasatya*, adj.).[11] The world, which consists of various pluralistic differetiated-appearances (*nāmarūpa*), is itself *Brahman*.[12] *Brahman* is the very principle that upholds "names and forms" (*nāmarūpa*) and so on.[13]

Brahman is a concrete universal and in manifesting differenciated appearances maintains its self-identity. Hence the phenomenal world cannot at all be illusory as the Advaita school asserts. It is "the actuality of the Absolute Truth expressed through dualistic appearances" (*paramārthavastubhūtaṃ dvaitarūpeṇa*).[14] He stated that it is because the pairs of opposites in the phenomenal world are in themselves actual that the sections concerning rituals in the scriptures (*karmakāṇḍa*) are to be trusted.[15]

Then by what method can the *Brahman*, of such a metaphysical constitution, be known? He demonstrates[16] this through a method based on the previously discussed epistemological theory. We cannot deny the actuality of our experiential knowledge in daily life as experience-in-general. This is his point of departure for the proof.[17] Yet, if we seek the most universal proposition concerning our experiences in daily life, it is that "all things possess both a differentiated and a non-differentiated essence" (*bhedābhedātmakaṃ sarvaṃ vastu*).[18] For example, if we take a cow as an individual thing, it possesses both the undifferentiated character of "cowness" and the particular differentiated characteristics of dewlap, horns, etc. For him this proposition is the major premise. Next it can be said of every metaphysical entity that it is in some sense a "thing" (*vastu*). This is also his minor premise. From these two premises, it is beyond doubt that even metaphysical entities possess both a differentiated nature and an undifferentiated nature. He cames to a conclusion of this kind. According to Śaṅkara, Bhartṛprapañca presented the following type of discussion concerning *Ātman*[19] :

> The entity *Ātman* has by nature both unity and plurality. For example, a cow has unity as the cow-substance (*godravyatā*) and mutual differences such as the dewlap. Just as there are thus unity and plurality in things gross [perceptible], so should it be inferred that there are unity and plurality in things partless and formless [space etc.].[20] Since [this rule] is found in all cases without exception, *Ātman* too has mutual plurality of such things as the function of sight[21] and unity as *Ātman*.

According to Ānandagiri the meaning of this passage can be summarized in the following manner:

> *Thesis*: What is at issue (= *Ātman*) is different and non-different (*bhinnābhinna*).
> *Reason*: Because it is a thing (*vastu*).
> *Example*: Like the case of a cow.[22]

Since the same can be said of Brahman, we reach the conclusion that *Brahman* is both differentiated and undifferentiated, both dual and non-dual.

We should be careful to note that here *Ātman* and *Brahman* are taken as objective "things". We must remark that such a view of *Ātman* is closer to the Nyāya-Vaiśeṣika philosophy than to Vedānta philosophy in general.

If it is held that *Brahman* thus possesses these two contradictory aspects, what is the relationship between the *Brahman* of undifferentiated appearances and the *Brahman* of differentiated appearances? In some cases, Bhartṛprapañca asserts that the *Brahman* of undifferentiated appearances is the cause (*kāraṇa*), with the *Brahman* of differentiated appearances as the effect (*kārya*), and that both are actual. In the previously presented simile of sea-water and waves, since the waves arise from sea-water we should state the day before new moon; Kuhū,[3] also called Guṅgū,[4] the new moon day; Anumati,[5] the day before full moon; and Rākā,[6] the day of new moon. The importance of the new and full moon days is seen in the Darśa-pūrṇamāsau, or festivals of the new and full moon days respectively.

One special day in the month, the **Ekāṣṭakā**, or eighth day after full moon, was important. In the Pañcaviṃśa Brāhmaṇa[7] there are stated to be in the year twelve such, mentioned between the twelve days of full moon and the twelve days of new moon. But one Ekāṣṭakā is referred to in the Yajurveda Saṃhitās and elsewhere[8] as of quite special importance. This was, in the accordant opinion of most commentators, the eighth day after the full moon of **Māgha.** It marked the end of the year, or the beginning of the new year. Though the Kauṣītaki Brāhmaṇa[9] places the winter solstice in the new moon of Māgha, the latter date probably means the new moon preceding full moon in Māgha,[10] not the new moon following

[3] Av. vii. 47; Taittirīya Saṃhitā, i. 8, 8, 1; iii. 4, 9, 1; Kāṭhaka Saṃhitā, xii. 8, etc.

[4] Rv. ii. 32, 8, where Sāyaṇa identifies it with Kuhū.

[5] Taittirīya Saṃhitā, i. 8, 8, 1; iii. 4, 9, 1: Kāṭhaka Saṃhitā, xii. 8; Vājasaneyi Saṃhitā, xxix. 60; xxxiv. 8. 9; Ṣaḍviṃśa Brāhmaṇa, v. 6.

[6] Rv. ii. 32, 4; v. 42, 12; Taittirīya Saṃhitā, i. 8, 8, 1; iii. 4, 9, 1. *Cf.* Nirukta, xi. 31; Weber, *Indische Studien*, 5, 228 *et seq.*; Ludwig, Translation of the Rigveda, 3, 189.

[7] x. 3, 11. *Cf.* Satapatha Brāhmaṇa, vi. 2, 2, 23; Av. xv. 16, 2.

[8] Taittirīya Saṃhitā, vii. 4, 8, 1; Pañcaviṃśa Brāhmaṇa, v. 9, 1. *Cf.* Taittirīya Saṃhitā, iii. 3, 8, 4; iv. 3, 11, 3; v. 7, 2, 2; Av. iii. 10; viii. 9, 10; Kāṭhaka Saṃhitā, xxxix. 10; Maitrāyaṇī Saṃhitā, ii. 13, 21, etc. See Kātyāyana Śrauta Sūtra, xiii. 1, 2, with the commentary; Pañcaviṃśa Brāhmaṇa, *loc. cit.*, with Sāyaṇa's notes; Weber, *Naxatra*, 2, 341, 342; *Indische Studien*, 17, 219 *et seq.*

[9] xix. 23.

[10] So Vināyaka on Kauṣītaki Brāhmaṇa, *loc. cit.*; Ānartīya on Śāṅkhāyana Śrauta Sūtra, xiii. 19, 1; Weber, *op. cit.*, 2, 345, 346, 353, 354. Weber accepts the scholiasts' view that Māgha is here regarded as beginning with the day after full moon in Taiṣa; but it is simpler to suppose the meaning to be that Māgha is regarded as commencing with, not after, the new moon and ending with the day before new moon. Several passages in the Baudhāyana Śrauta Sūtra (ii. 12; iii. 1; xxvi. 18; xxx. 3; see Caland, *Über das rituelle Sūtra des Baudhāyana*, 36, 37) and Kauṣītaki Brāhmaṇa, i. 3; Satapatha Brāhmaṇa, xi. 1, 1, 7, point to the full moon being the middle of the month, and the new moon being regarded as either the beginning or the end. Hopkins (n. 11) thinks Kauṣītaki Brāhmaṇa, v. 1; Śatapatha Brāhmaṇa, vi. 2, 2, 18, point to the commencement of the month with the full moon. If this could be accepted, then the Aṣṭakā would fall a week before the winter solstice in Māgha.

indicated in various passages in his commentary that it coincides with some one of them. This may be thought to be similar to the *Brahma-sūtra*, where the relationship between the Absolute and Self is defined in a great many ways.

How then would *Brahman* evolve differentiated appearances? To answer this a theory of eight States (*aṣṭāvasthā*) was proposed. Śaṅkara has the following passage:

> Some people have an explanation concerning this as follows:
>
> The 'inner ruler' (*antaryāmin*) is the slightly agitated state of the Imperishable (*akṣara*, *Bṛhad. Up.* III,8), i.e. *Brahman*, which corresponds to the great ocean, being of immovable nature. The individual self (*kṣetrajña*), which does not know the 'inner ruler', is the extremely agitated state [of It]. They go on to postulate five further states, and hold that there are thus eight states (*aṣṭāvasthā*) of *Brahman*.[30]

According to the sub-commentator Ānandagiri, the other five states mentioned are *piṇḍa*, *jāti*, *virāj*, *sūtra*, and *daiva*. Immediately after this, Ānandagiri presents three more — *avyākṛta*, *sākṣin*, and *kṣetrajña* — to complete the total of eight. The theory of the eight states is presented three times in Sureśvara's *Vārttika* and Ānandagiri's sub-commentary on it. They may be set out as in the following chart:

Eight States mentioned by Śaṅkara[31]	Eight States given in Ānandagiri's Commentary[32]	Eight States given in Ānandagiri's sub-commentary to Sureśvara's *Vārttika* (three separate passages)		
		(1)[33]	(2)[34]	(3)[35]
(*brahman*)	*avyākṛta*	*avyākṛta*	*brahman*	*avyākṛta*
antaryāmin	*sākṣin*	*antaryāmin*	*antaryāmin*	*antaryāmin* } *īśvara*
kṣetrajña	*kṣetrajña*	*sākṣin*	*sākṣin*	*sākṣin* } *īśvara*
daiva	*daiva*	*daiva*	*devatā*	*indriya* = *devatā*
sūtra	*sūtra*	*sūtra*	*sūtra*	*prāṇa*
virāj	*virāj*	*virāj*	*virāj*	*virāj*
jāti	*jāti*	*jāti*	*jāti*	*jāti*
piṇḍa	*piṇḍa*	*piṇḍa*	*piṇḍa*	*bhūta* = *vyakti*

The last five have been here supplied from Ānandagiri's sub-commentary.

Columns (1) and (2) are according to Sureśvara's *Vārttika* and Ānandagiri's sub-commentary, Column (3) appears only in Ānandagiri's sub-commentary.

Let us go on to examine the theory of the eight states with the aid of the chart.

(1) *Brahman itself or that which has not evolved* (*avyākṛta*)

Śaṅkara says of Bhartṛprapañca that he did not definitely present a principle of the Unevolved and he held only that one state is *Brahman* itself without any movement whatever. This was called the Unevolved (*avyākṛta*) by Sureśvara and Ānandgiri because it is the source of the evolution of the world. Then it is stated that Bhartṛprapañca called the evolution of the world "the evolution of the unevolved" (*avyākṛtavyākaraṇa*).[36] Then the ultimate to which return those who have attained complete release is called the unevolved one.[37] Hence this unevolved one must be posited at the head of the eight states.[38] According to Śaṅkara's philosophy, the unevolved one indicates *Brahman* united with ignorance, i.e. the world-principle, and should be differentiated from *Brahman* itself. According to Bhartṛprapañca, however, since *Brahman* itself evolves, there is no objection to holding that the unevolved one is *Brahman*.

(2) *The Inner-ruler* (*antaryāmin*)[39]

The Inner-ruler is discussed in detail in *Bṛhadāraṇyaka-Upaniṣad*, III,8. It is inherent in phenomena, yet is different from phenomena, being the principle which governs them. Bhartṛprapañca explains that it is "the state of the Highest *Brahman* which is slightly agitated". This probably approximates the concept of the governing-deity (*īśvara*) of the Advaita school. Hence, it belongs to the category of that which is evolved (*vyākṛta*).[40]

(3) *The individual-self* (*kṣetrajña*) *or the "witness"*

This is the individual spirit or soul.[41] When the movement of the Highest *Brahman* has reached its peak, the individual self is formed. The individual-self is a manifested form (*vikāra*)[42] of the Highest-self. At the same time, since the individual-self is a manifestation of a part (*aṃśa, ekadeśa*) of the Highest-self,[43] the individual-self is a part (*aṃśa, ekadeśa*) of the Highest-self. Hence the individual-self cannot be complete and universal (*vibhu*).[44] Yet since its essence is the Highest *Brahman*, the individual-self, just as the Highest *Brahman*, has "consciousness" (*vijñāna*) as its essence.[45] Hence, the individual-self is called "that which arises from consciousness" (*vijñānamaya*).[46] Since the result as a whole is real, the myriad individual-selves, being results of the evolution of *Brahman*, are real.

He therefore holds that the relationship between the individual-self and the Highest *Brahman* is not one of complete difference. It is neither identical nor yet different. That is, he holds that the various individual-selves are different to the extent that they are actually formed as real existences, but since they are all formed as manifestations of *Brahman*, on that point they are identical. Yāmuna, of the Qualified Advaita school, dissatisfied with this view, held that Bhartṛprapañca's ideas were heretical. Śaṅkara also makes vigorous attacks on the point.

The individual-self is alternatively called the "witness" (*sākṣin*) or the positive agent (*kartṛ*), i. e. the subject of action. Thus it is both the subject of pleasure (*bhoktṛ*) and the subject which is bound and released.[47] Functions like seeing are attributes (*guṇa*) of the individual-self, *ātman* ; and *ātman* is the "subject of attributes" (*guṇin*).[48] Since the function of seeing etc. belongs to the individual-selves, no transcendental principle can be posited as the subject of the seeing function etc. in general.[49]

Now in this case, why must any individual-self be posited as an existence separate from the physical body? Bhartṛprapañca answers that in the individual the various acts of perception (*upalabdhi*) do not appear simultaneously, but successively. This is the evidence (*liṅga*) of the existence of *Ātman*.[50]

He states that this individual-self does not know the inner ruler,[51] but constantly transmigrates accompanied by "a conglomerate of consciousness, actions and memories of the past" (*vidyā-karma-pūrvaprajñā-samudāya*).[52] This might be regarded as following directly the statement in the *Bṛhadāraṇyaka-Upaniṣad* (IV,4,2) explaining death: "The deceased's consciousness, actions, and memories of the past [of the life just ended] leave with that person" (*tam vidyākarmāṇi samanvārabhete pūrvaprajñā ca*). On this point his view thus agrees with that of the "opponent" presented in the *Brahma-sūtra* (III,4,5) and differs from the view of the *sūtra* itself (III,4, 11). According to other passages in Śaṅkara's account, Bhartṛprapañca further asserted:

> Lust (*kāma*) and latent desire (*vāsanā*) abide in the hearts [of human beings] and surround and cling to the *Ātman* in the heart. And when

> [*Ātman*] leaves the heart (dies), they remain in *Ātman*, It is, as it were, like the fragrance of flower petals [remaining as a trace in other things even after the flower has died].[53]

He probably held that even after death *kāma* and *vāsanā* remain attached to the *Ātman* of human beings and continue the process of transmigration.[54] "*Kāma*" may be thought of as the raw principle of life-energy of the individual-self and "*vāsanā*" as latent dynamic impressions remaining in the individual-self when it has completed some action. Hence he no doubt accepted in some sense the theory of a subtle body (*liṅgaśarīra*, *sūkṣmaśarīra*).

(4) *Divinity* (*daiva,devatā*)

As indicated previously, since Sureśvara uses the term "sense organ" (*indriya*) for it, this term means the divinity which governs the sense organs of human beings. Śaṅkara and others of the Vedānta school held that particular divinities governed and caused the activities of the sense organs of human beings. It is noteworthy that this view can already be seen in Bhartṛprapañca. It is probably that the divinities which govern natural phenomena are also included in his definition.[55]

(5) *Sūtra*

The expanded term is "the individual-self as *sūtra*" (*sūtrakṣetrajña*). In the *Bṛhadāraṇyaka-Upaniṣad* (III,7,2) the wind, as the world-principle which interweaves together worlds such as this one and the universal existence, is called *sūtra* and taught as a principle correlative with the Inner Ruler. Bhartṛprapañca goes further to identify it with *Hiraṇyagarbha* which since the time of the *Ṛg-veda* had been held to be the world-creating deity. He held that the spiritual and individual *ātman* (*cetana vijñānātman*) are first moved by wind and space, and with that movement as a basis (*ādhāra*), other phenomena are brought into action.[56] Hence he identifies it with *Prāṇa*, which is the breath of heaven and earth.[57]

(6) *Virāj*

According to Sureśvara's account, Bhartṛprapañca held that *Sūtra* (= *prāṇa*) is brought into being by a slight movement of *Brahman* but that by a violent movement *Virāj* is brought into being.[58] More explicitly, this indicates the *Brahman* which appears as the natural world manifested in heavenly bodies such as sun and moon and in basic phenomena such as fire etc.[59]

(7) *Jāti*

In the commentaries there are no explanations of the term "*jāti*". However, since it is a concept which is in contrast with "individual bodies" or "individual object", we may follow the usage common to Indian philosophy in general and take its meaning to be "genus". In that case it is intermediate between *Brahman* as the highest universal and individual objects, which may be held to be at the limit of particularity. Within the Vedānta school, Bhartṛprapañca holds this view in common with Bhartṛhari.[60]

(8) *Individual-selves* (*piṇḍa*)

"*Piṇḍa*" originally means a lump of earth, but subsequently comes to be used also to indicate the physical body. Bhartṛprapañca himself occasionally uses it in the sence of physical body.[61] However, as the last of the eight states, *piṇḍa* has a special meaning for Bhartṛprapañca. It may also be termed a "being" (*bhūta*) or "individual object" (*vyakti*).[62] The concept is the opposite of genus : *piṇḍa* is formed at the limit of particularization from genus. Or in his own words it is formed at the limit of movement of *Brahman*. Hence he compares it to the tips of waves which are caused by the movement of the wind.[63]

In this way *Brahman* evolves the eight states. Bhartṛprapañca held that in the universe which is manifested through these eight states, there is birth, continuity of existence, and death ; these are in eternal oscillation.[64]

Along with the theory of eight states, a theory of three strata (*rāśitraya-kalpanā*) has been recorded as characteristic of Bhartṛprapañca's views.[65]

(1) The lowest stratum (*adhama-rāśi*), also called "the stratum which both has form and has no form" (*mūrtāmūrtarāśi*). —— This probably indicates the natural world in general. It is "what is used" (*prayojya*) by the individual-self ; it is the means (*sādhana*) by which the innumerable individual-selves are able to receive various types of experiences.

(2) The middle stratum (*madhyama-rāśi*). —— This indicates the individual-self and the conglomerate of knowledge, action and memories of the past which are attached to it. The individual-self as agent (*prayoktṛ*) confronts the natural world. To emphasize the point that the individual-self

creates various actions through its continuous movement, this stratum is also called the stratum of action (*karmarāśi*).

(3) The highest stratum (*uttama-rāśi*). —— It is also called the superior stratum (*utkṛṣṭa-rāśi*) and the stratum of the highest-self (*paramātma-rāśi*). It indicates the highest-self.[66]

We do not know how Bhartṛprapañca related the these-stratum theory to the eight-state theory within his system, but it seems probable that in general the eight-state theory is a detailed exposition of the lowest stratum of the other theory.

Our next problem is this : What is the motive-power or cause which brings about the evolution of these appearances in the phenomenal world? According to Sureśvara, Bhartṛprapañca holds that it is solely Nescience (*avidyā*).[67] However, there is very little in the way of explanation of Nescience in Bhartṛprapañca as presented by Śaṅkara, and no difinite conclusion can be reached.[68] It may be considered that in what is attributed by Sureśvara to Bhartṛprapañca in regard to Nescience there are not a few ideas of Sureśvara's own.

At any rate Bhartṛprapañca held that *Brahman* itself evolves to bring into being the multifarious appearances of the phenomenal world. Further accounts of him by Śaṅkara have Bhartṛprapañca holding to "the hypothesis that the various potentialities such as the function of seeing existing within the highest-self are evolved variously as eye, colour etc. (*pariṇāmabhedakalpanā*)[69] ". Since he held to such a theory of evolution of phenomena (*pariṇāmavāda*), the basic tendency of his thought was extremely close to the Sāṃkhya theories.[70] Admitting this fact, Sureśvara at the same time attempts to explain how Bhartṛprapañca's ideas differ from the Sāṃkhya philosophy.[71]

Along with the above tendency, we can discern in his views a considerable leaning towards the Vaiśeṣika philosophy. One instance is his emphasis on the importance of demonstration through inference in problems of metaphysics. Then in his speculations on *Ātman*, he holds that *Ātman* is as much an objective thing (*vastu*) as other things and states that the essence which manifests objective things in general is also manifesting *Ātman*. This is in marked contrast to Śaṅkara, who distinguishes objective things from

Ātman and vigorously emphasizes the reasons why they must never be confused. If we consider the three-stratum theory or the eight-state theory, we see that what is being presented is a classification as of the objective world ; there is almost no consideration of the subjective significance of the spiritual principle. The philosophical standpoint is extremely objective. On these points, therefore, his philosophy resembles the Vaiśeṣika philosophy. Even Sureśvara clearly admits that Bhartṛprapañca in places adopted Vaiśeṣika theories.[72]

Thus, in the Vedānta philosophy of the early period, Bhartṛprapañca's metaphysics have a highly individual character of their own.

Notes

1) p.661, v. 1139, Also the *bhāṣya* fragment on this.

2) Ś. ad *Bṛhad. Up*. p.731, *Vārttika*, p.877, v. 48 ; *sarvaikatva* (p. 661, v. 1139).

3) *Vārttika*, p. 877, v. 48 ; p. 623, v. 948.

4) *paramātmā nitya iti bhāṣyārtha*/(*ibid*. p. 664, v. 1155.)

5) Ś. ad *Bṛhad. Up*. p.731.

6) Cf. The fragments cited in Ān. ad *Bṛhad. Up*. p.560 ; Ān. ad *Vārttika*, p. 1433, v. 318.

7) Ś. ad *Bṛhad. Up*. pp. 731, 733. Sureśvara also presents many terms with the same meaning : *bhinnābhinnātmakaṃ brahma* (p.876, v. 46), *dvaitādvaitātmakaṃ brahma* (p. 1934, v. 30 ; p. 1956, v. 48), *brahmaṇo dvaitādvaitātmakatva* (p. 1655, v. 1562).

8) *Vārttika*, p. 876, v. 46.

9) Ān. ad v. 48, p. 1957.

10) Ān. ad v. 36, p. 1955.

11) Ś. ad *Bṛhad. Up*. p. 730.

12) *yathoktaṃ-bhinnābhinnātmakaṃ brahmaiva jagad iti*/(Ān. ad v. 1562, p. 1655.) *brahmaṇo 'nyad⋯⋯vastu brahmaiva paramārthataḥ*/(*Vārttika*, p.664, v. 1153.)

13) *brahma nāmarūpādivad*/ *Vārttika*, p. 876, v. 46.

14) Ś. ad *Bṛhad. Up*. p. 731.

15) Ś. ad *Bṛhad. Up*. p.731.

16) As authority for the dual-nondual doctrine in the scriptures, he cites *Bṛhad. Up*. I,6, 3 ; II,4 (& IV,5). Cf. Kanakura : *op. cit*. pp. 36-38.

17) Cf. The previous Sub-Section.

18) *Vārttika*, p. 1168, v. 1640 ; "*bhinnābhinnātmakaṃ⋯⋯sarvaṃ vastu*" p. 877, v. 51. "*bhinnābhinnātmatā⋯⋯artheṣu*" p. 877, v. 50. "*samastavyastatā*", p. 1590, v. 1187.

19) Ś. ad. *Bṛhad. Up*. IV,3,24-30, p. 622. Cf. *Vārttika*, p. 1668, v. 1639 ff.

20) According to Ānandajñāna's *Ṭīka*.
21) According to the *Bṛhad. Up.* IV,3, 23-30, these refer to the functions of sight, smell, taste, speech, hearing, thought, touch and cognition.
22) Ān. ad Ś.'s *Bṛhad. Up. Bhāṣya*, p. 622.
23) Ś. ad *Bṛhad. Up.* p. 731. Cf. p. 492.
24) *Vārttika*, pp. 623-624, vv. 948-950 ; p. 572, v. 693.
25) In another passage it is stated that all "*viśeṣa*" are included in *Ātman* and that *Ātman* is "*sāmānya*". Cf. Ān ad v.952, p. 624. On this point his views resemble those of Bhartṛhari.
26) Ānandagiri explains this as "*aṃśin*" and "*aṃśa*".
27) This example appears in Sureśvara's main verses.
28) In another passage (p. 572, v. 694) this simile is used to explain "*avayava*" and "*avayavin*".
29) Cf. *Vārttika*, p. 572, v. 693. Also Ān. ad v. 1043, p. 643.
30) Ś. ad *Bṛhad. Up.* p. 492.
31) Ś. ad *Bṛhad. Up.* p.492
32) *ibid.*
33) *Vārttika*, p. 643, v. 1043.
34) *Vārttika*, p.662, vv.1142-1143.
35) *Vārttika*, p.532, v. 487.
36) *Vārttika*, p. 758, v. 1646. Cf. p. 1008, v. 92 ; p. 639, v. 1025 ; p. 647, v. 1065.
37) Cf. Sub-Section 3, Religious Practices.
38) *avyākṛtādipiṇḍāntam*···, *Vārttika*, p. 669, v. 1178.
39) From the chart we see that in one instance Ānandagiri substitutes "*sākṣin*" for "*antaryāmin*".
40) Ān. ad v. 1143, p. 662.
41) *kṣetrajña* = *jīva* (Ān. ad Ś.'s *Bṛhad. Up. Bhāṣya*. p. 492).
42) Ś. ad *Bṛhad. Up.* p. 560.
43) Cf. The fragments cited in *Vārttika*, p. 1013, v. 122 ; p. 1241, v. 11 ; Ān. ad v. 120, p. 1013.
44) Cf. The fragment cited in Ān. ad v. 1131, p.1580.
45) *vijñānaṃ paraṃ brahma, tatprakṛtiko jīvo vijñānamaya iti Bhartṛprapañcair uktam/* (Ān. ad Ś.'s *Bṛhad. Up. Bhāṣya*, p.560 ; Ān. ad *Vārttika*, v. 318, p. 1433).
46) Ś. ad *Bṛhad. Up.* p. 328.
47) Cf. The fragments cited in the sub-commentary to Ś. ad *Bṛhad. Up.* p. 328. *Vārttika*, p. 1236, v. 172 ; p. 1009, v. 97 ; p.1012, v. 120 ; pp. 1012-3, v. 115.
48) Cf. The fragment in the sub-comment to *Vārttika*, p.1653, v. 1548 ; also the fragments cited in the sub-comments to vv. 1549, 1550 (and the fragments in the sub-comment to

this), 1551, 1552 ; p. 1654, v. 1556.

49) Ś. ad *Bṛhad. Up.* p. 445.

50) *Vārttika*, p. 1581, v. 1136, and the fragments included there.

51) Cf. note 31.

52) Ś. ad *Bṛhad. Up.* p. 328. However, in the later Advaita school, his statement is wrongly transmitted, "*avidyā*" being substituted for "*vidyā*". Cf. Ān. ad Ś.'s *Bṛhad. Up. Bhāṣya*, p. 324. Further, Sureśvara states that the individual-self (*vijñānātman*) consists of *avidyā*, *bhāvanā* (= *pūrvaprajñā*) and *karman*. Śaṅkara's account, however, undoubtedly transmits Bhartṛprapañca's views more correctly. Deussen (Cf. Deussen : *SV*. S. 406) asserts that the term "*pūrvaprajñā*" in the previously cited *Bṛhad. Up.* IV,4,2 should be read "*apūrva-*⋯". We may hold that a similar type of mistake was made about Bhartṛprapañca's theories.

53) Ś. ad *Bṛhad. Up.* p. 614. Cf. *Vārttika*, p. 1012, v. 117.

54) Sureśvara has discussed the relationship between *kāma*, *bhāvanā* and *karman*. (*Vārttika*, p. 1590, vv. 1189-1191 ; 1195-1197 ; p. 1786, vv. 396-401.

55) *Vārttika*, p. 536, v. 511. Cf. *Vedāntasāra*, §140.

56) Ś. ad *Bṛhad. Up.* p. 323. ; Ān. ad *l. c.* ; *Vārttika*, p. 1000, v. 49.

57) *Vārttika*, p. 1957, v. 54 ; p. 532, v. 487.

58) *Vārttika*, p. 1957, v. 54.

59) *paramātmaiva*⋯⋯*vairājaṃ sthūlaprapañcātmakaṃ sthānaṃ prāpya virāḍ ucyate sa cāgnisūryādyavayavavān*/Ān. ad v. 511, p. 536.

60) Cf. Part VII, Chapter IV, Section II.

61) Cf. The fragmant cited in Ān. ad v. 65, p. 1369. For the example Sureśvara uses, Cf. *Vārttika* v. 98, p. 447.

62) Cf. note 27. Also *piṇḍabhāvaś caturvidhabhūtagrāmatvaṃ*, Ān. ad *Vārttika*, v. 54, p. 957.

63) *Vārttika*, p. 1957, v. 54.

64) Ś. ad *Bṛhad. Up.* p. 731. Cf. Ān. ad *Bṛhad. Up. Vārttika*, II,3, v. 148. p. 1017.

65) Ś. ad *Bṛhad. Up.* p. 328 ; *Vārttika*, p. 1011, v. 112 ff.

66) *uttamaḥ paramātmākhyo rāśiḥ*⋯/(*Vārttika*, p. 1011, v. 113), so that strictly speaking *paramātma-rāśi* should be taken as a *karma-dhāraya* compound.

67) *Vārttika*, p. 1090, v. 1093, p. 662, v. 1144 ; p. 661, v. 1141.

68) Śaṅkara (Ś. ad *Bṛhad. Up.* p. 416) also holds that the individual-self which has still not attained complete release is departed from the Highest-self through Nescience. Nescience is held to be an attribute of the individual-self and not of the Highest-self. (*avidyayoṣarasthānīyayā svātmaprabhavayā parātmanaḥ paricchinno*⋯⋯/) Cf. *Vārttika*, p. 1157, st. 55.

69) Ś. ad *Bṛhad. Up.* p. 625. Cf. *Vārttika*, p. 877, v. 48.

70) In expositions attributed to him there appear the term "*tāmasa*", "*sāttvika*" etc. (*Vārttika*, p. 827, v. 172). Resemblances to Sāṅkhya theories — though the thrust of the argument differs — has already been noted by Hiriyanna (*op. cit.* pp. 85-86).

71) *Vārttika*, p. 1012, v. 116 ; p. 1013, v. 124.

72) ……*iti Kaṇabhukcittam evaṃ samāśritāḥ*/ *Vārttika*, p. 1012, v. 120.

Sub-Section 3. Religious Practices

Bhartṛprapañca held that the ultimate goal of religious practice is release. Here he does not differ from other Vedāntins, but in his view of the methods and stages toward the attainment of release we can recognize his own particular theory. He asserted that in order to attain release both meditation on *Brahman* (*brahmopāsti*) and action (*karman*) are necessary.[1] That is, he objected to the view which holds that it can be attained through only the direct realization of *Brahman*. Meditation on the Absolute *Brahman* and progression to its true form is an indispensable condition for the attainment of release, but he emphasized that together with this it is necessary to practice the various acts enjoined by the scriptures, i.e. the various religious rites. He states that the religious rites must be observed throughout one's life.[2] That the observance of religious rites is a supplementary means toward the attainment of release is accepted by Śaṅkara's Advaita school, but they held that such actions have only an indirect effect and that the direct cause of release is in all cases the realization of *Ātman*. Bhartṛprapañca, however, held that both are of equal importance in as necessities for release. He further held that the chanting of the *mantras* in the Vedic scripture or the reading of sections of the *Brāhmaṇas* also aided in the realization of *Ātman*.[3] This is not accepted by the Advaita shool.

In this manner, since he evaluated highly the religious observances of the orthodox Brāhmin school, we may state (using an expression of a later age) that he held "the view which emphasizes both thought and action" (*jñānakarma-samuccaya-vāda*). In this he agrees with Bhāskara et. al. Hence, in contrast to Śaṅkara who thought only the *Upaniṣads* to be highly important among the Vedic scriptures, Bhartṛprapañca held the *karmakāṇḍa*, i. e. the section which define the observances of religious rites, to be of importance equal to the *Upaniṣads*.[4]

Further, in relationship with the observance of religious rites, he also viewed as important the education of one's progeny. Through bearing and raising children, people must strive to preserve the continuity of the ancestral religious rites. Since such actions are also laid down in the scriptures, progeny are also "one means toward the attainment of release" (*muktisādhana*).[5] Since carrying out religious rites and raising children are possible only in family-life, he probably felt that within such family life the mind should be made tranquil and meditation on *Ātman* carried out. Since he had such great respect for family life, we see that on the question of religious practice his standpoint was completely opposed to that of many Vedānta religious practitioners who disparaging family-life and praised the life of homeless wandering ascetic.

Release, then, is attained through long unbroken practice of religious rites and meditation[6]; hence it does not occur instantaneously. Bhartṛprapañca held that only after passing through special stages does one attain finally complete release. According to Śaṅkara's account,[7] Bhartṛprapañca states:

> Even if through religious one is separated from the world of experienced objects, even if having eliminated one's bonds (*graha, atigraha* = *bhandha*), one is completely without desires and actions, one still does not attain full release. Through Nescience he will still be separated from the highest-self. For him names (*nāman*) still remain. This condition is an intermediate state (*antarāla*) on the way to the attainment of complete release. It is called '*apavarga*'. After this, one finally knows the uniqueness of the highest-self, discards dualistic views, and attains direct realization of the highest-self.

The term "intermediate state" probably indicates a stage intermediate between transmigration and release. Since Bhartṛprapañca held that after death people who have observed religious rites enter a stage preparatory to release and subsequently attain full release, it is clear that he held to the theory of gradual release (*kramamukti*).

In another passage[8] explaining Bhartṛprapañca's views, Śaṅkara, explaining the boundary between the intermediate world and full release, uses the terms "lower Brahman" (*aparaṃ brahma*) and "higher *Brahman*" (*paraṃbrahma*). He explains that through the clear realization of the lower

Brahman, which accompanies religious rites, one attains to the conditions of the lower *Brahman*. Such a person, who is separated from the objects of experience, and who [further], because he has attained all, has cut off all bonds of desire and action, becomes the Highest *Brahman* by the power of "the clear realization of *Brahman*" (*brahmavidyā*). This agrees in general with the above presented theory, but the term "lower *Brahman*" is from Śaṅkara's own philosophical vocabulary. Bhartṛprapañca probably used the terms "intermediate world" or "*apavarga*". It may be thought, however, that Bhartṛprapañca probably uses the term "Highest *Brahman*".

In regard to this, however, it is stated in Ānandagiri's sub-commentary that lower *Brahman* here refers to "*Hiraṇyagarbha*". According to another passage in Śaṅkara's account[9], Bhartṛprapañca states:

> *Hiraṇyagarbha* is 'the seat of action which is in the state of being evolved' (*vyakṛtavāsthaḥ karmāśayaḥ*), or 'the world which has been evolved and is limited' (*vyākṛtaḥ paricchinno lokaḥ*). In contrast, the ultimate dimention is 'the still unevolved condition, the world of origin cause' (*loko 'vyākṛtāvasthaḥ kāraṇarūpam*). With the former as *Ātman*, the actions of the worshippers vanish; with the latter as *Ātman*, the actions of the worshippers do not vanish.

Summarizing the abqve discussion, the plan of release can be illustrated in this chart:

The Sphere of Ultimate Release	World Where Ascetics Go after Death
The Highest Self (*paraṃ brahma*)	*Hiraṇyagarbha*
	The intermediate state (*antarāla*)
mokṣa	*apavarga*
the unevolved (*avyākṛta*)	the evolved (*vyākṛta*)
cause (*kāraṇa*)	effect (*kārya*)[10]
unlimited(*aparicchinna*)	limited (*paricchinna*)
no individual names remaining	individual names remain
Highest *Brahman* (*paraṃ brahma*)	Lower *Brahman* (*apraṃ brahma*)

Virtually he admitted two kinds of *samuccaya* of knowledge (*vidyā*) and actions (*karman*,rituals). Human beings in the mundane world of transmigration attain the world of *Hiraṇyagarbha* by means of the first *sam-*

uccaya. Then, human beings in the world of *Hiraṇyagarbha* attain the world of *Brahman* by means of the second *samuccaya*.[11]

Hence, according to Bhartṛprapañca, through observing the religious rites and practicing meditation, people after death enter the intermediate state which is the world of *Hiraṇyagarbha*. After passing[12] through the process of union with *Hiraṇyagarbha*, they then are re-united with the Highest *Brahman*. Such a view is close to what is stated in the *Brahma-sūtra*, IV,3,10. It is also related that by directly worshipping the highest *Brahman* release can be attained before birth, but it appears that Bhartṛprapañca held that full release occurs after death.[13]

Notes

1) *Vārttika*, p.767, v.1692 ; p.768, v. 1700 ; p.769, vv.1702 ; 1706. Cf. Ś. ad *Bṛhad. Up*. p.190. A recent study — Shoun Hino : "Bhartṛprapañca on Liberation —— Sureśvara's Criticism of his Amalgamation of Knowledge and Action", *Journal of Indian and Buddhist Studies*, vol. XXXI, No.2, 1983. pp.761-764.(in Japanese)
2) *Vārttika*, p.851, v.302.
3) *Vārttika*, p.1890, v.1932f.
4) Ś. ad *Bṛhad. Up*. p.731.
5) Ś. ad *Bṛhad. Up*. p. 236. Also, Ānandagiri's sub-commentary.
6) *paraṃ brahma sadopāsīta yatnataḥ*/(*Vārttika*, p. 623, v. 948.)
7) Ś. ad *Bṛhad. Up*. III,2,13, p.416. Cf. *Vārttika*, p. 1154, vv. 41,42.
8) Ś. ad *Bṛhad. Up*. p. 151.
9) Cf. Ś. ad *Bṛhad. Up*. p. 190 ; *Vārttika*, p. 769, vv. 1704 ; 1705. Also, Ānandagiri's sub-commentary.
10) In the passages attributed to him this is not stated to be an "effect", but we feel no objection to so explaining it. Cf. *Brahma-sūtra*, IV,3,10.
11) *hiraṇyagarbha-vijñāna-karmaṇoḥ prathamaḥ kila*//(*Bṛhad. Up. Bhāṣya Vārttika* I,4. 1708.) *samuccayas tato 'nyo 'yam avyakta-brahma-vidyayā*/ *vyakta-sūtrātma-vidyāyāḥ paro 'py eṣa samuccayaḥ*//(*ibid*.)
12) Sureśvara refutes this view. *Vārttika*, p. 778, v. 1761.
13) Cf. The previously cited statement by Śaṅkara : The actions of those who worship *Brahman* as the Cause, do not vanish. Also *Vārttika* p. 1375, v. 102, and the fragment cited in the sub-comment : *yathāhur — dvividho mokṣo 'sminn eva śarīre sākṣātkṛtabrahmā mukta ity ucyate na brahmaṇi līnas, tasya śarīrapātottarakālaṃ brahmaṇi layo dvitīyo mokṣaḥ, sa tv āśāsitavya iti*/

CHAPTER VIII
ŚABARASVĀMIN

SECTION I. THE MAN, HIS WORKS AND HIS DATES

Śabarasvāmin is the author of the oldest extant commentary to the *Mīmāṃsā-sūtra*. Details of his life are completely unknown, but we may infer that he lived in around 550 A.D.

His name appears in Śaṅkara's commentary to the *Brahma-sūtra* III,3,53,[1] and the eighth-century Jain scholar Mallavādin also discusses his commentary.[2] The Mīmāṃsā scholar Kumārila and a younger scholar Prabhākara wrote a work called *Bṛhatī* (a sub-commentary to the commentary by Śabarasvāmin) based on a *Vārttika* by an unknown "author of the *Vārttika*" (*Vārttikakārapādāḥ*). This "author of the *Vārttika*" is different from Kumārila and is the person who wrote the sub-commentary to Śabarasvāmin's commentary.[3] Hence Śabarasvāmin was a person at least two generations earlier than Kumārila.

Further, the following legend has been transmitted among Indian scholars (*paṇḍit*).[4] The real name of Śabarasvāmin was Ādityadeva, but fleeing the persecution of Jain followers he became a forest hermit and took the name Śabara. Śabarasvāmin had six children. That is, from his union with a girl of the Brahmin caste was born the astronomer Varāhamihira; from his union with a girl of the Kṣatriya caste were born King Bhartṛhari and King Vikrama; from his union with a girl of the Vaiśya caste were born Haricandra and Śaṅku; and from his union with a girl of the Śūdra caste was born Amara.

brāhmaṇyām abhavad Varāhamihiro jyotirvidām agraṇīḥ/
rājā Bhartṛhariś ca Vikramanṛpaḥ kṣatrātmajāyām abhūt/
Vaiśyāyāṃ Haricandravaidyatilako jātaś ca Śaṅkuḥ kṛtī
Śūdrāyām Amaraḥ ṣaḍ eva Śabarasvāmidvijasyātmajāḥ//

(However, the 15th-16th-century poet Vidyāpat Thakkura, in his poem entitled *Puruṣaparīkṣā*, takes Śabarasvāmin to be the teacher of

Vikrama.)

Now then, we cannot use legend as a direct source, but the above "six children" may be considered to have existed at about the same time. It is known that Varāhamihira died in 587 A.D. and that Bhartṛhari was a person of about the late fifth century. In another poem transmitted in India, Amarasiṃha, Śaṅku and Varāhamihira are listed among the nine poets employed in the court of King Vikrama.[5] It has been shown that the words of this poem cannot be taken literally, but nonetheless can we not say that "the persons said to be Śabarasvāmin's children" lived at about the same time or the time that their dates are not too different? Bāṇa (early seventh century) in his preface (*śloka* 12) to the "*Life of King Harṣa*" praises his own predecessors, and among them he lists Haricandra. From these facts we may infer that Śabarasvāmin lived around 550 A.D.

The Śabarasvāmin who was the son of Bhaṭṭa Dīptasvāmin and wrote a commentary to the *Liṅgānuśāsana* of Harṣavardhana is a Mīmāṃsā scholar of the same name, but he was a different person. This Śabarasvāmin belongs to a later period.[6]

It is related that Śabarasvāmin's works include the following:

(1) A commentary to the *Mīmāṃsā-sūtra* (*Mīmāṃsā-sūtra-bhāṣya*).

(2) A commentary to the *Devatākāṇḍa* (*Devatākāṇḍa-bhāṣya*).

(1) is presently extant and has been published, but (2) is no longer extant. It is related that Mīmāṃsā scholars before him combined the *Mīmāṃsā-sūtra* and the *Devatākāṇḍa*, which concerns the rites of Mīmāṃsā, into one work consisting of sixteen chapters and wrote continuous commentaries to these. Śabarasvāmin, however, wrote separate commentaries to each and greatly abbreviated the annotations to the *Devatākāṇḍa*.[7] He did not write a commentary to the *Brahma-sūtra*, but as shall be discussed later, he was well-versed in Vedānta scholarship.

Notes

1) Cf. translation in Part V, Chapter III, Section I.

2) *Nyāyabinduṭīkāṭippaṇī*, p.16.

3) G. Jha : *The Prabhākara School of Pūrva-mīmāṃsā*, p.8.

4) The *ślokas* cited below are from G. Jha, *op. cit.*, p.7. Cf. also Ui Hakuju : *A Study of*

Indian Philosophy, vol. I, p.165.

5) Winternitz: *GIL*. III, S.42-43. Winternitz states that the person named 'Śaṅku' is completely unknown, but he is mentioned in Bhaṭṭotpala's commentary to the *Bṛhat-saṃhitā* (p.699, VizSS.).

6) Aufrecht: *CC*. I, p.632.

7) *Punar Dvikāṇḍe Dharmamīmāṃsāśāstre pūrvasya Tantrakāṇḍasya-Ācārya-Śabarasvāminā'tisaṃkṣepeṇa Saṃkarṣakāṇḍaṃ dvitīyam upekṣya kṛtaṃ bhāṣyam / tathā Devatākaṇḍasya saṃkarṣeṇa /* (*Prapañcahṛdaya*, p.39)

SECTION II. HIS THOUGHT: ŚABARASVĀMIN'S *ĀTMAN* THEORY

Sub-Section 1. Introduction

Śabarasvāmin's views are presented in his commentary to the *Mīmāṃsā-sūtra*, but there has not yet been any complete study of this bulky and difficult work. Gangānātha Jhā published a three-volume English translation of this work,[1] and so we look forward to further research on Śabarasvāmin's thought with the aid of this translation. We do not intend to present a complete discussion of his thought here. However, in the commentary to *sūtra* I,1,5, there exists a discussion of *ātman*; passages from the *Upaniṣads* are also frequently cited and discussed there. Since it is an important source which should not be overlooked, we shall examine it in the following pages.[2]

As has already been stated,[3] in the commentary to *sūtra* I,1,5, there is a lengthy quotation of the "author of the commentary"(*Vṛttikāra*), and, following the quotation, there is Śabarasvāmin's commentary.[4] After first stating that the scriptures state that those who observe the sacrifices receive the rewards of the heavenly world, there is presented a long account of a debate concerning *ātman*. The opponents in the debate appear to be "materialists," but in actuality they must be considered to be Buddhists who held Vijñānavāda views. Hence, not only must the following discussion be considered important in relation to research on Vedānta philosophy, but it must also be evaluated highly as one of the earliest attacks on the Vijñānavāda theories. Ānandajñāna views Śabarasvāmin as first among the scholars who attacked Buddhism.[5]

Notes

1) G. Jha : *Shabara-bhāṣya*, 3 vols., GOS. Baroda, 1933ff.

2) O. Strauss (*Die älteste Philosophie der Karma-Mīmāṃsā*) has presented a study of this section. An explanation is presented in S.21-28 and a translation in S.51-58.

3) Cf. Part V, Chapter IV, Section I.

4) *atha yad uktam animittaṃ śabdaḥ karmakāle* ..... (p.18, *l*.7ff. BI.) and after.

5) Ān. ad *Bṛhad. Up. Vārttika*, p.1460, ad v. 483.

Sub-Section 2. Characteristics of Śabarasvāmin's *Ātman* Theory

It may be said that there exist no previous examples of such a detailed discussion of *ātman* as in Śabarasvāmin's *Bhāṣya* I,1,5 (pp.50-60).[1] From a philosophical standpoint it is extremely interesting; it includes many problems which should be considered more thoroughly. But since our main objective is to explain the actual state of Vedānta philosophy in its early period, we shall not touch upon these various problems. Therefore, we shall here consider (1) the philosophical standpoint of the opponents of Śabarasvāmin, (2) the characteristics of Śabarasvāmin's *ātman* theory, and (3) the relationship between his view and Śaṅkara's.

Firstly, in considering the philosophic standpoint of Śabarasvāmin's opponents, we see that questions from a person who seems to be a *Lokāyata* are cited in p.50, line 5 and lines 7-8. The remaining criticisms are all concerned with theories of the Vijñānavāda school of Buddhism. (Commentators such as Kumārila and modern scholars accept this point.) From the above-mentioned discussion of Śabarasvāmin, we may summarize the assertions of the Vijñānavāda school in the following manner: — The contents of our consciousness change every moment, and it contains no permanent and unchanging element. The totality which consists of various contents of consciousness may be supposed to exist, but there is no substance as their unifying subject which transcends it. Hence there does not exist any *ātman* such as is posited in the philosophies of the Orthodox Brahmanical schools. That is, there is no *ātman*. — Various other problems are discussed in a supplementary sense, and it is a highly interesting discussion from which we can know one aspect of Vijñānavāda thinking of that time. It cannot be stated, however, that the Vijñānavāda assertions are presented here as they were. For example, the opponents quote Yājñavalkya's well-known teaching in the *Śatapatha-Brāhmaṇa* (i.e. the concluding portion which corresponds to the *Bṛhadāraṇyaka-Upaniṣad*) as a scriptural testimony for their own opinion, but it is absolutely unlikely that Buddhists would cite passages from Vedic scriptures as scriptural testimony. From the time of early Buddhism, it was not at all rare for views or passages from the Vedic scriptures to be introduced or cited in Buddhist texts, but these are always discussed as heretical theories which *should be refuted* and not as authority for Buddhist theories. Even in later periods, when intercourse with thinkers of Orthodox Brahmanical schools became more frequent, this remains the same. Hence, Śabarasvāmin does not introduce the Vijñānavāda theories as they were. It may be supposed that, in his own understanding, he presents Vijñānavāda views as the opponents' assertions (*pūrvapakṣa*) and subsequently refutes them. Hence he shapes the form of debate according to his own desires and answers self-posed questions. Since he takes up the problem of self-reflection concerning the contents of consciousness,[2] this is probably related to the concept of *saṃvid,* which constitutes a highly important problem in later Vijñānavāda theories. It is probable that such later Vijñānavāda theories are taken up for discussion here.

We shall next proceed to an examination of Śabarasvāmin's theory of *ātman*. Śabarasvāmin's purpose in presenting such a detailed discussion of *ātman* is to build a philosophical foundation for the Mīmāṃsā system as the science of the principles of religious rites. The Mīmāṃsā school has as its premise the belief that if one observes the religious rites which are prescribed in the Vedic scriptures, one will inevitably receive in this life or in the next such rewards as are cited in the scriptures. In this, of course, there is an acceptance of the basic philosophical proposition that the subject which observes some religious rite in the present is identical with that which receives some reward in the future. If the person who faithfully observes religious rites in the present cannot receive the relevant rewards in the future, and if some person who is completely unrelated receives those rewards, the scriptures of the Orthodox Brahmanical schools which state "Those who hope for such-and-such a good reward should observe such-and-such a religious rite" become meaningless and their authority is undermined. Rites in general have a *raison d'être* only upon the acceptance of the theory that there actually exists an *ātman*, i.e., soul, which is eternal and always one and the same entity. If *ātman* does not exist, rites in general become meaningless and worthless. The existence of *ātman* is accepted in general by most of the philosophical schools in India, but the Lokāyatas and Buddhists do not accept its existence. Hence, in order to build a basis for religious rites, the Mīmāṃsā school had to argue against these heretical views. Thus, an examination of *ātman* gradually came to occupy an important position in Mīmāṃsā philosophy.

In considering Śabarasvāmin's discussion, we may suppose that although in the previous section in his commentary "the *Vṛttikāra*" refers as the opponents' view to the argument that the Vedic scriptures cannot be a source of knowledge (*pramāṇa*),[3] Śabarasvāmin felt it necessary to supplement it, since there does not exist a sufficient refutation of that argument in the passage of the *Vṛttikāra*.[4] Śaṅkara takes special note that Śabarasvāmin took this argument of *ātman* from the *Brahma-sūtra* III,3,53 and discusses it here in the *Mīmāṃsā-sūtra*.[5] It may be said that in order to establish a philosophical foundation for Mīmāṃsā, Śabarasvāmin utilized Vedānta philosophy. At the time of the establishment of Vedānta school, the Vedānta was modeled on the system of Mīmāṃsā. A great many of its research methods and terminology were used.[6] In contrast, Mīmāṃsā had not at all adopted methods from the Vedānta. In the case of Śabarasvāmin, however, he came to use the philosophical views of Vedānta in order to establish a foundation for his own philosophy. Hence, with him we see clearly that in a sense contrary to the bases of the *Brahma-sūtra*, etc., Vedānta and Mīmāṃsā are two great mutually supplementary philosophical systems.

Now then, although Śabarasvāmin's *ātman* theory may be based on the ancient oral traditions or literature concerning the *Brahma-Sūtra* III,3,53, we may also suppose that it includes his own additions or revisions. Since it is impossible to differentiate these two aspects, we shall here simply examine the characteristics of the *ātman* theory as presented by him.

The concept which we usually and very generally express as "soul" or "spirit" is frequently indicated by Indians as "*ātman*." Śabarasvāmin follows this common usage, but occasionally he calls it "*puruṣa*" or "the inner self"(*pratyagātman*).[7] The nuances which these terms embrace are somewhat different, but they both indicate the same entity. According to Śabarasvāmin, for each individual existence there exists an *ātman* as its central principle. Each *ātman* is an independent and separate entity. The aspect of separateness from each other is not based on some special principle (e. g., *māyā*, etc.) but is basically an actually existent principle. There does not exist an identity relationship, such as Śaṅkara asserts to exist, between the mutually opposing "I" and "Thou." Hence the *ātman* which Śabarasvāmin discusses here is always the individual self and not anything like the universal self or highest self. There exist innumerable *ātman*. It is clear that he holds to the theory of a plurality of *ātman*.

Ātman is the subject of the individual's knowledge and action. It is the holder of various types of ideas (*vijñāna*), but, transcending individual ideas limited in time, it maintains a self-identity.[8] Individual ideas, as the content of consciousness, are created and perish instant by instant, but the *ātman* as their holder is eternal.[9] Hence, Śabarasvāmin maintains the theory that *ātman* is immortal. On this point his thought stands in direct opposition to the Buddhist non-soul (self) theory, in particular the Vijñānavāda. Further, according to Śabarasvāmin, *ātman* is a purely spiritual entity, and therefore it must be considered in a manner different from that concerning material elements. *Ātman* is separate from the physical body, yet it controls it. The physical body is formed as an agglomerate of material elements, and no spiritual quality can be seen in it. On this point he objects to the materialists, who regard the spirit as an attribute of the material physical body.

In such a case, how can it be demonstrated that *ātman* is different from the physical body? In general outline, his answer to this problem is as follows. While we are alive, our physical bodies constantly show movements, e. g., breathing, opening and closing of the eyes, etc. From this fact we first infer that there exists an *ātman* different from the physical body.[10] Since such movements cannot be recognized in the body of a dead person, it is not an attribute (*guṇa*) of the physical body.[11] We must suppose that the inner principle which is *ātman* makes possible such movements of the physical body. Further, the fact that we arouse desires by remembering past experiences proves that the same *ātman* constantly exists and that it is the subject which unifies our experiences which belong to separate times.[12] The activities of memory and recollection which are necessary conditions for the rise of our desires are possible only because *ātman* as the subject of consciousness is always an identical entity.[13] Further, the fact that others carry out the actions of daily life in a unified or planned manner indicates that *ātman* also exists in others.[14] Since such activities do not belong to the physical body, we must suppose that they are subordinated to *ātman*. This demonstrates that *ātman* is an entity which is separate from the physical body and exists eternally.

His *ātman* theory is presented in the form of a dialog or disputation with his opponent, and not in an organized discussion. However, in reading his discussion one becomes aware that his *ātman* theory, in particular his demonstration of its existence, greatly resembles Vaiśeṣika philosophy. Mīmāṃsā scholars of later periods were also aware of this.[15]

Firstly, they share a common demonstration of the existence of *ātman*. The Vaiśeṣika school states: "Inhalation, exhalation, the opening of the eyes, the closing of the eyes, life, the movement of the *manas*, changes in other sense-organs, happiness, unhappiness, desire, disgust, purposive effort are marks of [the existence of] the *ātman*."[16] Praśastapāda also presents a similar discussion.[17] In particular, concerning the existence of the *ātman* of others, it states: "Activity and inactivity observed in the inner self are the marks of [the existence of] the *ātman* of others."[18] The charge that "if *ātman* does not exist, it is impossible to explain the reasons for the establishment of memory," is one that is always used by various Indian schools[19] when attacking Buddhism. It is also used as *reductio ad absurdum* for the purpose of proving the existence of *ātman*. Śabarasvāmin was probably influenced by such ideas.

Beyond this, however, there is an astounding degree of agreement between his theory and the *ātman* theory presented in the *Carakasaṃhitā*.[20] The demonstration of the existence of *ātman* in both works agrees almost entirely. Hence, rather than holding that Śabarasvāmin here adopted Vaiśeṣika theory,[21] we should suppose that he expanded in detail the demonstrations of the existence of *ātman* which were widely accepted by naturalistic scholars of his period. According to Śaṅkara, Śabarasvāmin's discussion is based on notes of a Vedānta scholar who was active before him. Hence, it may be held that Mīmāṃsā scholar attempted to absorb the philosophy of thinkers who had modes of thought associated with the natural sciences (Vaiśeṣika, medicine, etc.).

It is highly interesting that we find the above type of discussion accepted by the scriptures of primitive Buddhism. When the king called Pāyāsi denied the existence of the soul and its transmigration, the Buddhist sage Kassapa refuted him. One of the points of his argument is as follows: — When this physical body has life (*āyu*), bodily warmth (*usmā*) and consciousness (*viññāṇa*), it is highly flexible and active. And when it does not have life, bodily warmth, or consciousness, it is heavy, stiff, and still. Just as no sound is emitted from a conch-shell until a person blows it and effort and "wind" are added to it, the body will not move unless life, bodily warmth and consciousness are active in the physical body of a living person. This can be seen by comparing the physical body of a living person and that of the dead. If such a difference is recognized, it cannot be said that human beings are only flesh. It must be supposed that other than the body, a subject of transmigration exists.[22] — It is highly interesting that this argument found in primitive Buddhist texts later came to be used by its opponents in order to refute Buddhism.

Now then, as previously stated, Śabarasvāmin asserts that the existence of *ātman* separate from the physical body can be established through inference from the various types of activities of *ātman*. However, when confronted with the question "What is *ātman* itself?," he answers, "It cannot be known through the teaching of another person." That is, it cannot be related to other persons through the use of concepts. Hence, *ātman* cannot be predicated through any concept. It exists at the innermost part of our existence; it is not the physical body, nor is it breath. The pleasures which we experience also are not *ātman*. It cannot be explained that *ātman* is manifested through some specific form.[23] It is something which can be only "self-known"(*svasaṃvedya*). It cannot be grasped through another person.[24] In a similar manner, the inner feelings of each individual, such as pleasure or displeasure, can be known only by each person himself.[25] The subject who reflects in such a manner and the *ātman* which is reflected upon are in actuality identical. The act of self-reflection is an essential activity of *ātman* itself.[26]

It was previously pointed out that the view that *ātman* is directly known through sense perception was advocated by Upavarṣa. Śabarasvāmin accepted it, and it was later transmitted to Kumārila and was also partially accepted by Śaṅkara. Vaiśeṣika school also states similarly: "Since the concept "I" indicates [one's own] inner self (*pratyagātman*) and not other things (e. g., the physical body, etc.), the object of sense perception is [*ātman* which is] different [from the physical body, etc.]."[27]

Śabarasvāmin calls the content of the direct perception of *ātman*, which is gained through self-reflection, "I" consciousness (*ahaṃpratyaya*). He thinks that for us this is of the highest degree of self-evidence and can absolutely not be doubted. Hence he clearly states: "It cannot be said that "I" consciousness is a delusion (*vyāmoha*)."[28] On this point, also, he agrees with Vaiśeṣika theories.

Further, the fact that his view concerning this problem is in clear opposition to Śaṅkara is extremely interesting from the standpoint of the history of Vedānta philosophy. According to Śaṅkara, "I" consciousness (*ahaṃpratyaya*) is the fundamental condition which makes possible the everyday activities of the individual self, but from a metaphysical standpoint it appears only after the highest self, as the Absolute, has been limited by ignorance (*avidyā*). Hence it is false and an illusion.[29] According to him, it is only after the disappearance of "I"consciousness that the true nature appears. However, according to Śabarasvāmin, "I" consciousness is absolutely true, certain and cannot be doubted. Through the philosophical theory that there exist individual *ātman* as the objects of "I" consciousness, he tries to establish a foundation giving a rational reason for practicing the rites and festivals maintained by the Orthodox Brahmanical school. In contrast, Śaṅkara, who emphasized the life-style of detached concentration which does not observe religious rites, had inevitably to assert that *ātman*, as the

Absolute, transcends "I" consciousness. We can see that the difference in the views of *ātman* between these two scholars is, in actuality, closely related to their standpoints concerning action.

Now then, if *ātman* is to be directly perceived by each individual, how does he know the *ātman* of other persons? As has been previously stated, according to Śabarasvāmin, the *existence* of the *ātman* of others can be known through inference. Since the *ātman* itself of other persons, however, cannot be directly known, it is held that there is no means of its knowledge other than analogy (*upamāna*).[30] That is, since we directly realize and know our own *ātman*, we transfer its contents to the *ātman* of others and know them by analogy. For example, he states that, when another person says "Ouch!", we recall previous experiences when we felt "Ouch!" in order to understand that person.[31]

According to Śabarasvāmin, such an *ātman* is the subject of action and also the subject of knowledge. However, he does not think that this *ātman* is a subject of knowledge which constitutes an object by its own naturally inherent powers. According to Śabarasvāmin, *ātman* is like a mirror which reflects objects as they are. The basic principle of his theory of knowledge is expressed in his statement "Just as something is perceived, so all exist."[32] *Ātman* does not constitute the object, but, to the contrary, the content of consciousness is formed dependent on the object. His theory of knowledge is realistic through and through. According to him, among the various means of knowledge (*pramāṇa*) which make knowledge possible, sense perception (*pratyakṣa*) is the most basic and other types of knowledge are derived from it.[33] This epistemological assertion has attracted the attention of later scholars of other schools as one of the characteristics of his thought.[34] On this point, too, he takes a standpoint that is diametrically opposed to the Buddhist Vijñānavāda.

In general, the main characteristics of Śabarasvāmin's *ātman* theory are as presented above. The *ātman* which he discusses corresponds to what is called the individual self (*jīva*) by Vedānta school in general. It resembles generally the individual self discussed in the *Brahma-sūtra*. But while the *Brahma-sūtra* posits "the principal vital air" (*mukhya prāṇa*) as the principle which makes possible the activity of life, Śabarasvāmin does not mention this at all. He attributes life-activity completely to *ātman*. Hence, as previously indicated, it must be said that his *ātman* theory is closer to Vaiśeṣika views. He thinks that there actually exist innumerable *ātman* and that each of them perceives in replica the object of an objective outer world. According to him, therefore, the individual self is true, and its knowledge and action are both true. Hence his position is quite contrary to Śaṅkara's. We do not know in what manner he conceived of the relationship between the highest self and the individual self, but it may be assumed that though he probably recognized a highest self, he did not place much importance on it. On this point, too, we may say that his view resembles Vaiśeṣika philosophy.[35] In terms of schools, he belongs to the two Mīmāṃsā schools which had existed since Upavarṣa. In order to further develop theoretically the *ātman* theory, however, he probably absorbed the *ātman* theories of the contemporary schools which had modes of thought close to that of the natural sciences (Vaiśeṣika school, medicine, etc.).

The conditions which made possible such an amalgamation already existed in the thought of Upavarṣa and Bodhāyana. For example, we may regard as forerunners of Śabarasvāmin's views Upavarṣa's theory of direct perception of *ātman* and Bodhāyana's view concerning the dominance of the object in knowledge. Further, since Śaṅkara states that Śabarasvāmin based his discussion on the *Brahma-sūtra* III,3,53, the synthesis of *ātman* theories in the above sense must have been probably undertaken by some scholar before Śabarasvāmin. Śabarasvāmin probably directly followed the theory of that scholar.

At any rate, it is known that in his view Vedānta and the Karma-Mīmāṃsā are mutually complementary. He recognizes the authority of Vedānta scriptures. He cites passages from the *Upaniṣads*[36] in order to prove his theory,[37] although, as Prof. Jacob has pointed out, his interpretations of the scriptures differ from Śaṅkara's.[38] He wrote annotations only to Mīmāṃsā works, but sought not at all to refute Vedānta.

Finally, I should like to discuss the relationship between Śabarasvāmin and Śaṅkara.

It is clear from the above discussion that Śabarasvāmin's *ātman* theory is markedly different from the thought of Advaita school of the Śaṅkara line. Yet Śaṅkara attaches the honorific term "master" (*ācārya*) to Śabarasvāmin's name.[39] This indicates that in Śaṅkara's time Śabarasvāmin was also considered an authority on Vedānta school.

From the standpoint of the history of thought, a particularly interesting point is the fact that in Śaṅkara's works some of his arguments are identical with Śabarasvāmin's. For example, as previously pointed out in the chapter on Upavarṣa, the argument that *ātman* is directly perceived is frequently presented. Besides, in demonstrating the existence of *ātman*, Śaṅkara says, "If there were no *ātman* different from the body, then there would be no room for Vedic injunctions that have the other world for their result."[40] This is a clear acceptance of the basic standpoint of Mīmāṃsā school. In showing that *ātman* is different from the body, he further says:

> …For [the attributes of *ātman*] differ in character from the attributes of the body. The attributes of the body, such as form, exist only as long as the body exists; but, even if the body exists, breath, movement, etc., do not exist in the state of death. Further, form and other attributes of the body can be perceived by others, but consciousness, memory and other attributes of *ātman* cannot be perceived by others.[41]

This is completely identical with Śabarasvāmin's demonstration. Further, in annotating the *Brahma-sūtra* II,2,25, Śaṅkara presents an extremely detailed argument that the existence of an eternal *ātman* must be accepted [42] because of the existence of memory which links the past and the present of each individual and that the Buddhistic "non-self" theory and "consciousness-only" theory are therefore in error. In essence, this argument is also completely identical with Śabarasvāmin's view.

In academic circles generally, Śaṅkara's philosophy is held to have strong spiritualistic or idealistic tendencies, but if his statements are closely examined, even on problems of epistemology he presents assertions which are identical with Śabarasvāmin's. He seeks the validity of the contents of knowledge in its agreement with objects.

> But knowledge arises through the right means of knowledge, and it agrees with the objects. It cannot be formed even with a hundred injunctions, nor can it be forbidden by a hundred prohibitions, since it

is not dependent on man, but on the existing thing.[43]

Hence, he says, "If the object to be known is one and the same, then the knowledge is also one and the same."[44] And he accepts that if the object is different, the contents of knowledge also differ.[45] It has been pointed out by scholars that the epistemology of the later Advaita school has marked realistic tendencies.[46] But such a tendency already exists in Śaṅkara's thought, and even in Śabarasvāmin and earlier thinkers. But more interesting is the fact that Śaṅkara posits *ātman*, the sense-organs, objects and *manas* as the four means which enable the formation of perception (*upalabdhisādhana*). In particular, he places *manas* in the leading role.[47] This is clearly what is presented in Vaiśeṣika philosophy.[48] Hence, it cannot be denied that there exists in Śaṅkara's thought a realistic tendency which is common to Vaiśeṣika philosophy and Śabarasvāmin.

How should we explain such an agreement in thought? Rather than holding that Śaṅkara followed Śabarasvāmin's theories, we should hold that both are based on traditional theories of the earlier Vedānta school. Śabarasvāmin probably reproduced fairly faithfully the Vedānta theories of an earlier period. Though Śaṅkara also reproduces the traditional theories of an earlier period, he asserts that these all are possible only from "the standpoint of daily life" or from "the standpoint of conceptualized expressions"(*vyavahāra-avasthā*) and that from "the standpoint of the Absolute Truth" or from "the standpoint of the Absolute"(*paramārtha-avasthā*) such a structure of the individual self and its functions is completely illusory. Hence, the ideas he held in common with Śabarasvāmin are those taught from "the standpoint of daily life" and the ideas which contradict these are those taught from "the standpoint of the Absolute Truth." If we understand it in this way, we can readily explain why Śaṅkara at times presents completely self-contradictory statements concerning *ātman*. Hence, Śaṅkara thinks that the *ātman* theory such as Śabarasvāmin presents is applicable to the individual self (*jīva*), but he also strongly emphasizes anew that it is not applicable to the highest self as the absolute, which is the essence of the individual self.

At any rate, we may explain the existence of identical arguments in the works of both thinkers as being related to the historical fact that from a period much earlier than Śabarasvāmin such an *ātman* theory had been propounded by a group of scholars within Vedānta school itself and that such a view was handed down for a very long period.

Notes

1) The edition on which my discussion is based is E.Frauwallner: *Materialien zur ältesten Erkenntnislehre der Karmamīmāṃsā*, Wien, 1968.

2) p.60, lines 5-15.

3) p.10, line 22-p.11, line 17. (Bl.).

4) O. Strauss: *op. cit.*, S.22.

5) Cf. Part V, Chapter III, Section I.

6) Cf. *A History of Early Vedānta Philosophy*, Part One, p.480f.

7) p.56, line 2.

8) p.56, lines 8-11.

9) p.56, lines 11-20.

10) p.50, lines 5-9.

11) p.50, lines 8-12.

12) p.56, line 14-p.58, line 3.

13) p.54, lines 14-16, p.56, lines 1-4, p.56, lines 7-20.

14) p.56, lines 21-24.

15) Pārthasārathimiśra notes that Śabarasvāmin's argument is based on Vaiśeṣika views. O. Strauss: *op.cit.*, S.24.

16) *Vaiśeṣika-sūtra* III,2,4.

17) *pravṛttinivṛttibhyāṃ rathakarmaṇā sārathivat prayatnavān vigrahasyādhiṣṭhātā 'numīyate, prāṇādibhiś ceti ...... sukhaduḥkhecchādveṣaprayatnaiś ca guṇair guṇy anumīyate/Praśastapādabhāṣya*, Kāśī Sanskrit Series, 3, pp.32-34.

18) *Vaiśeiṣika-sūtra*, III,1,19.

19) *Brahma-sūtra*, II,2,25; III,2,9; *Nyāya-sūtra*, III,1,14.

20) Cf. Part II, Chapter III, Section V of the present work (Part One, p.342f).

21) O. Strauss (*op. cit.*, S.26) states that Śabarasvāmin's argument is based on pre-Praśastapāda Vaiśeṣika theory.

22) *DN.*, Pāyāsi-suttanta, XVI; XVII; XVIII; XIX.

23) p.58, lines 13-20.

24) p.56, line 24-p.58, line 12.

25) p.58, lines 8-12.

26) p.58, lines 21-24.

27) *Vaiśeṣika-sūtra,* III,2,14.

28) p.56, lines 7-20.

29) Cf. Part V, Chapter III, Section III of the present work (p.38ff); also Deussen: *SV.*, S. 56.

30) p.58, line 25-p.62, line 1.

31) p.62, line 1-p.62, line 4.

32) p.60, line 7.

33) *pratyakṣapūrvakatvāc cānumānopamānārthāpattīnām apy akāraṇatvam iti/* Śabarasvāmin ad I,1,4. Cf. *Ślokavārttika, pratyakṣasūtra*, 87.

34) Mallavādin: *Nyāyabinduṭīkāṭippaṇī*, p.16. *l.*10. .... *yad uktaṃ Śabarasvāmiprabhṛtibhiḥ pratyakṣaṃ pramāṇaṃ, nānumānam .....*/

35) The Vaiśeṣika school holds to the theory of 'plural selves', but it also seems to have recognized a 'unique self'. Cf. Ui Hakuju: *A Study of Indian Philosophy*, vol. III, pp.522-523.

36) He cites it with the attribution "the *Brāhmaṇa* states." These are all passages in the *Śatapatha-Brāhmaṇa* (Mādhyaṃdina Rec.) which approximate those in the *Bṛhadāraṇyaka-Upaniṣad*.

37) p.58, lines 8-9, 9-10, 11-12, 13-14, p.60, lines 18-19, 20-22.

38) Hermann Jacobi: "Über die ältere Auffassung der Upaniṣad-Lehren," *Festschrift Ernst Windisch*, S.153-157. Prof. Jacobi states that there are not a few aspects of this argument which are simply imaginative speculations, but he feels that Śaṅkara's and Śabarasvāmin's explanations clearly differ concerning the passage "[*ātman*] is not intelligible, for [*ātman*] cannot be grasped" (*Bṛhad. Up.* III,9,26). Śaṅkara takes this statement as referring to the highest self, but Śabarasvāmin takes it as referring to the individual self which is held to be 'ungraspable' by another.

39) Ś. ad *BS.* III,3,53. Cf. Part V, Chapter III, Section I.

40) Ś. ad *BS.* III,3,53. Cf. Part V, Chapter III, Section I.

41) Ś. ad *BS.* III,3,54; vol. II, p.373, *ll.*1-4.

42) This argument is also seen in other works by Śaṅkara. Cf. Ś. ad *Bṛhad. Up.* p.733. This argument was used by various Indian schools against Buddhism. I have discussed this in more detail in "Arguments of Various Indian Schools against the Non-Ātman Theory," Miyamoto, S. (ed.): *Studies in the History of the Establishment of Mahāyāna Buddhism*, p.205ff.

43) *jñānaṃ tu pramāṇajanyaṃ yathābhūtaviṣayaṃ ca na tan niyogaśatenāpi kārayituṃ śakyate/ na ca pratiṣedhaśatenāpi vārayituṃ śakyate/na hi tat puruṣatantraṃ vastutantram eva hi tat*/Ś. ad *BS.* III,2,21; vol. II, p.220, *ll.*8-10.

44) *vedyaikyād vidyaikatvam*/Ś. ad *BS.* III,3,35; vol. II, p.336, *l.*12. Śaṅkara here discusses it in direct relationship with meditation (reverence). However, we may view it as a conclusion which was drawn from his basic standpoint concerning epistemological

problems.

45) Hence *vijñāna* is sometimes expressed in the plural form. Cf. Ś. ad *BS*. III,3,42; vol. II, p.349, *l*.7.

46) O. Strauss: *Indische Philosophie*, S.246.

47) Ś. ad *BS*. II,3,32; vol. II, p.63, *l*.3.

48) *Vaiśeṣika-sūtra*, III,2,1.

CHAPTER IX
BHARTṚMITRA

We know almost nothing of Bhartṛmitra's personality or biography, and none of his works is extant today. Hence, we are unable to discover too many details about him. But since his theories are discussed in works of later periods, we can gather some amount of information concerning his life and theories.

From the statements in Yāmuna's *Siddhitraya*,[1] Bhartṛmitra was a Vedānta scholar who lived before Śaṅkara. He was probably active in the period between Bhartṛprapañca and Bhartṛhari.

In the *Nyāyamañjarī*, a work by Jayanta-Bhaṭṭa, a tenth-century scholar of Nyāya school, Bhartṛmitra is mentioned twice as a "Mīmāṃsā scholar" (*Mīmāṃsaka*). There exists the following statement:

> *mīmāṃsakānāṃ tu nāvaśyam ākāśam eva śrotram/*
>
> Thus, for the *Mīmāṃsaka* scholars the organs of hearing cannot necessarily be said to be space.

Immediately following this there is a quotation from Bhartṛmitra:

> *tathā ca Bhartṛmitraḥ---pavanajanitasaṃskārapakṣo bhavatu tathāpi nātiprasaṅgaḥ, niyatadeśasyaiva tatra saṃskārāt/* (*Nyāya mañjarī*, VizSS, p.253)
>
> Bhartṛmitra states: Even if there may be the theory that [hearing] is an impression brought into being by wind, there is no error of *atiprasaṅga* (unwarrantable stretch of a rule), since it is only to the [organ of hearing], which is in a definite place, that the impressions of hearing occur.

Subsequent to this statement a debate occurs. From this debate we see that Bhartṛmitra opposed the view of Nyāya school which held that the aural organs (*śrotra*) can only be space. He asserted that hearing is an impression caused by wind. In other passages he also presents similar discussions and criticisms.

> *yat tu Bhartṛmitras tam eva saṃskāraṃ śrotreṇendriyam abhyupaiti*

tad idam apūrvakaṃ kim api pāṇḍityam/indriyasya hi saṃskāryasya kalpanam anupapannam/(*Nyāya mañjarī*, VizSS, p.226.)

Hence, we see that he was recognized generally in India as a Mīmāṃsā scholar. In the *Abhidhāvṛttimātṛkā*[2] by Mukulabhaṭṭa, he is referred to as "master" (*ācārya*), and the following *śloka* is attributed to him:

abhidheyena sāmīpyāt sārūpyāt samanvāyataḥ/
vaiparītyāt kriyāyogāl lakṣaṇā pañcadhā matā//

However, we must consider as particularly important the fact that his views are rejected as heretical by Kumārila. In the beginning of Kumārila's *Ślokavārttika* (*Ślokavārttika*,10, p.4) the following statement is found:

prāyeṇa sarvā mīmāṃsā hanta lokāyatīkṛtā/
tām āstikapathe kartum ayaṃ yatnaḥ kṛto mayā//

Ah! The entire Mīmāṃsā system has almost been made into the Lokāyata. In order to reset it on the path of the Orthodox school, I made this effort.

In Pārthasārathimiśra's *Nyāyaratnākara* (pp.3-4) there is the following annotation:

Concerning Mīmāṃsā studies, do there not already exist the old commentaries by Bhartṛmitra et. al.? What is the use of this [new commentary]? It is answered: —"almost" (*prāyeṇa*), etc. Though Mīmāṃsā system is really not the Lokāyata (*alokāyata*), Bhartṛmitra et. al. have made it into the Lokāyata by adopting [views] such as: the desired fruit is not derived from constant rites; the undesired [fruit] is not derived from the [performance of] prohibited [deeds]. Thus, in order to return Mīmāṃsā learning to the path of the Orthodox school, [Kumārila] endeavored to write the *Ślokavārttika*.

From this passage, we see that before Kumārila many commentaries to the *Mīmāṃsā-sūtra* had been written, and among these Bhartṛmitra's particularly had become a focus of attention. Mīmāṃsā philosophy of rites and the materialistic theories of the Lokāyata are diametrically opposed. It seems highly peculiar to hear that they were combined, but we can see from this and also from other sources that before Kumārila there existed the highly interesting attitude that Mīmāṃsā teachings, as well the Lokāyata, represented a heretical view. That is, in the *Yogayātrā* (IV, 24) by the great astronomer Varāhamihra (d. 587), it is stated that Mīmāṃsā followers (*Mīmāṃsaka*) and Buddhists destroy the virtue of holy places (*tīrthapuṇya*).[3] Concerning this, A.Weber explains that this shows that the *Mīmāṃsaka* teachings were regarded as heretical. We know very little about their circumstances, but, at any rate, before the time of Kumārila there existed a quite different type of Mīmāṃsā believer.

Now then, what is the significance of the fact that Bhartṛmitra transformed the *Mīmāṃsaka* teachings into those of the Lokāyata? It is a basic tenet of the Orthodox Brāhmaṇas that one attains good rewards if one faithfully observes the rites stipulated in the scriptures and that one receives bad results if one commits acts prohibited by the scriptures. But in the above passage it is held that Bhartṛmitra did not believe in this principle and his theory is criticized as being the same as that of the Lokātaya school. Such views, however, were held by some of the early Vedānta scholars. For example, Bhartṛhari[4] held that in terms of the Absolute Truth there can be no future rewards and asserted that the theory of rewards was a vulgar pedagogical theory propounded to convert the ignorant masses. The tendency to be condescending toward the general teachings of the Orthodox Brāhmaṇas can also be seen in the *Māṇḍūkya-kārikā*. Bhartṛmitra probably held views of the same genre. That is, he probably held that teachings such as those presented in the *Mīmāṃsā-sūtra* were vulgar pedagogical theories propounded for the sake of ignorant people who believed in the good effects of rites and that such rites had significance only in this sense. He probably explained the *Mīmāṃsā-sūtra* from such a standpoint. It may be assumed that for this reason Kumārila and Yāmuna rejected him as a heretic.

His works are now completely lost, but from the above considerations it may be held that he wrote a commentary to the *Mīmāṃsā-sūtra* and works concerning other Vedānta texts. His dates are before Kumārila and later than or about contemporaneous with Bhartṛprapañca. Thus, he was probably active in the period from 550 to 600 A.D.[5]

Notes

1) Cf. Part V, Chapter I, p.15.

2) p.14 (NSP.). This is according to V. A. Ramaswami Śastri, *IHQ*. vol. X, no. 3, p.452.

3) Weber: *Ind. St.*, XIV, S.315. Also, cf. the "Mīmāṃsaka" entry in the index of the same work.

4) Cf. Part VII, Chapter IV, Section VII.

5) With due consideration of other sources it is difficult to accept the statement in Yāmuna's biography which places him earlier than the grammarian Bhartṛhari. (Cf. Part V, Chapter II.)

[Addendum]

The main text and Umbeka's commentary to the *Ślokavārttika* have been published (*Ślokavārttikavyākhyā Tātparyaṭīkā of Bhaṭṭombeka*, ed. by S. K. Ramanatha Sastri, University of Madras, 1940). In this publication the first half of this *śloka* is presented as "*prāyeṇaiva hi Mīmāṃsā loke lokāyatī kṛtā*." Umbeka's comments are as follows: *nanu Vedārthagrahaṇāvismaraṇārtham api tattad Bhartṛmitrādiviracitatattvaśuddhyādilakṣaṇaprakaraṇam asty eveti gatārtham idaṃ vākyam ity āha — prāyeṇaiveti* / Hence, Bhartṛmitra's work was probably called "*Tattvaśuddhi*."

CHAPTER X
ŚRĪVATSĀṄKAMIŚRA

According to the previously cited passage in the *Siddhitraya* by Yāmuna,[1] Śrīvatsāṅkamiśra wrote a detailed commentary to the *Brahma-sūtra*. Yāmuna evaluated this commentary as "relating a principle as deep and profound as the great sea." Since the honorific "holy master" (*Bhagavat*) is attached to his name and since he was regarded as an authority second only to Dramiḍa, he probably held views resembling those of Dramiḍa and Yāmuna. The suffix "*miśra*" is also an honorific. Sudarśana-sūri, who wrote a commentary to Rāmānuja's *Vedārthasaṃgraha*, states that he is "a follower of Śrī-vatsāṅkamiśra" (Śrī-vatsāṅkamiśra-vaṃśya).[2]

Yāmuna presents Śrī-vatsāṅka as slightly later than Śaṅkara,[3] and states that he presented heretical theories which differed from those of the Orthodox Vedānta theories (i.e. theories of the Yāmuna school), confusing the people of the world. As noted by the editor of the *Siddhitraya*, this Śrīvatsāṅka is a different person. Their dates are different. The Śrī-vatsāṅka whom we will consider in this chapter is perhaps later than Dramiḍa but earlier than Śaṅkara. Thus, we probably commit no great error in placing him at about 600A.D. In contrast to this, the Śrī-vatsāṅka who propounded heretical views lived between the times of Śaṅkara and Bhāskara, and thus belonged to the period centering around 750A.D.

The works attributed to Śrī-vatsāṅka or Śrī-vatsāṅka-miśra are as follows.[4] (None have been published.)

(1) *Vaikuṇṭhastotra*
(2) *Śrīstava*
(3) *Sundarabāhustotra*
(4) *Yamakaratnākara*
(5) *Atimānuṣastava*
(6) *Kureśavijaya*
(7) *Varadarājastava*
(8) *Vaikuṇṭhastava*

Judging from these titles, they are probably all strongly tinged by the Hindu religion, in particular *Viṣṇu*-worship. It is not at all certain whether they are actually works by the Śrī-vatsāṅka whom we take to be the subject of this chapter.

The name "Śrī-vatsāṅka" literally means "the symbol of the blessed calf" and was an honorific for the god *Viṣṇu*. According to the myths of the Hindu religion, *Viṣṇu* interrupted the sage-hermit Bharadvāja when he was in mystical meditation. Angered, the sage threw water on the breast of *Viṣṇu*. The resulting mark became the symbol of the calf. Alternatively, it is held that the symbol was made by *Viṣṇu*'s three-pronged lance.[5] At any rate, since it is recognized in general as a symbol of *Viṣṇu*, it may be assumed that a scholar who possessed such a name probably revered the god *Viṣṇu*. In particular, since Yāmuna held Śrī-vatsāṅka to be a scholar in the direct lineage of his school, this inference would seem to have a considerable degree of certainty. Ultimately, the solution to this problem awaits an analysis of the contents of Śrī-vatsāṅka's works.

Notes

1) Cf. Part V, Chapter I, p.15.

2) At the end of the note to the *Vedārthasaṃgraha* the following statement is made: *iti śrīharitakulatilakaśrīvāgvijayisūnunā śrīvatsāṅkamiśravaṃṣyena śrīraṅgarājadivyājñāla-bdha-Vedavyāsāparanāmadheyena śrīmad-varadācāryapāda-sevā-samadhigata-vedārthasaṃg-rahatātparyeṇa śrīsudarśanasūriṇā vilikhitā tātparyadīpikā samāptā/*

3) Aufrecht: *CC*.III, p.127 places Śrī-vatsāṅka as a disciple of Rāmānuja, but does not cite the basis for this attribution. Since Yāmuna was the teacher of Rāmānuja it is unquestionable that this Śrī-vatsāṅka belonged to a period earlier than Rāmānuja.

4) Aufrecht: *CC*. I, p.674; II, p.231; III, p.139.

5) Cf. Hopkins: *Epic Mythology*, pp.184, 205, 213; V. Fausböll: *Indian Mythology*, p.104.

CHAPTER XI
SUNDARAPĀṆḌYA

It has recently been brought to light by Prof. Kuppaswāmi that before Śaṅkara there existed a person named Sundarapāṇḍya who was both a scholar of Mīmāṃsā rites and also a Vedānta scholar.[1] He is called "the Master Sundarapāṇḍya" (Ācārya-Sundarapāṇḍya). From the various comments concerning him, we may reach the following conclusions.

(A) At the very least, the following two works are attributed to him:[2]

1. A *Vārttika* to the *Brahma-sūtra*.
2. A *Vārttika* to the *Mīmāṃsā-sūtra*.

Both are composed in verse and are made up of *ślokas*.

(B) Dates: His dates are uncertain, but since *ślokas* from his *Vārttikas* are cited in Kumārila's *Tantravārttika* and in Śaṅkara's commentary to the *Brahma-sūtra*, he is unquestionably earlier than these two. He no doubt is a person of about 600 A.D. or earlier. During his time he was regarded as an authoritative scholar. Prof. Kuppaswāmi and other scholars have presented imaginative guesses which attach the name Sundarapāṇḍya to various persons, but it is difficult to reach a decisive conclusion about these.

Let us next examine statements attributed to Sundarapāṇḍya.

In the *Mīmāṃsā-sūtra* (III,3,14) it is stated: "In determining the meaning of the scriptures, the six types of pronouncements, i.e. *śruti*, *liṅga*, *vākya*, *prakaraṇa*, *sthāna*, *samākhyā*, are useful. But when they are used in conjunction with each other the latter are successively weaker, for the latter are successively further from the goal." In the passage explaining this there are the following *ślokas*:

āha ca

niḥśreṇyārohaṇaprāpyaṃ prāptimātropapādi ca/
ekam eva phalaṃ prāptum ubhāv ārohato yadā//
ekasopānavarty eko bhūmiṣṭhaś cāparas tayoḥ/
ubhayoś ca javas tulyaḥ pratibandhaś ca nāntarā//

virodhinos tadaiko hi tat phalaṃ prāpnuyāt tayoḥ/
prathamena gṛhīte 'smin paścimo 'vataren mudhā//
tena yady api sāmarthyaṃ pratyekaṃ siddham anyadā/
tathāpi yugapadbhāve jaghanyasya nirākriyā//
anyathaiva hi śūnyeṣu durbalair api caryate/
anyathā balavad-grastaiḥ sarvaśaktikṣaye sati//[3]

"When the two ascend in order to get the only one fruit that is to be reached only by ascending the stairs and is obtained only by reaching [it], [when] one of them is one step higher and the other stands on the earth, [when] their swiftness is the same and there is no obstacle on the way, then one of these hostile [men] will get that fruit. When this [fruit] is caught by the former, the latter would descend in vain. Therefore even if it is well-known that each has the same ability in another case, a man of lower class will be rejected when they exist at the same time. If there is none [who competes], even the weak in ability will fulfill in one way and those who are caught up by the powerful will fulfill in another way, when all the powers have perished."

Further in the *Vedānta-kalpataru* (ad III, 3, adhik. 15; VizSS., p.429) it is stated:

āha cātra nidarśanam ācāryasundarapāṇḍyaḥ/

Following this the first three of the above five *ślokas* are cited.

From this we can see that Sundarapāṇḍya explained Mīmāṃsā philosophy by using skillful similes.

Let us next examine his statements concerning Vedānta philosophy. Toward the end of his comments to the *Brahma-sūtra* I,1,4, Śaṅkara states that all the injunctions in the Vedic scriptures and all the other sources of knowledge (*pramāṇa*) have as their ultimate object the understanding of the significance of the sacred words "I am *Brahman*" (*Bṛhad. Up.* I,4,10). He asserts that once the non-dual *ātman* is known, neither the object nor the subject of cognition can exist, and therefore the source of knowledge also cannot exist. Subsequently, as scriptural basis for his theory, he cites the following three *ślokas*:[4]

gauṇamithyātmano 'sattve putradehādibādhanāt/
sadbrahmātmāham ity evaṃ bodhe kāryaṃ kathaṃ bhavet //

"When the metaphorical or false *ātman* is non-existent, [the ideas of my] child, [my] body are sublated. Therefore, when it is realized that 'I am the existent *Brahman*, *ātman*', how can any duty[5] exist?"

anveṣṭavyātmavijñānāt prāk pramātṛtvam ātmanaḥ/
anviṣṭaḥ syāt pramātaiva pāpmadoṣādivarjitaḥ//

"Before the *ātman* which should be sought is known, *ātman* is the subject of cognition.[6] [If] the subject of cognition itself is sought, [it] is free[7] from evils and defects, etc."[8]

dehātmapratyayo yadvat pramāṇatvena kalpitaḥ/
laukikaṃ tadvad evedaṃ pramāṇaṃ tv ātmaniścayāt//

"Just as the notion that the physical body is *ātman* is assumed as valid knowledge, this worldly [sense, etc.] are valid knowledge until *ātman* is actually known."[9]

From these short fragments we can infer the characteristics of Sundarapāṇḍya's views. If we now take into consideration the explanations of the *Bhāmatī* et al. to present his views in a systematic manner, they take the following form. Concerning *ātman*, Sundarapāṇḍya posited a principal *ātman* and a non-principal *ātman*; he further differentiated the latter into a metaphorical *ātman* and a false *ātman*.

(1) The principal *ātman* (*mukhya-ātman*) = Being (*sat*) = *Brahman*.

(2) The non-principal *ātman*

a. The metaphorical *ātman* (*gauṇātman*). This refers to one's own wife and children, etc. One's wife and children belong to one's self, yet they are different from one's self. This is a fact that can be readily understood by anyone. However, in a metaphorical sense people feel that the wife and children which belong to oneself are also one's self (*ātman*). When one's children are in pain or when they are happy, one feels that in the same manner one is in pain or happy. But the *ātman* of one's children and the *ātman* of one's self are not at all identical. To see both as identical is metaphorical.

b. The false *ātman* (*mithyātman*). This refers to the physical body, senses, etc. Everyone acknowledges that one's wife and children, wealth, etc., are different from *ātman* in its basic sense. However, some people (fools and the Cārvāka) hold that *ātman* can be none other than the physical body or the physical senses, etc., and loose sight of *ātman* itself. The *ātman* which they conjure is a false *ātman*.

In Sundarapāṇḍya's *ślokas* cited above, there appears the phrase "children and physical bodies, etc." It is not clear what the "etc." refers to, but in India generally, when listing a series of established ideas, it is common for only the first or the first and second to be specifically listed and the remainder relegated to an "etc." (*ādi*). In the later *Vedānta-sāra* (146-155) by Sadānanda there is presented a list of theories by people who mistakenly take *ātman* to be children, the physical body, the physical senses, breath, mind, perceptions, non-intelligibility (*ajñāna*), knowledge limited by non-intelligibility, and *śūnya*. Subsequently these are each discussed and refuted. Although it cannot be held to be identical, such a listing of mistaken views concerning *ātman* may be thought to be traceable to the earlier period of Sundarapāṇḍya.

According to Sundarapāṇḍya, our daily lives occur on the basis of these two types of mistaken views of *ātman* (*ātmābhimāna*).[10] He holds that in such daily life, the view that the physical body, etc., are *ātman* is correct knowledge and that to the extent that everyone recognizes it the experiences in general of daily life are actual. It is on such a basis that our actions occur. Yet, once one advances to the true form of *ātman,* one is able to understand that such knowledge and actions cannot be actual. The individual self which is held to be the subject of knowledge (and actions) in our daily experiences is also, in essence, completely without defects, separate from evils, defects, etc. When one has attained this principle, actions (*kārya*) no longer exist. At that stage one has already reached the dimension of emancipation. Hence, emancipation arises from attainment of this principle.

Explained in terms of the three *ślokas* previously cited and the various comments on these *ślokas*, Sundarapāṇḍya's views are as stated above. They are clearly in the same line of thought as Śaṅkara's Advaita theory. Indeed, it is because of this that Śaṅkara also cites Sundarapāṇḍya as a scriptural basis. From this, we can see that the Advaita theory was established about a century before Śaṅkara, or even earlier. We do not know exactly why such scholars also simultaneously studied the Mīmāṃsā teachings, but they probably did so simply because it was an ancient and traditional field of study.

Notes

1) S. Kuppuswāmi Śāstrī: "Problems of Identity in the Cultural History of Ancient India," *JORM*.1927, pp.5-15. Cf. pp.179-180. Prof. Śāstri has examined a large quantity of published and unpublished works and has collected many fragments.

2) In works of later periods he is simply called the author of the *Vārttika*. However, from the passages which quote him we may infer that he wrote *Vārttikas* to the *sūtras* of the two Mīmāṃsaka schools.

3) *Tantravārttika*, Benares edition, pp.852-853. Cf. G. Jha's Eng. Tr. pp.1184-1185.

4) According to Nārāyaṇa-Sarasvatī's (15th or 16th cent.) sub-commentary to Śaṅkara's commentary to the *Brahma-sūtra*, these three *ślokas* are by "*saṃpradāyavido Gauḍapādācāryāḥ*." Based on this, A. Venkatasubbiah asserts that Gauḍapāda's *Āgama-śāstra* was originally larger than its presently extant four chapters and that these three *ślokas* were cited from such a "lost" chapter (A. Venkatasubbiah: "On Gauḍapāda's *Āgama-śāstra*," *IHQ*. XI, 1935, p.789). However, from the passages which quote him we may infer that he wrote *Vārttikas* to the *sūtras* of the two Mīmāṃsaka schools. Since this assertion has not at all been substantiated, we must follow the various sources indicated by Prof. Kuppuswāmi and hold that the three *ślokas* are by Sundarpāṇḍya.

5) *vidhiniṣedhādivyavahāra (Ratnaprabhā), vidhividheyādivyavahāra* (*Nyāyanirṇaya*).

6) This indicates the differentiated perception which occurs on the basis of the subject-object dichotomy: "*pramātṛtvam ātmanaḥ*" / *upalakṣaṇaṃ caitat* / *pramāprameya-pramāṇavibhāga ity api draṣṭavyam* / (*Bhāmatī*).

7) This indicates the statement: "*yā ātmā'pahatapāpmā vijaro vimṛtyur viśoko — so 'nveṣṭavyaḥ*" *(Chānd. Up.*VIII,7,1).

8) *Ratnaprabhā* and *Nyāyanirṇaya* take this as indicating "the highest self."

9) Only this last *śloka* is also cited in *SDS*. XVI, *ll*.191-2 (p.409) as a scriptural source.

10) *tad evaṃ dvividho'yam ātmābhimāno lokayātraṃ vahati* / *Bhāmatī* ad *l.c.*

CHAPTER XII
BRAHMADATTA

According to Yāmuna[1] Brahmadatta was a Vedānta philosopher who appeared between Bhartṛmitra or Bhartṛhari and Śaṅkara. He is regarded as heretical by the Dramiḍa-Yāmuna school. Hence, his dates may be tentatively placed as generally between 600 and 700A.D.

A number of extant editions have been transmitted as Brahmadatta's works,[2] but it is highly doubtful that they are works by the Brahmadatta who lived before Śaṅkara. In the *Prapañcahṛdaya*,[3] which is a summary of the various types of learning occurring in India during the time of its compilation, it is stated that Brahmadatta wrote a commentary to the *Brahma-sūtra*. The *Prapañcahṛdaya* presents many names of scholars who wrote commentaries to the "Two Mīmāṃsas" or the "Ritual *Mīmāṃsā-sūtra*," but it associates Brahmadatta only with the *Brahma-sūtra*. Hence, he probably did not write a commentary to the "Ritual *Mīmāṃsā-sūtra*."

His views are presented in passages scattered in works of later periods. In the *Tattvamuktākalāpa* (II, 16) by Vedāntadeśika (14c.), after a certain heretical theory has been discussed, it is stated:

> *ekaṃ brahmaiva nityaṃ, tad-itarad akhilaṃ tatra janmādibhāg ity āmnātam. tena jīvo 'py acid iva janimān/*[4]
>
> "It is handed down in the scriptures that *Brahman* alone is one and eternal; everything else possesses birth, etc., in it. For this reason the individual self, like a non-conscious thing, also is created."

According to his own commentary to this passage, there are four types of scholars who hold this view: (1) The Vijñānavādins, who speak of the instantaneous birth and death of the individual self; (2) the Cārvāka school, which holds that the individual self exists when one is alive, but is destroyed at death; (3) some of the authors of the *Purāṇas* (*Paurāṇika*), who hold that the individual self continues to exist after death, but returns to nothingness at the time of the destruction (*pralaya*) of the universe; and (4) some of the Vedāntins, who hold that the individual self continues to exist until emancipation is attained. The last are called "those who appear to discuss, but do not really discuss the *Upaniṣad*s" (*Aupaniṣadābhāsa*). Among these Brahmadatta is included. Hence, Brahmadatta must have held that in terms of the Absolute Truth both *Brahman* and the individual self are actual and that to the extent that the individual self transmigrates both are different. But since the individual self returns to *Brahman* when it is emancipated, both become indivisible. It may be said that this is a very special type of theory. It agrees with the theory of Auḍulomi as presented in the *Brahma-sūtra* and also with the theories of some of the followers of the Pāñcarātra school.[5] Going back to an earlier period, such a view can also be found in the *Upaniṣads*. It may be that there exists no direct school connecting these two, but it cannot be doubted that such views were transmitted to some in each period of the early Vedānta school. Since the *Brahma-sūtra* does not recognize Auḍulomi's views as among the accepted theories (*siddhānta*) of its school, the Orthodox school of early Vedānta philosophy probably regarded such views as heretical.

Now then, how can emancipation of this kind be attained? Brahmadatta held that this is made possible by continuous repetition of meditation on *ātman*. In Sureśvara's *Naiṣkarmyasiddhi* (I, 67) his views are introduced.

> "Some people, based on the strength of their own traditional theories, state the following. —Even if the knowledge (*vijñāna*) that 'I am Brahman' arises from the sentence of the *Upaniṣad*s, the mere arising of the knowledge itself does not destroy ignorance (*ajñāna*). But for him who worships daily over a long period of time, the residual impression [of these exercises] increases, and thus ignorance is completely eliminated, for there is the passage: 'Having become a god, he goes to the Gods.' (*Bṛhad. Up*. IV, 1,2)"

According to the commentary entitled *Vidyāsurabhi* by Jñānāmṛta,[6] the "some people" mentioned here refers to "Brahmadatta et al." Hence, from the above passage we see that Brahmadatta did not believe, as Śaṅkara did, that simply by acquiring the knowledge of personal identity with the universe, i.e. "I am Brahman," emancipation is immediately attained. He felt that the attainment of such knowlege is insufficient and that, while always keeping that principle in mind, it had to be daily meditated upon over a long period of time. As the result of such practice, at a certain time ignorance is eliminated and emancipation is attained. Hence, he recognized as necessary for the attainment of emancipation the following two conditions: (1) metaphysical knowledge attained from the scriptures, and (2) meditation on *Ātman.* Since the latter are special actions or activities, we may say that in one sense Brahmadatta also held to the theory of "knowledge combined with action" (*jñānakarmasamuccayavāda*).

The above inferences concerning Brahmadatta's views can be confirmed in passages from other works by Sureśvara. In his *Bṛhadāraṇyakopaniṣad-bhāṣyavārttika*,[7] Sureśvara discusses Brahmadatta's views and refutes them.

> "The impossibility of injunction through the theory of *bhāvanā* in the case of oneness has already been explained in our examination of eligibility."
>
> "As to how the meaning of injunction is impossible following the doctrine of *niyoga* when oneness has been established is here explained with care."

Concerning the second *śloka*, Ānandagiri notes:

> "However, here, there is the suspicion that by using the theories of Brahmadatta et al., it is explained that [the passages in the *Upaniṣads*] order the somatic acquisition of knowledge (*jñānābhyāsa*)."

Hence Brahmadatta held that the various passages in the *Upaniṣads* ordered repeated meditation on *ātman.* On this there is a marked discrepancy in view with Śaṅkara and Sureśvara, who held that the main objective of the *Upaniṣad*s was the teaching of the true form of *ātman.* Concerning the basic nature of the commandments in the Vedic scriptures in general, the Kumārila branch of the Mīmāṃsā school takes them to be "purposive encouragement" (*bhāvanā*), while the Prabhākara branch takes them to be "doctrines" (*niyoga*).[8] Thus, Brahmadatta's view has this point in common with the Prabhākara sect.

At present, our knowledge of his life and views is limited to the above considerations. In the above manner, since he was criticized by both the Advaita school[9] and the Rāmānuja school, he had a distinctive philosophy which differed from that of these two schools. On this point he should be considered as an important thinker.

Notes

1) Cf. Part V, Chapter I of the present work. From the *Prapañcahṛdaya*, which will be discussed later, we see that he is earlier than Bhāskara. Further, as will also be discussed later, there is no evidence that he is also earlier than Sureśvara.

2) According to Aufrecht : *CCI*, p.381, as works of a person named Brahmadatta there exist the *Karaṇaprakāśa*subsequently (a work on astronomy) and the *Vedāntadīpikā*. Another work also cites his commentary to the *Śāṅkhāyanaśrautasūtra*.

3) *Brahmakāṇḍasya* [*bhāṣyam*] *Bhagavatpāda-Brahmadatta-Bhāskarādibhir matabheden-āpi kṛtam* (*Prapañcahṛdaya*, TrivSS. p.39). By examining foregoing passages, we see that in this case "Brahmadatta" indicates the *Brahma-sūtra*.

4) This is according to M. Hirīyanna, "Brahmadatta: An Old Vedāntin," *JORM*. 1928, p.2.

5) Cf. Part III, Chapter I, Section IV of the present work, Part One, p.382ff.

6) I am presently not able to examine the original. This is based on Hiriyanna: *op. cit*., p.4 ; Dasgupta, *HIPh*. vol.II, p. 99.

7) *Saṃbandhavārttika*, vv.796-797, p.219.

8) Hiriyanna : *op. cit*., p.6.

9) Puruṣottamamiśra's *Subodhinī* to the *Saṃkṣepaśārīraka*, III,217 : *māyāmātraṃ sarvam ity etan na sāṃpradāyikam iti cen na, Brahmadattādibhir uktatvād*. However, as previously stated, Brahmadatta clearly held views which differed from the Advaita theories. Hence, we may say either that the sub-commentator purposely made the false statement that Brahmadatta held Advaita views, or that Brahmadatta also accepted the term "*māyāmātra*," but, as in the first stanza of the *Māṇḍūkya-kārikā*, interpreted it from the standpoint of the "emanation" theory. It is probably the latter case.

CHAPTER XIII
GOVINDA

Govinda at times has an honorific attached to his name such that he is also called "Govinda-nātha."[1] In the addenda to various works by Śaṅkara, it is noted that Śaṅkara was Govinda's student.[2] The Indian traditions not only recognize this assertion, but also take Govinda to be Gauḍapāda's disciple.[3] If we accept that there is about a generational difference between each of these three scholars, we may state that in general Govinda's dates are from about 670 to 720 A.D. and Gauḍapāda's dates from about 640 to 690 A.D.

None of his works is presently extant. At the very least, however, he seems to have written a commentary (*Bhāṣya*) to the *Chāndogya-Upaniṣad*.

In the *Chāndogya-Upaniṣad* I,10,1 it is recorded that the region of the Kuru kingdom was afflicted by a disaster called "*maṭacī*." The meaning of the term "*maṭacī*" is not clear. Śaṅkara explains it as "thunder storms" (*maṭacyo 'śanayaḥ*), Raṅgarāmānuja takes it to be a "rain of stones" (*aśmavṛ-ṣṭi*), and Ānandagiri, using both explanations, states: *maṭacyo mardanahetavo 'śanayaḥ pāṣāṇavṛṣṭayo vā*. Most Western scholars take it to mean "hail." However, as Bhandarkar asserts, it seems best to explain it as a Sanskrit transliteration of the Dravidian word "*miḍice*" (damage by locust hordes).[4] The modern encyclopedia *Śabdakalpadruma*, which was published in Calcutta, uses the last explanation and states as follows:

raktavarṇakṣudrapakṣiviśeṣaḥ/ iti govinda-bhāṣyadhṛtac chāndogyaḥ/[5]

This agrees in general with the explanation "locust damage." I do not know what sources the editors of the *Śabdakalpadruma* used, but at any rate we can see from this that there previously existed a commentary by Govinda to the *Chāndogya-Upaniṣad*. It differed somewhat from the commentaries by Śaṅkara et al. and also contained accurate explanations.

There also is a tradition that he wrote commentaries (*Bhāṣya*) to the *Devatākāṇḍa* and the *Brahma-sūtra*.

In the *Sarvasiddhānta-saṃgraha* I,22, which is attributed to Śaṅkara, it is stated:

bhāṣyaṃ caturbhir adhyāyair Bhagavatpādanirmitaṁ/
cakre vivaraṇaṃ tasya tad Vedāntaṃ pracakṣate //

In the commentary by Śeṣagovinda (a disciple of Madhusūdana-Sarasvatī) the following statement is found:

"bhagavatpādaḥ" śrīmān śaṅkarācārya-gurur govinda-bhagavatpūjyaḥ/

Further, concerning the first half of the couplet, he states:

devatākāṇḍasya bhāṣyaṃ sūtrāṇāṃ vyākhyānaṃ bhagavatpādanirmitam ity āha/

And of the latter half:

uttaracatuṣkasyāpi bhāṣyam ācāryapraṇītam ity āha/[6]

An edition of the *Yogatārāvali* which is attributed to Govinda is presently extant, but it is not certain whether the attribution is accurate. It is said to be a work concerning Yoga.[7]

There is also mention of a Govinda who was a scholar of the Vedas. Ṣaḍguruśiṣya, who in the late twelfth century wrote commentaries to Śaúnaka's *Anuvākānukramaṇī* and Kātyāyana's *Sarvānukramaṇī*, lists Govinda as one of his predecessors.[8] Further, there is extant a commentary by Govinda to the *Śāṅkhāyana-śrauta-sūtra* XVII and XVIII (i.e. *mahāvrata*).[9] It is not clear, however, whether this Govinda is identical with the person who was Śaṅkara's teacher.

A study of the biographies of Śaṅkara written in later periods may provide some legendary source material concerning Govinda. However, we shall leave that task to a future occasion when we consider the biographies of Śaṅkara.

Notes

1) A traditional poem contains the term "Govinda-yogīndra" (Mahadevan: *GP*, p.2).
2) According to the *Śaṅkaravijaya*, Govindapāda is first and Śaṅkarācārya second in the lineage of heads of the Śringeri monastery. H. Wilson: "A Sketch of the Religious Sects of the Hindus," *Works*, vol. I, p.201.
3) Cf. Part VI, Chapter II, Section III of the present work.
4) D. R. Bhandarkar: *Lectures on the Ancient History of India*, Calcutta, 1919, pp.26–27. Cf. also Prof. Ui's Japanese translation of the *Chāndogya-Upaniṣad*, p.25, note.

5) Cf. *PW*. s.v. "*maṭacī*."

6) According to M. Raṅgācārya : *The Sarva-siddhānta-saṃgraha of Śaṅkarācārya*, Madras, 1909, Preface, pp.vii-viii.

7) No.4357 in the *Descriptive Catalogue of the Sanskrit Manuscripts in the Government Oriental Manuscripts Library at Madras* (according to M. Raṅgācārya : *op. cit.*, p.viii).

8) Weber : *HIL*, pp.61-62.

9) Weber : *HIL*, p.55. *Die Handschriften-Verzeichnisse der Königlichen Bibliothek zu Berlin*, I. Band,1853, No.109 (S.28).

CHAPTER XIV
MAṆḌANAMIŚRA

Maṇḍanamiśra was a disciple of Kumārila. Following Mādhava's account in his *Śaṅkaradigvijaya*, it was previously held in academic circles that Maṇḍanamiśra was a disciple of Kumārila who met and debated with Śaṅkara. After losing the debate he became Śaṅkara's disciple and changed his name to Sureśvara. Recent research,[1] however, has made it clear that he is not identical with Sureśvara. As was previously discussed,[2] his dates are approximately 675-725A.D. Hence, his dates are about the same as Śaṅkara's, but he was a bit older.[3]

The following works have been transmitted as his:

(1) *Vidhiviveka*, with the commentary *Nyāyakaṇikā* of Vācaspatimiśra; *The Pandit*, new series, 25-28 (1903-1906).

(2) *Sphoṭasiddhi*, with the *Gopālikā* by Ṛṣiputra Parameśvara, ed. by S. K. Rāmanātha Śāstrī, Madras, 1931; Madras University Sanskrit Series, no.6.

(3) *Mīmāṃsānukramaṇikā*, with an original commentary *Mīmāṃsāmaṇḍana* by Gaṅgānātha Jhā, ed. by Nyayopadhyaya Dhundhiraja Śastri, fasc. 1-5, Benares, 1928-30; ChowkhSS. nos.377, 380, 383, 389, 398.

(4) *Bhāvanāviveka*, with the commentary of Bhaṭṭa Umbeka, ed. with introduction by MM. Gaṅgānātha Jhā, 2 parts, Benares Library, 1922, 1923; Princess of Wales Sarasvatī Bhavana Texts, 6.

(5) *Vibhramaviveka*, ed. by S.Kuppuswami Sastri and T.V. Ramachandra Dikshitar, *Journal of Oriental Research Madras*, 1927 [Supplement to Journal, vol.I]. Also, Madras Oriental Series, 1 (1932).

(6) *Brahmasiddhi* with Śaṅkhapāṇi's commentary, ed. by Mm. S. Kuppuswami Sastri, Madras Government Oriental Manuscripts Series, no.4,1937. This work consists of a prose section and a verse section. There existed at least four commentaries to it, as listed below, but of these only the latter two are extant.[4]

(1) The *Tattva-samīkṣā* by Vācaspatimiśra.
(2) The *Brahmasiddhi-vyākhyā-ratna* by Ānandapūrṇa.
(3) The *Brahmasiddhi-ṭīkā* by Śaṅkhapāṇi.
(4) The *Abhiprāyaprakāśikā* by Citsukha.

Other than the above works, he is said to have written a commentary to Kumārila's *Tantravārttika*.[5]

From the above works, we may infer that he was conversant in both the Mīmāṃsā and Vedānta teachings. During his lifetime he appears to have been well-known as a Vedānta scholar. In the work entitled *Aṣṭasāhasrī*, the Jain scholar Vidyānanda mentions the "Vedāntavādin Maṇḍanamiśra,"[6] and later Vedānta scholars frequently cite him.[7] His Vedānta philosophy is presented mainly in the *Brahmasiddhi*.[8] It is known that Vācaspatimiśra wrote a commentary to this work called the *Tattvasamīkṣā*.[9] Since Vācaspatimiśra wrote commentaries to the most important works of the various sects which existed during his time, his selection of this work indicates that it was then considered highly important. It states that his views differed somewhat from Śaṅkara's.[10] At that time he seems to have been a Vedānta scholar equal in authority to Śaṅkara. It may be thought that since he was older than Śaṅkara and also a highly influential contemporaneous scholar, in order to clearly impress upon their readers the greatness of Śaṅkara's works, later biographers tried to show that even he was defeated by Śaṅkara. They thus came to imagine that he was identical with Sureśvara.

His Vedānta philosophy should be studied in conjunction with the views of Śaṅkara and Sureśvara. Thus, we will put aside a discussion of his thought until the publication of the *Brahmasiddhi*. We shall simply state here that he was a scholar who was active just a little earlier than Śaṅkara.

Notes

1) M. Hiriyanna: "Sureśvara and Maṇḍana-miśra," *JRAS*. 1923, p.259ff; 1924, pp.96-97. Dinesh Chandra Bhattacharya: "Maṇḍana, Sureśvara and Bhavabhūti, the Problem of their Identity," *IHQ*. vol. VII, 1931, pp.301-308. Amarnath Roy: "A Note on Sureśvarācārya and Maṇḍana-Miśra," *IHQ*. vol. VII, 1931, p.632. Dasgupta (*HIPh*.vol.II, p.82ff) also views them as being separate persons. Also, according to Prof. Kanakura's

introduction, Rāmasvāmi Śāstrī rejects the view that Maṇḍanamiśra and Sureśvara are identical (*Tattvabindu by Vācaspatimiśra with Tattvavibhāvanā by Ṛṣiputra Parameśvara*, edited by V. A. Rāmasvāmi Śāstrī, 1936, Annamalai University Sanskrit Series, no.3, Introduction, p.40ff). As a point of interest, the oldest source which views them as identical is the *Śaṅkaradigvijaya* (Cf. Aufrecht. *CC*. III, p.91).

2) Cf. Part I, Chapter II of the present work, Part One, p.88.

3) S. Kuppuswami has previously argued that Maṇḍanamiśra is pre-Śaṅkara (*Report of the Third Oriental Conference*, Madras, 1925, p.480). Unfortunately, I have not been able to see his report.

4) Dasgupta : *HIPh*. vol.II, p.83.

5) This is recorded in the *Śāstradīpikā* II,1,1 (G. Jhā: *The Prābhākara School of Pūrva Mīmāṃsā*, p.8).

6) Pathak: *JBRAS*, 1894, p.228.

7) Dasgupta: *HIPh*. II, p.83.

8) Dasgupta (*HIPh*. II, p.87ff) has previously introduced it.

9) Prof. E. Kanakura : "The Philosopher Vācaspatimiśra," *Studies in Religion*, new series, vol.14, part 1, p.80.

10) Cf. Hiriyanna: *op. cit*. According to the sub-commentary *Vedāntakalpataru*, there exist a number of passages in the *Bhāmatī* which discuss and refute Maṇḍanamiśra's views (T. R. Chintamani : *JORM*. III, 1929, p.43).

CHAPTER XV

FRAGMENTARY TRANSMISSIONS OF VARIOUS DIFFERING THEORIES

The scholars of the early Vedānta school whom we know lived in the period between the writing of the *Brahma-sūtra* and Śaṅkara are the thirteen persons discussed above and Gauḍapāda. Undoubtedly there existed many scholars other than these, but their names have not been transmitted down to us. Although their names are not known, we know that there were many who held differing theories within the Vedānta school in the period before Śaṅkara.

It was previously stated that in his commentary to the *Brahma-sūtra* Śaṅkara frequently attacks the theories of the "*Vṛttikāra*." He also discusses and refutes various different theories held by many other authors. Let us next list the most important of these different theories.

SECTION I. DIFFERENT THEORIES CONCERNING *ĀTMAN*

(1) After explaining in detail that although the individual self itself does not exist in terms of the Absolute Truth, it is actual in the sense that it is identical with *Brahman* (ad *BS.* I,3,19), Śaṅkara states:

> *apare tu vādinaḥ pāramārthikam eva jaivaṃ rūpam iti manyante asmadīyāś ca kecit/*[1]
>
> "Thus people of other schools and some among those of our own school think that the form of the individual self is [that] of the Absolute Truth."

Since he uses the term "some among those of our own school," he no doubt refers to one branch of the Vedānta school. We see that in the period before Śaṅkara there actually existed some who asserted not that the individual self exists temporarily because of attributes (*upādhi*) based on ignorance, but that the individual self in itself is actual and that it is an entity different from *Brahman*. Śaṅkara acknowledges that these people were members of the Vedānta school.

(2) As heretical theories, Śaṅkara lists along with Bhartṛprapañca's "eight-aspects" theory, the theory that the eight varieties are not aspects (*avasthā*) but potentialities (*śakti*), the theory that the indestructible (*akṣara*) *Brahman* is composed of limitless potentialities (*anantaśaktitva*), and the theory that the eight varieties are transformations (*vikāra*) of the "Indestructible." Ānandagiri calls the four theories the "aspect theory" (*avasthāpakṣa*), the "potentiality theory" (*śaktipakṣa*), the "branch theory" (*avayavapakṣa*), and the "transformation theory" (*vikārapakṣa*) respectively.

(3) Further, in explaining *Māṇḍūkya-kārikā* III, 20, the following statement is made:[2]

> *kecid upaniṣadvyākhyātāro brahmavādino vāvadūkā ajātasyaivātmatattvasyāmṛtasya svabhāvato jātim utpattim icchanti* /
>
> "Some verbose Brahmavādins who explain the *Upaniṣads* accept that 'birth', i. e. origination, belongs by nature to the 'non-originated', i. e. immortal *Ātman*-Truth."

Śaṅkara calls such theorists "believers in the origination of *Ātman*" (*ātmajātivādin*). They held that *Ātman* is the world-cause and that it becomes the phenomenal world after its origination.

(4) In the comment to II, 1, 14 of the *Brahma-sūtra* the following heretical view is discussed:

> "*Brahman* is composed of many natures (*anekātmaka*). For example, just as a tree has many branches, *Brahman* possesses many powers (*śakti*) and the actions (*pravṛtti*) dependent on those powers. For this reason, both its oneness (*ekatva*) and its plurality (*nānātva*) are true (*satya*). Thus, a tree considered in itself is one, but it is manifold if viewed as having branches; so the sea in itself is one, but manifold as having waves and foam; so the clay in itself is one, but manifold if viewed with regard to the jars and dishes made of it. Then activity towards final release resulting from knowledge will be established by the portion of oneness. On the other hand, the worldly activities and the Vedic activities which are based on the *Karmakāṇḍa* will be established by the portion of plurality."[3]

According to the annotation, this theory is a *Bhedābhedamata*[4] theory. Since this discussion in its entirety can be seen in fragments attributed to

Bhartṛprapañca, it is possible that his theories have been cited here.

Notes

1) Śaṅkara ad *BS*. vol. I, p.278, *l*.14.

2) The commentary to the *Māṇḍūkya-kārikā* attributed to him is probably not his work. However, there is no great error in assuming that it is close to his views.

3) Śaṅkara ad *BS*. vol. I, p. 459,*l*. 13 - p. 460, *l*. 5.

4) According to the *Ratnaprabhā*, the *Bhāmatī* and *Nyāyanirṇaya* are listed as "*anekāntavāda*."

SECTION II. HERETICAL THEORIES CONCERNING EMANCIPATION

(1) Śaṅkara attacks the views of people who explain that "since the *Upaniṣads* and other Vedic scriptures present injunctions (*vidhi*), the knowledge of *Brahman* (*Brahma-jñāna*) is proclaimed for those who desire to attain the reward of 'immortality' (*amṛtatva*)."[1]

(2) Śaṅkara also refutes the arguments of people who explain that emancipation is "that which should be originated" (*utpādya*), or "that which is originated through transformation" (*vikāra*).[2]

(3) *Prapañcavilayavāda* (Absorption of Phenomena theory).

In the *Upaniṣads* there are many commandments ordering meditation on *Ātman* as some type of thing. There existed theories which explained that this is an order to "absorb" phenomena. That is, since the phenomenal world which expresses dual opposition is "an obstacle to awakening to the knowledge of the true principle" (*tattvāvabodha-pratyanīkabhūta*), by absorbing it emancipation occurs. In later Vedānta works this theory is frequently discussed as a heretical theory, and Śaṅkara also discusses and refutes it.[3] According to Śaṅkara, if "absorption of phenomena" means destruction of the natural world, this is impossible; and if it means the destruction of illusions which arise from ignorance, it cannot be enacted through an order, but only through understanding (knowledge). However, the believers in the "absorption of phenomena" theory actually held that since the scriptures order that "*Ātman* should be regarded as A (e. g. breath)," or "*Ātman* should be seen as B (e. g. mind, *manas*)," in seeing *Ātman* as A, B is denied, and vice versa. Thus they held that a man should be known as without attributes (*nirguṇa*). Hence it may be held that the views concerning *Ātman* of these theorists were relatively close to Śaṅkara's.[4]

Notes

1) Ś. ad *BS*. I, 1, 4. vol. I, p. 53.
2) Ś. ad *BS*. I, 1, 4. vol. I, p. 67.
3) Ś. ad *BS*. III, 2, 21. vol. II, p. 217, *l*. 5ff.
4) Hiriyanna has examined later sources and presented a detailed discussion of them ("Prapañcavilayavāda: A Doctrine of Pre-Śaṅkara Vedānta", *JORM*. vol. I, 1927, p. 109 ff).

SECTION III. HERETICAL EXEGESES OF THE *BRAHMA-SŪTRA*

Although they contain no important philosophical differences, Śaṅkara discussed the heretical theories of his predecessors concerning individual passages of the *Brahma-sūtra*. We have already discussed the heretical theories presented by the "*Vṛttikāra*," but other than these, the heretical explanations concerning I, 2, 27; I, 2, 28; I, 3, 1; I, 3, 13; and I, 4, 12 are also discussed. Deussen explains these as later additions, but this is not correct.[1]

In explaining IV, 3, 7-14 of the *Brahma-sūtra*, Śaṅkara explains that concerning the *sūtra* which he regards as the accepted theory (*siddhānta*), others have explained it as a preliminary assertion (*pūrvapakṣa*).

The subject here is the ultimate fate of those who still have not attained knowledge of the Highest *Brahman*. Thus, it is clear that this is not simply a difference in linguistic explanation of the *sūtra*, but rather we see that important philosophic differences existed among the various commentators with regard to this problem.

We can also infer such a situation from Bhāskara's commentary. He clearly states that his commentary was written with the intent of positively criticizing the previous commentaries, which had hidden the true meaning (*abhiprāya*) of the *sūtras*.[2] Further, from his commentary we see that at that time there were numerous scholars who wrote commentaries which were very different from Śaṅkara's. Bhāskara is a person not far removed in time from Śaṅkara. And although he frequently attacks Śaṅkara's theories, he also attacks the theories of other commentators on the *sūtras* (I, 3, 10; III, 2, 4; III, 4, 32, etc.). When examining these passages, we see that they do not at all necessarily agree with Rāmānuja's explanation. Thus, we see that at that time there existed commentators on the *sūtras* who held explanations different from those of Śaṅkara, Bhāskara and Rāmānuja.

In previous chapters, I have presented commentators on the *Brahma-sūtra* who existed before Śaṅkara. It may be held that among them there existed large differences in their explanations of the *sūtras*.

Notes

1) For example, Bhāskara, who was not so far removed from Śaṅkara, also discusses and refutes the heretical view presented in I, 3, 1. Hence it cannot be considered a later addition.

2) At the beginning of his *Brahmasūtrabhāṣya*, Bhāskara states the following: *sūtrābhiprāyasaṃvṛtyā svābhiprāyaprakāśanāt vyākyātaṃ yair idaṃ śāstraṃ vyākhyeyaṃ tannivṛttaye//*

SECTION IV. COMMENTATORS ON THE *CHĀNDOGYA-UPANIṢAD* AND THE *BṚHADĀRAṆYAKA-UPANIṢAD*

The oldest extant commentary to the *Chāndogya-Upaniṣad* is Śaṅkara's, but as stated previously, there existed earlier commentaries by Ṭaṅka, Draviḍa, et al. Various "heretical theories" are introduced in Śaṅkara's commentary, but among them we should pay particular attention to the theories cited as the "*Vṛttikāra*'s." We find the following passage in the *Chāndogya-Upaniṣad*:

> "There are three branches of religious duty (*dharma*). The first is sacrifice, study of the *Vedas* and alms-giving. The second is indeed austerity. The third is a student who dwells in the house of his teacher and settles himself permanently in the house of a teacher. All these attain to the worlds of the virtuous. He who stands firm in *Brahman*

attains immortality." (*Chānd.Up.*, II, 23, 1)

In commenting on this passage, Śaṅkara refers to a different view:

"Concerning this, some people say as follows: — Here it is said that those who practice any of the four stages of life [which are prescribed in the Brahmanical codes] attain to the world of the virtuous without discrimination because of the performance of their own duty. Even if they lack knowledge (*jñāna*) [of *Brahman*], 'all these attain to the world of the virtuous.' In this case the wandering mendicants are not excluded. The austerity of the wandering mendicants is also knowledge, *yama* and *niyama*. Both wandering mendicants and ascetics are understood by the term 'austerity' in the [statement], 'The second is indeed austerity'.

For this reason [the meaning of the passage] is that, among those who practice the four stages of life 'those who abide in *Brahman*', i. e. those who believe in the sacred sound *OM* (*praṇavasevaka*), go to immortality, since the four are the same with respect to the point of having the qualification [of attaining immortality], since it is not prohibited [to anyone], and since it is reasonable that [anyone] is capable of abiding in *Brahman* at the break of one's activities. Further, the term 'those who abide in *Brahman*' is not conventionally used for the wandering mendicant unlike the terms such as barley and wild boars, for [the term] is used with reference to the mark which is 'abiding in *Brahman*'. In actuality, terms in conventional usage are not used with reference to the mark. It is possible for all to abide in *Brahman*. The term 'the one abiding in *Brahman*' denotes the one possessed of the mark which is 'abiding in *Brahman*'; therefore, it is not reasonable to limit it to the one object, i. e. 'the wandering mendicants', because of the absence of the reason for limitation. [It is possible to apply it to Vedic scholars, house-holders, forest-dwellers, etc.]

And immortality is not [attained] by the mere [performance of] the duty prescribed for the stage of life of 'the wandering mendicant', since [if it is so,] it would follow as the result that knowledge [as the means for attaining immortality] becomes useless. If [the opponents say that] knowledge combined with the duty for the life of the wandering mendicant alone is the means to [attain] immortality, [we reply:] that is not right, for [even the duty prescribed for the life of the wandering mendicant] is not different [from that for the other stages of life] with respect to the point that [it is] the duty for that stage of life. [Hence there is no reason for particularly honoring the life of the wandering mendicant.] Or, the [fact] that [the performance of] the duty characterized by knowledge is the means for [attaining] immortality is also common to the duties for all the stages of life. Moreover, there is no scriptural statement that final release occurs only to the wandering mendicant who abides in *Brahman* and to nobody else. It is the fixed doctrine of all the *Upaniṣads* that final release arises from knowledge. For this reason, he who abides in *Brahman* among those who [are performing] the duties prescribed for their own stages of life goes to immortality." (Ś. ad *Chānd. Up.*, pp. 116-117)

According to Ānandajñāna, the above is "the explanation of the *Vṛttikāra*" (*Vṛttikārīyaṃ vyākhyānam*). Śaṅkara appends objections to the above view, and of these the sub-commentator (Ānandajñāna) states: "He refutes the theory of the *Vṛttikāra*, which holds that he who dwells in *Brahman* is one who performs the combination [of knowledge and action]." (*brahmasaṃsthaḥ samuccayānuṣṭhāyīti Vṛttikāramataṃ nirākaroti.*) Thus, the *Vṛttikāra* held that people in any of the four stages of life prescribed by the Brahmanic codes can attain emancipation by meditation on *Brahman*. On this point he is in irreconcilable opposition to Śaṅkara, who honored and praised the life of the wandering mendicant. Rather, this view clearly resembles that of Bhartṛprapañca et. al.

At present the identity of this "*Vṛttikāra*" is completely unknown. The "*Vṛttikāra*" who wrote a commentary to the *Bṛhadāraṇyaka-Upaniṣad* existed before Śaṅkara, and it has already been explained that he is not Bhartṛprapañca.[1]

Note

1) Cf. Part V, Chapter VII, Section II, note 15.

SECTION V. PRE-ŚAṄKARA COMMENTATORS ON THE *BHAGAVAD-GĪTĀ* — PIŚĀCA, RANTIDEVA, GUPTA, ET AL.

The oldest extant commentary (*Bhāṣya*) to the *Bhagavad-Gītā* is that written by Śaṅkara. He was not, however, the first to comment on it. Many previous commentaries existed, and since their explanations differed, Śaṅkara, while taking a critical attitude toward them, wrote his "*Commentary to the Gītā*." Śaṅkara himself clearly records this.

> "The religious text called the *Bhagavad-Gītā* is the essence of the meaning of all the *Vedas*, but its meaning is difficult to understand. In order to explain its meaning many people have explained the meanings and principles of its vocabulary and of its statements. However, it came to my attention that some people state that its content is various and completely contradictory. In order to establish its meaning, by means of clear reasoning I shall present a concise explanation of it (*saṃkṣepato vivaraṇaṃ kariṣyāmi*)." (Ś ad *Bhag. G.* pp. 5-6)

Concerning this, we see in Ānandagiri's note that there existed many masters previous (*pūrvācārya*) to Śaṅkara and that they were "*Vṛttikāras*" who wrote commentaries to the *Gītā*. Śaṅkara criticized these earlier theories (*pūrvavyākhyāna, prācīna vyākhyāna*). Further, since Ānandagiri calls them *Samuccayavādins,* they probably held, as in the case of Bhāskara et al., that both knowledge and action were necessary for attaining final release. From Śaṅkara's statement, it appears that these commentaries were exceedingly voluminous.

But are the names of these earlier commentators not known? In a later period Vedāntadeśika, a scholar in the Rāmānuja tradition, listed many commentators to the *Gītā*. Toward the end of his comments on the *Gītā* XVIII, 66 he states the following:

> *evam anyeṣv api bhūteṣu bhaviṣyatsu ca Śrīmad-Gītā-bhāṣyeṣu bhagavad-yāmuna-āryabhāṣyakāramatānusāreṇa diṅmohaḥ praśamayitavyaḥ/ piśāca-rantideva-gupta-śaṃkara-yādavaprakāśa-bhāskara-nārāyaṇārya-yajñasvāmiprabhṛtibhiḥ svaṃ svaṃ matam āsthitaiḥ parahśatair bhāṣyakṛdbhiḥ asmatsiddhānta-tīrthakaraiś cāvigītaparigṛhīto 'yam atra sārārthaḥ //*[1]

"In this manner the errors in direction [of explanations] in other past and future commentaries to the sacred *Bhagavad-Gītā* must be eliminated in conforming with the explanation of the venerable commentator and master, Yāmuna. Piśāca, Rantideva, Gupta, Śaṅkara, Yādavaprakāśa, Bhāskara, Nārāyaṇārya, Yajñasvāmin, et al., over a hundred commentators and the various leading scholars of our school, each held to his own theories. But, concerning the following meaning, they all without presenting differing views agreed to it. . . "

From this statement we learn that before the appearance of Śaṅkara's commentary to the *Bhagavad-Gītā* three persons named Piśāca, Rantideva and Gupta wrote commentaries to the *Gītā*. We also see that their standpoints differed markedly from that of the Rāmānuja school.

(1) As a commentary to the *Bhagavad-Gītā*, we have presently available a work called *Piśācabhāṣya* or *Paiśācabhāṣya*.[2] In one edition its author is held to be the monkey-god Hanumat.[3] The edition seen by F. Hall consisted of 2300 *ślokas* on 163 pages, but there was no ascription of authorship.[4] We do not know what degree of relationship this work has with the commentator Piśāca who appears in Vedāntadeśika's statement. In Indian mythology Piśāca is a demon who eats raw and bloody meat: he is called an "eater of corpses" (*kravyād*). We do not know for what reasons and by what process the authorship of this work came to be ascribed to a mythological figure. But in India there are not a few ancient works which in later periods came to be associated with mythological figures.[5] There is probably no harm in holding this work to be one example of this.

(2) Rantideva's commentary is presently not extant. In Indian history there are a number of people named Rantideva. We know that there existed persons with that name who were a *yoga* practitioner, a poet, a student of sex (*kāmaśāstra*), and a compiler of a dictionary.[6]

(3) Gupta's commentary also is presently not extant. Several works mention a Gupta who was a grammarian,[7] but we do not know whether he was identical with the author of the *Gītā* commentary.

Since this is all we know, it is impossible to clarify the views held by each of these three scholars. However, since a number of pre-Śaṅkara heretical theories concerning the *Bhagavad-Gītā* are mentioned in Śaṅkara's commentary, we can attain some degree of understanding of the views held by pre-Śaṅkara commentators to the *Gītā*.

The views held by the "*Vṛttikāra*" to the *Gītā* are particularly worthy of notice.

(1) The view held by the "*Vṛttikāra*."

(Fragment 1)

After asserting that emancipation can be attained only by abandoning all action and achieving knowledge of *ātman*, Śaṅkara discusses the following heretical theory:

> "Concerning this [problem] some people state: — 'Individuation' (*kaivalya* = emancipation) cannot be attained simply by resting in 'realization of *ātman*', which is based on abandonment of all action. Rather, individuation is attained by the knowledge which is coordinate with the performance of actions (rites) such as the fire-ritual, etc., which are prescribed in the *śruti* and other ancient religious works. This is the meaning established in the *Gītā* as a whole. The pronouncement which explains this meaning states: 'If you do not engage in the battle for this truth (*dharmya saṃgrāma*)...' (II, 33). 'Thus, indeed, you must act' (IV, 15), etc. We must not doubt in the following manner: ' [Since] the rites prescribed in the *Vedas* [order offerings of animal sacrifice], they are sins of injury, etc. Thus, they are immoral (*adharma*).' For it is like the action of warriors whose essence is in fighting. They injure masters, brothers and children; it is indeed terrifying. But [for the warrior] because it is his *dharma*, it is not immoral. And if one does not act, 'one throws away his own essence, abandons honor, is deserving of punishment' (II, 32). [The god Kṛṣṇa,] who spoke thus, had previously determined that one's actions and rituals characterized by the killing of animals, etc. — as ordered by scriptures which state 'While in possession of life, one must act' (cf. *Chānd.Up.* VIII, 15, 1) — are not sins." (Ś. ad *Bhag.G.* II, 11, p. 41)

Following this, Śaṅkara presents his refutation. According to Ānandagiri, the above is the "theory of the *Vṛttikāra*" (*Vṛttikṛtām abhipretam*).

(Fragment 2)

At the beginning of Chapter Three of the *Bhagavad-Gītā*, Prince Arjuna poses the following questions to Kṛṣṇa:

> "Oh, Lord who excites people! If you think that action is superior to understanding, why, Oh Keśava, do you order of me such a fearful deed?"

For Śaṅkara, this passage is, of course, an indication of the superiority of knowledge to action, but he also mentions the following heretical interpretation:

> "Some people take the meaning of Arjuna's question in a different manner. They explain the Bhagavad's answer as being in opposition to it. Concerning the part where the connection is explained, in opposition to my explanation of the meaning of the *Gītā*, they explain the meaning here of questions and answers. That is, concerning that part, they state: — 'For all people who perform the actions of their stations (*āśrama*), the significance of the conjunction of thought and action (*jñānakarmaṇoḥ samuccayaḥ*) is taught in the *Gītā*.' They hold that this is re-affirmed [here]. [Hence,] the doctrine that emancipation is attained by abandoning the various actions which are ordered in the scriptural passage that states 'While in possession of life [one must act]' (cf. *Chānd.Up.* VIII, 15, 1) and is attained only by knowledge is completely prohibited.—"

Śaṅkara refutes such an explanation and Ānandagiri states that the heretical view is the "meaning held by the *Vṛttikāra*" (*Vṛttikārābhiprāya*).

(Fragment 3)

> "One who sees non-action in action and action in non-action is, among men, one who possesses understanding. While performing all actions he possesses unity of mind." (*Bhag.G.* IV, 18)

After commenting on this passage, Śaṅkara mentions the following heretical views:

> "Some people explain this *śloka* in a different manner. That is, according to their view, rites as performed for the Governing Deity and at the same time as rites which should be observed do not have any effect. They are expressed [in the *śloka*] as 'non-action' in a secondary (metaphorical) sense. 'Non-action' means that they are not performed. And that [the non-performance of rites which should always be observed] brings about the result of falling into hell. Thus, in the same

secondary (metaphorical) sense it is called 'action'. In this, *he who sees non-action in action* (rites) which should always be performed [creates no effects] because effects do not exist. It is like the milk-cow being a cow (*go*), but being called a non-cow (*ago*) if it does not produce the effect which is milk. In the same manner, *he who sees action* in 'non-action', i.e. the non-performance of rites which should always be performed, creates the bad effect of [falling into hell], etc. —"

Śaṅkara refutes this explanation. According to Ānandagiri, the above heretical view is the "explanation of the *Vṛttikāra*" (*Vṛttikāra-vyākhyāna*).

From the views expressed in the above fragments it is clear that the *Vṛttikāra* is a *Jñānakarmasamuccayavādin*. He emphasizes that in order to attain emancipation simple realization of *Brahman* is not enough : one must also perform the rites prescribed in the Brahmanic Codes.

(2) Other heretical views.

Views by other commentators who emphasized the importance of observing the rites prescribed in the Brahmanic scriptures are also occasionally mentioned.

(Fragment 1)

"*Brahman* is the offering ; *Brahman* is the oblation ; it is poured into the fire of *Brahman* by *Brahman* ; he must go to *Brahman*, dwelling in the contemplation which has *Brahman* as its object." (*Bhag.G.* IV, 24)

After explaining the above stanza, Śaṅkara refers to the following different view :

"With regard to this, some people say : — What is *Brahman* is the offering. *Brahman* is established by the fivefold case (*kāraka*)* such as the offering and that alone performs the action. In this case the idea of the offering does not cease to exist but the idea of *Brahman* is superimposed upon the offering and the like, just as the idea of *Viṣṇu* and the like is superimposed upon the image and the like or just as the idea of *Brahman* is superimposed upon the name and the like." (p. 218)

Ānandagiri notes that this is "an explanation by people belonging to our school" (*svayūthyavyākhyāna*). Śaṅkara opposes the above explanation and explains that in this passage knowledge is praised.

(Fragment 2)

"These actions, however, must also be performed with abandonment of attachment and fruits. Oh, son of Pṛthā, this is my definite and highest judgment." (*Bhag.G.* XVIII, 6)

After commenting on this stanza, Śaṅkara refers to the following different interpretation:

"Other people explain it as follows: — Because of the absence of the fruit in obligatory actions, it is not reasonable to say, 'with abandonment of attachment and fruit'. 'These also' — 'These' optional actions (*kāmya*), other than the obligatory (*nitya*) ones, 'also must be performed'; how much more so the obligatory sacrifice, giving and austerity. —" (p. 681)

Śaṅkara, of course, refutes the above explanation.

(Fragment 3)

In annotating *Bhagavad-Gītā* II, 21 Śaṅkara asserts that in terms of the Absolute Truth actions are not possible. He then states the following:

"With regard to this, some conceited pedants say: — The knowledge, at the time of the arising of which it is taught that there arises the renunciation of all actions, that 'I am *Ātman*, which is changeless, non-agent, one and free from the sixfold change of states beginning with birth', does not occur to anybody.— " (p. 74)

Śaṅkara refutes this by stating:

"If that be so, then the scriptures which teach non-birth are meaningless."

According to Ānandagiri, the above is "a theory of the Mīmāṃsā school" (*Mīmāṃsaka-mata*).

Other than the above there are explanations which are strongly tinged by Hinduism.

(Fragment 4)

anādimat paraṃ brahma na sat tan nāsad ucyate/(*Bhag.G.* XIII, 12)

Śaṅkara interprets this stanza as follows:

"It is the beginningless highest *Brahman*. It is neither said to be being nor non-being."

Moreover, he refutes another interpretation, according to which the above *pada* is split as: "*anādi matparaṃ brahma,*" which is interpreted as:

"It is *Brahman*, beginningless and superior to me."

Śaṅkara states as follows:

> "With regard to this, some people split the *pada* into *anādi matparam*. If the above-mentioned meaning is expressed by the *bahuvrīhi* compound (*anādimat*), there is the undesirable [result] that the suffix *-mat* is meaningless. [*anādi* alone would suffice.] They show that [*Vāsudeva* and *Brahman*] are distinct things by saying that the one of which I am the highest power *parā śaktiḥ* called *Vāsudeva* is superior to me."

Śaṅkara refutes such explanations. From this statement we see that previous to Śaṅkara there existed commentators who held that the highest potentiality of the Highest *Brahman* is *Vāsudeva*. These commentators had not yet reached the point of seeing *Vāsudeva* as the ultimate world-principle. Hence, Jayatīrtha, a dualistic Vedānta scholar of a later period, refuted this view by stating that *Vāsudeva* and *Brahman* are not different.[9]

Notes

1) According to B. N. Krishnamurti Sarma: "Bhāskara, a Forgotten Commentator on the *Gītā*," *IHQ*. vol. IX, 1933, p. 670.

2) Aufrecht: *CC*. I, p. 391. *The Paiśācabhāṣya*, ĀnSS. No. 44, Poona 1901.

3) Aufrecht: *CC*. III, p. 84.

4) Fitzedward Hall: *A Contribution towards an Index to the Bibliography of the Indian Philosophical Systems*, Calcutta, 1859, p. 120.

5) For example, it is related that there existed an old commentary called *Rāvaṇabhāṣya* to the *Vaiśeṣika-sūtra*.

6) Aufrecht: *CC*. I, p. 492; Winternitz: *GIL*. Bd. III, S. 541.

7) Aufrecht: *CC*. I, p. 155.

8) *kartṛkarmakaraṇasampradānādhikaraṇarūpeṇa pañcavidhena brahmaiva vyavasthitaṃ karma karotīti*//(Ānandagiri).

9) Sarma: *op. cit*., p. 676.

SECTION VI. JÑĀNANIDHI

The play-writer Bhavabhūti was well-versed in Vedānta philosophy.[1] He notes that his teacher was Jñānanidhi. He praises this teacher, saying: "His

Holiness . . . Jñānanidhi, [my] teacher, who is foremost among the great sages, Paramahaṃsas, like Aṅgiras, [and] who [is possessed of the store of wisdom] as his name indicates. (*śreṣṭhaḥ paramahaṃsānāṃ maharṣīṇām ivāṅgiraḥ/yathārthanāmā bhagavān . . . Jñānanidhir guruḥ//*)[2] Etymologically, the term "*paramahaṃsa*" means "best of the *haṃsa*-birds," and it is an honorific for religious practitioners who spend a life of wandering, exclusively meditating on *Brahman*. The *haṃsa*-bird moves with the changes of the seasons to find dwellings which are appropriate to itself. It is a metaphor for those who have no attachments. Those who are called "*paramahaṃsa*" are mainly believers in Vedāntic thought.[3] Hence, it is probable that Jñānanidhi also belonged to this group. It may be held that Bhavabhūti received his knowledge of Vedānta philosophy from Jñānanidhi.

Bhavabhūti's dates are approximately 690-740 A.D.[4] Hence, if we place Jñānanidhi a generation or so earlier, his dates would be about 630-700. Since his works are not extant, we do not know his views. However, if we hold that the Vedānta philosophy related by Bhavabhūti is that learned from Jñānanidhi, his views would be close to those of Bhartṛhari. (At any rate, it is difficult to believe that the playwright Bhavabhūti himself worked out such philosophic ideas to include them in his plays.)

Notes

1) Cf. Part II, Chapter III, Section VII of the present work, Part One, p.352ff.

2) *Mahāvīracarita*, Act I, v. 5.

3) This is well indicated in the *Paramahaṃsa-Up.*, *Paramahaṃsa-parivrājaka-Up*.

4) Cf. Part I, Chapter II, Section 2-B-3 of the present work, Part One, p.84.

SECTION VII. FORERUNNERS OF THE ADVAITA THEORIES

The theories that we introduced and examined above differ from the Advaita theories. On the other hand, however, there also exist theories which may be seen as forerunners of Advaita theories.

(1) In commenting on the *Bhagavad-Gītā* (XIII, 14), Śaṅkara states the following:

tathāhi saṃpradāyavidāṃ vacanam adhyāropa-apavādābhyāṃ niṣ-

prapañcaṃ iti//

"For instance there is the word of the knowledge of tradition : — 'By superimposition and denial, that which is free from phenomena is made phenomenal'."

"That which is free from phenomena" probably indicates *Brahman*. "Superimposition" (*adhyāropa*) and "denial" (*apavāda*) were originally ideas used in Buddhism, in particular Vijñānavāda philosophy. In Chinese they are rendered respectively as 增益 and 損減. The former indicates the mistake of believing something to exist which does not exist, the latter the mistake of regarding as non-existent something which does exist. Hence we see that even before Śaṅkara these two ideas were used by the Vedānta school. (Bhartṛhari also uses these two ideas, but we shall discuss this in a later chapter.[1])

(2) We have one passage by a scholar who influenced the ideas of Bhartṛhari. In chapter thirteen (the thesis of the Pāṇini school) of Mādhava's *Sarvadarśanasaṃgraha* where Bhartṛhari's theories are presented, it is stated that based on the most extreme universal, 'existence' (*sattā*), various class-concepts such as 'cow-ness' (*gotva*) are formed. Subsequent to this we have the following passage :[2]

tathā cāptavākyam —

sphaṭikaṃ vimalaṃ dravyaṃ yathā yuktaṃ pṛthak pṛthak/
nīlalohitapītādyais tadvarṇam upalabhyate//iti/

tathā hariṇāpy uktaṃ —

saṃbandhibhedāt sattaiva bhidyamānā gavādiṣu/
jātir ity ucyate tasyāṃ sarve śabdā vyavasthitāḥ //(= *Vākyapadīya* III, 1, 33, p. 29)
taṃ prātipadikārthaṃ ca dhātvarthaṃ ca pracakṣate/
sā nityā sā mahān ātmā tām āhus tvatalādayaḥ//iti/(= *Vākyapadīya* III, 1, 34, p. 29)

"For this reason a person of authority (one who can be relied upon) states : —

'Just as the crystal, [though in itself] pure, is perceived to possess each of the colors when it is connected with blue, red, yellow, etc.'

[Bhartṛ]hari also says similarly:

'Differentiated in the cow, etc., on account of different combinations, existence (*sattā*) itself is called a "class" (*jāti*). All words are established on existence.'

'[An earlier scholar] states that it (existence) has the meaning of the stem-form of nouns and has the meaning of verbal root. It is permanent. It is the Great Self. [The suffixes] -*tva*, -*tā*, etc., refer to it.'"

In this manner, Mādhava separates the statements of the 'authoritative person' (*āpta*) and those of Bhartṛhari. Since the latter is a supplementary explanation of the former we may assume that the former was by a person who lived considerably earlier than Bhartṛhari. As further evidence, we see that the above passage is also quoted in Helārāja's commentary to the *Vākyapadīya*.[3] In that work after the quotation it is stated: ". . . Concerning this problem, there is another reading of the *āgama*." (. . . *iti aparo 'trāgamapāṭhaḥ*.) Since Helārāja calls it an '*āgama*', he must have considered it a very authoritative statement. The comparison of the relationship between the Absolute *Brahman* and the phenomenal world to that between the pure and translucent crystal and that which is seen to have the various colors of things which are attached to it is well-known as a characteristic device used by Śaṅkara.[4] But before Śaṅkara, Bhartṛhari used this simile,[5] and even his use is based on an earlier tradition. The use of the 'crystal simile' is indeed a very old practice in the Vedānta school.

The names of those who proposed the ideas introduced above are not known, but it is unquestionable that such theories are pre-Śaṅkara. Some of these theories agree with the views of scholars discussed in previous chapters, but those which differ are far more numerous. From this we gain some idea of the wealth and variety of thought in the early Vedānta school.

Notes

1) Cf. Part VII, Chapter II, Section III.
2) Cf. *SDS*. XIII, *ll*. 205-212 (p. 304).
3) ad *Vākyap*. III, 3, 41 (p. 117).
4) Ś. ad *Bṛhad. Up*., p. 623; Ś. ad *BS*. I, 3, 9 (vol. I, p. 275, *l*. 8); III, 2, 11 (vol. II, p. 206,

ll. 1-2).

5) *Vākyap*. III, 3, 41 (p. 116).

PART VI

THE *MĀṆḌŪKYA-KĀRIKĀ*

INTRODUCTION

From the discussion in previous chapters it is clear that the Advaita branch of the Vedānta school had an extremely long historical tradition even before Śaṅkara, which had produced many thinkers and philosophers. But the works of such thinkers have been scattered or lost. We know of them only through fragments quoted in works of later writers. The Advaita school too regards the *Brahma-sūtra* as a fundamental text, but this was because at the time of its formation the authority of the *Brahma-sūtra* was already established and had perforce to be respected even by non-dualists. Moreover, statements in the *sūtra* being extremely simple, the Advaita school was able to explain them in a manner fitting its own views. The actual doctrine of the *Brahma-sūtra* itself is that of the Bhedābheda school, differing considerably from Advaita views. As a pre-Śaṅkara work which clearly presents the Advaita views, there now remains to us only the *Māṇḍūkya-Kārikā*[1].

Of course it is unquestionable that besides the *Māṇḍūkya-Kārikā* there exist many other pre-Śaṅkara works which presented the same type of teachings. Scholars occasionally assert that the *Kārikā* is the only pre-Śaṅkara work[2] which presents Advaita views ; but this is clearly wrong, as can be seen from the numerous sources we have already presented. Further, it cannot be stated that the *Māṇḍūkya-Kārikā* is the oldest work to present the Advaita views. The verses themselves and the early commentaries to them clearly show that the *Kārikā* is based on theories of previous thinkers. For example, *śloka* II.1 states :

> "The wise men explain the illusoriness of all phenomena which occur in dreams."

Śaṅkara glosses the phrase 'the wise men explain' (*āhur manīṣiṇaḥ*) as 'experts in the science of proof say' (*pramāṇakuśalāḥ kathayanti*) ; and Ānandagiri glosses it as : 'the teaching of the ancients says' (*vṛddhasam-matim āha*). It is highly unlikely that these refer to the scholars who studied the old *Upaniṣads*. Hence we may say suppose that the *Kārikā* itself, Śaṅkara and Ānandagiri accept that even before the compilation of the *Kārikā* text there existed Vedānta thinkers who held such views. Further, in *śloka* II,31 there is presented as the words of 'sages well-versed in Vedānata' (*Vedānteṣu vicakṣṇaiḥ*) a statement in words identical to that of the Mādhyamaka school of Buddhism. Thus we must conclude that even before the compilation of the *Kārikā*, there were Vedāntins influenced by Buddhistic thought.

But since there presently exists no independent work earlier than these *Kārikās*, the work is the most important source for clarifying the thought of the early Advaita school. In particular, we must carefully note how it at times presents an extremely systematic and organized exposition, and also on occasion is highly polemical. While absorbing the ideas and being influenced by the thoughts of various schools, it also sharply criticizes and attacks other philosophical standpoints. It profoundly influenced later Indian thought, and in subsequent periods was considered to be itself a *śruti*, thus having an authority equal to that of the *Upaniṣads*. It is not only an extremely important work in the history of the development of Indian thought, but apart from that, the work itself has the sparkle of genius. Very directly and loftily it proclaims with bold assurance that it is the Truth. Certainly it is one of the brilliant lights in the history of human philosophical thought.

The *Māṇḍūkya-Kārikā* consists of 215 *ślokas*, and is completely in verse form (first chapter, 29 ; second chapter, 38 ; third chapter, 48 ; fourth chapter, 100). It is also called the *Gauḍapāda-Kārikā*, and is attributed to Śaṅkara's master Gauḍapāda. Since its authorship and date of compilation have been discussed by many scholars, we shall first present a study in detail of some key *ślokas* and on this basis attempt a unified analysis. Without a complete primary analysis, no integrated theoretical interpretation is possible. Since the *Māṇḍūkya-Kārikā* is inseparably bound to the *Māṇḍūkya-Upaniṣad*, we shall also attempt a simultaneous examination of that. Thus in the first chapter of this Part, we present our analysis on these lines.

Notes

1) Vidhusekhara Bhattacharyya's work was criticized by orthodox scholars for the reason that his interpretations were too Buddhistic. Criticism of this kind was expressed by the following work,— *Gauḍapāda-Kārikā.* Edited with a complete translation into English, Notes, Introduction and Appendices by Raghunath Damodar Karmarkar. Poona, Bhandarkar Oriental Research Institute, 1953. A study of conservative character on Gauḍapāda is T.M.P.Mahadevan: The *Ajātivāda* of Gauḍapāda.(*B.C.Law Commemoration Volume,* part. I, p.308.)

2) Walleser: *DAV.*, S.14.

CHAPTER I

INTERPRETATIONS OF SOME WORDS AND PHRASES OF THE *MĀṆḌŪKYA-UPANIṢAD* AND *KĀRIKĀ*

The *Māṇḍūkya-Upaniṣad* and the *Māṇḍūkya-Kārikā* have been translated in full:

Paul Deussen: *Sechzig Upanishad's des Veda*. Leipzig 1897, S.573-604.

The Māndūkyopanishad with Gaudapāda's Kārikās and the Bhāshya of Śankara, tr. by Manilal N. Dvivedi. Bombay 1909.

Maṇḍūkya Upaniṣad with Gauḍapāda's Kārikā and Śaṅkara's Commentary, tr. by M. Srinivasa Rao. The Vedānta Kesari, Madras, vols. XVIII-XXI (1931-35).

The Māṇḍūkyopaniṣad with Gāuḍapāda's Kārikā and Śaṅkara's Commentary, tr. by Swami Nikhilananda. Maysore 1936.

The Āgamaśāstra of Gauḍapāda, tr. by Vidhushekhara Bhattacharyya. University of Calcutta, 1943.

Māṇḍūkyopaniṣad with Gauḍapādīya-kārikā and Śaṅkara-bhāṣya with a Hindi translation. Gita Press, Gorakhpur (Samvat 1993).

Part of the *Kārikās* was also translated into German:

Max Walleser: *Der ältere Vedānta*. Heidelberg 1910.

In the *Kārikās* there are words which do not appear in the Sanskrit dictionaries; there are also not a few cases where the meanings of words as given in the dictionaries are not applicable to the context of the *Kārikās*. In such cases the examples of these words have to be sought for over a wide range of Sankrit texts, and thereby the meaning has to be ascertained and also the historical associations have to be clarified. For instance, some words which does not appear in the general Sanskrit dictionaries may appear frequently in Buddhist texts, and in this case by an examination of its use there the meaning can be ascertained, and further one knows that this is originally a Buddhist term which has been incorporated into the *Māṇḍūkya-Kārikās*.

When in addition it is found that there were good many examples in the *Kārikās* of words which the ordinary Sanskrit dictionaries are giving as peculiar to Buddhist texts, the connection of the vocabulary with that of Buddhism becomes clear and particularly important.[1]

It was Vidhusekhara Bhattacharyya who brought to light the peculiar words and phrases of the *Kārikās* which show Buddhist influence.[2] His work is full of explanations and parallel passages so that it is needless to repeat the same results. In the following I have been concerned to point out some meanings of words and some parallel passages, which escaped his attention. In order to avoid prolixity I indicate the most noteworthy ones.

Notes

1) In this connection, the relationship between the Vedānta philosophy and Buddhism was discussed by Helmuth von Glasenapp in his *Vedānta and Buddhismus* (Verlag der Akademie der Wiessenschafter und der Literatur in Mainz. Wiesbaden, 1950).

2) See this Part Introduction note 1.

SECTION I. SOME NOTES ON THE VERSE VII OF THE *MĀṆḌŪKYA-UPANIṢAD*

In the Japanese original work I translated all verses of the *Māṇḍūkya-Upaniṣad* with critical annotations. But in the following I propose to comment on the verse VII which seems to be very important to me.

> *nāntaḥprājñaṃ na bahiṣprajñaṃ nobhayataḥprajñaṃ na prajñānaghanaṃ na prajñaṃ nāprajñam adṛṣṭam avyavahāryam agrāhyam alakṣaṇam acintyam avyapadeśyam ekātmapratyayasāraṃ prapañcopaśamaṃ śāntaṃ śivam advaitaṃ caturthaṃ manyante/ sa ātmā sa vijñeyaḥ/ Māṇḍūkya-Upaniṣad*, VII.

This contains words and expressions which are unusual and not found in the old *Upaniṣads* or in Sanskrit literature generally. The negative expressions recall phrases of Buddhist texts. Mere repetitions of negations are already found in *Bṛhadāraṇyaka-Upaniṣad* II,8,8 and in the Jaina scriptures, *Āyārangasutta* I,5,6,4 and elsewhere, but here we can recognize in addition traces of Mahāyāna influence: the doctrine of the Void.

(1) Here "*ayam ātmā* ··· *kṛtsnaḥ prajñānaghana eva*" (*Bṛhad. Up.* IV,5,13) (this self ··· a mass of consciousness alone) which is the concept of the *Bṛhadāraṇyaka-Upaniṣad* is negated. One must say that the concept of

Fourth State established a new standpoint which is an advance on the thought of *Ātman* as "mere consciousness"(consciousness alone).

(2) The notion that the Absolute is not to be seen or not to be experienced is expressed by the word *adṛṣṭa*.[1] There are examples in the Buddhist classics.[2]

(3) *avyavahārya* (not of *vyavahāra* — empirical life) does not appear in the old orthodox Brahmin works ; but in the *Prajñā-pāramitā-sūtra* the principle of the Void is called *avyavahāra*, which Xuan zang (玄奘) translates as "not to be argued about" (*Vajr.Pr*.30).

(4) *agrāhya* (not to be grasped). This word often appears in Buddhist texts.[3]

(5) *alakṣaṇa*. In the Chinese translation of Buddhist texts, this is translated into "without form" and is a very important concept. For instance in the *Madhyānta-vibhāga-śāstra*, the argument is "without form therefore without-I". And one of the three kinds of Non-I is *alakṣaṇa-nairātmya*, and again it is taught that *alakṣaṇa* is *nairātmya* as also frequently in other Buddhist texts.[4] In orthodox Brahmin philosophical works, on the other hand, the word *alakṣaṇa* does not come up as a philosophical concept. Śaṅkara in his note gives *alakṣaṇa* as *alinga* but this is forced interpretation to which there is probably no parallel. If it is taken in the Buddhist sense of "without form" then the interpretation becomes natural.

(6) *acintya*. this is a favorite expression in Chinese Buddhist translation there appearing as meaning "marvelous" or "unthinkable", but it hardly appears in the Vedic texts taken as a whole.

(7) *avyapadeśya* (indescribable). This word is in general used in Indian philosophy but hardly appears in Buddhist classics. Śaṅkara explains it here as *avyapadeśyaṃ śabdaiḥ* (indescribable by words). In the *Brahma-sūtra* commentary Śaṅkara uses this word *avyapadeśya* when setting out the views of the teacher Audolomi about *Ātman* (ad *BS*.vol.II,p.558,*l*.1).

(8) *prapañca upaśamam*. First, the word *prapañca* is used not only in Vedānta philosophy but generally in the orthodox Brahmin philosophical works in the sense of "the expanse of the world" or "the phenomenal world". As against this, in the Buddhist works it is normally translated by a Chinese compound meaning "fruitless verbiage", though there are a few

cases where it is rendered as "falsehood, fiction, fallacy" etc.[5] A number of meanings can be noted in examples of its use in Buddhism.

1. Word, *prapañco vāk* (*Mvṛ*. p.373,*l*.9). *prapañcair aprapañcitam* (*Mvṛ*. p.373,*l*.9).
2. = *nimitta* (*Mvṛ*. p.538,*l*.5).
3. Various phenomena (*Mvṛ*. p.350,*ll*.13-15).
4. Discriminating, *jalpaḥ prapañco vikalpa iti yāvat*. (*AAA*. p.122,*l*.14).
5. Distinguishing variously what should not be distinguished (*MadhyK*. — *TT*. vol.30, p.31 "vain to discuss whether Buddha dies or does not die" and again in *Mahāprajñāpāramitā-sūtra*, number 74 of the one-sided teachings: "deciding whether to define *dharma* as eternal or not eternal is vain verbiage").
6. The original thing giving rise to discriminations (*MadhyK*. XVIII,5).

Thus though the translation is the same, "verbiage", the content of its meaning varies quite a bit according to context.

On the other hand the word *upaśama* (*nirvāṇa*, annihilation) appears very frequently in Buddhist classics.

However the combination of the two words, *prapañcopaśama*, is a most unusual word and it appears that there is no other example in the orthodox Brahmin tradition.[6] It appears in later *Upaniṣads* which resemble this one.[7] But that will be the influence of the *Māṇḍūkya*. This word appears in Nāgārjuna's *Mādhyamika* in the hymn of reverence and in XXV,24. Kumārajīva translates it variously as "right annihilation of all vain talk" or "total extinction of vain talk". This peculiar expression is only known in these two books and we have to recognize in it an indication of the close connection between *Māṇḍūkya-Upaniṣad* and *Kārikās,* on the one hand Mādhyamika and its associated works. It may be that one cannot assert that there was borrowing by the former form the latter, but there seems no doubt that the former received it from Mahāyāna texts. Compare *prapañcasya uparama* (*Mvṛ*.p.11); *prapañcapravilaya* (Ś ad *BS*. III,2,21); *sarvaprapañcopaśamād bhrānto nābhipravartate* (*Laṅk*.X,230. p. 295).

(9) *śānta*. All the words from the root *śam* are frequently found in Indian philosophy generally and in Buddhist works. Here it is associated with the

word *śiva*, but there are similar examples in the Buddhist classics; *śāntaṃ śivaṃ sākṣikuruṣva dharmam* (*Saundarananda*, XVI,26. p.115).

(10) *śivaṃ pariśuddhaṃ paramānandabodharūpam iti yāvat* (Ān. ad *GK*. p. 46, *l*.2). Looking at Buddhist works, we find that Kumārajīva translates *śiva* by "peaceful tranquillity" (*MadhyK*. V,8). Again "pure" (Index to *Laṅk*.), "auspicious" (*Mhvyut*. I,57) and "*nirvāṇa*"[x] were also translations of this word. It is also used as an adjective for *nirvāṇa* and the supreme *bodhi* (*SaddhP*. 130; 290 = XVI,26).

[PARALLELS WITH *MĀDHYAMIKA*]

As far as the author's present researches have gone, the close conjunction of *prapañcopaśamam* with *śiva* is found, in a wide range of books studied, only in the *Mādhyamika-Kārikās* and the *Māṇḍūkya-Upaniṣad* and *Kārikās* — these two works alone.

prapañcopaśamaṃ śāntaṃ śivam advaitaṃ caturtham.../ *Māṇḍ*. *Up*. VII.

amātraś caturtho 'vyavahāryaḥ prapañcopaśamaḥ śivo 'dvaitaḥ.../ *Māṇḍ*. *Up*. XII.

amātro 'ntaramātraś ca dvaitasyopaśamaḥ śivaḥ.../ *GK*.I,12.

....

yaḥ pratītyasamutpādaṃ prapañcopaśamaṃ śivaṃ deśayām āsa.../ *MadhyK*. *maṅgala śloka*.

.....*bhāvānāṃ te na paśyanti draṣṭavyopaśamaṃ śivam*.../ *MadhyK*. V,8.

sarvopalambhopaśamaḥ prapañcopaśamaḥ śivaḥ/ *MadhyK*. XXV,24.ab.

(11) *advaita=bhedavikalparahita* (Śaṅkara). Of the old *Upaniṣads* this word appears only in *Bṛhad*. *Up*. IV,3,32, and instances in old literature are few, but in later Vedānta it became a very important concept. This word on the other hand hardly appears in Buddhist works. In them it is rather *advaya* which is popular.

(12) Calling the ultimate principle the Fourth had occurred before; in *Bṛhad*.*Up*. V,14,3-7 it is *turīya*, and in *Maitri Up*. VI,19; VII,11 and 8, it is called *turya*.

Notes

1) Compare *Bṛhad*. *Up*. II,7,23; III,8,11.

2) Cf. Indices to *Mhvyut.*, *MAVṬ* and *Laṅk.*
3) See Dr. Wogiwara's Sanskrit-Japanese dictionary.
4) See the Sanskrit-Japanese dictionary under *alakṣaṇa.*
5) See index to *Laṅk.*
6) Cf. *PW* ; Jacob : *Concordance* ; Dasguta : *HIP.*. Vol I, p.425.
7) *Nṛsiṃha-Pūrva-Tāpiny-Up.*IV,2 ; *Nṛsiṃhottara-Tāpiny-Up.*I ; *Rāmottara-Tāpiny-Up.*I.
8) Cf. Index to *Daśabhūmika.*

SECTION II. SOME NOTES ON THE *MĀṆḌŪKYA-KĀRIKĀ*

In the following section of the Japanese original work comes a Japanese complete translation of the *Māṇḍūkya-Kārikā*, with critical annotations based upon the commentary by Śaṅkara. But to render them all into English here is unnecessary, inasmuch as some good translations have been published and are now available in the West and India. So this part has been omitted from the English translation of this work.

In the following I propose to comment on some important verses relevant to the account of the thought of Vedānta which will come later.

Sub-Section 1. *Āgama*

I,3. *viśvo hi sthūlabhuṅ nityaṃ taijasaḥ praviviktabhuk/*
ānandabhuk tathā prājñas tridhā bhogaṃ nibodhata//

This verse is cited by Sureśvara in his *Bṛhad.Up.Vārttika* I,4,744 (p.582).

viśvo hi sthūlabhuṅ nityaṃ taijasaḥ praviviktabhuk/
ānandabhuk tathā prājña iti cāgamaśāsanam//

On this Ānandajñāna glosses — "*atrāpi śrutiṃ paṭhati*".

I,5. *triṣu dhāmasu yad bhojyaṃ bhoktā yaś ca prakīrtitaḥ/*
vedaitad ubhayaṃ yas tu sa bhuñjāno na lipyate//

[Parallel Passages]

triṣu dhāmasu yad bhogyaṃ bhoktā yaś ca prakīrtitaḥ/
ubhayaṃ brahma yo veda sa bhuñjāno na lipyate//Sūtasaṃhitā, IV,8,33 (p. 918).

triṣu dhāmasu yad bhogyaṃ bhoktā bhogaś ca yad bhavet/Kaivalya-Up. I,

18).

I,9. *bhogārthaṃ sṛṣṭir ity anye krīḍārtham iti cāpare/*
devasyaiṣa svabhāvo 'yam āptakāmasya kā spṛhā//

"Some say that the world-creation is for the sake of his enjoyment, whereas others say that it is for the sake of his amusement. It is, however, the nature of God, for how can desire be there in one (=God) whose desire has been satisfied?"

The idea that the world-creation is for his enjoyment is set forth in *Bṛhad. Up*. I,4,17 ; *Sāṃkhya-kārikā*, 17 ; *Pañcadaśī*, I,26. *avidyopādher jīvasya bhogārtham īśvaraḥ sṛṣṭyādi karoti*/Śrīdharasvāmin on *Bhāgavata-Purāṇa*, III,7,4. (Bhattacharrya : *AS*. p.294).

Cf. *BS*. II,1,33 ; *Maitri-Up*. VI,1,

Śaṅkara dstinguishes between *Īśvara* or *Brahman*, and *deva*. (Deussen : *SV*. S.68ff.). But in *GK*.(I,9 ; 10 ; II,12 ; 19) *deva* is Overlord, close to *Īśvara* in Śaṅkara's philosophy. In the *Pañcarātrarahasya* also *deva* is synonymous with *Īśvara* (*SDS*. IV, *ll*.308-39). The theory that world-creation is the nature of *deva* is set froth in *Nyāyavārttika*, IV,1,21. Cf. Sāyaṇa ad *Tait.Ār*. VIII,p. 570..

The thought that God is one whose desires are fulfilled (*āptakāma*) is set forth in *Bṛhad.Up*. IV,4,6 ; *Chānd.Up*. VIII,7,1 ; *Śvet.Up*. I,11. Bhartṛprapañca held the same idea. (Ś. ad *Bṛhad.Up*. p.156,*l*.16). Cf. *āptakāmaśruti* (Ś. ad *BS*. II,1,33).

The argument that the *āptakāma* cannot engage in world-creation is set forth in Ś. ad *BS*. II,1,32 (vol.I, p.503,*l*.10f. *pūrvapakṣa*). Cf. *SDS*. XI,*l*.196.

I,17. *prapañco yadi vidyeta nivarteta na saṃśayaḥ/*
māyāmātram idaṃ dvaitam advaitaṃ paramārthataḥ//

"If the phenomenal world were really existing, it would have to cease to exist, no doubt. But the world of duality is mere *māyā*. Viewed from the ultimate truth, it is non-duality."

The latter half of this verse is cited in *Vivekacūḍāmaṇi* 406 as *śruti*.

The term *māyāmātra* is quite often used in works of the Vedānta school. (e. g. *BS*.III,2,3 ; Ś. ad *BS*.II,1,9. vol. I. p.446,*l*.2 ; *Sarvasiddhāntasaṃgraha* XII,

77 ; *Pañcapādikā* p.10,*l*.8 ; *Bṛhad.Up. Vārttika,* II,1,266. p.931). The meaning of this term is heatedly debated by scholars. As the view attributing world-creation to *māyā* is refuted in *GK*.I,7 and the world-cause is in the first chapter of *GK*. regarded as *deva*. The term *māyā* in this verse must have meant "the wonderful power of a god" or "its manifestation", according to the ancient meaning of the word as in the *Vedas*. Madhva interprets *māyā* = *bhagavad-icchā* (*SDS*. V,*l*.122).

prapañca is a word introduced from Buddhism.

I,24. ***oṃkāraṃ pādaśo vidyāt pādā mātrā na saṃśayaḥ/***
oṃkāraṃ pādaśo jñātvā na kiṃcid api cintayet//

[Parallel Passages]

*ātmasaṃsthaṃ manaḥ kṛtvā na kiṃcid api cintayet/Bhag.G.*VI,25.

mano nirviṣayaṃ yuktvā tataḥ kiṃcana na smaret/Bhāgavata-Purāṇa II,1, 19.

Sub-Section 2. ***Vaitathya*** **(Illusoriness)**

II,1. ***vaitathyaṃ sarvabhāvānāṃ svapna āhur maniṣiṇaḥ/***
antaḥsthānāt tu bhāvānāṃ saṃvṛtatvena hetunā//

"The wise teach illusoriness of everything in the dream ; because their existence being covered up [in the veins], [in the dream all] the objects exist in the inner part [of the body]."

The words in brackets are supplied by Śaṅkara. In the second half of the verse, "exist in the inner part"(*antaḥsthāna*) alone would be insufficient as a reason, so covering-concealment (*saṃvṛtatva*) is supplied. Śaṅkara's comment adds that according to the view of an objector, we cannot say that the existence of a jar is false just because it is within a covering, and to explain in the same way that a thing is unreal it is not sufficient simply that it "exists within". The proposed reason, namely, is "*anaikāntika*". So to define the reason more narrowly, Śaṅkara supplies "because it exists covered up in the veins (*nāḍī*) within the body". Thus dream is a phenomenon of the inner part, within the veins, and as the mountains and elephants etc. seen in dream cannot be really within veins, they must be illusory. (So it can be taken that *antahsthāna* is a concept of wider scope than *saṃvṛtatva*.)

Compare *GK*.II,4 ; IV,33 ; *na tāvat svapne rathādīnām ucito deśaḥ saṃbhavati/na hi saṃvṛte dehadeśe rathādayo 'vakāśaṃ labheran*//(Ś. ad *BS*.III, 2,3. vol.II. p.181,*l*.4).

II,2. *adirghatvāc ca kālasya gatvā deśān na paśyati/*
pratibuddhaś ca vai tasmin deśe na vidyate//

The second half is the same as IV,34 and the first half is similar in meaning. Compare Śaṅkara on *BS*.III,2,3 : "It is not possible to conceive that in a moment a sleeping man can reach a place hundreds of miles away and return." *na hi suptasya jantoḥ kṣaṇamātreṇa yojanaśatāntaritaṃ deśaṃ paryetuṃ viparyetuṃ ca tatra sāmarthyaṃ saṃbhāvyate*/(Ś. ad *BS*.III,2,3. vol. II. p.181,*ll*.9-10).

II,3. *abhāvaś ca rathādīnāṃ śrūyate nyāyapūrvakam/*
vaitathyaṃ tena cai prāptaṃ svapna āhuḥ prakāśitam//

This refers to *Bṛhad.Up*.IV,3,10 ; "there are no chariots ..... but he himself makes chariots ...". According to the commentator Puruṣottama, the sacred text referred to is *Bṛhad.Up*.IV,3,14. Cf. V.Bhattacharyya, p.16.

II,4. *antaḥsthānāt tu bhedānāṃ tasmāj jāgarite smṛtam/*
yathā tatra tathā svapne saṃvṛtatve na bhidyate//

Śaṅkara does not give a word-by-word analysis. The objects in the waking state and the objects in the dream states have the common quality of "being seen" (*dṛśyatva*) which proves their illusoriness (*vaitathya*).

na hi saṃvṛte dehadeśe rathādayo 'vakāśaṃ labheran/(Ś. ad *BS*.III,2,3. vol. II. p.181,*l*.4). That the experience of the waking state should also be "covered" (*saṃvṛta*) is absolutely Buddhist. Cf. *saṃvṛtisatya*.

See *GK*.II,1 ; VI,33.

II,5. *svapnajāgarite sthāne hy ekam āhur maniṣiṇaḥ/*
bhedānāṃ hi samatvena prasiddhenaiva hetunā//

On *samatva* Śaṅkara glosses *bhedānām grāhyaghrāhakatva* ; in other words the perceived individual objects have their existence on the basis of the pair perceiver/perceived. The point is that waking and dream are the same in this regard.

Cf. *dve eva sthāne* (*Bṛhad.Up*.IV,3,9).

The doctrine that the waking state and dream state are not different can be seen putting out its first shoots in the *Upaniṣad* (*Bṛhad.Up*.IV,3,14) and it was particularly taught in the Vijñāna-vāda school of Buddhism. For instance, *na hy atītānāgatavartamānānubhave suptasya jāgrataś ca kaścid viśeṣo 'sti* /(*MAVṬ*, p.26.*l*.14). In later Vedānta and in the Grammarians who were influenced by Vedānta, the doctrine was taught. See *SDS*.XIII,*ll*. 269-270. In *Nyāya-sūtra* IV,2,31 the doctrine is presented and attacked.

II,6. *ādāv ante ca yan nāsti vartamāne 'pi tat tathā/*
vitathaiḥ sadṛśāḥ santo 'vitathā iva lakṣitāḥ//

The word *avitatha* is hardly used in orthodox Brahmanical texts (Cf. *PW*.). But in Buddhism it is frequently used from the time of the Pālī scriptures.

[Parallel Passages]

The first part of this verse occurs in *Yogavāsiṣtha* IV,45,45 and Śaṅkara uses the same argument. *pradhānapuruṣeśvarāṇāṃ caivam antavattve saty ādimattvaprasaṅgaḥ ādyantavattve ca śūnyavādaprasaṅgaḥ*/(Ś. ad *BS*.II,2,41. vol. I. p.608,*l*.8). Still, for the final proof in Śaṅkara's comment to *BS*.III,2, 3, see *Bhāgavata-Purāṇa* X, b 28,21.

The doctrine can be traced back to the *Mādhyamika-kārikā* XI,2 ; *naivāgraṃ nāvaraṃ yasya madhyaṃ tasya kuto bhavet*/(*MadhyK*.XI,2). "As there are no beginning and end, how could there be a middle ?" In the XIth chapter of the *MadhyK*. the fact that there is no beginning or end in *saṃsāra* is treated in detail. Bhattacharyya points out similar phrases in Jaina classics (Bhattacharyya : *AS*. p.142).

yassa n'atthi purā pacchā majjhaṃ tassa kuo siyā/*Āyāraṅga* I,4,4,3.
ādāv ante ca yan nāsti madhye 'pi ca na tat tathā/*Nayopadeśa* 14.

II,7. *saprayojanatā teṣāṃ svapne vipratipadyate/*
tasmād ādyantavattvena mithyaiva khalu te smṛtāḥ//

Bhattacharyya reads *svapne 'pi pratipadyate* without manuscript support.

According to Śaṅkara, food and drink satisfy man's hunger and thirst, and serve a purpose as an actual operation like the comings and goings of chariots etc.

The contradiction is for instance that a man goes to sleep after satisfying hunger and thirst, yet suffers them in a dream.

II,8. ***apūrvāḥ sthānidharmā hi yathā svarganivāsinām/***
tān ayaṃ prekṣate gatvā yathaiveha suśikṣitaḥ//

According to Śaṅkara, this is in answer to the objection that there are extraordinary experiences in dream which are never met in the waking state, and therefore the states are distinguishable. The answer is that these "extraordinary" or "miraculous" experiences are manifestations out of the state of the dreaming person, and so not extraordinary or miraculous at all. They are like the thousand eyes possessed by the god Indra in heaven. So the argument that experiences of dream are extraordinary but those of waking are real cannot be established. Examples of dream experiences are that one rides on an elephant with four tusks and eight legs.

II,9. ***svapnavṛttāv api tv antaścetasā kalpitaṃ tv asat/***
bahiścetogṛhītaṃ sad dṛṣṭaṃ vaitathyam etayoḥ//

bahiścetogṛhītam = *bahiścetasā gṛhītam* = *cakṣurādidvāreṇa upalabdham* (Śaṅkara). Cf. *bahiṣprajña* (*Māṇḍu.Up*. III).

II,10. ***jāgradvṛttāv api tv antaścetasā kalpitaṃ tv asat/***
bahiścetogṛhītaṃ sad yuktaṃ vaitathyam etayoḥ//

Cf. *GK*.IV,63-66.

II,11. ***ubhayor api vaitathyaṃ bhedānāṃ sthānayor yadi/***
ka etān budhyate bhedān ko vai teṣāṃ vikalpakaḥ//

The "one who can discriminate (*vikalpaka*)" means the Creator (=*nirmātṛ*) according to the commentators Ānandajñāna and Mitākṣarā. It can probably be also understood as one who discriminates in this thought.

Śaṅkara takes the verse as the words of questioner (*codaka*). If there is no subject to discriminate the individual things, it means a fall into the error of "Non-I" doctrine (*nirātmavāda*). To this, the next verse gives the answer that the subject is God the *Ātman*.

In the *Mādhyamika-kārikā* a similar difficulty appears (V,6):

"Again, when existence does not exist, of what can there be non-existence? And is there someone different from existence and non-existence to know existence and non-existence?"

But in the *Mādhyamika-kārikās*, after arguing that no discriminable object can be established, it says that no discriminator can be established either, and without discriminator nor discriminated, it is an ultimate void (*śūnya*). All this comes down to the distinction of the standpoints of doctrine of an "I" (Vedānta) and doctrine of "No-I" (Mahāyāna Buddhism).

II,14. ***cittakālāś ca ye 'ntas tu dvayakālāś ca ye bahiḥ/***
kalpitā eva te sarve viśeṣo nānyahetukaḥ//

Śaṅkara admits two kinds of time: (1)*cittakāla*, i.e., *kalpanākāla* that applies and operates within one's mind. (2)*dvayakāla*, i.e., *bhedakāla*, measurable time, which can be measured as 'that much (*tāvad*)' or 'this much (*etāvad*)'. The former is limited by mind (*cittaparicchedya*), whereas the latter is delimited mutually by objects (*anyonyaparicchedya*), and limited by two time-points (*kāladvayāvacchedena kṛtaḥ*, Ān.). The former is relevant to the stream of consciousness alone, the latter is the time that is measured in the objective, natural world. In Jaina works *Davvasaṃgraha*(21), *Pañcāstikāyasamayasāra and Prameyakamalamārtaṇḍa*(p.168), two kinds of time are recognized also.

V.Bhattacharyya (*AS*.pp.24-25) takes *dvaya* as meaning *grāhya* and *grāhaka*, based upon the use of this word in the fourth chapter of *GK*., which must be influenced by *Vijñānavāda* of Buddhism. But the second chapter of *GK*. must be examined separately from the fourth chapter of *GK*.

II,16. ***jivaṃ kalpayate pūrvaṃ tato bhāvān pṛthagvidhān/***
bāhyān ādhyātmikāṃś caiva yathāvidyas tathāsmṛtiḥ//

The commentary *Mitākṣarā* says on this verse: — *ataḥ sṛṣṭer vaiṣamyatve dharmādikāraṇasadbhāvān naikarasyam/yathākarma yathāśrutam iti śravaṇād ity arthaḥ*/"The Supreme Lord, considering the knowledge and *karman* of each individual soul in the previous *kalpa*, creates all the souls in accordance with them". Cf.*Bṛhad.Up*.IV,4,2; *BS*.II,1,34; II,3,42; III,4,11.

II,17. ***aniścitā yathā rajjur andhakāre vikalpitā/***
sarpadhārādibhir bhāvais tadvad ātmā vikalpitaḥ//

This *Kārikā* is quoted in *Bṛhad.Up. Vārttika* of Sureśvara, I,4. as a saying of Gauḍapāda.

II,18. ***niścitāyāṃ yathā rajjvāṃ vikalpo vinivartate/***
rajjur eveti cādvaitaṃ tadvad ātmaviniścayaḥ//

This four *Kārikās* II,17 ; 18 ; 19 ; 20 are quoted in the *Madhyamakālaṅkāra* of the Buddhist Śāntarakṣita. The snake-rope analogy was adopted from Buddhism.

The snake-rope analogy was adopted from Buddhism. It often appears in Vijñānavāda works and in the fundamental Mahāyāna scriptures (e. g. *Laṅkāvatāra-sūtra*) and latter Hīnayāna (e. g. *Abhidharmakośavyākhyā*) and Mādhyamika works (e. g. *Mādhyamikavṛtti*).

It seems that it was taught everywhere and all the time in Buddhism. It also appears in works like *Bhagavat-purāṇa*, though it is not clear whether this was direct from Buddhism or by way of Vedānta. Bhartṛhari opposed this way of explaining the phenomenal world (*Vākyap.* II,290).

II,19. ***prāṇādibhir anantais tu bhāvair etair vikalpitaḥ/***
māyaiṣā tasya devasya yayāyaṃ mohitaḥ svayam//

[Parallel Passages]

vādibhir darśanaiḥ sarvair dṛśyate yat tv anekadhā/
vedāntavedyaṃ brahmedam ekarūpam upāsmahe//

Sarvasiddhāntasaṃgraha I,1.

nirguṇo 'pi hy ajo 'vyakto bhagavān prakṛteḥ paraḥ/
svamāyāguṇam āviśya bādhyabādhakatāṃ gataḥ//

Bhāgavatapurāṇa VII,1,6 (ed. Burnouf).

mohayatīvātmānaṃ svamāyayā dvaitarūpayā devaḥ/
upalabhate svayam evaṃ guhāgataṃ puruṣam ātmānam//

Ādiśeṣa's *Paramārthasāra* v.32.

II,31. ***svapnamāye yathā dṛṣṭe gandharvanagaraṃ yathā/***
tathā viśvam idaṃ dṛṣṭaṃ vedānteṣu vicakṣaṇaiḥ//

[Parallel Passages]

yathā māyā yathā svapno gandharvanagaraṃ yathā/
tathotpādas tathā sthānaṃ tathā bhaṅga udāhṛtam//MadhyK.VII,34.
kleśāḥ karmāṇi dehāś ca kartāraś ca phalāni ca/
gandharvanagarākārā marīcisvapnasaṃnibhāḥ//MadhyK.XVII,33.
rūpaśabdarasasparśā gandhā dharmāś ca kevalāḥ/
gandharvanagarākārā marīcisvapnasaṃnibhāḥ//MadhyK.XXIII,8.
alātacakranirmāṇasvapnamāyāmbucandrakaiḥ/
dhūmikāntaḥpratiśrutikāmarīcyabhraiḥ samo bhavaḥ//
Catuḥśatikā XIII,800, p.503.
gandharvanagarasvapnamāyānirmāṇasādṛśāḥ/LaṅK., p.283,*l*.13.
māyāsvapnanibhā bhāvā gandharvanagaropamāḥ/LaṅK., p.374,*l*.12.
yathaiva gandharvapuraṃ marīcikā yathaiva māyā supinaṃ yathaiva/
svabhāvaśūnyā tu nimittabhāvanā tathopamān jānatha sarvadharmān//
Samādhirāja. (ed. Calcutta, 1896. p.38.)

Referring to the theory of Buddhists, Śaṅkara says: *yathā hi svapnamāyāmarīcyudakagandharvanagarādipratyayā vinaiva bāhyenārthena grāhyagrāhakākārā bhavanti*/(ad. *BS*.II,2,28).

II,32. *na nirodho na cotpattir na baddho na ca sādhakaḥ/*
na mumukṣur na vai mukta ity eṣā paramārthatā//

Śaṅkara recognized *sādhakāvasthā* (ad. *BS*.III,3,28. vol.II, p.320).

paramārthatā is originally the term of Buddhism and has the same meaning as *śūnyatā* (*MAV*. p.49,*l*.17. Cf. p.50,*l*.20).

[Parallel Passages]

sa(=utpanna-bodhicittaḥ) sarvadharmān anutpannān aniruddhān abaddhān amuktān atamo'ndhakārān aprakāśān paśyati/SaddhP. p.127,*ll*.10-11.

dṛṣṭaṃ hi tathāgatena traidhātukaṃ yathābhūtaṃ na jāyate na mriyate na cyavate nopapadyate na saṃsarati na parinirvāti na bhūtaṃ nābhūtaṃ na santaṃ nāsantaṃ na tathā nānyathā na vitathā nāvitathā/SaddhP. p.271.

na san na cāsan na tathā na cānyathā na jāyate vyeti na cāvahīyate/
na vardhate nāpi viśudhyate punar viśudhyate tat paramārthalakṣaṇam//
MSA.VI,1.

na badhyate na mucyate udayavyayadharmiṇaḥ/

saṃskārāḥ pūrvavat sattvo badhyate na na mucyate/*MadhyK*.XVI,5.

tad uktam abhiyuktaiḥ

dṛśis tu śuddho 'ham avikriyātmako/

na me 'sti bandho na ca me vimokṣaḥ//

Vedāntasāra, 210 (ed. Böhtlingk). Cf. *Vivekacūḍāmaṇi*, 503.

baddho mukta iti vyākhyā guṇato me, na vastutaḥ/

guṇasya māyāmūlatvān na me mokṣa na bandhanam//

Bhāgavata-purāṇa, XI,11,1.

na bandho 'sti na mokṣo 'sti nābandho 'sti na bandhanam/

aprabodhād idaṃ duḥkhaṃ prabodhāt pravilīyate//*Yogavāsiṣṭha*, IV,38,22.

II,35. *vitarāgabhayakrodhair munibhir vedapāragaiḥ*/

***nirvikalpo hy ayaṃ dṛṣṭaḥ prapañcopaśamo 'dvayaḥ*//**

The term "*advaya*" and "*prapañcopaśama*" are originally the term of Buddhism. Cf. *Māṇḍ.Up*. VII.

[Parallel Passages]

aparapratyayaṃ śāntaṃ prapañcair aprapañcitam/

nirvikalpam anānārtham etat tattvasya lakṣaṇam//(*MadhyK*. XVIII,9.)

II,36. *tasmād evaṃ viditvainam advaite yojayet smṛtim*/

***advaitaṃ samanuprāpya jaḍaval lokam ācaret*//**

"*jaḍaval lokam ācaret*". This ideal was formerly advocated by ascetics of early Buddhism.

Cf. *yathā jaḷo ca mūgo ca attānaṃ dassaye tathā*/

nātivelaṃ pabhāseyya saṃghamajjhamhi paṇḍito//

(*Theragāthā*, 582.)

[Parallel Passages]

ātmārāmo 'nanyavṛttyā vicarej jaḍavan muniḥ/

Bhāgavata-purāṇa, XI,11,17. (Cf. XI,11,16.)

gūḍhadharmāśrito vidvān ajñātacaritaṃ caret/

andhavaj jaḍavac cāpi mūkavac ca mahīṃ caret//

Vasiṣṭha-smṛti. (Cf. V.Bhattacharyya : *AG*. p.301).

Cf. *tasmād brāhmaṇaḥ pāṇḍityaṃ nirvidya bālyena tiṣṭhāset*/

Bṛhad.Up. III,5. (Cf. *Jābāla-Up*. VI).

II,37. ***niḥstutir nirnamaskāro niḥsvadhākāra eva ca/***
calācalaniketaś ca yatir yādṛcchiko bhavet//

calācala. Śaṅkara interprets this as *cala=śarīra, acala=ātmatattva.* However, this may be a reduplication of *cal-*. Cf. *bhavābhava, Suttanipāta,* 1068 etc.; *Udānavarga,* III,7. Native grammarians explained it as "*cal+āk+cal+ac>calācala−* (*Pāṇ.* VI,1,12. *Vārttika,*6)"; some modern linguists explain that the final vowel of the first member of the compound has been prolonged. Cf. Geiger, *Pāli.Lit. u. Spr.* §33. There are also some other explanations. (I owe this information to Prof. Hisashi Matumura.)

[Literature]

W. Stede: *Zeitschrift für Buddhismus,* VI, S.92f.

Debrunner's *Nachträge zu Wackernagel's Altindische Grammatik,* II-1, 148,5.

F. Edgerton: *BHSG,* §§23.12-13.

Speyer: *ZDMG.*65, S.316.

K. Hoffmann: *KZ.* 76 (1960), S.248.

[Parallel Passages]

nirdvandvo nirnamaskāro niḥsvadhākāra eva ca/

Nāradaparivrājaka-Up. 75.

idam antaraṃ jñātvā sa paramahaṃsa ākāśāmbaro, na namaskāro na svāhākāro na nindā na stutir yādṛcchiko bhavet, sa bhikṣuḥ/

Paramahaṃsa-Up.

na ..... namaskāro na svāhākāro na svadhākāraś ca ... nindāstutivyatirikto .../Paramahaṃsa-Parivrājaka-Up.

ni[ḥ]stutir nirnamaskāraḥ parityajya śubhāśubhe/
araṇye vicaraikākī yena kenacid āśitaḥ//

MBh. XII,242, v.9. Cf. *MBh,* XII,263, v.34.

II,38. ***tattvam ādhyātmikaṃ dṛṣṭvā tattvaṃ dṛṣṭvā tu bāhyataḥ/***
tattvībhūtas tadārāmas tattvād apracyuto bhavet//

Cf. *tattvabhāva* (*Śvet.Up.* I,10).

Cf. *ātmārāma* (*Bhāgavata-Purāṇa,* XI,11,7).

ātmaratir ātmakrīḍa ātmamithuna ātmānandaḥ ..../

*Chānd.Up.*VII,25,2.

[Parallel Passages]

śūnyam ādhyātmikaṃ paśya paśya śūnyaṃ bahirgatam/
na vidyate so 'pi kaścid yo bhāvayati śūnyatām//

Mvṛ. p.348,*ll.*11-12. (Cf. ibid., p.340,*l.*7).

Sub-Section 3. *Advaita*

III,4. *ghaṭādiṣu pralīneṣu ghaṭākāśādayo yathā/*
ākāśe saṃpralīyante tadvaj jīvā ihātmani//

[Parallel Passages]

ghaṭe bhinne ghaṭākāśa ākāśe syād yathā purā/
evaṃ dehe mṛte jīvo brahma saṃpadyate punaḥ//

Bhāgavata-Purāṇa, XII,5,5.

III,15. *mṛllohavisphuliṅgādyaiḥ sṛṣṭir yā coditā 'nyathā/*
upāyaḥ so 'vatārāya nāsti bhedaḥ kathaṃcana//

[Parallel Passages]

tat tathaiva samāśritya sādhyasādhanasaṃsthitiḥ/
paramārthāvatārāya vidvadbhir avakalpyate/Pramāṇavārttika.
lokāvatāraṇārthaṃ ca bhāvā nārthena deśitāḥ/BCA. IX,7.
ata eva lokāvatāropāyatvāt sadasadādideśanānām ..../

Catuḥśatikā, VIII,192. (p.478.)

upāya eṣo varadasya jñāne praveśanārthāya nidarśito me/SaddhP. p.42.

This opinion was inherited by Śaṅkara; *api ca parasmin brahmaṇi cittāvatāropāyamātratvenaite* [*dharmāḥ*] *parikalpyante na draṣṭavyatvena*/(Ś. ad *BS*. III,3,13. vol.II, p.274).

III,16. *āśramās trividhā hīnamadhyamotkṛṣṭadṛṣṭayaḥ/*
upāsanopadiṣṭeyaṃ tadartham anukampayā//

[Parallel Passages]

hīnotkṛṣṭamadhyama (*SaddhP*. p.116,*l.*22. Cf. ibid. p.316,*l.*7).

hīnotkṛṣṭamadhyamayogayogibhiḥ (*Laṅkāvatāra*, p.45,*l.*12. Cf. p.31,*l.*1; p. 347,*l.*9).

hīna, madhyama, udāra (*SaddhP*. p.309,*l.*2).

hīna, madhyama, uttama (*Bodhis*. p.57,*l*.2).
hīna, madhya, viśi[illegible] (*Laṅkāvatāra*, p.117,*l*.9).

III,20. ***ajātasyaiva bhāvasya jātim icchanti vādinaḥ/***
ajāto hy amṛto bhāvo martyatāṃ katham eṣyati//

The refutation of the theory of origination (*jāti=utpatti*) is set forth in *Tattvasaṃgraha*, v.140.

[Parallel Passages]

yasmāc ca tad anutpannaṃ na tasmād vipraṇaśyati/(*MadhyK*. XVII,21.)

III,21. ***na bhavaty amṛtaṃ martyaṃ na martyam amṛtaṃ tathā/***
prakṛter anyathābhāvo na kathaṃcid bhaviṣyati//

The term *anyathābhāva* is not used so often in Brahmanic literature (Cf. *PW*.), but quite often in Buddhist works. (Cf. *Mvṛ*. p.145, n.1 ; *MadhyK*. XIII, 3-6 ; XV,5 ; *Laṅkāvatāra*. p.76, *l*.4 ; p.159,*l*.6 ; etc.).

[Parallel Passages]

yady astitvaṃ prakṛtyā syān na bhaved asya nāstitā/
prakṛter anyathābhāvo na hi jātūpapadyate//

MadhyK. XV,8. (Cf. XV,2). (Cf. *Tarkajvālā* ad VIII,50).

In Vedānta works also,

svarūpasyānapāyāt/(Ś. ad *BS*.III,2,7. vol.I. p.194,*l*.11.)
agnyauṣṇyavat svabhāvasyāparihāryatvāt/
(Ś. ad *BS*.IV,3,14. vol.II, p.546,*l*.3 ; Cf. *SDS*.XVI, *l*.44).

Cf. *tad api nityaṃ yasmiṃs tattvaṃ na vihanyate*/
Patañjali : *Mahābhāṣya*, vol.I, p.7.*l*.22.

III,22. ***svabhāvenāmṛto yasya bhāvo gacchati martyatām/***
kṛtakenāmṛtas tasya kathaṃ sthāsyati niścalaḥ//

The same argumentation is set froth in *GK*.IV,8 and *Tattvasaṃgraha*, v. 130,ab.

III,27. ***sato hi māyayā janma yujyate na tu tattvataḥ/***
tattvato jāyate yasya jātaṃ tasya hi jāyate//

[Parallel Passages]

sataś cotpattir iṣṭā cej janitaṃ janayed ayaṃ/
Sarvasiddhāntasaṃgraha, IV.a,8.
saṃbhavaḥ kriyate yasya prāk so 'stīti na yujyate/
sato yadi bhavej janma jātasyāpi bhaved bhavaḥ//*Catuḥśatikā*, XI,257.
viruddhe cet phalaṃ hetau hetoḥ saṃkramaṇaṃ bhavet/
pūrvajātasya hetoś ca punarjanma prasajyate//*MadhyaK*.XX,9.

III,28. ***asato māyayā janma tattvato naiva yujyate/***
vandhyāputro na tattvena māyayā vāpi jāyate//

The simile of *vandhyāputra* is not found in pre-Śaṅkara Brahmanical literature, but quite often in Buddhist works:

vandhyāputra — *Laṅk*. pp.19,*l*.7; 104,*l*.10; 160,*l*.3; 188,*ll*.1-5; 371,*l*.3; *Mvṛ*. p.528,*l*.6; 591,*ll*.2-3.
vandhyāputravat — *MAVṬ*. pp.224,*l*.7; 234,*l*.15; 235,*l*.11; 241,*l*.8.
vandhyāyāḥ putra — *Laṅk*. pp.105.*l*.17; 322,*l*.5.
vandhyāsuta — *Mhvyut*. p.139,*l*.18; *Laṅk*. p.85,*l*.6. (Cf. p.266,*l*.11); p. 267,*l*.4.
vandhyāsūnu — *Mvṛ*. p.287,*l*.16.
vandhyātanaya — *Mvṛ*. p.578,*l*.5.
vandhyāduhitṛ — *Mvṛ*. p.350,*l*.19.
vandhyāprasūyata — *Laṅk*. p.9,*l*.2.
vandhyaurasa — *Laṅk*. p.96,*l*.14; p.289,*l*.13.
yathā vandhyā strī svatanayena nāpekṣyate — *Mvṛ*. p.382,*l*.14.

III,29. ***yathā svapne dvayābhāsaṃ spandate māyayā manaḥ/***
tathā jāgrad dvayābhāsaṃ spandate māyayā manaḥ//

dyayābhāsa is a peculiarly technical term of *Vijñānavāda*. It means "the object"(*grāḥya*) and "the subject"(*grāhaka*) of cognition.

svadhātuto dvayābhāsāḥ sāvidyākleśavṛttayaḥ/*MSA*. XI,32.
dvayābhāsā iti grāhyagrāhakābhāsāḥ/Comm.
advayābhāsa — *MSA*. XI,33 (*na punar dvayābhāsāḥ*, Comm.).
dvayābhāsatā — *MSA*. XI,22.
Cf. *dvayaprabhāsa* — *MSA*. XI,34; *MAVṬ*. p.227,*l*.14 (= *dvayapratibhāsa* = *grāhyapratibhāsaṃ grāhakapratibhāsaṃ ca*/Comm. ad *MSA*.

XI,34).

dvayena pratibhāsatvam — *MAVṬ*. p.217,*l*.20 ; p.219,*l*.23.

Śaṅkara interprets in the same way :

grāhyagrāhakarūpeṇa dvayābhāsaṃ spandate/
jātaṃ ghanaspandakramān manaḥ — *Yogavāsiṣṭha*, IV,44,17. (Dasgupta : *HIPh*. vol.II, p.235).

III,31. ***manodṛśyam idaṃ dvaitaṃ yat kiṃcit sacarācaram/***
manaso hy amanībhāve dvaitaṃ naivopalabhyate//

It is likely that *cara* means animals (*jaṅgama*), and *acara* means plants (*sthāvara*).

manodṛśyam = *manasā vikalpyamānena dṛśyam*. (Ś.) Cf. *cittadṛśya*, *GK*. IV, 28 ; 36 ; 77.

The term *amanībhāva* is mentioned in *Maitri-Up*.VI,34. Cf. *amanastā*, *GK*. III,32. In *Yogavāsiṣṭha* it is mentioned as *unmanībhāva* (Cf. Parallel passages mentioned below). The thought that *manas* should be negated ultimately is in common with the *Vijñānavāda* philosophy. In a Vedānta work, written in Prakrit, *unmanī*, the fifth *avasthā* is mentioned in addition to *jāgṛti*, *svapna*, *suṣupti*, *turīyā*. It is probably a feminine noun made from the adjective *unmana*. Whether it should be admitted or not is heatedly debated in a work by the twelfth century philosophical poet Mukundarāja (*Vivekasindhu*, III, 31 ; VI,87-90. Jacob : *Hindu Pantheism*, pp.61-62.)

[Parallel Passages]

manodṛśyam idaṃ sarvaṃ yat kiṃcit sacarācaram/
manaso hy unmanībhāvād dvaitaṃ naivopalabhyate//
Yogavāsiṣṭha (Cf. Radhakrishnan : *IPh*. vol.II, p.581, n.1).

manaḥ sṛjate vaidehān guṇān karmāṇi cātmanaḥ/
tan manaḥ sṛjate māyā tato jīvasya saṃsṛtiḥ//Bhāgavatapurāṇa, XII,5,6.

III,32. ***ātmasatyānubodhena na saṃkalpayate yadā/***
amanastāṃ tadā yāti grāhyābhāve tadagraham//

[Parallel Passages]

avidyamāne bhāve ca kasyābhāvo bhaviṣyati/
bhāvābhāvavidharmā ca bhāvābhāvam avaiti kaḥ//MadhyK.V,6.

na ca bhāvābhāvavisadṛśadharmā kaścit tṛtīyaḥ padārtho 'sti yo 'nayor avagamaka iti nāsti bhāvābhāvayoḥ parīkṣakaḥ/ Mvṛ. p.133.
vijñānam api nāsty eva jñeyābhāve samutthite/
ato mādhyamiko vakti sarvaśūnyaṃ vicāritam//
Sarvasiddhāntasaṃgraha, IV, a, 17.
nāsti cāsyārthas tadabhāvāt tad (=vijñānam) apy asat/ MAV. I,3.
yadā tv ālambanaṃ jñānaṃ naivopalabhate tadā/
sthitaṃ vijñānamātratve grāhyābhāve tadagrahāt//
Triṃśikā, XXVIII. (Cf. *Laṅk.* p.169.)

III,38. ***graho na tatra notsargaś cintā yatra na vidyate/***
ātmasaṃsthaṃ tadā jñānam ajāti samatāṃ gatam//
[Parallel Passages]
aprahīṇam asaṃprāptam ...... etan nirvāṇam ucyate/ MadhyK. XXV,3.
kāraṇavyatirekeṇa yadā kāryaṃ na vidyate/
pravṛttiś ca nivṛttiś ca tadā naivopapadyate// Catuḥśatikā, XV,350. p.513.
nāpaneyam ataḥ kiṃcit prakṣeptavyaṃ na kiṃcana/
draṣṭavyaṃ bhūtato bhūtaṃ bhūtadarśī vimucyate// MAVṬ. p.29.
Cf. *Bodhisattvabhūmi*, p.266.

III,39. ***asparśayogo vai nāma durdarśaḥ sarvayogibhiḥ/***
yogino bibhyati hy asmād abhaye bhayadarśinaḥ//
"What is called 'contactless concentration' is very difficult to be realized by all *yogins* ; the *yogins* shrink from it, seeing fear in what is not to be feared".

V.Bhattacaryya reads the first *pada asparśayogo namaisa.*

This verse is cited by Vidyāraṇya in his *Pañcadaśī* II,29.

The term *bhayadarśin* is Buddhistic. Cf. *Mahāvyutpatti* 126,61. *GK.* IV, 42.

In the third chapter, the ultimate objective is negation of *manas*, and the practice for it — *asparśayoga* — is given in detail.

In the fourth chapter, the teaching on practice is very different from the view of the Śaṅkara school. According to the latter, what is essential for liberation is to realize directly in the self that *Brahman* = "*ātman*" ; since

Brahma-realization is simply a function of recognition, no special laborious endeavour is needed. So Advaita commentators could not accept the doctrine of the *Kārikās* as it stood. According to the commentator Śaṅkara, liberation must be for each individual *svabhāvata eva siddha* or already attained, and Ānandajñāna comments:

> "In the sun itself there is neither day nor night, but according to the conception of a rising and setting [of the sun], day and night are thought to occur. In the same way, when *Brahman* is considered in itself, it is neither consciousness nor non-consciousness, but according to the *upādhi*, both are thought to be in it." (ad *GK*. III,36)

So all already have liberation; but for *yogis* of inferior or lower nature (*yogino ... hīnamadhyamadṛṣṭayaḥ*) liberation arises on the basis of control of *manas*.

Ānandajñāna is explaining this *asparśayoga* borrows Yoga terms, saying that by practice of *samprajñātasamādhi* one comes to unity facing the supreme *Brahman*, and by *asamprajñātasamādhi* he is one with the highest *Brahman*.

V.Bhattacaryya sees this *asparśayoga* as the same as Buddhist *samādhi*, in which there is complete extinction of sensation and thought(*AS*. p.94). But since the word *asparśayoga* is not found in Buddhist texts, the identification may be premature. The word does not appear in the *Upaniṣads* nor in the Yoga books, nor in Sanskrit dictionaries.

In a Sanskrit commentary on the latter Buddhist text *Bauddha Gana O Doha* (Sahityapariṣad Granthāvalī, 55, p.19), *asparśayoga* is referred to. and the Tibetan translation *Mi-reg-pahi sbyor-ba* was probably *asparśayoga* (Bhattacharyya). Some phrases of Āryadeva might be thought to have some connection, but as they deal with the illogicality of a conjunction between what can be touched (*sparśavat*) and what cannot be touched (*asparśavat*), there is no direct connection (Āryadeva's *Catuḥśatika*, v.308).

III,41. ***utseka udadher yadvat kuśāgreṇaikabindunā/***
manaso nigrahas tadvad bhaved aparikhedataḥ//

utseka udadher .... kuśāgreṇaikabindunā — This simile was adopted from Buddhism. Cf. *Dhammapada* LXX; *Sukhāvatīvyūha* XIII; T'ang version of the *Gaṇḍavyūhasūtra* (Taisho Tripiṭaka, vol. X, p.424).

III,44. *laye saṃbodhayec cittaṃ vikṣiptaṃ śamayet punaḥ/*
sakaṣāyaṃ vijāniyāt samaprāptaṃ na cālayet//

[Parallel Passages]

līnaṃ cittasya gṛhṇīyād uddhataṃ śamayet punaḥ/
śamaprāptam upekṣeta tasminn ālambane punaḥ//MSA. XIV,9-10.

Sub-Section 4. *Alātaśānti*

IV,1. *jñānenākāśakalpena dharmān yo gaganopamān/*
jñeyābhinnena saṃbuddhas taṃ vande dvipadāṃ varam//

"The one who, through wisdom which is like space and not to be separated from the known, rightly is aware of all the phenomena which are like space, I worship as the highest among men."

This is the verse of adoration, the *maṅgalācaraṇa* generally attached to a Sanskrit work, and one observes the markedly Buddhist flavour, a flavour of the whole chapter.

"Wisdom which is like space..." : This idea is probably borrowed from Buddhism. In Buddhist works it is emphasized that the mind is like space. Cf. *Madhyamakavṛtti*, p.518, *l*.3-4 ; *Bodhicaryāvatārapañjikā* (Poussin) p.277, *l*. 13 ; *Mahāvyutpatti* XXX,19.

"Known ..." : In the ideas of the fourth chapter, particularly the *vijñāna* (consciousness-only) doctrine, the known cannot have independent existence apart from knowledge. So knowledge cannot be "separated" (*abhinna*) from the known. The meaning of *jñeya* (known) seems to be somewhat different from the meaning in III,47. Śaṅkara glosses it as *jñeyair dharmair ātmabhiḥ* — but there are no other instances of this and it is forced.

"*dharma*" : Compare *Laṅkāvatāra*, p.203, *l*.8-9, where the *dharmas* are likened to space.

"*saṃbuddha*" : Śaṅkara renders it as *īśvara*, the highest Lord. But there are no instances of Indian divinities being called "*saṃbuddha*." On the other hand, the Buddha is called "*saṃbuddha*" in Buddhist texts (*Madhyamaka-Kārikā*, *maṇgalācaraṇa* XVII,12 ; *Mahāyānasūtrālaṅkāra* XI,3 ; 6 ; 54). Again "*buddha*" appears six times in Chapter IV (verses 19, 42, 80, 88, 98, 99). Of these, verse 98 and "*ādi-buddha*" in verse 92 are simply adjectives; ruling these out, all the others are used as special appellations. Śaṅkara renders as: *paṇḍita* (19), *advaitavādin* (42), *paramārthadarśin* (80, 99), *paramārthadarśin brahmavid* (88). So he takes one who has realized the truth as being called *buddha*. But since calling such a man *buddha* is a special point of Buddhism, one has to take this as a case of Buddhist influence. In fact there is really no reason not to take it as indicating the Buddha. It is a very interesting fact that in the *Kārikās* only in the fourth chapter does the word "*buddha*" appear frequently, and "*budh*" as a verb often appears too (75, 78, 79, 100). Śaṅkara in IV,19 glosses *buddha* as the *paṇḍits* of other sects who dispute among themselves, but it need not be taken in this way. Here too there is no obstacle to taking it as one who has realized truth.

"*dvipadāṃ varam*" : The meaning is "he who has surpassed all beings with two legs (=human beings)." Śaṅkara gives it as *puruṣottama* and understands it as referring to *Nārāyaṇa*. In the Epics, heroes are called by this phrase, but in Buddhism it is an appellation of the Buddha. Cf. *dvipadottama* (*SaddhP*. p.10, *l*.9; p.21, *l*.16; p.24, *l*.8; p.55, *l*.21; p.66, *l*.11; p.118, *l*.21; p.132, *l*.6, 11; p.136, *l*.9; p.139, *l*,6; p.150, *l*.14; p.151, *l*.9; p.171, *l*.26; p.183, *l*.15; p.257. *l*.28; p,260, *l*.7.); *dvipadānam uttama* (*SaddhP*. p.35, *l*.15; p.51, *l*.16; p.67, *l*. 17; p.142, *l*.5.); *dvipadendra* (*SaddhP*. p.168, *l*.13.); *Buddhaṃ śaraṇaṃ gacchāmi dvipadānām agryam* (*Mhvyut*. p.267, *l*.1).

[Parallel Passages]

yaḥ pratītyasamutpādaṃ prapañcopaśamaṃ śivam/
deśayāṃ āsa saṃbuddhas taṃ vande vadatāṃ varam//

MadhyK. salutation stanza.

buddhāna jñānaṃ dvipadottamānām udārarūpaṃ tatha vandanīyam/
SaddhP. p.85, *ll*.16-17 (III, *gāthā* 92).

IV,2. *asparśayogo vai nāma sarvasattvasukho hitaḥ/*
avivādo 'viruddhaś ca deśitas taṃ namāmy aham//

"To all people as a happiness, and a benefit, not making dispute [with other sects], not contradictory [to anything] — that unattached Yoga is taught. I revere [him who teaches] it."

The phrase "seek the welfare and happiness of all beings" is a set phrase often encountered in the texts of primitive Buddhism. It does not, however, seem to be found in Brahmanical texts.

"Not making dispute"(*avivāda*) : The concept of *avivāda* is discussed in a subsequent section. The conclusion is that it derives from Buddhism, being a doctrine of the Mādhyamikas held previously to the *Gauḍapādīya-Kārikā*. The idea of not contradicting other sects, and not disputing with them, is also emphasized in the Jain line, but in Buddhism it was established from the first. In texts of primitive Buddhism it is often stated : "Do not make dispute (*vivāda*)." There are a number of hymns in the *Suttanipāta* which express ideas very similar to those mentioned in the *Māṇḍūkya-Kārikās* (Hymns 891, 892, 893, 894). The very word "*a-vivāda*" is Buddhist ; in ordinary Indian philosophy it means only "something undisputed," "what everyone recognizes." This use is often found in Buddhist texts, but the idea of non-disputation is one of the concepts of the Mādhyamika.

IV,4. *bhūtaṃ na jāyate kiñcid abhūtaṃ naiva jāyate/*
vivadanto 'dvayā hy evaṃ ajātiṃ khyāpayanti te//

[Parallel Passages]

asan na jāyate loko na san na sadasan kvacit/Laṅk. III,21.
sataś ca tāvad utpattir asataś ca na yujyate/
na sataś cāsataś ceti pūrvam evopapāditam//MadhyK. VII,20.
na san nāsan na sadasan dharmo nirvartate/MadhyK. I,7.

The former half of *Gauḍapādīya-Kārikā* IV,4 reminds us of Mādhyamika argumentation, e.g. *gataṃ na gamyate tāvad agataṃ naiva gamyate/ MadhyK*. II,1.

IV,9. *sāṃsiddhikī svābhāvikī sahajāpy akṛtā ca yā/*
prakṛtiḥ seti vijñeyā svabhāvaṃ na jahāti yā//

[Parallel Passages]

svabhāvaḥ kṛtako nāma bhaviṣyati punaḥ katham/
akṛtrimaḥ svabhāvo hi nirapekṣaḥ paratra ca//MadhyK. XV,2.

IV,12. *kāraṇād yad ananyatvam ataḥ kāryam ajaṃ yadi/*
jāyamānād dhi vai kāryāt kāraṇaṃ te kathaṃ dhruvam//

[Parallel Passages]

hetoḥ phalasya caikatvaṃ na hi jātūpapadyate/ *MadhyK*. XX,20.

ekatve hi phalahetoḥ syād aikyaṃ janakajanyayoḥ/ibid. XX,21.

Cf. *kāryakāraṇayoḥ anyatvasyāsiddhatva*. *Mvṛ*., p.222, *l*.5.

IV,18. *yadi hetoḥ phalāt siddhiḥ phalasiddhiś ca hetutaḥ/*
katarat pūrvaniṣpannaṃ yasya siddhir apekṣayā//

[Parallel Passages]

yadīndhanam apekṣyāgnir apekṣyāgnim yadīndhanam/
katarat pūrvaniṣpannaṃ yadapekṣyāgnir indhanam// *MadhyK*. X,8.

IV,20. *bījāṅkurākhyo dṛṣṭāntaḥ sadā sādhyasamo hi naḥ/*
na ca sādhyasamo hetuḥ siddhau sādhyasya yujyate//

"The illustration of a seed and its sprout is to us always a fallacy of the thing that is yet to be proved (*sādhyasama*). And a reason (*hetu*) which is similar to the probandum cannot be used for establishing a thing in question."

"*naḥ*" : *saḥ* according to one manuscript.

This is an attack on the doctrine which assumes an unbroken succession of cause-and-effect relations — a sprout appearing from a seed and then the sprout giving birth to seeds. The doctrine of one who attacked this former doctrine is referred to in Bhāskara (on *Brahma-sūtra* II,1,39). Explanations on the basis of this analogy were originally put forward in one section of Buddhism, but the Mādhyamikas attack it (see commentary on verse 59). Candrakīrti (*Mahāvṛtti*, p.222) puts forward the same argument, that one cannot establish something by something else which itself needs to be established.

"*sādhyasama*" is a kind of fallacy (*Nyāya-sūtra* III,b,3). "Similar to the probandum" : "ist genau so erst zu beweisen, wie die Behauptung"(Ruben). Or "the unproved" (*pseudo-probans*) : "der 'mit dem zu Beweisenden auf gleicher Linie stehende' Scheingrund" (Ruben) (*Nyāya-sūtra* I,b,8).

IV,22. *svato vā parato vāpi na kiñcid vastu jāyate/*
sad asat sadasad vāpi na kiñcid vastu jāyate//

[Parallel Passages]

na svato nāpi parato na dvābhyāṃ nāpy ahetutaḥ/
utpannā jātu vidyante bhāvāḥ kvacana kecana//MadhyK. I,1.
na svato jāyate bhāvaḥ parato naiva jāyate/
na svataḥ parataś caiva jāyate jāyate kutaḥ//MadhyK. XXI,13.
na svato jāyate bhāvaḥ parato naiva jāyate/
na svataḥ parataś ceti viparyayagataḥ kutaḥ//MadhyK. XXIII,20.

IV,23. ***hetur na jāyate 'nādeḥ phalaṃ vāpi svabhāvataḥ/***
ādir na vidyate yasya tasya hy ādir na vidyate//

[Parallel Passages]

hetor ādir na ced asti phalasyādiḥ kuto bhavet/BCA. IX,123.

IV,27. ***nimittaṃ na sadā cittaṃ saṃspṛśaty adhvasu triṣu/***
animitto viparyāsaḥ kathaṃ tasya bhaviṣyati//

"In the three divisions of time (i.e. the past, the present and the future) the mind does not touch any cause (object); how is it then that a false notion would arise without any cause of it?"

The use of the word *adhvan* in this sense is only found in Buddhist Sanskrit. Cf. *PW*; Schmidt: *Nachträge* s.v. *adhvan*. In *Yoga-sūtra* IV,12 *adhvan* is used in this sense, but this too is probably Buddhist influence.

For the final phrase of the verse, see the same argument in *MadhyK*. XXIII,8; 9; *Laṅk*. X,123.

The term *viparyāsa* is peculiarly Buddhistic. According to the dogmatics of the Sarvāstivāda and the Mahāyāna, there are four kinds of false notions (*viparyāsas*), i.e. suppositions of being permanent (*nitya*), happy (*sukha*), ego (*ātman*) and pure (*śuddha*). This term must have been introduced by Gauḍapāda.

IV,28. ***tasmān na jāyate cittaṃ cittadṛśyaṃ na jāyate/***
tasya paśyanti ye jātiṃ khe vai paśyanti te padam//

"Therefore, the mind does not originate, nor does the object which is cognizable by it originate. Those who see the origination of it (i.e. the mind or the object) are those who see the footmark [of birds] in the sky."

Śaṅkara and Ānandajñāna take it that in IV,24 the *bāhyārthavādin* (who maintains the existence of external objects) is introduced, and in 25-27 the *vijñānavādin* has refuted him, negating the existence of external objects; and now in this verse the *vijñānavādin* himself is attacked, and both the "field" (object) and "consciousness" (subject) are negated. Many present-day commentators follow this line. However, if the previous verses are *vijñānavādin* teaching, with the present verse being an attack on it, it is inexplicable why at the beginning of this verse there occurs the word *tasmād* (and therefore). "Therefore" has to be taken as expressing the sense that the previously mentioned idea, and the idea to be expressed now, are from the same standpoint. Even if we take it that from the absolute viewpoint mind and object are both unborn, this point is already prominent in the *vijñānavāda* doctrine as transmitted to China by Paramārtha. He advocated the theory that, viewed from the ultimate standpoint of absolute deliverance, both the subject and the object should be annulled as empty (*śūnya*). This view is clearly expressed in Asaṅga's *Mahāyānasamparigrahaśāstra*, and most clearly in Paramārtha's Chinese translation of this text, and in other texts too, such as *tac cārthābhāvajñānaṃ tad eva vijñaptimātrajñānaṃ nivartayati, arthābhāve vijñaptyasaṃbhavād* (*MAVṬ*. p.247, *ll*.18-20. Cf. Hakuju Ui: *Indo Tetsugaku Kenkyū*, vol. VI, p.369). Therefore, IV, 25ff has the doctrine held by the author of this fourth chapter himself, and it is put forward as his, and it is not an attack on *vijñānavāda*. One concludes that the view of Indian scholarship in general, that this verse is, following Śaṅkara's note, an attack on *vijñānavāda*, is incorrect.

IV,33. *sarve dharmā mṛṣā svapne kāyasyāntar nidarśanāt/*
saṃvṛte 'smin pradeśe vai bhūtānāṃ darśanaṃ kutaḥ//

[Parallel Passages]

tan mṛṣā moṣadharma yad bhagavān ity abhāṣata/
sarve ca moṣadharmāṇaḥ saṃskārās tena te mṛṣā//MadhyK. XIII,1.
tan mṛṣā moṣadharma ..../ibid. XIII,2.
sarvasaṃskārāś ca mṛṣā moṣadharmāṇaḥ/Mvṛ. p.41, *l*.5 = p.237, *l*.12.
sarvadharmāṇāṃ moṣadharmatva/Mvṛ. p.44, *l*.8.

mṛṣāsvabhāvāḥ padārthāḥ/Mvṛ. p.45, *l*.8. Cf. ibid. p.50, *l*.4.
mṛṣārthatā bhāvānām/Mvṛ. p.44, *l*.12.
Cf. *Yuktiṣaṣṭikā* XXVIII.

IV,40. ***nāsty asaddhetukam asat sad asaddhetukaṃ tathā/***
sac ca saddhetukaṃ nāsti saddhetukam asat kutaḥ//

[Parallel Passages]

na bhāvāj jāyate bhāvo, bhāvo 'bhāvān na jāyate/
nābhāvāj jāyate 'bhāvo, 'bhāvo bhāvān na jāyate//MadhyK. XXI,12.
Cf. *MadhyK*. I,1 ; 6 ; 7 ; VIII,1 ; 8 ; 10.

IV,42. ***upalambhāt samācārād astivastutvavādinām/***
jātis tu deśitā buddhair ajātes trasatāṃ sadā//

This is the same as the astonishment of Hīnayānists on hearing *Mahāyāna-sūtras*.

[Parallel Passages]

uttraset saṃtraset saṃtrāsam āpadyet/SaddhP. p.202, *l*.28.
udārayāne ca samuttrasanti/ibid. VII, *gāthā* 92.
Cf. *SaddhP*. p.34, *ll*.21f ; VIII, *gāthā* 2 ; *Bodhisattvabhūmi* p.265, *ll*.9f ; p.323, *l*.27 ; *Laṅk*. p.167 ; *Kāśyapaparivarta* in *Mvṛ*. pp.337-338.
ete 'pi lokaprasiddhimātreṇotpādādayaḥ svabhāvenāvidyamānā api bhagavatā tathāvidhavineyajanānugrahacikīrṣuṇā nirdiṣṭā/Mvṛ. p.177, *ll*.7-8.

IV,45. ***jātyābhāsaṃ calābhāsaṃ vastvābhāsaṃ tathaiva ca/***
ajācalam avastutvaṃ vijñānaṃ śāntam advayam//

The word "*ābhāsa*" is used in philosophical texts of Brahmanism in the meaning of "fallacy." The meaning "manifestation" or "appearance" is quite Buddhistic.

[Parallel Passages]

amalādvayajñāna — Mvṛ. p.556, *l*.6.
bodhiś cādvayalakṣaṇā — BCAP. ed. Poussin, p.277, *l*.14.
tad eva cittaṃ paramārthataḥ prakṛtiprabhāsvaram anāgantukam abhūtaparikalpasam utthagrāhyagrāhakādidvayasamāropābhiniveśavāsanāśūnyam

advayasvabhāvam āgatadoṣavinirmuktam āśrayaparāvṛtter vyavadānam/ibid. p.269, *ll.*19-21.

IV,56. *yāvad dhetuphalāveśaḥ saṃsāras tāvad āyataḥ/*
kṣiṇe hetuphalāveśe saṃsāraṃ na prapadyate//

[Parallel Passage]

ya ājavaṃjavībhāva upādāya pratītya vā/
so 'pratītyānupādāya nirvāṇam upadiśyate//MadhyK. XXV,9.

IV,57. *saṃvṛtyā jāyate sarvaṃ śāśvataṃ tena nāsti vai/*
sadbhāvena hy ajaṃ sarvam ucchedas tena nāsti vai//

The theory of "neither *śāśvata* nor *uccheda*" is especially advocated in the Mahāyāna. (Cf. *Madhyamaka-śāstra* I,1 ; XIV,1 ; 3 ; XV,10 ; 11 ; XVII,7 ; 8 ; 10 ; 20 ; 22 ; XVIII,10 ; 11 ; XXI,14 ; 15 ; 16 ; 17 ; XXII,12 ; XXV,3 ; 21 ; 23 ; XXVII, 1 ; 12 ; 16 ; 17 ; 18 ; 20 ; 29. Cf. *Laṅk.* V,1. p.219 ; X,2.)

[Parallel Passages]

bhāvā jāyanti saṃvṛtyā paramārthe 'svabhāvakāḥ/
tayā sarvam idaṃ satyam, asatyaṃ paramārthataḥ//AAA. p.420, *ll.*13-14.
yasmāt pravartate bhāvas tenocchedo na jāyate/
yasmān nivartate bhāvas tena nityo na jāyate//Catuḥśataka X,25 (=*Mvṛ.* p. 376.)

IV,58. *dharmā ya iti jāyante jāyante te na tattvataḥ/*
janma māyopamaṃ teṣāṃ sā ca māyā na vidyate//

[Parallel Passage]

māyādayaḥ svabhāvenānutpannā avidyamānāḥ/Mvṛ. p.177, *l.*6.

IV,59. *yathā māyāmayād bījāj jāyate tanmayo 'ṅkuraḥ/*
nāsau nityo na cocchedī tadvad dharmeṣu yojanā//

[Parallel Passages]

bījasya sato yathāṅkuro na ca yo bīju sa caivāṅkuro/
na ca anyu tato na caiva tad evam anuccheda aśāśvata dharmatā//
Lalitavistara p.210, *ll.*4-5 (*Mvṛ.* ad II,25 ; XXI,21.)
yathā hi kṛtakād bījād aṅkuraḥ kṛtako bhavet/

Catuḥśataka X,24 (restoration into Sanskrit).
aṅkuro jāyate bījād bījaṃ tenaiva sūcyate/*BCA*. IX,115.
bījāṅkuravat -- *Mvṛ*. p.458, *l*.13 ; p.252, *l*.11. Cf. ibid. p.423, *l*.10.
aṅkurādisaṃtāna -- *Mvṛ*. p.313, *l*.3.
Śālistambha-sūtra. Cf. *BCAP*. pp.575 f.

This simile was adopted by later Vedāntins. Cf. Jacob : *Laukika-nyāyāñjali* vol.1. s.v. *bījāṅkuranyāya*.

IV,60. ***nājeṣu sarvadharmeṣu śāśvatāśāśvatābhidhā/***
yatra varṇā na vartante vivekas tatra nocyate//

[Parallel Passages]

nivṛttam abhidhātavyaṃ nivṛtte cittagocare/*MadhyK*. XVIII,7.
tattvaṃ hy akṣaravarjitam — *Laṅk*. p.48, v.119.
avāca anakṣarāḥ sarva śūnyāḥ śāntādinirmalāḥ/*Mvṛ*. p.539. Cf. p.493.
yasmāt pravartate bhāvas tenocchedo na jāyate/
yasmān nivartate bhāvas tena nityo na jāyate//
Catuḥśataka X,25 (=*Mvṛ*. p.376). Cf. *MadhyK*. XV,10 ; 11.

IV,62. ***advayaṃ ca dvayābhāsaṃ cittaṃ svapne na saṃśayaḥ/***
advayaṃ ca dvayābhāsaṃ cittaṃ jāgran na saṃśayaḥ//

[Parallel Passages]

cittaṃ paramārthataḥ .... advayasvabhāvam — *BCAP*. p.408, *ll*.11-13.
grāhyagrāhakādyākāravinirmuktam advayalakṣaṇaṃ cittam — ibid. p.410, *ll*.9-10.

IV,63. ***svapnadṛk pracaran svapne dikṣu vai daśasu sthitān/***
aṇḍajān svedajān vāpi jīvān paśyati yān sadā//
IV,64. ***svapnadṛkcittadṛśyās te na vidyante tataḥ pṛthak/***
tathā taddṛśyam evedaṃ svapnadṛkcittam iṣyate//
IV,65. ***carañ jāgarite jāgrad dikṣu vai daśasu sthitān/***
aṇḍajān svedajān vāpi jīvān paśyati yān sadā//
IV,66. ***jāgraccittekṣaṇīyās te na vidyante tataḥ pṛthak/***
tathā taddṛśyam evedaṃ jāgratas cittam iṣyate//

The theory advocated in IV,63-66 is cited by Śaṅkara as that of Vijñānavādins : *yathā svapnavijñānagrāhyaṃ ghaṭapaṭādivastu svapnavijñānavyatirekeṇānupalambhāt svapnaghaṭapradīpādeḥ svapnavijñānamātratā 'vagamyate, tathā jāgarite 'pi ghaṭapradīpāder jāgradvijñānavyatirekeṇānupalambhāj jāgradvijñānamātrataiva yuktā bhavitum*/Ś. ad *Bṛhad.Up*. p.571, *ll*.6-9. Hence it was not Vedāntic in his view.

IV,69. ***yathā māyāmayo jīvo jāyate mriyate 'pi ca/***
tathā jīvā amī sarve bhavanti na bhavanti ca//

[Parallel Passages]

sudurbodhāsi māyaiva dṛśyate na ca dṛśyate/Rāhulabhadra's *Prajñāpāramitāstava* XVI.

na niruddhā na cotpannā yathā māyāmayāḥ kvacit/
na niruddhā na cotpannā sarvasattvās tathā tvayi//Rāhulabhadra's *Saddharmapuṇḍarīkastava* (ed. by Wogihara, Introduction, p.39.)

IV,70. ***yathā nirmitako jīvo jāyate mriyate 'pi ca/***
tathā jīvā amī sarve bhavanti na bhavanti ca//

[Parallel Passages]

yathā nirmitakaṃ śāstā nirmimītarddhisaṃpadā/
nirmito nirmimītānyaṃ sa ca nirmitakaḥ punaḥ//
tathā nirmitakākāraḥ kartā yat karma tat kṛtam/
tad yathā nirmitenānyo nirmito nirmitas tathā//*MadhyK*. XVII,31 ; 32.

IV,75. ***abhūtābhiniveśo 'sti dvayam tatra na vidyate/***
dvayābhāvaṃ sa buddhvaiva nirmitto na jāyate//

[Parallel Passage]

abhūtaparikalpo 'sti dvayaṃ tatra na vidyate/*Madhyāntavibhāgaśāstra* I,1.

IV,76. ***yadā na labhate hetūn uttamādhamamadhyamān/***
tadā na jāyate cittaṃ hetvabhāve phalaṃ kutaḥ//

Cf. *MadhyK*. XIX,4 ; XX,22.

IV,77. ***animittasya cittasya yānutpattiḥ samādvayā/***
ajātasyaiva sarvasya cittadṛśyaṃ hi tad yataḥ//

On *ajāta*, Cf. *ajātāḥ sarvadharmāḥ* — *Mhvyut*. X,11 ; *ajātaṃ sarvatraidhātukaṃ samanupaśyati* — *Āryadhyāyitamuṣṭisūtra*, *Mvṛ*. p.298, *l*.14.

IV,80. ***nivṛttasyāpravṛttasya niścalā hi tadā sthitiḥ/***
viṣayaḥ sa hi buddhānāṃ tat sāmyam ajam advayam//

"*viṣayaḥ sa hi buddhānāṃ*" : This phrase is found in the T'ang version of the *Buddhāvataṃsaka-sūtra*, vol.19 (*Taisho Tripiṭaka*, vol.X, p.101b).

Cf. "*buddhabhūmi*, *Laṅk*. X, v.105 ; *Viṃśatikā* ad v.10, p.6, *l*.18 ; *MSA*. XX-XXI,26.

IV,81. ***ajaṃ anidram asvapnaṃ prabhātaṃ bhavati svayam/***
sakṛd vibhāto hy evaiṣa dharmadhātuḥ svabhāvataḥ//

[Parallel Passages]

prakṛtiś ca dharmāṇa sadā prabhāsvarā — *SaddhP*. II, v.102.

prakṛtiprabhāsvarasya dharmadhātor āgantukopakleśopakliṣṭatvāt — *MAVṬ*. p.261, *l*.19.

prakṛtiprabhāsvaradharmadhātu — *ibid*. p.261, *l*.19.

prakṛtiprabhāsvaraṃ cittam — *Laṅk*. p.358, *ll*.5 ; 11 ; 13.

tad eva cittaṃ prakṛtiprabhāsvaram — *BCAP*. p.269, *l*.19 (ed. by Poussin).

cittaṃ ca prakṛtiprabhāsvaratayā vyavadānasvabhāvatvān na praheyam — *ibid*. p.270, *l*.3.

IV,82. ***sukham āvriyate nityaṃ duḥkhaṃ vivriyate sadā/***
yasya kasya ca dharmasya graheṇa bhagavān asau//

bhagavat = *ātmādvayo devaḥ* = *paramātman* = *Aupaniṣadaḥ puruṣaḥ* — Ś. However, in Advaita works *Ātman* is never called *bhagavat*. The appellation *bhagavat* is peculiar to the Bhāgavatas (R. G. Bhandarkar : *Collected Works*, II, pp.192–193), and *Gauḍapādīya-Kārikā* does not reflect any Vaiṣṇava traits. Therefore, it is likely that this term was introduced from Buddhism.

[Parallel Passages]

paraṃ nirodhād bhagavān bhavatīty eva nohyate/
na bhavaty ubhayaṃ ceti nobhayaṃ ceti nohyate// *MadhyK*. XXV,17.
tiṣṭhamāno 'pi bhagavān bhavatīty eva nohyate/

na bhavaty ubhayaṃ ceti nobhayaṃ ceti nohyate//*ibid*. XXV,18.

Cf. *Aṣṭasāhasrikā* (ed. by Wogihara, pp.554-555) ; *MadhyK*. XV,6 ; 7; 8 ; 10 ; 11 ; XVIII,8 ; XXII,13 ; 14. Also Chinese versions of the *Mahāprajñāpāramitā-sūtra*, vol.442 ; 510 (*Taisho Tripiṭaka*, vol.7, p.229a ; p.603c).

IV,84. ***koṭyaś catasra etās tu grahair yāsāṃ sadāvṛtaḥ/***
bhagavān ābhir aspṛṣṭo yena dṛṣṭaḥ sa sarvadṛk//

[Parallel Passages]

prapañcayanti ye buddhaṃ prapañcātītam avyayam/
te prapañcahatāḥ sarve na paśyanti tathāgatam//*MadhyK*. XXII,15.

Cf. *Laṅk*. p.190 ; *MadhyK*. I,1 ; XII,1 ; 10 ; XVIII,6 ; 8 ; XXII,11 ; 12 ; XXV,4 -16 ; 17 ; 18 ; 21-23 ; XXVII,13 ; 14 ; 18 ; 20 etc.

na san nāsan na sadasan na cāpy anubhayātmakam/
catuṣkoṭivinirmuktaṃ tattvaṃ mādhyamikā viduḥ//Āryadeva's *Jñānasāra-samuccaya* (*Jhā Commemoration Volume*, p.86) ; widely quoted (e.g. *BCA*. BI. p.359 ; *Sarvasiddhāntasaṃgraha* ; *SDS*. II, *l*.159).

sad asat sadasac ceti nobhayaṃ ceti kathyate/
nanu vyādhivaśāt pathyam auṣadhaṃ nāma jāyate//
Catuḥśataka VIII,20 (reconstruit par P. L. Vaidya, p.74 ; *Mvṛ*. p.372.)

sad asat sadasac ceti sadasan neti ca kramaḥ/
eṣa prayojyo vidvadbhir ekatvādiṣu nityaśaḥ//*ibid*. XIV,21 (*ibid*. p.114.)

sad asat sadasac ceti yasya pakṣo na vidyate/
upālambhaś cireṇāpi tasya vaktuṃ na śakyate//
Catuḥśataka VIII,25 ; *Mvṛ*. p.16.

etayā catuṣkoṭikayā mahāmate rahitāḥ sarvadharmā ity ucyate — *Laṅk*. p. 122.

yac ca mahāmate na kāryaṃ na kāraṇaṃ tan na san nāsad yac ca na san nāsat tac cātuṣkoṭikabāhyam/cātuṣkoṭikaṃ ca mahāmate lokavyavahāraḥ/yac ca cātuṣkoṭikabāhyaṃ tad vāgmātraṃ prasajyate bandhyāputravat / bandhyāputro hi mahāmate vāgmātraṃ na cātuṣkoṭikapatitaḥ/*Laṅk*. p.188. Cf. pp. 96 ; 171.

IV,85. ***prāpya sarvajñatāṃ kṛtsnāṃ brāhmaṇyaṃ padam advayam/***
anāpannādimadhyāntaṃ kim ataḥ param īhate//

According to *PW*. the word "*sarvajñatā*" appears only in later literature after the tenth century. But in Buddhist literature it appears from early times : *sarvajñatva* = *buddhatva* (*Aṣṭasāhasrikā*, BI. pp.42-43). According to Haribhadra, the former means the state in which *jñeyāvaraṇās* are annulled, and the latter means the state in which *kleśāvaraṇās* are annulled (*AAA*. p. 167.) Śaṅkara's interpretation (ad *GK*. IV,89 : *sarvaś cāsau jñaś ca sarvajñas tadbhāvaḥ sarvajñatā*) seems to be twisted.

The term "*brāhmaṇya*" is interpreted by Ānandajñāna to mean "the state of one who knows *brahman*" (*brahmavid, mukhyo brāhmaṇa*). This interpretation is correct. But in early Jain and Buddhist literature the true Brahmin (*brāhmaṇa, māhaṇa*) is extolled and the Buddha or one who has perfected his religious practice is called a *brāhmaṇa* (e.g. *Dhammapada* XXVI ; *Suttanipāta* 594 f; *Vāseṭṭhasutta* ; *Uvāsagadasāo* 187 ; 193). *brāhmaṇya* is extolled in the dogmatic literature of later Buddhism. (e. g. *AKV*. p.578, *l*. 23 f.)

"*anāpannādimadhyānta*" is interpreted by Śaṅkara as "*utpattisthitilaya anāpanna aprāpta yasya*." Cf. *anādinidhanaṃ brahma* — *Vākyap*. I,1 ; *anādimadhyāvasānatvaṃ na svataḥ parato 'pi vā* — *Madhyamakasiddhānta* (*Mvṛ*. p.546, *l*.8.)

IV,86. ***viprāṇāṃ vinayo hy eṣa śamaḥ prākṛta ucyate/***
damaḥ prakṛtidāntatvād evaṃ vidvāñ śamaṃ vrajet//

About the original meaning of the word "*vipra*," Cf. Macdonell and Keith : *Vedic Index*, s.v. *vipra*. The word "*vipra*" does not necessarily mean "Brahmin." Bhāskara (ad *BS*. II,2,28) calls Dharmakīrti, the Buddhist logician, "*viprabhikṣu*" when citing his verse.

The terms "*śama*" and "*dama*" are often used together. "*śānto dāntaḥ*" (*Bṛhad.Up*. IV,4,23. Cf. *Vedāntasāra* 14 ; 26 ; Ś. ad *BS*. I,1,1). In Buddhism also — *dama-śamatha* (*SaddhP*. p.75, *l*.12.)

IV,87. ***savastu sopalambhaṃ ca dvayaṃ laukikam iṣyate/***
avastu sopalambhaṃ ca śuddhaṃ laukikam iṣyate//

IV,88. ***avastv anupalambhaṃ ca lokottaram iti smṛtam/***
jñānaṃ jñeyaṃ ca vijñeyaṃ sadā buddhaiḥ prakīrtitam//

"The standpoint that consists of the two, the object and [its] perception, is regarded as 'mundane'. The standpoint without the object, but with the perception, is regarded as 'pure mundane'. The standpoint without the object and the perception is said to be 'supra-mundane'. Knowledge and its object should be understood. This theory is always declared by the Buddhas."

Śaṅkara explains *laukika* to mean *jāgarita*, *śuddhaṃ laukikam* to mean *svapna*, *lokottara* to mean *suṣupta*, and *vijñeya* to mean *turīya*. But this interpretation is too farfetched. The state of *svapna* cannot be called *śuddha*. As *suṣupta* has *bījas* of afflictions in a dormant state (Cf. *GK*. I,13), it cannot be called *lokottara*. Chapters II, III, and IV of the *Gauḍapādīya-Kārikā* do not necessarily presuppose the theory of the four mental states. Here Śaṅkara had to give a forced interpretation, being influenced by the presupposition that all four chapters of this work must set forth the same theory.

The terms *laukika* and *lokottara* were originally of Buddhist origin, although the former was used quite often in Brahmanic literature. *Śuddhalaukika* is a term meaning *pṛṣṭhalabdhajñāna* (*MAVṬ*. p.22, *l*.15 ; p.118, *l*. 17 ; p.224, *l*.8). *pṛṣṭhalabdhajñāna* (i. e. *śuddhalaukikajñāna*) was regarded as being in opposition to *lokottaranirvikalpajñāna* (*Viṃśatikā* p.9, *l*.15. Cf. p.40, *ll*.23-26). This knowledge has *paratantralakṣaṇa* as its essence (*paratantrasvabhāvo hi śuddhalaukikagocaraḥ*/ *MAV*, p.22, *l*.15. Cf. *ibid*. p.118, *ll*. 15 f ; p.224, *l*.8). Some of the Vijñānavādins say that the three knowledges called *laukika*, *śuddhalaukika* and *lokottara* have respectively *parikalpita-svabhāva*, *paratantra-svabhāva* and *pariniṣpanna-svabhāva* for their objects (*MAVṬ*. p.112, *ll*.12 f.). There was a view maintaining three kinds of knowledge, i. e. *laukikaṃ jñānam*, *lokottaraṃ jñānam* and *lokottaratamaṃ jñānam* (*Laṅk*. pp.156 ; 157). Considering these facts, we are led to the conclusion that the theory of the three kinds of knowledge has nothing to do with the theory of the four mental stages as is set forth in the first chapter of the *Gauḍapādīya-Kārikā*, but was introduced from some Vijñānavādins.

"*laukika*" means cognition of an object in the state of confrontation of subject and object (*grāhyagrahaṇaviṣayo hi lokaḥ*/Ś. ad *GK*).

avastv anupalambhaṃ ca grāhyagrahaṇavarjitam ity etal lokottaram ata eva lokātītam/Ś. ad *GK*. Cf. *lokād uttīrṇam iti jñānaṃ lokottaraṃ ca tad iti*/ *Triṃśikā* p.44.

"*anupalambha*" is particularly a Buddhist term. Cf. *acitto 'nupalambho 'sau jñānaṃ lokottaraṃ ca tat*/*Triṃśikā* v.29 ; *muktiḥ parama upalambhasya vigamaḥ*/*MSA*. XI,47.

IV,90. *heyajñeyāpyapākyāni vijñeyāny agrayānataḥ*/
**   *teṣām anyatra vijñeyād upalambhas triṣu smṛtaḥ*//**

According to Śaṅkara, *heya* = *jāgarita-svapna-suṣupta*, *jñeya* = *paramārtha-tattva*, *āpya* = *pāṇḍitya-bālya-mauna*, *pākya* = *rāgadveṣamohādayo doṣāḥ kaṣāya*. But we can find better explanations in Buddhist works. *heya* = *parikalpitaḥ svabhāvaḥ*, *jñeya* = *tattva* = *pariniṣpannaḥ svabhāvaḥ*, *āpya* = *dharmadhātu* (Cf. *prāpyaṃ dharmadhātuḥ* — Sthiramati ad *MSA*. XIX,56), *pākya* = *sattva* (Cf. *paripācyaṃ vastu sattvadhātur aviśeṣeṇa* .... *paripācanayogyaṃ vineyadhātuḥ* — Sthiramati ad *MSA*. XIX,56 ; *bodhisattvasya prajñā sarvasattvānāṃ sarvaśukladharmān paripācayati* — *Kāśyapaparivarta* XXXI).

jñeya, *heya* and *viśodhya* (*MSA*. XI,13) are explained by Sthiramati : *satataṃ dvayena rahitaṃ tattvaṃ parikalpitaḥ svabhāvo grāhyagrāhakalakṣaṇenātyantam asattvāt*/*bhrānteḥ saṃniśrayaḥ paratantras tena tatparikalpanāt anabhilāpyam aprapañcātmakaṃ ca pariniṣpannaḥ svabhāvaḥ*/*tatra prathamaṃ tattvaṃ parijñeyaṃ dvitīyaṃ praheyaṃ tṛtīyaṃ viśodhyaṃ cāgantukamalād viśuddhaṃ ca prakṛtyā*//

"*agrayāna*" (*MSA*. XII,20 ; 23) is a synonym of *Mahāyāna*. Cf. *agre yāne* (*MSA*. II,2), as against *Hīnayāna* (*MSA*. p.53). Cf. *SaddhP*. p.60, *l*.12, v.1 ; p. 76, *l*.17 ; p.180, *l*.24 ; p.184, *l*.24 ; *Guhyasamāja* p.20 ; *Vajracchedikā* p.30, *l*.6 ; *agrayānika* (*SaddhP*. p.129, *l*.3, V, v.61) ; *agrayānī mahāmuniḥ* (*Lalitavistara* ed. by S. Lefmann, p.438, *l*.8).

IV,91. *prakṛtyākāśavaj jñeyāḥ sarve dharmā anādayaḥ*/
**   *vidyate na hi nānātvaṃ teṣāṃ kvacana kiñcana*//**

[Parallel Passage]

notpannā jātu vidyante bhāvāḥ kvacana kecana/*MadhyK*. I,1.

IV,92. *ādibuddhāḥ prakṛtyaiva sarve dharmāḥ suniścitāḥ/*
yasyaivaṃ bhavati kṣāntiḥ so 'mṛtatvāya kalpate//

[Parallel Passage]

yaṃ hi na vyathayanty ete puruṣaṃ puruṣarṣabha/
samaduḥkhasukhaṃ dhīraṃ so 'mṛtatvāya kalpate//Bhag.G. II,15.

IV,93. *ādiśāntā hy anutpannāḥ prakṛtyaiva sunirvṛtāḥ/*
sarve dharmāḥ samābhinnā ajaṃ sāmyaṃ viśāradam//

[Parallel Passages]

ādiśāntā hy anutpannāḥ prakṛtyaiva ca nivṛtāḥ/
dharmās te vivṛtā nātha budhyanta iti nāyakaḥ //Ratnameghasūtra (*Mvṛ*. p.225).

evaṃ ca bhāṣāmy ahu nityanivṛtā ādipraśāntā imi sarvadharmāḥ/SaddhP. p.45, *l*.12.

śāntāḥ kila sarvimi dharma 'nāsravā nirodhotpādavivarjitāś ca/ibid. p. 110, *l*.1.

yo hi niḥsvabhāvaḥ so 'nutpanno yo 'nutpannaḥ so 'niruddho yo 'niruddhaḥ sa ādiśānto ya ādiśāntaḥ sa prakṛtiparinirvṛtaḥ/Sthiramati ad *MSA*. XI,51.

sattvāḥ prakṛtyā parinirvṛtāḥ/BCA. IX,104.

sarvadharmāḥ .... anutpannāniruddhasvabhāvatvāc ca prakṛtiparinirvṛtā ādiśāntā ity ucyate/BCAP. ad IX,108.

IV,96. *ajeṣv ajam asaṃkrāntaṃ dharmeṣu jñānam iṣyate/*
yato na kramate jñānam asaṅgaṃ tena kīrtitam//

"*asaṅgaṃ jñānam*" is taught quite often in Mahāyāna literature. Cf. *asaṅgalakṣaṇaṃ jñānam* (*Laṅk*. p.157, *l*.14) ; *asaṅgasvabhāvalakṣaṇaṃ jñānam* (*ibid*. p.157, *l*.16) ; *asaṅgaṃ .... jñānadarśanam* (*Mhvyut*. IX,16-18) ; *asaṅgajñāna* (*SaddhP*.III,v.10 ; *Mhvyut*. X,32).

IV,98. *alabdhāvaraṇāḥ sarve dharmāḥ prakṛtinirmalāḥ/*
ādau buddhās tathā muktā budhyanta iti nāyakāḥ//

"*prakṛtinirmala*" : *ādiśuddhatvād ādipariśuddhatvāt sattvasya* (*Aṣṭasāhasrikā* p.47) ; *prakṛtivaimalya* (*MAVṬ*. p.122, *l*.10) ; *prakṛte kalpanārāgair vivi-*

ktaṃ cittaratnakam/ādiśuddham anutpannaṃ nijarūpam anāvilam// (*Cittaviśuddh-iprakaraṇa* XXVIII) ; *sarva* (sic) *śūnyāḥ śāntādinirmalāḥ* (*Mvṛ*. p.539, *l*.11).

[Parallel Passages]

ādiśāntā hy anutpannāḥ prakṛtyaiva ca nivṛtāḥ/
dharmās te vivṛtā nātha budhyanta iti nāyakaḥ//Ratnameghasūtra (*Mvṛ*. p.225).

IV,99. *kramate na hi buddhasya jñānaṃ dharmeṣu tāyinaḥ/*
sarvadharmās tathā jñānaṃ naitad buddhena bhāṣitam//

"The knowledge (*jñāna*) of the Buddha, the saviour, does not relate itself to objects. All the *dharmas* (objects) as well as *jñāna* — this has not been taught by the Buddha."

The ideal person is here called *tāyin*. This appellation can be traced not only to early Buddhism, but also to early Jainism (e. g. in the colophon of every chapter of the *Isibhāsiyāiṃ*).

The phrase "no teaching was taught by the Buddha" is quite commonly seen in Mahāyāna literature. Cf. *na kvacit kasyacit kaścit dharmo buddhena deśitaḥ/MadhyK*. XXV,24, cd ; *nodāhṛtaṃ tvayā kiñcid ekam apy akṣaraṃ vibho/kṛtsnaś ca vaineyajano dharmavarṣeṇa tarpitaḥ//Niraupamyastava* VII (*JRAS*. 1932, p.314) ; *dharmo naiva ca deśito bhagavatā pratyātmavedyo yata ākṛṣṭā janatā ca yuktivihitair dharmaiḥ svakīṃ dharmatām/MSA*. XII,2,ab ; *nāsti dharmo yas tathāgatena deśitaḥ/ Vajracchedikā* p.24 ; p.29 ; *yāñ ca rātriṃ tathāgato 'bhisaṃbuddho yāñ ca rātriṃ parinirvāsyati atrāntara ekam apy akṣaraṃ tathāgatena nodāhṛtaṃ na pravyāhariṣyati avacanaṃ bhuddha-vacanam/Laṅk*. pp.142-143 (Chinese translation, *Taisho* XVI, p.499a) ; *yasyāṃ ca rātryāṃ dhigamo yasyāṃ ca parinirvṛtaḥ/ekasminn antare nāsti mayā kiṃcit prakāśitam//Laṅk*. p.144 (Chinese translation, *l.c*. and *Taisho* XVI, p.376c ; 421c) ; *yāṃ ca rātriṃ śāntamate tathāgato 'nuttarāṃ samyak-saṃbodhim abhisaṃbuddho yāṃ ca rātrim anupādāya parinirvāsyati, atrāntare tathāgatenaikam apy akṣaraṃ nodāhṛtaṃ na vyāhṛtaṃ nāpi pravyā-harati nāpi pravyāhariṣyati/Tathāgataguhyasūtra* (*Mvṛ*. p.539) ; *nirakṣaratvād dharmasya/Laṅk*. p.194 ; *tattvaṃ hy akṣaravarjitam/ibid*. p.48 (cf. *Mvṛ*. p. 539) ; *na me yānaṃ mahāyānaṃ na ghoṣo na ca akṣarāḥ/ibid*. p.137 ; *anak-*

ṣarasya dharmasya śrutiḥ kā deśanā ca kā/śrūyate deśyate cāpi samāropād anakṣaraḥ//Mvṛ. p.264 ; *BCAP*. p.365.

So it is quite clear that this phrase in *GK*. IV,99 must have been influenced by Mahāyāna philosophy.

IV,100. *durdarśam atigambhīram ajaṃ sāmyaṃ viśāradam/*
buddhvā padam anānātvaṃ namaskurmo yathābalam//

[Parallel Passages]

adhigato kho me ayaṃ dhammo gambhīro duddaso duranubodho santo paṇīto atakkāvacaro nipuṇo paṇḍitavedanīyo/MN. vol.I, p.167 (Cf. p.487).

gambhīro vatāyaṃ mayā dharmo 'dhigato 'bhisaṃbuddhaḥ śāntaḥ praśānta upaśāntaḥ praṇīto durdṛśo duranubodho 'tarko 'vitarkāvacaraḥ/Lalitavistara p.392 (Cf. pp.395, 397).

ayaṃ dhammo gambhīro duddaso duranubodho/Mahāvagga I,5,2,8.

Appendix. INTERPRETATIONS OF SOME TECHNICAL TERMS THAT OCCUR OFTEN IN THE *MĀṆḌŪKYA-KĀRIKĀ*

I. *buddha, saṃbuddha*

The term *saṃbuddha* in the *Gauḍapādīya-Kārikā* IV,1 is explained to mean "*īśvaro .... Nārāyaṇākhyas*." But in Hindu tradition there is no instance where the Hindu Lord is called *saṃbuddha*. On the other hand, *saṃbuddha* is an appellation or epithet of the Buddha.[1] The word "*buddha*" appears six times in the fourth chapter of the *Gauḍapādīya-Kārikā* (19 ; 42 ; 80 ; 88 ; 98 ; 90). In verses 92 and 98 "*buddha*" is nothing but an epithet. In the other cases the word "*buddha*" is used as a special technical term. Śaṅkara explains it to mean "*paṇḍita*" (*anyonyapakṣadoṣam bruvadbhir vādibhir buddhaiḥ paṇḍitair ity arthaḥ* — v.19), *advaitavādin* (v.42), *paramārthadarśin* (vv.80 ; 99), and *paramārthadarśin brahmavid* (v.88). This means that he understood the word "*buddha*" to mean "one who has understood truth." This is peculiarly Buddhistic. The verb *budh* is also often used (vv.75 ; 78 ; 79 ; 100).

Note

1) *MadhyK. maṅgalācaraṇa*, XVIII,12; *MSA.* XI,3; 6; 54. Cf. *Indices to Laṅk.* and *MAVṬ.*

II. *dharma*

The word *dharma* appears frequently in this Chapter IV (vv.1, 6 [twice], 8, 10, 21, 33, 41, 46, 53, 54, 58, 59, 81, 82, 91, 92, 93, 96, 98, 99 [twice]). Of these, in 1, 10, 46, 53, 81, 91, 92, 96 and 99 Śaṅkara clearly glosses *dharma* as *ātman*. But here in the *Māṇḍūkya-Kārikā* it is being used in a special sense unexampled elsewhere in Vedānta literature. Śaṅkara generally glosses it as *ātman*, and the plural *dharmāḥ* as *ātmānaḥ*.[1] There is no example in the old *Upaniṣads* of the word *dharma* being used to mean *ātman*.

When it appears in the *Kāthaka-Upaniṣad* IV,14, Śaṅkara takes *dharma* as *ātman*, but this cannot be right.[2] Even in Śaṅkara's own commentary on the *Brahma-sūtra*, the word "*dharma*" is never used in the sense of *ātman*. There it always means either (1) rule of conduct, duty, ethical conduct, or else (2) either nature or attribute. This use is to be found in all the early Vedānta writers. In the Vedāntic schools generally there is no example of this word's being used as *ātman*, and so Śaṅkara's gloss on it in this fourth chapter can be taken as incorrect.

Looking at individual examples, we can see this. For instance in IV,1, *dharmān* (accusative plural) is glossed by him as *ātmānaḥ*. Though *ātman* is always non-dual, here Śaṅkara puts the word in the plural, so that it has to be taken in the sense of individual self.[3] But this interpretation is not consonant with the content of the word *gaganopama*, which compares the individual self to space. So Śaṅkara's rendering is not right. Here *dharma* must be understood in the Buddhist sense.

Again, the phrase *sarve dharmāḥ* (all *dharmas*) frequently occurs (vv. 10, 33, 91, 92, 93, 98, 99). This too is a familiar phrase in Buddhism, and it would be natural to take it in the normal Buddhist sense.[4]

That *dharma* in the fourth chapter is a Buddhist term can be recognized from other points too. III,20 and IV,6 have identical phrases except that *bhāva* in the former is changed to *dharma* in the latter. So we have to take it that *dharma* has the same sense as *bhāva*. Note that in Nāgārjuna's

Akutobhaya they are synonyms, but *dharma* is a special Buddhist term, whereas *bhāva* is a technical word common to the Indian schools.

Since *dharma* is thus being used in its Buddhist sense, there were cases where Śaṅkara could not gloss it as *ātman*, but perforce recognized it as being used in the Buddhist sense. For instance the *dharmān* of IV,41 he gives as *hastyādīn dharmān*, and in IV,54 *dharmāḥ* is glossed by him as *bāhyadharmāḥ*.[5]

The meaning of *dharma* in Buddhism has been much disputed, but here in the fourth chapter, since it is a synonym of *bhāva,* it can probably be understood as "thing," "what exists," "fact," "object," etc.

The use of the word "*dharma*" in a Buddhist sense in the *Kārikās* is confined to this fourth chapter. In the third and earlier chapters (II,25 ; III, 1) the general technical use in orthodox Brahmanism is followed.

Notes

1) In III.1 he glosses *dharma* as *sādhaka* or practitioner, a strange interpretation.

2) See Part One of the present work. p.19ff.

3) Ānandajñāna : *bahuvacanam upādhikalpitabhedābhiprāyam* /

4) An example, however, of a visible object's being called *dharma* exists in the Yoga school : *dṛśyā buddhisattvopārūḍhāḥ sarve dharmāḥ*/Vyāsa on *Yoga-sūtra* II,17. But in the Brahmanical schools of philosophy this is exceptional.

5) Ānandajñāna : *ghaṭādayo nātmanaḥ*/

III. *paramārtha*

This term is not found in older *Upaniṣads*. In the scriptures of early Buddhism the term *paramattha* is used in the sense of "ultimate truth," or "the highest truth."[1] This meaning is carried down into later Buddhist literature.[2] The Buddha is called *paramārthadarśin*.[3] In philosophical texts of the Mahāyāna, *paramārtha* is a synonym of *tattva, tathatā, śūnyatā, ānimitta, bhūtakoṭi* and *dharmadhātu*.[4] It is identified with *anutpāda*.[5]

This idea was introduced into the *Gauḍapādīya-Kārikā*. In Vedānta philosophy it is interpreted as meaning *Brahman*.[6] This word appears in the Great Epics and other literary works[7] as well as in Jain works.[8] So we cannot decisively assert that this term was introduced directly from Buddhism, but as the meaning of this word in the *Gauḍapādīya-Kārikā* is conspicuously Buddhistic, it is likely that the use of this word in the *Gauḍapādīya-Kārikā* is a trace of Buddhist influence.

Moreover Mahāyāna Buddhism admits two kinds of truth, i. e. *paramārthasatya* and *saṃvṛtisatya*, both of which are found in the *Gauḍapādīya-Kārikā* IV,73 and 74. It is likely that this is a trace of Buddhist influence, for this theory is set forth in connection with the theory of *trisvabhāva*, an idea peculiar to Vijñānavādins.

Notes

1) Cf. *Suttanipāta* 68 ; 219.

2) Cf. *SaddhP*, p.92, *l*.23 ; p.93, *l*.1 ; p.122.

3) *Ibid*. I, v.97 ; III, v.18 ; VII, v.60 ; XVI, v.5.

4) Cf. *MAV*. I,14 ; *BCAP*. p.528, *l*.13.

5) *Vajracchedika* 17.

6) Cf. *ekarūpeṇa hy avasthito yo 'rthaḥ sa paramārthaḥ*/Ś. ad *BS*. II,1,11. vol. I, p.452.

7) Cf. *PW*. s.v.

8) e.g. *paramaṭṭha*, *Uvāsagadasāo* CLXXXI etc.

IV. The Simile of *Alātacakra*

This simile is often used in Mahāyāna literature to teach the "*niḥsvabhāvatā*" of things.

alātacakranirmāṇasvapnamāyāmbucandrakaiḥ/
dhūmikāntaḥpratiśrutkāmarīcyabhraiḥ samo bhavaḥ//*Catuḥśatikā* XIII, 800, p.503 (Cf. *Mvṛ*. p.173, *l*.2).

tasmān nāsti saṃsāraḥ, pūrvāparakoṭyanupalambhāt, alātacakravad iti sthitam/*Mvṛ*. p.219, *ll*.7-8.

tad yathā mahāmate acakram alātacakraṃ bālaiś cakrabhāvena parikalpyate na paṇḍitaiḥ, evam eva mahāmate kudṛṣṭitīrthyāśayapatitā ekatvānyatvobhayān ubhayatvaṃ parikalpayiṣyanti sarvabhāvotpattau/ *Laṅk*. p.92, *l*.9.

It is mentioned in the *Satyasiddhiśāstra*, vol. X (*Taisho* vol. 32, p.316b).

CHAPTER II
TEXTUAL ANALYSIS

The authorship and date of composition of the *Māṇḍūkya-Kārikā* have been the subject of much controversy. In this chapter I shall first examine problems peripheral to the actual *Kārikā* verses, and then with the help of conclusions thus reached, tackle the central problems which have been most discussed.

SECTION I. VARIOUS NAMES OF THE *MĀṆḌŪKYA-KĀRIKĀ*

From the note at the end of each chapter in the published edition (BI. and ĀnSS.), the title of this work is *Gauḍapādīya-kārikā*.[1] This is sometimes abbreviated to simply *Gauḍapādīya*.[2] Indian scholars usually call it the *Māṇḍūkya-kārikā*, but the reason for this is not clear. The note at the end of the first chapter states: *Māṇḍūkyopaniṣad-arthāviṣkaraṇa-parāyāṃ Gauḍapādīya-kārikāyāṃ*..., while that at the end of the fourth chapter it says: *Gauḍapādācārya-kṛtā Māṇḍūkyopaniṣat-kārikāḥ*. Thus it was being taken that the *Kārikā* clarified the meaning of the *Māṇḍūkya-Upaniṣad*, and had been written by a person named Gauḍapāda. The name *Māṇḍūkya-kārikā*, as used by modern scholars, is probably an abbreviation of *Māṇḍūkya-Upaniṣat-kārikā*. The postscript of one edition states that the entire *Māṇḍūkya-kārikā* is *Śrī-Māṇḍūkyopaniṣad-Gauḍapāda-vyākhyāna*.[3]

The *Kārikā* is also called *Āgama-Śāstra*. In the postscript to the commentary to the *Kārikā*, written by Śaṅkara, the main text is called the *Gauḍapādīya-Āgama-Śastra* or simply the *Āgama-Śāstra*. Thus we know that at the time when this commentary was written, the *Kārikā* was also called the *Āgama-Śāstra*.[4] Originally this may have meant "a work on the scriptures," but later it seems to have acquired the meaning of "a work which itself has the authority of scripture."[5]

Then again, in some editions it is called *Upadeśagrantha*, *Āgamagrantha*, or *Māṇḍūkya-vārttika*.[6] Further, Kamalaśīla, citing passages from the *Kārikā*, calls it *Upaniṣad-śāstra*.[7] However, this probably should not be taken as a proper noun, its meaning being rather that the *Kārikā* clarifies the meaning of the *Upaniṣad*. The fact that the *Kārikā* is called a "*śāstra*" indicates that these verses held the position of a basic text for this school, in much the same way as we find the *Madhyamaka-śāstra* as a basic text for the Madhyamaka School.

Whatever this may imply, the most common names, which have also textual confirmation, are these :

1. *Gauḍapādīya-Kārikā*
2. *Māṇḍūkya-Upaniṣat-Kārikā*
3. *Āgama-Śāstra*

Of these three, the first is derived from the author's name, and the third purely from its contents ; they will be discussed later. The second is derived from the fact that the *Kārikā* is based on the *Māṇḍūkya-Upaniṣad*. As will be explained in detail below, the *Māṇḍūkya-kārikā* was frequently transmitted either in the form of the first chapter only, or with all four chapters placed together. In later periods the four chapters were considered in India generally as four independent *Upaniṣads*, and because of this, when Indian studies were first established in the West, it was thought that the *Kārikā* was made up of four *Upaniṣads*. However this was a mistake ; the four chapters of verses make up the *Māṇḍūkya-kārikā* and were not originally *Upaniṣads*.[8]

In general the *Māṇḍūkya-Upaniṣad* is considered to be one of the *Upaniṣads* attached to the *Atharva-veda*. However a work called *Caraṇavyūha* states that *Māṇḍūkya* means one of the branches attached to the *Ṛg-veda*. It is not clear why this *Upaniṣad* is called *Māṇḍūkya*. Madhva, in his commentary to the *Māṇḍūkya-Upaniṣad*, states that when the god Varuṇa had been transformed into a frog (*maṇḍūka*) he beheld this *Upaniṣad* called the *Māṇḍūkya* (*...iti maṇḍūkarūpī saṃdadarśa varuṇaḥ śrutim*).[9] On the other hand Sureśvara, citing passages from its sixth section, calls it the *Māṇḍūkeya-śruti*. Thus we do not now know by what process this *Upaniṣad* acquired its name ; what can be said with certainty is that from a relatively early period there was confusion about its name.[10]

Śaṅkara, in his *Chāndogyopaniṣadbhāṣya*(ad VIII,12), apparently refers to the *Gauḍapādīya-kārikā*:

tasmād idaṃ tyaktasarvabāhyaiṣaṇair ananyaśaraṇaiḥ paramahaṃ saparivrājakair atyāśramibhir Vedāntavijñānaparair eva vedanīyaṃ pūjyatamaiḥ prājāpatyaṃ cemaṃ saṃpradāyam anusaradbhir upanibaddhaṃ parkaraṇacatuṣṭayena/

Ānandajñāna comments:

pūjyatamair iti nityānuvādaḥ/ teṣām ātmavedanopāyaṃ prāktanam upadiśati.....prājāpatyaṃ ceti/ sthānatrayaṃ turīyaṃ cety etadviṣayaṃ prakaraṇacatuṣṭayam/(Ānandāśrama edition, p.500)

As the *Gauḍapādīya-kārikā* is referred to by Śaṅkara in this passage as an authoritative text, the author of the *Gauḍapādīya-kārikā* must have lived before Śaṅkara.

Notes

1) In the *Advaita-brahma-siddhi* two *ślokas* are also cited with this title (Walleser: *DAV*. S. 8).

2) Ānandajñāna calls Śaṅkara's commentary the *Gauḍapādīya-bhāṣya* (p.1, *l*.20).

3) Weber: *Indische Studien*, II, S.100-101.

4) In one edition examined by Weber, the *Māṇḍūkya-kārikā* is called simply the *Āgama-Śāstra*; and the term *Gauḍapāda* appears neither in the postscript nor in the commentary.

5) Sureśvara occasionally calls the main *ślokas* simply "*āgama*." Cf. notes to the main text I,3.

6) V. Bhattacharyya, *AS*. p.lxi, p.244.

7) Walleser: *DAV*. S. 21.

8) Weber: *HIL*. p.161.

9) *Ind. Ant*. vol. 62, p.188 (as cited in Venkatasubbiah's article). Further, one edition of this *Upaniṣad* is entitled the *Maṇḍūka-Upaniṣad* (R. G. Bhandarkar: *Collected Works*, II, p.95).

10) *Bṛhad. Up. Vārttika*, p.1294 (III, 8, 26).

SECTION II. COMMENTARIES ON THE *MĀṆḌŪKYA-UPANIṢAD* AND THE *KĀRIKĀ*

Among the commentaries and notes to the *Māṇḍūkya-Upaniṣad*, the

Māṇḍūkya-kārikā of Gauḍapāda is the oldest. But apart from this we have the following:[1]

(1) The Commentary (*Bhāṣya*) by Śaṅkara.

It provides notes to both the *Māṇḍūkya-Upaniṣad* and the *Gauḍapāda-kārikā*.

Editions:

The Māṇḍūkyopaniṣad with Gauḍapāda's *kārikā*, Śaṅkara's *Bhāṣya and* Ānandagiri's *Ṭīkā*, ed. by Ābājī Kāthavaṭe, ĀnSS. no 10. Poona, 1890.

Māṇḍūkyopaniṣad with Gauḍapāda's *Kārikā and* Śaṅkara's *Bhāṣya*. Memorial Edition of Śaṅkara's Works, Vani Vilas. Press, Srirangam. (Not consulted).

It has also been published in Calcutta as one volume of the Bibliotheca Indica.

As supplementary commentaries to this work we have the following:

(a) The Supplementary Commentary by Ānandajñāna. Ānandajñāna himself called his supplement the *Gauḍapādīyabhāṣyasya Vyākhyā*. It has been published as an appendix to Śaṅkara's Commentary cited above.[2]

(b) The Supplementary Commentary by Śuddhānanda.

(c) The Supplementary Commentary by Ānandātman.

(d) The Supplementary Commentary by Mathurānātha Śukla.

(e) The Supplementary Commentary by Raṅgarāmānuja.

Another work, probably also a supplementary commentary, is:

(f) *Gauḍapādīya-bhāṣya-ṭippaṇa* by Anubhūtisvarūpācārya.[3]

Of the above-mentioned, Ānandajñāna's is probably the oldest, but it appears that even before him supplementary commentaries had been composed by others (*ṭīkā-kāra*). He states in the benedictory stanza of his work: "The commentary to the *Gauḍapāda-kārikā* (*Gauḍapādīya-bhāṣya*) would seem to be clear, but I shall do my best to explain the profound meaning of its contents. Even though former savants (*pūrve vidvāṃsaḥ*) have composed commentaries (*vyākhyāna*) to this work, I am making a further attempt for the benefit of duller intellects."

Further, regarding the second *śloka* of the initial dedication in Śaṅkara's

Commentary, a tradition is recorded that previous to Ānandajñāna's there existed three different commentaries.[4] Thus, we may infer that Ānandajñāna made use of previously existing supplementary commentaries in his own commentary.

As a summary of the main points of Śaṅkara's commentary there exists:

(g) *Māṇḍūkyopaniṣad-bhāṣyārthasaṃgraha* by Rāghavānanda.[5]

(2) The Commentary by Brahmānanda-sarasvatī.

(3) The Commentary by Rāghavendra.

(4) The *Dīpikā* by Nārāyaṇa.

(5) The *Dīpikā* by Śaṅkarānanda.

Editions:

Published with the *Māṇḍūkya-Upaniṣad* in ĀnSS. no. 10; also published with Prakāśānanda's *Mitākṣarā* in Haridās Sanskrit Series, no.1.

(6) The *Māṇḍūkyopaniṣad-āloka* by Vijñānabhikṣu.

(7) The Commentary (*Bhāṣya*) by Madhva (=Ānandatīrtha).

Related to this work there exist the following three commentaries:

(a) The Supplementary Commentary by Vidyātīrtha.

(b) The Supplementary Commentary by Śrīnivāsatīrtha.

(c) The *Māṇḍūkyopaniṣad-bhāṣya-saṃgraha* by Rāghavendra.

(8) The *Māṇḍūkyopaniṣadarthaprakāśa* by Kūranārāyaṇa. The author belonged to the Rāmānuja School.

Edition: ĀnSS. no. 62.

(9) The Commentary by Doḍḍācārya (=Mahācārya). The author belonged to the Rāmānuja School.

(10) The Commentary by Nārāyaṇāśramin. The author belonged to the Advaita School. His date is uncertain, but since he refers to Śaṅkara and Ānandagiri, he is later than these two.[6]

(11) The Commentary by Upaniṣad-brahma-yogin.

Edition:

Māṇḍūkyopaniṣad and Gauḍapādīya-Kārikā, with the Commentary of Śrī Upaniṣad-brahma-yogin; *Daśopaniṣads*, Adyar Library, 1935.

(2)-(11) above may generally be taken to be commentaries on the *Upaniṣad* only. As a commentaries to the *Māṇḍūkya-kārika* only we have the following:

(12) The *Mitākṣarā* by Svayaṃprakāśānandasarasvatī (abbreviated as Prakāśānanda).

Edition:

Mitākṣarā, A Gloss on Śrī Gauḍapāda Ācārya's Māṇḍūkya kārikā, by Svayaṃprakāśānanda Sarasvatī; and *Māṇḍūkyopaniṣad-dīpikā* of Śaṅkarānanda, ed. by Pandit Ratna Gopal Bhatta, Kashi Sanskrit Series, no.48. 1910.

According to its postscript, other names for it are *Śrī-Gauḍapādīya-śloka-vṛtti* and *Śrī-Gauḍapādīya-vārttika-vṛtti*. Its author may be considered to have lived approximately during the latter half of the 16th century.[7] Its contents are almost identical with Śaṅkara's commentary and Ānandajñāna's supplementary commentary.

(13) The *Gauḍapādīya-viveka*.[8]

Of the above-cited works, the commentary ascribed to Śaṅkara is the earliest and most important. However, the question of whether it actually is a work by the Śaṅkara who wrote the commentary to the *Brahma-sūtra* has long been a problem to scholars. Other than the fact that in the postscript of one edition there is an attribution to Śaṅkara, we have no proof of authorship. The great majority of Indian scholars consider it the work of the same Śaṅkara and do not question this, but scholars who do critical research have always had doubts on the point. At a relatively early stage Walleser posed such questions,[9] but it was Jacobi and Vidhusekhara Bhattacharyya particularly who argued that this was not a work by Śaṅkara. Jacobi points out[10] that in the commentary to *Kārikā* II, 4 there is an argument which uses the five-part proof.[11] He finds it unthinkable that the author of the Commentary to the *Brahma-sūtra* would use in their exact form the technical terms and method of inference of the Nyāya School. It is indeed a fact that the author of the commentary to the *Māṇḍūkya-kārikā* was adept in logical inference.[12] But it is not possible to conclude immediately from this fact that its author and the author of the commentary to the *Brahma-sūtra* were different persons. In Indian philosophical circles of that time, although the three-part proof already was in wide use, the five-part proof had not yet been completely discarded. In fact, the five-part proof methodology is used in the Commentary to the *Brahma-sūtra*.[13] In this commentary Śaṅkara quotes from the *Nyāya-sūtra*, affirming and utilizing its assertions.[14] Thus it would not at all be strange if he used the five-part proof of the Nyāya School. It must be concluded that Jacobi's proposal has an extremely weak basis.[15]

Paṇḍit Vidhusekhara Bhattacaryya concluded that the commentary to the *Māṇḍūkya* was not a work by Śaṅkara for a variety of reasons. We no doubt should pay heed to his assertion that there are faults in its rhyme and rhythm patterns and that it has grammatical errors. But Bhattacharyya further cites as evidence several passages in the Commentary which are at odds with Śaṅkara's thought. But we must add that, on the contrary, since the Commentary is intended as notes to the *Māṇḍūkya-kārikā*, it is quite natural that they do not coincide with Śaṅkara's thought.

I feel it possible to conclude that the author of this commentary was not Śaṅkara for a number of different reasons. From the sections in the Commentary to the *Brahma-sūtra* which attack Buddhism, we know that Śaṅkara had a good knowledge of Buddhist teaching and of its technical terminology. Though there are of course not a few passages which miss the point, we may say generally that Śaṅkara understood Buddhist thought. In contrast, however, although an exceedingly large number of Buddhistic terms and modes of expression are found in the *Māṇḍūkya-kārikā*, the author of the commentary has added notes which are far from appropriate. To explain this, we might perhaps suppose that the author of the Commentary was aware of the influence of Buddhism on the *Māṇḍūkya-kārikā*, but in order to hide the fact deliberately wrote comments which miss the point. However, in such a case, he probably would have stated somewhere in the work that in commenting on the *Kārikā*, a Buddhist interpretation should not be followed. Since there is no such note, we may conclude that the author of the commentary was not well versed in Buddhist Sanskrit and Buddhist teachings.

Another point that merits attention is the fact that in the Commentary the Absolute Self (expressed in the first chapter of the *Kārikā* as the 'Fourth Stage') is called "*vijñapti*."[16] Ānandajñāna also follows this usage.[17] Another startling point is the fact that the essence of *Ātman* is explained as *vijñaptimātra*.[18] Ānandajñāna subscribes also to this.[19] This is exactly the same term, *vijñaptimātra*, that is used in Buddhism. The use of the term *vijñapti* in a philosophical sense is not seen in general Indian sources; it is a uniquely Buddhistic usage. The author of the Commentary explains it as a synonym of *vijñāna*.[20] Thus, he also explains that the actual existence of "higher truth" is *vijñānamātra*.[21] He occasionally calls it *vijñaptimātra*,[22] and also uses many other terms of this genre.[23] Such a mode of expression is not seen at all in Śaṅkara's Commentary to the *Brahma-sūtra*. Further, the author of the *Māṇḍūkya* Commentary frequently uses the term "*advaya*" as an adjective qualifying the term *Ātman*.[24] In meaning this term is used in practically the same sense as "*advaita*." However, in origin it is a term from Buddhist Sanskrit. As far as this author is aware, the term is not used at all in the Commentary to the *Brahma-sūtra*. Thus, in light of the use of this important technical term, it must be concluded that the author of the *Māṇḍūkya* Commentary is different from the Śaṅkara who wrote the commentary to the *Brahma-sūtra*. It may be considered that since the *Kārikā* uses many Buddhist terms its commentary would quite naturally use many such terms. Yet even if that be so, we must also note that in points quite independent of explanations of passages in the *Kārikā* such terms are used. Although the above-mentioned term "*vijñapti*" appears not even once in the *Kārikā*, the author of the Commentary uses it frequently. Thus, it may be judged fairly conclusively that the author of the Commentary himself felt it necessary to use the term.

Although the author of the commentary to the *Māṇḍūkya-kārikā* was not well-versed in Buddhist Sanskrit, he preferred to use terms that were characteristically Buddhist. At first glance this appears odd; we may explain it in the following manner. The Śaṅkara who wrote the commentary to the *Brahma-sūtra* was fairly well-acquainted with Buddhist teachings, and thus when he propounded his own theories he attempted to distance himself as far as possible by avoiding Buddhist terms. In contrast to this, the author of the Commentary to the *Māṇḍūkya-kārikā* was not well-acquainted with Buddhist teachings, but had studied in an atmosphere or tradition rather strongly influenced by Buddhism. Thus Buddhist terms were relatively familiar to him. Although he did not fully understand Buddhist thought, he unconsciously used Buddhistic terminology in his own theories.

That the author of the Commentary to the *Brahma-sūtra* and the author of the Commentary to the *Māṇḍūkya-kārikā* are different can also be seen from the texts cited by each. The latter quotes from the *Kaivalya-Upaniṣad*[25] and the *Nṛsiṃhottara-tāpanīya-Upaniṣad*,[26] but the former not at all. Thus it can be seen that there is some difference in the type of *Upaniṣad* recognized as their basic authority.[27]

From the above facts it must be assumed that the authors of the two commentaries were probably different. However, it is also probable that in time and in social circumstances and position, or in education, they were not far apart. The author of the commentary to the *Māṇḍūkya-kārikā*, like the author of the commentary to the *Brahma-sūtra*, believed in the worship of Viṣṇu and does not refer to the god Śiva.[28] Further, the literary style of the two works is quite similar. The works cited in both are mostly "old *Upaniṣads*." There are some citations from *Purāṇas*, but they are few. So on this point they are markedly different from works such as the commentary to the *Śvetāśvatara-Upaniṣad*, which is also attributed to Śaṅkara. Because of this, no doubt, the *Māṇḍūkya* Commentary was later taken to be a work by Śaṅkara, and the tradition that it was his work came to be unquestioned.[29] Thus, although the commentary to the *Māṇḍūkya* is not actually by Śaṅkara, it may be assumed that there is nothing drastically wrong in using it as a source when discussing early Vedānta philosophy.

Notes

1) As listed in Aufrecht : *CC*. III.

2) p.225, *l*.11. In Aufrecht : *CC*. the supplementary commentary attributed to Ānandatīrtha is probably an error for Ānandajñāna.

3) Mahadevan : *GP*. p.241.

4) p.4. *l*.18 — p.5. *l*.7.

5) Dasgupta : *HIPh*. II, p.78.

6) (8), (9), and (10) are listed in the previously cited article by Venkatasubbiah. (4) and (8) may be identical works. Since they have not yet been published, details about them are not clear.

7) Cf. Dasgupta : *HIPh*. vol. II, p 220 ; Farquhar : *Outline*, p.368.

8) Mahadevan : *GP*. p.241.

9) Walleser: *DAV*. S. 55, Anm. 1.

10) H. Jacobi: *JAOS*. 1913, p.52, n. 2.

11) "Phenomena seen in the state of waking are false" is the thesis (*pratijñā*); "because they are seen" is the reason (*hetu*); "like those seen in the state of dreaming" is the example (*dṛṣṭānta*); "Just as things seen in dreams are false, so in the state of waking also the things are not different [from those in a dream], inasmuch as they are seen" is the application of the reason (*hetūpanayana*); "Therefore it is declared that [the phenomena which are seen] are also not true" is the conclusion (*nigamana*)." (ad *GK*. II, 4.)

12) *hetuṃ dṛṣṭāntaṃ ca vakṣyāmi* (Ś. ad *GK*. p.105, *l*.25), *anaikāntiko hetuḥ* (*ibid*., p.65, *l* 21), *anvaya-vyatireka* (*ibid*., p.140, *l*.12), *pratijñā* (*ibid*., p.140, *l*.14.)

13) *paramāṇūnām aṇutva-nityatva-viparyayaḥ prasajyeta/...... kutaḥ/evaṃ loke dṛṣṭatvāt/ yad dhi loke rūpādimad vastu tat svakāraṇa-apekṣayā sthūlam anityaṃ ca dṛṣṭam/ tadyathā paṭas tantūn apekṣya sthūlo 'nityaś ca bhavati ....../tathā cāmī paramāṇavo rūpādimantaḥ...../tasmāt te 'pi kāraṇavantas.....sthūlā anityāś ca prāpnuvanti//......* (Ś. ad *BS*. II, 2, 15. vol. 1, pp.547-8.)

14) Ś. ad *BS*. I, 1, 4. vol. I, pp.62-63.

15) Paṇḍit Vidhusekhara Bhattacharyya: "Śaṅkara's Commentaries on the Upaniṣads," *Sir Asutosh Mookerjee Jubilee Volumes*, vol. III, 1925, pp.101 ff.; *AS*. p.xxxiii, n.3.

16) *.....paramārthavijñaptyā 'tmarūpeṇa/*(Ś. ad *GK*. p.139, *l*.14)

17) *paramātmā ...... nityavijñaptisvabhāvo/*(Ān. ad *GK*., p.4, *l*.17). *nityavijñaptirūpe turīye* (Ān. ad *GK*. p.49, *l*.24).

18) *svena viśuddhavijñaptimātrasattādvayarūpeṇa ......* (Ś. ad *GK*. p.81, *l*.8). As an explanation of "*sarvadharmeṣu*" in the main text IV.60, it is stated "*ātmasv ajeṣu nityaikarasavijñaptimātrasattākeṣu/*"

19) *brahmaṇo ... vijñāptimātratva* (Ān. ad *GK*. p.3, *l*.10). *turīye nitye vijñaptimātre* (*ibid*., p.17, *l*.13).

20) Śaṅkara explains "*vijñāna*" in *GK*. IV, 45 as "*vijñapti*" (p.188, *l*.20).

21) *paramārthasadvijñānamātrāviśeṣāt/*(Ś. ad *GK*. p.140, *l*.3), *ajaṃ vijñānamātraṃ tattvam/*(*ibid*., p.173, *l*.21). Other than these, this term appears on p.173, *l*.19; p.192, *l*. 6; p.197, *l*.9.

22) Ś. ad *GK*. p.141, *l*.24; Ān. ad *GK*. p.221, *l*.3.

23) *cittavikalpanāmātra* (Ś. ad *GK*. p.200, *l*.15); *manovikalpanāmātraṃ dvaitam iti siddham/*(Ś. ad *GK*. p.92, *l*.3); *dvaitasya mānasatva* (Ś. ad *GK*. p.92, *l*.2).

24) *advaya ātmā paramārthaḥ/*(Ś. ad *GK*. p.9, *l*.8). The term *advaya* is also used of *ātman* on p.187, *l*.14; p.186, *l*.25; p.81, *l*.9; p.91, *l*.22, etc.

25) p.16; "*sarvabhūtāni cātmani*" (= *Kaivalya-Up*. X).

26) p.118, *l*.5: "*mṛtyoḥ sa mṛtyum āpnoti*" (*Nṛs. Ut. Tāp. Up*. VIII). Or it may be a

corrupt form from the *Kāṭhaka-Up.* IV, 11 ; but even if that be the case, it should be regarded as important that such a corrupt form was used.

27) Prof. Belvakar emphasizes that in explaining *śloka* III,14 of the main text, the commentator would quite naturally be expected to refer to the *Chānd. Up.* VI, 3, 2 ; and that since he does not, he cannot be the "great Śaṅkara."

28) "*saṃbuddha*" in IV,1 is held to be *Nārāyaṇa*. Further, Ānandajñāna also relates that the author Gauḍapāda was a worshipper of the god *Viṣṇu* (ad *GK*. p.2, *l*.3). Ānandajñāna himself dedicated the initial and final *ślokas* to *Viṣṇu* (ad *GK* p.1, *l*.17 ; p.225, *l*. 7). Concerning the *Viṣṇu* worship of Śaṅkara, author of the commentary to the *Brahma-sūtra*, see my article in the Festschrift in honor of Professor Ui Hakuju.

29) There is a view that the *Gauḍapādīya-bhāṣya* was written by Śaṅkara himself (T. Vetter : *Festschrift E. Frauwallner*, *WZKSO*, 12/13, 1968 S.407ff ; S. Mayeda : "On the Author of the *Māṇḍūkyopaniṣad* and the *Gauḍapādīya Bhāṣya*," *The Adyar Library Bulletin*, vols. 31-32, 1967-68, pp.73-94). A detailed analysis of the work has been made: Paul Hacker: "Notes on the *Māṇḍūkyopaniṣad* and Śaṅkara's *Āgamaśāstravivaraṇa*." *Festschrift Gonda*, pp.133-115-132 ; see also : *Māṇḍūkya Upaniṣad et Kārikā de Gauḍapāda*. publiée et traduite par Em. Lesimple, Paris, Adrien-Maisonneuve, 1944.

SECTION III. CHANGES IN THE AUTHORITATIVENESS OF THE *MĀṆḌŪKYA-UPANIṢAD* AND THE *KĀRIKĀ*

In the theological traditions of orthodox Brahmanism, the *Veda* taken in the wide sense is "revelation" (*śruti*) and possesses absolute authority, and other traditional books (*smṛti*) and commentaries and so on are thought to have weight insofar as they are in accord with revelation in their content (and only insofar). It has been for long a question in India whether the *Māṇḍūkya-upaniṣad* and *Kārikās* on it are to be included among revealed works or not. Modern scholars have come to various conclusions. It is intended to set out here the various assessments of the value of these works by the Indians during their history, and by an examination of the results to clear up the differences in authority attributed to them. From this we can also assess their varying place in the history of Indian thought. Let us first see how they were regarded in primitive Advaita, and then how their authoritativeness changed.

Sub-Section 1. The *Māṇḍūkya-Upaniṣad* and the *Kārikās* as Viewed in Early Advaita

In his commentary on the *Brahma-sūtras* (I, 4, 14 and II, 1, 9), Śaṅkara twice quotes the text of a *Māṇḍūkya-kārikā* as the doctrine of "one who knows the traditional doctrine" (*Saṃpradāyavid*). Thus Śaṅkara considered that the *Kārikās* were a human production and not revelation.

In the *Chāndogyopaniṣadbhāṣya* (ad VIII,12,1) Śaṅkara seems to refer to the *Gauḍapādīya-kārikā*. He writes as follows:[1]

tasmād idaṃ tyaktasarvabāhyaiṣaṇair ananyaśaraṇaiḥ paramahaṃsaparivrājakair atyāśramibhir vedāntavijñānaparair eva vedanīyaṃ pūjyatamaiḥ prājāpatyaṃ cemaṃ saṃpradāyam anusaradbhir upanibaddhaṃ parkaraṇacatuṣṭayena/

Ānandajñāna comments on this as follows:

pūjyatamair iti nityānuvādaḥ/ teṣām ātmavedanopāyaṃ prāktanam upadiśati prājāpatyaṃ ceti/ sthānatrayaṃ turīyaṃ cety etadviṣayaṃ prakaraṇacatuṣṭayam/(ĀnSS. edition, p.500)

As the *Gauḍapādīya-kārikā* is cited as an authority by Śaṅkara in this passage, it is most likely that the composer of the *Kārikās* lived earlier than Śaṅkara.

Again Śaṅkara's pupil Sureśvara, referring to the *Māṇḍūkya-kārikā* II, 17, calls it the words of Gauḍapāda:

aniścitā yathā rajjur iti nyāyopabṛṃhitam/ sphuṭārthaṃ Gauḍapādīyaṃ vaco 'rthe 'traiva gīyate//(*Bṛhad. Up. Vārttika*, I,4,389. p.510)

Again in his own work *Naiṣkarmyasiddhi* IV, 41 and 42 he quotes *Kārikās* I,11 and 15, and in the same work in IV, 43 he quotes *Upadeśasāhasrī* XVIII, 26 and then says:[2]

evaṃ Gauḍair Drāviḍair naḥ pūjyair ayam arthaḥ prabhāṣitaḥ/(IV,44)[3]

From these facts, one can conclude that Sureśvara also considered the *Kārikās* as the work of a man named Gauḍapāda, and not as a *śruti* or part of one. So at the time of Śaṅkara and Sureśvara, the *Māṇḍūkya-Kārikās* did not yet possess the authority of *śruti*. However, Sureśvara, when quoting *Kārikā* I.3 in his *Bṛhad. Up. Vārttika* I.4.744, calls it '*āgama*' (traditional work), and so there is no doubt of his great reverence for it.[4]

What was the case with the *Māṇḍūkya-Upaniṣad* itself? Scholars have often voiced the suspicion that the *Māṇḍūkya* was recognized as an *Upaniṣad* only later, and in the time of Śaṅkara himself it was not credited with the authority of *śruti*.

Venkatasubbiah[5] argues with much erudition that the so-called *Upaniṣad* is the work of Gauḍapāda who wrote the *Kārikās*, and later extended his thesis even further to maintain that both are merely a part of a great work called the *Āgama-śāstra*.[6] On the other hand, Vidhushekhar Bhattacharyya argues that the so-called *Upaniṣad* did not exist at all at the time of Śaṅkara, but was composed later, on the basis of the first chapter of the *Kārikās*, and still later came to be an accredited *Upaniṣad*. The two theories agree that the *Māṇḍūkya-Upaniṣad* must not be put in the same category as the old *Upaniṣads*, but must have been composed later. However, it is then necessary to examine the reasons that are being given for supposing that it was composed at a later time.

A most important reason is that, in all of Śaṅkara's works, this *Upaniṣad* is not cited even once.[7] The fact that it is not quoted in the *Brahma-sūtra* commentary has previously attracted the notice of scholars, and according to Mr. Venkatasubbiah's researches, in Śaṅkara's commentaries on the nine principal *Upaniṣads* and the *Gītā*, the *Māṇḍūkya-Upaniṣad* is not quoted even once. Even in places where it would be very likely to be quoted, there is no reference to it at all. So one could conclude that at the time of Śaṅkara this *Upaniṣad* did not have the status of *śruti* authority. Again, looking at Śaṅkara's commentary to the *Upaniṣad*, it is not taken as *śruti*, for the opening says:

> "*om ity etad akṣaram idaṃ sarvaṃ tasyopavyākhyānam*" / *vedānta-arthasāra-saṃgrahabhūtam idaṃ prakaraṇacatuṣṭayam* "*om ity etad akṣaram*" *ityādy ārabhyate* /

And he calls himself "one who is to comment on the *prakaraṇa*" (*prakaraṇavyācikhyāsu*).[8] This commentator calls each book of the *Kārikās* a "*prakaraṇa*," and one has to consider that the words "*om ity etad akṣaram*," etc., of the *Māṇḍūkya-Upaniṣad* are included in the "four books (*prakaraṇa-catuṣthaya*)." So it is the *Gauḍapāda-kārikā*, which includes the *Māṇḍūkya-Upaniṣad*, that is taken as the "summary teaching the essence of the *Upaniṣads*" (*Vedāntārthasārasaṃgraha*). This is the theory which is being put forward.

This is the main evidence adduced to show that at the time of Śaṅkara the *Māṇḍūkya* was not recognized as *śruti*. But on this alone it is quite impossible to accept the conclusion. In the commentary on the *Upaniṣad* itself, the phrase "*ayam ātmā brahma*" (this self is *brahman*)[9] is quoted as *śruti*, and one has to conclude that this is a phrase from the *Māṇḍūkya Upaniṣad* II, quoted as authoritative. Again, it has to be noted that Sureśvara quotes a verse (6) of this *Upaniṣad* as *śruti*:

> *eṣo 'ntaryāmy eṣa yoniḥ sarvasya prabhavāpyayau/ Māṇḍūkeyaśrutivaca iti spaṣṭam adhīyate//*(*Bṛhad. Up. Vārttika*, III, 8, 26. p.1294)

Sureśvara was a direct disciple of Śaṅkara, indeed one who wrote commentaries on Śaṅkara's works, and if Śaṅkara had positively rejected the *Māṇḍūkya-Upaniṣad* as *śruti*, then it is unimaginable that Sureśvara would have quoted it as such. So it has to be admitted that already before the time of Sureśvara this *Upaniṣad*'s authority as revelation was accepted. But in view of the fact that Śaṅkara does not quote it, it is likely that he did not regard it as particularly important. Again, as has already been pointed out, the fact that the commentator refers to this short *Upaniṣad* as included in the "*prakaraṇa*" treatise shows that before the time of the composition of the commentary this small *Upaniṣad* had already been incorporated in the first chapter of Gauḍapāda's *Kārikās*. The later commentator Nārāyaṇāśramin thought that the first chapter of the *Kārikās* was made up of *śruti* and the commentary on it (*śruti-tad-vyākhyā-ghaṭitaṃ prathamaṃ prakaraṇam*).[10] And in that case there would be nothing contradictory in referring to the *Māṇḍūkya-Upaniṣad* as the *śruti* in question.

The *Māṇḍūkya-Upaniṣad*, then, was already recognized as *śruti* in the early Vedāntic schools, but not regarded as specially important. And therefore one can conclude that theories which hold the *Upaniṣad* to be the work of Gauḍapāda or some later author are untenable.

Thus, in the early Advaita, it was the prose part only which was the *Upaniṣad*, and the verse was thought to be a commentary to bring out its meaning. Later, Ānandajñāna inherited this view as it stood. According to him, the *Māṇḍūkya-Upaniṣad* is *śruti*,[11] and the *Gauḍapāda-kārikā* is an explanation (*vyākhyāna*),[12] an elucidation (*vivaraṇa*)[13] of it, aiming at making its meaning clear (*māṇḍūkyopaniṣad-arthāviṣkaraṇa-para*).[14] He also thought that to the *Upaniṣad* which is the "basic canon" (*mūlagrantha*)[15] the four chapters of the *Kārikās* had been added.[16] Again, there was a group who believed that the *Gauḍapāda-kārikā* was a *vārttika* commentary[17] to the *Māṇḍūkya-Upaniṣad*. This kind of view is followed by the *Advaitin* Nārāyaṇāśramin and the *Viśiṣṭādvaitin* Raṅgarāmānuja.[18]

Notes

1) I owe this information to Mr. T. Leggett.

2) Cf. Walleser: *Der älterer Vedānta.*

3) This means that Gauḍapāda was revered by Sureśvara as one of his predecessors. Jñānottama explains: *Gauḍair Gauḍapādācāryair* .....

4) In his note to the *Bṛhad. Up. Vārttika* Ānandajñāna says, "*atrāpi śrutim paṭhati*" (and here he quotes *śruti*).

5) "The *Māṇḍūkyopaniṣad* and Gauḍapāda," *Ind. Ant.*, vol. LXII, 1933, and "On Gauḍapāda's *Āgama-śāstra*," *IHQ*. XI, 1935.

6) "The *Māṇḍūkya-Upaniṣad* and the *Gauḍapāda-Kārikās*", *IHQ*. I,1925.

7) In the *Brahma-sūtra* commentary on I,1,9 there is "*prabhavāpyayāv*" *ity utpatti-pratyayayoḥ prayogadarśanāt*: "it is seen that origin and dissolution are referred to by the phrase *prabhava-apyayau*." But this should probably be taken as quoting *Kāṭhaka-Upaniṣad* IV, 11 rather than the *Māṇḍūkya-Upaniṣad*. Śaṅkara frequently quotes from the *Kāṭhaka-Upaniṣad*.

8) Compare Ānandajñāna on *GK*... *prakaraṇatvena* .... (p.5, *l*.21).

9) p.39.

10) Venkatasubbiah: *Ind. Ant.* LXII, *op. cit.*, p.188.

11) pp.12, *l*.1; p.12, *ll*. 9-10; p.22, *l*.1.

12) p.4, *l*.21; p.25, *l*.1.

13) p.46, *l*.20.

14) p.2, *l*.3.

15) p.18, *ll*. 18,21.

16) *prakaraṇacatuṣṭayaviśiṣṭasya śāstrasya*. See *Venkatasubbiah, Ind. Ant.* LXII, p.221; cf. p.5 and p.157.

17) *Pañcadaśī*, II,29. In his notes to this verse Rāmakṛṣṇa Paṇḍita quotes *Kārikā* III,39 and says it is the *Vārttika*. In one of the editions of Śaṅkara's commentary it says: *atha vārttika karoktam vākyam* (ĀnSS., p.25 n.)

18) See Venkatasubbiah, *op. cit.*, pp.189, 191.

Sub-Section 2. The Later Status of the *Māṇḍūkya-Upaniṣad* in India

As stated previously, although they did not evaluate it as highly as the "old *Upaniṣads*," the thinkers of the early Advaita school considered the *Māṇḍūkya-Upaniṣad* to be a *śruti*. With the passage of time, however, this *Upaniṣad* came to be regarded as an extremely important scripture and greatly influenced later Indian thought. It came even to surpass the authority of the "old *Upaniṣads*."

Firstly, in acknowledging the importance of the *Gauḍapāda-kārikā*, we must also recognize the indirect influence of the *Māṇḍūkya-Upaniṣad* itself since it was held that Gauḍapāda wrote the *Kārikā* based on this *Upaniṣad*, and thus that the two works are closely related. If the *Gauḍapāda-kārikā* is regarded as having had a permanent significance on Indian thought, the importance of the *Māṇḍūkya-Upaniṣad* cannot be ignored.

Further, the *Māṇḍūkya-Upaniṣad* greatly influenced other *Upaniṣads* which are subsidiary to the *Atharva-veda*.

1. The *Māṇḍūkya-Upaniṣad* I-VII appears in almost the same form in the *Nṛsiṃha-pūrva-tāpanīya-Upaniṣad* IV,1 (in one edition IV, 2) and the *Nṛsiṃha-uttara-tāpanīya-Upaniṣad* I. In the *Rāma-uttara-tāpanīya-Upaniṣad* III, except for one passage where the phrases are placed differently, it is included in exactly the same form. Further, in the *Yogacūḍāmaṇy-Upaniṣad* 72 ff. and in the *Nārada-parivrājaka-Upaniṣad* 7.3 ff., although the wording differs considerably, the contents are the same.
2. Although there is a considerable amount of difference, the *Māṇḍūkya-Upaniṣad* IX-XII appears in generally the same form in the *Nṛsiṃha-uttara-tāpanīya-Upaniṣad* II.

In this manner it influenced many of the "new *Upaniṣads*," in particular the *Nṛsiṃha-uttara-tāpanīya-Upaniṣad*, in which almost the entire *Māṇḍūkya-Upaniṣad* in included.

Now comes the question of whether the *Māṇḍūkya* existed as an independent work and was subsequently incorporated into other works, or whether it was put together out of passages extracted from other works. For the following reasons I feel that the *Māṇḍūkya-Upaniṣad* is earlier.

1. The *Māṇḍūkya-Upaniṣad* is structured as an organized work, and each chapter has its appropriate place in the developmental structure of the *Upaniṣad*. The *Nṛsiṃha-uttara-tāpanīya-Upaniṣad*, however, does not have a unified organization and its contents are extremely fragmentary. It may thus be considered to have been put together from various older works. In its explanation of various "sacred sounds" it is unmistakable that the *Māṇḍūkya-Upaniṣad* is relied upon. The case of the *Nṛsiṃha-pūrva-tāpanīya-Upaniṣad* is the same.[1)]

2. In the initial verse section of the *Rāma-uttara-tāpanīya-Upaniṣad* a half-syllable measure (*ardhamātrā*) other than *a*, *u*, and *m* is recognized. The quality of *Rāma* is taken as a half-syllable, but in the following prose section (i. e., the section that is almost the same as the *Māṇḍūkya-Upaniṣad*) the half-syllable sound is not discussed at all. This is clearly contradictory. However, if it is considered that the author of the *Rāma-uttara-tāpanīya* created this situation by forcibly seeking to explain sacred sound by citing the *Māṇḍūkya-Upaniṣad*, this difficult point is easily resolved.

3. Since the "new *Upaniṣads*" were composed on the basis of worship of *Nṛsiṃha* and *Rāma*, they embrace various types of popular beliefs and contain passages which bring to mind *Tantra* literature ; they have an extremely esoteric coloring. Thus they reflect the beliefs of the general populace and undoubtedly at the time of their composition were considered to be of (relatively) low value. (Śaṅkara, for example, does not once cite these "new *Upaniṣads*.") It is hardly conceivable that orthodox *Brahmins*, who formed the intellectual stratum in India, extracted passages from these works and revered them. On the contrary, it is probably more accurate to hold that the faithful among the general populace took passages from the Orthodox Brahmanical literature and composed these "new *Upaniṣads*, and that at a later period these eventually came to acquire the authority of *Upaniṣads*.

4. Since the *Yogacūḍāmaṇy-Upaniṣad* and the *Nāradaparivrājaka-Upaniṣad* are not included even in the *Oupnek'hat* and since in content they may be considered to be works of a later period, it goes without saying that they owe their very existence to the influence of the

Māṇḍūkya-Upaniṣad.

In this manner, since it influenced so many of the "new *Upaniṣads,*" the *Māṇḍūkya* came to be considered the most important of the *Upaniṣads*. In the *Muktikā-Upaniṣad* I, 26–29, it is stated:

> (Question:) Then by what means can this final release which is perfect isolation be attained?
>
> (Answer:) The *Māṇḍūkya* alone is sufficient for the final release of those who seek final release. But if your knowledge has not yet been established, read the ten *Upaniṣads*. .... And if your knowledge is still not firm, O son of Anjanā (mother of the monkey-god *Hanumat*), study the *Upaniṣads* called the Thirty-two, and perfect it. If you desire final release free from the body, read the 108 (*Upaniṣads*).

Thus the *Māṇḍūkya-Upaniṣad* came to be considered the most basic of all the *Upaniṣads*, and in fact the other *Upaniṣads* were considered to have only a supplementary significance in relationship to it. (Of course, the *Māṇḍūkya-Upaniṣad* indicated here may also include the first stanza of the *Māṇḍūkya-kārikā*). When we reflect on the fact that this *Upaniṣad* was neglected in earlier periods, this change in evaluation is indeed startling. Even in the Advaita school it came in later periods to be extremely highly regarded. For example, the "Outline of Teachings" in Sadānanda's *Compendium* of *the Upaniṣads* is based on the *Māṇḍūkya-Upaniṣad*. Upaniṣad-brahma-yogin, who wrote commentaries on the 108 *Upaniṣads*, calls it "the sum of all the *Upaniṣads*" (*Sarva-Vedānta-sāriṣtha*).[2]

What made this *Upaniṣad* particularly meaningful was the *Gauḍapāda-Kārikā,* which had been appended to it. Let us here examine the changes in evaluation of these verses.

Notes

1) T. M. P. Mahadevan is of the same opinion (*GP*. pp.38–39).

2). T. M. P. Mahadevan: *GP*. p.89.

Sub-Section 3. Changes in the Evaluation of the *Māṇḍūkya-Kārikā*

1. Schools other than the Advaita come to take the first chapter of the *Māṇḍūkya-kārikā* as a *śruti*.

The early Advaita school considered the *Māṇḍūkya-kārikā* the work of Gauḍapāda and not a *śruti*, but later the Vedānta schools other than the Advaita tended to take the view that both the prose section (i.e., the *Māṇḍūkya-Upaniṣad*) and the first chapter of the *Gauḍapāda-kārikā* (*Āgama-prakaraṇa*) formed the *Māṇḍūkya-Upaniṣad*, or, alternatively, that although only the prose section was the *Māṇḍūkya-Upaniṣad*, the first chapter of the *Kārikā* was also a *śruti*.

Madhva (1199-1278) and the scholars who followed him (Vyāsatīrtha, Śrīnivāsa et.al.) held that only the prose section was the *Māṇḍūkya-Upaniṣad*, but thought that the first chapter of the *Gauḍapāda-kārikā* was also a *śruti*. They relate the story of how the god *Varuṇa*, having assumed the form of a frog (*maṇḍūka*), was meditating on and honoring the god *Nārāyaṇa* by means of the sacred syllable *OM*, and was rewarded by receiving these holy texts, and further how *Brahmā* in the guise of a sage (*ṛṣi*) witnessed this.[1] Thus the *Kārikā* itself was accepted as a *mantra* (sacred verse) of *śruti*, and even the linking passage *atraite ślokā bhavanti* joining the *Upaniṣad* to the *Kārikās* was recognized as *śruti*.

Even Rāmānuja who followed the *Viśiṣṭādvaita* held that the first chapter was a *śruti*.[2] The two scholars who followed him, Kūranārāyaṇa and Doḍḍācārya (= Mahācārya), also wrote notes to the *Māṇḍūkya-Upaniṣad*. They both held that the first chapter of the *Gauḍapāda-kārikā* was a *mantra* and that this chapter together with the prose section formed the *Māṇḍūkya-Upaniṣad*.[3] It may be supposed that Rāmānuja himself also held this view.[4]

Appaya Dīkṣita,[5] who wrote commentaries to the 108 *Upaniṣads*, wrote a commentary to the *Māṇḍūkya-Upaniṣad* and to only the first chapter of the *Kārikā*. Thus he also may be considered to have held this view.[6] When one surveys the existing editions of the *Māṇḍūkya-Upaniṣad*, one finds a great many which include the first chapter of the *Gauḍapāda-kārikā*.[7] Finally, even the Vedānta scholar Sāyana calls this first chapter the *śruti* of the Māṇḍūkya school (*Māṇḍūkya-śākhā*).[8]

In this manner, during this period this work was recognized as having great authority, and it came about that scholars who followed in the lines of Rāmānuja and Madhva came to regard this work as a *śruti*. They commented on it in such a manner that it would agree with their own theories. (Since the contents of the first chapter, as will be explained in detail later, differ in not a few points from that of the second and subsequent chapters, it may be considered that followers of the above schools were able to relate it fairly easily to their own theories.) This tendency was prevalent only within the Vedānta school. Thus, it must be said that although the *Gauḍapāda-kārikā* was not regarded as a *śruti* by the early Advaita scholars, there is a relatively ancient basis for its being considered a *śruti* by people of other sub-sects of the Vedānta.

2. The later Advaita school also concurs that the first chapter of the *Māṇḍūkya-Kārikā* is a *śruti*.

As has already been stated, in the Advaita school, beginning with Śaṅkara followed by Ānandajñāna, Nārāyaṇāśramin et.al., only the *Māṇḍūkya-Upaniṣad* was considered to be a *śruti*. The *Māṇḍūkya-kārikā* was considered to be a work written by Gauḍapāda in order to clarify the meaning of the former. In later periods, however, there appeared those within the Advaita school itself who acknowledged that the first chapter of the *Māṇḍūkya-kārikā* was a *śruti*. Since this is inconsistent with Śaṅkara's attitude toward it, we must consider this to be an important development in the history of the Advaita school. At an early period Nārāyaṇāśramin relates that such scholars existed. At the beginning of his commentary to the *Māṇḍūkya-Upaniṣad* he states:

> The *Māṇḍūkya-Upaniṣad*, which begins with the sentence "This syllable *OM* is the entire universe," consists of four chapters (*khaṇḍa*). Saying four times [in the first chapter], "Concerning this point there are these *ślokas*" (*atraite ślokā bhavanti*), in four chapters [of his own] Master Gauḍapāda composed *ślokas* of explanation with the blessings of Nārāyaṇa. For this reason the first chapter, which consists of *śruti* and comments on it, has the *śruti* as the main thing. For this reason students of the *Veda* began treating it as an *Upaniṣad* (*chāndasānām Upaniṣad-vyavahāraḥ pravṛttaḥ*).[9]

Then, from approximately what period did the first chapter of the *Māṇḍūkya-kārikā* come to be regarded as a *śruti* by the Advaita school? As already pointed out, Sureśvara regarded it as a work by Gauḍapāda but

Ānandajñāna, who wrote a commentary to Sureśvara's *Bṛhadāraṇyaka-Upaniṣad-Bhāṣya-Vārttika*, took it to be a *śruti*.[10]

This does not agree with the fact that the Ānandajñāna who wrote a supplementary commentary (*ṭīkā*) to the *Māṇḍūkya-kārikā* did not regard the first chapter as *śruti*. However, that Ānandajñāna was presumably a different person. Just as all the works attributed to Śaṅkara are not by one person, the works attributed to Ānandajñāna probably are not all by the same author.

In about 1200 A.D. Vimuktātman also appears to have considered the first chapter of the *Māṇḍūkya-kārikā* to be a *śruti*.[11] Further, in the *Vedānta-kalpataruparimala* (a supplementary commentary to the *Bhāmatī*) written by Appaya Dīkṣita (latter half of the 16th century), the *Māṇḍūkya-kārikā* I,9 is quoted as from the *Māṇḍūkya-Upaniṣad*.[12] In the notes to the ten *Upaniṣads* written by Upaniṣad-brahma-yogin, a scholar of the Advaita school, it can be seen that he regarded only the first chapter of the *Kārikā* as a *śruti*, or *mantra*, and the remaining three as *prakaraṇa*.[13]

Another interesting point is that in works falsely attributed to Śaṅkara passages from the first chapter of the *Kārikā* are cited as being from the *Māṇḍūkya-Upaniṣad*. For example, in the *Vivekacūḍāmaṇi* (406), which is attributed to him, verse I,17 is quoted with the following comment:

> *māyāmātram idaṃ dvaitaṃ advaitaṃ paramārthataḥ/*
> *iti brūte śrutiḥ sākṣāt suṣuptāv anubhūyate//*

It may be possible to consider this to be a quotation from a text now lost. But speculations of such a nature disappear when one considers the following passage from Dvivedagaṅga's commentary to the *Bṛhadāraṇyaka-Upaniṣad*:

> *māyāmātram idaṃ dvaitam advaitaṃ paramārthataḥ iti Māṇḍūkya-śruteś ca/*[14]

In the *Viṣṇusahasranāmabhāṣya*,[15] which is also attributed to Śaṅkara, verses I,26-29 are quoted as from the "*Māṇḍūkyopaniṣad*." Further, in another attribution to Śaṅkara, the *Nṛsiṃha-pūrva-tāpanīya-Upaniṣad-bhāṣya*,[16] the first chapter of the *Kārikā* is held to be the *Māṇḍūkya-Upaniṣad*.

That is, in explaining passages of the *Nṛsiṃha-pūrva-tāpanīya*, they are compared with passages from the *Māṇḍūkya-Upaniṣad*, accompanied by the following explanation:

> *kiṃcobhayatrāpi bahutarapāṭhasāmye 'pi kvacit pāṭhabhedo' pi dṛśyate/ turīyamātrāṇirūpaṇāvasara "eṣo 'ntaryāmy eṣa īśāna eṣa prabhur" iti Māṇḍūkye pāṭhaḥ/ Tāpanīye tv "eṣo 'ntaryāmy eṣa yonir" itīśānaprabhupadadvayaṃ vihāya pāṭhaḥ/*[17]

The terms "*prabhu*" and "*īśāna*" considered here do not occur in the *Māṇḍūkya-Upaniṣad*, but appear in the *Kārikā*. In other words, here the prose section and the verses (first chapter) together are called the *Māṇḍūkya-Upaniṣad*.[18]

From the above facts we come to the following conclusions:

1. The first chapter of the *Māṇḍūkya-kārikā* was considered by the early Advaita school to be a work by Gauḍapāda. However, because it was transmitted to later scholars in a form interspersed throughout the *Māṇḍūkya-Upaniṣad*, the first chapter of the *Kārikā* came to be considered a part of the *Upaniṣad*, even by followers of the Advaita school. The content of the first chapter is almost the same as that of the *Upaniṣad*, and since it was not rare for verse to be interspersed in the prose sections of the "old *Upaniṣads*," it is not strange at all that later scholars came to regard the first chapter of the *Kārikā* as a *śruti*.

2. The citing of the first chapter of the *Kārikā* from the *Māṇḍūkya-Upaniṣad* in works attributed to Śaṅkara in fact contradicts Śaṅkara's own standpoint. Thus it is clear that the authors of such works cannot be the Śaṅkara who wrote the commentary to the *Brahma-sūtra*. It also must be considered that such authors are different from the author of the commentary to the *Māṇḍūkya-kārikā*. Thus, whether the first chapter of the *Kārikā* is regarded as a human work or as a *śruti* can be a test for the authenticity of various works attributed to Śaṅkara. In other words, we have established a criterion for determining the authenticity of works attributed to Śaṅkara

3. All four chapter of the *Māṇḍūkya-Kārikā* come to be regarded as *Upaniṣads*.

Furthermore, in later periods all four chapters of the *Māṇḍūkya-kārikā* came to be regarded as *Upaniṣads*. Puruṣottama, a grandson of Vallabhācārya (1479-1531 A.D.), regarded all four as *Upaniṣads* and wrote commentaries to each.[19] In this manner each separate chapter of the *Kārikā* came to be regarded in India generally as an independent *Upaniṣad*. Each was handed down with its own name. In other words, the four chapters of the *Kārikā* were considered to be four *Upaniṣads*.[20]

First chapter : There has been no edition of the first chapter alone transmitted as an independent *Upaniṣad*. Editions of the first chapter are invariably interspersed in parts throughout the prose *Māṇḍūkya-Upaniṣad* exist are in that form as the *Māṇḍūkya-Upaniṣad*. This is a highly interesting fact. Since it suggests avenues of approach to the problem of the process of compilation of the *Māṇḍūkya-kārikā*, we shall discuss it more fully in a later section.

Second chapter : The second chapter is transmitted under the name *Vaitathya-Upaniṣad* or *Dvaitavaitathyākhya-Upaniṣad*. (It is sometimes called the *Vaitathya-prakaraṇa*.)

Third chapter: The third chapter is known as the *Advaita-Upaniṣad*.[21]

Fourth chapter : The fourth chapter is known as the *Alātaśānti-Upaniṣad*. (It is sometimes called the *Alātaśānti-prakaraṇa*.)

These are considered to belong to the *Śaunakīya* branch of the *Atharva-Veda*.[22] There are also cases in which all four chapters are included in the *Māṇḍūkya-Upaniṣad*.[23] To the question of whether these are actual examples of the second and following chapters being considered *Upaniṣads* (*śruti*), we can say that there is evidence that the second chapter at least was considered to be a *śruti*.

That is, in the *Vidvanmanorañjanī*,[24] which is a commentary to the "*Vedānta Compendium*" (*Vedāntasāra*), and *Sāṃkhyapravacanabhāṣya*[25] of Vijñānabhikṣu, *Kārikā* II,32 is quoted as a *śruti*. However, since this verse also exists in the verse sections of the "new *Upaniṣads*,"[26] it may be from that source. It is a matter which merits investigation.

There are examples in which works other than the *Upaniṣads* have been called *śruti*,[27] but the *Māṇḍūkya-kārikā* is certainly the prime example.

The *Māṇḍūkya-kārikā* seems to have had great influence on the scriptures of Indian religions. A work attributed to Ādi-Śeṣa is the *Paramārthasāra*, which was later revised and supplemented from the standpoint of the Pratyabhijñā school by Abhinavagupta (late 10th c.- early 11th c.), with its former title being retained. These two works not only have doctrinal points in common with the *Māṇḍūkya-kārikā*, but even their phraseology is the same as or similar to the latter's. It may be supposed that Ādi-Śeṣa's work was based on the *Māṇḍūkya-kārikā*.[28] Further, since there exist shared or similar passages in the *Yogavāsiṣṭha* and the *Bhagavata-purāṇa*, these works also may be considered to have been influenced by the *Kārikā*.[29]

4. Conclusion.

a. It appears that in the Advaita school the *Māṇḍūkya-Upaniṣad* was considered a *śruti* even before Śaṅkara's time, although, of course, during his period it was not considered particularly important. In later periods, however, it came to be very highly evaluated, in fact, to be regarded as expressing the essence of *Upaniṣad* philosophy.

b. Concerning the *Māṇḍūkya-kārikā*:

1) In Śaṅkara's and Sureśvara's time the four chapters were considered to be a work by Gauḍapāda and not a *śruti*.

2) The Rāmānuja school and the Madhva school considered only the first chapter to be a *śruti*.

3) Because the first chapter of the *Kārikā* was transmitted in a form combined with the *Māṇḍūkya-Upaniṣad* in later periods within the Advaita school itself, many came to regard it as part of the *Māṇḍūkya-Upaniṣad*.

4) The dates are uncertain, but at some later period the four chapters each came to be regarded, by traditional scholars in general, as independent *Upaniṣads*.

c. The *Kārikā* is held to have been composed by Gauḍapāda of the Advaita school and is widely known as relating the views of the Advaita school. Notwithstanding this fact, it was highly respected by the opposing Rāmānuja and Madhva schools, even ultimately coming to be regarded as a *śruti* by these schools. In later periods, therefore, the view of it as a basic scripture, held in common among the schools of Vedānta philosophy, was not unlike that of the *Brahma-sūtra*. This is a fact that should be kept in mind when considering the significance of these chapters. It will not suffice to assume that this work relates only the thought of the Advaita school.

d. It is undeniable that the so-called *śruti* of the Indians were not regarded as such from their very beginnings; rather, they had to attain that authority only gradually. This is the case not only with the *śruti*, but also with other extremely old works. Among such works there are not a few with prose and verse sections, and thus we may infer that these also were not composed at the same time, but were subsequently edited into their present forms.

The problem is that at present the stages are usually not clear to us. The history of changes in the authority of the *Gauḍapāda-kārikā*, however, is clearly delineated by the process in which the verse section came to be interwoven with the prose section and also by the process whereby the supplementary sections came to attain as much authority as the original sections. In this respect, the history of the *Māṇḍūkya-Upaniṣad* and the *Kārikā* should be regarded as highly important.[30]

Notes

1) At the beginning of this commentary (*Bhāṣya*), Madhva cites the following *ślokas*: *Dhyāyan Nārāyaṇaṃ devaṃ praṇavena samāhitaḥ/ Maṇḍūkarūpī Varuṇas tuṣṭāva Harim avyayam//... Brahmadṛṣṭān ato mantrān pramāṇam salileśvaraḥ/ atra ślokā bhavantīti cakāraiva pṛthak pṛthak//*Madhva states that these *ślokas* are from the *Padma-purāṇa*, but in the presently extant edition they are not to be found. These are as presented in *Venkatasubbiah, op. cit.*, pp.171, 191; V. Bhattacharyya: *AS.* pp. xxxi-xxxii; Mahadevan: *GP.* pp.31-32.)

2) *Śrībhāṣya*, I. p.102 (BSS.); Mahadevan: *GP.* p.32.

3) According to the article cited in note 1.

4) In the *Śrībhāṣya*, Rāmānuja states as follows in a passage where he refutes the *brahmājñānavāda*, which states that *Brahman* itself is transformed into the individual self by an unintelligent (*ajñāna*) power: *jīvasyaiva hi māyayā nirodhaḥ śrūyate — "tasmiṃś cānyo māyayā saṃniruddhaḥ"*(*Śvet. Up.* IV, 9) *iti/"anādimāyayā supto yadā jīvaḥ prabudhyate"* (*GK.* I, 16) *iti ca/"indro māyābhiḥ pururūpa īyate"* (*Bṛhad. Up.* II, 5, 19) *ityatrāpi vicitrāḥ śaktayo 'bhidhīyante* /(*Śrībhāṣya*, BSS.p.102).

5) Not identical with the author of the famous *Siddhāntaleśasaṃgraha*.

6) V. Bhattacharyya : *IHQ*. vol. 1. 1925, p.121 ; ditto : *AS*. p.xxxii. n.

7) Sanskrit Manuscripts (The Adyar Library), vol. I, *Upaniṣads*, pp.116, 287-288. (However, this is according to the above-cited article by V. Bhattacharyya.) According to *A Descriptive Catalogue of the Sanskrit Manuscripts* in the Government Oriental Library, Mysore, by M. S. Basavalingayya, vol. 1. p.441 (Mysore, 1937), after *śloka* I, 29 of the *Gauḍapāda-kārikā* is presented, it is stated : *iti Māṇḍūkyopaniṣat samāptā*.

8) *māyāmātram idaṃ dvaitam advaitam paramārthataḥ*/(= *GK* I,17) iti. *māṇḍūkyaśākhāyāṃ śrutivākyam adhīyate*//— Sāyaṇa ad *Taitt.Ār*. ĀnSS. no. 36, VII, 1 (p.483).

9) According to *Venkatasubbiah, Ind. Ant*. LXII, p.188.

10) In the *Bṛhad. Up. Vārttika* (I, 4, 615. p.556), after citing *GK*.14 it is stated : *svapnanidrāyutāv ādyau prājñas tv asvapnanidrayā*/*ity ādisthāna-bhedo 'pi vedāntoktau viniścitāḥ*//615// In contrast with this, Ānandajñāna states : *sthānabhede śrutim pramāṇayati*. However, '*Vedāntokti*' in this case can probably be explained as 'statements concerning the *Upaniṣad*.' Ānandajñāna, in another passage, cites *GK* I, 16 as a *śruti* which indicates *avidyānāditva* ; he also notes *GK* I, 3 as a *śruti*.

11) In his work *Iṣṭasiddhi* (p.331. GOS.), he cites *GK* I, 16 and I, 14 before the passage from the *Ait. Up*. 3, 12 (according to B. N. K. Sarma, *Poona Orientalist*, Vol. I, No. 2, p.36).

12) *krīḍārthaṃ sṛṣṭir ity anye bhogārtham ity cāpare*/*devasyaiṣa svabhāvo 'yam āptakāmasya kā spṛhā*//*iti Māṇḍūkyopaniṣadi tātkālikānandaprayojanalīlātvam eva krīḍārthaṃ sṛṣṭir ity anya iti anenānabhimataṃ pradarśitaṃ na tu hāsagānāditulyaprayojana-udveśarahitaṃ līlātvam* //(p.406, VizSS.)

13) *himavatpṛṣṭhāsano gauḍapādācāryaḥ śrīśukamukhān māṇḍūkyopaniṣadgūḍhāśayaṃ vijñāya, ... atha sarvabhūtānukampayā tām evopaniṣadaṃ vyācikhyāsoḥ gauḍapādācāryasya māṇḍūkyagūḍhāśayānuvādinyaḥ śrutayaḥ khilaśrutayo mantrāś ca prādurbabhūvuḥ sahasraśaḥ*/ *tatra kāṃścin mantrān pradhānataḥ catuṣpādagocaracaturmātrālaṅkṛta-māṇḍūkyopaniṣadaḥ pratyaṃśaṃ vibhāgaśo yojayām āsā*/ *tasya āgama-pradhānatvena oṃkārayāthātmyanirṇāyakatvāt tad idam āgamaprakaraṇam ucyate*//*śiṣṭaṃ śrutimantrajātam arthataḥ saṃgṛhya kārikārūpeṇa prakaraṇatrayaṃ racayām āsa — Vaitathyādvaitālātaśāntibhedāt*// (from the above-cited article by B. N. K. Sarma)

14) Weber : *Indische Studien*, II, S. 102.

15) *Minor Works of Śaṅkarācārya*, p.516.

16) The author of this work is not identical with the Śaṅkara who wrote the commentary to the *Brahma-sūtra*. However, it has been shown by Vidhusekhara Bhattacharyya that he is identical with the author of the Tāntric work *Prapañcāgama-śāstra* (or *Prapañcasāra*). (*Śaṅkara's Commentaries on the Upanishads*, Sir Asutosh Mookerjee Silver Jubilee Volumes, vol. III, p.105 ff.)

17) p.46, AnSS.

18) This can be seen from the following passage: *ata ūrdhvam māṇḍūkya ukta evārthe ślokān paṭhitvā turīyaḥ pāda etasmiṃs tāpanīye tu tān vihāya turīyaḥ pādaḥ*. (*Nṛs. Pū. Tāp. Up. Bhāṣya*, p.48).

19) V. Bhattacharyya: *IHQ*.vol. I. 1925, p.122; Amarnath Ray: *IHQ*. vol. XIV, 1938, p. 564.

20) Walleser: *DA V*. S. 5; Deussen: *Sechzig Upanishads*, S. 574; Colonel Jacob: *Concordance*, Preface, p.8; V. Bhattacharyya: *AS*. p.xxxvii.

21) In one edition the alternative title *Upadeśagrantha* is added. In still another edition the entire *Māṇḍūkya-kārikā* is called the *Śrī-Upadeśagrantha* (ĀnSS. p.155. n. 1).

22) This explanation is according to Aufrecht *CC*.; Weber: *Indische Studien*, Bd. II. S. 102; Weber: *HIL*. p.161; R.G. Bhandarkar: *Collected Works*, II. p.95.

23) "I remember to have seen a printed edition of the 108 *Upanishads* in which it was stated at the end of each *prakaraṇa, iti Māṇḍūkyopaniṣadi prathamaṃ prakaraṇaṃ, dvitīyaṃ prakaraṇaṃ*, etc" (Venkatasubbiah: *Ind. Ant*. LXII, p.191).

24) p.135, ed. by Jacob.

25) pp.22, *l*.6; 28, *l*.11; 122. *l*.7; 159. *ll*. 8-9 (ed. by R. Garbe).

26) *Amṛtabindu-Up*. X; *Tripurātāpinī-Up*. X; *Avadhūta-Up*. VIII; *Ātma-Up*. XXXI. Cf. *Brahmabindu-Up*. X.

27) In the *Bhagavadgītārthasaṃgraha* (VII,7) by Abhinava, one *śloka* from the *Paramārthasāra* by Śeṣa is cited as a *śruti* (Mahadevan: *op. cit*., p.44, n). The *Bhagavad Gītā* is also called an *Upaniṣad*.

28) V. Bhattacharyya: *AS*. pp. lxxix-lxxxv. However, Mahadevan (*GP*. pp.15 f.) hypothesizes that this work is of the same period as Gauḍapāda.

29) V. Bhattacharyya: *AS*. pp. lxxxvi-lxxxviii; Mahadevan: *GP*. pp.21-28.

30) There exist other similar cases. For example, Śaṅkara (ad *BS*. III, 2, 18) cites a passage from the *Amṛtabindu-Up*., but states that it is from a *mokṣaśāstra*. Thus in his time, this work was still not considered to be part of the accepted scriptures. However, there probably exists no other work which shows as clearly as the *Gauḍapāda-kārikā* the process by which a work came to be regarded as a *śruti*.

SECTION IV. THE COMPILATION OF THE *MĀṆḌŪKYA-UPANIṢAD* AND THE *MĀṆḌŪKYA-KĀRIKĀ*

Sub-Section 1. The Compilation of the *Māṇḍūkya-Upaniṣad*

The *Māṇḍūkya-Upaniṣad* is a short prose work of eleven paragraphs. Among the 108 *Upaniṣads*, it is the shortest. Its prose is lucid and its organization well-structured.[1] In this regard it is very different from the early *Upaniṣads*, which are similar to the *Brāhmaṇas* in being verbose and repetitive, with an extremely unstructured mode of exposition. From this fact alone we may infer that this *Upaniṣad* differs considerably in time from the "old *Upaniṣads*" and that its author, trained in systematic thinking, was familiar with the philosophic modes of thought of a considerably later period.

Further, in examining the terms and modes of expression used in this *Upaniṣad*, we see many borrowings from the "old *Upaniṣads*."

Māṇḍ. Up.

I. *tasyopavyākhyānam* = *Chānd. Up.* I,1,1. (Among the "Old *Upaniṣads*," the term "*upavyākhyāna*" is used only in the *Māṇḍ. Up.* and the *Chānd. Up.*)

I. *trikālātīta* = *Śvet. Up.* VI,5.

V. *yatra supto na kathaṃcana kāmāṃ*
kāmayate, na kaṃcana svapnaṃ paśyati = *Bṛhad. Up.* IV,3,19.

X. *prajñānaghana eva* = *Bṛhad. Up.* IV,5,13.

X. *nāsyābrahmavit kule bhavati* = *Muṇḍ. Up.* III,2,9.

Other than these, as was shown previously in the section titled "Interpretation," its main concepts already exist in the "old *Upaniṣads*." It contains enumerated summaries which bring to mind the Sāṃkhya philosophy. In this regard it is similar to the later "old *Upaniṣads*" such as the *Kāṭhaka-* and *Śvetāśvatara-Upaniṣads*.[2] As was pointed out in detail in the section titled "Interpretation," many particular Buddhist terms or uniquely Buddhist modes of expression may be found in it. Thus, in form of exposition and in terminology or mode of expression, it must be concluded that this *Upaniṣad* was compiled at a relatively late period.

The above also holds true of its philosophical content. In this *Upaniṣad* the universe is explained as the syllable "*Om*." This syllable is divided into the sounds *a-u-m* plus a silent element.

These sounds are each held to be a stage (*pāda*) of *Brahman* and are explained to be respectively [1] the *Vaiśvānara*, [2] the *Taijasa*, [3] the *Prājña*, and [4] the *Caturtha*, which are successively the state of universality, the state of light, the state of wisdom, and the Fourth state.

On the basis of this foursome, the various concepts and ideas discussed in the "old *Upaniṣads*" are systematically allocated to the four stages.

What had been thought of in the "old *Upaniṣads*" as the basic principle of the universe, or again the concepts and attributes belonging to that basic principle, are in this *Upaniṣad* allocated to the third stage, of wisdom. (In fact terms from the old *Upaniṣads* such as *prajñānaghana*, *ānandamaya*, *ānandabh-uj*, *ekībhūta*, *prājña*, *sarveśvara*, *sarvajña*, *antaryāmin*, the origin of the universe and so on, are here epithets applied to the third state, of wisdom.) This *Upaniṣad* thus held that what was expressed by these concepts was not the absolute, and went on to determine an absolute beyond them, the Fourth state, as their basis. This Fourth state does not have any definition in positive terms of its true nature. This position is a step beyond the idea of *sat* (existence), *cit* (consciousness) and *ānanda* (bliss) which in general Vedānta philosophy are taken as the nature of *Brahman*. The nature of the Fourth is held to be expressible only by negation; it is the so-called ground of *atyanta-śūnyatā* (absolute emptiness). Thus what is held to be the Fourth is an idea more sophisticated than the various world principles postulated in previous *Upaniṣads*, and it is a stage more advanced than that of the *Upaniṣads* incorporating them. From the fact that many Buddhist terms are found in its explanation, it is clear that this view was established under the influence of the Mahāyāna Buddhist concept of "Void." It thus may be concluded that this *Upaniṣad* is later than the other "old *Upaniṣads*" and, further, later than the establishment of early Mahāyāna Buddhism.

Again, I feel also that the *Māṇḍūkya-Upaniṣad* was compiled after the *Maitri-Upaniṣad*.

> As reasons for this we may cite the following two facts. (1) Although both *Upaniṣads* discuss the sacred sound *Om*, the explanation in the *Maitri-Upaniṣad* is extremely simple and unorganized. In contrast, the explanation in the *Māṇḍūkya-Upaniṣad* is much more structured. (2) Although Buddhistic influence can be seen in the *Maitri-Upaniṣad*, the particular terms and modes of expression of Mahāyāna Buddhism do not yet appear, whereas the influence of the Mahāyāna concept of "Void" can clearly be recognized in the *Māṇḍūkya-Upaniṣad*. Thus,

there will probably be no objection to our concluding that it is later than the *Maitri-Upaniṣad*. Among the "old *Upaniṣads*," these two are of the late period and were not considered to be as important as the other "old *Upaniṣads*."[3] From the above facts it may be said that the *Māṇḍūkya* was the latest of the "old *Upaniṣads*."

The upper limits of the date of compilation of the *Māṇḍūkya-Upaniṣad* are as stated above ; concerning its lower limits, we may state the following. Although Mahāyāna Buddhism strongly influenced this *Upaniṣad*, neither the mode of exposition of the Mādhyamika school nor the characteristic terminology of the Vijñānavāda school appears. The explanation of the "Fourth stage" brings to mind passages from the texts of early Mahāyāna Buddhism.

Further, this *Upaniṣad* was compiled much earlier than the "new *Upaniṣads*."

It has been shown previously that it was compiled earlier than the *Nṛsiṃha-Tāpanīya-Upaniṣad* and the *Rāmottara-Tāpanīya-Upaniṣad*.[4] Among the *Upaniṣads* which are subsidiary to the *Atharva-Veda*, there are a few which discuss the sacred sound *Om*. These are the *Dhyānabindu*, *Yogatattva*, *Atharvaśikhā*, *Haṃsanāda*, *Brahmavidyā*, *Tāraka*, *Prāṇa* and *Śaunaka Upaniṣads*. (The "old *Upaniṣads*" also mention the sound *Om*, but still do not present any analytical explanation of it.) These *Upaniṣads* analyze *Om* into the sounds *a-u-m* plus the state without measure (*ardhamātrā*),[5] but, in contrast, the *Māṇḍūkya* explains it as *a-u-m* plus the silent element. Thus among the *Upaniṣads* subsidiary to the *Atharva-Veda* the *Māṇḍūkya* is the oldest and, in the development of theories concerning the sacred sound *Om*, may be placed in a middle period.

Reflecting on these facts, we may say that it is probably not too far out to consider the date of compilation of the *Māṇḍūkya-Upaniṣad* to have been about the first or second centuries A.D.[6]

Notes

1) The systematic character of this *Upaniṣad* will be discussed later.

2) Cf. Śaṅkara's gloss on *saptāṅga*, *ekonaviṃśatimukha* (*Māṇḍ. Up.* III ; IV).

3) The *Māṇḍūkya-* and *Maitri-Upaniṣads* are not once cited in Śaṅkara's commentary

to the *Brahma-sūtra* (Deussen : *SV*. S. 32 f.).
4) Cf. Sub-Section 3, Section II of this Chapter.
5) Weber : *Indische Studien* I, S. 251 ; Deussen, *Sechzig Upanishads*, S. 573.
6) This point will be discussed further in Sub-Section 3, Section III.

Sub-Section 2. Examination of the Characteristics of the Chapters of the *Māṇḍūkya-Kārikā*

The *Māṇḍūkya-Kārikā* is composed of four chapters (*prakaraṇa*). The first is called *Āgama-prakaraṇa*, the second *Vaitathya-prakaraṇa*, the third *Advaita-prakaraṇa*, and the fourth *Alātaśānti-prakaraṇa*. They consist respectively of 29, 38, 48, and 100 *ślokas*. Of these, it is only the *ślokas* of the first chapter that are interspersed among the prose lines of the *Māṇḍūkya-Upaniṣad*. *Ślokas* I-IX are placed between paragraphs 6 and 7 of the *Upaniṣad*, *ślokas* X-XVIII between paragraphs 7 and 8, *ślokas* XIX-XXIII between paragraphs 11 and 12, and *ślokas* XXIV-XXIX after paragraph 12.

Let us examine the contents of each of the chapters and consider the process of their compilation. Although these verses have been transmitted from ancient times as a work by a person named Gauḍapāda, one may question this traditional attribution. In the following sections we shall depart from that tradition and examine the contents independently. We shall then proceed to the problem of Gauḍapāda, to whom is traditionally ascribed the authorship of the *Kārikā*.

(1) Examination of the First Chapter.

The first chapter of the *Māṇḍūkya-Kārikā*, constituting a commentary to the *Māṇḍūkya-Upaniṣad*, was written in conjunction with the already extant *Upaniṣad*. The academic world in general accepts this fact.

In the modern period Vidhusekhara Bhattacharyya has, however, opposed this general view. He asserted that the *Māṇḍūkya-Upaniṣad* was written in order to explain the meaning of the first *Kārikā* chapter, and thus that the *Upaniṣad* is in reality a commentary to the first chapter.[1] His main reasons are as follows :

1. In the commentary to the *Brahma-sūtra*, Śaṅkara quotes the *Māṇḍūkya-Kārikā* but does not mention the *Upaniṣad*.

2. In general, commentaries explain important or difficult passages in the work commented upon, but the *Kārikā* does not explain terms such as "*saptāṅga*" and "*ekonaviṃśati*" in the *Māṇḍūkya-Upaniṣad*. If the *Kārikā* were a commentary, it would undoubtedly have explained these terms.
3. In the *Upaniṣad*, the first state is termed "*vaiśvānara*," but in the *Kārikā* the term "*vaiśva*" is used. If the *Kārikā* were a commentary, it of course would have used the term "*vaiśvārana*." It cannot be accepted that a commentary should have freely altered the terminology of its main text.
4. In the *Upaniṣad* (5) the term "*prajñānaghana*" appears, but in the *Kārikā* (1) the term is "*ghanaprajña*" ; the same reasoning applies.
5. The *jāgaritasthāna*, the *svapnasthāna*, and the *suṣuptasthāna*, constituting a central theme in the *Māṇḍūkya-Upaniṣad*, are not explained at all in the first chapter of *Māṇḍūkya-Kārikā*.

From these facts Bhattacharyya concluded that the prose *Upaniṣad* was written in order to explain the first *Kārikā* chapter. To make the specialized terminology of the first chapter more readily available to a wider readership, certain terms were altered in the prose section to those used generally in the *Upaniṣads*. The terms "*viśva*," "*ghanaprajña*" and "*ānandabhuj*" in the *Kārikā* were thus altered to "*vaiśvānara*," "*prajñānaghana*" and "*ānandamaya*."

However, I would suggest that these arguments do not really overturn the traditional view. The above points may be answered respectively:[2)]

1. Even if Śaṅkara did not quote from it, the *Māṇḍūkya-Upaniṣad*, as has already been shown,[3)] had already come to be considered a *śruti* in Śaṅkara's day.
2. Failure to explain difficult terms is a phenomenon frequent among Indian commentators ; it is not at all rare.
3. & 4. The fact that in expressing important concepts this *Upaniṣad* used terms shared with the "old *Upaniṣads*" and the *Kārikā* different terminology indicates that this *Upaniṣad*, in terms of content, is close to the "old *Upaniṣads*" and that the *Kārikā* was compiled in a later period. In particular the term "*viśva*," as will be shown later,[4)] was in

use in books of Hinduism, and so it is reasonable to suppose that the first chapter of the *Kārikā*, in terms of content and also of date, is close to the texts of Hinduism.

5. Concerning the three states of consciousness, the author of the *Kārikā* probably felt no particular need to explain them.

Thus the basis of Vidhusekhara Bhattacharyya's argument is not only weak, but the very facts cited in his argument lead per contra to an opposite conclusion. Over and above this, I feel that we can show from other viewpoints that the compilation of the *Māṇḍūkya-Upaniṣad* was the earlier.

1. In Indian studies, it is commonly held that if a work is called an *Upaniṣad*, even if only casually, it may be thought that the work was compiled earlier than other works which are related to it. The *Māṇḍūkya-Upaniṣad*, in particular, was accepted as such by the various Vedānta schools and was revered as conveying the essence of the *Upaniṣads*. Thus one cannot lightly dismiss its authority. (Ānandajñāna also considered the "sacred chapter," i. e., the first chapter of *GK*., to be an explanation (*vyākhyāna*) of the *Māṇḍūkya-Upaniṣad*.)[5]
2. The content of the *Māṇḍūkya-Upaniṣad* is simple; in contrast, the first chapter presents rather difficult explanations of it.
3. Although the "four states" are explained in separate sections in the *Upaniṣad*, in *ślokas* I.1-5 of the *Kārikā* the first three states are juxtaposed in one *śloka*. That is, the *Kārikā* assumes that an explanation of the four has already been presented. Thus it should be understood that the *Māṇḍūkya-Upaniṣad* was compiled first and that later someone well-versed in it arranged and re-organized it for the sake of students studying it, in the form of the first chapter of the *Kārikā*.
4. In this *Upaniṣad*, it is said of those who know the significance of the individual sounds "*ya evaṃ veda*." The rewards for those who have such knowledge are explained. In content and style this has the aura of Brahmanism. In the first chapter rewards in this life are not mentioned at all. Thus we must hold that the *Māṇḍūkya-Upaniṣad* is older.
5. In the first chapter the *prasaṅga* method of argument of the Mā-

dhyamika school can be recognized, but this does not appear in the *Māṇḍūkya-Upaniṣad*

From the above facts we may state that the *Māṇḍūkya-Upaniṣad* was compiled at a relatively early date and that there is a considerable difference in time between it and the first chapter of the *Kārikā.*

Let us now examine the contents of the first chapter. *Ślokas* I-V constitute a verse form of the explanation of the three states, *Viśvā, Taijasa,* and *Prājña* presented in the *Māṇḍūkya-Upaniṣad. Ślokas* VI-IX discuss, in relation to the third state, the creation of the world. At the same time it attacks other theories extant at the time, thus clarifying the cosmological view that it maintains. *Ślokas* X-XVIII explain the fourth state, while *ślokas* XIX-XXIII make clear the relationship between the four sound-elements which constitute the syllable *Om* and the four states of *Brahman. Śloka* XXIV and the following *ślokas* explain religious practices which reaffirm the sacred sound. Thus, in terms of content, the first chapter may be seen to be a commentary on the *Māṇḍūkya-Upaniṣad*. Although it occasionally contains passages which are the same or explanations which are similar to those in other *Upaniṣads*, it has no passage which clearly indicates or discusses other *Upaniṣads*. It has as its sole purpose the clarification of the essential meaning of the *Māṇḍūkya-Upaniṣad*.[6] It was for this very reason that it came to be closely associated with this *Upaniṣad* and to be handed down together with it.

This first chapter is called the "*Āgama-prakaraṇa*" because its function is the clarification of the *āgama*.[7] *Āgama* (tradition) is contrasted with "*upapatti*" (proof)[8] or "*tarka*" (logic).[9] Although there also exist "*pauruṣeyāgama*" (traditions originating from human beings),[10] what is indicated here is the "traditional" quality of the *Māṇḍūkya-Upaniṣad* as a *śruti*.[11] Thus it may also be said that the first chapter is a *vārttika* (authoritative commentary) to the *Māṇḍūkya-Upaniṣad*. In the strictest sense it should be regarded as such,[12] and in actuality there were many scholars in India who did.[13]

Thus at first glance the first chapter of the *Kārikā* does seem to follow the *Māṇḍūkya-Upaniṣad* scrupulously. Still, there are some differences to be seen in attitude and standpoint. As already pointed out :

1. The *Upaniṣad*, using usual Upaniṣadic terms, calls the first state

vaiśvānara and the fourth state *caturtha*. But in the first chapter, the words *viśva* and *turya* are used, which are terms found in the texts of Hinduism.

2. In the *Upaniṣad*, human consciousness is analyzed in detail into *jāgarita*, *svapna*, and *suṣupta*, whereas in the first chapter the explanation of these is completely omitted.
3. As to content, we must note that in *Kārikā* I,10 the fourth state is called *īśāna* (controller-lord), *prabhu* (lord), *deva* (god) and so on, while in the *Upaniṣad* itself these all apply to the third state. The *Upaniṣad* is following the line of the ancient orthodox Brahmanical school of philosophy, while further attempting to found it on the doctrine of the Void as its basis, whereas (as will be discussed later) the first chapter changes the line of thought slightly to fit the theology and realism of Hinduism, as exemplified in the present instance.
4. The influence of Buddhism is much stronger in the first chapter than in the other chapters. The concept of *paramārtha* or ultimate truth appears. Since the theory of higher and lower truths did not exist in orthodox Brahmanism, there is no question that it was adopted from Buddhism.[14]
5. In the *Kārikā* I,13, in order to differentiate the third and fourth states, the concept of "*bīja*" (seed) is used. The commentator Śaṅkara also relies heavily on it. As a philosophical concept which signifies the latent force within phenomena, "*bīja*" is used neither in the *Māṇḍūkya-Upaniṣad* nor in the older texts of Orthodox Brahmanism. Thus, the concept was probably taken from Buddhism, in particular from the Sautrāntikas and the "Consciousness-only" theory.[15]

In view of these points, it is difficult to say that the explanations in the first chapter are altogether the same as the thought of the *Māṇḍūkya-Upaniṣad*. From the fact that it had absorbed Buddhistic thought, and also attacks the cosmological theories of other schools, we may infer that from an early period there existed a religious group who revered the *Māṇḍūkya-Upaniṣad*, and that in a later period, because this group came in contact with various other different schools, a need was felt to understand more clearly the teachings of their own school and to establish more firmly its philosophical foundations. One of the scholars among them organized and rewrote into verse form the ideas contained in the *Māṇḍūkya-Upaniṣad*, while at the same time attacking the explanations of other schools. Further, it may be held that this school was in constant contact with Buddhists.

(2) Examination of the Second Chapter.

Although all four chapters of the *Māṇḍūkya-Kārikā* are considered to have been written by Gauḍapāda, the contents of the first chapter differ considerably from those of the other chapters. The first chapter must be considered from a different standpoint.

The first chapter, as has been shown, is clearly a commentary to the *Māṇḍūkya-Upaniṣad*. The remaining three chapters, however, are completely independent works. The first chapter has a close relationship with the *Upaniṣad*, but it is difficult to find any direct relationship between the *Upaniṣad* and the other three chapters.[16)] In these chapters, the main goal is to establish the assertions of the Advaita school through theoretical reasoning.

1. Firstly, in the *Māṇḍūkya-Kārikā* only the first chapter discusses the sacred sound *Om* and its significance. This is a marked characteristic of the first chapter. Thus, Ānandajñāna calls the first chapter specifically a "treatise on *Om*" (*Oṃkāraprakaraṇa*).[17)] The first chapter can clearly be differentiated in this regard from the others.
2. Similarly, the theory of the "four states" is discussed only in the first chapter and does not appear in the other chapters.[18)]

Thus there exists a basic difference in the method of presentation of doctrine between the first chapter and the other chapters. Further, the two parts do not agree on philosophical problems ; between the two, there can be seen contradictions in thought :

1. Firstly, there exists a clear difference in the handling of cosmological questions. In the first chapter it is stated that : — For all existing things there is a source of their existence. This is the "*puruṣa*" called "*prāṇa*," which creates all individual things in their separateness. It is like the sun which releases rays of sunlight (6th *śloka*). And the essence of the "*deva*" such manifesting activity. Since the *deva* has all

desires fulfilled, there is no reason for desire to exist in him (9th *śloka*). The simile of the source of phenomena and the sun releasing sunlight is in meaning completely the same as that of sparks scattering from a flame. The "fire-sparks" simile is found in the "old *Upaniṣads*" (*Bṛhad. Up.* II, 1, 20 ; *Muṇḍ. Up.* II, 1, 1) and the "sun-sunlight" simile is found in the *Brahma-sūtra* (III,2,25 ; 28 ; II,3,46), but in these the general standpoint is that of the "actual manifestation" theory (*pariṇāmavāda*), which is markedly different from the "phenomenal appearance" theory (*vivartavāda*) or the "illusion" (*māyā*) theory. From the latter standpoint, the *pariṇāmavāda*, as such, cannot be accepted. Thus the *Māṇḍūkya-Kārikā* (III,15), which rests on the *māyā* theory, states that the explanation of the creation of the world by means of the "fire-sparks" simile is merely illustrative, simply a convenient device, used to lead towards the truth. Śaṅkara, in the commentary to the *Brahma-sūtra*, also presents the same explanation.[19)]

As Śaṅkara states,[20)] the explanation which uses the "sun-sunlight" simile may be taken as signifying either the relationship between the whole and its parts or the relationship between a changing object and its essence. Yet in the *Kārikā* (III,7) the view that the individual self is a part of the Absolute Self or that it is a changing manifestation of it is denied. Further, as Śaṅkara states,[21)] the fire-sparks simile is meant to explain the origin (*utpatti*) of the world. Although the first chapter (I,6) clearly recognizes theories concerning cosmological origins (*prabhava*), the third and fourth chapters, in contrast, explicitly state that the world is "not born" (*ajāti*) and devote particular attention to attacking theories of cosmological origins.

It may be noted that the theory which explains that the world principle is "*prāṇa-puruṣa*" is common to the "old *Upaniṣads*" in general. In the second chapter (19,20), however, the theory which holds that *prāṇa* is the world principle is rejected as a lower teaching.

Reflecting on these points, we must conclude that the first chapter and the other chapters present completely contradictory ideas concerning the problem of cosmology. The creation theory in the first chapter is closely related to the "old *Upaniṣads*" and the thinking of the early Vedānta school. Contrarily, the third chapter and Śaṅkara himself explain it as a pedagogical device. Thus the philosophical standpoints of the two clearly differ, the latter being a step more advanced than the former.

2. The standpoint concerning objects in the phenomenal world is different. In the first chapter (I,7) the assertion that creation is similar to a dream or an illusion is rejected as a heretical theory.[22] The other chapters, however, make great efforts to show that phenomena are, indeed, similar to illusions and dreams (II,4 ff; 31 ff; III,10; 19; 24; 29; IV,44; 58; 59; 61; 69). Thus, although the first chapter rejects the *māyā* theory, the other chapters, in contrast, uphold it. Further, the first (I,6) takes the view that the various forms of existence of the phenomenal world are actual (*sat*). It may be said that this view takes the standpoint of the *satkāryavāda* theory, which holds that actuality is born only from other actualities. In contrast, however, the other chapters compare the objects of the phenomenal world to dreams and illusions, denying their actuality.[23] Thus, this latter standpoint may be seen to be that of the "phenomenal appearance" theory (*vivartavāda*).
3. The conception of the Absolute differs. In the first chapter (I,26) the differentiation of Absolute *Brahman* and Lower *Brahman* is accepted, while in the second chapter (II,27) the views which establish such a distinction are rejected.
4. The four states (*pāda*) of *Brahman* are discussed in the *Māṇḍūkya-Upaniṣad* and the first chapter of the *Kārikā*, but in the second chapter (II,21) such enumerative schemes are taken as inferior and the distinctive "four state" theory of the *Māṇḍūkya-Upaniṣad* is treated in the same way as the theories of other schools.
5. The second chapter asserts that insofar that both are illusory there is no difference between experiences in the states of wakefulness and dreaming and that these two states are one (*eka*).[24] Such a view is recognized neither in the *Māṇḍūkya-Upaniṣad* nor in the first chapter. The *Upaniṣad* and the first chapter differentiate the two states of

consciousness, and do not at all refer to their points of similarity. Thus the assertion in the second chapter that both states have the same nature clearly shows that its author was influenced by the Vijñānavāda views of Asaṅga and Vasubandhu. Other examples of the influence of Vijñānavāda theories in the second chapter may be seen, as for example the "snake-rope" simile (II,17).

From these facts, we must conclude that there is a wide difference in content between the first and the other chapters. The commentator Śaṅkara also recognized this fact. He states that reflection on the sacred sound *Om*, as taught in the *Māṇḍūkya-Upaniṣad* and the first chapter, is meant for those of "average or lower intelligence" (*mandamadhyamadhī*) and not for those of superior intelligence.[25] Meditation on the sacred sound *Om* is nothing other than a form of worship (*upāsana*), but in the latter chapters of the *Kārikā* such worship is looked upon as being for those of only average or lower endowment.[26] Thus, the commentator himself was aware that the sense of the first chapter and that of the others differ. It may be held that the Rāmānuja school and the Madhva school considered the first chapter a *śruti* because its contents accord well with their own theories. In contrast, the other chapters are clearly in opposition to their theories.

As shown above, there exist clear differences in thought between the first chapter and the other chapters. It now seems quite impossible to hold that all four chapters of the *Kārikā* were written by one person. The two parts (the first chapter and the other chapters) were undoubtedly written by different persons. Further, they were nor written during the same period ; the first should be considered earlier. The development of later chapters presupposes the ideas found in the first chapter. The teachings of the first chapter are evaluated as inferior, and the superiority of the teachings in the later ones is emphasized. Thus, the later chapters may be considered to have been composed at a later period.

Other than those indicated above, further examples of the influence of Buddhism may be seen. For example, phenomena are compared to dreams, illusions and mirages (*gandharvanagara*) (II,31). Outwardly, however, the author vigorously claims to be of a Vedānta school (*vedāntaniścayaḥ, vedānteṣu, vicakṣaṇaiḥ*/II,12 ; 31). He cites passages from the *Upaniṣads*,[27] but not once does he cite a Buddhist text.

(3) Examination of the Third Chapter.

The third chapter is in its entirety an independent work. Its first *śloka* and its last *śloka* both assert the doctrine of non-birth (*ajāti*). The philosophical basis of the entire chapter is the *Māyāvāda* or *Vivartavāda*. The "old *Upaniṣads*" are frequently cited in this chapter.[28] It asserts that although teachings which do not agree with the *Vivartavāda* theory are frequently seen in the "old *Upaniṣads*," these are all "expedients" presented for the sake of the attainment of the truth. It asserts that various teachings were used to meet differences in the capabilities of the believers and thus that they are not at all contradictory to the teachings of this work. Here we see a form of critical evaluation of the *Upaniṣadic* texts. Such thinking may be considered to have been influenced by Buddhism, in particular Mahāyāna Buddhism. Having compared passages from it with those in Buddhistic texts, one finds that influence undeniable. Such critical thinking is a peculiarly marked characteristic of the third chapter.

Although the influence of Buddhistic thought is strong, its basic standpoint is not at all identical with that of Buddhism. The Buddhist Kamalaśīla called the second and third chapters the "*Upaniṣadic* theory" (*gsaṅ baḥi bstan bcos*).[29] The position of the third chapter concerning general philosophical problems is generally the same as that of the second chapter. But where the second chapter abruptly states that the phenomenal world is an illusion, the third chapter critically attempts to establish a logical foundation for the Advaita theories. A particularly distinctive theory is its explanation of the creation of the world from *manas*. This is expounded neither in the *Upaniṣads* nor in the other chapters of the *Kārikā*. It is an idea which does not appear at all in Śaṇkara's *Brahma-sūtra-bhāṣya* nor in the works of scholars of the early Vedānta school. It is a theory unique to the *Kārikā*, and for examples similar to it one must turn rather to the *Yogavāsiṣṭha* or the *purāṇa* literature.[30] Thus the third chapter, different from the other chapters, may be considered from the standpoint of its thought to belong to the same current as the popular philosophies. (The second chapter states that the *deva* called *ātman* generated the world through *māyā*, an idea similar to that of the *Śvetāśvatara-Upaniṣad*. The fourth chapter states that the phenomenal world is created through the false appearance of *vijñāna*, a view similar to that of the Vijñānavāda school.)

From these facts, we are led to conclude that the author of the third chapter differed from those of the other chapters. From its contents, its date of compilation may be considered to have been about the same as that of the second chapter.

(4) Examination of the Fourth Chapter.

The fourth chapter of the *Māṇḍūkya-Kārikā* opens with an invocatory verse and similarly ends with a concluding verse of invocation. This shows that the fourth chapter is an independent work complete in just one hundred verses.[31] And the striking peculiarity of the fourth chapter is that throughout the whole work there is striking influence from Buddhism.

First in the invocatory verse the salutation is made to the "awakened one" (*saṃbuddha*), and throughout the whole work the one who is awakened to truth is called "*buddha*."[32] Such a term is not found in the previous three chapters. In the first three chapters the wise man or the man of knowledge is called *muni* (I, 29 ; II, 35), *tattvavid* (II, 34), *dhīmat* (III, 34), *vicakṣaṇa* (II, 31) and so on. But in this fourth chapter, instead of such traditional Brahmanical terminology, a Buddhist term is used. Calling a holy sage "*buddha*" appears not to be admitted in general traditional Brahmanical literature. Therefore, while in the first three chapters the fact of Buddhist influence is only hinted at, here is openly expressed a standpoint like that of a Buddhist. Not only this but he further emphatically proclaims his own standpoint as "the highest vehicle" (*agrayāna* = great vehicle, Mahāyāna).

In accordance with this standpoint, the phrasing is in general of remarkably Buddhist character. Admittedly in the fourth chapter there are fairly numerous *Kārikās* with wording almost identical with the second and third chapters.[33] It may be considered that these have been taken from the previous chapters and inserted. But there being extremely few gaps for the interpretations, the wording is altered. And where the wording is altered, the newly applied terms are invariably Buddhist. For instance IV, 6 and III, 20 are identical except that "*bhāva*" has been amended to "*dharma*." Both words may be understood in the same meaning, but as mentioned in Nāgārjuna's *Wu-wei-lun* (『無畏論』), "*bhāva*" is a word found generally running through Indian philosophy, while the word *dharma* in this meaning is a peculiarly Buddhist term.[34] The word *dharma* in the fourth chapter is used in this peculiarly Buddhist sense, whereas in the first three chapters the word in this sense does not appear. Again, IV, 60 and 61 are identical with III, 29 and 30, except that *manas* is given as *citta*. That *manas* reveals the phenomenal world of (or as) "two original oppositions" is taught in various Hindu religious books such as for instance the *Yogavāsiṣṭha*, *Bhāgavata-purāṇa,* etc.,[35] and it is not a Buddhist doctrine. But that the heart (mind, *citta*) reveals (manifests) phenomena is often taught in Buddhism too,[36] so that to set up the mind as the absolute being recognized generally as a peculiarity of the Buddhist teaching,[37] such an alteration of wording is not strange even as Buddhist doctrine.

In the light of these facts, it appears the author of the fourth chapter adopted some of the verses of the first three chapters, but in adopting them amended the usual Brahmanical terms to Buddhist terms. Such amendment is seen in other points also. For instance, in the first three chapters the Vedantic terms *dvaita* and *advaita* are much used, but in the fourth chapter these are not used and the specially Buddhist terms *dvaya* and *advaya* are used.

Again, looking at Nāgārjuna's works, almost the same arguments are everywhere countered as here.[38] They are provided with the special Mādhyamika *reductio ad absurdum* dialectic (*prasaṅga*). The destroying of the view of separate phenomena by the tetralemma, or too the thesis that the Buddha neither "is," "is not," "both is and is not," "neither is nor is not" (IV, 82-84), can be recognized in Mādhyamika works. The view of existence too is quite that of the Mādhyamika (IV, 27), and so the author of the fourth chapter must have read the works of Nāgārjuna and others.

Again the influence of Vijñānavāda appears no less. Even in the second and third chapters the influence of Vijñānavāda is clearly recognizable, though the changefulness of *vijñāna* (or mutation of *vijñāna*, consciousness) is not yet taught. But in the fourth chapter the evolutionary development of phenomena from *vijñāna* is majestically taught (IV, 45-52). We would not be wrong to say that the philosophical doctrine is that of Vijñānavāda. In explaining the status of the phenomenal empirical world, the simile of the revolving fire wheel (*alāta*) is used. This simile has been used from old in the orthodox Brahmanical tradition for various purposes, but to use it to explain the ground of the status of the phenomenal world is clearly due to Buddhist, and in particular Vijñānavāda, influence.[39] Again in the fourth chapter, the basic terms of the three natures spoken of in Vijñānavāda philosophy are clearly contrasted (*paramārtha*, IV, 73; 74; *paratantrāstitā*, IV, 24; *paratantrābhisaṃvṛti*, IV, 73; *paratantrābhiniṣpatti*, IV, 74; *kalpitasaṃvṛti*, IV, 73; 74). Again, the teaching relating to stages in the completion of the training (discipline) seems to come from some branch of the Vijñānavāda (IV, 87; 88). Again, there is something almost identical with the very first verse of the "Treatise on the Distinction between the Middle and the Extremes" (*Chung-pien fen-pieh lun* 『中辺分別論』 by Vasubandhu; according to dictionary no Sanskrit name, but said to be an explanation of the *Madhyānta-vibhāga-śāstra*) (IV, 75). These clearly we can take as the direct influence of various works of the Vijñānavāda school.

One point to be noted here is this: the Vijñānavāda which here appears in terms of language is certainly identical with the language of Vijñānavāda works of a comparatively early date, and the thought also accords with early Vijñānavāda philosophy. The language special to late Vijñānavāda (for instance as represented by Dignāga and Dharmakīrti) is not used at all. It should be noted that Śaṅkara is mainly attacking the doctrine of Dharmakīrti,[40] so that the Vijñānavāda which influenced the fourth chapter of the *Māṇḍūkya-Kārikās* and the Vijñānavāda which Śaṅkara is attacking are very different. And since in our fourth chapter there is no influence from the later Vijñānavāda, its date may be fairly early.

Besides, there are very many verses reminiscent of Mahāyāna scriptures and writings unconnected with the special doctrines of the Mādhyamikas or Vijñānavāda. Again, there are very many Buddhist technical terms. Besides those previously noted, there are the Buddhist Sanskrit words *acintya* (41; 52), *adhvan* (27), *avivāda* (2), *tāyin* (99), *nirmukta* (70), *paridīpita* (19), *prajñapti* (24; 25), *laukika* (87), *lokottara* (88), *saṃvṛti* (57; 74), etc. The incidence of the use of Buddhist Sanskrit is far more striking than in the preceding three chapters, and in fact without a knowledge of Buddhist technical terms, comprehension of this fourth chapter is hardly possible.

A Buddhist coloring thus appearing everywhere, does the standpoint of orthodox Brahmanical doctrine or the standpoint of Vedānta philosophy appear at all? The first thing to note is that in this fourth chapter almost no quotations from or references to the *Upaniṣads* are found.[41] In his commentary on the *Kārikās* Śaṅkara quotes many phrases from the *Upaniṣads*, but for the fourth chapter these quotations are very few, nor can it be said that the phrases quoted are necessarily texts on which the *Māṇḍūkya-Kārikās* are based. The *Kārikās* of the fourth chapter being largely based on Buddhist influence, this fact is rather natural. It is also in striking contrast to the previous three chapters, particularly the third chapter, where references to *Upaniṣad* texts were abundant.

On the other hand, the concept of eternality rejected in Buddhism is in fact rejected in Verse 59. Again it can be supposed that the use of the word *sukha* instead of using the "*ānanda*" of the *Upaniṣads* and later is on the contrary a Buddhist expression.[42] Beyond this, throughout the fourth chapter there is not a single instance of the rejection of Buddhist doctrine.[43]

On the contrary, ideas are everywhere taught in this fourth chapter which can be considered special to Buddhist writings. In the "*Bodhisattva*'s State" Maitreya says of the content of Mahāyāna writings, "Their writings say that all *dharmas* have no self-nature, that there is no entity, and they speak of birthlessness and deathlessness, that all *dharmas* are equally empty (or equal in emptiness), equally delusion or dream,"[44] and he mentions that when the Hīnayāna followers hear such teachings they fall into consternation and slander them. All these things are taught in the fourth chapter of the *Māṇḍūkya-Kārikās*. (On "consternation," see IV, 42.)

Altogether one could have very little difficulty in feeling that in this fourth chapter post-Upaniṣadic orthodox Vedānta philosophy has been completely swept away and that it is altogether a Buddhist book. Looking at Ānandajñāna's commentary, we can see that the criticism that there is no point of difference between the fourth chapter of the *Kārikās* and Buddhist doctrine existed in the world of thought at that time. Namely, the opponent inquires:

"In the highest truth, what exists is knowledge (consciousness) alone, and in this very consciousness are discriminated the knower, object of knowledge, etc.—in saying this, you too are really adopting Buddhist doctrine."

jñānamātraṃ pāramārthikaṃ tatraiva jñātṛjñeyādi kalpitam iti saugatamatam eva bhavatāpi samgṛhītam/[45)]

In reply to this, Ānandajñāna, after commenting on Śaṅkara's text, replies as follows:

"Apart from all different forms, perfect, beginningless, without end, pure consciousness (*jñaptimātra*), the truth attainable only through the *Upaniṣads* is here being taught. And so in the doctrines of other sects like this is not [taught anything]. How can there be room for the rise of doubts from confusion of doctrines [theft of Buddhist doctrine]?"[46)]

It is probably needless to say that Ānandajñāna's reply is here wide of the mark. The fact is that at that time the Hindus themselves detected the real nature of Chapter Four.

It is a significant fact that phrases of the first three chapters of the *Kārikās* are widely quoted not merely, as expected, in books of the orthodox Brahmanical tradition but also in Buddhist writings. But so far as my own investigation goes, I have not yet found an instance of a quotation from Chapter Four. The content and language of Chapter Four being too Buddhistic, the general Hindu scholars found it strange and did not follow its authority.

Was the author of Chapter Four with these characteristics not a Buddhist? — Scholars have often entertained this suspicion. But it has been transmitted as part of the literature of the Vedānta school and revered and commented upon by that school, and so one has to say that the author must have been a scholar and perhaps a practitioner of the Vedānta school. At the same time, though belonging to the Vedānta school, his cultural background and thought were, one can say, entirely Buddhist. Bhartṛhari, though a grammarian of the orthodox Brahmanical line, often lived in Buddhist temples and trained in Buddhist studies.[47)] It can be imagined that the author of the fourth chapter probably did the same.

The next question that arises is: why did the author, a Vedāntin, write a book with such Buddhist colouring? Probably the author, living at a time when the Mahāyāna was flourishing and which was so under Buddhist influence, could not help making use of their technical terms and concepts. It is just in the same way that those who teach Indian thought to Westerners cannot help resorting to traditionally Western terms and concepts.

If we now change our standpoint and view this book as a Buddhist work, it is not necessarily of very great value. One gets the impression that the whole fourth chapter is made up of extracts from or imitations of Mahāyāna scriptures and Mādhyamika and Vijñānavāda writings. Again, the special Mahāyāna doctrine of Perfect Compassion is not taught. The author has assembled special arguments from Buddhist works and constructed the chapter, and for this reason the work makes a most odd impression on the general reader. What is for us the most interesting is that the composition and transmission of such a book inside the Vedānta school is important material on the diffusion and permeation of Buddhist thought into that school.

(5) Conclusions.

After hitherto examining the characteristics of the separate chapters of the *Māṇḍūkya-Kārikās*, we can present the following summary of the whole.

(1) Chapter I is directly connected with the *Māṇḍūkya-Upaniṣad* and is a commentary on it. The second and other chapters, judging by their content, are separate works and it is hard to see any direct connection with the *Upaniṣad*. It may be supposed that this is the reason why the first chapter is called *Āgamaprakaraṇa* whereas the other three chapters are given philosophical and theoretical titles.

(2) Accordingly it is hard to see any systematic construction or close internal relationship running through the four chapters as a whole. In other words, there is no theoretical thread recognizable as running from the first to the fourth chapter. At the beginning of his commentary, Śaṅkara expounds the mutual relations between the chapters,[48] but one cannot say that this explanation is necessarily faithful in regard to the content of the separate chapters. Nor is the reason clear why these four chapters should have been put together.

(3) Looking at the content of the chapters, at the beginning of each there is given a theoretical explanation and discussion of metaphysics, and in the last part is taught the discipline for the realization of a practitioner. If one man had written the whole on a predetermined plan, he would surely not have displayed such disjointedness as to argue the same questions separately in four chapters. Again, in the various chapters cases where the same poetical phrase is substantially repeated are considerable.[49] But had the author been one man following a single plan, this would be meaningless. Would it not be more natural to suppose the existence of four basic religious works, teaching a combination of metaphysical speculation and practical discipline, which were later brought together to form one work?

(4) Again, we can simply express the central thought of the chapters as follows: Chapter I — *pariṇāmavāda* and again *satkāryavāda*. Chapters II and III — the *māyā* doctrine and the *vivarta* doctrine; Chapter IV — Buddhist doctrine. In this way the gist of the chapters differs.

(5) Chapter I in general follows the *Māṇḍūkya-Upaniṣad*, though there are instances where the teaching is slightly different. The views in the second and third chapters on many points contradict the view of the *Māṇḍūkya-Upaniṣad* and the *Kārikās* of Chapter I and rate it as an inferior doctrine. Again Chapter IV takes verses from Chapters II and III, but in so doing revises the technical terms in a Buddhist sense. Accordingly, when we examine the *Māṇḍūkya-Upaniṣad* and the four chapters of its *Kārikās* side by side, the later chapters presuppose the earlier ones, making them a precondition. One is therefore forced to conclude that the later the chapter, the later it was written.

(6) As for Buddhist influence, in the *Māṇḍūkya-Upaniṣad* early Mahāyāna influence can be seen, in Chapter I of the *Kārikās* Mādhyamika influence, and in Chapter II and the other chapters again on top of that Vijñānavāda influence. (Particularly in III, 32 can be seen the influence of the terminology of Vasubandhu's "Thirty Verses on Consciousness-Only," and so Chapter III would have been written after Vasubandhu.) By the fourth chapter, we can almost regard the

work as a Buddhist book. The later the chapter, the more striking the Buddhist influence.

It is therefore quite unreasonable to suppose that the four chapters were written by one individual at one time. It would be more natural to think of them as independently composed by separate people and afterwards assembled into a single work. And as to their date, it may be assumed that the earlier the chapter, the earlier the date of composition and the later the chapter, the later the date.

It was pointed out in the section on differences in the authority of the *Kārikās* that the separate chapters were regarded as independent *Upaniṣads* and that they were separately copied and transmitted. These facts show that the four chapters were also read and studied separately, and show that later generations thought that the chapters were capable of separation and independence. From these facts too the surmise is strengthened that each chapter was originally a separate work. Further, of the four chapters, the first alone is specially regarded as a revealed scriptural work, and in view of the fact that there are commentaries on this chapter alone, we can probably understand the first chapter as having been originally separate from the other chapters.

We cannot thus suppose that the four chapters of the *Māṇḍūkya-Kārikās* are all the work of one person.[50)] Nevertheless they are traditionally ascribed to Gauḍapāda and are believed to be by him. Is there then any relation between Gauḍapāda and the *Māṇḍūkya-Kārikās* ? This we shall discuss next.

Notes

1) Vidhusekhara Bhattacharyya : *IHQ*., vol. I, 1925, p.124 ff ; ditto ; *AS*. pp. xxxviii-xlvii.

2) Against Bhattacharyya's theses, Mahadevan (*GP*. pp.46-52) also presents opposing views.

3) Cf. the previous section.

4) Cf. note (16) for Sub-Section 1, Section II of the next chapter.

5) *Ṭīkā*, p.8. *Śrutyukte 'rthe tadvivaraṇarūpāñ ślokān avatārayati*/— *ibid*., p.46, cf. p.57.

6) In one edition the first chapter is named *Māṇḍūkya-vyākhyāna*: *āgamaśāstravivaraṇe prathamaṃ prakaraṇam Māṇḍūkya-vyākhyānaṃ samāptam*/— (Weber : *Indische Studien*, II, 100-101).

7) *prathamaṃ prakaraṇam āgamapradhānam*/(Ś. ad *GK*., p.8).
8) Ān. ad *GK*. p.66, *ll*.1-2 ; 7-8. *Bṛhad. Up. Vārttika*, III, 1. 4-5 (p.1137.)
9) Ś. ad *GK*. p.103, *l*.7 ; *Manu*, XII, 105-6.
10) Ān. ad *GK*. p.83, *l*.22. Bhartṛhari also used the term "*āgama*" in this sense. Cf. Part VII, Chapter III of this work.
11) Ś. ad *GK*. p.8, *l*.4. Cf. *yad adhyāyādau āgamamātreṇopanyastam,'nāsya jarayaitaj jīryatītyādi, tad iha nyāyenopapādayitum upanyastam*/(Ś. ad *Chānd. Up*. VIII,10,4. p.487.)
12) It is held that "*Vārttika* is consideration of matters which are discussed in the main text, matters not discussed, and those which are badly discussed" (*uktānuktaduruktacintā vārttikam*/— Rājaśekhara's *Kāvyamīmāṃsā*, GOS. 1916, p.1 ; from the above-cited article by V. Bhattacharyya). From an Indian standpoint, it is not possible that anything can be "badly discussed" in *śruti*.
13) In one manuscript the *Māṇḍūkya-Kārikā* is called the *Māṇḍūkya-Upaniṣad-Vārttika*. Gauḍapāda is considered to be the *Vārttika-kāra*. (Cf. *GK*. edition, ĀnSS. p.25, n. ; p.155, n. 1 ; Mitākṣarā edition, postscripts to chapters 3 and 4.)
14) Cf. the discussion on the term *paramārtha* in Appendix III to the previous chapter.
15) Other passages which indicate that the first chapter was influenced by Buddhism are as indicated in the Appendix to the previous chapter.
16) It is thought that Madhva et al. wrote their comments to only the first chapter, and not to the others, for this reason (V. Bhattacharyya : *AS*. pp. xxxvii-xxxviii.)
17) ad *GK*. p.8, *l*.11 ff. ; cf. *oṃkāranirṇayadvāreṇātmapratipattyupāyabhūtam ādyaṃ prakaraṇam ity uktam*/(Ān. ad *GK*. p.9, *l*.11).
18) Śaṅkara, the author of the commentary, explains *ślokas* IV, 87-88 of the main text in conjunction with the "Fourth State." However, in the comments to IV, 88 in the previous chapter, it has been explained that this is an error.
19) Cf. the comments to III,15 in the previous chapter.
20) ad *BS*. III, 2, 28. Cf. the comments to I, 6 in the previous chapter.
21) Cf. the comments to I, 6, 3, 15 in the previous chapter.
22) It may be possible to hold that I, 18 recognizes the existence of *vikalpa*.
23) *tasya dvaitasya hetuto vaitathyapratipādanāya dvitīyaṃ prakaraṇam*/(Ś. ad *GK*. p.8, *l*. 6.)
24) *GK*. II, 5.
25) Ś. ad *GK*. p.60, *ll*. 6-9 ; Ān. ad. *GK*. p.54, *ll*. 11-12.
26) Cf. *GK*. III, 1 ; 6. Also Śaṅkara's comments to this *śloka*.
27) For example, *GK*. II, 3.
28) See *ślokas* XI-XVI, *ślokas* XXIII-XXVI.
29) Walleser : *DAV*., S. 21.
30) Cf. the comments to III,31 in the previous chapter.

31) V. Bhattacharyya : *AS*. pp.lv-lvi.

32) Cf. Appendix I to the previous chapter.

33) *GK*. IV, 6 = III, 20 ; IV, 7-8 = III, 21-22 ; IV, 7 cd = IV, 29 cd = III, 21 cd ; IV, 31-32 = II, 6-7 ; IV, 34 = II, 2 ; IV, 61-62 = III, 29-30 ; IV, 71 = III, 48.

34) Cf. "*dharma*" in Appendix II to the previous chapter.

35) Cf. the comments to III, 31 in the previous chapter.

36) In the famous phrase : "The Three Worlds are false, being produced of mind." The term "produced of mind" is in the extant Sanskrit edition "*cittamātra*." In the *Śuklavidarśanabhūmi* (Bendall MSS.) we have "*cittamātraṃ bho jinaputra yad uta traidhātukam*" (Poussin : *JRAS*. 1908, p.889).

37) *duḥkhasvābhāvikatvavādibhir bauddhaiś cittasyaivātmatābhyuapagamāc ca*/(*Sāṃkhya-pravacanabhāṣya* p.10, *ll*. 12-13.)

38) *Ślokas* similar to IV,4 ; 7 ; 10 ; 12 ; 15 ; 16 ; 18 ; 20 ; 22 ; 33 ; 40 ; 55 ; 56 ; 59 ; 60 ; 70 ; 76 ; (82 ; 83) ; 84 ; 91 ; 99, etc., as presented in the previous chapter can be found in the *Madhyamaka-śāstra* and the *Vigrahavyāvartanī*.

39) Cf. "The simile of the *alātacakra*" in Appendix IV to the previous chapter.

40) H. Nakamura : *A History of Early Vedānta Philosophy*, Motilal Banarsidass, 1983, Part One, pp.75-79. Prof. David H. Ingalls has shown this in detail (*Philosophy East and West*, III, 1954, p.291 f.)

41) Deussen says that "*asaṅga*" in the 72nd verse is from *Bṛhad. Up*. IV, 3, 15, 16. But as pointed out in the translation, to understand it in this sense is inappropriate. "*prabhātaṃ bhavati svayam*" too, as pointed out previously, should be understood as Buddhist influence instead of in reference to *Bṛhad. Up*. IV, 3, 9 ; 14. Only "*sakṛdvibhāta*" in verse 81 can be considered to be based on *Chānd. Up*. VIII, 4, 1.

42) For instance in the *Sadddharma-Puṇḍarīka-sūtra* "*nivṛti*" is called "*paramaṃ saukhyam*." (*SaddhP* p.188, *l*. 13). Again in the "Uprising (breaking forth) Knowledge Classic" (reference to a Japanese edition) "*nirvāṇa*" is called "happiness."

43) As usual, Śaṅkara and Ānandajñāna in their notes make it that in *gāthās* 25-27 Vijñānavāda doctrine is raised, and *gāthā* 28 is an attack on this, and they again stress that in *gāthā* 99 "*jñānaṃ naitad buddhena bhāṣitam*" the Vedānta teaches a profound truth above that of Buddhism. Many scholars translate it in this way. I have noted in the "critical translation" that this translation is wrong.

44) *Bodhisattvabhūmi*, p.265, *l*.9 f.

45) Ān. ad *GK*. p.220, *ll*. 16-17.

46) Ān. ad *GK*. p.221, *ll*.3-4.

47) Discussed by the author in the next chapter of the present volume.

48) Ś. ad *GK*. p.8. See V. Bhattacharyya (*AS*. pp. xlvii-lvii) who asserts separate authorship of the chapters.

49) Cf. V. Bhattacharyya : *AS.* pp. liv-lv.

50) Formerly A. Venkatasubbiah (*Ind. Ant.* LXII, pp.181-193) argued that the *Māṇḍūkya-Upaniṣad* and the four chapters of the *Māṇḍūkya-Kārikās* were all by one author, but our study makes it clear that this thesis cannot be supported. For an opposing view, see Mahadevan (*GP.* pp.44-46). P. Deussen (*AGPh* 1. 2, S. 28f.) does not recognize this *Upaniṣad* as authoritative, but probably it was no less so than the later Minor *Upaniṣads*.

Sub-Section 3. Gauḍapāda and the Compilation of the *Māṇḍūkya-Kārikā*

The "*pāda*" in the name Gauḍapāda[1] is honorific, and at times it is abbreviated to leave simply the name "Gauḍa."[2] The person to whom the *Kārikā* is attributed is also called Gauḍacaraṇa,[3] Gauḍapādācārya,[4] or Gauḍācārya.[5] Information concerning the person called Gauḍapāda and details concerning his life are not available. It may be assumed that he was a person from the Gauḍa area, i.e., northern Bengal, but we have no positive evidence to support such an assumption. (In Sanskrit, not only those dwelling in the Gauḍa area, but also those who originated in that area and even those intending to go there may all be called "Gauḍa".)[6] According to one legend, there was a river called *Hirarāvatī* in the kingdom of *Kuru* (*Kuru-kṣetra*) and on its banks there dwelled the Gauḍa tribe (*Gauḍajāti*). Its chief (*śreṣṭha*) was Gauḍapāda. From the Dvāpara period, he absorbed himself in mystical meditation, and since people of that time did not know his personal name, he was known by the common name of his tribe, Gauḍa.[7]

According to what is accepted in the general traditions of India, Gauḍapāda was the teacher of Govinda, who in turn was Śaṅkara's teacher.[8] Since this lineage was generally accepted in India from an early date, there perhaps will be no objection to our accepting it. In this case, he would be a person about two generations removed from Śaṅkara (ca. 700-750 A.D.). Thus he could be considered to be a person of the middle and late seventh century, approximately 640-690 A.D. According to the same tradition, he was a disciple of a person called Śuka.[9] We have no information at all about Śuka, but we perhaps may conjecture that the mythical philosopher Śuka, who is mentioned in the epics, is being referred to here.

Earlier, Wallesser presented the view — causing a debate in academic circles — that Gauḍapāda was originally not the name of a person but signified "four stanzas of poetry which were composed by Vedānta scholars of the Gauḍa district." He held that these stanzas were each called "*pāda*," and in a later period were misunderstood as being the name of a person.[10] This theory, however, is not generally accepted. "*Pāda*" is an honorific ending, as in the case of *bhagavatpāda*, *ācāryapāda*, etc. As Wallesser indicated, Sureśvara and Mādhava in quoting Gauḍa used plural forms such as "Gauḍair"[11] or "Gauḍācāryāḥ."[12] However, these are cases of the honorific plural and do not indicate that Gauḍa actually signified several people. Thus, Wallesser's argument is insufficient. Further, Sureśvara, in quoting the *Māṇḍūkya-Kārikā* in his *Bṛhadāraṇyaka-Upaniṣad-Bhāṣya-Vārttika*,[13] uses the personal names Gauḍapāda and Gauḍācārya. He states that the *ślokas* are "the words of Gauḍapāda (*Gauḍapādīyaṃ vacas*)." There thus is no doubt that he recognized Gauḍapāda as an actual historical person.

However it cannot be assumed on the mere grounds — as just shown — that Gauḍapāda was a historical figure (instead of a group in the Gauḍa region, as postulated by Wallesser) that he was the author of the *Kārikās*. As already pointed out, there are mutual contradictions of doctrine and ideological standpoint between the chapters of the *Kārikās*, and it would be extremely difficult to take them all as the work of the same author. On the other hand, there are references by Sureśvara and others to verses of these *Kārikās* as the "words of Gauḍapāda," and so it is impossible to suppose that there is no connection at all.

Should we not then make this supposition? — that the *Māṇḍūkya-Kārikās* were put together as separate works at a fairy early date among Vedānta ascetics who revered the *Māṇḍūkya-Upaniṣad*, but they were not yet in their present form. It was Gauḍapāda who, adding a good deal of supplementary material of his own to bring them to their present form, put them together as one work, the *Māṇḍūkya-Kārikās*. This could provide a good explanation of how it is that there are contradictions in doctrine between the various chapters of the *Kārikās*, and yet they are all credited with being the work of Gauḍapāda. Gauḍapāda would then be the editor and compiler rather than the author.

In any case there is no question that the *Māṇḍūkya-Kārikās* were finally established in their present form by Gauḍapāda. There is the fact already pointed out by Walleser[14] that Śāntirakṣita in his own notes to his work *Madhyamakālaṃkāra* quotes *Māṇḍūkya-Kārikās* III, 4 ; 6 ; 8 ; II, 17 ; 18 ; 19 ; 20 ; III, 30 in that order. The quoted order follows mainly the order in the present *Kārikās*, and so it must be assumed that the *Kārikās* were established in their present form before Kamalaśīla. Since Kamalaśīla's date is about 680-740,[15] the supposition becomes a certainty that the work had already been put in its final form by Gauḍapāda by the middle of the seventh century.

Yet questions remain. If we take it that *Kārikās* of the individual chapters had been composed separately even before Gauḍapāda, how much earlier were they written? At present no definite answer can be given to this question. But perhaps it is possible to make some inferences.

Taking the final Chapter Four first, the influence of Nāgārjuna's *Madhyamaka-kārikā* is marked, and it must have been written after Nāgārjuna (150-250 A.D.). *Kārikā* LXXV in particular is almost the same wording as the opening verse of the *Madhyānta-vibhāga-śāstra*, and so it must be considered to have been composed after that. (It is unimaginable that Maitreya would have picked out a verse from a book of the Vedānta school and made it his opening verse.) Maitreya's work was disseminated mainly by the commentary on it by Vasubandhu, so that if we take Vasubandhu's dates (320-400)[16] as an upper limit, we can take it that most of the fourth chapter was written between 400 and 600 A.D.

As for the third chapter, a similar doctrine to what is contained there often appears in the works of Bhavya (Bhāvaviveka). *Kārikā* V of the third chapter of the *Māṇḍūkya-Kārikās* is almost word for word *Kārikā* XIII of Chapter Eight of Bhavya's *Madhyamaka-hṛdaya-kārikā* (literally *Middle-view Heart-doctrine Kārikās*). So one can suppose that most of the third chapter was already written by the time of Bhavya, 490-570.[17] Again, *Kārikā* XLIV matches very closely a *Kārikā* in the *Mahāyāna-sūtrālaṅkāra* and can be thought to show the influence of Maitreya. In the light of this evidence it is permissible to suppose that most of the third chapter was completed by 400-500.

As the previous detailed analysis has shown, the first chapter must have been written before the second, which presupposes it. In particular, it was often only the first chapter that was recognized as revelation (*śruti*), and so we may assume that the first chapter must have preceded the second by a good time.

But among the technical terms of Chapter I, as already noted, there are a fair number which are common to Hinduist works rather than the old *Upaniṣads*, and so it is difficult to place it very early. Moreover Mādhyamika influence is recognizable in Chapter I, so that it has to be placed later than Nāgārjuna (150-250). Almost nothing of Vijñānavāda influence is to be seen. Accordingly the composition of most of it can be put at 300-400.

Our examination has shown that the *Māṇḍūkya-Upaniṣad* itself was later than the *Maitrī-Upaniṣad* but before other "new" *Upaniṣads* attached to the *Atharva-Veda*. The influence of the Mahāyāna — particularly the doctrine of the void — is recognizable. It has already been shown that it must have been composed considerably earlier than the first chapter of the *Māṇḍūkya-Kārikās*. On the evidence, it would have been written probably about 1-200 A.D.

Perhaps one may speculate a little further. The *Māṇḍūkya-Upaniṣad* was composed by a Brahmin in an area where there were opportunities for contact with Mahāyāna Buddhism in about the first or second century A.D. Later, someone of a school which revered the *Upaniṣad* wrote the first chapter of the *Kārikās* as a commentary on it. Brahmin philosophers of the same tradition later on successively wrote Chapters II, III and IV in the name of clarifying the real essence of the *Upaniṣad*.

There was a close scholastic connection between these authors and they had a common inclination to fill out the Vedānta doctrine with borrowings from Buddhist philosophy, which was in their time very developed. So it was that the group of works came to be treated as a set and handed down together with the *Māṇḍūkya-Upaniṣad* to posterity. The four books, differing in time of composition and with differences also in doctrinal content, in the middle of the 7th century were edited and put together by Gauḍapāda, who added some material, in their present form as the *Māṇḍūkya-Kārikās*.

The phrase "*atraite ślokā bhavanti*"[18] ("here there are these verses"), which often appears when the first chapter of the *Kārikās* is quoted, would have been inserted by the editor when the first chapter of the *Kārikās* was put together with the *Upaniṣad*.[19] After this they were handed down without further amendment in the form in which we have them today.

In any case there is no doubt that this is a Vedāntic work. Sureśvara appraised Gauḍapāda as "one who knows the established doctrine of all Vedānta" (*nihśeṣavedasiddhāntavidvas*).[20]

Ānandajñāna relates a very interesting tradition about him : The Teacher (Gauḍapāda) formerly in Badarikā *āśrama*, where Nārāyaṇa (= Viṣṇu) dwells, performed great *tapas* meditating on Nārāyaṇa. Then the Lord, being pleased, gave him Vidyā. Therefore the highest Lord (*parameśvara*) is known as "teacher of the Teacher"[21] (*paramaguru* ; the second "teacher" would be "teacher Gauḍapāda")[22] (Ānandajñāna on *GK*). The *Mahābhārata*[23] speaks of Badarī *āśrama* where Nārāyaṇa and Nara together retired to practice *tapas* ; it is in the deep Himalayas at the source of the Ganges. It is not clear how far this story refers to fact. Again, Ānandajñāna says about the *Kārikās*, "holy Gauḍapāda made clear the meaning of the *Māṇḍūkya-Upaniṣad*, having understood it by grace of Nārāyaṇa," and says these were the *Kārikās* he wrote.[24] However, this account makes Gauḍapāda a devotee of Viṣṇu, whereas in the *Kārikās* themselves faith of Viṣṇu is not mentioned.

Gauḍapāda is credited with commentaries on the following works:

(1) *Bṛhadāraṇyaka-Upaniṣad*[25]

(2) *Nṛsiṃhatāpanīya-Upaniṣad*[26]

(3) *Anugītā*

(4) *Uttaragītā*

(5) *Devīmahātmya*

(6) *Śrīvidyāratnasūtra* (Tantra-associated, to which there is a *Dīpikā* commentary by Vidyāraṇyamuni)

(7) *Subhagodaya*

The *Uttaragītā-bhāṣya*[27] has been published (1910, Vanivilas Series, Sri rangam). Neither from the point of view of ideas, nor as a commentary does it seem outstanding. It is close to the *Māṇḍūkya-Kārikā* doctrine, but also says, "rituals, charity, etc., hearing, etc., are indeed means to realize truth," and phrases like "*lokasaṃgrahārtha karman*" imply a standpoint of "action combined with knowledge," and so on this point it differs from the *Māṇḍūkya-Kārikā*. Still it would involve no contradiction to suppose him the author if Gauḍapāda is regarded as the editor of the *Kārikās*.

Since works other than those mentioned above are still unpublished, we are not able to present any positive opinions on them.

There exists a tradition that Gauḍapāda authored an "appreciation" of the *Durgāsaptaśatī*.[28] In the line of scholars belonging to the Tantra religion the existence of two Gauḍapādas is recognized.[29] However, it is probable that the works pertaining to Tantra were written by entirely different Gauḍapādas. Further, it is possible that in order to heighten the authority of a work it was attributed to Gauḍapāda at a later period.

Notes

1) E.g. Sureśvara's *Bṛhad. Up. Vārttika* IV, 4, 886 (p.1866). Occasionally, because of rhyme considerations, he is called Gauḍapāda (*Jagadgururatnamālāstava*; V. Bhattacharyya : *AS*. p.lxiv.)

2) *Naiṣkarmyasiddhi* IV, 44.

3) *Śārīrakamīmāṃsābhāṣyavārttika*, ed. Anantakṛṣṇa Śāstri and Aśokanātha Bhattacharyya, p.5f. (As cited in V. Bhattacharyya : *AS*. p.lxiv ; Mahādevan : *GP*. p.3. Incidentally, according to Bhattacharyya, it is clearly recorded on page 6 of this work that his name was Gauḍa.)

4) Ś. ad *Śvet. Up.* I, 8.

5) *Pañcadaśī* II, 23 (V. Bhattacharyya : *AS*. p.lxiv) ; Sāyaṇa ad *Tait. Ār.* VII, 2 (ĀnSS., p.565); Sureśvara's *Bṛhad. Up. Vārttika*, II, 1, 386, p.951.

6) V. Bhattacharyya : *AS*. p.lxvi.

7) *Śārīraka-mīmāṃsā-bhāṣya-vārttika* (Asutosh Sanskrit Series No. 1), p.6. (As quoted by T. M. P. Mahadevan : *GP*. p.3 ; Bhattacharyya : *AS*. p.lxvii.)

8) The *ślokas* cited in *Dvādaśamahāvākyavivaraṇa* by Vaikuṇṭhapurī (Aufrecht: *Bodl. Cat*. p.227), *Śaṅkaravijaya* by Mādhava (*ibid*., p.255b ; cf. Walleser: *DA V*., S. 10 ; Colebrooke : *Misc. Ess*., *Collected Works II*, p.93), the edition with Śaṅkara's dates recorded discovered by Pathak (*Ind. Ant*. XI, 1882, p.174) ; Aufrecht : *CC*., I, p.170 ; Mahadevan : *GP*. p.2.

9) Other than the works cited in note 8, it also appears in Śaṅkara's commentary to the *Śvet. Up*. I, 8 (cf. Walleser : *DA V*. S. 8).

10) Walleser : *DA V*. S. 1 ff.

11) *Naiṣkarmyasiddhi*, IV, 44. In the same passage Śaṅkara's *Upadeśasāhasrī* XVIII, 26 is

quoted with the words "*Drāviḍair ... prabhāṣitaḥ.*" It is clear that Śaṅkara as one individual is indicated here. Thus, "Gauḍair ..." can also be explained in the same manner.

12) *Pañcadaśī*, II, 23.

13) (a) "*aniścitā yathā rajjur*" (=*GK*. II, 17) *iti nyāyopabṛṃhitam/sphuṭārthaṃ gauḍapādīyaṃ vaco 'rthe 'traiva gīyate//Bṛhad. Up. Vārttika*, I, 4, 389 (p.510). Ānandajñāna calls this quotation "*saṃpradāyavidāṃ vākyam*" and calls Gauḍapāda an "outstanding person" (*viśiṣṭa-puruṣa*). (b) It is stated: *gauḍācāryair idam vastu yathā 'smābhiḥ prapañcitam/— Bṛhad. Up. Vārttika*, II, 1, 386 (p.951). (c) It is stated: *ślokāṃś ca gauḍapādāder yathoktārthasya sākṣiṇaḥ/adhīyate 'tra yatnena saṃpradāyavidaḥ svayam//— Bṛhad. Up. Vārttika*, IV, 4, 886 (p.1866), and *GK*. II, 38; III, 46 are quoted.

14) Walleser: *DA V*. S. 20.

15) The author's *A History of Early Vedānta Philosophy*, Part One, pp.79-87.

16) Ui Hakuju: *A Study of Indian Philosophy*, vol. I, p.414.

17) *Ibid*., vol. 5, p.149.

18) Ānandajñāna also takes this passage as being by Gauḍapāda. Ān. ad. *GK*. p.25, *l*.4.

19) Ānandajñāna takes these as the words of Gauḍapāda — see Ānandajñāna's commentary on *Gauḍapāda-Kārikās*.

20) *Bṛhad. Up. Vārttika*, II, 1, 5, 386 (p.951).

21) Probably the meaning is "master" as in the appellation "Master Gauḍapāda."

22) Ānandajñāna ad *GK*., p.157, *ll*. 22-24; cf. p.2. It is recorded in the notes (*ṭīkā*) by Nārāyaṇa to the *Māṇḍūkya-Upaniṣad* that Gauḍapāda underwent severe religious practices in a cave in the Himalayas and, having written the four stanzas of the *Kārikā*, presented them to Śuka (V. Bhattacharyya: *AS*, p. lxxiii, n.2).

23) *MBh*. XII, 336, 10 (=12659); 341, 111 (=12975); 345, 10 (=13314); 345, 27(=13330).

24) Ān. ad *GK*., p.2, *ll*. 3-4.

25) However, the citation in the bibliography may be in error. "Report on Search for Sanskrit MSS., 1883-84" (= *Coll. Works of Sir R. G. Bhandarkar*: vol. II, pp.69-70).

26) As stated in Aufrecht, *CC*., vol. III. Concerning the notes to the *Nṛsiṃha-tāpanīya-Up*., cf. V. Bhattacharyya: *AS*. pp.291-292.

27) *Uttaragītābhāṣya*, published in the Vani Vilas Series, Srirangam, 1910. However the author was not able to see this work. His comments are based on Belvalkar: *Lectures*, p.189. Also, cf. Mahadevan: *GP*. p.26 f.

28) This is discussed by Bhāskararāya in his notes to the *Durgāsaptaśatī* (V. Bhattacharyya: *AS*., p.lxxxix).

29) It appears in the *Śrīvidyārṇava* by Pragalbhācārya (V. Bhattacharyya: *AS*. p.lxxxx).

CHAPTER III
THOUGHT

As has already been shown, if the *Māṇḍūkya-Upaniṣad* and the four chapters of the *Kārikā* are held to have been composed not at the same time, but to have been composed at successively different periods, there can be no doubt that there exist between them shifts or developments in thinking. Keeping this point in mind, let us examine the views discussed in the *Upaniṣad* and in each of the four chapters of the *Kārikā*.

SECTION I. THE STANDPOINT OF THE *KĀRIKĀ*

Since the *Māṇḍūkya-Upaniṣad* is early enough to be included among the "Ancient Upaniṣads" and since it claims itself to be an *Upaniṣad*, there can be found in it nothing like logical argument.

The first chapter of the *Kārikā* presents comments on the *Upaniṣad* and, as part of the commentary, some demonstrative explanations. However, it still shows no reflection on the relationship between the scriptures and logical thinking.

In the second and following chapters of the *Kārikā*, however, this problem comes to hold extreme importance. The second chapter in outward form also takes the traditional position of the Vedānta school and has as its purpose the explanation of the true purport of the *Upaniṣads*. Thus, its theories are held to be not the result of independent thinking by the author but "the fixed theories of the *Vedānta* (*Vedāntaniścaya*)" (II,12), the thought of "the sage who has reached the innermost meaning of the *Veda* (*muni vedapāraga*)" (II,35), or that of "the wise man who is versed in the *Vedānta* (*Vedānteṣu vicakṣaṇa*)" (II,31). In this manner, since the author himself asserts that his theories are equivalent to the true meaning of the *Upaniṣads*, he makes special efforts to quote many passages from the *Upaniṣads* as references in order to show that his views are not at all independently created or heretical views. In order to establish the legitimacy of his assertions, logical proof and proof based on references to the scriptures are presented. This is a tendency common to many Indian philosophical works. A theory had to be rational and possess a purely logical foundation, but at the same time also had to have a basis in the scriptures of its school. It is held that "what is learnt from the *Śruti* and based upon reason" (II,3) is truth. (This is equivalent to the "theoretical proof" and "scriptural proof" required in Buddhism.) However, what should one do in the case where, concerning the same point, several contradictory passages exist in the scriptures? For example, in the scriptures some passages explain that the phenomenal world is actually created, while contrarily others state that it is a temporary manifestation and that its creation is not an actual fact. In such a case, which view should one accept? Here, standards for determining this question no longer exist in the scriptures; only logical investigation can determine our choice. Thus, the *Māṇḍūkya-Kārikā* (III,23) states:

> That which is ascertained [in the scriptures] and also connected with reason is [the truth] and not the other. (Cf. also III,26)

It opts for the latter view that the phenomena of this world are temporary manifestations. Here, we have already reached the stage where the deciding factor is reason.

Further, this attitude which emphasizes reason reaches the point at which scriptural passages which contradict the author's own views are explicated in a manner which unduly forces agreement. The third chapter of the *Kārikā* takes the position that the individual self and absolute self are not separate, yet in the scriptures it is stated that even before the origination of the universe the individual self and the absolute self are separate. This is a clear contradiction. Concerning this, the *Kārikā* states that the individual self and absolute self are differentiated after the creation of the phenomenal world, and explains this by stating that although their differentiation is attributively presented in a secondary sense in the scriptures, this should not be taken literally (III,13). In particular, Ānandajñāna states in explanation that he who understands in the above manner is no longer a slave of the *Vedas*, but the meaning of the *Vedas* which he states is in truth the meaning of the *Vedas* (*yathoktavijñānavān vedakiṃkaro na bhavati kiṃ tu sa yaṃ vedārthaṃ brūte sa eva vedārtho bhavaty ity arthaḥ*).[1] Here we have an assertion of the superiority of free and independent thinking over that of traditional authority. Here, philosophy is no longer the handmaiden of theology; rather, the scriptures are made the handmaiden of philosophy.

Thus, its attitude toward the scriptures is actually extremely liberal. The authors of the *Kārikā* were dissatisfied with the attitude of general theologians who simply collected organized passages from the scriptures or who simply commented on them. Such scholars no doubt paid attention to outstanding philosophical constructions of other schools, and even if they were heretical theories, willingly followed those theories which they felt agreed with "reason." It may be considered that this attitude is one of the reasons for the marked influence of Mahāyāna Buddhism on the *Kārikās* as a whole.

Throughout the four chapters of the *Kārikā*, we can see a strong desire to approach the truth. In its theoretical proposals there is always a strong respect for "reasonableness" (*yujyate*) (II,27 ; 8). Those points which "cannot be proved" (*nopapattir vidyate*) (III,10) cannot be believed. The truth must be stated on the basis of logical reason (*hetu*) (II,1 ; 5 ; III,26), and a wrong reason[2] must not be used (IV,20). This attitude which emphasizes logical demonstration led even to the point where in this work we find the use of the tetralemma (*catuṣkoṭi*),[3] which is thought to have originated in Buddhism, and the *prasaṅga* method (*reductio ad absurdum*).[4]

In view of the above characteristics, the four chapters of the *Kārikā*, in particular the second and third chapters, while claiming to be based on the scriptures, are in actuality each a type of philosophical discussion which develops its own distinctive philosophical system. In the fourth chapter the *Upaniṣads* are hardly mentioned at all, the discussion being developed almost entirely on the basis of Buddhistic theories. Here we have a scholar belonging to the Orthodox Brahman school who disregarded the scriptures of his own school and, based on his own philosophical beliefs, used Buddhistic doctrines and thought structures. Thus, it may be said that the theories presented here are a type of philosophical discussion. In terms of content, it is a pure critique of opposing theories.

Hence, concerning the problem of "proof based on the scriptures and logical proof," the chapters of the *Māṇḍūkya-Kārikā* successively become richer in distinctive philosophical thinking, and evidence of reflective consciousness of this problem becomes gradually more pronounced. Concerning the scholastic standpoints of this *Kārikā*, we can also see a development (probably historical) running through the four chapters.

Notes

1) Ān. ad *GK*., II, 30, p.90.

2) Here the *sādhyasama* is discussed.

3) IV,40 ; 83 ; 84. Cf. also IV,22.

4) I,17 ; 18 ; III,22. This approximates what is called *tarka* in the systems of logic of later periods.

SECTION II. THE ABSOLUTE AND THE PHENOMENAL WORLD

Sub-Section 1. The Four States (*pādas*) of *Brahman*

A. The Theory Presented in the *Māṇḍūkya-Upaniṣad*

The central teaching is the explanation of the absolute *Brahman* (namely *ātman*) in correlation with the sacred syllable *Om*. *Om* was the holy syllable which originally Brahmins recited at the time of sacrifice with reverence to concentrate their devotion.[1]

It is thought that this syllable possessed from ancient times a sort of occult significance, and later it became the object of theological concepts, and among *yogis* practice of meditation on *Om* flourished. And so it came about that a special kind of philosophical speculation developed in regard to the letter-sound *Om*. Already in the *Chāndogya-Upaniṣad* (II,23,4) *Om* is regarded as one with the universe (*idaṃ sarvam*) and again it is called "the essence (*rasa*) of the whole *Veda*" (I,1), and "the deathless fearless syllable" (*svaram amṛtam abhayam*) (I, 45). Thus exalted, *Om* soon came to be considered as no other than the absolute, as where it is declared "*Om* is *Brahman*" (*Tait. Up*. I,8). Thereafter *Om* is seen as the symbol of *Brahman*.

Accordingly the Brahmin ascetics of that time believed that by meditation on this *Om* they would be able to attain *Brahman*.[2]

This sacred syllable was often treated by the later Brahmin thinkers[3] and the *Māṇḍūkya-Upaniṣad* is also in the tradition of this philosophical speculation. The Brahmin who composed this *Upaniṣad* would have been one devoted to the practice of *Yoga* by taking the sacred syllable as his object of meditation. And to explain the significance of his practice he sets out briefly a philosophical doctrine about it, linking it with various Upaniṣadic doctrines and fitting them together in one organized hole.

His doctrine is as follows:

> All is no other than *Brahman* and this *Brahman* is our "this self" (*ayam ātma*). All things have their basis of existence in the absolute *Brahman* (=*ātman*); all the phenomena stand on *Brahman* as their basis. The word which symbolizes *Brahman* is the sacred syllable *Om*. It can be regarded as identical with *Brahman*. And so the syllable *Om* is the symbol of all things.[4] In *Om* all beings have their materialization. All temporal existence relating to past, present and future is no other than *Om*, and again transcendental existence beyond time is no other than *Om*.

What is specially noteworthy in this doctrine is that this *Brahman* or *ātman* is not a principle contrasted with the phenomenal world or the separate forms. In the *Śvetāśvatara-Upaniṣad* (VI, 5) the One who is contrasted with all phenomenal existence conditioned by time, who is existence transcending time and who transcends the three world is the Highest Lord. But here, temporal existence and trans-temporal existence are both taken to be no more than one aspect of the Absolute.

The Absolute includes and synthesizes all that is. All that is, just because it is, can be the Absolute expressed as *Brahman* or *ātman*. In the old thought, the Absolute was sought in a state transcending the phenomenal world, but here it comes to be thought of as including it. To make clear how an Absolute of this kind sets up the phenomenal world, a doctrine of four *pādas* (four feet) is propounded. According to the *Māṇḍūkya*, *Brahman* consists of four *pādas*, namely an association of four *pādas* (quarters). A doctrine of four quarters had already been found in the *Ṛg-Veda*,[5] and in the *Maitrī-Upaniṣad*[6] the four states are described one by one corresponding to states of human consciousness, but in this *Māṇḍūkya-Upaniṣad* the idea of the four states is the backbone of the system, and postulated as four states of the Absolutes. They can be set out systematically (as in the diagram), which fact shows that the doctrine is itself systematic.

The statement that *Brahman* possesses these four states does not, according to Śaṅkara's commentary, mean that *Brahman* has four parts. Each of the four is successively a substratum and related as being the basis (of the preceding). It is not for instance as with the four feet of an animal which are independent of each other, but to be thought of as with the four parts of the *Kārṣāpaṇa* coin.[7] Namely, for facilitating trade (*vyavahāraprācuryāya*), for convenience one quarter of it is thought of, but the one-quarter *Kārṣāpaṇa* is swallowed up in the half-*Kārṣāpaṇa*, and this latter again is swallowed up in the whole coin. In the same way the four states of All-pervading (*viśva*) etc. are successively swallowed up by the succeeding one. Accordingly, a succeeding state is the substratum of the preceding one. And since the Absolute symbolically is one with the syllable *Om*, the four states of *Brahman* are taken as one with the different *mātrās*[8] (syllable-measures) of *Om*.[9]

Thus pre-supposing *Om* as the symbol of *Brahman*, each of the three out of the four states of *Brahman* is allocated to a measure of *Om* and a mutual relation is in each case stressed. The *yogins* of that time were practicing their *yoga* by meditating on *Om* and doubtless the purpose was to show the meaningfulness of their meditation, and the explanation is extremely systematic. In the old *Upaniṣads*, *ātman* or a similar principle was taken to be located in various parts of the body, but here the locating of the first three of the four-quarters is given according to a synthetic system: "the all-pervading state is in the hollow of the right eye, the radiant state is in the inner part of the mind, and the wisdom state is in the space in the heart" (I, 2). As in the case of the *Om* this can be taken as a means to facilitate meditation on *ātman*.

Though the presentation is indeed systematic, it was not simply fitting together former views and concepts; it goes one step further than the notions of the old *Upaniṣads* in establishing its system. The basis which makes the systematization possible we can find in the establishment of the fourth state. The *Māṇḍūkya-Upaniṣad* specifies the third state as "Lord of all beings", "omniscient", "inner controller", "source from which arise the origin and dissolution of all beings" and in the old *Upaniṣads* all these concepts meat the Absolute, the supreme principle of the universe.

And the *Māṇḍūkya*, in taking them as specifying the third state, now postulates the fourth state behind that. Namely it finds a principle which is the support of what had been taken as the supreme principle in previous *Upaniṣads*. Even as regards the three states, waking, dreaming and dreamless state, these were recognized in previous *Upaniṣads* but it is the originality of the *Māṇḍūkya-Upaniṣad* to discover the fourth state which supports them.[10] But here the ultimate new revealed as the fourth state could not be specified as "existent" or affirmatively and positively as a principle ; it is an absolute of negation, ultimate void (*śūnya*). It is expressed merely in negative terms. Even "auspicious" and "peace" are in fact negative concepts. Previously Yājñavalkya, the Upaniṣadic philosopher, had specified the nature of *ātman* as "pure consciousness (knowledge) alone" (*prajñānaghana*)[11] but here this is denied "not pure consciousness (knowledge) alone". An actual Upaniṣadic doctrine has to be denied.

After all, if a principle is asserted as the origin of the universe, and then it is sought to find some yet more fundamental principle than that, the logical chain could extend without end, and would fall into the fallacy of infinite regress (*anavasthā*). What can, without falling into this fallacy, be established as the substratum of the principle which in the old *Upaniṣads* is the origin of the universe, must be an absolute negation differed from it. Against an origin of the universe which is a principle positively and affirmatively specified, the forth state has to be a principle negatively defined. Just in so far as it is "not to be seen, not to be grasped" it can make possible all activity.

In the case of human consciousness it was understood in this way. In previous *Upaniṣads*, the waking, dreaming and dreamless state are considered, and it is taught that in dreamless state there is oneness with *Brahman* and that it was seen as the absolute. But here this *Upaniṣad* has a separate fourth state which establishes the other three states (*pādas*) and this is said to be the basis of the three states. Namely the fourth state has no specific "field" (*sthāna*) as an aspect of consciousness (as the others have), and for that reason it can make the other three states of consciousness possible.[12]

In this way the *Māṇḍūkya-Upaniṣad* in setting up a fourth state, continues the general metaphysic of the old *Upaniṣads*, but in seeking to go beyond it makes an inevitable change in the theoretical development. What occasioned the specification of the fourth state in this way must have been the *Śūnya* (void) concept of Mahāyāna Buddhism.[13] Expressions which are startlingly identical or similar are found in Mahāyāna.[14]

In another sense, recognition of the negatively defined absolute, which is behind the principle recognized generally by the old *Upaniṣads* and different from it, led to setting up two kinds of highest principle : the highest principle from the standpoint of existence and the highest principle from the standpoint of the void. The development of this probably in later centuries came out in the concepts of "Highest *Brahman*" and "Lower *Brahman*". The concept of two kind of *Brahman* already appears in the *Kārikās* (I,26), and the peculiar view of *Īśvara* afterwards in the Advaita school may be supposed to have its source here.

The ideas of the sacred syllable *Om* has a special place in the history of Indian thought, and the doctrines of the four states of *Brahman* and the four *mātrās* of *Om* were adopted in various sects of Hinduism[15] and by the Yoga school.[16] Among philosophers of Vedānta in later centuries were those who postulated a fifth state (without-mind, *unmanī*) beyond the fourth and the point was debated.[17] It is not clear how far all these doctrines were directly influenced by the *Māṇḍūkya-Upaniṣad* and the *Kārikās* on it, but it is a very interesting point in the history of thought.

Notes

1) Scholars often compare this to the "A-men" used in Christianity. In Buddhism, too, when being ordained the recipient vows to maintain the requlations in answer to questions of the ordainer and then says "*Om*". *Bodhisattvabhūmi*, p.153, *l*. 23.

2) Cf. *Bhag. G*. VIII, 12-13; XVII, 24.

3) For examples, Cf. *Kāṭhaka-Up*. II, 15-17 ; *Muṇḍ. Up*. II, 2,3 ; *Maitri-Up*. VI, 4, 5 ; 23 ; 24 ; 37 ; VII ; *Praśna-Up*. V, 2-7 (Cf. *BS*. I, 3, 12) ; *ĀpDhS*. I, 4, 137.

4) Just as the image (*pratimā*) of *Viṣṇu* is the symbol of *Viṣṇu*, *Om* is a device for the realization of *Brahman* (Ān. ad *GK*. p.9, *l*. 20).

5) "Thus is his greatness. But *Puruṣa* is even greater. All things are one-fourth of him ; the immortals in heaven are the other three quarters" (*ṚV*. X, 90, 3 = *Chānd. Up*. III,

12, 6). *Ṣoḍaśakalāvidyā*'s theory (*Chānd. Up.* IV, 4-9) also seems to have absorbed the idea of four *pādas*. However, it may be said that in contrast to the introspective and subjective theories in the *Māṇḍūkya-Upaniṣad*, these older theories explain the *pādas* objectively.

6) "He who sees with the eye [the self in the waking state], he who moves in dreams [the self in the dreaming state], he who is in deep sleep [the self in the state of deep sleep] and he who is beyond the deep sleep [the self in the fourth state], these are his four distinct conditions. Of these the fourth is greater [than the rest]". (*Maitrī-Up.* VII, 11, 7. Cf. VI, 19). As a point of interest, if we compare the terms used for the various stages of consciousness in the *Chānd. Up.* VIII, 7-12, and the terms used by Śaṅkara for the four stages, we have the following: *viśva akṣipuruṣa, cākṣuṣapuruṣa, chāyāpuruṣa, chāyātman / taijasa svapnātman / prājña suṣuptashta / caturtha uttamapuruṣa //* (Mahadevan: *GP*. p.72).

7) Ś. ad *GK*., p.13, *ll.* 4-5. Ānandavana's commentary to the *Rāma-tāpanīya-Up.* (Weber: *Indische Studien* II, S. 107) and Nārāyaṇa's *Dīpikā* (ĀnSS. p.576) also explain it in the same manner.

8) The mora (*mātrā*) is the unit that may be considered when the individual syllables (*akṣara, varṇa*) have been dissected.

9) Cf. *Māṇḍūkya-Upaniṣad* VIII-XII; *Māṇḍūkya-Kārikā* I,16; 19-21; 24.

10) It was thought that *turīya* is a shortened form of *caturīya*. (*Vārttika* on Pāṇini, VII, 51).

11) A good example is *Bṛhad. Up.* IV, 5, 13.

12) The view that the true *ātman* is different from the state of deep sleep appears in the *Chānd. Up.* VIII,11-12.

13) In Śaṅkara's commentaries it is stated that his opponents raised the difficult question of whether the fourth state is not *śūnya*. Śaṅkara's answers are a reflection of his own standpoint and are not necessarily true to the intent of the *Māṇḍūkya-Upaniṣad*. Contrarily, the views of his opponents are probably more accurate. (Ś. ad *Māṇḍ. Up.* p.41, *l.* 9.).

14) Cf. Part VI, Chapter I ,Section I of this book.

15) In the *Bhāgavata-Purāṇa* VII, 15,54 (pub. par Burnouf), too, after discussing *oṃkāra*, it is stated that *Ātman* consists of four states. *indriyāṇi manasy ūrmau vāci vaikārikaṃ manaḥ / vācaṃ varṇasamāmnāye tam oṃkāre svare nyaset //53// agniḥ sūryo divā prāhṇaḥ śuklo rākottaram svarāt / viśvaś ca taijasaḥ prājñas turya ātmā samanvayāt //54//* However, the terms used for the four states agree with those used in the first chapter of the *Kārikā* and not with those in the *Māṇḍūkya-Upaniṣad* (i.e., in the *Upaniṣad* we have *vaiśvānara, caturtha*).

16) In the chapter on *sphoṭa* in the *Yogasārasaṃgraha* the fourth state is explained as

sphoṭa. praṇavasyākārokāramakārarūpamātrātrayaṃ brahmādidevatātrayātmakatvam uktvā praṇavadevatātrayātiriktaparabrahmātmakacaturthamātrāṃ śrutaya āmananti. sā ca caturthī mātrā varṇatrayād atiriktaḥ sphoṭa eva saṃbhavati/ (Cf. Abegg : "Die Lehre vom Sphoṭa im Sarvadarśanasaṃgraha", *Festschrift Windisch*, S. 190.)

17) In the *Vivekasindhu* III, 31 ; 87-90 by Mukundarāja, a philosophical poet of the late twelfth century, the fifth state is discussed. (Jacob : *Hindu Pantheism*, pp.61-62). Also, Upaniṣadbrahmayogin, an Advaita scholar of a later period, divided each of the four states into four parts to establish sixteen states. Cf. Mahadevan : *GP*. p.101-106.

B. The Theory in the First Chapter of the *Kārikās*

The first chapter of the *Kārikās* is a commentary on the *Māṇḍūkya-Upaniṣad*, but whereas the *Upaniṣad* treats the *pādas* and the syllables of *Om* successively, the *Kārikās* explain the *pādas* by taking them in relation to particular points. As has already been pointed out in the analysis of the particular *Kārikās* individually, the explanation is in general at one with the *Upaniṣad*, but again a fair number of new explanations are added which have to be reckoned as new doctrine not taught by the *Upaniṣad*.

The first chapter of the *Kārikās* goes yet further than the *Upaniṣad*, and illustrates the distinction of the four *pādas* of the *Brahman* in a special way. According to *Kārikā* 15 of the first chapter, "cognition of the truth wrongly" "cognition different from the true form" (*anyathāgrahaṇa*) are called figuratively "dream"(*svapna*), and "ignorance regarding truth" (*tattva-ajñāna*) is called "sleep" (*nidrā*). In dream, representations different from true forms arise, and in sleep there is no awareness of anything in the outer world, hence such terms may be used. Again the former is called "effect" (*kārya*) and the latter is called "cause" (*kāraṇa*) (11). The mistaken cognition have ignorance regarding truth as their pre-condition, and they are thus called result and cause respectively. As cause, the sleep is again called "seed" (*bīja*) (13).

As has been indicated, the all-pervasive state (*viśva*) and the radiant state (*taijasa*) are bound by effect (dream) and by cause (sleep), the wisdom state (*prajñā*) being bound by cause (sleep) alone. But the fourth state is not bound by either of them (11 and 14). The first three states are in fact our life of illusion, what is fundamentally only one being divided into three (1 and 2).

The principles which cause the manifesting of the three states are false cognition of truth and ignorance of truth. The principle of *māyā* is also considered (16) and probably it indicates the two. It is beginningless (*anādi*). Since our daily life manifests on the basis of this false cognition of truth and ignorance of truth, when they vanish, we attain the fourth state and come to abide in peace in the fourth state.

But what is this "abiding in peace in the fourth state"? The first three states of waking, dream and sleep are each made to have their field of action (*sthāna*) and a state of consciousness different from these three could not be physiologically or psychologically human. And so the field of action of fourth state is itself rather these three human states. This is why no special field of action for the fourth state is specified. And so when we look the "person abiding in the fourth state" outward, in his action there does not appear any symptom or tendency of an occult kind different from any ordinary man ; he is performing actions like an ordinary man. But since he has reached the truth of the absolute, though in outward form he is the same as an ordinary man, yet he transcends the world. Therefore it is taught "though enjoying, he is not tainted" (5). This is clearly in the same line as the doctrine of the *Īṣa-Upaniṣad* (2). So the "dissolution of phenomena" is not a total unawareness as in the third state, but he realizes in practice the negation of relative distinctions while possessing consciousness. From the point of view of the *yogi* who has opened up this realization, everything is without distinctions and the same. For the people of the world, the relative duality exists, but for the one who has realized truth, it does not (18). The sage transcends them though he is in the separate forms.

The concept, taught in the first chapter of the *Kārikās*, of the fourth state is not necessarily at one with the same in the *Upniṣad*. Here the fourth is explained as the supreme principle as "the Lord who is the controller of eradication of all pains" (*nivṛtteḥ sarvaduḥkhānām īśānaḥ prabhuḥ*) and "omnipresent being the god (*deva*) of all." (10), but the *Māṇḍūkhya-Upaniṣad* calls the third state "the Lord of all" (*sarveśvara*), so on this point there is a considerable difference of doctrine apparent. Again, in the same *Upaniṣad*, the third state is specified as the "omniscient one" (*sarvajña*), but in the first chapter of the *Kārikās* the fourth state is called "the one who sees all" (*sarvadṛś*) (12). In the *Upaniṣad* the negative nature of the fourth state is stressed, whereas here in the *Kārikās* in speaking of its true nature there is a return, at least in form of expression, to the standpoint of the old *Upaniṣads* generally. It is a complete reversal from the new philosophical standpoint seen to be taken by the *Māṇḍūkya-Upaniṣad*. And in the second chapter of the *Kārikās* and the others, there is once more a stress on the negative character of the absolute.

However in the *Māṇḍūkya-Upaniṣad*, what the old *Upaniṣads* taught as "the origin of all beings" and "the source of the production and destruction of all beings" is simply allocated to the third state of *Brahman*, and the question is not yet touched as to how this production and destruction are brought about. But in this first chapter of *Kārikās*, after expounding the comparisons of the three states, this question is discussed in some detail. The *Kārikās* from (6) onward teach that there must be a source for the origin of all the objects of the phenomenal world which is ruled by space and time. Then how do all the beings arise from that source ? The answer is that "*Prāṇa* as *Puruṣa*", namely "the Lord" (*deva*) creates all the spiritual existences separately. The illustration is given that it is like the sun emitting rays. And this creative operation is said to be the fundamental nature (*svabhāva*) of the Lord (*deva*).

Puruṣa in the *Ṛg-Veda* and *Prāṇa* in the *Atharva-Veda* have been set up as the root principle of the world. Here also in line with those concepts, they are proposed as the ultimate principle. The theory of creation of the world taught in this first chapter is one kind of emanation theory. Accordingly since the creation is something which has come forth from God, it is endowed within its limits with divine nature. The individual "I" too is something possessing real existence. Here the *māyā* doctrine is not yet being taught.[1] Both origin and dissolution of the world are accepted (17). It is never taught that the separate forms of the phenomenal world are empty illusions.

Again since the analogy of light and the light-source as explanation for world creation is also accepted in the *Brahma-sūtra* (III, 2, 28), on this point the above mentioned creation theory is at one with the doctrine of the *Brahma-sūtra*. Śaṅkara, when he comes to explain this doctrine of the

Kārikās, uses the analogy of sparks coming from a fire.[2] This analogy appears not only in the *Upaniṣads* but in the primitive Vedānta schools, and had already been used by Āśmaratya[3] and Dravida,[4] so that it can be said that the author holds the same idea as these philosophers.

This kind of view, as Śaṅkara himself admits, clearly recognizes the origin of the world.[5] And inasmuch as it teaches the world creation by the kind of analogy, the author of this first chapter of the *Kārikās* no doubt thought that the individual "I" is one part (*ekadeśa*) of the supreme self.[6] This philosophical standpoint can be considered to be the Not-one-not-different doctrine. And so the world creation theory taught here is quite different from the general non-dualist thinking, and is also different from what is taught in the second chapter of the *Kārikās*.[7]

In connection with the question of creation, here several theories about creation of the world are mentioned, and they are rejected. Some people, for instance, regard creation of all beings as the divine power (*vibhūti*) of the highest Lord, other people think of it as "like a dream or a illusion", and yet others believe it is the "mere desire of God" (*icchāmātraṃ prabhoḥ*), and again the theorists of time maintain that it "arises from time" (*kālāt prasūti*), whereas others teach that it is "for the enjoyment" (*bhogārtha*) of a transcendent anthropomorphic god and still others teach it is "for sport" (*krīḍārtha*). But the author of the first chapter of the *Kārikās*, does not express approval of these various teachings. Since according to his view God is "one who has attained all desires" (*āpta-kāma*), he cannot have any aspirations (*spṛhā*), and so the action of the world creation cannot be for the sake of any purpose whatever.

From this listing of the various doctrines we can get to know what were some of the creation theories of that time, and at the same time realize that the author of this first chapter of the *Kārikās* holds a special position in the history of Vedānta philosophical thought. The fact that he rejects the analogy of creation as dream or illusion means that the doctrine of the first chapter is different from Buddhist doctrines, and also different from the same doctrine held by Vedānta schools too and set out in the *Kārikās* from the second chapter onwards,[8] and also different from the thought of Śaṅkara himself. The rejection, furthermore, of the doctrine of creation as based on the desire of the Lord is at variance with the teaching generally in the *Upaniṣads* that *ātman* of *sat* (existence) conceived a desire to create the world and created it.

In its rejection of the doctrine of "origination through time", it denies the Bhartṛhari doctrine.[9] Again the rejection of the doctrine "for enjoyment" is not at one with Sāṃkhya-style Vedānta. Since the doctrine of "for the sake of sport" is rejected, there is a denial of the teaching of the fundamental classic (authority) of the Vedānta schools, the *Brahma-sūtra* itself. It has to be acknowledged that in rejecting, in connection with the theory of purpose of creation, all the various theories deriving from branches of the same Vedānta sect, the author is maintaining a quite original view. And it can be said that the doctrine of Uddyotakara of the Nyāya sect most closely resembles his doctrine.[10]

The creation doctrine here taught is not merely special within the Vedānta sect, but differs from that of the *Kārikās* themselves in the second chapter onwards. In the first chapter, as has already been noted *prāṇa* is made the fundamental principle which manifests the world, but in the second chapter (19 ; 20) the doctrine of recognizing *prāṇa* as the ultimate principle is rejected. Again according to the first chapter, the individual self is projected from the world-cause, namely is no other than a transformation of it, but in the third chapter (7) the doctrine which takes the individual self as a transformation (*vikāra*) of the supreme self is rejected.

However the origination and dissolution of the world, in this first chapter of the *Kārikās* as in the *Māṇḍūkya-Upaniṣad*, can be manifest only in the third state of *Brahman*, and in *Brahman* itself namely the fourth state it cannot manifest. The first chapter calls the vision standing in the fourth state, vision "in the highest sense" (*paramārthatas*) (17). Here there is clearly an influence from Buddhist concepts, when the author of the first chapter seeks to clarify the nature of the fourth state, as the absolute, by using this concept. "It is non dual, seen in the highest sense" (17) this doctrine can be understood as already a first step in the direction of an illusionistic doctrine.

Notes

1) In I, 17 it is explained that dualistic opposition in the world is simply "*māyā* only"

(*māyāmātra*). But here this does not have the meaning of the *māyā* theory as discussed by the Advaita school of later periods. Rather, it is meant to indicate the inconceivable and mysterious powers of the deity who created the world. Cf. notes to I,7 in Part VI, Chapter I, Section II, Sub-Section 1 of this book.

2) Ś. ad *GK*. I, 6.

3) Cf. *A History of Early Vedānata Philosophy*, part I. p.384f.

4) Cf. supra.

5) *kāsucic chrutiṣv agnivisphuliṅgādinidarśanair jīvātmanaḥ parasmād brāhmaṇa utpattir āmnāyate*/ (Ś. ad *BS*. II, 3, 17, vol. II, p.38, *ll*. 13-14)

6) *baddhaḥ kaścid ātmā .... parasyātmanaḥ .... prakāśāśrayanyāyena caikadeśabhūto 'bhyupagamyeta....* (Ś. ad *BS*. III, 2, 29)

7) The term *advaita* is used (I,10; 16; 17), but it is meant to indicate the non-differentiation of the Absolute itself. It is probably not accurate to relate it directly to the theories of the Advaita school of later periods.

8) It contradicts the theories in the *GK*. II, 1 ff.; 31; III, 10; IV, 58, etc.

9) Cf. the subsequent parts.

10) Cf. notes to I,9 in Part VI, Chapter I, Section II, Sub-Section 1 of this book.

Sub-Section 2. The Doctrine of *Māyā*

In the second and third chapters of the *Kārikās*, the doctrine is taught that the individual soul comes into being and the world into manifestation through *māyā*. But the doctrine is presented quite differently in the two chapters.

A. The Theory Presented in the Second Chapter of the *Kārikās*

In the second chapter of the *Māṇḍūkya-Kārikās*, the concept of the four states (*pāda*) is completely abandoned. The doctrine of "those who teach the *pādas*" (*pādavid*) is in this chapter made one of the doctrines which are of a lower grade and inferior (II,21). Thus the metaphysics of the second chapter differ markedly from what is taught in the *Māṇḍūkya-Upaniṣad* and the *Kārikās* on it.

In the *Māṇḍūkya-Upaniṣad*, the four states of *Brahman* are each invested with their own special significance, and none of them is treated as an illusion. The *Kārikās* on the *Upaniṣad* follow this. It is true that they point out the common element shared by the waking state and the dreaming state

(I,11 and 14), but they do not go so far as to dismiss the waking experience as illusory. But this second chapter emphasizes that the whole waking experience is illusory and that there is no essential difference between dreaming and waking. Hence in the end the final conclusion was reached that:

> "Verily the wise teach that dreaming and waking are one." (II,5)[1)]

This expression is often clearly repeated in the Mahāyāna classics. In the first chapter of the *Kārikās*, the doctrine of the phenomenal world as comparable to a dream or an illusion is rejected as being heretical, but in this second chapter this very doctrine, just as it was rejected there, is here accepted.

The view that there is not the slightest difference between the experience of the waking state and the experience of the dreaming state does not only strike modern people as strange, but also aroused violent opposition from Indian philosophers of the time. But the real meaning of those who propounded this theory was that both of these kinds of experience are unreal in *paramārthatā*, and intending to say that it is insofar as the Absolute is covered (*saṃvṛta*) and this everyday experience is set up that these two are not different, they probably made use of such a stimulatingly strange expression. (Compare, however, II, 9 ; 10.)

Since thus all the forms of the phenomenal world are illusion, in the highest sense they cannot come to be. In the highest sense, the real truth can only be expressed by negations.

> "No destruction and again no birth, none bound and again none assiduous in practice, none seeking liberation, none liberated. This highest truth (= *paramārthatā*) is auspiciousness." (II,32 ; 33)

What is called highest truth (*paramārthatā*) or non-duality (*advayatā*) in the second chapter means essentially just the same as the Fourth State taught in the *Māṇḍūkya-Upaniṣad*. But such technical expressions were, needless to say, borrowed from Mahāyāna Buddhism.

Well, how did the phenomenal world's distinct forms come into existence — in opposition to the essence of the highest truth as described? This second chapter teaches that the god (*deva*) *Ātman* by his self-development created the phenomenal world.

"The god *Ātman* by his own power-of-illusion (*māyā*) himself made distinctions of himself. He (*Ātman*) knows all the individual things." (II, 12)

The creative principle is *Ātman*-god or the Lord (*prabhu*)(II.13). Himself non-dual (*advaya*) (II.33), he nonetheless discriminates and creates (*kalpayati*) everything (II, 12 ; 13 ; 14 ; 16 ; 33). (Here the word *kalpayati* possesses both the meaning "thinking-discriminating" and "creating".) So according to the second chapter, *Ātman* is the god that creates the world, and that god's mere thought produces the phenomenal world of distinctions as it is. The origin of the world is the same thing as the thought of the Absolute himself.

As to the course of the production by the thought of the Absolute, a fairly detailed description is given. The apparent world of distinct opposites is considered to arise from the individual soul ("I") as the subject of cognition and action and as the things which are objects over against the subject. Thus they are all caused to exist, just as they appear, as discriminations of the Absolute.

"[The god *Ātman*] first of all discriminates and creates the individual soul, and then discriminates and creates the external and also internal objects." (II,16)

The individual soul has spiritual existence and is subjective, and so is near to the *Ātman*-god, whereas the external objects are rather objective and phenomenal and to be regarded as distanced from *Ātman* itself and far removed from it. Thus it came to be thought that *Ātman* first produced the individual self which is near and then the objective phenomenal things.

These objective things too are divided into "internal things" (*ādhyātmikā bhāvāḥ*) and "external things" (*bāhyā bhāvāḥ*). The process by which these two come to be is set out in detail in this chapter. In the Lord as absolute spirit are two "minds": the inner mind (*antaścitta*) and the outer mind (*bahiścitta*). With the inner mind he creates everything that exists within the mind, namely all ideas; with the outer mind he creates things existing in the outer world in a definite order (II,13). What exists within the mind is the Unmanifest (*avyakta*), and what exists without the mind is the "clear" (*sphuṭa*) (II,15). It is no doubt meant that whereas the former cannot be perceived by another, the latter can be perceived objectively by sense organs. Again, the former is restricted by inner time (*cittakāla*), the latter by discrete time (*dvayakāla*) (II,14). The author of the chapter was probably thinking that time which can be reckoned by spatial quantification is appropriate only to the objective phenomena external to the mind, and that time concerned with the phenomena of consciousness is something different.[2]

Thus there is a difference in nature between the things which exist in the outer world and the ideas which are latent in the mind, but they are the same insofar that they have been created by the "discriminating" of the *Ātman*. The distinction of "inside" and "outside" the mind cannot in the highest sense exist, and it is understood that the distinction of "outer" and "inner" is made with reference merely to our sense organs.

As has been said above, everything comes into being on the basis of the discrimination (thought) of the god *Ātman*. The primal generative power of world creation exists in god himself. This is a power which is miraculous, transcending human conceptual thinking, and so it is referred to by the word *māyā*, which was the word used to express, in ancient times, the miraculous power of god. The power called *māyā* is in god himself, but it obscures god. God also has delusion (*moha*). The thought which god under delusion makes is the manifestation of the world (II,19). This idea would derive directly from the *Śvetāśvatara-Upaniṣad*, but it is here that the *māyā* doctrine clearly comes onto the stage.

God as the cause of the world, who has this nature, is not identical with the absolute principle in the highest sense. The principle of the highest truth is something absolutely negative which does not allow of any positive statement at all. *Ātman* as the cause of the world, on the other hand, namely god, is of himself naturally possessed of delusion, and so has become the cause of world manifestation. God stands as the direct negation of the truth in the highest sense. It is needless to point out how this idea of god conforms to the controller-god (*īśvara*) put forward by Śaṅkara. If we compare it also with the *Māṇḍūkya-Upaniṣad* and the first chapter of the *Kārikās*, the truth in the highest sense and god can probably be taken to correspond to the Third and Fourth States respectively.

When the world comes into existence in this way, how is liberation to be obtained? The author of the chapter borrows some similes from *Vijñānavāda* for his explanation. A man at dusk sees a rope across his path and mistakes it for a snake or a current of water. But once he has ascertained what it really is, that it is a snake, the water or snake disappears as a false discrimination. Similarly a man from ignorance does not know the truth and is deluded, but if he perceives what *Ātman* really is, he destroys ignorance and attains liberation (II,17). However, various questions arise — (1) With this simile, ignorance would reside in the individual. But according to the afore-mentioned doctrine, god too has ignorance. Then is it in the individual or in god, or if it is in both, is it the same ignorance or a different ignorance? (2) Again, when the true form of the rope is known, the snake is annihilated as a false discrimination, but in the world the forms remain as before, and so can it be said they are not destroyed? No replies are given in this second chapter, and it was the concern of the third and fourth chapters, and the later Vedānta, to resolve them.

Notes

1) Cf. *GK*. II,4; 11. "The various notions in the waking state are untrue like those in the dreaming state." *Upadeśasāhasrī*, II,109.

2) Concerning the difference between these two types of time, cf. notes to II, 14 in Part VI, Chapter I, Section II, Sub-Section 2 of this book.

B. The Theory Presented in the Third Chapter of the *Kārikās*

In the third chapter the theories are further advanced. In the first chapter, creation is presented as derived from the essence (*svabhāva*) of the deity, and in the second chapter as arising through the *māyā* of *Ātman* as the deity. But in the third chapter, non-origination, i. e. the denial of creation in the Absolute Truth, is emphasized. It is stated that *Ātman* is not originated nor does it originate anything. In the initial *śloka* of this chapter it is stated:

> "Although [things] are being born on all sides, [in actuality] nothing is originated." (III,2)

It is postulated that all things are non-originated. The final *śloka* concludes:

> "No individual self is born. There is no possibility of its [birth]. This

is the highest truth where nothing is born." (III,48)

Thus the purpose of the entire chapter is to explain the significance of "non-origination." The idea of "non-origination" was discussed in the previous chapter (II,32), but here we have a positive attempt to prove that the individual self and the [phenomenal] world are not created.

Firstly, according to the author of this chapter, the non-birth and non-death of the individual self signifies that "the individual self and the absolute self are not different (*jīvātmanor ananyatva*)" (III,13). He explains this with the simile of space.

Ātman (the absolute self) is compared to space-in-general and the individual self (smaller self) to the space enclosed in a bottle. The space in a bottle is basically not different from space-in-general, but simply because of the restriction of the bottle it exists temporarily in that manner. In the same manner, when the absolute self is restricted by the physical body, etc., what is called the individual self comes into being (III,3). Further, when the bottle is broken, the space within it returns to space-in-general. It is held that in the same manner when the conglomerating factors of the physical body, etc., are destroyed, the individual selves merge into the absolute self (III,4). From this simile we may infer that it was thought that the individual self is in essence identical with the absolute self.

Since the individual self and the absolute self are identical, from the standpoint of Absolute Truth opposition cannot exist among the individual selves. Differences of form, potentiality, names, etc., exist among the individual bottles, but there exist no differences in the spaces enclosed by each. In the same manner, differences exist among the physical bodies, etc., of the individual selves, but there exists no difference in the *Ātman* which is the essence of the individual selves (III,6). Thus, the essence of the individual self is illusion. It is thought that people or the individual selves transmigrate, that they are born, die, arrive, dwell, leave, etc., but these are temporary shapes; in terms of the Absolute Truth there are no changes (III, 9). In terms of the Absolute Truth, the individual self does not transmigrate, it is not soiled by mud. Those who have not realized the true principle think that *Ātman* is soiled with impurities; they are like children who think that space is painted in various colors (III,8).

Against such a view of *Ātman*, however, the following type of criticism can be raised. — If the individual self and the absolute self are the same and thus if the *Ātman* which resides in the bodies of all things is the same, when one individual self is born, dies, and feels pleasure or pain, all the other individual selves should also be born, die, and feel pleasure or pain. Such a situation is impossible; thus the numerous individual selves must be absolutely different. — According to the commentator, this is the criticism of the Sāṃkhya[1] and Yoga schools which hold to the theory of pluralistic selves. In answer to this, the author of this chapter states: "When the space within one bottle is combined with dust or smoke, the space within other bottles is not necessarily also combined with dust or smoke. In the same manner, when one individual self is born, dies, enjoys pleasure, etc., it does not follow that the other individual selves are born, die, enjoy pleasure, etc." (III,5).

Here the *Brahman-Ātman* theory is presented with clear self-awareness. The author, rejecting the views of other sects within the Vedānta school, asserts that just as the space within a bottle is not a "transformation" (*vikāra*) of space-in-general nor a "part" of it, the individual self is not a "transformation" of the highest self nor a "part" of it (III,7). The view that the individual self is a "transformation" (*vikāra*) of the highest self was widely held in early Vedānta philosophy. According to the commentator Śaṅkara, this is to be considered in the sense that a necklace is a transformation of gold[2] or foam and froth are transformations of water.[3] The first chapter of the *Māṇḍūkya-Kārikā* also holds to this view. The view that it is a "part" (*avayava* = *aṃśa*)[4] of the absolute self is presented in the *Brahma-sūtra* (II,3,43). The commentator Śaṅkara notes that this is to be understood in the same manner that a branch is thought to be part of a tree. This simile is used not only by Bhartṛprapañca,[5] but was widely used by the early Vedānta school.[6] Yet, in this third chapter, these views are refuted and it is asserted that the individual self and absolute self are identical. This is a noteworthy turning point in the history of early Vedānta philosophy.

If the individual self and the absolute self are considered to be identical, however, what is the condition which produces mutual opposition among the individual selves? This can be none other than the conglomerates of the physical body and senses. These conglomerates are "created by the *māyā* of

Ātman." In the same manner that physical bodies, etc., appear in dreams, physical bodies, etc., are temporary creations of *māyā* and do not actually exist. It is asserted that although there may exist evaluative differences among the physical bodies of Heaven (the deity), human beings, animals, etc., all physical bodies are illusions (III,10).

In the same manner as the individual selves are created, so too are the various things in the phenomenal world created through the *māyā* of *Ātman*.

As in the second chapter, the third chapter of the *Kārikās* discusses the creation of phenomena through *māyā*.

> "In truth, this non-originated thing is differentiated only through *māyā* [and] never in any other way." (III,19)

> "It is indeed reasonable that the being is born through *māyā*." (III,27)

That is to say, since it originates through *māyā* from the essential *Ātman*, what is created is not real (III,27). The development of the world is no more than a temporary manifestation. Thus the creation of the world is in actuality non-originated. Here we reach a point where what in later periods was called the *māyā* theory or temporary-manifestation theory (*vivartavāda*) is clearly discussed.

This view shows an irreconcilable opposition to the theories of the old *Upaniṣads*[7] and the traditional old Vedānta school,[8] which assert that phenomena are actually created from the non-originated *Ātman*. "[Some] theorists recognize the creation of a non-originated thing" (III,20). In opposition to this, the author of this chapter asserts that for *Ātman* any "transformation" in a real sense is impossible. He has here abandoned the older traditional theories of his school. He repeatedly shows by the following types of arguments that in terms of the Absolute Truth the development of *Ātman* is not possible.

(1) The essence of actuality absolutely cannot be transformed. *Brahman* in essence is non-originated, non-dying. Thus it is impossible that *Brahman* should abandon this essence to become the perishable objects of the phenomenal world (III,20 ; 21).

(2) If, as those who assert the development from *Brahman* state, *Brahman* itself can be transformed, *Brahman* cannot be held to be undying and immovable. If understood thus, *Brahman* loses its significance as the

Absolute (III,22).

(3) Further, if phenomena are created in a real sense, from the essential *Brahman* other essential things are created. Therefore the latter can become the base for the creation of still other things. One thus falls into a reductive argument. According to the *māyā* theory, only *Ātman* is real and the phenomenal world is illusory. In this manner, one does not fall into the error of reduction (III,27).

In order to establish this assertion, the author of this chapter uses many arguments from the Mādhyamaka school.[9] His use of heretical theories in order to refute theories held by other sects within his own school is highly interesting. His use of such theories, however, is only partial and his basic standpoint is the pure temporary-manifestation theory. Here, *Ātman* is taken to be pure existence and this existence is considered to be the base from which the appearances of the phenomenal world are created. This is a highly distinctive philosophical standpoint which is irreconcilably opposed to the views which are developed from the concept of *śūnyatā*. "If *Ātman* is *śūnyatā*, in terms of the Absolute Truth not only is creation impossible but even creation through *māyā* is impossible. A son of a barren woman, so to speak, in actuality or even through *māyā* cannot be born. Only if *Ātman* is existent, creation is through *māyā* possible." (III,28) This is indeed a [basic] criticism against the "non-disputants" (*asadvādin*)[10] of the Nyāya-Vaiśeṣika school.

This view is in complete agreement with the assertions of the Advaita school of later periods. In the second chapter of the *Kārikā*s, the concept of *māyā* appears, but it is still not accompanied by this clear line of thinking. Thus, here in the third chapter the *māyā* theory (or temporary-manifestation theory) is logically completed. In the third chapter, in an attempt to present a scriptural basis for the view that the development of the [phenomenal] world is through *māyā*, many points in the *Upaniṣads* are discussed and many *ślokas* are cited (III,24 ; 25 ; 26).

Since *Ātman* in this manner develops the [phenomenal] world through *māyā*, it is in itself undifferentiatedly equal and is the absolute negative. The indication of "the non-inferior, non-originated absolute principle which attains equality" is the purpose of the third chapter.

> "[The state of union with *Brahman*] is non-originated, without sleep, without dreams, without names, without form ; it always illuminates and is all-knowing. It is not accessible in any way." (III,36)
>
> "[It] is beyond all expression, above all thoughts, very calm, and always brilliant. [It] is the contemplation which is immovable and free from fear." (III,37)

Thus the concept of *Brahman* itself is the same as that in the second chapter.

Together with the theory that *Ātman* creates the temporary manifestation of phenomena through *māyā*, it is also stated that the dualistically opposed phenomenal world arises (*spandate*) through *manas* (cf. III,29 ; 30 ; IV,61 ; 62). That is, just as *manas* produces dualistic phenomena through *māyā* in dreams, in the wakeful state *manas* also produces dualistic phenomena through *māyā*. It is stated that although *manas* from the standpoint of Absolute Truth is non-dualistic (*advaya*), in the period of wakefulness and in dreams it produces dualistic opposition (*dvayābhāsa*).

The problem now moves to the question of the relationship between *manas* and the previously discussed *Ātman*. Here, *manas* is probably the nuclear principle which produces the individual self. Thus it is an actualization of *Māyā*. In general Indian philosophy, *manas* is considered to be the organ which is the "unifying sponsor" of the consciousness and action of the individual self. But here it is not simply an organ ; rather, it is the active principle which resides at the base of the individual self. All objective phenomena are constructed and manifested through *manas* ; they do not actually exist in the form that appears in consciousness. Thus, when one reaches the stage where *manas* is not active, one does not perceive the dualistically opposed world (III,31). The creation of the world through *māyā* (III,10) means, in strict terms, that is "arises" (*spandate*) through the activity of *manas*. When this activity ends, the phenomenal world also disappears.[11)]

In other words, *manas* has *māyā* as the basis of its potentiality and is established by the concealment of *Ātman* itself which is the Absolute Truth. Thus, when we realize the true form of *Ātman*, we must negate *manas*. *Manas* disappears and with this disappears the objective world which it constructs.

> "When [*manas*] does not imagine by dint of the realization of *Ātman*-Truth, [it] goes to the state of non-*manas*, since in the absence of the objects to be perceived it does not perceive." (III,32)

Ātman, as the true principle of reality is undying, but *manas* is to be abandoned.

When *manas* is abandoned, there appears basic, pure reason. "The undifferentiated and non-originated reason" is inseparable from the intuitive (*jñeya*) *Brahman*. That is, the "non-originated and eternal *Brahman*" comes to be realized through the similarly "non-originated reason" (III,33). This may be seen to be the Absolute returning to itself. Thus, there exists no separate area of liberation; liberation is no more than *Ātman* itself returning to itself. It is asserted that, in terms of the Absolute Truth, transmigration and "liberation" do not exist (III,4).

But what do we mean when we say that when *manas* is negated "we are led to a state which is without *manas*"? Does it simply mean that *manas* is not active? Does this not mean that we reach a state which is the same as deep sleep? In answer to such questions it is stated:

> "[The state of *manas*] in deep sleep is different from [it]. It is not like that." (III,34)

Thus, it does not mean that there is no activity or that nothing is perceived, as when one is in deep sleep. The abandoned *manas* is "without differentiation, a *manas* which is suppressed" (III,34). It is released from all restrictions, it is self-existent and indestructible.

> "Although [*manas*] disappears in the state of deep sleep, the suppressed [*manas*] does not disappear." (III,35).

In the state of emancipation it is everywhere in a state of primary liberation. At this point human beings are in complete union with the Absolute.

> "That is indeed fearless *Brahman* who is radiant as knowledge on all sides." (III,35).

In the Vedānta school, this idea of the activity and end of *manas* is a completely distinctive one. Such views do not exist in the old *Upaniṣads*. There, *manas* is considered the product of the development of the highest principle.[12] Śaṅkara also holds similar views. Rather, the above views are held in common with Indian scriptures such as the *Yogavāsiṣṭha*, *Bhāgavata-purāṇa*,[13] etc., and appear in later periods in the new *Upaniṣads*.[14] On the other hand, in the Vijñānavāda philosophy it is held that *manas* is the principle which through the differentiation of the *ālayavijñāna* produces attachment to self and that it should be eliminated through ascetic practices.[15] On this point it has a commonality with the above described concept of *manas*. Thus it should be understood that the ideas in the third chapter of the *Māṇḍūkya-Kārikā* were formed under the influence of the Buddhistic Vijñānavāda theories, and that this was passed on to later works of the Hindu religion.

Notes

1) Cf. *Sāṃkhya-Kārikā*, XVIII.

2) Bhartṛhari used this explanation (cf. Part VII, Chapter IV, Section IV).

3) Bhartṛprapañca and Bhavabhūti used this explanation. Cf. infra.

4) *Ān*. ad *GK*., p.114, *l*. 9. On this point there are some semantic differences with the *Brahma-sūtra*. (Cf. *A History of Early Vedānta Philosophy*, Part One, p.500f.)

5) *Ibid*., p.486f.

6) Śaṅkara cited the following as heretical theories and refuted them (supra): *nanv anekātmakaṃ brahma yathā vṛkṣo 'nekaśākha evam anekaśaktipravṛttiyuktaṃ brahma/ ata ekatvaṃ nānātvaṃ cobhayam api satyam eva/* (ad *BS*. II, 1, 14. vol. I, p.459, *ll*. 13-14). In the sub-commentary *Ratnaprabhā* this is explained as *bhedābhedamata*. In other passages it is stated similarly : *yathānekātmako vṛkṣaḥ śākhā skandho mūlaṃ cety evaṃ nānāraso vicitra ātmety āśaṅkā saṃbhavati tāṃ nivartayituṃ sāvadhāram āha — "tam evaikaṃ jānatha ātmānam" iti/* (*Ś*. ad *BS*. I, 3, 1. vol. I, p.236, *l*. 13ff.). Cf. also *Ś*. ad *Bṛhad*. *Up*. p.293, *l*. 13.

7) *Tait*. *Up*. III, 1, 1 etc.

8) *Brahma-sūtra*, I,1,2.

9) Cf. notes to the above *ślokas* in Part VI, Chapter I, Section II, Sub-Section 3 of this book.

10) *asadvāda* (*Ś*. ad *GK*. p.139, *l*. 2). *asadvādin* (*Ś*. ad *GK*. p.139, *l*. 1). *asadvādibhir asataḥ sajjanmābhyupagamād* ... (*Ān*. ad *GK*., p.139, *l*. 4). These are in opposition to the Sāṃkhya theories (*Ś*. ad *GK*., p.159, *ll*. 16, 17).

11) Such expressions may be seen in the *Yogavāsiṣṭha* : *spandāt sphurati citsargo niḥspandād brahma śāśvatam/— Yogavāsiṣṭha*, NSP. III, 67, 8. (Cf. article by V. Bhattacharyya : *Proc*. *II*. *OC*.)

12) E. g., *Muṇḍaka-Upaniṣad*, II,1,3.

13) Cf. notes to III,29-31 in Part VI, Chapter I, Section II, Sub-Section 3 of this book and also note 11 of this section.

14) *yan manas trijagatsṛṣṭisthitivyasanakarmakṛt/tan mano vilayaṃ yāti tad viṣṇoḥ paramaṃ padam//*— *Maṇḍalabrāhmaṇa-Up*. V. Cf. also *Brahmabindu-Up*. I-VIII; *Nāradabindu-Up*. XLVII. The early forms of these views appear in the *Kāṭhaka-Upaniṣad* VI,10 and the *Maitrī-Upaniṣad* VI,34.

15) Such theories not only appear in general Vijñānavāda literature, but also appear in the *Laṅkāvatāra-sūtra*: *vikalpakasya manovijñānasya vyāvṛttir nirvāṇam ity ucyate/*— *Laṅk*. p.126.

Sub-Section 3. The *Vijñānavāda* Theory as Presented in the Fourth Chapter of the *Māṇḍūkya-Kārikā*

In the fourth chapter of the *Māṇḍūkya-Kārikā* the metaphysical standpoint is further changed from the preceding chapters; there is a shift from the *Māyā* theory to the *Vijñānavāda* theory. The fourth chapter is of course influenced by the second and the third chapters but it is free from the views presented there. Having absorbed Buddhist philosophy, it forms a new metaphysics. It may be said that its nucleus is the *Vijñānavāda* theory. It is asserted that all objective phenomena exist as manifestations of Consciousness (*vijñāna*) and that there is nothing which can exist objectively and independently apart from Consciousness.

In order to clarify this principle of Consciousness-only, it is necessary first to negate the reality of things external. The author of the fourth chapter tries to prove this with various types of arguments. They may generally fall into the following three types:

1. The non-origination of everything is clarified. If everything is non-originated and non-existent in the external world, then it must be considered to be falsely manifested.
2. Things external are experienced in the waking state. It is, however, demonstrated that the experience in the waking state are untrue like those in the dreaming state.
3. Things external do not exist separately from the mind. It is explained that since they are dependent on the mind for their existence they are no more than false manifestations.

Let us examine each of these arguments.

1. Non-origination.

In the fourth chapter the author clearly declares that the theory of non-origination (*ajāti*) is the basis of his thought (IV,4 : 5). Immediately following this declaration, he demonstrates that origination in its true sense is impossible. The arguments of this type can be classified in three kinds :

(1) The negation of origination in general.

(2) The negation of the view that cause and effect are not different.

(3) The negation of the view that cause and effect occur in co-ordinate measure, i.e. the view that effect occurs as a reward to cause.

Among those argument (1), which negates origination in general (IV,6-10), is entirely the same as that in *Māṇḍūkya-Kārikā* III,20-22.(IV,9-10 are merely a supplementary explanation).

Argument (2) (IV,11-13) is a refutation of the view of the *Satkāryavādins* who assert that as far as the evolution of the world is concerned, the cause transforms itself into the effects, being not different from the latter. In terms of schools the Sāṃkhya and those Vedānta scholars who accept the real origination of the world from *Brahman* are here primarily attacked. If we summarize this sharp refutation which is based on the *prasaṅga* method of the Mādhyamika school, it is as follows :

(a) The case in which the cause is non-originated (*aja*).

1. If the effect is a transformation of the cause or if the cause is in itself the effect, there is no difference between cause and effect. Therefore, if the cause is non-originated and eternal, the effect must also be non-originated and eternal. However, this contradicts our actual experience. Since this world is actually being originated and variously differentiated, it cannot be eternal. If we admit our empirical knowledge, everything as the effect is actually being originated and is non-eternal. Therefore, if one holds the theory that cause and effect are not different, then one must also accept that *Brahman* as the cause is actually being orginated and is non-eternal (IV,11 ; 12).

2. There is no example with which to support the argument that something is originated out of the principle which is non-originated.

Therefore, the *Pariṇāmavāda* theory is without proof. (IV,13ab).

(b) The case in which the cause is something originated (*jāta*).

If the cause which has the phenomenal world as its effect is "something originated," then there must exist a more fundamental cause for that cause. Thus, one falls into the error of *regressus ad infinitum* (*anavasthā*,IV,13cd; III,27).

Argument (3) (IV,14ff.) is a refutation of such a generally accepted view of causality that good and bad actions as causes result in obtainment of the physical body, etc, as their effects and further that the physical body, etc. cause good and bad actions; thus one continues to transmigrate endlessly. Therefore, this argument is concerned with the causal relationship among things phenomenal and not with the causal relationship between the universal cause and the phenomenal world as in the previous case.

Firstly, in using the term causality, one must accept the successive occurrence of cause and effect. If cause and effect occur simultaneously, then cause and effect are mutually unrelated like left and right horns. Thus they lose their characteristics as cause and effect (IV,16).

However, even if successive occurrence is accepted, there remain the following difficulties unsolved:

(a) If cause gives rise to effect and further effect gives rise to cause, the successive relationship between cause and effect is not fixed. Then, it must be accepted that a child gives birth to its father (IV,15).[1]

(b) If cause gives rise to effect and further effect gives rise to cause, then both cause and effect are in the relationship of mutual dependence. It is, therefore, difficult to say that the either of them is definitely established. Thus it is also difficult to hold that effects result from causes (IV,17[2]; 18; 21).

(c)[3] If it is held that since there exists the example of seeds producing sprouts and sprouts producing seeds, there is no objection to accepting the mutually dependent relationship between cause and effect, the argument falls into the error of *sādhyasama*, i.e. the error of "taking as the premise that which is to be established" (IV,20).

(d) It may be stated that since the continuous line of cause and effect is without beginning the mutually dependent relationship between the two is possible. But, still, the causal relationship cannot be established. If the effect is without beginning, then it cannot give rise to the cause since the former is something which has not yet been originated. It is also true of the cause (IV,23).[4]

These arguments which negate the causal relationship are in large part taken from the works of the Mādyamika school.[5]

Having thus shown the reason why origination is impossible, all possible cases of origination are negated.

> "Nothing is produced either from itself or from other than itself, nor is anything produced which is existent, non-existent, or both existent and non-existent." (IV,22)
>
> "No non-existent has the non-existent as its cause, nor does any existent have the non-existent as its cause. No existent has the existent as its cause. And how can the non-existent have the existent as its cause?"(IV,40).[6]

Here we find a complete negation of the view of the early Vedānta school that the existent produces the existent and also the view of the false appearance theory of the second and third chapters of the *Māṇḍūkya-Kārikās* according to which the phenomenal world appears falsely from the existent through *Māyā*.[7] The assertion of non-origination which is presented in the earlier portions of these *Kārikās* is here pursued to its very limits.

The theory of non-origination has finally brought about an important change even in the concept of the Absolute. In previous Vedānta philosophy the Absolute was postulated as existent (*sat*) whereas in the fourth chapter the Absolute is said to be not any one of the existent, the non-existent, both existent and non-existent, and neither existent nor non-existent. This ontological view is clearly in complete agreement with that of the Mādhyamika school of Buddhism.[8] The author of the fourth chapter has finally passed beyond the boundaries of the basic doctrines of the Vedānta school.

In this manner, since origination is impossible in any way, the Absolute Truth is non-origination.

> "In truth, everything is non-originated." (IV,57)[9]
>
> "The things which [are thought to be] originated, in truth, are not originated."[10] (IV,58)[11]

Thus the origination and destruction of the various things in the phenomenal world which we experience daily are not actualities. They are similar to origination and destruction of illusion.

> "The origination of these (things) are like illusion, and that illusion does not exist." (IV,58)

In the view of ordinary people things external appear to continuously exist, which is, in actuality, just as an illusory sprout comes forth from an illusory seed and from that sprout comes forth a similarly illusory seed (IV, 59). The painful fact of birth and death of the individual self, in truth, is like the birth and death of the individual self which is seen in dreams, made of illusion. or of supernatural power (IV,68-70).[12] Thus, from the standpoint of the highest truth, it is impossible that the individual self is born or dies (IV, 71). Transmigration is empty (*śūnya*).

In this manner, since the existence of all things is not true, they cannot be said to be eternal. Since the death of anything does not actually occur, annihilation is also impossible. Eternality or annihilation can only be said of actually existent things. Therefore, it must be said that all things are non-eternal and non-annihilated (IV,57[13]; 59[14]; 60).[15]

Here we see the author borrowing the ideal of emptiness (*śūnyatā*) or the middle path free from both the theories of eternality and annihilation, which has been advocated in the Buddhist philosophy from an ancient period. This is probably a direct influence from *Mahāyāna*,[16] especially from the Mādhyamika school.[17]

2. The falsity of experiences in the waking state.[18]

In the fourth chapter, as in the previous chapters, it is asserted that the things experienced in the waking state are false like those experienced in the dreaming state.

> "Like the body (experienced in dream) everything seen by the mind (in the waking state) is unreal (*avastuka*).[19]" (IV.36).

In order to explain this point, the author firstly demonstrates, as in the second chapter, that the things experienced in dream are false (IV,31-36) and then he asserts that the experiences in dream are not based on those in the waking state. The ordinary people think that the experiences in the dreaming state are based on those of the waking state and that although the things experienced in the dreaming state are false, those in the waking state, which are their causes, are real (IV,37). But, this view is in error. As has already been demonstrated, origination in general is impossible and everything is non-originated. Therefore, it is impossible to maintain that things real in the waking state give birth to things unreal in the dreaming state (IV,38). Generally speaking, there is in no way origination of the unreal from the real (IV,40).[20] Thus the author of the fourth chapter thinks that since the relationship between the states of dreaming and waking as conceived by the ordinary people is impossible, the two states which are in such relationship are both false and that the things experienced in both states are also false. He states that the view which holds that various things, whether in the dreaming state or in the waking state are real, is an inverted one (*viparyāsa*, IV,41).

Of course, the things in the waking state definitely have some effect on us and are perceived as such but they are not actually real. They are comparable, for example, to an elephant as a magical illusion[21] which is actually perceived and performs actions but which cannot be said to be real (IV,44). Thus, the author of the fourth chapter indeed admits that there is difference between the two states, dreaming and waking, but holds that "to see the unreal" is common to both states.

These arguments seem to come mainly from the *Vijñānavāda*.

3. The mutually dependent relationship between things external and the mind.

Firstly, the argument which accepts the reality of external objects is presented in the following manner: the perceiving action of the perceiver must have its real object. If there is no object, the perceiving action could not take place because of the absence of the subject and the object. Our psychic affection and perception, dependent on real objects, have them as their causes (IV,24 ; 25).[22] In reply to this the author of the fourth chapter maintains that no object actually exists independently outside the mind (*citta*).

His argument is as follows: when we penetrate into the actuality of the

Absolute Truth, we are able to see that the objects which are taken to be the causes or our psychic affection and perception are not their causes (IV, 25).[23] What we regard as objects (*artha*) are, in truth, "false appearance as objects" (*arthābhāsa*)[24] and "non-existent" (*abhūta*). Thus the mind has no contact with its object which is independent and real nor with its false appearance (IV,26). This is the truth which holds good in the threefold time, past, present, and future. (IV,27).[25]

If that be the case, why is the object nothing but false appearance? Why must its reality be negated? Because everything is dependent on the mind. In other words it is "the object to be seen by the mind" (*cittadṛśya*, IV,77). Therefore, we can argue as follows;

> "These (objects) do not exist apart from the [mind]" (IV,64; 66).[26]
>
> "The false appearance as the objects (*arthābhāsa*) is not different from the mind" (IV,26).

On the contrary, the mind cannot exist independent and separate from the object. Therefore, they are in mutually dependent relationship.

If one annuls this relationship, then it must be said that neither the mind nor its object could exist independently.

> "In truth, both (=the mind and its object) should be seen mutually.[27] How can it be said [with regard to either of them] that "it exists"? Both are devoid of [stable] essence[28] and perceived only as that whic one has been conscious of." (IV,67)

In this manner both the object and the perceiving subject are in a mutual relationship, and thus if the object seen by the mind is empty, then the mind must also be empty.[29]

> "Thus neither the mind nor the object seen by the mind is originated."[30] (IV,28).
>
> "Thus the mind is not originated. And thus the objects are declared to be non-originated." (IV,46).

The author states that those who see the origination of both are like those who see the foot-prints of birds[31] in the sky (IV,28). These views clearly coincide with the true *Vijñānavāda* which negates the reality of both the consciousness and its object.[32] As can also be seen from other points, the author of the fourth chapter here brings in the *Vijñānavāda* views which are based on Maitreya and Asaṅga.

From this fact we can see that the author of the fourth chapter of the *Māṇḍūkya-Kārikā* occupies a unique position in the history of the Vedānta philosophy. Upavarṣa and Śaṅkara assert that, even if we negate all objects, we cannot doubt the existence of the self, as far as we possess self-consciousness and are aware of it.[33] This is the philosophical standpoint of the Vedānta school in general. The author of the fourth chapter, however, completely abandoning such a standpoint, asserts that the subject which is the nucleus of the existence of the individual self is, in truth, empty like the object. Such an assertion is originally made by the Mahāyāna Buddhism and is quite exceptional in the Vedānta school.

The author of the fourth chapter uses the above-discussed argument to demonstrate the substancelessness (*dravyatvābhāva*) of the things external and to lead one to the theory of Consciousness-only by negating the distinction (*nānātva*) of things (IV,91[34] ; 94). But even if one accepts this theory and holds that things external are merely false appearances, the question would remain : How do they appear though they are unreal ? Even if they be false appearances, there must be some principle to explain their occurrence. According to the author of the fourth chapter, all phenomena falsely appear through the movement of *Vijñāna*. "*Vijñāna*" is not necessarily the same as the above-discussed *manas* (mind) in the previous chapters, but rather it may be considered to be the principle which exists as the basis of the mind and its objects. The movement of this *Vijñāna* makes the object (*grāhya*) and the subject (*grāhaka*)[35] falsely appear (IV,47). It is stated that *Vijñāna* "appears to have an origin" (*jātyābhāsa*), "appears to admit movement" (*calābhāsa*) and "appears to be an object" (*vastvābhāsa*)[36] (IV,45).

The author presents an outstanding explanation of the process of false appearance by using the simile of moving the fire-brand (*alāta*).[37] When one places a flame to the end of a torch or piece of wood and moves it in the air, it appears to be straight or crooked and so on (IV,47ff.). The circle of the fire-brand is no more than a false appearance in the form which is perceived but "substancelessness" is recognized in it. A similar explanation is used of the false appearance of the object. Since it is nothing but a false appearance (*ābhāsa*) due to the movement of *Vijñāna*, it is also devoid of substance. It is not based on anything other than *Vijñāna*. Such a false appearance can only be said to be unthinkable (*acintya*).

Hence, the opposition of the subjective "mind" (*citta*) and the objective things (*dharmāḥ*), i. e. the opposition of the subject and the object is due to the movement of *Vijñāna*. Therefore, we cannot regard either of them as a more fundamental principle. It is stated that:

> "The things are not born from the mind (*citta*), nor the mind from the things" (IV,54).

Thus the philosophical tendency to get one from the other is rejected.

Now, when the *Vijñāna* ceases to move, the false appearances of phenomena also completely return to nothingness. This is comparable to the fact that when a fire-brand ceases to move, the various forms which have been falsely appearing also cease to exist. The nature of *Vijñāna* itself is "unborn, immovable, non-material, quiescent and non-dual" (IV,45). Hence it is thought that for *Vijñāna* itself there exists the state of movement and the state of rest (IV,48). And the main objective of the fourth chapter is to teach that the calm state of final release results from the cessation of the movement of *Vijñāna*. This is the reason why this chapter is entitled "the cessation of the fire-brand (*alāta-śānti*).

It is a unique fact in the history of the Vedānta philosophy that the author regarded such *Vijñāna* as the Absolute. In the Vedānta school in general *Brahman* or *Ātman* is looked upon as the ultimate principle; yet these are not discussed at all in the fourth chapter. On the point that it regards *Vijñāna* as the ultimate principle, it is rather closer to the theory of *Aupaniṣads*[38] referred to in Śāntarakṣita's *Tattvasaṃgraha* or in some of the *Purāṇas*.[39] It is needless to say that such a theory came into existence under the influence of the *Vijñānavāda*. Yet, the point that the movement (spand) of *Vijñāna* is stressed reminds us of the cosmological theory of the Śaiva sect of Kashmir (the *Pratyabhijñā* theory).

Immediately after the discussion of false appearance due to the movement of *Vijñāna*, we find the theory that things experienced in the waking state and those experienced in the dreaming state are both false appearances of the Mind (*Citta*) through *Māyā* (IV,61-66). This argument is entirely the same as that in the third chapter, which states that all phenomena are false appearances of the *Manas* through *Māyā*. Here, however, *Manas* is replaced by *Citta*. (The replacement of *Manas* with *citta* probably occurred through the infuence of the mind-only theory of the Mahāyāna Buddhism. In India it is generally accepted that the placement of *citta* as the ultimate principle is a uniquely Buddhistic theory).[40] This argument at first glance appears to contradict the above-presented theory which sees *citta* and things as equal (IV,54). But here the argument borrowed from the third chapter is probably used to impress upon the reader the fact that all phenomena arise through *citta*. Therefore, the *citta* discussed here has approximately the same meaning as the above-cited *Vijñāna*. In other places *citta* is held to be the ultimate principle.

> "The duality which consists of the subject and the object is nothing but the vibration of the *Citta*. *Citta* has no object. It is, therefore, said that [*Citta*] is eternal and free from attachment" (IV,72).

Thus *Citta*, which is the substratum of the subject and the object, cannot be merely the subject of cognition. In the *Vijñānavāda* philosophy, also, *Citta* is occasionally used as a synonym of *Vijñāna* and a *sūtra* passage which states that "the three-fold world is nothing but the Mind"[41] is sometimes considered to be a scriptural testimony of the *Vijñānavāda*. It is, therefore, not at all strange that the two terms are thought to be synonymous in the fourth chapter, which has the *Vijñānāvāda* doctrine as its nucleus.

What then is the principle which causes movement in *Vijñāna* or *Citta*? It is called *Māyā*,(IV,61), false attachment (*abhūtābhiniveśa*, IV,79), or covering (*saṃvṛti*, IV,57). In the orthodox Brahmanical tradition "*Māyā*" has been considered to be the mystical power of the god from an ancient time. In the second and third chapters of these *Kārikās* it is held to be the efficient cause of the evolution of the world. The concepts of "false attachment" and "covering" (practical truth) are taken from Buddhism. These correspond to the idea of "nescience" (*avidyā*) in Śaṅkara's philosophy. "Covering" is an idea which stands in opposition to that of the "absolute truth" (*sadbhāva*). The birth, death and change in the phenomenal world which falsely appear through the covering of truth must be negated from the stand point of the absolute truth (IV,57). We clearly see here that in particular the Buddhist idea of the twofold truth as found in the Mahāyana Buddhism is absorbed in the Advaita philosophy or the fourth chapter of these *Kārikās*.

It is said that there is the twofold covering: "covering due to false construction" (*kalpitasaṃvṛti*) and "covering dependent upon another" (*paratantrābhisaṃvṛti*) (IV,73). It is not clear how the former differs from the latter. However, *Kārikā* IV,74 indicates that the former is the principle which causes knowledge different from the truth whereas the latter is the principle which establishes the things in the phenomenal world, making possible the daily lives of human beings. Both of them stand in opposition to the highest truth (*paramārtha*). Therefore, the things which exist through either of the two kinds of coverings are unreal from the standpoint of the highest truth. It is needless to say that this view is influenced by the *Vijñānavāda* theory of three fold nature (*trisvabhāva*).

Roughly speaking, we may show it as follows:

Covering due to false construction -- False construction } Practical
Covering dependent upon another -- Dependent origination } truth

Absolute truth ——————— -The highest truth—— Highest truth

It may be considered that these three correspond to the three truths (*satya*) or three kinds of existences (*sattva*) recognized by the later Advaita school.[42] The three are shown as follows:

[I] The truth as false appearance (*prātibhāsika-satya*)

The existence which has *avidyā* as its limiting adjunct (*avidyopādhikasattva*).

For example, the idea derived from mistaking mother of pearl for silver. Since it contradicts the valid knowledge, it must be denied even in the sphere of daily life.

[II] Practical truth (*vyāvahārika-satya*)

The existence which has *māyā* as its limiting adjunct (*māyopādhikasattva*).

For example, the things in the natural world such as space. They have practical efficiency (*arthakriyā*) and it is accepted that they are true in daily life. However, from the standpoint of the highest truth, they are false and must be negated.

[III] The hightest truth (*pāramārthika-satya*)

The existence in the highest truth (*paramārthasattva*).

Only Brahman can be called thus.

[A] Seen from the viewpoint of time, truth [I] is momentary truth. [II] exists as long as there exists the perceiving subject, and truth [III] is eternal. [B] If we see truth [I] from the standpoint of truth [II] the object is false whereas the subject is true, and if we see truth [II] from the standpoint of [III] both the subject and the object in truth [II] are false. [C] Truth [III] does not have any limiting adjunct but truths [I] and [II] do. The later Advaita Vedānta School generally holds this view.

The above-mentioned threefold truth corresponds the above threefold standpoint found in the fourth chapter of the *Māṇḍūkya-Kārikā*. ("*Saṃvṛti*" may be considered to be equivalent to the "*upādhi*".) Therefore, it is likely that the theory of threefold nature in the *Vijñānavāda* philosophy was thus adopted by the *Māṇḍūkya-Kārikā* and later the same idea was expressed in different technical terms, giving rise to the above-mentioned theory of threefold truth with some alterations in the Adyaita Vedānta school of later period.

Now, our transmigratory existence is due to this covering. Since we are attached to the differentiated appearances of the phenomenal world without knowing the truth, we cannot obtain "peace of mind" (*vaiśāradya*, IV,94). Hence, in order to achieve final release, the covering must be eliminated. It is said that if we once realize the truth, transmigration also ceases to exist since the covering is ignorance of the truth.

> "As long as there is a strong attachment to cause and effect, transmigration persists. But when that strong attachment to cause and effect is destroyed, transmigration is no longer possible" (IV,56. Cf.IV,55).

In other words, by realizing non-origination, one "does not fall into an inverted view" (IV,46) and "enters into the non-origination of cause and effect" (IV,54). To realize non-origination is to become non-originated. One who realizes non-origination is no longer born (*na jāyate* ; IV,75 ; 76). And the state of final release achieved in this manner is in direct opposition to the differentiated appearances of the phenomenal world. It is non-originated, equal, non-dual, non-separated, quiescent, pure and un-injured

(IV,77 ; 93 ; 98). It can be expressed only negatively or statically.

According to the author of the fourth chapter, the differentiated appearances of birth and death in the phenomenal world are all false and untrue but they play their own roles as the true in this world, for human beings mistakenly regard them as true. It is, however, known to one who has realized the theories of non-origination and Consciousness-only that all differences and origination are false. Therefore, even if they occur to him in the same manner as to the ordinary people, they do not have any raison d'être, that is, they have perished. In other words, it is considered that the awakened one is in the state of non-origination.

Therefore, final release and transmigration falsely appear owing to the difference between knowledge and ignorance of the truth. The ordinary people and the scholars think that, though transmigration is beginningless, final release from it can be obtained through religious practices and that the highest pleasure of final release continues eternally. However, these two states are not independent (IV,30). Transmigration is ultimately empty from the standpoint of the highest truth and not different from final release.[43] There is no inverted view from the standpoint of the highest truth (IV,27). For this reason transmigration can be transformed into final release. In the fourth chapter the possibility of final release is grounded on the theory of undifferentiated Consciousness-only.

It is particularly noteworthy that the author of the fourth chapter quotes many passages from the Mahāyāna Buddhist scripture and that he lays stress on the point that all things (*sarve dharmāḥ*) are by nature enlightened, released, and quiescent (IV,92 ; 93 ; 94 ; 98).[44] According to the Buddhist philosophy, that which the ordinary people and philosophers regard as *ātman* is in actuality merely a composite of many elements of existence (*dharma*). Mahāyāna Buddhism emphasizes in particular that because these elements of existence are by nature pure, final release is possible. In the fourth chapter, these ideas are directly adopted. Therefore, the fourth chapter accepts the non-self theory and abandons the traditional *ātman* theory of the orthodox Vedānta school.[45] The fourth chapter does not refer to *Brahman* or *Ātman* at all. Here, non-self, emptiness and the non-differentiated Consciousness-only constitute the basic doctrines.

Notes

1) The *argumentum ad absurdum* : "a child would give birth to its father" (*GK*.IV,15) was originally set forth by the Mādhyamikas; *Vigrahavyāvartanī* V,50; its Chinese version, V,28: *Taisho Tripiṭaka*, Vol. XXXII,p.20 bc. Cf. *Vigrahavyāvartanī* V,51; *Bodhicaryāvatāra*, IX,114. Refutation against it is forth in *Nyāya-sūtra*, II,1,41. (Cf.ibid.IV,1,39).

2) The argument in the *Māṇḍūkya-Kārikā* IV,17 should be compared to that in the *Mādhyamika-Kārikā* X,10 and 11, also *Prasannapadā* on them. The argument in the *Māṇḍūkya-Kārikā* IV,18 should be compared to the *Mādhyamika-Kārikā* X,8 which runs as follows: *yadīndhanam apekṣyāgnir apekṣyāgnim yadīndhanam/katarat pūrvaniṣpannam yadapekṣyāgnir indhanam//*"The absolute ignorance of cause and effect" (*pūrvāparāparijñāna*)(*Māṇḍūkya-Kārikā* IV,21) is also discussed in *Nyaya-sūtra* II,18,11, *Mādhyamika-Kārikā* XI,2-6.

3) *bījāṅkurākhyo dṛṣṭāntaḥ sadā sādhyasamohi naḥ/na ca sādhyasamohetuḥ siddhau sādhyasya yujyate//*(*Māṇḍūkya-Kārikā* IV,20) Those who criticized the theory based upon the simile of *bījāṅkura* are referred to in Bhāskara (ad *Brahma-sūtra* II,1,36). The explanation resorting to this simile, which was originally set forth by some Buddhists, was refuted by the Mādhyamikas (*Mādhyamika-Kārikā* XVII,7-10; *Catuḥśataka* X,24, rendered version; *Lalitavistara* p.210, *ll*.4-5, cited in *Prasannapadā* ad II,25; XXI,21). This simile is often mentioned by the Mādhyamikas. *aṅkuro jāyate bījād bījaṃ tenaiva sūcyate* (*Bodhicaryāvatāra*, IX,115). *bījāṅkuravat* (*Mādhyamika-vṛtti*, 458, 1.13; p.252,*l*.11. Cf. ibid., p.423, *l*.10; *aṅkurādisantāna* (ibid. p.313, *l*.3); *Śālistamba-sūtra*; *Bodhicaryāvatāra*, pp.575f.) It was adopted by the Vedāntins also. Cf. G. Jacob: *Laukikanyāyāñjali* vol.I, s.v. *bījāṅkura-nyāya*.

4) *hetur na jāyate 'nādeḥ phalaṃ vāpi svabhāvataḥ/ādir na vidyate yasya tasya hy ādir na vidyate//*(IV,23). Cf. *hetor ādir na ced asti phalasyādiḥ kuto bhavet/*(*Bodhicaryāvatāra*, IX,123); *svato vā parato vāpi na kiñcid vastu jayate/sad asat sadasad vāpi na kiñcid vastu jāyate//*(*Māṇḍūkya-Kārikā*, IV,22). This argumentation must have been adopted from the Mādhyamika school. Concerning the first half of the stanza, Cf. *na svato nāpi parato na dvābhyāṃ nāpy ahetutaḥ/utpannā jātu vidyante bhāvāḥ kvacana kecana//* (*MadhyaK*. I,1); *na svato jāyate bhāvaḥ parato naiva jāyate/na svataḥ parataś caiva jāyate kutaḥ//*(ibid. XXI,13); *na svato jāyate bhāvaḥ parato naiva jāyate/na svataḥ parataś ceti viparyayagataḥ kutaḥ//*(ibid. XXIII,20). Concerning the latter half of the stanza, Cf. *sataś ca tāvad utpattir asataś ca na yujyate/na sataś cāsataś ceti pūrvam evopapāditam//*(ibid. VII, 20); *na san nāsan na sadasan dharmo nirvartate/*(ibid. I,7). The same argumentation is mentioned in the *Dvādaśamukha-śāstra*[*Taisho Tripiṭaka*, vol.XXX, p.160b]; the *Śata-śāstra*[ibid. vol.XXX, p.178a-c]. *asan na jāyate loke na san na sadasan kvacit/* (*Laṅk*. III,21).

5) See my former notes.

6) *nāsty asaddhetukam asat sad asaddhetukaṃ tathā / sac ca saddhetukaṃ nāsti saddhetukam asat kutaḥ* // (*Māṇḍūkya-Kārikā*. IV,40). Cf. *na bhāvāj jāyate bhāvo, 'bhavo bhāvān na jāyate / nābhāvāj jāyate 'bhāvo bhāvān na jāyate* // (*MadhyaK*. XXI,12). Moreover, ibid. I,1 ; 6 ; 7 ; VIII,1 ; 8 ; 10.

7) Cf. *Kārikā*, IV,3 ; 4.

8) See Notes 1-6.

9) *sadbhāvena* [or *svabhāvena*] *hy ajaṃ sarvam* / (*Māṇḍūkya-Kārikā*, IV,57) *aja* or *anutpatti* of all things is emphasized throughout all *Mahāyāna* literature.

10) *dharmā ya iti jāyante jāyante te na tattvataḥ / janma mayopamaṃ teṣāṃ sā ca māyā na vidyate* // (*Māṇḍūkya-Kārikā*, IV,58). Cf. *māyādayaḥ svabhāvenānutpannā avidyamānāḥ* / (*Mādhyamaka-vṛtti*, p.177,*l*.6).

11) Cf. *Kārikā*, IV,60.

12) *yathā māyāmayo jīvo jāyate mriyate ca / tathā jīvā amī sarve bhavanti na bhavanti ca* // (*Māṇḍūkya-Kārikā*, IV,69). Cf. *sudurbodhāsi māyaiva dṛśyate na ca dṛśyate* / (Rāhulabhadra's *Prajñāpāramitā-stava*, v.16.H.Ui : *Indo Tetsugaku Kenkyu*, vol.1, p.347) ; *na niruddhā na cotpannā yathā māyāmayāḥ kvacit / na niruddhā na cotpannā sarvasattvās tathā tvayi* // (Rāhulabhadra's *Saddharmapuṇḍarīka-stava*, in the *Saddharmapuṇḍarīka-sūtra* ed. by Wogihara, preface, p.39) ; *yathā nirmitako jīvo jāyate mriyate 'pi ca / tathā jīvā amī sarve bhavanti na bhavanti ca* // (*Māṇḍūkya-Kārikā*, IV,70). Cf. *yathā nirmitakaṃ śāstā nirmimitardhisampadā / nirmito nirmimītānyaṃ sa ca nirmitakaḥ* // *tathā nirmitākāraḥ kartā yat karma tat kṛtam / tad yathā nirmitanānyo nirmitas tathā* // (*MadhyK*. XVII,31 ; 32). The term *nirmitaka* is a term peculiar to Buddhism. Cf. s.v. *nirmitaka* in O. Böhtlingk and R.Roth's *Sanskrit-Wörterbuch nebstallen Nachtraegen* (St.Petersburg, 1855-75. and O.Böhtlingk's *Sanskrit-Wörterbuch* in Kurzerer Fassung, (St.Petersburg, 1879-89).

13) *saṃvṛtyā jāyate sarvaṃ śāśvataṃ tena nāsti vai / sadbhāvena hy ajaṃ sarvaṃ ucchedas tena nāsti vai* // (*Māṇḍūkya-Kārikā*, IV,57) ; *saṃvṛti* = *saṃvaraṇa*, *avidyāviṣayo laukiko vyavahāraḥ* (Ś. ad *l.c.*). In Buddhist literature it is a term contrary to *tattva* (Cf. *Mādhyamaka-vṛtti* 54,1,10). *Saṃvṛtisatya* is a concept contrary to *Paramārthasatya*. *saṃvṛti* etymologically derived from the meaning : "to cover (truth)". It is supposed that the term *sadbhāva* does not necessarily mean "existence" or "the existent", but synonymous with *bhūta* (*Māṇḍūkya-Kārikā* IV,25). Cf. *sadbhūta*, Vyāsa ad *Yoga-sūtra* I, 35. *Sadbhāvena* is likely to be synonymous with *tattvataḥ* (IV,58) in contrast to *saṃvṛtyā*. Here we can locate an influence of the Buddhist concept of *satya-dvaya*. The teaching that all things are non-eternal and non-annihilated is peculiar to Buddhism. It is found throughout all *Mahāyāna* literature. e. g. *MadhyK*. Salutation stanza ; XIV,1 ; 3 ; XV,10 ; 11 ; XVII,7 ; 8 ; 10 ; 20 ; 22 ; XVIII,10 ; 11 ; XXI,14 ; 15 ; 16 ; 17 ; XXII,12 ; XXV, 3 ; 21 ; 23 ; XXVII,1 ; 12 ; 16 ; 17 ; 18 ; 20 ; 29. *Laṅk*. V,1, p.219 ; X,2). However, here in this verse (IV,

57) of the *Māṇḍūkya-Kārikā* it is taught that in the practical truth there is nothing eternal ; on the other hand there is no annihilation in the ultimate truth. Therefore the Buddhist theory of *satya-dvaya* has been adopted in a highly twisted form. (However, the theory in IV,59 is different from this.)

14) IV,59 was discussed in the above.

15) *nājeṣu sarvadharmeṣu śāśvatāśāsvatābhidhā/yatra varṇā na vartante vivekas tatra nocyate//*(*Māṇḍūkya-Kārikā*, IV,60). *varṇa* means *śabda* (Śaṅkara). *viveka* is explained by Śaṅkara as: *idam evam iti viveko viviktatā.* Throughout Indian philosophy in general *viveka* means the knowledge which leads us to salvation, as is explained here by Śaṅkara. This meaning has been preserved till later days (e.g. *Vedāntasāra* XV). However, in this stanza *viveka* is rejected, which must be a Buddhist influence. Cf. *nivṛttam abhidhātavyaṃ nivṛtte citta-gocare/*(*MadhyK*. XVIII,7) ; *tattvaṃ hy akṣaravarjitam/*(*Laṅk*. p.48, v.119) ; *avāca anakṣarāḥ sarve śūnyāḥ śāntādinirmalāḥ/*(*Mādhyamaka-vṛtti*, p.539. cf.p.493). Concerning *śāśvata* and *aśāśvata*, Cf. *yasmāt pravartate bhāvas tenocchedo na jāyate/yasmān nivartate bhāvas tena nityo na jāyate//*(*Catuḥśataka* = *Mādhyamaka-vṛtti*, p.376. Cf. *MadhyK*. XV,10 ; 11). Although Śaṅkara cites *Tait.Up*.II, 4.1 and II,9,1 to explain this verse, it is quite clear that this verse is influenced by Buddhist expressions and ideas.

16) Non-birth (*ajāti*) was emphasized in Mahāyāna scriptures. (J.Takasaki : *The Ratnagotravibhāga*, p.167.)

17) See my notes to these *ślokas* in the above.

18) The assertion that the experiences in the waking state and those in the dreaming state are not different is seemingly expressed in *Bṛhad.Up*.IV,3,14 in its incipient state, but it was especially set forth by the *Vijñānavādins*. e.g. *na hy atītānāgatāvartamānānubhave suptasya jāgrataś ca kaścid viśeṣo 'sti/*(*MAVT*. p.26,*l*.14). Later such opinion was expressed by Advaitins and Grammarians who were placed under such an influence (Cf. *Sarvadarśanasaṃgraha*, ed. Abhyankar, XIII, *ll*.269-270). The *Nyāya-sūtras* IV,2,31f. refutes such an opinion.

19) *avastuka* is a peculiarly Buddhist term. e. g. *avastukāḥ sarvadharmāḥ* (*Mahāvyutpatti*, X,10). *avastuka eva bālānāṃ prapañcaḥ* (*Mādhyamaka-vṛtti*, p.224,*l*.11). *grāhyaṃ grāho grahītā ca nāsti, nāma hy avastukam* (*Laṅk*. p.299,*l*.12). *avastukaṃ cittam*. (ibid. p.335,*l*. 6). *avastukatā* (*Abhisamayālaṅkārāloka*, p.925,*l*.18) ; *avastukatva* (*Bodhicaryāvatāra*, ed. by Poussin, p.333,*l*.22) ; *avastu* (*Māṇḍūkya-Kārikā*, IV,87 ; 88) ; *avastukatva* (ibid.IV,45).

20) *nāsty asaddhetukam asat sad asaddhetukaṃ tathā/sac ca saddhetukaṃ nāsti saddhetukam asat kutaḥ//*(*Māṇḍūkya-Kārikā*, IV,40). The purport of this verse is the same as the following : *na bhāvāj jāyate bhāvo, bhāvo 'bhāvān na jāyate/nābhāvāj jāyate 'bhāvo bhāvān na jāyate//*(*MadhyK*. XXI,12). Cf. *MadhyK*. I,1 ; 6 ; 7 ; VIII,1 ; 8 ; 10.

21) The simile of *māyā* is already mentioned in scriptures of early Buddhism

(*Therīghāthā* 394 ; the Chinese version of the *Saṃyuktāgama-sūtra*, vol.X, *Taisho Tripiṭaka*, vol.II, p.69a ; No.265). In *Wisdom Sūtras* it often mentioned, e.g. *sarvadharmā api*........... *māyopamāḥ svapnopamāḥ* (*Aṣṭasāhasrikā*, ed. by Wogihara : p.159). In some *Mahāyāna Sūtras* it is said that *māyā* is the essence of all things (*māyālakṣaṇa-svabhāva*, *Śālistambha-sūtra*, cited in *Mādhyamaka-vṛtti*, p.567,*l*.6 ; p.568,*l*.15). *yat tu dṛṣṭipatha-prāptaṃ tan māyaiva sutucchakam*/(Poussin *JRAS*. 1908, p.889.) ; *yaś ca dharmān vijānāti māyā-svapna-svabhāvakān/ kadalīskandhaniḥsārān pratiśrutkā-samānakān//* (*Saddharmapuṇḍarīka*, ed. by Wogihara and Tsuchida : p.130,*ll*.15-16). It is said that the simile of *māyā* is adopted to make clear the theory of "neither existence, nor non-existence" of all thing (*Bodhisattvabhūmi*, p.266,*l*.17ff.). Those things which were created by *māyā* do not exist, but can be perceived (*na saṃvidyata upalabhyate ca*, *Madhyāntavibhāgaṭīkā*, ed. by Yamaguchi, p.230,*ll*.11-13). The *Māṇḍūkya-Kārikās* adopted such ideas. The simile or *māyāhastin* is often mentioned in Mahāyāna scriptures (*Laṅk*. X,v.126 ; *Trisvabhāva-nirdeśa* 27). Moreover, *māyāpuruṣa* (*Aṣṭasāhasrikā*, p.63 ; *MadhyK*. XXIII,9 ; *Madhyāntavibhāgaṭīkā*, p.113,*l*.4), *māyāturaga* (*Mādhyamaka-vṛtti*, p. 237,*l*.6), *māyārājā* (*Mahāyāna-sūtrālaṅkāra*, XI,29). All actions of man can be compared to those of a man created by a magician (*māyākāra*), being attached to a woman who was also created by the magician (*Mādhyamaka-vṛtti*, p.46,*l*.2 ; p.463,*l*.10 ; *Bodhicaryāvatāra*, IX,31 ; Cf. *māyāyuvati*, *Mādhyamaka-vṛtti*, p.45,*l*.9 ; *māyākāranirmitā strī*, ibid. p.463,*l*.11). The simile of dreams and *māyā* is refuted in the first chapter (I,7) of the *Māṇḍūkya-Kārikās*, whereas it is adopted in the second and sequent chapters or this work. In this respect we can find the difference of the philosophical standpoints of both sections of this work. Śaṅkara ascribes this simile to the *Vijñānavādins* of Buddhism in his (*Brahma-sūtra-bhāṣya*, II,2,28. ĀnSS. vol.I, p.580,*ll*.8-12). Or it is said that this simile is held by the *pracchanna-Bauddhas*, *māyins* (*Śrinivāsīya*, p.12 ; mentioned in T. M.P.Mahadevan's *Gauḍapāda*, p.41,n.) Such a theory is obviously refuted by Śaṅkara (ad *Brahma-sūtra* II,2.29) and by Bhartṛhari (*Vākyapadīya*, II,297). Such a refutation is introduced into works of Buddhist *Vijñānavādins* as was set forth by opponents (e. g. *Viṃśatika*, p.1,*l*.17-p.2,*l*.6). Although the simile of *māyā* and *māyin* is mentioned in the *Śvetāśvatara-Upaniṣad* IV,9-10, it was generally regarded by Indian intellectuals as was advocated by Buddhists, especially *Vijñānavādins*. Therefore we have to conclude that the simile of dreams of *māyā* in the second and fourth chapters must have been introduced from Buddhism, especially the *Vijñānavāda*.

22) Opponents to the Mādhyamikas set forth arguments to the same effect—*atrāha vidyanta eva skandhyatanadhātavaḥ/ kutaḥ/ tad āśrayasaṃkleśopalabdheḥ// iha yan nāsti na tadāśrayasaṃkleśopalabdhir asti vandhyāduhitur iva vandhyāsūnoḥ/ santi ca rāgādayaḥ kleśāḥ saṃkleśanibandhanam*/(*Mādhyamaka-vṛtti*, p.137).

23) *nimittasyānimittatvam iṣyate bhūtadaśanāt*//(*Māṇḍūkya-Kārikā* IV,25cd). In this sen-

tence *Vijñānavāda* is clearly set forth as is explained by Ānandajñāna. *bhūtadarśana*, which means *paramārthadarśana* according to Śaṅkara, is a peculiarly Buddhist term. It means "to see reality"'. It is the same as *lokottaraprajña* (*Madhyāntavibhāgaṭīkā*, p.29, *l*.8). "*bhūtadarśin*" is explained as "one who sees reality"'("Buddha-nature Treatise"; *MAVT*. p.29,*l*.8). *draṣṭavyaṃ bhūtato bhūtaṃ bhūtadarśī vimucyate*/*Abhisamayālaṅkāra*, V,21. p.885; *draṣṭavyaṃ bhūtato bhūtam*/(*Saundarānanda*, XIII,51, p.94). *bhūta* does not mean "existence", but "reality", "truth". Cf. *bhūtanaya yathābhūta*, *bhūtakoṭi*.

24) *arthābhāsa* is a technical term of *Vijñānavādins*. *vāsanair luḍitaṃ cittam arthābhāsaṃ pravartate* (*Laṅk*. p.285,*l*.5). Cf. ibid. p.283,*l*.16; p.284,*l*.4; 336). *svabījaparipākād arthābhāsaṃ vijñānam utpadyate* (*MAVT*. p.11,*l*.22. Cf. ibid. p.26,*l*.17). Śaṅkara comments—*cittam eva hi ghaṭādyarthavad avabhāsate yathā svapne*. It is quite clear that the thought of Buddhist Idealism is expressed here in this stanza.

25) It is likely that in verse IV,27 a certain kind of realism, such as that of the *Sarvāstivādins*, is criticized. The argumentation to the same effect is set forth in *MadhyK*. XXIII,8; 9; *Laṅk*. X,123. The use of the term *adhvan* in this sense peculiarly Buddhist. Cf. Böhtlingk's and Roth's *Wörterbuch*, and Schmidt's s.v. *adhvan* in Nachtrage. The term *adhvan* in *Yogasūtra* IV,12 seem to be a borrowing from Buddhism.

26) The same argumentation as in vv.IV,63-66 is set forth by Śaṅkara as the theory of *Vijñānavādins*. (ad *Bṛhad. Up*. p.571,*ll*.6-9). In the *Mahāyānaśraddhotpādaśāstra* a similar notion is expressed. Such terms as *citta-dṛśya*, *cittamātra* are used often in *Mahāyāna* literature (Cf. Index to *Laṅkāvatāra*).

27) *anyonyadṛśya* = *parasparāpekṣasiddhika* = *anyonyāśraya* = *itaretaragrāhya* (Ānandajñāna). Śaṅkara also explains it in a similar way. Such a thought is expressed in *Mahāyāna* literature, *atha yad evālambanaṃ tad eva cittam*/*yadi tāvad anyad ālambanam anyac cittaṃ tad dvicittatā bhaviṣyati*/(*Āryaratnacūḍaparipṛcchā*, cited in *Mādhyamaka-vṛtti*, p.62).

28) *lakṣaṇaśūnya*. Cf. *alakṣaṇa*, *Māṇḍ.Up*.7; *lakṣyalakṣaṇavarjitam*, *Laṅk*. p.190, III,v.79; p.294, X,224. Cf. ibid. X,21; *MadhyK*. V,5.

29) This represents the ultimate standpoint of the perfect *Vijñānavāda*, as is represented in the *Mahāyāna-saṃparigraha* etc. *tac cārthābhāvajñānaṃ tad eva vijñaptimātrajñānaṃ nivartayati, arthābhāve vijñapty-asaṃbhavād*/(*MAVT*. p.247,*ll*.18-20). "Apart from *vijñāna*, there is no *traidhātuka*. Apart from *traidhātuka*, there is no *vijñāna*. "*Hsien-shih-lun*,. H.Ui: *Indo Tetsugaku Kenkyu*, vol.VI, p,369).

30) Non-origination of Mind is set forth in *Mahāyāna* literature. e.g. *cittaṃ hi Kāśyapa pari-gaveṣyamānaṃ na labhyate. yan na labhyate tan nopalabhyate tan nātītam, nānāgatam, na pratyutpannam. yan nātītaṃ nānāgataṃ na pratyutpannaṃ tat tryadhvasamatikrāntam. yat tryadhvasamatikrāntaṃ tan naivāsti naiva nāsti svabhāvaḥ. yasya nāsti svabhāvaḥ tasya nāsti utpādaḥ yasya nāsty utpādaḥ tasya nāsti nirodhaḥ*/(*Kāśyapa-*

parivarta, 102. *Mādhyamaka-vṛtti*, p.45. Cf. ibid. p.62,*l*.4f.).

31) The simile of the footprints of birds is often mentioned in Buddhist literature. *Dhammapada* 93; *Therag*. 92; *Āryaratnākara-sūtra* in *Mādhyamaka-vṛtti*, p.90; *Vimalakīrtinirdeśa, sattvaparīkṣā* etc.

32) See my notes to these *ślokas* in the previous chapter, Prof. H.Ui pointed out that the views of the *Kārikā* agree in certain aspects with the theories in Asaṅga's *Mahāyānasaṃparigrahaśāstra* (H.Ui: *Yuishin-no-Jissen*. pp.146-153).

33) supra.

34) *vidyate na hi nānātvaṃ teṣāṃ kecana*/(*Māṇḍūkya-Kārikā*, IV,91). There is a parallel passage: — *notpannā jātu vidyante bhāvāḥ kvacana kecana*/(*MadhyK*. I,1).

35) *grāhya* and *grāhaka* are the terms which are used often in the literature of *Vijñānavāda*.

36) *ābhāsa* in the meaning of "appearance" or "manifestation" is a technical term of *Vijñānavāda* (Cf. Index to *Laṅk*.; Index to *MAVT*.; Śaṅkara as *BS*.II.2,28).

37) The simile of the fire-brand (*alātā*)-*cakra* is resorted to in *Mahāyāna* literature to teach the theory of *niḥsvabhāvatā* and *śūnyatā* of all things. *Catuḥśatikā*, XIII,800. p.503. *Mādhyamaka-vṛtti*, p.173,*l*.2; p.219,*ll*.7-8; *Laṅk*. p.92,*l*.9; *Satyasiddhi*, vol.X, (*Taisho Tripiṭaka*, vol.XXXII, p.316b). *Mahāvyutpatti*, 139,21.

38) Cf. *Tattvasaṃgraha, Aupaniṣadātmaparīkṣā*.

39) See, for example, *Viṣṇupurāṇa* II,12,42 (Wilson, *Collected Works*, Vol.VII,310).

40) *duḥkhasvābhāvikatvavādibhir bauddhaiś cittasyaivātmatābhyupagamāc ca* (*Sāṃkhya-pravacanabhāṣya*, p.10, *l*.12). Buddhist scholars of later period admit that the nature of this *Citta* can be nothinig but what is called *Brahman* in the orthodox Brahmanical tradition (*ekaikasya cittasya brahmatādikaṃ*. *Bodhicaryāvatāra*, V,15).

41) *cittamātram idaṃ yad idaṃ traidhātukam* (*Daśabhūmika-sūtra*. ed. by Kondo, p.98); *cittamātraṃ bho jinaputra yad uta traidhātukam* (*Śuklavidarśanabhūmi*, Poussin: *JRAS*. 1908, p.889).

42) *Sarvadarśanasaṃgraha*, XVI, *ll*.656-670.

43) See also *Kārikā* II,32.

44) This is probably the meaning of IV,1 and IV,91 where all things are compared to space.

45) If *Ātman* is admitted, the following assertion is rendered meaningless: "Since all things are by nature pure, the individuals are also by nature released".

SECTION III. PRACTICE

Looking at the spiritual practice taught in the *Māṇḍūkya-Upaniṣad* and the four chapters of the *Kārikās*, a tendency can be made out which is common to all of them, but again each chapter has its own peculiar doctrines. Here we consider the doctrines on practice, giving due regard to the special colour of each chapter of the *Kārikās*.

Sub-Section 1. Meditation on *OM* (The Theory Presented in the *Māṇḍūkya-Upaniṣad* and the First Chapter of the *Kārikās*)

In the *Māṇḍūkya-Upaniṣad*, there are no positive rules spoken of in connection with the life of practice of the religious aspirant. But as can be easily known from its content, this text is teaching to a *yogi* practicing the *yoga* of meditation on *OM* the mystical significance of his meditation. Accordingly, those who follow the practice of the *Upaniṣad* would be concentrating on meditation on *OM*. This meditation on *OM* had from ancient times been generally practiced among *yogis*,[1] and here it is gone into in detail. We find that the various states (*pāda*) of *Brahman* and the syllables (*mātra*) of *OM* have appropriate connections, and the common nature of each pair is displayed, and the man who knows each one is able to attain a specific result. This is the style of thinking of the *Brāhmaṇas*, and doubtless the author of the *Upaniṣad* thought along these lines. So the meditation taught here, though it is a meditation on *Brahman*, is still seeking various results in the world, and from the point of view of the Vedānta philosophers of later times it is of very little worth. At the beginning of the third chapter of the *Kārikās*, this kind of meditation-aiming-at-results (*upāsanā*)[2] is rejected as a shallow and low-grade method of spiritual practice. The practice of the ascetics who were originally practicing (honouring) the *Māṇḍūkya-Upaniṣad* cannot yet be called wholly of the Vedānta school.

The first chapter of the *Māṇḍūkya-Kārikās*, being a commentary on the *Māṇḍūkya-Upaniṣad*, is centered on an exposition relating to *OM* and its method of practice is this meditation on *OM*. In this chapter *OM* is particularly emphasized as a symbol of *Brahman*. It is said that the holy word is "the fearless *Brahman*" (I,25), "the pervader of all things," "the Lord abiding in the hearts of all [being]" (I,28). Thus all the special qualities which are spoken of relating to *Brahman* can be applicable just as they are to the holy syllable. The holy syllable should be expressed only negatively: "The holy syllable has no before, no after, no inner, no outer, and is indestructible" (I,26). "The holy syllable as the destruction of duality is auspicious" (I,29a).

And since it is thus a negative principle, the holy syllable includes all and makes everything possible. Whatever is, it exists within *OM*. "The holy syllable is truly the lower *Brahman* and again the holy syllable is the highest [*Brahman*], so it is taught" (I,26). "Truly the holy syllable is the beginning, the middle and the end of all" (I,27). Thus the holy syllable while in itself incapable of being determined in any way, being absolutely negative, still it is absolutely positive inasmuch as it makes all determinations possible by its power.[3]

"The sound *OM* does not possess any *mātras* (syllables), yet it possesses infinite syllables" (I,29). To meditate on the holy syllable as this kind of absolute, to realize the holy syllable is the practice of the *yogi* (I,26). Knowing the holy syllable is the way to become one with the absolute (I,27). If one has known the holy syllable, the state of liberation appears of itself. "The one who meditates always on the holy syllable, wherever he may be, is without fear" (I,25). "Realizing the sound *OM*, the wise man does not grieve" (I,28).

The man who has realized the real form of *OM* is called a "sage" (a pure silent one, *muni*) (I,29).

This holy syllable *OM* is divided into the three syllables A, U, and M, and also the soundless, and each of these corresponds to the four states of *Brahman* (pervading state, radiant state, wisdom state, and fourth state).[4]

"The sounds are undoubtedly the states" (I,24). Thus to know the true meaning of the holy syllable *OM* is to know the meaning of its various syllables. "Let him know the sounds of *OM* as the respective states" (I,24). And to know the respective correspondences between sounds and states is to penetrate to the absolute. "He who can know the common qualities which are equivalent to the three states" is called "the great sage" (*mahāmuni*) (I,

22).

In the *Māṇḍūkya-Upaniṣad*, the one who has known these correspondences is described as obtaining various special results, and these results are almost the same as those taught in the *Brāhmaṇas* generally, but here in the *Kārikās'* first chapter it is taught that if a man knows the common nature shared by a particular state of *Brahman* and its corresponding syllable, he attains to that particular state of *Brahman*, the all pervading state and so on (I,23). Again it stresses that one should know the sound *OM* annihilates duality and is auspicious (I,29). Thus the result of meditation which is taught in this first chapter of the *Kārikās* is *Brahman*, and very different from the results which are taught in the *Brāhmaṇas* generally. The object here being simply the attainment of *Brahman*, there is no question of the various worldly results as taught in the *Brāhmaṇas*. The exclusive teaching is meditation on *OM* and realization of *Brahman*. On this point, the doctrine is on the same lines as that of the meditation on *OM* in the *Gītā*.[5)] Thus the *OM* meditation taught in the *Kārikās'* first chapter goes a step further than what is taught in the *Upaniṣad*, being purer in content and more Vedāntic.

Still, even this kind of *OM* meditation, when viewed with the eye of a thoroughgoing Vedāntin of later times, was after all not the highest practice. In the *Kārikās* from the second chapter onward, such meditation is discarded and the teaching of the states (*pāda*) of *Brahman* is rated as a lower teaching.[6)] Moreover, Śaṅkara's verdict is that by *OM* meditation only the lower *Brahman*, namely *Hiraṇyagarbha*'s realm, can be reached, it being only on the ladder of gradual realization, and it cannot directly give ultimate liberation.[7)]

Notes

1) For example, the *Yoga-sūtra* I,27 decrees that the presiding deity should be meditated upon through the sacred sound (*praṇava*). Cf. also Chapter III, Section II, Sub-section 1. The recitation of the holy syllable *OM* is enjoined in *Manu* II, 74-84 and XI, 249 ; 266.

2) Bhattacharyya asserts that *upāsana* or *upāsanā* should not be translated as "reverence" but as "meditation" (*dhyāna*) (V. Bhattacharyya : *AS*. pp. 295-298).

3) According to Śaṅkara's commentary, all words (*śabda*) are developed on the basis of the sound *OM* (*vikāra*) (Ś. ad *GK*., p.10, ll. 16 ; 23).

4) Concerning this equivalency relationship, cf. previous section I.

5) "He who practices the *yoga*-concentration, controlling all the gates (senses), confining the mind in the heart and putting the breath on his own head, he who goes abandoning the body, uttering the *Brahman* which is the one syllable *OM* and recollecting me goes to the highest state" (*Bhag*. G. VIII, 12-13).

6) Cf. *ślokas* II,21; III, 1; 16 of the *Kārikās*.

7) *trimātreṇoṃkāreṇāvalambanena paramātmānam abhidhyāyataḥ phalaṃ brahmalokaprāptiḥ krameṇa ca samyagdarśanotpattir iti*/(Ś. ad *BS*. I, 3, 13)

Sub-Section 2. The Life of Ascetic Wandering Dedicated to Meditation on *Ātman* (The Theory Presented in the Second Chapter of the *Kārikās*)

The religious practice discussed in the second chapter of the *Māṇḍūkya-Kārikā* is the direct realization of the true *ātman*, i.e. "the cessation of the expansion of the universe, devoid of duality and false construction" (II,35). The practitioner is required to be always in meditation on *ātman* and to live in the ultimate state.

> "Having thus known this (cessation of the universe), one should fix one's memory on non-duality." (II,36)
>
> "Having seen the truth inwardly, and having seen the truth outwardly, one should become the truth, delighting therein and being such one should be unmoved from it." (II.38)

Thus, meditation on the sacred sound *OM* is not mentioned here at all; only the realization of the true form of *ātman* is taught. This is the inevitable conclusion resulting from the fact that the metaphysical basis of the second chapter is the *māyā* theory.

However, if the *māyā* theory is subscribed to, the differentiated appearances of the phenomenal world must be considered to be illusions. Hence, the path which leads to a return to actuality must be said to lie in the negation of the differentiated appearances of birth, death, and change. Thus the theorist here necessarily sought escape from the pain of change, disturbance, and impermanence which occur in the daily life of actual society; he sought the dimension of quiescence and death. In the second chapter rather detailed regulations on the actual lives of the practitioners are presented.

The person who realizes *ātman* is "the sage who has reached the innermost meaning of the *Veda*" (*muni vedaparāga*) (II,35). Having been enlightened and being knowledgeable, he is "free from attachment, fear, and anger" (II, 35). Having eliminated all human emotions, like the dead tree and eternal stones, he is completely without interest in all phenomena.

> "Having reached non-duality, he should behave like a fool (*jaḍa*) in the world." (II,36)[1]

He is a practitioner who has abandoned his home, he is completely free of the ceremonies and etiquettes of the layman, which he has transcended. He does not praise anything or pay homage to anybody.[2] He does not perform any sacrifice as the custom of a *Brāhmaṇa* (II,37).[3] He is clothed only in his simple robes, begs, and leads a life of wandering from village to village. He has no attachments and is completely without possessions. He has as his home this changing, non-eternal world, acting at random.

Among the works of the early Vedānta school, the second chapter of the *Kārikās* is probably the most detailed concerning the wandering mendicant.[4] The life of the wandering mendicant had frequently been praised as an ideal in the old *Upaniṣads* and other scriptures. In the *Mahābhārata* it is discussed in phrases identical with those in the *Māṇḍūkya-Kārikā*.[5] Among the early Vedānta scholars there were probably not a few who led such lives.[6] Such an ideal life also came to be praised in later periods by the various sects of the Hindu religion. For example, the tale of King *Bharata* (*Bharataupākhyāna*) in the *Viṣṇupurāṇa* (II,13-16), the "Biography of the Idiot *Bharata*" in the *Bhāgavatapurāṇa* (V,9-10),[7] etc., praise the life of wandering asceticism which is described in the second chapter of the *Māṇḍūkya-Kārikā*.[8] The wandering mendicants were important members of the Vedānta school and in later periods came to occupy a central position within the school. Yet, on the other hand, there continued to exist from an ancient period persistent views which opposed such a life of wandering asceticism. The clash between the view that honored the householder in order to maintain the ancient traditional Brahmanical rites and the view which praised the life of wandering asceticism is apparent in the famous "Dialogue between Father and Son" in the *Mahābhārata*.[9] The view which recognizes the ideal of union with *Brahman* in this world is greatly emphasized in the tale of the "Man Who

Holds the Scales" (*Tulādhara*).[10] The subject here is no more than a peddler, but he finds the absolute meaning in his own daily and honest tradesman's life. In Tantric works, also, it is taught that carrying out a correct moral life in actual society is union with *Brahman*, and the life of a wandering ascetic is criticized.[11] Such views of life continued to exist, and in later periods thinkers such as Kabir and Tukārām, objecting to severe asceticism, recognized God in daily productive life.[12]

Thus among those who held to the philosophic viewpoints of the same Vedānta school there long existed a difference between two types of completely opposing views concerning the basic problem of actual life. It may be supposed that within the Vedānta school at about the time of the compilation of the *Māṇḍūkya-Kārikā* there was a gradual increase in the number of people practicing lives of wandering asceticism.

Notes

1) *jaḍaval lokam acaret*/This ideal was set forth in *Manu* II, 110. The ideal of living like a senseless thing (*GK*. II, 36) was advocated already in early Buddhism : *yathā jaḷo ca mūgo ca attānaṃ dassaye tathā*/(*Theragāthā*, 582).

2) *nirstuti nirnamaskāra* (*GK*. II, 37). This idea was already expressed in *Mahābhārata* XII, 263, 34. Cf. the discussion of "the sraman who does not honor the king" among monks of ancient China.

3) The interpretation of *calācala* (*GK*. II, 37) as duplication can be justified by a form such as *bhavābhava* (*Suttanipāta*, 1068, etc.)

4) Among the new *Upaniṣads* which discuss the life of wandering asceticism, there are probably some which are earlier than Śaṅkara. Many of these, however, are of indeterminate date.

5) Cf. notes to II,37 in Part VI, Chapter I, Section II, Sub-Section 2 of this book.

6) The *Upaniṣad* states that Yājñavalkya also entered such a life.

7) In the *Mārkaṇḍeya-Purāṇa* also those who have abandoned the Brahmanical rites and festivals for the life of wandering asceticism are called *jaḍa* (Winternitz : *HIL*. vol.I, p. 561).

8) Winternitz : *HIL*. vol. I, p.548ff.

9) *Mahābhārata* XII, 175 ; XII, 277 ; *Mārkaṇḍeya-Purāṇa* 10-44.

10) *Mahābhārata*, XII, 261-264.

11) Winternitz : *HIL*. vol. I, pp. 597-599.

12) Winternitz : *GIL*. Bd. III, S. 586 ; 589.

Sub-Section 3. *Asparśayoga* (The Theory Presented in the Third Chapter of the *Kārikās*)

In the third chapter of the *Māṇḍūkya-Kārikā* the ultimate objective of religious practices is taken to be the negation of *manas* and "the attainment of the state that is not *manas*." This is actualized by "the control of *manas*" (*manaso nigrahaḥ*)[1], and the exercise is called *asparśayoga*. We may say that all the religious exercises presented in the third and fourth chapters can be summarily called *asparśayoga*.

Among the works of the orthodox Brahmanical schools this type of *yoga* is discussed only in this work. The term itself appears neither in the *Upaniṣads*[2] nor in the scriptures of the Yoga school. It appears, however, in Buddhist texts of later periods.[3] Śaṅkara explains its meaning as "*yoga* which has no restrictions."[4] In the *Gauḍapāda-Kārikā*, however, the recognition by the mind of phenomena as actual and its subsequent activity or its forming a relationship with phenomena is expressed by the term "to touch" (*spṛśati, saṃspṛśati*).[5] Thus, *asparśayoga* probably was meant to indicate "deep meditation" in which one sees that all phenomena are not real but only false appearances and that everything is the same and equal.[6] Mādhava calls this *yoga* "*samādhi* free from judgement" (*nirvikalpasamādhi*) and holds it to be fundamentally different from "*samādhi* with forms" (*sākāradhyāna*).[7] But "*samādhi* free from judgement" is what is explained by Maitreyanātha as the essence of Mahāyāna Buddhism.[8] It is likely that the idea of *asparśayoga* derived from Mahāyāna Buddhism. "*Na, bhagavan, kleśās tac cittaṃ spṛśanti.*"[9] Thus the idea of a special type of *yoga* was probably borrowed from Buddhism, or was formed under its influence. This discussion in the *Kārikās* themselves is in content highly Buddhistic. That is, this *asparśayoga* is said to be "*samādhi* that is immovable and without fear" (III,37); it is union with the absolute. Its virtues are highly negative: "[It] conduces to happiness of all beings and is beneficial and free from dispute [with other schools], and it does not contradict [anything]" (IV,2).

This *asparśayoga* was markedly different in purpose from the type of *yoga* undertaken by the general religious practitioner of its period.[10] At that time most religious practitioners meditated on the Lord, worshipped the various gods, or revered other natural and supernatural existences. There were many who meditated on *Brahman* and *ātman*, but they depended on some symbol (e.g. the sacred sound *OM*) in carrying out their meditation. Here, in contrast with such tendencies, the theory of *asparśayoga* is propounded. As opposed to the fact that at that time the meditation of most of the practitioners was "*samādhi* with forms," here it is "*samādhi* free from judgement." No doubt this new view must have impressed the average practitioner as rather odd. According to the *Kārikās*, *asparaśayoga* "is difficult to be acquired by all *yogins*" (III,39). They could not understand its true significance and viewed it with fear.

> "Those *yogins* are afraid of it (=*asparśayoga*), seeing fear where in fact there is no fear." (III,39)

According to the commentator Śaṅkara, the *yogins* think that this *yoga* brings about the annihilation of *ātman* (*ātmanāśa*) and are afraid of it. That is, *asparśayoga* destroys the lower self which is in opposition to others and leads one to the state of non-self. This concept of *asparśayoga*, influenced by Buddhism, may be seen to have been an entirely new creation within the Vedānta school. We can see that within that school it was originally regarded as somewhat alien or foreign. The author of the third chapter explains that this *samādhi* is higher than the "worship" (*upāsanā*) which was taught in the Vedānta school in general. The traditional practices of "worship" (*upāsanā*, meditation) are evaluated as shallow (*kṛpaṇa*)(III,1).

The specific exercises for the perfection of *asparśayoga* are explained in detail in the third chapter of the *Kārikās*. Its essence is in the control of *manas*. Through this *yoga*, one is able to attain "fearlessness, elimination of pain, awakening, indestructible tranquility" (III,40). But one must realize the control of *manas* through tireless, inrepressible efforts. It requires an almost inconceivably firm resolve, one which may be likened to the resolve needed to drain the ocean by drops with the point of a blade of *kuśa* grass [11] (III,41).

Firstly, as preparation, two means (*upāya*) are necessary: removal of desire (*vairāgya*) and repetition of knowledge (*jñānābhyāsa*). The former is to turn back *manas* from desires and enjoyments, repeatedly remembering that all is misery. The latter is to see nothing born, repeatedly remembering that all is unborn (III,43). When practicing *yoga*, one must not allow the mind to be distracted or to rest. Both are obstacles to religious exercises. Hence, the mind must be controlled by these two methods in order that, on the one hand, the mind is not distracted because of desires and enjoyments, while on the other it does not rest. If the mind is distracted, it must be made tranquil; if it is in a state of rest, it must be awakened (III,43,44). This corresponds to the Buddhist teaching that when practicing *samādhi* indolence (*auddhatya*) and depression (*styāna*) must both be avoided.

By undertaking the exercises with due attention to these matters, the mind gradually reaches a state of equanimity. When the mind reaches this one must strive not to upset it (III,44). And when such *yoga* exercises have been completed, *Brahman* is present.

> "When the mind is not in the state of rest nor is distracted again, when it is free from movement and manifestation [of the object], then it is the perfect *Brahman*." (III,46)[12)]

> "[The wise] say that [the mind] dwells in itself, calm, having *nirvāṇa*, and that it is the unspeakable highest bliss, unborn, all-knowing, [identical] with the knowable (=*Brahman*) which is unborn." (III,47)

In this manner when *asparśayoga* is completely carried out, the activity of *manas* is controlled and all differentiated appearances are eliminated. At that point appears "the knowledge which is not separate from the knowable" (*jñeyābhinnaṃ jñānam*; III,33,IV,1). It is emphasized, however, that this state is different from the simple non-differentiation which occurs in deep sleep. Rather, it is the state of equanimity of mind acquired through purposeful effort.

In the *Kārikās* it is stated in the above manner that union with *Brahman* occurs after undergoing religious exercises with minute attention to the above details. Hence it was not thought that final release could be attained through the simple rational knowledge that *Brahman* is *ātman*.

On this point the theories of the third chapter of the *Kārikās* differ markedly from the view concerning religious exercises held by the branch of the Advaita school which follows Śaṅkara. According to Śaṅkara, final release occurs immediately upon acquiring the knowledge that *Brahman* is *ātman*. Concerning the cognition which is the "knowing of *Brahman*," no special extreme effort is necessary. Thus, the commentators on these *Kārikās* who held to the theory of the Advaita school could not accept that of these *Kārikās*. According to the commentator Śaṅkara, final release is by nature established (*svabhāvata eva siddhaḥ*) for such individuals. According to Ānandajñāna, concerning the sun in itself, there exists no day or night, but by positing its rising and setting, day and night can be considered. In the same manner, concerning *Brahman* in itself there is no cognizance or non-cognizance of it, but through its limiting adjunct both can be considered.[13] Therefore, we are already in a state of final release, but those poor in spiritual sensitivity or the shallow *yogins* (*yogino... hīnamadhyam-adṛṣṭayaḥ*) think that final release arises from the control of *manas*. Thus in commenting on the following *śloka*:

> "All *yogins*' absence of fear depends upon the control of *manas*" (III, 40)

Śaṅkara gave it a different meaning: The absence of fear, all *yogins* who are devoid of knowledge of the truth of *ātman*....(*ātmasatyānubodhara-hitānāṃ...sarveṣāṃ yogināṃ*).[14] Concerning the significance of religious exercises in order to attain "final release," it is known that the Advaita school of later periods held a different view which went beyond that of the *Māṇḍūkya-Kārikā*.

Notes

1) III, 34; 35; 40; 41.

2) Śaṅkara notes this as *prasiddham upaniṣatsu*, but this term does not appear in the *Upaniṣad*. Further, it does not appear in any of the Sanskrit dictionaries.

3) In the Sanskrit commentary to a later Buddhist work, *Bauddha Gāna O Dohā* (Sāhityapariṣad Granthāvalī, 55, p.19), *aspṛśayoga* is discussed, but since in the Tibetan commentary we find *mi-reg-paḥi sbyor-ba*, the correct form is probably *asparśayoga* (Bhattacharyya: *AS*. p.305). The following passage by Āryadeva appears at first glance to have some relationship with it, but here we have a discussion of the irrationality of combining "something which can be touched" (*sparśavat*) and "something which cannot be touched" (*asparśavat*), and there is probably no direct relationship: *na hy asparśavato nāma yogaḥ sparśavatā saha/ rūpādīnām ato yogaḥ sarvathāpi na yujyate//* (Āryadeva's *Catuḥśatikā*. v. 308, p.507).

4) *sarvasaṃbandhākhyasparśavarjitatvād asparśayogo nāma vai smaryate prasiddham*

upaniṣatsu/(Ś. ad *GK*. III, 39); *sparśanaṃ sparśaḥ saṃbandho na vidyate yasya yogasya kenacit kadāpi so 'sparśayogo brahmasvabhāva eva*/(Ś. ad *GK*. IV, 2). Furthermore, Śaṅkara has substituted the term *advaitadarśanayoga*.

5) *cittaṃ na spṛśaty artham* (*GK*. IV, 26); *nimittaṃ na sadā cittaṃ saṃspṛśaty adhvasu triṣu*/(*GK*. IV, 27); *viparyāsād yathā jāgrad acintyān bhūtavat spṛśet*/(*GK*. IV, 41).

6) There are some who explain *yoga* to mean "union." "The touch of untouch, — probably referring to *Nirvāṇa*" (Dasgupta: *HIPh*., vol. I, p.423). However, since in the explanation of *asparśayoga* the term *yogin* appears three times, it is probably best to regard it as a type of *dhyāna*. Further, it may be held to mean "*yoga* which is not stained (not influenced) by phenomena." We have the following examples: *mātrāsparśās tu kaunteya śītoṣṇasukhaduḥkhadāḥ/āgamāpāyino nityāḥ tān titikṣasva bhārata*//(*Bhag. G*. II, 14; cf. V, 27); *na tena* [*upabhogena*] *paramārtharūpasya brahmaṇaḥ saṃsparśaḥ*/(Ś. ad *BS*. I, 2, 8, vol. I, p.148, *l*. 5). However, it is probably best to explain it according to the material in the *Kārikās*, as cited in note 5. Cf. also *asparśa* (*Upadeśasāhasrī*, p.343).

7) *Pañcadaśī* II, 24 (Walleser: *DAV*. S.4).

8) *yogaś ca nirvikalpaḥ samastam idam uttamaṃ yānam*/(*MSA*. XVI, 5). The term *nirvikalpa* is Buddhist Sanskrit.

9) *Ratnagotravibhāga*, p.15.

10) Ānandajñāna uses the terms of the Yoga school to explain *asparśayoga*. He teaches that one should endeavor to converge the mind through *saṃprajñātasamādhi* and to unite with *Brahman* through *asaṃprajñātasamādhi*. This is his own explanation and is not related to the *Māṇḍūkya-Kārikā* (p. 152, *l*. 5; p. 153, *ll*. 14-15). V. Bhattacharyya views *asparśayoga* as identical to the Buddhistic *nirodhasamāpatti* (V. Bhattacharyya: *Proc. II, OC*. p.445f; *AS*. p.95f.), but since the term *asparśayoga* does not appear in Buddhist scriptures, it is a little rash to say that both are identical.

11) It is likely that the simile of a *kuśa* leaf (*GK*. III, 41) was introduced from Mahāyāna Buddhism. "All oceans can be dried drop by drop by a leaf" (*Taishō Tripiṭaka*. vol. X, p.424c; *Gaṇḍavyūha*, p.476, *ll*. 15-18; *Sukhāvatīvyūha*, published by Daitō Shuppansha, p.64).

12) Cf. also *śloka* III, 45.

13) Ān. ad *GK*. III, 36.

14) Ś. ad *GK*. III,40. This note probably is not Śaṅkara's, but there is no doubt that it follows his line of thinking.

Sub-Section 4. The Practice of Consciousness-Only (The Theory Presented in the Fourth Chapter of the *Kārikās*)

In the fourth chapter, too, the religious exercises are called *asparśayoga*.

Thus, the religious exercise in the fourth chapter is the same as that in the third chapter. However, because the philosophic content of the fourth chapter is almost entirely the same as the Consciousness-only philosophy of Buddhism, a number of special characteristics can be seen in its theories concerning religious exercises.

The author of the fourth chapter proclaims that his own position concerning religious exercises is that of the "highest path" (*agrayāna*) (IV,90). Since *agrayāna* is another name for the Mahāyāna, he is here stating that his own standpoint concerning religious exercises is that of Mahāyāna Buddhism. He calls the person who has completed three exercises and whom we should take as our teacher the "*Buddha*." The initial and final *ślokas* of the fourth chapter are both dedicated to the "enlightened one" (*saṃbuddha*). In works of the orthodox Brahmanical schools, these are complete exceptions.

In what manner was the *Buddha* or "enlightened one" considered? Concepts such as *saṃbhogakāya* and *nirmāṇakāya* established in Buddhism are not discussed in the fourth chapter. What is discussed is that which approximates what is called *dharmakāya* in Buddhism. According to the theory presented, the ignorant in this world say that "*Bhagavat*"[1] is existent, non-existent, both existent and non-existent, or neither existent nor non-existent, etc., and conceal its true form. The true form of the *Bhagavat*, however, transcends these four attributes. Thus, it states that the person who sees that "the *Bhagavat* is not touched by these four attributes" is a person who sees all (IV,82). This is in complete agreement with the view of the *Buddha* in Nāgārjuna's *Mādhyamaka-śāstra*.[2]

The absolute which is called "*Buddha*" or "*Bhagavat*" is held to be "the equalness which is non-originated and non-dual" (IV,80), "the state of non-origination and equality" (IV,95), "the state without fear" (IV,78), "immortality" (IV,92), "the state which is difficult to be seen, very profound, unborn, equal, fearless and which is the absence of difference" (IV,100), "the state of complete omniscience, the state of being [true] *Brahman* and the state which is non-dual, without beginning, without middle, and without end" (IV,85). These do not necessarily differ from the concepts of the absolute presented in the previous chapters, but it should be noticed that here they are placed within the range of the vocabulary of Buddhist modes of expression.

Such explanations are highly similar to those of the Mādhyamika school, but since the Consciousness-only theory presented in this chapter is, as has already been discussed, the *Vijñānavāda* which maintains that both the object and the subject of cognition are unreal, it does not contradict such a conception of the absolute at all.

To actualize the state of the absolute the *asparśayoga* must be practiced: namely, seeing that all objective phenomena have no real existence, controlling the self, he must exert himself to make the heart pure, be free from grief, cut off desire, and be without attachment so that desire does not arise (IV, 78; 79; 85; 86). In this practice the greatest care and unremitting circumspection are necessary. There must not be the slightest falling away (IV,97). This is not fundamentally different from what was taught in previous chapters, but the metaphysics is different.

Until the absolute is realized, there is a noteworthy doctrine of stages. In this fourth chapter the metaphysics is according to *Vijñānavāda*, so the ascending stages of practice are in line with *Vijñānavāda* (IV,87; 88):

(1)Dualist world view (*dvayaṃ laukikam*): here external objects exist and also awareness exists. Remaining in the world of opposing duality, attached to the existence of eternal objects, this is called the standpoint of the ordinary man of the world who is aware of objects.

(2)Pure world view (*śuddhaṃ laukikam*): here external objects do not exist, but awareness exists. Having realized external objects do not exist, still the standpoint is bound to consciousness concerned with external objects. It is regarded as the state of a practitioner who has not yet attained.

(3)Beyond the world view (*lokottara*): here external objects do not exist, nor does awareness. It is realizing the non-existence of external objects and being not bound by a consciousness in relation to them. This is the state of success.

It is stated that in these three stages, when knowledge and the known have successively been understood, the practitioners become "those who are possessed of the great knowledge" (IV,95) and reach "spontaneously the state of omniscience[3] everywhere in this world" (IV,89). This ultimate state is not death, but occurs in this world. These three stages were originally discussed by a group of *Vijñānavādins*, and they may correspond to (1) existence produced from imagination, (2) existence arising from dependent origination, and (3) existence as the highest truth. The author of the fourth chapter absorbed these into his own theory.[4]

Now then, in the state in which the religious exercises have been completed, both subjective knowledge (*jñāna*) and objective things (*dharma*) are non-originated. Knowledge does not function toward the external objects, and things do not act toward knowledge (IV,99). Both are inseparable (IV, 1). And the "knowledge" which appears here is free from attachment (IV,96 ; 72). Since it is beyond discrimination (IV,60), it is said that "this knowledge has not been taught by the *Buddha*" (IV,99). It is the silence of the absolute; it is *śūnya*.

As has been shown above, each chapter of the *Māṇḍūkya-Kārikā* presents a particularly distinctive discussion of religious exercises. Yet we can see a unifying thread running through each chapter, i.e. the teaching to *yoga* practitioners of the ideal form of religious exercises. Although the theories differ in each chapter, the target of the teachings is *yoga* practitioners. Hence it was possible for the *yoga* practitioner Gaudapāda to compile and unify the *Māṇḍūkya-Upaniṣad* and the *Kārikās* at a later period. Yet, despite this common point, we should not overlook the fact that, as explained above, concerning the theories of religious practices there exists a process of historical development among the chapters of the *Kārikās*.

Notes

1) Concerning the fact that the term *Bhagavat* is used in the *Kārikās* in the Buddhistic sense, cf. note to IV,82 in Part VI, Chapter I, Section II, Sub-Section 4 of this book. The appellation *tāyin* (*GK*. IV,99) was used in early Jainism too. A sage is always called *tāyin* in the colophon of every chapter of the *isibhāsiyāim*.

2) Cf. note to *GK*. IV, 82 in Part VI, Chapter I, Section II, Sub-Section 4 of this book.

3) The phrase "*Buddhas* alone know truth" (*GK*. IV, 80) is used in Mahāyāna literature, e. g. the Tang version of the *Buddhāvataṃsakasūtra*, chüan 19, *Taishō Tripiṭaka*, vol. X, p.101b ; cf. *Buddhabhūmi*, *Laṅkāvatāra* X, v. 105, p.278.

4) Cf. note to IV,87 in Part VI, Chapter I, Section II, Sub-Section 4 of this book.

SECTION IV. OPPOSITION AND RECONCILIATION OF WORLD-VIEWS

The fact that in the real world various opposing world-views exist in competition came to be an extremely important problem for the Vedānta school.

The Vedānta school invariably postulates a monistic metaphysical principle such as *Brahman* or *ātman* and asserts that all phenomena devolve from it alone. But in the actual human world differing and contradictory philosophical theories exist in opposing rivalry. If we subscribe to the thoroughgoing monistic standpoint of Vedānta philosophy, we must hold that all heretical theories arise from *Brahman*. If it is stated that they arise from some principle other than *Brahman*, the monistic or absolute quality of *Brahman* is abandoned. Why then do various types of philosophical theories coexist? Further, what significance does this fact have? How should we explain this fact, and what attitude should we take toward it? Vedānta philosophy was forced to confront such difficult questions. This problem was taken up from an extremely early period. Let us examine this problem in the following sections.

Sub-Section 1. The Unified Standpoint

As previously stated, the Vedānta school from its very beginnings took as its object philosophical investigations concerning the Upaniṣadic scriptures. Hence we can recognize a tendency toward striving to unify and co-ordinate the various views discussed in the scriptures. Needless to say, we shall not point out every example of this within the Vedānta school, but we can recognize such tendencies within the *Upaniṣads* themselves. For example, such a tendency toward unification and co-ordination can be seen to some degree in the *Kāṭhaka*, *Śvetāśvatara*, and *Maitrī Upaniṣads*. In the "*Adhyātmapaṭala*" of the *Āpastambīya-Dharmasūtra*, there is clearly taken an attitude of selecting and unifying theories from the *Upaniṣads* from a particular standpoint.[1]

We can also recognize such tendencies in the *Māṇḍūkya-Upaniṣad*. In the sixth *śloka* of this *Upaniṣad* the concepts which previously had been held as the highest principle in the old *Upaniṣads* — i. e., "the Lord of all" (*sarveśvara*), "the omniscient" (*sarvajña*), "the inner regulator" (*antaryāmin*), "source of all things" (*yoniḥ sarvasya*), "the source from which all things arise and to which they return" (*prabhavāpyayau bhūtānām*) — are all placed within the third stage of *Brahman*, i. e. the stage of *Prajñā*. These each had been postulated as the ultimate world-principle by earlier philosophers, and each is a concept with differing significance. Yet here they are all taken as being equivalent in that they belong to the third stage. There is postulated an ultimate Fourth Stage (*caturtha*) as their base. The previous metaphysical theories are all recognized and unified, but their significance as the ultimate principle is negated. We may say that there is presented here one method of solving the problem of opposition of qualitatively different world-views. This attitude of including and synthesizing previous theories but placing them on a lower stage in order to assert the superiority of one's own theory can be seen not only to run through the chapters of the *Māṇḍūkya-Kārikā*, but, indeed, is an attitude found throughout the two-thousand-year history of the Vedānta school.

Notes

1) Hajime Nakamura: *A History of Early Vedānta Philosophy*, Part One (Motilal Banarsidass, 1983), pp. 306-313.

Sub-Section 2. The Raison d'Etre of Heretical Theories

Although various and sundry views are presented in the Upaniṣadic scriptures, there can be seen among them a common intellectual tendency or mode of thought. Thus, in order to unify them the method used in the *Māṇḍūkya-Upaniṣad* may be held to be sufficient. In actual philosophical circles, however, contradictory theories or those which will absolutely not allow any other exist in opposition. How are we to explain this fact?

In the first chapter (I.7 ff.) of the *Māṇḍūkya-Kārikā* the existence of such differing theories is considered. They are listed and attacked, but here they are only refuted and beyond this the problem is not treated more thoroughly. This problem is first discussed in detail in the second chapter.

In the second chapter of the *Kārikā*, after the process of the evolution of the world is discussed, the various then existent theories concerning the world-principle are discussed. According to the *Kārikā*, when viewing the world, scholars have taken the following types of principles to be the ultimate principle — i. e., "breath" (*prāṇa*), "structural elements" (*guṇa*), "truth" (*tattva*), "[four] quarters [of *Brahman*]" (*pāda*), "object" (*viṣaya*), "world" (*loka*), "gods" (*devāḥ*), "the *veda*", "sacrifice", "the enjoyer" (*bhoktṛ*), "the objects of enjoyment" (*bhogya*), "thing subtle" (*sūkṣma*), "thing gross" (*sthūla*), "things with forms" (*mūrta*), "formless things" (*amūrta*), "time", "direction", "discussion" (*vāda*), "the universe" (*bhuvana*), "mind" (*manas*), "enlightenment" (*buddhi*), "mind" (*citta*), "merit and demerit", "the twenty-five principles", "the twenty-six principles", "the thirty-one principles", "infinity", "the various worlds" (*lokāḥ*), "the stages of life" (*āśrama*), "the feminine, masculine, and neuter genders [of nouns]", "the highest *Brahman* and the lower *Brahman*", "creation" (*sṛṣṭi*), "dissolution" (*laya*), "subsistence" (*sthiti*), etc. It is stated that the numerous schools stand in opposing competition because they each take one of these as the Absolute (II, 20 ff). According to the author of the second chapter, however, these principles or things are not the true Absolute. They are no more than false construction (*vikalpita*) as the world-principle (II, 19). The true Absolute is *Ātman*. Since the above philosophers do not know the true form of *Ātman*, they mistake such particular principles or things for *Ātman* and do not part from such attachments (II, 29). Because of this many differing types of thought systems are established.

Hence, although the above-listed theories cannot be said to be true teachings, these principles or things are in actuality established on the basis of *Ātman*. Each is no more than one form of manifestation of *Ātman*. Thus, they cannot be anything other than *Ātman*. To think that they are other than *Ātman* is also a delusion of human beings.

> "Although it (*Ātman*) is not different from them [breath, etc.], [the fools] think that they differ [from *Ātman*]. Those who truly know it thus may imagine without doubt." (II, 30)

Thus, although the above-presented principles and things in themselves are not *Ātman*, they each have their raison d'être in being based on *Ātman*. Since the various philosophical theories in the world are developed on the basis of taking one of the above as the Absolute, if we press the point, we may say that all heretical and differing theories in actuality are also formed on the basis of *Ātman*.

In this manner the second chapter of the *Kārikā* rejects all previous philosophical theories — among which are many that are discussed in the *Upaniṣads* — as incomplete ; but at the same time it recognizes that since they are established upon the basis of *Ātman*, they each possess partial truth. Here we reach a point where the raison d'être of all types of philosophical thinking is recognized. This is an epochal development in the intellectual history of the orthodox Brahmanical schools.[1] The Buddhist scholar Bhavya also relates that such views existed in the Vedānta school of his time.[2)]

Tracing it back to an earlier period, we may see that such intellectual tendencies had begun to take form in the theistic views of the *Ṛg-Veda*. The Vedic religion is clearly a polytheistic teaching, but at rites and festivals the deity which is being particularly honored and revered is for that period considered to be the principal deity. Thus some scholars call it henotheism or, because the principal deity is changed according to the rite, kathenotheism. Thus, the theism of the *Vedas* holds that the primary nature of the absoluteness of the deity does not exist in the deity itself, but exists rather behind the various deities. If that be the case, the question immediately arises : What is the Absolute that exists as that background ? And, indeed, the search for the answer to this question commenced. Even in the ancient *Ṛg-Veda* there appears, for example, the view that the various Vedic deities — i. e., *Indra*, *Mitra*, *Varuṇa*, *Agni*, *Yama*, *Mātariśvan* — are different names of the sun-god.[3)] It is also declared that the various gods are each none other than aspects of the god *Agni*.[4)] It may be said that these views each hold that in their actual form the separate and mutually opposing deities can be nothing other than manifestations of the Unique, and are attempts at establishing a synthesis within the theism of the *Vedas*. The tendency toward viewing the deities as manifestations of the Unique and toward accepting this as their raison d'être becomes markedly more pronounced in the *Brāhmaṇas* and *Upaniṣads*. In such a manner, that which in earlier times had been held to be the absolute principle came to be considered as mere deities, and with development in thought various ultimate principles other than such "deities" came to be postulated. The Vedānta school came to provide a philosophic basis for the raison d'être of all such theories. It may be said that such a method of handling the problem existed within a tradition subscribed to from an extremely early period. This mode of thinking also influenced the world-view of the theologians of the Hindu religion in later periods.[5)]

Notes

1) Together with this, similar views appear from an early period in the Jain religion. However, there it is asserted from the standpoint of indeterminism (relativism, *anekāntavāda*). I hope to discuss this on another occasion.

2) Hajime Nakamura : *A History of Early Vedānta Philosophy*, Part One, p.215f.

3) *ṚV*. I, 164, 46.

4) *ṚV*. V, 3, 1.

5) For example, in the *Kūrma-purāṇa* I, 22 ff. it is stated that each of the seven deities is worthy of reverence ; thus all religions are recognized (Winternitz : *HIL*., vol. I, p. 574).

Sub-Section 3. The *Avivāda* (Non-Disputation) Theory

In the second chapter of the *Māṇḍūkya-Kārikā* it was emphasized that the various types of differing theories concerning the ultimate world-principle are all derived from *Ātman*. In the third chapter this view is further developed to reach the standpoint which emphasizes non-contradiction with the philosophical theories of other schools, i. e. the "non-disputation" theory. It holds that although the theories of various other schools are mutually contradictory, the theories of Vedānta philosophy do not contradict the theories of other schools.

> "The dualists, firmly fixed in the viewpoint of their own theories, mutually contradict each other. But this [our view] does not contradict them." (III,17)

In this case the term "dualists" covers all scholars other than the Vedānta school, i. e. all those in opposition to the Advaita view of the Vedānta school. It can be readily understood that the theories of scholars who held to dualistic views contradicted each other, but why is it possible to say that the Vedānta theories do not contradict those of the dualistic theorists?

Śloka III, 18 of the *Kārikā* provides an explanation in the following manner. According to the theorists who hold to the dualistic view, "in Absolute Truth, and also in that which is not Absolute Truth," that is, from the metaphysical standpoint and also from the worldly standpoint, there exist the differentiated appearances of dualistic opposition. Thus, because they attach themselves to one of the principles among the phenomena which are established upon such opposition, it is natural that the theories of these dualistic theorists are mutually contradictory. However, according to the theorists who belong to the Advaita group of the Vedānta school, "the highest truth is non-dual (*advaita*) and dualism is its differentiated appearance" (III, 18). When seen from the standpoint of Vedānta philosophy, the various concepts or things which the dualistic theorists hold to be the highest principle can only be manifestations of *Ātman* as the Absolute. Among things which are manifested appearances there exist contradictory relationships, but this contradictory relationship does not exist between them and *Ātman*, for *Ātman* is their source and they are different in their dimension. Thus, the theories of the dualists who stick to one of the manifested appearances contradict each other, but the standpoint of the Vedānta school which teaches *Ātman* does not contradict any other philosophical theory. Śaṅkara compares it to the fact that one's own arms and legs do not contradict oneself.[1] This view is absorbed by the fourth chapter of the *Māṇḍūkya-Kārikā*. The *asparśayoga* which is taught is described as "free from dispute and contradiction [of anything]" (*avivādo 'viruddhaś ca*) (IV, 2).

Now then, in the third chapter there is presented the general viewpoint that the views of other schools contradict each other but Vedānta philosophy does not contradict them. In the fourth chapter this is demonstrated with particular emphasis on the problem of ontology.

> "Some disputants really assert the birth of a thing which is already existent [while] other men of wisdom [assert the birth] of a thing which is non-existent. They dispute with each other." (IV,3)

The fact of the philosophical world that they dispute with one another presents in itself a type of philosophy.

> "That which is already existent does not come into being and that which is non-existent also does not come into being. While thus disputing, these dualists assert non-origination." (IV,4)

The various schools dispute and debate about the basic problem of the evolution of the world. Those who assert that existence creates, i. e. that the world develops from existence, reject the theoretical premises of those who hold that the world develops from non-existence. On the other hand, those who assert creation from non-existence attack the premises of the former. Since each school nullifies the theoretical basis of the other school, we can no longer recognize creation. The fact of opposition in the intellectual world teaches us non-origination.

> "We rejoice that they assert non-origination. We do not dispute with them. Know non-disputation." (IV,5)

Thus the theory of "non-origination" of the Advaita theorist does not especially assert any opposition to the theories of other schools. It is held that since it is the true form of Absolute Truth it does not contradict the assertions of other schools, and accordingly disputes or debates do not arise.

We can recognize here a special type of philosophy which holds that the fact of opposition of theories in the philosophical world presents in itself a certain philosophy. In the West such a philosophical viewpoint also existed. For example, Hegel may be seen as one who held such a view. Hegel recognizes a movement of logic in the history of the exchange and development of philosophical views and emphasizes that the history of philosophy is in itself philosophy. In Vedānta philosophy, however, there is no concept of the history of philosophy. Vedānta philosophy abstracts the historical changes of the various philosophical systems and places emphasis simply on the opposition of the various philosophical types. In contrast with the Western philosophers placing a philosophical significance on the historical origins of various philosophical views, Indian philosophy recognizes a type of philosophy in the fact of the spatial co-existence of various philosophical types (or contemporaneous existence of opposition). In the Vedānta school of later periods, many works which may be called "Introductions to Philosophy"— works which discussed various philosophical systems — were produced. These were all written from such a standpoint. From the standpoint of intellectual history it is extremely interesting that even before Śaṅkara this was discussed in the *Māṇḍūkya-Kārikā* and also by Bhartṛhari.[2]

Now then, in the fourth chapter, the "non-disputing" standpoint concerning the problem of "origination" is made clear, and the explanation "actuality is not originated; non-actuality is not originated," etc., is clearly taken from Buddhistic theories, in particular those of the Mādhyamika school.[3] The "non-disputing" standpoint which is based on such ontological views is thus derived from Buddhism. The standpoint of not contradicting and disputing with other schools is also emphasized by the Jain school,[4] but in Buddhism it was discussed from the very beginnings of this school. In early Buddhist scriptures we already find frequent admonitions such as "do not dispute" (*avivāda*).[5] We see that the following *Ślokas* in the *Sutta-nipāta* present views which remarkably resemble the previously presented *Ślokas* of the *Māṇḍūkya-Kārikā*.

> Those who proclaim teachings other than this (= our own) miss purity and are not perfect (*kevalin*) — thus assert the diverse followers of the various other schools (*tithya*). For they are affected with attachment to their own views. (*Suttanipāta*, 891)
>
> They say that only here [in their own views] is there purity, while there is no purity in other teachings. Thus are the diverse followers of other teachings attached, and they, firmly standing on their path, argue (*sakāyane tattha daḷahṃ vadānā*). (*ibid.* 892)
>
> And, firmly standing on their own path and arguing, whom should he call a 'fool'?
>
> If he says that their theory is foolish, impure, he himself would get into strife. (*ibid.* 893)
>
> Standing on the decision (*vinicchaya*) [of theories], he measures by himself and comes to dispute (*vivāda*) [with others] in the world.
>
> Having abandoned all the decisions of theories, people do not cause strife in the world. (*ibid.* 894)[6]

The term "non-disputation" (*avivāda*) is in origin Buddhistic. In the general philosophical literature of India the term "*avivāda*" has the meaning "no room for argument, everywhere recognized, certain,"[7] but in the

Māṇḍūkya-Kārikā it has the meaning "not disputing."[8] Terms with such a meaning are frequently seen in Buddhist scriptures, and the standpoint of "non-disputation" is a central view of Buddhism.[9] The characteristically Buddhistic term "non-argument" (*araṇā*) is synonymous. The concept of "non-argument" is frequently emphasized in Buddhist scriptures. The Buddha is called "one who has abandoned disputation" (*raṇaṃjaha*),[10] and Subhūti is praised as "first among the non-disputants" (*agro 'raṇāvihāriṇām*).[11]

From these facts we may conclude that although scholars belonging to the Vedānta school assert that the standpoint of non-disputation is particular to that school,[12] this standpoint is derived from Buddhism.

Notes

1) ad. *GK*. III, 17.

2) Cf. infra.

3) Cf. notes to IV,4 ; 22 ; 40 in Part VI, Chapter I, Section II, Sub-Section 4 of this book.

4) For example, the great scholar Hemacandra asserts the following : *anyonyapakṣapratipakṣabhāvād yathā pare matsariṇaḥ pravādāḥ / nayān aśeṣān aviśeṣaṃ icchan na pakṣapātī samayas tathārhatāḥ// Vītarāgastuti*, v, 30 (= *SDS*. III, *ll*.409-412).

5) For example, the following phrase is frequently repeated : *mā āyasmanto appamattakehi vivādaṃ āpajjitthāti/* (*MN*. vol. II, p.240).

6) These verses have been translated in most part according to the Japanese translation of the *Tripiṭaka* of the Southern Transmission. Passages with the same meaning can be found in the *Suttanipāta*, 824 ; 887 ; *Mahāniddesa*, XII, 280 f.

7) Unbestritten, worüber Alle einig sind ; Comm. zu *Nyāyasūtra*, I, 18, 24. *KF*. Cf. *SDS*. XI, *l*.107.

8) *viruddhavadanaṃ vivādaḥ pakṣapratipakṣaparigraheṇa yasmin na vidyate so 'vivādaḥ/* (Ś ad *GK*. IV, 2) ; *avivāda = vivādarahitaṃ paramārthadarśanam/*(Ś ad *GK*. IV, 5).

9) *vivādaprāptyā na duḥkhaṃ praśāmyate avivādaprāptyā ca duḥkhaṃ nirudhyate /— Samādhirāja-Sūtra* (*Mvy*. pp.136, *ll*.1-2 ; p.270, *ll*. 17-18) ; *tena hy āyuṣmantaḥ saṃgāsyāmo na vivadiṣyāmaḥ avivādaparamo hi śramaṇadharmaḥ — Āryaratnakūṭasūtra* (*Mvy*. p.338, *ll*. 13-14). Cf. a famous stanza of Guṇavarman (5th century), Taishō Tripiṭaka, vol. 50, p.342a.

10) Cf. *Avadānaśataka* II, 131, no. 3 ; *KF*. III, 253 ; IV, 295. Further, in the *Divyāvadāna*, p. 401, *l*. 4 the Buddha is called *araṇāvihārin*.

11) *Mahāvyutpatti*, 244, 103 ; *Avadānaśataka* II, 131, 5-6.

12) Nikhilānanda: *The Māṇḍūkyopaniṣad*, foreword, p.ii ff.

Sub-Section 4. Synthesis and Reconciliation of Differing Theories in the Scriptures

In the second chapter of the *Māṇḍūkya-Kārikā* all heretical theories were held to be manifestations of *Ātman* and this was accepted as their raison d'être. However, this was no more than a formal solution. The Vedānta students subsequently were confronted with the problem of how to explain the varying theories discussed in the scriptures. Since the Vedic scriptures — including the *Upaniṣads* — are absolute authorities for the Vedānta school, the scholars of this school had to show clearly that their own theories were in agreement with the theories of the scriptures. The theories of the Advaita school, however, clearly contradict passages in the *Upaniṣads*. How is this to be explained and reconciled? These scholars were all troubled by this problem. The *Brahma-sūtra* itself is a crystallization of attempts to solve this problem. The early Vedānta scholars also expended much energy on this problem.[1]

In the *Māṇḍūkya-Kārikā* this problem is taken up in particular detail in the third chapter. That is, here various explanations have been appended to the scriptural passages which contradict the Advaita theories. Firstly, in the *Taittirīya-Upaniṣad* the fivefold sheath (*pañca-kośa*) theory is presented, but it is explained that the "*Ātman* consisting of Bliss," which is the innermost, is in actuality the "highest individual self" (*paro jīvaḥ*) and that this is equivalent to the sky (III,12).

In the scriptures it is stated that even before the origin of the world the individual self and the absolute self were separate, but it is now held that this is no more than a temporary teaching (*gauṇa*) and should not be understood literally (III, 14). It is thought that the scriptures recognize the origination of the world because in the *Upaniṣads* the creation of the world is likened to pottery being made of clay, implements from copper, or sparks arising from bonfires; but these are temporary pedagogical devices used to make persons in this world aware[2] of the principle of non-duality and also should not be understood literally. It is emphasized that in terms of Absolute Truth differentiated appearances do not exist (III,15).

If that be the case, why is it that in the scriptures not only the principle of Absolute Truth is presented, but many pedagogical devices are also used? Why is it that various contradictory passages exist?

In answer to these questions the authors of the *Kārikā* state that this is because the "spiritual state" of the religious practitioners who receive the teachings differ variously. Among the practitioners there are those in the higher, middle, and lower states. For those in the higher state, i. e. those who excel in spiritual sensitivity, the actual theory of Absolute Truth is directly presented. However, for those in the middle and lower states, i. e. those of middling or dull sensitivity, it is not possible to present the actual theory directly. If that is done, they will resist it and not accept it, or they will destroy it to produce unwanted results. In order to prevent this, readily understandable pedagogical devices must be used. They are thus gradually led up to the actual theory. Hence, it is with compassion for those in the middle and lower states that these pedagogical devices are used. The various teachings concerning reverence (*upāsanā*) presented in the *Upaniṣads* should be understood as having this significance (III,16).

Here one type of solution to the problem of contradictory theories in the *Upaniṣads* is reached. This mode of solution is clearly taken from Buddhism. The idea of pedagogical devices is frequently emphasized in Mahāyāna texts,[3] and the Mādhyamika[4] and Vijñānavāda[5] schools subscribe to it. Hence, it may be surmised that the *Māṇḍūkya-Kārikā* absorbed the Buddhistic idea of pedagogical devices and made it the structural basis for scriptural exegeses in the Vedānta school. This attitude was continued by Śaṅkara,[6] who in his time simply recognized this attitude as quite normal for the Vedānta school.

A similar view is briefly taken up in the fourth chapter. It is asserted that the theory of the origination of the world which exists in the scriptures is temporarily presented for the sake of the realists (*astivastuvādin*) who think that the phenomena which we experience exist in exactly the manner that we experience them.

> "The *Buddhas* taught origination for those who because of their attachments and religious exercises hold that things exist in reality and are afraid of the doctrine of non-origination." (IV,42)

According to Śaṅkara's note, because the *astivastuvādins* are scholars who faithfully follow the scriptures (*śrotriya*), when they hear the theory of non-origination (*ajāti*) they are greatly disturbed because they think it to be a theory which teaches "the destruction of *Ātman*" (*ātmanāśa*). (They are also afraid of the theory of *asparśayoga* — III,39.) Thus, in order to prevent this agitation their attachments are taken into consideration, and in order to help their religious exercises the theory of the creation of the world is temporarily presented. Thus, this theory of origination is, of course, not the true teaching.

Here we can see an attitude similar to that in the Mahāyāna scriptures with regard to their evaluation of Hīnayāna Buddhism. The scholars who literally follow the theories of creation presented in the scriptures approximate the *śramaṇas* (the sages of the Hīnayāna, *śrāvakas*) who are viewed condescendingly in the Mahāyāna scriptures. That they are afraid when they hear the theory of non-origination is similar to the followers of the Hīnayāna who are much disturbed by hearing the Mahāyāna theories.[7] The above-presented *śloka* (IV,42) agrees completely with the theories of the Mādhyamika school.[8] Here there can be no doubt that these ideas and modes of expression in the *Māṇḍūkya-Kārikā* were taken from Mahāyāna texts.

The scripturalists literally follow the passages in the scriptures and believe that the world is actually created from *Ātman*. Is it acceptable to leave them in that state of belief? Since they still do not know the actual teaching is there nothing that can be done? It is quite natural that such questions arise, and the authors of the *Kārikā* answer thus:

> "Those who go astray owing to attachment, being afraid of non-origination, will not be affected in [being attached to] origination. Even if there be faults, they would be small." (IV,43)

Even if they are followers of a shallow view which teaches the creation of the world, they are, in terms of Absolute Truth, within the correct path like those who have acquired the true teaching, i. e. the principle of non-origination. It is held that they are not in error, and even if they are in error, it is only a small one and thus emancipation is possible. Here it is held that all views presented in the scriptures have their own significance and all religious practitioners follow the one true path. "Means are the same as the ultimate end." Here the idea of reconciliation is clearly presented.

This attitude of reconciliation toward the realists who are attached to creation is in the same line of reasoning as the "One Vehicle" idea of the *Saddharma-puṇḍarīka-sūtra*. The *Saddharma-puṇḍarīka-sūtra* is representative of the scriptures which present such ideas of reconciliation (*Versöhnung*). In its introduction, with a grand plot and using an elegant literary style, it proclaims that here the *Buddha*'s "Discourse on the Great *Dharma*" (*mahā dharmanirdeśa*)[9] is presented. But no abstract philosophical thinking is to be recognized in the first half of the *sūtra*. Only the fact that all the various teachings of the *Buddha* arrive at the One Vehicle is repeated in elegant style and through various similes. Thus one attempts in vain to find in it a particular philosophical system.[10] The famous passage on the ten factors of existence is not, as has been frequently maintained in China and Japan, a discussion of ten categories; it is no more than an emphasis on the fact that the true nature of the *dharmas* is known only to the *Tathāgata*.[11] (In *śloka* IV.80 of the *Māṇḍūkya-Kārikā* it is stated similarly that the unborn and non-dual sameness is "the field of activity of the *Buddhas*" [*viṣayaḥ buddhānām*].) In the fact that the *Saddharma-puṇḍarīka-sūtra* does not present any particular philosophical theory we can conversely recognize the great philosophic standpoint of the *Saddharma-puṇḍarīka-sūtra*. The first half of the *Saddharma-puṇḍarīka-sūtra* places extraordinary emphasis on the fact that the three vehicles of the *śrāvakas*, *pratyekabuddhas*, and *bodhisattvas* are really one vehicle and expends great energy in expounding only this fact. These "three vehicles" may be seen as the three leading teachings in existence at the time of compilation of this *sūtra*, and the *Saddharma-puṇḍarīka-sūtra* recognizes the role and significance of each, emphasizing that each is a vehicle of salvation offered by the compassion of the *Buddha*. Its basic view is that "there is only One Vehicle, not two or three." That is, it had previously been generally understood that the three vehicles were separate, but this is only a superficial view. Each is a pedagogical method presented by the *Buddha* to lead his followers, and in truth there is only one vehicle. This contrasts markedly with early Buddhism, which strongly criticizes Hīnayāna Buddhism. The attitude of reconciliation in the

Saddharma-puṇḍarīka-sūtra is a thorough going one. Even the *Śrāvakas* who have heard and accepted only one *śloka* will no doubt be able to become *Buddhas*.[12] Those who build *stūpas* or worship *Buddha* relics or statues are all on the *Buddha*-path and can attain enlightenment. Even more, even those who in play pretend to build *stūpas* in the sand and children who scratch out pictures of the *Buddha* on walls are all saved by the compassion of the *Buddha*. Even if their minds are in confusion, if they once recite "salutation to the *Buddha*" (*namo 'stu buddhāna*) before a *Buddha* image or *stūpa*, they attain highest enlightenment (*agrabodhi*).[13]

In this manner, it may be said that insofar that it recognizes that there is absolute significance in those who follow lower theories, the previously presented *śloka* IV,43 of the *Māṇḍūkya-Kārikā* is compatible with the views of the *Saddharma-puṇḍarīka-sūtra*. In that *śloka* the mistaken evaluation and attachment to lower pedagogical methods as Absolute Truth is called an error (*doṣa*). In the same manner the *Saddharma-puṇḍarīka-sūtra* holds that Śāriputra and the five hundred *arhats* revering Hīnayāna teachings were in error (*atyaya, aparādha*).[14] Hence, on this point too one can see agreement between the two.[15] Thus, I feel that there is no objection to holding that the views of the *Saddharma-puṇḍarīka-sūtra* or views similar to them influenced the *Māṇḍūkya-Kārikā*.

However, we must note here that the reconciliatory views of the *Saddharma-puṇḍarīka-sūtra*, which recognize an absolute significance in all paths, are limited to theories within Buddhism. The *Saddharma-puṇḍarīka-sūtra* vigorously refutes non-Buddhistic systems of religious practice. The *sūtra* repeatedly emphasizes that other systems must not be approached.[16] Thus the reconciliatory views of the *sūtra* are applicable only within Buddhism, and it is held that all other systems should be abandoned, their truth being not even partially accepted. In this lies a pronounced difference with the views of the second chapter of the *Māṇḍūkya-Kārikā*. As previously stated, according to the second chapter of the *Māṇḍūkya-Kārikā* all thoughts appear through the self-differentiation of *Ātman*. Thus, it is stated that their truth can be accepted to this degree, but that no concept can fully grasp the true form of *Ātman*. According to the standpoint of the second chapter, heretical views such as Buddhism, Jainism, Lokāyata, and the

Vedic scriptures which determine rites and festivals are essentially not different from each other. They are all based on the illusion (*māyā, saṃmoha*) of the deity as *Ātman*. The metaphysics of the *Māṇḍūkya-Kārikā* was to this degree able to explain the reason for the existence of heretical theories which contradict the scriptures. But as a result it was placed in a position in which it became impossible to demonstrate the reason for any special absolute significance in the Vedic scriptures which it reveres. The *Saddharma-puṇḍarīka-sūtra,* on the other hand, clarifies the raison d'être for the various theories within Buddhism and is able to establish the absoluteness of the "One Path" teaching, but it does not at all touch on the problem of why many other non-Buddhistic teachings were formed. It simply leaves the problem in its unsolved state. That is, the solution of this problem was left for Buddhistic scholars of later periods. The Mādhyamika school sees the reason for the formation of various non-Buddhistic views in the fact that they do not comprehend the true meaning of "*śūnya*" and posit various particularistic actualities. The Consciousness-only school, on the other hand, explains that because such schools theorize about self and *dharmas* various types of heretical theories are formed.

However, both the Mādhyamika and the Consciousness-only schools are explicit in regarding non-Buddhistic systems as heretical and view them as false theories which do not reach the true principle. Thus, in this regard they are identical with the *Saddharma-puṇḍarīka-sūtra* in holding that only the theories within Buddhism are accurate. Their attitude of reconciliation did not extend beyond Buddhism. The work which advanced from this position to evaluate the significance of non-Buddhistic views was the *Mahā-nirvāṇa-sūtra*.

> "And the Buddha admonished Kāśyapa: The various differing theories, cults, charms, words, etc., are all the teaching of the *Buddha*; they are not heretical."[17]

Here we reach a point where all alien theories are considered to be essentially Buddhistic.[18] Here Buddhism is no longer a particular philosophy in opposition to other systems; here Buddhism is the absolute principle itself. That which is called "alien theories" is no more than manifestations of one point or aspect of its ultimate principle. The view that there is a difference between Buddhism and other theories is a relative view, and it is held that from the standpoint of the Absolute, there exists in the universe only the one teaching of Buddhism. We may say that this view rests on a line of thinking identical with that of the second chapter of the *Māṇḍūkya-Kārikā.*

From the above discussion it is clear that long before Śaṅkara there was formulated the view which holds that those who revere the scriptures — even if they follow different theories or undertake different religious exercises — ultimately come to the same point. It is said that this view was first formulated by the late Vedānta school -- for example by Kṛṣṇamiśra (11th cent.) in his *Prabodhacandrodaya*— but in actuality its early developments reach back to a fairly ancient period.[19]

In earlier sections we treated the *Māṇḍūkya-Upaniṣad* and each of the four chapters of the *Kārikā* as separate units and conducted a textual analysis of them. There we hypothesized that each was compiled successively. Here, as a result of our examination of their philosophical content and from the perspective of the separate problems examined, I feel that we have made clear the historical development in thought among the separate units.

Notes

1) For example, cf. the fragment by Draviḍa (12). supra.
2) In I, 18 there appears the view that in explanations passages are cited in order to teach the people.
3) This view appears in a particularly strong form in the chapter "*Upāya-kauśalya*" of the *Saddharma-puṇḍarīka-sūtra*. Further, in Mahāyāna Buddhism the idea of complete and incomplete manifestation of the true principle is based on this mode of thinking.
4) According to Candrakīrti, the *Madhyamaka-śāstra* of Nāgārjuna also accepts that the Buddha's teachings are adjusted to the listener (XVIII,6 ; XXII,11). That is, in accordance with the high, middle, and low abilities of the followers, different teachings are propounded in order to bring them to the truth (*hīnamadhyotkṛṣṭavineyajanānujighṛkṣayā*) (*Mvṛ*. p.357, *l*.2- p.358, *l*.6 ; p.444, *ll*.4-6 ; p.371, *l*.14 ; p.547, *l*.14). *buddho 'vadat tathā dharmaṃ vineyānām yathākṣamam*/— *Mvṛ*. p.359, *l*.12 (Poussin takes this to be a citation from Nāgārjuna's works ; cf. n. 5.) Cf. also Part VII, Chapter II, Section 1, Sub-Section 4, where Nāgārjuna is cited.
5) For example, cf. *MSA*. XVI, 69 ; 76.

6) *na hy avikāre 'nante brahmaṇi sarvaiḥ puṃbhiḥ śakyā buddhiḥ sthāpayituṃ mandamadhyamottamabuddhitvāt puṃsām iti*/(Ś. ad *BS*. III, 2, 33, vol.II, p.237, *ll*.8-10); *hīnamadhyamottamabhāvena hi prāṇibhedān vidadhata īśvarasya* (Ś. ad *BS*. II, 2, 37. vol. I, p.603, *l*.1).

7) For examples from Mahāyāna scriptures, cf. notes to IV, 42 in Part VI, Chapter I, Section II, Sub-Section 4 of this book.

8) Cf. notes to *GK* IV, 42 in Part VI, Chapter I, Section II, Sub-Section 4 of this book.

9) *Saddh. P*. p.15, *l*.10.

10) Cf. Tominaga Nakamoto's *Shutsujō Kōgo*, "Zatsu" 25. Tominaga (1715-46) was the first intellectual in Japan to study Buddhist scriptures without being guided by traditional religious views or by anti-Buddhist views, said of the *Saddharma-puṇḍarīka-sūtra* as cited above.

11) The fact that the passages of the *jūnyoze* of the *Saddharma-puṇḍarīka-sūtra* are extremely different in the Sanskrit version and the various translations indicates that they do not discuss categories. The emphasis in the Chinese versions that only the *Buddha* realizes them does not differ from p.116, *l*.16 ff. in the *Saddharma-puṇḍarīka-sūtra*.

12) *Saddh. P*. II, *gāthā*, 53.

13) *Saddh. P*. II, *gāthā*, 76 ff.

14) *Saddh. P*. p.59, *l*.15; p.185, *l*.7.

15) Other examples concerning great disciples cite Draviḍa, etc. Cf. Part V, Chapter VI. The beginnings of such reconciliatory views may be seen in the *Bhagavad-Gītā* VII,21; IX,23. However, there are no expressions of rejoicing that there is deep reflection or solution of the problem of overcoming the opposition in world-views.

16) "When the *Bodhisattva Mahāsattva* Mañjuśrī does not serve, not court, not wait upon kings; does not serve, not court, not wait upon princes; when he does not approach them; when he does not serve, not court, not wait upon persons of another sect, *carakas, parivrajakas, jīvakas, nirgranthas*, nor persons passionately fond of fine literature; when he does not serve, not court, not wait upon adepts of worldly spells, and votaries of a worldly philosophy, nor keep any intercourse with them" —(*Saddh.P*. XIII, "Sukhavihāra").Further, admonitions with the same meaning are presented in the chapter "*Aupamya*" (*Saddh. P*. III, v. 148) and the chapter "*Samantabhadrotsāhana*."

17) "*Mahā-nirvāṇa-Sūtra*" (Southern recension), Chapter VIII (Taishō Tripiṭaka, vol. 12, p.653c).

18) However, the view that all theories which are accepted in this world are Buddhistic theories existed before Nāgārjuna. See Taishō Tripiṭaka, vol. 25, p.66b.

19) Farquhar: *Outline*, p.228. Such views are also conspicuous in the "Various Paths" (*Prasthānabheda*). Cf. Madhusūdana-sarasvatī.

PART VII

THE VEDĀNTA PHILOSOPHY OF THE GRAMMARIAN BHARTṚHARI

INTRODUCTION

The philosophy of language was initiated in India, and it is needless to discuss Bhartṛhari's thought as a whole anew. In the following I would like to point out and discuss some features of his thought which seem to be relevant to the development of pre-Śaṅkara Vedānta philosophy.

Since the present work was published in Japanese, some studies on the Indian philosophy of language, especially on the thought of Bhartṛhari,[1] have been published. Their details are as follows:[2]

[On Indian Philosophy of Language]

BROUGH, John

1951 "Theories of General Linguistics in the Sanskrit Grammarians," *Transactions of the Philological Society*, 1951, Oxford, pp.27-46. [Reprinted in *A Reader on the Sanskrit Grammarians*, edited by J. F. Staal, Massachussets Institute of Technology, 1972. Indian edition: Delhi, Motilal Banarsidass 1985, pp.402-414.]

1953 "Some Indian Theories of Meaning," *Transactions of the Philological Society*, 1953, Oxford, pp.164-167. [Reprinted in *A Reader on the Sanskrit Grammarians*, edited by J. F. Staal, Massachussets Institute of Technology, 1972. Indian edition: Delhi, Motilal Banarsidass 1985, pp.414-423.]

CARDONA, George

1976 *Pāṇini. A Survey of Research*, The Hague, Mouton & Co. [Indian reprint: Delhi, Motilal Banarsidass 1980.]

1983 *Linguistic Analysis and Some Indian Traditions*, Pandit Shripad Deodhar Memorial Lectures (First Series), BORI Post-Graduate and Research Department Series, No.20, Poona.

CHATTERJEE, Chinmayi

1983 *Pāṇinidarśanam as Included in the Sarvadarśanasaṃgraha of Mādhavācārya along with Bengali and English Translations*,

Sanskrit Commentary by Mahāmahopādhyāya Vasudev Śāstrī Abhyankar, and Expository Editorial Notes, Calcutta, Jadavpur University.

CHOUDURI, M. N.

1959 *Kāvya Tattva Samīkṣā, Philosophy of Poetry*, Delhi, Motilal Banarsidass. (Rhetoric has close relation to the philosophy of language.)

COWARD, Harold G., and K. Kunjunni RAJA(ed.)

1990 *Encyclopedia of Indian Philosophies, Vol. V : The Philosophy of the Grammarians*, Delhi, Motilal Banarsidass.

JAINI, Padmanabh S.

1959 "The Vaibhāṣika Theory of Words," *BSOAS*. vol.XXII, part 1, 1959, pp.95-107. (The philosophy of language among the Sarvāstivādins is noteworthy.)

MATILAL, Bimal Krishna

1985 *Logic, Language and Reality : An Introduction to Indian Philosophical Studies*, Delhi, Motilal Banarsidass.

1990a *The Word and the World : India's Contribution to the Study of Language*, Delhi, Oxford University Press.

ORUI, Jun

1965 *Toyogaku Kenkyū*, vol.I, p.17. (This is an article on the essence of the word.)

PANDEYA, R. C.

1963 *The Problem of Meaning in Indian Philosophy*, Delhi, Motilal Banarsidass. (Reviewed by V. Varadachari : *Adyar Library Bulletin*, vol. 37, part 1, 1965, pp. 162-164.)

RAJA, K. Kunjunni

1956 *Adyar L.B.* vol.XX, pp.345-348.(In some texts of the Vijñānavādins the transfer of meanings was admitted.)

1963 *Indian Theories of Meaning*, Adyar, Adyar Library and Research Centre. (Reviewed by J. C. Wright : *BSOAS*. vol. XXVIII, part 1, 1965, pp. 162-164.)

RUEGG, David Seyfort

1959 *Contribution à l'histoire de la philosophie linguistique indienne*,

Publications de l'Institut de Civilisation Indienne. Fascicule 7. Paris, E. de Boggard, Éditeur. (Reviewed by B. Sheft : *JAOS*. vol. 80, 1960. pp. 259-60 ; reply by Ruegg : *JAOS*. vol. 81, 1961, pp. 65-68 ; other reviews : M. Biardeau : *Indo-Iranian Journal*, vol. 4, 1960. pp. 170-172 ; J. F. Staal : *Philosophy East and West*, vol. 10, 1960, pp. 53-57 ; C. Pensa, *East and West*, vol. 14, 1963, pp. 105-107.)

SASTRI, Gaurinath

1959 *The Philosophy of Word and Meaning : Some Indian Approaches with Special Reference to the Philosophy of Bhartṛhari*, Calcutta Sanskrit College Research Series, No. 5. Calcutta, Sanskrit College. (Reviewed by D. Seyfort Ruegg : *Indo-Iranian Journal*, vol. 4. 1960, pp. 173-179.)

SASTRI, P. S.

1958/59 "Nature of Meaning," *Journal of the Ganganatha Jha Research Institute*, part 1-2, pp.5-38.

SCHARFE, Hartmut

1977 *Grammatical Literature*, vol. 5.2 of *A History of Indian Literature*, Wiesbaden, Otto Harrassowitz.

STAAL, J. F.

1969 "Sanskrit Philosophy of Language," *Current Trends in Linguistics*, 5, edited by Thomas A. Sebeok. The Hague, Paris, Mouton & Co, pp.499-531.

1976 "Sanskrit Philosophy of Language," *History of Linguistic Thought and Contemporary Linguistics*, edited by Herman Parret. Berlin, New York, Walter de Gruyter, pp.102-136.

1988 *Universals : Studies in Indian Logic and Linguistics*, Chicago, The University of Chicago.

[On the Thought of Bhartṛhari]

CHAKRAVARTI, P.

1934 *Journal of the Department of Letters, University of Calcutta*, vol. XXV.

COWARD, Harold G.

1976 *Bhartṛhari*, Boston, Twayne Publishers. (In this work Bhartṛhari is located and evaluated in the history of philosophy in general. Reviewed by T. K. Mahadevan: "A Wittgenstein too Early: Bhartṛhari and Indian Linguistic Philosophy," *Indian and Foreign Review*, vol. 15, No. 19, 15 July 1978, p.24.)

DESHPANDE, Madhav M.

1992 "Bhartṛhari," *Philosophy of Language: An International Handbook of Contemporary Research*, edited by M. Dascal, D. Gerhardus, K. Lorenz & G. Meggle. Berlin - New York, Walter de Gruyter. Vol. 1, pp.269-278.)

GANGULI, Hemanta Kumar

1963 *Philosophy of Logical Construction: An Examination of Logical Atomism and Logical Positivism in the Light of the Philosophies of Bhartṛhari, Dharmakīrti and Prajñākaragupta*, Calcutta.

HERZBERGER, Radhika

1986a *Bhartṛhari and the Buddhists: An Essay in the Development of 5th and 6th Century Indian Thought*. Studies of Classical India, vol. 8, Dordrecht, Reidel.

IYER, K. A. Subramania

1982 *The Vākyapadīya: Some Problems*, Professor K. V. Abhyankar Memorial Lectures (First Series), BORI Post-Graduate and Research Department Series, no 14, Poona.

PANDEY, Sangam Lal

1974 *Pre-Śaṃkara Advaita Philosophy*, Allahabad, Darshan Peeth, pp. 330-359. (In the tradition of the philosophy of language, Bhartṛhari is an outstanding figure. His Vedāntic thought is discussed comprehensively in this study.)

PATNAIK, Tandra

1994 *Śabda: A Study of Bhartṛhari's Philosophy of Language*, New Delhi, D. K. Printworld.

SASTRI Gaurinath

1991 *The Philosophy of Bhartṛhari*, Delhi-Varanasi, Bharatiya Vidya Prakashan.

VARMA, Satya Kam

1968 *Bhāṣātattva aur Vākyapadīya*, Dillī, Bhāratīya Prakāśan. (In Hindī.)

1976 *Studies in Indology*, New Delhi, Bharatiya Prakashan.

[On *Pratibhā* or Sentence-Meaning]

AKAMATSU, Akihiko

1992 "The Evolution of Linguistic Theory in Classical India," *Jinbun Gakuho*, Kyoto University, no.60, pp.203-227. [In Japanese.]

1993 "*Pratibhā* and the Meaning of the Sentence in Bhartṛhari's *Vākyapadīya*," *Asiatische Studien/Études Asiatiques*, no 47.1, pp.37-43. [Indian reprint: *Bhartṛhari, Philosopher and Grammarian*, edited by Saroja Bhate & Johannes Bronkhorst. Delhi, Motilal Banarsidass 1994.]

DRAGONETTI, Carmen and Fernando TOLA

1990 "Some Remarks on Bhartṛhari's Concept of *Pratibhā*," *Journal of Indian Philosophy*, Dordrecht, No.18, pp.95-112.

GONDA, Jan

1963 *The Vision of the Vedic Poets*, The Hague, Mouton & Co. [Chapter XV: "*Pratibhā*," pp.318-348.]

HARADA, Waso

1987 "Intuition and Self Cognition as the Denotation of a Word (I): Dignāga vs. Bhartṛhari (1)," *Bukkyo Gakkaiho*, Koyasan, No.13, pp.22-39. [In Japanese.]

1989a "Intuition and Self Cognition as the Denotation of a Word (II): Dignāga vs. Bhartṛhari (1)," *Bukkyo Gakkaiho*, Koyasan, No.14, pp.69-83. [In Japanese.]

1990 "Intuition and Self Cognition as the Denotation of a Word (III): Dignāga vs. Bhartṛhari (1)," *Bukkyo Gakkaiho*, Koyasan, No.15, pp.27-53. [In Japanese.]

1991 "Intuition and Self Cognition as the Denotation of a Word (IV): Dignāga vs. Bhartṛhari (1)," *Bukkyo Gakkaiho*, Koyasan, No.16, pp.29-53. [In Japanese.]

1992 "Intuition and Self Cognition as the Denotation of a Word (V): Dignāga vs. Bhartṛhari (1)," *Bukkyo Gakkaiho*, Koyasan, No.17, pp.25-57. [In Japanese.]

HATTORI Masaaki

1977 "The Sautrāntika Background of the *Apoha* Theory," *Buddhist Thought and Asian Civilization* (Essays in Honor of Herbert V. Guenther on his Sixtieth Birthday), edited by Leslie S. Kawamura and Keith Scott, Emeryville, California, Dharma Publishing, pp.47-58.

1980 "*Apoha* and *Pratibhā*," *Sanskrit and Indian Studies* (Essays in Honour of Daniel H. H. Ingalls), edited by M. Nagatomi et al., Studies of Classical India, vol.2, Dordrecht, D. Reidel, pp.61-73.

1987 "Indo Gengo Tetsugaku ni okeru Ningenkan" ("The Concept of Man in the Linguistic Philosophy of Classical India"), *Toyo ni okeru Ningenkan*, edited by S. Mayeda, Tokyo, The University of Tokyo Press, pp.181-200. [In Japanese.]

1993a "Kamalaśīla's Interpretation of Some Verses in the *Vākyakāṇḍa* of Bhartṛhari's *Vākyapadīya*," *Asiatische Studien/Etudes Asiatiques*, no. 47.1, Proceedings of the First International Conference on Bhartṛhari, Pune, January 6-8, 1992, pp.135-140. Indian reprint: *Bhartṛhari, Philosopher and Grammarian*, edited by Saroja Bhate & Johannes Bronkhorst. Delhi, Motilal Banarsidass, 1994.

1993b "The Verses Quoted from the *Vākyapadīya* I in the *Tattvasaṃgraha* XVI," *Chi no Kaiko - Bukkyo to Kagaku*, Tokyo, pp.365-375.

IYER, K. A. Subramania

1941 "*Pratibhā* as the Meaning of a Sentence," *Proceedings of the All-India Oriental Conference*, 10, Tirupati, 1940, Madras, pp.326-332.

1980/1 "Bhartṛhari on the Sentence," *Adyar Library Bulletin*, Madras, No.44/45, pp.15-49.

JOSHI, S. D.

1977 "Bhartṛhari's Concept of *Pratibhā*: A Theory on the Nature of Language Acquisition," *Some Aspects of Indo-Iranian Cultural Traditions* (Commemoration Volume of Dr. V. G. Paranjpe), Delhi, pp.71-76.

KAVIRAJ, Gopinath

1924 "The Doctrine of *Pratibhā* in Indian Philosophy," *Annals of the Bhandarkar Oriental Research Institute*, no. V, pp.1-18 & 113-132. [3 : "*Vyākaraṇa*," pp.11-18.]

KUANPOONPOL, Priyawat

1991 *Pratibhā : The Concept of Intuition in the Philosophy of Abhinavagupta*, Doctoral Dissertation, Harvard University. [Available on microfilm.]

MURTI, P. Srirama

1992 "*Pratibhā, Sphoṭa* and *Dhvani*," *Language and Text* (Studies in Honour of Ashok R. Kelkar), Delhi, Kaliṅga Publications, pp.51-56.

PATNAIK, Tandra

1988 "Language, Thought and Communication : An Appraisal of Bhartṛhari's Theory of Language," *Indian Philosophical Quarterly*, Poona, no.15 (3) : pp.349-368.

1989 "Some Reflections on Bhartṛhari's Notion of Sentence Meaning," *Visva Bharati Journal of Philosophy*, nos.24.2 (Feb. 1988) & 25.1 (August 1988), pp.118-129.

RAJA, K. Kunjunni

1961 "Bhartṛhari's List of Sentence-Definitions : The Textual Problem," Summaries of Papers, All India Oriental Conference 21, (Srinagar 1961), Srinagar, pp.197-198.

1962 "Bhartṛhari's List of Sentence-Definitions," *Adyar Library Bulletin*, Madras, no.26, pp.206-210.

RUKMANI, T. S.

1987 "Patañjali's *Prajñā* and Bhartṛhari's *Pratibhā* : A Comparative Study," *Indian Philosophical Quarterly*, Poona, no.14 (1), pp.81-90.

SHRIRAMAMURTI, P.

1980a "Grammarians and Literary Critics on *Pratibhā* in Sanskrit," *Proceedings of the All-India Oriental Conference*, 29 (Poona 1978), Poona, pp.301-305.

1980b "The Meaning of the Sentence is *Pratibhā*," *Proceedings of the Winter Institute on Ancient Indian Theories on Sentence-Meaning*, (Held in March 1979), edited by S. D. Joshi, Pune,

University of Poona, pp.9-16.

VARMA, Satya Kam

1980 "Sentence-Meaning according to Bhartṛhari," *Proceedings of the Winter Institute on Ancient Indian Theories on Sentence-Meaning*, (Held in March 1979). edited by S. D. Joshi, Pune, University of Poona, pp.17-37

1984 "Definition of Sentence: Bhartṛhari's View," *International Journal of Dravidian Linguistics*, no.13.1, pp.171-176.

[On *Sphoṭa*]

BHATTACHARYA, Ram Shankar

1958 "Some Broad Aspects of Indian Grammar and the Theory of *Sphoṭa*," *Journal of the Gangānātha Jhā Research Institute*, Allahabad, No.15, pp.83-92.

BRONKHORST, Johannes

1991a "Studies on Bhartṛhari 3: Bhartṛhari on *sphoṭa* and Universals," *Asiatische Studien/Études Asiatiques*, No.45.1, pp.5-18.

COWARD, Harold (G.)

1980 *Sphoṭa Theory of Language*, Delhi, Motilal Banarsidass.

1994 "Kumārila's Theory of Word Meaning in Relation to the *Sphoṭa* Theory of Bhartṛhari," *Studies in Mīmāṃsā*, Dr. Mandan Mishra Felicitation Volume. Ed. R. S. Dwivedi. Delhi, Motilal Banarsidass, pp.215-219.

DANGE, Sadashiv A.

1980 "*Sphoṭa* - A Reappraisal," *Proceedings of the Winter Institute on Ancient Indian Theories on Sentence-Meaning* (Held in March 1979), Edited by S. D. Joshi. Pune, University of Poona, pp.69-78.

DASH, Narendra Kumar

1988 "*Sphoṭatattvasamīkṣā*," *Viśva-saṃskṛtam*, Hoshiapur, No.25. [In Sanskrit.]

IYER, K. A. Subramania

1937 "Who are the *anityasphoṭavādins*?," *Proceedings of the All-India Oriental Conference* 8 (Mysore 1935), Bangalore, pp.258-263.

1947 "The Doctrine of *Sphoṭa*," *Journal of the Gangānātha Jhā*

Research Institute, No.5, pp.121-147.

JOSHI, S. D.

1967 *The Sphoṭanirṇaya of Kauṇḍa Bhaṭṭa*, Centre of Advanced Study in Sanskrit, University of Poona, Class C, No.2.

KAPILA DEVA Śāstrī

1968 "*Vaiyākaraṇānāṃ sphoṭavādāḥ*," *Viśva-saṃskṛtam*, Hoshiarpur, No.4, pp.40-51. [In Sanskrit.]

MATILAL, Bimal Krishna

1992 "The *Sphoṭa* Doctrine of the Indian Grammarians," *Philosophy of Language : An International Handbook of Contemporary Research*, edited by M. Dascal, D. Gerhardus, K. Lorenz & G. Meggle. Berlin - New York, Walter de Gruyter. Vol.1, pp.609-620.

MISHRA, K. K.

1986 "Bhartṛhari's Theory of *Sphoṭa*," *Indologica Taurinensia*, No.13, 1985-86, pp.115-121.

MURTI, P. Srirama

1992 "*Pratibhā*, *Sphoṭa* and *Dhvani*," *Language and Text* (Studies in Honour of Ashok R. Kelkar), Delhi, Kalinga Publications, pp.51-56.

PALSULE, G. B.

1993 "Points of Agreement and Difference between the *Vākyapadīya* and the *Mahābhāṣya-Dīpikā* in the Matter of *Sphoṭa*," *Asiatische Studien/Études Asiatiques*, No.47.1, pp.215-220. [Indian reprint : *Bhartṛhari : Philosopher and Grammarian*, edited by Saroja Bhate & Johannes Bronkhorst. Delhi, Motilal Banarsidass 1994.]

1994 "*Sphoṭa* in Bhartṛhari's Linguistic Philosophy," *Vācaspatyam* (Pt. Vamanshastri Bhagwat Felicitation Volume), Pune, Vaidika Samshodhana Mandala, pp.128-131.

PATHIRAJ, R.

1995 "The *Sphoṭa* Doctrine of Bhartṛhari," *Indian Philosophical Quarterly*, Poona, No.22 (1), pp.67-74.

PATNAIK, Tandra

1991 "A Note on Bhartṛhari's Theory of *Sphoṭa*," *Prajñā* (*Research*

Bulletin of the Department of Philosophy, Uktal University, Bhubaneswar, No.11, pp.59-65.

PUSHPENDRA, Kumar

1984 "Bhartṛhari's Theory of *Sphoṭa*," *Linguistic Thought in Ancient India*, ed. by Pushpendra Kumar, Delhi, Nag Publishers, pp.117-124.

SASTRI, Gaurinatha

1937 "A Study in the Dialectics of *Sphoṭa*," *Journal of the Department of Letters*, No.29, University of Calcutta. [See 1980 for a rewritten version.]

1980 *A Study in the Dialectics of Sphoṭa*, Delhi, Motilal Banarsidass.

[On *Dhvani*]

IYER, K. A. S.

1956 *ABORI*. vol.46, pp.49-65.

KAMIMURA Katsuhiko

1974 *Tohogaku*, No.48, July, pp.1-12.

[On Time]

VRAT, S.

1958 *ABORI*. vol.39, pp.68-78.

[On the Simile]

CHATURVEDI, Kākatālīya Mithilesh

1974 *Śri Venkateswara University Oriental Journal*, Tirupati, vol.17, parts 1 and 2, Jan.- Dec., pp.93-99.

[On Compounds]

CHATURVEDI, Mithilesh

1975 "Bhartṛhari on the Number of Words to be Compounded Simultaneously," *Indological Studies, Journal of the Department of Sanskrit*, University of Delhi, vol.3, Nos.1-2, Dec. pp.31-38.

[On the *Vākyapadīya*]

1. Editions

(1) *Vākyapadīya* (*3rd Kāṇḍa*) *with the Commentary of Helārāja*, ed. by K. Sāmbaśiva Sāstrī. Trivandrum Sanskrit Series, no. CXVI. Trivandrum, 1935. (*Sādhana-samuddeśa* up to *Liṅga-samuddeśa* of *Prakīrṇaka*.)

(2) *The Vākyapadīya, with the Commentary of Helārāja* (*3rd Kāṇḍa*), ed. by Vaidyaśāstanipuṇaḥ L. A. Ravi Varmā. University of Travancore Sanskrit Series, no. CXLVIII. Trivandrum 1942. (Vṛttisamuddeśa)[3]

(3) *The Vākyapadīya. A Treatise on the Philosophy of Sanskrit Grammar by Bhartri Hari* [sic]. (*Brahma Kāṇḍa*). Edited with the *Bhāvapradīpa* commentary and notes by Sūryanārāyaṇa Śukla [sic]. Kashi Sanskrit Series 124, Benares 1937. [Reprinted with Hindī commentary etc. by Rāmagovinda Śukkla. Varanasi 1961.] (*YR-List*. No.6 [No.7].)[4]

(4) *Vākyapadīya Part I* (*Brahmakāṇḍam*), with the Commentaries *Svopajñaṭvṛtti* by Harivṛṣabha & *Ambākartrī* by Padmaśrī Pt. Raghunātha Śarmā. Sarasvatī Bhavana Granthamālā, vol. 91, Varanasi, Sampūrṇānanda Saṃskṛta Viśvavidyālaya, 1963. (*YR-List*. No.8a.)

(5) *Vākyapadīyam Part II* (*Vākyakāṇḍam*), with the Commentary *Ambākartrī* by Raghunātha Śarmā. Sarasvatī Bhavana Granthamālā, vol. 91, Varanasi, Sampūrṇānanda Saṃskṛta Viśvavidyālaya, 1968. (*YR-List*. No.8b.)

(6) *Vākyapadīyam Part III* (*Pada Kāṇḍa*) (*Jāti, Dravya and Saṃbandha Samuddeśa*), with the Commentary *Prakāśa* by Helārāja and *Ambākartrī* by Pt. Raghunātha Śarmā. Sarasvatī Bhavana Granthamālā, vol. 91, Varanasi, Sampūrṇānanda Ṣaṃskṛta Viśvavidyālaya, 1974. (*YR-List*. No.8c.)

(7) *Vākyapadīyam Part III, Vol. II*, (*Bhūyodravya-Guṇa-Dik-Sādhana-Kriyā-Kāla-Puruṣa-Saṃkhyā-Upagraha-and Liṅga-Samuddeśa*), with the Commentary *Prakāśa* by Helārāja and *Ambākartrī* by Pt. Raghunātha Śarmā. Sarasvatī Bhavana Granthamālā, vol. 91, Varanasi, Sampūrṇānanda Saṃskṛta Viśvavidyālaya, 1979. (*YR-List*. No.8d.)

(8) *Vākyapadīyam Part III*, (*Padakāṇḍa*) (*Vṛttisamuddeśa*), with the Commentary *Prakāśa* by Helārāja and *Ambākartrī* by Pt. Raghunātha Śarmā. Sarasvatī Bhavana Granthamālā, vol. 91, Varanasi, Sampūrṇānandasaṃskṛtaviśvavidyālaya. 1977. (*YR-List*, No.8e.)

(9) *Vākyapadīya of Bhartṛhari with the Commentary of Helārāja. Kāṇḍa III*,

Part I. Edited by K.A. Subramania Iyer. Deccan College Monograph Series 21, Poona, 1963 [III.1.1- III.7 end]. (*YR List*. No.9a.)

(10) *Vākyapadīya of Bhartṛhari with the Commentaries Vṛtti and the Paddhati of Vṛṣabhadeva, Kāṇḍa I*. Critically edited by K.A. Subramania Iyer. Deccan College Monograph Series 32, Poona, 1966. (*YR-List*. No.9b.)

(11) *Vākyapadīya of Bhartṛhari with the Prakīrṇaprakāśa of Helārāja. Kāṇḍa III, Part II*. Critically Edited by K.A. Subramania Iyer. Poona, 1973. [III.8. 1 - III.14 end]. (*YR-List*. No.9c.)

(12) *Vākyapadīya of Bhartṛhari (An Ancient Treatise on the Philosophy of Sanskrit Grammar). Containing the Ṭīkā of Puṇyarāja and the Ancient Vṛtti*. Edited by K. A. Subramania Iyer. With a Foreword by Ashok Aklujkar. *Kāṇḍa* II, Delhi, Motilal Banarsidass, 1983. (*YR-List*. No.18.)

(13) *Bhartṛhari. Vākyapadīya Brahmakāṇḍa. Avec la Vṛtti de Harivṛṣabha. Texte Reproduit de l'édition de Lahore*. Traduction, Introduction et Notes par Madeleine Biardeau. Publications de l'Institut de Civilisation Indienne, Serie in-8, fascicule 24, Paris, de Boccard, 1964. (*YR-List*. No.10.)

(14) *Vākyapadīya of Bhartṛhari*. Edited by K.V. Abhyankar and V. P. Limaye. University of Poona Sanskrit and Prakrit Series, Volume II, Poona, 1965. (Annotations are detailed, and the index is convenient.) (*YR-List*. No.11.)

(15) *Śrīmadbhartṛhariviracitaṃ Svopajñaṭīkāsamanvitaṃ Vākyapadīyam (Brahmakāṇḍam)*. Ed. by Pandit Vāmana Bālakrishna Bhagavata. Grantha-Saṃśodhana-Prakāśana-Maṇḍala, Publication No.2, Tilak Maharashtra Vidyapeeth, Poona, 1965. [Text and Marathi translation.] (*YR-List*. No.12.)

(16) *Vākyapadīyam* (*Brahmakāṇḍa*) *of Shri Bhartṛhari, The Great Linguist & Grammarian, with Trilingual Commentary* by Dr. Satyakam Varma. New Delhi, Munshi Ram Manohar Lal, 1970. [Sanskrit - English - Hindi.] (*YR-List*. No.13.)

(17) *The Vākyapadīya. Critical Text of Cantos I and II [with English Translation, Summary of Ideas and Notes]*. By K. Raghavan Pillai. Delhi, Motilal Banarsidass, 1971 (Studies in the *Vākyapadīya*, vol.I). (*YR-List*. No. 14.)

(18) *Bhartṛharis Vākyapadīya. Die mūlakārikās nach den Handschriften herausgegeben und mit einem Pāda-Index*, versehen von Wilhelm Rau.

Abhandlungen für die Kunde des Morgenlandes XLII, 4, Wiesbaden, Franz Steiner, 1977. (*YR-List*. No.16a.)

(19) *Bhartṛharis Vākyapadīya. Vollständiger Wortindex zu den mūlakārikās*, von Wilhelm Rau. Akademie der Wissenschaften und der Literatur, Abhandlungen der Geistes- und Sozialwissenschaftlichen Klasse, Jahrgang 1988, No. 11, Stuttgart, Franz Steiner Verlag, 1988. (*YR-List*. No.16b.)

(20) *Bhartṛharis Vākyapadīya II : Text der Palmblatt-Handschrift Trivandrum S. N.* 532 (=*A*), von Wilhelm Rau. Akademie der Wissenschaft und der Literatur, Abhandlungen der Geistes- und Sozialwissenschaftlichen Klasse, Jahrgang 1991, No.7, Stuttgart, Franz Steiner Verlag, 1991. (*YR-List*. No.23.)

(21) *Vākyapadīyaprameyasaṃgraha. Ein anonymes Scholion zum Zweiten Kāṇḍa des Vākyapadīya*, von Wilhelm Rau. Abhandlungen der Marburger Gelehrten Gesellschaft, Jahrgang 1978, No.2, München, Wilhelm Fink Verlag [in collaboration with PERI Sarveswara Sharma].

(22) *Word Index to the Vākyapadīya of Bhartṛhari (together with the Complete Text of the Vākyapadīya)*, by Saroja Bhate and Yashodhara Kar. Delhi, Eastern Book Linkers, 1992. (*YR-List*. No.25.)

2. Translations

(1) English

BERGDAHL

1988 *The Sādhanasamuddeśa (Ka. 1-44) of Bhartṛhari's Vākyapadīya with the Commentary Prakāśa of Helārāja*, Doctoral Dissertation, University of Pennsylvania. Ann Arbor, UMI 8804883. [III-7-1-44 (*Sādhana*), *kārikā*, *Prakāśa* of Helārāja]

HOUBEN, Jan E. M.

1995 *The Saṃbandha-samuddeśa (Chapter on Relation) and Bhartṛhari's Philosophy of Language, A Study of Bhartṛhari's Saṃbandha-samuddeśa in the Context of the Vākyapadīya, with a Translation of Helārāja's Commentary Prakīrṇaprakāśa*, Gonda Indological Studies, volume II. Groningen, Egbert Forsten. [III-3 (*Saṃbandha*), *kārikā*, *Prakāśa* of Helārāja]

IYER, K. A. Subrahmania

1965 *The Vākyapadīya of Bhartṛhari with the Vṛtti. Chapter I, English Translation*, Poona, Deccan College, Postgraduate and Research Institute, 1965. [I, *kārikā*, *Vṛtti*]

1977 *The Vākyapadīya of Bhartṛhari, Chapter II, English Translation with Exegetical Notes*, Delhi, etc., Motilal Banarsidass. [II, *kārikā*, Notes]

1971 *The Vākyapadīya of Bhartṛhari, Chapter III, Part I, English Translation*, Poona, Deccan College, Postgraduate and Research Institute. [III-1, *kārikā*, Summary of the *Prakāśa*]

1974 *The Vākyapadīya of Bhartṛhari, Chapter III, Part II, English Translation with Exegetical Notes*. Delhi, etc., Motilal Banarsidass. [III-2, *kārikā*, Summary of the *Prakāśa*]

PILLAI, K. Raghavan

1971 *The Vākyapadīya. Critical Text of Cantos I and II* [*with English Translation, Summary of Ideas and Notes*]. Delhi, Motilal Banarsidass, (Studies in the *Vākyapadīya*, vol.I). (*YR-List*. No.14.) [I, II *kārikā*] (Reviewed by Katsuhiko Kamimura : *Annals of Oriental Research*, University of Madras, 1973, pp. 10–13. In this review its relevance to Indian literature is clearly pointed out.)

SHARMA, Peri Sarveswara

1972 *The Kālasamuddeśa of Bhartṛhari's Vākyapadīya, together with Helārāja's Commentary Translated from the Sanskrit for the First Time*, Delhi, Motilal Banarsidass. [III-9 (*Kāla*), *kārikā*, *Prakāśa* of Helārāja]

(2) German

BANDINI, Giovanni

1980 *Die Erörterung der Wirksamkeit. Bhartṛharis Kriyāsamuddeśa und Helārājas Prakāśa zum ersten Male aus dem Sanskrit übersetzt, mit einer Einführung und einem Glossar*. Beiträge zur Südasienforschung. Südasien-Institut Universität Heidelberg, Band 61, Wiesbaden, Franz Steiner. [III-8 (*Kriyā*), *kārikā*, *Prakāśa* of Helārāja]

1982 "Die Erörterung der Person. Bhartṛharis *Puruṣasamuddeśa* und Helārājas *Prakāśa* zum ersten Male übersetzt und mit einem

Kommentar versehen," *Zeitschrift der Deutschen Morgenländischen Gesellschaft*, Wiesbaden, No.132, pp.150-173. [III-10 (*Puruṣa*), *kārikā*, *Prakāśa* of Helārāja]

(3) French

BIARDEAU, M.

1964 *Bhartṛhari Vākyapadīya Brahmakāṇḍa. Avec la Vṛtti de Harivṛṣabha*. Publications de l'Institut de Civilisation Indienne, fascicule 24, Paris, de Boccard. [I, *kārikā*, *Vṛtti*]

(4) Japanese

AKAMATSU Akihiko

1998a *The Philosophy of Language in Classical India, Vol.1. Translation and Annotation of the First Kāṇḍa of Bhartṛhari's Vākyapadīya with the Vṛtti* (Koten Indo no Gengo-Tetsugaku 1), July 1998, Tokyo, Heibon-sha (Toyo-Bunko 637). [I]

1998b *The Philosophy of Language in Classical India, Vol.2. Translation and Annotation of the Second Kāṇḍa and of the Kriyāsamuddeśa of Bhartṛhari's Vākyapadīya* (Koten Indo no Gengo-Tetsugaku 2), August 1998, Tokyo, Heibon-sha (Toyo-Bunko 638). [II, III-8 (Kriyā)]

HONDA Yoshichika

1994-7 "A Study of the *Vākyapadīya* II (1)-(3)," *The Hiroshima University Studies*, Faculty of Letters, (1)=Vol. 54, 1994 ; (2)=55, 1995 ; (3)=57, 1997. [II. 1-12]

TANIZAWA Junzo

1991 *Bhartṛhari's Vākyapadīya 3-14, Vṛttisamuddeśa, Japanese Translation and Notes (1)*, Tokyo, The Sankibo Press. [III-14 (*Samāsa*)]

UNEBE Toshiya

1995 "Bhartṛhari no suiri-kan (1)," *Reseach Report in the Graduate School of Otani University*, No.12.

1998 "Bhartṛhari no suiri-kan (2)," *Journal of the Kyushu Ryukoku Junior College*, No.44. [I. 1-43]

3. Studies

BIARDEAU, M.

1964 *Théorie de la connaissance et philosophie de la parole dans le Brahmanisme classique*, The Hague, Mouton. (Reviewed by Shinjo Kawasaki : *The Journal of Intercultural Studies*, Intercultural Research Institute, The Kansai University of Foreign Studies, Hirakata, Osaka, 1974, pp. 43-46. In this review a history of studies on the philosophy of language in India is briefly set forth.)

IYER, K. A.

1969 *Bhartṛhari : A Study of the Vākyapadīya in the Light of Ancient Commentaries*. Poona, Deccan College, Postgraduate and Research Institute.

RAU, Wilhelm Rau

1971 *Die handschriftliche Überlieferung des Vākyapadīya und seiner Kommentare*. München.

SHARMA, P. S.

1972 *The Kālasamuddeśa of Bhartṛhari's Vākyapadīya*.

[On the *Mahābhāṣyadipikā*]

1. Editions[1] and Translations

(1) Partly edited by Brahmadatta Jijñāsu, Suprabhātam saṃvat 1991 [= 1933]. [Covers only the first *Āhnika* up to p.11, l.19 in the 'critical edition', ed. Bronkhorst.] (*YR-List*. No.1.)

(2) Partly edited by V. Svaminathan under the title *Mahābhāṣya Ṭīkā* (*Āhnikas* 1-4). Hindu Vishvavidyalaya Nepal Rajya Sanskrit Series, vol. 11, Varanasi, Banaras Hindu University, 1965.1. (*YR-List*. No.2.)

(3) Partly edited by V. Swaminathan, Tirupati, Kendriya Sanskrit Vidyapitha. (Reviewed by S. D. Joshi : *ABORI*, vol. 46, 1965, pp.178-180.)

(4) Edited by K. V. Abhyankar and V. P. Limaye. Post-Graduate and Research Department Series, No.8, Poona, Bhandarkar Oriental Research Institute, 1970. [=K. V. Abhyankar and V. P. Limaye (ed.) : *ABORI*. Poona, vol. 43, 1962, pp. 1-48 ; vol. 44, 1963, pp. 49-80 ; vol. 45, 1964, pp. 81-112 ; vol. 46, 1965, pp. 113-144 ; vol. 47, 1966, pp. 145-188 ; vol. 50, 1969, pp. 189-312]. (*YR-List*. No.3.) This edition is based on the same manuscript, but the editing is different, and the final outcome is fairly different. On the manuscript, Cf. Wilhelm Rau : *Die handschriftliche Überlieferung des Vākyapadīya*

und seiner Kommentare, München, 1971, S. 44.

(5) *Mahābhāṣyadīpikā* of Bhartṛhari. [manuscript reproduced]. Poona, Bhandarkar Oriental Institute, 1980. (*YR-List*. No.4.)

(6) "Critical edition" with English translation. Bhandarkar Oriental Research Institute, Poona. (*YR-List*. No.5.)

Āhnika I (Fascicule IV), critically edited by Johannes Bronkhorst, Post-Graduate and Research Department Series, No.28, 1987.

Āhnika II (Fascicule V), critically edited by G. B. Palsule, Post-Graduate and Research Department Series, No.31, 1988.

Āhnika III (Fascicule I), critically edited by G. B. Palsule, Post-Graduate and Research Department Series, No.22, 1985.

Āhnika IV (Fascicule VI), critically edited by G. V. Devasthali and G. B. Palsule, Post-Graduate and Research Department Series, No.32, 1989.

Āhnika V (Fascicule II), critically edited by V. P. Limaye, G. B. Palsule, and V. B. Bhagavat, Post-Graduate and Research Department Series, No.23, 1985.

Āhnika VI, Part I (Fascicule III), critically edited by V. B. Bhagavat and Saroja Bhate, Post-Graduate and Research Department Series, No.25, 1986.

Āhnika VI, Part II (Fascicule VII), critically edited by V. B. Bhagavat and Saroja Bhate, Post-Graduate and Research Department Series, No.34, 1990.

Āhnika VII (Fascicule VIII), critically edited by G. B. Palsule and V. B. Bhagavat, Post-Graduate and Research Department Series, No.37, 1991.

(7) "*Mahābhāṣyadīpikā* wayaku" (a Japanese Translation of the *Mahābhāṣyadīpikā*, Abhyankar & Limaye, p.2, l.1-p.4, l.25), by Naomichi Nakada, *Okuda Jiō Sensei Kinen Bukkyo Shiso Ronshu*. Kyoto, Heirakuji Shoten, pp.1195-1203.

2. Studies

AKLUJKAR

1971 "*Mahābhāṣya-dīpikā* or *Tripādī*?," *Adyar Library Bulletin*, Madras, No.35, pp.159-171.

DWIVEDI, S. S.

1974 *Bhartṛhari-kṛta Mahābhāṣya-dīpikā : eka adhyayana* [*A Study of Bhartṛhari's Mahābhāṣya-dīpikā*], Doctoral Dissertation, Gujarat University. [In Gujarati, unpublished.]

FILLIOZAT, Pierre-Sylvain

1991 *An Introduction to Commentaries on Patañjali's Mahābhāṣya*, Professor K. V. Abhyankar Memorial Lectures (Fourth Series), BORI Post-Graduate and Research Department Series, no 35, Poona.

HOUBEN, Jan E. M.

1997 "*Sūtra* and *Bhāṣyasūtra* in Bhartṛhari's *Mahābhāṣya-Dīpikā : On the Theory and Practice of a Scientific and Philosophical Genre*," *India and Beyond : Essays in Honour of Frits Staal*, ed. by D. van der Meij. London, Paul Kegan, pp.271-305.

KUDO, Noriyuki

1997 "*Vākyabheda* as Technique of Interpretation in Bhartṛhari's *Mahābhāṣya-Dīpikā*," *Journal of the Association of Studies in Indology and Buddhism*, vol.46, part 1, pp.461-457 [pp.(60)-(64)]. [In Japanese.]

PALSULE, G. B.

1991-92 "Problems of Text Reconstruction in the *Mahābhāṣya-Dīpikā*," *Annals of the Bhandarkar Oriental Research Institute*, Poona, No. LXXII/LXXIII, Amṛtamahotsava (1917-1992) Volume, pp. 395-408.

1993 "Points of Agreement and Difference between the *Vākyapadīya* and the *Mahābhāṣya-Dīpikā* in the matter of *Sphoṭa*," *Asiatische Studien/Études Asiatiques*, No.47.1, pp.215-220. [Indian reprint : *Bhartṛhari, Philosopher and Grammarian*, edited by Saroja Bhate & Johannes Bronkhorst. Delhi, Motilal Banarsidass, 1994.]

PANDA, Ramesh Chandra

1983 *The Mahābhāṣya-dīpikā : A Critical Study*, Doctoral Dissertation, University of Poona. [Unpublished.]

1990 "*Śabda* as presented in the *Mahābhāṣya-dīpikā*," *Jagannāthajyoti*,

Puri, No.4, pp.125-129.

RAJA, K. Kunjunni

1990 Chapter on Bhartṛhari's *Ṭīkā* on Patañjali's *Mahābhāṣya*, in *Encyclopedia of Indian Philosophies*, Vol. V : The Philosophy of the Grammarians. ed. by Harold G. COWARD and K. Kunjunni RAJA, Delhi, Motilal Banarsidass, pp.172-174.

SVAMINATHAN, V.

1963 "Bhartṛhari's Authorship of the Commentary on the *Mahābhāṣya*," *Adyar Library Bulletin*, Madras, No.27, pp.59-70.

Notes

1) Those who admire Bhartṛhari established an association in 1974 (Bhartri Hari Smarak Mission [in Hindī : Bhartṛhari Smārak Miśan], 9, Janpath, New Delhi - 1).

2) An international conference on Bhartṛhari was held on January 6-8, 1992 in Pune, under the joint auspices of the University of Poona and the University of Lausanne (Switzerland). Its proceedings were published as *Asiatische Studien/Études Asiatiques*, no 47.1 (1993), or, in its Indian reprint, *Bhartṛhari, Philosopher and Grammarian* [Proceedings of the First International Conference on Bhartṛhari], edited by Saroja Bhate & Johannes Bronkhorst, Delhi, Motilal Banarsidass, 1994. Most of the following bibliography is based on and selected from Yves Ramseier's "A Bibliography on Bhartṛhari" (updated version 16 Feb. 1999) available on the internet, with several additions by Mr. KUDO Noriyuki. Its printed form appeared first in the above-mentioned *Asiatische Studien/Études Asiatiques*, pp.37-43. The URL is :

http : //www-orient.unil.ch/E-Texts/Bharhari/Bibliography.html

3) The number of *kārikās* is almost the same in both the Benares Sanskrit Series edition and the Trivandrum edition, with a slight difference that the number of *kārikās*. (*Kāla-samuddeśa*, 114 ; *Saṃkhyā-samuddeśa*, 32 ; *Upagraha-samuddeśa*, 27 ; *Vṛtti-samuddeśa*, 624.) Prof. Varma points out the fact that Helārāja's explanations are in many cases based on Kaiyaṭa, so that Helārāja must be contemporaneous with, or posterior to, Kaiyaṭa, and that the dates of Helārāja must fall in the 13th or 14th century (*Vākyapadīyam*, *Brahmakāṇḍa*, New Delhi, 1970, Introduction, pp.4-6). Helārāja was also called Puṇyarāja or Phullarāja (ibid. p.4).

4) This number is given in Yves Ramseier's list ("Bibliography on Bhartṛhari," [abbreviation : *YR-List*.]).

5) Cf. K. Swaminathan : *Adyar L.B.* vol. XXVII, 1963, pp.59-70.

CHAPTER I

THE GRAMMARIAN BHARTṚHARI: THE MAN AND HIS WORKS

SECTION I. HIS WORKS

Of the works by Bhartṛhari, there is no doubt that at least the following two are his authentic writings:

(1) *Vākyapadīya*

(2) *Mahābhāṣyadīpikā*

(1) *Vākyapadiya*

It is certain that this work is an authentic work.[1] The publication of this work took nearly fifty years and was finally completed in 1937.[2] The title "*Vākyapadīya*" means "A Treatise on Sentences (*vākya*) and Words (*pada*)."[3] Because this work is composed of three chapters, it is also called "*Trikāṇḍī*" (Three Chapters Edition).[4]

The first chapter was given the name "*Brahmakāṇḍa*" or "*Āgamasamuccaya*" (Collection of Sacred Traditions).[5] According to the article by Kielhorn,[6] this chapter consists of 183 stanzas in most manuscripts, but the published work (Benares Sanskrit Series) has 157 stanzas. His philosophical thoughts are, for the most part, set forth in this chapter. That is, he discusses Brahman, the real nature and function of language, the significance of grammar, and so forth. Consequently, scholars who attack the philosophical thought of Bhartṛhari criticize it as a rule by quoting from this chapter.[7]

The second chapter is entitled "*Vākyakāṇḍa*" (Section on Sentences) and sets forth a treatise on sentences. According to the article by Kielhorn, it contains 487 stanzas, but the published work has 493 stanzas.

The third chapter is entitled "*Prakīrṇaka*" or "*Padakāṇḍa*."[8] According to Kielhorn's report, it consists of 1315 stanzas, but the published version has 1319 stanzas. In this chapter he minutely treats the subject of words (*pada*). This chapter is extremely detailed, and is further divided further into fourteen sections.

The numbers of stanzas included in the three chapters are as follows. (In my original Japanese work, only the numbers of stanzas in the BenSS edition were listed, but in this English version I also list those of Rau's and Iyer's editions for reference.)

Chapter and Section	Numbers of Stanzas BenSS		Rau	Iyer
I. *Brahmakāṇḍa*	157		183	147
II. *Vākyakāṇḍa*	493		490	485
III. *Padakāṇḍa*				
1. *Jāti*	106	(pp.1-84)	110	106
2. *Dravya*	18	(pp.85-95)	18	18
3. *Saṃbandha*	86	(pp.96-138)	88	88
4. *Dravya*[9]	3	(pp.139-144)	3	3
5. *Guṇa*	9	(pp.145-156)	9	9
6. *Diś*	28	(pp.157-172)	28	28
7. *Sādhana*	165		167	167
a. *Kāraka*			44	
b. *Karman*	88	(pp.173-236)	45	
c. *Karaṇa*	10	(pp.237-242)	11	
d. *Kartṛ*	24	(pp.243-256)	24	
e. *Hetu*	4	(pp.257-261)	4	
f. *Saṃpradāna*	7	(pp.262-267)	7	
g. *Apādāna*	12	(pp.268-276)	12	
h. *Adhikaraṇa*	8	(pp.277-282)	8	
i. *Śeṣa*	7	(pp.283-289)	7	
Concluding Verses	5	(pp.290-297)	5	
8. *Kriyā*[10]	63	(pp.298-342)	64	63
9. *Kāla*	113	(pp.342-390)	114	114
10. *Puruṣa*	9	(pp.391-394)	9	9
11. *Saṃkhyā*	31	(pp.395-414)	32	32
12. *Upagraha*	28	(pp.415-428)	27	27
13. *Liṅga*	31	(pp.429-446)	31	31

14. *Vṛtti*	629(pp.447-743)	625	624

The three chapters altogether have 1969 verses in the published edition or, according to the article by Kielhorn, 1985 verses.

Although the *Vākyapadīya* is composed of the above three chapters, it seems that, in ancient times, the first chapter, *Brahma-kāṇḍa*, and the second chapter, *Vākya-kāṇḍa*, were combined and handed down as one work, which was called the *Vākyapadīya*. The third section, *Prakīrṇaka*, on the other hand, was handed down as a separate work and was known only as *Prakīrṇaka*.

Vardhamāna (c. 1140), in his own work, *Gaṇaratnamahodadhi*, calls Bhartṛhari's work "*Vākyapadīya-Prakīrṇakayoḥ kartā Mahābhāṣyatripadyā vyākhyātā ca.*"[11] Hence the so-called *Trikāṇḍī* (Three Chapters Edition) (today called *Vākyapadīya*) of Helārāja was created by combining the *Vākyapadīya* and the *Prakīrṇaka*. One may ascertain this assumption especially if one considers the fact that the first two chapters were commented upon by Puṇyarāja and the last chapter by Helārāja. Moreover, the interesting account in the *Nan-hai chi-kuei nei-fa chuan* by I-ching offers more cogent grounds than the above for this.

> Next, there is the *Vākyapadīya*; it comprises 700 stanzas and its commentary comprises 7000 stanzas. This is also a work by Bhartṛhari. It describes the meaning of scriptural testimony and inference. Next, there is the "鞞拏" (*Prakīrṇaka*); it comprises 3000 stanzas and its commentary contains 14000 stanzas. Its stanzas were composed by Bhartṛhari and its commentary is a work by Dharmapāla. It penetrates into the secret of the universe and reaches the truth of human reasoning. If one studies it, one will understand grammar very well.[12]

The *Vākyapadīya* mentioned here refers to the first and second chapters of the extant *Vākyapadīya*, and as the number of their verses is nearly 700, this coincides with the account by I-ching. Now, what "鞞拏" indicates has been vigorously discussed by scholars, but to this day, however, it is said generally in academic circles that it is a transliteration of "*Paīṇṇa*," which is a Prakrit form of *Prakīrṇaka*.[13] Not only is there the difficult problem that the number of verses does not coincide, but Kielhorn explains that the corresponding part may have been lost as Puṇyarāja writes that the *Padakāṇḍa* was not handed down perfectly either because of the fact that the period of Puṇyarāja has not been investigated, or because of some carelessness on the part of the person who copied the text, or because of some other reason.[14]

This supposition may perhaps be correct. Of the poems of Bhartṛhari, at least 19 were handed down in Tibetan translations of the works of Dignāga, Bhavya, Asvabhāva, and Jñānaśrībhadra, and of these at least 10 fragments are in the *Vākyapadīya* of Bhartṛhari, but the remaining nine are not to be found either in the *Vākyapadīya* or in his collection of lyrical poems. Although two corresponding Sanskrit texts have been discovered, these are not found in the *Vākyapadīya*.[15] Again, one text is quoted in the ancient commentary "*Vākyapadīya*," published by Cārudeva.[16] If so, it is to be surmised that the remaining nine may be in the part of the *Vākyapadīya* which was not published.

Now, if such an explanation is accepted, it seems obvious that although the first two sections and the last section were handed down as separate works immediately after Bhartṛhari's death, later generations eventually combined them and regarded them as one work. However, there is no doubt that both of them were written by the same person.[17] Perhaps Bhartṛhari, after he had written the first two sections, in later years again began to write and wrote the third section.

Although the *Vākyapadīya* has been hitherto considered by scholars[18] to be a commentary on the *Mahābhāṣya* of Patañjali, this is a mistake and it is not a verbatim commentary. Rather, according to the critical remarks of recent grammarians, it is "stanzas which reveal the purport of the *Mahābhāṣya*" (*Mahābhāṣya-arthatātparya-jñāpikāḥ kārikāḥ*).[19] Puṇyarāja called Bhartṛhari, the writer of this work, "the annotator" (*ṭīkākāra*, *ṭīkākṛt*),[20] but perhaps, as will be explained later, this may mean that Bhartṛhari wrote a commentary on the *Mahābhāṣya* apart from this.

As for the commentaries on the *Vākyapadīya*, the *Prakāśa* of Puṇyarāja was handed down for the first and second sections, and the *Prakīrṇaka-prakāśa* of Helārāja for the third section,[21] and both of them have already been published.[22] The character and dates of Puṇyarāja are completely obscure. According to the concluding stanza of Helārajā's commentary,

Helārajā was a descendant of Lakṣmaṇa, a premier of the king Muktāpīḍa in Kashmir, and was said to be the son of Bhūtirāja. According to the history book *Rājataraṅgiṇī* (I, 17-18), he was a believer in Pāśupata, and it is said that he wrote the history *Pārthivāvali*, composed of 12000 stanzas. He may perhaps be considered to have lived during the period from the 9th century to the 10th century.[23] Although the commentaries of these two scholars are a great reference for reading and understanding the main work, nevertheless, it cannot be said that they faithfully elucidate the real intention of Bhartṛhari. Both commentaries give a markedly non-dualistic (*advaita*) interpretation.

Furthermore, according to the account by I-ching noted earlier, it is said that Bhartṛhari himself wrote a commentary for the *Vākyapadīya*, and Dharmapāla (late 6th century) wrote a commentary on the *Prakīrṇaka*. This perhaps may have occurred. We know from other sources[24] that Dharmapāla was well-versed in grammar. Moreover, what can be regarded as a verse which existed in Bhartṛhari's own commentary is also quoted in other works.[25]

The ancient commentary on the first section, the *Vākyapadīya,* and a sub-commentary (*Ṭīkā*, the *Vṛṣabhadeva*) have been published in recent years.[26] This ancient commentary is longer than that of Puṇyarāja, and according to its publisher Cārudeva, it is said that the commentary by Puṇyarāja is supposed to have originated with Bhartṛhari himself.[27] However, since the theories of the later Advaita School are brought together in this section, research is necessary in order to conclude that it is Bhartṛhari's own commentary.

Now, in connection with this problem, I wish to point out an interesting fact. In the *Tattvasaṃgrahapañjikā* (ad v.128, p.67), the very first stanza of the *Vākyapadīya* is quoted, and directly after it the following comment is made:

> *tatra — ādiḥ — utpādaḥ nidhanam — nāśaḥ, tadabhāvād anādinidhanam / akṣaram iti / akārādyakṣarasya nimittatvāt / etenābhidhānarūpeṇa vivarto darśitaḥ / arthabhāvenetyādinā punar abhidheyavivartaḥ / prakriyeti bhedāḥ / brahmeti nāmasaṃkīrtanam /*[28]

On the other hand, the work *Prameyakamalamārtaṇḍa* by the Jaina scholar

Prabhācandra, after having quoted the same verse from the *Vākyapadīya*, says the following:

anādinidhanaṃ hi śabdabrahma, utpādavināśābhāvād, akṣaraṃ cākārādyakṣarasya nimittatvād / anena vācakarūpatārthabhāvenety anena tu vācyarūpatāsya sūcitā / prakriyeti bhedāḥ / śabdabrahmeti nāmasaṃkīrtanam iti /

The similarities between these two passages are astonishing. On the other hand, the commentary by Puṇyarāja on the same verse is written in a style which is greatly different from these two passages. If so, how should the similarity in the passages from the two commentaries above be interpreted? As there is a passage of five verses from the *Tattvasaṃgraha* (vv. 910-914) of Śāntarakṣita in the *Prameyakamalamārtaṇḍa* by Prabhācandra, in which he quotes the passage,[29] perhaps Prabhācandra had read the annotated passage by Kamalaśīla. If so, it can be thought that with this passage he revised and inserted the words of Kamalaśīra. However, on the other hand, both Kamalaśīra and Prabhācandra had seen the ancient commentary on the *Vākyapadīya*, and it can be thought that in order to copy in general as it was, the wording which explained this was coincidental. That is to say, before Kamalaśīra, the ancient commentary already existed immediately after Bhartṛhari's death, and it was widely read not only among orthodox Brahmins, but also among the followers of Buddhism and Jainism, and it may be considered rational to assume that later it was scattered and lost. In this matter, further research is needed.

At any rate, that the ancient commentary first existed, and was afterwards scattered and lost, is a fact. The reason it was scattered and lost is not clear, but since in the commentaries of both Puṇyarāja and Helārāja the non-dualistic interpretation is quite pronounced, and in later times such a tendency came to flourish, both commentaries were whole-heartedly accepted, and it may be supposed that the ancient commentary which did not have this tendency was discarded. (Furthermore, the circumstances under which the commentary by Dharmapāla was not handed down in India can be easily understood.)

(2) *Mahābhāṣyadipikā*[30]

This is a commentary on the *Mahābhāṣya* of Patañjali. The manuscript exists only in the National Library in Berlin, and it is said that it cannot be found in India.[31] The manuscript itself is almost non-existent, and in recent years it has become impossible to read it. According to the accounts of later grammarians, this work comments only on the first three *pādas* of the *Mahābhāṣya*, and nothing further than that has been handed down.[32] However, the single extant manuscript stops at the seventh lesson (*āhnika*) of the first *pāda*.[33] Thus it is a manuscript filled with imperfections. Regarding its contents, it is an extremely minute and detailed commentary, and since it alludes to some ancient commentaries on the *Mahābhāṣya* which have already been scattered and lost today, what makes it remarkable may be the fact that it refers to these. The text of the *Mahābhāṣya* which is annotated in this work is in general the same as the present manuscript, but there are passages which preserve readings which do not exist anywhere in the present manuscript. Therefore, compared with the commentary by Kaiyaṭa, it amounts to an exceedingly sparse selection from the commentary by Bhartṛhari, at least insofar that it is concerned only with the opening seven lessons. The commentary by Bhartṛhari is at least four times as voluminous as that by Kaiyaṭa. Judging by this then, in its entirety the written commentary by Bhartṛhari must have had as many as approximately 25000 stanzas. If it did, then it would coincide with the account by I-ching.

> There is also a commentary on the *Vṛtti-sūtra*, which is called the *Cūrṇi* and has 24000 stanzas. It was composed by the scholar Patañjali, and thus greatly elaborates on the former *sūtra*, piercing the skin [explaining the obscure points] and analyzing the reasoning; it explains in great detail the latter commentary, dissecting the hairs and rushes in clarifying the *sūtra*, and studying it took three years. This great work is similar in its merit to the Spring and Autumn Rites of the Chou. Next, there is the *Bhartṛhari-śāstra*, which is a commentary on the former *Cūrṇi*. It was written by the great scholar Bhartṛhari, and has 25000 stanzas. It discusses fully the essentials of the human facts as well as of grammatical science. It describes the reason for the rise and the decline of various families. It profoundly explains the *Vijñānavāda*

and well discusses *hetu* (reason) and *udāharaṇa* (example).[34]

The *Cūrṇi* is the *Mahābhāṣya* for Pāṇini's *Sūtra*, and according to Kielhorn, Bhartṛhari, in this commentary, calls Patañjali the author of the *Cūrṇi* (*Cūrṇikāra*). It nearly coincides with the number of 25000 stanzas. Consequently, the treatise of Bhartṛhari mentioned by I-ching is the commentary by Bhartṛhari on the *Mahābhāṣya* of Patañjali. In view of this fact, it is evident that one can adequately rely on the account by I-ching also.

There are a great number of sub-commentaries on the *Mahābhāṣya*, and as this work by Bhartṛhari is at present the oldest, one should be fully aware of this point.

In view of the present manuscripts and the account by I-ching, the works by Bhartṛhari are limited to the above two.[35] Furthermore, although it may be supposed that he might have written a commentary on the *Mīmāṃsā-sūtra*,[36] the authenticity of this is not clear. But it is certain that Bhartṛhari was well-versed in the study of Mīmāṃsā religious matters.[37]

Furthermore, besides this there exists a collection of lyrical poems called the *Bhartṛhariśataka*. As a collection of lyrical poems, it is an extraordinary manuscript, and because of its fecund rhetorical and poetic flourishes and its graceful poetical phrasing, it has been fondly regarded since ancient times. It is made up of three sections.

(1) *Śṛṅgāra-śataka* (Hundred Stanzas on Love). With elegant and charming verses he sings of the charms of his lady love and of the pleasures of love, and discarding completely distressful affliction, he recommends the path of tranquillity and silence.

(2) *Nīti-śataka* (Hundred Stanzas on Conduct in Life). He explains the cardinal points of conduct in life and practical morality, alternating between adroit similes and bitter cynicism. The underlying tone is utilitarian.

(3) *Vairāgya-śataka* (Hundred Stanzas on Renunciation of Desire). Arriving at liberation, the supreme goal of humanity, he teaches that one may attain supreme bliss by means of faith in god (in either *Śiva* or *Brahman*).

Besides these, the *Vijñāna-śataka* (Hundred Stanzas on Knowledge) and *Viṭavṛtta* have also been handed down as his works, and there are in addition to these a great number of lyrical poems attributed to him, which with the above-mentioned total 1039 stanzas.[38]

Now, it is a problem which among these are really the works of Bhartṛhari. Winternitz maintains that since the individualistic colouring in the "Hundred Stanzas on Love" is extremely strong, it and a part of the other two "Hundred Stanzas" were original with a poet called Bhartṛhari,[39] and Professor Renou is in agreement with this.[40]

According to Professor Kosambi, who has critically studied his lyrical poems, 76 stanzas of the "Hundred Stanzas on Conduct in Life," 71 stanzas of the "Hundred Stanzas on Love," and 53 stanzas of the "Hundred Stanzas on Renunciation of Desire," altogether 200 stanzas, which appear in all of the manuscripts, are probably, at any rate, derived from the original author, but the rest are thought to be doubtful. If so, is the author of the prototype two hundred stanzas then the same person as the grammarian Bhartṛhari? Regarding this, Professor Kosambi explains that later editors probably recorded all the poems which were believed by later generations to have been composed by Bhartṛhari,[41] but the prototype 200 stanzas were made in the early centuries after the birth of Christ,[42] and these writers were Brahmins.[43] Perhaps there were originally the works by the poet Bhartṛhari himself, and in later centuries verses of the same sentiment were appended, until finally the great number of transmitted and accepted works we have today came into existence.

Well now, whether or not the author of these prototypes was the same person as the grammarian Bhartṛhari is considered a problem among scholars. Clear confirmation does not exist on the dates of the poet Bhartṛhari.[44] As the account by I-ching on the grammarian Bhartṛhari and the Indian tradition on the poet Bhartṛhari are alike to a remarkable extent, both presume that they are perhaps the same person, but whether they are the same is still a difficult problem.[45] In particular, in this prototype of the "Hundred Verses Edition," some verses which praise the god Śiva are included. However, in the *Vākyapadīya* the concept of worship of Śiva cannot be found. Again, among the poems of this "Hundred Stanzas Edition," there are a great number which either are the same as poems in other literary works or resemble them. When we add together and think about these facts, the "Hundred Stanzas Edition" may perhaps have been a compilation and collection by the poet Bhartṛhari of the lyrical poems which had been handed down at the time as the nucleus of his own works.

Notes

1) This is based on the postscript in this work, the account in the "Records of the Buddhist Religion" (*Nan-hai chi-kuei nei-fa chuan*) by I-ching which is given later, and the *SDS*. XIII, *ll*. 113, 193, 208, etc.

2) This work was published from 1887 to 1907 as vol. II, Fasc. III (to p.288) of the Benares Sanskrit Series. Publication was afterwards suspended for some time, but from 1928 to 1937 vol. II, Fasc. IV — Fasc. VIII was published, and the work was thereby completed. This edition includes in the First and Second *Kāṇḍa* the commentary by Puṇyarāja, and in the Third *Kāṇḍa* the commentary by Helārāja. In addition, the Third *Kāṇḍa* and the commentary by Helārāja were published in the Trivandrum Sanskrit Series, no. 116 (1935), and it and the commentary by Bhāvapradīpa have been published in the Kashi Sanskrit Series, no.124 (*Vyākaraṇa* Section, 15) (1937) ; together with the ancient commentary by Cārudeva Śāstrī, they were published in Lahore in 1934, but I have not been able to see any except the BenSS. Cf. following explanations on the commentaries.

3) "Nach dem Schol. zu. P.4, 3, 88 bedeutet *Vākyapadīyam* ein vom *vākya*, Satz und vom *pada*, Wort behandelndes Werk" (Weber : *Indische Studien*, V. S. 158, Anm. 2).

4) According to the verse in the conclusion of Helārāja's commentary. Because *SDS*, XIII, *l*. 192 calls the first chapter '*prathama-kāṇḍa*', in the time of Mādhava at least the first and second parts had already been combined to form a single work. And Colebrooke says that there are instances where *Vākyapadīya* has been quoted under the name '*Harikārikā*' (*Collected Works*. *II*, p.40).

5) According to all postscripts of Puṇyarāja. The title '*Brahmakāṇḍa*' is adopted by both Helārāja (p.629) and Mādhava (*SDS*. XIII, p.114).

The following description is based on Aklujkar (Ashok Narahar Aklujkar : "An Introduction to the Study of Bhartṛhari," *Asiatische Studien/Études Asiatiques*, No.47. 1, 1993. p.33. Appendix [Indian reprint : *Bhartṛhari*, *Philosopher and Grammarian*, edited by Saroja Bhate & Johannes Bronkhorst. Delhi, Motilal Banarsidass, 1994]).

〈Title of each *Kāṇḍa*〉

I) *Āgama-samuccaya* or *Brahmakāṇḍa*

II) *Vākyapadīya* or *Vākyakāṇḍa*

III) *Prakīrṇa(ka)kāṇḍa* or *Padakāṇḍa*, *Prakāśa* (by Helārāja).

6) F. Kielhorn, "On the Grammarian Bhartṛhari," *Ind. Ant*. 1883, pp.226-227.

7) E. g. cf. the quotations in the *Śabdabrahmaparīkṣā* in the *Tattvasaṃgraha*, the *Prameyakamalamārtaṇḍa* of Prabhācandra, the *Tantravārttika* of Kumārila, the *Nyāyamañjarī* of Jayanta, the *Sarvadarśanasaṃgraha* XIII of Mādhava, etc.

8) Kielhorn says that it is also called '*Prakīrṇa*'.

9) The *dravya* which is discussed in this part is mutually opposed to *guṇa*.

10) This name is missing in the published edition, but Helārāja, in the beginning of this *samuddeśa*, comments "*idānīm......kriyāyāḥ śāstrīyaṃ lakṣaṇam āha*," and Mādhava (*SDS*. XIII. *l*.221), quoting the 21st verse ("*jātim anye kriyām āhur anekavyaktivartinīm*") of this *samuddeśa*, records that it is explained in the "Kriyāsamuddeśa." Consequently, "*samuddeśa*" must have been its name.

11) According to Kielhorn's article, ibid.

12) *Taisho*, LIV, 229b.

13) Kielhorn, ibid., and B. Liebich : *Das Datum Candragomin's und Kālidāsa's*. Breslau, 1903, p.7. See also Tanaka "The *Vākyapadīya* of Bhartṛhari," in *Philosophy* (Annual Journal of Philosophy), Faculty of Letters, Waseda University, VII, p.76 ff.

14) According to Professor Louis Renou, the late Dr. S. Dasgupta actually checked the manuscript of the *Vākyapadīya* and found that the verse in the Benares Sanskrit Series work had been left out.

15) See Part V, Chapter II of this book.

16) *Brahmakāṇḍa* edited, with *Vṛtti* and Vṛṣabhadeva's *Ṭīkā*, by Cārudeva Śāstrī. Lahore, 1934.

17) Cf. *Vākyapadīya*, II,491.

18) Macdonell : *History of Sanskrit Literature*, p.431 ; Abhyankar : *Sarvadarśanasaṃgraha*, Appendix, p.529.

19) It appears in the recent grammatical work *Śabdārtharatna* (A. Weber : *Indische Studien*, V. S, 161, Anm.)

20) ad *Vākyapadīya*, II, 484 ; 486 etc.

21) Th. Aufrecht : *Catalogus Catalogorum* (I, p.557 ; II, pp.131, 224 ; III, p.118) also lists only these two.

As regards the commentator of the second section of the *Vākyapadīya* ascribed to Puṇyarāja or Phullarāja, Aklujkar insists that the commentary of Puṇyarāja is not original, but a short recast of the commentary of Helārāja (nonexistent) (Ashok Narahar Aklujkar : "The Authorship of the *Vākya-kāṇḍa-ṭīkā*," *Charudeva Shastri Felicitation Volume*, Delhi, 1974. pp.165-188 ; "An Introduction to the Study of Bhartṛhari," *Asiatische Studien/Études Asiatiques*, No.47.1, 1993. p.23, fn.12. [Indian reprint : *Bhartṛhari, Philosopher and Grammarian*, edited by Saroja Bhate & Johannes Bronkhorst. Delhi, Motilal Banarsidass 1994]). He also says that the name of Puṇyarāja and Phullarāja is derived from a misreading of the *Śāradā* script.(Akuljkar : "An

Introduction to the Study of Bhartṛhari," p.23). On the other hand, Peri Sarveswara Sharma and Houben refute Aklujkar's views (Peri Sarveswara Sharma : "Puṇyarāja's *Ṭīkā* on the *Vākya-kāṇḍa* of the *Vākyapadīya* of Bhartṛhari," *Bhāratīya Vidyā*, No.42, 1983, pp.1-21 ; Jan E. M. Houben : *The Saṃbandha-samuddeśa (Chapter on Relation) and Bhartṛhari's Philosophy of Language, A study of Bhartṛhari's Saṃbandha-samuddeśa in the Context of the Vākyapadīya, with a Translation of Helārāja's Commentary Prakīrṇaprakāśa*, Gonda Indological Studies, volume II. Groningen, Egbert Forsten. 1995, p.13, fn.32). For details on this point, see Jan E. M. Houben : "Bhartṛhari's *Vākyapadīya* and the Ancient *Vṛtti* (2) : The Vedic Background of the Author of the *Vākyapadīya-Vṛtti*," *Studien zur Indologie und Iranistik*, Reinbeck, Band 21, 1997, pp.71-77 ; "Bhartṛhari's *Vākyapadīya* and the Ancient *Vṛtti* (1) : The *Vṛtti* and Vṛṣabhadeva's *Paddhati* on *Vākyapadīya* 1.46a *ātmabhedam/ātmabhedas*," *Annals of the Bhandarkar Oriental Research Institute*, Poona, No.LXXVIII, 1997, pp.177-200 ; "Bhartṛhari's *Vākyapadīya* and the Ancient *Vṛtti* (3) : On Syntactic and Stylistic Evidence regarding the Authorship of the *Vākyapadīya-Vṛtti*," *Wiener Zeitschrift für die Kunde Südasiens*, Wien (forthcoming).

22) However, both commentaries published in the Benares Sanskrit Series, since they are not critical publications, have a great number of misreadings of the manuscripts and typographical errors. Opposed to this, there is the account in the *SDS*. XIII based upon both commentaries which is quite accurate.

The following description is based on Aklujkar (Ashok Narahar Aklujkar : "An Introduction to the Study of Bhartṛhari," *Asiatische Studien/Études Asiatiques*, No.47.1, 1993, p.33. Appendix. [Indian reprint : *Bhartṛhari, Philosopher and Grammarian*, edited by Saroja Bhate & Johannes Bronkhorst, Delhi, Motilal Banarsidass, 1994).

〈Commentaries on each *Kāṇḍa*〉

I) *Vṛtti* by Hari-vṛṣabha or Bhartṛhari
Paddhati by Vṛṣabhadeva

II) *Vṛtti* by Hari-vṛṣabha or Bhartṛhari
Ṭīkā by Puṇyarāja (= Phullarāja?)
Vākyapadīya-Prameyasaṃgraha (unknown)

III) *Prakāśa* by Helārāja [two gaps in it filled by Phullarāja)

Raghnātha Sharma composed his own commentary *Ambākartrī*. (see Editions, *YR-List*. No.8).

23) The king Muktāpīḍa is the same person as the king Lalitāditya. He reigned until c. 732. Consequently, Helārāja must have lived after the ninth century. On the other hand, since Kalhaṇa, the author of the *Rājataraṅgiṇī*, lived at the beginning of the 12th century, Helārāja must have lived before then. Further, concerning Helārāja and allusions to his academic theory, one can cite *SDS*. XIII, *l*. 121 ; *Vedāntakalpatarupari-*

mala, p.549.

24) Dr. Ui : "Researches on Indian Philosophy,' V. p.130.

25) *tathā coktaṃ Vākyapadīye — 'na hi gauḥ svarūpeṇa gauḥ, nāpy agauḥ, gotvābhisaṃbandhāt tu gauḥ'* (cf. M. Winternitz : *GIL*. Bd III, S.395) in the *Kāvyaprakāśa*, II, 8, of Mammaṭa may have been a passage in the self-commentary of the *Vākyapadīya*, according to K. G. Subrahmanyam. (*JORM*. vol. I. 1927, pp.185, 187). However, this might have recorded in this way the purport of Bhartṛhari's theory.

26) Bhartṛhari : *Vākyapadīyam. tatra Hari-upajña-vṛtti-sanāthaṃ Vṛṣabhadeva-ṭīkāsaṃkṣepa-saṃyutaṃ prathamaṃ kāṇḍaṃ, tac ca...... Śrī-Cārudeva-śāstriṇā...... saṃśodhya...... ṭippaṇaiś copabṛṃhitam, tad etat lavapure...... saṃmudrya prākāśyaṃ nītam*. Vikrama-vatsarāḥ, 1991. (Lahore 1937).

27) P. Hacker : *Vivarta*, S. 201-205. Once Dr. Biardeau told me that there are some important discrepancies between the *Kārikā*s and the *Vṛtti* so that we are not quite sure whether the *Vṛtti* was written by Bhartṛhari himself. To illustrate, in the *Vṛtti* the four phases of *śabda* are set forth, whereas in the *Kārikās* seemingly three phases are set forth, perhaps under the influence of Kaśmīr Śaivism. This problem requires further investigations (Bhartṛhari's own commentary, vol. IV, p.11).

On the author of the *Vṛtti* on the First Section of the *Vākyapadīya*, scholars have different opinions. The following scholars say that Bhartṛhari is the author of the *Vṛtti*.

Ashok Narahar Aklujkar : "The Authorship of the *Vākyapadīya-vṛtti*," *Wiener Zeitschrift für die Kunde Südasiens*, Wien, No.16, 1972. pp.181-198.

Ashok Narahar Aklujkar : "Once again on the Authorship of *Trikāṇḍī-Vṛtti*," *Asiatische Studien/Études Asiatiques*, No.47.1, 1993, pp.45-57. [Indian reprint : *Bhartṛhari, Philosopher and Grammarian*, edited by Saroja Bhate & Johannes Bronkhorst, Delhi, Motilal Banarsidass, 1994].

Wilhelm Halbfass : *Tradition and Reflection. Exploration in Indian Thought*. Albany, State University of New York Press. 1991 ; *On Being and What there is. Classical Vaiśeṣika and the History of Indian Ontology*. Albany, State University of New York Press. 1992.

Jan E. M. Houben : *The Saṃbandha-samuddeśa (Chapter on Relation) and Bhartṛhari's Philosophy of Language, A study of Bhartṛhari's Saṃbandha-samuddeśa in the Context of the Vākyapadīya, with a Translation of Helārāja's Commentary Prakīrṇaprakāśa*, Gonda Indological Studies, volume II. Groningen, Egbert Forsten. 1995.

K. A. Subrahmania Iyer : *The Vākyapadīya of Bhartṛhari with the Vṛtti. Chapter I, English Translation*, Deccan College Building Centenary & Silver Jubilee Series 26, Poona. 1965 ; *Bhartṛhari. A Study of the Vākyapadīya in the Light of the Ancient*

Commentaries, Deccan College Building Centenary and Silver Jubilee Series: 68, Poona. 1969.

Hartmut Scharfe: *Grammatical Literature*, vol. 5.2 of *A History of Indian Literature*, Wiesbaden, Otto Harrassowitz. 1977. [Chapter XI: "The later Pāṇini school," pp.170-175].

Charudeva Shastri: "Bhartṛhari: A Critical Study with Special References to the *Vākyapadīya* and its Commentaries," *Proceedings of the Fifth Indian Oriental Conference* (Lahore, 1928), Lahore. Vol.1, 1930. pp.630-655.

On the other hand, the following scholars say that Bhartṛhari is not the author of the *Vṛtti*.

Madeleine Biardeau: *Bhartṛhari Vākyapadīya Brahmakāṇḍa. Avec la Vṛtti de Harivṛṣabha*. Publications de l'Institut de Civilisation Indienne, fascicule 24, Paris, de Boccard. 1964.

Johannes Bronkhorst: "Études sur Bhartṛhari 1: L'Auteur et la Date de la *Vṛtti*," *Bulletin d'Études Indiennes*, Paris, No.6, 1988. pp.105-143.

28) Cf. Part VII, Chapter II, Section III, Sub-Section 3 of this book.

29) Cf. K. B. Pathak: *ABhI*, vol. XIII, 1930-31, pp.81-83.

30) According to the Berlin manuscript, its title is *Bhartṛharitīkā* or *Śrīmahābhāṣyaṭikā Bhartṛhariviracitā* or *Śrīmahopādhyāyabhartṛhariviracitā Śrīmahābhāṣyadīpikā*. (Kielhorn: *Mahābhāṣya*, vol. II, preface, p.12).

31) Th. Aufrecht, *CC*, I, p.440. Kielhorn has reported that although he endeavoured to find this manuscript, he was unable to discover even one edition in India. (Preface to edition of *Mahābhāṣya*, vol. I, p.9). Kielhorn first published the beginning of this part from the manuscript in Berlin. (Kielhorn: *Mahābhāṣya*, vol. II, preface, pp. 12-21).

32) Helārāja called this work '*Tripadī*' in the concluding verse of the *Prakīrṇaka-prakāśa*. See also the words of Vardhmāna previously noted.

33) The following comments follow the report of Kielhorn. (*Ind. Ant.* 1883, p.226; *Mahābhāṣya*, vol. II, p.12).

34) *Taisho*, LIV. 229b.

35) Based upon the words of Vardhamāna previously noted, his work is also given in addition as the *Mahābhāṣya-tripadīvyākhyāna*, in Aufrecht: *CC*. I, p.440, but this really means *Mahābhāṣyadīpikā*, and a book with such a title does not exist.

36) According to G. Jhā: *The Prabhākara School of Pūrva Mīmāṃsā*, pp.6-7, the *Śāstradīpikā*, X, 2, 59-60 alludes to the ancient commentary by Hari.

37) Cf. *Vākyapadīya*, p.100.

38) *The Epigrams Attributed to Bhartṛhari*, ed. by D. D. Kosambi: Singhi Jain Series, vol. 23. Bombay, 1948. Both the text and an English translation have been published. *Bhartṛhari: Poems. With the Transliterated Sanskrit Text of the Śatakatrayam*. Trans-

lated by Barbara Stoler Miller. New York and London, Columbia University Press, 1967.

39) Winternitz: *GIL.* III, S. 137-140.

40) Louis Renou et Jean Filliozat: *L'Inde Classique*, tome II. Paris, 1953, pp.232-233.

41) D. D. Kosambi: *Bhartṛhari*, Introduction, p.78.

42) *ibid.* p.78.

43) *ibid.* pp.80-81.

44) However, many of the poems of Bhartṛhari are quoted in the *Sūktimuktāvali* of Jalhaṇa in the 13th century. (R. G. Bhandarkar: *Collected Works*, vol. II, p.389).

45) J. Hertel: *WZKM*. XVI, 1902, S. 202-205; D. D. Kosambi: *Bhartṛhari*, p.79.

SECTION II. THE MAN

Bhartṛhari is also called Hari for short.[1] According to Indian tradition, it is said that he was the son of Śrīdharasvāmin. He probably lived around 450-500 AD.[2] Exact details on the country of his birth and the land where he lived are not clear, but perhaps it can be thought that it may have been in Central India along the River Ganges, particularly around the region of Avantī.[3] According to the *The History of Buddhism* of Tāranātha, Bhartṛhari is described as a person who became king as a member of the royal family of Mālava,[4] but this is a strange coincidence. (Avantī is the country inhabited by the tribe Mālava.) In the *Vākyapadīya*, the place-names Kuru,[5] Pañcāla,[6] and Mathurā[7] appear, but one should probably understand that these are not allusions to place-names in his homeland and amount only to the reappearance of places which have been given as examples in the literature of old. This point is the same as in the case of Śaṅkara's works.[8]

Concerning his character, I-ching has recorded it in detail. I-ching's account of his writings has already been quoted, and concerning his character, he says the following:

> This scholar was very famous throughout the five parts of India, and his virtues were known everywhere (lit. 'to the eight quarters'). He believed deeply in the Three Jewels (i. e., *Ratnatraya*) and diligently meditated on the 'twofold nothingness (*śūnya*)'. Looking for the excellent Law he became a homeless priest, but overcome by worldly desires he returned again to the secular world. In the same manner he became

seven times a priest and seven times returned to the laity. Unless one believes well in the truth of cause and effect, one cannot act strenuously like him. He wrote the following verses, full of self-reproach:

Through the enticement of the world I returned to the secular world. Being free from secular pleasures again I wear the priest's robe. How do these two impulses play with me as if a child?

He was a contemporary of Dharmapāla. Once when a priest in a monastery, being harassed by worldly desires, he was disposed to return to the laity, he remained, however, firm and asked a student to get a carriage outside the monastery. On being asked the reason, he replied: 'It is the place where one performs meritorious actions, and it is designed for the dwelling of those who keep the moral precepts (*śīla*). Now, passion already predominates within me, and I am incapable of adhering to the excellent Law. Such a man as myself should not intrude into an assembly of priests come here from every quarter.'

Then he returned to the position of a lay devotee (*upāsaka*), and wearing a white garment continued to exalt and promote the true religion, remaining in the monastery. It is forty years since his death (AD. 651-652).

Next after having explained about the *Vākyapadīya*, he says:

The above-mentioned books are well studied by both monks and laymen. If they do not study them, they cannot gain the fame of "the well-informed."

Judging from this passage, Bhartṛhari was a famous grammarian who excelled in learning and virtue, but he frequently went back and forth between a life at home and a life as a penitent, and could not be consistent in either of them.

The above-cited poem recorded by I-ching gave some impetus to a Japanese philosopher. Miura Baien (1723-1789), in his work on poetics, referring to the above-cited poem of Bhartṛhari, asserted that there is a universal sense of beauty in Sanskrit, Chinese and Dutch poems.[9] Holland was the only Western country with which trade was permitted by the government of Japan in those days.

On the other hand, even in India the traditions about Bhartṛhari have been handed down in various forms in later centuries,[10] but the common aspects of these legends are either his royal family or his birth in a royal tribe,[11] and that as a youth he enjoyed the merriment of human life and enjoyed a passionate life, but in later years, leaving these afflictions, he discarded the world and entered a life of asceticism. This legend closely resembles the account by I-ching. Consequently, it may perhaps be supposed that such biographies give a truth account of the character of Bhartṛhari. If so, it is not in the slightest mysterious that he, who experienced two kinds of life, should have either composed or compiled the apparently contradictory collections of poems, the "Hundred Stanzas on Love" and the "Hundred Stanzas on Renunciation of Desire." Now, according to the account by I-ching, since he was a person of poetic genius, even though one presume that perhaps the grammarian Bhartṛhari and the poet Bhartṛhari are perhaps the same person, there is at least the possibility. However, as will be realized in the following, when one examines the contents of the *Vākyapadīya*, since the contents of the "Hundred Stanzas of Bhartṛhari" contain quite a few contradictory points, it may be thought that to explain both of them as different persons is not difficult. At least, in the extant "Hundred Stanzas of Bhartṛhari," it can be firmly asserted that there are included many poems which are not original with Bhartṛhari himself.

His faith and accomplished learning will be discussed later.

At any rate, the grammarian Bhartṛhari was a man of wide and many-sided accomplishments. According to the endorsement of the *Vākyapadīya*, it is said that Bhartṛhari was a great grammarian, a great poet, a great yogic practitioner, a great warrior, and the ruler of the region of Avantī.[12] During the time when I-ching was in India, his celebrated name as a scholar had already been sung far and wide.

Notes

1) Cf. *SDS*. XIII, *ll*. 113; 208; 256; *Vedāntakalpataruparimala*, p.549 (VizSS.); and the concluding verses of *Prakīrṇaka-prakāśa*, etc. This is exactly the same as Dharmakīrti, whose name was abbreviated to Kīrti.

2) See Part V, Chapter II of this book. Sadhu Ram asserts that his dates cannot be later than the 3rd century AD. (*Journal of the Ganganatha Jha Research Institute*, vol. IX,

parts 2-4, Feb-Aug. 1952, pp.135-151).

3) Cf. The account by I-ching and the postscript to the *Vākyapadīya*.

4) A. Schiefner: *Tāranātha's Geschichte des Buddhismus*, St. Petersburg, 1869. S. 195. However, the original has Bhartṛhari, and Schiefner thinks that this might be a dialect form for Bhartṛhari.

5) *Vākyapadīya*, III, 7, a, 4 (p.177).

6) III, 14, 483 (p.679).

7) III, 14, 533 (p.699), 534 (p.700), 535 (p.700), 542 (p.703), 544 (p.703).

8) Cf. "The Philosophical and Social Position of Śaṅkara's Philosophy," in *Collection of essays in honor of the sixty-first birthday of Dr. Hakuju Ui*: *Problems in Indian Philosophy and Buddhism*, p.357ff.

9) R. H. van Gulik: "Miura Baien on Indian and Dutch Poetry," *Monumenta Nipponica*. vol. I, 1938, pp.173-177.

10) pp.75-76 of the thesis by Mr. Tanaka previously noted. D. D. Kosambi: *Bhartṛhari*, p.80.

11) "Bhartṛhari-bhūmipati", (*Saṃkīrṇaśloka*, v. 626, ed. by D. D. Kosambi, p.176).

12) ...... *iti Mahāvaiyākaraṇa-Mahākavi-Mahāyogi-Mahārāja-Avantīśvara-Śrī-Bhartṛhariviracitaṃ Vākyapadīyam*. However, it is not clear when the postscript was appended.

CHAPTER II
THE POSITION OF BHARTṚHARI IN THE HISTORY OF THOUGHT

SECTION I. THE TRADITION OF GRAMMAR AND ITS REVIVAL BY BHARTṚHARI

Sub-Section 1. Introduction

Bhartṛhari was first of all a grammarian, and then a grammarian of the orthodox Brahmanic line. Because in later centuries the very mention of the philosophy of grammar would immediately bring to mind the name of Bhartṛhari, so great was his reputation, he must have been an important figure of epochal significance in the history of grammar too. Because adequate and detailed research has already been conducted by scholars especially on the three great grammarians of ancient times (Pāṇini, Kātiyāyana and Patañjali), whereas the history of grammar in the middle ages up to Bhartṛhari has been left in a completely dark state, an examination of this point in particular should serve as a preparatory guide for acquainting us with the historical significance of Bhartṛhari.

In India, the investigation of words has been carried out from extremely ancient times.[1] Since words are the most important element in prayer, it would seem quite natural that those who performed the religious rituals should have regarded the investigation of words as important. Consequently, from ancient times there appeared one after another specialist in the interpretation, etymology and grammar of the Vedic scriptures, which are the collected hymns, lyrical poems, funeral addresses, etc., used in rituals. The germination of such a scholastic tendency can be found already in the *Brāhmaṇas*, *Āraṇyakas* and *Upaniṣads*, but in the Vedic scriptures it reached in the point of establishing grammar as an independent field of learning among Brahmanic scholars. It was considered to be one of the six supplementary sciences for the study of the Vedas. It seems that even during the period of the rise of Buddhism Brahmins were vigorously engaged in the study of grammar. For instance, whenever a Brahmin is praised in early

Buddhist scriptures for his learning and virtue, it is always emphasized that he was a person who had training in grammar.[2]

On the subject of the etymology and interpretation of the Vedas, Yāska (ca. 500 BC.) wrote the *Nirukta*, which has been transmitted down to the present day. In addition the *Prātiśākhyas*, composed for different schools of the Vedas, also had some bearings on this. But as a work of grammar, the grammar of Pāṇini is the oldest extant work. Of course, grammarians had appeared one after another from extremely ancient times, but although their names have been handed down, their works have been lost and have not survived down to the present day. Perhaps it was because Pāṇini's grammar had been completed earlier than any other grammar adopted the rules of ordinary speech (*bhāṣā*), which differs from the language of the Vedas of the ancient period, and it included not only rules for compounds, but also ritual related to everyday conversion from Sanskrit. These rules set out to indicate the standard for correct Sanskrit. Consequently, grammar was liberated by Pāṇini from its position of being merely one of the supplementary sciences for Vedic studies and firmly established itself as an independent science. The content of his grammar was recorded in an extremely succinct *sūtra* style using algebraic symbols. It afterwards became the supreme authority on classical Sanskrit not only for scholars of orthodox Brahmanism, but also for scholars of Buddhism and Jainism, serving as a basic authority for them all.

In this manner the grammar of classical Sanskrit was firmly established by Pāṇini, and later it was minutely revised and supplemented by the annotations (*Vārttika*) of Kātyāyana (ca. 250 BC.) and the commentary (*Mahābhāṣya*) of Patañjali (ca. 150 BC.). Everything was laid down in very fine detail, and Sanskrit grammar was perfected for once and for all.

Then, many years later, the study of grammar was revived by Bhartṛhari and began to flourish once again. This is a well-known fact. But in what manner had the schools of grammar continued to exist until the time of Bhartṛhari? And how had the tradition of grammar been preserved and maintained before the appearance of Bhartṛhari? Since nothing conclusive has been recorded, and since historical research by resent scholars has not yet been completed, we find ourselves in an extraordinarily unclear position.

In order to understand the historical significance of Bhartṛhari in the history of Indian thought, one must clarify the historical background prior to him, and when doing so one is confronted with the difficult question of how to shed light on the actual state of grammar and its history. What is extremely fortunate in this regard is the highly interesting account found at the end of the second section of the *Vākyapadīya*, dealing with the tradition of grammar before Bhartṛhari[3] and the circumstances of its revival by him. This section has been carefully noted by scholars since early times as source material describing the actual state of grammar in the middle ages, and ever since this work was published, it has been discussed with reference to excerpts from the manuscripts.[4] Since it is extremely important for understanding the significance of Bhartṛhari in the history of Indian thought, we shall in the following present a translation of this section, referring at the same time to other materials that may offer clues to its meaning, as well as considering the history of the grammatical schools.

Notes

1) On philological and grammatical research by Indians up to the time of Pāṇini, Cf. B. Liebich : *Zur Einführung in die indische einheimische Sprachwissenschaft*,II. *Historische Einführung und Dhātupāṭha*, SHA. 1919.
2) *DN*. vol. I, pp.88, 114, 129, 141 ; *MN*. vol. II, pp.133, 147, 165, 210 ; *AN*. vol. I, pp.63, 166 ; vol. III, p.223 ; *Suttanipāta*, p.105.
3) *gurupūrvakrama* (Puṇyarāja ad *Vākyap*.II, 484.)
4) This is discussed in Goldstücker : *Pāṇini*, 273, f. ; Kielhorn : *NGGW*, 1885, 188, but I have not been able to consult it. A.Weber, in *Indische Studien* V, S.158 ff., has read the proofs of some of the manuscripts and has translated them using revised sentences ; he has, moreover, mentioned a refutation which is contrary to the interpretation by Goldstücker. Again, in the same work (S.447-8), there is appended a critique by Stenzler of Weber's translation and interpretation. R. G. Bhandarkar has also discussed the passage (*JBRAS*. XVI, 1885, 266 f. ; *Collected Works*, vol. I, p.166 f.). However, none of these experts has referred to the commentary by Puṇyarāja.

Sub-Section 2. Bhartṛhari's Account of the Tradition of Grammar

prāyeṇa saṃkṣeparucīn[1] *alpavidyāparigrahān*/

saṃprāpya vaiyākaraṇān Saṃgrahe 'stam upāgate//(*Vākyap*. II, 484)

"When the Compendium (*saṃgraha*),[2] having reached the grammarians who were fond of conciseness and possessed of little knowledge, was about to fail into oblivion."[3]

kṛte 'tha Patañjalinā guruṇā tīrthadarśinā/
sarveṣāṃ nyāyabījānāṃ Mahābhāṣye nibandhane//(*ibid*., II, 485)

"Then, the master Patañjali, seer of the ford, composed the 'Great Commentary', a work on the essential outline of the seeds of all logic [as well as Grammar]."[4]

alabdhagādhe gāmbhīryād uttāna iva sauṣṭhavāt/
tasminn akṛtabuddhīnāṃ naivāvāsthita niścayaḥ//(*ibid*., II, 486)

"Which is bottomless because of profundity[5] and, as it were, clear[6] because of skillfulness,[7] and those who were [of little knowledge and][8] of untrained understanding did not have firm conviction in it."

Baiji[9]*-Saubhava-Haryakṣaiḥ śuṣkatarkānusāribhiḥ/*
ārṣe viplāvite granthe saṃgrahapratikañcuke[10] *//*(*ibid*., II, 487)

"When the book (= Great Commentary), which was the armour of the Compendium, was distortedly understood[11] by Baiji, Saubhava, and Haryakṣa who were devoted to dried up logic [which was not based upon the scriptures]."

yaḥ Patañjaliśiṣyebhyo bhraṣṭo vyākaraṇāgamaḥ/
kāle sa Dākṣiṇātyeṣu granthamātre vyavasthitaḥ//(*ibid*., II, 488)

"The tradition of grammar was lost from the pupils of Patañjali, and in the course of time this tradition was preserved only in the book among the people of the Deccan."[12]

parvatād āgamaṃ labdhvā Bhāṣyabījānusāribhiḥ/
sa nīto bahuśākhatvaṃ Candrācāryādibhiḥ punaḥ//(*ibid*., II, 489)

"After the master Candra and others who were devoted to the seeds[13] [of logic] in the '[Great] Commentary' obtained the sacred work (*āgama*) from the mountains,[14] the tradition of grammar came back to consisting of many schools."[15]

nyāyaprasthānamārgāṃs tān abhyasya svaṃ ca darśanam/
praṇīto guruṇā 'smākam ayam āgamasaṃgrahaḥ//(*ibid*., II, 490)

"Studying these ways of the science of logic as well as his own view (the established doctrine in the study of grammar),[16] the master (i. e. Vasurāta)[17] wrote a synopsis of the sacred work for us."

Notes

1) Weber reads '*saṃkṣeparatān,*' but both Stenzler and BenSS now together follow the *Ṭīkā*.

2) On the *Saṃgraha* in this verse, Goldstücker interprets it as indicating the work *Saṃgraha* (said to be by either Vyāḍi or Dākṣāyaṇa) based upon the *Mahābhāṣya* of Patañjali, but Weber has refuted this; it is an ordinary noun meaning a collection merely related to grammar (*āgamasaṃgraha*, die Zusammenfassung alles Zusammengehörigen), and it is contrasted to *saṃkṣepa*. Puṇyarāja has commented in the following manner: *iha purā Pāṇinīye 'smin vyākaraṇe Vyāḍy-uparacitaṃ granthalakṣaparimāṇaṃ Saṃgrahābhidhānaṃ nibandhanam āsīt / tac ca kālavaśāt sukumārabuddhīn vaiyākaraṇaṃ prāpyāstam upāgatam / tasmāt kleśabhīrutatvāt saṃkṣeparucayas te janāḥ /*. In this verse, since it is expressed in the singular as a work earlier than Patañjali, it might be interpreted as a proper noun indicating the '*Saṃgraha* of Viyādi' of Puṇyarāja. Now it is known that this was a voluminous work.

3) Since *upa* is appended, it is different from *astaṃ gate* (Weber).

4) Supplemented by Puṇyarāja.

5) The word '*gāmbhīrya*' is employed throughout Sanskrit literature, but the meaning "the contents of the instruction are profound" does not appear in the dictionary. Such usage is a characteristic of Buddhist Sanskrit. In general Sanskrit Buddhist scriptures, it is employed in the meaning that the truth of the doctrine cannot be easily understood (e. g. *SaddhP*. p.28, *l*.2 ; p.225, *l*.18). 'Extremely deep' has almost become an established translation in Buddhist scriptures translated into Chinese.

6) *sauṣṭhava* is the same as *paripāṭī* (Puṇyarāja). It may mean that the 'Great Commentary' (*Mahābhāṣya*), being set up in sequence, was methodological and systematic.

7) *uttāna*: oben schwimmend, od. schwimmen auf der Oberfläche (Weber) ; offen daliegend (Stenzler). On the other hand, Puṇyarāja has noted it as *uttānaṃ spaṣṭam*, but the meaning 'clear and distinct' cannot be immediately found in the dictionary. In India, in general, it is employed in the sense "it has expanded," "the mouth of the vessel has become turned upwards," etc. Further, the special use of *uttāna* as 'clear' or 'distinct' is a characteristic of Buddhist Sanskrit. Cf. U.Wogihara: *Lexikalisches aus der Bodhisattvabhūmi* (Dissertation). S. 18 ; *Mvy*. ed. by Poussin, p.2, n.3. For further materials not given by these two, Cf. *uttānīkaroti----prakāśayati* (*BCA*. PBI., p.59, *l*.11) ; *Bodhisattvabhūmi*, p.82, *l*.18 (translated by Xuanzang: 'coarse and shallow'). It frequently appears in the *Saundarananda*. For *uttānakriyā*, Cf. *Bodhisattvabhūmi*, p.81, *l*.11

(translated by Xuanzang 'The Clearly Understood'). Moreover, to regard the opposing concepts of *uttāna* and *gambhīra* as having been already demonstrated is a special peculiarity of Buddhist works.

8) Supplemented by Puṇyarāja. *svalpaprajña.*

9) Weber : *Vaiji.*

10) Weber : However both BenSS. and Stenzler follow *kañcukaiḥ* (that is, the adjective *granthe*). Weber translates *pratikañcuka* as "Widersacher des *saṃgraha,*" but perhaps it has almost the same meaning as *kañcuka*. Cf. *graha* : *pratigraha.*

11) *viplāvita*. The meaning of this word has been discussed vigorously by scholars, but Puṇyarāja interprets it as *ābhāsīkṛta* ('to be made false'). As Kielhorn (*Ind. Ant.* vol. V, 1876, p.241f.) has asserted that this interpretation is correct, I have followed it here.

12) This means that a living tradition of the study of grammar does not exist.

13) *nyāyabīja* (Puṇyarāja).

14) Weber interprets *parvata* as "der himmlische Genosse des Götterboten *Nārada*." Bhandarkar also regards it as a proper noun. However, Puṇyarāja : *parvatāt trikūṭaikadevavartitriliṅgaikadeśād iti. tatra hy upatale.../*. It is not absolutely necessary that it be interpreted mythologically, but at any rate one might interpret it as 'mountain'. It is also related that Nāgārjuna, who brought about the rise of Mahāyāna Buddhism, also entered the snow mountains and received the Mahāyāna scriptures from a monk in a *stūpa* (see *Taisho*., v.50, p.317c). Further, Sylvain Lévi (*BEFEO* III, 1903, p.50, n.) asserts that he received instruction in grammar from the mountains of Kashmir, but this is perhaps based upon a late quote from the *Rājataraṅginī*. I would rather, judging from the *Vākyapadīya*, think that it should be interpreted as : "he obtained them from the mountains of the south country."

15) On *VākyaP.* II, 489 (=486 [Rau's edition] ; 481 [Iyer's edition]). See the following articles:

Ashok Narhar·Aklujkar : "The Concluding Verses of Bhartṛhari's *Vākya-kāṇḍa*," *Annals of the Bhandarkar Oriental Research Institute*, Poona, No.LVIII/LIX (Diamond Jubilee Volume), 1978, pp.9-26 ; "Interpreting *Vākyapadīya* 2.486 Historically (part 1)," *Adyar Library Bulletin*, Madras, No.44/45 (Dr. K. Kunjunni Raja Felicitation Volume), 1980/81, pp.581-601 ; "Interpreting *Vākyapadīya* 2.486 Historically (part 2)," *Indological and Buddhist Studies* (Volume in Honour of Professor J. W. de Jong on his Sixtieth Birthday), edited by L. A. Herscus et al., Canberra, Faculty of Asian Studies, 1982, pp.1-10 ; "*Rāja-taraṅgiṇī* 1.176," *Ancient Indian History : Philosophy and Culture. Essays in Memory of Prof. Radhagovinda Basak Vidyavacaspati*, ed. by Pratap Bandhopadyay and Manabendu Banerjee, Calcutta, Sanskrit Pustak Bhandar, 1987, pp.224-245 ; "Interpreting *Vākyapadīya* 2.486 Historically (part 3)," *S. D. Joshi Felicitation Volume*, edited by M. Deshpande & S. Bhate, Ann Arbor, 1991, pp.

1-47.

Johannes Bronkhorst: "On the History of Pāṇinian Grammar in the Early Centuries Following Patañjali," *Journal of Indian Philosophy*, Dordrecht, No.11, 1983, pp.357-412.

George Cardona: *Pāṇini. A Survey of Research*, The Hague, Mouton & Co., 1976 [Indian reprint: Delhi, Motilal Banarsidass, 1980], p.97, n.36.

Shivram Dattatray Joshi: "Sanskrit Grammar," *Ramakrishna Gopal Bhandarkar as an Indologist: A Symposium*, Ed. by R. N. Dandekar, Poona, Bhandarkar Oriental Research Institute, 1976, pp.113-142.

S. D. Joshi and J. A. F. Roodbergen: *Patañjali's Vyākaraṇa Mahābhāṣya: Anabhihitāhnika* (P.2.3.1-2.3.17), Publications of the Centre of Advanced Study in Sanskrit Class C, No.11, 1976 [Introduction 1: On Patañjali's Date, the Composition of the *Mahābhāṣya* and its Early Tradition, pp.i-xxxiv].

S. D. Laddu: "A Reconsideration of the History of the *Mahābhāṣya*," *Centre of Advanced Study in Sanskrit Studies*, Poona, No.6, 1981, pp.187-197; "Contribution towards the Date of the Grammarian Patañjali," *Ṛtam*, 16-18, 1984/86, pp.193-195.

M. Ramakrishna Kavi: "The Discovery of the Author's *Vṛtti* on the *Vākyapadīya*," *Journal of the Andhra Historical Research Society*, Rajamundry, No.4, 1930, pp.235-241.

16) *Vyākaraṇasiddhānta* (Puṇyarāja).

17) According to Puṇyarāja.

Sub-Section 3. The Conditions of the Study of Grammar up until Bhartṛhari

With the above account of Bhartṛhari as a basis, when we again refer to the annotations and commentaries by Puṇyarāja and reflect upon various other materials, we can trace in outline the historical vicissitudes of grammar from the age of Pāṇini up until Bhartṛhari in the following manner.

I. The Completion of the *Saṃgraha* of Vyāḍi (c.300 BC.)

Before even the appearance of Kātyāyana, there had existed the grammarian Vyāḍi, also known as Dākṣāyaṇa. The relation between his dates and those of Pāṇini is not clear, but it is generally thought that he came after Pāṇini. It seems that he lived in a period not too distant from Kātyāyana.[1]

This Vyāḍi wrote a work called the *Saṃgraha* (or *Saṃgraha-sūtra*), which exhaustively explained numerous items related to the study of grammar. This work was indeed a huge work, and according to the account of Nāgeśa it is said to have consisted of 100,000 verses,[2] but it has not been handed down to the present. Patañjali, who revered and esteemed Pāṇini, quoted from this *Saṃgraha* in the *Mahābhāṣya*. It is said that Patañjali called people who studied the *Saṃgraha* the *Sāṃgrahasūtrika* and the *Sasaṃgraha*, and also *Paramadākṣāyaṇa*.

According to what has been handed down by Patañjali, in this *Saṃgraha* the question of whether words are permanent or a result (that is, impermanent) is the essential subject under consideration, and Vyāḍi refuted the theory which asserted that words are the result of being formed and consequently impermanent. On this point, one can say that the theory of Vyāḍi was inherited by Patañjali as well as Bhartṛhari.[3] Again, the question of whether words mean an individual thing or a class was considered a problem among the scholars of that time, and Kātyāyana has recorded that Vyāḍi asserted the former and Vājapyāyana the latter.[4] One should perhaps say of this tnat Bhartṛhari was closer to the thought of *yāyana*.[5]

Further, there is also a tradition that the *Paribhāṣā*, which indicates the method of interpretation of the grammar of Pāṇini, was Vyāḍi's own work,[6] but the details are not clear.

Notes

1) According to the *Kathāsaritsāgara* (*taraṅga* 4) of later centuries, Vyāḍi lived at the same time as Kātyāyana and Indradatta, and together they studied under the Teacher Upādhyāya Varṣa. It is said that they are all classified under the Indra Schools (Aindra school) (Belvalkar : *SSG*, pp.10, 19).

2) Weber : *HIL*. p.227, n.

3) According to the previously noted verses of the *Vākyapadīya* and vol.I pp.68-69 of Dr. Ui's *Studies on Indian Philosophy*, this argument appears in *Mahābhāṣya*, vol.I, p.6, 1.12 ff.

4) *Vārttika*, 35 ; 45, under *Pāṇini*, I, 2, 64.

5) Cf. Part VII, Chapter IV, Section II, Sub-Section 2 of this book.

6) Belvalkar : *SSG*. pp.27 ; 54.

II. From Vyāḍi to Patañjali (c.300–150 BC.)

Bhartṛhari has recorded that after the *Saṃgraha* of Vyāḍi had been composed, research on the study of grammar fell into decline, and there no longer appeared any great investigations, with schools merely writing works which recorded extracts or summaries of the *Saṃgraha* and maintaining the tradition of study. As mentioned by Bhartṛhari, great works comparable to the *Saṃgraha* or the *Mahābhāṣya* were not written in this period. However, it was not the case that the study of grammar had fallen into complate decline. The appearance of Kātyāyana and his writing of the *Vārttika* on the Grammar by Pāṇini occurred in this period. His dates are supposed, for the most part, to have been c. 250 BC., and he composed a short annotation (*vārttika*) on an important section from the grammar of Pāṇini in which, with an extremely critical attitude, he either accepted or rejected the rules of Pāṇini's grammar.

As a work on grammar from this period, this *Vārttika* is unique among those now extant, but grammarians of that time succeeded one another in great numbers. As for grammarians besides Vājapyāyana, previously noted, and Vyāḍi, Kātyāyana gives Pauṣkarasādi, and when he quotes the theories of some scholars, he says "some people" (*eka,kecit*).[1] Again, Patañjali, in the *Mahābhāṣya*, has handed down the view that, besides these scholars, there were the scholars Gonardīya and Goṇikāputra. One may assume that these scholars lived at the time of Vyāḍi and Kātyāyana, and carried out their independent critical research. Consequently, even in this period one may suppose that the investigation of grammar was carried out as actively as before.

Note

1) *Vārttika* 4 ad II, 1, 1 etc.

III. The Composition of the *Mahābhāṣya* by Patañjali

Following such a state of activity, Patañjali appeared around 150 BC. and produced the *Mahābhāṣya* on the *Vārttika* of Kātyāyana. This work is not a mere commentary; he minutely and critically examined the rules of the critical interpretation by Kātyāyana, and either criticizes them or corrects them. The grammar of Sanskrit is prescribed in fine detail. Since it perfected and systematized Sanskrit as a cultural language, this work later came to receive great respect in later centuries. Bhartṛhari called it 'the work of a saintly sage' (*ārṣa grantha*)[1] and he chiefly endeavoured to explain the purport of this work.[2] The grammarians of later generations called themselves "those who scoop up the current of Patañjali (*pīta-Patañjala-jala*)."[3] Furthermore, as something which should be noted in particular in the history of philosophy, he engaged in a philosophical consideration of the essential quality of words, and that is should even be called linguistic philosophy became apparent as it progressively took on a distinctive form.

Well now, the study of grammar in India up until Patañjali had had a complicated history; and at present only the grammar of Pāṇini, the *Vārttika* by Kātyāyana, and the *Mahābhāṣya* by Patañjali have survived. The other writings have all been dispersed and lost. This fact shows again that only these three works had a decidedly dominant influence on later Sanskrit. One could say that the study of Sanskrit grammar in India was perfected once and for all by these three works. In later years, the authority of these three scholars was regarded as absolute. Even Bhartṛhari, who brought a revival to the study of Sanskrit, considered the above works as the foundation of his own theory.[4] In the detailed rules of the grammar of Sanskrit, the scholars who came after have not, for the most part, added any substantially new ones. Thus in this way, it reached the point where the free modification of Sanskrit was blocked.

Notes

1) *Vākyap*. II, 487.

2) For example : III, 8, 63 (p.341) ; III, 13, 16 (p.438) ; III, 14, 34 (p.466) ; 160 (p.532) ; 168 (p. 537) ; 459 (p.669), etc.

3) *SDS*. XIII, *l*. 2.

4) *Vākyap*. I, 23. However, Patañjali was not quite an authority to Bhartṛhari. Some Vedic passages on which Patañjali gave explanations were not understood in the same way by Bhartṛhari, so there must be some distance between these two scholars (Yutaka Ojihara : *Sur une Formule Patañjalienne, "na cedānīm ācāryāḥ sūtrāṇi kṛtvā nivartayanti," Indologica Taurinensia*, vol. VI, 1978, Torino, pp.219-234). From this we are led to the conclusion that the date of the *Mahābhāṣya* must be placed earlier than has

been done by most scholars. On the other hand, other scholars think that Patañjali's date should be placed later, (Cf. S. D. Joshi : *Sanskrit Grammar*, in R. N. Dandekar (ed.) : *R.G Bhandarkar as an Indologist, a symposium*, Poona, 1976).

IV. The Rise of Heterodox Grammar and the Decline of Orthodox Grammar (150 BC.-200 AD.)

The history of the grammatical schools up until Bhartṛhari has been comparatively well investigated, but the state of affairs after him is not clear. According to Bhartṛhari, the study of grammar by orthodox Brahmins, which had originated with Patañjali, conspicuously declined after the death of Patañjali. Now, a great number of scholars appeared who ignored the rules of the *Mahābhāṣya* by Patañjali, and who advanced independent theoretical research on grammar. These included, among others, Vaiji, Saubhava, and Haryakṣa. Their writings are not extant, but it seems that because they succeeded in cutting off their academic tradition, they had superior power in the extreme at that time. Bhartṛhari reports that their learning swept over all of India, extinguished the tradition of the grammar of Patañjali, until finally it no longer existed as a school, but was only preserved in the inner regions of the mountains in the southern Deccan region as a manuscript.[1]

Be that as it may, it is not the case that the rules of Pāṇini's Grammar were completely ignored. There were still some scholars in other areas who continued to preserve and follow these rules, who dismembered the ancient study of grammar, and who, by a fresh system, endeavoured to formulate a rational study of grammar. The oldest writing to indicate such attempts was the *Kātantra* of Śarvavarman, a Buddhist, and it is thought that the nucleus of this work was perhaps formulated in the first century AD.[2)] It is a commentary which offers an explanation of how Sanskrit grammar could be easily understood, and was warmly welcomed by the people of that time, and afterwards it was rapidly propagated throughout the broad area from Kashmir to Ceylon. Again, it also exerted a remarkable influence on the formation of Tibetan grammar.[3)]

An interesting episode which points to the actual conditions of the study of grammar at that time has been handed down by Hsüan-tsang.[4)] He says that Pāṇini was born in a village called Śalātura in Gandhāra, and immediately after the reign of King Kaniṣka, when a certain Buddhist "Great *Arhat*" came to the village for diversment, a Brahmin says that they "taught by the whip" their own children. Thereupon, the *Arhat* asked the Brahmin why he was making the child suffer like that. The Brahmin answered that it was because, although he was teaching the child "the treatise of statements" (i. e., the study of grammar), the child had not progressed in the slightest. Thereupon the *Arhat*, it is said, enlightened the Brahmin on that fact that the endeavour to learn such a "grammar of worldly works" was insignificant, and had the child leave home for the monastery.

If one considers that this includes even a small amount of historical fact, then even in this period there was no relinquishing of the tradition of the science of grammar, and among the Brahmins it was handed down, chiefly from father to son, as a hereditary study. Now, in order to faithfully cause this tradition to be inherited, a sternness even to the point of whipping a child was considered necessary. At this point, the Buddhists thought that such an academic transmission was insignificant, and caused it to be abandoned. Bhartṛhari lamented that the study of grammar in this period had become decadent, but it might rather have been the result of the influence of the laissez-faire attitude of the Buddhists, who had risen to prosperity this time, towards the academic traditions of the Brahmins.

Notes

1) The ancient grammars have been somewhat neglected, but they were handed down to later centuries in nearly the same form as they existed originally. It can be assumed that the texts handed down to the present of the grammar of Pāṇini and the *Mahābhāṣya* of Patañjali, are, for the most part, not at all different from the texts of the original authors themselves (F.Kielhorn : "On the *Mahaabhāṣya*", *Ind. Ant.*, vol.V, 1876, pp.241-251).

2) L. Renou et J.Filliozat : *L'Inde Classique*, II, 1953, p.93. All of the extant text waş not by Śarvavarman, but the appropriate part of it did originate with him (Winternitz : *GIL*, Bd. III, S.397 ; Belvalkar : *SSG*, pp.81 ff.).

3) Inaba : "The Influence of Indian Grammar on the Development of Tibetan Classical Literature," *Journal of Indian and Buddhist Studies*, vol. III, 2, p.50 ff.

4) *Ta t'sang hsi yü chi*, vol. II.

V. The Revival of Orthodox Grammar by the Master Candra (Latter Half of the Third Century)

That the study of orthodox grammar, which originated with Patañjali, was revived in this period was due to the Master Candra. He obtained the texts on the study of grammar from the mountains of the southern country, investigated them, and finally caused them to be propagated throughout India.

There is a detailed explanation of this matter in the work on the history of India, *Rājataraṅgiṇī*. According to this work, Abhimanyu ascended to the throne in Kashmīra in a period later than King Huviṣka of the Kuṣāṇa Dynasty and Nāgārjuna but prior to King Mihirakula. His strength and authority were comparable even to that of the god Indra. He built the city of Abhimanyupura, which he had crowned with his own name, and constructed inside the city temples for the God Śiva. It is said that he had such scholars like the Master Candra study the *Mahābhāṣya*.

> "The Master Candra and others, having received instruction to come there from him (=King Abhimanyu) and having already obtained the sacred traditional writings [of the study of grammar] at that time, then reached Kashmīra and popularized the *Mahābhāṣya* and also wrote their own grammar." (I, 176)[1]

Because King Abhimanyu is considered to have been a person of for the most part the third century AD., it is to be inferred that in the latter half of the third century, in Kashmīra of Northwest India, the study of orthodox grammar of the line of Patañjali was introduced.[2] It is not clear what kind of person this "Master Candra" was, but he was probably a different person from the Grammarian Candragomin famous in later centuries.

Following this, the study of grammar came to be intensively studied in Kashmīra. It seems that even as a school of study, it had considerable influence. At the very end of the "Chapter on the Refutation of the Self" (Vol.30) of the *Abhidharmakośa* by Vasubandhu, the theory of the Vātsiputrīya that the self is not the same and not different from the elements, the *ātman* theory of the Vaiśeṣika, and the *ātman* theory of the

Vaiyākaraṇa (grammarians) are refuted in detail. Concerning Vasubandhu's real intention in writing the *Abhidharmakośa,* there have been various suggestions since ancient times, but at least on the surface, because it takes as its principal objective the discussion covering the academic theories of the Kashmīra Sarvāstivādins, it can be seen that in the Kashmīra of that time the grammarians' school was a powerful adversary in thought and debate. That is, in the early half of the fourth century[4] the grammarians' school had built a firm foundation in Kashmīra.

It is not clear up until what time the grammarians' school continued to exist in Kashmīra, but for a time grammatical research became decadent, and then in the eighth century it is said that research on the *Mahābhāṣya* was once again initiated. At this time also, the king Jayāpīḍa (reigned 755-786)[5] summoned grammarians from foreign countries.

> Bringing [competent] expositors from other countries, the King restored in his own country [the study of] the *Mahābhāṣya* which had been interrupted [for a long time].[6] (*Rājataraṅgiṇī*, IV, 488)

Notes

1) *Candrācāryādibhir labdhvādeśaṃ tasmāt tadāgamam/pravartitam Mahābhāṣyaṃ svaṃ ca vyākaraṇaṃ kṛtaḥ//*(*Rājataraṅginī*, I, 176). The interpretation of this verse has been vigorously debated among former Indian scholars. Many scholars have emended the text, but I myself have followed the interpretation by Leibich, who followed the text as it stood. Since this verse greatly resembles a passage in the *Vākyapadīya*, II, 489 (Cf. previous part in this book), he surmised that Karuhana may have written it by copying the latter (B. Leibich: *Das Datum des Candragomin, WZKM* 1899, S.308 ff).

2) R. G. Bhandarkar: *Collected Works*, Vol.I, p.167; Winternitz: *GIL*, III, S.399, Anm. 2.

3) Yaśomitra: *AKV*. p.712, *l*. 26. According to Yaśomitra, there are passages in the *Abhidharmakośa* which refer to theories of grammarians other than these, and he attacks these (*AKV*. p.294, *l*.27).

4) Vasubandhu probably lived 320-400 AD., and the *Abhidharmakośa* was a work in his early period. Cf. Dr.Ui: *History of Indian Philosophy*, p.387.

5) R. G. Bhandarkar: *Collected Works*, vol.I, p.166.

6) *deśāntarād agāmayya vyācakṣaṇān kṣamāpatiḥ/prāvartayata vicchinnaṃ mahābhāṣyaṃ svamaṇḍale//vicchinna* means "researches had been suspended for a long time" (F. Kielhorn: "*On the Mahābhāṣya*," *Ind. Ant*, vol.V, 1876, p.241 f.).

VI. The Restoration of the Study of Grammar by Vasurāta (c.400-450)

After the Master Candra appeared, the scholar Vasurāta studied not only grammar but general theoretical learning and wrote a work which might have been entitled "A Synopsis of Scripture" (*Āgamasaṃgraha*). Bhartṛhari called the author of this work "Teacher" (*guru*),[1] while the commentator Puṇyarāja frequently referred to Vasurāta as the "Teacher" (*guru*) of Bhartṛhari, and the scholar of Jainism Siṃhasūrigaṇi (beginning of the sixth century)[2] called Vasurāta the "Teacher" (*upādhyāya*)[3] of Bhartṛhari. Even in a recent work, *Śabdārtharatna*,[4] the tradition is recorded that works on the study of grammar which had fallen into oblivion for a long time came into the hands of Vasurāta, and from him they were again handed down to his pupil Bhartṛhari, whereupon Bhartṛhari wrote the *Vākyapadīya*. Consequently, even before the appearance of Bhartṛhari, it is evident that the scholar Vasurāta had endeavoured to revive the study of grammar.

Extremely interesting in this regard is the account given in Paramārtha's translation, *The Biography of the Buddhist Monk Vasubandhu*,[5] according to which this Vasurāta continued through his entire life a logical dispute with Vasubandhu.

According to this account, Vasurāta was the husband of the younger sister of the "New Sun King,"[6] that is, King Bālāditya. This king was the crown prince of Vikramāditya,[7] and it is said that from Vasubandhu he received the Buddhist precepts on the orders of his father. Consequently, Vasurāta was about the same age as Bālāditya and was from a Brahmin household with a position high enough to marry the daughter of a king. Again, Vasubandhu and Saṃghabhadra were contemporaries, but Vasubandhu was much older. Since it is to be surmised that Vasubandhu probably lived c.320-400, while Bhartṛhari lived c.450-500, Vasurāta may perhaps be regarded as having lived around the years 400-450.

At any rate, an interesting legend has been handed down relating to the circumstances whereby grammar, which had fallen into decline for a long period of several hundred years, was revived in this way by the Master Candra and Vasurāta. That is, according to Puṇyarāja:[8]

> "The fundamental scriptures of the study of grammar, having been written and recorded by the (evil demon) Rāvana, existed on top of a

rock on the three-peaked mountain, and these were carried out by the *Brahmarakṣas*[9] and given to the Master Candra and the Master Vasurāta."

Another legend similar to this has also been preserved in the *Śabdārtharatna*.[10] It is not clear, as might be expected, what historical reality this legend indicates.[11] But does it not perhaps point to the fact that the study of grammar, which had been discontinued for a long time, was revived, and emphasize its important historical significance? The legend perhaps arose as the result of an attempt to impress this fact upon people.

Even the followers of Buddhism could not ignore the fact that the grammatical school had come to occupy an important position in the intellectual circles of that time. For example, even in the *Triṃśikāvijñāptimātratābhāṣya* by Sthiramati (c.470-550),[12] the philosophical theories of the grammarians are alluded to and refuted.

In a passage which discusses the metaphor (*upacāra*) at the beginning of this work (p.17, *l*.11), he says that the metaphor that the schoolchild is fire is possible when the color red or a strong disposition is common both to a schoolchild and to fire. Then he says, "Because in this case the class (*jāti*) or the substance (*dravya*) is transferred by saying that the schoolchild is fire," and next he attacks the metaphor in general. Vinītadeva, commenting on this, considers this to be the theory of the grammarians (Vaiyākaraṇa).[13]

Again, Bhavya (c.490-570) has also recorded the fact that grammarians of that time asserted the existence of *ātman,* which is maintained by the Vedānta School.[14]

It is not difficult to imagine that various grammars had existed either in this period or earlier. When one mentions the revival of the study of grammar in India in general or the origins of linguistic philosophy, one immediately calls to mind the name of Bhartṛhari, but even before his appearance a number of grammarians had appeared one after another and had exerted themselves in pioneering roles. His commentary on the *Mahābhāṣya* was written with reference to the commentaries which had existed already before him, and he himself refers to "other grammars" (*vyākaraṇāntara*) and to "other grammarians" (*anye vaiyākaraṇāḥ*) in his work.[15] Again, phrases such as "other traditional works" (*smṛtyantara*) and "other grammars" (*vyākaraṇāntara*), by which he refers to other grammars in his *Vākyapadīya*, were interpreted by commentators to indicate the grammars of Āpiśali and Kāśakṛtsna. Furthermore, in the *Mahābhāṣya* he quotes "the disciple of Āpiśali" and a passage from Kuni, who was a commentator on the *Aṣṭādhyāyī*.[16] Although the theory of Āpiśali was referred to by Pāṇini in the *Aṣṭādhyāyī* (VI, 1, 92) and the theory of Kāśakṛtsna was referred to in the *Mahābhāṣya* of Patañjali and the *Brahma-sūtra* (I, 4, 22), it is not clear whether the grammars of Āpiśali and Kāśakṛtsna were transmitted down to the time of Bhartṛhari and their successors existed. However, judging from the fact that so many works and writers were referred to by Bhartṛhari, there can be no doubt that he critically analyzed the theories of many grammarians.

Thus there were so many different theories in Sanskrit grammar and grammarians adhered to different theories. In addition to this, the study of the grammar of Prākṛt was also gradually flourishing. As Bhartṛhari frequently stated himself, the social influence of Prākṛt, the vulgar language of that time, was extremely great and was a continual threat to the historical tradition of Sanskrit. A structural systematization of the grammar of Prākṛt was also frequently attempted. However, it is to be regretted that all the grammars of the vulgar language of that time have been lost, and the oldest extant grammar which relates to the vulgar language, the *Prākṛtaprakāśa* by Vararuci, is presumed to perhaps date from the time before Bhartṛhari or from about the same period.[17]

Bhartṛhari, accepting such a historical tradition of grammar, and in such circumstances, appeared on the stage in the history of Indian thought.

Notes

1) Puṇyarāja ad *Vākyap*. II, 486 ; 489 ; 490.

2) *so 'bhijalpo 'bhidheyārthaparigrāhī bāhyāc chabdād anya iti bhartṛharyādimatam / vasurātasya bhartṛhary upādhyāyasya mataṃ tu*....(*Nayacakraṭīkā*, folio 272a). Cf. *evaṃ tāvat Bhartṛharyādidarśanam uktam / Vasurātaḥ Bhartṛharer upādyāyaḥ* (ibid. folio 277a). This work is a commentary by Siṃhasūrigaṇi on the *Nayacakra* by Mallavādin. This Mallavādin is a different person from the author of the *Nyāyabinduṭīkāṭippaṇī*. The above text is quoted from H. R. Rangaswamy Iyengar : *Bhartṛhari and Dignāga*

(*Śrī-ātmānanda-Prakāśa*, ed. by Jain Atmananda Sabha, Bhavnagar, Saurastr, 1952, p. 28).

3) *Manu* II, 140f ; *Yājñavalkya-smṛti*, I, 2, 34-35. In addition, the words "*guru*," "*ācārya*," and "*upādhyāya*" are distinguished in the codes of Brahmanism, and even in Buddhism a similar distinction was made (Cf. Dr. Nakano Gisho : *The Codes of Yājñavalkya*, p. 145), but such a distinction may perhaps not have been clearly made in the studies on grammar.

4) A. Weber : *Indische Studien*, Bd. V. S. 161, *Anm.*; *ZDMG*, XIV (1860), S. 566.

5) *Taisho Tripiṭaka*, vol.50, p.190b-c.

6) *Taisho Tripiṭaka*, vol.50, p.189c.

7) *Taisho Tripiṭaka*, vol.50, p.190b.

8) ad *Vākyap*. II, 489.

9) The name of a *Rākṣas*. It can be interpreted as "a *Rākṣas* who has been transformed from a *Brahmin* who has committed evil actions" or "a *Rākṣas* who can assume the form of a *Brahmin*."

10) Weber : *Indische Studien*, Bd. V. S.161, Anm.

11) Further, a legend which resembles this has also been preserved on the *Mahānāṭika* (Cf. Winternitz : *GIL*. Bd. III, S.244). That is, the god of monkeys, *Hanumatto*, who is said to be the author of this work, wrote it down on a rock and threw it into the ocean, but afterwards it was discovered and came to spread throughout the world.

12) Dr. Ui : *History of Indian Philosophy*, p.434.

13) Cf. Mr. Seishoo Nozawa : "On the hypothesis in *the Treatise on the nature of the existent self and in the Treatise on Consciousness-only*," in the Shi edition, *Studies on Religion*, vol.25, no. 4, p.345 ff. That this is considered a theory of the Vaiśeṣika school in the account of the *Treatise on Consciousness-only* (*Ch'eng wei-shih lun*『成唯識論』) is not correct.

14) *Tarkajvālā* ad VIII, 30 (Cf. Part II, Chapter IV, Section VII, Sub-Section 2 of *A History of the Early Vedānta Philosophy*, Part One, p.184ff).

15) On the early explanation of the *Mahābhāṣyadīpikā*, Cf. the previously noted thesis by Kielhorn (*Ind. Ant.* 1883) and the *Mahābhāṣya*, vol.II, preface, p.21. Further, the occasions when Bhartṛhari refers to conflicting theories are mainly when he says 'other person' or 'the theories of others' (*eke varṇayanti, anye varṇayanti, apare varṇayanti, anyeṣāṃ darśanam, apareṣām vyākhyānam*, etc.), and he does not concretely record the names of the assertors of these conflicting theories.

16) Kielhorn, *IA*. 1883, p.227. See Part III, Chapter VIII, Section II of *A History of the Early Vedānta Philosophy*, Part One, p.372ff.

17) The rhetorician Bhāmaha wrote a commentary on this work by Vararuci (Winternitz : *GIL*. III, S.405). The verses in the *Kāvyālaṅkāra* by Bhāmaha have been quoted in

the *Tattvasaṃgraha* of Śāntarakṣita, and since Kamalaśīla considered these to be the words of Bhāmaha, Bhāmaha lived before Śāntarakṣita. On the other hand, in the sixth verse of the fifth chapter of the same work by Bhāmaha, since he refers to the definition of *pratyakṣa* by Dignāga, and in the same work, verse 22, to the three aspects of cause, Bhāmaha lived after Dignāga. Furthermore, Benoytosh Bhattacharyya says that Bhāmaha is also earlier than Dharmakīrti (*Tattvasaṃgraha*, Foreword, p.lxxix), while Jacobi considered him to be later than Dharmakīrti (Winternitz : *GIL*. III, S.641), but the grounds for both of these arguments are rather weak. Consequently, since he lived some time between Dignāga and Śāntarakṣita, Bhāmaha must have occupied a position roughly between 500-650 AD. Since Vararuci lived even earlier than him, it may perhaps be assumed that he is approximately of the same period as Bhartṛhari or earlier.

Appendix. The Date of Candragomin[1)]

It has been generally thought by academic circles up until now that Candragomin was a grammarian who lived prior to Bhartṛhari. But since there seem to be several questions regarding this point, I did not give a general conspectus of the history of grammatical schools before Bhartṛhari in the above account. I shall now give my reasons.

Candragomin was a follower of Buddhism. The grammar, *Cāndravyākaraṇa*, which he wrote, was disseminated throughout Buddhist countries, from Nepal and Tibet to Ceylon and Java, and was exceedingly important in the history of Indian grammatical studies.

The dates of his life have been frequently discussed in academic circles up to the present, and as a rule scholars have considered the Teacher Candrācārya to be the same person as Candragomin. However, that which has been transmitted about the Master Candra and that which has been transmitted about Candragomin do not coincide. Rather, it would seem that only by considering that there were different persons can the various traditions be reasonably interpreted.

First, the accounts about the Master Candra, as previously noted, have only been recorded in the *Rājataraṅgiṇī* and the *Vākyapadīya*, and according to these, he came after the King Huviṣka and Nāgārjuna and was of the same period as the King Abhimanyu. On the other hand, he was earlier than Vasurāta and the King Mihirakula (first half of the sixth century). Consequently, as has already been mentioned, it may be assumed that he was probably a person of around the latter half of the third century. Vasurāta was senior to Vasubandhu of the same period and lived, probably, c.400-450.[2)]

Consequently, the Master Candra and Candragomin lived in different periods and, further, the spheres of activity of both were different. The Master Candra, according to the *Rājataraṅginī*, engaged in the essential activity of reviving and disseminating the study of grammar in Kashmīra. Furthermore, Candragomin[3)] was born in the Bengal region of eastern India, came to Nālandā, received the protection of the king of that region, and wrote his works on the study of grammar chiefly there. He then went to Kashmīra, and his relations with the king Abhimanyu have not been recorded.

Now, Candragomin was a person somewhat later. First, as pointed out by Liebich,[4)] the example *ajayaj japto Hūṇān*, which is given in his grammar, can perhaps be interpreted as a scribal error for *ajayad Gupto Hūṇān*. This may be thought to point to the fact that King Skandhagupta (reigned to 480 AD.) crushed the invasions of the Huns (465-470), or to the fact that King Yaśodharman completely drove out the Huns in 544. Liebich holds that this may perhaps refer to the victory of Skandhagupta. In that case, Candragomin cannot have lived, under any circumstances, before the latter half of the fifth century.

Further, according to Tibetan sources, e. g., *The History of Buddhism* by Bu-ston[5)] and the *History of Indian Buddhism* by Tāranātha, Candragomin engaged in logical disputes with Candrakīrti.[6)] As Candrakīrti refuted[7)] the theories of Bhāvaviveka (c.490-570),[8)] it has been thought that he lived for the most part around 650.[9)] Now, according to the *History of Buddhism* by Bu-ston, this logical dispute was conducted after the writing of the various studies of grammar which were transmitted as his work had been completed. If such is the case, then his dispute can be thought to have probably occurred in the later years of his life. Again, according to the Tibetan tradition in the same way, Candragomin lived in the period of Śīla, the son of Harṣadeva,[10)] and if the Harṣadeva mentioned here is considered to be the same person as Harṣavardhana, Candragomin would have lived a little before c.700 AD. Again, I-ching, in the fourth volume of his *Nan-hai chi-kuei nei-fa chuan*, has reported on a person called "The Great Master Yüeh-kuan (月官)," and when I-ching went to India (673) he lived in eastern India and had a direct interview with him. This could be considered to perhaps indicate the Candragomin mentioned above.[11] I-ching has reported the following on him :

"Again, [I came across] the great master 'Yüeh-kuan' in Eastern India. He wrote the poems of the prince Viśvantara. All the poets sing and dance through the five heavens. This is the prince who used to be called Sudāna."[12]

"In Eastern India there is a great being whose name is 'Yüeh-kuan (月官)'. He is a *Bodhisattva* of great genius and bravery. When I-ching arrived there, this person was still alive. Some asked, 'Which is more severe in hurting, poisonous objects or poison?' He answered according to his inquirer, 'The poison is far removed from the poisonous objects. If the poison is taken, it causes injury, [while] if the poisonous objects are meditated on, they are burned up.'"[13]

First, it is thought that "Yüeh-kuan (月官)" here is a translation of Candragomin.[14] The "Great Being" is, in this case, a title of respect. "Great Being" is a Chinese translation of *Bodhisattva*, and this coincides well with the legend in Tibet which says that Candragomin was a believer and follower of lay Buddhism (who could not become priest). (The word '*gomin*' when attached to the end of a name generally indicated that the person was a lay follower [*upāsaka*] of Buddhism). Further, the words 'poison sphere' and 'poison medicine' recorded above can be found in the poem *Śiṣyalekhā*, which is a work by Candragomin.

viṣasya viṣyāṇāṃ ca dūram atyantam antaram/
upabhuktaṃ viṣaṃ hanti viṣayāḥ smaraṇād api//[15]

This has a phonetic resemblance to this *viṣa* and *viṣaya*, and this phrase, in the collection of poems *Subhāṣitāvalī*.(v.3368) has been listed as a poem by Candragopin, but this may clearly be a mistake for Candragomin. Consequently, this verse, even in India in later centuries, was evidently considered to be a particular characteristic expression of Candragomin.

Next, according to I-ching's account, when Candragomin made into verse the real life story of Prince Viśvantara, that is Prince Sudāna, it became popular throughout all India. According to Lēvi, this may refer to the *Lokānanda*, a work by him. Now, since the hero in only the latter is *Maṇicūḍa*, and in both they are thinking of the moral ideal of discarding the body, there may have been such commingling and confusion. This point makes necessary further research, but such confusion is possible.

These accounts are not contradictory in the least on the dates of Candragomin. Consequently, it may be well to regard Candragomin as having lived approximately between 620 and 680 A.D. He must have been later than Bhartṛhari.

However, the following points have been raised against such a supposition:

1. The example *ajayaj japto Hūṇān* has been given as an example of the imperfect, which indicates the fact had arisen during the life of the speaker, but since this may perhaps be a mistake for the sentence *ajayad Gupto Hūṇān*, it has been arqued that Candragomin must have been a person directly after the victory against the Huns. This has been particularly emphasized by Liebich. However, among the grammarians, the usage of such an example was probably in that period, but it was recorded and handed down by the grammarians, and if it is assumed that it was handed down to the period of Candragomin, there is no hindrance at all. Now, as Lēvi has pointed out, the kings whose names end in Gupta were many in number, and since the confrontations with the Huns occurred afterwards until the 12th century, this example cannot necessarily be interpreted as referring to the victory of King Skandhagupta.

2. In the *Kāśikāvṛtti* by Jayāditya on the grammar by Pāṇini, rules which exist only in the grammar of Candragomin, and neither in the *Sūtra* by Pāṇini nor in the *Mahābhāṣya* by Patañjali, are included.[16] In this regard I-ching has recorded that Jayāditya lived over thirty years before the actual time when I-ching was in India.[17] Consequently, this means that Candragomin must have lived even before Jayāditya. However, even if the commentary by Jayāditya is considered to include the rules of Candra's grammar, one cannot conclude that he quoted

them directly from the latter. After Candra's grammar had been formulated, the academic lineage of the study of grammar continued for a long time without interruption. Now, it must have explained the various rules. Candragomin probably collected and unified these. This is exactly the same as in the case of Pāṇini's grammar. Consequently, even if one considers that the commentary by Jayāditya includes the rules of Candrā's grammar, there would be no objection at all if the former were of a more ancient age than the latter.

Further, in the Tibetan Tripiṭaka there exists the *Varṇa-sūtra,* which has been handed down as a work by Candragomin, and Dharmapāla (Chos-skyoṅ) wrote a commentary (*Varṇa-sūtra-vṛtti*) on this, and this has been preserved down to the present day (*Northeast Catalog*, Nos.4272-4273). Dharmapāla, to the extent that one follows the account of Hsüan-tsang, must be considered to have lived between 530-561. In this case, Candragomin must be considered to be a person previous even to him. However, since the Tibetan tradition is conspicuously different from the account on Dharmapāla handed down by Hsüan-tsang, it is highly doubtful whether the Dharmapāla reported by Hsüan-tsang wrote this commentary.

At any rate, it may be assumed that the chronological contradictions[18] pointed out by scholars could be settled by distinguishing between the Master Candra and Candragomin. There is a possibility that this Master Candra may have been called Candragomin, but if that is the case, then it would be well to assume that the two persons called Candragomin existed in different periods.[19]

Notes

1) I may add in passing that according to the established academic view down to the present day, the "Master Candra," previously noted, has been interpreted as the same person as Candragomin. But as I think that he cannot have followed him, I shall utilize this opportunity to publish my opinion as an appendix.

2) Cf. Belvalkar: *SSG*. p.59. However, there are no clear grounds that one could conclude that the teacher Candra was the direct teacher of Vasurāta, although Vasurāta is the teacher of Bhartṛhari.

3) *History of Buddhism* by Bu-ston, tr. by Obermiller, II, 132-134. Cf. Schiefner: *Tār-*

anātha, S. 148.

4) B. Liebich : *Das Datum des Candragomin* (*WZKM*. 1899, 308-315).

5) Tr. by Obermiller, Part II, p.132.

6) Schiefner : *Tāranātha* S.154-5. Further, according to *Tāranātha*, Candragomin is recorded after Dharmakīrti and is considered to have been the pupil of Sthiramati (S.150), but this is not recorded in Bu-ston's *History of Buddhism*.

7) *Mvṛ*., pp.36 ; 351.

8) Dr. Ui : *Studies on Indian Philosophy*, V.5, p.149.

9) Dr. Ui : *History of Indian Philosophy*, p.541.

10) S. Ch. Vidyābhūṣana : *A History of Indian Logic*, Calcutta. 1921, p.335 ; Schiefner : *Tāranātha*, S.145.

11) S. Lévi : "Notes chinoises sur l'Inde, III, La date de Candragomin," *BEFEO*, III, 1903, p.41 f.

12) *Nan-hai chi-kuei nei-fa chuan*, V.4 (*Taisho Tripiṭaka*, p.228a).

13) ibid., p.229.

14) Sylvain Lévi : op. cit., pp.38-53. The refutation by Liebich (*Das Datum Candragomin's und Kālidāsa's*. Breslau, 1903) cannot be thought to include the assertion by Lévi. That Candragomin was translated as "Miao-yüeh (妙月)" in the *Mahāvyutpatti* is an important translation from the Tibetan translation *bTsun-pa zla-ba*. Consequently, it is not a disproof to regard him as the same as Yüen-kuan (月官).

15) However, in the *Śiṣyalekhā*, *pāda* b has become *dūram atyantagocaram*. This is according to the thesis of Lévi previously noted (p.39).

16) Kielhorn : *Ind. Ant.*XV, pp.183-185.

17) Cf. Note 12.

18) Winternitz : *GIL*, III, S.400.

19) S. Ch. Vidyābhūṣana (op. cit. pp.333-336) assumes that there were two Candragomins. One wrote the *Candravyākaraṇa* in c.700 AD., and the other lived in c.925 and wrote works on logic.

[Recent studies on Candragomin]

BRONKHORST Johannes

1983 "On the History of Pāṇinian Grammar in the Early Centuries Following Patañjali," *Journal of Indian Philosophy*, Dordrecht, No.11, pp.357-412.

1985 "On the Chronology of the *Tattvārtha Sūtra* and Some Early Commentaries," *Wiener Zeitschrift für die Kunde Südasiens*,

No.29, pp.155-184.

1990 *The Cāndra-vyākaraṇa : Some Questions*. Vortrag gehalten auf der VIII. WSC, Wien.

1990a "*Vārttika*," *Wiener Zeitschrift für die Kunde Südasiens*, No.34, pp.123-146.

DASH, Prafulla Chandra

1986 *A Comparative Study of the Pāṇinian and Cāndra Systems of Grammar*. Delhi, Ramanand Vidya Bhawan.

HAHN, Michael

1993 "Notes on Buddhist Sanskrit Literature : Chronology and related Topics," *Studies in Original Buddhism and Mahāyāna Buddhism in Commemoration of Late Professor Dr. Fumimaro Watanabe*, Kyoto, pp.31-58.

OBERLIES, Thomas

1989 *Studien zum Cāndravyākaraṇa. Eine kritische Bearbeitung von Candra IV.*4.52-148 *und V.*2. Stuttgart [Studien zum *Cāndravyākaraṇa* I].

1992 "Verschiedene neu-entdeckte Texte des *Cāndravyākaraṇa* und ihre Verfasser (Studien zum *Cāndravyākaraṇa* II)," *Studien zur Indologie und Iranistik*, Band16/17, pp.161-184.

1996 "Das zeitliche und ideengeschichtliche Verhältnis der *Cāndra-Vṛtti* zu anderen *V(ai)yākaraṇas* (Studien zum *Cāndravyākaraṇa* III)," *Studien zur Indologie und Iranistik*, Band 20, pp.265-317.

RADICCHI, A.

1985 "Notes on *Cāndravyākaraṇa*," *Proceedings of the First International Sanskrit Conference*, edited by V. Raghavan. New Delhi, pp.242-247.

TATZ, M.

1976 "On the Date of Candragomin," *Buddhism & Jainism*, ed. by H. Ch. Das, Ch. Das and Shri Satya Ranjan Pali, Cuttack, pp. 281-297.

VERHAGEN, P. C.

1994 *A History of Sanskrit Grammatical Literature in Tibet*. Vol. 1,

Leiden.
VISALAKSKY, P.
1981 "The Influence of Cāndra and Kātantra Grammars on *Kāśikāvṛtti*," *Veshveshvaranand Indological Journal*, No.7, pp.45-49.

Sub-Section 4. The Position of Bhartṛhari in the History of the Study of Grammar

The appearance of Bhartṛhari was of epochal significance for the tradition of the study of grammar in India. In this respect, the school of grammar which derived from Pāṇini and Patañjali developed further to the point of becoming one of the schools of philosophy. Now, Bhartṛhari himself was the very person who caused such a transition. The grammarians afterwards, in regard to the problems of linguistic philosophy, chiefly followed Bhartṛhari and revered him as an authority.[1] Works which discuss chiefly linguistic philosophy have appeared in great numbers in India, but among them his *Vākyapadīya* is the oldest extant work. Again, in the study of grammar in a narrow sense, his influence was exceedingly great.[2] Consequently, scholars of later centuries expressed their respect for Bhartṛhari by considering him a person who ranked second only to Pāṇini, Kātyāyana, and Patañjali.[3]

Because of this, later scholars of other schools, whenever they attack the philosophy of the grammarians, quote in particular the *Vākyapadīya* of Bhartṛhari and criticize this work. Beginning with the Buddhist philosophers Śāntarakṣita and Kamalaśīla,[4] the Jaina philosopher Prabhācandra,[5] Kumārila of the Mīmāṃsā,[6] Jayanta[7] of the Nyāya school, and a great many other scholars attack him, regarding him as a representative of the grammarians.[8] Again, the *Sarvadarśanasaṃgraha* regards the academic theories of the grammarians as one of the philosophical systems and has made the theories of Bhartṛhari representative of this system.

What kind of philosophy did he who was the reviver of the study of grammar and also the creator of linguistic philosophy advocate? To explain this will be the topic of the following chapter. Bhartṛhari, by including the philosophy of the Vedānta within the study of grammar, accomplished such a development in ideas. At the same time that he was a grammarian, he was also a scholar of the Vedānta. Consequently, I shall also make clear in the next section the fact that he was considered a scholar of the Vedānta.

Notes

1) e. g. Cf. Kaiyata's commentary on the *Mahābhāṣya*.

2) That Kaiyata's commentary on the *Mahābhāṣya* is chiefly based upon that of Bhartṛhari is as has already been noted. Again, the *Saṃkṣiptasāra*, a grammar written by Kramadīśvara (13th century) was written with the *Mahābhāṣya-dīpikā* as its model (Belvalkar : *SSG*. p.109).

3) Aufrecht : *Bodl. Cat*. p.175b.

4) *Tattvasaṃgraha*, p.67ff. ("Śabdabrahmaparīkṣā").

5) It is frequently referred to in the *Prameyakamalamārtaṇḍa*.

6) *Ślokavārttika*, sphoṭavāda.

7) *Nyāyamañjarī*, p.531 ff.

8) Further, it is said that his theories are discussed in the *Sammatitarkaprakaraṇa*, p.379 f., *Nyāyakaṇikā*, p.286 f., Nāgojibhaṭṭa, *Laghumañjūṣā* p.173, etc.

SECTION II. BHARTṚHARI AS VEDĀNTIN

As grammarian, or as author of the *Bhartṛhariśataka*, Bhartṛhari is a great figure in the history of Indian thought, but the fact that at the same time he was also a Vedānta philosopher seems to have been overlooked. Perhaps the fact that the publication of the *Vākyapadīya* was incomplete for so long was the reason that scholars of the world generally did not remark that his position is Vedāntic. But it is a solid and indubitable fact that he is an important figure in the history of early Vedāntic philosophy.

Among the sects of Vedānta, he was regarded as one of the ancient scholars of their school. The later Yāmuna counts Bhartṛhari as one of the old philosophers of the Vedāntic school before Śaṅkara, and from the Viśiṣṭa (limited) Advaita tradition he regards him as teaching a heretical doctrine.[1] But even in this same Viśiṣṭa Advaita tradition, in later times, Bhartṛhari is seen as an authority on Vedānta. Raṅga-Rāmānuja in the 16th century quotes him :

> But Bhartṛhari teaches: The spontaneous preservation of itself is what is meant by 'Existence'. Namely, Existence, being the special characteristic of things animate or inanimate to preserve themselves, is an evidence for the existence of the Supreme Self, — such is the meaning.
>
> *uktaṃ ca Hariṇā : ātmānam ātmanā bibhrad astīti vyapadiśyate*(= *Vakyap*. III, 3, 47, p. 120) *iti cetanācetanayor ātmabharaṇalakṣaṇasattā paramātmasattādhīnety arthaḥ*/[2]

If we look elsewhere in Advaitic works, we find in the *Bhāmatī* of Vācaspati Miśra a quotation from Bhartṛhari as an authority (*Bhāmatī* ad *BS*. II, 1, 11).

> In regard to things which are to be known simply on the authority of scripture and which are not the objects of independent theorizing, the arguments by which the Sāṃkhyas for instance seek to postulate a primordial substance, *pradhāna* and so on, developing in accordance with all-pervading nature and distinctions, — cannot hold. So it is said: "What is inferred by a skilled logician with much labour, by those yet more adept is established to be the contrary."(*Vākyap* I. 34).

Again in Mādhava's *Sarvadarśanasaṃgraha* in the 16th chapter where he speaks of his own sect's doctrine, Bhartṛhari's verses are quoted as authority for his own teaching. So it is clear that Bhartṛhari's position is adopted and approved as it stands by Vācaspati Miśra and Mādhava. In the *Sarvadarśanasaṃgraha*, Bhartṛhari's doctrine is mainly discussed in the 13th chapter, on the doctrine of Pāṇini, and this is because it is closely connected with Pāṇini. Mādhava himself considered it essentially the same as that of "those versed in the Vedānta" (*Vedāntavādanipuṇāḥ, SDS*. XIII, *l*.267). The latter Advaitin Pratyagrūpa also recognized him as a Vedāntin.[3] Further, writers of the Kashmir Shiva sect (Somānanda, Utpala), when crticizing the *Sphoṭa* theory, call Bhartṛhari an Advaitin.[4]

So that Vedānta schools themselves went so far as to recognize Bhartṛhari as a precursor of their own doctrines, while other schools thought of his doctrine as Vedānta or a variety of it. The Buddhist Śāntarakṣita (*Tattvasaṃgraha*, v. 152) recognizes his doctrine as *Brahma*-doctrine (*Brahma-darśana*), and the Buddhist Jñānaśrībhadra calls him a teacher of *Brahman* (*tshaṅs par smra ba*).[5] Again the Jaina scholar Prabhācandra calls him *Śabdādvaitavādin*, and Abhayadeva calls his doctrine *Śabdādvaitavāda*.[6] This term would be because Bhartṛhari understood *Brahman* as arising from Word (*śabda*). In view of this appellation it is probable that he was viewed as a Vedāntin in the broad sense, with his stress on *Brahman* as having Word for its essence forming the special peculiarity of his thought. However this kind of idea is recognized by the *Brahma-sūtras* and by Śaṅkara himself, and is not a doctrine special to Bhartṛhari.[7] We can say that on this point he is not apart from the main current of Vedānta.

He is, therefore, widely recognized in India generally as a Vedāntin and furthermore he himself declares that his standpoint is that of "one who knows the inner secret of the three *Vedas*", namely a Vedāntin.

> "On this point it is just the not making of distinctions between perceiver, thing perceived and function of perception that the knowers of the inner secret of the three *Vedas* declare to be Truth."
>
> *yatra draṣṭā ca dṛśyaṃ ca darśanaṃ cāvikalpitam/*
> *tasyaivārthasya satyatvaṃ āhus trayyantavedinaḥ//*(*Vākyap*. III, 3, 70).[8]

The "inner secret of the three *Vedas*" means Vedānta.[9]

Bhartṛhari calls himself (III, 1, 43. p. 36) a monist(*ekatvadarśin*) and the commentator Helārāja glosses this as "non-dualist" (*advaitin*). Further, according to Helārāja, Bhartṛhari's doctrine was non-duality(*advaitavāda*,[10] *advaitanaya*)[11] and he also calls it "existent non-duality"[12] (In a fair number of verses, probably later, which could go back to him, the standpoint of Vedānta philosophy is expressed.)[13] Again the *Yoga Vāśiṣṭa*, which has a peculiar character as a classic of Hinduism, quotes phrases of the *Vākyapadīya* and shows traces of its influence.[14]

Thus Bhartṛhari was regarded as a Vedāntin not only in the orthodox Brahminical world but also by Buddhists and Jains, and in addition he himself was a professed orthodox Vedāntin. He is known as a Grammarian, and as we shall see, he was influenced by Buddhism, but in philosophy he was a Vedāntin.

Such being the case, how did he combine his Grammarian's and Vedāntin's philosophy? And what sort of metaphysics did he construct out of them? In what sense can his philosophy be called Vedāntic? — let us reply to such questions in the next part. But before turning to them, we give a general examination into his connections with Buddhism, in the succeeding section.

Notes

1) *Siddhitraya* p.5 -- see this book, Part V, Chapter I.
2) Raṅgarāmānuja : *Chāndogya Upaniṣat prakāśikā* ad VII, 24, 1. p.554. (AnSS.).
3) In his notes on the Advaitin Citsukha's *Tattvapradīpikā*, Pratyagrūpa calls Bhartṛhari a *Brahmavitprakāṇḍa*.
4) Mahadevan : *GP*. p.228.
5) See Part V, Chapter II, Fragment 2 of this book.
6) *Prameyakamalamārtaṇḍa*, p.11b : after quoting a verse from *Vākyapadīya* he says, *ye'pi śabdādvaitavādino nikhilapratyayānāṃ śabdānuviddhatvenaiva savikalpakatvaṃ manyante*.
7) *Brahma-sūtra* I, 3, 28-30 and Śaṅkara's commentary.
8) According to the quotation in *Sarvadarśanasaṃgraha* of Sāyana-Mādhava, XIII, *ll*. 254-6 ; the text published of *Vākyapadīya* gives *vā vikalpitam* for *cāvikalpitam* but this is incorrect. See Helārāja's commentary. The text also gives *śritās* for *āhus*.
9) Helārāja remarks : *Ṛg-yajuḥ-sāmātmako Vedas trayī, tasyā antaḥ sārabhūtārthanir-*

ṇayamaya *Upaniṣadbhāgaḥ* / Cf. *trayyantair brahmavijñānam aparokṣam vibhāvyate*/ (*Ahirbudhnya-saṃhitā* XIII, 26.).

10) For instance Helārāja ad III, 9, 46. p.359.

11) Helārāja ad III, 2, 7. p.89.

12) *sattādvaita darśana*, Helārāja ad III, 8, 35. p.326.

13) *Saṃśayita-Ślokas of Bhartṛhari*, ed. by D. Kosambi, v. 662, p.181. Cf. Vedānta, v. 287, p. 112 ; *brahmadhyāna*, v. 239 ; *brahmajñānavivekin*, v. 283 ; *Vedāntapraṇihitadhī*, v. 287 ; *parabrahman* v. 301, p.479 ; *Yājñavalkya*, v. 634.

14) Glasenapp : *Zwei philosophische Rāmāyaṇas*, Akademie der Wissenschaften und der Literatur. Abhandlungen der geistes-und sozialwissenschaftlichen Klasse. Jahrgang 1951. No.6 Wiesbaden. S. 435 f.

SECTION III. BHARTṚHARI AND BUDDHISM

Sub-Section 1. The Legend that Bhartṛhari was a Follower of Buddhism

As has been made clear in what was discussed in the preceding section, Bhartṛhari himself adopted a position as a Vedānta philosopher, and even in Indian circles of thought in general in later centuries he was evaluated in this way. Consequently, he was a person who should be regarded as a Vedānta philosopher, but in present-day academic circles it has been argued for some time whether or not Bhartṛhari was a follower of Buddhism. The emergence of such a problem is due to I-ching's report that he was a follower of Buddhism.

According to the words of I-ching, Bhartṛhari was an ardent Buddhist believer ("a man of the pure faith"): "he believed in the three gems," "he reflected upon the two emptinesses," and frequently lived in Buddhist temples ; his work, the *Vākyapadīya*, is said to be a work which "clarified deeply consciousness-only and superbly discussed the reason (*hetu*) and example (*udāharaṇa*)." Since he traveled throughout India shortly after Bhartṛhari's death — 40 years after his death, according to his own account — it may be assumed that the account in his work *Nan-hai chi-kuei nei-fa chan* can be adequately relied upon. Again, I-ching recorded that Dharmapāla, who was a Buddhist scholar, wrote a commentary on the *Prakīrṇaka*, a work by Bhartṛhari. Consequently, based upon these accounts, scholars down to the present day have asserted that Bhartṛhari was a follower of Buddhism[1] and have thus tried to read Buddhist ideas into even the *Bhartṛhariśataka*.

Be that as it may, Bhartṛhari was not a follower of Buddhism. He admitted the absolute authority of the Vedic scriptures and clearly stated that his study of grammar was a learning for the sake of maintaining, preserving, and understanding the *Vedas*. Such an attitude for a follower of Buddhism could not have been permitted under any circumstances. A follower of Buddhism never respected and obeyed the *Vedas*. Furthermore, his philosophical thought was highly Vedāntic, and he even called himself "the one who can know the inner meaning of the three *Vedas*" (*trayyantavedin*), and even scholars in India in later centuries, as I have already mentioned, regarded him as a Vedānta philosopher. Consequently, there is no room for doubt that he was not a truth follower of Buddhism. Academically, he had adopted the position of a pure, orthodox Brahmin.

If so, why did I-ching report that Bhartṛhari was a follower of Buddhism? In order to give an answer to this question, I shall first consider the following two issues:

1. How did the followers of Buddhism of later centuries regard, in general, Bhartṛhari? Did they, like I-ching, regard him as a follower of Buddhism?
2. What kind of attitude did Bhartṛhari himself adopt towards Buddhism?

I shall discuss the first issue in Sub-Sections II and III and the second issue in Sub-Sections IV and V, and lastly I shall give my conclusion.

Note

1) Further, the eminent scholar Pathak, apart from the account by I-ching, has separately asserted that Bhartṛhari must have been a follower of Buddhism (K. B. Pathak: "Was Bhartṛhari a Buddhist?", *JBRAS*, XVIII, 1894, pp. 341-349). According to his line of reasoning, Vācaspatimiśra, in his work, quotes a verse from the *Vākyapadīya* with the words "those of other teachings," (*bāhyāḥ*), and since the word "one of other teachings" in his work *Bhāmatī* (ad I, 1, 1, p. 25, B.I.) is used to mean a follower of Buddhism, Vācaspatimiśra must have regarded the author of the *Vākyapadīya* as a follower of Buddhism. However, *bāhya* is not a word which means only a follower of Buddhism. E. g. judging from the phrase *bāhyā apy āhuḥ* ... "*śāstracintakāḥ khalv evaṃ vivecayanti na pratipattāraḥ iti*" (*Bhāmatī* ad *BS*. I, 1, 1. p. 8, NSP.), an almost identical

phrase appears also in the *Sarvadarśanasaṃgraha*, and as in the commentary by Abhyankar, it should probably be considered to indicate the scholars of rituals or the scholars of the Mīmāṃsā, etc. Therefore, the assertion by Pathak is not valid.

Sub-Section 2. Bhartṛhari as Seen by the Buddhists

There is no instance of Bhartṛhari's name being mentioned in Chinese translations of the Buddhist *sūtras*, and the account by I-ching noted above is the sole source. Therefore, except for this, Chinese translations of the Buddhist *sūtras* cannot serve as any clue whatsoever. But in the Sanskrit originals of Buddhist works which have not been translated into Chinese there are passages which refer to Bhartṛhari. That is, Dharmottara wrote the *Nyāyabinduṭīkā* on the *Nyāyabindu* of the famous logician Dharmakīrti, and Mallavādin further wrote a supplementary commentary (*Ṭippaṇī*), which is extant and has already been published. There are passages in it which refer to the ideas of Bhartṛhari. In presenting various theories[1] on the problem of knowledge, he says as follows:[2]

> Again, in the same way, the grammarians (*vaiyākaraṇa*) say: "The meaning (*vācya*) associated with its indicator (*vācaka*) manifests itself in the perception through the sense organs. Therefore, [everything] has connection with the word as its nature."
>
> "If the eternal nature of knowledge having the word as its essence were to disappear, the light [of the spirit][3] would not shine forth, since it indicates[4] [the various meanings]." (*Vākyap*, I, 125)
>
> "There is no notion in the world which the word does not follow. All knowledge appears, as it were, to be pierced by the word." (*Vākyap*, I, 124)

That is, since these passages have been given as one of the heretical theories along with the Mīmāṃsā and the Nyāya school, etc., as seen from the standpoint of a Buddhist theory, Bhartṛhari's linguistic philosophy is understood as something which is thought to be other than a theory of Buddhism.

However, since it has been said that the commentator Mallavādin was a scholar classified as a Jain,[5] it might be thought that the value as a source of the above account is slight; however, on the contrary, the direct opposite can hold true. There is a tendency, in general, that if the thought of school 'A' and the thought of school 'B' are analogous, when their difference is not too great, those who are grouped in both schools themselves fully know the differences between the two schools and emphasize contrary points, but a third person who is not grouped in the two schools ignores the differences between the two schools and ends up concluding that they are of an identical kind. If it had been questioned whether the thought of Bhartṛhari was close to the theories of Buddhism, or if it had been admitted in general that it was near, Mallavādin probably would not have regarded the theories of Bhartṛhari as a heretical theory as seen from the standpoint of Buddhism. Furthermore, he did not regard Bhartṛhari as a Buddhist, but as a 'grammarian'.[6]

Mallavādin lived at the end of the eighth century,[7] and it is evidently clear that it was thought in India in general during this period that the academic theories of Bhartṛhari were different from the theories of Buddhism.

However, to the extent that it is not compared with that, that which might make this situation clear for us is the account in the *Tattvasaṃgraha*, a work by Śāntirakṣita in the middle of the eighth century. This work critically attacked from a Buddhist standpoint the system of thought which was then prevalent through India in general. There is a chapter called "Examination of *Brahman* as words"(*śabdabrahmaparīkṣā*), in which the academic theories of Bhartṛhari are introduced and criticized. This chapter may be the most important source — and up to now among those published, it is perhaps the only one — by which one might know how the Buddhists regarded the thought of Bhartṛhari. Consequently, a close investigation of this may perhaps show clearly in what respects his thought differs from Buddhism, and also in what respects it resembles it. Again, to know what points of the academic theories of Bhartṛhari were attacked is an immensely interesting issue. I shall translate and produce in the following all the verses (together with the commentary by Kamalaśīla). (The commentary by Kamalaśīla was also written in the same period as Śaṅkara, and should be regarded as unusually important.)

A favourable circumstance regarding the translations is that Tibetan translations have been preserved in the Tanjur of the Tibetan *Tripiṭaka*, and it is convenient to be able to refer to them. Because the Tibetan translations are almost direct word-by-word and phrase-by-phrase translations, comparing them is easy. By this means one can revise the scribal errors in the Sanskrit works and the typographical errors in the printed works, and also interpret clearly and accurately the passages which are unclear in meaning. Major differences have been recorded in the annotations. Even on the structure of the sentences, passages which were translated following the interpretation of the Tibetan translation are not few. However, since there are passages in which the Tibetan translation appears to have misunderstood the original work, these have been noted in the annotations.

Notes

1) *asti cātra vipratipattiḥ.*

2) *tathā ca Vaiyākaraṇā āhuḥ/ vācakasaṃsṛṣṭaṃ vācyam indriyajñāne pratibhāsate/ tena śabda-saṃyojanātmakam iti/ vāgrūpatā ced utkramed avabodhasya śāśvatā/ na prakāśaḥ prakāśeta sā hi pratyavamarṣiṇī//* (= *Vākyap* I, 125. p. 47) ; *na so 'sti pratyayo loke yaḥ śabdānugamād ṛte/ anuviddham iva jñānaṃ sarvaṃ śabdena bhāsate//* (= *Vākyap*, I. 124) — *Nyāyabinduṭīkāṭippaṇī*, p. 20, *ll.* 2 - 7 (ed. Th. Stcherbatsky, B. B.)

3) According to the commentary by Puṇyarāja, *caitanya, jñāna.*

4) *pratyavamarṣiṇī.* Among linguistic philosophers in general, *pratyavamarṣa* was employed to indicate the object of meaning. Cf. Śaṅkara ad *BS.* I, 3, 28 (Vol. I, p. 305, 1. 6, ĀnSS) : Logical disputes on *sphoṭa.* Betastung (Deussen), a comprehensive consciousness (Thibaut).

5) M. Winternitz : *GIL.* Bd. III, S. 468.

6) According to the Index, the word *Vaiyākaraṇa* was used in this passage.

7) Cf. note 5.

(Appendix) I referred to the Tibetan translation of the *Pañjikā*, borrowing the microfilm of the sDe-dge edition stored in the library of Tohoku University from my esteemed friend, the late Mr. Tanden Kasamatsu. I would like to take this opportunity to express my deep gratitude to him.

Sub-Section 3. "Examination of *Brahman* as Words" (*Śabda-brahma-parīkṣā*) in the *Tattvasaṃgraha*

In the Japanese original work I translated all the verses of the *Śabda-brahma-parīkṣā* into Japanese with critical annotations. But in the following

I propose to translate into English as far as verse 143.

Contents Verse No.

I. Assertion of the Philosophers who Hold that *Brahman* is Words

[Tib.184a] The philosophers who hold that *Brahman* is words (*śabda-*

brahma-vādin)[1] by such words as "perishing and arising" declare:
[Verse 128]

"It is thought that the concurrence of these things is the evolution (*pariṇāma*) of *Brahman*, the highest being uninfluenced by "perishing and arising"[2] and consisting of words (*śabda*)."

It is recognized[3] that the concurrence of objects such as visible forms, etc., is the evolution[4] of "*Brahman*, which is free from the distinctions of before and after, etc.,[5] is unborn and indestructible, and is formed from words." As it is explained next:

"*Brahman*, [which is the source] from which arises the creation[6] of the world, imperishable, the fundamental nature of that which is words, with neither beginning nor end,[7] evolves[8] as objects (meaning, *artha*). (*Vākyapadīya*.I.1)[9]

Here, "beginning" (*ādi*) refers to "arising" (*utpāda*), and "end" (*nidhana*) to "perishing" (*nāśa*). Because they do not exist, it is "with neither beginning nor end." "Imperishable" (*akṣara*) is thus mentioned because it is the cause of letters (*akṣara*) such as '*a*'. By this (word, *akṣara*), evolution[10] is denoted as indicator (*abhidhāna*). Furthermore, by means of "as objects" (meaning), evolution is denoted as that which is designated (indicated, meaning, *abhidheyavivarta*). Creation (*prakriyā*) means all individual things (*bhedāḥ*). That which is called "*Brahman*" is given the appellation [of the major subject].

[This verse in the *Tattvasaṃgraha*] explains the meaning of this verse [appearing at the beginning of the *Vākyapadīya*]. — It is said, "uninfluenced by 'perishing or arising'," etc. The words "perishing or arising" also contain other implicit meanings.

[That is to say,] it should be known that in this verse the meaning is also [included] that "it is apart from the spacial distinctions of before and after." For in this case it is explained that "without beginning or end" is held to also be apart from the spacial distinctions of before and after.

"Consisting of Words" means "that the word is held to be its original nature." For that reason, it is said that Words are the original nature of it (=*Brahman*), that is to say, it (=*Brahman*) is that which has words as its fundamental nature. [In other words] it means that the Word is its unmistaken (correct) fundamental essence.

"The Highest" refers to the fact that the sacred sound (*praṇava*=*om*) is held to be the fundamental essence. In the final analysis, the sacred sound is the substance (*prakṛti*) of all words (*śabda*) and all meanings (*artha*), and it is said that it is the *Vedas*. Furthermore, these *Vedas*, which have come into being by the order and arrangement of sounds and vocabulary, are the means to communicate it (=the Highest). [Now, the *Vedas*] exist by means of the principle that they are a reflection of it (=the Highest). [That is to say, the *Vedas* are the reflection of *Brahman*, as it were.] Now, the purport is that men who perceive its inner organ (i. e., the mind) by means of the *dharma*, which brings prosperity (*abhyudaya*) and supreme bliss (*niḥśreyasa*) as the fruits of its action, shall perceive this highest self, *Brahman*.[11]

Now, in order to establish this purport, the proof is offered that: "Anything, no matter what it is, which is penetrated by the form (*ākāra*) of a certain thing,[12] is made up of that thing. For example, it is acknowledged in general by the world that a thing made from the transformation of clay, such as a jar, saucer, cup, etc., is a physical substance which conforms to the form of the clay, and these things are composed of clay (Tib. 185a). And the fact that "all things are penetrated by the form of words" is, in this case, the cause of their self-nature (*svabhāva-hetu*).[13] (And it is not an unestablished cause [*asiddha-hetu*]).[14] And it is indeed admitted in the general world [by direct perception] that ultimately all things conform to the form of words. That is to say, since all concepts (*pratyaya*)[15] are born in relation to things (*artha*, meaning), they arise only as an accompaniment of the representation of words (*śabda*).[16] For, as it is next explained:

> "A concept which does not accompany words does not exist in the world. All concepts appear as if they were pierced by words, as it were." (*Vākyap*. I.124)
>
> (French Trans.: "En ce monde, il n'y a pas d'idée qui ne prenne la forme de la parole; toute connaissance apparaît comme pénétré de la parole." — Biardeau, V.123, p.157)

Now, the supposition (*prajñapti*) of the original nature of all physical substances is based upon the form of concept. For that reason, it is established that all things are penetrated by the form of words. And since this fact is established, it is also naturally established that they are composed of these [words]. For "their being composed of that" (*tanmayatva*) is "their having only that as their fundamental essence" (*tanmātrabhāvitva*).[17]

II. The Refutation of the Philosopers who Hold that *Brahman* is Words

II-A. Refutation of Evolution

[The following] will refute the matter which is asserted [by these who assert that *Brahman* is words] by means of such phrases as "one should cross-question [in the following manner] [those] people."

[Verse 129]

One should cross-question in the following manner those people who argue in this way. — Does it (i. e. *Brahman* as words) itself (1) discarding its fundamental essence as words, enter into appearance such as blue, etc. [of the phenomenal world]?

[Verse 130]

(2) Or does it not? —

(1) If one considers that it has adopted the first case, and if it is so, [*Brahman*] must become separate from indestructibility. For it would be to destroy the fundamental essence which existed from before.

[Verse 131]

(2) If one considers that it has adopted the latter case, and if it is so, when blue, etc. have been cognized, the perception of the fundamental essence of words, even in one who does not have the sense of hearing (i. e., a deaf person), should clearly arise.

In regard to this problem, (A) in certain cases, because [the world] is the evolution[18] of words, [the formation of the world of words] can be thought to be the condition (that which is established, *sādhya*) which should be logically demonstrated. (B) Again, in certain cases, because [the world] arises from words, ['the formation of the world from words' is thought to be the condition which should be logically demonstrated.] E. g. there is the case that "life is that which is formed from food (*annamayāḥ prāṇā iti*)."[19] For the rule exists that the suffix [formed from *mayat*] means the cause (*hetu*).[20] Consequently, in this it means that "food is the cause in order that life may arise."

II-A-1. The Impossibility of Evolution when the World is held to have evolved from Words.

II-A-1-a. General Introduction

Here, (A) first, in the first case, it cannot be established. For the self-substances of evolution[21] are impossible. That is, if *Brahman*, who has as its fundamental nature words, were to enter into the state of blue, etc,[22] (1) at some time it would enter by discarding "the fundamental essence, which is words, " [of itself], (2) or it would enter without discarding its fundamental essence.

II-A-1-b. The case in which *Brahman* discards its own Substance

Among these : (1) if the first case should be adopted, that *Brahman* [enters into the state of blue, etc.] by discarding the fundamental essence, it would be that the "indestructibility," viz. "the imperishability," that had been hypothesized by these passages that "it has neither beginning nor end" (*Vākyap.*I,1) does not coincide. For, [if this is considered to be the case,] the fundamental essence which exists from before already[23] would be extinguished and perish.

II-A-1-c. The case in which *Brahman* Does not discard its own Substance

II-A-1-c-i. The Fallacy that the Sense of hearing arises even in a Deaf Person

(2) Again, if the latter case should be adopted, that *Brahman* [enters into the state of blue, etc.] without discarding its fundamental essence, if it would be that sounds arise in the consciousness, even for 'those who do not have the sense of hearing', that is, the deaf,[24] at the time when one is cognizant of blue, etc. For, in the same way as the consciousness of blue, etc. [the consciousness of words, also] is not separate from it (i. e. words).

[On this point, the following] argument form (*prayoga*) is established — if it is the case that A is not separate from B, when A is in the consciousness, B is in the consciousness. E. g. in the case when blue, etc., are in the consciousness, the fundamental essence (*ātman*) of this blue, etc., must be in the consciousness. Now, that words[25] are something which is not separate from blue is the self-essence-cause (*svabhāva-hetu*). If this were not the case, since [blue, etc., and words] would become independent existences which are mutually different,[26] it probably would not[27] be established that [this individual thing which is blue, etc.] has words as its fundamental essence. [Consequently, based upon the above presupposition, when blue, etc., are in the consciousness, the conclusion would be reached that sounds should be heard even by one who does not have the sense of hearing.] — The above fact is the logical demonstration which makes, in this case, the argument of the logical opponent invalid.[28]

Teaching in detail this fact, he says, "For," etc.

[Verse 132]

> For, [you have taught] that all things are brought into existence as composed from words in their verbatim meaning. If one does not discard the fundamental essence of words, then there is no determination of all evolution.

For (*yena* = *yasmāt*) you teach that the world has its fundamental essence in words in their verbatim meaning. Why is this? Saying this, he says, "If one does not discard the fundamental essence of words."

II-A-1-c-ii. The Fallacy that the Sense of hearing arises at the same time as the Sense of Sight, etc.

If, in the verbatim meaning, it [the word] exists as something formed from words, what kind of thing would it become?[29] Asking this, he says, "Furthermore, ...in the meaning which is not metaphorical," etc.

[Verse 133]

> Further, in this way, if what blue, etc., are identical [with words] are established in the meaning which is not metaphorical (i.e. the original meaning), when one perceives that (i.e. blue, etc.), how can the perception of words not exist?

"Blue, etc., are identical" should be interpreted by supplementing the phrase "with words." "When one perceives that" means "in the state in which one perceives the blue, etc., of those things." "How can the perception of words not exist?" that in the same as the perception of the fundamental essence of blue, etc., since the word has also the special essence oı being perceived,[30] it is quite nature that one should perceive the word also.

Additional Discussion: *Reduction ad Absurdum* in the case in which the Sense of hearing does not arise

[Verse 134]

> "Really, if it is considered that words have not been perceived, the perception of blue, etc., also must not exist. For [blue, etc., and words] would be of identical fundamental essence. If it were the case that [blue, etc., and words] caused the special essence to be different, [both of them] should be absolutely separate and different."[31]

If [when you have perceived blue, etc.] the perception of words should arise, if one does not admit that, and if it is so, blue, etc., also, in the same way as the fundamental essence of words, would become something which cannot be perceived. "For they would be something of identical fundamental essence" means [according to your theory] "since blue, etc., are something of identical fundamental essence with words." If this were not the case, if one were to hypothesize that blue, etc., possess a special essence which is different from words, and if this were so, [in opposition to your theory] you would admit the absolute separateness and differentness [of both of them].

Asking why, he says:

[Verse 135]

> "For the fact that a mutually contradictory special essence accompanies both is the special quality which indicates the separate difference of many things. If it is not so [and if further the identical nature of these things exists],[the discrimination] of others which can be posited in the various individual things should not be able to also exist."

Really, to say that the same thing is both perceived and not perceived by the cognitive prime substance of identity is not correct. For it would be to discard the identity [of those things when one considers that there are such things]. If this is not the case, and if, really, even if the essential qualities which are mutually contradictory [in all things], after all, if one considers that the identity [in all these] exists, and if so, in the [various individual things][32] such as the pot, it can be thought that is the contrariness [Tib. 186 a] among the individual things which it has been admitted probably could not exist. "Contrariness in self-substance is not that which cannot exist only in *Brahman* alone. [In the same way even in other things the contrariness in the self-substance would be something which cannot exist]" the meaning is, and he would have used the word ("and also," *api*). For discrimination (*bheda*) does not exist for that thing which is existent in only its own-substance (i. e. *Brahman*). Discrimination[33] because it belongs to the spheres of things which are evolved. — Because this is the established theory [of the Vedānta School]. That is, it is not the case that the nature of beginninglessness and endlessness is admitted as the basic substance (*ātman*) of the pot, etc., but as the supreme self (*paramātman*). For the pot, its arising and perishing can actually be experienced, and as something which is limited spatially, it can be perceived. Now, the method of argument which points out the fallacy (*prasaṅga*), which runs "the clear and distinct perception of words, even in one who does not have the sense of hearing, would probably arise," has already been explained, but it could be thought that the special essence in which the fundamental essence[34] of *Brahman* is perceived[35] is obtained, and if so, we must regard that this method of argument to point out the fallacy can be appropriately employed. Furthermore, if one teaches that "[this fundamental essence of *Brahman*] is unusually subtle and is supersensible," this argument [to that extent] has no room for criticism. However, [according your theory] since the substance of blue, etc. that (i. e. words) , [if one considers that the perception of words does not arise] in the same way as [blue, etc.] and the fundamental substance of itself [that is, *Brahman* which is words], one must turn to the criticism that it would be that it cannot be perceived. Therefore, one could [not say that, and vulgar] people who embrace a shallow view know only the things which possess arising and perishing.[36]

The following can probably be said [as a cross-questioning of those who advocate the word-*Brahman*] : Although momentariness is not separate from blue, etc., in the perception of blue, etc., also, as you (Buddhists) do not have the perception of that momentariness itself, in the same way as this you do not perceive the fundamental essence of words also [when you perceive blue, etc.].

[The answer of the Buddhists :] This argument is not valid. For whenever one perceives blue, etc., it is not the case that momentariness cannot be perceived. Otherwise, it is taught, although [momentariness] would be known by means of the mind which is non-discriminate,[37] because, based upon illusion, he would commit the essential quality of others to this, he could not be firmly cognizant. Therefore, that momentariness must be perceived by intuition (*anubhava*), but it is never perceived by valid cognition (*niścaya-jñāna*). Consequently, since the difference between the concept (*jñāna*,knowledge) [of the non-discriminated and the discriminated] exists [in our theory], to say that the same momentariness [in the same time and place] is perceived and [in another place] is not perceived is not contradictory. However, in your theory [when one perceives blue, etc.], to say that words, in this way, are both perceived and not perceived [at the same time] is not valid. For you have set up the theory that all concepts (*jñāna*) are discriminated [Tib. 186b]. [Now, according to your theory] because it (i. e. words) can be perfectly[38] known by means of only one cognition (*jñāna*), the fundamental essence of others which has not yet been perceived is supposed not to exist. The following is the exact way it is explained.

How can that which cannot be determined (firmly cognized) by all determinations (firm cognitions) be the object of these (i. e. discriminated concepts)?

Again, if something be hypothesized as an undiscriminated concept (*avikalpaṃ jñānam*), and if so, one must not say that "the concept which does not accompany words does not exist in the world"(*Vākyap*.I,124ab). Now, the reason (*hetu*, cause) that "therefore [all things] are pierced and joined together by the shape and aspect of words," [which is advocated by you,] could not be established. Therefore, since the proof cannot be established, the academic position which asserts that all things have words as their fundamental quality would be merely a groundless argument.

Moreover, it is explained that because the momentariness of all things is established based upon other cognitive grounds (*pramāṇa*), although they are intuited, they are not firmly cognized. Furthermore, how can it be said that "all things have words as their fundamental essence" is established? The very fact that this can be said in this way would be to be able to firmly establish that the world also has words as its fundamental essence.

II-A-1-c-iii. The incidental Identity of the World

The explanation of another method of attack says, "Furthermore, in each of the respective things," etc.

[Verse 136]

> "Furthermore, if one considers that it can be thought that the unique '*Brahman* which is words' (*śabdātman*) is divided among each of the respective things, the result would be that all things are included in the same place, and yet [these] concepts must be that which possesses an identical form."

Really, when such a *Brahman* which is words [as in your assertion] goes towards the state of evolution,[39] (1) does each of the respective things enter into a condition which is different? or (2) do they not enter into such a condition?

Among these, (2) if one asserts that it does not become something different, and if so, it would be that "all" blue, etc., occupy the same place. "to occupy the same place" includes implicitly another meaning also. That is, it should be understood that time, the discriminations of change,[40] process,[41] and condition are also included. [These also become one.][42] Now, the concept (*vit*), that is, the appearance (*pratibhāsa*) [of the word in the consciousness] would become that which possesses the same form (*bhavet* – *prāpnoti*). For all things as blue, etc., would not be apparent from that fundamental essence which is the word 'identical'.

II-A-1-c-iv. The incidental Plurality of *Brahman*

[Verse 137]

> "Furthermore, if one considers that it (i. e. *Brahman* which is words) is different from each of the respective things, [it would be that] *Brahman* would then be that which is plural. For [*Brahman*] would possess the fundamental substance from which are formed the many things which are divided mutually."

Again, if one admitted that in each of the respective "its," that is, *Brahman* which is word (*śabdātman*) would be different [in relation to its own fundamental quality], if so, *Brahman* would become that which exists as a plurality. "For [it would be that] which possesses the fundamental substance which is form from the plurality of things which are mutually divided." [that is,] its 'fundamental substance' (*rūpa*), that is, fundamental essence (*svabhāva*), is those which are "mutually separated" and "which are formed from a plurality of things," that is, they have a plurality of things as their fundamental essence, one should analyze[43] and understand [this compound word]. 'That which is that' (*tat-tva*) is 'its essence' (*tadbhāva*). Furthermore, the supreme *Brahman* has been thought to be unique. Therefore,[44] by the acceptance of [your] assertion, its major import would be to establish the contradictory theory [to your theory].

II-A-1-c-v. The incidental Eternality of Objects of the phenomenal World

[Tib. 187a] An explanation of another refutation also says, "Furthermore, if one considers that the world is formed from eternal words," etc.

[Verse 138]

> "Furthermore, if one considers that [the world] is formed from eternal words, then all things also should arise as an incidental eternality.[45] Therefore, because [all things] are established and exist at the same time [as words] (*tadyaugapadyataḥ siddheḥ*), [the theory of] evolution is not appropriate."

"If one considers that the world is formed from eternal words," that is, if it were the case that it has eternal words as its essence, that is, if you should say that the fundamental substance of the world is words, then it would be the case that [fundamental essence of words]. Therefore, because all things in all times are being established at the same time[46] as words (*siddheḥ*, i. e., *siddhatvāt*), [the theory] of the evolution [of *Brahman* which you teach] cannot be established.[47] The '*tad*' [in the verse] means 'therefore' (*tasmād*). Or, again, [it means 'those' (*teṣām*)]. One may analyze[48] and explain that '*tadyaugapadya*' means that 'the blue, etc., of these exists at the same time [as words].'

If one says that evolution,[49] after all, cannot arise for things which are established at the same time, why is it? The answer is, "One aspect the differentia of oneness, etc."

[Verse 139]

> "Really, if the characteristic of oneness is hidden and the characteristic which is different arises in the present, evolution must be able to be

established. Just as if it is in clay, etc. But evolution of [the things which exist at the same] without having order cannot arise."

The word "but" (*tu*) has the import "But in relation to things [which exist at the same time], without order evolution could not be established," and it indicates [that that which has] order [of another] is different.[50] Because of this reason, it is not correct to say, first, that all things which have been formed from words have been formed by evolution.[51]

II-A-2. The Impossibility of Evolution in the case in which the World is held to occur as a Phenomenon from Words

II-A-2-i. An immutable Substance cannot give rise to Effect

[Verse 140]

"Again, even if one supposes that the world, by the aspect which is an effect, is something which can be formed from *Brahman* which is words because further [*Brahman* which is that word] cannot possess change, [the world] which progressively arises from it (i.e. words) cannot exist."

In this way [considering even the second case] again, because words are permanent [according to your theory], consequently, since they do not have change,[52] it is not the case that the result, etc., arise progressively from it (i. e., words). [On the other hand] because the cause is a perfect, complete and unobstructed potentiality, it would be that all things arise at the same time.[53] Really, [when one reflectively considers all things,] because of the very fact that the cause is not perfect and complete, [the arising of] the effect is delayed.[54] If one supposes that that cause is perfect and complete, and if so, why would it be that, by relying upon other things, [the effect for their sake] cannot arise at the same time?

II-A-2-ii. *Brahman* cannot give rise to an Aspect which contradicts its own Substance

[Verse 141]

"If one supposes that from that whose fundamental essence is the same the various fundamental essences which are mutually different arise, why could one not say that it (i. e. *Brahman*) is evolved as that which is all things?"

Moreover, again, if it is admitted that the various fundamental essences which are mutually different of *Brahman* which is the word arise from that which fundamental essence is the same, and if so, the theory that "it," that is, *Brahman* evolved as that which is all things (*artha*),[55] could not be established. For in the case when B arises, it is not correct that A, which does not enter into that fundamental essence of B [in actuality], evolves[56] as that which is an aspect of B. Therefore, in whatever case you may mention, the purport of the assertion [of the theorists who teach that *Brahman* is words] cannot be established.[57]

II-B. Refutation of the Assertion that all Things are pierced and bound by the form of Words.

Again, explaining that the reason that 'because [all things] are pierced and bound by the form of words' cannot be established, he says, "It cannot have that as its fundamental essence," etc.

[Verse 142]

> "The case can be posited that, because one can perceive "the quality making earth as its fundamental quality" which detaches from what cannot have it (i. e. clay) as its fundamental essence, the fundamental essence of the same clay exists in the individual things as the pot, the vessel, etc."[58]

[Verse 143]

> "But concerning all the things of blue, yellow, etc., in this way, [that same fundamental essence as words] one cannot perceive. Therefore, the supposition also that [of the identical fundamental quality] it is detached from what cannot have words as its fundamental essence is without grounds."

Really, that all things obey the same aspect in the supreme truth (*paramārthena*) cannot exist. For, because all things are caused to exist by their own fundamental essence (*svasvabhāva*)[Tib. 187b], it possesses the fundamental essence which is detached from the same kinds of things [and from the different kinds of things].[59] Rather, for these things, [the fundamental essence which is] "that which has been pierced and bound by the same formal aspect which was formed by detachment from things of a different kind" can only be established conceptually (imaginatively, *kālpanika*). [They are not something which is identical with the state of affairs of real actuality.] For example, although the pot, the plate, the water-pot, etc., in actuality, are mutually different, it is supposed[60] that 'the fundamental essence of earth' which was formed by the detachment from things of a different kind which does not possess the fundamental essence of earth.

Notes

1) Tib. *sgraḥi tshaṅs par smra ba.*
2) *nāśotpādāsamālīḍha-* : Tib. *skye ḥjig dag daṅ mi ldan pa.*
3) *pratīyate* : Tib. *...shes ṅes par bya ḥo.*
4) *pariṇāma* : Tib. *yoṅs su ḥgyur ba.*
5) *pūrvāpara* : Tib. *śar daṅ nub.*
6) *prakriyā* : Tib. *tha sñad ḥbyuṅ.*
7) The expression "*anādinidhana-*" is often used for *Viṣṇu* and *Brahmā* in the *Mahābhārata* (Cf. Sorensen's Index). It is also used with regard to *vāc*. *anādinidhanā nityā vāg utsṛṣṭā svayaṃbhuvā/ādau vedamayī divyā yataḥ sarvāḥ pravṛttayaḥ//* — *Mahābhārata* XII, 233, 24, quoted by Śaṅkara ad *BS.* I,3,28 (Vol.I, p.298, ĀnSS).
8) *vivartate* : Tib. *yoṅs gyur pa.* This shows that the Tib. translator regarded *vi-vṛt* as synonymous with *pari-nam*.
9) This stanza is *Vākyapadīya* I, 1, which is famous and quoted in *SDS* XIII, *l.* 115-6 (p. 298) and *Prameyakamalamārtaṇḍa*, p.11b.
10) vivarta- : *Tib. yoṅs su ḥgyur ba.*
11) "*taṃ tu paramaṃ brahmāṇam ... paśyantīti.*" must be corrected to "*taṃ tu paramaṃ brahmātmānam ... paśyantīti.*" *Brahman* as the absolute principle is not used as a masculine noun anywhere in the *Vākyapadīya* nor in Vedic literature in general. Further, the Tib. translation also reads: *tshaṅs pa mchog gi bdag ñid de ni ... mthoṅ ba yin no.*
12) *yadākārānusyūtās* : Tib. *gaṅ gi rnaṃ pa daṅ ldan pa.*
13) Tib. *raṅ bshin gyi gtan tshigs.* This is a technical term in Dharmakīrti's logic which is used in contrast with *kāryahetu.*
14) After *svabhāvahetu*, the Tib. translation reads: *gtan tshigs ma grub pa yaṅ ma yin te.*
15) "*śabda eva pratyayo*" must be corrected to "*sarva eva pratyayo*" according to Tib. *śes pa thams cad.*
16) *śabdollekhānugata-* : Tib. *sgraḥi rnam pa daṅ ldan pa.*
17) Tib. *de tsam gyi ṅo bo yin pa.*

18) *pariṇāma* : Tib. *yoṅs su gyur pa*. This Tib. translation indicates the result of evolution ; the action or process of evolution is translated as : *yoṅs su ḥgyur ba*.

19) As for *annamayāḥ prāṇā iti*, see *annamayo hy ayaṃ prāṇaḥ* (*Maitri. Up.* VI, 11) ; *annād bhūtāni jāyante* (*Tait. Up.* II, 2 ; *Maitri. Up.* VI 12) ; *annād bhavanti bhūtāni* (*Bhag. G.* III, 14 ; *Maitri. Up.* VI, 37 ; *Praśna Up.* I, 14).

20) The Tib. translation lacks the portion corresponding to *yathā 'nnamayāḥ prāṇā iti hetau mayadvidhānāt*. Instead it has *rgyuḥi don la rgyu ma yin pa brjod paḥi phyir daṅ/ rgyu las byuṅ baḥi rkyen du brjod paḥi phyir ro/*. At the time of Kamalaśīla there may have existed the idea that "the word *annamaya* means a modification (*vikāra*) of food as cause." Cf. *BS* I,1,13 and Śaṅkara's commentary on it ; *Mahābhāṣya* ad IV, 3, 155, Vol. II, p.324.

21) See note 4.

22) *nīlādirūpatāṃ pratipadyamānaṃ* : Tib. *sṅon po la sogs paḥi ṅo bor ḥgyur ba na/*

23) *paurastyasvabhāva-* : Tib. *sṅon gyi raṅ bshin*. The discussion is the same in its purport as *Māṇḍūkyakārikā* III, 22.

24) The Tib. translation lacks the word *badhirasya*.

25) *śabda-* : Tib. *sgraḥi bdag ñid* (=*śabdātman*).

26) *bhinnayogakṣematvāt* : Tib. *grub pa daṅ bde ba tha dad paḥi phyir*. Since the Tib. translation is too faithful, it cannot be of help for interpretation. *P.W.* gives for the compound *samānayogakṣematva* the translation "gleichen Wert habend mit, Nichts mehr seiend als." This compound occurs in *SDS.* IV, *l*.68 ; XII, *l*.146 ; XVI, *l*.578 and is used in the sense of "being of the same meaning," "having the same value"; Abhyaṅkar interprets it as *tulyatva*. Further, the compound *tulyayogakṣematva* is used as its synonym (*Sāṃkhyapravacanabhāṣya* ad I,43,p.20). The term *yogakṣema* is used in the sense of "security of wealth," "well-being" or "welfare," and in Pāli texts *yogakkhema* it is synonymous with *nirvāṇa*. As for this term, see Rai Bahadur Amarnath Ray's article, "*yogakṣema*" (*BSOS*, vol.VII, 1933, pp.133-136). According to him, *yogakṣema* originally meant "the highest good" or "summum bonum" and should be interpreted as *yogeṣu* (among gains) and *kṣemaḥ* (what is good or auspicious). Since *yogakṣema* means the most important thing that human beings seek or the most fundamental thing in human existence, *samānayogakṣema* and *tulyayogakṣema* mean "being of, or common in, the same existence, meaning or value," and *bhinnayogakṣema* has the opposite meaning (Sthiramati uses the term *ekayogakṣematva* twice. See *Madhyāntavibhāgaṭīkā*, p.33, *l*.6 ; *Triṃśikāvijñaptibhāṣya*, p.19, *l*.17.

27) *na* should be inserted before *prasidhyet* in light of Tib. *mi ḥgrub bo*.

28) *bādhakaṃ pramāṇam* : Tib. *gnod par byed paḥi tshad maḥo*.

29) *tataḥ kim* : Tib. *de las cir ḥgyur*.

30) *upalabdhilakṣaṇaprāptatvād* : Tib. *dmigs paḥi mtshan ñid du gyur paḥi phyir ro*.

31) Cf. *Tattvasaṃgrahapañjikā* ad stanza 331.

32) There must have been the compound *vyaktibhedānām* before or after *ghāṭādīnām* in light of Tib. *deḥi tshe bum pa la sogs paḥi gsal ba tha dad pa brtag par ḥdod paḥi gsal ba tha dad pa gaṅ yin pa der yaṅ mi ḥgyur ro.*

33) For "*vikāraviṣayatvād asyeti siddhāntaḥ*" the Tib. translation reads: *ḥdi ni ḥgyur ba med paḥi raṅ bshin yin paḥi phyir daṅ/tha dad pa med paḥi raṅ bshin yin paḥi phyir ro shes bya ba grub paḥi mthaḥ yin no//*

34) *rūpa*: Tib. *ṅo bo.*

35) *upalabdhilakṣaṇaprāpta-*: Tib. *dmigs paḥi mtshan ñid du gyur pa.*

36) *tataś cāyaṃ niyamo nopapadyate/udayavyayavatīm evārthamātrām aparadarśanāḥ pratiyantīti*: Tib. *de lta yin daṅ tshu rol mthoṅ ba rnams kyis skye ba daṅ ḥjig pa daṅ ldan paḥi don tsam śes so shes bya baḥi ṅes pa ḥdi mi ḥthad do/*

37) *nirvikalpena cetasā*: Tib. *rtog pa med paḥi śes pas.*

38) *sarvātmanā*: Tib. *deḥi bdag ñid thams cad ṅes pas ...*

39) See note 18.

40) See note 4.

41) *-vyāpāra-*: Tib. *bya ba.*

42) After *grāhyam*, the Tib. translation reads: *ḥdi rnams khyaṅ gcig tu ḥgyur ro.*

43) *vigrahaḥ*: Tib. *tshig rnam par sbyar ro.*

44) *ato 'bhyupetabādhāpratijñāyā iti bhāvaḥ?*: Tib. *des na dam bcaḥ ba la khas blaṅs pas gnod pa yin no sñam du bsams paḥo.*

45) The same argument appears in *Tattvasaṃgrahapañjikā* ad stanza 381; *Māṇḍūkya-kārikā* IV, 12.

46) *yaugapadyataḥ*: Tib. *cig car.*

47) "*pariṇāmātmā na prāpnoti*" must be corrected to *pariṇāmo na prāpnoti* in light of Tib. *yoṅs su ḥgyur bar mi ḥgyur ro.*

48) See note 43.

49) See note 4.

50) *nākrame tu vastuni pariṇāmaḥ siddhyed iti bhinnakramas tu-śabdaḥ*: Tib. "*ni*" *ḥi sgra ni go rims med pa la ni dṅos po yoṅs su ḥgyur ba ḥgrub par mi ḥgyur ro shes rim pa gshan du bya ḥo.*

51) See note 4.

52) *avikāritvāt*: Tib. *ḥgyur ba med paḥi phyir.*

53) The same argument occurs in *Tattvasaṃgraha*, stanza 331.

54) *kāraṇavaikalyād dhi kāryāṇi pratilambante*: Tib. *rgyu ma tshaṅ baḥi phyir ḥbras bu stoṅ pa yin na.*

55) *vivṛttam artharūpeṇa*: Tib. *don gyi ṅo bor rnam par ḥgyur ba.*

56) *vivarta*: Tib. *rnam par ḥgyur ba.*

57) *nāvakalpate*: Tib. *brtag par mi bya ḥo*.
58) *kalpate* must be corrected to *kalpyate* in light of the *Pañjikā*.
59) *samānajātīyavijātīyavyāvṛttasvabhāvatvāt*: Tib. *rigs mthun pa daṅ mi mthun pa las ldog paḥi raṅ bshin yin paḥi phyir ro* (=*samānajātīyavijātīyavyāvṛttasvabhāvatvāt*).
60) *kalpyate*: Tib. *rtog pa*.

Sub-Section 4. Bhartṛhari's Criticism of the Buddhist Theory

Our investigations in the *Śabdabrahmaparīkṣā* of the *Tattvasaṃgraha* clearly indicate that the Buddhist philosophers attacked the thought of Bhartṛhari as being heretical in nature and now it would be appropriate to look at the other side of the coin and see how Bhartṛhari regarded Buddhist doctrine. There is a great deal of controversy in academic circles about whether or not Bhartṛhari's *Vākyapadīya* is Buddhistic in content[1] and I made my investigation of the text with this in mind. The general conclusion was that, although Bhartṛhari did not make a sweeping denunciation of Buddhist doctrine, he did attack it as being heretical. Let us now examine some of the passages of the *Vākyapadīya* which pertain to this problem, making use of the various commentaries.

In the *Vākyapadīya* there are passages which deals with the problem as to whether or not there is a fundamental distinction between the original meaning of a word (*mukhya-artha*) and the secondary meaning of a word (the metaphorical meaning — *gauṇa-artha*). For example, if one sees a lion and says, "That is a lion," the word 'lion' is used in its original sense; whereas, when one says, "That man is a lion," the word 'lion' means something like 'a man who is fierce like a lion' and is thus used in its secondary or metaphorical sense.

However, someone who holds a philosophical position different from that of Bhartrhari might say something like the following with regard to this point:

> "When a [secondary] meaning [of a word] is ascertained even though diametrically opposed [to the original meaning of the word] then the word following the conception [of the secondary meaning] functions as its original meaning."
>
> *atyantaviparīto 'pi yadā yo 'rtho 'vadhāryate/*

yathāsaṃpratyayaṃ śabdas tatra mukhyaḥ pravartate//(*Vākyap*. II, 287).

In other words, it is impossible to draw a hard and fast distinction between the primary and secondary (metaphorical) meanings of words. The meaning of words is established by us completely subjectively and there is no 'original meaning' which has an independent existence transcending our subjectivity. This is the claim that a word which is used in one sentence must be understood as expressing its original meaning within those limits.[2]

Bhartṛhari would, however, counter this claim, saying "Although the meaning of a word belongs to subjectivity, the distinction of original and secondary meaning is fixed [from the very first]".[3] Further he emphasizes that the secondary meaning is based on the original meaning and it is established through postulating the original meaning.

> "Truly metaphorical expression is established because of the existence of the original meaning."
>
> *upacāro hi mukhyasya saṃbhavād avatiṣṭhate*/ (*Vākyap*. III, 8, 13. p. 313).

While attempting to prove that the distinction of these two meanings can be established, he first asserts the existence of a distinction of *satya* (truth) and *asatya* (untruth).[4]

> "Although the ascertainment of the Truth of the meaning [of a word] depends on [our subjective] notions, none of the notions arises [unrestrictedly] with this [word] as something arbitrary."
>
> *yady api pratyayādhīnam arthatattvāvadhāraṇam*/
> *na sarvaḥ pratyayas tasminn asiddha iva jāyate*// (*Vākyap*. II, 288).

There is no explanation of this passage in the commentaries but I think the following would be an adequate interpretation. Given the word 'lion', for example, aside from the original meaning (something like 'carnivorous, ferocious feline with a mane') we can distinguish various metaphorical meanings such as 'ferocious person' or 'kingly individual'. These are all formed in our subjectivity but there is clearly a distinction between the original meaning and the metaphorical meaning. Moreover, since there is a fixed relation between the two, the metaphorical meaning could not possibly be something which is established in a purely arbitrary manner. Pursuing this point in more detail, Bhartṛhari continues:

"The act of seeing with respect to water is identical with the seeing of a mirage [in both cases]. Although the act of seeing and the like are the same in both cases, water is not a mirage."

darśanaṃ salile tulyaṃ mṛgatṛṣṇādidarśanaiḥ/

tulyatve darśanādīnāṃ na jalaṃ mṛgatṛṣṇikā// (*Vākyap*. II, 289).

It sometimes happens that a mirage, reflecting the water of an oasis, suddenly appears in the desert. The claim being made is that when one compares the seeing of the water of a mirage and the seeing of actual water one finds that the act of seeing is in both cases the same but the objects of our seeing are different i.e., actual water and the water of a mirage are not the same. This is clearly in opposition to Budhist doctrine, for the metaphor which compares all worldly phenomena to mirages is used quite extensively in Buddhist literature and in works influenced by this literature such as the *Māṇḍūkya-Kārikā* (II,31). With respect to attacking the explanation based on this metaphor, at least Bhartṛhari is in agreement with Bhartṛprapañca and Śaṅkara.[5]

"Since it is universally well-known that there exists a function which is not common to both a rope and a snake, even though the seeing of both is the same, a distinction of the two must be clearly made."

yad asādhāraṇaṃ kāryaṃ prasiddhaṃ rajjusarpayoḥ/

tena bhedaḥ paricchedyas tayos tulye 'pi darśane//(*Vākyap*. II, 290).

Just as a person may see a rope lying in the road at dusk, mistake it for a snake and become frightened, so people become perplexed and troubled by mistaking the various aspects of the phenomenal world for reality. In *Vijñaptimātratā* philosophy the snake is explained as corresponding to imagination and the rope as corresponding to interdependence. Further, this metaphor is found in the *Māṇḍūkya-Kārikā* (II, 17 ; II, 18) and is often used by Śaṅkara.[6] Bhartṛhari, however, rejects this interpretation and claims that both in the case of seeing an actual snake and also in the case of seeing what one mistakes for a snake, the act of seeing is identical but the rope and the snake are two completely different objects and the two must be clearly distinguished. On this point then, Bhartṛhari is at odds with the Vijñānavāda school.

"And when a cause [is a defect in the object or the sense organ] of the perverted view [error] concerning things well-known [the true thing][7] is seen and if the difference (e. g., two moons) from the [true thing which is due to this cause] is recognized, then people call this [difference] 'untrue' (*asatya*)."

prasiddhārthaviparyāsanimittaṃ yac ca dṛśyate/

yas tasmāl lakṣyate bhedas tam asatyaṃ pracakṣate// (*Vākyap*. II, 291).

Since errors in knowledge are due to defects in the objects or sense organs, for example, our mistake of a rope for a snake which is due to insufficient light and the existence of the two moon which is due to the eye-sickness, it is not right to regard everything as false by identifying it with its mistaken forms. This argument of Bhartṛhari is also given in the beginning of the *Viṃśatikā-vijñaptimātratā-siddhi* where people or other schools criticize the Vijñānavādins.

It reads, "Just as, though those who suffer *timira*-eye sickness see hairs, rope and the like, such cognition does not occur to those who are free from *timira*-eye sickness."[8] Therefore, Bhartṛhari's argument comes from the views of opponents of the Vijñānavādins.

"Although a wall painting[9] with an uneven surface may resemble mountains and the like, these do not function as obstacles in the way that mountains do."

yac ca nimnonnate citre sarūpaṃ parvatādibhiḥ/

na tatra pratighātādi kāryaṃ tadvat pravartate// (*Vākyap*. II, 292).

This means that actual mountains have the function of impeding our progress but painted mountains do not.

"If one touches a [real] wheel by hand, the uninterrpuptedness of the tactile sensations continue to be. But this is not the case with a wheel of fire-brand since if one touches it, it is interrupted."

sparśaprabandho hasena yathā cakrasya saṃtataḥ/

na tathā 'lātacakrasya vicchinnaṃ spṛśyate hi tat//(*Vākyap*. II, 293).

This comparison of the phenomenal world to a wheel of fire-brand is found quite often in Buddhist texts. It is the central thought of the fourth chapter of the *Māṇḍūkya-Kārikā*, but it is precisely this view which Bhartṛhari is attacking.[10]

"And in the cities the earthen embankment, the rampart, and the upper stories give rise to tactile sensations and covering, but in the case of 'Gandharva city (= a mirage)' there is nothing of the sort."

vapra-prākāra-talpaiś ca sparśanāvaraṇe yathā/

nagareṣu tu te tadvad gandharvanagareṣv api// (*Vākyap*. II, 294).

The likening of the phenomenal world to Gandharva city (= a mirage) is quite common in Buddhist works and is also found in the second chapter of the *Māṇḍūkya-Kārikā* (II,31). Bhartṛhari, however, staunchly opposes such a view, and it is of particular interest that an argument quite similar to Bhartṛhari's is given in the beginning of the *Viṃśatikā-vijñaptimātratā-siddhi* as an example of the criticisms of the Vijñaptimātratā doctrine put forth by other schools. "Gandharva castle cannot be used as a castle."[11]

"There do not exist in a thing made from clay so much efficiency as accomplished by true (real, *mukhya*) wild beasts, domestic animals, etc. Therefore these beasts, domestic animals and the like are objects desitgnated by the suffix-*ka*."

mṛgapaśvādibhir yāvān mukhyair arthaḥ prasādhyate/

tāvān na mṛnmaye 'py asti tasmāt te viṣayaḥ kanaḥ//(*Vākyap*. II, 295).

"A vast area is covered by well-known mountains but it is seen that [their] reflction (*pratibimba*) is located within a small area."

mahān āvriyate deśaḥ prasiddhaiḥ parvatādibhiḥ/

alpadeśāntarāvasthaṃ pratibimbaṃ tu dṛśyate//(*Vākyap*. II, 296).

This also can be taken as a criticism of the comparison of everything to its reflection on the surface of a mirror or water[12] which is found in various *Mahāyāna Sūtras*[13] and the adoption of such doctrine by one of the Vedānta school.[14]

"Moreover, true (real, *mukhya*) poison and the like are the cause of death but the poison and the like in a dream do not accomplish their own end."

maraṇādinimittaṃ ca yathā mukhyā viṣādayaḥ/

na te svapnādiṣu svasya tadvad arthasya sādhakāḥ//(*Vākyap*. II, 297).

This metaphor which likens the phenomenal world to a dream is also one which appears quite frequently in Buddhist works and in the *Māṇḍūkya-Kārikā* after chapter 2.

As has been discussed before, this view is in sharp contrast to that of

Bhartṛhari and is rather in agreement with the criticisms offered by other schools in the *Viṃśatikā-vijñaptimātratā-siddhi* (i. e., "The food, drink, swords, staffs, poisons, medicines and garments etc. to be found in dreams cannot be used to assuage thirst and so forth.").[15] Moreover, it is known that within the Vedānta school itself his position is quite similar to that of the *Brahma-sūtra* (II, 2, 29) and Bodhāyana.[16]

Bhartṛhari summarized the above argument in the following:

> "Anything which is seen untruly due to differences of place, time, and the sense organs are determined in the way that it is generally acknowledged by ordinary people."(*Vākyap*. II, 298).

Acccording to Puṇyarāja's commentary, mistakes in cognition occur in the following instances:

(1) Differences of place. That is to say that mistakes sometimes occur because of a difference of distance. For example, mistakes which arise because the object seen is a great distance away.

(2) Differences of time. For examples, in summer one sees from a distance the haze caused by subterranean heat and mistakes it for water.

(3) Differences relating to the sense organs. For example, one who has a certain affliction of the eyes may see two moons in the sky.

Since one must decide about such matters in the way that people acknowledge as being generally correct the distinction of truth and falsity with regard to cognition is clear cut. Thus, according to Puṇyarāja, it is a mistake to regard even true cognition as being false or illusory.

In addition there are arguments, which we will investigate later, which can be interpreted as defending the Mādhyamika thesis that all is void, although it is not clear whether in these instances he had in the doctrine which interprets *śūnyatā* purely negatively. At any rate, it is obvious that Bhartṛhari's assertions are diametrically opposed to the assertions of at least the *Vijñaptimātratā*, i. e. it is indisputable that he is in agreement with the claims of opposing schools. Moreover, when one turns to his relation to the other schools of Vedānta while keeping the above points in mind one finds that he attacked the doctrine expressed in the *Māṇḍūkya-Kārikā* (chapter 2ff.) and in part at least the thought of Śaṅkara. On the other hand, with regard to this particular point at least, he is in agreement with Bodhāyana, Bhartṛprapañca and chapter 1 of the *Māṇḍūkya-Kārikā*.

According to Helārāja's commentary there are still more references to the *Vijñaptimātratā* in the *Vākyapadīya*. In the passages which discuss the 'meaning of words'(*padārtha*) the following statement succeeds the presentation of the argument of the Vaiśeṣikas:

"Certain people know that what is called [form] has pervasion as its nature and explain as a thing (*dravya*) [the form] which has separation [from others] as its nature.[17]

anupravṛttirūpāṃ yāṃ prakhyātām ākṛtiṃ viduḥ/

kecid vyāvṛttirūpāṃ tu dravyatvena pracakṣate//(*Vākyap*. III, 1, 19).

Helārāja takes this passage to be an expression of the doctrine of the *Vijñānāvāda*. After presenting this heresy Bhartṛhari proceeds to develop his own theory.

"'It is the different limiting adjunct (*upādhi*) of the highest Being. The same is true of 'It is not different.' Such expression (*prapañca*)[18] arises with reference to the various *ātman* of things which are connected [with the limiting adjunct]".

bhinnā iti paropādhir abhinnā iti vā punaḥ/

bhāvātmasu prapañco 'yaṃ saṃsṛṣṭetv eva jāyate// (*Vākyap*. III, 1, 20).

Thus, if one follows Helārāja's interpretation, one must understand Bhartṛhari as viewing *Vijñānavāda* philosophy as the heresy of 'certain people' not of his school on a par with Vaiśeṣika philosophy, which is to say that it occupies a position inferior to the Vedānta thought to which he subscribed. However, the *Vijñaptimātratā* thesis given here is not to be taken as the traditional thesis asserted by Asaṅga and Vasubandhu. It is rather the thesis asserted by the later scholars of the *Vijñānavāda* who were primarily interested in logical investigations.

It is evident that he was not a Buddhist for he paid great reverence to the *Vedas* and followed the principles of Vedānta philosophy, but it is worth noting that he expounded a thesis which is in direct opposition to the statements and intentions of Mahāyana Buddhism.

Notes

1) Radhakrishnan (*IPh.* Vol.II, p.465) maintains that the *Vākyapadīya* is Buddhistic in content, but W. Ruben (*ZII*. VIII, 1931, S.53, Anm. 2) claims that there is no evidence to show that Bhartṛhari was a Buddhist.
2) *bauddha eva śabdārtho nāsti kaścic chabdeṣu gauṇamukhyavibhāga iti* .... *vākye na śabdeṣu gauṇamukhyavibhāgaḥ kaśct.* (Puṇyarāja ad *Vākyap*. II,287).
3) *bauddhe 'pi śabdārthe vyavasthita eva gauṇamukhyavibhāgam iti*/(Puṇyarāja ad *Vākyap*. II, 299).
4) *idānīm atrāpi gauṇamukhyavibhāgaṃ samarthayituṃ satyāsatyavibhāgaṃ tāvad upakramitum āha*/. — (Puṇyarāja).
5) Cf. Ś. ad *Bṛhad*. Up. p.731,*l*.17. According to Śaṅkara's Commentary on the *Brahmasūtra* (II,2,28) Śaṅkara rejected the Buddhists comparing even the experience of their waking hours to things like *gandharvanagara*. Moreover the metaphor of *mṛgatṛṣṇā* is referred to at *Vākyap*. III,13,8 (p.434).
6) Deussen : *SV*. S.290.
7) *prasiddhaḥ satyarūpo 'rthaḥ* — Puṇyarāja.
8) *yathā taimirikānāṃ saṃtāne keśādyābhāso nānyeṣāṃ*. (*Viṃśatikā-Vijñaptimātratāsiddhiḥ*, p.3, *l*.12).
9) *citrabhitti* — Puṇyarāja.
10) The metaphor of the wheel of fire is referred to in other places as well. See the next Sub-Section.
11) *gandharvanagareṇāsattvān nagarakriyā na kriyate.* (*Viṃśatikā-Vijñaptimātratāsiddhiḥ* p.3, *l*.15).
12) The *pratibimbaka* metaphor is also used at *Vākyap*. I,100 but since there an active manifestation (i. e. *nāda*) opposed to a passive manifestation (i. e. *sphoṭa*) is compared to the water surface it must be considered separately from the present use. At *Vākyap*. I,20 the fact that grammar manifests the nature of various words is compared to *pratibimba* but in this case the problem is completely different.
13) For example : *Laṅk*. p.20, *l*.15 ; p.42, *l*.9 ; p.72, *l*.16 ; p.94. *l*.4 ; p.106, *l*.6 ; p.375, *l*.4.
14) Cf. Śaṅkara ad *BS*. vol.II, p.85, *l*.3ff ; p.90, *l*.10. cf. *BS*. III, 2, 18.
15) *Taisho Tripiṭaka*, vol.31, section 74 : *yad annapānavastraviṣāyudhādi svapne dṛśyate tenānnādikriyā na kriyate* (*Viṃśatikā-vijñāptimātratā-siddhiḥ* p.3, *l*.14).
16) See Part V, Chapter IV, Section III of this book.
17) For an interpretation of this passage, consult *Vākyap*. III,1,14.
18) In the annotation the word *vyavahāra* occurs.

Sub-Section 5. Buddhist Influence upon the *Vākyapadiya*

As we have previously seen, Bhartṛhari rejects the doctrine of Mahāyāna Buddhism, but if one scrutinizes his view carefully, one can see that he is well-informed of Buddhist thought. It appears that he was thoroughly familiar with Buddhist literature. Throughout the *Vākyapadīya* he unconsciously adopts Buddhist expressions and modes of explanation.

The commentator Helārāja says that Bhartṛhari sometimes adopts Buddhist doctrine. At *Vākyapadīya* III,3,72 (p.133), after referring to the doctrine of regarding non-existence as a substance, he says ;

> "Since that which transcends[1] the objects of expression is not a substance, one cannot speak of the distinction which exist in substances."
>
> *avastutvād atītaṃ yad vyavahārasya gocaram/*
> *tatra vastugato bhedo na nirvacanam arhati//*(*Vākyap*. III, 3, 75. p.134).

According to Helārāja, this stanza is composed in accordance with 'the Buddhist viewpoint' (*Bauddhadṛṣṭi*) ; it expounds the view that 'there is no independent non-existence separated from existence.' This view is indeed found in Buddhist literature, for example in the *Mādhyamika Śāstra* (XXV, 7) one finds out :

> "Where there is not existence there is not non-existence."
>
> *yatra bhāvo na nābhāvas tatra vidyate.*

The passage from the *Vākyapadīya* cited above is so Mahāyāna Buddhistic in expression that it would not at all seem strange to find it in a Buddhist text. Bhartṛhari takes a position with similar import in various other passages as well.[2] He maintains that it is impossible to establish the real types and distinctions of 'non being' and here too one can see the influence of Buddhist doctrine. Although the theories of the grammarians of antiquity were quite similar to Vaiśeṣika doctrine, Bhartṛhari here differs or it would be better to say that he expressed a theory which was more advanced. Since this conceptual reform was effected through the influence of Buddhism it assumes an even greater significance.

Another example of what Helārāja regards as the adoption of Buddhist doctrine is the reference made to 'various changing forms' (*ākārair apāyibhiḥ...*) at *Vākyapadīya* III, 2, 4.[3]

In the preceding section we took up the question of metaphors but did not give an exhaustive account. For example, the metaphor of the wheel of fire-brand was referred to in many places other than those heretofore cited.

> "It is based upon the *Śrutis* that one has the experience of perceiving forms of things [even] in the wheel of fire-brand etc. which are the causes of absolutely false [words]."
>
> *atyantam atathābhūte nimitte śrutyapāśrayāt/*
> *dṛśyate 'lātacakrādau vastvākāranirūpaṇā//*(*Vākyap*. I,131), (Iyer's edition: I, 12 (p.198).

That is to say, the wheel of fire is, in itself, non-being (non-existent) but since it is discussed in the sacred books it is possible to treat it as something which has the character of a material object. In other passages also[4] the wheel of fire is referred to as something which does not actually exist but merely manifests itself temporarily. The using the metaphor of the wheel of fire in this sense is clearly the result of Buddhist influence.[5]

The mode of expression peculiar to Buddhist works can be seen in various places throughout the *Vākyapadīya*. For example, Bhartṛhari says of Patañjali's *Mahābhāṣya*.

> "[It is] bottomless because of profundity clear, as it were, because of skillfulness."
>
> *alabdagādho gāmbhīryād uttāna iva sauṣṭhavāt/*(*Vākyap*. II, 486).

The two words 'profundity' (*gāmbhīrya*) and 'clear' (*uttāna*) are used in this sense only in Buddhist works[6] and further putting these concepts in opposition is also peculiar to Buddhist texts.

In the section on Buddhism of his *Sarvadarśanasaṃgraha* Mādhava cites a stanza from Nāgārjuna's *Bodhicittavivaraṇa* and comments on it as follows:

> And it should not be taught that 'the distinction of the teachings according to [the difference in] intention of the people who are to be guided is not based on orthodox tradition.' For the *Bodhicittavivaraṇa* says as follows:
>
> "The teachings of the Lord of the world (*lokanātha*) in this world, following the intentions and abilities of people, are multifariously divided through many expediencies. The teachings are distinguished

owing to the difference of 'profound' and 'clear' (*gambhīrottānabheda*), being characterized by both in some cases. [However,] *śūnyatā* which is of non-dual character is not differentiated.[7]"

Since this sort of explanation does not appear in other parts of the *Sarvadarśanasaṃgraha* it would seem that in Mādhava's eyes the contrast of 'profound' (*gambhīra*) and 'clear' (*uttāna*) was expounded explicitly only in Buddhism.[8]

The view which recognizes the opposition of these two modes of preaching the law finds expression not only in the *Mādhyamika* writing of Nāgārjuna but also in works of the *Vijñānavādins*. For example, in the *Yogācārabhūmi* 'shallow' (*uttāna*) and 'profound' (*gambhīra*) are regarded as two opposing concepts and in the passage which explains the pure acts of beneficence of the *bodhisattva* the same claim is made.

> *punar bodhisattaḥ pūrvaṃ bālaprajñānāṃ sattvānām uttānāṃ dharmadeśanāṃ karoti. uttānāṃ avavādānuśāsanīm anupravartayati. madhyaprajñāṃś caināṃ viditvā madhyāṃ dharmadeśanāṃ madhyāvavādānuśāsanīṃ anuprvartayati. pṛthuprajñāṃś caināṃ viditvā gaṃbhīrāṃ dharmadeśanāṃ sūkṣmām avavādānuśāsanīm anupravartayaty anupūrveṇa kuśalapakṣasamudāgamāya. iyam asyānupūrvaṃ sattveṣu arthacaryā.*[9]

These two terms *uttāna* and *gambhīra* are used in a specialized sense even in the sacred works of primitive Buddhism.[10] Thus there would seem to be nothing which stands in the way of concluding that Bhartṛhari's use of such expressions is attributable to Buddhist influence.

However, the Buddhist influence is not restricted to mere details of style and vocabulary but penetrates to the very core of the thought of the *Vākyapadīya*. Mahāyāna Buddhist texts emphasize that the absolute state, considered as truth, transcends our discursive thought and thus can only be expressed in a negative way, and consequently negative terms are repeated over and over. However, in the *Vākyapadīya* also the same sort of explanation is given. The absolute is explained thus.

> It (Truth, *tattva*)[11] is neither existent nor non-existent. It is neither one nor different. It is not connected nor it is divided. It is not changed nor it is otherwise (non-changed).[12]

na tad asti na tan nāsti na tad ekaṃ na tat pṛthak/
na saṃsṛṣṭaṃ vibhaktaṃ vā vikṛtaṃ na ca nānyathā// (*Vākyap.* III, 2, 12, p.91).

This passage brings to mind the famous dedicatory verse of the *Mādhyamika-Śāstra*. Moreover, if we think of the meaning of the phrases we can see that the negative expressions of this verse correspond in order to the *Mādhyamika-Śāstra*'s 'no production, no extinction, no annihilation, no permanence, no unity, no diversity, no coming and no departure.' But this alone is not sufficient to warrant the conclusion that this passage is the result of the direct influence of the *Mādhyamika-Śāstra*. (The reason being that expressions arranged in the form of eight negations are to be found quite often in other Mahāyāna texts.) Nonetheless, it cannot be doubted that this form of expression was borrowed from some *Mahāyāna sūtra* or *śāstra*.

This verse is also very similar to the first verse of *Tattvādhikāra* 7 of the *Mahāyānasūtrālaṅkāra*.

na san na cāsan na tathā na cānyathā na jāyate vyeti na cāvahīyate/
na vardhate nāpi viśudhyate punar viśudhyate tat paramārthalakṣaṇam// (*Mahāyānasūtrālaṅkāra* VI, 1).

Translation: "No existence and no non-existence, no similarity and no difference, no birth and no extinction, no increase and no decrease, no purity and no impurity — these five pairs of negations express the highest truth. Aspirants must, above all, know this."[13]

If one compares this verse to the verse of Bhartṛhari cited above it is obvious that 'no existence and no non-existence', 'no similarity and no difference', 'no increase and no decrease' are expressions common to both verses. However, this is only a similarity of linguistic expression and it does not necessarily mean that the two verses are identical in conceptual content.

According to Vasubandhu this verse can be interpreted in the following manner. This passage gives five classes of characteristics of *paramārtha* i.e., *advayārtha* or *dharmadhātu*. (1) No existence and no non-existence. *Paramārtha* or pure (*anāsrava*) *dharmadhātu* is not existent because, in the final analysis, that which is produced from imagination or dependent origination is not real. In contrast, it is not non-existent, for the highest truth (*tathatā*) truly exists even though it is not recognized by the confused and foolish. (2) No identity and no difference means the same as 'no unity and no otherness'. Imagination is false and dependency is that which harmonizes truth and falsity. Since both are not absolutely identical with *tathatā*, *paramārtha* is said to be 'not one'. However, imagination and dependency, in actual fact, do not exist completely independently, for both are ultimately traceable to *tathatā*. Thus, they are not different from *tathatā*. (3) No birth and no extinction. Since *dharmadhātu* is "that which is not produced" in any way (*anabhisaṃskṛta*) it is indestructible. (4) No increase and no decrease. Through study and discipline the defiled portion of our nature (*saṃkleśapakṣa*) decreases and the purified portion (*vyavadānapakṣa*) increases to the same degree, yet the *dharmadhātu* itself remains as it was i.e., no increase and no decrease. (5) No purity and no impurity. The true nature of *dharmadhātu* is without defilement, and even if we should attain this state through study and training the *dharmadhātu* has not thereby been particularly purified. On the other hand, from our point of view as human beings the *dharmadhātu* is covered and hidden by worldly passions, and since these defilements and illusions are removed only through our study and practice it is possible to say that the *dharmadhātu* is "not without being purified".

In contrast to this the previously cited passage from the *Vākyapadīya* must, according to Helārāja, be interpreted in the following manner. Truth is not something which exists as the essence of the various forms of change, but since that which has 'non-existence' as a determining attribute is not real it can also be said that 'it is not that it is not'. Since it is something prior to division one cannot even call it 'one' and yet, since nothing can exist separated from it, it is 'not different (differentiated)'. Further, since there is nothing which exists in contrast to it, neither combination nor division constitute its essence. Since it does not admit of development (*pariṇāma*) but does admit of temporary manifestation (*vivarta*) it can be said to be 'not a changing thing'. However, since it manifests itself through the characteristics of a variety of phenomena one cannot say that it is unchanging.

I have some rather grave doubts about the validity of this interpretation given by Helārāja.[14] These negative expressions do not, it seems to me, have the meaning that Helārāja attributes to them but are rather the means used to express the notion of *karma* resulting from the relation of mutual dependency, such as is found in the *Mādhyamika-Śāstra*, which Bhartṛhari had adopted. One can cite as evidence for this view the fact that both the opposition of unity and difference and that of existence — non-existence in the *Vākyapadīya* are established in the relation of interdependency and by the argument that these aspects cannot subsist independently. The idea that these concepts are established in the negation of the concepts which stand in opposition to them was first stressed by the Mahāyāna Buddhist, especially the *Mādhyamika* school. In this line by line investigation I have omitted any reference to the concept of the 'absolute *Brahman*' but nonetheless I am convinced that the interpretation of the above passage from the *Vākyapadīya* must be made along the lines indicated. It is undeniable that the passage is quite similar to one of the most essential and central passages in all *Mahāyāna* literature. Moreover, one cannot but acknowledge that this similarity is not mere coincidence but is the result of the influence of Buddhist, literature on Bhartṛhari.

Not only does the thought and mode of expression of the *Mādhyamika* school make their appearance in the *Vākyapadīya* but there are also passages which make use of the thought characteristic of the *Vijñānavādins*. At one point he explains that the reality of the highest truth is nondiscriminable although it manifests itself through the forms of discrimination. He then goes on to say:

> "Just as the various qualities of objects of knowledge are not possible to exist [for they are not real]; [15] even though it is established that it (= the real, *tattva*) is, as it were, of the nature of these various qualities, it is not of the nature of them at all [from the highest truth]."
> *yathā viṣayadharmāṇāṃ jñāne 'tyantam asaṃbhavaḥ/*
> *tadātmeva tat siddham atyantam atadātmakam//* (*Vākyap*. III, 2, 9, p. 90).

According to Helārāja's commentary 'Just as ...' is the statement of the *Vijñānavādins* (*Vijñānavāde viṣayākārasya tāvato 'satyatvān nīlādis tadgato dharmo jaḍo jaḍe jñāne 'saṃbhavo 'tyantam iti*). As this commentary suggests there seems to be no reason not to regard these words as being *Vijñānavāda* doctrine. Thus it would seem that Bhartṛhari adopted the

Vijñānavāda theory also, at least in so far as it agreed with or was capable of corroborating his own theory.

There is also the following lyric poem, which, although it does not appear in the *Vākyapadīya*, is attributed to Bhartṛhari.

> This world is mere thought, falsely originated. But, Oh *Brahman*, where does it dissolve through the mere absence of thought?
> *saṃkalpamātram evedaṃ jagan mithyāsamutthitam /*
> *asaṃkalpanamātreṇa brahman kvāpi vilīyate //*[16)]

Whether this poem is actually Bhartṛhari's work or not is not known, but at least it shows that his name has been traditionally linked with *Vijñānavāda*-type thought.

In addition, he often uses words which are related to the original terms for the two truths and the three modes of existence.

First let us consider the concept of 'the highest truth' *paramārtha*. Since this concept appears in the *Māṇḍūkya-Kārikā* and in the works of Śaṅkara it has aroused the interest of many scholars as the evidence of Buddhist influence on these works. Bhartṛhari also made use of this concept in his works.

(a) *nityeṣu tu kutaḥ pūrvaṃ paraṃ vā paramārthataḥ/*(*Vākyap*. II, 22, p.77).

"But how could there truly be any before and after in the eternal from the standpoint of the highest truth?"

(b) *paramārthe tayor eṣa bhedo 'tyantaṃ na vidyate/*(ibid. III, 6, 26, p. 172).

"In the highest truth the distinction of both [identity and difference] does not at all exist."

(c) *paramārthe tu naikatvaṃ pṛthaktvād bhinnalakṣaṇam /*
pṛthaktvaikatvarūpeṇa tattvam eva prakāśate // (ibid. III,7,a,39, p. 200).

"However, in the highest truth there is no identity which has an essence different from difference. The truth itself shines forth in the form of difference and identity."

(d) *na vākye 'sti vibhāgaḥ paramārthataḥ/*(ibid. III, 8, 45 p.331).

"There is no division in a sentence from the standpoint of the highest truth."

Further, the term *vyavahāra*, which is opposed to *paramārtha*, is also used often in the *Vākyapadīya*[17] although there is no example of it being used in explicit contrast to *paramārtha*.

Moreover, in the *Vākyapadīya* one frequently encounters terms which are very similar to the original terms for the threefold nature in *Yogācāra* philosophy. First of all, the meaning 'perfection' or 'accomplishment'.[18] is denoted by the term '*parinispatti*' and which is used only in Buddhist literature.[19] Kumārajīva interprets this word as 'achievement'[20] and Xuan zang interprets it as 'perfection'[21] or 'completion'.[22] In general, words derived from the root *pari-niṣ-pad* are to be found·lonly Buddhist works.[23] Although Bhartṛhari does not refer to *parinispannalakṣaṇa* it should be kept in mind that he does use terms which are intimately connected with it.

Further, he often uses terms which correspond to the '*paratantra*' of *paratantralakṣaṇa*. Now the word '*paratantra*' had been in general used in India since the time of the *Mahābhārata* and its meaning was something like 'to be dependent on another'. Nonetheless, it would seem plausible that Bhartṛhari's predilection for using this word[24] to express this particular meaning rather than the many other available terms is attributable to a suggestion he received from the technical language of the *Vijñānavāda* philosophy.

Word which resemble the term '*parikalpitalakṣaṇa*' are also used profusely. The words '*parikalpa*' and '*parikalpita*' are normally used only as Buddhist Sanskrit[25] but the frequency of their occurrence in the *Vākyapadīya* is exceedingly high.

parikalpa III, 3, 64. (p.130) (Helārāja annotates this as *vikalpa*).
parikalpita saṃyogidharmabhedena deśe ca parikalpite/
teṣu deśeṣu sāmānyam ākāśasyāpi vidyate//(III, 1. 15. p.20).
ekasya buddhyavasthābhir bhede ca parikalpite/
karmatvaṃ karaṇatvaṃ vā kartṛtvaṃ vopajāyate/(III,7,102. p.244).
lṇlḷtor grahaṇe bhedo grāhyābhyāṃ parikalpitaḥ/(II,101. p.124).

There are, in addition, innumerable other passages which could be cited.[26]

Böhtlingk-Roth's dictionary gives only two meanings for the word '*parikalpanā*', 'perfecting' and 'calculation'. So its use in the *Vākyapadīya* is clearly Buddhistic.

(III, 6, 18, p.168) (III, 7, a, 57, p.209) (II, 91, p.121) (II, 133, p.137) (III, 7, a, 6, p.178) (III, 7, 119, p.252).

Further, the neuter form '*parikalpana*' does not appear at all in the aforementioned dictionary but it is used in the *Vākyapadīya* in the same sense as the above term.

(II, 57, p.90) (III, 7, a, 65, p.214).

The verbal forms are used in the meanings of 'to discriminate' or 'to imagine' *parikalpayet* [II,221 (p.171)], *parikalpyate* [I,62 (p.25)] ; II,73 (p.96) ; II,139 (p.139) ; II,249 (p.184) ; III,13,10 (p.435) ; III,14,255 (p.574) ; 391 (p.632) ; 617 (p.737). Cf. III,3,14 (p.104).

Thus, although the various terms which resemble the original terms for the threefold nature in the *Vijñānavāda* are not found together in any one section of the work, nonetheless one must take careful note of the fact that these terms are used in the *Vākyapadīya* with surprisingly greater frequency than the general trend in Sanskrit works, and that these terms were used in a special sense usually restricted to Buddhist works. We may conclude that this is a clear example of the influence of the *Vijñānavāda* on this work in the usage of terms.

The terms '*adhyāropa*'[27] which is more or less similar in its meaning to '*parikalpa*' is also used (Helārāja glosses it as *samāropa*).[28] This is originally a technical term of the *Vijñānavāda*, which has the meaning 'to imagine that something (e. g. demons, delusions) exists even though it does not actually exist.'[29] It is translated as "increase"[30] in Chinese Buddhist texts. This concept is opposed to that of *apavāda* (i. e. to deny the existence of something which actually exists). Theses terms were formerly[31] thought to be technical terms peculiar to the *Advaitavādin*, but as I have attempted to show above, they are originally Buddhist, especially *Vijñānavādin*, terms and it is from these sources that Bhartṛhari adopted them and incorporated them in his philosophy. In fact, Bhartṛhari's use of these terms is the first example[32] of their use in the extant *Vedānta* literature. Bhartṛhari also uses the term '*adhyāsa*'[33] which has the same meaning as '*adhyāropa*'.[34]

Bhartṛhari describes the origination of the various forms of the phenomenal world as manifest '*pratyavabhāsate*'.[35] This term is used as a technical and philosophical term in '*Vijñānavādins*' doctrine with the meaning 'Various things manifest as if they were existent.'[36] Moreover, in *Vijñānavāda* the noun '*pratyavabhāsa*' is used with the meaning 'The six senses illuminate six objects separately.'[37] Similarly, *avabhāsa* and *pratibhāsa* are also technical terms of the *Vijñānavādins*.

By the term *prapañca* Bhartṛhari means "to express by dint of such the method of concepts as 'one', 'different' the absolute which is by nature beyond verbal expression" (*Vākyap*. III, 1, 20). This is a typically Buddhist usage. In contrast, the term is used in the Indian philosophic world as a whole to mean 'the phenomenal world' or the 'extent of the world'. There are in addition numerous other terms which are traceable to Buddhist Sanskrit.

advaya	III, 3, 64, (p.129).
grāhya	*grāhyatvaṃ grāhakatvaṃ ca dve śaktī tejasaḥ* (I, 55, p.23); also II, 63 (p.93); II, 101 (p.124); II, 107 (p.127).
viparyāsa	I, 17, (p.8); II, 276 (p.196); II, 291 (p.202).
viparyasta	II, 257 (p.188); II, 258 (p.189).
viparyaya	I, 156 (p.61); II, 440 (p.265); III, 3, 52 (p.123); III, 3, 59 (p. 126); III, 6, 19, (p.168); III, 7, 118 (p.252); III, 10, 7 (p.394).
viparīta	III, 7, 118 (p.252).
vikalpita	II, 229 (p.176), III, 14, 74 (p.487); 146 (p.524).
avikalpita[38]	III, 3, 70 (p.132).
ābhāsa	*ābhāsopagamo vyaktiḥ*, III, 7, a, 53 (p.206).
avabhāsa[39]	*arthāvabhāsarūpā hi śabdebhyo jāyate smṛtiḥ*/(II, 424, p. 260).
adhvan	*trayo 'dhvānaḥ* III, 9, 52 (p.361). Cf. III, 9, 101 (p.384).

I have only discussed those terms and passages where the Buddhist characteristics are evident on even the most cursory examination but if one enters into a detailed examination of Bhartṛhari's thought the evidence of Buddhist influence increases overwhelmingly. In terms of research into the history of philosophic speculation it is just this point which deserves greatest attention but I will reserve discussion of it for a later time and will confine myself here to pointing out the enormous Buddhist influence which must be acknowledged to exist merely on the basis of terminology and language.

Notes

1) *sarvavyavahārātīta* — Helārāja.
2) For example III, 3, 67-68 (p.131).
3) *"cāpāyibhir" iti hetunirdeśaḥ śākyasamakakṣyatayā kṛtaḥ.* — (Helārāja ad *Vākyap*. III, 2, 4).
4) *alātacakravad rūpaṃ kriyāṇāṃ parikalpyate*/(III, 8, 8. p.308).
5) Cf. Part VI, Chapter I, Appendix IV of this book.
6) Cf. Notes 5) and 7) of Section I, Sub-Section 2 of this Chapter.
7) *Tohoku Catalogue* No. 1800. According to Poussin's French translation of the second chapter of *Outline of Philosophical Systems*, this verse is in Tandjour, Rgyud XXXIII. fol. 45b and is quoted at *Bhāmatī*, ad II,2,18. (Cf. Ānandajñāna ad *l.c.*).
8) *SDS*. II, *ll*.341-347.
9) *Bodhisattvabhūmi*, p.224. *The Opinions of Yoga Masters*. Book 43 (*Taisho Tripiṭaka*, vol. 30, p.531). Moreover the contrast of these two concepts appears at other places in this work also. *Bodhisattvabhūmi* pp.262, *l*.24 - 263, *l*.2 ; p.283, *l*.19.
10) e. g. *Aṅguttara-Nikāya*, vol. I, p.70.
11) Supplemented by Helārāja.
12) *avikṛta* — Helārāja.
13) *Taisho Tripiṭaka* Vol. 31, p.598b.
14) For example, Helārāja and the later *Vedānta* scholars make a distinction between *vivarta* (temporary, apparitional manifestation) and *pariṇāma* (development) while Bhartṛhari and Śaṅkara use the two terms with almost the same meaning. I will discuss this in detail later.
15) Supplemented by Helārāja.
16) *Saṃkīrṇaśloka* v. 769. D. D. Kosambi ; *Bhartṛhari*, p.196.
17) For example III,8,18 (p.313) ; 26 (p.320).
18) III, 7, a, 89 (239), III, 8, 53, (p.334).
19) An observation of *MW*. *KF*. yields only *Vajracchedikā*, p.40, *l*.8f. as positive evidence for this term.
20) *Saddharmapuṇḍarīka* (ed. by Wogihara and Tsuchida, p.202, *l*.27).
21) *Bodhisattvabhūmi*, p.273, *ll* 16 ; 24, *Taisho Tripiṭaka* Vol. 30, p.543.
22) *Bodhisattvabhūmi*, p.101, *l*.18.
23) Cf. *PW*. The fact that Śaṅkara (ad *BS*. II,1,6) uses the word '*pariniṣpannatva*' must rather be attributed to Buddhist influence.
24) *paratantra*, II, 198 (p.162) : III, 1, 87 (p.66) : III, 13, 6, (p.433) : *paratantratva*, I, 62 (p.25) :

III, 3, 4 (p.99) : III, 7, a, 8 (p.179).

25) From *PW*.

26) *Vākyap*. III, 3, 86, (p.138) ; III, 13, 28 (p.444) ; III, 14, 19 (p.456) ; 75 (p.487) ; 264 (p.578) ; 589 (p.722).

27) *Vākyap*. III, 1, 6 (p.12) ; III, 11, 10 (p.399).

28) Even in Buddhism the two words *samāropa* and *adhyāropa* are used in the same way. For example, Candrakīrti annotates the word '*nirvāṇasamāropa*' which appears at *Mādhyamika-Śāstra* XVI, 10 as *nirvāṇādhyāropa*.

29) For example, *Madhyāntavibhāgaṭīkā* (ed. by S. Yamagudhi, pp.79, *l*.20 ; 246, *l*.17 ; 239, *l*.2 ; *Madhyamakavṛtti*, p.264, *l*.11 ; 299, *l*.4 ; 364, *l*.9 ; *Abhisamayālaṅkārāloka* (ed. by Wogihara), p.52, *l*.4.

30) The verb '*adhyārohati*' means 'to increase' in Buddhist Sanskrit (Cf. *Bodhisattva-bhūmi*, p.171, *l*.6). Its causative form means "to superimpose" and its past participle '*adhyāropita*' is also used quite often. *Triṃśikāvijñaptibhāṣya*, pp.28, *l*.29 ; 35, *l*.11 ; *Abhisamayālaṅkārāloka*, p.66, *l*.8 ; *Madhyāntavibhāgaṭīkā*, p.140, *l* 12 ; 247, *l* 10. Cf. Ś. ad *BS*. I,2,17. (vol. I, p.203, *l*, 4).

31) Cf. *Madhyāntavibhāgaṭīkā*, pp.79, *l*.22 ; 209, *l*.19. *Abhisamayālaṅkārāloka*, p.22, *l*.23. It also appears in various other Chinese translations of *Vijñānavāda* works.

32) As a pre-Śaṅkara example there is the phrase quoted at Ś. ad *Bhag. G*. XIII, 14. See Part V, Chapter XV, Section VII of this book.

33) *Vākyap*. III, 8, 11 (p.310) ; III, 9, 33 (p.353) ; *adhyasta*, III, 8, 107 (p.387).

34) Cf. *PW*. *adhyāropa*. Also Cf. *Vedāntasāra* 33 ff. falsche Übertragung (Böhtlingk), Aufbürdung (Deussen), illusory attribution (Jacob).

35) *Vākyap*. III, 1, 36. In *MW*. the verb form is not given, only the noun form *pratyava-bhāsa* (becoming visible, appearance) is given, and mentioned that it is used in *Uttara-rāmacarita*.

36) *Madhyāntavibhāgaṭīkā*, p.232, *l*.20.

37) *Triṃśikā-vijñaptibhāṣya*, p.18. *l*.18.

38) Following Helārāja and *Sarvadarśanasaṃgraha* XIII, *l*.255.

39) Cf. *rūpasyāvabhāsa iti ... avabhāso hi rūpamātrasyābhivyaktikāraṇam*. (*Madhyāntavibhāgaṭīkā*, p.86, *l*.6).

Sub-Section 6. Conclusion

Our investigations conclusively demonstrate that there is a strong element of Buddhist influence in the *Vākyapadīya* which manifests itself quite conspicuously both conceptually and linguistically. Bhartṛhari carefully scrutinized Buddhist works, listened to the preaching of the Law, and at time as I-ching relates, even resided for short periods in Buddhist temples. Thus I-ching's claim that Bhartṛhari was well versed in Buddhist doctrine is seen to well founded. Yet at the same time it must be noted that I-ching's discussion refers only to one aspect of Bhartṛhari as a thinker, for it is undeniable that Bhartṛhari saw himself as firmly implanted in the traditional orthodox Brahmin position and thus it is that he devoted such immense energy to the revitalization of grammar which is the foundation of that position. Further, his philosophical position must, as I have noted, be catalogued as part of Vedānta philosophy. I-ching merely placed special emphasis on one feature of Bhartṛhari's thought, namely that he had studied and been influenced by Buddhist thought.

Even the fact that Dharmapāla wrote a commentary[1] on Bhartṛhari's *Prakīrṇaka* is not due to his regarding the latter's theory as Buddhistic but rather because he regarded traditional grammar as a cultural asset which the various schools could all utilize to advantage. Since grammar, in this sense, was the discipline concerned with the rules of Sanskrit, which was the common language of the educated class in India, it had a character which placed it above religious or academic sectarianism.

There were also not a few Buddhist scholars who were well versed in grammar. The most famous is Candragomin, but it is also related that Dharmakīrti devoted some time to the study of grammar.[2] Candrakīrti, who wrote a commentary on the *Mādhyamika-Śāstra*, and Yaśomitra, who wrote a commentary on the *Abhidharma-kośa*, were both quite familiar with Pāṇini's work and the same can probably be said for Dharmapāla.

It has been customary in academic discussion to cite Gauḍapāda and Śaṅkara as classic examples of *Vedānta* scholars who were influenced by Mahāyāna Buddhism. As a result of our investigations, however, we see that there was a thinker of the same stamp, a thinker who was profoundly influenced by Buddhism even though he denounced and criticized it, who existed some time before Śaṅkara.[3]

Notes

1) Cf. Chapter I, Section I of this Part.

2) E. Obermiller: *History of Buddhism by Bu-ston*, part II, p.152.

3) My opinion that Bhartṛhari was not a Buddhist fundamentally was agreed to by Dr. S. L. Pandey (*Pre-Śaṃkara Advaita Philosophy*, op. cit., p.335). An English translation of this chapter of the original book was published formerly under the title "Bhartṛhari the Scholar" (*Indo Iranian Journal*, vol. IV, 1960, Nr. 4, pp.282-305). Later an article to correct the above-mentioned article was published -- "Nakamura on Bhartṛhari" (*Indo Iranian Journal*, vol. XIII, No. 3, 1971, pp.161-175). The English translation of this chapter in the present work was done independently of the above-mentioned articles.

CHAPTER III

BHARTṚHARI THE SCHOLAR

SECTION I. BHARTṚHARI'S THEORY CONCERNING THE SACRED BOOKS

Bhartṛhari declared himself to be a grammarian and contemporary scholars of India looked upon him as one. But on the study of grammar originated in the interpretation of the *Vedas* orthodox Brahmanic scholars had included grammar in the six *aṅgas* which were supplementary to the *Vedas*, and from ancient times it had held an important and revered place.

Bhartṛhari was also held in high esteem as a Vedānta philosopher and since this philosophy was founded on various orthodox Brahmanic sacred books, in particular the *Upaniṣad*, it clearly follows that Bhartṛhari, in addition to being a grammarian and a Vedānta philosopher, was also a believer in those sacred books. The question arises as to whether he really believed in the authority of those sacred books. The historical fact, which grammar originally developed out of the *Vedāṅgas*, prejudiced his thinking, so that he was obliged to declare that the grammar which he taught was based on the *Vedas* and that he himself was a follower of the Vedic lore.

Thus in his writings he referred frequently to the *Vedas*. Though he recognized the authority of the four *Vedas*[1] and the existence of various Vedic schools based on the same ritualism,[2] he asserted that the *Vedas* were of one entity, so to speak, they were taught by many saints in various ways and this rise to the opinion that there were several versions of the *Vedas*.[3] This illustrates clearly the general attitude towards the *Vedas* in Bhartṛhari's day.

The *Vedas* are the sacred scriptures of orthodox Brahmanism and are known as the *śruti*. Brahmanic scholars hold that the *Vedas* are not the work of man but revelations from time immemorial acquired by various *ṛṣis* through mystic inspiration and were handed down by them from generation to generation. In order to differentiate between the *Vedas* and the compositions of the later sages, the latter were called *smṛti* and were supposed to be based on the *śruti*, i. e. the *Vedas*. Both *śruti* and *smṛti* were handed down from father to son in an unbroken chain through ages, and the Indians in general accorded to both authority and veneration. Bhartṛhari accepted this view of the orthodox Brahmins:

> "It is said that the words of the *śruti*, though their author and their origin is unknown to us, go on forever without interruption ; so does the *smṛti*[4] though it was composed by scholars."[5]
>
> "The words of the *śruti* were composed a long long time ago."[6]

At the *Mahāpralaya* (the destruction of the whole world, especially at the end of a *kalpa*) the world, dissolving into the *Brahman*, reverts to nothing and is reborn as a new world again. This process of annihilation and rebirth continues in an eternal cycle while the *Vedas* remain unchanged ; they are unaffected by the process of birth, duration and annihilation of the world. Thus they are without beginning and without end. (In this respect the thought of Bhartṛhari is precisely the same as that contained in the *Brahma-sūtra*,[7] which was also shared by the Mīmāṃsā school.) On the other hand, however, the *smṛti*, though of human conception and origin, was handed down from ancient times in an unbroken sequence. And here Bhartṛhari makes a point of emphasizing the fact that the composition of the *smṛti* writings are multifarious : some are clear as to their aim and purpose (for instance the writings on medicine) ; some are vague and difficult to follow (as for example the writings on what foods should and should not to be eaten). But all the *smṛti* writings were propounded by the Vedic scholars (*Vedavid*) following the special characteristics (*liṅga*) of the *Vedas*.[8]

Bhartṛhari calls the *śruti śāstra*[9] or *āgama*[10] as well as the *smṛti*. Frequently however the term *śāstra* refers to the *Vedas* in a broad sense,[11] and the term *āgama* stands for the *smṛti*[12] and in particular the books which give the basic rules on grammar.[13] The intrinsic meaning of the term *āgama* suggests something which has been handed down from ancient times ;[14] therefore[15] it can stand for books such as those of the Vaiśeṣika school as well as the *śāstra*. But in the *Vākyapadīya* the term *āgama* refers to the books of the pure orthodox Brahmanic schools and can therefore include the *śruti* and the *smṛti*. As we have already stated, the former was of non-human creation and the latter compiled by human effort ; but the latter found its source and origins in the former. In the concept of the transmigration of the world it is believed that the *śruti* perishes only to grow like seeds (*bīja*) out of the *Vedas* again.[16]

> "It is our fixed belief that the *āgama* was produced out of some source or other. When all the *āgama* have perished, the three *Vedas* will remain like seeds to give new birth to the *āgama*."[17]

As we can clearly see from the above quotation, Bhartṛhari regarded the *Vedas* as the absolute source of all knowledge. He studied them diligently and was well versed in them. He was also familiar with the subtle differences which existed between the various Vedic schools.[18] His work clearly reflects his veneration for the *Vedas*.

His views on the *śruti* and the *smṛti* are much similar to those of the Mīmāṃsā school. It is not possible to go deeply into this matter in this article, but short reference must be made to it as it has given rise to many questions. To modern scholars it may seem illogical that Bhartṛhari held the *Vedas* in such profound veneration ; but when we realize the circumstances which led to the establishment of grammar as a branch of studies in ancient India, Bhartṛhari's attitude can be easily understood. In the beginning, grammar like the study of phonetics (*śikṣā*), prosody (*chandas*) and etymology (*nirukta*), was only an auxiliary science or one of the *Vedāṅgas*. It was taken for granted that the scholars who applied themselves to these studies were convinced of the absolute sanctity of the *Vedas*. Accordingly, up to a much later period, all grammarians adhered unconditionally to the *Vedas*. Since he grew up in such an atmosphere of tradition, the sanctity of the *Vedas* was an accepted and undisputed fact which he believed had been handed down through the ages. The important place accorded to their sanctity in his writings arises from the fact that, as a grammarian, he was loyal to historical traditions and beliefs.

Bhartṛhari does not make an effort to explain clearly and in detail why the *Vedas* were regarded as holy. To one of a faithful Brahmin of the orthodox school, their holiness was without question ; in other words he took it for granted. This does not mean, however, that he did not give the matter his thought and consideration, for he was, after all, a philosopher. Traces of his speculations, though they may be few, can be found in his writings. To him the *Vedas* were "the convenient road (expediency) leading to the *Brahman*" or "the imitation[19] of the *Brahman*". These phrases which were used in the Vedānta philosophy express his veneration of the *Vedas*. But when we analyze them we see that the only absolute principle which he accepted was the *Brahman* existing behind the *Vedas*, although these were traditionally considered to have a holiness of their own. His idea suggested, consequently, that the authority of the *Vedas* is dependent on the *Brahman*. According to Bhartṛhari the *Brahman* is high and the *Vedas* is low. In other words, although Bhartṛhari was an orthodox Brahmin scholar who professed profound veneration for the *Vedas*, in actual fact he transcended this generally accepted belief. In terms of his own doctrines, parts of the *Vedas*, which deal with various rituals, lose their significance,[20] and the *Vedānta* (*Upaniṣad*), which deals with the *Brahman*, is the only adequate one. Therefore we can say that Bhartṛhari's doctrines were based on the Vedānta philosophy although on the surface he appears to be an ordinary Brahmin scholar professing the same Vedic ideas as all other scholars of his time.

Notes

1) *atharvaṇām aṅgirasāṃ sāmnām ṛgyajuṣasya ca/yasminn uccāvacā varṇāḥ pṛthak sthitaparigrahāḥ//* (*Vākyap*. I, 21). But in some cases the term *trayī* is found. Cf. ibid. I, 134; III, 3,70.

2) *bhedānāṃ* (*śākhānām*) *bahumārgatvaṃ karmaṇy ekatra cāṅgatā/śabdānāṃ yataśaktitvaṃ tasya śākhāsu dṛśyate//* (*Vākyap*. I, 6). The word in brackets are supplemented by the commentator.

3) *prāptyupāyo 'nukāraś ca tasya* (= *brahmaṇaḥ*) *vedo maharṣibhiḥ/eko 'py anekavartmeva samāmnātaḥ pṛthak pṛthak//* (*Vākyap*. I, 5).

4) In some cases the words *śruti* and *smṛti* are used in combination. (*Vākyap*. I, 135).

5) *anādim apy avicchinnāṃ śrutim āhur akartṛkām/śiṣṭair nibadhyamānā tu na vyavacchidyate smṛtiḥ//* (*Vākyap*. I, 146). The text has *avacchinnām* for *avicchinnāṃ* and the present writer changed it to the above reading according to the commentary of Puṇyarāja. According to the information by Prof. de Jong, Charudeva Shastri's edition (Lahore, 1934) gives the reading: *avyavachinnāṃ*, which must be right.

6) *śāstram atidūre vyavasthitam*, ibid. III, 14, 74, p. 487.

7) Refer to *A History of Early Vedānta Philosophy*, Part One, pp.477 ff.

8) *smṛtayo bahurūpāś ca dṛṣṭādṛṣṭaprayojanāḥ/ tam evāśritya liṅgebhyo vedavidbhiḥ prakāśitāḥ//* (*Vākyap*. I, 7).

9) Puṇyarāja refers to the *smṛti* as *smṛtiśāstra* (ad *Vākyap*. I, 43).

10) *śrutismṛtilakṣaṇāgama* (Puṇyarāja ad I, 41).

11) *Vākyap*. I, 43 ; I, 137. But in a certain case he refers to the grammar of Pāṇini as *śāstra* (III, 13, 23, p. 441).

12) *sarvapravādeṣv āgamavākyānāṃ smṛtivākyānāṃ praṇetṛparigraheṇa pauruṣeyatvam upagamyate* — (Pūṇyarāja ad *Vākyap*. I, 134).

13) Cf. *Vākyap*. II, 484 f.

14) *vṛddebhya āgamaḥ*, III, 7, 2 (p. 294) ; *pūrvebhya āgamaḥ*, III, 14, 20 (p. 456).

15) *Vākyap*. III, 11, 9. See also the commentary of Helārāja (p. 399).

16) *tāni (Vedavākyāni) pūrvāgameṣu vicchinneṣu anyeṣu praṇetṛṣu āgamāntarānusaṃdhāne bījavad avatiṣṭhante/* (Puṇyarāja ad *Vākyap*. I, 134).

17) *na jātv adartṛkaṃ kaścid āgamaṃ pratipadyate/ bījaṃ sarvāgamāpāne trayy evādau vyavasthitā//* (*Vākyap*. I, 134).

18) In his commentary on the *Mahābhāṣya* he refers to and quotes from *Taittirīyāḥ*, *Vājasaneyinaḥ*, *Āśvalāyana- and Āpastamba* (*-śrauta*) *-sūtra*, *Bahvṛca-*(*śrauta*)*-sūtrabhāṣya*, *Nirukta*, *Prātiśākhya* and *Śikṣā* (Kielhorn in *Indian Antiquary*, 1883, p. 227). It is likely that he had no specific connection with any Vedic school. However, Prof. Rau asserts that Bhartṛhari may have belonged to the Maitrāyaṇīya school. The reason for his assertion is that among 109 Vedic passages which he cites in his *Mahābhāṣyaṭīkā* and *Vākyapadīya*. 34 are cited from texts of the Maitrāyaṇīya school. (Wilhilm Rau : "Bhartṛhari und der *Veda*", *Studien zur Indologie und Iranistik*, herausgegeben von Verlag A. u. J. wezler, Heft 516 : *Festschrift Paul Thieme*, 1980, S. 167-180).

19) *prāptyupāyo 'nukāraś ca tasya (brahmaṇaḥ) vedaḥ* ... (*Vākyap*. I, 5). Cf. *Tattvasaṃgrahapañjikā* ad v. 128 — *varṇapadakrameṇāvasthito vedas tadadhigamopāyas tasya praticchandakanyāyenāvasthitaḥ/*

20) For further details of his views on the *Vedas* see *Vākyap*. I, 8-10 ; 24 ; II, 240 ; 392 f. etc.

SECTION II. THE SIGNIFICANCE OF BHARTṚHARI'S SCHOLARSHIP AS A GRAMMARIAN

As there is a tendency in the Vedic ideas of Bhartṛhari to evaluate the *Vedas* from a Vedānta standpoint rather than from the usual Brahmin one, his attitude as a grammarian must differ from that of the other grammarians of his time. Before discussing this point, it may be well to examine his conception of grammar.

This branch of study was, in ancient India, one of the six *aṅgas*, called *vyākaraṇa*; the *aṅgas* were second in importance to the *śruti*. Therefore grammar-books giving the rudiments of grammar were a part of the *smṛti*. It is said that the various grammar-books written by ancient scholars were based on the *śruti* and the *smṛti*, a point acknowledged by Bhartṛhari:[1]

> "Therefore the excellent scholars began to teach the significance of words according to the *Vedas* which were not created by man, and, according to the *smṛti*, which laid down the rules [on the usage of words]."[2]

We are inclined to believe that the grammarians of those days, despite the interest they had in their subject and the pleasure they derived from it, would not have devoted their energies to such a complicated and elaborate study as grammar, if it were only one of the six *Vedāṅgas*. But scholarship in the field of grammar was second in importance only to the *Vedas* themselves as is clearly shown by some Buddhist *sūtras*.[3] Bhartṛhari emphasized its importance as a study in its own right. According to him scholarship in grammar should be placed higher than the others of the six *Vedāṅgas* (*prathamaṃ chandasām aṅgam*)[4] and elsewhere he praises it as the highest among the studies of the three *Vedas* which are made up of many branches of study.[5] He also speaks of it as the foundation of all other studies.

> "As the species of the meanings of all words are subject to their forms (*ākṛti*), the study of grammar is the original source of all studies (*vidyā*) in the world."[6]

It is the foundation on which all other studies are based and can be likened to a purifying fire.[7]

> "Being a purifying fire to all study, it shines brightly over all branches or learning."[8]

Sometimes it is likened to a light in the darkness (*tamasi jyotis*). Likewise Bhartṛhari considers the study of grammar to be the most excellent of all the ascetic trainings (*tapasām uttamaṃ tapaḥ*)[9] and therefore it deserves the highest praise.

The original aim of grammar was to study the structure of the sacred language of Sanskrit and thereby codify the various rules applied in the language, thus preserving its purity and preventing its corruption. As Vedic literature was written in Sanskrit, the endeavor to preserve the purity of the language meant the preservation of the *Vedas* themselves.

Patañjali's statement that grammar should be studied in order that the *Vedas* be preserved[10] (*rakṣārthaṃ Vedānām adhyeyaṃ vyākaraṇam*) illustrates this point. Bhartṛhari inherited this traditional attitude towards grammar. As grammar aimed at checking the corruption and confusion of the language of the sacred *Vedas*,[11] Bhartṛhari called it counteracting linguistic corruption[12] (*vāṅmalānāṃ cikitsitam*).

What is actually meant by the right usage of a language? The grammatical rules of Sanskrit had been established by the *sūtras* of Pāṇini, the "*Vārttika*" of Kātyāyana and the "*Mahābhāṣya*" of Patañjali. The works of these three came to be regarded by the scholars who came later as representing the very highest authority. Bhartṛhari confirms this in his work.[13]

Thus the duty of the grammarians who came after those three pioneers lay not in codifying new rules but in preserving and propagating the rules which had already been fixed. This reflects the attitude of Indian society at this period, 100 BC. and onwards, which gradually took on a tolerably stable character. What this society cherished was not the novelty of things but the durability of tradition. Therefore things which had been handed down from the immemorable past were treasured and valued. The study of grammar claimed to be age-old and a part of the historical traditions. The correct usage of words (*sādhutva*) meant faithful conformation with the traditional rules of language. The usage held to be the correct one was that given in the traditional rules of grammar. Therefore it followed that "being right" meant "being old" ; one was related to the other just like the back of something is related to its front.

According to Bhartṛhari the sacred study of grammar aimed at continuity (*nitya*) and correctness of language.[14]

> "The aim of grammar is the knowledge of correctness of words. The rules of this sacred study have been handed down in an unbroken chain

to the educated."[15]

His attitude towards language as a social phenomenon is as thoroughly conservative as that of any other orthodox Brahmin scholar.

What were his reasons for ranking the study of grammar so high, calling it the foundation of all other studies? The answer, we think, lies in the fact that all studies can be brought into existence only through the medium of language, either the written or the spoken word. The semantic relation can only be classified and expressed logically by means of words. At present grammar is the only study wherein the sole object is the analysis of words.[16]

> "Without grammar the understanding of the real nature of various words cannot exist."[17]

Bhartṛhari illustrates this point by means of the simile of the mirror which reflects the images of various objects.[18] Supposing that it is only by studying grammar that the nature of words can be understood, then it is for grammarians to devote their energies to this study. With this in view, Bhartṛhari enters into philosophical speculations and adopts a philosophical attitude to language which is quite separate from mere defense of grammatical rules and their propagation. He delved much deeper into linguistic problems than any of his predecessors had done and came to the conclusion that words were component parts of the *Brahman* and therefore on the same level as it.

As this metaphysical attitude formed the nucleus of Bhartṛhari's philosophical ideas, his grammatical ideas transcended those of the grammarians before him. According to him, grammar leads the way to the *Brahman* (*āsannaṃ brahmaṇas* I, 11). He goes on to assert that grammar is a direct road (*āñjasa* I, 12) and that finally the highest *Brahman* can be reached through scholarship in grammar (I, 22 cd). Since reaching the *Brahman* means arriving at spiritual liberation, the study of grammar may be called the gate leading to spiritual liberation.[19] Therefore Bhartṛhari elevates grammar from a mere study in which rules on grammar are discussed to a study of the inner-self (*adhyātmaśāstra*).

> "It is the first step towards perfection. It is the truly royal road for those who deserve enlightenment".[20]

Thus he praised the merits of grammar.

"The knowledge of the inner self cleans dirt from the body, from speech,[21] from the mind and can be compared to a healing process."[22]

Bhartṛhari's theory which describes grammar as a study of the inner-self (*adhyātmaśāstra*) which brings about spiritual liberation was of epoch-making importance in the history of grammar in India.

The various rituals described in the *Vedas* aim at prosperity in the present world and heavenly rebirth in the next. The aim of grammar is to understand the language of the Vedic scriptures and from it prosperity in this and the other world can be attained. Kātyāyana put into words his belief that the use of the language of grammatical *sūtras* leads to prosperity (*śāstrapūrvake prayoge 'bhyudayaḥ*).[23] And Patañjali endorsed this view too and other later grammarians believed they would find rebirth and happiness in heaven through their study of grammar.[24] But Bhartṛhari's belief was based on philosophical ideas. He claimed the aim behind the study of grammar to be much higher than rebirth in heaven. For him, it meant the acquirement of Brahmanic wisdom and the study of grammar was a quest for spiritual liberation.

This theory brought on a new significance to the study of grammar and one which differed from the theories of his predecessors. And of course, it was his adoption of the Vedānta philosophy that brought about this great change in the study of grammar.

In what way is the study of grammar a quest for spiritual liberation? To find an answer to this question we must refer to his ideas on metaphysics. With this in mind, a study of his metaphysics will be made in next chapter and, as an introduction to this, his theory concerning knowledge in general will be discussed first.

Notes

1) Cf. *Vākyap*. I, 143.

2) *tasmād akṛtakaṃ śāstraṃ smṛtiṃ vā sanibandhanām/āśrityārabhyate śiṣṭaiḥ śabdānām anuśāsanam//* (*Vākyap*. I, 43).

3) In the various traditional sciences of India "*Vyākaraṇa*" is mentioned next to the *Vedas*. '*Ch'eng-shin-lun*' X, Miscellaneous Impurities, 136 (*Taisho Tripiṭaka,* vol. 32, p. 321 b); '*Mahāparinirvāṇa-sūtra*' XIX (*Taisho Tripiṭaka,* vol. 12, p. 730 ab).

4) *Vākyap*. I, 11. *SDS*. XIII, *l*.87 (p. 295). This idea was shared by Patañjali — *'pradhānaṃ ca ṣaṭsv aṅgeṣu vyākaraṇam/pradhāne ca kṛto yatnaḥ phalavān bhavati'* (*Mahābhāṣya*, p. 1, *ll*.19-20 ; Cf. *SDS*. XIII, *l*.84).

5) *anekatīrthabhedāyās trayyā vācaḥ paraṃ padam* (*Vākyap*. I, 144).

6) *yathārthajātayaḥ sarvāḥ śabdākṛtinibandhanāḥ/tathaiva loke vidyānām eṣā vidyā parāyaṇam//* (*Vākyap*. I, 15).

7) *Vākyap*. I, 14. cd.

8) *pavitraṃ sarvavidyānām adhividyaṃ (= vidyāsu) prakāśate.* (*Vākyap*. I, 14).

9) *Vākyap*. I, 11.

10) *Mahābhāṣya*, I, p. 1 (ed. by Kielhorn).

11) *bhavati ca śabdasaṃskāro vyākaraṇaśāstrasya prayojanam.* (*SDS*. XIII, *l*.59, cf. *ll*.61).

12) *Vākyap*. I, 14 (the aim of grammar is also said to be the perfection of words).

13) *Vākyap*. I, 23.

14) *Vākyap*. I, 29.

15) *sādhutvajñānaviṣayā saiṣā vyākaraṇasmṛtiḥ/avicchedena śiṣṭānām idaṃ smṛtinibandhanam//* (*Vākyap*. I, 143).

16) Cf. *Vākyap*. I, 13 ab.

17) *tattvāvabodhaḥ śabdānāṃ nāsti vyākaraṇād ṛte/* (*Vākyap*. I, 13. cd).

18) *Vākyap*. I, 20.

19) *dvāram apavargasya*, I, 14. Cf. *śabdānuśāsanaśāstrasya niḥśreyasasādhanatvaṃ siddham.* *SDS*. XIII, *ll*.275-6. *tasmād vyākaraṇaśāstraṃ paramapuruṣārthasādhanatayādhyetavyam iti siddham.* (*SDS*. XIII, *l*. 284).

20) *idam ādyaṃ padasthānaṃ siddhisopānaparvaṇām/iyaṃ sā mokṣamāṇānām ajihmā rājapaddhatiḥ//* (*Vākyap*. I, 16). *siddhi* = *kaivalya-prāpti* (Puṇyarāja). He means spiritual liberation.

21) = *apabhraṃśānāṃ nivṛtti* (Puṇyarāja).

22) *kāyavāgbuddhiviṣayā ye malāḥ samavasthitāḥ/cikitsālakṣaṇādhyātmaśāstrais teṣāṃ viśuddhayaḥ//* (*Vākyap*. I, 148).

23) *Mahābhāṣya*, 1, p.10.

24) "Also others say thus : if one word is known and used correctly, it will be a cow in the heavenly realm that brings about things one desires. And again others say thus : they ride on the wagon that are made of words well combined and well regulated and go to the heavenly realm where desirous pleasures are. But those who talk such wrong words as *cikkamita* go there troubled" (*SDS*. XIII, *ll*.92-96).

SECTION III. BHARTṚHARI'S THEORY ON KNOWLEDGE

As Bhartṛhari's grammatical scholarship was based — albeit superficially — on the preservation of traditional usage, his scope in the realm of philosophy was consequently restricted. He was a staunch supporter of traditions(*āgama*) and was strongly opposed to scholars who aimed at forming their philosophical ideas around a nucleus of logic(*tarka*).

Though he admitted the existence of perception(*pratyakṣa*) and inference(*anumāna*) applied by men in general, Bhartṛhari advocated the existence of something which could not be proved by either of these.

> "Various divine powers such as demons, *pitṛs* and vampires which exist outside the realm of perception and inference [employed by the ordinary man] are the result of certain processes such as asceticism in the past lives."[1]

What he means is that, though we cannot ascertain the powers of demons, *pitṛs* and vampires etc. through perception or inference, nevertheless we cannot deny their existence. How then do we know that they exist? Through the *āgama*, that is, through the source of the scriptures.

> "There is no ordinary *linga* to prove the existence of the universal, the form, the essence and the species. Therefore some other source (i. e. that of the sacred books) is used."[2]

It hardly calls for mention that all philosophic schools belonging to the orthodox Brahmanical religion recognized the various sources of tradition, especially the *Vedas*, besides perception and inference ; therefore no special mention is called for. But Bhartṛhari stressed with emphasis the importance of the *āgama* and as he held it in profound veneration he was strongly opposed to schools which resorted to philosophical thinking. Here again we get a glimpse of Bhartṛhari's particular attitude as a scholar. He holds that the meaning of things is indeed determined by the sacred scriptures.[3] And again, at the end of the second book of his *Vākyapadīya* where he discusses in detail the tradition of the study of grammar,[4] he adds that only through the teachings of various *āgamas* can the mind reach clear understanding. How much can those who follow their own reasonings discover?[5] And further :

"Those who are full of illusions without the *āgamas* and do not follow the teachings of the ancients will never attain to lucid wisdom.[6]"[7]

In other words, as far as Bhartṛhari was concerned, only the *śruti* and the *smṛti* carried real authority. Therefore he criticized philosophers who formulated their own ideas which are independent of tradition.

Although there is, in this verse, no reference to any school of thought to which he was opposed, we are of the opinion that the materialists, the Buddhists, Jains, the Nyāya-Vaiśeṣika school and the Sāṃkhya school were among those which he combatted. Bhartṛhari, turning a bold front, proved that even if the orthodox Brahmanic school is attacked and challenged by liberal thinkers who flourish logic as a weapon, it can suffer no harm because of its long traditional superiority.

"Therefore as the spirit [in the doctrine of subjectivity is not harmed by anything], so will those who follow the ways of the *āgama* handed down to us without interruption meet with no refutation from the argumentations by means of logic (*hetuvāda*)."

His thinking was not confined to the field of metaphysics but extended to his activities as a member of society. He held that the laws(*dharma*) which regulated the lives of citizens in Indian society could neither be established nor refuted by theory(*tarka*) as they were based on the sacred *āgama*.

"The *dharma* is not founded on theory [alone] without the sacred *āgama*. Even the wisdom of various *ṛṣis* was derived from the sacred *āgama*."[9]

"No one can refute by [mere] theory the uninterrupted ways[10] of *dharma*, as they are generally acknowledged."[11]

According to Bhartṛhari even something which is rejected by the public or considered to be contrary to all reason should be obeyed and carried out if it is so stated in the sacred *āgama*. He holds, too, that something which may be quite difficult to exist in actual life must be acknowledged if it is laid down in the sacred *āgama*.[12] His veneration of the sacred scriptures may be regarded as conservative in the extreme, even blindly enthusiastic.

Thus, as we have shown, Bhartṛhari's charasteristics as a scholar were his veneration of the traditional *āgama* and his refutation of logic. On what grounds did he refute logic? The following lines sum up these reasons.

He stresses the fact that men may come to unexpected danger when they reflect and act purely according to logic.

> "Even as a blind man who hurries over a cliff by measuring his way step by step and releases his hold falls off that cliff, so it can easily happen that a man falls into a pit when he acts chiefly on inference [without the eyes of the *āgama*]."[13]

He likens the *śāstras* to the eyes as they enable us to have knowledge.[14]

It is interesting to note that this argument was used by the Vātsīputrīya school which was a branch of Hīnayāna Buddhism. In commenting on the *Madhyamaka-kārikā* IX,3 of Nāgārjuna, Bhavya, a philosopher of the Mādhyamika school, makes the following statement in the *Prajñā-pradīpamūla-madhyamaka-vṛtti* :

> And yet some of the Vātsīputrīyas believe the contrary. We cannot approve of the theory which, according to the *āgama*, holds that one who clings to existence(*upādātṛ*) expiates the *karmas* of what looks to be the former existence and becomes one who clings to existence(*upādātṛ*) of the [five] *upādānaskandha*. However, what the *upādātṛ* does not exist is an established fact. Therefore we do not mean to assert by inference(*anumāna*) that the *upādātṛ* does not exist. This can be likened to the following :
>
> "As a blind man hurries along a dangerous road by measuring his way step by step, thus when one acts chiefly by inference one easily runs into the danger of falling into a pit." (*Vākyap.* I, 42).

This argument is not sound, because the gods themselves on account of their various *upādānaskandhas* are designed as *devas*, because the inference is not correct as 'to measure one's way step by step' is found in negative instances (*vipakṣe sattva*) and because those who chiefly make use of false inference (*anumānaprabhāsa*) fall into a pit. As doubts arise, the sacred scriptures being open to followers of all beliefs, it is not right to draw a conclusion(*avadhāraṇa*) based on this fact alone (*pratijñā*). It must be taken into account that the sacred scriptures have the same significance as the method of inference has *hetu*. For that which is not the direct object of perception(*pratyakṣa*) may be a cause of discriminative knowledge (*dṛṣṭānta*). For instance, the inference is by nature(*svabhāva*) a cause of discriminative knowledge."[15]

Commenting on the above passage, Avalokitavrata remarks as follows:

> "In order to make the meaning clear the *ācārya* Bhandrihari resorts to a simile of a blind man so as to point out the reason why inference should be refuted …"[16]

Bhavya's above statement[17] is exactly the same as Bhartṛhari's in the *Vākyapadīya*. As the statement comes from a Buddhist work we can take it that the idea was fairly popular in ancient India as typical of Bhartṛhari.

Why is it then not safe to have recourse to inference as a guiding principle? He claims that there are roughly two arguments. In the first place he declares that it is absolutely impossible to ascertain precisely the *vyāpti* which is an integral part of inference. In other words he doubts the existence of a proper subsumptive relationship of ideas.

> "Because of the fact that the nature of all things varies[18] according to conditions, place and time, it is difficult to ascertain the nature of things by inference."[19]

This statement is further commented on by Puṇyarāja:

> "Even the one and the same thing may assume a different function or character under different conditions or in different places. For instance, water is cold in a snow-bound place but hot in a heated pot. The same applies to difference in time; for example a fire feels very hot in the summer, but not so in the winter. Consequently the *svabhāva* of water cannot be known by inference; only by *āgama*. — Even the thing whose functions are clearly known [like fire for instance] will be impeded in this when brought into contact with another thing"[20]

To illustrate this point Puṇyarāja writes:

> "For example the burning of a fire is impeded in a cloud; it can also be prevented by incantations and medicine."

This idea of Bhartṛhari's was made use of by Śaṅkara in his writings:

> "Even certain ordinary things such as gems, spells, herbs and the like possess powers which, owing to difference of time, place, occasion and so on, produce various opposite effects, and nobody unaided by instruction is able to find out by mere reflection(=logic) the number of these powers, their flavouring conditions, their objects and their purposes

etc. ; how much more impossible is it to conceive without the aid of Scripture the true nature of *Brahman* with its powers unfathomable by thought!"[21]

In this connection it is interesting to note that the doctrine "Just as the subsumptive relationship of two ideas cannot be absolutely established, inference in general cannot exist" was in circulation throughout India as the theory propounded by the Lokāyata school of materialists.[22] It is ironical that Bhartṛhari, who advocated the sanctity of the orthodox Brahmanic *āgama*, should have something in common with a school of materialists who were little better than heathens in his eyes.

And, in the second point, he asserts that in actual life no inference can exist which will meet with the approval of everyone.

> "A fact verified after much thought by those skilled in inference may be interpreted in quite a different way by those who are even more skilled in inference."[23]

Thus as far as logical reflections are concerned Bhartṛhari has reached an attitude of relativism or skepticism. His arguments refuting logic became famous in later years and various writings of the Vedānta school refer to these arguments.[24]

Having assumed this attitude of relativism, Bhartṛhari declares inference to be incapable of persuading. According to him logic is powerless to move a person who is firmly convined of the truth of some fact and a person who believes that fact to be as true as his senses tell him ; therefore logical argumentation is powerless when it comes to persuading someone of something.

> "When a person does not doubt his knowledge even as he does not doubt his senses, how can anyone persuade him?"[25]

This theory of relativism or skepticism was not new in India. It had been propounded by Sañjaya as early as Buddha's time and the Jain belief had had similar philosophical inclinations from its inception. But the fact that an orthodox Brahmin should take up this attitude is remarkable indeed.

It is interesting to note in passing that Śaṅkara adopted Bhartṛhari's philosophy as it was. This can be seen from the tone in which he propounded his doctrine in the following extracts from his writings.

> "In matters to be known from Scripture mere reasoning is not to be relied on for the following reason also. As the thoughts of man are altogether unfettered, reasoning which disregards the holy texts and rests on individual opinion only has no proper foundation. We see how arguments, which some clever men had excogitated with great pains, are shown, by people still more ingenious, to be fallacious, and how the arguments of the latter again are refuted in their turn by other men; so that, on account of the diversity of men's opinions, it is impossible to accept mere reasoning as having a sure foundation."
>
> "But that cognitions founded on reasoning do conflict is generally known; for we continually observe that what one logician endeavours to establish as perfect knowledge is demolished by another, who, in his turn, is treated alike by a third."[26)]

Here again Śaṅkara is in agreement with Bhartṛhari's views. Bhartṛhari's doctrine brought much influence to bear on the later school of Advaitins. The great scholar of the school, Mādhava, accepted his views unreservedly.[27)] (We may point out that a similarity exists between the views of Bhartṛhari and Śaṅkara and those of the French philosopher Blaise Pascal as expressed in his *Pensées* where he holds that the philosophical reflections of men are always one-sided and contradictory; that the Christian truth should be reverted to.)

The next step is to discuss Bhartṛhari's arguments in refutation of inference. His two chief ones have been discussed earlier on; the first, objective and based on pure theory, the second based on the social and individual point of view. As the second one does not refute the essentials of inference they may be considered irrelevant. But "to rely on inference" is decidedly a social phenomenon and since he is opposed to it his arguments have points in them which merit attention. But do his statements prove inference to be false? Was Bhartṛhari truly opposed to it? To answer these questions we have to discuss his statements and his arguments.

As his first point Bhartṛhari holds that in some cases A can be B, in others A cannot be B and that therefore no subsumptive relationship can exist between the two. But Bhartṛhari admits that in cases where A can be B and the conditions(*upādhi*) which make this possible are represented by C, then there must be a subsumptive relationship between A, C and B. Then of course it can be imagined that in combining A with C conditions represented by D may be necessary to bring about the subsumptive relationship between A, C and B ; and this *ad infinitum*.

The very fact that he considered such problems proved that Bhartṛhari himself presupposed the existence of subsumptive relationship. Indeed his argument to refute it[28] is based on inference. Therefore Bhartṛhari failed in his effort to refute inference for the simple reason that he could not unfold his own opinion without it. Consequently we may add that his arguments to refute inference are weak and faulty.

As for his second statement, his assertions that the conclusions drawn by different philosophers conflict with one another is quite correct as a factual statement, but his conclusion "Therefore one should not rely on inference" is evidently derived from inference. For the proposition "One should not rely upon that which is not accepted by all" is presupposed as the major premise to the above statement. Here we come face to face with the interesting case of a philosopher who negates inference, taking recourse to it himself. Therefore the relativist and dubitative attitude of Bhartṛhari was contradictory in itself. Since skepticism or the theory of doubt is full of difficult points as is noticed in the history of Eastern and Western philosophy, he had to acknowledge the difficulty of being absolutely skeptical.[29] However Bhartṛhari's real aim in refuting the power of inference was to minimize its importance and exalt the sanctity of the orthodox Brahmin *āgama*. Thus all his statements quoted above point to the one conclusion that "all inferences include falsehood" and he really believed this.

> "When one wishes to convey to others that what one said was untrue, when one declares that one's sayings were nothing but lies, one does not mean the actual stating of that statement. For if the saying itself be false, the words fail to convey the meaning that they were meant to convey."[30]

The above statement can be taken to mean that he refutes the argument that "an assertion that all is falsehood is self-contradictory and therefore cannot exist". In other words an assertion "all is false" can be either true or false. If it is true, he cannot possibly declare that "all is false" as the very assertion is true. On the other hand, however, if the assertion itself is false, it cannot exist.

We know that a similar problem was discussed by European philosophers but in so far as it concerns Indian philosophy it was propounded by the opponents to the Mādhyamika philosophy. In the *Vigrahavyāvartanī* of Nāgārjuna we find the following argument:

> "If [as the Mādhyamika asserts] the essence (nature) of things escapes us and cannot be found anywhere, then the very words that thou utterest lack their own essence and all things cannot be deprived of their nature."
>
> "If thou assetest that only this sentence of thine has its essence (i. e. it is not false) then the very previous assertion will mean nothing when it is heard."[31]

These arguments were brought forward in order to refute the doctrine of the Mādhyamika that all things are void. Similar arguments were also found in the *Nyāya-sūtra* (II,1,13-14).[32]

Bhartṛhari was against adding the statement "··· is false" to an assertion. In other words, though he maintained that all things were false, he tried to find truth in that assertion at least. This can be traced in his statement that "inference is wrong and therefore the *āgama* is not wrong" thus totally refuting inference.

As in his refutation of inference, Bhartṛhari had finally to betray the fact that he virtually resorted to reasoning, although he ardently expressed his absolutely orthodox attitude in his arguments for the sacred scriptures. He held them in profound veneration maintaining that disobedience of their laws to be evil without questioning whether this was really right or wrong. But the sacred books, which Bhartṛhari believed in so absolutely, were collections of the wise words of philosophers who had lived hundreds, even a thousand years before his time so that there were many phrases which were meaningless and their obvious or superficial meanings were found to be doubtful on philosophical and theological grounds. Sometimes scholars interpreted them in such a way that the original meaning was lost. Bhartṛhari himself admitted that this had happened.

> "Though all men are able through the *āgama* to understand things the

fruit of which is yet to be experienced, what is stated in the *āgama* can be interpreted in the contrary meaning."[33]

The above extract makes it clear that Bhartṛhari himself acknowledged the fact that various interpretations differed occasionally from and contradicted what was stated in the sacred books. Therefore when confronted with cases of this kind, it was logical reasoning on the part of scholars engaged in the elucidation of the text and not the sacred scriptures themselves which led to a final decision. This opinion was confirmed by Puṇyarāja.[34] In addition Bhartṛhari had the following to say on this point:

"There is a possibility that in interpreting the phrases of the sacred books the opinions of the monogenists and the dualists may differ as each derives his opinions from his own judgement."[35]

It is indeed true that many of the interpretations of words and phrases in the sacred books contradicted each other. Even those who profoundly venerate the sacred books have to admit this. When confronted with such problems, we have to resort to human logic to decide which interpretation is to be used. The following words written by Bhartṛhari illustrate this clearly.

"Logical argument (*tarka*) which does not contradict the sacred *Vedas* is as an eye to those who have not yet seen the truth. For the meaning of the sentences cannot be construed from the colour (that is the tangible, material contents of the sacred books) alone.[36]

Even as colour which is a material thing can be perceived by the eyes, so can the contents of the sacred books only be comprehended by logical reflection. Therefore, though he appears to be a profound venerator of the sacred books, Bhartṛhari had to resort to logical reflection in the end. Puṇyarāja makes this point quite clear in the following lines:

"Logic which does not conflict with the *āgama* is indeed a proper foundation on which knowledge is built. And contrarily *āgama* which is not tempered with logic is meaningless."[37]

After all Bhartṛhari was virtually a philosopher and a free thinker who delved into metaphysical reflections while on the surface keeping *āgama* as the basis of his philosophy.[38] (Śaṅkara also admits that logic is necessary for the interpretation of the sacred books.)[39]

Scholars who came after him were fully aware of Bhartṛhari's ambiguous attitude. His veneration of the sacred books was disregarded as being common to other schools of thought and the metaphysical side of his studies which he had built up so carefully was examined with great interest.[40] This led to his being called a logician (*naiyāyika*) by the great scholar Vācaspatimiśra. The irony of this is of course obvious because Bhartṛhari had always opposed the logicians of other schools of thought.

And now we come to a discussion of his doctrine as a true believer in the sacred scriptures. Arguments which refute logic do not necessarily support the sacred books. And scriptures or sacred writings are not confined to the Brahmin belief alone. They are found in the Buddhist and Jain beliefs as well. Therefore Bhartṛhari must have had some good reason for insisting that only the sacred writings of the orthodox Brahmin belief should be honoured and revered. As we have discussed earlier, he acknowledged two classes of sacred books: those collected by the ancient *ṛṣis* (*Vedas*) and those complied by scholars who came later (*smṛti*). Bhartṛhari insisted that the minds of the *ṛṣis* and the scholars in question were perfect and flawless, transcending the past and the future and it was not for shallow human understanding to refute what they had said and written.

> "The knowledge of the wise, lucid and unscathed in their minds, with knowledge concerning the past and the future, is as sound and reliable as that which we acquire through our senses."[41]
>
> "The truths, which are told by those who see with the sacred eye things which are unperceivable because they are beyond perception, cannot be denied by inference."[42]

Of course he did not admit the sensory perceptions to be correct in themselves. To prove this Bhartṛhari gave the following answers to the question as to whether things are really what our senses tell us they are.[43]

> "The empty sky appears to have a surface just like fire-flies seem to be made of fire. Seen from a different aspect, the empty sky has no surface and the fire-fly no fire."[44]
>
> "Therefore the wise observe correctly with the mind even those things which can be directly perceived by the senses. As intuition should be true knowledge, we should not represent the things which we

perceive."[45]

Bhartṛhari was very critical of perceptive recognition but respected intuition which the *ṛṣis* esteemed so highly. And as the sacred writings were full of intuitive knowledge Bhartṛhari insisted that they should be observed. He held that a certain knowledge exists in our daily life which cannot reach us through inference but only through our own perceptive experience.

> "Knowledge regarding jewels and gold which belongs to those who have made a study of these things cannot be fully conveyed to those who have made no study of them, except through learning and training; it cannot be derived from inference."[46]

He then adds that the contents of the sacred scriptures are understood by the *ṛṣis* who practised Yoga.[47]

What was the object of the intuition of the *ṛṣis*? According to his philosophy it was without doubt "the *Brahman* consisting of words". This point will be dealt with later. According to Bhartṛhari's philosophy too, the *Vedas* possess the highest authority because they are the reflection or image of the *Brahman*. Therefore his profound belief in the *Vedas* can be attributed to the fact that the *ṛṣis* in ancient times held the intuition of the *Brahman* in profound veneration. Bhartṛhari accorded a place of primary importance to the training and discipline through which the intuition of the *Brahman* could be attained. But even in his philosophy, the *Brahman* is a state which transcends words; the *ṛṣis* attained their intuition through Yoga, a word-less and thought-less realm; and this is the reason why the *Brahman* cannot be explained in words. The teaching of the *Brahman* is simply the expediency of the imparting of truth to men.

> "Because the descriptions of things in the sacred writings are made in order to explain things by means of words, the *avidyā* itself is set forth by means of certain descriptions."[48]

According to Puṇyarāja the contents of the sacred books are explained for the benefit of the stupid and to explain truth itself is an impossibility.[49] His statement that the explanations of the sacred scriptures is based on the *avidyā* is a bold one for a Brahmanic scholar; Śaṅkara shares his opinion in this. Bhartṛhari's view on this point will be discussed in full later.[50]

Therefore as a scholar of traditional lore Bhartṛhari has a deep veneration for the sacred scriptures but as a philosopher he accords them little real value. In fact[51] from the point of view of philosophy the sacred scriptures were only of secondary importance.

In conclusion we can sum up the following facts about Bhartṛhari: He professed to restore orthodox Brahmanic studies, especially the study of grammar; he attacked the general tendency in the schools of philosophy in his day to depend on logic alone at the same time advocating the sanctity of the sacred books. But in order to do this (refute logic and advocate the sanctity of the sacred books) he had to propound certain arguments and in so doing was obliged himself-albeit unconsciously-to resort to logical reflections. His fragmentary views regarding knowledge reveal that he recognized three ways in which knowledge could be obtained:

1) Perception through the senses (*pratyakṣa*);
2) Thinking by inference (*anumāna*);
3) Intuition of the Brahman (*āptavacana*).

The first and second methods are those applied by ordinary men and according to one view-point of his, perception is stable and inference subsists on it.[52] While emphasizing, however, the fact that inference is unstable, he resorts to it in his own writings.

The third method is to be found only in the ancient *ṛṣis* and the *Yogins* who through a system of abstract meditation and rigid asceticism aim to become united with the *Brahman*. While the first two methods are earth bound, the last is not of this world. The sacred books are based upon the third method which is described and known as *āptavacana* in India. The term *pratyakṣa* is something used for the third as well as the first method since both methods base their experience on clear evidence.[53] Needless to say, however, the first and third methods differ from each other fundamentally. Though Bhartṛhari revered the *āptavacana* above all, in point of fact he made use of the three methods. The three methods, according to Bhartṛhari, are nothing but the self-manifestation of the absolute *Brahman*.

Notes

1) *pratyakṣam anumānaṃ ca vyatikramya vyavasthitāḥ/ rakṣaḥpitṛpiśācānāṃ karmajā eva siddhayaḥ//* (*Vākyap*. I, 36). Instead of *karmajā*, the Benares edition reads *karmāntā*. I

adopted the reading of the Lahore edition according to the information by Prof. de Jong.

2) *sāmānyam ākṛtir bhāvo jātir ity atra laukikam/liṅgaṃ na saṃbhavaty eva tenānyat parigṛhyate//*(*Vākyap*. III, 14, 323. p. 605).

3) *tayā*(= *śrutyā*) *hy artho vidhīyate*(= *niścīyate*), I, 130d. Puṇyarāja's interpretation was followed.

4) Cf. A. Weber: *Indische Studien*, V. S.158 ff.; *Vākyap*. II, 484 ff.

5) *prajñā vivekaṃ*(= *vaiśāradyaṃ*) *labhate bhinnair āgamadarśanaiḥ/kiyad vā śakyam unnetuṃ svatarkam anudhāvatā//*(*Vākyap*. II, 492).

6) Commenting on this statement, Puṇyarāja calls academic knowledge *bhagavatī vidyā, bhagavatī prajñā*. There must be something in common with the Buddhist term of *bhagavatī prajñāpāramitā* in so far as expression is concerned.

7) *tat tad utprekṣamāṇānāṃ*(= *vikalpayatām*) *purāṇair āgamair vinā/anupāsitavṛddhānāṃ vidyā nātiprasīdati//* (*Vākyap*. II, 493).

8) *caitanyam iva yaś cāyam avicchedena vartate/āgamas tam upāsīno hetuvādair na bādhyate//* (*Vākyap*. I, 41).*hetuvāda* = *tārkikapravāda* (according to Harivṛṣabha).

9) *na cāgamād ṛte dharmas tarkeṇa vyavatiṣṭhate/ṛṣīṇām api yaj jñānaṃ tad apy āgamahetukam//* (*Vākyap*. I, 30).

10) With regard to the last part of the statement Puṇyarāja declares: *āgamād dhi lokaviruddhaṃ tarkaviruddham apy ācaraṇaṃ pratipadyante śiṣṭāḥ*.

11) *dharmasya cāvyavacchinnāḥ panthāno ye vyavasthitāḥ/na tāṃl lokaprasiddhatvāt kaścit tarkeṇa bādhate//* (*Vākyap*. I, 31).

12) See *Vākyap*. I, 131.

13) *hastasparśād ivāndhena viṣame*(= *girimārge, Comm.*) *pathi dhāvatā/anumānapradhānena vinipāto na durlabhaḥ//* (*Vākyap*. I, 42). The Benares edition reads: *hastasparśādibādhena*. But we adopt the reasoning of the Lahore edition, which coincides with the reading of the Tibetan citation.

14) See *Vākyap*. III, 14, 81 (p.490).

15) (1-*yaṅ na gnas ma buḥi sde pa dag las kha cig phyïr zlog par byed de*-1)/........ (2 - *lu ṅas ñe bar len pa po ltar gyur pa sṅa na gnas pa yod pa ltar ḥgyur baḥi las yoṅs su zad pas/mi la sogs paḥi phuṅ po ñe bar blaṅ baḥi ñe bar len pa po ñid du ḥgyur bar grags pas rjes su dpag pas ñe bar len pa po med pa ñid du bstan pa kho bo cag mi ḥdod de*-2)/....... (3-*loṅ ba rkaṅ paḥi* [*rkaṅ pa-Sde dge*] *tshod dpags kyis/ñam ṅaḥi lam du rgyug pa ltar/rjes su dpag pa gtsor ḥdsin pa/rnam par ltuṅ ba mi dkaḥo//* - 3) *shes bya ba lta bur ḥgyur ro shes na/*................. *de ni rigs pa ma yin te/*.......... *lha yaṅ lhaḥi ñe bar blaṅ ba dag ñid la brten nas lha ñid du gdags par bya ba yin paḥi phyir daṅ/rkaṅ paḥi tshod dpags pa ni mi mthun paḥi phyogs la yaṅ yod paḥi rjes su dpag pa ñid du ma grub paḥi phyir daṅ/rjes su dpag pa ltar snaṅ ba gtsor ḥdsin pa ni ltuṅ*

bar ḥgyur baḥi phyir ro/ liṅ spyi yin pas the tshom skye baḥi phyir yaṅ de ñid las ṅes par gzuṅ bas mi rigs te/ luṅ ni rjes su dpag pa las doṅ tha dad pa ma yin par gzuṅ bar bya ste/ mṅon sum ma yin paḥi don rtogs paḥi rgyu yin paḥi phyir/ dper na/ rjes su dpag paḥi raṅ gi bdag ñid bshin no/ (125 a) (I cited the passage by courtesy Prof. J. Nozawa ; Cf. The *Tibetan Tripiṭaka*, Peking Edition, ed. by D. T. Suzuki. Tokyo-Kyoto 1957, vol.95, p.193, fol.153a, *l*.7f. Later I checked this with the reprint edition of the Sde-dge. Tripiṭaka, (Dbu Ma)2, published by the Sekai Seiten Kanko Kyokai, 1977, p. 63, fol.125 a, *ll*.3-7.

16) *don de ñid bsal bar bya baḥi phyir slob dpon bha ṅdri ha ris rjes su dpag pa sun phyuṅ baḥi khuṅs bstan paḥi phyir/* (3-3) *shes bya ba smras te/ dper na loṅ ba rkaṅ paḥi tshod dpag gis lam bde ba spaṅs te ñam ṅaḥi lam du rgyug pa śiṅ la sogs pa dag gis brdos pa la rdeg ḥchaḥ śiṅ rnam par ltuṅ ba mi dkaḥ ba de bshin du/ yid ches paḥi luṅ spaṅs pa rjes su dpag paḥi tshod dpag gis rtog ge skam poḥi lam du rgyug pa dag kyaṅ tshe ḥdi la yaṅ ḥkhrul paḥi gnod par ḥgyur la/ tshe phyi ma la yaṅ ḥbras bu mi ḥdod par rnam par ltuṅ bar ḥgyur ro shes zer ro/* [vol.97, p 92, fol.225b, *l*. 2f.] (The author is deeply grateful to Dr. Josho Nozawa, through whose kindness he was able to obtain the extracts from the Tibetan text quoted above.)

17) This verse is not found in the corresponding passage in the Chinese version of the *Prajñā-pradīpa-mūla-madhyamaka-vṛtti* translated by Prabhākaramitra. Dr. Nozawa informs the writer that it may have been omitted when translated into Chinese.

18) This verse is incorporated in the *Tattvasaṃgraha* under the heading v. 1460.

19) *avasthā-deśa-kālānāṃ bhedād bhinnāsu śaktiṣu/ bhāvānām anumānena prasiddhir atidurlabhā//* (*Vākyap*. I, 32).

20) *nirjñātaśakter dravyasya tāṃ tām arthakriyāṃ prati/ viśiṣṭadravyasaṃbandhe sā śaktiḥ pratibadhyate//* (*Vākyap*. I, 33). This verse is incorporated in the *Tattvasaṃgraha* under the heading v.1461. The first *pāda* reads as *vijñātaśakter apy asya*.

21) Ś. ad *Brahma-sūtra* II, 1, 27.

22) *SDS*. I, *ll*.70-102.

23) *yatnenānumino 'py arthaḥ kuśalair anumātṛbhiḥ/ abhiyuktatarair anyair anyath-aivopapādyate//* (*Vākyap*. I, 34).

24) *Bhāmatī* ad *Brahma-sūtra* II, 1, 11 ; *SDS*. XVI, *ll*.820-821. This statement is also quoted in the Anumāna-parīkṣā of the *Tattvasaṃgraha* as a doctrine of Bhartṛhari (p. 426, v.1462).

25) *yo yasya svam iva jñānaṃ darśanaṃ nābhiśaṅkate/ sthitaṃ pratyakṣapakṣe taṃ katham anyo (tarkaśaraṇaḥ) nivartayet//* (*Vākyap*. I, 39).

26) Ś. ad *Brahma-sūtra* II, 1, 11 (ĀnSS. vol.1, pp.449 ; 452).

27) *SDS*. XVI, *l*. 818f.

28) *Vākyap*. I,32

29) See Paul Deussen: *Allgemeine Geshichte der Philosophie*, II, 1, S.212.

30) [*svavākyānām asatyārthatāpratipādanāya*] *sarvaṃ mithyā bravīmīti* [*ukte*] *naitad vākyaṃ vivakṣyate* (= *vyarthatā na prasañjanīyā*) / *tasya* (= *satyavākyasya*) *mithyābhidhāne hi prakrānto 'rtho na gamyate*// (*Vākyap*. III, 3, 25, p. 108).

31) The *Vigrahavyāvartanī of Nāgārjuna* with the author's commentary ed. by E. H. Johnston and Arnold Kunst (Bruges, 1951), vv.1-2. Also see part III of *Hui-cheng-lun* (*Rtsod-pa bzlog-paḥi tshig-leḥur-byas-pa shes-bya-ba. Vigrahavyāvartanīkārikā*).

32) This argument is in some ways similar to "*nityasamā jātiḥ*" recognized by the Nyāya school (*Nyāya-sūtra* IV, 1, 25-26); Cf. no. 74.

33) *sarvo 'dṛṣṭaphalān arthān āgamāt pratipadyate*/ *viparītaṃ ca sarvatra śakyate vaktum āgame*// (*Vākyap*. I, 142).

34) *tasmād āgamaṃ pramāṇīkṛtya kācid yuktir ucyamānā upodbalakatvaṃ labhate*. — (Puṇyarāja ad *Vākyap*. I, 142).

35) *tasyārthavādarūpāṇi niścitya svavikalpajāḥ*/ *ekatvināṃ dvaitināṃ ca pravādā bahudhā matāḥ*// (*Vākyap*. I, 8).

36) *vedaśāstrāvirodhī ca tarkāś cakṣur apaśyatām*/ *rūpamātrād dhi vākyārthaḥ kevalān nāvatiṣṭhate*// (*Vākyap*. I, 137).

37) *āgamāvirodhī tarka eva pramāṇam atarkaś cāgamo viphala iti* (ad *Vākyap*. I, 137); Cf. ibid. I,138.

38) The argument which Bhartṛhari employed to advocate the sacred *Vedas* was used by the materialists to refute them (*SDS*. I, *ll*.46f.).

39) "Just as in the case of several conflicting scriptural passages we explain all of them in such a manner as to make them accord with one, so *Śruti*, if in conflict with other means of right knowledge, has to be bent so as to accord with the latter. Moreover, reasoning, which enables us to infer something not actually perceived in consequence of its having a certain equality of attributes with what is actually perceived, stands nearer to perception than *Śruti* which conveys its sense by tradition merely" (Ś. ad *BS*. II,1,4). This problem is discussed more boldly in the *Yogavāsiṣṭha*. The author says that a *śāstra*, though it is derived from men, deserves to be accepted, if it is reasonable. One must follow reason. A speech, if reasonable, must be accepted even from a child, but that which is not reasonable should be rejected like a piece of straw though it might be uttered even by *Brahman*, the creator. That man is certainly not wise who rejecting the beautiful water of the Ganges flowing before him drinks from a well thinking only that it belongs to his father: *api pauruṣam ādeyaṃ śāstraṃ ced yuktibodhakam*/ *anyat tv ārṣam api tyājyaṃ bhāvyaṃ nyāyaikasevinā*// *yuktiyuktam upādeyaṃ vacanaṃ bālakād api*/ *anyat tṛṇam iva tyājyam apy uktaṃ padmayoninā*// *yo 'smattātasya kūpo 'yam iti kaupaṃ pibaty apaḥ*/ *tyaktvā gāṅgaṃ purasthaṃ taṃ ko na śāsty atigarhitam*// (*Yogavāsiṣṭha* II, 18, 2-4; Vidhushekhara Bhattacharya, *The Āgamaśāstra of*

Gauḍapāda, University of Calcutta, 1943, p.303).

40) Vācaspatimiśra comments on the *Brahmasūtra-bhāṣya* by Śaṅkara as follows in I, 3, 28 where Śaṅkara refutes the *sphoṭa* theory: *diṅmātram atra sūcitam. vistaras tu Tattvabindāv avagantavya iti/alaṃ vā naiyāyikair vivādena/*(p.260). Here *Tattvabindu* is the name of a book written by Vācaspatimiśra in accordance with the theory of the Bhāṭṭas. See also Th. Stcherbatsky: *Buddhist Logic*, II, p.403.

41) *āvirbhūtaprakāśānām. anupadrutacetasām/atītānāgatajñānaṃ pratyakṣān na viśiṣyate//* (*Vākyap.* I, 37).

42) *atīndriyān asaṃvedyān paśyanty ārṣeṇa cakṣuṣā/ye bhāvān vacanaṃ teṣāṃ nānumānena bādhyate//* (*Vākyap.* I, 38).

43) *vayaṃ yathāvad artho dṛṣṭaḥ tathaiva ca vyavahariṣyāmaḥ*/Puṇyarāja's interpretation was followed.

44) *talavad dṛśyate vyoma khadyoto havyavāḍ iti/na cen nāsti talaṃ vyomni na khadyote hutāśanaḥ//* (*Vākyap.* II, 142, p.140).

45) *tasmāt pratyakṣam apy arthaṃ vidvān īkṣeta yuktitaḥ/na darśanasya prāmāṇyāt dṛśyam arthaṃ prakalpayet(= vyavahāraṃ nirvāhayet)//*(*Vākyap.* II, 143. p.140).

46) *pareṣām asamākhyeyam abhyāsād eva jāyate/maṇirūpyādivijñānaṃ tadvidāṃ nānumānikam//* (*Vākyap.* I, 35).

47) *tathā ṛṣīṇām api yogajapratyakṣagamyam eva.* (Puṇyarāja ad I, 35).

48) *vyavahārāya manyante śāstrārthaprakriyā yataḥ/śāstreṣu prakriyābhedair avidyaivopavarṇyate//* (*Vākyap.* II, 234). The latter half of this statement is again recorded in III, 14, 78.(p.489).

49) *śāstrārthaprakriyāḥ kevalam abudhānāṃ vyutpādanāya ato na śāstrāṇi tattvaṃ vaktuṃ pārayanti.* Puṇyarāja ad *Vākyap.* II, 234.

50) *Vākyap.* I, 74; II, 240; II, 322f.

51) According to a fragment ascribed to him and cited in a Tibetan text, Bhartṛhari thought even the sacred books were based on the *parikalpa*. The author's article: "Tibetan citations of Bhartṛhari's verses and the problem of his date", (*Yamaguchi Commemoration Volume* (Kyoto, 1955), p. 125). By courtesy of Rev. Jain Muni Jambuvijay the author came to know that the following verse is cited in Bhartṛhari's own commentary on v.I. 1 (Lahore ed.): *sarvaparikalpānām ābhāse 'py anavasthitaḥ/tarkāgamānumānena buddhyā parikalpitaḥ//*

52) "If the words were founded upon the *darśana*(= *pratyakṣa*) there would be no need for inference. Indeed when the *darśana* is established why should be need for inference?" (*na cālam anumānāya śabdo darśanapūrvakaḥ/siddhe hi darśane kiṃ syād anumānaprayojanam//* (*Vākyap.* III. 13, 12. p. 436).

53) In the *Brahma-sūtras* the *Vedas* are called *pratyakṣa*. Cf. *BS.* I,3,28; III, 2, 24; IV, 4, 20.

APPENDIX. WESTERN PARALLELS

Some of Bhartṛhari's dogmatical statements illustrate the mediaeval trends of thought which can be traced in other countries. In the following appendix the writer would point out certain parallels in mediaeval West.

To page 514.

Al-Mansur a Muslim Caliph published an edict in which he declared that God had decreed hell fire for those who believed that truth could be found by means of unaided reason. All books on logic and metaphysics were burnt.

Algazel a Muslim philosopher wrote a book called "The Destruction of the Philosophers" pointing out that, since all the truth necessary to life is to be found in the Koran, speculation independent of revelation is pointless.

Abelard in his famous book "Sic er Non", ("Yes and No") states that nothing outside the scriptures is infallible ; even Apostles and Fathers may err.

To page 519.

Eubalides said as follows :

> "Wenn ich sage : ich lüge, lüge ich dann oder sage ich die Wahrheit? Wenn ich dabei die Wahrheit sage, so lüge ich ; wenn ich aber lüge, so sage ich eben die Wahrheit. Die Lösung liegt darin, dass in diesem Falle die Form des Urteils, welche den Anspruch involviert, etwas als seiend als wahr auszusagen, zufälligerweise mit dem Inhalt des Urteils in Widerspruch steht. Als Curiosum mag in Erinnerung gebracht werden, dass es ... von den Kretern heisst : "..Die Kreter sind immer Lügner." (P. Deussen : *Allgemeine Geschichte der Philosophie*, II,1, Leipzig, 1911, S. 212.)

To page 521.

According to the Muslim mystics, every text of the Koran had seven or seven hundred layers of interpretation, the literal meaning being only for the ignorant and the vulgar. It would seem to follow that a philosopher's teaching could not possibly conflict with the Koran ; for among seven hundred interpretations there would surely be at least one that would fit what the philosopher had to say. (B. Russell : *A History of Western Philosophy*, New York, 1945, p.426.)

To page 524.

The three kinds of knowledge, as were set forth by Bhartṛhari, were mentioned in nearly the same way by Thomas Aquinas; according to him there are three ways of knowing God: by reason, by revelation and by intuition of things previously known only by revelation, although he says almost nothing about the third way. (B. Russell: op. cit. p.460.)

CHAPTER IV
METAPHYSICS

SECTION I. ABSOLUTE *BRAHMAN*

Sub-Section 1. *Brahman* in the True Sense

In Bhartṛhari's philosophy also the absolute is *Brahman*. The common Indian philosophical terms used to elucidate this absolute are *dravya* or *vastu*[1] (substance, noumena). In other words, it is that which is *nitya*[2] (constant) despite changes in the phenomenal world.

The fact that Bhartṛhari interpreted *dravya* as *Brahman* is of momentous significance for the history of Indian linguistic philosophy. Although *dravya* was the term commonly used throughout Indian philosophy to express the notion of noumenon or substance there were various interpretations of just what this substance was and these divergent interpretations gave rise to the different philosophical positions of the various schools. Even within the same school there were quite often several different interpretations, for example, in the school of grammarians there was a long tradition of interpreting *dravya* as 'individual'. Thus, according to the older grammarians such as Patañjali 'substance' was the 'individual' in opposition to *ākṛti* (form) or *jāti* (genus).[3] By introducing Vedānta philosophy into grammar, however, Bhartṛhari caused a change in the grammarian's view of substance. According to him, particular things are what are real or substantial in the everyday world but they are not real or substantial in the ultimate sense. Substance is the supreme genus, the limit of a quest for an ever higher genus in particular things; it is nothing other than *Brahman* as existence. Thus the concept of substance is radically altered; it changes from particulars to *Brahman*.

Brahman as noumenon is also called *'Tattva'* (truth).[4] *'Tattva'* has the sense of actual fact or things[5] just as they are in the ordinary world but it had also been used as a technical philosophical term from quite ancient times. The Vedānta school took it to refer to *Brahman* while Bhartṛhari called it *'para'*[6] (the highest one) which was also a term in general use throughout Vedānta philosophy.[7]

Brahman as the absolute is characterized in the early part of the *Vākyapadīya* as *'anādinidhana'* (without beginning or end).[8] This adjectival phrase was originally used in the *Mahābhārata* to apply to *Viṣṇu* and *Brahmadeva* as well as to *vāc* (the word) as the world principle.[9] Since Bhartṛhari assumed *Brahman* to be the absolutely highest principle, he applies the phrase to *Brahman* rather than to *vāc* and thus it becomes a term reserved for *Brahman* alone. Then, since *'anādinidhana'* means having no *utpāda* (origination) and no *nāśa*[10] (destruction) it follows that *Brahman* is both *akṣara*[11] (indestructible) and *amṛta* (eternal).[12]

However, since the phenomena of production and destruction are possible only in time, the denial of production and destruction implies that *Brahman* is not bound by the conditions of time. Elsewhere Bhartṛhari says that absolute truth is *"paurvāparyavivarjita"* (free from the relation of before and after). If one can interpret this spatially then it becomes *"pūrvāpara-deśavibhāga-rahita"*[13] (free from the spatial distinction of before-after). Thus *Brahman* transcends the conditions of both space and time. This characteristic of *Brahman* is in direct opposition to the nature of particular things. Particular things exist only when they are conditioned spatially and temporally. "Jars and the like are perceived as things, the production and destruction of which is experienced and as being limited spatially."[14]

This claim, made at the very beginning of the *Vākyapadīya*, is a direct conscious attack on the common sense view of the man in the street. He speaks of the vulgar philosophic view of the common man as follows:

> "It is judged in the world that the world[15] is [quantitatively] limited since jars and the like are seen [to be quantitatively limited]. It is said that because, the various things are formed, *Brahman* also has its beginning even though it be eternal"[16] (*Vākyap.* II, 239).

The common man tries to apply the principles which are appropriate in the phenomenal world of his daily experiences to the unlimited which absolutely transcends this phenomenal world and even to transexperiential reality. He maintains that such naive speculation is a grave mistake.

Since *Brahman* is in no way the recipient of either special or temporal limitations, its essence is absolutely undifferentiable. It is impossible to attach to it any particular characterizing stipulation. Thus there can be no term which could be predicated of it; it is above conceptual stipulations. Even if one tries to express it in order to convey it to another person one can do nothing but rely on negative expressions. Concerning *'tattva'* he says "It neither is nor is not; it is neither one nor differentiated; neigher combined nor separated; neither changing nor unchanging."[17] All of the linguistic expressions (*vyavahāra, prapañca*) referring to *Brahman* are nothing other than *upādhi* applied to the absolute.

> "'To be different' is limiting adjunct (*upādhi*) of the highest one and the same is true of 'not being different." (*Vākyap*. III, 1, 20).

Thus it naturally follows that the distinction of subject-object does not exist in *Brahman*.

> "That in which there is no distinction to be made among the seer, the seen, and the act of seeing is truth. This is related by those who know the secrets of the three Vedas"[18] (*Vākyap*. III, 3, 70).

Brahman in the true sense is really absolute negation.

Notes

1) *Vākyap*. III, 2, 1 ; 2 is called *Dravyasamuddeśa* and it is here that the nature of *Brahman* is discussed in greatest detail.
2) *Vākyap*., III, 2, 1.
3) *dravyam hi nityam ākṛtir anityā*/(*Mahābhāṣya* p.7, *ll*.11-12, ed. by Kielhorn).
4) *Vākyap*. III, 2, 1 ; 6 ; 7 ; 10.
5) *Vākyap*. III, 3, 3.
6) *Vākyap*. III, 1, 20.
7) In the *Brahma-sūtra* also the absolute is generally referred to with the term *'para'*.
8) *Vakyap*. I,1. The expression *'anādinidhanamadhya'* also appears in the *Prajñāpāramitānayaśatapañcaśatikā*. See *Jisshū Bongogaku* (in Japanese) by Unrai Wogihara : p. 156.
9) Cf. Sprensen's Index. For an actual example concerning the word *'vāc'* see *Mahābhārata* XII, 233, 24(quoted by Ś. on *BS*. I, 3, 28).
10) *Tattvasaṃgraha*, v.128. See PartV, Chapter I, Section I of this work for an explanation of the interpretation in *Prameyakamalamārtaṇḍa*. In *Vākyap*. III, 2, 18. *tattva* is said

to be '*ajanman*' (not originated).

11) *Vākyap.* I, 1.

12) *Vākyap.* I, 133.

13) *Tattvasaṃgrahapañjikā* ad V, 128.

14) ibid. ad VI, 135.

15) *ayaṃ viśvaprapañcarūpaḥ lokaḥ*/Puṇyarāja.

16) This sort of vulgar philosophic view already made its appearance among the sixty-two views of Buddha's time. See *Dīgha-nikāya, Brahmajālasuttanta.*

17) *Vākyap.* III, 2, 12. See Section III of this Chapter.

18) Cited according to the quotation in *SDS*. XIII, *ll*.254-6. In the Benares edition of the *Vākyapadīya cāvikalpitam* is written as *vā vikalpitam*, which is wrong (see Helārāja's commentary). Also in this edition '*āhus*' is '*śritās*'.

Sub-Section 2. The Argumentation to Prove the Unlimitedness of *Brahman*

If *Brahman* in the true sense is this sort of thing, then why is it that the absolute can only be transmitted to men by way of negative expressions? Why is it that *Brahman* cannot have positive conceptual determinations? He gives a detailed account of the reasons for this in Chapter three of the *Vākyapadīya.*

As we have already noted, he maintains that the absolute *Brahman* transcends all spatial and temporal determinations. Now the simplest and most basic form of spatial determination which makes it possible for things to be in opposition to each other is the opposition of identity and difference. The Law of Identity and Law of Non-Contradiction are fundamental principles which must be conformed to when projecting temporal change or when representing objects spatially. Thus the identity-difference relation is fundamentally preserved. Furthermore, if one considers the question of whether A is identical to or different from B from an ontological point of view, it becomes a question of whether A exists as B or not. The logical relation of identity-difference can be ontologically transformed to a relation of being-non-being. Thus it is that Bhartṛhari took the modes of identity, difference, existence, and non-existence to be the fundamental forms of spatial determination. In contrast, the most fundamental form of temporal determination can be said to be 'change'. Thus, in order to clarify the character of the absolute, Bhartṛhari examined the oppositional relation obtaining between the most fundamental of spatial forms, identity (Law of Identity), difference (Law of Contradiction), existence, and non-existence, and concluded that the Law of Identity and the Law of Contradiction were not applicable to the absolute. Taking up the question of change, the most fundamental form which makes temporal discrimination possible, he maintained that there is no change in the ultimate sense and thus that the true absolute transcends change.

I. The Negation of Identity-Difference, Being-Non-Being

Bhartṛhari first examined the problem of the identity-difference dichotomy and pointed out that the structure of these concepts was such that neither could be established by itself but only in the negation of the concept opposed to it. In other words, these concepts can be established only in a relation of mutual dependence.

> "Without *nānātva* (difference) there is no *ekatva* (identity) and without *ekatva* there is no *nānātva*. In the highest truth the distinction between these concepts does not exist at all." (*Vākyap*. III, 6, 26, p.172).

According to Helārāja the two concepts, identity and difference, are *anyonyāśraya* (interdependent). "It would follow that one cannot be established without the other being established." (*ekāsiddhāv itarāsiddhiprasaṅgaḥ*).

Bhartṛhari further expands on the above comment in the following way:

> "If one does not conceive of difference, it is impossible for identity to exist: if identity is not supposed, then difference must also be discarded." (*Vākyap*. III, 6, 28).

According to Helārāja, this is because they have *parasparāpekṣā* (mutual dependence).

Being and non-being are also, like identity and divergence, mutually dependent. For non-being to be established as non-being the negation of being is indispensable. Non-being is the negation of being (*bhāva*) or deficiency (*abhāva*). Moreover, for being to be established as being there must be the covert negation of non-being. In short, being and non-being do not exist separately but both arise out of *ātman*.

> "On the basis of the unique *ātman*, being and non-being, which are not different, are imagined." (*Vākyap.* III, 3, 60).

Their foundation is *ātman*. The two are not unrelated and independent; on the contrary, it is only when they are established in a tense relation as the mutually opposing concepts of being and non-being that they are able to function as expressions (*vyavahāra*) of the essential elements of daily life.

> "Being and non-being follow the ordinary expressions as non-different [as mutually dependent]." (*Vākyap.* III, 3, 59).

The point which must be most carefully attended to here is the attack on the philosophical view which takes non-being to be substantial.[1]

> "Non-being cannot be established either as being in contradiction [to being] or as not being in contradiction [to it], either as actually existing or as not actually existing, either as being ordered or as not being ordered." (*Vākyap.* III, 3, 66).

Furthermore, no matter whether non-being really exists or not, true being is neither produced nor annihilated.

> "Even if non-being were to be existent, the nature of being would not be discarded. Or even though non-being were non-existent, the nature of being would not [thereby] be created." (*Vākyap.* III, 3, 72).

With this ontological view as a foundation, Bhartṛhari rejected the four types of non-being propounded by the Vaiśeṣika.[2] According to Helārāja the four types,[3] i. e. *prāgabhāva* (non-existence of anything which may yet be), *pradhvaṃsābhāva* (non-existence in consequence of annihilation), *atyantābhāva* (absolute non-existence) and *itaretarābhāva* (mutual non-existence), are all *'kālpanika'* (based on imaginative construction). In other words, these four types do not have objective existence but are nothing more than subjective phantasms. Bhartṛhari claimed that, in the same fashion, the opposition of being and non-being and all the dualistic oppositions based on this are established only as the result of pure subjective imagination.

> "Just as four distinct states could be discriminated with respect to what is called *nīrūpa* (non-substantial), so is the duality based on being and non-being." (*Vākyāp.* III, 3, 65).

This is clearly a doctrine advocated by the Mādhyamikas. The Mādhyamikas expended every effort to show that all things and concepts are established in a relation of mutual dependency (*parasparāpekṣatva*).[4] There is also widely assumed in Mādhyamika works the general principle that two things which are established in a relation of mutual dependency are such that if one does not exist neither can the other (*itaretarāśrayaṇād ekābhāvād anyatarābhāvaḥ syād iti*).[5] The rejection, on the basis of this principle, of the separate and independent existence of the objects or concepts which stand in this relation of mutual dependency is expounded in the *Mādhyamika-śāstra* and many other works of the Mādhyamika school. Some examples are the following:

> "Impurity does not exist without being dependent on purity. We explain purity with reference to impurity. Thus purity is inconceivable" (*Mādhyamika-śāstra*, Chap. XXIII, verse 10).
>
> "Purity does not exist without being dependent on impurity. We explain impurity with reference to purity. Thus, impurity does not exist." (*Mādhyamika-śāstra*, Chap. XXIII, verse 11).

Arguments of this sort are so numerous throughout Mādhyamika literature that it would be simply impossible to enumerate them here. With this evidence, however, I think it can be safely concluded that the previously noted quotations from the *Vākyapadīya* related to the opposition of being and non-being as well as identity and difference were most probably the result of the influence of Mādhyamika thought.

Thus, since he saw that it was essential to identity and difference, being and non-being to be established in a relation of mutual dependency, Bhartṛhari contended that these concepts were not applicable to the absolute.

> "There is no oneness nor diversity, no existence (*sattva*) nor non-existence (*nāstitā*) in the *Ātman*-principles of things which are not connected [with the limiting adjunct]." (*Vākyap.* III, 1, 21).

In Buddhism these concepts of identity, difference, being and non-being are said to be the basis for the occurrence of various metaphysical speculations. In the *Saddharmapuṇḍarīka-sūtra*,[6] for example, it is said that the common man is led to embrace sixty two different views by adhering to these four concepts. Since Bhartṛhari thoroughly rejects their fundamental opposition, he can, to this extent, be said to be following Buddhist doctrine. This position is often given expression in Nāgārjuna's *Mādhyamika-śāstra* but the following line from the *Awakening of Faith śāstra* is the one that most closely resembles Bhartṛhari's words.

> "The truly self-born has no aspect of being, no aspect of non-being, no aspect of not being and no aspect of not non-being. It has no identity, no differentiation, non-identity, no non-differentiation and no identity-differentiation."

Thus, if the states of identity, difference, being, and non-being cannot be attributed to the absolute, then all differentiations based on these cannot exist in *Brahman* either. For these reasons Bhartṛhari concluded that diversity and multiplicity could not really be part of the essence of *Brahman*.

Notes

1) Helārāja (on III, 3, 72) interprets this as a discussion of the seventh category, i. e. the 'non-being' expounded by the Vaiśeṣika philosophy. It is well known that Udayana wrote a short work, *Lakṣaṇāvalī*, in which in 984 seven categories are set up. But the doctrine of the seven categories had existed before Udayana. Before that some of the Mīmāṃsakas adopted the theory of non-category. Also Maticandra (550-650) sets up "non-declaration of categories" in his *sheng-sung-shih-chü-i-lun* (= *Vaiśeṣika-daśa-padārtha-śāstra*). It is not clear which doctrine Bhartṛhari is attacking specifically, but it is clear that he rejects a philosophy which tends to substantialize non-being.

2) See *Vaiśeṣika-sūtra* IX, 1, 5.

3) See *Vaiśeṣika-sūtra* IX, 1, 5.

4) *hetuphalayor anyonyāpekṣatva* (*Mvṛ.* p.55, *l*.1); *tāni ca paraspara-apekṣayā sidhyanti* (*Mvṛ.* p.75, *l*.10); *parasparāpekṣā siddhiḥ* (*Mvṛ.*, p.67, *l*.11; p.200, *l*.3); *parasparāpekṣikī siddhiḥ* (*Mvṛ.*, pp.189, *ll*. 8, 9; 190, *l*. 8; 213, *l*. 11; 345, *l*. 2); *anyonyāpekṣikī siddhiḥ* (*Mvṛ.*, p.190, *l*.130); *parasparāpekṣā* (adj. *Mvṛ.*, p.189, *l*.15).

5) *Bodhicaryāvatārapañjikā*, p.538, *l*.5.

6) *vilagna dṛṣṭī-gahaneṣu nityam astīti nāstīti tathāsti nāsti/dvāṣaṣṭidṛṣṭī-kṛta-niśrayitvā asantabhāvaṃ parigṛhya te sthitāḥ//* (*SaddhP.* II, gāthā 65). One can by the way trace this view back to early Buddhism. For example, in the Pali Texts (*Saṃyutta-Nikāya* XII, *Nidānasaṃyutta* 48. vol.II, p.77, Buddha rejects the extreme views that all is being or that all is nothing-ness and explains the Law of *Karma* by means of the middle path.

II. The Negation of Change

Bhartṛhari, along with rejecting multiplicity, also claimed that change in any ultimate sense was impossible. Change can be said to be the replacement of one aspect of a thing by another but if we express this in terms of the most abstract and general form of the modalities of individual objects then what we have is being becoming non-being or non-being becoming being. (being becoming being or non-being becoming non-being do not represent change but simply continuations of the same state). However, it is just these two forms which he most clearly and emphatically rejects.

> "No non-being is produced and then becomes being. Being does not go to non-substantiality."[1] (*Vākyap.* III, 3, 60).

He follows this with the explanation:

> "Since non-being is substanceless, there is no cause which produces it. What cause will be made that could affect being with substance." (*Vākyap.* III, 3, 61).

In other words, since non-being is substanceless it is impossible to bring it into existence and since being has substance it is impossible to destroy it.

> "If the acquisition of the thing itself is called 'birth' and the existence which is to be obtained is attained, then from what is being produced and how is non-being produced?" (*Vākyap.* III, 3, 43. vol.II, p.118).

These arguments were often propounded by the Mādhyamika School and an argument quite similar to it can be found in the *Māṇḍūkya-kārikās.*[2] Bhartṛhari takes a position similar to that of these arguments in that he denied the production of both being and non-being.

He thus concludes that the arguments of various philosophers who attempt to make either being or nothingness the ultimate world principle are grossly mistaken and that only the absolute *Brahman* is real.

> "For this reason, there are some who say 'All is non-being,' or 'All is being'. But there exists no other state than the one reality." (*Vākyap.* III, 3, 62).

Here again we have an instance of the confluence of the thought of Bhartṛhari and the Buddhists. In fact, the claims that 'All is being' or 'All is non-being' were already rejected in the scriptures of primitive Buddhism[3] as being two opposing but equally heretical doctrines. Not only is this argument preserved and repeated in the *Mahāyāna sūtras*[4] but also Nāgārjuna[5] later followed out this position, rejected both of these heresies and attempted to clarify the true meaning of 'the middle path' which was different from either of these extremes. It can thus be concluded that here is another instance of Bhartṛhari inheriting some of the central concepts of Buddhist thought.

According to Bhartṛhari the proponents of the metaphysics of being and the proponents of the metaphysics of non-being were continually preoccupied with attacking each other and this fact indicated that neither of these philosophies was truly philosophy at all.

> "Thus those who assert that [all is] being (*bhāvavādin*) do not acknowledge non-being and those who assert that [all is] non-being (*abhāvavādin*) do not recognize being as a character of reality[6] (*tattvalakṣaṇa*)" (*Vākyap.* III, 3.63).

This is clearly identical with the view expressed in the fourth chapter of the *Māṇḍūkya-kārikā*:

> "There are actually some disputants who assert the origination of a thing which is already existent; there are other wise men who admit the origination of a thing which is non-existent. They dispute with each other." (*Māṇḍūkya-kārikā* IV, 3).
>
> "That which is already existent does not come into being. That which is not non-existent does not come into being ··· while contending [with each other] in this fashion the dualists actually make clear non-origination" (ibid. IV, 4).

As a result of our investigations, there is no room for doubt that Bhartṛhari's argument which denies the reality of change in the phenomenal world as well as the creation of the world is the same as the arguments of the Mādhyamika school and the *Māṇḍūkya-kārikā*, but there is not sufficient evidence available to determine whether he inherited this mode of thought directly from the Mādhyamikas or indirectly through the *Māṇḍūkya-kārikā*. Both I-ching's description and the content of the *Vākyapadīya* clearly show that he was quite well versed in Buddhist philosophy and it is quite probable that Bhartṛhari came to this position after reading and studying both the works of the Mādhyamika school and the Vedānta scholars. (Just because his presentation resembles that of the *Māṇḍūkya-kārikās,* one cannot jump to the conclusion that he was directly influenced by that work. One reason for this is that it is now generally believed that there were at the time a large number of other works which were similar to the *Māṇḍūkya-kārikā*).

In any case, I think it is clear from the above investigation that the view of *Brahman* in the absolute sense and the theoretical foundation for this view were both derived, directly or indirectly, from Mahāyāna Buddhism and particularly the Mādhyamika school. Moreover, the introduction of this theory brought a marked qualitative change in the thought of the Vedānta schools.

Notes

1) *anupākhyatā. anupākhya* is 'that which cannot be perceived' but this comes to 'that which has no substance'. Cf. Ś. on *BS* II, 1, 14. vol, 1, p.459, *l*.11.

2) See *Māṇḍūkya-kārikā* IV, 4 ; 38 ; 40 : and the annotations for these verses in *Māṇḍūkya-kārikā-bhāṣya.*

3) *śabbaṃ atthīti. kho Kaccāyana, ayaṃ eko anto. sabbaṃ natthīti ayaṃ dutiyo anto. ete te, Kaccāyana, ubho ante anupagamma majjhena tathāgato dhammaṃ deseti* ··· *Saṃyutta-Nikāya,* XII, 15 (vol.II, p.17) "Oh Kaccāyana, the doctrine that 'All is being' is one extreme view. But, Kaccāyana, the Buddha accepts neither of these views and expounds the Law by means of the Middle Path." Also see vol.12 of the Chinese translation of the *Saṃyuktāgama,* the section relating to Kātyāyāna (*Taisho Tripiṭaka* vol. 2, p.85c). Further all metaphysical positions are said to be based on the two views 'the ens position' and the 'non-ens position' (See *Madhyamāgama* 26 *Taisho Tripiṭaka,* vol.1, p.591a ; *Abhidharmamahāvibhāṣā-śāstra* vol.200, *Tisho Tripiṭaka* vol. 27, p.1002c, etc.).

4) *astīti, Kāśyapa, ayam eko'ntaḥ, nāstīty ayaṃ dvitīyo'ntaḥ/yad anayor dvayor antayor madhyam iyam ucyate, Kāśyapa, Madhyamā pratipad bhūtapratyavekṣā//*Kāśyapaparivarta, *ed. Staël*-Holstein, 60, Cf. 52-59. Further, the same argument also appears in *Samādhirāja-sūtra* (ed. Calcutta, p.30). (Cf. *Mvṛ.*, p.135). Here, being apart from the views of ens and non-ens is called *'avivāda'* and is thus in accord with the *Māṇḍūkya-kārikā,* chapter 4. Also see *SaddhP*. II, gāthā 65, *Laṅkāvatāra* III, 22 (p.152).

5) "Again, Buddha, who knew being both ens and non-ens prohibited both the doctrines ; 'all is being' and the 'all is non-being' in the *sūtra* which is the instruction to Kātyāyana. (*Mādhyamika-śāstra,* XV, 7). See *Mādhyamika-śāśtra,* V, 8.

6) The expression *'tattvasya lakṣaṇam'* is the *Mādhyamika-śāstra* (XVIII, 9) but

Kumārajīva translates this as 'true form'.

III. Comparison with the Traditional Definitions of *Brahman*

As I have already remarked, the use of negative expressions and adjectives is encountered quite frequently even in the *Upaniṣads* and there is nothing strange about an orthodox *Brahman* scholar adopting such a mode of explanation. However, if one accepts his definition at face value, then there would seem to be three points at which it contradicts the definition of *Brahman* given most generally in the *Upaniṣads* and the Vedānta schools. First, Bhartṛhari time and again insists that *Brahman* is 'not one and not diverse' while the *Upaniṣads* and the Vedānta schools in general regarded *Brahman* as 'the One (*eka*)'. Not only this but Bhartṛhari himself actually refers to the *Brahman* as '*eka*'.[1] Thus while it may be permissible to apply 'not divergent' to *Brahman*, does it not seem that to apply 'not one' would be in direct contradiction to the fundamental teachings of Vedānta? Second, he interprets *Brahman* as 'not being and not non-being' but in Vedānta thought in general *Brahman* is defined as being. For this reason he should not be able to say 'not being and not non-being'. Third, he says *Brahman* 'neither changes nor is unchanging' but this seems to contradict his own claims that *Brahman* is above the forms of production and destruction.

These are quite legitimate doubts but I think they can be resolved satisfactorily. First, with reference to the argument for 'not one and not diverse' Bhartṛhari's ground for making this claim is this argument[2] :

> "Without diversity there is not identity and without identity diversity does not exist. Both are mutually dependent on the other and it is inconceivable that either could exist separately. Each is established only on the assumption of another which stands opposed to it as its negation. Thus both are in reality empty. Ultimately neither identity nor diversity can exist".

This summarizes the foundation for his position and as I indicated previously we can see in this the adoption of the ontology of Mahāyāna Buddhism, especially that of the Mādhyamikas. The doctrine of *karman*, according to which all things are established in a relation of mutual dependency (*parasparāpekṣā*), is quite strongly emphasized in Mahāyāna Buddhism but is not found in other Indian schools. Bhartṛhari incorporated this doctrine into his own thought and used it to provide the foundation for the doctrine of the *Upaniṣads* that no contemplative determinations whatever were applicable to the absolute *Brahman*. In other words, he borrowed from Buddhist philosophy to demonstrate the validity of the doctrine propounded in the sentences of the holy scriptures, the *Upaniṣads*. If we stop to think of what reasons he could have had for adopting these expressions and this mode of proof, it seems clear that he wanted to say that *Brahman* was completely above and apart from the multiplicity and diversity of all things. He expounded the doctrine of 'not identical and not diverse' by examining unity and diversity as the most fundamental logical relations existing between any two things in opposition.

However, the '*eka*' expounded in the *Upaniṣads* is something which transcends all relations of opposition and sometimes the world cause prior to the development of the multifarious phenomenal world is referred to by this term. Its true meaning is something which is apart from all forms of discrimination. In other words, '*eka*' is not a positive, determining numeral but is rather a negative term by virtue of its meaning. This term has a character which negates its own primary meaning. Interpreted this way, 'non identity and non-diversity' and '*eka*' are synonymous and thus Bhartṛhari felt no contradiction in applying both to the *Brahman*. There is, however, quite a difference in nuance between these expressions and while '*eka*' was a term which had been used among *Brahman* thought from times past, the expression 'not identical and not different' was borrowed from Buddhism.

Reasoning along these lines the second and third problems are easily solved. To think of *Brahman* itself as 'being' or 'unchanging' is in accord with the ancient orthodox Brahman thought while the expressions 'not being and not non-being' and 'not changing and not unchanging' were borrowed from Buddhism, but it is clear that he thought of both modes of expression as indicating the freedom of *Brahman* from all forms of discrimination. This being the case, it follows that, in his works, 'one' and 'being' are not used in their literal sense (*mukhya artha*) but in a secondary sense (*gauṇa artha*), in particular, a metaphysical sense to show absolute negation. He most clearly states that *Brahman* absolutely transcends the forms of the phenomenal world.

> "In the same way the various forms of changes can in no way be established in true reality (*tattva-brahman*). Moreover, this reality seems to have these forms as its essence but [in the highest truth] it is something whose nature is not at all comprised of these forms." (*Vākyap.* III, 2, 10).

Well then, if the absolute *Brahman* is something which admits of no conceptual restriction and repudiates all attempts to express it, then there arises the question that perhaps the whole enterprise of philosophical inquiry into the nature of *Brahman* is meaningless from the start. In order to form a philosophical doctrine and convey it to others one must resort to the medium of language. Bhartṛhari himself was faced with this doubt and thus subjected himself to severe self-criticism. As a result, he declared that even though the absolute itself rejected any sort of conceptual limitation yet a philosophy which used language to investigate the absolute was both possible and necessary.

> "Real substance (*vastu*, =*Brahman*) is known through its untrue form. The truth itself can be expressed by words which are untrue limiting adjuncts." (*Vākyap.* III, 2, 2).[3]

For the absolute words are no more than *upādhi*, they are not real,[4] but by using them it is possible to express what sort of thing *Brahman* is. He explains the ground of this possibility by a metaphor. 'Just as Devadatta's pure house' which is grasped by the term 'house' is expresed by means of an unstable mark (*Vākyap.* III, 2, 3).[5] According to Helārāja this passage has the following meaning. In order to tell someone which house is 'Devedatta's house' one can use an expression like 'the house on which the crow has alighted'. The crow may, of course, leave immediately, for it is after all an unstable representation which is not part of the house itself but it is possible to refer to it for convenience's sake. In just the same way it is possible to refer to and teach someone about *Brahman* by means of language. In this instance, 'Devadatta's house' corresponds to *Brahman* and the 'crow' corresponds to *'vāc'*. This explanation along with Śaṅkara's metaphor of the *arundhatī*[6] star, which it resembles, is ingenious devices to evoke consent and a measure of understanding. But they are, after all, merely metaphors and, as such, are insufficient to explain how the absolute which transcends language can be discussed linguistically in Vedānta philosophy.

It is probable that for Bhartṛhari this was not the sort of question which could be answered by giving a straightforward proof but rather a question which evoked the whole course of his philosophical development as an answer. As will be explained later, he regarded philosophy as the self-development of the absolute. At this point all we want to show is that he was engaged in self-criticism in response to these various methodological doubts and that he was thoroughly confident of validity of his position as a whole.

Notes

1) *Vākyap.* I,2 ; I, 4 ; III, 1, 22.
2) *Vākyap.* III, 6, 26 ; 28 previously given translation and *Vākyap.* III, 1, 21 ; III, 7, a, 39.
3) *SDS.* XIII, *ll.*230-231 also quote this.
4) The principle of *upādhi* was generally recognized throughout Indian philosophy but one group which opposed Śaṅkara maintained that *upādhi* was real (*SDS.* XIII, *ll.*800 f, 865 f.). Since Bhartṛhari regarded *upādhi* as unreal, he is on this point quite close to Śaṅkara.
5) *SDS.* XIII, *ll.*232-233 also cite this.
6) In order to teach someone which star is *arundhatī* it is first necessary to locate a nearby large star and from this indicate which star is *arundhatī*. Ś. on *Brahma-sūtra*, I, 1, 8 ; 1, 12. Nṛsiṃhasarasvatī on *Vedāntasāra* XX, p. 28.

Sub-Section 3. *Brahman* as the Basis of Differentiated Aspects

Although *Brahman* itself, as it has been stated, cannot be conceptually defined and expressed only negatively, we must understand the differentiated aspects of the phenomenal world which we experience as based upon *Brahman*. An absolute which fails to form the differentiated aspects of our world lacks the significance of being an absolute. When we consider this matter, we must admit that *Brahman* has some form of connection with the differentiated aspects. Thus, Bhartṛhari, as previously mentioned, states :

"That (truth, *tattva*)" is neither existent nor non-existent, that is neither one nor different, that is neither united nor separate and that is nither changing nor not different from it (i. e. changeless)." (*Vākyap.* III, 2,12)

And immediately afterwards he states the opposite:

"That does not exist and yet exists, that is one and yet different, that unites and separates, that changes and is different from it (i. e., does not change)." (*Vākyap.* III, 2, 13).

The commentator Helārāja states in a later verse that "*ātman* within ignorance" (*ātmaivāvidyāyām*) is here being taught. Such a concept reminds us of the *tathāgata-garbha* or *ālaya-vijnāna* theory in Mahāyāna Buddhism. Therefore, truth or *Brahman* was thought to possess two aspects: one aspect transcends all words and is expressed only through negation, and the other aspect establishes words and is manifested positively. Bhartṛhari compares both aspects and further states:

"[In the highest truth] the truth itself which is not discriminated receives the forms (aspects) of discrimination. And differentiation in time does not exist in that truth, yet differentiation in time is perceived." (*Vākyap.* III, 2, 8).[1]

Judging from these quotations, there is no doubt that Bhartṛhari believed that the self-same *Brahman* possessed two aspects which were completely opposite to each other. One was *Brahman* in the sense of highest truth, and the other was the aspect which formed the differentiated aspects of the phenomenal world. Both are mutually contradictory, but because of the contradiction the two are united in an absolute. For the very reason that the *Brahman* from the ultimate standpoint is absolute negation, it is believed that the differentiated aspects can be formed.

That Bhartṛhari conceived of these two contradictory aspects of *Brahman* is worthy of our attention. In later ages these contradictory and opposing aspects were grasped as two completely separate principles, and they eventually became formed into the two concepts of "highest *Brahman*" (*paraṃ brahma*) and "lower *Brahman*" (*aparaṃ brahma*). Bhartṛhari, however, merely saw that there were two aspects to *Brahman* and did not call them by special technical names. His belief was that the "highest *Brahman*" (*paraṃ brahma*) itself separated into multi-varied forms and unfolded the phenomenal world.[2]

Now, the problem arises that is how the *Brahman* which can be expressed only negatively can become the basis of the differentiated world. *Brahman* itself is permanent, singular, undifferentiated and pristine wisdom, but how can this manifest the phenomenal world which is complex, many-sided and impermanent? Since the *Brahman* is of only one form, the effect which it unfolds can also be thought of as having only one form, one place, one time, one appearance, one function and one situation. And since the *Brahman* is also permanent, the effect which it unfolds must also be permanent. If the source which unfolds the differentiated aspects of the phenomenal world is in *Brahman* itself, the essence of the *Brahman* in the ultimate sense must also be plural, because the potentiality of differentiation resides within *Brahman*. If such is the case, the idea that the highest *Brahman* is an absolute one is contradicted. Such was the criticism[3] directed against the theory of world-emanation in the Vedānta philosophy of the age.

In order to solve this difficulty the central concern of the Vedānta scholars turned towards explaining the relationship between *Brahman* and the phenomenal world. All of them faced problems in attempting the explanation, and Bhartṛhari tried to solve the theoretical impasse by positing that the *Brahman* as world-cause "consists of words."

That *Brahman* is independent of all differentiated aspects and that it is the basis of all existence are views expressed by the Vedānta school in general, and they cannot be considered as original with Bhartṛhari. His method of expression and proof, however, were under the influence of Buddhism, and this alone accounts for the variation in his thought. In contrast to the other philosophers, Bhartṛhari especially emphasized the fact that *Brahman* as the basis of differentiated aspects "consists of words" (*śabdamaya*)[4], that is, it has "words as the essence" (*śabdatattva*).[5] According to him, words are no different from *Brahman*,[6] and words form the essence of all things. This idea is generally regarded by the scholars of India as the greatest characteristic of Bhartṛhari's philosophy and has frequently been subjected to criticism. He has, therefore, been called *śabdabrahmavādin*[7] or *śabdādvaitavādin*[8]

Notes

1) Cf. *Gauḍapādīya-Kārikā*, II, 14.
2) *Vākyap*. I, 22 ; *Tattvasaṃgraha*, v.128.
3) *Tattvasaṃgraha*, vv.136–138 ; 141 (translated in Part VII, Chapter II, Section III, Sub-section 3 of this book).
4) *Tattvasaṃgraha*, v.128.
5) *Vākyap*. I. Cf. *Vākyap*. III, 2, 11. According to Kamalaśīla, *paraṃ brahma* is *śabdamaya* (*Tattvasaṃgraha*, v.128). Since *Brahman* is also formed by sounds, he is also called *akṣara* (*Vākyap*. I, *Tattvasaṃgrahapañjikā* ad v.128). A group of later scholars stated that his *śabdabrahman* refers to the same thing as *Īśvara* (*Nyāyamañjarī*, p.535).
6) Cf. *Vākyap*. III,2,16. Also, *brahmatattvaṃ śabdāt pāramārthikāt na bhidyate* (Halārāja ad *Vākyap*. III, 2, 11, p.91).
7) *Tattvasaṃgrahapañjikā* ad v.128, p. 67 (see also Part VII, Chapter II, Section II of this book).
8) *śabdādvaitavādin* (*Prameyakamalamārtaṇḍa*, p.11 b). The Jain scholar Abhayadeva also calls his theory *śabdādvaitavāda* (F. O. Schrader : *Über den Stand der indischen Philosophie zur Zeit Mahāvīras und Buddhas*, Strassburg, 1902, Diss. S.55). Such ideas as *śabdabrahman* and *parabrahman* were introduced into Hindu theology, as can be seen in *Viṣṇu-purāṇa* V, 1, 35 ; Vol.IV, pp.207–8.

SECTION II. WORDS

Bhartṛhari postulated the "*Brahman* consisting of words" as the fundamental principle of all things, but such an idea did not suddenly appear in the history of Indian philosophy. The scholars of India before him had conducted a rather detailed, philosophical investigation into the essence of language. Influenced by this long and complicated tradition of speculation into the nature of language, Bhartṛhari perfected the metaphysics of language. Thus, in order to fully understand the concept of words in Bhartṛhari, we must first glance at the history of the metaphysics of language before him. It is only through understanding this historical background that we can properly evaluate and appreciate the significance of Bhartṛhari's linguistic philosophy in the history of thought.

What, then, are the "words" that he considered to be the essence of *Brahman*? And what does it mean to say that the world unfolds from "words"? We shall consider these two questions in the following.

Sub-Section 1. The Pre-History of the Metaphysics of Language

I. Words as the Highest Principle in the *Vedas*

The idea of conceiving words as the highest principle of all things appears already in the oldest literature of India, the *Ṛg-Veda*, which contains meaningful philosophical insights and reflections on the nature of language.

Ṛg-Veda X, 17 and X, 125, which are philosophical verses on the subject of words formed in the latter period of this work, both established words as the highest principle of all things. In the *Ṛg- Veda* X, 125 it states that words as the highest principle are the support of all the gods, controller of all things, and exist universally in all things. But, rather than being regarded as the ultimate principle of the world, they were seen as *Īśvara*. Since it states that words originated from water in the earliest beginnings, this is closer to the concept of creator (*prajāpati*) or golden womb (*Hiraṇyagarbha*) of later ages. They were also given the position of a supreme being who controls grace and salvation, for as he states,

"Whomsoever I desire to, I make a *Brahman*, a hermit, a sage."

In contrast to verse X, 125, which sings of words as the world principle, verse X, 71 considers the socio-ethical significance of words. What is especially stressed in ethical action is the friendly relationship (*sakhya*) in society ; for example, when people perform rituals with a united heart, good results can be obtained, but when this is not done, words do not help the evil-doer in any way.

> "Whomsoever has abandoned a loyal friend, he does not have any part in word (*vāc*). No matter what he hears, he hears in vain. Truly, he does not know the path of righteous action."

The essence of words is sought in the proper performance of rituals brought about by mutual trust and cooperation of the people. Thus, the subjective character of words in ethics is here noticed.

> "Many people who are seeing do not truly see word (*vāc*). Many people who are hearing also do not hear it."

The nature of words transcends the realm of human experience, and it possesses a subjective value characterized by the idea that though one hears one may not truly hear. It does not refer to the signs used by human beings, but to something akin to the *ātman* which was grasped by the later Upaniṣadic philosophers. The poets of the *Ṛg-Veda* reflected on the socio-ethical significance of language and exerted efforts to understand its subjective, fundamental nature. There are naive and coarse elements in the poetic expressions, but the intent of the poet is understandable.

In this way the function of language is highly regarded and it is considered to be the ultimate principle in the two verses on words (*vāc*), but the words used in our human society and the words as world principle must be distinguished. What, then, is the relationship between the two? A clear answer is not found in the two versed cited above, but some reflections on this problem are found in another verse (*Ṛ. V.* I, 164, 45).

> "Speech has been measured out in four 'one-fourths' (*pada*). The wise *Brahmans* know them. [Among the four] the three which are kept in close concealment do not move. Men speak the fourth 'one-fourth' of speech."

Although words as principle are formed of four parts, consisting of four one-fourths, the language understood and used by human beings is nothing more than the last one-fourth. This corresponds to the verse on *puruṣa* (X, 90,3).

> "One-fourth of Him is all creatures. Three-fourths of Him are the immortal in heaven."

This shows that the essence of words was thought to transcend human experience and cognition.[1]

When we look at these poems, we notice that words were thought to be a metaphysical principle already in the *Ṛg-Veda*. Thus, we can trace the tendencies of later philosophers, such as Bhartṛhari and other orthodox Brahmin scholars, to form a unique metaphysics with words as the world principle in the *Ṛg-Veda*.

In this way, language as a metaphysical principle can be considered identical with *Brahman* and *ātman*. It was thus that the *Brāhmaṇa* explicitly states, "The word is *Brahman*" (*brahma vai vāk*) (*Ait. Br.* IV, 211). The tendency to consider words as the principle forming all things is prominent throughout the whole *Brāhmaṇa* literature, and the significance of words in the creation of the world was especially highly regarded. In the *Ṛg-Veda* the "creator of all things" (*Viśvakarman*) was called the "Master of Words" (*Vācaspati*),[2] and in *Brāhmaṇa* literature also the Creator (*Prajāpati*) is regarded as the "Master of words" (*Vācaspati*).[3] Thus, words were believed to be the essence of the creator,[4] and sometimes they were thought to be identical with the whole world.[5] In fact, at times words were considered to be a higher principle than the creator itself.[6]

In particular, words (*vāc*) and mind (*manas*) are frequently referred to together in *Brāhmaṇa* literature,[7] but at times their superiority or inferiority are discussed.[8] From this fact, we can know that there were two traditions among the theologians of the time — one recognizing words as the world principle, and the other advocating mind. This opposition also appears in later *Vedānta* philosophy in a more systematic and complex form. Bhartṛhari and other scholars, for example, emphasize world emanation from words, but the *Māṇḍūkya-kārikā* (Chapter 3), *Yogavāsiṣṭha*, etc., teach emanation from the mind.

Although in *Brāhmaṇa* literature there is a general tendency to treat all things concerning human matters and nature as spiritual or divine existence, and, therefore, words too are placed in the same category, the theologians who taught the ideas noted above undoubtedly recognized words as a unique fundamental principle.

In this way, since words are regarded identical with the world principle throughout the *Vedas*, which are the basic scriptures of orthodox Brahmanism, the union of grammar and *Vedānta* philosophy must have been rather easily effected by Bhartṛhari, in spite of the fact that early grammarians did not think along the lines of *Vedānta* philosophy. Furthermore, since such ideas existed in the *Vedas*, Bhartṛhari and others could legitimate their Vedantic interpretation and give it scriptural authority.

Notes

1) *Śat. Br.* IV, 1, 3, 16 states that the "one-fourth" which is human language is clear (*nirukta*) but that the other "three-fourth is not clear (*anirukta*)." The latter is said to consist of the speech of animals, birds, and small insects. This is definitely a farfetched interpretation made by the *Brāhmaṇa* theologians. For a detailed study on this subject,

see Louis Renou and Liliane Silburn: *Nirukta and Anirukta in Vedic* (Dr. Lakshman Sarup Memorial Volume, Hoshiarpur, 1954).

2) *R.V.* X, 81, 7.

3) *Śat. Br.* V, 1, 1, 16.

4) *Pañcav. Br.* XX, 14, 2.

5) *Śat. Br.* XI, 1, 6, 18.

6) *Śat. Br.* V, 1, 3, 11.

7) For example, there is the myth which states that Prajāpati gave birth to the world by achieving union with words (*vāc*) as *manas*. (*Śat. Br.* VI, 1, 2, 7).

8) *Śat. Br.* I, 4, 1, 8-12; *Tait. Saṃh.* II, 5, 11, 4.

II. The Concept of *śabdabrahman* in Later *Upaniṣads* and Epics

As it has already been pointed out, Bhartṛhari considered *śabdabrahman* (*Brahman* as voice) as the ultimate principle of all things, but the expression *śabdabrahman* existed before his time, although its connotation differed slightly from that of Bhartṛhari.

When we seek the origin of the concept of *śabdabrahman*, we discover that it is already found in the *Maitri Upaniṣad* (VI, 22).

> Now, it has been said elsewhere 'there are truly two *Brahman* to be meditated upon: *Brahman* as sound, and *Brahman* as non-sound. Now, *Brahman* as non-sound is revealed only by *Brahman* as sound.'
>
> Now, in this case sound-*Brahman* is the sacred sound *Om*. Ascending by it, one comes to an end in the non-sound-*Brahman*. So one says: 'This is the way. This is immortality. This is complete union, and also peacefulness.'
>
> Now, as a spider ascends by means of his thread and obtains free space (*avakāśa*), thus, assuredly, indeed does that meditator, ascending by means of *Om*, obtain independence (*svātantrya*).
>
> [But] others expound the sound-*Brahman* in a different way. By closing both ears with the thumbs, they hear the sound of space within the heart. Of it there is this sevenfold comparison: like rivers, a bell, a brazen vessel, a wheel, the croaking of frogs, rain, and whispering in a hidden place. By transcending sound-*Brahman* which has many characteristics, they enter into the *Brahman* which is ultimate, no-sound, and unmanifest. There they are unqualified, indistinguishable, like the

various juices which have reached the condition of honey. For thus has it been said:

There are two *Brahman* to be known: sound-[*Brahman*] and Highest [*Brahman*].
Those who know sound-*Brahman* reach Highest *Brahman*. (*Maitri-Up*. VI, 22)

Now, it has been said elsewhere: 'Sound-*Brahman* is the syllable *Om*. That which is its acme is quiescence, soundless, fearless, sorrowless, blissful, satisfied, steadfast, immovable, immortal, unshaken, enduring, called *Viṣṇu*. In order to gain paramountly, one should worship these two *Brahmans*. For thus has it been said:

> The higher and lower god who is known by the name of *Om* is soundless and empty. Thereupon concentrate in the best place.[1] (ibid. VI, 23)

In these quotations the word *śabda* is used in the sense of "voice" or "sound," but the meaning of "speech" is also thought to be contained within it.

This theory of *śabdabrahman* in the *Maitri Upaniṣad* is included just as it is in the epics and newer *Upaniṣads*.

> "One should know two types of *Brahman*, sound-*Brahman* and Highest *Brahman*. Those who have fully realized sound-*Brahman* reach Highest *Brahman*.[2]" (*MBh*. XII, 233, 30=XII, 8540)

Verse 17 of the *Brahmanbindu Upaniṣad* contains almost the same wording, and verse 17 of the *Amṛtabindu Upaniṣad* states the same thing in regard to two kinds of knowledge (*dve vidye*).[3]

When we consider this *śabdabrahman* taught in these verses in their respective context, they probably refer to "the words of the *Veda*" or "the sentences of the *Veda*," rather than to a world cause. "*Brahman* as not voice" or "Highest *Brahman*" juxtaposed with this is the ultimate principle. A similar usage of *śabdabrahman* is found in the *Bhagavad-Gītā* (VI,44):

> He is carried on by the former practice without his wish. Even one who [merely] wishes to know *yoga* transcends the word-*Brahman*.

The *śabdabrahman* referred to here is interpreted as "the effect of the performance of rituals taught in the *Veda*" (*Vedoktakarmānuṣṭhānaphala*) by

Śaṅkara and as "the ritual section of the *Vedas*" (*Karmakāṇḍa Veda*) by Nīlakaṇṭha. Thus, it was understood as religious practices in general or the results specified in the Vedic scriptures, and *śabdabrahman* denoted the supernatural powers inherent in the performance of rituals, rather than a world principle.

In these later *Upaniṣads* and epics, *śabdabrahman*, which meant the *Vedas* in general, was distinguished from the Highest *Brahman* as the absolute, and the former possessed significance as the steps leading to the latter. The distinction between the two would be dissolved once the idea that the words which form the essence of *Vedas*[4] are none other than the highest principle. Such an interpretation was advocated by Bhartṛhari, who claimed that words are the essence of *Brahman*. Thus he elevated the content of *śabdabrahman*, inherited from the later *Upaniṣads* and epics, from one of lesser significance to one of the highest implications.

Notes

1) According to Rāmatīrtha's commentary, it refers to the heart or the brow.
2) Cf. *MBh.* XII, 271, 30 (=XII,9708).
3) *dve vidye veditavye tu śabdabrahma paraṃ ca yat/śabdabrahmaṇi niṣṇātaḥ paraṃ brahmādhigacchati //Amṛtabindu-Up.* XVII (ĀnSS. p.77). *SDS*. XIII, *l*.274 quotes only the latter half of the above verse as "the words of a person of knowledge" (*abhiyuktokti*). Thus, Mādhva did not consider it to be a passage from the *Upaniṣads*.
4) However, Bhartṛhari considered the words of the *Vedas* to possess the preliminary significance of serving as a means to the highest principle, and he called them "expediences to reach *Brahman*" and "reproduction of *Brahman*": *prāptyupāyo 'nukāraś ca tasya* (=*brahmaṇaḥ* Comm.) *vedaḥ/ Vākyap*. I, 5. Cf. *varṇapadakrameṇāvasthito Vedas tadadhigamopāyas tasya praticchandakanyāyenāvasthitaḥ/ Tattvasaṃgrahapañjikā* ad v.128. He considers the *vāc* which forms their essence to be absolute.

III. The Theory of World Evolution from Word in Orthodox Brahmin Tradition

As we have seen, there are not a few cases in the *Vedas* where words are considered to be the highest principle of the world. When we examine them, we see that this concept is very complex and confusing. Words are sometimes represented variously as the creator of the world, as the material cause of the world, as the formal cause of the world, as unlimited and undefined *Brahman*, as the fundamental self, and so on.

However, when philosophical thought developed after the *Vedas* and various concepts became the common property of the different schools, the content of the concept of words (*śabda*, *vāc*) as the highest principle came to be extremely limited. That is, with the definition of *Īśvara*, *Brahman*, *ātman*, material cause (*upādānakāraṇa*), ultimate cause (*nimitta-kāraṇa*) and so forth becoming final, it was necessary to conceive of words as having none of these meanings. What, then, could be the content of words, different from and not applicable to any other philosophical concepts? The answer would be the denotation of 'meaning': to grasp various things by their respective forms which differentiate them from all other forms. Thus, words as the world principle came to be regarded as attaching form to things and as being the formal cause of the world.

We can see such a method of speculation in the philosopher Uddālaka of the *Upaniṣads*. He advocated that the various aspects of the phenomenal world were established through "comprehension by meaning" (*vācāraṃbhaṇa*).[1] The idea of considering words as the formal cause of world creation appears frequently in the subsequent works of the orthodox tradition. The *Mahābhārata* and the *Laws of Manu* state that *Īśvara* created the world according to the words of the *Vedas*.[2]

> "In the earliest beginnings that great creator (*Maheśvara*) created the names, forms, and activity of functions of various things (*bhūta*) from the words of the *Vedas* only." (*Mahābhārata* XII, 233, 25)
>
> "But in the beginning he created individually the names, functions, and various conditions of all created beings from the words of the *Vedas* alone." (*Manu*, I, 21)

Just as the master craftsman conceives in his mind the form of his work to be created in the future and exerts great effort, so *Īśvara* conceives of words and performs the activity of world creation. Such an idea reflects the true intent of the author of the *Brahma-sūtra* (I, 3, 28), or so state the various interpreters.

Although the idea that words are the formal cause of world creation became influential among Indian intellectuals, this did not completely stamp out the primitive and naive views on linguistic philosophy that exist in the *Ṛg-Veda*. They remained as strong as ever among the popular religious teachers, as for example revealed in *Tantra* literature with its definite esoteric characteristics, which teaches world evolution from words, and in the *Śiva* sect of Kashmir, which teaches that the various forms of impurities in the phenomenal world are manifested by the Voice (*nāda*) as the creative force of *Śiva*.[3)] To be sure, the philosophers of the various schools of Hinduism systematized variegated forms of the "metaphysics of language." The study of this topic would prove to be extremely fascinating, but it will be omitted here, for the majority appear after Bhartṛhari. It should be noted, however, that the intimate connection between grammar and Hindu theology is a subject which will require future elucidation.

Notes

1) The meaning of this word was elaborated upon in interpreting *Brahma-sūtra* II, 1, 14.
2) Cf. Ś. ad *BS*. I, 3, 28.
3) Bhandarkar: *Vaiṣṇavism, Śaivism etc*., p. 130.

Sub-Section 2. Bhartṛhari's Theory of Words

The Sanskrit term for "word" is *śabda*, which can also be translated as "voice." It denotes the voice emitted by man, and sometimes it also includes the sounds of the natural world. In Buddhist philosophy "voice" is enumerated as one of the twelve *āyatanas* and eighteen *dhātus*, and it denotes the object of the auditor faculty. In Bhartṛhari, however, *śabda* does not refer to natural sounds but is rather a unique metaphysical principle.

I. The Relationship between Words and Meaning

According to Bhartṛhari, all words (*śabda*) denote meaning (*artha*). And in order for meaning to be understood as meaning, the essential condition is that it be denoted by words.

> "Now, the meaning which is denoted whenever a word may be pronounced — people call it the meaning of that word. Nothing else is

the characteristic of meaning." (*Vākyap*. II, 329)

"[The word] which has previously been conceived in the mind (*buddhi*) is chosen to denote a certain meaning." (*Vākyap*. I, 47ab)

He also compares the denotation of meaning by words to the illumination of things by lamp light. A word is that which illuminates (*prakāśaka*) and meaning is that which is illuminated (*prakāśya*); the word is also the cause[1] (*kāraṇa*) and meaning an effect (*kārya*).

Words, therefore, are a medium which is absolutely indispensable in understanding meaning. Meaning is not something which can be directly perceived by the senses; it establishes a relationship with the subject only through the medium of words.

"Therefore, since the own form [of the pronounced word] is not understood, one asks, 'What have you[2] said?' When the meaning is to be revealed, the own form of the senses is not similarly perceived." (*Vākyap*. I, 57)

In another place,[3] words are said to reveal form (*ākāra*). According to Bhartṛhari, for example, when work is done on the material called gold, various types of accessories are made, and the various forms and appearances it manifests are called form (*ākāra*). Form was thought to be a concept which opposed the material, and it was believed to undergo "change" (*apāyin*).[4] Thus, the "form" he refers to can be understood as the "meaning" which denotes the various individual things in our world of experience.

Now, since words denote meaning, the differences in the various meanings can be ultimately reduced to differences in words.

"The difference among '*ṣaḍja*'[5] and others is manifested when explained by means of words; therefore, it is well ascertained that all divisions of meanings depend upon nothing but the denotative powers of the words."[6] (*Vākyap*. I, 120)

On the other hand, however, in order for words to be established in their uniqueness, "meaning" becomes the basic condition; therefore, meaning can be said to be the *dharma* of words.[7]

In regard to the fact that words denote meaning, there is not the slightest difference between the words which are used in the daily life of the people and the words found in the *Vedas*.[8] Although grammar in general believed that words such as "cows, horses, people, elephants, birds," etc., used by the people were auxiliary (*upakārin*)[9] to the words in the *Vedas* and that the Vedic words were of fundamental importance, such a distinction was completely negated when Bhartṛhari conducted his philosophical inquiry into the nature of language.

Bhartṛhari said that when we carefully examine the fact that words denote meaning, we are implying that the potential power (*śakti*) inherent in each word manifests meaning. According to him, since it is this potential power that makes possible the understanding of things, the potential power is the bond that maintains and controls all things.

> "The denotative powers (*śakti*) that depend upon words are the combining links of all the universe. This [meaning] which has power as its eye, has appearance as its nature and has various forms is cognized." (*Vākyap*. I, 119)

Now, although this potential power manifests meaning, there is an inseparable connection (*sambandha*) between each word and its meaning which cannot be replaced by other inseparable connections. He argued that unless this relationship endures, it becomes impossible for a given word to always express the same meaning. The grammarian Kātyāyana[10] stated that this inseparable connection was a determined relationship both permanent and immutable. Patañjali[11] also believed that words, meanings, and their relation were permanent and immutable, and the *Mīmāṃsā* school affirmed this interpretation. Bhartṛhari inherited this traditional view from the past.

> "It has been handed down by great sages who are the authors of *sūtras*, *anutantras* (*vārttikas*), and the *Bhāṣya*[12] that words, meanings, and their relation are permanent." (*Vākyap*. I, 23)

Among the three listed as permanent in this quotation, no one would question the fact that meaning (*artha*) is eternal. Meaning always expresses the selfsame content in the subjective minds of all people, and it transcends all temporal distances. But the problem of whether the "word" and the "relation of word and meaning" are permanent and immutable or are subject to change has been a crucial matter in the history of Indian philosophy. With regard to the relation between word and meaning, Bhartṛhari believed it to be permanent and "not man-made."[13] He also stated that "the potential power (*śakti*) of various words is determined,"[14] and he explained that this relation remains unchanged from the eternal past.

> "Just as the suitableness of the various senses for their respective objects is beginningless, likewise the suitableness,[15] i. e. the relation of words to their meanings, is beginningless." (*Vākyap*. III, 3, 29)

How, then, are we able to know that such a relation exists? He explains that when we hear a given word, a set idea immediately arises in our minds and thus we know that their relationship is determined ; therefore, we must see that the relation between the two is permanent.

> "When [the word] is the cause of the idea, it is possible for the word to be related to its meaning. Then it is inferred that there is a relation [between the two]."[16] (*Vākyap*. III, 3, 37)

Bhartṛhari then criticizes those who argue that the connection between the two is only a matter of convenience and custom and states as follows :

> "In no way can a man create the relation to the external object, eternal (e.g. *jāti*,[17] etc.) or non-eternal (e.g. a jar), by means of [the words], the relation of which has not yet been created [it]." (*Vākyap*. III, 3, 38)

A word and its meaning are inseparable ; therefore, the relation between the two must be considered as being determined from the eternal past. Since the relation between the word and its meaning is thus determined and not confused, a mutual causal relationship between the two is established (*śabdārthayoḥ kāryakāraṇabhavaḥ*).[18]

> "The word is the cause of meaning. Because meaning is produced by means of word. Likewise, the word is understood according to the meaning, which is the object of the cognizing subject (*buddhi*)." (*Vākyap*. III, 3, 32)

In other words, we are able to understand the meaning of a word upon hearing the word, but at the same time, since the word carries a certain meaning, it is understood as the particular word and no other.

Now, if the meaning is permanent and if the relation between the word and its meaning is also permanent,[19] then the word by necessity must also be permanent. The fact that the word is permanent and that the relation between the word and its meaning is permanent refer to the same fact. Bhartṛhari maintains that the word has been established from the eternal past and that it is impossible for the word to have a beginning.[20]

> "The scholars of the word know that there are two words among the words in use : one is the cause (*nimitta*) of the words [which become the basis of understanding meaning], and the other is used in the sense of meaning (*artha*) [which is to be expressed]." (*Vākyap*. I, 44)

That is, both "the cause which leads to understanding meaning" and the "meaning" itself are both expressed by words (*śabda*). Are the two different in their essence then? Or are they originally one but understood as separate? This question naturally poses a problem, and Bhartṛhari recognizes that the two views had opposed each other from ancient times.

> "Some ancient people say that there is an essential difference between the two. Others, on the other hand, declare that though they are non-different, they are different owing to differences in the cognizing subject." (*Vākyap*. I, 45)

When Bhartṛhari uses "word" (*śabda*) in the narrow sense, he clearly distinguishes it from "meaning."[21] We then may surmise that he stipulated the sound which is the object of our auditory sense to be "word." But this is not exactly true, because the "word" is to be perceived by means of "sound."

> "That [word] is perceived by the sound (*dhvani*) which evolves from various causes."[22] (*Vākyap*. I, 47cd)

When, for example, we hear the sound "fire," we immediately recall the idea of fire, but if we analyze the process further, we see that the word "fire" is manifested by the sound "fire" and the word expresses the concept of fire.[23] We may think that when someone says "fire," that sound immediately disappears and, therefore, impermanence common to all created effects may be recognized in the word. But, according to Bhartṛhari, even though the sound may disappear, the word which is manifested will by necessity denote meaning, since it is originally permanent.[24]

Bhartṛhari next explains how understanding immediately arises when we hear words, as follows :

> "By means of various pronounced words are understood the idea held

by the speaker, the [external meaning which is independent of the subject], and the own form [of the word]. Their relation has been established [from the beginning]." (*Vākyap*. III, 3, 1)

The *Nyāya* scholars[25] held that since one can immediately understand the meaning upon hearing the word (meaning and word being eternally connected), all knowledge based upon words is inference. This argument has something in common with the above thesis.

The understanding that words and their sounds are separate is an essential point in Bhartṛhari's philosophy, and it is extremely important for a proper appreciation of his ideas. The Buddhist philosopher Śāntarakṣita criticized Bhartṛhari's philosophy, saying that if, as Bhartṛhari advocates, all phenomena have word as their essence, the perception of the word must also simultaneously occur when the colors such as green, etc., are perceived and appear in consciousness, the hearing of sound must occur in the deaf who have lost the auditory faculty.[26]

He misunderstood the significance of Bhartṛhari's concept of words by identifying it with sound. Although the *Nyāya* and *Vaiśeṣika* schools claim that words are none other than sounds and Buddhist philosophy also uses the original term for word, *śabda*, to mean "the object in general of the auditory faculty" among the twelve *āyatanas* and eighteen *dhātus* (which may have accounted for the misunderstanding), such criticism reveals a lack of proper appreciation for Bhartṛhari's philosophy.

What, then, is the "word" which is neither "meaning" nor "sound"? According to Bhartṛhari, it is none other than *sphoṭa*. The *sphoṭa* theory is considered to be the most prominent characteristic of his philosophy, and any reference to *sphoṭa* theory in later Indian philosophy inevitably refers to Bhartṛhari's linguistic theory. *Sphoṭa* means the true word or the essence of words, and it is to be manifested by sound and at the same time denotes the super-sensory principle which manifests meaning. His unique theory on *sphoṭa* will be discussed later, and we will further analyze Bhartṛhari's own views on the direct relation between words and their meanings.

Now, if we accept the fact that words express meaning, then the next problem is what the meaning expressed by an individual word is — whether it is a particular thing or a generality. This problem had been debated by grammarians from very ancient times, and Kātyāyana's *Vārttika*[27] notes a detailed controversy on this subject. According to this work, the conflict between disputants who interpreted the meaning denoted by an individual word as generality[28] and those who interpreted it as a particular thing existed before Kātyāyana. "The philosophers who taught that generality is the meaning denoted by individual words" (*jātipadārthavādin*)[29] were represented by Vājapyāyana,[30] and in contrast "the philosophers who taught particular things as the meaning denoted by individual words" (*dravyapadārthavādin*)[31] were represented by Vyāḍi.[32] After describing minutely and examining carefully the controversy between these two scholars before his time, Kātyāyana sides with Vājapyāyana, slightly modifying his theory.

Patañjali next comments upon the passages concerning the debate which appears in Kātyāyana's *Vārttika*, but his own theory is highly eclectic. At the beginning of the *Mahābhāṣya* he states:

> Question: "Now, does the meaning (*padārtha*) of a word refer to class (*ākṛti*)? Or does it refer to an individual object (*dravya*)?"
>
> Answer: "Both."
>
> Question: "How can that be known?"
>
> Answer: "[Because] the master (Pāṇini) teaches *sūtras* in two ways. [On the one hand] thinking that the meaning of a word is class, he says, "In cases of expressing class, in denoting the singular, the plural is optionally employed."[33] [On the other hand] with the view that the meaning of a word is an individual thing, he deals with [the rule of] *ekaśeṣa* (retention of one): "of words having the same form, and all in the same one case-termination, only the last one is retained."[34] (*Mahābhāṣya*, vol. I, p.6, *ll*.8-11)

According to this passage, Patañjali asserted that Pāṇini believed that individual words express both generality and particular things, but it seems that Pāṇini himself merely noted grammatical rules and had no clear realization of this problem. What Patañjali did was read such an interpretation into Pāṇini, and what is noted here is the view of Patañjali himself.

Patañjali's view, however, was not a conclusion he had reached through his own philosophical inquiry, but a compromise theory which resulted from his eclectic approach. After introducing the theories that the meaning denoted by individual words is either generality or particular things, he states as follows:

> "Truly, for those who advocate that generality is the meaning denoted by individual words, particular things are not the meaning denoted by individual words. Again, for those who advocate that particular things are the meaning denoted by individual words, generality is not the meaning denoted by individual words. [Then] for both disputants [ultimately] both are the meanings denoted by individual words. But for each disputant one is the main thesis and the other is subservient. For those who advocate that generality is the meaning expressed by individual words, generality is the main thesis and particular things are subservient. For those who advocate that particular things are the meaning denoted by individual words, particular things are the main thesis and generality is subservient."[35]

Patañjali affirmed the existence of truth in both theories and, taking a kind of synthetic position, he attributed it to Pāṇini.

In this way there were three different theories[36] concerning the meaning denoted by individual words among the ancient grammarians, but it also came to be discussed widely among philosophers in general. The medieval philosophical texts provide a detailed description of the course of the controversy. For example, the *Mīmāṃsā-sūtra* (I, 3, 33) concludes that individual words express generality, but the *Nyāya-sūtra* (II, 2, 65) opposes this and teaches that an individual thing (*vyakti*), form (*ākṛti*), and class (*jāti*) are the meanings denoted by individual words.

Bhartṛhari himself already knew of the existence of these two theories and mentions this fact. Pāṇini stipulates that "when a word [used for grammatical rules] is not a technical term, it [denotes] its own form" (*svaṃ rūpaṃ śabdasyāśabdasaṃjñā*, I, 1, 68), and Bhartṛhari comments in regard to this as follows:

> "Just as words like *vṛddhi*, manifesting their own forms, enter into relation with their named, i. e. the words conveyed by *ādaic* (*ā*, *ai*, *au*)." (*Vākyap*. I, 59)
>
> "In the same way, the word *agni* (in the *Aṣṭādhyāyī*, IV, 2, 33),

manifesting its own form *agni*, enters into the relation [of name and named] with the word *agni* [used in speech] and conveyed by the word *agni* [in the *sūtra*]." (*Vākyap*. I, 60)

"Whatever word is uttered does not necessarily become the object of grammatical operation. Its power to bring another similar word to the mind is not taken away." (*Vākyap*., I, 61)

What, then, is the own form of the word?

"According to some, [when Pāṇini says in his *sūtra* I, 1, 68] 'the own form.....' the individual thing (*vyakti*) is shown as the name (*samjñā*), and grammatical operations are concerned with the individual thing. The general form as existing in a particular one undergoes grammatical operations...." (*Vākyap*. I, 68)

"Others, on the other hand, consider the particular form to be understood as the named in this *sūtra*; in particular places, the particular form conveyed by the general form comes up [for grammatical operations]." (*Vākyap*. I, 69)

In regard to the significance of the above statement from the standpoint of linguistic philosophy, Professor Brough comments as follows:[37]

"It is, of course, easier to be clear in such discussions where the grammar of one language is described in another language. Thus, a translation into English of a Sanskrit passage on Sanskrit grammar shows at once which words are autonomous, since these, of course, remain in Sanskrit. This is also obvious in the case of a two-language dictionary : the heading-words, in the first language, are clearly autonomous (*svaṃ rūpam*), while the defining words in the second language express their own meanings. The distinction, though not so immediately apparent, is, of course, equally present in a one-language dictionary, and in logical and mathematical definitions, as well as in everyday usage ("what does 'x' mean?" ; "what did you say?" —— "I said 'x'"). The importance of this for logic is very considerable.[38] It is fundamental in the discussion of the possibility of stating the syntax of a logical language in that language itself, and is important for the theory of a hierarchy of languages.[39] But these matters must be reserved for a later discussion."

What attitude, then, did Bhartṛhari take concerning this problem? He discusses the problem of generality in *Vākyapadīya*, Chapter 3, Section 1 (*Jātisamuddeśa*), in which he clearly states as follows:

> "Their own generality is first expressed by all the words. Then there arises the thought of superimposing the generality upon the form of the generality of the meaning". (*Vākyap*. II I, 6)

By the word "cow," for example, the generality of the word "cow" itself, i.e., "cow-word-ness" (*gośabda-tva*),[40] is first denoted, and next the generality of the meaning "cow," i. e., "cow-ness" (*gotva*) is denoted. Based upon the cow as generality, the individual cows are finally denoted, and the cognition or intent concerning them arises; therefore, the particular thing ranks third when counted from the original "word." The statement that "all generalities of meanings depend upon the form of their words" (*Vākyap*. I, 15) indicates the same thinking. On this point, therefore, Bhartṛhari, while inheriting the views of Vājapyāyana and Kātyāyana, advocated a very unique theory which differs from theirs.

Notes

1) *Vākyap*. II, 32. In this case "cause" (*kāraṇa*) probably means the cause which awakens understanding (*jñāpakahetu*). Cf. Ruben: *Die Nyāya-sūtras*, Anm. 296.
2) *bhavān* (Puṇyarāja).
3) *Vākyap*. III, 2, 6.
4) *Vākyap*. III, 2, 4.
5) The first of the seven sounds.
6) Biardeau's edition reads "*śabdamātrāsu niśritāḥ*" for "*śabdamātrāḥ suniścitāḥ*."
7) *Vākyap*. I, 58. Also Cf. *Vākyap*. I, 13ab; II, 121.
8) *Vākyap*. II, 121.
9) *Mahābhāṣya*, vol. I, p. 1. *SDS*. XIII, *l*. 11 ff.
10) *siddhe śabdārthasaṃbandhe*, p.6 (ed. by Kielhorn). Cf. *SDS*. XIII, *l*. 234.
11) *siddhaḥ śabdo 'rthaḥ sambandhaś ceti* (*Mahābhāṣya*, vol. I, p.7).
12) *Anutantra* (= *Vārttika*, Puṇyarāja).
13) *akṛtrimo 'bhisambandho viśeṣaṇa-viśeṣyavat* (*Vākyap*. II, 370).
14) *śabdānāṃ yataśaktitvam* (*Vākyap*. I, 6).
15) Compatibility forms the essence of the connecting relationship: *śabdārthayoḥ sambandho yogyatālakṣaṇaḥ* (Helārāja ad *Vākyap*. III, 3, 37).

16) A similar view is also found in *Vākyap*. III, 3, 3 and *Nyāyasūtra* II, 1, 49 ; 52.

17) Parentheses indicate supplements made by Helārāja.

18) Helārāja ad *Vākyap*. III, 3, 32.

19) That words are permanent (*nitya*) means that words are a supersensory reality which can be cognized by the subject through sounds at anytime, and it does not mean that words are always existing.

20) "Whether words be permanent or things produced, there is no beginning of them just as [there is no beginning] of living beings. The permanence of this rule is now taught." *nityatve kṛtakatve vā teṣām ādir na vidyate/prāṇinām iva sā caiṣā vyavasthānityatocyate//*(*Vākyap*. I, 28). According to Puṇyarāja, the former is the theory of *abhivyaktivādin*, and the latter the theory of *janmavādin*. Cf. *anādivṛddhavyavahṛdvyutpattyaiva ca tatsthiteḥ / śabdasyārthena saṃbandha ādimattā na śaṅkyate //* — Sureśvara : *Bṛhad. Up. Vārttika*, p. 240, v, 874.

21) Cf. I, 47ab. The sections comparing words and meanings have already been listed.

22) Biardeau's edition reads "*karaṇebhyo*" for "*kāraṇebhyo*." *anugṛhyate=upalabhyate* (Puṇyarāja).

23) *Vākyap*. I, 59 ; 60.

24) *Vākyap*. I, 61 ; 65.

25) Vātsyāyana ad *Nyāya-sūtra*, II, 1, 51.

26) *Tattvasaṃgraha*, vv.131-135.

27) *Vārttika* 35-59 under I, 2, 64 (ed. by Kielhorn, vol. I, p.242, *l*.10 - p.247, *l*.16). The translation of this portion is found in Otto Strauss : "*Altindische Spekulationen über die Sprache und ihre Probleme*," *ZDMG*, 1927, S.137-151. The disputation between both theories is also introduced in *SDS*. XIII, *ll*.237-251.

28) For the grammarians Patañjali and Śabarasvāmin *ākṛti* and *jāti* are synonymous, but the *Nyāya* school distinguished the two. According to Vātsyāyana (ad II, 2, 67), form (*ākṛti*) is the set patterns of a thing and it is the symbol of generality (*jātiliṅga*). Thus, man is able to grasp generality by means of form. The generality called "hand" has form, but the generality called "clay" does not possess form.

29) *SDS*. XIII, *l*. 237.

30) *ākṛty-abhidhānād vaikaṃ vibhaktau vājapyāyanaḥ* (*Vārttika* 35, under Pāṇini, I, 2, 35). *ākṛty-abhidhānād vaikaṃ śabdaṃ vibhaktau vājapyāyana ācāryo nyāyyaṃ manyate/ekākṛtiḥ sā cābhidhīyata iti//*(*Mahābhāṣya*, vol. I, p.242).

31) *SDS*. XIII, *ll*.228 ; 244.

32) On Vyāḍi, see Part VII, Chapter II, Section I of this book. *dravyābhidhānaṃ Vyāḍiḥ* (*Vārttika* 45, under Pāṇini I, 2, 64) ;— *dravyābhidhānaṃ vyāḍir ācārya nyāyyaṃ manyate/dravyam abhidhīyata iti//*(*Mahābhāṣya*, vol. I, p.244).

33) *Pāṇini*, I, 2, 58 : e. g., it is possible to say it in the singular, *sampanno yavaḥ*, or in the

plural, *sampannā yavāḥ*.

34) *Pāṇini*, I,2,64 : e. g., instead of saying 'tree and tree and tree' (*vṛkṣaś ca vṛkṣaś ca vṛkṣas*), one says, 'various trees' (*vṛkṣāḥ*).

35) *Mahābhāṣya* (vol. I, p.246, *ll*.14-17 ; under *Vārttika* 53 ad Pāṇini I, 2, 64). Śabarasvāmin also introduces the same idea, but he himself does not subscribe to it (ad I, 3, 33; Cf. Strauss : *Die älteste Philosophie der Karmamīmāṃsā*, S.61).

36) These three different theories are also listed in *Tattvasaṃgrahapañjikā* ad v.883 ; *SDS*. XIII, *ll*.237-251.

37) John Brough : *Theories of General Linguistics in the Sanskrit Grammarians*, Transactions of the Philological Society, 1951, p.31.

38) See, for example, Carnap : *The Logical Syntax of Language*, p.156.

39) Bertrand Russell : *An Inquiry into Meaning and Truth*, p.62.

40) According to Helārāja.

II. The Essence of Generality

According to Bhartṛhari, the meaning denoted by individual words, as it has been explained, refers to nothing other than generality. But what does he mean by "generality"? Generality is not a mere abstract concept but something which has objective reality. The various forms of generality mutually form a relationship between that which is higher and universal and that which is lower and particular, and at the same time they prevail universally in all particular things.[1]

> "The *Smṛti* also says that [generalities in the form of] various things, such as '*Brāhmaṇa* in general' (or '*kṣatriya* in general') exist, are manifested, and effect their own functions by themselves in all living beings." (*Vākyap*. III, 1, 44)

Thus, according to him, the special features of particular things are formed on the basis of generality. But what then is generality itself formed of? Even though we speak of generality, since it becomes a particular in relation to the generality which encompasses it, when we expand its relationship infinitely to a higher generality, it ultimately becomes nothing other than "being-ness" (*sattā*). According to Bhartṛhari, the various forms of generality, such as "cow-ness" (*gotva*), etc., are ultimately established in being-ness. The meaning of all words, therefore, is ultimately none other than being-ness.

Now, if the meaning of all words is none other than being-ness in essence, then a problem arises : all words would then become synonymous, and the limitations and distinctions among words would be destroyed.[2] According to grammarians such as Bhartṛhari and others, this criticism is invalid, because although being-ness itself is absolutely without content, rejecting all material prescriptions, it forms the various forms of generality, such as *gotva*, etc., by receiving limitations. If we were to describe this relationship by a analogy[3] used by scholars before Bhartṛhari, it would be like the relationship between a crystal and its colors. Although the crystal itself is absolutely pure and immaculate, the various colors make it appear as if the crystal itself possesses the colors of green, red, yellow, etc. In the same way, according to the same principle, being-ness, which is the unconditioned, absolute truth, receives the limitations of external attachments (*upādhi*)[4] and manifests itself in the form of diverse generalities. That is, although the meaning of various words forms the ultimate standpoint in nothing other than the selfsame being-ness, it becomes formed into various things by attachments[5] and, therefore, no confusion arises between the various words in the present, real world.

> "On account of the difference in the related, being-ness (*sattā*) itself is divided variously into 'cow[, horse]', etc., and is called generality. All words are established in that being-ness." (*Vākyap*. III, 1, 33)

When we read such explanations concerning generality and being-ness we cannot help being surprised at its similarity to Vaiśeṣika philosophy. The *Upaniṣads* already considered "that which is" (*sat*) to be the world cause, but it is not a concept discovered at the limits of universalization beyond generality. Being-ness in the latter sense was greatly studied in the Vaiśeṣika system. The *Vaiśeṣika-sūtra* explicitly states that "since being-ness (*bhāva*) is the cause of comprising [all things], it is only the universal (*sāmānya*)" (I, 2, 4), and asserts that being-ness is a concept superior to all other concepts and that it never becomes the seed for other concepts. That which is conceived opposite to this being-ness is "the particular at the limits" (*antyāḥ viśeṣaḥ*)(I, 2, 6). This is the particular (*viśeṣa*) and it can never become the universal. All other concepts are found between the two extremes of being-ness and "the particular at the limits" ; to higher concepts they become particulars and to lower concepts they become universals.

In Vaiśeṣika philosophy this being-ness is not merely the highest concept, but it was also considered to be a form of metaphysical principle: "Being-ness (*sattā*) is a thing different (*arthāntara*) from substance, quality, and movement" (*Vaiśeṣika-sūtra*, I, 2, 8). The reason that it is recognized as a significant, special principle is that "when we face substance, nature, and movement and can express them as being existent (*sat*), their basis is being-ness (*sattā*)"(I, 2, 7). That is, being-ness is the principle which establishes the above three categories (*padārtha*). Furthermore, being-ness can be predicated by neither the universal nor the particular (I, 2, 10); it merely has the characteristic (*liṅga*) of existence (*sat*), and since it has no characteristic which distinguishes it from others, it is the single one (*eka*).

When we turn to the *Praśastapādabhāṣya*, it divides the universal into the highest universal (*paraṃ sāmānyam*) and the lower universal (*aparaṃ sāmānyam*). Since the universal is basically a principle which establishes generalization, the highest universal is the universal in its original, fundamental sense, and this is nothing other than being-ness (*sattā*). On the other hand, the lower universal includes substance-ness, quality-ness and movement-ness, and since they each possess particularity, it also possesses the aspect of the particular.[6] The *Daśapadārthaśāstra* by Maticandra of a later period clearly distinguishes between the highest universal and lower universals, limiting the universal only to the highest universal (i. e., being-ness) and the particular to the particular at the limit. He posits the lower universals located between the two as a separate category and calls it "*sāmānyaviśeṣa* (general-particular)."[7]

In this way being-ness (*bhāva*, *sattā*) is an important concept in Vaiśeṣika philosophy, and Bhartṛhari's theory is very close to it. We know for other reasons also that Bhartṛhari was well-versed in Vaiśeṣika philosophy; consequently, we believe that he was influenced by the Vaiśeṣika on this point.

However, Bhartṛhari, who stands in the tradition of Vedānta philosophy, interprets the concept of being in an entirely different manner from the Vaiśeṣika. In Vaiśeṣika philosophy being-ness as a metaphysical principle is the ultimate concept derived by objectively pursuing abstraction upon abstraction in the direction of the higher forms of generality, and it stands opposite to the cognizing subject.[8] "Being-ness" is invariably an object of the cognizing subject, and the opposition between the two is radical. But in the case of Bhartṛhari being-ness has the character of being the subject and is one with wisdom in the ultimate sense.[9] His true intention is expressed in the statement that "the meaning of all words is none other than generality characterized by wisdom in the ultimate sense."[10] And this wisdom in the ultimate sense is nothing other than *Brahman-ātman*.

According to Bhartṛhari, therefore, while the meaning of the stem or root of a noun directly reveals generality, it ultimately denotes being-ness. Furthermore, being-ness prevails in all things, and since there is nothing opposing it, it is permanent (*nitya*) and it is also the great self (*mahān ātmā*).[11]

> "[The ancients] teach that it (being-ness) is the meaning of the stem and the meaning of the verbal root. It is permanent. It is the great self (*mahān ātmā*). [The suffixes] -*tva*, -*tā*, etc., refer to this." (*Vākyap*. III, 1, 34)

Mādhava gives the following explanation concerning this verse.[12] First, it is generally accepted that the meaning expressed by the stem (*prātipadika*) of a noun is being-ness. In regard to the verbal root there are two theories: one is that it expresses things (*bhāva*, existing things in general), and the other is that it expresses action (*kriyā*). In the former theory "existing things in general" are nothing but being-ness, and in the latter theory too the meaning of the verbal root is being because such actions as scholars teach ultimately mean "the generality which exists in many individual things" (*jātiḥ......anekavyaktivartinī*). Thus, regardless of which theory we take, the verbal root means being-ness. The word "cow-ness" (*gotva*) has the suffix -*tva*, and since Pāṇini prescribes that "-*tva*" and "*tā*" indicate its existence in general (*Pāṇini* V, 1, 119), "cow-ness" (*gotva*) means "the fact of being a cow in general," and the correct interpretation would be that it expresses being-ness. Mādhva then concludes with the following statement: "And that being-ness is permanent, since it is free from origination and extinction. Since all phenomena are the false appearance of being-ness, and [being-ness itself] is free from all limitations of place, time, and substance, it is taught that this being-ness is the great self."(*SDS*. XIII, *ll*.224-5)

All generalities, therefore, are being-ness in the ultimate sense.[13] When we compare the highest form of generality called being-ness with the generality of "cow-ness," etc., being-ness may be considered as the generality called the "great universal" (*mahāsāmānya*) and, in contrast, cow-ness may be thought of as the lower universal (*aparasāmānya*). The latter, however, is no different from being-ness as the great universal in the ultimate sense (*par amārthatas*) ; the only difference is that as the connecting element (*sambandh-in*) in regard to being-ness differs, so being-ness becomes distinguished as cow-ness, horse-ness, etc.[14] Thus, cow-ness is established as the being-ness which is possessed by the cow as a particular thing, and it never appears attached to other particular things. Bhartṛhari states, after giving the analogy that the crystal itself is clear but manifests various colors according to its limitations, as follows:

> "Likewise, although the word was previously established in this being-ness, it approaches the connection with qualities, compatible or incompatible." (*Vākyap*. III, 3, 41)

Although the meaning of all words is *Brahman* as being-ness, the "meaning" refers to the *Brahman* which is hidden by limitations, that is the *Brahman* which possesses differentiated aspects. Mādhava[15] explains this point as follows: "Verbal expression (*vyavahāra*) is that which is falsely imagined only by ignorance (*avidyā*) as abundant in difference falsely constructed by limiting adjuncts of each ; therefore, the *Brahman*-truth with different forms which are imposed by the forms fixed for each single case is the object of every word. And although there is no difference in the absolute truth, various phenomena falsely appear through covering in the state of daily life as in the dreaming state." (*SDS*. XIII, *ll*.264-267)

The fact that words are able to denote meaning is because the generality which is directly manifested by words exists in being-ness. "In the generality [called] being-ness which is differentiated by the various [things] such as 'cow', all words such as 'cow' are established as denoting meanings."[16] That is, being-ness forms the meaning and is the basis which makes possible the connection between words and their meaning. In fact, being-ness is ultimately the foundation which makes possible understanding and communication by means of words.

Bhartṛhari, furthermore, determined that only being-ness (*sattā*) is the true absolute, and that which establishes generality as general is untruth. The relationship between truth and untruth is also conceivable between the higher generality which embraces and the lower generality which is embraced; therefore, all concepts are untruth in relation to the universal and truth in relation to the particular.

> "Now, the two things (*bhāva*), truth and untruth, reside in each respective thing (*bhāva*). It is said that of the two truth is generality (*jāti*) and the individual thing is untruth." (*Vākyap*. III,1,32)

The being-ness which is conceived at the upper limits of universalization is absolute truth, and the particular thing which is conceived at the opposite limits of particularization is absolute untruth, but everything that exists in between is truth in one direction and untruth in the opposite direction, thus possessing both aspects. Furthermore, although we speak of truth and untruth, they are ultimately expressed within the relationship of relativity. Everything which can be described as existing in whatever sense possesses an aspect of being-ness, and this being-ness does not exist transcendentally and independently of things.[17)]

> "Therefore, being-ness which is one exists within the various transformations of things." (*Vākya*. III,8,28)

Consequently, Bhartṛhari's philosophy does not negate the multi-complex phenomenal world. It asserts that as the complexity increases, the reality of a particular thing decreases and weakens, and in contrast as the complexity and particularity decrease, its reality increases and strengthens. Bhartṛhari recognized merely the difference in degrees of reality between various things. It is on this point that his theory of being differs greatly from the *Māṇḍūkya-kārikā* and Śaṇkara, and thus secures him a unique position in the history of Vedānta philosophy.

According to him, therefore, since untruth is a defective state of truth, it is impossible to establish independent substance or the principle of untruth together with truth.[18)] Since the real nature of truth is misunderstood and not clearly revealed, people merely imagine a separate substance or principle called untruth.

"It is the tradition from the ancients that there is no distinction between truth (*tattva*) and untruth (*atattva*). The truth which has not yet been thoroughly examined is called 'untruth' [by those who maintain their difference]." [19] (*Vākyap*. III,2,7)

Since the statement "that truth and untruth cannot be distinguished" is a notion of the *Mādhyamika* and *Mahāyāna* Buddhism in general,[20] we can recognize here the influence of Buddhist thought. The commentator Helārāja explains the relationship between the two by the analogy of light and darkness — since an independent entity called darkness does not exist and since it appears only when light is dimmed, darkness can be dispelled by light.

Now, since generality is an intermediary existence, both the universal and the particular which are aspects of generality are established by limitation by others, and consequently we must admit that they are untruth.

"It is said that both the universal (*sāmānya*) and the particular (*viśeṣa*) are distinct from [other universals and particulars]; therefore, the various words are established with the mere reference to differentiated aspects which are untrue." (*Vākyap*. III, 3, 71)

According to Bhartṛhari, therefore, the generality which is implied by words is all untrue from the standpoint of ultimate truth. Generality, of course, contains a certain degree of reality, but the basis on which the various forms of generality claim uniqueness is in the highest sense untrue. But at the same time, even though generality is untrue in the ultimate sense, it is the actual principle which manifests the differentiated aspects of the phenomenal world.

"Anything which generality does not belong to does not originate." (*Vākyap*. III, 1, 25)

Generality makes possible the various things and occurrences in the phenomenal world,[21] and it is never affected by the changes of the phenomenal world. "The complexity of words is permanent" (*vācaś copaplavo* [= *bhedo*] *dhruvaḥ*),[22] he asserts. Even if the universe is destroyed, generality will not be destroyed. According to the common view of the people of India, the universe originates and is destroyed in cycles, but even in the time of destruction, generality will not lose its self-identity. Bhartṛhari quotes the opinion of "certain people" (*eke*) on this matter:

> "Certain people teach that the substratum (*āśraya*) of all generality (*jāti*) is never destroyed [in the great dissolution, *mahāpralaya*]. And they have established that all things are not dissolved at the same time." (*Vākyap*. III, 1, 42)

Although there is a problem with the statement "all things are not dissolved at the same time," the commentator Helārāja gives the following two interpretations. First, even in a single universe (*brahmāṇḍa*) the dissolution of all things does not occur simultaneously.[23] Second, since there are innumerable universes, even if one universe is destroyed, all the other universes remain; therefore, the dissolution of all things does not take place simultaneously.[24] Although it is not clear which interpretation we should accept, Bhartṛhari gives his own theory as follows:

> "According to people who espouse the theory of oneness, when the various individual things have been dissolved into *prakṛti* (primary matter), the various generalities, being self-dependent, arrive at the state of substance (*dravyasattva*)." (*Vākyap*. III, 1, 43)

That is to say, generality is self-dependent and does not lose its independent existence even in the great dissolution. That the generalities arrive at "the state of substance" means precisely that "generalities exist by nature as the substance"[25] (*dravyātmanā jātīnāṃ sattvam*). The tendency to regard generality or concepts as substantial is prominent especially among the Nyāya-Vaiśeṣika in Indian systems of philosophy, but they do not consider generality to be substance (*dravya*) directly. Generality is understood as a universal (*sāmānya*), and it is differentiated from substance. The fact that they regard concepts and generality as substance agrees rather with the doctrines of the *Sarvāstivādins* in Buddhism. According to the *Sarvāstivādins*, the various *dharmas* that are categorized into 75 elements of existence are real as substance (*dravyasat*=*dravyataḥ sat*), and these *dharmas* do not refer to particular things, but, evolving from the meaning of norm, point to the basis by which the various forms of particular things are established. Consequently, on the surface the thesis is similar to what the *Sarvāstivādin* teaches. That "generality comes to have its own reality in the extinction of the universe" is not, of course, taught by Buddhists. This is probably unique with Bhartṛhari. According to his philosophy, *Brahman* as the world cause is the true existence, and the various forms of generality which have been established as the result of emanation are the decreasing of that true existence. Therefore, extinction would mean the revival of true existence itself, and consequently generality also becomes true existence in the extinction of generality. That is, true existence is being-ness, and to become true existence is to become truly real.[26]

In this way, according to Bhartṛhari, generality is a metaphysical principle and is not something postulated by the abstract thinking process. The generality he speaks of is neither an ethical nor an epistemological concept, but a principle which exists prior to particular things in the sense of world emanation or ontology. He, therefore, states that the essence of generality cannot be grasped by logical thinking but only by the intuitive power of the sages which is far beyond ordinary beings.

> "People know that the knowledge concerning them (generalities) is [directly] gained by means of all the senses on account of practice by those who are superior to us,[27] just as people with discerning sight can [directly] perceive the distinction between precious stones, silver, etc." (*Vākyap*. III, 1, 46)

"Those who are superior to us," according to Helārāja, include the ancient masters, Patañjali, and their god *Īśvara*. They are all *yoga* practitioners, and they intuited the various forms of generality, transcending the correspondence between the senses and their objects. The knowledge thus gained is intuitive perception (*sākṣātkāra*).[28] According to the transmitted text (*āgama*) quoted here by Helārāja, "Now they do not see with the various senses. Through the olfactory sense he hears sound, through the back he sees colors, and by the tips of the fingers he perceives all the objects of the senses."[29]

Notes

1) *vyakti-sarvagatatva* (Helārāja).

2) *SDS*. XIII, *ll*.197-202.

3) Cf. Helārāja ad *Vākyap*., p.117; *SDS*. XIII, *ll*.205-207. See Part V, Chapter XV, Section VII of this book.

4) Bhartṛhari himself frequently uses the word *upādhi*, e. g., III,13,24 (p.442) ; III,14,126 (p. 513) ; and 127 (p.514). He calls the words (*śabda*) used by man *asatya-upādhi* (*Vākyap*. III, 2,2).

5) *SDS*. XIII, *ll*.203-205.

6) *Praśastapādabhāṣya*, pp.4 ; 164-167 (ChawkhSS).

7) H. Ui : *Indo Tetsugaku Kenkyu*, vol.III, pp.461-462.

8) For example the following statement is found in the *Daśapadārthaśāstra*: "What is *sattā*? It is that which is inherent in all categories, substance, quality and action, and is perceived by all the sense organs. It is the cause of the recognitions with respect to substance, quality and action that are *sattā*".

9) Cf. *saṃvillakṣaṇaṃ tattvam eva sarvaśabdārtha iti* (*SDS*. XIII, *l*.228) ; *advayaṃ satyaṃ brahma-tattvam. sarvaśabdārtha iti sthitam* (*SDS*. XIII, *ll*.250-251).

10) *paramārthasaṃvillakṣaṇasattājātir eva sarveṣām śabdānām artha iti.....jātisamuddeśe pratipāditam* (*SDS*. XIII, *ll*.194-196).

11) The idea of regarding the absolute as the highest universal agrees with the *Vedānta* philosophy criticized by Kumārila and Mallavādins (*Ślokavārttika*, *pratyakṣasūtra*, v. 114 ; *Nyāyabinduṭīkāṭippaṇī*, ed. by Stcherbatsky, BB. XI, p.35). This kind of thinking can also be seen in one aspect of Vijñaptimātratā philosophy (*Bodhisattvabhūmi*, ed. by U. Wogihara, p.212, *l*.12f.; *Yogācārabhūmi* [『瑜伽師地論』]vol. 43, *Taisho* 30, pp.528 ff.) For ideas preceding Bhartṛhari on this subject, see *SDS*. XIII, *ll*.205-212 ; Helārāja ad *Vākyap*. III,3,41. p.117.

12) *SDS*. XIII, *l*.218 ff.

13) Follows Helārāja ad *Vākyap*. III, 1, 33; *SDS*. XIII, *l*.213ff.

14) *SDS*. XIII, *ll*.216-218.

15) *SDS*. XIII, *ll*.264-267. Helārāja ad *Vākyap*. III,2,16 also has almost the same passage.

16) *SDS*. XIII, *l*.216ff.

17) *na cātra darśane sadbhyaḥ sattā vyatiriktā bhāvata iti sarvaṃ tanmayam* (Helārāja ad *Vākyap*. III, 1, 35. p.30).

18) *nehādvaitanaye satyāsatye dve rūpe staḥ, advaitahāniprasaṅgāt* (Helārāja ad *Vākyap*. III,2,7).

19) *bhedadarśanavyavasthitaḥ* (Helārāja).

20) "*Saṃsāra* is not at all different from *Nirvāṇa* ; *Nirvāṇa* is not at all different from *saṃsāra*." (*Mādhyamaka-śāstra*, XXV, 19) ; "What is the limit (*koṭi*) of *Nirvāṇa* is also the limit of *Saṃsāra*. There is not the subtlest [difference] between the two." (*Mādhyamaka-śāstra*, XXV, 20) ; "This world has as its nature what the *Tathāgata* has as his nature."(*Mādhyamaka-śāstra*, XXII, 16) ; "Do not see *nirvāṇa* and *saṃsāra* as having different natures. There is no distinction between the two natures of *nirvāṇa* and *saṃsāra*."(『六十如理論』 v.5, *Taisho* 30, pp.254ff.) The *Vijñaptimātratā* school also

makes the same point : '*Saṃsāra* and *nirvāṇa* are not two and have not the slightest difference. Since one dwells in the state of non-self, one gains *nirvāṇa* after exhausting life.' Interpretation : "There are no two things called *saṃsāra* and *nirvāṇa*. Nor is there the slightest difference. Why? Because all things are without self and equal."(「大乘荘厳経論」 II, *Taisho* 31, pp. 598 ff.) Cf. *Mahāyānasūtrālaṅkāra*, p. 23.

21) *prayojaka* (*Vākyap*. III, 1, 25 ; 27) ; *sādhana* (ibid. III, 1, 27) ; *sādhaka* (ibid. III, 1, 44).

22) *Vākyap*. I, 87.

23) *ekasminn api brahmāṇḍe yugapad bhāvānām pralayo nāstīti darśanāśrayeṇoktam/*

24) *yadvā brahmāṇḍāntare vinaṣṭe 'pi brahmāṇḍāntarasambhavād yugapat pralayo nāsti/ tathā cāhuḥ/aṇḍānām īdṛśānāṃ tu parisaṃkhyā na vidyata iti /*

25) Helārāja ad *l.c.*

26) *sattaiva sattvaṃ dravyam ity ucyate* (Helārāja ad *Vākyap*. III, 1, 35).

27) *asmadviśiṣṭa* appears in *Vaiśeṣika-sūtra* II,1,18. Upaskāra states that it refers to *Īśvara* and *maharṣi*, but it does not include *Īśvara* and means *siddhadarśana* and *yogin*.

28) *indriyapratiniyamānapekṣaṃ ca sākṣātkārarūpaṃ teṣāṃ jñānam......yoginaḥ sarvā gotvabrāhmaṇatvādijātīr adhyakṣayantaḥ* (Helārāja ad *Vākyap*. III, 1, 46. p.40).

29) A similar explanation is made in *Vijñaptimātratā* philosophy when explaining *kṛtyānusthāna-jñāna* (成所作智) (e.g. *Ch'eng wei-shih lun* 10, 10T).

SECTION III. *SPHOṬA*

Sub-Section 1. The Origin of the Concept of *Sphoṭa*

The *sphoṭa*[1] theory is the most characteristic of Bhartṛhari's philosophy. When Indian philosophers of other schools criticize the *sphoṭa* theory they generally refer to Bhartṛhari as the object of their arguments. Not only that, but the later grammarians also looked up to him as their authority. We will, therefore, pay special attention to his *sphoṭa* theory.

Now, the reason that the concept of *sphoṭa* came to be the most important in Bhartṛhari's philosophy of language is to be seen in a historical movement of philosophy before him in which this concept was established. We shall, accordingly, examine the way in which the concept of *sphoṭa* came to be formed before we discuss Bhartṛhari's *sphoṭa* theory.

Note

1) *Sphoṭa* is discussed in the following works —

John Brough : *Journal of the Philological Society*, 1951, p. 37 f.

K. A. Subrahmania Iyer : *Journal of the Ganganatha Jha Research Institute*, vol.V, part 2, Feb. 1948, pp. 121-147.
K. Kunjunni Raja : *Adyar Library Bulletin*, vol.XX, 1956, pp. 84-116.
R. S. Bhaṭṭāchārya : *Journal of the Ganganatha Jha Research Institute*, vol. XV, parts 1-2, Nov. 1957-Feb. 1958, pp.83-92.
Cf. Maṇḍanamiśra's *Sphoṭasiddhi*. It is also discussed in Vācaspatimiśra's *Tattvabindu* (Shōren Ihara: *IBK*, vol.8, No.2, 1960, pp.170f.). It has been published and translated into French (*Le Tattvabindu de Vācaspatimiśra*, ed. and translated into French by Madeleine Biardeau, Pondicherry, Institut Français d'Indologie, 1956). This is not a Vedāntic text (Dasgupta : *HIPh*. II, p. 107). The Yoga school also maintained the idea of *sphoṭa* (S. Ihara : *Mikkyo Bunka*, No.74, Feb. 1966, pp.1-11).

I. Formation of the Concept of *Sphoṭa*

The concept of *sphoṭa* was established by grammarians who inquired into the essential nature of the word for the sake of building the foundations of the theory that the word is permanent. The question of whether or not the word is permanent[1] had already been discussed in the *Nirukta* of Yāska (c. 500 B.C.). He firstly gave the theory expounded by Audumbarāyaṇa and then criticized that theory :

> "According to Audumbarāyaṇa, speech is permanent in the sense organ [of a perceiver] (*indriyanityaṃ vacanam*). In that case, it is not reasonable that there is the fourfold division [of words]. Further, it is also unreasonable that the words uttered at different times are related to each other and that they are analyzed etymologically by this science (=etymology). However, since the word is universally pervasive [among people] and the word is subtle, the grammatical specific names are set up by the word itself with the purpose of using the words [rightly] in our daily life in this world. Gods as well as human beings are expressed by words. Since human knowledge is impermanent, the sacred verse (*mantra*) in the *Vedas* is the accomplishment of sacrifice."[2]

The portion quoted above is the oldest example which is likely to refer to the problem of whether the word is permanent. According to Audumbarāyaṇa as quoted above, the word first of all continues to exist so long as we can hear it in speech through the organ of hearing, while the essential substance of the word which is permanent beyond it does not exist. Contrary to this, Yāska maintains that it is necessary for men to learn grammar in order to teach the right usage of words, admitting the word to be universal (i. e., permanent) in our ordinary life.

Next to the Yāska's work on etymology, we might examine Pāṇini's grammar. This work, however, does not treat in detail of problems in the philosophy of language, such as the essential nature of the word.

It is in the *Vārttika* of Kātyāyana that the question of the essential nature of the word is discussed in detail. At the beginning of this work, he says, "The connection (*saṃbandha*) between the word (*śabda*) and the meaning (*artha*) is established (*siddha*)." 'To be established' (*siddha*) is a synonym of 'to be permanent' (*nitya*).[3] We thus see that the assertion that the word is permanent is here clearly expressed. Kātyāyana, however, does not discuss the question "What is the word?" fully. He discusses only the essential nature of the word here and there in the *Vārttika*. He recognizes in one place that the letter (*varṇa*) possesses its own existence, independent of the sound of a speaker. There he says, "It has, however, been established that the letters are fixed; as a speaker talks slowly and long, or quickly and short, the way of pronouncing [them] is differentiated" (*siddhaṃ tv avasthitā varṇā vaktuś cirācira-vacanād vṛttayo viśiṣyante*).[4] To wit, such letters as '*a*' and '*i*' are pronounced slowly and long or quickly and short in accordance with the way of pronouncing by a speaker, but the letters themselves are fixed and unchangeable. He, therefore, definitely distinguished the letter itself from the sound which we hear through the ears. This view is taken over by the Mīmāṃsā and the Vedānta, too. But he does not consider the letter itself as the word. He admits that the letter perishes immediately after it is pronounced (*uccaritapradhvaṃsitva*), and further asserts that the word (*vāc*) exists in each letter.[5] In this manner he holds that the word is a transcendental entity, different from the letters, that it manifests itself in each of the letters, and that the letters are pronounced with various tones according to the mental and physical conditions of a speaker.

Then, what on earth is the word which emerges from these sounds? To this question Kātyāyana does not give any answer. It was Patañjali who, having inquired more deeply into the problem, established the view of language of the grammarians. At the start of the *Mahābhāṣya*,[6] he explains the essential nature of the word as follows:

Question: In the case of 'cow' (*gauḥ*), what is the word (*śabda*)? Is it the word — that which possesses a dewlap, a tail, a lump on the back, claws and horns?

Answer: No. That is what is called a substance (*dravya*).

Question: Then, is it the word — that which is gesture, behaviour or blinking?

Answer: No. That is what is called action (*kriyā*).

Question: Then, is it the word — that which is white, blue, black, red or gray?

Answer: No. That is what is called quality (*guṇa*).

Question: Then, is it the word — that which is universality (*sāmānya-bhūta*), not different in different things and undestructible in the destroyed things?

Answer: No. That is what is called form (*ākṛti*).

Question: Then what is on earth is the word?

Answer: That which, when pronounced, generates a notion (*saṃpratyaya*) of a possessor of a dewlap, a tail, a lump on the back, claws and horns — this is the word.

Or in our ordinary life[7] the sound (*dhvani*) which conveys the meaning of a word (*pada*) is called the word (*śabda*). For example, "Make a noise" (*śabdaṃ kuru*), "Do not make a noise" (*mā śabdaṃ kārṣīḥ*), "This student makes a noise" (*śābdakāry ayaṃ māṇavakaḥ*), etc. Because he makes sounds , it is thus said. Therefore, the word (*śabda*) is sound.[8]

We here find that he manifestly shows two definitions concerning the word. The first is that the word is a basic model which causes a perceiver to have an idea through sounds, and the second is that the word is sound. Patañjali accepts both of these two definitions. However, the fact that he presents us these two definitions at the beginning of his work merely means that he just realizes the actual circumstance in which both of them are generally held according to common sense, but it does not mean that he accepts them on the same level. The latter definition that the word is sound does not in any way accord with the former one that the word is a basic model which causes an idea. How, then, did Patañjali himself think on this matter? What is his position towards these two definitions? Since he, having made comments upon Kātyāyana's view, dealt clearly with this problem, I shall here examine it.

Kātyāyana, as stated above, explains as follows:

"The letters are fixed; as a speaker talks slowly and long or quickly and short, the way of pronouncing [them] is differentiated."

Patañjali, too, accepts this view and Comments on it as follows:

"[Here] is a certain speaker who speaks quickly; he speaks letters quickly. Someone [speaks] slowly, another speaks more slowly. For example, someone goes quickly, another walks slowly, and another advances the same way more slowly. And a charioteer proceeds quickly, a horse-rider advances slowly, and a walking man goes more slowly.

[An opponent says:] It is not suitable to give these instances. In these cases the way is the [unchanged] substratum of the action of going. [In the case of pronouncing a word] it is not reasonable that its substratum [i. e. the sound] is long and short.

Answer: In that case, [too, we can take it] in the same way. The word is *sphoṭa*; the sound is the quality of the word (*sphoṭaḥ śabdo dhvaniḥ śabdaguṇaḥ*). How is it so? It is like a drum beating. For example, after beating a drum, someone proceeds twenty steps, and another thirty and another forty while its sound is heard. Likewise the *sphoṭa* has the constant length of duration, [its] prolongation is made by the sound (*sphoṭaś ca tāvān eva bhavati dhvanikṛtā vṛddhiḥ*). Words have *sphoṭa* and sound. And the sound indeed appears short for some people and long for others. Both (*sphoṭa* and sound) are [established] by the nature.[9]"

According to this passage, Patañjali tentatively accepts Kātyāyana's theory that the word is the letter (*varṇa*). But as he encountered criticism from his opponents, he further came to define the essential nature of the letter as *sphoṭa*. In this manner, Patañjali, taking a more advanced position than Kātyāyana, grasped the features of the word more clearly, and consequently the concept of *sphoṭa* appeared for the first time in the history of Indian philosophy.[10] The *sphoṭa* mentioned above is, however, largely different in its content from Bhartṛhari's, though both have the same name. *Sphoṭa* as explained by Bhartṛhari has metaphysically a deeper meaning, while *sphoṭa* as expounded by Patañjali is rather considered to correspond to the original sound (*prākṛto dhvaniḥ*) explained by Bhartṛhari.[11] From the standpoint of the theory of language, Patañjali adopts as his own theory the first of the two definitions mentioned at the beginning of the *Mahābhāṣya*, and we might say that he just accepted the second as the popular view in the world at large.[12]

What, then, does the word in truth or *sphoṭa* explained by Patañjali mean metaphysically? What kind of relation does it have with the word which is often regarded as the highest principle in the *Vedas*? He does not specifically inquire into these problems. He just explains the verse in the hymn of the *Ṛg-veda* IV,58,3 which says, "The great god has entered into the mortals" (*maho devo martyāṃ āviveśa*) as denoting the sense that the word as the universal principle has entered into mortal men, and he maintains that we human beings are identical with this universal principle.[13] The idea that the creator of the world entered into created beings after finishing the work of creation is often found in the *Vedas*, and Patañjali applied this idea to the word as the universal principle.

By the way, the concept of *sphoṭa* had thus been formed at the latest in the second century B. C. In later times this concept also had an influence on schools other than the grammarians. Even in the *Mahābhārata*, though in the portion added later, it appears at least twice.[14] And in later times *sphoṭa* is highly regarded as an object of meditation among *yogins* in general. *Yogins* generally meditate upon the holy syllable '*om*', and this can be, according to scholars of later times, divided into four sound components, namely, *a*, *u*, *m* and silence. This division has already been shown in the *Māṇḍūkya Upaniṣad* and *Kārikā*. The Yoga school of later times takes the fourth one, i. e., silence, as *sphoṭa* and as being identical with the highest *Brahman*.[15] Such a conception of *sphoṭa* is known to be characteristic of the Yoga school.[16] Moreover, the *Bhāgavata Purāṇa*, which has been held in high esteem in recent times, treats of *sphoṭa* in association with the holy syllable '*om*'. According to this work, *sphoṭa* is "the specific mark of the Lord *Brahmā*, the highest self" (*liṅgam Bhagavato Brahmanaḥ paramārmanaḥ*), and "that by which the word appears" (*yena vāg vyajyate*).[17]

Consequently, in consideration of these facts, we see that the concept of *sphoṭa* has been widely held generally in India among *yogins* who contemplate upon the holy syllable '*om*'. Nevertheless, it was the grammarians who deeply investigated the meaning of *sphoṭa* and developed in earnest the concept of *sphoṭa*. There have been so many scholars[18] who held that *sphoṭa* was a principle maintained exclusively by the grammarians (*vaiyākaraṇa*). The concept of *sphoṭa* is indeed characteristic of the grammarians, and almost all the schools of Indian philosophy except the Yoga school criticize the grammarians' *sphoṭa* theory. Not only Buddhist[19] and Jain scholars,[20] who oppose the Brahmanical standpoint, criticize the *sphoṭa* theory, but the Nyāya,[21] the Vaiśeṣika and the Sāṃkhya[22] do not recognize the principle of *sphoṭa*. Furthermore, even in such Brahmanical schools as the Mīmāṃsā[23] and the Vedānta[24] the *sphoṭa* theory is refuted by argument too.

Here the *sphoṭa* theory which was subject to criticism from other schools is mainly concerned with Bhartṛhari's views. Bhartṛhari is indeed regarded as the advocator of the *sphoṭa* theory. The grammarians of later ages looked upon him as the authority for their *sphoṭa* theory.[25] Thus, Bhartṛhari is, we might say, the person who was thorough and exhaustive in thinking about the essential nature of the word among the grammarians.

The grammarians of the middle ages, as explained below, also made comments about *sphoṭa*. Furthermore, it is plain in the light of Bhartṛhari's writings that the concept of *sphoṭa* maintained by them is different in its content from Bhartṛhari's. However, the names of these scholars have been lost in the limitless stream of the history of Indian thought, and only the name of Bhartṛhari came to be widely known in later ages.

Notes

1) On the problems of the philosophy of language in the *Nirukta*, see Max Müller: *ASL*, pp.161-168. Cf. O. Strauss: "Altindische Spekulationen über die Sprache und ihre Probleme," *ZDMG*. Bd.81, 1927, S.99-125.

2) *The Nighaṇṭu and Nirukta*, ed. by Lakshman Sarup, p. 29. As to the portion quoted here, Prof. Brough has studied it in detail, and so I have translated this portion largely on the basis of his study (John Brough: "Audumbarāyaṇa's Theory of Language,"

BSOAS. XIV, pt.1, pp.73-77). As pointed out by Prof. Brough, this portion is fully explained in *Vākyap*. II,345-349:

sarvaṃ sattvapadaṃ śuddhaṃ yadi bhāvanibandhanam/
saṃsarge ca vibhaktasya tasyārtho na pṛthag yadi// (*Vākyap*. II, 345)
kriyāpradhānam ākhyātaṃ nāmnāṃ sattvapradhānatā/
catvāri padajātāni sarvam etad virudhyate// (ibid. II, 346)
vākyasya buddhau (=pratipattṛ-buddhau) nityatvam arthayogaṃ ca laukikam/
dṛṣṭvā catuṣṭvam nāstīti Vārtākṣaudumbarāyaṇaḥ// (ibid. II, 347)
vyāptimāṃś ca laghuś caiva vyavahāraḥ padāśrayaḥ/
loke śāstre ca kāryārthaṃ vibhāgenaiva kalpitaḥ// (ibid. II, 348)
na loke pratipattṝṇām arthayogāt prasiddhayaḥ/
tasmād alaukiko vākyād anyaḥ kaścin na vidyate// (ibid. II, 349)

Verse II,345 is based on Prof. Brough, who follows the India Office Malayalam manuscript which has *vibhaktasya*, while the Benares edition and a manuscript have *vibhakto'sya*.

3) *nityaparyāyavācī siddhaśabdaḥ* (*Mahābhāṣya*, p.6, *l*.17).

4) *Vārttika* 5, under I,1,70.

5) *ekaikavarṇavartitvāt vāca uccaritapradhvaṃsitvāc ca varṇānām* (*Vārttika* 10, under I, 4, 109, p.356).

6) *Mahābhāṣya*, vol.I, p.1. Cf. *Vākyap*. II, 329.

7) The punctuation of the following sentences is based on J. Brough: *Theories of General Linguistics*, etc., p. 32.

8) *Mahābhāṣya*, vol.I, p.181.

9) It is unclear what the last verse is quoted from. Presumably it is quoted from Vyāḍi's *Saṃgraha*.

10) The theory of a scholar called Sphoṭāyana is quoted in Pāṇini's Grammar. In later times there arose a view which interpreted this name as a common noun, meaning "one who relies on *sphoṭa*" (*sphoṭa eva ayanam arthabodhakatayāśrayaṇam yasya*, s.v. in *Vācaspatya, Śabdakalpadruma*). However, in Pāṇini's grammar, this name is mentioned as a scholar's name regardless of the *sphoṭa* theory. Therefore, it cannot be clearly decided whether this person advocated the *sphoṭa* theory or not.

11) J. Brough: *Linguistics*, etc., p. 36.

12) Kaiyaṭa and Mādhava hold that the first theory indicates *sphoṭa*. Kaiyaṭa ad *Mahābhāṣya* (*NSP*.), p.16; *SDS*. XIII. *l*.140.

13) *Mahān devaḥ/śabdaḥ/martyā maraṇadharmāṇo manuṣyāḥ/tān āviveśa/mahatā devena naḥ sāmyaṃ yathā syād ity adhyeyaṃ vyākaraṇam//* (*Mahābhāṣya*, vol.I, p.3, *l*.21; cf. *SDS* XIII, *ll*.110-111). But Yāska interprets 'great god' here as a sacrifice (*yajña*); Sāyaṇa says that, besides this interpretation, it also refers to the god of the sun (*Sūrya*)

(Sāyaṇa ad *Ṛ.V.* IV, 58, 3).

14) *M.Bh.* III, 11, 58 ; *Harivaṃśa* (bhaviṣyaparvan), 16,52 (based on Dr. Ui : *Indo Tetsugaku Kenkyu*, or *Study of Indian Philosophy* I, p. 92). But we cannot find it in the *Harivaṃśa* (Poona Ed.).

15) *praṇavasyākārokāramakārarūpamātrātrayaṃ brahmādidevatātrayātmakatvam uktvā praṇavadevatātrayātiriktaparabrahmātmakacaturthamātraṃ śrutaya āmananti sā ca caturthī mātrā varṇatrayād atiriktaḥ sphoṭa eva saṃbhavati.* — *Yogasārasaṃgraha*, ed. by G. Jha, Bombay, 1894, p.67.

16) Bhoja ad *Yogasūtra*, I, 42 ; Vijñānabhikṣu ad *Sāṃkhya-sūtra* V, 57.

17) *Bhāgavata-Purāṇa* (XIII, 6, 37) (but according to Munir : *Original Sanskrit Texts*, vol. III, p. 43).

18) *Vaiyākaraṇādyupakalpitaṃ dhvanibhyo 'rthāntarabhūtam vācakaṃ śabdātmānaṃ sphoṭam... nirācikīrṣann āha.* — *Tattvasaṃgrahapañjikā* ad v.2704 (p.720). Cf. Bhāskara ad *BS*. I, 3, 10.

19) *Tattvasaṃgraha*, pp.67-75. Here there is no mention of the word '*sphoṭa*', but of '*śabdabrahman*'.

20) *Prameyakamalamārtaṇḍa*, pp.11ff. ; 131ff. etc.

21) *Nyāyasūtra* II, 2, 35 and the portions of the *Bhāṣya* and the *Vārttika* which show their opposition.

22) Also in *Sāṃkhya-sūtra* V,57, where the meaning of a word is said to come out through the sound itself, *sphoṭa* is rejected.

23) *Ślokavārttika*, *sphoṭavāda*. Besides, it is criticized in the *Tattvabindu* by Vācaspatimiśra too. Of this he himself makes a clear assertion (*Bhāmatī* ad I, 3, 28). I note in parentheses that Maṇḍanamiśra wrote a book called *Sphoṭasiddhi* (see Part V, Chapter XIV of this book).

24) Ś. ad *BS*. I, 3, 28.

25) *sphoṭo nādābhivyaṅgyo vācako vistareṇa Vākyapadīye vyavasthāpitaḥ* (Kaiyaṭa ad *Mahābhāṣya*, p.16, NSP. ; *SDS*. XIII, *l*.145).

II. Views on the Essence of the Word before Bhartṛhari

Bhartṛhari, who accepted the idea of *sphoṭa* mentioned above, systematized a metaphysics of the word of his own. However, in describing his own theory he was led to refute other views on the essence of the word. He describes three views on the essence of the word in the *Vākyapadīya* :

> "Someone says that (1) the wind, (2) atoms or (3) knowledge is transformed into the word. However, since there is a difference in

views among the doctrines of various schools, there is no fixed view [on the subject]."

According to the first view, the wind (or the air) is transformed into the word.

"Activated by the effort following the desire of the speaker, the wind is struck at the different places of articulation and is transformed into the word." (*Vākyap.* I,109)

The reason why the wind is capable of appearing as letters such as '*a*', '*i*', '*u*' is explained as follows:

"Since [the wind] which is characteristic of increasing speed by the power of the cause meets with [the cause called endeavour],[1] even the solid forms [called letters] are separated." (*Vākyap.* I, 110)

Probably he holds that because the word is necessarily accompanied by expiration when it is uttered, it is air in motion, and thus a transformation of the wind. Such an idea is referred to and at the same time refuted in the *Mīmāṃsā-sūtra* (I,1,22). Śabarasvāmin, who calls them "those who assert that the wind is the cause" (*vāyukāraṇaka*), reports that such an idea is held by scholars who are engaged in the science of *śikṣā* (the science which teaches proper articulation and pronunciation of Vedic texts), one of the six limbs of the *Vedas*.[2] But on the other hand he himself recognizes that the word which we actually utter in speaking is a transformation of the wind.[3] Vātsyāyana of the Nyāya school,[4] as well as Praśastapāda of the Vaiśeṣika school,[5] are also of the same opinion.

According to the second view, the essence of the word is explained as "the atoms of words":

"The atoms, which have the function of separation and conjunction on account of being possessed of all powers, transform themselves into shadow, sunlight, darkness and the word." (*Vākyap.* I, 111)

"The atoms called words, when their power is being manifested, are set in motion by effort and gathered [to come into existence] , [small pieces of cloud] are gathered [to come into existence] as cloud." (*Vākyap.* I, 112)

Vātsyāyana also mentioned a theory, although it is unknown who advocated it, that the word arises from the vibration of elements.[6]

According to the third view, knowledge (*jñāna*) is the word.

"And this inner knowledge, which exists as the subtle word, transforms itself into the word in order to manifest its own form."

athedam āntaraṃ jñānaṃ sūkṣmavāgātmanā sthitam/

vyaktaye svasya rūpasya śabdatvena vivartate[7] // (*Vākyap.* I, 113)

"Having become *manas*, the [word] comes to be fully matured by heat and enters into the wind called breath. Then it is driven out."

sa manobhāvam āpadya tejasā pākam āgataḥ/

vāyum āviśati prāṇam athāsau samudīryate// (*Vākyap.* I, 114)

"The wind becomes the substratum of the principle, inner organ, is influenced by its attribute, and is transformed by the very heat."

antaḥkaraṇatattvasya vāyur āśrayatāṃ gataḥ/

taddharmeṇa samāviṣṭas tejasaiva vivartate// (*Vākyap.* I, 115)

"The breath, after splitting its own knot in the form of sounds and after manifesting letters, is merged into them."

vibhajya svātmano granthīn śrutirūpaiḥ pṛthagvidhaiḥ/

prāṇo varṇān abhivyajya varṇeṣv evopalīyate// (*Vākyap.* I, 116)

Here the idea that "inner knowledge ..... is transformed into the word" is similar in content to the view of Bhartṛhari himself.[8]

Now, if we summarize the above presentation by Bhartṛhari concerning the process whereby subtle word, or inner knowledge, comes to be actually heard through our ears, we may explain it like this:

1) *Manas*, the faculty of apperception, gives an impetus to heat, an energy inside the body.[9] Then the word in a latent or potential state is connected by that power with the wind existing inside the body.

2) That wind, being controlled by *manas*, begins to appear as inner wind by the power of heat, an efficient cause.

3) This inner wind, which causes a sound to manifest, produces a sound, an object of hearing.

Probably there had existed in older times the idea that heat becomes an efficient cause so that the word may transform itself. According to the *Chāndogya-upaniṣad* (III, 18, 3), the word is itself transformed by *Agni*, who is light (*jyotis*).

Now, Bhartṛhari next quotes two more theories (*matāntara, pakṣāntara*).[10]

The first is :

"The word which is perpetually in motion is not perceived because it is subtle. Just as the wind is perceived through [its] tanning, so the [word] is perceived through its own cause."

ajasravṛttir yaḥ śabdaḥ sūkṣmatvān nopalabhyate/
vyañjanād vāyur iva sa svanimittāt pratīyate// (*Vākyap.* I, 117)

According to Puṇyarāja's commentary, the subtle wind mentioned above is the subtle sound (*sūkṣmo dhvaniḥ*), and it is, according to some theories, the ether (*ākāśa*). The expounders of this theory, therefore, think that the word is only the vibration of ether which fills the physical world, and that we cannot perceive the vibration by our ordinary senses since it is extremely subtle, and it presents itself only to our ears. They maintain, as it were, a kind of wave-motion theory. According to the Vaiśeṣika[11] and Nyāya schools,[12] word (or sound) is a quality (*guṇa*) of space. They also hold the same view as the above.

The second theory is :

"And the power of that [word] which is in the breath and in the intellect, while evolving, is differentiated at the different points of articulation."

tasya prāṇe ca yā śaktir yā ca buddhau vyavasthitā/
vivartamānā sthāneṣu saiṣā bhedaṃ prapadyate// (*Vākyap.* I, 118)

The potentiality of the word is, according to this theory, contained in our apperception as well as in inner wind, and it is transformed into the word in the external world, motivated by the efficient cause of the organ of pronouncing. But it is not known who the expounder of this theory was.

Bhartṛhari was well-versed in these earlier theories. But being unsatisfied with them, he established a metaphysics of his own. After criticizing these different theories, he maintains that the essence of the word is *sphoṭa*.

Notes

1) *saṃnipātāt = prayatnaviśeṣarūpakāraṇasaṃbandhāt* (Puṇyarāja).
2) *tathā ca śikṣākārāḥ āhuḥ — vāyur āpadyate śabdatām iti* (ad *Mīmāṃsā-sūtra* I, 1, 22).
3) Śabarasvāmin ad *Mīmāṃsā-sūtra* I, 3, 25.
4) Vātsyāyana ad II, 2, 18 (p.162).

5) *Praśastapādabhāṣya*, Śabdaprakaraṇa (p.145).

6) *mahābhūtasaṃkṣobhajaḥ śabdo 'nāśrita utpattidharmako nirodhadharmaka ity anye* — Vātsyāyana ad *Nyāyasūtra* II, 2, 12.

7) The edition has *nivartate*, but it should be read *vivartate* or *nirvartate*.

8) Part V, Chapter II of this book.

9) *manaḥ kāyāgnim āhanti* — *Pāṇinīya-śikṣā* (P. Chakravarti : *Linguistic Speculations of the Hindus*, p. 90).

10) According to Puṇyarāja's commentary.

11) *śabdo 'mbaraguṇaḥ śrotragrāhyaḥ kṣaṇikaḥ* — *Praśasrapādabhāṣya* (p.144).

12) *Nyāyasūtra* I, 1, 14 ; III, 1, 56 ; 67 ; III, 2, 24 ; IV, 2, 21.

Sub-Section 2. The Meaning of *Sphoṭa*

As mentioned above, there was for a long time a controversy in India between the proponents of the word's permanence (*nitya*) and the proponents of the word's impermanence or artificial existence (*kṛtaka*). Bhartṛhari also declares that these two groups existed together.[1] If we borrow the terminology of Puṇyarāja, the former are the adherents of the manifestation theory (*abhivyaktivādin*),[2] who maintain that the permanent word manifests itself through sound, while the latter are the adherents of the production theory (*janmavādin*), who assert that the word is created and produced by men. If we assign each of these two groups to schools, we may say that the grammarians, Mīmāṃsā and Vedānta belong to the former, while the Nyāya, Vaiśeṣika, etc., belong to the latter. The proponents of the word's permanence must prove that the word is permanent so that they may assert their own theory against the opposite assertion that the word undergoes change and destruction.

It was in the Mīmāṃsā school[3] that people made efforts to prove this. In this school the word is distinctly separated from the sound (*nāda*), and it is determined to be permanent, while the sound is impermanent. According to this assertion, the sound, which is a physical and physiological phenomenon, manifests the word, which is a special substance, and moreover this word indicates meaning. The word is, as it were, an intermediary between sound and meaning. But the *Mīmāṃsā-sūtra* does not mention anything about the essence of the word. Upavarṣa declares later that the word is the sound (*varṇa*).[4] As stated above, Śabarasvāmin accepts this, and the later

Vedānta school follows him.

However, if an individual syllable such as '*a*', '*i*', '*u*', etc., is the essence of the word, how can these syllables indicate a meaning? Each of these syllables is alone unable to show the meaning. In order to state the structure in which the word indicates the meaning, we need an explanation well based upon fact. It was a success in a way for Brahmanism that the Mīmāṃsā school proved the word to be permanent. However, it can hardly escape the charge of being insufficient for explaining the connection with the meaning. It was Bhartṛhari who gave afresh a conclusive answer to this problem. He primarily accepts as a presupposition of his own the theory of the Mīmāṃsā school that the word is permanent. Just advancing one step more than the Mīmāṃsā, he relies on the concept of *sphoṭa*.

As Bhartṛhari declares that the word is *sphoṭa*, the stipulations about the word as presented in the previous section might be applied exactly to *sphoṭa*. But on the other hand it should be considered that *sphoṭa* contains a special and distinctive meaning beyond what the simple word means, because he especially adopts and emphasizes the principle of *sphoṭa*.

Sphoṭa is the essence of the word (*śabdatattva*,[5] *śabdātman*[6]), or the word itself,[7] which is clearly distinguished from the sound (*dhvani*).[8] It is called "the permanent word which does not have any divisions."[9] Although the word as sound changes incessantly in arising and perishing, *sphoṭa* as the essence of the word is beyond the changes which the sound undergoes in arising and perishing. *Sphoṭa* is eternal and imperishable. It is neither newly established nor destroyed. It has no beginning and no end. It has no distinction of before and after. It is eternal, imperishable, unitary, undivisible, and exists of itself. According to his philosophy, the absolute, *Brahman*, is the word, and therefore *sphoṭa* is identified with *Brahman*. Later philosophers call it the cause of the world (*jagannidāna*).[10]

As we can see in such expressions, *sphoṭa* seems to be highly regarded as a metaphysical principle. But in fact it is taken from our everyday experience. This fact will gradually be clarified in the following.

The word *sphoṭa* is etymologically a noun derived from the verb root '*sphuṭ*'[11] (to split open, to crack, to appear suddenly). It has two meanings: (1) *sphoṭa* itself appears through sound, and (2) *sphoṭa* causes a meaning to appear. The reason why this term is especially formed from the verb root '*sphuṭ*' is that the fact of appearance is very rapidly accomplished in both cases. *Sphoṭa* is different from sound, and at the same time it is distinguished from meaning. It is an intermediary between sound and meaning. Bhartṛhari does not say anything about the etymology of the word '*sphoṭa*', but Mādhava explains it as follows:

> (1) *Sphoṭa* means "to be burst open, i. e., to be manifested by letters." So it is a thing to be manifested by letters. (2) *Sphoṭa* [further] means "the meaning bursts open (*sphuṭati*), i. e., becomes manifest (*sphuṭībhavati*) from this." So it is a thing which makes a meaning understood. In this manner, [scholars] explain to us the meaning of the word '*sphoṭa*' in two ways.[12]

It is regarded as indispensable for an explanation of the characteristics of *sphoṭa* to say that these two meanings are included in it.

> *Sphoṭa* is different from the letter and is to be manifested by letters, and it is the eternal word which makes the meaning understood, say the *sphoṭavādins*.[13]

We, therefore, experience two processes when we hear someone speak and understand what he says. (1) Firstly *sphoṭa* is expanded. (2) Secondly the expanded *sphoṭa* expresses the meaning which leads to understanding. By passing through these two processes we can finally understand what is said.[14] Of these two, the second process, i. e., the connection of the word with its meaning, has already been considered in the previous section. The 'word' here is indeed the true word. Namely, it is none more than *sphoṭa*. That being so, I will here consider especially the first process.

According to Bhartṛhari, the *sphoṭa* which is the essence of the word is revealed by sound (*nāda*),[15] and this sound is not a mere sound, but is to be reduced to one of the Sanskrit syllables (*varṇa*) so far as it is pronounced in a word. Therefore, *sphoṭa* is, it is said, revealed by the syllables.[16] The relation between *sphoṭa* and sound is like that between a thing to be revealed and a revealer.

> "Just as the fixed fitness is established between a sense organ (e. g., the eye) and its object, so [the fixed fitness] between *sphoṭa* and sound [is established] as the relationship between a thing to be revealed and

a revealer."

grahaṇagrāhyayoḥ siddhā yogyatā niyatā yathā/
vyaṅgyavyañjakabhāvena tathaiva sphoṭanādayoḥ// (*Vākyap.* I, 98)

Metaphorically speaking, sound is like an image of *sphoṭa*.[17]

Now if *sphoṭa* is in this manner revealed by sound, a question arises: Is it not impermanent and easy to destroy? To take an example, although the form of a pot is already established in the mind of a potter, it is revealed by an actual pot which is made of the material of clay, and the pot is impermanent. Likewise it must be said that *sphoṭa* is impermanent too.[18] To this opposing view Bhartṛhari replies as follows:

"And it is not necessarily established that non-eternal things manifest themselves. The permanent classes are also thought to manifest themselves by [their impermanent] substrata."

na cānityeṣv abhivyaktir niyamena vyavasthitā/
āśrayair api nityānāṃ jātīnāṃ vyaktir iṣyate// (*Vākyap.* I, 96)

A class is permanent and unchangeable, but it manifests itself in impermanent things. If you say that *sphoṭa* is impermanent because it manifests itself, then you should say that a class is also impermanent.[19] This is what Bhartṛhari means to say.

Since *sphoṭa* is the true word, it has no distinctions inherent in itself and is beyond the distinctions of temporal sequences. However, it is, he says, misunderstood to have a possibility of distinction in itself, only for the reason that it is revealed by sound, which belongs to the temporal domain.

"Because sound is produced in sequence, it [=*sphoṭa*] has no before, nor after. It has no order, but it is perceived as differentiated, as it were, by the form of sequence."

nādasya kramajātatvān na pūrvo nāparaś ca saḥ/
akramaḥ kramarūpeṇa bhedavān iva gṛhyata // (*Vākyap.* I, 48)

Metaphorically speaking, *sphoṭa* is the moon in the sky, and sound is an image of the moon reflected in water. The image of the moon moves and changes incessantly, while the moon itself has no change in the sky.

"Just as a reflection existing in other place [than where the real thing stays], as it were, follows the motion of water because of the action of water, so *sphoṭa* and sound are related."

pratibimbaṃ yathānyatra sthitaṃ toyakriyāvaśāt/
tatpravṛttim ivānveti sa dharmaḥ sphoṭanādayoḥ// (*Vākyap.* I, 49)

The *sphoṭa* which is revealed, therefore, is wholly without distinction and without limitation. But it manifests itself in various ways in accordance with the distinctions of its revealers.

"And a thing to be manifested follows the distinctions of its manifesters. It is evident in the case of reflections in such various reflectors as oil and water."

prakāśakānām (=*abhivyañjakānām*) *bhedāṃś ca prakāśyo* (=*abhivyaṅgyo*) *'rtho 'nuvartate/*
tailodakādibhede tat pratyakṣaṃ pratibimbake// (*Vākyap.* I, 100)

Sphoṭa is originally different from sound, and the former is in a sense quite opposed to the latter. Therefore, *sphoṭa* simply manifests itself in sound, which is compared to a reflected image. But it does not arise in it.

"It is not possible for things like mountains to come into existence on a diamond, the surface of a mirror, etc., which are incompatible in size [with those objects].[Therefore, *sphoṭa* does not come into existence but manifests itself.]"

viruddhaparimāṇeṣu vajrādarśatalādiṣu/
parvatādisarūpāṇāṃ bhāvānāṃ nāsti saṃbhavaḥ// (*Vākyap.* I, 101)

Sphoṭa itself exists in a realm which is beyond our perception. Nevertheless, this *sphoṭa* is perceived and manifests itself with various forms. Why is this so? Because it is, he says, due to an adjunct (*upādhi*).

"They declare that, although temporarily indivisible in itself, *sphoṭa*, when it follows the duration of sound, has distinction of duration due to differences in limiting adjuncts for perception."

sphoṭasyābhinnakālasya dhvanikālānupātinaḥ/
grahaṇopādhibhedena vṛttibhedaṃ pracakṣate// (*Vākyap.* I, 75)

In other words, the *sphoṭa* which is the essence of the word is beyond our perception, and at the same time exists in perceiving (*buddhistha*, *Vākyap.* I, 46)

In this manner, Bhartṛhari thinks of two processes in which firstly sound reveals *sphoṭa* and secondly *sphoṭa* indicates meaning. Why does he come to think of these two processes? Is he not justified in thinking that the sound (or the syllables) directly reveals the meaning? As a matter of fact, the Mīmāṃsā and Vedānta schools in general, which follow the theory of Upavarṣa, define the essence of the word as a syllable denoting meaning. Why, then, is it that Bhartṛhari especially propounded the principle of *sphoṭa*? How can this *sphoṭa* be proved to exist? He does not particularly refer to these questions in the *Vākyapadīya*. However, in Mādhava's *Sarvadarśanasaṃgraha,* Chapter XIII, we see that the grammarians prove the existence of *sphoṭa*.[20] In the same chapter, the opponents assert that, because there is no means of knowledge (*pramāṇa*) by which to prove the existence of *sphoṭa*, they cannot accept this principle, while the grammarians assert that they can directly prove the existence of *sphoṭa*.

> "To these problems he replies: — (A) Concerning this point, the sense-perception (*pratyakṣa*) is certainly the means of knowledge, because it is common to all (*sarvajanīnatvāt*)[21] to cognize a word apart from various letters, thinking that 'cow' is a word. For [you] cannot say, in the absence of any contradiction, that the perception of the word is false."

That is to say, everyone knows the fact by his direct perception that apart from sounds and syllables the word exists as a symbol. Therefore there is, he says, no doubt that *sphoṭa* exists.

> "(B) Otherwise it is not reasonable that the meaning of the word is understood. For this reason as well [the existence of] *sphoṭa* should be accepted.
>
> And [the assertion] that the concept of 'cow' appears only from letters cannot bear examination, since it cannot bear either of the following dilemmas: Do the letters (e. g., '*g*', '*au*', and *visarga*) produce the concept of meaning (1) unitedly (e. g., in the form of '*gauḥ*') or (2) separatedly? (1) Not the first, since letters, which are momentary,[22] cannot form a united whole. (2) Not the second, since the conception of the meaning cannot arise from separate letters. And there is no other alternative than separation or union. Therefore, since letters are incapable of expressing the meaning, that by dint of which the meaning is understood is *sphoṭa*."

In connection with the reason for the latter alternative, Kaiyaṭa also says,

"If each of the letters indicates the meaning, it is of no use to pronounce the second and subsequent letters [after the first letter that indicates the meaning]."[23]

Furthermore, Mādhava refers to the rebuttal made by adherents of the *sphoṭa* theory against the assertion of those who maintain that the word is the syllables:

> All this argument is like 'a drowning man's catching at a straw',[24] since either of the alternatives is impossible in the following dilemma: Is the substratum of the conception of a word (A) merely a single letter (*varṇa*), or (B) an aggregate of letters?
>
> (A) It is not the former, because it is impossible that a series of letters which are different from one another, without any uninterrupted cause produces the idea of a word just as flowers do not produce the idea of a flower garland without a string.
>
> (B) And it is not the latter, either, because it is not possible that letters which are destroyed immediately after they are pronounced combine into an aggregate. (1) For the expression 'aggregate' (*samūha*) is applied to many things perceived as existing together at one place, for example to the trees such as *dhava*, *khadira* and *palāśa* which are perceived as existing together at one place, or again to elephants, men, horses, etc. [existing together]. Those letters, however, are not perceived in such a way [existing together at one place], because [the letters] are destroyed as soon as they arise. Further, in the assertion that [the letters] reveal [*sphoṭa*], [*sphoṭa*] is revealed simply by the order of sequence, since [they] cannot form an aggregate. (2) And with regard to letters, no imaginary aggregate should be imagined, because as the result this would involve a "mutual dependence" (vicious circle) for [on the one hand], when it is established that [letters] convey a meaning, letters produce the idea of a word under this condition; and [on the other hand], when it is established that [letters constitute a word], it is established that [they] convey a meaning. Therefore, it is not possible that letters express a meaning; so the existence of *sphoṭa* should be accepted [as an intermediary for those two].[25]

As defined in the above quotation, the grammarians presuppose the principle of *sphoṭa* so that they may explain the fact that they understand the meaning immediately after hearing syllables. Since the grammarians regard the meaning expressed by the word as a metaphysical substance, they are forced to think of an intermediary between the syllables and the meaning. In this philosophy of the word they entirely ignore the role of a perceiver who grasps the sound and expresses the meaning, and they take the meaning or *sphoṭa* simply as objective. This is a remarkable fact in the history of philosophy.

The grammarians, in this way, devote themselves to proving the reason why they have to posit *sphoṭa*. It is, however, a point of utmost difficulty to explain the relationship between *sphoṭa* and syllables. *Sphoṭa* is a super-temporal and permanent principle, while syllables are impermanent since they arise and perish in a moment and are thus temporarily limited. Then, how can these two, which are contrary in nature, be related to each other? Or how can impermanent syllables reveal the permanent and supertemporal *sphoṭa*? This difficult problem is to be solved. If a syllable alone reveals *sphoṭa*, then it is not necessary to arrange many syllables to construct a word or sentence. And if a collection of many syllables reveals *sphoṭa*, then the collection of syllables can, as stated above, not be formed in itself. In other words, the expounders of the *sphoṭa* theory censure the adherents of the syllable theory (*Varṇavādin*) in terms of the argument of dichotomy, but this time they incur the same reproach. The grammarians of this period were well aware of this.[26] Making great efforts to get rid of this difficult point, they had got to create their ideas independently. According to Mādhava's *Sarvadarśanasaṃgraha*, Chapter XIII, the expounders of the *sphoṭa* theory, who maintain that it is one thing for the syllables to indicate the meaning and another for the syllables to reveal *sphoṭa*, explain the process in which *sphoṭa* is revealed as follows.

> The first sound reveals *sphoṭa*, but not clearly. Each successive manifeste [sound] makes [it] more and more clear just as the *Veda*, after one reading, is not retained but is made sure by repetition, or just as the real nature of a jewel does not shine clearly when it is first known [as a jewel] but is, in its final splendour, revealed as it is,[27] since there is the following authoritative statement :[28]

"When the idea (*buddhi*) of [a hearer], the seed of which is implanted by sounds, attains maturity by successive repetition, the word is determined with the last sound."

nādair āhitabījāyām antyena dhvaninā saha/
āvṛttaparipākāyāṃ buddhau śabdo 'vadhāryate// (*Vākyap*. I, 85)

To wit, *sphoṭa* has already been revealed by the first syllable, but this *sphoṭa* is still in an obscure condition, and so it becomes clearer and clearer through the second and following syllables, and is finally ascertained by the last one. Such being the case, the first syllable is the revealer of *sphoṭa*, and the second and following syllables are merely subsidiary to it. According to the *Vākyapadīya*, Chapter I, this first syllable is called the primary sound (*prākṛto dhvaniḥ*) and the following syllables modified sounds (*vaikṛto dhvaniḥ*).[29] The former has a form of cause (*kāraṇarūpa*) since it reveals *sphoṭa* (*sphoṭavyañjaka*), while the latter have forms of effect (*kāryarūpa*). The *sphoṭa* mentioned by Patañjali is indeed considered to correspond to the primary sound. Now, when we cut off halfway a series of certain syllables which compose a word, we can gain another word. (For example, when we cut off halfway the word 'manage' in English, we have another word, i. e., 'man'.) Bhartṛhari explains it thus:

"It is the incapability of a comprehender (=hearer) that one thinks as existing the [actually] nonexisting verbal elements in the middle. They are only a means to the understanding [of the actually pronounced words]."

asataś cāntarāle yāñ chabdān astīti manyate/
pratipattur aśaktiḥ sā grahaṇopāya eva saḥ// (*Vākyap*. I, 86)

Thus, *sphoṭa* is revealed by the first syllable. *Sphoṭa* itself is supertemporal, but provisionally the time of the first, or primary sound is ascribed to *sphoṭa* as the time of *sphoṭa*.

"Since the long, short, and protracted sounds, etc., are different in nature [from *sphoṭa*], when [*sphoṭa*] is permanent, the time of the primary sound is applied figuratively to that of the word."[30]

svabhāvabhedān nityatve hrasvadīrgaplutādiṣu/
prākṛtasya dhvaneḥ kālaḥ śabdasyety upacaryate// (*Vākyap*. I, 76)

"The primary sound is regarded as the cause for perceiving the letters. The modified [secondary] one is considered to be the cause of distinctions in the function [of the actual utterance]."

varṇasya grahaṇe hetuḥ prākṛto dhvanir iṣyate/
vṛttibhede nimittatvaṃ vaikṛtaḥ pratipadyate[31] // (*Vākyap.* I, 77)

"But after the manifestation of the word (*sphoṭa*), the modified [secondary] sounds produce the difference in the function [of the utterance]. The nature of *sphoṭa* is not differentiated by them."

śabdasyordhvam abhivyakter vṛttibhede tu vaikṛtāḥ/
dhvanayaḥ samupohante sphoṭātmā tair na bhidyate// (*Vākyap.* I, 78)

Prof. Brough has given us a detailed explanation of this, which helps us understand it. For example, when we hear the utterance 'shita', it happens that we cannot know whether it is '*śita*' or '*śīta*'. After understanding the meaning, we can know which is meant. I pronounce differently the English words 'poor', 'pore', and 'paw', but people in South England pronounce them without distinction, saying 'pho:'. The latter, he says, corresponds to the modified sound.[32]

Thus, the so-called time of *sphoṭa* is limited always to the first moment of the sound of any word, and the modified sounds which follow it are different in each word.

"The time of *sphoṭa* is not different in a word, short or long. But the series of the other sounds is subject to increase or decrease."

alpe mahati vā śabde sphoṭakālo. na bhidyate/
paras tu śabdasaṃtānaḥ pracayāpacayātmakaḥ// (*Vākyap.* I, 104)

Thus, the first or primary sound bears a special meaning, and it regulates and conditions all the sounds which follow it.

"But, just like the light of a lamp, only the sound is perceived from a long distance. And in the sounds [for example,] of bells, etc., the difference is seen conspicuously."

dūrāt prabheva dīpasya dhvanimātraṃ tu lakṣyate/
ghaṇṭādīnāṃ ca śabdeṣu vyakto bhedaḥ sa dṛśyate// (*Vākyap.* I, 105)

To take an example, it is like this: A bell, when once struck, retains reverberation thereafter, and the nature of this reverberation depends upon that of the bell; likewise there occur, it is suggested, the differences between words. Puṇyarāja gives this explanation, saying that it is the theory of some teachers (*kecid ācāryāḥ*). Presumably Bhartṛhari accepted this explanation. (Puṇyarāja explains it by using the simile of beating an musical instrument and its sound in his commentary on the *Vākyapadīya* I, 104.)

Thus, we have to consider distinctly that the word as vaguely referred to by worldly people has the following three phases: (1) *sphoṭa* or the essence of the word, (2) the primary sound or the original form of the sound, and (3) the sound pronounced in an actual way, namely, the modified sound as the secondary sound. (Here it is to be noted that there is a problem which is common to Gestalt theory.) Generally in our daily conversation we are not conscious of the distinctions between these three.

> "(1) Some consider that the sound is perceived as identical with *sphoṭa*'s form. (2) [Others consider that] the sound is not perceived [by other organs]. (3) Others [consider] that the sound is [perceived] independently. (4) And others say that the sound is a manifester."[33]
>
> *sphoṭarūpāvibhāgena dhvaner grahaṇam iṣyate/*
> *kaiścid dhvanir asaṃvedyaḥ svatantro 'nyaiḥ prakāśakaḥ//* (*Vākyap.* I, 82)

Moreover, it is often taught in later grammatical and tantric texts that the word's form is divided into four kinds in the physical process of the manifestation of the word.[34] Bhartṛhari endroses this too.

1) *Parā vāk*. This is the essence of the word, abiding in the innermost part of the body (*mūlādhāra*).

2) *Paśyantī*. This is the form in which the above *parā vāk* has slightly started to manifest. At this moment the internal breath arrives from the innermost part of the body (*mūlādhāra*) at the navel. However, the word is not yet divided into parts.

3) *Madhyamā*. This is the form in which the word has manifested itself further, and the internal breath arrives at the heart.

4) *Vaikharī*. This is the form in which the word is spoken by men. In this case, the breath comes up to the mouth through the throat.

Bhartṛhari does not give us any detailed explanation of these four forms. But there is no doubt that he accepted these four forms as well known by worldly people.[35] For this reason, we can see that these four forms had already been established before Bhartṛhari.

Notes

1) *Vākyap*. I, 28.

2) In the *Yin-ming ju cheng-li lun* (因明入正理論, *Nyāyapraveśa*) *śabdābhivyaktivādin* is translated *sheng-hsien-lun* (声顕論, theory of word manifestation).

3) Cf. *Mīmāṃsā-sūtra* I, 1, 6-23.

4) Ś. ad *BS*. I, 3, 28 ; Bhāskara ad *BS* I, 3, 29, pp.62-63 ; Śabarasvāmin ad *Mīmāṃsā-sūtra* I,1,5 ; *Prameyakamalamārtaṇḍa*, p.136, a. See Part V, Chapter III of this book.

5) *niravayavam arthapratyāyakaṃ śabdatattvaṃ sphoṭākhyam* (*SDS*. XII, *l*.193).

6) *Tattvasaṃgrahapañjikā*, p.720.

7) According to the commentator Puṇyarāja, *sphoṭa* is explained to be the true word, while sound is only a quality (*sphoṭaḥ śabdo dhvaniḥ śabdaguṇaḥ.*—Puṇyarāja ad *Vākyap*. II, 1, p.64).

8) Moreover in later rhetoric *dhvani* means a word (*śabda*), a resound, or a noise, up to a hint, or a suggestion, and it is identified with *lakṣaṇā*. Mahimabhaṭṭa maintains that *dhvani* is included in reasoning (*anumāna*). (Louis Renou : "Le *dhvani* dans la poêtique sanskrite," *The Adyar Library Bulletin*, vol. XVIII, p.1f.)

9) *sphoṭākhyo niravayavo nityaḥ śabdo* (*SDS*. XIII, *l*.113) ; *sphoṭātmā nityaḥ śabdaḥ* (*SDS*. XIII, *l*.126).

10) *SDS*. XIII, *ll*.113-114. According to Puṇyarāja (ad *Vākyap*. I, 119), Bhartṛhari, who rejects other theories, maintains that the word is the root of the world (*śabdasyaiva jaganmūlatva*).

11) Particularly it means 'to start opening (a bud)'. It is etymologically identified with the German verb *spalten*. In contemporary Hindī explosives such as gunpowder are called *visphoṭaka vastu*. As for the etymological meaning of *sphoṭa*, Manfred Mayrhofer explains it as follows : — Sphuṭati Springt auf, birst, platzt, spaltet sich/bursts, splits (Br., usw. ; Br., ep. *sphoṭati*)..... Sphoṭaḥ m. Blase, Beule, Pustel/blister, boil, pustule (kl.) (*Kurzgefasstes etymologisches Wörterbuch des Altindischen*, Band III, Heidelberg, Carl Winter, 1976, S.543 ; 546).

12) *sphuṭyate vyajyate varṇair iti sphoṭo varṇābhivyaṅgyaḥ sphuṭati sphuṭībhavaty asmād artha iti sphoṭo 'rthapratyāyaka iti sphoṭaśabdārtham ubhayathā nirāhuh* (*SDS*. XIII, *ll*. 137-139).

13) *varṇātirikto varṇābhivyaṅgyo 'rthapratyāyako nityaḥ śabdaḥ* (*SDS*. XIII, *ll*.135-7). According to the *Nyāyakośa*, the same phrase is seen in Śrīkaṇṭha's *Tarkaprakāśa*. Kaiyaṭa also refers to it : *tad*(=*varṇa*)-*vyatiriktaḥ sphoṭo nādābhivyaṅgyo vācako* (Kaiyaṭa ad *Mahābhāṣya*, p.16. NSP.). Cf. *SDS*. XIII, *l*.144.

14) *abhivyaktaḥ sphoṭo 'rthaṃ pratyāyayati* (*SDS*. XIII, *l*.152).

15) *nādavyaṅgyaḥ sphoṭaḥ* (Puṇyarāja ad *Vākyap*. I,48).

16) *sphuṭyate vyajyate varṇair iti sphoṭo varṇābhivyaṅgyaḥ* (*SDS*. XIII, *l*.137).

17) Cf. *Vākyap*. I,49.

18) *anityaḥ śabdo, abhivyaṅgyatvāt, ghaṭādivat* (Puṇyarāja ad *Vākyap*. I, 96).

19) *uktam anumānaṃ jātau vyabhicaratīti bhāvaḥ* (Puṇyarāja ad *Vākyap*. I, 96).

20) *SDS*. XIII, *l*.127ff.

21) *SDS*. IX, *ll*.127-129. Nāgeśabhaṭṭa also explains it in the same way : "We understand that 'this is a word' or 'this is a sentence', and this understanding is a proof of knowing that the *sphoṭa* exists and keeps its essential form." (*Mahābhāṣya-pradīpoddyota*, BI. vol. I, p.11 ; here I quote from Brough, *Linguistics etc*., p.42.) Other scholars also understand it in the same way : "that from which the meaning bursts forth, i. e., shines forth, in other words, the word-as-expressing-a-meaning (*vācaka*)" (Koṇḍabhaṭṭa : *Vaiyākaraṇa-bhūṣaṇa*, Bombay, 1915, p.236) ; "*sphuṭati prakāśate 'rtho 'smād iti sphoṭo vācaka iti yāvat*" (Nāgeśabhaṭṭa : *Sphoṭavāda*, Adyar Library, 1946, p.5). The latter two examples are quoted from Brough, *Linguistics etc*., pp.33-34. *pratyeka-varṇebhyo 'tiriktaṃ 'kalaśa' ity-ādirūpam akhaṇḍam ekapadaṃ sphoṭa iti Yogair abhyupagamyate* (Vijñānabhikṣu's *Sāṃkhya-pravacana-bhāṣya* ad V,60, ed. by R. Garbe, HOS., vol.2, p.129).

22) *ekaikavarṇavartitvāt vāca uccāritapradhvaṃsitvāc ca varṇānām* (Kātyāyana's *Vārttika* 10, under Pāṇini I, 4, 109).

23) ad *Mahābhāṣya*, NSP. p.12 ; *SDS*. XIII, *l*.143.

24) Cf. *SDS*. III, *l*.22.

25) *SDS*. XIII, *ll*.169-181.

26) *SDS*. XIII, *ll*.182-183. The *sphoṭa* theory and its criticism presented by Vācaspatimiśra are found in his *Tattvabindu* (Cf. Prof. Ensho Kanakura : "Vācaspatimiśra's Tattvabindu," *Bunka* XI, 7, 1944, July, p.5f.).

27) *SDS*. reads *āvṛtti-*.

28) *SDS*. XIII, *ll*.184-191.

29) *tatrādayaḥ prākṛtaḥ paro vaikṛta iti bodhyam* (Puṇyarāja ad *Vākyap*. I, 104).

30) Puṇyarāja ad *Vākyap*. I, 104.

31) In Biardeau's edition, this is the stanza quoted in the commentary of Harivṛṣabha.

32) John Brough : *Linguistics etc*., p.40.

33) This translation is mainly based on Puṇyarāja's commentary. Prof. Brough gives us a rather different interpretation : "Some consider that the perception of the *dhvani* is indissolubly linked with (the perception of) the form of the *sphoṭa* ; others hold that the *dhvani* itself is not perceived (as such) (i. e. we are not normally aware of the phonemes when we hear a word) ; and others consider the *dhvani* to be an independent manifesting agent (as is clearly seen in the speech of a parrot or a gramophone record)."

(*Linguistics* etc., p. 41) It reads in the *Laghumañjūṣā* : *sphoṭasyābhivyaktau prākṛto dhvaniḥ kāraṇam, cira-ciratara-sthitau tu prākṛtadhvanijātavaikṛtadhvaniḥ kāraṇam* (Based upon the *Nyāyakośa*).

34) Chakravarty : *Linguistic Speculations of the Hindus*, pp.48-51 ; G. Kaviraj : "The doctrine of Pratibhā," *ABhI*, vol. V, p. 114f.

35) *Vaikharyā Madhyamāyāś ca Paśyantyāś caitad adbhutam / anekatīrthabhedāyās trayyā vācaḥ param padam //* (*Vākyap.* I, 144).

Sub-Section 3. Sentence and *Sphoṭa*

Thus, Bhartṛhari establishes the special principle of *sphoṭa* and considers it to be the essence of the word. By what structure, then, is the language (word) whose essence is considered to be *sphoṭa* formed? The language (word) in daily usage consists of sentences (*vākya*), words (*pada*), and letters (*varṇa*) such as alphabets. It also has a mora (*mātrā*) found in each letter when it is analyzed. Each of the subsequent elements constitutes part of each of the preceding ones. Then, it should be asked what the primary form of language is. Bhartṛhari answers this by saying that only the sentence[1] is true language, while a word, a syllable, or a sound-element is merely imagined to exist or established in our imagination by extracting it from a sentence. In the same way *sphoṭa* is, strictly speaking, only a sentence. At this point we see a characteristic of the *sphoṭa* theory asserted by Bhartṛhari.

The theory that the word is permanent is equally accepted by the three schools closely related to the *Vedas* among the traditional Brahmanical schools, i.e., the Mīmāṃsā, the Vedānta, and the grammarians. However, these three schools hold different views on the structure of the word which is permanent. Bhartṛhari also refers to this subject, and in the first place he presents his view that the true nature of the so-called word is letters (*varṇa*).[2]

"Even if the word is differentiated, the identity of letters does not disappear. And even if sentences are differentiated, a word is perceived as one and the same. That word does not exist differently apart from letters. There is no sentence apart from letters and words."

pade bhede 'pi[3] *varṇānām ekatvaṃ na nivartate /*

vakyeṣu padam ekaṃ ca bhinneṣv apy upalabhyate// (*Vākyap.* I, 71)
tad varṇavyatirekeṇa[4] *padam anyan na vidyate/*
vākyaṃ varṇapadābhyāṃ ca vyatiriktaṃ na kiṃcana// (*Vākyap.* I,72)

According to scholars who hold this view, only syllables are true, and words and sentences are merely what is formed together by syllables. This view had, as mentioned above, been maintained by Upavarṣa, and Śaṅkara followed him too. Bhartṛhari, however, finally rejects this view.[5]

"Just as there are no parts in letters, so there are no letters in a word. No words exist apart from a sentence in any way."

pade na varṇā vidyante varṇeṣv avayavā iva/
vākyāt padānām atyantaṃ praviveko na kaścana//(*Vākyap.* I, 73)

According to him, letters and words were invented by men out of necessity in their daily lives, and thus they are unreal, while only sentences are real.[6] Even a word was just provisionally devised for enlightening the stupid.[7] The letter (*varṇa*) and the mora (*mātrā*) were invented by the imagination (*kālpanika*) as parts of the word and as parts of the syllable respectively, and thus each of them does not exist in an absolute sense.[8] Thus, he says, some grammarians (*vaiyākaraṇa*) make the mistake (*viparyaya*) of considering a letter as well as a word to be an ultimate reality.[9]

In particular, we have to attach great importance to his assertion that the primary form of language is not the word but the sentence. From ancient times there had coexisted two theories among grammarians. The first was that the indicator of meaning is the word, and the second that it is the sentence.[10] Bhartṛhari, however, rejected the former and adopted the second. With regard to the division of words, there had existed different views from older times too. Some divided them into two kinds, namely, nouns (*nāman*) and verbs (*ākhyāta*).[11] Grammarians of the traditional line such as Yāska, etc.,[12] who added two further kinds, namely, the prefix (*upasarga*) and the particle (*nipāta*), divided them into four. Still others divided them into five by adding a fifth, namely, *karmapravacanīya*.[13] Helārāja is said to have adopted the last view.[14] Contrary to these views, Bhartṛhari asserts that, in whatever way words are divided, they are invented by extracting them from a sentence, and that it is like when a word is analyzed into a word-root and a word-ending.

"Being separated from[15] a sentence, a word is divided into two by some, four or five by others, just as the root, endings, etc.[, which are separated from the word, are examined]."[16]

dvidhā kaiścit padaṃ bhinnaṃ caturdhā pañcadhā 'pi vā/
apoddhṛtyaiva vākyebhyaḥ prakṛtipratyayādivat// (*Vākyap.* III, 1, 1)

According to Bhartṛhari, only the sentence is real among the linguistic expressions of human beings. People in the first place comprehend words and letters which are in themselves parts of sentences. These words and letters, however, are merely means by which people grasp the meaning presented by sentences. But simply because philosophers in general do not know this structure of language, they believe the opposite. In reality words and letters are merely created temporarily through our imagination.

"Just as one perceives an object differently from its true form by having previously seen [it] from a distance or in the dark, and determines it differently from its true form,[17] so, when the sentence is manifested by the causes of manifestation, firstly the intellect (*buddhi*) takes action in the form of distinguishing parts [of a sentence]."

yathaiva darśanaiḥ pūrvair dūrāt saṃtamase 'pi vā/
anyathākṛtya viṣayam anyathaivādhyavasyati//
vyajyamāne tathā vākye vākyābhivyaktihetubhiḥ/
bhāgāvagraharūpeṇa pūrvaṃ buddhiḥ pravartate// (*Vākyap.* I, 90 ; 91)

Hence, as the word is, in the absolute sense, nothing other than a sentence, *sphoṭa*, which is the essence of the word in a strict sense, functions as the sentence too.[18] In India there are two groups among those who assert the *sphoṭa* theory : (1) the adherents of the word-*sphoṭa* theory (*padasphoṭavādin*), who consider each word to express meaning, and (2) those of the sentence-*sphoṭa* theory (*vākyasphoṭavādin*), who consider that a sentence as *sphoṭa* accomplishes the whole sense, while a word is nothing but a part of a sentence and a syllable a part of a word. As viewed from the above discussion, Bhartṛhari is undoubtedly to be included among the adherents of the sentence-*sphoṭa* theory.

Well, when one wants to get to *sphoṭa* as a sentence, one cannot immediately perceive and understand it. Only when parts which compose a sentence are arranged into a definite order can one reach *sphoṭa* through the medium of this process. Bhartṛhari insists urgently on this point.

" Just as there is a definite rule of sequence in the change by which milk [becomes curd] and a seed [becomes a sprout], so there is a settled sequence in [*sphoṭa*-]apprehenders' cognitions."

" So there arises the difference of nature even in those [words] which have parts according to the sequence of sounds [to take an example, as in the case of *nadī* and *dinā*]. The supposition of the difference of parts is a means to [arrive] at the partless [essences of words, *śabdātman*]."

yathānupūrvīniyamo vikāre kṣīrabījayoḥ/
tathaiva pratipattṝṇām niyato buddhiṣu kramaḥ// (*Vākyap*. I, 92)
bhāgavatsv api teṣv evaṃ rūpabhedo dhvaneḥ kramāt/
nirbhāgeṣv apy upāyo vā bhāgabhedaprakalpanam// (*Vākyap*., I, 93)

Thus, when viewed from the sequence of cognitions, a syllable or a word is first, and a sentence is second. On the other hand, when viewed from the ontological sequence of *sphoṭa* in manifestation, the sentence is first and the word or the syllable is second. In other words, the sentence is the basic thing from the viewpoint of metaphysics, while the word or the syllable is merely its derivative. The latter, however, plays an important role as the means of comprehending *sphoṭa,* which is the sentence, and only in this sense is it valuable.

" It is the incapability of a comprehender (=hearer) that one thinks of the [actually] nonexisting verbal elements in the middle as existing. They are only a means to the understanding [of the actually pronounced words]."

asataś cāntarāle yāñ chabdān astīti manyate/
pratipattur aśaktis sā grahaṇopāya eva saḥ// (*Vākyap*. I, 86)

Thus, Bhartṛhari holds that, logically speaking, a proposition or a conclusion indicated by it is the most primary among the linguistic expressions of human beings. But in other places he says, as mentioned above, that the meaning expressed by a word is a class. And he clearly says in another place that *sphoṭa* is a class.[19] A class is logically considered to be an idea. If this is the case, a question may arise : "Are both of them contradictory to each other?" Probably he does not see any contradiction between them. The word which he believes to exist is the word making up the absolute, "the word in function" or "the word in manifestation." Thus, the class expressed by it, too, is not the class made up only of non-objective imagination but "the class in function" or "the class in manifestation" which exists as a metaphysical principle. The class which is dependent upon the absolute and shares with it comes to manifest itself in the phenomenal world, and it produces various forms and changes in the phenomenal world. The self-manifestation of class creates a conclusion, and hence a sentence. The function of class shows a conclusion. The class is, in his philosophy, not a logical but a metaphysical or an ontological idea which is considered to be an idea of fact. Therefore, it does not seem to be contradictory for Bhartṛhari to think that the word whose essence is the sentence indicates a class as the medium of *sphoṭa*.

The *sphoṭa* theory developed further in later ages. At least apparently it was classified into eight types.[20]

1) The letter-*sphoṭa* (*varṇa-sphoṭa*)
2) The word-*sphoṭa* (*pada-sphoṭa*)
3) The sentence-*sphoṭa* (*vākya-sphoṭa*)
4) The *sphoṭa* of the undivided word (*akhaṇḍa-pada-sphoṭa*)
5) The *sphoṭa* of the undivided sentence (*akhaṇḍa-vākya-sphoṭa*)
6) The *sphoṭa* of the letter-class (*varṇa-jāti-sphoṭa*)
7) The *sphoṭa* of the word-class (*pada-jāti-sphoṭa*)
8) The *sphoṭa* of the sentence-class (*vākya-jāti-sphoṭa*)

The reason why these eight kinds of *sphoṭa* have to be considered is explained as follows:

1) In the first place, each suffix, for example, *-ḥ* in *rāmaḥ*, or *-ti* in *pacati*, has a meaning of its own. In addition, for example, *kar-*, *kār-*, *kur-*, and *cakar-*, which are derived from the same root "*kṛ*," are possessed of different functions.

2) But on the other hand, in the case of, for example, *rāmāya*, *rāmeṇa*, *haraye*, *harau*, *harīn*, etc., it is hard to tell exactly what part of each word signifies what is meant and what indicates the case. For this reason we must posit *sphoṭa*.

3) Similarly, since in the case of "*dadhīdam* (this is thick milk)" two words are combined into one sentence by reason of *saṃdhi*, we must posit the

sentence-*sphoṭa*.

4) However, in actual practice it is grammarians who divide a word into a root and an ending, analyze it into syllables, or sort a sentence into words,[21] while a word in its actual usage conveys its meaning as a unit. Therefore, we have to posit the *sphoṭa* of the undivided word.

5) But this is insufficient too, because each word does not show alone any meaning in an ordinary sentence (except when a sentence is made up of one word). Thus, we have to admit the existence of the *sphoṭa* of the undivided sentence. The former four kinds of *sphoṭa* are merely formed in the imagination (*kālpanika*).

6), 7), 8) The next problem is whether *sphoṭa* is an individual (*vyakti*) or a class (*jāti*). Hence we have to posit the final three kinds of *sphoṭa* of classes. In ancient times people held, it is said, the theory of the class-*sphoṭa* (*jāti-sphoṭa*), while in more recent times they (Nāgeśa and his contemporaries) maintained the theory of the individual-*sphoṭa* (*vyakti-sphoṭa*).[22] However, there is no great difference between them, but merely the difference of whether *sphoṭa* is perceptible in an individual case or not. Bhaṭṭoji-dīkṣita says[23] that Bhartṛhari maintained the theory of class-*sphoṭa*, and this can be accepted also from the explanation given above.

Prof. Brough provides the following explanation of the philosophical meaning of the theory of class-*sphoṭa*:[24]

> Thus the class-*sphoṭa* theory is closely similar to a modern view put forward by Kaplan and Copilowish, who define a sign (including a linguistic sign) as "a class of sign-vehicles all having one and the same law of interpretation." Merely as terminology, this is extraordinarily awkward — Russell, for example, stumbles[25] over this awkwardness and talks of the loudness of a "sign," forgetting for the moment that a "class of sign-vehicles" cannot have loudness. But the authors themselves have not taken their definition seriously, for they discuss the conditions under which a sentential sign may be true. Clearly a class cannot be true or false. Thus they have propounded a *jāti-sphoṭa* theory, but implicitly assume in their discussion a *vyakti-sphoṭa* view. It would seem, in fact, that the *jāti-sphoṭa* view is philosophically unworkable.

Sphoṭa[26] is thus an idea possessing the meaning stated above. Scholars are often perplexed as to how it is to be translated. It is hard for us to identify it with any concepts in Western philosophy of language. It has, because of its metaphysical character, many aspects which are similar to concepts such as logos, idea, etc. But on the other hand we should not overlook that it has some aspects which are different from them. In philosophical thinking about the idea of *sphoṭa* Indian scholars are concerned with the universal problems of symbolism. The idea of *sphoṭa*, however, cannot be fully understood by means of the preconceived ideas of Western philosophy, and for this very reason we see that our thinking about the *sphoṭa* theory will bear much fruit.

Thus, the essence of the word is, according to Bhartṛhari, *sphoṭa*, and it shows its most fundamental form when it appears as a sentence. The sentence, when viewed from formal logic, indicates a "conclusion," and all conclusions are really the manifestation of the absolute, *Brahman*, or, it should be said, *Brahman* itself.

Further, the conclusion is indistinct from reasoning in the actual thinking of a human being. He, therefore, goes on to say that logical reasoning exercised by men is also the self-manifestation of the word-as-the-absolute.

"Reasoning which is based upon human beings is the power of words."

śabdānām eva sā śaktis tarko yaḥ puruṣāśrayaḥ// (*Vākyap.* I,139ab)

Thus, according to him, reasoning itself is the work of the absolute. This idea is extraordinarily remarkable in the history of Indian philosophy. According to the Nyāya-Vaiśeṣika school, which is situated in the main current of Indian logic, reasoning is nothing other than a thinking or demonstration which each individual (*ātman*) performs by using words as a means for expressing ideas. Bhartṛhari's interpretation is quite opposed to this. According to him, reasoning is nothing other than the work of self-manifestation in the word which constitutes the absolute, and each individual is only a locus where the manifestation of the absolute occurs. His idea of logic is thus opposed to that of the Nyāya-Vaiśeṣika school.

Thus, since all logical thinking is, in the final analysis, based upon *Brahman*, it is impossible for *Brahman* to be proved to exist by logical thinking. *Brahman* is the basis on which formal logic can be established in our ordinary life, but it is in itself the absolute being which is beyond formal logic. A Buddhist philosopher, Śāntarakṣita, criticizes him, saying that the principle of "*Brahman* which consists of the word" cannot be proved to exist by our reasoning. But it should be said that he has not properly understood Bhartṛhari's idea of logic, and rather gives an impertinent criticism.

In this manner Bhartṛhari's idea of logic illustrates a special type which appeared in the history of Indian philosophy. However, he only started to develop this idea, and he did not leave any trace of having thought of it more deeply. It is unknown to us, too, whether this current of thought was further developed afterwards. Anyway, we should pay special attention to his idea of logic.

Notes

1) The definition of the 'sentence' is given by K. K. Raja : *Adyar L.B.*, vol.XXVI, 1962, pp.206-210. The cognition of the structural unification of words in a sentence is done by *ākāṅkṣā* (K. K. Raja : *Adyar L.B.*, vol.XXI, 1957, pp.282-295). When two words are put in apposition (*sāmānādhikaraṇya*) it is a universal that limits a substance in the first place, and a quality delimits it later (Kapila Deva Sastri : *Adyar L.B.*, vol.XXVIII, 1964, pp.41-54).

2) On this point we should take note of the following discussion :

"The content of a text is shown in the sense that the letters hold the meanings. The conventional meaning does not exist in the pure word-roots, etc."

śāstrārtha eva varṇānām arthavattve pradarśitaḥ/

dhātvādīnāṃ viśuddhānāṃ laukiko 'rtho na vidyate// (*Vākyap.* II, 212)

According to Puṇyarāja's commentary, the above verse is, it seems to me, connected with the argument in the following passage — *arthavanto varṇā dhātuprātipadika-pratyaya-nipātānām ekavarṇānām arthadarśanād varṇavyatyaye cārthāntaragamanād varṇānupalabdhau cānarthagateḥ anarthakās tu prativarṇam arthānupalabdheḥ* (*Mahābhāṣya*, I, 220).

3) Biardeau's edition reads *padabhede 'pi* for *pade bhede 'pi*.

4) Biardeau's edition reads *na varṇa-* for *tad varṇa-*.

5) *paramatam uktvā svamatam āha* (Puṇyarāja ad *Vākyap.* I, 73).

6) *tāni (padāni) asatyāni vākyam eva satyam ity arthaḥ* (Puṇyarāja ad *Vākyap.* I, 74) ; *tasmān manyāmahe padāny asatyāni, ekam abhinnasvabhāvakam vākyam* (Punyarāja ad *Vākyap.* II, 57).

7) *abudhabodhanāya padavibhāgaḥ kalpita iti* (Puṇyarāja ad *Vākyap.* II, 57).

8) Cf. *Vākyap.* I, 73 : *evaṃ niravayaveṣv api varṇapadavākyeṣu mātrāvibhāgo varṇavibhāgaḥ*

padavibhāgaś ca tat-kṛta eva kālpaniko mithyeti bhāvaḥ (Puṇyarāja ad *Vākyap.* I, 89).

9) *Vākyap.* I, 74.

10) *vaiyākaraṇā varṇavyatiriktasya padasya vākyasya vā vācakatvam icchanti* (Kaiyaṭa ad *Mahābhāṣya*, p.11, NSP).

11) *SDS.* XIII, *l.*117.

12) The classification of four kinds is found also in the *Prātiśākhya* (Max Müller: *ASL.* p.161).

13) *SDS.* XIII, *l.*121.

14) "*Karmapravacanīya*" is a preposition which independently governs the case not included in a compound. For example, in the sentence "*Śākalyasaṃhitām anu prāvarṣat*" (He caused it to rain after the *Śākalyasaṃhitā*), the preposition '*anu*' (after) implicitly means 'after hearing' (*niśamya*), and therefore it shows that there is a causal relationship between the *Śākalyasaṃhitā* and the rainfall (Cf. Helārāja ad *Vākyap.* III, 1, 1. p. 3). In this case, '*anu*' is a *karmapravacanīya*. Here there is a problem as to whether this *karmapravacanīya* is to be recognized as a kind of word or not. Mādhava, opposing its recognition as such, regards it as a prefix which modifies a special verb (*SDS.* XIII, *ll.* 122-5).

15) *apoddhṛtya=kalpanābuddhyā pṛthak padaṃ nikṛṣya* (Helārāja).

16) *SDS.* XIII, *ll.*119-120. It is also quoted in the *Prameyakamalamārtaṇḍa*, p.136.

17) According to Puṇyarāja's commentary, it means that when someone sees trees, etc., he mistakes them for elephants, etc., and that when seeing a rope, etc., he mistakes them for a snake, etc.

18) *akhaṇḍa eva sphoṭalakṣaṇaḥ śabdo vākyam iti darśitam* (Puṇyarāja ad *Vākyap.* II, 1. p. 64). Besides, *sphoṭa*-as-sentence is also admitted by the Yoga school.

19) "It is taught that *sphoṭa* is the class revealed by many individuals. And some suppose that the individuals of this class are the sounds [which reveal *sphoṭa*]."

anekavyaktyabhivyaṅgyā jātiḥ sphoṭa iti smṛtā/
kaiścid vyaktasya evāsya dhvanitvena prakalpitāḥ// (*Vākyap.* I, 94)

Puṇyarāja refers to this verse as *matāntara*. However, since he refers to this verse as *siddhāntisaṃmata* in his comment on the next verse, it is unquestionable that the thought of Bhartṛhari himself is expressed in this verse.

20) The following discussion is based on J. Brough: *Theories of General Linguistics etc.*, p.44f. In addition, Cf. Radhakrishnan: *IPh.*, vol.II, p.106. According to a modern text, the *Vaiyākaraṇabhūṣanasāra*, there are eight kinds of *sphoṭa*, namely, *varṇasphoṭa*, *padasphoṭa*, *vākyasphoṭa*, *akhaṇḍapadasphoṭa*, *akhaṇḍavākyasphoṭa*, *varṇajātisphoṭa*, *padajātisphoṭa*, and *vākyajātisphoṭa*. Among these, it says, "*tatra vākyasphoṭa eva vāstavaḥ, anyeṣāṃ tv avāstavatvam iti vaiyākaraṇānām siddhāntaḥ*" (*Nyāyakośa*).

21) Nāgeśa: *Laghumañjūṣā*, p.5: *tat tad arthavibhāgaṃ śāstramātraviṣayam.*

22) Introduction to V. Krishnamacharya's edition of Nāgeśa's *Sphoṭavāda*, p.24.

23) *Śabdakaustubha*, p.9.

24) John Brough: *Theories of General Linguistics etc.*, p.45.

25) *Mind*, Oct. 1939; discussed by Russel, *Inquiry into Meaning and Truth*, p. 184.

26) The *Mahāvyutpatti* reads *'sphoṭam'*, which is a neuter form. P. Deussen (SV. S. 80) interprets *sphoṭa* as 'Begriff', and is followed by a scholar (e. g. der durch den Buchstabencomplex dem Verständnis vermittelte Begriff. — R. Garbe: *Sāṃkhya und Yoga*, S.50-51). However, since *sphoṭa* is, as already discussed, revealed by sounds, and at the same time manifests the meaning (as it is called *vācaka* or *abhidhāyaka*), we cannot identify *sphoṭa* with 'Begriff' (Cf. Thibaut: *Vedānta-sūtra*, vol.I, p.204, n.). R. Garbe translates it "der Träger der Wortbedeutung" (*Sāṃkhya-Philosophie*, 2. Aufl. S. 152), but this is not satisfactory. Prof. Renou explains, "le substrat phonique du mot, le prototype éternel, imperceptible, indivisible, qui est à la source de l'émission sonore momentanée, et qui, une fois appréhendé par l'esprit, exprime la signification du mot lorsqu'il est manifesté par le son, littéralement lorsqu' il "éclate" (*L'Inde Classique*, tome II, p.80).

SECTION IV. EVOLUTION OF THE WORLD

Like other Vedāntins, Bhartṛhari determined the cause of world evolution to be absolute *Brahman*. The opening verse of the *Vākyapadīya* declares *Brahman* to be "that [source] from which arises world creation." This is exactly the same definition as in the *Brahma-sūtra* I, 1, 2:

"[*Brahman* is] that from which this [world's] origin, etc., arise."

His concept of *Brahman* as world cause is to this extent common to all the Vedāntic schools. Now, what does it mean to say that *Brahman* is the cause of the world? And how does the world evolve? Let us examine his ideas in detail.

Sub-Section 1. The Potential of World Evolution

The statement that *Brahman* has Word as its essence, as previously noted, is well-known to be a basic idea of Bhartṛhari's philosophy. It is expressed as "Word is the source of the world" (*śabdasya jaganmūlatva*).[1]

Bhartṛhari declares in the opening verse of the *Vākyapadīya* as follows:

"That [source] from which arises world creation, *Brahman* which is indestuctible, with word as its nature, without beginning or end, evolves as objects (meaning)."[2]

anādinidhanam brahma śabdatattvaṃ yad akṣaram/
vivartate 'rthabhāvena prakriyā jagato yataḥ// (*Vākyap.* I, 1)

Thus he thought that Word, of the nature of *Brahman*, is the cause of the world. As to the evolution of the world from Word, he adds that it is born of the Word of the *Veda*.

"These phenomena in the beginning evolved from the *Veda*."
chandobhya eva prathamaṃ etad viśvaṃ vyavartata/(*Vākyap.* I, 121cd)

Again the *Veda* is symbolized by the holy syllable *Om*, and Bhartṛhari held further that the holy syllable *Om* is the fundamental source of all words and all meanings, and is the very essence of the highest *Brahman*; he called the holy syllable (*praṇava*) the creator of all worlds (*vidhātā lokānām*, I,10). Not all words are included in Vedic scriptures, and moreover Word in Bhartṛhari's doctrine has not at all the meaning of the words used in those scriptures. Still, inasmuch as orthodox Brahmanic tradition views the ancient *Veda* as absolute, as eternal and imperishable Word, and frequently teaches that the world evolves from the Word of the *Veda*, Bhartṛhari too would have been generally in line with traditional doctrine.

Then in what sense does the world evolve from Word? As has been pointed out, the reality of word is *sphoṭa*, which expresses meaning (*artha*), and he thought that the evolution of the world is the patent manifestation of the relation expressing the meaning of words. So the evolved phenomenal world stands on the mutual relation between the "word" expressing meaning and the "meaning" expressed by it.[3] That word can express meaning is through the potency (*śakti*) of word,[4] and this potency is also that whereby Word, the nature of *Brahman* in its latent state, can make patent the phenomenal world. Thus it can be said that world evolution is founded on a similar basis to that by which the multiplicity of objects in the phenomenal world is manifested by the potencies of words.

These potencies are things existing in *Brahman* the absolute. *Brahman* possesses the totality of these countless potencies. Though in itself it is one alone and without difference, yet there is the capacity to manifest the different forms of the world from these potencies.

"Though declared to be One alone, as [many] potencies repose [in it] it is differentiated [variously]. Though without difference, because of the many potencies it appears just as if it became different."

ekam eva yad āmnātaṃ bhinnaṃ śaktivyapāśrayāt/

apṛthaktve'pi śaktibhyaḥ pṛthaktveneva vartate// (*Vākyap.* I, 2)[5]

As *Brahman* in itself transcends all the different forms, it is one alone, but as it is also the substratum in which rest infinitely many yet mutually distinct potentialities, it manifests in the phenomenal world as if endowed with separate natures. It is also termed "the substratum of all the potentialities."

"Regarded as one alone, *Brahman* can be defined as the essence which is the substance of all the potentialities."

sarvaśaktyātmabhūtatvam ekasyaiveti nirṇayaḥ/ (*Vākyap.* III, 1, 22ab)

So existence which is the nature of *Brahman* is also regarded as comprehending all the different forms.

"Existence, being in union with its own potentialities, is comprehended as all the forms."

sattā svaśaktiyogena sarvarūpa vyavasthitā (*Vākyap.* III, 8, 35 ; p.326)

This potentiality of evolution, as the power to materialize phenomena, is called by analogy "seed" (*bīja*) ; *Brahman* as comprehending the potentiality of the evolution of phenomena is termed "seed of everything" (*sarvabīja*).[6] In *Vijñānavāda*, *Ālaya-vijñāna*, which is the principle of change in all things, is called *sarvabījaka*.[7] Bhartṛhari was probably taking a hint from this when he called *Brahman* the seed of all. Here again the influence of *Vijñānavāda* is recognizable.

Notes

1) Puṇyarāja ad *Vākyap.* I, 119. The notion of Word as the cause of the world should be compared especially with the idea of logos, in the first place in the Gospel of John.

2) Cf. *param iti praṇavātmakam/praṇavo hi kila sarveṣāṃ śabdānāṃ cārthānām prakṛtiḥ sa ca Vedaḥ//* (*Tattvasaṃgrahapañjikā* ad v.128).

3) Kamaraśīla glossing *Vākyap.* Head-verse says: *akṣaram iti/... etenābhidhānarūpeṇa vivarto darśitaḥ/arthabhāvenetyādinā punar abhidheyavivartaḥ/* (*Tattvasaṃgrahapañjikā*, p. 67). Therefore, *vivarta* has to be taken as including these two aspects.

4) He thought of *śakti* even in regard to letters (Cf. *Vākyap.* I, 89). On *śakti* as the prime mover of evolution, there is a parallel in Anaxagoras' *spermata*, but in Bhartṛhari the potency is something spiritual.
5) Tibetan fragment 13 attributed to him (See Part V, Chapter II of this book).
6) *Vākyap.* I, 4.
7) See *Triṃśikāvijñaptimātratā*, Stanza II. Already in the *Saṃdhinirmocanasūtra* (『解深密経』) *ālaya* is called *sarva-bījaka-vijñāna*. On the idea of Word (*śabda*) as seed (*bīja*) comparison needs to be made with the concept of *logoi spermatikoi* in Stoic philosophy.

Sub-Section 2. Material Cause of World Evolution

Thus, as the capacity which is latent in "*Brahman* composed of the word" comes into action and manifests the phenomenal world, the diversity of the phenomenal world is previously contained in "*Brahman* composed of the word" in its latent state. Accordingly, the word in its latent state is, it should be said, the formal cause of the effect of its evolution. However, since words which are, as capacities, added to and stored in *Brahman* do not yet manifest their specific forms, they are all one and the same in their latent state, although, since their effects in evolution reveal the specific characters of each word, they are manifold and diverse. Therefore, when we see *Brahman* which is the sum of capacities, we can say that the one and same *Brahman* to which the adjunct is added is transformed in character from nondifference to difference. If this is the case, *Brahman*-as-the-cause will be considered to be the material cause of the phenomenal world in evolution.

Bhartṛhari compares the relationship between *Brahman* and the world of diversity to pure gold and a person's ornaments, since the former, when divided and worked on, becomes the latter.

> "Just as pure gold, etc., differentiated by their own perishable forms, come to be called by names such as ornaments."
> *suvarṇādi yathā bhinnaṃ svair ākārair apāyibhiḥ/*
> *rucakādyabhidhānānāṃ śuddham evaiti vācyatām//* (*Vākyap*. III, 2, 4 ; p.87)

He also says that just as ornaments such as earrings, etc., when melted down, are restored to their original gold, so too the phenomenal world, when it is destroyed, returns to the highest cause, *Brahman*, and as a result there appears the true (*satya*) form of *Brahman*.

"They say that just as, when a modification is gone, gold in an earring is true, so, when a modification [such as the earth] is gone, the highest material cause is true."[1]

vikārāpagame satyaṃ suvarṇaṃ kuṇḍale yathā/
vikārāpagame satyāṃ tathāhuḥ prakṛtiṃ parām// (*Vākyap*. III, 2, 15 ; p. 93)

In other words, when all things in the world go to ruin, all forms are dissolved into a fusion, and there appears only "*Brahman* consisting of the word," which remains undivided with no mark of diversity.

"The truth which remains at the end [of world dissolution], when a form is dissolved, is permanent and called the word. The true essence of this word is not differentiated."

satyam ākṛtisaṃhāre yad ante vyavatiṣṭhate/
tan nityaṃ śabdavācyaṃ tac chabdatattvaṃ na bhidyate// (*Vākyap*. III, 2, 11 ; p.90)

He also explains in another place that all things devolve into the Being at the time of world dissolution.[2] Since all things thus evolve from and devolve into *Brahman*, he explains:

"It is useless to imagine the difference in the nature of things."

bhāvānām ātmabhedasya kalpanā anarthikā/ (*Vākyap*. III, 1, 22cd)

The essence of all things is, he says, ultimately none other than *Brahman*. Therefore, there is no distinction among them. All things are not different in the absolute sense.[3]

Now it is also said in the Sāṃkhya school that the relationship between the absolute principle and the phenomenal world is taken as the highest material cause[4] and its modified effects. A Buddhist philosopher, Śāntirakṣita, observes that the refutation of the Sāṃkhya doctrine of evolution (*pariṇāmavāda*) is, as it stands, directed also against Bhartṛhari's philosophy.[5] Bhartṛhari, however, does not maintain in his philosophy the duality of *puruṣa* and *prakṛti* as the Sāṃkhya school does. So we must say that there is a clear difference in this point between both theories. Helārāja also defends himself so that he may eliminate any risk of this misunderstanding, saying, "This is not the doctrine of evolution like that of the Sāṃkhya school, but the doctrine of false appearance" (*nedaṃ Sāṃkhyanayavat pariṇāmadarśanam, api tu vivartapakṣaḥ*, ad *Vākyap*. III, 2, 25). I shall consider later whether this assertion is right or not, but now we have to accept that there is a clear difference as well as a close similarity between philosophies of Bhartṛhari and the Sāṃkhya school.

Rather, when we seek in the past a theoretical type well fitted to the simile of evolution from a material cause, we find that it would be Uddālaka's theory on the manifestation of Being.[6] Furthermore, his theory that *Brahman* is regarded as the highest material cause is similar in its theoretical standpoint to the *Brahmasūtra*.[7] Particularly, it attracts our deep interest in that Bhartṛhari adopts the simile of a snake's coiling as in the *Brahmasūtra* in order to explain the relationship between the evolved world and its material cause (*Brahman*).

> "Just as a snake coils itself, or scattered things meet together, so the existing (things) have, some say, the form of birth."
> *yathāheḥ kuṇḍalībhāvo vyagrāṇāṃ vā samagratā/*
> *tathaiva janmarūpatvaṃ satām eke pracakṣate//* (*Vākyap*. III, 7, 105; p. 246).

Since he says here "some say," it is clear that scholars other than Bhartṛhari had used the above simile in their explanation before him. This simile is similar to that of gold and its ornaments, and Helārāja takes the above theory as authority for his own theory (*svasiddhānta*).[8] It would seem, therefore, that Bhartṛhari quotes here the explanation with the above simile. This simile is quoted also in the *Brahma-sūtra*.

> "[The relationship between the highest Self and an individual self is] like a snake and its coils." (*Brahma-sūtra* III, 2, 27)

Commenting upon this, Śaṅkara also says, "Just as there is no distinction in 'snake', while there are distinctions [in a snake's state] like coils, expanded hood, erect posture, etc., so is this case." In other words, a snake whose body is extending, crooking, or coiling is no different as far as it is a 'snake', although it has distinctions since it shows various states (*saṃsthāna*). Likewise, between *Brahman* and an individual self there is a relationship which is neither identical nor different. Since this idea of "neither identical nor different," we must see, belongs to the *Brahma-sūtra*.[9] Bhartṛhari seems to hold the same view as in the *Brahma-sūtra* with regard to the relationship between *Brahman* and the evolved world.

But on the other hand, being influenced by *Vijñānavāda* theory, Bhartṛhari expounds a theory of world evolution which seems to belong to this theory. To wit, he says that oneness (*ekatva*) is the ultimate basis (*kāṣṭhā*), and that it shows its modes in every case.[10]

> "The heaven, the earth, the wind, the sun, the sea, the water, and the directions are parts of the inner organ itself, and they exist as external."[11]
>
> *dyauḥ kṣamāvāyur ādityaḥ sāgarāḥ sarito diśaḥ/*
> *antaḥkaraṇatattvasya bhāgā bahir avasthitāḥ//* (*Vākyap*. III, 7, 41 ; p. 200)

According to Helārāja, the heaven, the earth, the wind, the sun, which is the material cause of all fires and heavenly fire (*sakalatejasāṃ pradhānaṃ divyatejaḥ*), the water, and the sea are all elements, are the life of all the world (*mahābhūtāni sakalajagajjīvitabhūtāni*), and belong to the inner organ. In other words, they are manifesting themselves as inner beings (*antararūpatayā pratibhāsamānam*). "These things are only the reflected images, false appearances, and existing as external" (*ete bhāvāḥ pratibimbakāḥ, ābhāsā bahir avasthitāḥ*). But in the absolute truth (*paramārthe*) he comprehends that "The Word *Brahman*, which is the one, the highest, and consists of being and intelligence, exists as each of the things" (*ekam eva saccinmayaṃ paraṃ śabdabrahma yathātathāvasthitam iti kārikārthaḥ*).

Now, he holds that what is to be called the true self, throwing its image on the external world, reveals the forms (aspects) of the phenomenal world as real and external things, and that since external things are in their true forms none other than manifestations of the absolute intelligence, they do not have any independent existence apart from it.

He clearly adopts here ideas from *Vijñānavāda* theory. On the Buddhist side, too, Asvabhāva, a scholar who upheld *Vijñānavāda* theory, did not overlook its similarity to *Vijñānavāda* theory. He quotes the above verse from Bhartṛhari in his writing, and there he explains, "Therefore, all things manifested as objects are regarded as the mind only, and the objects are not regarded as different from the mind." For this reason, we can see that Asvabhāva himself observed the similarity to *Vijñānavāda* theory in Bhartṛhari's work. A Tibetan translator interprets Bhartṛhari's idea of the inner organ (*antaḥkaraṇa*) as inner knowledge (*naṅ gi śes pa*).[12]

Notes

1) It is also quoted in *SDS*. XIII, *l*.258.
2) *kramarūpasya saṃhāre tat sattvam iti kathyate* (*Vākyap*. III, 1, 35).
3) Helārāja glosses as follows: *advaitadarśanāśrayeṇāpi prāha* (ad *Vākyap*. III, 1, 22).
4) In another place (*Vākyap*. III, 1, 43 ; p.36), too, Bhartṛhari calls the highest *Brahman* '*prakṛti*'.
5) *Tattvasaṃgraha*, v.152.
6) *Chāndogya-upaniṣad*, Chapter VI.
7) *Brahma-sūtra*, I,4,23. Cf. ibid. II, 1, 19-20.
8) Ś. ad *BS*, vol.II, p.232, *l*.9.
9) Ghate: *The Vedānta*, pp.128, 133.
10) Helārāja ad III, 7, 41.
11) About the following discussion, see the source materials listed in Part V, Chapter II of this book.
12) In the Tibetan fragment (6) ascribed to him, it is called "the inner cause of beings" (Part V, Chapter II of this book).

Sub-Section 3. Change in the Phenomenal World

The capacities of the word depending upon *Brahman* become the formal causes and establish the individual forms of the phenomenal world. Moreover, this phenomenal world does not stay unchanged, but always continues to change. Bhartṛhari defines the nature of motion (*kriyā*) as follows:

> "As far as it is expressed as a thing to be accomplished, it is, whether established or unestablished, considered to be 'action' because it has the nature of depending upon the sequence."[1]
>
> *yāvat siddham asiddhaṃ vā sādhyatvenābhidhīyate/*
> *āśritakramarūpatvāt sā kriyeti pratīyate//* (*Vākyap*. III, 8, 1 ; p 298)

Accordingly, time is here considered to be the essential moment of motion. Generally the verb is formed on the basis of such a structure.

Now, he asserts that, although *Brahman* itself is beyond temporal limitation, it is the basis where temporal limitation is formed.

"That one exists limited by time. The part without before and after is indicated by another form [fast and slow, etc.]."

kālavicchedarūpeṇa tadevaikam avasthitam/
sa hy apūrvāparo bhāgaḥ pararūpeṇa lakṣyate// (*Vākyap*. III, 7, 42 ; p. 201)[1]

Time is "that which is the cause which forms restrictions upon the worldly expression" (*lokavyavahāraniyamanimittabhūta*).[2]

Although the conditions through which things change are very complicated, a certain mode in which the change takes place is observed in them. Bhartṛhari assumes that the changes in the phenomenal world can be summed up under the six kinds of changes such as birth, etc. (*janmādayo vikārāḥ ṣaṭ*),[3] and that these six kinds of changes become the capacities, forming the complicated changes in the phenomenal world.

"It (=Being) itself assumes the six states in the [six] modifications of becoming. Thus, it manifests itself gradually by those powers."

saiva (=sattā) bhāvavikāreṣu ṣaḍ avasthāḥ prapadyate/
krameṇa śaktibhis tābhir evaṃ pratyavabhāsate// (*Vākyap*. III, 1, 36)

These "six modifications of becoming" are, as commented by Helārāja, the six forms of transformation in phenomenal things expounded by an ancient philosopher of language, Vārṣyāyaṇi, namely, birth, existence, alteration, growth, decay, and destruction. This theory is quoted in Yāska's *Nirukta*, the oldest work of etymology which is extant.

"According to Vārṣyāyaṇi, there are six modifications of becoming: to be born, to be, to alter, to grow, to decay, and to perish.[4] 'To be born' means the commencement of the former state, but it neither means nor negates the later state. "To be" is the affirmation of the existence of what has already been born. "To alter" is the change of a non-decaying being from [its] true state. "To grow" [means] the fattening of one's own limbs or the increase of things which are associated [with one's self]. For example, he grows [prospers] by means of victory or he grows with his body. "To decay" means the opposite. "To perish" means the commencement of the later state. It neither means nor negates the former state. Hence, he always said other modifications of becoming are only the [further] modifications of these [six]."

It is said that Yāska was a man of far older times than Pāṇini,[5] and Vārṣyāyaṇi was a man of a more ancient period than Yāska. On this account we vaguely assume this to be the case, but he was a man of about the 5th century BC. Patañjali also quotes the theory of the Venerable (*Bhagavān*) Vārṣyāyaṇi in his *Mahābhāṣya*.[6] Accordingly the theory of the six forms of transformation had been maintained as an authoritative theory in tradition for about one thousand years until Bhartṛhari among the grammarians. Following this traditional theory, Bhartṛhari went a step further to consider the basis on which these six forms were established, and perceived them as the manifestation of Being, which is pure and unmixed.

Now, the Being which is their basis is nothing but *Brahman*. The sacred text (*Tait. Up*. III, 1) says that *Brahman* is the basis upon which birth, continuance and destruction are established, and the *Brahma-sūtra* (I,1,2) adopts this theory as a definition of *Brahman*. On account of this, it became later the basic teaching of the Vedānta school. Thus, according to this school, the forms of a thing are only of three kinds, namely, birth, continuance, and destruction. Thus, it seems that the above theory at first sight is inconsistent with the theory of Vārṣyāyaṇi. Bhartṛhari does not mention anything about this contradiction. The academic world of those times, however, could not neglect this problem. A disputant against Śaṅkara says as follows:

> "It is suspected that, if [the six modifications of becoming] such as origination and subsistence which were enumerated by Yāska be taken [here], the origination of the world from the root cause, its subsistence, and its destruction could not be understood in the *Brahmasūtra* I, 1, 2, since those [six modifications of becoming] are possible [only] during the period of subsistence [of the world]."[7]

To this criticism Śaṅkara replies as follows:

> "Do not doubt it; the origination from *Brahman*, the subsistence in it, and the dissolution into it are understood [here]."

And he also explains:

> "Since other modifications of becoming as well are included in origination, subsistence, and dissolution, [only] the three are referred

to in the *Sūtra*."

Thus, Śaṅkara eventually rejected the theory of six forms expounded by Vārṣyāyaṇi and Bhartṛhari as incomplete, and limited the number of transformations to three, saying that the fundamental forms of all the transformations are arising, continuance and perishing. In Buddhist philosophy, too, this problem had been discussed among scholars of the Hīnayāna since ancient times in terms of the problem of the form of the conditioned (*saṃskṛtalakṣaṇa*).[8] These three forms expounded by Śaṅkara are literally consistent with the theory of three forms of the conditioned. On the other hand, the disputant of Śaṅkara followed the theory of six forms expounded by Vārṣyāyaṇi, and moreover believed that this theory was applicable only to the transformation in the *kalpa* of continuation of the world. Therefore in this respect it seems that his theory is identical with that of Bhartṛhari.

Thus, according to Bhartṛhari, the capacities of the six forms such as birth bring about all the transformations in the phenomenal world, and these capacities of six forms are in fact at work on the basis of a capacity called time (*kāla*).

> "The six forms of transformation such as birth, though they are undestructible parts (capacities) of that (*Brahman*) and the sources of various things, depend upon the capacity of time."
>
> *avyāhatāḥ* (=*nityāḥ*) *kalā* (=*śaktayaḥ*) *yasya* (*brahmaṇaḥ*) *kālaśaktim* (=*kālākhyam svātantryam*) *upāśritāḥ*/
> *janmādayo vikārāḥ* (=*pariṇāmāḥ*) *ṣaṭ bhāvabhedasya yonayaḥ*// (*Vākyap*. I, 3)

All the capacities depending upon *Brahman* are ultimately subordinate to time when they manifest themselves in existence. Although *Brahman* is itself beyond time, it takes time as the opportunity for world evolution. Just relying upon the capacity called time, *Brahman*, the totality of all capacities, is capable of evolving the various forms of the world.[9] This capacity called time,[10] which is characteristic of the sequence (*krama*) expressed by priority and posteriority (*paurvāparya*), etc., does not exist apart from *Brahman*. The adherents of other schools (*tīrthāḥ*) interpret time as what is different (*pravibhakta*=*padārthāntara*) from *Brahman*, but this is wrong, and he asserts that because of the particularity of the capacity called time, it only looks as if it were so.[11]

We find here an interesting feature of his theory of time. Time as expounded by him is neither that which is regarded as an independent entity nor time diagramed into space. Nor is it time whose essential contents are lost and which is abstractly separated from the experiential world which is changing in transmigration. But it is in fact the driving force of world evolution on the basis of *Brahman* itself. Time is in itself merely a capacity of *Brahman*, the principle of the world, but merely because of it all the capacities are capable of manifesting themselves and evolving the world. In other words, time is equal in its character to other capacities in the sense that time is a capacity, but it is the capacity which is the principle making all other capacities into capacities themselves. In his philosophy *Brahman* is itself the material cause, and the word, the composing element, is characteristic of the formal cause, while time is seen to be the efficient cause.

It is quite unusual for a scholar of the Vedānta school to take time as having such implications. For example, in Śaṅkara's philosophy time is one of the conditions forming the phenomenal world, and at the same time a concept going together with space (*deśa*) and causality (*nimitta*).[12] Śaṅkara considered rather the lord (*īśvara*) or, in a strict sense, *māyā* (illusion) of the lord as the efficient or instrumental cause. This is said to be in accord with time expounded by Bhartṛhari. In the sense that he regarded time as important, his philosophy is rather close to the theory of those who adhered to Time (*kālavādin*).

But on the other hand the theory of evolution through nescience is mentioned in other places. A verse which is ascribed to Bhartṛhari says as follows:

> "Just as one who is afflicted with the *timira* eye sickness falsely imagines the pure sky as full of various kinds of objects [such as blue, yellow, etc.], so this immortal and changeless *Brahman*, entering, as it were, into the impure state, through nescience (*avidyā*), manifests itself in differentiated forms."[13] (A Buddhist philosopher, Dignāga, quotes this verse in order to explain almost the same thing with regard to consciousness.)[14]

The *Vākyapadīya* also says in the same way:

> "Although a place is [differently] imagined because of the difference

in attributes of those which are connected [with the space], the generality of the space exists in these places."[15]

saṃyogidharmabhedena deśe ca parikalpite/
teṣu deśeṣu sāmānyam ākāśasyāpi vidyate// (*Vākyap.* III, 1, 15 ; p.20)

Further he says in another place:

"Although reality is not what is falsely imagined, it assumes the [various] forms which are imagined."

vikalpa-rūpaṃ bhajate tattvam evāvikalpitam/ (*Vākyap.* III, 2, 8)

This idea is, it would seem, equivalent to the idea that manifestation is due to ignorance. In this case, he says, that which reveals the capacities as objective things is ignorance (*avidyā*). To take an example, although space itself is pure, one who suffers from blindness in his eyes considers that space is of various colors. Likewise, although *Brahman* is in itself beyond distinction, it manifests individual forms of various kinds by the power of ignorance. Then, is the principle of ignorance a part of or different from *Brahman*? Does ignorance exist as absolute intelligence? Or does it exist as an individual self? — These difficult questions have been discussed extensively in later Vedānta and other schools. But in this case we find only a few explanations of ignorance. Therefore, it is quite unclear what the detailed contents of ignorance are for him.

The idea that manifestation is due to ignorance was thereafter explained as the essence of the doctrines of the Non-duality school (*Advaita-vādin*). Anyway, the simile of defilement in space had often been employed in the same school.

"Just as the sky appears to be soiled with dirt to the ignorant, so *Ātman* also appears to be defiled with dirt to the non-enlightened." (*Māṇḍūkya Kārikā*, III, 8)

Śaṅkara also says in the same way:

"Just as the dirt on the surface of the earth and the like appear to exist in the sky, so the nature of non-*Brahman* (*abrahmatva*) and non-identity with all (*asarvatva*) are superimposed (*adhyāropita*) [upon *Brahman*] through nescience."[16]

Moreover, he who interpreted the manifestation of the phenomenal world in this way was allied to a scholar of the *Vijñānavāda* school, Dignāga.[17]

But, according to the *Vākyapadīya*, Bhartṛhari, although he recognizes ignorance (*avidyā*), does not give any detailed explanation, nor does he explain directly that the manifestation of the phenomenal world is due to the force of ignorance. Rather he imagines that the principle of the manifestation of the world is time (*kāla*) as a special power (*śakti*) of *Brahman*. And he does not hold that the phenomenal world is unreal, but admits that it retains a rather weakened reality. Contrary to this, it is said in the above verse that the phenomenal world is manifested by the power of ignorance. So it accords with the theory of non-duality (*advaitin*) among the Vedānta schools. For this reason, Sureśvara quotes the above verse almost verbatim.[18] The simile that space which is in itself pure is seen as if it were polluted is, as already pointed out, mentioned in the *Māṇḍūkya-kārikā*, III, 8 as well as in Śaṅkara's writings, and particularly in this regard his theory is almost in accordance with the theory of the Non-duality school. The idea that "*Brahman* is the word" is also consistent with the ideas of Śaṅkara.[19] Anyway we here find that the fundamental ideas of Śaṅkara had already been established about three hundred years before.

Now, accepting these different views concerning world manifestation, the grammarians of later ages came in the last analysis to conclude as follows: — *Brahman* called the word is possessed of innumerable powers (*śakti*). Among them ignorance (*avidyā*) as well as time (*kāla*) are the most important. The former manifests the various forms by the strength of covering the essence which is the one and only without distinction, while the latter has the power of reflecting by order the eternal parts (*kalā*) existing in *Brahman* called the word. Both of these powers are closely related to each other.[20] — We may regard this view as a synthesis of both theories mentioned above, and if both theories stated above derived from Bhartṛhari alone, then it would follow that Bhartṛhari expounded two theories which were more or less different with regard to world evolution. (In this regard the *Brahma-sūtra* is the same.)

Notes

1) I have already examined the original text and its Tibetan translation in Part V, Chapter II of this book.

2) Helārāja ad *l.c.* (p.200).

3) *Vākyap*. I, 3. The same work, III, 8, 26 (p.320), refers to "*ṣaṭsu bhāvavikāreṣu.*"

4) *Nirukta* I, 2 (p.29), ed. by L. Sarup — *ṣaḍbhāvavikārā bhavantīti Vārṣyāyaṇiḥ jāyate 'sti vipariṇamate vardhate 'pakṣīyate vinaśyatīti.*

5) Winternitz : *HIL*. vol.I, pp.69-70.

6) *Mahābhāṣya* under *Vārttika* 11 (ad Pāṇini I, 3, 1). Further, his name appears in the *Mahābhāṣya* ad *Pāṇini* IV, 1, 155 (p.263) too.

7) Ś. ad *BS*. I, 1, 2.

8) The *Tseng-i a-han ching*, vol. 12 (*Taisho* vol.2, p.607c) says that there are three in the property (the form of the conditioned) which forms conditioned things as conditioned things : arising, changing, and perishing. The *Pa chien-tu lun*, vol. 3 (*Taisho*. vol.26, p. 780c) also says the same. The Sarvāstivāda school lists the four kinds : birth, continuance, changing and destruction. They are expounded in the *Po-sha lun* (*Mahāvibhāṣā*), vol. 39, the *Shun-cheng-li lun* (*Nyāyānusāra*) vol.23, the *Chü-she lun* (*Abhidharma-kośa*, tr. by Hsüan-tsang), vol. 5, etc. The *Chung-lun* , Chapter 7 criticizes the listing of *utpāda*, *sthiti*, and *bhaṅga*.

9) *kā sā kālaśaktir, ata āha/ekasya sarvabījasya yasya ceyam anekadhā/bhoktṛbhoktavyarūpeṇa bhogarūpeṇa ca sthitiḥ//* (*Vākyap*. I, 4).

10) Further, the problem of grammatical tense is discussed in detail in the *Vākyapadīya*, chap. 3, *kālasamuddeśa*.

11) Cf. *Vākyap*. III,1,37 and Helārāja's commentary on it.

12) P. Deussen : *SV*. S.341.

13) Cf. Part V, Chapter II of this book.

14) *ibid*.

15) *ibid*.

16) Ś. ad *Bṛhad. Up*. p.152, *l*. 24. For a detailed explanation, see Part V, Chapter II of this book, n. 18.

17) *Trikālaparīkṣā*, vv.31-32.

18) See Part V, Chapter II of this book. Sureśvara as well as the commentator Ānandajñāna regard these two verses as of their own school.

19) Cf. Ś. ad *BS*. I, 3, 28.

20) Gopinath Kaviraj : "The Doctrine of Pratibhā in Indian Philosophy," *ABhI*, vol.V, p.12.

Sub-Section 4. The Cause of the World and Its Relation to the Phenomenal World

Bhartṛhari uses the verb "to evolve" (*vivartate*) to describe how the phenomenal world evolves from *Brahman*. But he does not employ the noun "*vivarta*" (false appearance, false manifestation), and the verb "*vivartate*" does not yet mean "to falsely appear" as in the later Advaita school. It cannot be said that he particularly emphasizes that the phenomenal world appears as an illusion which is opposed to the absolute.

First, I shall collect and examine instances of this word in the *Vākyapadīya*.

> "The beginningless and endless, the word-truth, the imperishable *Brahman*, from which the creation of the world proceeds, evolves as things (meanings)."[1]
>
> *anādinidhanaṃ brahma śabdatattvaṃ yad akṣaram/*
> *vivartate 'rthebhāvena prakriyā jagato yataḥ//* (*Vākyap*. I, 1)
>
> "Through the sound evolved from causes, that [word] is perceived."
> *kāraṇebhyo vivṛttene dhvaninā so 'nugṛhyate/* (*Vākyap*. I, 47cd)

Further, he introduces an explanation of the formation of the word expounded by a scholar of a certain school.

> "Having become the substratum of the principle, the inner organ (*manas*), and having been affected by the latter's property, the word is evolved by the very energy."
>
> *antaḥkaraṇatattvasya vāyur āśrayatāṃ gataḥ/*
> *taddharmeṇa samāviṣṭas tejasaiva vivartate//* (*Vākyap*. I, 115)

A verb "*vivartate*" in the instances mentioned above does not directly have the meaning that it becomes an illusory or false entity. For this reason, I tentatively translate it "to evolve." It is synonymous with "transformation"[2] (*pariṇāma*), a philosophical term since ancient times. He distinctly uses the word "*pariṇāma*." (In this point his theory is similar to the theory of the *Vijñānavāda* school.)

> "The scholars of sacred texts know that this [universe] is the transformation of the word. In the beginning all this was evolved from the *Vedas*."[3]
>
> *śabdasya pariṇāmo 'yam ity āmnāyavido viduḥ/*
> *chandobhya eva prathamam etad viśvaṃ vyavartata//* (*Vākyap*. I, 121)

Thus Bhartṛhari holds that both the verb "*vivartate*" and the noun "*pariṇāma*" mean the action of evolving (turning around) and are completely synonymous. He, like scholars of the later Advaita school, does not take them as different. Not only that, but Śaṅkara himself, the founder of the Advaita school, considers both to be synonymous. Therefore, it seems that scholars of the early Vedānta school did not generally admit any distinction between them.[4]

Furthermore the above can be proved by another means. The *Tattvasaṃgraha* refers to a criticism of Bhartṛhari's theory. According to this work, Śāntirakṣita as well as Kamalaśīla undoubtedly recognized Bhartṛhari as an expounder of the evolution doctrine. Furthermore, in the Tibetan translation of this text, *vivarta* and *pariṇāma* are translated by the same Tibetan word.[5] Thus we might guess that these scholars of a Buddhist school took these two words as synonymous.

Originally the word "evolving" (*pariṇāma*) was interpreted in two ways. Firstly, if A takes B as its essence, A is called the evolution of B. In this case, B shows a potential state, while A displays a patent state. Secondly, if A is a change of B, or if A arises from B, A is also called the evolution of B. In the first case, the cause and the effect are simultaneous, while in the second case, the cause is temporarily prior to the effect, and there is a development or a change between them. The philosophers of that time clearly noticed that they might define it as evolving (*pariṇāma*) in both cases. On the contrary, a Buddhist philosopher, Kamalaśīla, demonstrates that "evolving" cannot be proved to signify either of these two cases.[6] As is known from the statement that "three entities turn around and their cause and effect are simultaneous," the evolution (*pariṇāma*) of consciousness expounded by scholars of the *Vijñānavāda* school is included in the first case. But it seems that the original meaning of the word "*pariṇāma*" takes the idea of temporal sequence as its momentum. Śāntirakṣita asserts that the relation of evolving (*pariṇāma*) cannot be formed between two things which exist simultaneously without temporal sequence.[7]

Now, if we examine the cases where Bhartṛhari uses the word "*vivartate*," we find that, as shown in the examples cited above, he uses it in both senses. That being so, Bhartṛhari uses the word "*vivartate*," but only in the sense of "evolving" (*pariṇāma*). Thus we conclude that he did not expound the doctrine of illusory appearance (*vivartavāda*). According to him, world evolution does not mean that a being arises from another being, nor does it mean that a being arises from non-being.[8] It merely means that *Brahman* moves, as the same being, from the single, indiscriminate to the complicated, various, individual forms, and the complicated, various, individual forms are reduced to the single, indiscriminate form,[9] but it expresses an idea which is opposed to "destruction" (*saṃhāra*). To use Bhartṛhari's words, world evolution means that the "single, highest *Brahman*" (*ekaṃ paraṃ brahma*)[10] is itself "divided in various ways" (*bahudhā pravibhajyate*) by many "actions of creation" (*prakriyā*).[11] Thus, the prefix "*vi*" of *vivarta* is interpreted as signifying "divided in various ways." Therefore, world evolution does not, as Śaṅkara maintained, mean that lower *Brahman* (*aparaṃ Brahma*) evolves. The standpoints of these two philosophers are plainly different. Nor do we find in Bhartṛhari, like in the later Advaita school, the view that the matters of the phenomenal world are unreal. He emphasizes that experiences in our actual life should be esteemed. He rather[12] presents a criticism of Mahāyāna Buddhism, particularly the *Vijñānavāda* school, and he was, we might say, strongly inclined to realism.

However, we can see that he also had something to do with the Advaita theory of Śaṅkara's school. *Brahman* which is regarded as the basis of world evolution is *Brahman* restricted by adjuncts and possessed of powers, but it is not the absolutely negative *Brahman* in the absolute sense. Thus in this point of view he is similar to Śaṅkara who maintains that the world evolves from *Brahman* restricted by ignorance (*avidyā*). Accordingly, as the Advaita school flourished in later times, they deemed this point to be important, and there arose a strong tendency for his philosophy to be interpreted as the doctrine of illusory appearance (*vivartavāda*). A commentator of the *Vākyapadīya*, Puṇyarāja,[13] the grammarian Kaiyaṭa, and the author of the *Sarvadarśanasaṃgraha*, Mādhava,[14] also regard Bhartṛhari as the advocator of the doctrine of illusory appearance. But on the other hand it seems that there disappeared a school in which he was regarded as an expounder of the evolution doctrine.

However, among the verses ascribed to him there are some which clearly express the doctrine of illusory appearance (*vivartavāda*). Therefore, the excellent scholar Vācaspatimiśra knew well that there were two theories for one who expounds *Brahman* as the word (*śabdabrahmavādin*).[15]

Notes

1) A Tibetan fragment (15) ascribed to him. Cf. Part V, Chapter II of this book.

2) Further with regard to the word "*pariṇāma*," see *Vākyap*. I, 111 ; II, 187 ; 7,a,47(p.203), etc. Kamalaśīla, summarizing Bhartṛhari's philosophy, also says as follows : *yac chabdamayam brahma tasyāyaṃ rūpādir bhāvagrāmaḥ* pariṇāma *iti* (ad *Tattva-saṃgraha*, v. 128, p. 67).

3) A Tibetan fragment (14) ascribed to him. Cf. Part V, Chapter II of this book.

4) *triguṇaṃ pradhānam mṛdvad acetanaṃ cetanasya puruṣasyārthaṃ sādhayituṃ svabhāvenaiva vicitreṇa vikārātmanā vivartata iti* (Ś. ad *BS*. II, 2, 1, vol.I, p.514, *l*.5). In this case the word "*vivartate*" definitely means *pariṇāma*.

5) *Tattvasaṃgraha*, *Śabdabrahmaparīkṣā*.

6) *Tattvasaṃgrahapañjikā* ad v.129.

7) *Tattvasaṃgraha*, v.139.

8) Cf. present chapter, section I.

9) *Vākyap*. III, 2, 11 (p. 90).

10) *Vākyap*. I, 22.

11) It is a characteristic of the *Vākyapadīya* to use the word "*prakriyā*" in the sense of creating action (Cf. *Vākyap*. I, 1). This cannot be seen generally in Indian works (Cf. *PW*. s. v. *prakriyā*).

12) Especially see *Vākyap*. II, 287-298 ; III, 3,25 ; III, 8, 13 (present work, Part VII, Chapter II, Section III, Sub-Section 3).

13) For example, see the comment on *Vākyap*. I, 1.

14) Cf. *SDS*. XIV, *ll*.1-2.

15) He says in the *Nyāya-kaṇikā*, "*ye punar abhinnasya śabdabrahmaṇo vivartaṃ vā pariṇāmam vārtham ācakṣate...*" (based on G. Jhā's Commemoration Volume, *Śrīhārāṇa Candraśāstrī, śabdabrahmavāda*, p.91).

Sub-Section 5. The Problem of Contradiction

Now, since *Brahman* is composed of innumerable words and forms the world through its evolution, and since words exist innumerably and contradict each other, we here come to a noteworthy conclusion. That is to say, all the contradictions in the phenomenal world are based upon the absolute. The highest one which contains the words is itself filled with contradictions. For this very reason *Brahman* "which is not different from words" is "expressed by all words."[1] *Brahman* might be expressed by statements which are quite contradictory, saying that it exists as well as it does not exist, it is identical as well as it is different, it is united as well as it is separated, and it changes as well as it does not change (*Vākyap*. III,2,13). The evolution of contradictory forms in the phenomenal world just means that the contradiction which exists within *Brahman* itself comes out from its latent into its operative state.

> "The highest *Ātman* is the beloved, the hated, a speaker, the expressed or a motive. Just as contradictory forms are [perceived] to belong to a single mind in a dream, so contradictory forms such as birth, etc., are perceived in the truth which is without birth, permanent, and free from the relation of prior and posterior."
>
> *ātmā paraḥ priyo dveṣyo vaktā vācyaṃ prayojanam / viruddhāni yathaikasya svapne rūpāṇi cetasaḥ // ajanmani tathā nitye paurvāparyavivarjite / tattve janmādirūpatvaṃ viruddham upalabhyate //* (*Vakyap*. III, 2, 17-18; p.94)

He also says that various oppositions such as separation and connection, being and non-being, continuity and cessation, truth and untruth, etc., really "arise from the truth of *Ātman*."[2] In one place he also says that the truth is not different from the untruth (*na tattvātattvayor bhedaḥ*, *Vākyap*. III, 2, 7).

Generally and abstractly speaking, the common feature of these relations of contradiction contained by *Brahman* is seen in the relation between A and non-A. Ontologically speaking, it is the relation between being and non-being. This primary relation of contradiction, which is the basis of the relations of contradiction, really forms the essence of *Brahman*, which is the basis of world evolution. Thus the manifestation of various forms can be established.

"Therefore the one and only permanent thing which is of the nature of being and non-being, when expressed by word, appears in various forms by the distinctions of powers."[31]

tasmāc chaktivibhāgena nityaḥ sadasadātmakaḥ/

eko 'rthaḥ śabdavācyatve bahurūpaḥ prakāśate// (*Vākyap*. III, 3, 85; p. 138)

The principle which is characteristic of being and non-being is, according to the philosophy of the later Advaita school, *māyā* or ignorance. It is not *Brahman*. Therefore, there is a striking difference between them in this regard. That is to say, Bhartṛhari is led to say that the absolute itself contains within it contradiction as a momentum because he seeks the principle of world evolution within the absolute itself, while in the later Advaita school it is held that *Brahman* is beyond contradiction and that *māyā* or ignorance contains contradictions because those who maintain the doctrine of illusory appearance seek the principle of establishing the formation of the phenomenal world within the absolute of the negative state. If he had regarded the absolute as the absolutely inactive being, he would have reached the standpoint of the Advaita school. But since he took the absolute as active, he recognized the affirmative meaning of contradiction.

It was an unprecedented fact in the history of the philosophy of traditional Brahmanism that the assertion that the absolute itself contained contradictions within it was thus made in a clear way. Other scholars of the Vedānta school merely emphasize that the absolute of the negative state is opposed to the absolute itself. In this manner we can see a special feature of Bhartṛhari's philosophy.

Notes

1) That (=*Brahman* which is the highest cause) is the referent of all words, and these words are not different from that (=*Brahman*). Further, because there is no difference between them, there is a relation between them [that the words denote *Brahman* as the object], just as between the two different *ātmans*.

vidyā sā sarvaśabdānāṃ śabdāś ca na pṛthak tataḥ/

apṛthaktve ca sambandhas tayor nānātmanor iva/ (*Vākyap*. III, 2, 16; p.93)

This verse is quoted in *Sarvadarśanasaṃgraha* XIII, *ll*.262-3, where the first *vidyā* is *vācyā*. Helārāja also makes a comment on this point, saying, *sarvaśabdavācyatvaṃ tasyaiva (brahmaṇaḥ) nigamayitum āha*. Therefore, I follow the reading in *SDS*. The word *sā* refers, as Cowell mentions in a note, to *parā prakṛti* in the previous verse. *nānātmanor* is, according to *SDS*, *jīvātmanor*, but it is often the case in *Vākyap*. that the word *ātman* is used in the plural. Therefore, there would be no problem in leaving the dual as it stands.

2) Cf. Tibetan fragment (5) ascribed to Bhartṛhari (See Part V, Chapter II of this book).

3) *SDS*. XIII, *ll*.252-253 also quotes almost the same sentence.

SECTION V. THE INDIVIDUAL SELF

In Indian philosophy, particularly in Vedānta philosophy, it is generally common that the individual self is expressed by words such as *jīva*, *jīvātman*, *vijñānātman*, and *śārīra*. But Bhartṛhari does not use these words in particular. Did he, then, not consider the problem of the individual self? Seeing that it is a social activity to study, support and teach grammar, it is inconceivable that he did not think of the individual self, which is the subject of practicing this. Simply without using technical terms or conceptions such as *jīvātman*, *vijñānātman*, *śārīra*, etc., of Vedānta philosophy in general, he addressed the problem of the individual self in a different way. Since he often refers to *ātman* in general, I shall inquire into his notion of the individual self with reference to his statements about *ātman*.

Sub-Section 1. *Ātman*

In Bhartṛhari's as well as Vedānta philosophy in general, *Brahman* is identical with *ātman*[1] or the highest self (*paramātman*,[2] *ātmā paraḥ*[3]). The Being (*sattā*) which is the essence of *Brahman* is called the mighty self (*mahān ātmā*).[4] As *Ātman* is the self in its original sense, it is unable to create and destroy by its own power or the power of any others. On the contrary, it is the basis upon which creation and destruction are established.

> "The abandonment of the *Ātman*-truth does not take place from another. And the *ātman*-truth is neither [newly] established from its own nor from another."
>
> *ātmatattvaparityāgaḥ parato nopapadyate/*

ātmatattvan tu parutaḥ svato vā nopakalpate// (*Vākyap*. III, 3, 68; p.131)

This idea of *ātman* is identical with Śaṅkara's. According to Śaṅkara, *Ātman* is the own-form (*svarūpa*),[5] it is neither to be taken nor to be abandoned[6] (*aheyānupādeya*) : we cannot negate *ātman*, since it is the *ātman* itself of the person who negates it.[7]

Since this idea of *ātman* is generally common to the Vedānta school, there should be no need to explain it in detail. But it is characteristic of his idea of *ātman* that he defines the essence of *ātman* as the word. According to him, *Brahman* is the word, and so *ātman* is regarded as identical with the word. *Ātman* which is the word is mentioned in the *Ṛg-veda*.

"And the word which exists as *ātman* inside a speaker is, [the ancient sages] say, 'the great cow' with which the communion is desired."

api prayoktur ātmānam śabdam antaravasthitam/
prāhur mahāntam ṛṣabhaṃ yena sāyujyam iṣyate//(*Vākyap*. I, 132)

The interpretation that 'the cow as the great god' mentioned in the *Ṛg-veda* (IV,58,33) is the word was first presented by Patañjali.[8] Bhartṛhari, furthermore, regards it as identical with *ātman*. We see, accordingly, that he does not regard the word merely as a method or an instrument used by men, but as the essence of man, and that he is conscious of its subjective meaning. According to the commonsense view of worldlings, each individual hears as a perceiver the word through the ears, and the word is an objective entity. However, according to Bhartṛhari, this conventional view is false. In fact, the word which exists inside a perceiver makes our hearing possible.

"Just as the fire lighting in a piece of wood is the cause of another light, so the word existing in the intellect (*buddhi*) is individually the cause of hearing."

araṇisthaṃ yathā jyotiḥ prakāśāntarakāraṇam/
tadvac chabdo 'pi buddhisthaḥ śrutīnāṃ kāraṇaṃ pṛthak//(*Vākyap*. I, 46)

ātman as the word like this is no longer a mere perceiver, nor an imagined substance as a result of self-reflection, but is the comprehensive absolute on the basis of which the subject and the object are established. According to him, when *ātman* evolves, its subjective aspect still remains as the word (*śabda*), while its objective, external aspect becomes the meaning (*artha*).

"The word and the meaning are the two different parts of the one and only *Ātman*, and exist inseparably."

ekasyaivātmano bhedau śabdārthāv apṛthak sthitau/(*Vākyap*. II, 31cd)

"Just as the own-form [of knowledge] and that of the known are seen in knowledge, so the own-form [of the word] and the meaning are revealed in the word."

ātmarūpaṃ yathā jñāne jñeyarūpam ca dṛśyate/
artharūpaṃ tathā śabde ṣvarūpam ca prakāśate// (*Vākyap*. I, 50)

Ātman is the word, and the word is ultimately subjective in itself, but the word casts a reflection of its own upon the meaning. Although the word itself is beyond the opposition between subject and object, it is brought to stand against the objective meaning once it accomplishes self-evolution. That being so, the subject as well as the object are nothing other than the manifestation of the Absolute. If we know this structure of evolution, we come to understand without any contradiction that the word and the meaning are two different parts of *ātman*. Bhartṛhari clearly explains this metaphysical structure as follows:

"This word-truth which is the *Ātman* of the inner mora is always the manifester (i.e. word) and the manifested (i.e. meaning), the effect (= meaning) and the cause (=word)."

prakāśakaprakāśyatvaṃ kāryakāraṇarūpatā/
antarmātrātmanas tasya śabdatattvasya sarvadā// *Vākyap*. II, 32)

Seeing that Bhartṛhari thus compares the relation between the word itself (=*ātman*) and the meaning to the revealed and a thing to be revealed, he seems, as commented by Puṇyarāja, to have considered *ātman* to be 'made of light' (*jyotīrūpa*). It seems in this way that he follows the idea appearing in the old *Upaniṣads*, which say that *ātman* is light. By using the simile of light, Bhartṛhari often explains the principle that the word indicates the meaning.

"Just as light has two powers, that of being the perceiver and of being perceived, so all words have these two, which are, as it were, separate."

grāhyatvaṃ grāhakatvaṃ ca dve śaktī tejaso yathā/
tathaiva sarvaśabdānām ete pṛthag iva sthite[9] //(*Vākyap*. I, 55)

Light is the principle by which cognition is possible, and thus it is the cause (*kāraṇa*) of cognition. At the same time, light is the object of cognition. Considering that these two opposite characteristics can be applied similarly to the word, the basis of cognition, he seems to explain it in such a way.

We earlier introduced Bhartṛhari's idea that the word indicates the meaning. However, this merely means that he has just explained it that way in accordance with the views of the grammarians as well as Indian philosophers in general. According to his metaphysical theory of the word, the fact is that the word as the absolute indicates the meaning[10] when it has entered into the object (*viṣayatvam āpanna*). In other words, the word which is beyond the opposition between subject and object evolves itself, and it becomes in one aspect the word as the subjective *ātman*, and is formed in another aspect into the word as an objective entity, and then for the first time the latter comes to indicate the meaning. Therefore he says:

> "No meaning is conveyed by the words which have not become the objects. If not perceived, those words do not manifest the meanings by their mere existence."
>
> *viṣayatvam anāpannaiḥ śabdair nārthaḥ pratīyate/*
>
> *na sattayaiva te 'rthānām agṛhītāḥ prakāśakāḥ//* (*Vākyap.*I, 56)

Thus he claims that the word as the object is indispensable for perceiving the meaning.

Now, since the word is *ātman*, there arises a specific problem of philosophy. When the word is *ātman*, or the self which is the absolute entity, how can the diversity of the word be formed? If the words which retain their individual being different from each other are really temporary existents, then the word cannot be called *ātman*. Rather the word in general or 'wordness' (*śabdatva*) would be *ātman*. If so, the words would be deprived of selfhood (*ātman*hood). Bhartṛhari, however, holds in his philosophy that there must be many *ātmans* in accordance with many words since he has to insist on the idea that the word is *ātman* in order to avoid falling into the above conclusion. Bhartṛhari uses the plural form in the expression 'the true nature of *ātman*' (*ātmatattva*).[11] He also says, "*ātmans* connected to (adjuncts)..."[12] It is quite rare in the writings of the Vedānta school for *ātman* to be expressed in its plural form, and it is worth noticing. But even in Bhartṛhari's philosophy *Brahman,* which is the absolute and single truth, is after all *ātman* and cannot be expressed in the plural form. Therefore theoretically, in the final analysis, Bhartṛhari recognizes two kinds of *ātman,* namely, *ātman* which is the absolute (the highest self) and *ātman* which is the word. The former is *Brahman* in the absolute sense, while the latter is *Brahman* connected to adjuncts. Bhartṛhari does not clearly mention the distinction between these two kinds of *ātman,* but he himself persistently maintains that *Brahman* is the word, or that *ātman* is the word. Thus, it seems to me that he did not want to show clearly the reason stated above. Nevertheless, we are forced to draw such a conclusion when we investigate and analyze his theory logically.

The fact that he thus admits two kinds of *ātman* corresponds to the fact that Vedānta philosophers generally recognize the highest and the individual self (*jīvatman*). Bhartṛhari's idea of the highest self is common to other Vedānta philosophers, while his idea of '*ātman* as the word' is largely different in content from the 'individual self'. For example, I could compare his idea with Śaṅkara's. The individual self expounded by Śaṅkara — and further, it might be said, by all philosophers of the Advaita school — has been tentatively formed by adding the adjuncts (*upādhi*) such as body and sense-organs to the highest self and is void of its own-being. Then, what meaning does the word have with regard to the individual self? The word is the object of a sense-organ, the ear, and it is also transmitted to others by a behavioral organ, speech (*vāc*, language faculty). This is all the meaning that it has. (The Sāṃkhya school also holds the same view.) Śaṅkara regarded the word as a formal cause at the time of world creation, but he never called it *ātman,* and he considered that it was not related to the individual self. Thus, he did not attach great importance to the question of the word. He exclusively regarded the establishment of the individual self as important in philosophical problems. But Bhartṛhari, on the other hand, hardly discussed the problem of the individual self. What, then, did he think of the existence of an individual, especially of the activity of an individual self in the system of cognition and behavior? I shall consider this issue in the following.

Notes

1) *Vākyap*. III, 2, 1.
2) *Vākyap*. I, 133.
3) *Vākyap*. III, 2, 17.
4) *Vākyap*. III, 1, 34.
5) Ś. ad *BS*. vol.1, p.100, *l*.5. Cf. vol.1, p.107, *l*.13.
6) Ś. ad *BS*. vol.1, p.87, *l*.10. Cf. vol.1, p.599, *l*.1; *GK*.III, 38.
7) Ś. ad *BS*. vol.1, p.75, *l*.7 ff.; vol.1, p.76.
8) *Mahābhāṣya*, p.3, *l*.15 ff. *SDS*. XIII, *l*.98 ff. Cf. present chapter, Section III, Sub-Section I.
9) The edition has *pṛthagavasthite*. However, I here correct it to *pṛthag iva sthite* on the basis of v.1 and Puṇyarāja.
10) The meaning of *pratibhā* is discussed by Dr. Pandey (All India Sanskrit Sahitya Sammelan, Golden Jubilee Celebrations, Presidential Address: Sahitya Parishad, by Kanti Candra Pandey, Lucknow University). According to him, *pratibhā* is psychologically "the meaning of a sentence, which determines the action and behaviour of the being in which it arises." Viewed from a metaphysical standpoint, all the world that we experience is nothing but *pratibhā* (op. cit. p.9).
11) *Vākyap*. III, 1, 21. In addition, *Vākyap*. III, 2, 16 says, "for two different *ātmans*."
12) *Vākyap*. III, 1, 20.

Sub-Section 2. Human Activities

Bhartṛhari emphasizes, as a grammarian, the social function of language. If someone is completely excluded from society, he will not possess a language. Language presupposes human existences which are dependent on each other in their establishment, and a language is meaningful as a medium for making human activities social. Men can transmit their wills and understand each other by means of words. Bhartṛhari clearly comprehends this nature of language.

> "Just as the intellect (*buddhi*) of the speaker turns towards the words before [he speaks them], so the determination of the hearers also is directed towards those words."
>
> *yathā prayoktuḥ prāg buddhiḥ śabdeṣv eva pravartate/*
> *vyavasāyo grahītṝṇāṃ evaṃ teṣv eva jāyate//* (*Vākyap*. I, 53)

To wit, he says that when words function as words they have already been understood.

As a grammarian, he discussed the problem of the word and inquired into philosophical problems by way of the social nature of the word. On account of this, although it was quite rare for a scholar of the early Vedānta school, he proceeds, in his view of man, to the problem of social existence.

According to him, the world where our daily life operates, presenting three forms, namely, the enjoyer (*bhoktṛ*), the thing to be enjoyed (*bhoktavya*) and enjoyment (*bhoga*), is established to manifest in various ways.[1] Judging from enjoyment in ordinary life when an enjoyer aims at the object, the words necessarily come to his mind. Whatever the idea conceived in his mind, it is always characterized by the word.

> "There is no idea in the world which does not take the form of the word. All knowledge appears as if it were penetrated by the word."[2]
> *na so 'sti pratyayo loke yaḥ śabdānugamād ṛte/*
> *anuviddham iva jñānaṃ sarvaṃ śabdena bhāsate//*(*Vākyap*. I, 124)

Strictly speaking, all things presented to our minds are penetrated by the aspects (*ākāra*) of the word.[3]

The assertion that all things are composed of the word, and that our sensory contents are characterized by the word have given a peculiar feeling to Indian philosophers in general. Śāntirakṣita criticizes Bhartṛhari's philosophy, saying, "As for the things of our daily experience like blue, yellow, etc., we do not see the fact that they are characterized by the word. Hence it cannot be proved that all things are penetrated by the aspects of the word."[4] The expression 'characterized by the word' is indeed strange, but Bhartṛhari is probably arguing that all things as well as our ideas contain meaning in some way, and for this very reason the word which indicates the meaning constructs the essence of our existence.

Then, how can the philosophical meaning of the word be known? According to the doctrine of the expounders of the word-*Brahman* (*śabdabrahmavādin*) reported by Kamalaśīla, it is proved directly by our perception that all things are accompanied by aspects of the word.[5] It means, to explain it in more detail, that there is no room for doubt since we are able to know it from the sense perception which is self-cognizance (*svasaṃvedanapratyakṣataḥ*), i. e. from the direct experience of our own selves.[6]

Against this doctrine Śāntirakṣita and Kamalaśīla give their refutation: When we see a blue thing, etc., with our eyes, and at the same time think of another thing with the mind, we do not perceive 'blue' consciously even though we have a feeling of the blue in our minds. In other words, although we have the feeling of color, we do not hold the consciousness of the word. Therefore, it cannot be said that we directly perceive the word in a clear way with regard to all things. And even if the word were directly perceived in a clear way, this would not be proof for claiming that the word is regarded as the absolute.[7]

If we confine the expression 'it is to be known from our direct perception' only to meaning that 'it is known from our sensitive feeling', we will certainly fall into the mistake pointed out by Kamalaśīla. Bhartṛhari, however, seems to have used it in the sense that it is directly proved by our daily experience.[8] Accordingly it should be seen in the assertion of Bhartṛhari that our daily life is established with the self-evident presupposition that 'whatever is experienced in our daily life is characterized by being expressed by the word'.

Now, Bhartṛhari analyses and elucidates our consciousness on the basis of a fundamental standpoint like this. He thus says that the basic structure of consciousness in which our ideas are characterized by the word is permanent and unchangeable, and that we are able to hold our perceptions in this structure.

> "If the eternal nature that 'knowledge has the word as its essence' were to disappear, the light [of knowledge] would not shine. The eternal nature is the indicator [of various meanings]."[9]
>
> *vāgrūpatā ced u(t)krāmed avabodhasya śāśvatī/*
>
> *na prakāśaḥ prakāśeta sā hi pratyavamarśinī//* (*Vākyap*. I, 125)

Although consciousness itself has no content, it reflects the object like a mirror. Therefore, it is also said that "the idea (*jñāna*) is identical with the individual form (i. e. the object)", or that "the idea is dependent upon the thing to be known (the object: *jñeya*)."[10] For this very reason he considers that all of our ideas are also determined to cover with discrimination (*sarvavijñānānāṃ savikalpatā*).[11] Then according to him, since it is the word which constitutes the essence of the object in consciousness, our cognition is based on the word which is the objective being, and the subjective being of our cognition is meaningful only for reflecting it. We do not find in his thought the idealistic assertion that the perceiver presents the idea by the power of his imagination.

We can see here that Bhartṛhari, like other Vedānta scholars,[12] takes the position of the realistic theory of knowledge. However in his epistemology it is not intended, as the sensualists (*Lokāyata*) or Nyāya-Vaiśeṣika school, etc., maintain, that the external thing which exists independently from a perceiver is copied as it stands to be the object. In his philosophy cognition[13] means perceiving the forms of the word which penetrate the things in close touch with the things themselves. It is the direct perception of the universal form which is shown concretely in each individual thing.

Now, since the word or the form of the word expounded by him is universal being, if he defines cognition merely as perceiving its form, then a question will arise. How can an individual thing which exists solely as one, i. e. which cannot be replaced by any other thing, be known? According to him, all is one, and the differences between things should be avoided. How, then, is it possible that we recognize (*pratyabhijñā*) an individual thing just as it is in actual life? He might as well have asked these questions, but in fact he did not touch on them at all. It seems to me that while he was aware that an individual thing came into being for the reason that various forms were realized by some qualified materials, he persistently emphasized solely the direct perception of the form of the word without touching on the problem of recognizing an individual thing. We can see here one of the characteristics of his theory of knowledge.

Now, if our knowledge thus comes from reflecting the form of the word, then what is the knower who reflects it? Indian people of ancient times considered that the organ of cognition is thought (*manas*), intelligence (*buddhi*), mind (*citta*), etc. Its faculty and structure are explained in various ways by schools and scholars who present us with different arguments. It is, however, common to all schools except Buddhist ones that *ātman* is regarded as the supreme soul which exists in the depths of such an organ. Moreover, the various schools and theories appeared because there arose differences in interpreting what this *ātman* was. Bhartṛhari defines this *ātman* as the word, and because of this Bhartṛhari has been placed in a remarkable position in the history of Indian philosophy.

According to him, while the object of cognition is the form of the word, the self (*ātman*) or the subject of cognition is the word. Thus, the word expounded by him is possessed of a subjective character. This has already been stated. In this manner, since the word is *ātman* and ultimately the subject of cognition, it is the cognition that the word, which is subjective, reflects itself onto the word, which is the object. He explains this structure by using a simile.

> "Just as an image of another solid body [like a human being, etc.] is drawn on cloth as the object of knowledge, so is the triad in the case of the word."
>
> *yathaikabuddhiviṣayā*[14] *mūrtir ākriyate paṭe/*
> *mūrtyantarasya tritayam evaṃ śabde 'pi dṛśyate//* (*Vākyap*. I, 52.)

Just as the image of a human being is projected upon cloth or a wall, so too does the word as a subject, projecting itself on an object, perceive the word as an object, and the place where the cognition takes place, namely, cloth, a wall, etc., is just the mind (*buddhi*) or the inner organ (*antaḥkaraṇa*).[15] Generally philosophers imagine that the mind works independently. On the other hand, Bhartṛhari says that the mind is, in the absolute sense, only the place where the absolute projects itself and that active movement is not perceived there. Cognition is that the objectified word is just perceived by the original self (*śabdasya svagrāhyatva*).[16] Thus cognition is, in the last analysis, only the movement of the self-evolution whereby the word as the absolute is divided into the subject and the object, forming a relative opposition. In this case, the philosophical notion generally accepted by Indian scholars that the subject of cognition is the individual self[17] is completely disregarded. Regarding the word as absolute, he steps towards an idea closely linked to a kind of non-self theory in a different sense from Buddhism.

The idea concerning the problem of cognition which is regarded as characteristic of his philosophy is also seen to be concerned with the problem of action. Our action (*pravṛtti*) is necessarily performed for a purpose (*prayojana*). If it does not possess a purpose, the intended action will not be performed, the grammarians say. The purpose of this action is, according to Bhartṛhari, none other than the word. He says that the activities of us individuals, bodily beings, are ultimately governed by the word.

> "It is the word that prompts the corporeal self (*dehin*) to desire actual activities. If it is gone, this is near to being unconscious like a piece of wood or a wall."
>
> *arthakriyāsu vāk sarvā samīhayati dehinaḥ/*
> *tadutkrāntau visaṃjño 'yaṃ dṛśyate kāṣṭhakuḍyavat//* (*Vākyap*. I, 128)

The individual self, as generally viewed in philosophy, neither makes an image, nor acts on purpose, and the word causes the desire and action. This is what he means. Since the essential form of a thing makes us create the desires for conduct when we begin to act with the desire for a thing, he ought to maintain that the word causes our actions, giving special attention to the structure of our conduct.

Thus the word becomes for him the essence of action. He also says that our activity depends upon the word at the time of birth, and that such a character is innate.

> "The first movement of the [vocal] organs, the rending of the breath upward, and the striking of the places of articulation are not possible without the residual impression of the word."
>
> *ādyaḥ karaṇavinyāsaḥ prāṇasyordhvaṃ samīraṇam/*
> *sthānānām abhighātaś ca na vinā śabdabhāvanām//* (*Vākyap*. I, 123)

Immediately after birth, a man governed by the potentiality of the word begins to act,[18] and for this reason the word is the essential nature of man.[19]

If we could find in the behaviour of a baby the simplest and blindly or instinctively performed conduct of human beings, then conversely we can assume that the technique is the systematized or defined form of man's conduct on purpose. He further proceeds to the problem of technique.

> "Every mode of action in the world depends upon the word. Given in advance [in the past life] residual impression [by the word], even a child realizes this mode of action."[20]
>
> *itikartavyatā loke sarvā śabdavyapāśrayā/*
> *yāṃ pūrvāhitasaṃskāro bālo 'pi pratipadyate//* (*Vākyap*. I, 122)

To wit, the transmission as well as the maintenance of technique is all dependent upon the word, and the word is the fundamental and indispensable condition for all productive activities. In particular, reflection has a very important meaning: — "If one gives in advance instruction based upon the word, even a foolish man realizes this method." It is considered generally in the oriental arts that it is important that intuition or direct perception be based upon the accumulation of personal experiences. However, they make little effort to place the experiences generally on a social basis by arranging and systematizing them in a rational manner. If a technical skill does not pass through reflection by means of the word, it will be only an expert's skill. On the contrary, if it is rationalized by the word, it will be a universal one, and even a foolish man could learn it. The underdevelopment of technique generally in the East (— and the underdevelopment of the social economy that derives from this) is largely due to a lack of the above reflection. Bhartṛhari rightly refers to this weak point. As a matter of fact, he himself might not be clearly conscious of it; but we can discover here an important, meaningful assertion from our present standpoint. (Among the Eastern thinkers of the past times, how many of them have pointed out this weakness?)

> "It [=the word] is the foundation of all sciences, arts and crafts. All things [such as a bottle, etc.] are analyzed by the strength of the word at the time of their accomplishment."
>
> *sā sarvavidyā śilpānāṃ kalānāṃ copabandhanī/*
> *tadvaśād abhiniṣpattau*[21] *sarvaṃ vastu vibhajyate//* (*Vākyap*. I, 126)

To take an example, when a potter wants to make a pot, he holds an idea of the word 'pot', i. e. a form (*śabda*=*ākāra*), and therefore a pot, etc., have already existed in the mind of the potter apart from another before they are actually made. Therefore, the production which is accomplished by an art is, he held, only a movement whereby the potential or latent word is materialized into the world of actual experience. Śaṅkara was also aware of this problem. As for the problem of world creation, he gives a simile in explaining the process whereby the lord creates the world by taking the word as the formal cause, saying that one who gets to work with the desire of accomplishing an object (meaning) first of all imagines the word which signifies it, and then undertakes it. This fact is directly proved to all of us.[22]

Furthermore, he explains that when the creator (*Prajāpati*) created the world the Vedic words first appeared to his mind, and then he created the things of the world which correspond to them. Nevertheless, it is regarded as important that Bhartṛhari had already been aware of this structure of production before Śaṅkara. However, Bhartṛhari does not discuss more deeply the problem of the arts.

Anyway, he persistently emphasizes that daily life in this world is based upon the word. "The word is the foundation of the world,"[23] he explains.

Thus according to his theory of conduct, conduct is the movement of proceeding and identifying itself by which *ātman*-as-the-word proceeds to the form-as-the-word. The common view in Indian schools that an individual self (possessed of thinking and sense faculties) begins to move towards objects other than the self is in this case completely disregarded. According to Bhartṛhari, conduct as well as cognition is only an aspect of the word, the absolute in its self-evolution. And we cannot, in his philosophy, recognize his intention for explaining that conduct arises from the correlation between a self and another or from the counteraction between a subjective self and the objective surroundings. What we conventionally or philosophically call counteraction, i. e. the identification and separation between an individual and another self, according to him, only reveals the movement of various forms by way of the evolution of the word, the absolute.

In this manner, Bhartṛhari strongly maintains that the word as the formal cause restrains us in the actualities of human life. But if we examine the process through which he reached such a conclusion, we find that the tradition of the sacred language 'Sanskrit' had been firmly held among the intellectual communities of India and that there strongly remained a social environment and custom of holding the word in esteem. Encouraged by this tendency, he undertook such a philosophical investigation so that he might prove that this social tendency was reasonable. In other words, he was as a grammarian led to that conclusion because of his social and personal circumstances, but he did not enter the study of grammar through a philosophical investigation of the word. Thus, 'Bhartṛhari as a philosopher' was born from 'Bhartṛhari as a grammarian'. It is one of the reasons for emphasizing the importance of the study of grammar that he explains metaphysically the word playing as the formal cause an important role in actual life. For this reason, he exerts himself even to the extent of presenting other reasons in order to emphasize the importance of the study of grammar or the word. He also attaches importance to the magical power contained in the word.

> "Just as color and others [=color, taste, smell, touch] are seen to have fixed powers with regard to each thing, so too the words [of magical spells] are seen to be [effective] for dispelling poisons."
> *rūpādayo yathā dṛṣṭāḥ pratyarthaṃ yataśaktayaḥ/*
> *śabdās tathaiva dṛśyante viṣāpaharaṇādiṣu//*(*Vākyap*. I, 140)

In the arguments of someone who wants to base himself upon the social meaning of the word, the magical beliefs held by primitive people for some thousands of years go side by side with philosophical investigations which are hard to understand.

Now, life in the conventional world which has thus been established is, in the absolute sense, merely an imagined evolution. The fact that the primary form or the word which builds conventional life has meaning is only 'imagination based upon superimposition' (*adhyāropakalpanā*).[24] In other words, it means that people provisionally superimpose a class of word on a class of meaning. The words exist only as signifying the distinguished forms, which are unreal.[25] So the meaning (thing, *artha*), the word (*śabda*), and the notion (knowledge, *jñāna*) which is formed between them are, it might be said, all perverted (*viparyaya*). Furthermore, the thing to be seen (*dṛśya*), the seer (*draṣṭṛ*) and the seeing (*darśaṇa*) which is formed between them are all falsely imagined (*vikalpita*),[26] and do not exist in the absolute sense. Thus his view of all conventional activities is in this sense somewhat similar to that of Nāgārjuna of an earlier age and the *Māṇḍūkya-kārikā* of a later age.

He thus recognizes that conventional activities are unreal in the absolute sense. But considering that conventional activities were to the utmost seen to be real in a conventional sense, he maintained that the distinction between the real and the unreal (*satyāsatyavibhāga*)[27] is to be formed in a conventional sense. It is just with this intention that he rejects one after another all the similes which are often used in *Vijñānavāda* philosophy. For this reason, when Bhartṛhari and the grammarians of his school speak of both the real and the unreal in a conventional sense, these are different in meaning from the real and the unreal in the absolute sense. All specific or distinguished forms are in the absolute sense unreal, and then it can be said, as stated above, that the nearer a class comes to universal being, the more real it becomes, while the nearer it comes to the specific, the more unreal it becomes. In a conventional sense, the principle and the fact which are universally approved are real, while the errors which occur under the limitations of personal and specific circumstances such as injured sense-organs, incomplete reasoning, etc., are unreal. In the former case, the reverse of the notion 'real' (*satya*) is only lack of reality (*a-satya*);[28] in the latter it is said to be error (*viparīta*).[29] In the later Advaita school it is said that there are three kinds of truth, truth in appearance (*prātibhāsikasatya*), truth in a conventional sense (*vyāvahārikasatya*), and truth in the absolute sense (*pāramārthika-* or *tāttvika-satya*).[30] It is explained that the former two, as compared with the last, are unreal. It can also be said that the germ which evolved into such a definite theory of truth had already existed in Bhartṛhari's mind.

Notes

1) *Vākyap*. I, 4.

2) This verse is well known as one of Bhartṛhari's sayings and is quoted in many writings of later ages: *Tattvasaṃgrahapañjikā* ad v.128; *Nyāyabinduṭīkāṭippaṇī*, p.20; *Nyāyamañjarī*, p.80; *Prameyakamalamārtaṇḍa*, p.11b.

3) *Tattvasaṃgrahapañjikā* ad v.128, p.68, *l*.7ff.

4) *Tattvasaṃgraha*, v.143.

5) *Tattvasaṃgrahapañjikā* ad v.128.

6) *Tattvasaṃgrahapañjikā* ad v.147.

7) *Tattvasaṃgrahapañjikā* ad vv.146, 147.

8) Cf. *Vākyap*. I, 124.

9) As for the interpretation of this verse, see Part VII, Chapter II, Section I, Sub-Section 2.

10) *bhedānukāro jñānasya vācaś copaplavo dhruvaḥ/kramopasṛṣṭarūpāyā jñānaṃ jñeyavyapāśrayam//* (*Vākyap*. I, 87).

11) *Tattvasaṃgrahapañjikā* ad v.135.

12) Śabarasvāmin, Bhartṛprapañca, Śaṅkara, etc., maintain the realist theory of knowledge (Cf. Part VII, Chapter III, Section III of this book).

13) The cognition discussed here is knowledge of the daily life of experience, i.e. discriminating knowledge. The cognition of the nature of the Absolute (non-discriminative knowledge) will be explained later. *sā hi vāgrūpatā hi pratyavamarśaḥ savikalpakajñānam* (Puṇyarāja ad *Vākyap*. I, 125).

14) The original text has *ekabuddhiviṣayā*, but it is not clear. Here I translate it on the basis of the commentary of Puṇyarāja : *mūrtir...ekabuddhiviṣayatvam prāptā.*

15) Based upon the commentary of Puṇyarāja.

16) Puṇyarāja ad *Vākyap*. I, 52.

17) In Nyāya-Vaiśeṣika philosophy too, which is a different system, *ātman* signifies the individual self as the essence of personal existence.

18) A similar discussion is found in the *Nyāya-sūtra* (III, 1, 18-21). "[There is the *ātman* which continues to exist after death,] because a newly-born [baby] also understands joy, fear, and grief on account of being connected with the remembrance of what he has repeatedly experienced in the former life." (18) "After leaving [the former body] at death, [*ātman* enters into another body and exists] because [there is the fact that a baby in this world] desires for the breasts owing to [the remembrance] that he had meals repeatedly [in the former life]." (21) Moreover, the same discussion is also seen in the theory of recollection expounded by Plato (*Menon* 81 ; *Phaedo* 75).

19) Why is it that Patañjali mentioned '*atha śabdānuśāsanam*', but not '*atha vyākaraṇam*' at the beginning of the *Mahābhāṣya*? Discussing this problem, Mādhava introduces the following discussion in the chapter on Pāṇini's theory in the *Sarvadarśanasaṃgraha* (XIII, *ll*.45-48). "Objection : The activity [toward Vedic study] will be effected merely at the command of the obligation of learning —— The *Veda* with six limbs should be studied as *dharma* without any special end (Cf. '*niṣkāraṇa*' ; Abhyankar interprets it as *dṛṣṭaphalābhisaṃdhirahito nitya ity arthaḥ*). Answer : You should not think so, because, even though there be such an injunction, it would not be possible for the students to act [toward Vedic study] if no end [of 'the exposition concerning words'] is mentioned which teaches that it [=the grammar] is a limb of the *Veda*."

20) *loka-vyavahāra* — Punyarāja.

21) Biardeau's edition reads *-niṣpannaṃ* for *-niṣpattau*.

22) Ś. ad *BS*. vol.1, p.299. Cf. the idea of Demiourgos in Plato.

23) *śabdā lokanibandhanāḥ* (*lokavyavahāranimittabhūtāḥ* — Puṇyarāja) (*Vākyap*. II, 299). Mādhava considered that the word 'word' can also mean the extension of the world. *iha śabdaśabdena prapañco vivakṣitaḥ* (*SDS*. XIII, *l*.109).

24) *Vākyap*. III, 1, 6.

25) *Vākyap*. III, 3, 59.

26) *Vākyap*. III, 3, 70.
27) Puṇyarāja ad *Vākyap*. II, 288.
28) Also *atattva*. Cf. *Vākyap* III, 2, 7 ff.
29) Cf. *Vākyap*. II, 431.
30) Manilal N. Dvivedi: *The Māṇḍūkyopanishad*, Preface, p.xxi; *SDS*. XVI, *l*.656 ff.

SECTION VI. PRACTICE

Sub-Section 1. Esteem of Regulations in the Sacred Texts

Since Bhartṛhari was a scholar of the authorized school of Brahmanism, he expounded a theory of practice based upon the standpoint of this school. According to him, the ultimate standard for discerning good from evil is the sacred texts. Whatever in human behavior is conformable to the regulations of the sacred texts is 'good', while that which is not is 'evil.' Whatever class a man belongs to, he should follow unconditionally the regulations of the sacred texts.

> "'This is good (virtuous).' 'This is evil.' — In these two expressions the purpose of the text is one and the same to human beings up to *caṇḍālas* (men of the lowest tribes)."
>
> *idaṃ puṇyam idaṃ pāpam ity etasmin padadvaye/*
> *ā caṇḍālaṃ manuṣyāṇāṃ samaṃ śāstraprayojanam//* (*Vākyap*. I, 40)

Thus, he considers that the praise and reproach of various things stated in the texts seem to show the regulation of conduct, saying, "It should be done" or "It should not be done."[1] This regulation, which is the standard of conduct, is generally called *dharma* among Indian people. He regards this *dharma* as a human principle which is permanently unchangeable. Manu, etc., who are said to have written the law texts to provide for *dharma*, are considered by Indians to be historical persons who once lived in this world. As the law text is a human writing, it did not appear in this world for some periods like other writings, but on the other hand, since the expounded *dharma* is in itself the eternal and unchangeable principle, a righteous and excellent man always acts in accordance with the regulation of *dharma* even without the law text.

"Even if the doctrines perish and there be no other authors [to compose it], people [=the wise men[2]] do not abandon the *dharma* expounded in the *śrutis* and the *smṛtis*."

astaṃ yāteṣu vādeṣu kartṛṣv anyeṣv asatv api/

śrutismṛtigataṃ dharmaṃ loko na vyativartate// (*Vākyap*. I, 135)

It reminds us of the Buddhist doctrine which says, "*Dharmatā* is permanent, whether the *Buddha* appears or not." He emphasizes the eternity or permanency of the ever-lasting *dharma*. This idea of ethics is, it would seem, common to authorized Brahmanism in general. It is not specific to Bhartṛhari. Rather, the special character of his theory of practice might be seen in the fact that he was a grammarian of the authorized school of Brahmanism. How did he, who was a grammarian and the founder of the metaphysics of the word, develop a specific doctrine of practice? We shall examine this in the following.

Notes

1) *Vākyap*. II, 325.

2) *loka*. Puṇyarāja replaces it with the word '*śiṣṭāḥ*' in his commentary.

Sub-Section 2. The Correct Use of Language

Bhartṛhari, who deplored deeply of the situation of his time when the correct use of language had fallen into confusion, held that he was obliged to protect the correct use of the word.

"By the violation [of their obligation] some men speak like women, and some women talk like men. On account of that, their obligation is again taught."

kecit pumāṃso bhāṣante strīvat puṃvac ca yoṣitaḥ/

vyabhicāre svadhamo 'pi punas tenopadiśyate//(*Vākyap*. III, 14, 580; p. 719)

Probably it is an extremely difficult task for us to speak the correct language. Even a grammarian did not speak following the regulations of grammar in those days.

"A grammarian does not always speak like a grammarian. [He sometimes uses vulgar expressions.] Therefore, even a grammarian is told [by one who knows the correct use of the word] to speak like a grammarian."[1]

vaiyākaraṇavad brūte na vaiyākaraṇas sadā/
vaiyākaraṇavad brūṣvety ataḥ so 'py abhidhīyate// (*Vākyap*. III, 14. 579; p.719)

In this way it is shown that there was great confusion of language in those days and that the regulations of the sacred language called Sanskrit had been almost forgotten among people, while the vernacular languages had become influential in social life.

Classical Sanskrit had become fixed as a language since Pāṇini (c. 350 B.C.) composed its grammar, Kātyāyana (BC. 250 c.) revised it, and Patañjali (c. 150 B.C.) commented on it in detail. Afterwards it was prevented from being unrestrictedly transmitted since only those who were in the upper class used it in their conversation and composed poems and literature in it. Thus, the most valuable products of Indian culture in the form of words were mostly written in Sanskrit. Moreover, while the Sanskrit language was limited in its use to the ruling classes in India, the vernacular languages derived from it were used among most people, and some prose and poetry written in vernacular languages were transmitted. Particularly the Buddhists and the Jains engaged in their mission work by using many vernacular languages. Grammatical works on the vernacular languages have also been transmitted. So long as a vernacular language is used only among the lower classes of society, and so long as it is despised and neglected as a vulgar language, there does not arise any problem. However, when its influence became culturally great and when those speaking in the vernacular in opposition to the use of Sanskrit came to insist upon the importance of their language, the followers of authorized Brahmanism who had taken Sanskrit as the one and only scriptural language were brought to feel a great sense of threat. They had to reject the vernacular languages and insist on the superiority of Sanskrit so that they might protect their own cultural tradition. Bhartṛhari, who had set himself up as a restorer of traditional grammar, concentrated his efforts on this very point.

Originally the attitude of the Brahmins who considered that their own language Sanskrit was the one and only accomplished and genuine language went back to the age of the *Ṛg-Veda*. For them, Sanskrit in the Vedic scriptures was genuine and accomplished (*saṃskṛta*) "like the grain passed through a sieve" (*ṚV*. X,71,2). They had never accepted other languages as true or real. Although this attitude ran through the scholars of later authorized Brahmanism, Bhartṛhari, who had been influenced particularly by the social and cultural circumstances of his day, similarly emphasized this point, and delivered a strong attack on a vernacular language, *Apabhraṃśa* ('corrupted language').[2]

He mentions the fact that generally people of his day spoke only in vernacular languages, and that Sanskrit was a classical language which was hard to understand.

> "For those corrupted forms of the word (*apabhraṃśa*), which have been established through conventional habit among vicious speakers, the correct form does not convey the meaning directly."
>
> *pāraṃparyād (=abhyāsāt) apabhraṃśā nirguṇeṣv abhidhātṛṣu/*
> *prasiddhim āgatā ye tu teṣāṃ sādhur avācakaḥ//* (*Vākyap*. I, 155)

According to Puṇyarāja, 'vulgar tongues' means 'those who are women, *śūdras*, the immature, etc., or idle persons.' Therefore, their number probably amounted to seventy percent of all Indians of his day. When they heard their vernacular language, they immediately understood its meaning; when they heard Sanskrit, they did not directly grasp its meaning but just guessed it after interpreting it in accordance with their vernacular language. For them, Sanskrit was a forgotten language. In these circumstances Bhartṛhari declared that however influential the preponderance of vernacular languages was, it was nothing but a corruption, and he deplored it:

> "The divine language [Sanskrit] has been mixed up [with the corrupted forms] by the incapable speakers."
>
> *daivī vāg vyavakīrṇeyam aśaktair abhidhātṛbhiḥ/* (*Vākyap*. I, 156a)

For him, like for other scholars of the authorized school of Brahmanism, Sanskrit was 'the sacred word' (the language which belongs to the gods, *daivī vāk*),[3] while all other languages were just corrupt forms derived from it. Puṇyarāja[4] admired the ancient ages as ideal for the reason that in those days the sacred word remained genuine without being mixed with corrupt languages.

But on the other hand, there were quite a few scholars from ancient times who had maintained that the word was impermanent because it was incessantly changing, and there were many different languages among nations. Bhartṛhari, however, charges this argument to be false, saying,

"But those who consider [the word] impermanent are wrong in their view with regard to this discussion."

anityadarśinām tv asmin vāde buddhiviparyayaḥ/ (*Vākyap*. I, 156cd)

However, no one denies the fact that language is incessantly changing, and it is after all a dream to imagine a time when the sacred word, it is fancied, had remained genuine. Whatever ancient time we might go back to in the history of the Sanskrit language, we cannot find a period when there is no influence from the vernacular languages. Then why did he regard Sanskrit as sacred or right, and why did he consider other languages to be corrupt? He first charges the vernacular languages as follows. For instance, 'cow' is called '*gauḥ*' in Sanskrit, while in a vernacular language it is called '*goṇī*'. So he considers that the word '*goṇī*' is the word '*gauḥ*' become corrupt without assuming its accomplished form.

"They think of such a word (i. e. '*goṇī*') as a corrupted form, as denoting a particular meaning, that is devoid of perfection and is [uttered] when wanting to say 'cow' (*gauḥ*)."

śabdas saṃskārahīno yo gaur iti prayuyukṣite/
tam apabhraṃśam icchanti viśiṣṭārthaniveśinam//(*Vākyap*. I, 149)

The words '*go*' (cow) and '*aśva*' (horse) are called '*goṇī*' and '*asva*' in a vernacular language, but it does not mean that a vernacular language is the proper way of saying it. It merely indicates that the meaning of the vernacular word can be understood for the first time after restoring it to Sanskrit. However in this case, we should not consider that the words pronounced '*goṇī*' and '*asva*' cannot exist in Sanskrit. In this language the word '*goṇī*' means a particular receptacle and the word '*asva*' a man deprived of his properties.[5] In this way these words indicate the meaning of different things. If they use these words in the meanings of 'cow' and 'horse', then these words, it must be said, become corrupt.

"In the same way, [if] an incorrect form of a word is used when the correct form should be used, it indicates a certain meaning different from the correct one."[6]

evaṃ sādhau prayoktavye 'paśabdaḥ prayujyate/
tena sādhuvyavahitaḥ kaścid artho 'bhidhīyate// (*Vākyap*. I, 154)

"The words '*asva*', '*goṇī*', etc., are correct when they mean other things (i. e. a man deprived of his properties, receptacle, etc.). In all cases correctness is determined through different causes."[7)]

asvagoṇyādayaḥ śabdāḥ sādhavo viṣayāntare/
nimittabhedāt sarvatra sādhutvaṃ tu vyavasthitam// (*Vākyap*. I, 150)

Generally speaking, if a word uttered with the wish to indicate the meaning of A shows the meaning of B, then it cannot be said that it indicates the meaning.[8] Accordingly, when a word is uttered in order to indicate the meaning of A, the hearer has to restore it to a Sanskrit word. In this case he is just like one who understands the words uttered by a child.

"These [incorrect words] are the causes for producing an understanding of the correct words by inference. By identifying themselves [with the correct words], they, as it were, manifest the meaning of the [correct] words."

te sādhuṣv anumānena pratyayotpattihetavaḥ/
tādātmyam upagamyeva śabdārthasya prakāśakāḥ// (*Vākyap*. I, 151)

"When a child who is learning a word pronounces indistinctly the words '*amba, amba*', those who know his speech understand the meaning clearly thereby."[9]

ambāmbeti yadā bālaḥ śikṣyamāṇo 'pabhāṣate/
avyaktaṃ tadvidāṃ tena vyakte bhavati niścayaḥ// (*Vākyap*. I, 153)

It is said from the standpoint of those who speak *Apabhraṃśa* that the word '*goṇī*' immediately indicates the meaning of 'cow'. So the word '*goṇī*' is equivalent to the Sanskrit word '*go*' (nominative: *gauḥ*). But criticizing this view, Bhartṛhari says,

"The correct [words in Sanskrit] are not explained by scholars as if they were synonyms [of the corrupted words]. They are not [synonymous even] in the texts of the *smṛtis*, either. Therefore, [the corrupted words] do not directly indicate the meaning."

na śiṣṭair anugamyante paryāyā iva sādhavaḥ/
na[10] *yataḥ smṛtiśāstreṇa tasmāt sākṣād avācakāḥ//* (*Vākyap*. I, 152)

In this way, he raised an objection to regarding *Apabhraṃśa* as an independent language. He considers that *Apabhraṃśa* is, as the verb root *apabhraṃś* shows, nothing but a corrupt form of the sacred language Sanskrit.

Thus it is one of the remarkable characteristics of his theory that Bhartṛhari argued for protecting the genuineness of the sacred language called Sanskrit, rejecting *Apabhraṃśa* by force. Then why is only Sanskrit the sacred and genuine language, and why are other languages to be rejected? According to him, it is good to utter the correct word, while it is bad to utter the corrupt one. The former brings *dharma* to its maturation, while the latter destroys it.

> "The correct [words] acquired from scholars [like Manu, etc.] through tradition are the means to *dharma*. But the incorrect [words], although not different [from the former ones] in conveying the meaning, are of the opposite nature."[11]
>
> *śiṣṭebhya āgamāt siddhāḥ sādhavo dharmasādhanam/*
> *arthapratyāyanābhede viparītās tv asādhavaḥ//* (*Vākyap*. I, 27)

He acknowledged an ethical meaning in uttering the correct word. It is rather reasonable that he considered that the correct use of the Sanskrit language in ancient times was incomparably important, because he bases himself on the standpoint of conservatism, emphasizing the absolute superiority of Brahmanical culture.

Now, Indian people generally held that the practice of *dharma* brought about good merit, while the opposite brought about a bad retribution. On account of this, they also held the same view on speaking the word, which is an aspect of practice. Bhartṛhari claimed that good fortune was obtained by speaking the correct word, while calamity was brought about by speaking the incorrect and corrupt word.

> "Some think that the incorrect word can also indicate the meaning through inference. Although there is no difference in denoting the meaning [between the correct word and the incorrect one], it is fixed that [the correct word induces to] merit and [the incorrect one induces to] evil."
>
> *asādhur anumānena vācakaḥ kaiścid iṣyate/*
> *vācakatvāviśeṣe vā niyamaḥ puṇyapāpayoḥ//* (*Vākyap*. III, 3, 30; p.110)

And, after explaining that the word is possessed of magical power, he says as follows:

> "Just as these [words] have the capability of [producing] those [effects], so are they understood [to have the capability] of [producing] merit. Therefore, the good men who wish for prosperity (*abhyudaya*) should speak correct [words]."
>
> *yathaiṣāṃ tatra sāmarthyaṃ dharme 'py evam pratīyate/*
> *sādhūnāṃ sādhubhis tasmāt vācyam abhyudayārthibhiḥ//*(*Vākyap*. I, 141)

According to him, when one utters the correct word, one brings about prosperity, i. e. happiness in this world, and goes to heaven in a future life. The idea that one can obtain happiness in this life by uttering the correct word appeared already in the *Ṛg-Veda* (X,71). But the following saying of the grammarian Kātyāyana is the first instance of declaring its merit to be prosperity (*abhyudaya*): "If one utters the word in relying upon the text [of grammar], he brings about prosperity. This (uttering the correct word) is similar to [the study of] the Vedic words [which brings about excellent merit]."[12] It is seen that Bhartṛhari follows this traditional thought of the grammarians.

Now, the above are all the passages which mention the reasons for the command of obligation to utter the correct word. The virtue (*puṇya*) or prosperity (*abhyudaya*) acquired from uttering the correct word is the opposite to sin (*pāpa*). And yet it is reported that Bhartṛhari was a Vedānta philosopher who taught us liberation beyond such virtue and vice. Then what is liberation as expounded by him? I shall consider this next.

Notes

1) *-vat* means 'suitable' or 'conformable to' (Pāṇini V, 1,117).

2) *Apabhraṃśa* is one of the middle Indo-Aryan Languages, and is used in opposition to Sanskrit and Prākrit. As viewed from its name, it is clearly a kind of modified popular language, but it had already been adopted as a literary language in prose and poetry since about 6th century AD. However, it seems that the *Apabhraṃśa* which Bhartṛhari criticizes does not mean such a special language, but rather a language corrupted from a sacred one, i. e. the colloquial language in general. Puṇyarāja uses *apabhraṃśa* in its

plural form (ad I, 155).

3) Cf. *saṃskṛtaṃ nāma daivī vāg anvākhyātā maharṣibhiḥ/* (Daṇḍin's *Kāvyādarśa* I, 33).

4) *śrūyate hi purākalpe svaśarīrajyotiṣām manuṣyāṇām yathaivānṛtādibhir asaṅkīrṇā vāg āsīt evaṃ sarvair apabhraṃśaiḥ/* (ad *Vākyap*. I, 156).

5) *āvapane goṇīti svaiyogābhidhāne ca asva iti sādhv eva* (Puṇyarāja ad *Vākyap*. I, 150).

6) This verse is quoted also in *Tattvasaṃgrahapañjikā* ad v.2668 (p.713).

7) This verse is quoted also in *Tattvasaṃgrahapañjikā* ad v.2668 (p.713).

8) Cf. *Vākyap*. I, 157.

9) This verse is quoted also in *Tattvasaṃgrahapañjikā* ad v.2668 (p.713).

10) Biardeau's edition reads *te* for *na*.

11) = *śāstrānanugata* (Puṇyarāja).

12) *Vārttika* 9, under 1,1,1, p.10.

Sub-Section 3. Liberation

Bhartṛhari expounds liberation too. He says, "Liberation means that he is saved and liberated, and it is proclaimed by one who wishes for liberation."[1]

It is generally accepted in India that he asserted that liberation is attained by the direct perception of the absolute, *Brahman*.[2] He himself explains that a scholar (*śiṣṭa*) is "one who immediately perceives the nature of things"[3] (*bhāvatattvadṛś*),[4] and that "only the knowledge concerning *Brahman* is said to be true and pure."[5] He also says that *Brahman*, which is *ātman*, 'is known to be calm.'[6] Then how can one gain direct perception of this *Brahman*? He states that one can get it on the basis of the *Veda* (*āmnāya*).

> "If knowledge were spontaneous, there would be no use for the composition of the scriptures. If merit (*dharma*) is the cause of knowledge, then the *Veda* is the foundation of the former."
>
> *jñāne svābhāvike nārthaḥ śāstraiḥ kaścana vidyate/*
> *dharmo jñānasya hetuś cet tatrāmnāyo* nibandhanam// (*Vākyap*. I, 136)

To wit, he here asserts that the scriptures or the *dharma* expounded therein are effective for knowledge to arise, and in this respect his view is almost in accord with the theory of the Vedānta school in general.

However, because he holds in particular to the view that "*Brahman* is composed of the word," he differs from other Vedānta scholars in proclaiming direct perception of *Brahman*. He emphasizes direct perception by the power of the word.

> "Those who know the nature [of the word] see the powers of the word belonging to things."
>
> *svabhāvajñaiś ca bhāvānāṃ dṛśyante śabdaśaktayaḥ*/(*Vākyap*. I, 145)

Then what is it that they know the essence of the word to be? It is, he says, that language is always becoming vulgar in accordance with the changes of time. This means that, preventing it from falling into *Apabhraṃśa*, they keep the sacred language Sanskrit (*saṃskṛta*), handed down from ancient times, in its natural and genuine condition.

> "Therefore, the purification of the word (i. e. the elimination of *Apabhraṃśa*) is the accomplishment of the highest self. Those who know the essence of its function reach the immortal *Brahman*."
>
> *tasmād yaḥ śabdasaṃskāraḥ sā siddhiḥ paramātmanaḥ*/
>
> *tasya pravṛttitattvajñas tad brahmāmṛtam aśnute*//(*Vākyap*. I, 133)

'To know' means 'to control'. And he says that the accomplishment of the highest self or attainment of *Brahman*, which is liberation, means that one faithfully obeys the obligations in the study of grammar, such as the elimination of stains in the word, the learning of the correct meaning and usage of the word, and its practice. From his assertion we can discern a highly distinctive view on liberation in the history of Indian philosophy. In Vedānta, and in the Advaita school in particular, liberation means that one directly perceives *Brahman*, which is the unmarked truth beyond all expressions. Bhartṛhari, however, asserts that liberation means that one knows as it really is another aspect of *Brahman*, namely, the form of *Brahman* composed of the word, which is qualified by adjuncts and its expansions, while he recognizes, in the absolute sense, *Brahman* as unborn, imperishable, unmarked or inexpressible. In the Advaita school they argue for the realization of the undifferentiated form, while Bhartṛhari attaches importance to knowledge of the various forms of diversity.

Now I shall consider in greater detail the meaning of knowing the true form of the word. As the word is possessed of a social function merely as a medium of conveying the contents of communication from one person to another, it does not exist as a physical object, but it must be a thing which is understood by men and is at their disposal. If it is destitute of such meaning, then it will not be the word, but merely a sound. That being so, 'to know the true form of the word' means that we take the word as having a social function and learn the technique of speaking the word freely and accurately, and the grammarians are primarily responsible for teaching the technique of speaking the word correctly. That we know the word means that we understand the word practically and that, in the final analysis, we learn the technique of speaking the word. Thus, according to him, liberation, which means identification with the absolute, means that we learn and practice this technique in our social activities. For this very reason grammar is called 'the doctrine of the inner self', 'the door to liberation' or 'the right royal path for those who want to be liberated'.[9] Thus, liberation as expounded by him does not mean that we, like many Vedānta philosophers, are liberated from our secular life, but that we accomplish in practice the correct utterance of the word in our secular life. After all, liberation is, for him, in the range of practical observance, and for this reason he is in striking contrast to Śaṅkara.

The reason why Bhartṛhari, in the wide-ranging scope of human activities, particularly regarded the correct utterance of the word as liberation is directly concerned with the fact that he was a grammarian who followed the tradition of his school. We have to recall in his attitude of regarding enthusiastically the study of grammar as supreme the deeply rooted grammarians' tradition in India or the absolute supremacy of the Sanskrit language which helps it to continue to be the one and only continuous unifying factor in the history of Indian culture and society. He who had been brought up in a historical tradition like this and had become a scholar advocated a movement for purifying the language to keep the above tradition protected.

Here the problem is that, while he states that the correct utterance of the word brings about wealth or prosperity, he says here that the study of grammar leads to liberation. According to the general view of Indian philosophy, good fortune such as wealth, prosperity, etc., are relative things which are destined to disappear at some time, while liberation is something ultimate and absolute which cannot be surpassed by anything else. If this is so, we could say that there is a contradiction in Bhartṛhari's assertion. Then how can these two assertions be reconciled? It seems to me that, although these two assertions are contradictory to the end, it is the traditional view[10] of the study of grammar from ancient times that we obtain good fortune when we utter the correct word, while the assertion that we attain to liberation when we are well-versed in the word is stated on the basis of Bhartṛhari's belief in Vedānta philosophy. And thinking that if one is acquainted with the correct utterance of the word he anyhow acquires merit, he himself seems to define in some cases this merit as prosperity in accordance with the traditional theory of grammar from ancient times, and in other cases as 'arriving at *Brahman*' or 'liberation'. Thus, without establishing a strict distinction between them, he vaguely thinks of them in this way. However, it should be carefully noticed that he found a close relationship between 'the correct utterance of the word' and 'liberation'.

Now, the assertion that only extant Sanskrit is the language and at the same time in itself the essence of the absolute might make a very strange impression on modern people. But if one thinks of the strong traditional power of Sanskrit in India, one can easily understand a situation where such an idea might have formed. Even the language of the *Brāhmaṇas*, which had been composed about three thousand years ago, is not largely different from Classical Sanskrit at the time of Bhartṛhari. Furthermore, even the language of the *Ṛg-veda* is only slightly different from Classical Sanskrit. While the Sanskrit language thus has such a long and unchanged tradition or history, the vernacular language is of many kinds, of a short tradition, possessed of few literary sources, spoken by men of low class, easy to disappear, and shows signs of having been handed down in various ways. Considering that there existed such a situation, we should not necessarily be surprised that this scholar of Brahmanism held that Sanskrit was based upon the absolute, *Brahman*.

Notes

1) Tibetan fragment (6) ascribed to Bhartṛhari (PartV, Chapter II of this book). The present work, *supra*. The science of grammar is the means to spiritual liberation (K. A. Subrahmania Iyer : *AdyarL.B.*, vol. XXVIII, 1964, pp.112-131).

2) Kamalaśīla explains the view of liberation held by those who maintain the word-*Brahman* (*śabdabrahmavādin*): *taṃ tu paramaṃ brahmātmānam abhyudayaniḥśreyasa-phaladharmānugṛhītāntaḥkaraṇā yogina eva paśyanti* (*Tattvasaṃgrahapañjikā*, ad. v.151, p.74; cf. *Pañjikā* ad v.128, *ll*.3-4). "In the state of being a *yogin* the *yogins* contemplate upon their own or that (*brahman*) which is characteristic of light and shining itself." (*Pañjikā* ad v.151) Against the above view Kamalaśīla gives a detailed refutation. His discussion is almost the same as the criticism made by other Indian scholars about the Vedāntic view of liberation. Mādhava also states in the *Sarvadarśanasaṃgraha*, XIII, *ll*. 271-3, which explains the grammarians' view of liberation: "In this manner, when it has been understood that the highest *Brahman* which is permanent and of being, intelligence, bliss and is not different from the inner self the beginningless *avidyā* is destroyed, then the highest good (*niḥśreyasa*) characterized by the state of being of the nature of such *Brahman* will be established." As viewed from these facts, it seems to me that the grammarians' view of liberation became more and more Vedāntic after Bhartṛhari and in particular was strongly influenced by the Advaita school.

3) *Vākyap*.III, 13, 21 (p.440) = *vastuparamārthasākṣātkārin* (Helārāja).

4) *Vākyap*. III, 14, 52 (p.476), *tattvadarśin*.

5) *Vākyap*. I, 9: *satyā viśuddhis tatroktā vidyaivaikapadāgamā'*.

6) Fragment (10) ascribed to Bhartṛhari (Part V, Chapter I of this work).

7) Biardeau's edition reads *tasyām*- for *tatrām*-.

8) Literally it means 'the accomplished language'.

9) See Part VII, Chapter III, Section II of this work.

10) The Mīmāṃsā school also holds the same view (G. Jha: *The Prābhākara School of Pūrva Mīmāṃsā*, pp.322-325).

SECTION VII. CONFRONTATION AND RECONCILIATION IN VIEWS OF THE WORLD

According to Bhartṛhari, *Brahman*, the absolute, is made up of the word. He also claimed that the essence of the word is *sphoṭa*, which was assumed to be a special principle, and that *sphoṭa* is indeed the sentence. Accordingly, the sentence, or the conclusion which is the meaning indicated by it, is itself signified as the absolute, *Brahman*. Each of the conclusions given by us to events is as it is the appearance of the absolute. Our actual thinking is based upon the absolute. Thus, all the sciences and arts can also, according to him, be built on the basis of the absolute.

"From this [holy syllable], which is the creator of the worlds, proceed the various sciences based upon the major and minor limbs of the *Veda*, which are the causes of knowledge and of purification."

vidhātus tasya [*praṇavasya*] *lokānām aṅgopāṅganibandhanāḥ/ vidyābhedāḥ* [= *sāṅgopāṅgaśrutismṛtitrayyantā vidyāḥ*] *pratāyante* [= *prabhavanti*] *jñānasaṃskārahetavaḥ* [= *samyagjñānapuruṣasaṃskārahetavaḥ*]//(*Vākyap*. I, 10).

The limbs (*aṅga*) for studying the Vedic Scriptures, i. e. phonetics, ritual science, grammar, etymology, metric science and astronomy, and the minor limbs (*upāṅga*) such as physical science[1] etc., had, he said, been explained by the creator of the worlds to be the causes by which men were led to correct knowledge and were purified.

Sometimes in our actual life we are faced with conflicting or opposite conclusions about the same event. In such cases, we have to adopt either of them, concluding that one is true and the other is false, and in some cases both might be false. However, there are not a few cases where, if these conclusions are given for the same event, we are able to decide which is true and which is false by some way or another, and in such cases we can know clearly the reason why it is false. However, when we are faced with the fact that there are many different views of life and the world which conflict with one another with regard to philosophical problems of the world, the universe, or life into which those things are summed up, how can we conclude whether it is true or false? If, following Bhartṛhari, we consider that all conclusions and theories are manifestations of the absolute, we will have to say that even a heretical theory has the foundation of its existence on the absolute. If all metaphysical conclusions and theories are really manifestations of the absolute, then they cannot, even if heretical, be forcibly rejected merely because they are false. Even these theories are possessed of a reason for their existence. Then how can many metaphysical views which are in mutual conflict be formed? We are forced to clarify the reason for this. Thus in Bhartṛhari's philosophy he was forced to investigate the special problem of conflict between different systems of thought and the reason for their existence. In this respect the situation here is the same as in the case of the *Māṇḍūkya-Kārikā*.

In actual human society the various views of the world are opposed to, repel and contend with one another. Most of these theories may be false. Nay, all of them may be false. But even if they are false, it is an undoubted fact that our actual life is motivated by various views of the world or philosophical theories which are mutually different from each other. Bhartṛhari clearly observes this fact.

"The ordinary life is led on the ground of various views."

bhinnaṃ darśanam āśritya vyavahāro 'nugamyate/(*Vākyap*. I, 74ab)

Thus he observes the fact that the various philosophical theories are opposed to one another and insists that we should follow the sacred books. However, in the sacred books, which he regards as absolute truth, there are various different theories, and they are in conflict with or opposite to one another with regard to the same event. Furthermore, most of the Brahmanic scriptures explain events (e. g. religious rites) which are so different from his Vedānta philosophical theory or are not so important from his position. On this point, he says as follows:

"[The Brahmanic scriptures] are devised for unwise students and are provisional."

upāyāḥ śikṣamāṇānām bālānām apalāpanāḥ/ (*Vākyap*. II, 240ab)

According to him, the retribution theory was devised.

"Just as, when one refers to a tiger, a child stops crying, so damnation, though it is unreal, is prescribed [in the scriptures]."

vyāghrādivyapadeśena yathā bālo nivartyate/
asatyo 'pi tathā kaścit pratyavāyo vidhīyate// (*Vākyap*. II, 322)

A commentator, Puṇyarāja, annotates this verse in the following manner: — When one says, "A crying boy is eaten by a tiger," the fact that a tiger eats a crying boy does not actually occur, but one just stops a little boy's crying with the intention of saying, "You do not cry." The teaching presented (in the scriptures) that, if one violates the regulations, one falls into hell (*narakapāta*) is to be seen in the same way. So Bhartṛhari holds that, in the highest sense, hell, heaven, and transmigration do not exist, but they are meaningful in a therapeutic way. Bhartṛhari considers that all the Vedic scriptures have this same basis.

Now, the fear might arise in the minds of Indian people in general that if the idea of transmigration is thus taken away, then morality will be destroyed. To this Bhartṛhari gives the following answer:

"Even if an intelligent man determines that damnation is such, he does not perform those things which are prohibited by the scriptures."

na saṃvidhānaṃ kṛtvāpi pratyavāye tathāvidhe/
śāstreṇa pratiṣiddhe 'rthe vidvān kaścit pravartate// (*Vākyap*. II, 323)

To wit, even when one who has reached the truth knows that the retribution theory is provisional and devised, he never violates the principle of morality.

Besides, among later Mahāyānists, there was a person who held the same view as Bhartṛhari: "Hells are what have been falsely created by foolish men through wrong belief in the existence of non-being and what have been produced through one's own false imagination."

In this manner, he holds, as may be inferred from Bhartṛhari's statement, that things which are prescribed and prohibited in almost all scriptures are all temporarily devised, and that his own theoretical standpoint is situated in a higher position. Moreover, Vijñānabhikṣu of a later age (16th century) also held the view that the devised theory (*abhyupagama-vāda*) is stated in the scriptures.[3)]

The problem of conflicting opposition between the various theories of the scriptures presented by the Vedānta school was thus tentatively solved in the *Māṇḍūkya-Kārikā* and by Bhartṛhari. This method of solution[4)] was adopted from the expedience theory of Buddhism. Not only is the expedience theory often emphasized in the sūtras of Mahāyāna Buddhism,[5)] but it is also upheld by the Mādhyamika[6)] and *Vijñānavāda* schools.[7)] Accordingly, the *Māṇḍūkya-Kārikā* and Bhartṛhari, adopting the expedience theory from Buddhism, and making it a main point in interpreting the scriptures of the Advaita school, tentatively complete the explanation of the reason why theoretical contradictions and oppositions exist among the scriptures of traditional Brahmanism. This attitude was also inherited by Śaṅkara[8)] (first half of 8th century), who recognized it as a matter of fact. Supported by this view; he posited the twofold truth, two kinds of knowledge perceiving it, and two kinds of absolute in accordance with it. The theory of twofold truth is used by Vijñānabhikṣu for avoiding the theoretical contradictions between Sāṃkhya and Vedānta. In other words, Sāṃkhya theory is, he says, established from a conventional standpoint, while Vedānta theory is expounded in the absolute sense.[9]

He deals also with the theoretical confrontations among schools from the same point of view. According to him, their philosophical views which are in conflict with and critical of one another contain a partial truth, but on the other hand they have a one-sided bias. Even the scriptural teachings are, as stated above, merely devised for reaching the true Law. On the other hand, "the knowledge of *Brahman*"[10] expounded by him is the one and only true way, and it does not , he says, conflict with any theories since it is beyond the confrontation between schools.

> "Having decided [one-sidedly] [the sentences] in the form of the explanatory passages of it (= *Veda*), [they] have thought in many ways of the opinions of the Monists and the Dualists which have been derived from their own judgement."
>
> *tasyārthavādarūpāṇi niścitya*[11] *svavikalpajāḥ/*
> *ekatvināṃ dvaitināṃ ca pravādā bahudhā matāḥ//*(*Vākyap*. I, 8)

And also,

> "It is said that knowledge of it (=*Brahman*) alone is true purity, transmitted through one word, connected with the form of the sacred syllable and compatible with all theories."
>
> *satyā viśuddhis tatroktā vidyaivaikapadāgamā/*
> *yuktā praṇavarūpeṇa sarvavādāvirodhinī//* (*Vākyap*. I, 9)

To wit, he does not hold that he himself is an exponent of either Monism or Dualism, but he takes a standpoint beyond the confrontation between these two and with no conflict with any school. The grammar which he devoted himself to was originally a science for teaching the correct utterance of the word, and so it is beyond all confrontations between schools.[12] Also it naturally follows that this science is possessed of the above feature. He further states that his philosophical view is also possessed of the character of non-contradiction (*avirodha*).

Then why does his theory not conflict with any others? Bhartṛhari does not give any answer to this. However, the sacred syllable (*om*), regarded as the symbol of *Brahman*, nay, as *Brahman* itself, is, according to the commentator Puṇyarāja[13] that which has all forms (*sarvarūpa*), the origin which all theories arise from and are reduced to (*sarvadarśanodayapratyastamayayoni*), and the possessor of meaning in no way conflicting with anything else (*sarvāviruddhārthopagrāhin*). In other words, each theoretical standpoint is nothing but a form of manifestation of the absolute, *Brahman*, which is symbolized by the sacred syllable *Om*, and *Brahman* is capable of manifesting itself in any form ; many exponents, who adhere to one of these forms, merely regard it as absolute, while he who is well-versed in the truth and the foundation of establishing all forms does not conflict with them. Bhartṛhari here claims that any of the highest principles maintained in different schools is finally nothing but a form of *Brahman*.[14] We can here see a theory quite similar to the *Māṇḍūkya-Kārikā* as well as Buddhism insofar that he thus clearly presents his philosophical standpoint.[15]

Since Bhartṛhari holds this standpoint, he is very tolerant in his attitude towards the theories of other schools and observes that there are relative positions in the various systems of thought. He seems to recognize a partial truth in the Buddhist theory, since he adopts, as we have already stated, ideas, methods of expression, and logical arguments from it.[16] And although he rejects, in an absolute sense, the individual and independent existence of the six principles expounded in Vaiśeṣika philosophy, which is originally different in its thinking from Vedānta philosophy, he admits them as real, in a conventional sense, because he explains that they are the powers (*śakti*) of *Brahman*.

> "Therefore, all [the six categories] such as substance are the powers which are of different character. [These powers,] being collected together, accomplish the aim of life, while an individual [category, being separated from the other,] does not [do so]."[17]
>
> *tasmād dravyādayaḥ sarvāḥ śaktayo bhinnalakṣaṇāḥ/*
> *saṃsṛṣṭāḥ puruṣārthasya sādhikā na tu kevalāḥ//*(*Vākyap*. III, 1, 23)

In some limited sense he recognizes that Vaiśeṣika philosophy has a reason for its existence, and he also admits a practical value such that the aim of life can be achieved by it.

The attitude that Nyāya-Vaiśeṣika philosophy also has a reason for its existence can be seen also in Bhartṛprapañca, a philosopher of Early

Vedānta.[18] He holds that Nyāya-Vaiśeṣika philosophy can also prove logically (*upapattitaḥ*) what is purported in the scriptures. This attitude continues throughout the Vedānta school thereafter. Śaṅkara also does not hesitate to borrow a theory from Vaiśeṣika philosophy in order to criticize, for example, the Buddhist theory.[19] In some cases he also quotes a verse from the *Nyāya-sūtra* as an authority for his theory.[20] Also Ānandajñāna, although he rejects, in an absolute sense, the six principles of Vaiśeṣika philosophy, approves of them in a conventional sense.[21]

In the long run, the absolute, *Brahman*, gives, according to Bhartṛhari, a conclusion to itself by manifesting its own essence, the word. Whatever is a conclusion about the absolute is indeed nothing but a self-manifestation of the absolute. It seems to me that his idea of the reconciliation of various views of the world is based on this point.

The above are the main points of Bhartṛhari's philosophy. According to him, philosophy is the reflection made by the absolute or the subjective word through the word itself. But it is not that one who speculates philosophically carries out theoretical thinking, having the absolute as its object confronting him.

> "The word means such forms [which are of the nature of the mere adjuncts]; since [these adjuncts] are of the nature of the truth, a thing eternal is also denoted by this [word]."
>
> *teṣv ākāreṣu yaḥ śabdas tathābhūteṣu* [=*upādhimātrasvabhāveṣu*] *vartate/*
> *tattvātmakatvāt* [=*paramārthatas tattvād avyatirekād*] *tenāpi nityam evābhidhīyate//* (*Vākyap*. III, 2, 6. p.88).

Bhartṛhari discovers in the absolute itself the reason why the philosophical argument as stated above is possible.

Notes

1) Based upon Puṇyarāja's comment on the above verse.
2) *pratyavāya*. It is translated as "sin" or "reverse course" in the dictionaries, but here we may translate it as "falling into hell." Puṇyarāja glosses it "*narakapāta*." It is the opposite of "going to heaven" (*abhyudaya*). Cf. Deussen : *System des Vedānta*, S.534.
3) *Sāṃkhyapravacanabhāṣya*, p.4.

4) The idea of expedience (*upāya*) is also seen elsewhere. He holds that only a sentence is true, while a word and a syllable are tentatively constructed by us in perceiving. So he says, "The imaginary construction of divisions of parts (of the word) is the means to [reach] the partless [essence of the word, *śabdātman*]." *nirbhāgeṣv apy upāyo vā bhāgabhedaprakalpanam*/ (*Vākyap*. I, 93) It means that although a syllable and a word are false and tentatively constructed, they are the means for a sentence or *sphoṭa* (Cf. *Vākyap* I, 86).

5) See Part VI, Chapter III, Section IV, Sub-Section 4 of this book.

6) In *SDS*, II, *ll*.341-347, the author quotes a verse from Nāgārjuna's *Bodhicittavivaraṇa*: "You should not say, 'The distinction of teaching in accordance with [the distinction of] intentions of those who are to be guided (*vineya*) is not based on "The teachings of the Lord of the world (*lokanātha*) in this world, following the intentions and abilities of people, are multifariously divided owing to the difference of "profound" and "clear" (*gambhīrottānabheda*), being characterized by both ["profound" and "clear"] in some cases." [However], emptiness (*śūnyatā*), which is of a non-dual character, is not differentiated.'"

7) To take an example, *MSA*. XVI, 69; 76.

8) See Part VI, Chapter II, Section IV, Sub-Section 4 of this book. Anyway, Śaṅkara claims that the passages of the scriptures are meaningful and must be all accepted: *na hi Vedavākyānāṃ kasyacid arthavattvaṃ kasyacid anarthavattvam iti yuktaṃ pratipattuṃ pramāṇatvāviśeṣāt*/— Ś. ad. *BS*. III, 2, 15.

9) See the beginning of the *Sāṃkhyapravacanabhāṣya*.

10) *puruṣabuddhivikalpa* — Puṇyarāja.

11) Biardeau's edition reads *niśritāḥ* for *nicritya*.

12) "Grammar is to be accepted by all schools" (*vyākaraṇasya sarvapārṣadatva*, *SDS*. XIII, *l*.249). Grammarians may be followers of different religions. A great number of grammarians such as Pāṇini, Kātyāyana, Patañjali, etc., belonged to traditional Brahmanism, while Candragomin and Amarasiṃha, who compiled a dictionary, were Buddhists, and the famous grammarian Hemachandra was a Jain.

13) The comment on the above two verses.

14) *Vākyap*. III, 2, 1.

15) In the *Māṇḍūkya-Kārikā*, Chapter 4, it is said that it is not the exponents of Monism, but those of Dualism who contend with one another. Bhartṛhari is different from this in stating that the exponents of Monism and Dualism contend with one another. (See Part VI, Chapter III, Section IV, Sub-Section 4 of this book.)

16) See Part VII, Chapter II, Section III of this book.

17) The words in parentheses are supplemented by Helārāja's commentary.

18) See Part V, Chapter VII, Section III, Sub-Section 1 of this book. In the portion where

he quotes a statement by Bhartṛprapañca, he who intends to say that the highest self is different from an individual self, states after quoting many passages from the scriptures. — *Kaṇādākṣapādāditarka-śāstreṣu ca saṃsārivilakṣaṇa Īśvara upapattitaḥ sādhyate* (*Ś.* ad *Bṛhad. Up.* p.155).

19) Rejecting the Buddhist theory that the essence of space is unobstructibility and intending to show that space exists substantially (*vastu*), Śaṅkara relies on Vaiśeṣika philosophy.— *vipratipannān prati tu śabdaguṇānumeyatvaṃ vaktavyam, gandhādīnāṃ guṇānām pṛthivyādivastvāśrayatvadarśanāt.* (See Śaṅkara's commentary on *BS*. II, 2, 24.) Moreover, this is also accepted by the Sāṃkhya school (Cf. Garbe : *Sāṃkhya-Philosophie*, S.303). See Śaṅkara's commentary on *BS*. II, 2, 4.

20) Deussen : *System des Vedānta*, S.36.

21) Ānandajñāna's sub-commentary says, "(Question :) The Vaiśeṣika school says that there are six principles from substance to concomitance in an absolute sense, doesn't it?.... (Answer :) According to the expression of the technical terms in the Vaiśeṣika school, the six principles from substance to concomitance have been taught. However, these things do not exist in an absolute sense, but appear in a conventional sense (*saṃvṛtyā*)." (*An.* ad *GK*. IV,73; p.202, *ll*.2-5)

PART VIII
CONCLUSION

In the preceding chapters we have gathered and studied as many works and fragments as possible of pre-Śaṅkara Vedānta scholars, and we have discussed them in their historical order to bring this investigation to a close. In conclusion, the following two topics will be discussed:

1. The position of Śaṅkara in the history of Vedānta philosophy.
2. A summary of the history of early Vedānta philosophy.

CHAPTER I

THE POSITION OF ŚAṄKARA IN THE HISTORY OF VEDĀNTA PHILOSOPHY

It is generally recognized that the representative philosophy in the history of Indian thought is Vedānta and that its most well-known philosopher is Śaṅkara. The high esteem for Śaṅkara may be ascribed to two factors. First, the majority of scholars with classical training in India, called *paṇḍits*, belong to the tradition of Śaṅkara, and Śaṅkara's philosophical thought is prevalent among contemporary Indian intellectuals. It is only natural that the founder of such an influential school should be highly regarded as a great philosopher. Furthermore, in the early period of Western research on Indian philosophy, it was Śaṅkara's thought that first attracted wide attention. When Western scholars first began their studies on India, they investigated diverse fields, and the first to specialize in Indian philosophy was Paul Deussen of Germany. He became deeply engrossed in Śaṅkara's Vedānta philosophy and soon became its ardent admirer. He went to extremes in praising Śaṅkara and regarded him as one of the three greatest philosophers in history, the others being Parmenides and Kant.[1] The scholars of Indian philosophy who followed him also considered Śaṅkara to be the most important figure in Indian philosophy. Owing to these reasons, Śaṅkara is known today as the greatest philosopher in the history of Indian thought.[2]

A question, however, remains: was Śaṅkara a truly great philosopher? It is true that he developed ideas different from the other systems and other philosophers. Many works ascribed to Śaṅkara have also been transmitted to this day, and his school is undoubtedly the greatest philosophical tradition in medieval and modern India. These facts testify to the impact of Śaṅkara on Indian thought as a whole and to the pervasive influence of his scholastic tradition, but they are not conclusive proofs that he was an original thinker of great stature. Many people come into contact with Śaṅkara's thought and they express awe and respect, but are the ideas contained in his works unique and original with him? In the past when research on pre-Śaṅkara philosophy was non-existent, all the ideas discussed in his works were thought to have originated with him. As discussed in our study, however, we know that complex and varied developments took place within Vedānta philosophy, and this by necessity forces us to alter the traditional evaluation of Śaṅkara's significance in the history of Vedānta. We shall now examine the various points which are generally thought to be characteristics of Śaṅkara's philosophy, and their relevance to the early Vedānta school will be clarified.

(1) Śaṅkara believed that *Brahman* was an actual substance which was undiscriminated, equal, permanent, universal, and could not be predicated in any way, except negatively. This was taught generally in the early Vedānta school and is not an especially unique idea. Śaṅkara, however, distinguished between 'highest *Brahman*' (*param brahma*) and 'lower *Brahman*' (*aparam brahma*), and this is famous as one of the chief characteristics of his thought. But this concept of two types of *Brahman* existed from ancient times; as terms they are found in *Praśna-Upaniṣad* V, 2, and *Māṇḍūkya-kārikā* I,26; and in *Māṇḍūkya-kārikā* II, 27, it is said that the distinction between the two is not the highest truth.

According to Śaṅkara's transmission, furthermore, Bhartṛprapañca was also thought to have distinguished between these two types of *Brahman*.[3] If we should go further back, the possibility of its connection with Bādari's thought is also conceivable. Bādari recognized *Brahman* as a cause and *Brahman* as an effect, and these two are almost identical with the two types of *Brahman* conceived by Śaṅkara. The teaching that *Brahman* itself cannot be the ultimate goal for people who have gained spiritual liberation is also similar to that of Śaṅkara. Consequently, Śaṅkara understands Bādari's teaching to be the standard interpretation of the *Brahma-sūtra*, even going to the extent of negating the intentions of the compiler of the *sūtra*.[4] Although Bhartṛhari did not use these two expressions as technical terms, he recognized *Brahman* as the principle of absolute negation and *Brahman* as the basis of the unfolding of distinctions; therefore, these two may be said to correspond to the two concepts mentioned above.[5]

Now, according to Śaṅkara, the highest *Brahman* is *Brahman* itself, but the lower *Brahman* is formed by the addition of ignorance (*avidyā*) to the former and is *Īśvara*. Thus, *Īśvara* itself is a being of untruth. An idea similar to this is taught in the *Māṇḍūkya-kārikā*, Chapter II, according to which it is said that God possesses illusion (*saṃmoha*) and manifests this phenomenal world by the power of *māyā*.

(2) According to Śaṅkara's theory, the relationship between the phenomenal world and *Brahman* is such that it is not *Brahman* but *māyā* or ignorance that manifests this phenomenal world, but *Brahman* itself never undergoes change. He probably reached such a conclusion because he attempted to explain the emanation of the world by inheriting and advancing the monistic standpoint which had been traditional since the *Upaniṣads*. This view, however, is already found in a poetic verse[6] ascribed to Bhartṛhari approximately 300 years before Śaṅkara, and it is also taught in the *Māṇḍūkya-kārikā*, Chapter II *infra*. The theory of world emanation generated by ignorance is also introduced and rejected in Kumārila's work.[7] It is clear, therefore, that the idea of world emanation by means of ignorance was quite prevalent prior to Śaṅkara.

Also the term *'anirvacanīya'*, which is peculiar to the Vedānta school, was not coined first by Śaṅkara, but had already been used by Maṇḍanamiśra for the first time in his *Brahmasiddhi*.[8] Padmapāda used this term as a term of the philosophy of Śaṅkara.[9]

Śaṅkara proceeds to state that the phenomenal world is manifested owing to ignorance, but (a) it is to be considered like defilements in the air, or (b) it is like misjudging a piece of rope to be a snake.[10] However, the former is an analogy taught by Bhartṛhari and others, and the latter is cited in *Māṇḍūkya-kārikā*, Chapter II, and frequently alluded to in the Vijñaptimātratā philosophy of Buddhism of an even earlier period.

Besides the above, Śaṅkara explains the relationship between the world cause, *Brahman*, and the phenomenal world by various analogies, but the majority were conceived by people prior to Śaṅkara. (c) One of the famous analogies used by Śaṅkara to explain the relationship between *Brahman* and the phenomenal world is the example of the pristine and clear crystal which reflects the colors of the impure matter attached to it, but Bhartṛhari gave this as an example before Śaṅkara, and even this was based upon a transmission (*āgama*) prior to Bhartṛhari.[11] This had also been taught in the Vijñaptimātratā school. (d) The analogy of the ocean and the waves to explain the phenomenal world as unfolding from *Brahman* was used by Ṭaṅka, Bhartṛprapañca, and others before Śaṅkara, and the literatus Bhavabhūti considers it to be a Vedāntic analogy well-known among the people.[12] (e) The idea of comparing the manifestation of the world to the magical acts produced by a sorcerer[13] is frequently alluded to in the *Māṇḍūkya-kārikā* (especially IV,44), and it is found even earlier in the *Śvetāśvatara-Upaniṣad* (IV,9-10). (In this case, however, it is naturally important to remember the different connotations of *māyā*.) (f) The notion of comparing the phenomenal world to dreams and illusions, as well as the rejection of such thinking, occur frequently in the *Māṇḍūkya-kārikā* and in the writings of Kumārila.[14]

(3) Next, in regard to the *ātman* theory of Śaṅkara, he states that *ātman* is our original self which can be neither grasped nor abandoned, but such an idea was already taught by Bhartṛhari.[15] We may also be able to find this view in the earlier works of Mahāyāna Buddhism.

Śaṅkara's arguments concerning the existence of *ātman* were also inherited from previous scholars. He proved the existence of *ātman* from the self-evident fact that self-consciousness (*ahaṃkāra*) exists in all people, but this coincides with the Vaiśeṣika theory (Cf. *Vaiśesika-sūtra* III, 2, 14 f.), and among Vedānta schools it is thought to inherit the ideas of Upavarṣa.[16] The idea that since the attributes of *ātman* differ from the attributes of the body, *ātman* exists separately from the body and never dies, even though the body may die, is in complete agreement with the theories found in the old *Caraka-saṃhitā* and the later Śabarasvāmin.[17] And the argument which establishes the existence of an eternal *ātman*, based upon the fact that there exists the function of memory which unites past and present within the individual spirit, agrees with the theory in the *Nyāya-sūtra*, and it is also found in common with Śabarasvāmin.[18]

We must, however, remember that although Śaṅkara inherits the pre-existing arguments for the existence of *ātman*, *ātman* in his philosophy always denotes the individual self and not the Highest Self. Consequently, the existence of this individual self is conceivable from the standpoint of everyday life (*vyavahāra-avasthā*), but it is inconceivable from the standpoint of highest truth (*paramārtha-avasthā*). Thus, while Śaṅkara followed the older arguments for the existence of *ātman*, he limited its scope by applying them to the individual self only.

The term *paramārtha* was already used by Draviḍa, as can be seen in his fragment.[19]

Śaṅkara's theory concerning *ātman* viewed from the ultimate standpoint is the non-duality of *Brahman* and *ātman*, and the individual self is a mere illusion and not a real existence from this ultimate standpoint, although it is one with the Highest Self in the true sense. This is a famous characteristic of Śaṅkara's thought, but it was already taught by Sundarapāṇḍya.[20] Bhavya, furthermore, briefly mentions and criticizes the idea that the individual self is not different from the Highest Self.[21] The analogy of space within the jar which Śaṅkara frequently uses to advocate the non-distinction of the Highest Self and great self[22] is explained in detail in *Māṇḍūkya-kārikā*, Chapter III, and Bhavya cites it as a Vedāntic theory.

According to Śaṅkara, our daily life, composed of conflicting activities of individuals, is formed by our ignorance and is therefore illusory, but this idea also existed prior to him. Sundarapāṇḍya, for example, stated earlier that the knowledge recognized as true in daily life is not recognized as truth from the ultimate standpoint. And Kumārila comments critically upon the idea[23] that the subject of cognition is as illusory as a mirage.[24]

Śaṅkara also rewords this and states that illusions in our daily life arise from the false ascription (*adhyāsa*) of *ātman* to that which is not *ātman*; for example, misinterpreting the body as *ātman*. This view had already been considered by the Vedānta school before Śaṅkara. Śaṅkara himself relates that the two concepts of false ascription (*adhyāropa*) and false negation (*apavāda*) were used by the old Vedāntic scholars.[25] Bhartṛhari also uses both concepts.[26] Both are originally concepts of Buddhism, especially of the Vijñaptimātratā philosophy, and their usage was later adopted by the Vedānta school. Such a concept of false ascription of *ātman* was also considered by Sundarapāṇḍya,[27] from whom Śaṅkara probably derived his ideas. The idea of limitation of external attachment (*upādhi*) of *ātman* is already found in Bhartṛhari, who clearly states that such a limitation is not truth (*asatya*).[28]

When we inquire into the beginnings of the thesis that the phenomenal world is illusory, we can find similar ideas in the period almost identical with that of the *Upaniṣads*. Buddhism classified the idea that all change is illusory and that there is no change from the ultimate standpoint as a heretical doctrine which clings to annihilationism (*uccheda-vāda*), and Jainism describes such thinking as characteristic of the *akriyāvādin*.[29] The Abhidharma scholars regard this as the theory advocated by followers of *ātman* theory. This does not mean that Śaṅkara directly inherited these ideas but that the sources of such thought can be traced to a relatively early period.

(4) Thus, according to Śaṅkara, the activities of the individual self and the changes in the phenomenal world are considered illusory ; therefore, *saṃsāra* from the ultimate standpoint was inconceivable. Although Śaṅkara recognized the existence of *ātman* separate from the body and taught that good results could be obtained in present or future lives[30] insofar as Vedic rituals were performed according to the prescribed rules in the scriptures, which makes it similar to the Mīmāṃsā, he did not approve of this principle from the highest standpoint. According to his philosophy, the law of causality, which advocates that good *karman* results in good effects and bad *karman* results in bad effects, is not truth in the highest sense. Such thinking which implied the negation of the law of causality was found in previous thinkers. Bhartṛmitra[31] interpreted the *Mīmāṃsā-sūtra* according to this view and was criticized as having become a Lokāyata, and Bhartṛhari also states that the theory of hell was an uncouth expedience to guide the ignorant masses. That *saṃsāra* is not truth is reiterated in the *Māṇḍūkya-*

kārikā, and the literatus Bāṇa reports of the *Brahmavādin* who taught the groundlessness of *saṃsāra* (*saṃsārāsāratva*).[32]

(5) The characteristics of Śaṅkara's concept of spiritual liberation lie in the stress he placed on liberation by means of knowledge (*vidyā*). According to him, the performance of rituals is not necessarily required for gaining liberation, for it is the cognition of the true nature of *ātman* which leads to liberation. This idea, however, was expressed in the *Māṇḍūkya-kārikā* and by Sundarapāṇḍya, and it can be traced even earlier to the thought of Bādarāyana. Therefore, the idea that the performance of rituals and the cognition of *Brahman* (and consequent liberation) are entirely different matters existed from very ancient times. The fact that repeated life in *saṃsāra* could be sundered by knowledge was well-known among the intellectual class is found in the writings of the literati Bhāravi (6th century), Bhavabhūti (late 8th century), and others.

Śaṅkara's theory that there is nothing to be done when the realm of spiritual liberation is realized had already been advocated by Sundarapāṇḍya.[33] And non-action had been admired in the *Māṇḍūkya-kārikā* as the ideal stage of the ascetic.

Furthermore, the indispensability of devotion (*bhakti*) to the Supreme God for gaining liberation, which is emphasized by Vedānta schools other than the Śaṅkara school, has been regarded as one of the characteristics of the theories of Śaṅkara because he does not refer to it. In the early Vedānta school, however, the theory of devotion to and grace from the Supreme God can hardly be found.[34] Therefore we can judge from this point that Śaṅkara follows the general theory of this school in those days.

(6) Liberation is gained by means of knowledge. Śaṅkara conceived of two forms of knowledge, i. e. 'higher knowledge' (*parā vidyā*) and 'lower knowledge' (*aparā vidyā*), according to the two types of *Brahman*. Although this has been regarded as one of the characteristics of his thought, these two forms of knowledge had been mentioned in the *Ahirubudhnya-saṃhitā* and the *Viṣṇu-purāṇa* before him.[35] And that Śaṅkara interprets the theory of the *Upaniṣads* as either corresponds to what Gauḍapāda and Bhartṛhari said, namely, that there was both a 'truth theory' and an 'expedient theory' in the scriptures.

The characteristics of Śaṅkara's thought are almost exhausted by the various items listed in the above.[36] From the above examination, however, it becomes clear that all of these characteristics were advocated by someone before Śaṅkara. Adopting various previous scholars' ideas, he completed such a great achievement. In additon to these, there are many other characteristics of Śaṅkara's thought inherited from previous scholars.[37] Therefore it follows from the above examination that there are few original ideas of Śaṅkara himself. He was the person who synthesized the *Advaitavāda* which had previously existed before him.

The academic position of Śaṅkara himself was completely conservative. He advocated that all problems concerning metaphysical knowledge should be referred to the sacred scriptures, which are the final reference, because the theoretical speculations of the philosophers are contradictory and lack a positive basis. This shows complete agreement[38] with Bhartṛhari, and it is possible that it was directly inherited from him, since it is famous throughout India as Bhartṛhari's idea. He interpreted the contradictory theories within the scriptures as the result of diverse spiritual capacities to whom the teachings were given in response to their respective needs. This reason for the lack of unity within the scriptures[39] appears already in the *Māṇḍūkya-kārikā*, and it is found still earlier in Buddhism.

Śaṅkara proclaimed himself to be a theologian who clarified the true message of the *Upaniṣads,* and he did not set himself up to be the advocate of new views. He called himself 'an Upaniṣadic scholar (*Aupaniṣada, Upaniṣadvādin*)' or 'a *Brahman* scholar (*Brahmavādin*)' and never claimed a special role for himself. He criticized others within the same Vedānta tradition as 'people who call themselves Upaniṣad scholars'[40] and, in contrast, believed himself to be an authentic *Upaniṣad* interpreter. For this reason his basic attitude to the *Upaniṣad* was extremely submissive. Although his standpoint is often referred to as monism (*advaitavāda*) or representationism (*vivartavāda*), he never claimed any such scholastic theory for his view. Although he used the term *advaita*, the word was frequently employed before him;[41] and although he uses the verb *vivartate*, he interprets it as synonymous with 'developing' or 'unfolding' (*pariṇamate*).[42] Śaṅkara never took the initiative to coin new terminology nor advocated new theories; his standpoint is conservative, and he lived within the framework of traditional learning.[43] His knowledge of Sanskrit was perfect.[44]

Śaṅkara, therefore, was not an original philosopher who advocated a radically new theory; rather, he was a synthesizer of existing Advaita and the rejuvenator, as well as a defender, of ancient learning. It was due to his great efforts and contributions that the Vedānta school after him assumed a dominant position in the world of Indian philosophy, and in this sense his greatness is to be fully recognized. And since the *Brahma-sūtra-bhāṣya* and the commentaries he wrote on the older *Upaniṣads* were excellent works, concise and to the point,[45] his writings were revered exclusively at the expense of the works of other scholars before him. This was the reason that the actual condition of the early Vedānta school came to be obscured and neglected.

Thus, if such is the case, Śaṅkara's greatness was not that of an original thinker but that of an unequalled commentator. In the past the mutual contradictions of ideas within Śaṅkara's *Brahma-sūtra-bhāṣya* have often been pointed out,[46] and discrepancies in explanations or phraseology among the works of Śaṅkara which are beyond any doubt as to their authorship have been questioned, but they appear inexplicable only because he is esteemed highly as an original philosopher. If we were to see him only as an outstanding commentator with a rich philosophical background, there would be nothing strange in our discovering contradictions in his explanations. Sometimes he quotes entirely opposite interpretations in commenting upon a given *sūtra* or phrase[47] without settling which view is desirable. This clearly shows that he is nothing more than a compiler of ancient interpretations and not a philosophical thinker in the true sense. Another feature of Śaṅkara's commentaries which has been frequently pointed out by scholars is the contradiction between his commentaries on the *Upaniṣads* and the explanations in the *Brahma-sūtra-bhāṣya* regarding the same Upaniṣadic phrases.[48] We may understand this problem in the following manner. As I have discussed earlier, a considerable number of scholars wrote commentaries on the *sūtras* and *Upaniṣads* before Śaṅkara, and it is believed that Śaṅkara wrote his own interpretation by sifting materials from the existing commentaries. If this is true, when the views in the commentaries on which his work was based differed, it would only be natural to find diverse interpretations of the same phrase occurring in certain instances.

As a result of our investigation of early Vedānta philosophy, therefore, we must revise the traditional evaluation concerning Śaṅkara which has been generally accepted.

If we accept the fact that a great number of original philosophers appeared before Śaṅkara and that his efforts were mainly directed to synthesizing their achievements, what is the reason for their works being lost and only Śaṅkara's works being transmitted to posterity?

As we have seen, Śaṅkara was an interpreter rather than a thinker who made a systematic inquiry into his subject. His commentaries, furthermore, are said to have been brief compared to those of earlier scholars, and they were by no means superior in scholarship to the various existing commentaries. Thus, the reason that posterity reveres him is not due to his philosophical or scholarly significance but must be due to institutional factors.

According to the unified opinion of various legends of India, Śaṅkara traveled extensively throughout various parts of India, propagated Vedāntic thought, and built many monasteries (*maṭha*). These monasteries exist even today, and they form the centers of Vedāntic learning. Prior to Śaṅkara, however, nothing is known about the monasteries of the Vedānta school. According to the *Laws of Manu*, only those who have fulfilled the role of the householder can renounce the world and become recluses to concentrate on the truth of *Brahman* as taught in the *Upaniṣads*. Vedāntic ideas were mainly transmitted by many wandering monks. During the time of Bhavya (6th century), small monasteries were probably built and students of Vedānta maintained a community life to pursue their studies, but no description of their life remains to this day. This shows how insignificant their existence was. Bāṇa (7th century) also briefly alludes to the communal life of Vedāntic and other students, but he does not mention anything about a monastery exclusively for students of Vedānta.

Śaṅkara, however, built great monasteries anew exclusively for the students of Vedānta. This is a fact worthy of our attention. In their way of life they approached very closely the life of the Buddhist practitioners (*bhikkhu* and *bhikkhunī*) whom they criticized. The Vedāntic students called themselves recluses (*parivrājaka*) as before and they were so called by others, but it was in name only. Instead of wandering through various places, they settled down in a given monastery, and though they may have traveled to other monasteries, it was a matter of changing residence rather than of wandering from place to place. It was only natural for those who practiced religious austerities and received spiritual influence at monasteries founded by Śaṅkara to revere and respect him. And the Vedānta school probably became influential in society after the time of Śaṅkara. When we consider these historical facts, we can understand why Śaṅkara's works came to be specially revered, while the writings of other scholars before him came to be forgotten with the passage of time.

Notes

1) Deussen: *SV*. S.49.

2) "Man stellt Śaṅkara wohl dar als den grössten 'Filisophen' Indiens" (Rudolf Otto: *West-Östliche Mystik*, Gotha, 1926, S.22); "le philosophe qui joua peut-être le plus grand rôle dans l'ensemble de la spéculation indienne" (Masson-Oursel: *Esquisse*, p.209).

3) See Part V, Chapter VII, Section III, Sub-Section 3 of this book.

4) See Part III, Chapter I, Section VI of *A History of Early Vedānta Philosophy*, Part One, p.28f.

5) See Part VII, Chapter IV, Section I of this book.

6) See Part V, Chapter II of this book.

7) See Part II, Chapter III, Section V of *A History of Early Vedānta Philosophy*, Part One, p.495f.

8) Paul Hacker: *ZDMG*. Bd.100, 1950, S.255, Anm. 1.

9) Paul Hacker: *Untersuchungen über Texte des frühen Advaitavāda*, 1. *Die Schüler Śaṅkaras*. Abhandlungen der Geistes und Sozialwissenschaftlichen Klasse, Jahrgang 1950, Nr.26. Akademie der Wissenschaften und der Literatur, S.1931.

10) Ś. ad *BS*. vol.I, pp.363, *l*.19ff.; p.446, *l*.2; p.278, *l*.14; p.461, *l*.1; p.463, *l*.9.

11) See Part V, Chapter XV of this book.

12) See Part II, Chapter III, Section VI of *A History of Early Vedānta Philosophy*, Part One, p.516f.

13) Ś. ad *BS*. vol.I, p.122, *ll*.8-9; p.279, *ll*.1-2; p.445, *l*.12ff.; p.498, *l*.10. etc.

14) See Part II, Chapter III, Section VII of *A History of Early Vedānta Philosophy*, Part One, p.519f.

15) See Part VII, Chapter IV, Section V of this book.

16) See Part V, Chapter III, Section III of this book.

17) See Part V, Chapter VIII, Section II, Sub-Section II of this book ; Part II, Chapter III, Section V of *A History of Early Vedānta Philosophy*, Part One, p.474f.

18) See Part V, Chapter VIII, Section II, Sub-Section II of this book.

19) Śaṅkara's *Bhāṣya* ad *Chāndogya-upaniṣad* III, 10.1.

20) See Part V, Chapter XI of this book.

21) See Part II, Chapter I, Section V, Sub-Section 3 of *A History of Early Vedānta Philosophy*, p.339f.

22) Ś. ad *BS*. vol.I, p.97, *l*.6 ; p.181, *l*.1 ; p.122, *l*.10 ; p.209, *l*.8 ; p.243, *l*.8ff. ; p.459, *l*.10 ; p. 287, *l*.4 ; vol.II, p.41, *l*.19 ; p.85, *l*.7 ; p.457, *ll*.4-5 ; p.549, *ll*.4-5 (Cf. vol.I, p.182, *l*.7 ; vol.II, p.239, *l*.4).

23) See Part V, Chapter XI of this book.

24) See Part II, Chapter III, Section VI of *A History of Early Vedānta Philosophy*, p.493f.

25) See Part V, Chapter XV of this book.

26) See Part VII, Chapter II, Section I, Sub-Section 4 of this book. Bhartṛhari also uses the word *adhyāsa*.

27) See Part V, Chapter XI of this book.

28) See Part VII, Chapter IV, Section I, note 15 of this book.

29) See Part II, Chapter II, Section II of *A History of Early Vedānta Philosophy*, Part One, p.185 ; 409f.

30) See Part V, Chapter III, Section I and Part V, Chapter VIII, Section II, Sub-Section 2 of this book.

31) See Part V, Chapter IX of this book.

32) See Part II, Chapter III, Section VII of *A History of Early Vedānta Philosophy*, Part One, p.511f.

33) See Part V, Chapter XI of this book.

34) However, Draviḍa is an exception probably. See PartV, Chapter VI of this book, Fragment 5.

35) See Part II, Chapter III, Section VI of *A History of Early Vedānta philosophy*, Part One, p.489f. These two forms of knowledge are also listed in *Muṇḍaka Up*. I, 1, 4, but the meaning is slightly different, for 'lower knowledge' refers to the acquaintance with the *Vedas* and rituals and 'higher knowledge' to the awareness of *Brahman*.

36) G. Thibaut : *The Vedānta-Sūtras*, Introduction, pp. xxx-xxxi, and Ghate : *The Vedānta*, pp. 26, 40, list various items which are characteristic of Śaṅkara's thought and cannot be found in other Vedānta schools. They are all included in the above summary.

37) For example, (1) he believed that cognition depends upon the object and that the validity of cognition is to be sought in the correspondence with the object. This realism

concerning epistemology agrees with that of Śabarasvāmin. (See Part V, Chapter IX, Section II, Sub-Section 2 of this book.) (2) The discussion on the relationship between action and purpose reveals a complete agreement between Śaṅkara and Bhartṛhari. (See Part VII, Chapter IV, Section V of this book.) (3) His theory that the essence of words is *varṇa* inherits the view of Upavarṣa. He also criticizes the *sphoṭa* advocates, but his arguments are a collection of existing criticisms, and his own standpoint is somewhat vague. (See Part V, Chapter III, Section III of this book.) (4) Śaṅkara also believed that the various senses were ruled and controlled by divinity, but this idea is already found in the *Brahma-sūtra*, and Bhartṛprapañca also held similar views. (See Part IV, Chapter III, Section IV, Sub-Section 3 of *A History of Early Vedānta Philosophy*, Part One, p.458; Part V, Chapter VII, Section III, Sub-Section 2 of this book.) (5) His criticism of the Buddhist theory of *anātman* and Vijñaptimātratā is identical with that of the *Brahma-sūtra*, Bodhāyana, and Śabarasvāmin. (6) Śaṅkara's view that words are the formal cause of the origination of the world is found in the Vedānta philosophy transmitted by the *Brahma-sutra*, Bhartṛhari, and Bhavabhūti.

38) See Part VII, Chapter III, Section III of this book.

39) See Part VI, Chapter III, Section IV, Sub-Section 4 of this book.

40) See Part I, Chapter III, Section IV of *A History of Early Vedānta Philosophy*, Part One, p.157.

41) The appellation *Advaita* was already used by the Jaina scholars Samantabhadra and Akalaṅka, as well as by the Buddhist Kamalaśīla, but their interpretation of *advaita* does not necessarily agree with that of Śaṅkara.

42) See Part II, Chapter I, Section VIII, Sub-Section 2 of *A History of Early Vedānta Philosophy*, Part One, p.390; Part VII, Chapter IV, Section IV of this book. P. Hacker: *Vivarta*, S.24f.

43) When showing concrete examples, for instance, he did not cite an actual example from contemporary life but cited a name of a city contained in a classic which was approximately a thousand years old. See Part I, Chapter II, Topic A, Section VI of *A History of Early Vedānta Philosophy*, Part One, p.78f.

44) Paul Deussen points out some strange wordings in Śaṅkara's *Brahma-sūtra-bhāṣya*. "As stylistic curiosities from Śaṅkara's Commentary may be quoted: *prathama-tara*, p. 137, IV, 148, 12 (also on *Bṛih.* 273, 5); *upapadyate-tarām* 144, 6; *na-tarām* 931, 8; *akalpate* 815, 2 and *avyācakshīta* 819, 8 (a privative with a verb) and, to read it so, also *avirudhyeta* 265, 3; *janimataḥ* 833, 14; *janyate* 844, 7; *akiñcitkaratvāt* 141, 5; *arddhajaratīya* 122, 13, 176,11 (read so); *mukhya' eva prāṇasya dharmaḥ* (for *mukhyaprāṇasya eva dharmaḥ*) 161, 3; *śrutarahasyasya vijñānasya* (for *śruta-rahasya-vijñānasya*) 191, 7. Frequent enough is the use of the 3rd pers. sing. pres. as substantive: *caratiḥ* 762, 4; *sṛijatiḥ* 707, 10; *dhyāyatiḥ* 1071, 11; *īkshati-ādi-śravaṇam* 109; 7. *karoti-artha* 381, 4; *dhyāyati-artha* 1071,

10; also in the genitive: *sambhavater* 630, 3; *āpater* 1132, 9; *tarateḥ prāpnoti-arthaḥ* 834, 14 and even *prapañcayishyater* 99, 5, which is, however, retracted in the *Śuddhipatram*." (Paul Deussen: *The System of the Vedānta*, 1912; reprint, Motilal Banarsidass, 1972, p. 38, n.26) But these are not wrong usage. About *pramathatara*, Cf. Speyer: *Vedische und Sanskrit syntax*, 119, Anm. About *upapadyatetarām*, Cf. Speyer: op. cit., 121; Whitney: *Sanskrit Grammar*, 473, c. Grammatical explanations are given by these scholars. *arthajaratīya* is a quite common saying in the philosophical literature of India (Cf. Colonel Jacob: *Laukikanyāya*, I, p.6; Colonel Jacob: *The Vedāntasāra*, note p,171; *SDS*. ĀnSS. p.11, *l*.11, etc.). *caratiḥ* is grammatically quite correct, and can be seen often in Indian literature. It is the form of a finite verb, which is used as a masculine noun. *Janimataḥ, janyate, akiṃcitkaratvāt* are grammatically quite all right. Others are mere misprints. In other editions such as the Ānandāśrama Sanskrit Series and that of the Nirṇaya-Sāgara Press correct readings are given. Accordingly, all instances which Deussen pointed out can be explained away. We are led to the conclusion that Śaṅkara used classical Sanskrit correctly through and through.

45) It is said that his commentary on the *Chāndogya* was shorter than that of Draviḍa, and that his commentaries on the *Bṛhadāraṇyaka* and *Kāṭhaka* were briefer than those by Bhartṛprapañca. See Part V, Chapter VI and VII of this book.

46) Belvalkar: *Lectures*, pp.169-170.

47) For example, he presents three theories for interpreting *Brahma-sūtra* II, 4, 12, but he does not indicate which one is preferable. In some cases he lists both the interpretation of the *Vṛttikāra* and his own view, but does not clearly state which one should be adopted (I, 1, 19; I, 1, 25; I, 1, 31; I, 2, 23; I, 4, 3; See Part V, Chapter IV, Section I of this book). In many instances he also lists two interpretations (I, 1, 3; I, 1, 7; I, 3, 27; I, 4, 26; II, 1, 15; II, 2, 35; II, 2, 39; II, 2, 40; II, 4, 6; III, 1, 7; III, 2, 22; III, 3, 17; III, 3, 26). He also enumerates and criticizes different theories regarding the interpretation of *sūtras* (III, 3, 57; IV, 3, 14).

48) For example, Deussen: *SV*. S.150-151, 158, Anm, 73. Marschner discusses eleven instances where Śaṅkara's *Bhāṣya* and the *Brahma-sūtra-bhāṣya* do not agree on the explanations of scriptural passages in the *Bṛhadāraṇyaka-Upaniṣad* (Kathe Marschner: *Zur Verfasserfrage des dem Śaṅkarācārya zugeschriebenen Bṛhadāraṇyakopanisad-bhāṣya*, Diss. 1933, especially S.75-82).

CHAPTER II

A SUMMARY OF THE HISTORY OF EARLY VEDĀNTA PHILOSOPHY

According to our research discussed in this work, we can summarize the historical evolution of early Vedānta philosophy as follows:

(1) Prior to Gotama Buddha

Before the appearance of Gotama Buddha (approximately 463-383 BC.)[1] the main contents of the older *Upaniṣads* of the initial period were generally formed. During this time, the thinkers who belonged to the orthodox *Brāhmaṇa* lineage held various ideas taught in the older *Upaniṣads* of the initial period, and their philosophical thought revealed a manifold tendency. They belonged primarily to the *Brāhmaṇa* class, but there were some of *Kṣatriya* origin also. Among the *Brāhmaṇa* thinkers there were two types: priests and laymen.

(2) 400-200 BC.

This is the period approximately from the time of Gotama Buddha to the end of the Maurya Dynasty. During this time, the first unified country in the history of India appeared and epoch-making changes occurred. The *Brāhmaṇa* scholars transmitted the older *Upaniṣads* of the initial period, and at the same time they were developing the ideas contained in them. Furthermore, the older *Upaniṣads* in verse, belonging to the middle period, were compiled.

The Vedānta thought which is found in contemporary texts, such as Buddhist scriptures, Jain scriptures, etc., generally agrees with the ideas presented in the older *Upaniṣads*. That which is transmitted by the Greek Megasthenes (c. 300 BC.) as unique *Brāhmaṇa* ideas is also the teachings contained primarily in the older *Upaniṣads*.

This does not mean, however, that there were no individual philosophical reflections. The people whose names are given in the *Brahma-sūtra*, such as Kārṣṇajini, Kāśakṛtsna, Ātreya, Auḍulomi, Āśramathya, Bādari, and others belong to this period. They held different views concerning the various sections of the older *Upaniṣads* of the initial period, and they were also well-versed in sacrificial ceremonies, Karma-mīmāṃsā, and grammar. Thus, in the very same period that poets were singing the praises of *Brahman* and *Īśvara* on the one hand, the theologians were engaged in interpreting the *Upaniṣads* and conducting speculation on the other. It should, however, be noted that the works of these Vedānta theologians are almost never found in other sources.

Since the realization of Vedānta thought clearly appears in the older *Upaniṣads* of the middle period compiled at this time, the authors must have noticed the special significance of the *Upaniṣads*. In this period there also appeared attempts to form a single, unified interpretation of the *Upaniṣads* by selecting ideas suited to individual predilection and thought. (See, for example, the *Āpastamba-dharma-sūtra*.) Thus, Vedānta studies must have already existed from this time, although its systematic philosophy was yet to be formulated. For this reason, we can trace the origin of the Vedānta school to this period, but since other sources, such as Buddhist texts, do not mention the tendency to especially emphasize the *Upaniṣads* among the *Vedas*, we must conclude that the existence of Vedānta as a unique school was not generally known in India. Among contemporary scholars of Vedānta, it seems that the lay *Brāhmaṇas* were the principal figures, and a considerable number of recluses who had renounced the world were also found.

(3) 200 BC. to AD. 200

During this period, the repeated invasions of other races from the northeast occurred, and as a result a unique and distinctive culture was born. Although its influence upon the Vedānta school is not clear, we can definitely recognize the transformations that Vedānta underwent.

The *Upaniṣads* which belong to the later period of the older *Upaniṣads* (*Maitri*, *Māṇḍūkya*) were first compiled, and in them we can clearly see the influence of Buddhism.

The older *Upaniṣads* of the initial and middle periods took final shape as we know them today during this period, and their authority as part of the Vedic scriptures was recognized generally in India. But the attitude of emphasizing only the *Upaniṣads* among the *Vedas* as done by the Vedānta school of later ages was not yet known at this time.

When we look at the Brahmanical law books of the period, they prescribe that while the *Upaniṣads* should be studied together with the *Veda-Saṃhitā* during the period of studentship under a *Brāhmaṇa* master who leads a household life, the upholding and practicing of Upaniṣadic thought for the sake of liberation should be conducted in later age after renunciation. Consequently, the *Brāhmaṇa* laymen and priests transmitted the *Upaniṣads*, and communities specializing in the Vedānta school were not yet established.

During this period also the upholders of the *Upaniṣads* literally believed in the words of the *Upaniṣads*, and they concentrated on hermeneutical studies of the texts. They had yet to attempt the formulation of a synthetic and unified system of thought based upon the ideas of the *Upaniṣads*. Generally speaking, Vedānta thought combined with Sāṃkhya philosophy was quite popular. Such a tendency is strongly reflected in the epics, law books, medical works, and literary works of this period.

It was in the early part of this period that Jaimini and Bādarāyana appeared and expressed completely different views on the practical theory of the *Upaniṣads*. The former taught that people should perform ceremonies within the home, and the latter praised the life of the recluse. These two types of practical theory remained in opposition for a long time within the orthodox *Brāhmaṇa* world.

(4) AD. 200 to 400

This period covers the time from the height of the Kuśana Dynasty to the height of the Gupta Dynasty.

This was the period when Mahāyāna Buddhism flourished, but it was also a time when orthodox *Brāhmaṇa* culture began to be rejuvenated by the patronage of the Gupta Dynasty. As far as Vedānta thought was concerned, however, no significant changes occurred and the situation was the same as in the preceding period. The *Brāhmaṇas* of India upheld the *Upaniṣads* as faithfully as they had always done, and they stressed the importance of a single idea among the many ideas taught in the *Upaniṣads*. A systematic, unified study on the whole of the *Upaniṣads* did not yet appear at this time. The authors of practical books and the logicians believed that the philosophical studies of the Vedānta should be embraced within Vedic theology. The

Vedānta school was not an influential current in the intellectual world of India.

However, philosophical speculations based upon the *Upaniṣads* were gradually being pursued, riding on the wave of the renaissance of *Brāhmaṇa* culture, and such movements were being noticed by the other schools. It is believed that the main contents of the *Brahma-sūtra* were compiled at this time.

Together with this trend, the popularized Vedānta which incorporated Sāṃkhya ideas was enjoying wide acceptance. The Vedānta theology of the various branches of Hinduism was also being developed, and in the next period the *Brahma-sūtra* was to especially criticize these views.

(5) AD. 400 to 500

The Gupta Dynasty remained politically dominant in India as in the previous period. It was during this time that the *Brahma-sūtra* was compiled, an epoch-making event in the Vedānta school. With this achievement the Vedānta received a definite philosophical orientation, and it now had the power to counter the other philosophical schools prevalent at this time.

On the other hand, the theories of the Vedānta school of this period did not necessarily agree with that of the *Brahma-sūtra*, as introduced in detail by the work of Bhavya, for it was a conglomeration of primitive and native ideas of the *Upaniṣads*, as well as of highly sophisticated theories concerning *ātman*. While the *Brahma-sūtra* considers the *Chāndogya-Upaniṣad* to be the principal scripture, the Vedānta school transmitted by Bhavya reveres the *Upaniṣads* which tend toward the worship of *Śiva*. It is also believed that the original form of the *Māṇḍūkya-kārikā* was established at this time. Moreover, this *kārikā* itself admits the appearance of several thinkers who were influenced by Mahāyāna Buddhist philosophy and who were forerunners of the *māyā* theory of later ages.

During this period, there were several different traditions within the Vedānta school, which presents a complex picture. Ideas which are not found in the existing *Brahma-sūtra* were very popular also, and several commentaries on this sūtra were in the process of being written.

In the light of these facts it is believed that small-scale monasteries were built in various localities and that groups of Vedānta students studied and practiced while leading a communal life. Vedānta philosophy became widely known among the cultured classes, and its influence can be seen in the works of the poet Kālidāsa and in some portions of Mahāyāna Buddhist scriptures.

(6) AD. 500 to 700

Generally speaking, during this period small countries contended with each other for political supremacy, and the Vedānta school was on the path to achieving prominence. The names of approximately ten Vedānta scholars of this period have been handed down to us, and as their divergent views reveal, Vedānta philosophy was becoming very complex.

The school itself became very influential. Its existence was fully recognized by other religious groups and philosophical schools, and it became the object of a considerable amount of criticism. Frequent references to this school appear in the literary works of the period, and various Vedānta ideas were prevalent among the educated people. The majority of Vedānta scholars, however, held views different from those of Śaṅkara. The theory of Advaita is introduced in the literature of various schools, but it is not identical with the view of Śaṅkara.

It seems that there were a considerable number of Vedānta students who led a communal life during this period, and among them some must have become renunciants after concluding the householder's period of life, and others must have become renunciants directly from the period of studentship. The stipulation that one should become a renunciant after the householder's period of life, as prescribed in the *Laws of Manu*, was no longer observed. The various *Upaniṣads* and the *Maṇḍūkya-kārikā* which teach the life of wandering recluses clearly violate this stipulation.

When the Vedānta students began communal life together as an independent school, they came to sever themselves from the study of Karma-mīmāṃsā. The Mīmāṃsā school naturally could not accept this tendency, and the division and opposition between the Karma-mīmāṃsā and Vedānta schools become clearly manifested at the end of this period.

Among Vedānta scholars, however, there were some *Brāhmaṇas* who taught and upheld the complete *Vedas* as done earlier, and in their eyes the Vedānta and Mīmāṃsā ideas were not contradictory. It is believed that many of them were of the laity.

(7) AD. 700 to 750

During the time of Śaṅkara, various philosophical theories were advanced within the Vedānta school, and Śaṅkara advocated his views in opposition to these theories. From this period on there is a gradual increase in references to Advaita in the writings of Buddhists and Jains, and Śaṅkara's tradition came to be regarded as representative of Vedānta philosophy. Thus, while the Advaita had existed from very ancient times, as described in the previous chapter, it was after Śaṅkara's time that it suddenly became a powerful influence in the intellectual world.

The tendency of the Vedānta students to live in large monasteries and lead a communal life as an independent school became increasingly noticeable after the time of Śaṅkara. Such monastic life made possible their detailed and scholastic theological studies, and it formed the ideal condition for transmitting their writings to posterity. Thus, the works of Vedānta scholars increased greatly from this period, and many of them have been handed down to this day.

This concludes the outline of the evolution of the early Vedānta school. We can thus know that this school slowly and gradually developed over a very long period of time in an extremely complex form.

We shall now turn to a discussion of the characteristic features of this school. Although the views of the various scholars and the contents of the various works belonging to early Vedānta are multifarious and cannot be subsumed under a single description, the general tendency is to stress the *bhedābheda* theory. This is the theory that *Brahman* and the individual self are neither one nor different, but the interpretations of *bhedābheda* differ according to the scholar.

In contrast to this, Śaṅkara's concept of Advaita existed without any doubt prior to Śaṅkara, as examined in the previous section, but his view never occupied a dominant position. In fact, the people who held views directly opposite to Śaṅkara regarding the major problems in Vedānta philosophy were incomparably greater in number. Among pre-Śaṅkara writings and scholars, those relatively close to Śaṅkara are Sundarapāṇḍya and the *Māṇḍūkya-kārikā*, Chapter 2 *infra*. If we seek earlier sources, it is believed that Bādari held ideas similar to his, and Śaṅkara's master Govinda must have advocated identical views, although the details of his life are not clear. The works and scholars other than these all taught views considerably different from those of Śaṅkara. When we study other sources, we notice that there is almost no reference to *māyā* when introducing Vedānta philosophy. This means that the theory of *māyā* and of Advaita were so insignificant that they did not attract much attention. According to various sources, it was primarily during and following Śaṅkara's time that the Advaita as taught by Śaṅkara finally became popular. What happened was that this situation was obscured as the ideas in Śaṅkara's tradition later became popular and the early thinkers who expressed quite different views were completely forgotten.

On the other hand, dualism (or actually pluralism), such as that of Madhva, did not exist in the early Vedānta school.

The scholars of the early Vedānta school, as a rule, were also scholars of Karma-mīmāṃsā, for the Vedānta philosophy was closely related to Karma-mīmāṃsā and developed from a common basis. The *Brahma-sūtra* recognizes the learning of the Mīmāṃsā as a preliminary study. Based upon such a situation, the Vedānta scholars before and after the *Brahma-sūtra* were almost all versed in sacrificial ceremonies and Karma-mīmāṃsā. Among those before[21] the *Brahma-sūtra* Kārṣṇājini, Kāśakṛtsna, Ātreya, Āśramathya, Bādari, Jaimini, and Bādarāyana, and among those after the sūtra Upavarṣa, Bodhāyana, Bhartṛmitra, Śabarasvāmin, Sundarapāṇḍya, and Maṇḍanamiśra are noted in the sources as having been Karma-mīmāṃsā scholars. Thus, the majority of early Vedānta scholars had mastered both forms of Mīmāṃsā.

The scholars of early Vedānta were at the same time also well-versed in grammar. It is clearly known that especially Kāśakṛtsna, Auḍulomi, Bhartṛhari, and Maṇḍanamiśra were scholars of grammar and linguistic philosophy.

Although in later ages the theologians of the various sects of Hinduism utilized Vedānta philosophy to a greater or lesser degree to form the basis of their doctrines, such a close connection was non-existent before the time of Śaṅkara, and, in fact, the two were completely independent.

At least, there is almost no Hindu coloring in the Vedānta school in its narrow sense. Even when we look at the works or fragments of the Vedānta school before Śaṅkara, there is no reference made to *Viṣṇu* or *Śiva*. Even in non-Vedānta sources which introduce the thought of this school, there is almost no mention of *Viṣṇu* or *Śiva*, and the sects of Hinduism are even listed as opposing the Vedānta school. It is true that there was partial agreement between the philosophy of early Vedānta scholars and the theology of certain Hindu sects, but it was merely a coincidence, and no fundamental connection between them existed.[3] However, since the majority of thinkers of early Vedānta assumed the existence of *Īśvara* and considered it to be *Brahman* or the highest self, it would have been extremely simple to attach the names of *Viṣṇu* and *Śiva* to *Īśvara*.

The relationship between the Vedānta school and Buddhism should be carefully noticed. Although the Vedānta scholars of the initial period generally held an antagonistic attitude to Buddhism, the latter's influence on their thought cannot be glossed over. Hitherto the general opinion is that Śaṅkara's view has been criticized by other schools as Buddhist in disguise, but there were many early Vedāntic scholars who incorporated Buddhist ideas to a much greater extent than Śaṅkara. We can find the influence of Buddhism even in the classics of this school, such as the *Māṇḍūkya-kārikā*, *Māṇḍūkya-Upaniṣad*, and *Brahma-sūtra*. And as has been shown by the present writer, the problem of the similarities and differences between Buddhism and Vedānta philosophy was debated before the time of Śaṅkara. When the Vedānta developed from a mere interpretation of scriptures to a philosophical system, the incorporation of Buddhist philosophy played a central role. Therefore, the view that Śaṅkara was the first to incorporate Buddhist ideas is incorrect, for the Vedānta school had already completely embraced Buddhist philosophy prior to his time. Although Śaṅkara criticized Buddhism and attempted to eliminate the traces of Buddhist influence, there was nothing he could do with the influence which had crept into the essence of his philosophy.

When we consider the practical life of the early Vedānta scholars, it is noteworthy that they led a life of renunciation and wandering from ancient times. On the other hand, there must have been quite a few *Brāhmaṇas* who lived a lay life, but they were also strict upholders of ethical living, or at least it was required of them.

They were from the upper classes of society and educated in traditional learning and culture. Being mainly *Brāhmaṇas*, they looked down upon the untouchables of the *Śūdra* caste. (The Vedānta school which Bhavya transmits as transcending caste was probably an exception.) The doctrines were esoterically transmitted among a small number of selected intellectuals, and this school was especially secretive and conservative in the ancient period. Thus, on the matter of social class, they are to be sharply distinguished from the general practitioners and theologians of Hinduism. The scholars of early Vedānta themselves were aloof and withdrawing and never came into contact with the masses, but as their philosophy came to be incorporated into the theology of the various sects of Hinduism, its theoretical influence upon the whole of Indian society became final and definitive.

Notes

1) There are various conflicting opinions concerning the date of Buddha's *parinirvāṇa*, but this calculation is based upon the author's dating of the Maurya Dynasty based upon sources of the northern transmission. (See my article in Japanese, "On the Dates of the Maurya Dynasty," in *Tohogaku*, vol.X.)

2) The scholars of Karma-mīmāṃsā were also Vedānta scholars in reverse. Among the scholars listed in the *Mīmāṃsā-sūtra* only the following four are not found in the *Brahma-sūtra*: Aitśāyana (*Mīm. sūtra* III, 2, 43; III, 4, 24; VI, 1, 6), Kāmukāyana (XI, 1, 61; XI, 1, 62), Ālekhana (IV, 5, 17), and Lābukāyana (VI, 7, 37). All the other scholars are listed in the *Brahma-sūtra*. (For details, see Part III, Chapter I of *A History of Early Vedānta Philosophy*, Part One, p.3f.)

3) The agreement between the theories of Āśramathya and Pāñcarātra is frequently mentioned (See Part III, Chapter I, Section V of *A History of Early Vedānta Philosophy*, p.24f.). Śaṅkara alludes to *Viṣṇu* faith and quotes the *Purāṇa* literature, as I have pointed out, but it is difficult to find inevitable connections between them and Śaṅkara's philosophy. It is true that the *Bhagavad-Gītā* had a great influence upon early Vedānta philosophy, but this is primarily in its philosophical aspects. There are also similarities in thought between the *Māṇḍūkya-kārikā* and the works of the Hindu sects, but they are limited to ideas and having nothing to do with the aspect of religious faith.

APPENDICES

A. SUPPLEMENT TO *A HISTORY OF EARLY VEDĀNTA PHILOSOPHY*, PART ONE

I. THE PART OF "THE VEDĀNTA CHAPTER OF BHAVYA'S *MADHYAMAKAHṚDAYA*"

In Part One (pp.184ff.), I published only the *gāthās* of the Vedānta chapter of the *Madhyamaka-hṛdaya*. In order to understand the Vedānta thought revealed therein, the Tibetan version of the *Tarkajvālā*, the commentary by the author on the *Madhyamaka-hṛdaya* is needed. So, I publish the *pūrvapakṣa* portion of the chapter preserved only in Tibetan.

Madhyamaka-hṛdaya-vṛtti-tarkajvālā
(*dbu-maḥi sñiṅ-poḥi ḥgrel-pa rtog-ge ḥbar-ba*)
—*pūrvapakṣa*—

Abbreviations

D.	The Sde-dge Edition.
DK.	The Sde-dge Editon of the *Madhyamaka-hṛdaya-kārikā*.
Mhk.	*Madhyamaka-hṛdaya-kārikā*.
N.	The Snar-thaṅ Edition.
NK.	The Snar-thaṅ Edition of the *Madhyamaka-hṛdaya-kārikā*.
P.	The Peking Edition.
PK.	The Peking Edition of the *Madhyamaka-hṛdaya-kārikā*.
T.	*Tarkajvālā*

[D.251a ; P.282b6 ; N.270b4] *de nas da ni rig byed kyi mthaḥ smra baḥi de kho na ñid gtan la dbab pa la ḥjug pas leḥu brgyad pa brtsam par byaḥo// de la*

1) *rig byed mthar smras smras pa ni/*
ḥdus byas stoṅ par smra ba yi/
phyi rol pa la bdag rig dkon/
bdag sdaṅ[1] *thar pa ga la yod//*

(1) *Vedāntavādinaḥ prāhur ātmavid durlabho bahiḥ/*
kuta ātmadviṣām mokṣaḥ śūnyasaṃskāravādinām[2] *//*

rig paḥi mthar phyin pa ni rig byed mthaḥ pa ste/chags pa med par ṅes par rig paḥo//de smra baḥi[3] *ṅan tshul ga la yod pa ḥam/tshig de gaṅ la yod pa ni rig byed kyi mthar smra baḥo//de dag ni ḥdi skad smra*[4] *ste/rig byed kyi mthar lta ba las gshan pa phyi rol gyi bstan bcos la bdag rig pa yaṅ śin tu dkon//bdag la sdaṅ baḥi saṅs rgyas pa* [P.283a] *rnams gaṅ la brten nas thar pa thob par ḥgyur/gaṅ gi phyir de dag ni ḥdus byas thams cad stoṅ paḥo sñam du sems śin ḥdus byas stoṅ pa ṅo bo ñid daṅ bral ba ni skad cig skad cig la ḥjig pa yin pas su shig bciṅs śin grol bar ḥgyur//bdag rtag* [N. 271a] *paḥi ṅo bo ni deḥi rten yin paḥi phyir bciṅs pa daṅ grol bar rig paḥi ṅo bo yin pas des na rig byed las grags paḥi skyes bu ni ñe bar bsṅags par bya ba yin pas/*

2) *mun pa las gshan skyes bus*[5] *ni/*
chen por gyur pa[6] *ñi maḥi ḥod//*
dbaṅ phyug chen po bdag de ñid/
mkhas pas śes na ḥchi med ḥgyur//

(2) *tamaḥparastāt puruṣam mahāntaṃ sūryavarcasam/*
mṛtyum atyeti matimān matvā'tmānaṃ maheśvaram[7] *//*

mi bde bar gyur ciṅ mi bde bar byed pas na mun pa ste/rgyu daṅ ḥbras buḥi cha bsags pa ñid kyi khams gsum du srid paḥo//khams gsum shes bya bar grags paḥi mun pa de las gshan pa ni khams gsum las ḥdas pa shes bya baḥi tha tshig go[8] *//saḥi dkyil ḥkhor las śin tu ḥdas pa na mun paḥi dkyil ḥkhor ro//mun paḥi dkyil ḥkhor las śin tu ḥdas pa na/skyes bu gnas pa yin te/*

skyes bu draṅ sroṅ chen po ñi maḥi mdog/
mun pa las gshan gyur pa de rig na/
ḥchi ba med par ḥgyur te bdag gis rtogs/
skye med gnas ḥgro ba la lam gshan med//[9]

shes bya baḥo//ḥjig paḥi sṅon rol nas yod pa ḥam/gñid [D. 521b] *log pa las gshan yin paḥi phyir skyes bu ḥam/skyoṅ bar byed pa ḥam/ḥgreṅs par byed pas na skyes buḥo//chen por gyur pa ni thams cad las*[10] *lhag pa yin paḥi phyir ro//kha dog sna tshogs can yin paḥi phyir ñi maḥi ḥod do//ñi ma ni ḥod sna tshogs can yin te/ḥdi ltar dkar po daṅ/sṅon po daṅ/ dmar po daṅ/ ba*[11] *bla daṅ/yuṅ ba daṅ/phug ron daṅ/btod daṅ/ki bi tsa laḥi*[12] *kha dog ḥdsin paḥo*//[P.283b] *ciḥi phyir ñi maḥi ḥod zer ḥdi dag daṅ ldan ce na*[13] / *lha thams cad kyi bdag ñid yin pa ḥam*/*dbaṅ phyug chen poḥi ṅo bo yaṅ ḥdi yin paḥi phyir ro*//*gaṅ ḥdir ñi maḥi dkar poḥi ṅo bor ḥdug paḥi ni zla baḥi bdag ñid yin no*//*gaṅ me lha daṅ ẓla ba gñis las ni chuḥi mdog go*//*gaṅ nor* [N.271b] *lha dag gis brten pa las ni de dmar poḥo*[14] //*gaṅ ru dra bde byed pa dag*[15] *gi bdag ñid yin pas ni dkar la dmar baḥo*//*gaṅ dbaṅ po yin pa las ni du ba lta buḥo*//*gaṅ bśes gñen yin pa las ni yuṅ gi mdog go*//*gaṅ bśes gñen daṅ chu lha yin paḥi bdag ñid las ni rdul daṅ yuṅ gi mdog go*// *gaṅ dgar ka ñid kyi ni smug por ro*//*gaṅ sna tshogs kyi lha yin pas ni myur baḥo*//*gaṅ dbaṅ phyug yin pa de las ni tshaṅs paḥi mdog go*//*a ta*[16] *shes bya ba rtag tu ḥgro ba ste*/*ḥbyuṅ po thams cad rtag tu ḥdir ḥgro ba ḥam*/ *ḥbyuṅ po thams cad la rtag tu ḥdir ḥgro bas bdag go*//*de .jid ni kun la khyab pa yin paḥi phyir chen poḥo*//*dbaṅ phyug ni ḥjig rten thams cad las ḥdas paḥo*//*de lta buḥi rnam*[17] *pa can ñid kyi skyes bu rnal ḥbyor pa gaṅ gis lhaḥi mig gis mthoṅ ba de ni ḥchiṅ ba las śin tu ḥdas nas rga ba daṅ ḥchi ba med pa thob par ḥgyur ro*//*skyes bu ni kha dog sna tshogs can yin na yaṅ de lta na yaṅ grol*[18] *bar gyur paḥi dus na rnal ḥbyor paḥi mtshan ma ḥdi yin te*/

3) *byed po dbaṅ phyug gser mdog tu*/
gaṅ shig[19] *mtoṅ shiṅ lta*[20] *ba de*/
sdig daṅ bsod nams las ḥdas nas/
mchog tu shi ba thob par ḥgyur//

(3) *rukmavarṇaṃ yadā paśyan paśyet kartāram īśvaram*/
vihāya pāpam puṇyañ ca paraṃ sāmyaṃ[21] *tadā 'pnuyāt*//

gser ni sa le sbram ste/*de daṅ ḥdra baḥi mdog can gyi bdag gaṅ yin pa de yaṅ dag par brtags nas bsam gtan gyi mig gis mthoṅ bar gyur* [D.252a] *pa na bdag gis dbaṅ phyug chen po mthoṅ ṅo shes ḥdi ltar ṅes par byaḥo*//*de lta bur* [P.284a] *mtoṅ ba na sdig pa daṅ bsod nams kyi bdag ñid daṅ*/*gñi gaḥi ṅo boḥi ḥchiṅ ba rnams bcad nas mchog ste*/*khyad par can ni shi ba ste*/*shi baḥi ṅo bo ñid bya ba thams cad log pa rnam par mi rtog pa ñid ḥthob*[22] *par ḥgyur ro*[23] //*ḥdi ḥjig rten gsum las śin tu ḥdas pa yin na byed pa po ji ltar yin*/*riṅ nas gnas pa yin na gaṅ gi dbaṅ phyug yin she na*[24] / *riṅ na gnas su* [N.272a] *zin kyaṅ kun la khyab pa ñid du smras pa*/

4) *byuṅ gyur byuṅ daṅ ḥbyuṅ*[25] *ba dag*/

thams cad skyes bu yin ḥdod de/
de ni phyi naṅ riṅ ba daṅ/
de ni ñe daṅ de[26] *las byed//*

(4) *bhūtam bhavat bhaviṣyac ca sarvam puruṣa iṣyate/*
so 'ntar bahiś ca dūre ca so 'ntike sa ca karmakṛt[27] *//*

gaṅ mi la sogs pa ḥdas par gyur pa daṅ/da ltar byuṅ ba mthoṅ bar gyur paḥi gzugs daṅ/gaṅ phyis ḥbyuṅ bar ḥgyur ba de thams cad skyes bus byin gyis brlabs nas gnas pa ḥam/khams gsum thams cad la ḥdis khyab pa[28] *yin te/gaṅ gi phyir steṅ gi phyogs ni ḥdiḥi mgo boḥo//ḥog gi phyogs ni rkaṅ paḥo//nam mkhaḥ ni ltoḥo*[29] */phyogs rnams ni lag paḥo//gzaḥ daṅ rgyu skar rnams ni*[30] *skraḥo//ri bo rnams ni braṅ ṅo//riḥi phreṅ ba ni rus paḥo//chu kluṅ rnams ni rtsaḥi dra baḥo//nags tshal rnams ni spu daṅ sen moḥo//rgyab ni mtho ris kyi ḥjig rten no//dpral ba ni tshaṅs paḥo*[31] *//chos daṅ chos ma yin pa ni smin ma gñis so//khro gñer ni ḥchi bdag go//ñi zla ni mig gñis so//dbugs ḥbyuṅ*[32] *ba daṅ rṅub pa ni rluṅ ṅo//ri bran rnams ni soḥo//lce ni dbyaṅs can maḥo//om*[33] *shes bya baḥi yi ge daṅ/ba śa tha shes bya baḥi yi ge ni mchu*[34] *gñis so//mig phye ba daṅ btsums pa ni dus so//gyon paḥi phyogs ni bud med do//gyas paḥi phyogs ni skyes paḥo//ḥjig rten daṅ ḥjig rten ma yin pa ni nu maḥi bar ro//ser mo*[35] *rnams ni riḥi* [P.284b] *bar ro//pus mo gñis ni gser ḥdab gñis so//rje ṅar gñis ni tha skar gyi bu gñis so//rked smad ni ñin shag go//mje rlig ni dbaṅ poḥo// dgaḥ baḥi raṅ bshin ni skye dguḥi bdag poḥo//rkaṅ pa gñis ni khyab* [D.252 b] *ḥjug go/kha dog rnams ni khrag go//de ni phyi daṅ naṅ daṅ riṅ ba daṅ ñe ba na gnas pa yin pas dus thams cad du ḥgro ba daṅ ḥoṅ ba daṅ smin par bya ba la sogs pa rnams la ḥjug pa ñid yin no//gal te gcig ñid yin na bya ba du ma rnams la ḥjug pa daṅ/mi zad par ḥgyur ba ñid* [N.272b] *ji lta bu yin she na/dpeḥi sgo nas sgrub par byed de/*

5ab) *srid pa sna tshogs de las skyes/*
dar gyi srin[36] *buḥi skud pa bshin//*

(5ab). *viśve bhāvās tato jātā ūrṇanābhād ivāṃśavaḥ/*[37]

ji ltar srin bal byed paḥi srin bu srin bal gyi snal ma maṅ po skyed par byed kyaṅ ḥgyur ba yaṅ med la/zad pa yaṅ med pa de bshin du skyes bus khams gsum du skyed par byed du ziṅ kyaṅ ḥgyur ba yaṅ med la/zad pa yaṅ med pa yin no//ḥdi ni srid pa ḥbaḥ shig gi rgyur ma zad kyi/srid pa daṅ bral baḥi yaṅ byed pa po yin no shes smras pa[38] /

5cd) *mkhas pa de yi*[39] *char thim pa/*

yaṅ srid len par mi ḥgyur ro//

(5cd) *tasmin pralīnā vidvāṃso nā 'pnuvanti punarbhavam//*

gaṅ gi tshe mkhas pa bsam gtan la rnal ḥbyor pas blo gros kyi mig gis de mthoṅ bar gyur pa na/de ñid du thim par ḥgyur gyi/de ni sdig pa thams cad spaṅs pa yin pas yaṅ srid kyi ḥgro bar skye shiṅ sdug bsṅal gyi snod du ḥgyur ba ma yin no//yaṅ gaṅ gi phyir rnal ḥbyor pas skyes bu ma mthoṅ na bdud rtsi ḥthob pa ma yin pas/ḥdiḥi rgyu smras pa/

6) *ḥchi bcas rnams la bdud rtsi med/*

me la graṅ ba[40] *ji bshin no/*

des na[41] *bdud rtsi skyes by ñid/*

ma rtogs bdud rtsi yod mi rigs//

(6) *amṛtatvaṃ na martyasya vahneḥ śaityam iveṣyate/*

tasmād amṛtatā 'yuktā 'prabodhāt puruṣe 'mṛte[42] //

ḥchi bar ḥos paḥam/ḥchi ba yin pas na ḥchi bcas te ḥjig rten thams cad do//de ni ṅo bo ñid kyis rtag tu ḥchi ba yin pas bdud rtsi ñid yin par mi rigs te/[P.285a] *deḥi ṅo bo ñid ma yin paḥi phyir meḥi raṅ bshin tsha ba ñid la*[43] *graṅ baḥi ṅo bo ma yin pa bshin no//deḥi phyir na ḥchi bdag gi yul las ma*[44] *ḥdas paḥi skyes bu rtog*[45] *par ma gyur pa ḥchi ba daṅ bcas pa rnams kyis*[46] *bdud rtsi ḥthob par mi rigs so//ḥdi ni mthu che ba ñid bsṅags par bya baḥi phyir/*

7. *gaṅ las mchog gyur gshan med phyir/*

gaṅ las dam pa gshan med la[47] /

ḥdi las phra gyur gshan med pas/

sna tshogs ḥdi dag rgyu gcig ñid//

(7) *yataḥ param paraṃ nā'sti yato jyāyān na vidyate/*

aṇīyān nā'pi tenedaṃ viśvam ekena saṃtatam[48] //

gaṅ gi phyir mchog tu [D.253a] *gyur pa ñid daṅ/dam par gyur pa ñid daṅ gtso bor gyur pa ñid daṅ/phra bar gyur pa ñid ḥdi las gshan med do//*[N. 273a] *de lta buḥi yon tan brgyad*[49] *daṅ ldan pas phyug par gyur paḥi rnal ḥbyor pa ñid bstan*[50] *pa/*

de ni phra daṅ rags daṅ ldan/

yaṅ ldan gtso bo dbaṅ sgyur ba/

rab phye ḥdoḍ paḥi mthar thug gaṅ/
rnal ḥbyor ji ltar ḥdod par ḥgro[51] //

de ni gcig ñid yin yaṅ khams gsum sna tshogs bsdus paḥi bdag ñid yin no//

8ab. *der ni ḥbyuṅ ba thams cad kyaṅ/*
bdag ñid du ni ḥdus par mthoṅ/

(8ab) *tasmin sarvāṇi bhūtāni bhavaty ātmaiva paśyataḥ*[52] /

gyo ba daṅ mi gyo baḥi ḥbyuṅ ba thams cad kyaṅ bdag de ñid kyi[53] *khoṅs su ḥdus par gyur pa yin no//gshaṅ yaṅ bdag de ñid mthoṅ na/*

8cd. *byis daṅ mkhas*[54] *daṅ gdol pa daṅ/*
bram ze sogs rnams mñam pa ñid//

(8cd) *bālapaṇḍitacaṇḍālaviprādīnāñ ca tulyatā*[55] //

sdig daṅ bsod nams khyad par med par gyur pas mñam pa yin no shes bya bar sbyar ro//gal te ḥbaḥ shig ḥdi skad du/gaṅ skyes bu ni thams cad du khyab pa gcig ñid yin la/[56] *de las lha daṅ mi la sogs pa ḥgro ba rnam pa sna tshogs kyi lus rnams ḥbyuṅ bar ḥgyur ba yin na/ji ltar lus can bshin du mi rtag pa daṅ/thams cad du ma khyab paḥi ṅo bor mi ḥgyur she na/de la lan gdab par bya baḥi phyir smras pa/*

9. *bum pa ḥbyuṅ śiṅ ḥjig pa ltar/*
[P.285b] *nam mkhaḥ de yi bdag ñid min/*
lus can ḥbyuṅ shiṅ ḥjig pa ltar/
de bdag yin pas bdag mi ḥdod//

(9) *ghaṭotpattau vināśe vā 'kāśasya tadātmatā/*
tadātmatā 'tmano 'pīṣṭā na dehādyudayavyaye[57] //

ji ltar bum pa daṅ rdsas[58] *la sogs pa ḥbyuṅ shiṅ ḥjig par ḥgyur ba na nam mkhaḥ ni bum paḥi raṅ bshin du ḥgyur ba ma yin pa ltar de bshin du skyes bu yaṅ lus can rnam pa sna tshogs kyi dbye ba skye shiṅ ḥjig pa ñams su myoṅ du zin kyaṅ lus can gyi ṅo bo ñiḍ du ni gyur pa ma yin no//gshan the tshom za ba bzlog par bya baḥi phyir nam mkhaḥi dpe grub par ston pa/*

10. *bum paḥi nam mkhaḥ bshin du gcig/*
du maḥo she na bum pa dag/
chag[59] *na dbyer*[60] *med gcig ñid du/*
thams cad mñam[61] *par* [N.273b] *ḥgyur bar ḥdod//*

(10) *ghaṭākāśavad ekasya nānātvaṃ ced abhedataḥ/*
ghaṭabhedena caikatvaṃ sāmye sarvasya janmavat[62] //

gaṅ khyod kyi nam mkhaḥ gcig ñid yin yaṅ bum pa che chuṅ la sogs paḥi dbye bas tha dad pa ñid du ḥgyur [D.253b] *ba ltar bdag kyaṅ de daṅ ḥdraḥo she na/de ni mi rigs te/bum pa thams cad kyi nam mkhaḥ la khyad par med pa ñid yin te/bum pa gcig chag par gyur paḥi nam mkhaḥ daṅ/bum pa gshan chag paḥi nam mkhaḥ khyad par med pa de bshin du bum pa thams cad kyi nam mkhaḥ yaṅ yin la/de bshin du bdag kyaṅ lus can thams cad la khyad par med pa yin pas lus tha dad na yaṅ bdag ni thams cad la mñam par yod paḥi phyir bum paḥi nam mkhaḥi dpe ma grub pa ma yin no//*

yaṅ tshul gshan gyis bdag gcig pa ñid du sgrub paḥi phyir/

11. *ji ltar bum sogs tha dad kyaṅ/*
sa la tha dad ḥgaḥ yaṅ med/
de bshin lus ni tha dad kyaṅ/
bdag la tha dad ḥgaḥ yaṅ med//

(11) *yathā ghaṭādibhede 'pi mṛdbhedo nā 'sti kaś cana/*
(ththaiva dehabhede 'pi nā'tmabhedo 'sti kaś cana[63] //)

ji ltar bum pa daṅ kham phor la sogs pa rdsas tha dad du yod du ẓin kyaṅ/ deḥi rgyur pas[64] *yin pa la dbye ba ḥgaḥ yaṅ med pa de bshin du lha la sogs paḥi lus kyi dbye ba yod du zin kyaṅ/bdag la ni dbye ba ḥgaḥ yaṅ med do// gshan yaṅ/*

12. *ji ltar bum paḥi nam mkhaḥ gcig/*
rdul daṅ du bas [P.286a] *bsgribs pa na/*
thams cad de bshin ma yin ltar/
bde sogs de bshin bdag la min//

(12) *ghaṭākāśe yathaikasmin rajodhūmādibhir vṛte/*
tadvattā na hi sarveṣāṁ sukhāder na tathā'tmanaḥ[65] //

gaṅ saṅs rgyas pas bdag tu smra ba rnams la sṅar smras paḥi skyon bdag thams cad du khyab pa yin na/gcig bde bar gyur pa na thams cad kyaṅ bde bar ḥgyur ro//shes bya ba la sogs pa ḥdir spaṅ ba[66] *bya baḥi phyir smras pa/nam mkhaḥ ni kun la khyab pa yin na*[67] *yaṅ/bum pa gcig gi naṅ gi*[68] *nam mkhaḥ rdul daṅ du ba la sogs pas bsgribs pa na bum pa thams cad kyis*[69] *nam mkhaḥ bsgribs par gyur pa ma yin shiṅ/gcig bsgribs pa daṅ bral bar gyur pas thams cad bsgribs pa daṅ bral ba ma yin pa de bshin du/ḥdir skyes bu gcig bde ba daṅ ldan par gyur* [N.274a] *pa na thams cad bde ba daṅ ldan par gyur pa ma yin shiṅ/gcig sdug bsṅal bar gyur pa na thams cad kyaṅ sdug bsṅal bar gyur pa ma yin pa bshin no//yaṅ ji ltar ḥdi dag so soḥi rgyud la bde ba daṅ/sdug bsṅal ḥbyuṅ bar ḥgyur ba yin she na/smras pa/*

13. *bdag ma śes śiṅ ma rtogs pas/*
rmi lam [D.254a] *loṅs spyod ṅa rgyal bshin/*
las rnams sogs śiṅ dge ba daṅ/
mi dgeḥi ḥbras bu spyod pa yin//

(13) *aprabodhād anātmajñaḥ svapne bhogābhimānavat*[70] /
cinoti karma bhuṅkte ca tatphalam yac chubhāśubham//

ji srid du ḥdis bdag mthoṅ bar ma gyur ciṅ bdag ma śes pa de srid du/rmi lam gyi naṅ du mi bden paḥi gzugs la sogs pa la ñe bar loṅs spyod par ṅa rgyal byed pa de bshin du/bdag kun nas mi śes pa ñid kyaṅ dge ba daṅ mi dge baḥi las bsags[71] *nas/dge ba daṅ mi dge ba deḥi ḥbras bu ñe bar loṅs spyod par byed pa yin no//dbu maḥi sñiṅ poḥi ḥgrel pa rtog ge ḥbar ba// bam po ñi śu gñis pa//skyes bu ni byed pa po daṅ spyod pa po ñid yin te/ sdig pa daṅ bsod nams ñe bar sogs par byed pa daṅ/ñe bar spyod par byed pa yin paḥi phyir/sdig* [P.286b] *pa la sogs paḥi byed pa po yod paḥi skyon yod par ḥgyur ro*[72] *she na/*

14. *lus la gnas kyaṅ ma chags daṅ/*
spyod par byed kyaṅ mi gos[73] *te/*
ḥdod bshin spyod kyaṅ rgyal po bshin/
sdig pas gnod par mi ḥgyur ro//

(14) *dehasaṃstho 'py asaṃgatvād bhuñjāno nopalipyate/*
rājavat kāmacārī ca pāpenā 'naparādhy asau//

ji ltar ḥdis lus thams cad la gnas pa yin du zin kyaṅ de lta na yaṅ ma chags pa ñid yin pa daṅ/yul rnams la spyod du zin kyaṅ yul gyis kyaṅ gos pa med de/ji ltar rgyal po ḥdod pa bshin du spyod du zin kyaṅ phyir gnod pa byed pa med pa de bshin no//ḥdi yaṅ thams cad kyi dbaṅ phyug yin paḥi phyir sdig pa spyod du zin kyaṅ sdig paḥi ḥbras buḥi snod du ni mi ḥgyur ro// de bshin du ji skad bstan paḥi rim pas/

15. *gcig pu* [N.274b] *kun khyab rtag pa ste/*
tshaṅs mchog ḥchi ba med paḥi gnas/
rnal ḥbyor pa yis[74] *goms byas nas*[75] /
de ni yaṅ srid len mi ḥgyur//

(15) *ekaṃ sarvagataṃ nityam param brahmā 'cyutam padam/*
yogī yuñjāna (āve)tti[76] *na tadaiti punarbhavam//*

lus thams cad kyi dbaṅ phyug yin paḥi phyir gcig puḥo[77] *//ḥgro ba thams cad la khyab pa yin paḥi phyir kun khyab po//ñams pa med paḥi phyir rtag paḥo//mya ṅan las ḥdas paḥi bdag ñid yin paḥi phyir tshaṅs paḥo//phul du byuṅ ba yin pas mchog go//thog ma daṅ tha ma med paḥi phyir ḥchi ba med paḥo//dmigs paḥi gnas yin paḥi phyir gnas so//rnal ḥbyor pa ni bsam gtan gyi sbyor bas dmigs par byed pa ste/ḥdi ltar ṅes par* [D.254b] *goms par byas pa na ḥdi lta buḥi tshaṅs pa kun tu*[78] *rtogs pa yin te/des na deḥi yaṅ srid ldog par ḥgyur ro//dge ba daṅ mi dge ba la*[79] *sogs pa daṅ ñe bar spyod pa log par gyur paḥi bdag deḥi mtshan ñid ñe bar bsṅags pa ni/*

16. *de ni rtag par rtog med pa/*
ṅag[80] *gi spyod yul gaṅ mi gyur/*
blo ni dbye bas phrogs[81] *rnams kyis/*
de la tshig tu sbyor bar byed//

(16) *nityaṃ tad avikalpañ ca yatra vācām agocaraḥ/*
giras tatra prayujyante bhedāpahṛtabuddhibhiḥ//

tshaṅs pa de ni dus thams cad du rnal ḥbyor pa rnams kyis dmigs par bya ba yin [P.287a] *paḥi phyir rtag paḥo//dbaṅ po daṅ rnam par śes pa las gshan ñid yin paḥi phyir rtog pa med paḥo//blo dag gi spyod yul du gyur pa ni tshig brjod pa rnams kyi yaṅ yul yin par ḥgyur la/bloḥi spyod yul du ma gyur pa de ñid de ni tshig gi*[82] *spyod yul yaṅ ma yin no//ḥon kyaṅ dbye bas phrogs pa ni dbye ba la ñe bar soṅ baḥi blo ste/de gaṅ la yod pa ni blo ni dbye bas ḥphrogs paḥo//des de la tshaṅs paḥo//shes tshig sbyor bar byed de/ḥdi lta ste/bdag daṅ/skyes bu daṅ/dbaṅ phyug daṅ/kun la khyab pa daṅ/rtag pa shes bya ba la sogs paḥi*[83] *bar ro//ciḥi phyir she na/kun tu*[84] *tha sñad du bya baḥi phyir te/gshan dag gi*[85] *don*[86] *ji ltar bdag gi don ji lta ba bshin du*[87] *rtogs par ḥgyur shes bya bar ro//ḥdiḥi ṅo bo ni brjod par* [N. 275a] *bya ba ma yin pa ñid yin te/rig byed las raṅ byuṅ byed pa med pa boṅ tshad med pa ste/mun pa las gshan paḥi skyes bu ni/*

skyes bu draṅ sroṅ chen po ñi maḥi mdog/
mun pa las gshan gyur pa de rig[88] *na/*
ḥchi ba med par ḥgyur te bdag gis rtogs/
skye med gnas ḥgro ba la lam gshan med//

ces bya ba daṅ/de bshin du

de ni phra gyur skye gnas rnams na gcig pu nas/
de ni rgyas pa ḥdi dag yaṅ dag bsags pa yin/
de ni gtso bo mchog daṅ lha daṅ bstod bya ste/
bdag ṅes bzuṅ nas śin tu shi bar ḥgro bar ḥgyur//
gaṅ las mchog tu gyur pa gshan pa ḥgaḥ yaṅ med/
gaṅ las phra daṅ gtso bor gyur pa gshan[89] *ḥgaḥ ḥaṅ*[90] *med/*
ma bkag bsgribs pa med par lha de gcig pu gnas/
skyes bu de yaṅ kun la khyab ciṅ rgyas//
phra ba las[91] *kyaṅ* [D.255a] *phra shiṅ che bas che//*
ḥgro rnams bdag gi[92] *yon tan khyab nas gnas/*
mya ṅan bral bas mchod sbyin med par mthoṅ/
khams [P.287b] *rnams daṅ ba gtso boḥi che ba ñid//*

de bshin du/

lus med pa yi lus la ni/
kun tu[93] *gnas med gnas pa ni/*
chen por gtso boḥi bdag ñid de/
śes nas mkhas pa mya ṅan med//

de bshin du/

gyo ba de yin mi gyo de/
riṅ ba de yin ñe ba de/
naṅ yaṅ de yin thams cad kyi[94] */*
gñi ga de yin phyi rol ñid//

de bshin du/

dar gyi srin buḥi snal ma bshin/
chu śel nor buḥi chu bshin du/
nya gro yan lag zug rgyu bshin/
de ni lus can kun gyi rgyu//

shes bya ba la sogs pa rig byed kyi luṅ las mthoṅ baḥi tshad mas skyes bu mthoṅ ba shes bya ba ni de kho na ñid yin te/gshan gyis ñams par bya bar mi nus so shes bya ba ni rig byed kyi mthaḥ smra ba rnams kyi[95] *bkod paḥi phyogs sṅa ma yin no//*

[N.275b] *de la lan brjod par bya baḥi phyir bstan bcos byed pas smras pa/......*

Notes

1) *dań*, PK., NK.

2) In accordance with the Skt. text, the order of the four feet of this stanza in *T.* should have been: *a, c, b, d* [Gokhale].

3) *smras paḥi*, N.

4) *smraṅ ste* (*smra ba*?), N.

5) *bus*, D.; *bu*, N.

6) *ba*, P.

7) Hand-copy of the Ms.(=Mc.) shows: *purastāt* in *a*, *mṛtyubhyeti* in *c* and *satvā* in *d* (for '*matva*'=having known or perceived; cf. *Kaṭha-Up.* (=*KU*) 2. 12; *Śvetāśva.Up.* (=*ŚU*) 1. 6; 1. 12; *ĀŚ.* I, 28 etc.) [Gokhale].

8) *tha tshigs so*, P.

9) Quatation from *ŚU* 3. 8: *vedā 'ham etam puruṣaṃ mahāntam ādityavarṇaṃ tamasaḥ parastāt / tam eva viditvā 'timṛtyum eti nā'nyaḥ panthā vidyate 'yanāya //*, which is again found in the comm. to verse 16 below. Tib. translation of *ayana* here=*skye med gnas ḥgro ba* (*ajātisthānagamana*), which seems to suggest the *ajāti-vāda* of Gauḍapāda, treated at length in *ĀŚ.* III-IV [Gokhale].

10) *las pas*, D.

11) *tha*(?), D.

12) *ka pi dsa laḥi*, D.; *ka bi tsa laḥi*, N.

13) *she na*, D.

14) *poḥo*, D.; *baḥo*, N.

15) *ru tra bde byed dag*, D., N.

16) *ya ta*, N.

17) *rnams*, P.

18) *grol ḥgro*, D.

19) *gis*, PK.

20) *blta*, NK.

21) Mc. reads: *sātmyaṃ*. From the following *T.*, the Skt. reading would appear to be neither *sātmyaṃ* nor *sāmyaṃ*, but *śāntaṃ*, but it may be noted that *ĀŚ* uses both *sāmya* and *śānta* in the same sense for describing the Absolute; comp. III, 47, IV, 45 with IV, 80, 93, 95, 100. *Muṇḍaka-Up.* (=*MuU.*), 3. 1. 3 (cf. *Maitri-Up.* (=*MU.*) 6. 18) of which the present stanza is a virtual reproduction, also reads *sāmyam* thus: *yadā paśyaḥ paśyate rukmavarṇaṃ kartāram īśaṃ brahmayonim / tadā vidvān puṇyapāpe vidhūya nirañjanaḥ paramaṃ sāmyam upaiti //* [Gokhale].

22) *thob*, N.

23) *ro* omits in N.
24) *na*, D.; *nas*, N.
25) *byuṅ*, N.
26) *des*, PK.
27) Cf. *Ṛg-Veda* X. 90. 2: *puruṣa evedaṃ sarvaṃ yad bhūtaṃ yac ca bhavyam* = *ŚU.* 3. 15 [The v. l.: *evaitat* for *evedaṃ*, found in Kamalaśīla's comm. on Śāntarakṣita's *Tattvasaṃgraha*, p. 76 (Baroda, 1926) has already been pointed out by H. Nakamura in his article "A note on Pre-Śaṅkara Philosophy," *Proceedings of the Okurayama Oriental Research Institute*, vol. 1, p.3 (Yokohama, 1954); also v. l. *bhāvyam* for *bhavyam* (ibid.).] Further Cf. *IU.* 1. 5; *Bhag.G.* 13. 15 [Gokhale].
28) *pa* omits in P.
29) *stoḥo*, N.
30) *ni* omits in P., N.
31) *cha ṅas baḥo*, N.
32) *dbyuṅ*, P., N.
33) *auṃ*, P.
34) *chu*, P., N.
35) *sor mo*, D., N.
36) *srid*, PK.
37) For the simile of a spider cf. *BU.* 2. 1. 20; *ŚU.* 6. 10; *MuU.* 1. 7 etc. *T.* has "*dar gyi srin bu*" (=*kośakārakīṭa*, silkworm) and "*srin bal byed paḥi srin bu*" (hair-making insect) in the stanza and the commentary respectively. For the second half of the stanza cf. *ŚU.* 1. 7: *līnā brahmaṇi tatparā yonimuktāḥ* [Gokhale].
38) *smras ba*, N.
39) *de yi*, D. (Prosodically better); *deḥi*, P.
40) *graṅs pa*, N.
41) *dės ni*, P., N.
42) Mc. reads: *tamabhyasya* for *na martyasya* and does not write any of the *avagrahas* in the second line of the stanza. Numerous passages are found in the Upaniṣadic literature expressing this thought, continued from the preceding stanza. See: *ŚU.* 3. 7; 5. 6; 6. 17; *Kena-Up.* (=*KnU.*) 2. 4; *KU.* 6. 8; cf. *BU.* 4. 4. 7=*KU.* 6. 14-15; *ĀŚ.* III. 21, IV. 7, etc [Gokhale].
43) *la* omits in N., P.
44) *ma* omits in N., P.
45) *rtogs*, D.
46) *kyi*, N., P.
47) *med pa*, NK., PK.
48) See *ŚU.* 3. 9: *yasmāt paraṃ nāparam asti kiṃcid yasmān nāṇīyo na jyāyo 'sti*

kaścit/...... *tenedaṃ pūrṇaṃ puruṣeṇa sarvam.*

49) *bgyad*, D.

50) *stan*, N.

51) The Sanskrit text of this verse is not contained in the Sanskrit MS. published by Prof. Gokhale. It is likely, however, that this verse was regarded as composed by Bhavya himself, for this verse is contained in the Tibetan version of the *Madhyamaka-hṛdaya-kārikā*, Cf. *The Tibetan Tripiṭaka*, ed. by Department of Indian Philosophy and Indian Literature, vol. 200, 1977, fol. 253a, *l.* 2, and by D. T. Suzuki (Tokyo-Kyoto, The Tibetan Tripiṭaka Institute, 1957), vol. 96, p.14, fol. 31a, *l.* 3. *rab phye* should be read as *rab phyi*. A close relation between the Yoga and the Vedānta schools can be seen here.

52) Cf. *TU.* 7 : *yasmin sarvāṇi bhūtāni ātmaivābhūd vijānataḥ* (Śaṃkarānanda's *Dīpikā*).

53) *gyi*, D.

54) *mkhas pa*, N., P.

55) The thought to advocate 'equality' in the Vedāntic tradition can be noticed in the *Bhag.G.* V, 18.

56) N. has full stop after *pa* and no comma after *la*.

57) Mc. reads : *dehādyudayavyayam* in (d), where *dehādi* corresponds to Tib. *lus can* (= *dehin*) both in *Mhk.* and *T.* Cf. *ĀŚ.* III. 3 and 4 (corresponding respectively to *udaya* and *vyaya* of the *jīva*) with further references on pp. 301-302 ; *Brahmabindu-U.* 13-14. It is made clear by Bhavya that the adversary here and in the following argument is the Buddhist (see stanza 1 above and *T.* on 12 below). However, cf. also the *Sāṃkhya-kārikā* 10, which describes the characteristics of the *vyakta* and the *avyakta*, which are found mixed up here in the description of the *Puruṣa*, i. e., his being 'active' (cf. *kartṛ* in st.3 ; *karmakṛt* in st.4 etc.) and at the same time 'one' (*eka* in st.7), 'eternal and omnipresent' (*nitya*, *sarvatraga* in st.16 and *T.*) etc. This apparent incongruity which is sought to be removed by the Vedāntin by giving this example of 'the ether in the pot' (*ghaṭākāśa*) should therefore be equally objectionable to the Sāṃkhya [Gokhale].

58) *rdsa so*, D.

59) *chags*, PK., NK.

60) *dbye*, PK., NK.

61) *ñams*, PK., NK.

62) Mc. reads : *deha-* for *ceda-* in (b) and *caikasya* for *caikatvam* in (c). Mc. being the single source for the Sanskrit text, which sometimes makes no sense, I have ventured to emend it here rather heavily. The (d) of this stanza also seems doubtful. On the basis of *T.* I might suggest : *sāmyaṃ sarvasya siddhavat* (= [Hence] the state of sameness of everything is as good as proved).

63) The second line of this stanza is missing in Mc. and has therefore been reconstructed

from the Tibetan. For a different reconstruction, see *ĀŚ.*, pp.52-53. The loss of this line may be due to the homoeographic *'sti kaś cana* (either in the original ms. or in the copy). Cf. *ĀŚ.* III. 6, which is also found quoted in the Tibetan version of Śāntarakṣita's *Madhyamakālaṃkāra* (see Walleser, *Der ältere Vedānta*, p.20) [Gokhale].

64) *rgyur gyur pas*, D., N.

65) In (d), *sukhādir* would seem better than *sukhāder* of Mc. The first line is almost identical with *Āgamaśāstra* III. 5 (*yathaikasmin ghaṭākāśe rajodhūmādibhir yute*); the editor suggests the following reconstruction of the second line from the Tibetan: *na bhavanti tathā sarve na sukhādi tathātmanaḥ* (p.52) [Gokhale].

66) *spaṅ par*, D.

67) *na* omits in P., N.

68) *naṅ gi* omits in D.

69) *kyi*, P.

70) In the *Upaniṣads* there are many passages which refer to the state of dreaming.

71) *byas*, D.

72) *ro* omits in P.

73) *dgos*, P., N.

74) *yi*, P., N.

75) *na*, NK., D.

76) Mc. shows here a lacuna of two letters, which I have tried to restore after *T* : *kun tu rtogs pa yin te*, as in the stanza itself no translation of the missing term is given. With a slight emendation the original reading might as well be: *yuñjan yadā vetti* [Gokhale].

77) *paḥo*, P., N.

78) *kun tu kun du*, D.

79) *la* omits in P., N.

80) Sic. PK.; *gaṅ*, N., P., D.

81) *phrog*, N., P.

82) *gi* omits in P.

83) *paḥi* omits in D.; *la sogs par ro*, D.

84) *kun tu kun du*, D.

85) *gis*, D.

86) *don* omits in D.

87) *ji lta ba bshin du*, in N. and P., instead of *ji ltar bdag gi don ji lta ba bshin du*.

88) *rigs*, P., N.

89) *gshan pa*, N., P.

90) *yaṅ*, N., P.

91) *las bas*, D.

92) *gis*, N., P.
93) *kun tu kun du*, D.
94) *kyis*, N., P.
95) *kyis*, D.

II. THE PART OF "THE VEDĀNTA AS PRESENTED BY BHAVYA IN HIS *MADHYAMAKAHṚDAYA* AND *TARKAJVĀLĀ*"

When I wrote this section in the Japanese original version, the Tibetan text alone was available ; the Sanskrit original was not yet published. Now since the Sanskrit original of the *Madhyamaka-hṛdaya* has been published in the first volume of this work (pp.206ff.), I shall make some additional remarks, being based upon the Sanskrit original.

(1) The *Ātman* of the Vedānta school is called *puṃs* (*pumān* in nominative) in the Sanskrit verse after verse 76. This is a rather rare expression in the Vedānta school. Ordinarily it is called *puruṣa*. (In verses 2 and 4, the term *puruṣa* is used, being identified with *Ātman*.)

(2) The highest self is simply called *ātman* (v.58). It is the Highest (*para*, v.57). It is not a substance nor thing (*dravya*, v.58).

dravyaṃ yadi bhaved ātmā dravyatvāt sarvago na saḥ/
ghaṭavan nāpi nityaḥ syāt tena pūrṇaṃ kuto jagat//(v.58)

On the other hand, the individual self is called *antarātman* (vv.50 ; 51) as in the case of Yājñavalkya. In the Tibetan version it is translated as *tsheḥi bdag*, which means *jīvātman*.

(3) In verse 23 the Vedānta school admits two kinds of *Ātman*, i. e. the *Ātman* bound in body and the *Ātman* situated in the highest stage.

rig byed smra bas bdag de ni/rnam ba gñis su ḥdod byed de//
lus shes bya ba bciṅs bdag daṅ/mchog na gnas pa grol paḥi bdag//

This may be a later interpolation by somebody else. In the *Tarkajvālā* there is explanation on this verse.

(4) Among the later Vedāntins there was a controversy whether the *prapañca* is the *pariṇāma* or *vivarta* of *Brahman*. Bhavya does not use either term. It is likely that he did not know that there was such a controversial issue.

(5) In those days the fact that there existed a lot of common features (*bāhusādharmya*, v.87) between Mahāyāna and the Vedānta school was noticed and discussed. Bhavya thought that the latter (*tīrthyas*) adopted the thought of the former.

tāthāgatīm avitathā(ṃ) matvā nītim imāṃ śubhām/
tasyā jātaspṛhais tīrthyais kṛtaṃ tatra mamāpi tat//(v.78)

It is interesting to us that 'Buddhism' is called here '*tāthāgatī nītiḥ.*' Although Bhavya was a highly sophisticated theoretician, he admitted Buddhism as a practical teaching, using the appellation '*nīti.*' [Although in the manuscript it is written as *tīvrais*, I correct it to *tīrthyais*, according to the Tibetan version of the text and also to the explanation in the *Tarkajvālā.*] Later Buddhists asserted that Brahmins stealt Buddhist teachings. [The Southern Chinese version of the [*Mahāyāna*] *Mahāparinirvāṇa-sūtra*, vol. 16, *Taisho Tripiṭaka*, vol. XII, p.716c. ; Cf. ibid. p.382a.]

(6) Bhavya admitted that in Buddhism there were many different teachings (*deśanāyā vaicitryam*, v.80), but that they were nothing but expediencies to attract common people (*ākarṣaṇārtham*, v.80) to Buddhism.

(7) Although Bhavya admitted that there were common elements between Mahāyāna and Vedāntic teachings, he firmly asserted the teaching of 'Non-Self', which is, according to him, the ultimate truth of Buddhism.

nairātmyād eva bhītānām bhītvā tatraivāvasthitiḥ/
ākāśād iva bhītasya kvacanānyatra sthitir bhavet//

The fear in hearing the ultimate truth is referred to in the *Gauḍapādīya-kārikā* IV,42 (Cf. III,39) as well as in the *Prajñāpāramitā* literature. This expression originally derived from Mahāyāna texts.

(8) In one of the verses (after v.76) which seems to be a later interpolation the term *advaita* is used :

khapuṣpāt tadabhedaś ced asatpakṣaparigraha ....../
...... *spatte bhedaś ced advaitaṃ na prasidhyati//*

It is clear that Buddhists of those days already knew the term '*advaita*', probably not in the sense understood in the school of Śaṅkara, but just in the monistic sense. The term '*advitīya*' (v.72) which was originally used in the *Upaniṣads* (Cf. *Chānd.Up.* IV) is mentioned.

(9) Bhavya asserts that *Ātman* must be something that is not originated.

ajātatā hi bhāvānāṃ svabhāvo 'kṛtrimatvataḥ/
anapāyitvataś cāsāv ātmany api nigadyate//(v.81) (Cf. v.83)

The following verse also explains *Ātman* according to the *Tarkajvālā* (Tibetan) :

eko 'sāv ekarūpatvād bhāvabhede 'py abhedataḥ/
sarva[gaḥ] sarvadharmatvā[n] nityaś cāpy avināśataḥ//(v.82)

It is likely that the teaching of 'Non-Origination' was adopted here by Vedāntins, being influenced by the Mādhyamika school. This kind of influence can be noticed most conspicuously in the *Gauḍapādīya-kārikā*.

(10) The ultimate truth is set forth naturally as that in the Mādhyamika school. The last verse of the eighth chapter is set forth as follows:
savikalpāvikalpā[ṃ]ś ca yadā buddhir nivartate/
dhiyām aviṣaye tasmiṃ prapañcaśamaḥ śiva[ḥ]//(v.96)

The cognizing subject is referred to as *buddhi* or *dhī*, both of which are terms commonly used in Indian Philosophy in general. Both were translated as *blo* in Tibetan versions. Dignāga and Dharmakīrti also often use the term *buddhi*. It means that Bhavya was influenced by Brahmanistic philosophical systems.

On the other hand the expression '*prapañcaśamaḥ śivaḥ*' seems to have derived from the *Madhyamaka-kārikās*, and the later is adopted by the Śaiva-Siddhānta school.

Generally speaking, Bhavya used Brahmanistic philosophical terms to a greater extent than Nāgārjuna.

III. "*upāsana*"

The term *upāsana* is very difficult for foreigners to understand. Once I had an opportunity to see Śaṅkarācārya of Kāñcīpura, late at night, 10 : 30 p. m., on Jan. 22, 1960. He spoke in Sanskrit or Tamil; Prof. T. M. P. Mahadevan of the University of Madras took the trouble of interpreting. Questions and answers in the interview were recorded by Mr. Aiyer and published in his book :

> *The Acharya's Call*, H. H. Jagadguru's Madras Discourses [1957-1960], Part I. Compiled by V. Ramakrishna Aiyer (Madras : B. G. Paul & Co., 1964), pp.227-237, Appendix V : "Japanese Professor's Interview."

As I think the interview may be helpful for understanding the Vedānta teaching, I take the liberty of citing the passage :

> The Japanese Professor then asked His Holiness whether he will be permitted to put one or two questions. On receiving permission, he said that he was anxious to know what exactly is the meaning of "*upāsana*," a term he met with in Śrī Śaṅkara Bhagavatpāda's works, was it any special practice, and whether it was practiced in the Mutt?
>
> "*dhyānam eva upāsana*," His Holiness replied in Sanskrit. *upāsana* is *dhyāna* or concentration or meditation. A form is required for concentration. For example, you can meditate on a God with two hands or on a God with eight hands. Reality is always the same and changeless, God, as the ultimate Reality, is Formless. But *upāsana* of a Form is done with a purpose, namely, the attainment of a given benefit. The purpose to be attained by worshipping or concentration on a Form with two hands is not the same as that to be attained by worshipping a Form with eight hands. The scriptures tell you how to meditate, and on what all Forms and with what results. For *upāsana*, you have to follow the *śāstras* or Scriptures. The different *upāsanas* are all aids in the path to the ultimate Goal, namely, understanding Reality. Scriptures prescribe *upāsana* in order to train the mind to concentrate.
>
> The Professor asked whether the Mutt observed *upāsana* and what they were.

His Holiness said that in the scriptures we meet with varieties of *upāsana*. It is not necessary or possible to follow all of them. Usually one or two methods of *upāsana* are chosen and followed and worship offered at a fixed time. *upāsana* is the affair of the individual ; there is nothing collective about it. The *upāsana* followed depends on the family tradition of the individual or the initiation given to him by a Guru.

"What work will Swāmijī recommend to foreigners to understand Advaita Vedānta?" the Professor asked.

His Holiness : You can study *Viveka Cūḍāmaṇi*.

The Professor said that he found it to be an easy work and that it had impressed him.

His Holiness said that *Viveka Cūḍāmaṇi* is the best introductory work. The next step is to study *Aparokṣa-anubhūti*. If you study these two, you will get a general idea of Advaita Vedānta. (pp.228-229)

Reverting to the topic of knowledge of Reality or *jñāna*, and *upāsana*, the Jagadguru said that the two are entirely different. While *upāsana* is mental action, *jñāna*, which also belongs to the realm of the mind, is not action. Action is something done in obedience to the injunction. When the knowledge of Reality is comprehended, the mind continues to dwell in that Reality and does not respond to any injunction whether that injunction comes from any external agency or is the result of the prompting of the senses. The concept of action can be explained by a simple illustration. Here is a bunch of fruits, yellow in colour. When I say, "See, this is yellow," you concur and manifest no reaction, because in reality, it is yellow. On the other hand, if I say, "See, this is red," or "See, this is black," you react immediately and reply, "No, it is yellow." But if I say "Imagine this to be red," you are able to follow that direction. Therefore, action is related to the sphere of injunction. *upāsana* belongs to this category of mental action. You concentrate on God, imagining He is like this or that, until real *jñāna* dawns on you and you understand God as He really is. Thereafter you do not react to any direction to worship this or that form. (pp.236-237)

IV. OTHER

(Pages refer to the English version, Part One.)

p.32, n.10) Cf. Th. Stcerbatsky: *The Central Conception of Buddhism*, p. 73.

pp.48f) [Śaṅkara's date, c.700-750 AD.]

Daniel H. H. Ingalls: *Philosophy East and West*, vol.III, No.4, 1954, p. 292.

pp.48ff) [The Dates of Śaṅkara] I was told that J. Vorenne's study on the *Mahānārāyaṇa-upaniṣad* and P. B. Chakravartin's study on Pre-Sāṃkhya refer to the dates of Śaṅkara. Also,

L. P. Briggs: "The Genealogy and Successors of Śivāchārya; Suppression of the Great Sacerdotal Families by Sūryavarman I," *BEFEO*., vol.XLVI, 1, 1952, pp.177-185.

It has been made clear that Vidyānanda refers to Sureśvara.

Nathmal Tālia: *A Compendium of Vidyānanda's Satyaśāsana-parīkṣā*, reprinted from *Satyaśāsanaparīkṣā*, edited by Sri Gokulchandra Jain and published by Bhāratīya Jñānapīṭha, Varanasi, 1964.

To my regret all these works were not accessible to me. Dr. Pandey (*Pre-Śaṅkara Advaita Philosophy*, op. cit., p.69) fixes the date of Śaṅkara as c. 605-637 AD. Sources for his argumentation should be examined.

p.65) [The Date of Vācaspatimiśra] P. Hacker (*Festschrift Schubring*, S. 160-169) thinks that Vācaspatimiśra was most active in c. 970-980.

pp.65f) [Vācaspati's references to Bhāskara]

Daniel H. H. Ingalls: *Philosophy East and West*, vol.III, No.4, 1954, p. 292.

pp.75f) [Quotations of Dharmakīrti's verses]

Daniel H. H. Ingalls: *Philosophy East and West*, vol.III, No.4, 1954, p. 300.

p.77) [The Date of Sroṅ btsan sgam po] According to recent studies by Prof. Zuiho Yamaguchi, Sroṅ btsan sgam po was born in 581 AD. at the latest and died in 649 when he was 69 years old. The last three years he spent in matrimonial life with a Chinese princess. The date of his marriage with her was 646 AD. The year of her arrival in Tibet must have been 640

AD. (Zuiho Yamaguchi : *Toban Okoku Seiritsu-shi Kenkyū* [= *A Study on the Establishment of the Tu-fan Kingdom*], Tokyo : Iwanami Press, 1983, p.507 f.)

p.79) [The Date of Kumārila] Verses of Kumārila's *Ślokavārttika* are often cited in Arcaṭa's *Hetu-bindu-ṭīkā*, while Arcaṭa's theory was cited in works of Śālikanātha (c. 750-800). The assumption of Kumārila's date as c. 650-700 is justified. (Yusho Miyasaka : *IBK*, vol.II, No.1, p.300f.)

p.80) [The Date of Bhartṛhari] It should be corrected according to recent studies. (Hajime Nakamura : "Tibetan Citations of Bhartṛhari's Verses and the Problem of his Date," *Susumu Yamaguchi's Commemoration Volume*, pp.122-126.) This has been discussed in more detail by myself in the second volume of this work.

p.86) [The Date of Kamalaśīla] This has been controversial among Western and Japanese scholars for many years, and their opinions are not unanimous. They cite from many Tibetan and Chinese sources, and I shall refrain from going into greater detail.

p.93) [*Vedānta* meant *Āraṇyakas* in some cases] Moreover, *SDS.* V, *ll.*87-88. In one case *Vedānta* meant *rahasyamantra* and *brāhmaṇa* (*Baudhāyana-dharmasūtra*, p.258).

p.97) [Upaniṣadic texts were also recited] Cf. *Manu* VI, 83.

p.98) [*Vedānta* in the broad sense] Ānandajñāna interpreted *Vedāntakṛt* (*Bhag.G.* XV, 15) as *tad(= Vedānta)-arthasaṃpradāyapravartaka*, Madusūdana-sarasvatī as *Vedāntārthasampradāyapravartaka*, and Nīlakaṇṭha as *Vedānto-ktavidyāsaṃpradāyakṛt*.

p.117) [Appellations of the Vedānta School] In the Sāṃkhya school *vedānta* meant 'the end of the Veda'.

Vedānām avasāneṣu paṭhyate (*Yuktidīpikā*, ad I, 5)

The appellation *advaitavādin* is rarely used (*SDS.* XVI, *l.*96). *advayavādin* means *Buddha*, according to the *Amarakośa*. Cf. the above-cited passage in Bhāskara's *Bhāṣya* (*A History of Early Vedānta Philosophy*, Part One, p. 260).

p.118) [*Aupaniṣadika*] *Aupaniṣadika* means 'secret teaching of poetics' (*Kāvya-mīmāṃsā* I). Also, 'secret teaching' in the science of the erotic (*Kāma-sūtra* I,1,12).

p.121) [*Māhāyānika-pakṣa*] Cf. *Māhāyānika-pakṣānupraveśinām brahmavādinām* (Śālikanātha : *Prakaraṇapañcikā*, Benares, 1903, p.156, 15 [cited from P. Hacker : *Vivarta*, S.201]).

p.123, n.22) [*brahmavādin*] Cf. *Bhag.G.* XVII, 24.

pp.131ff) [References to Vedānta in Buddhist Works]

Daniel H. H. Ingalls : *Annals of the Bhandarkar Oriental Research Institute*, vol.XXXIII, p.12.

L. Renou : *Journal Asiatique*, 1955, tome CCXLIII, fasc.2, pp.249-251.

p.142) [colors of the spirit] The notion that the color of the spirit differs with persons was held by the Jains and the Ājīvikas (A. F. R. Hoernle, *ERE*. I, p.262a).

p.143) [a string through pure gems] This simile was used by the Sāṃkhyas also (*A History of Early Vedānta Philosophy*, Part One, p.335). Cf. *mayi sarvam idaṃ protaṃ sūtre maṇigaṇā iva* (*Bhag.G.* VII, 7).

p.147) [criticism of *Īśvara*] Cf. Guṇaratna ad *Ṣaḍdarśanasamuccaya*, ed. by L. Suali, Calcutta, 1905, pp.12ff.

p.165) [*The Śāstra by the Bodhisattva (Ārya-) Deva on the Explanation of Nirvāṇa by (Twenty) Heretical and Hīnayāna (Teachers) Mentioned in the Laṅkā(-avatāra)-sūtra*, Nj. 1260] This Chinese version was translated by Giuseppe Tucci into English (*T'oung Pao*, XXIV, pp.16-31). However, this translation was not accessible to me.

p.168) [*Brahmā* arose from a golden egg, and then caused the entire world to evolve] This idea was set forth in *Viṣṇu-Purāṇa* I, 2, 58f. (Works by the Late H. H. Wilson, vol.VI, London, 1864, pp.38f. ; *The Vishnu Purana*, Translated by H. H. Wilson, Calcutta, Punthi Pustak, 1961, p.17 ; Cf. n.30).

p.172) [*kāla*] In Jain texts *kālavāda* is referred to as a heretical doctrine (Guṇaratna ad Haribhadra's *Ṣaḍdarśanasamuccaya*, ed. by L. Suali, Calcutta, 1905, p.10). Some people regarded *kāla* as the principle for world evolution (*Śvet.Up.* I, 2 ; VI, 1). In *Viṣṇu-Purāṇa* I, 2 Brahmā evolves two forms : *puruṣa* and *kāla*.

p.178, n.17) Another possible interpretation is that the author of the text associated *mukha* with *kha* by means of Volksetymologie.

p.184, *l*.7 from bottom). Cf. *tenedaṃ pūrṇaṃ puruṣeṇa sarvam* (*Śvet.Up.* III, 9).

p.185, *l*.1) [*bhavaty*] This follows Gokhale's emendation. The manuscript reads *bhavaṃty*, which seems to be better.

p.202, v.80) [*deśanāyās tu vaicitryād*] In the [Tibetan] *Tarkajvālā* on this verse the opponent says, "the Madhyamakavādins teach self and non-self, *śūnyatā* and non-*śūnyatā*, *utpāda* and *anutpāda*, substantiality and non-substantiality. This is contradictory." In the [*Mahāyāna*] *Mahāparinirvāṇa-sūtra* contradictory teachings are all admitted (*chüan* 27 ; *Taisho Tripiṭaka*, vol. XII, p.523b).

p. 223) [Vedavādin] Candrakīrti mentions the term *rig byed du smra pa* in the 6th chapter of the *Madhyamakāvatāra* (Bibliotheca Buddhica, p.240).

p.249, *ll*.14-17) This verse is a citation from the *Madhyāntavibhāgaśāstra* (Sthiramati's *Madhyānta-vibhāgaṭīkā*, publiée par S. Yamaguchi, Nagoya, 1934, pp.51 ; 59-60).

p.292) [*Dvādaśāranayacakra*] References to the Vedānta school in this work are found in the commentary portion: *advaitajñatva*, *darśanam advaitam*, p.222 ; *advaita*, p.223 ; *advaitavāda*, pp.271, 279 ; *advaita*, *advaitārtha*, p.288.

p.313) [Mīmāṃsā and Vedānta] Very rarely were Mīmāṃsakas called 'Vedāntins'. Maṇibhadra, a later Jain scholar, called Jaimini Pūrva-Vedāntavādin (Maṇibhadra's *Laghuvṛtti* on Hemacandra's *Ṣaḍdarśana-samuccaya*, v.72, Chowkhamba Sanskrit Series, No.95, 1929, p.70). It is likely that Patañjali (2nd century BC.) relied on the scholarship and texts of earlier Mīmāṃsakas (E. Frauwallner : *WZKSO*. IV, 1960, S.92-118).

p.315) [The three debts] "A twice-born man who, with collected mind, follows the tenfold law and has paid his (three) debts may, after learning the Vedānta according to the prescribed rule, become an ascetic." (*Manu* VI, 94)

p.354) [*śabdabrahman* in *Bhavabhūti*] Discussed by Hacker : *Vivarta*, S.205-207.

p.355, *ll*.14-19) This verse is occasionally ascribed to Bhartṛhari (D. D. Kosambi : *Bhartṛhari*, p.181, v.662).

p.404) It has been held in general in India that the author of the *Brahma-sūtra* is Bādarāyaṇa. In this connection Śaṅkara himself regards Vyāsa as the authority on the traditions of the Vedānta school.

tyaktvāto hy anyaśāstroktīr matiṃ kuryād dṛḍhāṃ budhaḥ // 66 //

śraddhābhaktī puraskṛtya hitvā sarvam anārjavam/
vedāntasyaiva tattvārthe vyāsasyāpi matau tathā // 67 //

(Śaṅkara's *Upadeśasāhasrī*, ed. by Sengaku Mayeda, Tokyo, Hokuseido Press, 1973, I, 16, 66-67, pp.128-129)

"Therefore, having abandoned the teaching of other scriptures, a wise man should make firm his understanding [66] of the true meaning of the *Vedānta* (=Upaniṣads) and also of Vyāsa's thought, with faith and devotion and without any crookedness." [67] (*A Thousand Teachings, The Upadeśasāhasrī of Śaṅkara*, Translated by Sengaku Mayeda, University of Tokyo Press, 1979, p.156)

It is not quite clear whether Vyāsa meant Bādarāyaṇa or not. Ordinarily in Śaṅkara's works Vyāsa indicates the author of the *Smṛtis* and not Bādarāyaṇa, the author of the *Brahma-sūtra*.

p.425) Studies on parts of the *Brahma-sūtra* have been published.

P.M. Modi : *A Critique of the Brahmasūtra* (III 2. 11-IV), Part I. *Intrepretation of the Sūtras* (Baroda, 1945, Published by the author); Part II. *System of the Sūtras* (Baroda, 1956, Published by the author).

pp. 525-526) The theory of the Two Paths : *pitṛyāna* and *devayāna* seem to be relevant to the practice of *yajñas* (Cf. *Manu* III, 76).

B. SOME NEW LIGHT ON ŚAṄKARA

I. COMFLICT BETWEEN TRADITIONALISM AND RATIONALISM: A PROBLEM WITH ŚAṄKARA[1]

1. THE SIGNIFICANCE OF THE VEDIC SCRIPTURES

Insofar as his Commentary on the *Brahma-sūtra* goes, Śaṅkara was not a rationalistic philosopher who, disregarding tradition and carrying on speculation freely and independently, set forth his own argument. He claimed, through and through, to be a faithful expositor of the purport of the scripture (authoritative texts). For him, the *Veda* was of utmost significance[2] and of absolute authority.[3] Any part of the *Veda* can be an authority; no part can fail to be an authority.[4] The *Veda* is absolute concerning what it says; it does not depend on anything else; it is like the sun which shines throughout the universe.[5] (Actually, the Vedic texts which he cited were mostly the older *Upaniṣads*.)

The authority of the *Veda* is higher than that of the gods. It is by means of the *Veda* that even the gods are brought to spiritual liberation.[6] The *Veda* was not composed by men; it is authoritative in the sense of being self-revealing; it does not rely on any source.[7]

Then how is it that the *Veda* came to be known to men? The *Veda* had already existed in a latent condition in the world-creator who breathed it out. And the sages (*ṛṣis*) of antiquity *saw* it.[8] Or *Brahman* is the source (*yoni*) of the existing scriptures.[9] This thought is set forth by Śaṅkara following the *Bṛhadāraṇyaka-Upaniṣad* (II, 4, 10), whereas, on another occasion,[10] different from that explanation, he says that the whole world was produced from the words of the *Veda*, that is to say, the creator shaped the whole world with the words of the *Veda* as the formative causes. These two explanations seem to be contradictory to each other. However, we might be able to construe them as follows: the coming into existence of the *Veda* is a primordial production, whereas the creation from the words of the *Veda* means the creation at the beginning of each aeon (*kalpa*) ; the two creations have different significance.[11] Anyway, being established on *Brahman*, the *Veda* is eternal and everlasting — such must have been his thought.

The authority of the Vedic scripture is beyond the theories and inferences which are derived from the thinking of mankind.[12] Inference or analogy, which is based on worldly experiences, cannot apply to the content of the *Veda*.[13] Any augment which is not based on the *Veda* is worth refuting only for the reason that "it has not evidence in the *Veda*."[14]

Notes

1) This is a translation, somewhat abbreviated, of the author's "Dento to Gorishugi no Koso : Śaṅkara ni okeru Ichimondai," *Indogaku Bukkyogaku Kenkyū* (*Journal of Indian and Buddhist Studies*), vol.VIII, no.1, 1960, pp.9-18.

2) The opinion that man should not act arbitrarily apart from the prescripts of the scriptures is set forth in the *Bhagavad-Gītā* (XVI, 23).

3) *prāmāṇyam vedasya*, *BS*. vol.II, p.79, *l*.12 ; *āgamaprāmāṇya*, p.570, *l*.9 ; *pramāṇabhūtaṃ śāstram*, vol.I, p.103, *l*.1. *N.B.* All the Sanskrit citations have been, unless specifically mentioned, taken from Śaṅkara's *Brahmasūtrabhāṣya*, Hari Nārāyaṇa Āpṭe, ed., 2 vols. Poona, Ānandāśrama Press, 1900. The English translations have been cited chiefly from G. Thibaut's translation, occasionally with slight alteration.

4) *na hi vedavākyānāṃ kasyacid arthavattvaṃ kasyacid anarthavattvam iti yuktaṃ pratipattum, pramāṇatvāviśeṣāt*, vol.II, p.209, *ll*.8-9.

5) *vedasya hi nirapekṣaṃ svārthe prāmāṇyaṃ raver iva rūpaviṣaye. puruṣavacasām tu mūlāntarāpekṣaṃ vaktṛsmṛtivyavahitaṃ ceti viprakarṣaḥ*, vol.I, p.426, *ll*.2-4.

6) vol.I, p.291, *l*.9, to p.292, *l*.1.

7) *apauruṣeye vede vaktur abhāvāt*, vol.I, p.176, *l*.7.

8) vol.I, p.42, *l*.3 to p.43, *l*.3. Cf. Paul Deussen : *Das System des Vedānta*, Vierte Auflage, Leipzig, F. A. Brockhaus, 1923, S.72-73, Anm.57 ; *The Vedānta-sūtras with the Commentary of Śaṅkarācārya*, Translated by George Thibaut. Part I, Oxford, Clarendon Press, 1890, p.222 ; J. Muir : *Original Sanskrit Texts*, 3rd edition, London, Trübner, 1868-1884, vol.I, p.394 ; vol.III, p.85 : *atīndriyārtha-draṣṭāraḥ ṛṣayaḥ teṣāṃ vedadraṣṭṛtvaṃ smaryate yugānte 'ntarhitān vedān setihāsān maharṣayaḥ lebhire tapasā pūrvam anujñātāḥ svayambhuvā/ Vedārthaprakāśa* on *Tait. Saṃh.* Cf. Śāntiparva, 7660. Cf. Ś. on *BS*., I, 3, 33. To the gods also the Veda is revealed without learning it. (*teṣāṃ ca svayaṃ pratibhātavedatvāt*, and *BS*., I, 3, 26 ; Vol. I, p.291, *l*.10).

9) *BS* I, 1, 3, vol.I, p.41, *l*.3, to p.43, *l*.3.

10) On *BS*. I, 3, 28.

11) Cf. Jadunạth Sinha : *History of Indian Philosophy*, vol.II, Calcutta, Calcutta Central Book Agency, 1952, p.571.

12) "Nor, finally, can the authoritativeness of the *Veda* (*śāstra*) be proved by inferential reasoning so that it would be dependent on instances observed elsewhere. From all which it follows that the *Veda* possesses authority as a means of right knowledge of *Brahman*" (On *BS*. I, 1, 4. vol.I, p.50, *ll*.4ff).

13) "Nor can the analogies of ordinary experience (*sāmānyato dṛṣṭa*) be applied to something to be learned from scripture." (vol.II, p.559, *ll*. 9-10).

14) *pradhānādikāraṇavādāś cāśabdatvena nirākṛtāḥ*, vol.I, p.417, *ll*.14.) "We will hereafter refuse the so-called authority of the *smṛtis* and ratiocination (in support of the Sāṃkhya doctrine)" (*smṛtinyāyaprasiddhī tu parihariṣyete*, vol.I, p.379, *l*.9).

2. TRADITIONALISM AND RATIONALISM

Even Śaṅkara did not completely deny free and independent thinking on the part of men. However, he admitted its value and significance, allegedly at least, only insofar as it is helpful for understanding the thought of the scriptures and laying a theoretical foundation for it.[1]

This standpoint cannot but come into conflict with the rationalistic standpoint, which regards theoretical thinking as fundamental. The conflict between traditionalism and rationalism is clearly noticed in the following passage in a work of Śaṅkara :

> "In matters to be known from scripture mere reasoning is not to be relied on for the following reason also. As the thoughts of man are altogether unfettered, reasoning which disregards the traditional authoritative texts and rests on individual assumption alone has no proper foundation. We see how arguments, which some clever men had excogitated with great pains, are shown, by people still more ingenious, to be fallacious, and how the arguments of the latter, again, are refuted in their turn by other men ; so that, on account of the diversity of men's opinions, it is impossible to accept mere reasoning as having a sure foundation."[2]

The relativistic or skeptical opinion about the thinking of men was formerly asserted by Sañjaya in the period of the rise of cities in India, and partly shared by Mahāvīra and the Buddha ; so, it was not unusual in Indian thought. However, the above-mentioned assertion by Śaṅkara is simply a replica of the assertion by Bhartṛhari, the Vedāntic grammarian ; it is likely that Śaṅkara inherited the assertion of Bhartṛhari.[31]

When opponents point out the fact that rationalistic thinking could virtually have been launched in India by the Sāṃkhya and the Vaiśeṣika philosophers, Śaṅkara asserts that the diversity of their opinions evidences the fact that none of their opinions is the only true one.

> "Nor can we get over this difficulty by accepting as well-founded the reasoning of some person of recognized mental eminence, may he be Kapila or anybody else, since we observe that even men of the most undoubted mental eminence, such as Kapila, Kaṇāda and other founders of philosophical schools, have contradicted one another."

Against this opinion the rationalists say that the argument which is used to refute theoretical thinking cannot be established by itself.

> "But we will fashion our reasoning otherwise, i. e., in such a manner as not to lay it open to the charge of having no proper foundation. You cannot, after all, maintain that no reasoning whatever is well-founded. [1] You yourself can found your assertion that reasoning has no foundation on reasoning alone, your assumption being that, since some arguments are seen to be devoid of foundation, other arguments belonging to the same class are likewise devoid of foundation. [2] Moreover, if all reasoning were unfounded, the whole course of practical human life would have to come to an end, for we see that men act, with a view to obtaining pleasure and avoiding pain in the future, on the assumption that the past, the present, and the future are uniform. [3] Further, in the case of passages of the Vedic texts [apparently] contradicting each other, the ascertainment of the real sense, which depends on a preliminary refutation of the apparent sense, can be effected only by an accurate definition of the meaning of sentences, and that involves a process of reasoning. Thus, Manu also expresses himself : 'Perception, inference and the *Śāstra* according to the various traditions — this triad is to be known well by one desiring cleanness (or purity) in regard to right. He who applies reasoning not contradicted by the *Veda* to the

Veda and the [*Smṛti*] doctrine of law, he and no other knows the law' (*Manu Smṛti* XII. 105, 106). And that 'want of foundation,' to which you object, really constitutes the beauty of reasoning, because it enables us to arrive at unobjectionable arguments by means of the previous refutation of objectionable arguments. [There is no fear that because the one opinion is ill-founded the other opinion should be ill-founded too ;] for there is no valid reason to maintain that a man must be stupid because his elder brother was stupid. For all these reasons the want of foundation cannot be used as an argument against reasoning."

Against such an argument Śaṅkara points out the limit of rationalism, to the effect that, whereas the rationalistic way of thinking can apply to things in the empirical world, it is quite impossible to apply it to the metaphysical realm, which is beyond our experience.

"Against this argument [by rationalists] we remark that thus also there results 'want of release.' For, although with regard to some things reasoning is observed to be well founded, with regard to the matter in hand there will result 'want of release,' in other words, of the reasoning from this very fault of ill-foundedness (i.e., reasoning will not be exempt from the fault of not having a sound basis). The true nature of the cause of the world (*bhāvayāthātmya*) on which final emancipation depends cannot, on account of its excessive abstruseness, even be thought of without the help of the traditional or authoritative texts; for, as already remarked, it cannot become the object of perception, because it does not possess qualities such as form and the like, and, as it is devoid of characteristic signs, it does not lend itself to inference and the other means of right knowledge."

The assertion that inference cannot apply to metaphysical problems was held by Kant in the West ; even contemporary rationalists set forth the same opinion. That is why such a predecessor of analytical philosophy as Wittgenstein went almost to such a length as might be called mysticism.

However, to define (make clear) the limit (scope) of rationalism does not necessarily imply that abandoning the rationalistic attitude we must acknowledge the authority of scriptures. The attitude of applying the rationalistic attitude to its fullest extent presupposes abandoning the authority and prestige of scriptures in general. However, in Śaṅkara a sort of confusion in thinking can be noticed. The main point of his assertion is: "By way of rationalism one cannot apprehend the Absolute. Therefore, rely upon the *Veda*."[4] Here is an instance of going beyond logic. For Śaṅkara, who was a Brahmanistic philosopher, the main concern was to lay a firm and solid foundation for the authority and prestige of the traditional scriptures; various arguments were presented simply to bring about theoretical discussions which were favorable for his purpose.

Accordingly, his philosophical standpoint rather lacked in thoroughness (or consistency). Stressing the authority of the scriptures on the surface, he had to acknowledge in actuality the value of theoretical thinking. This situation can be noticed very well in the following passage:

> "Or else [if we adopt another explanation of the phrase 'want of release' (*avimokṣa*) in *sūtra* II, 1, 11], all those who teach the final release of the soul are agreed that it results from perfect knowledge. Perfect knowledge has the characteristic mark of uniformity, because it depends on actually existing things; for whatever is permanently of one and the same nature is acknowledged to be a true or real thing, and knowledge conversant about such a thing is called perfect knowledge, as, for instance, the knowledge embodied in the proposition, 'fire is hot.' Now, it is clear that in the case of perfect knowledge a mutual conflict of men's opinions is impossible. But that cognitions founded on reasoning do conflict is generally known, for we continually observe that what one logician endeavors to establish as perfect knowledge is demolished by another, who, in his turn, is treated similarly by a third. How, therefore, can knowledge, which is founded on reasoning, and whose object is not something permanently uniform, be perfect knowledge?[5] Nor can it be said that he who maintains the *pradhāna* (fundamental matter) to be the cause of the world (i. e., the Sāṃkhya) is the best of all reasoners, and is accepted as such by all philosophers, which would enable us to accept his opinion as perfect knowledge. Nor can we collect at a given moment and in a given place all the logicians of the past, the present and the future, so as to settle [by their agreement] that their opinion regarding some uniform object is to be considered

perfect knowledge."

"The *Veda*, on the other hand, which is eternal and the source of knowledge, may be allowed to have for its object firmly established things, and therefore the perfection of that knowledge which is founded on the *Veda* cannot be denied by any of the logicians of the past, present or future. We have thus established the perfection of this our knowledge which reposes on the *Upaniṣads*, and, since apart from it perfect knowledge is impossible, its disregard would lead to 'absence of final release' of the transmigrating souls. Our final position, therefore, is that on the ground of traditional scripture and of reasoning subordinate to traditional scripture, the intelligent *Brahman* is to be considered the cause and substance of the world."[6)]

Notes

1) The thought that ratiocination is to support the scriptures is found in Rāmānuja also. *ato 'tīndriye 'rthe śāstram eva pramāṇam ; tad upabṛmhaṇāyaiva tarka upādeyaḥ*/ Rāmānuja on *BS*. II, 1, 11).

2) Ś. on *BS*. II, 1, 11.

3) *Vākyap*. I, 34 ; I, 39. Cf. Part VII, Chapter III, Section III of this book.

4) That *Brahman* can be known only by means of the scriptures is set forth also in *Svātmanirūpaṇa*, 44 f.

5) The argument cited here also is inherited from Bhartṛhari. Cf. *Vākyap*. I, 34. See Part VII, Chapter III, Section III of this book.

6) "Even if those 'perfect' men (possessing supernatural powers) were accepted as authorities to be appealed to, still, as there are many such perfect men, we should have, in all those cases where the *smṛtis* contradict each other in the manner described, no other means of final decision than an appeal to *śruti*" (*siddha-vyapāśraya-kalpanāyām api bahutvāt siddhānām pradarśitena prakāreṇa smṛtivipratipattau satyāṃ na śrutivyapāśrayād anyan nirṇayakāraṇam asti*, vol.I, p.423, *l*.2).

3. THE STANDARD OF KNOWLEDGE

This sort of lack of thoroughness as is noticed in Śaṅkara seems to have been traditional to the Vedānta school. The *Brahma-sūtra* (II, 1, 18) had made Vedic passages (*śabda*) and reasoning (*yukti*) the two requirements necessary for establishing an assertion, and this attitude was inherited by

Śaṅkara.[1] Here the following question must arise. Is there not a case in which a Vedic passage is in contradiction to reasoning? Thinking that all Vedic passages must always be justifiable theoretically, Śaṅkara did not admit the possibility of any contradiction between the two.[2]

Then, what is the real nature of the scriptures which were endowed with such an authority? Speaking for the scriptures, the *Veda* was thought of as the supreme authority. The *Veda*, in contrast to daily experience (*loka*), was regarded as something beyond the world (*aloka*).[3]

Besides the *śruti* (i. e., the *Veda*), the *smṛti* were regarded as authorities second [only] to the *śruti* in significance. Accordingly, it was occasionally supposed that to be founded by the three, i.e., the *śrutis*, *smṛtis* and *nyāya* (ratiocination) is the mark of a truth.[4] Here ratiocination nearly amounts to the same as the above-mentioned 'daily experience.' The *smṛtis* were supposed to have the characteristics of both the *śruti* and daily experience.[5]

Perception (*pratyakṣa*) and inference or inferential reasoning (*anumāna*), which are mentioned quite a few times as the basis for argument in the *Brahma-sūtra*, mean, respectively, the *śruti*s and the *smṛti*s according to Śaṅkara.[6] The reasons they are called such are not explicitly explained in the *Brahma-sūtra*, and we have to surmise them. Śaṅkara explains them as follows: the *śrutis* are called 'perception' because they do not depend on anything else for their being a source of knowledge, and the *smṛtis* are called 'inference' because they depend on something else for their being a source of knowledge.[7] That is to say, the *śrutis* can be the absolute source [of knowledge], just in the same way as perception is self-evident and causes no doubt in the process of cognition.[8] For this reason they are called 'perception.' The *smṛtis* can be a source of knowledge insofar as they coincide with the *śrutis*, just in the same way as inference can be established insofar as it is based on perception. For this reason, they are called 'inference.' In the use of such terms as 'perception' and 'inference' instead of such terms as the '*śrutis*' and '*smṛtis*,' we perceive the *Brahma-sūtra*'s fondness for enigmatic expression. Anyway, as the *smṛtis* are inferior to the *śrutis* in authority, it is ruled out that, when there is contradiction between these two, the teaching of the *śrutis* should be adopted.[9]

The enumeration of the sources of knowledge (*pramāṇa*)[10] by Śaṅkara is not fixed as a formula. Needless to say, the *śrutis* are regarded as a source of knowledge.[11] In some cases the *Mantras* (magical formulas), *Arthavādas* (explanatory passages), *Itihāsas* (historical tales) and *Purāṇas* (old legends) are thought to be the authoritative sources for argumentation.[12] Among these four, the *Mantras* and *Itihāsas* are substantially included in the *śrutis*, and the *Itihāsas* and *Purāṇas* are included in the *smṛtis*. In some cases, as the fifth source 'daily experience' is enumerated in addition to the above-mentioned four.[13] In this case, 'daily experience' ranges from the experience of ordinary men up to rational theories. According to the information by Śaṅkara, Jaimini asserted that the above-mentioned five cannot be sources of authoritative knowledge concerning such problems as, e. g., whether gods keep their own bodies.[14] This betrays that Jaimini admitted that the above-mentioned five could be the sources.

Be that as it may, Śaṅkara in fact admitted daily experience or the thinking of ordinary men as an independent source of knowledge. "The conceptions of ordinary life (*lokaprasiddhi*) also must not be declared to be unfounded, if it is at all possible to accept them."[15] What is called 'ordinary life' or 'daily experience' (*loka*) is tantamount to the sources of knowledge, i. e., 'perception' (*pratyakṣa*), etc., in terms of Indian philosophy in general.[16] It was a customary practice for Śaṅkara to designate the sources of knowledge (*pramāṇa*) as 'perception,' etc.[17] And to be contradictory to perceptions, etc., was regarded as a fallacy.[18] However, he thought that man did not need to understand things as perception represents them, and that, insofar as metaphysical problems are concerned, man should accept what the scriptures teach, for perception is of no use concerning them.[19] It is not clear what is implied by the term 'etc.' when he said 'perception, etc.' It is certain that inference at least is implied.[20] He thought that inference is a secondary function, established on the base of perception by means of the senses.[21]

In some cases, Śaṅkara admitted four sources of knowledge, i. e., perception, inference, comparison (*upamāna*) and the scriptures,[22] and, in other cases, five, i. e., assumption (*arthāpatti*) in addition to the above-mentioned four.[23] The latter theory is the same as that of the Prābhākara school of the Mīmāṃsakas. (If we add non-perception to the above-mentioned five, the theory becomes just the same as that of the Kumārila school of the Mimāṃsakas.) Anyway, Śaṅkara was not too clear on the theory of knowledge. His standpoint was rather similar to that of the early Mimāṃsakas, who did not clearly distinguish the sources of knowledge and increased them (their number) more and more with the lapse of time. Later Advaitins came to recognize the six sources of knowledge accepted by the school of Kumārila.[21]

Notes

1) *nyāyataḥ śrutito vā*, vol.I, p.504, *l*.12; *śrutyanumānābhyām*, vol.II, p.20, *l*.10. *evaṃ hi śrutivākyaśataiḥ sabāhyābhyantaram ajam ātmatattvam advayaṃ na tato 'nyad astīti niścitam etat. yuktyā cādhunaitad eva punar nirdhāryat*, (on *Gauḍapādīya-kārikā* III,27. Poona, Ānandāśrama Press, 1928, p 137, *ll*.14-15).

2) *tad ātmaikatvapratipādanaparair vākyair nyāyopetair dvaitavādapratiṣedhaiś cāpaneṣyāmīti* (vol.I, p.279, *l*.8).

3) For example, he says that *pradhāna, mahat*, etc., are *aloka-Vedaprasiddha* (vol.I, p. 427, *ll*.8-9). The use of words in the *Veda* is made in contrast to that of words in ordinary daily life (vol.I, p.138, *l*.10).

4) *śrutismṛtinyāyaprasiddham*, vol.I, p.57, *l*.9. [In the assertion of the *pūrvapakṣa* it is said in the same way. Cf. vol.I, p.345, *l*.3.] Having cited many scriptural passages, he says: *ityādiśrutismṛtinyāyebhyo* (vol.II, p.540, *l*.12).

5) "Now things of the nature of the elements and the sense organs, which are well known from the *Veda*, as well as from experience, may be referred to in *smṛti*" (on *BS*. II, 1, 2. *bhūtendriyāṇi tāval loka-Veda-prasiddhatvāc chakyante smartum*, vol.I, p.426, *l*. 9).

6) Cf. Part IV, Chapter III, Section II of *A History of Early Vedānta Philosophy*, Part One, p.413; Paul Deussen: *Die Sūtra des Vedānta*, Zweite Auflage, Leipzig, F. A. Brockhaus, 1920, S.171; Thibaut: *The Vedānta-sūtras with the Commentary of Śaṅkarācārya*, p.203. Cf. Paul Deussen: *Das System des Vedānta*, Vierte Auflage, Leipzig, F. A. Brockhaus, 1923, S.95.

7) *prāmāṇyaṃ praty anapekṣatvāt*, vol.I, p.297, *l*.8. Cf. *vedasya hi nirapeksaṃ svārthe prāmāṇyam*, vol.I, p.426, *ll*.2-3.

8) *prāmāṇyaṃ prati sāpekṣatvāt*, vol.I, p.297, *ll*.8-9.

9) vol.I, p.422, *l*.1.

10) The passages in which Śaṅkara refers to *pramāṇa* are collected by P. Deussen (*Das System des Vedānta*, S.95, Anm.54).

11) *pramāṇam vedas*, *Upadeśasāhasrī*, II, 17, 8 ; *śāstrapramāṇataḥ*, ibid. II, 18, 40 ; *gatiśūnyaṃ na vedo 'yaṃ pramāṇaṃ saṃvadaty uta*, ibid. II, 18, 62.

12) *mantrārthavādetihāsapurāṇaprāmāṇyāt*, vol.I, 491, *l*.8. *mantrārthavādetihāsapurāṇādibhyo 'vagamyate*, vol.I, p.436, *l*.13 [*pūrvapakṣa*]. *mantrādi*, vol.I, p.323 *l*.8.

13) *mantrārthavādetihāsapurāṇalokebhyo*, vol.I, p.291, *l*.8 ; vol.I, p.315, *l*.5.

14) On *BS*. I, 3, 32 ; vol.I, p.315, *l*.6f.- p.316, *l*.5.

15) *lokaprasiddhir api na sati saṃbhave nirālambanā 'dhyavasātuṃ yuktā*, vol.I, p.323, *ll*. 6-7.

16) *pratyakṣādīni laukikāni pramāṇāni*, vol.I, p.462, *l*.3. (*pūrvapakṣa*.) "We say, rather, that a thing is known from ordinary life (*lokāt prasidhyati*), if it is known by the (acknowledged) means of knowledge (*pramāṇa*), perception, and so on." With Śaṅkara, *pratyakṣa* is the same as *dṛṣṭa* in common diction. This holds true with the Sāṃkhya school also. R. Garbe : *Die Sāṃkhya-philosophie*, 2 Aufl. Leipzig, H. Haessel Verlag, 1917, S.209.

17) *pratyakṣādipramāṇaviṣayavastujñāna*, vol.I, p.65, *ll*.6-7. *pratyakṣādiviṣaya*, vol.I, p.45, *l*. 3 ; p.49, *l*.9. *pratyakṣādīni pramāṇāni*, I, p.209, *l*.9. *pratyakṣādīnām anyatamenāpi pramāṇena*, vol.I, p.582, *l*.14. *pratyakṣādyabhāve śruter apy abhāvaprasaṅga*, vol.II, p.468, *l*.10, [*pūrvapaksa*]. *pratyakṣādipramāṇāni śāstrāṇi ca*, vol.I, p.12, *ll*.6-7. "The phenomenal world with forms (*rūpaprapañca*) is the object of perception, etc.," vol.II, p.224, *l*.3, (*pūrvapakṣa*). *pratyakṣādibhiḥ pramāṇaiḥ*, *Upadeśasāhasrī* I, 2,51. *pratyakṣādipramāṇa*, ibid. I, 2, 107. *pratyakṣādipratyaya*, ibid. I, 2, 108.

18) *pratyakṣādivirodhaś ca*, vol.II, p.466, *l*.10 ; p.468, *l*.6, (*pūrvapakṣa*) — *pratyakṣādipramāṇavirodhād*, *Vedāntasāra* 175.

19) *api cāgamabalena brahmavādī kāraṇādisvarūpaṃ nirūpayatīti nāvaśyaṃ tasya yathādṛṣṭam eva sarvam abhyupagantavyam iti* (on *BS*. II, 2, 38. vol.I, p.605, *ll*.1-3).

20) *anumānādipramāṇāntara*, vol.I, p.36, *l*.3. *śabdād vānumiter vāpi vā*, *Upadeśasāhasrī*, II, 18, 133.

21) Inferential reasoning is to present what is not directly perceived by means of relating it to what has already been perceived by us. That is to say, to infer what has not yet been perceived on the basis of what has been already perceived. Accordingly; where perception exists, inferential reasoning does not take place (*pratyakṣatvād anumānāpravṛtteḥ*, vol.II, p.53, *l*.11, to p.54, *l*.1). "Inferential reasoning is dependent on instances observed elsewhere." (vol.I, p.50, *ll*.4 f).

22) *pratyakṣānumānopamānāgamaiḥ sarvato yathātmyenāvadhārya*, on *Muṇḍ*. *Up*. I, 2,12. ĀnSS. Poona, Ānandāśrama Press, 1925, p.17.

23) *viṣayāntare sāmarthyāstitve pramāṇaṃ na pratyakṣaṃ nānumānaṃ nopamānaṃ nārthāpattir na śabdo 'sti*, (on *Bṛhad*. *Up*. III, 3, 1. ĀnSS. Poona, Ānandāśrama Press, 1927, p.423).

24) The *Vedāntaparibhāṣā* admits the six *pramāṇas*, i.e., *pratyakṣa, anumāna, upamāna, śabda, arthāpatti, anupalabdhi*. (Introduction 10).

II. MEDITATION IN ŚAṄKARA

1. MEDITATION AND *YOGA*

Śaṅkara, in his commentary on the *Brahma-sūtra*, speaks in detail about meditation (*upāsana*),[1] because the *sūtras* therein discuss various meditations taught in the *Upaniṣads* and also refer to *yoga*. *yoga* as the practice of spiritual aspirants in India generally is far wider than meditation, and Śaṅkara too accepts the practice of *yoga*.[2] He seems to have taken *yoga* as a synonym of *dhyāna*.[3] As against Śaṅkara the opponent (*pūrvapakṣin*) understands *yoga* as the means for obtaining right vision (*samyagdarśanābhyupāya*).[4]

It was generally believed that practice of *yoga* brought to its practitioner various occult powers, and Śaṅkara accepted the popular belief of this kind generally held. He thought, for example, that the *yoga* practitioner (*yogin*) can take on several bodies at the same time,[5] and he records this as a self-evident fact for the people of that time, recognized in proverbs and accepted principles:

> "Some persons when the previous body is destroyed [after dying] take on another body, but there are others who though their bodies go on as before, by the unobstructed power obtained by *yoga* take on several bodies — according to this accepted principle other bodies are taken on."[6]

Again, he accepted that by the power of *yoga*, particular stations, for instance the sun itself, can be reached,[7] and he thought that one could enter into various objects:

> "Since even the practitioner of *yoga*, if his practice is perfected, is able to enter into various objects, the existence of an Inner controller is possible."[8]

Further, since he refers to "some *yoga* practitioners who have obtained the [eight kinds of] unobstructed powers of *yoga*", he did accept the eight kinds of power spoken of by the Yoga sect; thus the Advaita (non-dualist) sect probably had no differences from the Yoga sect in regard to method of practice. So it would not have been necessary for Śaṅkara as a follower of the Vedānta to reject the *yoga*, as had been urged by a fair number of scholars.

It is doubtful, however, in the case of Śaṅkaras school how far they believed in the eight-fold powers or not. Perhaps it was simply mechanical repetition of what was written in the *Yoga-sūtra* and elsewhere. Followers of the Śaṅkara school today do not honestly credit such things. In the present day India the practitioners and followers of the Śaṅkara school, when they travel in parties, hire a bus, and the Śaṅkarācārya rides in his official car.

Notes

1) Śaṅkara generally takes it as a neuter noun, *upāsana*, but in the *Bhāmatī* it is used as a feminine, *upāsanā*. This was at first always translated by Japanese Indologists as *sūhai* (worship) but that is too far away from the root meaning of the word. Perhaps it derived from Böhtlingk. Deussen in his German translation of the *Brahma-sūtra* commentary translated it as Verehrung, but he himself probably came to realize that this was not exact. In his *System des Vedānta*, there is the exact translation "devout meditation." Strauss says of this word: (1) In various *Upaniṣads*, where the magical nature of the sacrificial texts is accepted, it has the meaning "sich zu einer Substanz oder Wesenheit setzen, indem man sie umwirbt, bedrängt, um sich ihrer zu bemächtigen, sie für sich zu gewinnen" (to seat oneself near to a substance or being, by way of wooing it, urging it, in order to gain power over it, to acquire it for oneself). But (2) in Śaṅkara the magical meaning recedes into the background and as *upa-ās* it is: "meditieren im Sinne hingebungsvoller bzw, verehrungsvoller Konzentration auf eine zu realisierende Vorstellung" (to meditate in the sense of devotion, i.e. reverent concentration on a visualization to be realized). Otto Strauss, *Udgīthavidyā*, S.249. The most detailed and accurate discussion of *upāsana* appears on pages 295-298 of Vidhushekhara Bhattacharyya: *The Āgamaśāstra of Gauḍapāda*, University of Calcutta, 1943. He says that *upāsana has the meaning "meditation."* The *upāsana* of practiser of the Vedānta school is spoken of in *The Brahma-sūtra with Śaṅkara-bhāṣya*, Ānandāśrama Sanskrit Series, Poona, vol.IV. *l*.1-12.

2) Ś. ad *BS*. vol.I, p.350, *l*.7.

3) ibid. IV, 1, 11; vol.II, p.482, *l*.9. But according to *Saundarananda* XVIII, *dhyāna* and *yoga* are clearly distinguished in their use, *dhyāna* being a state of the mind, and *yoga* the means to attain it. XVI, 2: *ṛddhipravekaṃ ca bahuprakāraṃ parasya cetaścaritāvabodham/atītajanmasmaraṇaṃ ca dīrgham divye viśuddhe śruticakṣuṣī ca*//XVI, 83; *dante 'pi dantam praṇidhāya kāmaṃ tālvagram utpīḍya ca jihvayāpi/cittena cittaṃ*

parigṛhya cāpi kāryaḥ prayatno na tu te 'nuvṛttāḥ//XVII, 3; *sa pādayos tatra vidhāya śaucam śucau śive śrīmati vṛkṣamūle/mokṣāya buddhvā vyavasāyakakṣāṃ paryaṅkam aṅkāvahitaṃ babandha*//XVII, 4; *ṛjuṃ samagraṃ praṇidhāya kāyaṃ kāye smṛtiṃ cābhimukhīṃ vidhāya/sarvendriyāṇy ātmani saṃnidhāya sa tatra yogaṃ prayataḥ prapede*// The formal method of sitting is a proper seat in a quiet place, setting one's thought on oneself, restraining the five senses within (Cf. *Buddhacarita* II,45), setting the teeth against each other and pressing the palate with the tongue, controlling mind by mind, concentrating on either the nose-tip or the forehead between the brows; (first) remedying the defects of passions active in the mind, he destroys them at the right time by bringing against them right ideas opposed to them. This is the principal means to reach liberation. Cf. v. 49; *tad yāvad eva kṣaṇasamnipāto na mṛtyur āgacchati yāvad eva/yāvad vayo yogavidhau samartham buddhim kuru śreyasi tāvad eva*//(In the above I have made use of an article by Professor Matsunami Seiren, page 120 of *Shūkyō Kenkyū* (*Religious Studies*) vol.XIII, no.3).

4) Again elsewhere the *pūrvapakṣin* saying "*samyagdarśanābhyupāyo hi yogo vede vihitāḥ*" cites explanations of *yoga* in the *Upaniṣads*.

5) Ś. ad *BS.* vol.II, p.326, *l*.11.

6) ibid.

7) ibid. vol.II, p.514, *l*.2.

8) ibid. vol.I, p.205, *ll*.5-6.

2. SPECIAL CHARACTER OF MEDITATION

The meditation with which Śaṅkara in his commentary on the *Brahmasūtra* is most concerned is called *upāsana* or *upāsanā* (and we shall normally mean this when the word is used without further qualification). In two places he mentions a definition of it.

In one place he defines it by saying: "What is called meditation consists of a continuation of thought of the same kind."[1] It is thus continuing to hold in the mind always the same thought. This view of it was passed down to the Vedānta schools of later centuries, which taught that the ultimate aim of meditation is concentration of the spirit (*cittaikāgrya*).[2] Probably in the Mīmāṃsā schools they thought that the *Upaniṣads* are not expounding oneness of *Brahman* with *Ātman*, but teaching meditation.

> "Again when it is said 'worship' (meditation, *upāsana*) or 'contemplation' (*nididhyāsana*), what is being spoken of is an action (*kriyā*) implying the quality of repetition (*āvṛtti*). For in ordinary usage, when a man

with an attitude of self-dedication attends on a teacher and so on, he is said to 'worship the teacher' (*gurum upāste*) or 'worship the king'. In the same way, when a wife is thinking uninterruptedly about her husband, burning with expectation, it is said that the wife, whose husband is away on a journey and who is alone, meditates (*dhyāyati*) on him."[3]

From this we can extract two interesting special points about meditation :

(i) Looking at these passages, we see that the word *upa-ās* includes both service done in an attitude of self-dedication as well as the sense of continuity through repetition. Certainly through this attitude there is a link connecting it to the notion of worship ;

(ii) the root *dhyai* is used in the same sense as *upa-ās* and *nididhyāsana* in the same sense as *upāsana*.

Elsewhere[4] he speaks of the meaning of *dhyāna* and *dhyāyati*, and there too he takes *dhyāna* and *upāsana* in the same sense. In one case, his idea seems to be that *dhyāna* = *ekāgratā*.[5]

Notes

1) Ś. ad *BS*. vol.II, p.480, *l*.5. *upāsanaṃ nāma samānapratyaya pravāha karaṇam*. Deussen breaks *samāna* into *sa-māna*, translating mit Ehrfurcht verbunden (*System des Vedānta*, S. 472). But Thibaut translates "by meditation we understand the lengthened carrying on of an identical train of thought", and Strauss prefers to accept Thibaut's translation (Otto Strauss: *Udgīthavidyā*, S.10).

2) *Vedāntasāra*, XI.

3) Ś. ad *BS*, II, p.548, *ll*.12ff.

4) ibid. IV, 1, 8 ; IV,1 ,9-10.

5) ibid. IV,1,11.

3. TEACHING

Now in connection with the above, a specially noteworthy concept in Śaṅkara is that of the knowledge called *vidyā*. *vid* and *upa-ās* have been used in the same sense, and there are passages explaining *vidyā* as nothing other than *upāsana*.

"Again, it is recognized that in all the *Upaniṣads* the two words 'know' (*vidi*) and 'meditate' (*upāsti*) are used without distinction. Thus for this reason too we can know that the word 'know' includes a sense of repetition."[1]

So saying he then cites some examples out of the holy texts. This teaching is not simply information, but it is 'knowledge' which carries the power of controlling humans morally.

Again, Śaṅkara has used the word *vijñāna*. In some cases he seems to use it in the same sense as *upāsana* and *nididhyāsana*.[2] It is only *samādhi* that seems to have been a little different from meditation (*upāsana*) and contemplation (*dhyāna*). Vedāntins too were practising the spiritual one-pointedness of *samādhi*.[3] The difference lay in this that *dhyāna* or *upāsana* came to an end as soon as the practiser attained a teaching, whereas *samādhi* existed unchanged even in the enlightened man.[4] In the later Advaita school the two were sharply distinguished, *samādhi* being called the means to attain liberation, whereas meditation (*upāsana*) brings its practitioner to the world of the gods (*devaloka*).[5]

Notes

1) Ś. ad *BS*. IV, 1, 1 ; vol.II, p.459, *ll*.4ff.
2) ibid. vol.II, p.291, *ll*.14-15.
3) ibid. II, 3, 39 ; vol.II, p.75, *ll*.5ff.
4) P. Deussen : *Das System des Vedānta*, S.444.
5) *Vedāntasāra*, XVII ; XXII.

4. THE VARIETIES OF MEDITATION

This meditation is continuous unwavering thought of a principle which functions within the heart and can be called the so-called 'Zen-with-thoughts'. They fall into different classes. Śaṅkara, discussing the posture and seat for meditation, analyses them into three :

(1) meditations (*upāsana*) connected with various parts of the rituals.
(2) right vision (*samyagdarśana*).
(3) other meditations (*upāsana*).

How is the division made into these kinds? 'Right vision' is not itself meditation, but it is probably included here, because it arises on the basis of meditation.

Now meditation on 'lower *Brahman*' is much discussed in Śaṅkara's commentary on the *Brahma-sūtra*, and probably this would come into section (3) above.

In the later Vedānta school 'higher meditation' (*utkṛṣṭopasati*) and 'lower meditation' (*mandopāsanā*) came to be distinguished.[1]

It was generally believed then at the time of Śaṅkara that worship of *Brahman* brought great results. In the words of the *prima facie* view (presented by the *pūrvapakṣin*, an opponent):

> "For meditation on *Brahman* is spoken of as for the purpose of obtaining great results."[2]

But meditation on *Brahman* itself is again divided into two kinds: the case where meditation is made by way of attributes (*guṇa-viśeṣa*) of *Brahman*, and the case where meditation is made by way of a symbol (*pratīka*).

What is called meditation by way of a symbol is when some particular thing is made into a symbol of *Brahman*, and one meditates on it. The fact of mental concentration is not different from worship by way of some attribute. For instance, the hymn called *gāyatrī* is taken as a symbol, and he performs recollection of the mind (*cetaso'rpaṇa*), namely mental concentration (*citta-samādhāna*).[3]

In various *Upaniṣads* here and there the phrase occurs "··· let him meditate that ··· is *Brahman*," and he understands this to mean "let him superimpose the idea of *Brahman* onto ···"[4]

Superimposition is also taught of concrete things other than *Brahman*. For example, he comments:

> "The idea of the sun and so on which have as basis some thing not an accessory part of the ritual, should be superimposed on the *Udgītha* and so on which are accessory parts of the ritual."[5]

Thus anything may become the occasion of meditation, namely a basis on which can be superimposed the idea '*Brahman*.' Through the form of the thing, he meditates on *Brahman*. "It is accepted that there is meditation on *Brahman* through individual things."[6] For instance, according to the *Aitareya-Āraṇyaka* which is cited in the discussion, it is taken that the great hymn (*mahat uktham*), the sacrificial fire, the *mahāvrata* sacrifice, are each of them *Brahman*.

Such a view was passed on down to the later Advaita schools also. The various gods, *yakṣas*, *rākṣasas*, people of the four castes, various animals, various plants··· "all these are worshipped as gods and it brings results."[7]

But in various *Upaniṣads* various symbols (*pratīka*) are taught in relation to *Brahman*, and it is said that one must not take the view that these symbols are *Ātman*.[8]

Meditation or view (*dṛṣṭi*) and worship (*upāsana*) are synonyms, but here we come up against a new question. Meditation or view is seeing that A is B, but in this case the view of higher must not be imposed on to an inferior thing.[9]

As to the judgement "A is B", or the operation of mentally making A to be B, Śaṅkara holds that intellectual formulation is of four kinds:

(1) superimposition (*adhyāsa*).

(2) negation (*apavāda*).

(3) identity (*ekatva*).

(4) limitation (*viśeṣaṇa*).

(1) Superimposition is mentally making A to be B. "Superimposition (*adhyāsa*) is when, in regard to two things, the idea of one is transferred on to the idea of the other, which still remains. Namely, though the idea of B is transferred into A, in A which has had the idea B transferred to it, the idea A still remains as before. For instance, when the idea *Brahman* is transferred into 'name,' the idea 'name' still continues as before and is not extinguished by the idea *Brahman*. Or again for example the idea of Viṣṇu and so on are carried over into an image of Viṣṇu."[10]

(2) Negation is when A has been mistakenly understood as B, by the knowledge of its true nature A is A the idea B is removed. When it has been ascertained that an idea previously imposed on to a thing was really a mistaken one, the subsequently arising veridical idea destroys the mistaken one previously imposed — this is negation. For example, the idea *Ātman* (formerly) superimposed on the aggregate of body and senses is destroyed by the arising of the true notion "thou art that",[11] namely that the idea *Ātman* is applied only to *Ātman*. Or again as in the case when a mistaken idea of the directions is destroyed by the true understanding of them.

(3) Identity means the case when A is absolutely identical with B, and would thus have needed no particular discussion. Śaṅkara says nothing about this case.

(4) Limitation (*viśeṣaṇa*) can be taken as a special case of superimposition. They do not differ in bring indirect expressions (*lakṣaṇā*), but whereas superimposition views A as B which is completely different from it, limitation is a case of the word expressing the whole now indicating only a part of it. So in limitation the indirect expression is in fact very close to the literal meaning.

> "But in indirect expression, the meaning indirectly expressed may be very distant from the literal meaning, or it may not. Namely in the case of superimposition (*adhyāsa*), the idea of what is B is transferred into what is B, and in that case the indirect expression becomes very distant from the literal meaning. But in the case of limitation (*viśeṣaṇa*), by a word expressing the whole (for instance *udgītha*), a part of it (for instance the syllable *om*) is indicated, and the indirect expression comes to be close to the literal meaning. In fact in ordinary experience the word for a collective whole does have the meaning also of a part of it, as for example they say when a part of a cloth or of a village has been burnt, "the cloth is burnt" or "the village is burnt."

Notes

1) *Vedāntakalpataru*, p.459.
2) Ś. ad *BS*. vol.I, p.149, *l*.16.
3) ibid. vol.I, p.155, *ll*.10-13.
4) ibid. IV, 1, 5.
5) ibid. IV, 1, 6.
6) ibid. vol.I, p.156, *l*.6.
7) *Pañcadaśī*, VI, 206-209.
8) *BS*. IV, 1, 4.
9) ibid. IV, 1, 5; vol.II, p.472 *ll*.4ff.
10) ibid. vol.II, p.266, *ll*.5ff.
11) *Chāndogya-Upaniṣad*, VI, 8, 7.

5. MEDITATION IS ACTION

For Śaṅkara meditation is action. Meditation is a different thing from knowledge (*jñāna*). Śaṅkara discusses in detail the difference between knowledge and meditation (*dhyāna*).[1] Both of them are functions relating to mind (*manas*), but meditation (*dhyāna*) is an action (*kriyā*) whereas knowledge is not action.[2]

Since Śaṅkara held this sort of view, here and there he contrasts knowledge (*jñāna*) and meditation (*dhyāna*). It is however doubtful whether before him a contrary of this kind was clearly recognized. According to Auḍulomi : "If the means such as knowledge (*jñāna*) and meditation (*dhyāna*) have been practiced and thereby (the individual self *vijñānātman* itself) has returned to calmness, it is loosed from the aggregate of body etc. and then has identity with the Highest Self."[3]

So even in the case of meditation on *Brahman* possessed-of-attributes (*saguṇa-vidyā*), the meditating subject does not escape from the condition of being an acting subject (*kartṛtva*) and is bound by action (*karman*). Thus in the case of meditation on *Brahman*-with-attributes, performance of duties is enjoined.

Thus knowledge cannot be enjoined but teaching (=meditation) is something that can be enjoined. And he seems to have thought that *vijñāna*, being a synonym of *vidyā*, can also be enjoined. "Wisdom must be cultivated in the right way."[4] "Various texts (*śruti*) declared in the *Upaniṣads* are not intended as glorification of some particular thing but intended to enjoin meditation,"[5] so he explains.

Since meditating like this is teaching (*vidyā*), logically there must be meditation on things to be affirmed and glorified, and also things to be negated and rejected. Śaṅkara recognizes that there exist two kinds of meditations : meditations enjoined and meditations forbidden.[6] What do these specifically refer to? There is no explanation in his own commentaries, but according to [other] commentaries there are enjoined meditations on hymn (*udgītha*) which are symbolic, and forbidden meditations are "studying wrong learning" and again "dwelling in thought on naked women" and "looking at naked women," and so on.

Again he thought *samādhi* practice too to be action.[7] However, in

Śaṅkara's view, one who has opened up realization still performs *samādhi*, and though he is called a saint living in the ideal state of liberation, it is certainly not that he is apart from action. Though discarding certain actions, he is still clearly performing action in the course of seeking to become completely actionless. This point is particularly made by Bhāskara. But his course of action can be said to negative in relation to social life. But such negative behaviour itself is in fact only possible on the basis of the existence of society.

In the case of meditation it is possible to think on a form other than the true form of the object, and there the will has freedom to choose. But in the case of knowledge, content of knowledge cannot differ from the object. 'Right vision', having the Highest Self as its object, receives its form just as it is.

> "In this case, something that does not exist may become the object for the operation of thinking, for even things conceived by fancy still become objects of that operation. But it is generally accepted in the world that in the operation of 'seeing', it is only really existing things that are the objects of sight. Thus it is known that the Highest Self, being the object of perfect direct vision, is indicated as object of an operation of seeing."[8]

In terms of historical developments, the various teachings (*vidyā*) for meditation were originally closely associated with the rituals. But certain teachings were not subsidiary to ritual, but when practiced on the occasion of the ritual helped towards its success.[9] If, namely, the ritual was accompanied by the teaching, it would be more fruitful than one not so accompanied. So that on ritual occasions it is recommended that teaching (meditation) must be performed.

> "Again [the text] so '[sacrifice] which a man does with knowledge, with faith and with secret teaching, has far more effects' has the verbal suffix, *tara* (more), from which it can be known that even sacrifice done without teaching has some effect. This is possible just because teachings are not always joined with the sacrifice. Otherwise if teaching were always joined with the sacrifice, how could it be known that a sacrifice without teaching does have some result? For it is an acknowledged

principle that when all component essentials are perfectly fulfilled, sacrifice does have a result."[10)]

But when it is a question of the teaching as to *Brahman* (*brahmavidyā*), teaching is independent of rituals.[11)]

Notes

1) Ś. ad *BS*. vol.I, p.71, *ll*.4ff.
2) *Vedāntasāra*, X.
3) Ś. ad *BS*. I, p.399, *ll*.5-6.
4) ibid. vol.I, p.423, *l*.7 — *sanmārge prajñā saṃgrahaṇīyā*.
5) ibid. vol.II, p.417, *l*.5; II, p.415, *l*.3.
6) ibid. II, 4, 11.
7) ibid. II, 3, 39.
8) ibid. vol.I, p.257, *ll*.3-5.
9) ibid. III, 3, 42.
10) ibid. II, p.351, *ll*.14ff.
11) For instance, since *vidyā* is enjoined for a celibate (*ūrdhvaretas*), *vidyā* is independent [of rituals]" — ibid. II, p.414, *l*.8.

6. THE REWARDS OF TEACHINGS

It is declared that there are rewards of teaching (meditation). Now of what sort would these be?

In Śaṅkara's time it was generally believed that there were two kinds of meditations: (1) those which bring results, and (2) those which do not. Among those which bring results, there are meditations which cause perfect direct vision (*samyagdarśana*) in the next world and allow liberation-by-stages.

> "For as in the case of *karman*, so here with meditation, it can be established as distinct or as without distinction. And exactly as in the case of *karman*, meditation is to be of two kinds: (1) causing experience of results, and (2) not causing such experience. Again certain meditations, as producing [in the next world] perfect direct vision (*samyagdarśana*) bring liberation-by-stages as their results."[1)]

Since, however, this passage appears as voiced by a questioner, it may not be the view of Śaṅkara himself. Probably it is the following opinion, expressed in other passages, that should be attributed to him. According to this, meditations are to be classified into three according to the rewards of worship :

(1) bringing about destruction of sins.
(2) bringing acquisition of superhuman powers.
(3) bringing liberation-by-stages.

> "The rewards of meditation on *Brahman*, as is known from various teachings, in some cases is destruction of sin (*duritakṣaya*), in some cases attainment of super-human powers (*aiśvaryaprāpti*), and in some cases liberation-by-stages (*krama-mukti*). It is accordingly proper to think that the texts which teach meditation and the texts which teach [what is] *Brahman* have differing purposes, and not correct to take their purpose as the same."[2]

Parallel to this is the statement that teaching (*vidyā*) is of two kinds : (1) by the teaching with *Brahman*-with-attributes as its object comes attainment of superhuman powers (*aiśvaryaprāpti*) and again annihilation of sin (*pāpanivṛtti*).[3] As against this, (2) by the teaching with the attributeless *Brahman* as its object, *karma* is burnt up entirely.[4] In this case he seems to think that both good and bad *karmas* are burnt up altogether.

Again in another place he says that (1) some meditations bring liberation-by-stages, (2) some meditations bring prosperity (*abhyudaya*, good fortune, especially life in heaven), and (3) some meditations bring success in the rituals (*karmasamṛddhi*).[5]

In still another place he says : (1) seeing that the Highest *Brahman* is *Ātman* brings liberation, and (2) seeing *Brahman* associated with attributes or symbols, one can attain various rewards connected with the field of reincarnation.

> "When it is declared that the Highest *Brahman* free from association with any of the separate forms is *Ātman*, it should be known that there is only one reward, namely release. But when *Brahman* is declared associated with the distinction of attributes, or the distinction of a symbol, we understand that [some reward high or low, connected with the field of reincarnation] is being taught. Namely, according to the holy text : "He is the eater of food, the giver of wealth. He who knows

thus obtains wealth."[6] (*Bṛhadāraṇyaka-Upaniṣad*, IV, 24)

Taking the above as statements meaning roughly the same thing, the two kinds of meditation may be supposed to be as follows : (1) that which has as its purpose the attainment of perfect direct vision (*samyagdarśana*). After this has been again and again repeated when once he has had the perfect direct vision, there is no necessity to perform it again. (2) that which has its purpose attainment of prosperity (*abhyudaya*). For this meditation, there has to be repetition by visualization (viewing in thought, *pratyaya*) until death. Even at the very moment of death this visualization must be repeated.[7]

He says furthermore that *Ātman* is to be meditated upon, and symbols (*pratīka*) are not to be meditated upon.[8] Meditation on symbols, especially the accessories of the rituals, has been performed from ancient times to the present day.[9]

What Śaṅkara himself is teaching is rather fragmentary and is not systematized, but if we put together the above, we can classify meditation in the following way :

A. That which brings no reward at all.

B. That which brings reward.

- I. that which brings success in ritual (*karmasamṛddhi*).
- II. that which brings prosperity (*abhyudaya*).
  - (1) annihilation of sin.
  - (2) acquisition of superhuman powers.
  - (3) rise of perfect direct vision in the next world, namely the possibility of liberation-by-stages.
- III. that which causes perfect direct vision to arise in this world. By this teaching all *karman* is burnt up entirely, making liberation possible.

Of these, I probably corresponds to meditation by means of a symbol (*pratīka*), and it may well be that II corresponds to meditation by means of attribute (*guṇaviśeṣa*), though it is not absolutely clear.

Sometimes one of the three is particularly favoured with a detailed explanation.

A teaching (*vidyā*) of *Brahman*-with-attributes causes attainment of prosperity (*abhyudaya*) as its result.[10] Again the result of meditation on *Brahman*-with-attributes (*saguṇa-vidyā*) is said to be the heaven-world etc.[11]

Again, it is said that meditation on the Highest Self (*paramātman*) comes to bring a reward of release from sin (*pāpavinirmokṣaphala*).[12] And in meditation on *Brahman*-with-attributes, the attributes meditated upon may be increased or lessened, bringing correspondingly different rewards.[13] (*Chāndogya-Upaniṣad*, III, 14, 2)

On the other hand, he who meditates on *Brahman* on the basis of some symbol (*pratīka*, for example *manas*, space, the sun etc.) cannot attain the world of *Brahman*, but it is said to get the rewards set out in the *Chāndogya-Upaniṣad* (VII, 2, 14).[14] Others, who perform meditation on *Brahman*-with-attributes, pass along the path of the gods (*devayāna*) and enter the *Brahman*-world, so Bādarāyaṇa thinks.[15]

Now what is the meaning of prosperity (*abhyudaya*)? According to Deussen[16] the word has two senses, instances of both of which are said to occur in texts :

(1) liberation by stages.

(2) temporary happiness in the path of ancestors (*pitṛyāna*).

Again it is said that there are places where the rewards of the "path of the ancestors" and those of the "path of the gods" are included.[17]

In any case, prosperity is contrasted with the Highest Good (*niḥśreyas*), and Śaṅkara explains the distinction.[18]

Now there are places where he thinks that the highest meaning of meditation is that it becomes the means for attaining perfect direct vision. And therefore, the seeker of liberation must practice meditation.

> "In this passage, meditation being taught only for the sake of attaining perfect direct vision (*samyagdarśana*), meditation is not itself the main subject of the passage."[19]

He also says that "perfect direct vision arises on a basis of meditation."

But as to when this direct vision will arise, that time is not fixed. Śaṅkara says that there are cases when the knowledge (*vidyā*) arises in this world, and cases where it arises in the next world.[20]

> "Therefore depending on the destruction of the obstacles, knowledge (*vidyā*) arises in this world or in the next world."[21]

To the question how this difference comes about, he replies that it corresponds to the degree of power employed by the one who practices.

"In the case of those who would attain liberation by means of teaching (*vidyā*), according to the varying degrees of power employed by them, in regard to the reward which is special to the teaching, it is recognized that there are definite distinctions as to whether the reward is attained in this world or the reward is attained in the next world."[22]

Notes

1) Ś. ad *BS*. vol.II, p.247, *ll*.2ff.
2) ibid. vol.II, p.216, *ll*.11-14.
3) ibid. vol.II, p.488, *ll*.2ff.
4) ibid. II, p.488, *ll*.5ff.
5) ibid. vol.I, p.113, *ll*.3-5.
6) ibid. vol.I, pp.153-54.
7) ibid. IV, 1, 12 ; vol.II, p.483.
8) ibid. IV, 1, 4.
9) E. Carpenter : *Theism in Medieval India*, p.127, fn.2.
10) Ś. ad *BS*. vol.II, p.323, *l*.9.
11) ibid. vol.II, p.565, *ll*.18-19.
12) ibid. vol.I, p.258, *l*.14 - p.259, *l*.2.
13) ibid. vol.II, p.554, *ll*.14ff.
14) ibid. IV, 1,4 ; vol.II, p.550, *l*.4.
15) ibid. IV,3, 15 ; vol.II, p.350, *l*.4.
16) P. Deussen : *Das System des Vedānta*, S.472. The material he presents still needs examining.
17) ibid. S. 450. But according to *Vedāntasāra*, XIII, by *upāsana satyaloka* (= *devaloka*) is attained. According to Jacob's edition, p.142, this is the fifth world. As authority he cites *Bṛhadāraṇyaka-Upaniṣad*, I, 5, 16 ; *Śatapatha-Brāhmaṇa*, XIV,4, 3, 24. Again he says, by *nityanaimittikaprāyaścitta*, the world of the ancestors (*pitṛloka*, the first world according to Jacob) is attained.
18) Ś. ad *BS*. vol.I, p.362, *l*.14. From the preceding and following context, it seems that the reference is to *Kāṭhaka-Upaniṣad*, II, 1-11.
19) Ś. ad *BS*. vol.II, p.278, *ll*.1-2.
20) ibid. III, 4, 51 ; vol.II, p.450 *ll*.11ff. (but this needs examining).
21) ibid. vol.II, p.452, *l*.18.
22) ibid. vol.II, p.453, *ll*.5-6.

7. PRACTICE OF MEDITATION

Let us look at the rules for practice of meditation. For its practice, there is no restriction as to direction (orientation), place or time.[1]

As to posture there seems to have been some debate at the time, and Śaṅkara[2] directs as follows:

(1) meditation in connection with the various parts of the rituals — these depend on the rituals and he says that forms of seated posture do not matter.

(2) perfect direct vision (*samyagdarśana*) : as to this, posture does not come into question.

(3) other meditations: these have to be done seated, and must not be performed walking or standing. He discusses this in detail.

Of the above three kinds, (2) and (3) are clearly done on a basis of individual self-realization and are coloured by post-Upaniṣadic views, whereas (1) is tied to *Vedic* rituals and is something magical before individual self-realization. Here there arises a difference of view among the really *Vedantic* thinkers. Of these, Ātreya held that the various meditations to bring rewards were performed by the sacrificer himself,[3] but Auḍulomi held that the priest of the sacrifice performed them, the rewards of the meditation going to the sacrificer.[4] The sacrificer, as the organizer of the sacrifice, pays their fees to the Brahmin priests, and therefore it is he who receives the reward. Śaṅkara seems to have agreed with the second view.

Śaṅkara's doctrine on the actual practice of meditation is probably the traditional method of its cultivation as handed down, but it seems that Śaṅkara did not practice meditation (*dhyāna*) necessarily according to the rules of the *Śvetāśvatara-Upaniṣad*.[5]

There is no deep discussion on the psychological stages of progress in meditation. Explanations in the psychological realm as to stages of progress till the heart is pacified are few. Only in the commentary on the *Kāṭhaka-Upaniṣad* (III, 13) he says:

"The meaning is as follows: — A man should restrain words within the mind (*manas*), namely, discarding the operation of the outer senses, speech organ and so on, they should exist as mind (*manas*) alone. Again, seeing that discriminating is an error, the mind also which directly discriminates the objects, he should restrain in the faculty of apperception (*buddhi*) which is called knowledge (*jñāna*) as having ascertainment as its essence. And he should, by making this faculty of apperception enter into a subtle condition, restrain it within the Great *Ātman* — which would be the experiencer or the supreme (matured by the *samādhi*) faculty of apperception of the Embryo (*hiraṇyagarbha*). And again that Great *Ātman* let him establish in the serene *Ātman*, namely the Highest *Puruṣa* which is the subject of this present passage, namely the highest ultimate goal — this is the meaning."[6]

Further, a class-nature of meditation is dimly disclosed. Meditation was something entrusted to the three classes of the top stratum, and the *śūdra* was excluded. (Those studying at Śṛṅgeri, the main center of the Śaṅkara school today, are high-caste Brahmins alone.)

Notes

1) Ś. ad *BS*. IV, 1, 11.
2) ibid. IV, 1, 7.
3) ibid. III, 4, 44.
4) ibid. III, 4, 45, 46.
5) ibid. vol.II, p.482, *ll*.6ff.
6) ibid. vol.I, p.350, *ll*.11ff.

8. IDENTIY AND DIFFERENCES IN TEACHING

The object to be meditated on is the form (*rūpa*) of the teaching (*vidyā*), and distinction between various teachings is founded on the difference between their objects of meditation. When the objects are different the teachings also come to be different, so that there exist a number of teachings. Accordingly the plural forms are used in speaking of teachings and meditations (*vijñānāni*).[1] If the object is not different, then teachings about it cannot be different.

"Now the object to be meditated upon is the form of the teaching, and when there is no distinction of form, no distinction between teachings can be established. Further if the teachings do not differ, distinction cannot be made of their attributes."[2] (*Bṛhad. Up*., III,8,8 ; *MuṇḍakaUp*.,

I, 1, 6).

"Since the object to be known is identical, the teachings also are identical."[3] (*Kāṭhaka Up*., III, 1; *Muṇḍaka Up*., III, 1)

These conclusions lead to a noteworthy conclusion: in regard to the Highest Self, it is always an identical teaching.

"Again as to the teaching of the Highest Self, there is no room for doubt to arise as to whether the teachings are one and the same or perhaps different — this has already been made clear."[4] (*Bṛhad. Up*., V, 4-5)

Even though there may be a few differences or contradictions between two teachings set out in the holy texts, he brushes them aside with the remark that they are not to be regarded, because the two form one and the same teaching.

This principle, however, was not an absolute basis for determining identity or difference of teachings. Where the object of meditation taught in two places in the holy texts is the same, still if the attributes of that object differ in the two places, they are in fact separate teachings.

"(Prima facie view proposed by an opponent): Again since the object of the knowledge (*vedya*) is not different, no distinction can be made of the teachings as separate. The object of knowledge is in fact the essence (*rūpa*) of a teaching. It is just as in the sacrifice, the divinities who are served with the offerings and the material of the sacrifices are the essence of the sacrifice." (*Chāndogya Up*., VIII, 1, 1, 5; *Bṛhad. Up*., III 3, 39).[5]

"And [since in these passages] the object to be known is the same, the teaching must be the same."[6]

Against this Śaṅkara says in refutation:

"Though the object to be known is not different teachings like this must be different. For though in the passages the object is the same, the attributes of that object are different, and therefore they are separate teachings of meditation."[7]

At any rate in accordance with this principle, the *Brahma-sūtra* takes a number of passages appearing in separate *Upaniṣads* as one and the same teaching, and it is said that those passages are to be taken as bound together.

However, he emphasizes that the *prāṇasaṃvāda* of *Chāndogya-Upaniṣad* (I, 3) and the *prāṇasaṃvāda* of *Bṛhadāraṇyaka-Upaniṣad* (I, 3) are said to be separate teachings of meditation.

Again, he says that in the tradition of a single *Vedic* school, it is possible that two passages make up a single teaching, or again that attributes (*guṇa*) may be summarized.[8] As an actual example, he says that the teaching of the sage Śāṇḍilya given in two passages (*Śatapatha-Brāhmaṇa*, X, 6, 8; *Bṛhadāraṇyaka-Upaniṣad*, V, 6) must, as being the same teaching, be combined.

Again he lays it down that the various teachings based on various elements making up the rituals may be good for all the *Vedic* schools (*śākhā*).[9] Then the various meditations on *Brahman*-with-attributes (*saguṇa-vidyā*) should be taken as one, and there are no contradictions between the various descriptions given in various *Upaniṣads*.[10] "The supplementary qualities of knowledge mentioned in one passage may be included in similar meditations given in other passages."[11] As to the reason why one can take the various passages together, he cites in explanation the example of the courage of Devadatta.

> "For example, it is not that Devadatta, famous in the place where he lives for possessing the virtues of courage and the like, loses his virtues when he has gone to another place, even though the people of that place do not recognize courage. In this case too, when they come to have specially good acquaintance with him, his good qualities do become recognized in the other place also."[12]

But just because the teaching is the same, it does not necessarily follow that the same meditation is performed. For instance what is taught in the *Bṛhadāraṇyaka-Upaniṣad* (I.5, 21-23) and in the *Chāndogya-Upaniṣad* (IV, 3) are, as teaching, one and the same, but as meditation they are distinguished as two. These are, namely the two aspects, viewed as individual body (*adhyātman*) and as cosmic divinities (*adhidaivatam*).

> "In regard to the question under discussion, as teaching (*vidyā*) there is thus no distinction. For looking at the opening and concluding sentences in these passages, in the teaching of the individual body and

again the cosmic divinities, it is recognized that it is only one teaching that is enjoined. Though the teaching is one, however, since there is the distinction between the aspect regarding the individual body and that regarding the cosmic divinities, the activity of the meditation is distinguished into two (*pravṛttibheda*)."[13]

Again he says that when meditation is done on *Brahman*-with-attributes, then even though two teachings are given in near-by passages in the holy texts, where the basis is different they must be taken as separate teachings. As example he gives the passage from the *Bṛhadāraṇyaka-Upaniṣad* (V.5).[14] Again on the same reasoning, the 'power' (*vibhūti*) taught in the *Rāṇāyanīya-khila* and the various attributes taught in the *Chāndogya-Upaniṣad* (III, 14) cannot be combined.[15] Again, the *Puruṣa* teaching (*puruṣavidyā*) of the Tāṇḍin school, that of the Paingin school, and that of the Taittirīyaka school, though having the same name, cannot be combined as the same teaching.[16]

So it is that the various teachings are given in the holy texts; but is it that we may combine or select them at will, or is it that some one of them must be selected? On this point Śaṅkara discusses in detail the statement that some one of the teachings must be selected, and that it is useless to perform a second meditation.[17] However, teachings performed on the basis of a desire (*kāmya*) may be combined at will, or not combined. For they, like the rituals, cause attainment of rewards and do not necessitate direct realization (*sākṣātkaraṇa*).[18] Again, various implements of the ritual or its component parts can be conjoined, but one cannot conjoin the meditations performed in regard to each of them. Various meditations chosen freely should be respectfully carried out without conjunction.[19] There is freedom of choice both in conjunction of meditations and also in selection of them.[20]

Notes

1) Ś. ad *BS*. vol.II, p.349, *l*.7.
2) ibid. III, 3, 33. vol.II, p.293, *ll*. 8-10.
3) ibid. III, 3, 34. vol.II, p.316, *l*. 12.
4) ibid. III, 3, 38. vol.II, p.335, 2.3.
5) ibid. vol.II, p.382, *ll*.4-6.

6) ibid. vol.II, p.382, *l*.13.
7) ibid. II, 3, 5.
8) ibid. vol.II, p.294, *l*.6.
9) ibid. III, 3, 55-56.
10) ibid. III, 1, 4.
11) ibid. vol.II, p.257, *l*. 9.
12) ibid. III, 3, 10.
13) ibid. vol.II, p.359, *ll*.5ff.
14) ibid. III, 3, 20-22.
15) ibid. III, 3, 23.
16) ibid. III, 3, 23.
17) ibid. vol.II, p.385, *ll*.14ff.
18) ibid. III, 3, 60.
19) ibid. III, 3, 65.
20) ibid. III, 3, 66.

9. CONCLUSION

The above discussion on teachings is probably very hard to follow, but if it is compared to the question in Zen as to what *koan* to take up, will it not become fairly easy?

Finally, there is meditating on the Highest *Brahman* and attaining the true *satori* — but the allotted space is already exceeded and we must discuss it on some other occasion.

10. SOME REMARKS IN COMPARISON WITH ZEN MEDITATION

Meditation is a form of religious practice universally admitted in various religions Eastern and Western. However, there must be some differences in their forms.

In Chinese and Japanese Zen Buddhism meditation is practiced in the cross-legged posture. It is called Zazen ("sitting meditation") in Japanese. Among Zen masters the following items were discussed.

At the time of Zazen meditation, what do they think? Or are they not thinking or anything? How do they seat themselves?

It is interesting to know that questions corresponding to these are discussed by Śaṅkara, reputed as the greatest philosopher of India, and this is what we have examined.

III. THE PRACTICE OF *YOGA* AS IS REPRESENTED IN ŚAṄKARA'S *YOGASŪTRABHĀṢYA VIVARAṆA*[1]

***Yoga-sūtra* II, 47 :**

"A stable seated posture arises from relaxation of strenuous effort, and identification with the infinite (*ānantyasamāpatti*)".

Vyāsa explains the words of the second half of the *sūtra* as "for the seated posture, the mind is made identified with the infinite."

On this, Śaṅkara takes identification with the infinite to mean "identification with everything in the universe",[2] whereas Vācaspati Miśra, after explaining that it is to "relax the innate tension (*svābhāvika-prayatna-śaithilya*)" takes it asidentification into the serpent king Ananta who upholds the universe and all things.[3]

This is clearly a Hinduistic interpretation, and here too there is little colour of Hinduism in Śaṅkara's comment, which can again be said to preserve an older form than that of Vācaspati Miśra.

***Yoga-sūtra* II, 48 :**

"From that (=from attaining the seated posture) there is no affliction by the pairs of opposites (heat and cold etc.)".

In Vyāsa's comment it says: "On attainment of the seated posture, there is no affliction from the opposites like heat and cold."

Śaṅkara here simply takes the prima facie meaning of the *sūtra* and Vyāsa's comment, but Vācaspati Miśra adds, "The seated posture is mentioned in the *Viṣṇu-Purāṇa*: 'remaining in the *bhadrāsana* etc. which embrace all the virtues'." (*Viṣṇu-Purāṇa* VI, 739) Śaṅkara hardly ever cites the *Purāṇa* scriptures whereas Vācaspati Miśra frequently quotes them. The latter again knows various postures like the 'auspicious posture (*bhadrāsana*)'.

***Yoga-sūtra* II, 49 :**

"When that (=seated posture) has been attained, inhalation (indrawn air) and exhalation (outgoing air) are finally cut off. This is regulation of breath".

Vyāsa's commentary is: "When the seated posture is perfected (breath regulation is effected). Inhalation (indrawn air) means drawing in the wind (=external air) which is outside. Exhalation (outgoing air) means expelling the wind (=air) in the abdomen. 'Breath regulation' means cutting off the functioning of both of them, namely that both (exhalation and inhalation) cease to exist."

As to inhalation and exhalation, Śaṅkara's comments are very brief. "Just as water, being dispersed outside, is sucked in through a tube, so the wind (=air) outside is dispersed, and through the orifices of the nostrils is sucked in as joined with the inhalation (*apāna*). This operation of sucking in is 'inhalation'. In the same way … the wind in the abdomen is joined to the operation of exhalation (*prāṇa*) and this emission is 'exhalation'."[4)]

But Vācaspati Miśra explains by using technical terms of *yoga*. "*recaka* (suspension of exhalation), *pūraka* (suspension of inhalation) *kumbhaka* (suspension of exhalation and inhalation)[5)] all have the common point of cutting off the operation of exhalation and inhalation. Ultimately, in the sucking in of the external wind and holding it within, which is *pūraka*, there is cutting off of the operation of exhalation and inhalation; in the emission of the abdominal wind and keeping it outside which is *recaka*, there is also cutting off of the operation of inhalation and exhalation; and also in *kumbhaka* there is cutting off of the operation of inhalation and exhalation. These things are in fact set out in the commentary."

***Yoga-sūtra* II, 50 :**

> "Control of breath is [of three kinds], as its operation has regard to the external or regard to the internal or is a rigid state; [with practice] it becomes long and fine".

Vyāsa's commentary: "Absence of operation of the breathing after exhalation (emission of air) is external control of breath.[6)] Absence of the operation of breathing after inhalation (taking in the breath) is internal control of breath.[7)] The third breath-control is a rigid state without operation of exhalation or operation of inhalation, sudden, and coming about [at a stroke] as a result of a sudden effort.[8)] Just as water dropped on a heated stone shrivels up everywhere, so the operation of exhalation and the operation of inhalation disappear at once. All these three are regulated in regard to place,[9] in the sense that their place, meaning their extent, is just so much. Again each [of the three] is regulated as to time,[10] in the sense, namely, of being delimited as defined by a particular number of moments. Again each is delimited as to number,[11] in the sense that the first uprising[12] [of the life-breath from the navel up to the palate] is a particular number of breaths. When that (rising life-breath) is held down, a second life-breath is delimited by the number of the individual breathings. The third uprising is similar. The mild breath-control is defined as so many, the medium breath-control as so many, and the intense breath-control as so many. In this way they are delimited by number. Breath-control when properly practiced in this way becomes long and fine."

Thus in his explanation of *Yoga-sūtra* II, 50, Vyāsa makes no use at all of *haṭha yoga* terms. But Vācaspati Miśra explains the three kinds of breath-control as *recaka*, *pūraka* and *kumbhaka* respectively. Śaṅkara on the other hand explains by simply analyzing various compounds which appear in the Vyāsa commentary, and does not add anything substantially new. He explains the phrase "breath-control whose operation is in regard to the exterior [wind]" (*bāhyavṛtti*) as: "others teach that breath-control in regard to the exterior is *pūraka*"[13] Again, as to "breath-control whose operation is in regard to the interior [wind]" (*ābhyantara*), he says: "they teach that it is *recaka*."[14]

So Śaṅkara knew the terms *pūraka* and *recaka* in use among some of the *yoga* practitioners of the time, but he simply mentions them as one doctrine and does not adopt them himself. He would have thought of them as unorthodox methods not in conformity with the ancient tradition of the Yoga school.

***Yoga-sūtra* II, 51 :**

"The forth breath control has discarded (transcended) external and internal objects".

Vyāsa's commentary: "What is delimited as regards place, time and number, as an external object, is discarded (transcended). Again what is delimited as an internal object is discarded (transcended). In both these, the breath-control becomes long and becomes fine. Next, based on a progress through mastery of all the stages, is absence of the operation of breath exhalation and inhalation, this being the fourth breath-control. Whereas the third breath-control has no regard to any object, has no operation [of breath], and is brought into being abruptly, is delimited as regards place time and number, and is long and fine, the fourth breath-control (restraint), being a conquest of all the stages in order, is based on an accurate knowledge of the objects of both inhalation and exhalation, and discarding (transcending) both [object], the operation ceases. This is the distinction."

Śaṅkara comments on this passage of Vyāsa simply by supplying some words, but Vācaspati Miśra adds various explanations. "The distinction is that the third breath-control comes about by a sudden effort regardless of anything else, but the fourth breath-control is based on having regard, and comes about through many efforts. It has no regard to the objects of *pūraka* and *recaka*, but has regard for place, time and number." This explanation does not appear in Śaṅkara. We do not know why he has said this sort of thing, but he may well have been thinking of ideas of *haṭhayoga*.

Again let us see what is said as to the control of the senses.

Vyāsa : "What is control of the senses? What is called control of the senses in *sūtra* II, 54 is when all the sense organs are disengaged from their respective objects, and are like an imitation of the mind itself."

Śaṅkara : "When they are not engaged with their respective objects, they become like an imitation of the mind itself" means that when the mind is controlled, then all the sense organs are controlled like the mind. As in the case of conquest of the senses, no other means is necessary.[15]

Just as when the king of the honey-bees flies up, the other bees too fly up in imitation of him, and when the king of the bees descends and settles, the other bees descend and settle in imitation of him, in the same way when the mind is controlled, all the senses are controlled. This is control of the senses.

***Yoga-sūtra* II, 55 :**

"From that (perception of sense control) arises perfect docility of the sense organs".

Vyāsa's comment : (1) Some teach that control of the senses means [that the various senses like the ear are] not addicted to their objects like sound: (2) [others that] practices not in conflict [with scripture etc., i. e. permitted by scripture] are proper: (3) some say that to engage in the objects like sound just as one desires [is allowable]; (4) some say that control of the senses is when desire and aversion having disappeared, the knowledge of sound etc. is without pleasure or displeasure. (5) Jāgīśavya says that it is the non-apprehension [of things] on account of the mind's being concentrated on one thing. Therefore he is saying that when the mind has been controlled all the senses are controlled, and other [external] methods laboriously devised for the occasions of controlling the senses are not necessary to the *yogin*.

There is no great difference between Śaṅkara and Vācaspati Miśra in commenting on this *sūtra*.

However it cannot be said that Śaṅkara is always the more faithful to the Vyāsa text. Where Vyāsa says '*kuśara-akuśarāni karmāṇi*' — *karmans* are good or bad — Śaṅkara insists that besides the good and the bad there must be recognized those which are 'a mixture of good and bad'. Śaṅkara has interpreted in his own way with distinct ideas of his own, whereas Vācaspati Miśra follows the Vyāsa text.

The usual word in the Yoga school to express the state of liberation is *kaivalya* (isolation), but there are instances where Śaṅkara uses the word *nirvāṇa*.[16]

On the whole Śaṅkara's commentary is terse, whereas that of Vācaspati Miśra is detailed; but on essentials there is no great difference between them. The great change in the fundamentals of *yoga* came later.

In the primitive Yoga school, prerequisites to *yoga* practice were the five Restraints (*yama*) namely non-violence, straight-forwardness, non-stealing, continence and absence of greed (*YS*. II, 30); the five Injunctions (*niyama*) namely purity, contentment, austerity, sacred recitation and worship of God (*YS*. II, 23). These are common to Jainism also, and taught in the *Manu-smṛti* (IV, 204), *Viṣṇu-purāṇa* (VI, 7, 36-38) etc. as also in the later Vedānta (for instance in *Vedāntasāra*). Śaṅkara pre-supposes them.[17] But where Vyāsa explains 'recitation' as "recitation of the sacred texts teaching liberation, or else recitation of the sacred syllable *Om* verbally"[18] Śaṅkara glosses "recitation of the sacred texts teaching liberation" as "recitation of *Upaniṣads* etc."[19] Many teachings of the *Upaniṣads* cannot be made to agree with the *Yoga-sūtra*, and why does he nevertheless deliberately explain it as '*Upaniṣads* etc.'? It is clearly because the commentator Śaṅkara is expressing a Vedānta standpoint.

Analyzed in detail in this way, the Śaṅkara commentary is seen to differ on a number of point of emphasis, but looked at broadly the differences are not great. The practice is retirement, solitary without any social aspect. *Yoga* with a social side was advocated in the Yoga school in later centuries by the Nātha school.

The stress on morality in latter-day Indian religions has made quite some change in *yoga* also. The *yoga* of ancient times was concerned with individual liberation and also the acquirement of miraculous magical and spiritual powers through *yoga* practice, and even today it has many practitioners; but *yoga* of the Nātha school of recent times differs considerably and has come to stress the ethical and social sides.[20] It is represented by the figures of Matsyendranāth and Gorakhnāth (or Gorakṣanāth) of the late 14th or 15th centuries.[21] Previous to that the *yoga* had laid down the five Restraints, namely non-violence, straight-forwardness, non-stealing, continence and absence of greed (possession but on the ground that absence of possessions) was impracticable and unrealistic, they were revised, and a group of six was substituted, namely sympathy (fellow-feeling, *dayā*), uprightness (*ārjava*), endurance (*kṣamā*), firmness (*dhṛti*), moderation in diet (*mitāhāra*) and to make up ten Restraints (*yamadaśa*).[22] (The *dayā* mentioned here is understood in India generally to mean a sympathy which protects the weak as circumstances and ability permit.) With this, *yoga* has developed into something ethical and social. The *yoga* taught by the modern Vivekānanda was also on these lines. It may be remarked that Gorakhnāth attacks the Śaṅkara doctrine of *Māyā*.[23]

When we look at these great changes of the later *yoga*, Vyāsa, Śaṅkara and Vācaspati look very much out of the same stable.

The above is no more than a partial examination, but this much can be said:

(1) So far as the *Brahma-sūtra* commentary goes, Śaṅkara accepts

yoga. There is a rejection of *yoga* in the *Brahma-sūtra* itself, and Śaṅkara comments on this *sūtra* as it stands, but he does so only because he is commenting on the *Brahma-sūtra* in which this appears. Furthermore the *sūtra* author is only rejecting metaphysical doctrines of the Yoga school and does not necessarily reject the *yoga* practice. Śaṅkara in fact accepts *yoga* practice.

(2) Thus it is possible that Śaṅkara wrote a commentary on the one by Vyāsa on the *Yoga-sūtra*.

(3) In the *Yoga-sūtra* commentary attributed to Śaṅkara, words and phrases reminiscent of Advaita ideas and their expressions are not few.

(4) However further study will be needed to determine the authenticity or otherwise of the work, or again it may prove impossible to settle the point.

(5) As far as I have observed so far, Vācaspati Miśra's interpretations appear to have a stronger Hinduistic colouring.

Notes

1) Śaṅkarācārya's *Pātañjalayogasūtrabhāṣyavivaraṇa*. Published as no.94 in the Madras Government Oriental Series, Triplicane, Madras, 1952.

2) *anantaṃ viśvam, anantabhāva ānantyam, tasmin samāpannam vyāpya viśvabhāvaṃ sthitam cittam āsanaṃ nirvartayati draḍhayati* / *YSViv*. p.227. *ll*.15-17.

3) *anante vā nāganāyake sthirataraphaṇāsahasravidhṛtaviśvabharāmaṇḍale samāpannaṃ cittam āsanam nirvartayatīti* /

4) *YSViv*. p.227.

5) For *recaka* "exhalation through one nostril" ; for *pūraka*, "inhalation through the left nostril alone"; for *kumbhaka*, "the way of restraining the breath by closing nostrils and mouth with the right hand", according to the account of various methods of restraining the breathing in V. S. Apte: *Practical Sanskrit-English Dictionary*. Cf. *Vedānta-sāra* 217; P. Deussen: *All gemeine Geschichte der Philosophie* I. 2. S.348; I. 3. S.566-567. These restraints of breathing are given in detail in *Haṭhayogapradīpikā* II. Woods translates *recaka* as 'emission', *pūraka* as 'inhalation' and *kumbhaka* as 'suspension', the mistakes deriving from the attitude of the old Sanskritist who sought to expound logically from bare etymology without regard to *yoga* practice.

6) This is *pūraka* (Vācaspati Miśra). "A control of breath whose operation is to bring in wind which is outside" (Śaṅkara).

7) This is *recaka* (Vācaspati Miśra). "A control of breath whose operation is to expel outside wind which is within" (Śaṅkara).

8) "It is neither sucking in nor expelling [the breath]" (Śaṅkara). "As a result of an effort to stop abruptly both exhalation and inhalation, the two cease. It is not as in the previous cases where there is an effort by which the flow of the effort to fill up is checked, nor where the effort necessary to check the flow of the effort of *recaka*. Instead, just as water dropped on to a hot stone shrivels and shrinks to nothing, so the wind, which is naturally mobile, having its operation dammed by a powerful effort of checking it, and becoming fine, remains in the body. There is no filling up as in *pūraka* nor expulsion as in *recaka*." (Vācaspati Miśra)

9) Again Vācaspati has this to explain 'in regard to place'. "The place [of the breath-control] is an extent measured in terms of the distance (*prādeśa*) between the tips of the outstretched thumb and index finger, of the distance (*vitasti*) between the index and little fingers, or the distance of a 'hand', and so on. Just as one looking at a blade of grass or piece of cotton etc. in a windless place infers from a slight movement in it the presence of wind, in the same way from a slight sensation like the feeling of ants creeping, from the soles of the feet to the crown of the head, the operation of the wind internally is inferred" (Vācaspati). However Śaṅkara takes 'delimited in regard to place' as meaning pervading the body of the practitioner. "When the operation of the external wind is drawn into the body, it fills the space from the nose-tip to the great toes; in the same say when the operation of the wind within is expellees outside, the wind fills the space from the great toes to the nose-tip. Or again in regard to the exterior, filling the space is understood in terms of the distance between the index and little finger and so on." This last is a glancing reference to some such idea as that of Vācaspati Miśra.

10) 'regulated as to time' is taken by Śaṅkara as 'taking up so many moments for the breath-control' corresponding exactly to Vyāsa, but Vācaspati piles on explanations and it is not clear just what he is saying: "An instant (*kṣana*) is one quarter of the time measured by the action of blinking. This (breath-control) is delimited by determining how many instants it takes. A moment (*mātrā*) is the time taken to rub the hand round the knee three times and then snap the fingers. The first uprising (*udghāta*) measured as thirty-six moments (*mātrā*) is the mild uprising. The second uprising, being double that, is the medium; the third uprising, being triple that, is the intense. The time of the finger-snapping as described before is equal to the time taken for the operation of a complete breath by a healthy man. The uprising action which is the object of the first uprising action is subdued, controlled, suppressed. How many instants of time (the above takes) is what is being referred to."

11) Again Vācaspati Miśra explains 'delimited as to number': " 'number' means how

many breaths, and there is some difference [between the number of moments and the number of breaths]. This breath-control, practiced daily for a day, half a month, a month and so on, increasing in place and time, becomes long. The attainment being in the form of extreme fineness and not dullness, it is called 'subtle'." But Śaṅkara's understanding of what 'number' means here is close to the Vyāsa original: "For instance, when all the winds, excited by the suppression, suddenly strike against the top of the head, suppression of the action is the first uprising. This is the mild one. When once more the wind suddenly strikes and is suppressed, the action of this second striking is determined by the number of exhalations it has taken. And this is called breath-control of the medium grade."

12) Woods takes this to mean "rising up of the vital current from the navel to the palate", but this interpretation is not to be found in the commentaries of Śaṅkara and Vācaspati Miśra.

13) *bāhyam anye pūraka ity ācakṣate*/ *YSViv*. p.227, *l*.30.

14) *taṃ recaka ity ācakṣate*/ *YSViv*. p.228, *l*.13.

15) The *ĀnSS* edition has *netarendriyajavad*. In the text as quoted in Śaṅkara's commentary, the *bhāṣya* has *nopāyāntaram*, which is clearer.

16) *YSViv*. ad I, 24 p.53 *l*.24.

17) *yamaniyamavidyābhyāsātmakasya sukṛtaduṣkṛtakṣayahetoḥ puruṣaprayatnasya*/Ś. ad *BS*. vol.II, p.320, *ll*.6-7.

18) *svādhyāyo mokṣaśāstrāṇām mokṣaśāstrāṇām adhyayanam*/ad *YS*. II, 32.

19) *upaniṣadādy adhyayanam*/ *YSViv*. p.216 *l*.25. Vācaspati gives no gloss on this.

20) R. D. Ranade: *Pathway to God in Hindi Literature*, Allahabad etc., Adhyatma Vidya Mandir, 1954, p.9f.

21) According to the view of G. A. Grierson in *ERE*. vol.6 pp.328-329. J.N. Farquhar(*An Outline of the Religious Literature of India*, p.254) puts him in the 12th century. The town of Gorakhpur, near where Śākhyamuni died, was the birth place of Gorakhnāth, and probably took its name from his temple there. A certain Indian intellectual once told me that the saint was called Gorakh (protector of cows) because he opposed the slaughter of cows by the English for their beef. This is probably not a fact, but that it is believed to be true is a fact. The book by Banerjea, quoted in the last note here, deals only with his philosophy and does not raise the question of his date. This strikingly exhibits the typical Indian attitude that the question is after all whether what he thought is true, and his date simply does not matter.

22) *Gorakṣavacanasaṃgraha* v. 78 (published in the work noted next).

23) Akṣaya Kumar Banerjea: *Philosophy of Gorakhnath with Gorakṣa-Vacana-Saṃgraha*, Gorakhpur, Mahant Dig Vijay Nath Trust, 1961, p.xvi; pp.242-243.

IV. THE VIEW OF *YOGA* IN ŚAṄKARA'S *BRAHMA-SŪTRA* COMMENTARY AND ITS MEDIAEVAL CHARACTER

In his commentary on the *Brahma-sūtra*, Śaṅkara discusses at length the question of meditation (*upāsana*). This is because the *Brahma-sūtra* is itself a discussion of the various meditations taught in the *Upaniṣads*. But *yoga* is also referred to. As a method actually practiced by aspirants in India generally, *yoga* is for wider than meditation, and Śaṅkara recognized *yoga* practice (Ś. ad *BS*. vol.I. p.350, *l*.7). He seems to have taken it as a synonym of *dhyāna*[1] (Ś. ad *BS*. IV, 11. vol.2, p.482). As against Śaṅkara, an opponent (*pūrvapakṣin*) takes *yoga* to be a means for attaining right knowledge (*samyagdarśanābhyupāya*) (Ś. ad *BS*. vol.I. p.428, *l*.9).[2]

It was generally believed that *yoga* practice would bring its practitioner various occult powers, and Śaṅkara accepts this sort of belief so commonly held. For instance, he thought that a *yoga* practitioner could take on several bodies at the same time.[3] And he relates that this was a self-evident fact to the people of the time, attested by sayings and maxims (*nyāya*).

> "Some people take on another body when the previous body perishes (=after death), but there are others who, though their body persists as before, take on another body according to the maxim (*nyāya*) that through the power of *yoga* one takes on many bodies." (Ś. ad *BS*. vol. II. p.236, *l*.11.)

Again, he accepted that through the power of *yoga* one could attain a special station, even the sun itself (Ś. ad *BS*. vol.II. p.514, *l*.2), and also that it is possible to penetrate to the center of anything. "Some practitioner of *yoga* (*yogin*) also, when his practice reaches perfection, can enter into the center of anything, and so it is possible to become its controller."[4]

Then since he refers to "some *yoga* practitioner who has acquired the [eight-fold] powers of making the body very small and so on",[5] he would have accepted the eight-fold powers spoken of by the Yoga school. Accordingly the Advaita school had no difference with the Yoga school as regards the practice. So there was no need for Śaṅkara to have repudiate the Yoga school in joining the Vedānta school.

There is just a doubt as to how far in the case of the Śaṅkara school there was real belief in the eight-fold powers. Perhaps it was a case of mechanically repeating what was written in the *Yoga-sūtra*. Followers of the Śaṅkara school today do not believe in such things; when in modern India practitioners and followers of the Śaṅkara school travel in groups, they hire a coach, and the Śaṅkarācārya goes in his personal car.

But Śaṅkara, commentator on the *Yoga-sūtra*, did at any ratio recognize a distinction between the Sāṃkhya and Yoga school. On the question of the supreme Lord he says: ' "The Lord who is different from primordial substance and also from *Puruṣa*, what in fact would He be?" Since in the Sāṃkhya classics generally no Lord is recognized, there is bound to be this question from those who do not yet understand as to what is the proof of the existence of the Lord, and what are his characteristics'.[6]

But in regard to the *yoga* practice, Śaṅkara's commentary has only a faint colouring of religion, whereas Vācaspati Miśra's explanations are Hinduistic and Haṭhayogic.

Notes

1) But according to *Saundarānanda* XVIII, *dhyāna* and *yoga* are used in clear distinction, *dhyāna* being the mental state and *yoga* the means to it. *ṛddhipravekaṃ ca bahuprakāraṃ parasya cetaścaritāvabodhaṃ/atītajanmasmaraṇaṃ ca dīrghaṃ divye viśuddhe śruticakṣuṣī ca//*XVI, 2; *dante 'pi dantaṃ praṇidhāya kāmaṃ tālvagram utpīḍya ca jihvayāpi/ cittena cittaṃ parigṛhya cāpi kāryaḥ prayatno na tu te'nuvṛttāḥ//* XVI, 83; *sa pādayos tatra vidhāya śaucaṃ śucau śive śrīmati vṛkṣamūle/mokṣāya buddhvā vyavasāyakakṣāṃ paryaṅkam aṅkāvahitaṃ babandha//*XVII, 3; *ṛjuṃ samagraṃ praṇidhāya kāyaṃ kāye smṛtiṃ cābhimukhīṃ vidhāya/sarvendriyāṇy ātmani saṃnidhāya sa tatra yogaṃ prayataḥ prapede//*XVII, 4. The formal method of sitting is a proper seat in a quiet place, setting one's thought on oneself, restraining the five senses within (Cf. *Buddhacarita* II, 45), setting the teeth against each other and pressing the palate with the tongue, controlling mind by mind, concentrating on either the nose-tip or the forehead between the brows; (first) remedying the defects of passions active in the will, he destroys them at the right time by bringing against them right ideas opposed to them. This is the principal means to reach liberation. (In the above I have made use of an article by Professor Matsunami Seiren, page 120 of *Shūkyo Kenkyū* (*Religious Studies*), vol.13. no.3).

2) Elsewhere again the *purvapakṣin*, saying "*samyagdarśanābhyupāyo hi yogo vede*

vihitāḥ" cites the expositions of *yoga* in the *Upaniṣads* (Ś. ad *BS*. vol.I p.427, *l*.11 f).

3) *eṣaiva ca yogaśāstreṣu yoginām anekaśarīrayogaprakriyā*/(Ś. ad *BS*. vol.II, p.564, *ll*.10-11. Cf. B.I. edition, p.284).

4) *yogino vā kasya cit siddhasya sarvānupraveśena yamayitṛtvaṃ syāt*/Ś. ad *BS*. vol.I, p. 205, *ll*.5-6.

5) *prāptāṇimādyaiś varyaḥ kaś cid yogī*/Ś. ad *BS*. vol.I, p.204, *l*.6.

6) *sāṃkhyaśāstre prasiddhyabhāvād īśvarasadbhāve copapattim avaśyanavagateśvaraviśeṣo vā pṛcchati*/ *YSViv*. ad I, 23. p.53, *ll*.18-19.

V. ŚAṄKARA'S *VIVARAṆA* ON THE *YOGASŪTRA-BHĀṢYA*

A work declared in the colophon to be by Śaṅkara, namely a gloss (*Vivaraṇa*) on the *bhāṣya* on the *Yoga-sūtra* has been discovered and published in Madras.[1] Hitherto unknown to the academic world, it is an important basic text for the history of Indian thought. In my article in the *Okuda Festschrift* in 1976, I have already pointed out a number of noteworthy words and citations, etc. which appear in it; I propose here to discuss some noteworthy ideas in the *Yogasūtrabhāṣyavivaraṇa* attributed to a Śaṅkara.

Vyāsa says simply in his commentary on *Yoga-sūtra* I, 1.

"What is called *yoga* is *samādhi*".

Vācaspati Miśra however says:

"It is accepted generally in *śruti* and *smṛti*, histories, *purāṇas* and so on that *samādhi* is the cause of bliss (*niḥśreyasa*=liberation)".[2]

But Śaṅkara discusses in detail how it is knowledge attained by means of *yoga* that is the cause of liberation.[3] In explaining the structure of the *Yoga-sūtra* he says:

"What is to be obtained is other than the result which is discarding [passions] on the basis of discriminative wisdom, and again the means to discarding is none other than discriminative wisdom. And thus the mutual relation of what is to be attained and the means to it is determined ··· As an example, the relation is well known that the result of medical remedies is none other than attainment of health, and again the means to health are none other than medical remedies".[4]

In other words the objective is to get rid of passions, etc. and discriminative wisdom is the means to it.[5] Here one can say that Śaṅkara lays the emphasis on knowledge. He presents an interpretation which appears markedly Advaitic.

Vyāsa says:

"Liberation (*apavarga*) is the experiencing subject's (*bhoktṛ*) knowing with certainty himself. There is no different [third] knowledge other than these two (experience of pain and pleasure, and liberation)".

Śaṅkara however says:

> "As long as ignorance (*avidyā*) exists, what is unpleasant and what is pleasant exist. And therefore experience [of pain and pleasure] exists. But since *puruṣa* in its essence can neither accept nor reject anything, when *puruṣa* is accurately known, how could there be experience [of pain and pleasure]? Therefore the idea which subdues the ideas which are essentially ignorance and take the form of pain and pleasure, is the knowledge of *puruṣa*. For no third separate knowledge can be conceived apart from and different from these two".[6]

If in this passage *puruṣa* is taken in the sense of *Ātman*, it is an Advaitic Position that is being put forward.

According to Śaṅkara's commentary:

> "Our bondage arises on the basis of ignorance".[7]
>
> "By destroying ignorance by knowledge, liberation is attained".[8]

The Yoga school traditionally have held that *puruṣa* is the experiencer, but Śaṅkara in commenting even on the *yoga*, abandons this traditional view and brings in the Vedānta Advaitic interpretation that *ātman* is not an experiencer.

> "*Puruṣa* takes a form identified with the various operations of the mind".[9]

To this *sūtra* Śaṅkara adds an Advaitic interpretation:

> "The opponent says: If *puruṣa* takes a form identified with the various operations, then he undergoes a change of state and it entails *puruṣa* being something changing. Will it not thus entail many errors?"
>
> "The reply is: It has been pointed out in the previous topic and already answered. The taking on of the various forms is a superimposition (*adhyāropa*) of the various operations of the mind on *puruṣa*. *Puruṣa* in its essence does not change.[10] It is as when something is placed against a crystal; its colour appears in it".[11]

This 'superimposition' (*adhyāropa*) concept and the example of the crystal are often employed in the Advaitic school.

Again, Vyāsa quotes Pañcaśikha: '*ekam eva darśanaṃ khyātir eva darśanam*'. Knowledge (*khyāti*)[12] in the Yoga school is the discriminating knowledge that knows the difference between *puruṣa* and fundamental causal substance, and Pañcaśikha takes *darśana* and *khyāti* as identical, but

Śaṅkara's view limits *khyāti* to an operation of *buddhi*, and the self-nature of *puruṣa* and *buddhi* are known by this knowledge.[13]

And in that case, the knowledge which discriminates has no connection with *puruṣa*. In fact a point which neither Pañcaśikha nor Vyāsa made clear, Śaṅkara makes clear-cut on the basis of his own ideas.

Again, Vyāsa says:

> "Just as the victory and defeat existing in the army are finally attributed to the king, because the king is the one who experiences the results of the fighting, in the same way it is said that bondage and liberation exist only in the *buddhi*, but are attributed to *puruṣa*. Because *puruṣa* is one who experiences those results".

Commenting on this passage, Śaṅkara interprets:

> "The one who experiences those results is the person who is aware of right idea and wrong idea".[14]

And again he says of the relation between bondage and liberation:

> "In so far as *buddhi* thinks experience of pain and pleasure, which have something to be done, and liberation something already completed, *buddhi* is bound …. Fulfillment of *buddhi*'s goal is completion of what had to be done. *Puruṣa* when seeing that is not involved in bondage or liberation, which are things apart from itself, and thinking that there is nothing for *puruṣa* to do, that completion of what was to be done is the liberation of *buddhi*".[15]

Again after listing the various operations of the human mind, perception, memory, inference and so on, he says:

> "Since these operations of the mind do not differ in so far as they are notions, the various attributes of *buddhi* exist only within *buddhi*, and are created by *buddhi*, and their existence in *puruṣa* is something superimposed (*adhyāropita*). *Puruṣa* being aware of them, adopts them, and in this way they are superimposed on *puruṣa* (*adhyāropyante*)".[16]

When the essential nature of A does not really exist in a thing B, yet is mistakenly supposed to exist there, it is called 'superimposition' and in Śaṅkara's *Brahma-sūtra* commentary the word *adhyāsa* is used for it; here the word *adhyāropa*. The Vyāsa commentary[17] uses the word *adhyāropita-sadbhāva*.[18] In any case it cannot be maintained that because the words for superimposition are different, the Śaṅkara who wrote the *Yoga-sūtra* commentary is other than the author of the *Brahma-sūtra* commentary.[19]

According to this interpretation, it comes to saying that the conjunction between *puruṣa* and primary matter does not cause mundane existence (*saṃsāra*) but superimposition is the cause. This is absolutely Advaitic.

In some places even technical terms of Vedānta are used. For instance *sūtra* IV,4 is:

> "When the *yogin* conjures up transformation bodies (*nirmāṇakāya*) their minds are produced from the pure I-am notion (*asmitāmātra*)."

Śaṅkara says:

> "Produced from the sense-organs and the pure 'I-am' notion alone".[20]

This pure 'I-am' notion he takes as *ahaṃkāra*[21] so far it is Sāṃkhyan. But Śaṅkara takes *asmitā*[22] as identical with the idea of 'I' (*ahaṃpratyaya*).[23]

Puruṣa has always the nature of awareness.[24] *Puruṣa* is what has awareness, and that is not experience (*bhoga*) of pleasure and pain.[25]

According to Vyāsa, the operations of the mind (*cittavṛttayaḥ*) are already known by *puruṣa*, but according to Śaṅkara they are brought about in accordance with the nature of *puruṣa* as one eternally aware (*nityopalabdhṛ*).[26]

Now Śaṅkara often uses of *Brahman* the expression 'having eternal awareness as its nature'.

Again, in the concluding verses of Śaṅkara's commentary :

> The syllable *Om* is the expression of the Lord;
> From the Lord the various results of all *karman*-s are manifested;
> In him himself there are no passions, no *karman*-s, no fruition of their results;
> He causes to appear all beings along with the results of their *karman*.
> The Lord (*Īśvara*) who is ruler (*īśa*) of all, creator who acts in the maintenance, creation and dissolution of the worlds.
> May that Kṛṣṇa think of our white (=good karma) and remove our black[27] (=bad karma).

Here the sound *Om* is taken as expressing the Lord. This is taught in *Yoga-sūtra* I, 27 and is a teaching of the Yoga school, and again is taught in the first chapter of the *Māṇḍūkya Kārikā* and is also a Vedāntic doctrine.

However, to call the Lord 'the creator who acts in maintenance, creation and dissolution of the worlds' is absolutely Vedāntic; no such idea is expressed in the *Yoga-sūtra*. But again the concept of God which Śaṅkara gives in this commentary is in some cases clearly different from that of the Advaita school. For example there is the view that the Lord (*Īśvara*) is not omniscient[28] but in the *Brahma-sūtra* commentary he takes it that the Lord is omniscient — but the position about omniscience in the Yoga school is not at all clear and further research is needed.

Again it is noteworthy that the Lord is called Kṛṣṇa. Śaṅkara in the *Brahma-sūtra* commentary refers to worship of Viṣṇu but does not refer to Kṛṣṇa. In the *Yoga-sūtra* of course there is no such reference. Śaṅkara's *Yoga-sūtra* commentary here takes a step in the direction of the *bhakti* faith of Hinduism; in explaining *yoga*, Śaṅkara thought it was the purification of the mind.

> "For taints (*kleśa*) are not operations of the mind. Really the various taints are not of the nature of [pure] ideas. But operations [of the mind] are of the nature of [pure] ideas. The various taints are impurities [dirt — *mala*] of the mind, just as cataract (*timira*) is an impurity of the eye. For when the mind is separated from the impurity of the passions, the fluctuations of [pure] ideas, and the opposing ideas, do not exist".[29]

Here he speaks a doctrine recalling that of *Mahāyāna* of the essential purity of the essence of mind. In the *Māṇḍūkya Kārikā* (IV, 62; 64; 72) what is taught about 'mind' (*citta*) is close to Śaṅkara's understanding of the *Ātman* doctrine. In particular, '*kleśa*' in the sense of 'passion' is peculiar to Buddhism, and it is the Śaṅkara of *yoga* who accepts it as having entered the thought of the Yoga school. As against that, not merely in Śaṅkara's *Brahma-sūtra* commentary but in Indian philosophy generally, *kleśa* is used in the sense of suffering and pain. Here Śaṅkara is immersed in the spiritual atmosphere of the practicing *yogins* who were influenced by Buddhism, and here too is the influence of the fact that the Yoga school from ancient times was using Buddhist technical terms.

The standpoint of this Śaṅkara is realism and he rejects the Consciousness-only doctrine.[30] Introducing the doctrine of other schools he says:

"The mind itself is something which takes an appearance (*ābhāsa*) of itself and an appearance as an object.[31] For in the various operations [of the mind] their forms are attested spontaneously. For instance a light illumines jars, etc. (objects of the external world) and also itself. Is it necessary to suppose a *puruṣa*, who is supposed as a subject and who knows the operations of the mind?" — this is said.[32]

To this the *Yoga-sūtra* replies in IV,19, as Śaṅkara explains it:

"Mind cannot illumine its own self, for mind is something seen."

Then he says:

"Nihilists (*vaināśika*) hold the mistaken view that the perceiving subject (*grāhaka*) and perceived object (*grāhya*) are nothing but mind itself".[33]

Then he explains:

"No single thing, called the succession of knowledge, exists".[34]

From this standpoint the *ālaya* consciousness is naturally rejected. The point of rejecting Consciousness-only doctrine is the same in the *Brahma-sūtra* commentary. Accordingly Śaṅkara, though adopting technical terms and so on from Vijñānavāda, yet rejects the doctrine itself.

The realist position can be recognized in other points. Śaṅkara, expatiating on Vyāsa's teaching, says that the sense organs receiving operations of forms of sounds, etc. of the outer world, are, the changing channels (*praṇāḍikā*) to the mind, namely portals (*dvāra*).[35] He says that direct perception (*pratyakṣa*) is established through them.[36]

Again looking at technical terms, in the same way there are expressions recalling those peculiar to Śaṅkara: "All things from *mahat* to a post".[37] This recalls '*brahmādi stambaparyanta*' which appears in the *Brahma-sūtra* commentary.[38] There are also to be found special technical terms not used too much in Indian philosophy generally; for instance *upasthāpita* occurs in the sense of 'caused to manifest' and 'caused to be manifested',[39] which Śaṅkara glosses as *pratyupanīta*.[40] Incidentally he calls something which manifests a result *pratyupasthāpaka*[41] and he seems to use the expression *avidyāpratyupasthāpita* 'manifested through ignorance' habitually in the *Brahma-sūtra* commentary.

Notes

1) Śaṅkarācārya's *Pātañjalayogasūtrabhāṣyavivaraṇa*, Published as no.94 in the Madras Government Oriental Series, Triplicane, Madras, 1952.

2) *Tattvavaiśāradī*, p.2. *ĀnSS*.

3) Cf. *avidyāmūlatvād asmitādīnāṃ kleśānāṃ vidyāyāś cāvidyocchedarūpatvād vidyodaye cāvidyādi-kleśamucchedo* … /Vācaspatimiśra ad *Vyāsabhāṣya* I, 1. p.3. *ĀnSS*.

4) *YSViv*. p.2, *ll*.18-23. ad *YS*. I, 1.

5) *YSViv*. p.2, *l*.23.

6) *YSViv*. p.180, *ll*.19-23, ad *YS*. II, 18.

7) *avidyānimitto hi bandhaḥ*/ *YSViv*. p.4, *l*.2, ad *YS*. I, 1.

8) *khyātir eva sādhanam avidyānivṛttidvāreṇa*/ *YSViv*. p.4, *l*.2, ad *YS*. I, 1.

9) *YS*. I, 4.

10) That *puruṣa* does not change is argued in other places also (*YSViv*. p.190, *l*.19f.; p. 191, *l*.13; p.349).

11) *YSViv*. p.14, *ll*. 15-17, ad *YS*. I, 4.

12) *YS*. I, 16; II, 5, 26, 28; III, 49; IV, 29.

13) *buddhivṛttir eva darśanam*/ *khyāyate puruṣeṇeti ca khyātiḥ, khyāyate anayā (buddhyā) ca buddhipuruṣayoḥ svarūpam iti khyātiḥ*/ *YSViv*. p.14, *ll*. 22-23, ad *YS*. I, 4.

14) *YSViv*. p.181, ad *YS*. I, 15-18.

15) *YSViv*. p.181, *ll*.17-20.

16) *YSViv*. p.181, *ll*.22-24.

17) *YBh*. p.181, ad *YS*. I,9.

18) The word *adhyāropa*, originally used in Vijñānavāda Buddhism, was adopted by the Yoga and Vedānta. *adhyāsa* is purely Vedāntic and not used in Buddhism.

19) The words *adhyāropayati and adhyāropaṇā* are used freely in the *Upadeśasāhasrī*, undoubtedly a genuine work of Śaṅkara. (Śaṅkara's *Upadeśasāhasrī* ed. by Sengaku Mayeda, Tokyo Hokuseido, 1973, p.302.)

20) *YSViv*. IV, 4, p.320, ad *YS*. I, 22.

21) *YSViv*. p.320, *l*.20.

22) *asmibhāvo 'smitā asmīti pratyayaḥ*/ *YSViv*. p.184, *ll*.22-23, ad *YS*. II, 19.

23) *so 'yam ahaṃpratyayo 'smitākhyakleśa ucyate*/ *YSViv*. p.138, *ll*.10-11. ad *YS*. II, 6.

24) *nityopalabdhisvarūpatva* — *YSViv*. p.191, *l*.27 ad *YS*. II, 20.

25) *YSViv*. p.191, *l*.15.

26) *YSViv*. p.348, *l*.24. ad *YS*. IV, 18.

27) According to the dictionaries, *śukliman* (m.) for 'white' occurs in *Harṣacarita*, and it also appears in *Prakaraṇapañcikā* IV, 49 (*SDS* XVI, *l*.444). Again *kṛṣṇiman* (m.) for black comes, according to the dictionaries, in *Mudrārākṣasa*. But when in this commen-

tary it is said *vyapanudatutarām kṛṣṇimānam sa kṛṣṇaḥ*, it is a kind of play on words of a kind which is not seen in the *Brahma-sūtra* commentary.

28) *YSViv*. p.64, *l*.154.

29) *YSViv*. p.126, *ll*.6-8, ad *YS*. II, 3.

30) Cf. the Fourth Chapter of *Māṇḍūkya-Kārikā*.

31) According to him, *svābhāsa=grāhaka, viṣayābhāsa=grāhya*.

32) *YSViv*. p.344, *l*.14-17, ad *YS*. IV, 19.

33) *YSViv*. p.356 ad *YS*. IV, 23.Śaṅkara's *Brahma-sūtra* commentary also calls Buddhist schools like the *Vijñānavādin* 'nihilist' — *vaināśika*.

34) *YSViv*. p.359, *l*.9, ad *YS*. IV, 24.

35) *YSViv*. p.19, *ll*.8-10.

36) *YSViv*. p.19, *l*.12.

37) *mahadādistambaparyantā mūrtayaḥ*/ *YSViv*. p.177, *l*.21, ad *YS*. II, 18.

38) Ś. ad *BS*. B.I. p.604, *l*.2 ; P. Deussen : *Das System des Vedānta* S.257.

39) *YBh*. III,17, p.266, *l*.10.

40) *YSViv*. p.267, *l*.12.

41) *YSViv*. p.22, *l*.12 ad *YS*. I, 6-7.

VI. A REVIEW OF V.M. APTE (trnsl.): *BRAHMA-SŪTRA SHANKARA-BHĀSHYA*

Brahma-sūtra Shankara-bhāsya, Bādarāyaṇā's Brahma-Sūtras with Shankarācārya's Commentary, Translated into English by V. M. Apte, pp.xxxvii + 2 + 888. Bombay, Popular Book Depot, 1960.

The most authoritative and best known work in the Vedānta philosophy, Śaṅkara's *Brahma-sūtra-bhāṣya*, was translated into English by Mr. V. M. Apte, B.A., LL.B., Advocate Dhulia, West Khandesh, India. Formerly there had been published two complete translations of the whole work in Western languages many years ago, one in English by George Thibaut (Sacred Books of the East, vols. XXXIV, XXXVIII, Oxford University Press, 1890, 1996), the other in German by Paul Deussen (*Die Sūtras des Vedānta oder die Śārīraka-mīmāṅsā des Bādarāyaṇa nebst dem vollständigen Commentare des Śaṅkara*, Leipzig, F. A. Brockhaus, 1887). These two have been regarded as standard translations for the students of Śaṅkara's philosophy. Part of the work was also translated into English by Dr. S. K. Belvalkar (The *Brahma-sūtras of Bādarāyaṇa with the comment of Śaṅkarāchārya*, chapter II, quarters I and II. Poona, Oriental Book-supplying Agency, 1923), and by Prof. Louis Renou (*Śaṅkara. Prolégomènes au Vedānta*, Paris, Imprimerie Nationale, 1951). In comparison with these foregoing translations, it may be safely said that the author of the present volume has made available to the reader an English translation of the original text in Sanskrit, as far as possible, word by word, in easy understandable English. The author modestly says in the introduction (p.xxxvii):

> "I hope that this English translation would be of some help to a student of the *Brahma-Sūtra-Bhāṣya* in the original, and if it does so, I shall consider it as quite adequate compensation for my labours."

The sentences of the translation are accurate. The way of translating the text is literal and faithful to the original. The style is easy to understand. The use of parentheses to make technical terms understandable is quite all right and very adequate; the author did not put unnecessary explanations in parentheses; the use of them is limited only in necessary cases. Wording of this translation is occasionally the same as that in Dr. Belvalkar's translation, and it is not strange, for both translations are aimed at being literal rendering which is faithful to the original text.

In many cases this translation is better than the foregoing ones. E. g., the author translated *kathamcit* as 'in some way or other' (p.412), which seems to be more easily understandable. However, in other cases former translations seem to be better. E. g., the author explains *anvaya* as 'logical continuance' in a bracket (p.346), but in this passage it seems that 'Gleichartigkeit' (Deussen) or 'homogenious constitution' (Belvalkar) got to the point.

It would not impair the value and prestige of this work, if the reviewer should mention some desirable points. It is regrettable that occasionally some careless mistakes or misprints in giving diacritical marks have crept in. In the front of the book the title is mentioned as: Bādarāyaṇā's *Brahma-sūtrās with Shaṅkarāchāryā's Commentary*, which should be corrected as: Bādarāyaṇa's *Brahma-sūtras* (in English; *Brahmasūtrāṇi*, and not *Brahmasūtrās*, in Sanskrit) with *Shaṅkarāchārya's* (or *Śaṅkarācārya's*) Commentary. The reviewer does not understand why the author always gave the word *sūtrās*, and *Brahma-sūtrās* instead of *sūtrāṇi* (in Sanskrit) or *sūtras* (in English).

The *Brahma-sūtras* is a copious work in which so many notions of various religious and philosophies are discussed, and it may have been unavoidable that the translation occasionally gives inadequate renderings in the passages referring to other philosophical systems of ancient India. For example, *dharma* and *adharma* as two of the five Astikāyas assumed by the Jains are translated as 'merit' and 'demerit' (p.406), which mistakes were also shared by Thibaut (part I, p.429) and Deussen ('die Entität des Guten' and 'die Entität des Bösen,' op. cit. S.365). They should be corrected as, say, 'the principle of motion' and 'the principle of rest.' The Jain technical term: *syād* was just translated as 'may be' (p.406), which is rather misleading. The word does not represent the form of a finite verb, but an indeclinable. The meaning of the technical term is: 'von gewähltem Standpunkt aus gesehen' (W. Schubring: *Die Lehre der Jainas*, S.108) or 'in gewisser Hinsicht' (F. O. Schrader: *Über den Stand der Philosophie*, usw., S.50-51). *syād ity anaikāntikatvadyotako nipātaḥ* (*Sarvamatasamgraha*, p.17.) Cf. *SDS*. III, *l*.379; *Bhāmatī*, II, 2, 33; *Nyāyanirṇaya*, *l. c.*, *Āptamīmāṃsā*, 105; *SDS*. III, *ll*.381-

382. It is a synonym of *kathaṃcit*. (*SDS*. III, *l*.385 ; *Nyāyanirṇaya*, ĀnSS., vol. I, p.594, *l*.1. *l*.383f.) Śaṅkara himself paraphrases *syād*···, *syād*··· with *pakṣe* ···, *pakṣe*··· (ĀnSS., vol.I, p.595, *l*.8).

It is likely that the author deliberately avoided overburdening the book with many lengthy and abstruse notes, but in order to make clear some obscure passages, it is advisable that footnotes should occasionally be added in due length. What does 'the eight-fold actions' (p.410) mean? It is well known to students of Jainism, but not to readers at large. On p.414 the two concepts of *tādātmya* and *tadutpatti* in the logical system of Dharmakīrti are implied.

The author mentions the sources of the Upaniṣadic citations in this work, but he did not include all the necessary remarks about the citations traced by Deussen. In the prospect that, as this translation is such an excellent and voluminous one that there would be no other attempt in the near future to publish another translation of this scale, the reviewer, taking advantage of this occasion, would like to give some supplementary remarks, skipping those which were already made by Deussen or Thibaut :

The verses cited at the end of Śaṅkara's Commentary on I, 1, 4 (p.35 of Apte's translation) were composed by Sundarapāṇḍya. (Cf. S. Kuppuswami Śāstrī : *Journal of Oriental Research Madras*, 1927, pp.5-15 ; pp.179-180 ; A. Venkatasubbiah : *Indian Historical Quarterly*, vol.XI. 1935, p.789 ; H. Nakamura : *Vedānta Tetsugaku no Hatten*, Tokyo, 1955, pp.231-238). One verse is cited in *SDS*. XVI, *ll*.191-192.

p.392 (ad II, 2, 26) : "Without the destruction of the cause···" is the citation from the *Nyāya-sūtra*, IV, 1, 14.

p.826 (ad IV, 2, 16) : A verse referring to Śuka, Cf. *Mahābhārata*, XII,8485 ; 12044.

p.732 (ad III, 4, 9). The first scriptural declaration cited there is also found in the *Vidvanmanorañjanī*, p.69.

The reviewer is afraid that the part in which Buddhism is criticized is rather difficult to understand or often misleading, unless it is explained with some detailed annotations. Here just some citations or references alone will be identified.

II, 2, 20. The same argument as is set forth here can be noticed in

Nāgārjuna's *Madhyamaka-śāstra*, XX, 15; XXI, 7.

Bhāva asya vyāpāraḥ. The verse cited here by the commentators to explain this phrase was composed by Dharmakīrti. (Poussin: *Prasannapadā*, p.116, n. 1. *Upadeśasāhasrī*, II, 18, 143).

II, 2, 21. The *prasaṅga* method of the Mādhyamikas was adopted by the *sūtrakāra* who was due to refute Buddhism. Cf. *Madhyamakaśāstra*, XX, 6; 7.

II, 2, 23. Something like Śaṅkara's criticism was set forth by King Milinda (*Milindapañho*, p.263, ed. by Trenckner).

II, 2, 24. *āvaraṇābhāvamātram ākāśam*. Cf. *Abhidharmakośa*, 1, 5; *Abhidharmakośavyākhyā*, ed. by U. Wogihara, p.15, *l*.11.

The Buddhist *sūtra* cited here is referred to in *Dīghanikāya*, vol.II, p.107, *Abhidharmakośavyākhyā*, ed by U. Wogihara, p.15, *l*.27f.; *Tarkajvālā* of Bhavya, ad VIII, 65.

II, 2, 28. *pramāṇa-prameya-phala-vyavahāra*. This is a phrase by Dharmakīrti. E.g., *Pramāṇa-vārttika*, III,305-306 (*SDS*. II, *ll*.249-250); 366, etc.

sahopalambhaniyamād abhedo··· This verse is often cited in philosophical works, but originally this is part of a verse of Dharmakīrti's *Pramāṇaviniścaya*. (The *Tibetan Tripiṭaka*, vol.130, Tokyo-Kyoto, 1957. *Bstan-ḥgyur*, *Gtan-tshigs rig-pa*, Ce 263 B 4-6.) I owe this information to Mr. Isshi Yamada.

na hy anayor ekasyānupalambhe 'nyasyopalambho 'sti. na caitat svabhāvaviveke yuktaḥ pratibandhakāraṇābhāvāt. This is a sentence of the *Pramāṇaviniścaya*. (ibid. 263 b 6).

yad antarjñeyarūpaṃ tad bahirvad avabhāsate. This is *Ālambanaparīkṣā* 6 a-b. (S. Yamaguchi: *JA*. 1929, Janvier-Mars, p.9; The *Tibetan Tripiṭaka*, vol. 130, Ce 178, *ll*.2-3).

These are just examples of remarks on the Buddhist part. On other parts, also, the same procedure should be followed, a task which must be up to the efforts of the forthcoming students of the future. It is impossible to translate adequately, unless we trace the citations and references to the sources.

Despite the above-mentioned points, readers will be benefited greatly in reading the original Sanskrit text with the aid of this translation, and nobody would deny the fact that this is a great contribution to the study of not only Vedānta but also Indian philosophy in general.

VII. AN INTERVIEW WITH ŚAṄKARĀCĀRYA OF KĀÑCĪPURAM

When I paid a visit to Śṛṅgeri, I was so very glad to have the opportunity of seeing the headquarters of the traditional scholarship and supreme wisdom of India. I could see many *paṇḍits* and even children who were learning Sanskrit literature. I took much interest in finding so many similarities between Śṛṅgeri and Koyasan (高野山), the headquarters of Japanese *Vajrayāna*. It was a great pleasure and also a great privilege to have the opportunity of seeing the present Śaṅkarācārya in a suburb of Madras on January 20, 1960. His personality is indeed very impressive and inspiring ; he convinced me that he was a man of earnest asceticism and true wisdom. I talked with him over so many things. But here I want to set forth details of our discussion about some technical problems.

I asked him :

"What is the significance of *upāsana*?"

The Svāmījī replied :

"*Upāsana* and *dhyāna* mean the same thing. *Upāsana* is to practice the injunctions as are ordained in the Scriptures, e. g. : You should meditate upon *Brahman* as such and such a thing. *Brahman* is one, but *upāsanas* are many. The *upāsana* is a mental action (*mānasa karma*), but cognition (*jñāna*) is not. Then what is the difference? For example, when we see something blue in colour, to know that "it is blue" is a cognition, but not a mental action. However, to meditate upon it, thinking that "it is in actuality red," is an *upāsana*, namely, a sort of action."

I asked him :

"Do they still observe the practice of *upāsana*, getting together in a group?"

The Svāmījī replied :

"It is still observed at fixed times. However, it is up to each individual whether to participate or not. There is no coercion. There is no custom of practicing it in groups."

Then I was reminded of a comment by an Indian intellectual that in India there has existed no congregation in the Western sense. I think his comment was corroborated by this authority.

I asked the Svāmījī:

"In the authoritative works which are supposed by scholars to have been virtually written by Śaṅkara himself, there are some references to the god *Viṣṇu*, but no reference to the god *Śiva*. And yet the followers of Śaṅkara are all *Śaivas*. What is the reason for that?"

The Svāmījī asked me in return:

"Tell me the reason that you take us all for *Śaivas*."

I thought that it is a universally admitted fact that the Śaṅkaraites are closely connected with Śaivism, and I was reminded of the fact that even Indian intellectuals think that the Śaṅkaraites are *Smārtas* and *Śaivas* at the same time. It seemed to be beyond doubt. But, as I was quizzed by him, I pointed out the following two points. — Don't you practice the *linga* worship? And second, all the ascetics who have gathered here today have three white lines in ashes on their foreheads. Is this not good evidence? There appeared to be nobody who had the three vertical lines of the Vaiṣṇavas among those who participated in the *pūjā* there and then.

The Svāmījī answered:

"Some Śaṅkaraites are *Vaiṣṇavas*; they bear the mark in three white vertical ash lines on their foreheads. But many others are *Śaivas*; they bear the mark of their own. Some others bear no mark. After Śaṅkara there came many *tīrthaṅkaras*: Rāmānuja, Madhva, Vallabha, etc. They were mostly followers of the *Viṣṇu* cult. So, as a counteraction to them, most of the Śaṅkaraites became *Śaivas*. This is why we find so many *Śiva* worshippers among the Śaṅkaraites. I myself am just indifferent to these distinctions. (The Śaṅkarācārya bore only one white horizontal line on the forehead then.) For example, when a devout believer prostrates all his body on the ground, I confer benediction upon him, touching him on the forehead with my hand, saying: '*Nārāyaṇa*!' On that occasion I have the god *Viṣṇu* in mind. But when I observe the *linga*-worship, I am a worshipper of *Śiva*. I am neither *Śaiva*, nor *Vaiṣṇava*. However, some of my followers belong to either of them. The *Viṣṇu*-worshippers among the Śaṅkaraites do not pay visits to the temples of *Śiva*. They dislike the *Śaivas* among the Śaṅkaraites with much more intensity than the *Vaiṣṇavas* at large dislike the *Śaivas*. On the other hand, the *Śiva*-worshippers among the Śaṅkaraites dislike the *Viṣṇu*-worshippers among them. That is to say, there are *Śaivas* and *Smārtas* among the *Śiva*-worshippers who are exclusive to the *Vaiṣṇavas*."

Our discussion covered so many interesting problems, some of which I presented at the twelfth general assembly of the Japanese Association of Indian and Buddhist Studies, which was held at Waseda University, Tokyo, in May 1960. Many participants there listened to my lecture very enthusiastically. There is much interest in the philosophy and school of Śaṅkara among Japanese scholars. I do hope that cultural exchange between both countries will be enhanced.

My visit to Tiruvannamalai on January 21, 1960 was also a very impressive one. When I was in America, Professor Frederic Spiegelberg and others had told me of their spiritual experience at the sage's ashram. The book *Der Weg zur Selbsterkenntnis* by the late Heinrich Zimmer was, so to speak, a revelation to me. Only this year was I able to fulfill my long cherished desire to visit the holy place, which struck me very much. There prevails a calm, serene and yet spiritual atmosphere in the ashram. As my stay there was too short, I can not pass any judgement or form any opinion. What I can say right now is that everything there was striking and fascinating. The time-honored big temple there is more grand, magnificent and imposing than I had expected. There remain so many things which attract me.

INDEX

B

F

G

I

J

O

Q

R

T

U

V

POSTSCRIPT

It was indeed 25 years ago, in 1976, that *A History of Early Vedānta Philosophy,* Part One was published by the Motilal Banarsidass Publishers, Delhi, India. As is stated in the Preface of the book, this was originally the doctoral dissertation submitted to the University of Tokyo by the late Dr. Hajime Nakamura in 1942, the manuscript of which was said to have been so bulky and heavy that he could not carry it by hand to the University and that he had to use a bicycle trailer for that purpose.

Because of the difficulties to publish the manuscript just after World War II, it was only in 1956 that it was finally published as *Shoki no Vedānta Tetsugaku* (*A History of Early Vedānta Philosophy*) in 4 volumes of 2410 pages in total by the Iwanami Shoten Booksellers, Tokyo. In 1957 it received the Imperial Award from the Japan Academy. Nearly 60 years have already passed since the publication of this great tome.

It seems, however, that during this long period, Dr. Nakamura was preparing for the publication of the second volume of the English version of *A History of Early Vedānta Philosophy*, translating portions into English for publication in various foreign journals, and obtaining the help of other scholars as well. Unfortunately Mr. Trevor Leggett, who played a significant role in translating Part One, could no longer assist him due to failing eyesight. It seems to me that Dr. Nakamura could not, thereafter, find any other gifted person like Mr. Leggett with the three important conditions necessary for the task, the English language as his native language and being well versed in Japanese as well as in Vedānta philosophy. Hence the translation progressed very slowly. I myself was asked to help in a small portion of the project relating to Part One. However, I did not participate in translating Part Two, being uninformed of the state of the project after the publication of Part One.

On the 2nd of September, 1999, I unexpectedly received a telephone call from the late Dr. Jion Abe, then Executive Secretary of the Eastern Institute, Inc., who had just visited Professor Nakamura as requested. He reported that Dr. Nakamura was very anxious about the English translation of his book *A History of Early Vedānta Philosophy* and wished me to bring the task to completion. I therefore visited him with my wife the following morning to inquire after his health and to convey to him my willingness to comply with his request. .But alas, lying in his bed, his eyes and mouth remained closed, with only a slight reaction to the calling of his family, my wife and myself. On the 10th of October, he quietly breathed his last breath, attended to by his family and his pulse taken by Mrs. Nakamura, a medical doctor.

Dr. Nakamura had originally planned to publish this Part Two only through the Motilal Banarsidass Publishers, as was in the case of Part One. However, he in all likelihood noticed that his last day was quickly approaching, and he decided to first publish it in a special issue of *Toho*, the Bulletin of the Eastern Institute, Inc., in haste, and thereafter to have Motilal Banarsidass Publishers publish it in book form. He entrusted Dr. Hiroyuki Sato, a specialist in Vedānta philosophy and a researcher at the Institute, with the task of publishing Part Two, handing him the bulky manuscript in English in February, 1999.

The various sets of translated manuscripts handed to Dr. Sato were not of equal quality, for they had been prepared not only by Dr. Nakamura himself but also with the help of various scholars. Therefore, several sections had to be completely retranslated into English at the 2nd proofreading. These circumstances caused to further delay the work of editing Part Two which was already far behind schedule.

However, this prolonged work is now about to be completed. There are three books which Dr. Nakamura could not see in print before he passed away, among the great number of works written by himself or closely related to him in some way or other. They are 1. *The Structure of Logic* in two volumes (Seidosha Publishing House, May, 2000), 2. *An Encyclopaedia of Comparative Philosophy* (Tokyo Shoseki Publishing House, August, 2000), and 3. *A Grand Dictionary of Buddhist Terms* (Tokyo Shoseki Publishing House, June, 2001). The fourth will be this present publication. It is indeed regrettable and inexcusable that I could not complete the task and show him a new book in his lifetime, but it is, at least, a pleasure for me to realize his last wish in the second anniversary of his death.

As noted above, nearly 60 years have already passed since the 4 volumes of *A History of Early Vedānta Philosophy* was published in Japanese. Meanwhile, new researches have been reported in such fields as Bhartṛhari and the like. Nevertheless none can take the place of Dr. Nakamura's achievements in the field of pre-Śaṅkara Vedānta. Furthermore, publications in this area have been a significant and priceless literature only to students able to read Japanese. With the publication of this Part Two in English with many additions and revisions done by the author himself, I believe that *A History of Early Vedānta Philosophy* will be an important literature indispensable not only to those who are specialists in the study of Vedānta but also to those engaged in the study of Indian thought in general.

Acknowledgement must be made to the many scholars and graduate students without whose aid this Part Two would not have been realized. I would here like to express my deepest gratitude to the following, their names in the alphabetical order and without titles: Takayoshi Aono, Koki Aruga, Tan Saw Chye, Takamichi Fujii, Ikuro Hattori, Keijin Hayashi, Kuniko Hosono, Kazuyosi Hotta, Iwao Ishikawa, Kei Kataoka, Takahiro Kato, Han Ik Kim, Noriyuki Kudo, Michitoshi Manda, Kazuya Mori, Shinya Moriyama, Shuichi Nara, Ruriko Sakuma, Hiroyuki Sato, Kouju Sato, Maho Shibazaki, Taisei Shida, Ikkei Suzuki, and Hirohisa Toda.

Furthermore, the late Mr. Trevor Leggett, who played a truly important role in the publication of Part One, might also have edited the English of two thirds of Part V and a portion of Part VI, although this can not be ascertained. When the editorial work started, Professors Hiroshi Marui, Ryozun Mitomo and Yoshifumi Mizuno gave valuable advice. Especially Professor Marui kindly gathered competent graduate students of the University of Tokyo to help with the work. Finally, the late Professor Jion Abe, Mrs. Sumiko Miki, Administrator and elder daughter of Dr. Nakamura, Mrs. Hiromi Oikawa and Mr. Shinji Horiuchi, Executive Secretaries, and other researchers of the Eastern Institute made great efforts to realize Dr. Nakamura's last wish. As for the publication, Mr. Makoto Toshima of Tokyo Shoseki and Mr. Koichiro Inoue, who succeeded Mr. Toshima were also most helpful. My sincerest gratitude is due to them all for their warm-hearted cooperation and utmost dedication to the fulfillment of

Dr. Nakamura's dream of seeing his works published in English.

January 13, 2002

Sengaku Mayeda

Note: Dr. Nakamura attached supplements to the end of each volume of *A History of Early Vedānta* Philosophy in Volumes I-IV, in the third edition of 1981. In 1989, he added another bulky book of 916 pages, entitled *Śaṅkara's Thought*, to the 4 volumes, naming them all collectively *Indian Philosophical Thought*, Volumes I-V. His present English translation, which is based upon the first edition, does not include the 5th volume nor his additional new supplements attached to each volume in the third edition.